Spurgeon's Devotional Bible

Selected passages from the Word of God with running comments

C. H. Spurgeon

BAKER BOOK HOUSE
Grand Rapids, Michigan 49516

Reprinted 1990 by
Baker Book House Company

ISBN: 0-8010-8043-6

Printed in the United States of America

PREFACE

There is an encouraging trend toward the restoration of daily devotions, both on an individual and family basis. This book is the perfect answer to anyone who has this aim in view. The emphasis in this volume is on Scripture, with comments interspersed where questions are apt to arise, or where desirable application comes natural.

The gist of the entire Bible is contained between the covers of this book. The passages omitted are almost always summarized wherever possible. To reduce a passage to the proper length, verses are naturally omitted in whole or in part, but in such a way that the narrative or teaching remains clear and unimpaired.

The book will be read through in one year where morning and evening devotions are maintained. Where only one devotional per day is possible, observance of the second date, which is inserted below the first in smaller type, will render the volume useful for two full years.

It is hoped that the enjoyment of the selected extracts may lead the reader to establish or to continue the excellent practice of daily devotions and Bible reading.

— The Publishers

THE *mere reading of the holy Scriptures will be of no avail to us, unless the Holy Spirit sanctify the truth to our souls. Let us pray that (in commencing this year's Family Reading) he who commanded light to shine out of darkness may shine into our hearts and give us to know the inner meaning of his word. We shall begin at the opening page of revelation.*

GENESIS I. 1—5.

1 In the beginning God created the heaven and the earth.

2 And the earth was without form, and void; and darkness *was* upon the face of the deep. *(Thus dark are we by nature, thus disordered are all our powers through sin. We are nothing but confusion and emptiness.)* And the Spirit of God moved upon the face of the waters.

The Spirit of God is the first efficient mover in the new creation. He visits the dead and dark heart, and begins the work of salvation within.

3 And God said, Let there be light: and there was light. *(See the power of the word of God! He speaks and it is done. Thus powerful is the word of the gospel when heard in the soul. May its enlightening power be felt by us all.)*

4 And God saw the light, that *it was* good: *(Wherever God puts his grace he looks upon it with pleasure)* and God divided the light from the darkness. *(Grace also makes a separation, for what fellowship has light with darkness?)*

5 And God called the light Day, and the darkness he called Night. And the evening and the morning were the first day.

Thus the first day of the week, the day of our Lord's resurrection is a day of light. May it ever be so to us.

IT *is interesting to notice how the New Testament, as written by John, opens in the same manner as the Old Testament, with "In the beginning." Let us add to our reading the first fourteen verses of John's Gospel. Jesus, the Lord our Saviour, is called "the Word," or the uttered mind of God.*

JOHN I. 1—14.

1 In the beginning was the Word, and the Word was with God, and the Word was God.

2 The same was in the beginning with God. *(Jesus was in existence when all created things began; he was with God in nature, in love, and in co-operation, and he is himself essentially God.)*

3 All things were made by him; and without him was not any thing made that was made.

4 In him was life; and the life was the light of men. *(If we live unto God, and have any spiritual light, it comes to us by Jesus Christ.)*

5 And the light shineth in darkness; and the darkness comprehended it not.

6 ¶ There was a man sent from God, whose name *was* John.

7 The same came for a witness, to bear witness of the Light, that all *men* through him might believe.

8 He was not that Light, but *was sent* to bear witness of that Light.

9 *That* was the true Light, which lighteth every man that cometh into the world. *No one can get light from any other source, and all who desire light may have it from him.*

10 He was in the world, and the world was made by him, and the world knew him not.

11 He came unto his own, and his own received him not. *(The Jews, who were his own kinsmen, rejected him; and, alas! too many of the children of godly parents refuse the Saviour. May it not be so in this house.)*

12 But as many as received him, to them gave he power to become the sons of God, *even* to them that believe on his name: *(This is the essence of the gospel, Christ is the giver, we are only receivers. Faith like a hand receives Christ, and with him the privilege of adoption.)*

13 Which were born, not of blood, nor of the will of the flesh, nor of the will of man, but of God.

14 And the Word was made flesh, and dwelt among us, (and we beheld his glory, the glory as of the only begotten of the Father,) full of grace and truth. *(The Lord grant unto us to receive of his grace and to know his truth. Amen.)*

Ere the blue heavens were stretch'd abroad,
From everlasting was the Word:
With God he was; the Word was God,
And must divinely be adored.

But lo! he leaves those heavenly forms,
The Word descends and dwells in clay,
That he may hold converse with worms,
Dress'd in such feeble flesh as they.

Mortals with joy beheld his face,
Th' eternal Father's only Son:
How full of truth! how full of grace!
When through his eyes the Godhead shone!

2   " 𝕮reate in me a clean heart."   JANUARY 1.—EVENING.

[*Or January 2.*]

GENESIS I. 6—13.

AND God said, Let there be a firmament in the midst of the waters, and let it divide the waters from the waters.

The expanse of the atmosphere separates the vapours above from the waters below. Luther used to wonder at the arch of heaven, which stands unsupported by pillars. He saw in it a lesson for his faith, teaching him that the Lord could uphold him by unseen power. He who creates with a word can sustain in the same manner.

7 And God made the firmament, and divided the waters which *were* under the firmament from the waters which *were* above the firmament: and it was so. *(What the Lord in the former verse commanded he in this verse creates: in the same manner one Scripture bids us believe, and another tells us that faith is the work of God.)*

8 And God called the firmament Heaven. And the evening and the morning were the second day.

9 And God said, Let the waters under the heaven be gathered together unto one place, and let the dry *land* appear: and it was so.

Note the frequent repetition of those little words, " and it was so." We may gather from them that none of God's words of promise or threatening will fall to the ground.

10 And God called the dry *land* Earth; and the gathering together of the waters called he Seas: and God saw that *it was* good.

God's care in naming " day " and " night," and " earth," and " sea," should teach us to call things by their right names; let us never call sin pleasure, or the Lord's service a weariness.

11 And God said, Let the earth bring forth grass, the herb yielding seed, *and* the fruit tree yielding fruit after his kind, whose seed *is* in itself, upon the earth: and it was so.

12 And the earth brought forth grass, *and* herb yielding seed after his kind, and the tree yielding fruit, whose seed *was* in itself, after his kind: and God saw that *it was* good.

When God has put light into a soul, and divided its sin from its new life, he next looks for fruit, and ere long it is brought forth to his glory.

13 And the evening and the morning were the third day. *(So far, we have considered the second and third day's work of creation: it may be well for us now to be reminded that our Lord*

Jesus was there, and " without him was not anything made that was made.") Let us read—

PROVERBS VIII. 22—36.

22 The LORD possessed me in the beginning of his way, before his works of old.

23 I was set up from everlasting, from the beginning, or ever the earth was.

24, 25, 26 When *there were* no depths, I was brought forth; when *there were* no fountains abounding with water. Before the mountains were settled, before the hills was I brought forth: While as yet he had not made the earth, nor the fields, nor the highest part of the dust of the world.

27, 28, 29 When he prepared the heavens, I *was* there: when he set a compass upon the face of the depth: When he established the clouds above: when he strengthened the fountains of the deep: When he gave to the sea his decree, that the waters should not pass his commandment: when he appointed the foundations of the earth:

30, 31 Then I was by him, *as* one brought up with him: and I was daily *his* delight, rejoicing always before him; rejoicing in the habitable part of his earth; and my delights *were* with the sons of men.

32, 33 Now therefore hearken unto me, O ye children: for blessed *are they that* keep my ways. Hear instruction, and be wise, and refuse it not.

34 Blessed *is* the man that heareth me, watching daily at my gates, waiting at the posts of my doors.

35 For whoso findeth me findeth life, and shall obtain favour of the LORD.

36 But he that sinneth against me wrongeth his own soul: all they that hate me love death.

May we hearken to him who is " made of God unto us wisdom," and find life and favour in him.

I sing th' almighty power of God
    That made the mountains rise;
That spread the flowing seas abroad,
    And built the lofty skies.

There's not a plant or flower below,
    But makes his glories known;
And clouds arise, and tempests blow,
    By order from his throne.

GENESIS I. 14—23.

AND God said, Let there be lights in the firmament of the heaven to divide the day from the night; and let them be for signs, and for seasons, and for days, and years: and let them be for lights in the firmament of the heaven to give light upon the earth: and it was so. *(There was light before the appearance of sun or moon; but God made these the bearers thereof, that they might declare his glory. He could have done without them, but he did not please so to do. He could enlighten men's minds without his ministers or his church; but, if he chooses to use them as lights in the world, let us be thankful for them, and pray for them.)*

16 And God made two great lights; the greater light to rule the day, and the lesser light to rule the night: *he made* the stars also.

Thus a chaos of light was reduced to order. Order is a law of God. Families are unhappy without it.

17 And God set them in the firmament of the heaven to give light upon the earth,

18 And to rule over the day and over the night, and to divide the light from the darkness: and God saw that *it was* good.

The delightful alternation of the day so suitable for labour, and the night so proper for rest, is certainly "good" for us in many ways, and we ought to adore the goodness of God therein.

19 And the evening and the morning were the fourth day.

20 And God said, Let the waters bring forth abundantly the moving creature that hath life, and fowl *that* may fly above the earth in the open firmament of heaven.

Thus the Lord's work of creation advanced to higher stages each day, and we shall find it so in grace; he will yet reveal choicer mercies to us.

21, 22 And God created great whales, and every living creature that moveth, which the waters brought forth abundantly, after their kind, and every winged fowl after his kind: and God saw that *it was* good. And God blessed them, saying, Be fruitful, and multiply, and fill the waters in the seas, and let fowl multiply in the earth.

23 And the evening and the morning were the fifth day. *(The inconceivable numbers of fish and fowl in the earth show how potent was this primeval blessing. Let but the Lord bless his church in the same manner, and her converts shall*

be as the stars of heaven for multitude. Such wonders of creation ought not to be rehearsed without a song of praise: let us therefore turn to—

PSALM CXLVIII.

1 Praise ye the LORD. Praise ye the LORD from the heavens: praise him in the heights.

2 Praise ye him, all his angels: praise ye him, all his hosts.

3 Praise ye him, sun and moon: praise him, all ye stars of light.

4 Praise him, ye heavens of heavens, and ye waters that *be* above the heavens.

5 Let them praise the name of the LORD: for he commanded, and they were created.

6 He hath also stablished them for ever and ever: he hath made a decree which shall not pass.

7 Praise the LORD from the earth, ye dragons, and all deeps:

8 Fire, and hail; snow, and vapours; stormy wind fulfilling his word:

9 Mountains, and all hills; fruitful trees, and all cedars:

10 Beasts, and all cattle; creeping things, and flying fowl:

11 Kings of the earth, and all people; princes, and all judges of the earth:

12 Both young men, and maidens; old men, and children:

13 Let them praise the name of the LORD: for his name alone is excellent; his glory *is* above the earth and heaven.

14 He also exalteth the horn of his people, the praise of all his saints; *even* of the children of Israel, a people near unto him. Praise ye the LORD. *(All this day let us praise God with our hearts, words, and actions; for he has dealt very kindly with us as a family. Blessed be his name.)*

Praise him, ye gladdening smiles of morn;
Praise him, O silent night;
Tell forth his glory all the earth;
Praise him, ye stars of light!

Praise him, ye stormy winds, that rise
Obedient to his word;
Mountains, and hills, and fruitful trees,
Join ye and praise the Lord!

Praise him, ye heavenly hosts, for ye
With purer lips, can sing—
Glory and honour, praise and power
To him, the Eternal King!

GENESIS I. 26—31.

THE *Lord first prepared the world for man, and then placed him in it. He fitted* up the house before he made the tenant. *This is an instance of his thoughtful care for our race.*

26 ¶ And God said, Let us make man in our image, after our likeness: and let them have dominion over the fish of the sea, and over the fowl of the air, and over the cattle, and over all the earth, and over every creeping thing that creepeth upon the earth.

Note the words, " Let us make." The three divine persons hold a council; let us learn to adore Father, Son, and Spirit, as the One God. Man was the highest work of the six days' creation, and was not fashioned without special consideration. He was made to be lord of the world; and if now the beasts rebel against him, it is only because he also has rebelled against his God.

27 So God created man in his *own* image; in the image of God created he him; male and female created he them.

29 ¶ And God said, Behold, I have given you every herb bearing seed, which *is* upon the face of all the earth, and every tree, in the which *is* the fruit of a tree yielding seed; to you it shall be for meat. (*Before he sinned man did not kill animals, but lived on fruits; every meal of flesh should remind us of our fall.*)

31 And God saw every thing that he had made, and, behold, *it was* very good. And the evening and the morning were the sixth day.

GENESIS II. 7—25.

AND the LORD God formed man *of* the dust of the ground, and breathed into his nostrils the breath of life; and man became a living soul.

8 ¶ And the LORD God planted a garden eastward in Eden; and there he put the man whom he had formed.

9 And out of the ground made the LORD God to grow every tree that is pleasant to the sight, and good for food; the tree of life also in the midst of the garden, and the tree of knowledge of good and evil.

10 And a river went out of Eden to water the garden; and from thence it was parted, and became into four heads.

Thus there was abundance of food and drink, and a pleasant variety of prospect: the garden was a paradise of comfort. *" No herb, no flower, no tree was wanting there that might be of ornament or use; whether for sight, or for scent, or for taste. The bounty of God wrought further than to necessity, it provided for comfort and recreation."*

15 And the LORD God took the man, and put him into the garden of Eden to dress it and to keep it. (*Some occupation is necessary to happiness. Lazy people would not enjoy even Eden itself. A perfect man is a working man.*)

16 And the LORD God commanded the man, saying, Of every tree of the garden thou mayest freely eat:

17 But of the tree of the knowledge of good and evil, thou shalt not eat of it: for in the day that thou eatest thereof thou shalt surely die.

This was an easy yoke. Only one tree out of thousands was denied him as a test of his obedience. The Lord's commandments are not grievous.

18 ¶ And the LORD God said, *It is* not good that the man should be alone; I will make him an help meet for him.

Before Adam knew that he wanted a companion, his tender Creator knew it, and resolved to find him one. Thus with gracious foresight does the Lord supply our needs.

21 And the LORD God caused a deep sleep to fall upon Adam, and he slept: and he took one of his ribs, and closed up the flesh instead thereof;

22 And the rib, which the LORD God had taken from man, made he a woman, and brought her unto the man.

23 And Adam said, This *is* now bone of my bones, and flesh of my flesh: she shall be called Woman, because she was taken out of Man.

We ought dearly to love mother, and wife, and sister, and aunt. These dear friends greatly minister to our happiness; and boys and young men should always treat them with tender respect.

24 Therefore shall a man leave his father and his mother, and shall cleave unto his wife: and they shall be one flesh.

25 And they were both naked, the man and his wife, and were not ashamed.

We ought never to be proud of our clothes, for our weakness makes us need them; and they prove that we are sinful, since until we are covered we are ashamed to be seen. May Jesus cover us with his glorious righteousness.

O UR *last reading showed us man fresh from the hand of his Maker. It will be well to pause and consider the Lord's goodness to our race. We cannot find a fitter assistance for our meditation than David's joyful vintage hymn.*

PSALM VIII.

1 O LORD our Lord, how excellent *is* thy name in all the earth ! who hast set thy glory above the heavens.

2 Out of the mouth of babes and sucklings hast thou ordained strength because of thine enemies, that thou mightest still the enemy and the avenger. *(It is a part of the excellence and glory of God that he magnifies himself by means of insignificant creatures. Though his name is excellent in all the earth yet babes may praise it, and though his glory be above the heavens sucklings may proclaim it. It needs a great orator to win men's admiration for a doubtful character ; but so surpassingly glorious is the Lord, that even a child's tongue suffices to baffle his foes, and charm his friends.)*

3 When I consider thy heavens, the work of thy fingers, the moon and the stars, which thou hast ordained ;

4 What is man, that thou art mindful of him ? and the son of man, that thou visitest him ? *(The heavens are so vast and he so small; the moon so bright and he so mean ; the stars so glorious and he so grovelling; Lord, how canst thou stoop from the sublimities of heaven to visit such a nothing as man ? The study of astronomy is calculated to humble the mind as well as to enlarge it : and at the same time it excites adoring gratitude when we see the Lord lavishing his love upon creatures so insignificant as ourselves.)*

5 For thou hast made him a little lower than the angels, and hast crowned him with glory and honour.

Since he is mortal and angels are immortal, man is a little lower than they ; yet it is but for a little time and then man's coronation with glory and honour shall have come. Then shall it be seen that angels are but servants to the saints, and that all creatures work for their benefit.

6 Thou madest him to have dominion over the works of thy hands ; thou hast put all *things* under his feet :

7 All sheep and oxen, yea, and the beasts of the field ;

8 The fowl of the air, and the fish of the sea, *and whatsoever* passeth through the paths of the seas. *(All these creatures he either tames to his hand, or slays for his use. His fear and dread are on them all. Marred as man's dominion is, he still walks among the inferior animals with something of that awe, which, as a poet saith, " doth hedge a king." In Adam's innocence man's rule of the lower races was no doubt complete and delightful ; one imagines him leaning upon a tawny lion, while a fawn frisks at the side of Eve. In the Lord Jesus, however, we see man most eminently in the place of honour, exalted in the highest. We know that the position of our Lord Jesus is a representative one for all his people, for the members are like the Head. In Jesus man is indeed " crowned with glory and honour." It is both our duty and our privilege to rise superior to all the things of earth. We must take care to keep the world under our feet, and the creatures in their proper place. Let none of us permit the possession of any earthly creatures to be a snare unto us ; we are to reign over them, and must not permit them to reign over us.)*

9 O LORD our Lord, how excellent *is* thy name in all the earth !

Lord, what is man, or all his race,
 Who dwell so far below,
That thou shouldst visit him with grace,
 And love his nature so ?

That thine eternal Son should bear
 To take a mortal form,
Made lower than his angels are,
 To save a dying worm ?

Let him be crown'd with majesty
 Who bow'd his head to death ;
And be his honours sounded high
 By all things that have breath.

We raise our shouts, O God, to thee,
 And send them to thy throne ;
All glory to the united Three,
 The undivided One.

'Twas he, and we'll adore his name,
 That form'd us by a word ;
'Tis he restores our ruin'd frame :
 Salvation to the Lord !

WE *have grouped together a few of the texts which refer to the Sabbath, in order that at one reading we may have the subject before us. In the history of the creation, we have the institution of the sacred day of rest.*

GENESIS II. 1—3.

1 Thus the heavens and the earth were finished, and all the host of them.

2 And on the seventh day God ended his work which he had made ; and he rested on the seventh day from all his work which he had made.

3 And God blessed the seventh day, and sanctified it : because that in it he had rested from all his work which God created and made.

This primitive institution was confirmed at the giving of the Law upon Sinai ; and is therefore surrounded by as solemn sanctions as any other precept of the Decalogue.

EXODUS XX. 8—11.

8 Remember the sabbath day, to keep it holy.

9 Six days shalt thou labour, and do all thy work :

10 But the seventh day *is* the sabbath of the LORD thy God : *in it* thou shalt not do any work, thou, nor thy son, nor thy daughter, thy manservant, nor thy maidservant, nor thy cattle, nor thy stranger that *is* within thy gates :

11 For *in* six days the LORD made heaven and earth, the sea, and all that in them *is*, and rested the seventh day : wherefore the LORD blessed the sabbath day, and hallowed it.

WE *are not, however, to regard this law as forbidding the doing of works of piety, charity, or necessity, for our Lord Jesus has awarded us full liberty on these points. He corrected Jewish misconceptions, and taught us not to make a bondage of the day of rest.*

MARK II. 23—28.

23 And it came to pass, that he went through the corn fields on the sabbath day ; and his disciples began, as they went, to pluck the ears of corn.

24 And the Pharisees said unto him, Behold, why do they on the sabbath day that which is not lawful ?

25 And he said unto them, Have ye never read what David did, when he had need, and was an hungred, he, and they that were with him ?

26 How he went into the house of God in the days of Abiathar the high priest, and did eat the shewbread, which is not lawful to eat but for the priests, and gave also to them which were with him ?

27 And he said unto them, The sabbath was made for man, and not man for the sabbath :

28 Therefore the Son of man is Lord also of the sabbath.

OUR *Lord performed many of his noblest cures on the Sabbath, as if to show that the day was ordained to glorify God by yielding benefit to man. If at one time more than another the healing virtue flows freely from our Lord, it is on that one day in seven which is reserved for holy uses, and is called " the Lord's Day." In the passage which we are about to read he shows how suitable it is that a holy day should be crowned with holy deeds of mercy and love.*

LUKE XIV. 1—5.

1 And it came to pass, as he went into the house of one of the chief Pharisees to eat bread on the sabbath day, that they watched him.

2 And, behold, there was a certain man before him which had the dropsy.

3 And Jesus answering spake unto the lawyers and Pharisees, saying, Is it lawful to heal on the sabbath day ?

4 And they held their peace. And he took *him*, and healed him, and let him go ;

5 And answered them, saying, Which of you shall have an ass or an ox fallen into a pit, and will not straightway pull him out on the sabbath day ?

O day of rest and gladness,
　O day of joy and light,
O balm of care and sadness,
　Most beautiful, most bright !
Thou art a cooling fountain
　In life's dry, dreary sand ;
From thee, like Pisgah's mountain,
　We view our promised land.

May we, new graces gaining
　From this our day of rest,
Attain the rest remaining
　To spirits of the blest ;
And there our voice uпраising
　To Father and to Son,
And Holy Ghost, be praising
　Ever the Three in One.

THE *present portion of Scripture contains the sad record of the Fall, in which through our first parents we all fell,*

GENESIS III. 1—19.

1 Now the serpent was more subtil than any beast of the field which the LORD God had made. And he said unto the woman, Yea, hath God said, Ye shall not eat of every tree of the garden? *(The devil often begins as if he were an enquirer.)*

2 And the woman said unto the serpent, We may eat of the fruit of the trees of the garden :

3 But of the fruit of the tree which *is* in the midst of the garden, God hath said, Ye shall not eat of it, neither shall ye touch it, lest ye die. *(She should have been more precise. God did not say, " lest ye die," but " ye shall surely die." Error commences in little departures from truth.)*

4 And the serpent said unto the woman, Ye shall not surely die :

5 For God doth know that in the day ye eat thereof, then your eyes shall be opened, and ye shall be as gods, knowing good and evil. *(He cruelly slanders God. He hints that God was afraid that man would grow too great.)*

6 And when the woman saw that the tree *was* good for food, and that it *was* pleasant to the eyes, and a tree to be desired to make *one* wise, she took of the fruit thereof, and did eat, and gave also unto her husband with her; and he did eat. *(See the progress of sin, she listened, she saw, she took, she gave to Adam. She had been wiser if she had turned away at first.)*

7 And the eyes of them both were opened, and they knew that they *were* naked; and they sewed fig leaves together, and made themselves aprons.

8 And they heard the voice of the LORD God walking in the garden in the cool of the day: and Adam and his wife hid themselves from the presence of the LORD God amongst the trees of the garden.

9 And the LORD God called unto Adam, and said unto him, Where *art* thou ?

10 And he said, I heard thy voice in the garden, and I was afraid, because I *was* naked; and I hid myself.

11 And he said, Who told thee that thou *wast* naked ? Hast thou eaten of the tree, whereof I commanded thee that thou shouldest not eat ?

12 And the man said, The woman whom thou gavest *to be* with me, she gave me of the tree, and I did eat. *(He throws the blame on God for giving him a wife. Alas ! what wretched ingratitude.)*

13 And the LORD God said unto the woman, What *is* this *that* thou hast done ? And the woman said, The serpent beguiled me, and I did eat. *(Sinners are ready with excuses, and yet they have never a good one. Open confession of our wrong-doing is far better.)*

14 And the LORD God said unto the serpent, Because thou hast done this, thou *art* cursed above all cattle, and above every beast of the field; upon thy belly shalt thou go, and dust shalt thou eat all the days of thy life :

15 And I will put enmity between thee and the woman, and between thy seed and her seed; it shall bruise thy head, and thou shalt bruise his heel. *(Here a blessed promise lies like a pearl in a shell. The serpent's curse is for us a blessing, for Jesus our Saviour is therein foretold.)*

16 Unto the woman he said, I will greatly multiply thy sorrow and thy conception; in sorrow thou shalt bring forth children; and thy desire *shall be* to thy husband, and he shall rule over thee.

17 And unto Adam he said, Because thou hast hearkened unto the voice of thy wife, and hast eaten of the tree, of which I commanded thee, saying, Thou shalt not eat of it : cursed *is* the ground for thy sake; in sorrow shalt thou eat *of* it all the days of thy life. *(See how obliquely the curse falls. It glances rather on the ground than on man. Wondrous is God's mercy.)*

18 Thorns also and thistles shall it bring forth to thee; and thou shalt eat the herb of the field;

19 In the sweat of thy face shalt thou eat bread, till thou return unto the ground; for out of it wast thou taken : for dust thou *art*, and unto dust shalt thou return. *(Thus sin when it is finished bringeth forth death.)*

Yet, mighty God, thy wondrous love
Can make our nature clean,
While Christ and grace prevail above
The tempter, death, and sin.

The second Adam shall restore
The ruins of the first,
Hosanna to the sovereign power
That new creates our dust.

T HE *New Testament is the key to the Old. There we find an explanation of the position of Adam in reference to the race of man. He represented us all, and we all share the sad effects of his transgression. He was the door through which both sin and death entered into our world. So the apostle Paul teaches us in*

ROMANS V. 12—21.

12 Wherefore, as by one man sin entered into the world, and death by sin; and so death passed upon all men, for that all have sinned: *(All men sinned in Adam who stood as representative for them all, and therefore all men die.)*

13 For until the law sin was in the world: but sin is not imputed when there is no law.

14 Nevertheless death reigned from Adam to Moses, *(It is clear that there was sin in the world before the law because men died; that sin came in through the fall,)* even over them that had not sinned, after the similitude of Adam's transgression, *(even infants die through Adam's sin, though without personal guilt,)* who is the figure of him that was to come. *(For Jesus is the second head of the race, the second representative man. As we fell by our union with Adam, so if we are in Christ we shall rise by virtue of our union with the Lord Jesus, who is here intended by the term, " him that was to come." But he is the Head and Leader of a believing people: the great question is, are we believers in him?)*

15 But not as the offence, so also *is* the free gift. For if through the offence of one many be dead, much more the grace of God, and the gift by grace, *which is* by one man, Jesus Christ, hath abounded unto many. *(Note that salvation is not the reward of merit, but a free gift; and mark how God's grace outruns human sin. The apostle speaks of "much more," as if he meant, more likely, more easily, more abundantly. It was God's strange work when he condemned the race for Adam's sin; but it is his delight to accept men for the sake of his dear Son.)*

16 And not as *it was* by one that sinned, *so is* the gift: for the judgment *was* by one to condemnation, but the free gift *is* of many offences unto justification. *(One sin destroyed us, but grace blots out many sins.)*

17 For if by one man's offence death reigned by one; much more they which receive abundance of grace and of the gift of righteousness shall

reign in life by one, Jesus Christ. *(Ruined by one man's sin, restored by one man's righteousness. The rise will be greater than the fall.)*

18 Therefore as by the offence of one *judgment came* upon all men to condemnation; even so by the righteousness of one *the free gift came* upon all men unto justification of life. *All in Adam fell by Adam, all in Christ are restored by Christ.*

19 For as by one man's disobedience many were made sinners, so by the obedience of one shall many be made righteous. *This is the fundamental doctrine of the gospel; Jesus makes us righteous in his righteousness. We are accepted in the Beloved.*

20 Moreover the law entered, that the offence might abound. *(The law of Moses makes us conscious of sin, it probes our wounds, it brings out into action the evil which lurks in our hearts, and so by the blessing of the Holy Spirit it drives us from self-dependence, and compels us to look to the grace of God in Christ Jesus.)* But where sin abounded, grace did much more abound: *(The floods of grace prevail above the mountains of our sins. Almighty love paints a rainbow on the blackest clouds of human transgression.)*

21 That as sin hath reigned unto death, even so might grace reign through righteousness unto eternal life by Jesus Christ our Lord. *Happy are those in whom reigning grace has implanted spiritual life, for the same grace will sustain, increase, and perfect that life till it melts into glory. Are all the members of this family saved in Christ Jesus? Endeavour every one of you to answer the question. Let us not be divided, but let us together seek the Lord, and may we all meet in heaven.*

We were lost, but we are found,
Dead, but now alive are we;
We were sore in bondage bound,
But our Jesus sets us free.

Strangers, and he takes us in,
Naked, he becomes our dress,
Sick, and he from stain of sin
Cleanses with his righteousness.

Therefore will we sing his praise
Who his lost ones hath restored,
Hearts and voices both shall raise
Hallelujahs to the Lord.

HAVING *by our last reading been taught our own connection with Adam's fall, we will now attentively consider a passage of Scripture which shows the consequent corruption of human nature in all times and places. Let us read:*

ROMANS III. 9—26. ✓

In this portion Paul quotes the words of several Old Testament authors, puts them all together, and presents them to us as a terrible, but truthful, description of fallen man. Of the boastful Jews the apostle asks the question—

9 What then ? are we better *than they ?* No, in no wise: for we have before proved both Jews and Gentiles, that they are all under sin ; *(As an old divine puts it, "whole evil is in man, and whole man in evil.")*

10 As it is written, There is none righteous, no, not one: *(What the prophet said of one is here applied to the whole race, for the nature of man is in all cases the same. Note how strong are the three negatives here, how they quench all hope of finding a natural righteousness in man.)*

11 There is none that understandeth, there is none that seeketh after God.

12 They are all gone out of the way, they are together become unprofitable ; there is none that doeth good, no, not one.

13 Their throat *is* an open sepulchre; with their tongues they have used deceit ; the poison of asps *is* under their lips :

14 Whose mouth *is* full of cursing and bitterness:

15 Their feet *are* swift to shed blood :

16 Destruction and misery *are* in their ways :

17 And the way of peace have they not known :

18 There is no fear of God before their eyes.

See how in character and nature, without and within, in every faculty, in mouth, feet, heart, and eyes, the disease of sin has affected us. We may not actually have committed all the evils here mentioned, but they are all in our nature. Circumstances and education prevent our being so bad in practice as we are in heart, but as the poison is in the viper even when it stings not, so is sin always within us.

What crimson sins are these which defile us ! How divinely powerful must that medicine be which can purge us from such deadly diseases. After this indictment of human nature there

follows *a declaration that by the works of the law none can be saved, since all are already guilty, and the book of the law itself contains the evidence of their guilt and condemnation.*

19 Now we know that what things soever the law saith, it saith to them who are under the law : that every mouth may be stopped, and all the world may become guilty before God.

20 Therefore by the deeds of the law there shall no flesh be justified in his sight: for by the law *is* the knowledge of sin. *(We use the law rightly when it convinces us of sin and drives us to the Saviour, but we altogether abuse and pervert it if we look to be saved by obedience to it.)*

21 But now the righteousness of God without the law is manifested, being witnessed by the law and the prophets ;

22 Even the righteousness of God *which is* by faith of Jesus Christ unto all and upon all them that believe : for there is no difference.

There is no difference in the fact of guilt, in the impossibility of salvation by merit, and in the plain and open way of justification by faith.

23 For all have sinned, and come short of the glory of God ;

24 Being justified freely by his grace through the redemption that is in Christ Jesus :

25 Whom God hath set forth *to be* a propitiation through faith in his blood, to declare his righteousness for the remission of sins that are past, through the forbearance of God ;

26 To declare, *I say*, at this time his righteousness : that he might be just, and the justifier of him which believeth in Jesus.

What a precious gospel verse. May every member of this family understand it, and be a partaker in the substitution of the Lord Jesus. We are all fallen; may every one of us be justified freely by God's grace through faith in the blood of the Lord Jesus. Let us earnestly pray to be cleansed by the atoning death of him who bore for his people all the curse of the law.

To the dear fountain of thy blood,
  Incarnate God, I fly ;
Here let me wash my spotted soul
  From crimes of deepest dye.

A guilty, weak, and helpless worm,
  On thy kind arms I fall ;
Be thou my strength and righteousness,
  My Jesus, and my all.

GENESIS IV. 1—15.

AND Adam knew Eve his wife; and she conceived, and bare Cain, and said, I have gotten a man from the LORD. (*She probably hoped that this was the Messiah. Alas! how often are parents' hopes deceived. It was not "a man—the Lord" who had come to Eve's bosom, but a man of sin, a child of the wicked one.*)

2 And she again bare his brother Abel. (*Her second child she called "Vanity," and yet he was precious in the sight of the Lord. What mistakes we make about our children.*) And Abel was a keeper of sheep, but Cain was a tiller of the ground.

3 And in process of time it came to pass, that Cain brought of the fruit of the ground an offering unto the LORD.

4 And Abel, he also brought of the firstlings of his flock and of the fat thereof. And the LORD had respect unto Abel and to his offering:

5 But unto Cain and to his offering he had not respect. (*Cain had no faith, and he had no eye to the blood of atonement: Abel had both. These should be main points in all our religious duties.*) And Cain was very wroth, and his countenance fell. (*Wroth not with himself as he ought to have been, but with his brother and with God.*)

6 And the LORD said unto Cain, Why art thou wroth? and why is thy countenance fallen?

7 If thou doest well, shalt thou not be accepted? and if thou doest not well, sin lieth at the door. (*It is sin which blocks the way.*)

8, 9 And Cain talked with Abel his brother: and it came to pass, when they were in the field, that Cain rose up against Abel his brother, and slew him. And the LORD said unto Cain, Where is Abel thy brother? And he said, I know not: Am I my brother's keeper? (*We shall either be our brother's keeper or our brother's murderer. If we do not labour to save others, we shall be guilty of their blood.*)

10, 11, 12 And he said, What hast thou done? the voice of thy brother's blood crieth unto me from the ground. And now art thou cursed from the earth, which hath opened her mouth to receive thy brother's blood from thy hand; When thou tillest the ground, it shall not henceforth yield unto thee her strength; a fugitive and a vagabond shalt thou be in the earth.

13 And Cain said unto the LORD, My punishment is greater than I can bear. (*He makes no confession of his sin, but only murmurs at his punishment. We know many whose minds are in a similar state. They cavil at hell, but they persevere in sin.*)

14, 15 Behold, thou hast driven me out this day from the face of the earth; and from thy face shall I be hid; and I shall be a fugitive and a vagabond in the earth; and it shall come to pass, that every one that findeth me shall slay me. And the LORD said unto him, Therefore whosoever slayeth Cain, vengeance shall be taken on him sevenfold. And the LORD set a mark upon Cain, lest any finding him should kill him.

This ancient record of the first murder is used by John as a picture of the action of the unregenerate in all time. Love marks the children of God, and hate is the sure ensign of the heirs of wrath. Thus writes the beloved apostle:—

I JOHN III. 10—15.

10 In this the children of God are manifest, and the children of the devil: whosoever doeth not righteousness is not of God, neither he that loveth not his brother.

11 For this is the message that ye heard from the beginning, that we should love one another.

12 Not as Cain, *who* was of that wicked one, and slew his brother. And wherefore slew he him? Because his own works were evil, and his brother's righteous.

13, 14 Marvel not, my brethren, if the world hate you. We know that we have passed from death unto life, because we love the brethren. He that loveth not *his* brother abideth in death.

15 Whosoever hateth his brother is a murderer: and ye know that no murderer hath eternal life abiding in him.

O for grace to purge our hearts of all anger, envy, malice, and bitterness of every kind, that like Jesus we may be full of love and gentleness.

Lord, from anger purge my heart,
Bid all enmity depart;
New-created from above,
Let my very life be love.

Quench in me each evil fire,
Envious thought or fierce desire.
Flame from heaven upon me fall!
Love of God be all in all.

GENESIS V. 21—24.

OUR *reading leads us to think upon that eminent saint of the antediluvian church, Enoch, the seventh from Adam.*

21, 22, 23, 24 And Enoch lived sixty and five years, and begat Methuselah: And Enoch walked with God after he begat Methuselah three hundred years, and begat sons and daughters: And all the days of Enoch were three hundred sixty and five years : And Enoch walked with God: and he *was* not ; for God took him.

Here it is worthy of notice that the sacred writer says once that Enoch " lived ; " but he changes the word and writes Enoch " walked with God;" thus teaching us that communion with God was Enoch's life, and truly so it ought to be ours. He was not a mere talker about God, but a walker with God. This holy patriarch lived in unbroken intercourse with the Lord for three hundred years, not now and then visiting with God, but habitually walking with him. This is a point of great difficulty. To draw near to God is comparatively easy ; but to remain in undivided fellowship, "this is the work, this is the labour." Yet the Holy Spirit can enable us to accomplish even this. Continued communion is what we should aim at, and we should not be content with anything short of it.

Some excuse themselves from seeking after unbroken fellowship with God because of their calling, their circumstances, and their numerous engagements. Enoch had the cares of a family upon him, and he was also a public preacher, and yet he kept up his walk with God: no business or household cares should make us forget our God. Society with God is the safety of saints, it is their solace and delight, it is their honour and crown. More to be desired is it than gold, yea, than much fine gold. Happy was Enoch to enjoy it so sweetly, and so continuously. The long intercourse of this good man with his God ended in his being borne away from earth without death to that place where faith is lost in sight. He did not live like others, and therefore he did not die like others.

Paul tells us a little more concerning this holy man, and we will gather up the fragments of his history which remain on record, that nothing may be lost.

HEBREWS XI. 5, 6.

5, 6 By faith Enoch was translated that he should not see death ; and was not found, be-cause God had translated him : for before his translation he had this testimony, that he pleased God. But without faith *it is* impossible to please *him :* for he that cometh to God must believe that he is, and *that* he is a rewarder of them that diligently seek him.

Faith was the spring from which his communion was derived. Works do not make us walk with God; but faith brings us into his presence, and keeps us there. It is very likely that Enoch's pious conversation did not please men, but that little mattered since it pleased God.

FROM *Jude we learn that Enoch had an eye to the coming of Christ. The pure in heart who see God are the seers of their age, and look far ahead of others. What Enoch saw he told forth for the warning of others, and it is our duty to do the same, that sinners may be led to flee from the wrath to come.*

JUDE 14, 15.

14 And Enoch also, the seventh from Adam, prophesied of these, saying, Behold, the Lord cometh with ten thousands of his saints,

15 To execute judgment upon all, and to convince all that are ungodly among them of all their ungodly deeds which they have ungodly committed, and of all their hard *speeches* which ungodly sinners have spoken against him.

How important is the doctrine of the advent of the Lord from heaven, since so early in the world's history one of the holiest of prophets proclaimed it. There must surely be some very powerful influence in this truth, since the greatest teachers of it mentioned in Scripture were also among the most eminent for close fellowship with heaven. Enoch "walked with God," Daniel was a "man greatly beloved," and John was "that disciple whom Jesus loved." O Lord, if the expectation of thy coming will make us walk with thee, be pleased to fill us with it.

Sun of my soul, thou Saviour dear,
It is not night if thou be near,
Oh ! may no earth-born cloud arise
To hide thee from thy servant's eyes.

Abide with me from morn till eve,
For without thee I cannot live ;
Abide with me when night is nigh,
For without thee I dare not die.

A T *first men lived for hundreds of years,
but a few generations of long-lived men
sufficed to make the race very wicked ; and, when
the holy seed of Seth intermarried with the
graceless race of Cain, the people of God degenerated, the salt lost its savour, and the whole
earth became corrupt.*

GENESIS VI. 5—22.

5 ¶ And GOD saw that the wickedness of man
was great in the earth, and *that* every imagination
of the thoughts of his heart *was* only evil continually. *(What a charge against man, and it is
true of us all still.)*

6, 7 And it repented the LORD that he had
made man on the earth, and it grieved him at
his heart. And the LORD said, I will destroy
man whom I have created from the face of the
earth; both man, and beast, and the creeping
thing, and the fowls of the air ; for it repenteth
me that I have made them.

8 But Noah found grace in the eyes of the
LORD. *(What a blessed but was that. In the
midst of wrath the Lord remembered mercy; even
as in punishing sin he remembers Christ and all
those who are of his family. The distinction
made was the fruit of grace. It is not said that
Noah deserved preservation, but Noah found
grace.)*

9 ¶ These *are* the generations of Noah :
Noah was a just man *and* perfect in his generations, *and* Noah walked with God. *(In this he
was a worthy descendant of Enoch.)*

10 And Noah begat three sons, Shem, Ham,
and Japheth.

11 The earth also was corrupt before God,
and the earth was filled with violence. *(Those
who are corrupt towards God are sure to be
violent towards men.)*

12, 13 And God looked upon the earth, and,
behold, it was corrupt; for all flesh had corrupted
his way upon the earth. And God said unto
Noah, The end of all flesh is come before me ;
for the earth is filled with violence through
them ; and, behold, I will destroy them with
the earth.

14 ¶ Make thee an ark of gopher wood ;
rooms shalt thou make in the ark, and shalt
pitch it within and without with pitch.

15 And this *is the fashion* which thou shalt
make it *of:* The length of the ark *shall be* three
hundred cubits, the breadth of it fifty cubits, and

the height of it thirty cubits. *(In all our
actions we must follow the divine rule. If our
religious observances have not this inscription
upon them—" Thus saith the Lord," they will
profit us nothing.)*

16 A window shalt thou make to the ark,
and in a cubit shalt thou finish it above; and
the door of the ark shalt thou set in the side
thereof; *with* lower, second, and third *stories*
shalt thou make it. *(Noah must make the ark
after God's plan, and those who expect to be
saved must receive salvation in God's way. Not
our whims but God's word must guide us.)*

17 And, behold, I, even I, do bring a flood
of waters upon the earth, to destroy all flesh,
wherein *is* the breath of life, from under heaven;
and every thing that *is* in the earth shall die.

18, 19, 20 But with thee will I establish my
covenant; and thou shalt come into the ark,
thou, and thy sons, and thy wife, and thy sons'
wives with thee. And of every living thing of
all flesh, two of every *sort* shalt thou bring into
the ark, to keep *them* alive with thee; they shall
be male and female. Of fowls after their kind,
and of cattle after their kind, of every creeping
thing of the earth after his kind, two of every
sort shall come unto thee, to keep *them* alive.
*(As Noah was the preserver of life so is Jesus;
and as he became the new head of the saved race,
so our Lord is the Head of his church, which is
the seed saved out of the world.)*

21 And take thou unto thee of all food that
is eaten, and thou shalt gather *it* to thee; and
it shall be for food for thee, and for them.

22 Thus did Noah ; according to all that God
commanded him, so did he. *(Noah's faith led
him to obedience. If we would be saved from the
destruction which is coming upon the world, we
must submit ourselves without reserve to the commands of our Lord Jesus. We shall not be
saved for keeping the commands of God, but if we
have true faith we shall prove it by following the
Lord's directions.)*

O Lord, we praise thy sovereign grace,
Grace o'er the raging flood supreme.
How well didst thou secure the race
Thou hadst determined to redeem.

They in the ark serenely housed,
Smiled on the universal wreck.
Fierce were the waves by vengeance roused,
But mercy held them all in check.

GENESIS VII.

AND the LORD said unto Noah, Come thou and all thy house into the ark; for thee have I seen righteous before me in this generation. *(When the Lord said, " Come," it was a gracious intimation that he was already in the ark, and meant to be there with his servant. It is also a type of the gospel invitation, " the Spirit and the bride say, Come.")*

2 Of every clean beast thou shalt take to thee by sevens, the male and his female : and of beasts that *are* not clean by two, the male and his female.

3 Of fowls also of the air by sevens, the male and the female; to keep seed alive upon the face of all the earth. *(In Christ, the ark of our salvation, the unclean shall be sheltered as well as the clean. Noah was to bring them in, and such is the privilege of every believer; he is to labour for the saving of the souls of others.)*

4 For yet seven days, and I will cause it to rain upon the earth forty days and forty nights; and every living substance that I have made will I destroy from off the face of the earth.

5 And Noah did according unto all that the LORD commanded him.

¶ 11, 12, 13, 14 In the six hundredth year of Noah's life, in the second month, the seventeenth day of the month, the same day were all the fountains of the great deep broken up, and the windows of heaven were opened. And the rain was upon the earth forty days and forty nights. In the selfsame day entered Noah, and Shem, and Ham, and Japheth, the sons of Noah, and Noah's wife, and the three wives of his sons with them, into the ark; They, and every beast after his kind, and all the cattle after their kind, and every creeping thing that creepeth upon the earth after his kind, and every fowl after his kind, every bird of every sort. *(It was wonderful that all these creatures should willingly enter the ark; and it is even more wonderful that sinners of all kinds should be led by sovereign grace to find refuge in the Lord Jesus. They must come when grace calls.)*

15 And they went in unto Noah into the ark, two and two of all flesh, wherein *is* the breath of life.

16 And they that went in, went in male and female of all flesh, as God had commanded him : and the LORD shut him in. *(What a blessed thing for Noah. Those whom God brings into Christ, he takes care to shut in, so that they shall go no more out. God did not shut Adam in Paradise, and so he threw himself out; and we should every one of us get out of Christ, if the Lord had not in mercy closed the door.)*

17 And the flood was forty days upon the earth; and the waters increased, and bare up the ark, and it was lift up above the earth.

18 And the waters prevailed, and were increased greatly upon the earth; and the ark went upon the face of the waters.

19 And the waters prevailed exceedingly upon the earth; and all the high hills, that *were* under the whole heaven, were covered.

20 Fifteen cubits upward did the waters prevail; and the mountains were covered. *(It was then too late to look to the ark. Dear friends, may we never put off faith in Jesus until it is too late. It will be an awful thing to find ourselves lost in a flood of wrath, with no eye to pity and no arm to save. Yet so it must be if we neglect the great salvation.)*

21 And all flesh died that moved upon the earth, both of fowl, and of cattle, and of beast, and of every creeping thing that creepeth upon the earth, and every man:

22 All in whose nostrils *was* the breath of life, of all that *was* in the dry *land*, died.

23 And every living substance was destroyed which was upon the face of the ground, both man, and cattle, and the creeping things, and the fowl of the heaven; and they were destroyed from the earth: and Noah only remained *alive*, and they that *were* with him in the ark. *(As there was no safety out of the ark, so is there no salvation out of Christ. The Lord grant that every member of this family may flee to Jesus at once, and be saved by faith in him.)*

Come to the ark, come to the ark,
　To Jesus come away :
The floods of wrath are bursting forth,
　O haste to Christ, to-day.

Come to the ark, all, all that weep
　Beneath the sense of sin :
Without, deep calleth unto deep ;
　But all is peace within.

Come to the ark, ere yet the flood
　Your lingering steps oppose ;
Come, for the door which open stood
　Is now about to close.

O UR *last reading showed us Noah saved from amidst a drowning world. This may well lead us to consider the special protection which the Lord grants to his own people, of which the psalmist sings so sweetly in—*

PSALM XCI.

1 He that dwelleth in the secret place of the most High shall abide under the shadow of the Almighty. *(When through the blood of Jesus a soul is brought into sweet fellowship with God, its real dangers are all over: it is, and must be, for ever safe. Noah was secure the moment he entered the ark, and so are we so soon as we are in Christ.)*

2 I will say of the LORD, *He is* my refuge and my fortress: my God; in him will I trust.

3 Surely he shall deliver thee from the snare of the fowler, *and* from the noisome pestilence.

4 He shall cover thee with his feathers, and under his wings shalt thou trust : his truth *shall be thy* shield and buckler. *(What a tender picture. We, like the little birds, hide beneath the wings of God.)*

5 Thou shalt not be afraid for the terror by night; *nor* for the arrow *that* flieth by day;

6 *Nor* for the pestilence *that* walketh in darkness; *nor* for the destruction *that* wasteth at noonday. *(As from apparent dangers so from concealed evils God's people are preserved. There are heresies which would, if it were possible, deceive even the very elect; but they shall not be deceived, for the Lord is their keeper.)*

7 A thousand shall fall at thy side, and ten thousand at thy right hand; *but* it shall not come nigh thee.

8 Only with thine eyes shalt thou behold and see the reward of the wicked.

Noah saw the utter ruin of the ungodly world, and this, no doubt, led him the more devoutly to bless the grace which had rescued him from the like sin and doom.

9 Because thou hast made the LORD, *which is* my refuge, *even* the most High, thy habitation;

10 There shall no evil befall thee, neither shall any plague come nigh thy dwelling.

11 For he shall give his angels charge over thee, to keep thee in all thy ways.

12 They shall bear thee up in *their* hands, lest thou dash thy foot against a stone.

13 Thou shalt tread upon the lion and adder: the young lion and the dragon shalt thou trample under feet. *(Those who sought our destruction shall themselves be overthrown. Their power and subtlety shall not avail them.)*

14 Because he hath set his love upon me, therefore will I deliver him: I will set him on high, because he hath known my name.

15 He shall call upon me, and I will answer him: I *will be* with him in trouble; I will deliver him, and honour him. *(Trouble we must experience, there is no immunity from that, but prayer meets every case, and brings suitable succours under all dangers. Conquered trials honour the Lord who helps us through them, but they also put the honours of experience upon those who have been exercised by them.)*

16 With long life will I satisfy him, and shew him my salvation.

The years of the righteous may be few, and yet they may live long, for men's lives are not to be measured by the years through which they breathe, but by the good they accomplish, the favour of God which they enjoy.

Let us, as a family, thank God that our lives have been preserved from infectious diseases, from sudden death, and from fatal accidents. God's providence is our inheritance. The throne of grace and a promise of being accepted when we approach it are among our choicest treasures. If we be indeed God's children, angel guards are hovering over us at this hour ; and we may rest assured that whatever ills may be abroad, we are safe beneath the wings of God. We ought, therefore, as Christians, to be very calm in troublous times, and show by our holy courage that we have a sure ground of confidence.

Parents, store this Psalm in your hearts, and ye children and young people treasure it in your memories; it is more precious than the much fine gold.

He that hath made his refuge God
Shall find a most secure abode,
Shall walk all day beneath his shade,
And there at night shall rest his head.

Then will I say, " My God, thy power
Shall be my fortress and my tower :
I, that am form'd of feeble dust,
Make thine almighty arm my trust.

GENESIS VIII.

AND God remembered Noah, and every living thing, and all the cattle that *was* with him in the ark : *(The Lord did not forget the saved ones. He thought on Noah first, and then on those with him, and even thus he remembers his dear Son, and us for his sake.)* and God made a wind to pass over the earth, and the waters assuaged;

2 The fountains also of the deep and the windows of heaven were stopped, and the rain from heaven was restrained; *(How readily are all things ordered by the Lord's providence. Winds and waters move at his bidding, as well for the deliverance of his people as for the destruction of his foes.)*

3 And the waters returned from off the earth continually: and after the end of the hundred and fifty days the waters were abated.

4 And the ark rested in the seventh month, on the seventeenth day of the month, upon the mountains of Ararat.

5 And the waters decreased continually until the tenth month: in the tenth *month*, on the first *day* of the month, were the tops of the mountains seen.

6 ¶ And it came to pass at the end of forty days, that Noah opened the window of the ark which he had made:

7 And he sent forth a raven, which went forth to and fro, until the waters were dried up from off the earth. *(This foul bird could light on carrion; just as wicked men find delight in sin.)*

8 Also he sent forth a dove from him, to see if the waters were abated from off the face of the ground;

9 But the dove found no rest for the sole of her foot, and she returned unto him into the ark, for the waters *were* on the face of the whole earth: then he put forth his hand, and took her, and pulled her in unto him in the ark. *(Even thus our weary souls when renewed by grace find no rest in polluted things, but return unto Jesus their rest; and he graciously draws us in to himself when we are too faint to come.)*

10 And he stayed yet other seven days; and again he sent forth the dove out of the ark;

11 And the dove came in to him in the evening; and, lo, in her mouth *was* an olive leaf pluckt off: so Noah knew that the waters were abated from off the earth.

12 And he stayed yet other seven days; and sent forth the dove; which returned not again unto him any more. *(In the new and renovated world the dove could live at liberty, as regenerated souls dwell amid holy things.)*

15 ¶ And God spake unto Noah, saying,

16 Go forth of the ark, thou, and thy wife, and thy sons, and thy sons' wives with thee.

17 Bring forth with thee every living thing that *is* with thee, of all flesh, *both* of fowl, and of cattle, and of every creeping thing that creepeth upon the earth; that they may breed abundantly in the earth, and be fruitful, and multiply upon the earth.

18 And Noah went forth, and his sons, and his wife, and his sons' wives with him:

He did not come forth till he was bidden to do so by the same voice which called him into the ark. The steps of a good man are ordered by the Lord.

19 Every beast, every creeping thing, and every fowl, *and* whatsoever creepeth upon the earth, after their kinds, went forth out of the ark.

20 ¶ And Noah builded an altar unto the LORD; and took of every clean beast, and of every clean fowl, and offered burnt offerings on the altar. *(Before he built a house he built an altar. God must be first worshipped in all things.)*

21 And the LORD smelled a sweet savour; and the LORD said in his heart, I will not again curse the ground any more for man's sake; for the imagination of man's heart *is* evil from his youth; neither will I again smite any more every thing living, as I have done.

22 While the earth remaineth, seed-time and harvest, and cold and heat, and summer and winter, and day and night shall not cease.

Thus Noah's sacrifice was pleasing to the Lord and the ground of a new covenant; and so the offering of the Lord Jesus is evermore a sweet savour, and for his sake the covenant of grace is made with all the saved ones. Have all of us an interest in it?

O Jesus, Saviour of the lost,
Our ark and hiding place,
By storms of sin and sorrow toss'd,
We seek thy sheltering grace.

Forgive our wandering and our sin,
We wish no more to roam;
Open the ark and take us in,
Our soul's eternal home.

IN *this portion we have fuller particulars of the gracious covenant made with Noah and his seed.*

GENESIS IX. 8—17.

8 ¶ And God spake unto Noah, and to his sons with him, saying,

9 And I, behold, I establish my covenant with you, and with your seed after you;

10 And with every living creature that *is* with you, of the fowl, of the cattle, and of every beast of the earth with you; from all that go out of the ark, to every beast of the earth.

11 And I will establish my covenant with you; neither shall all flesh be cut off any more by the waters of a flood; neither shall there any more be a flood to destroy the earth.

To those who have been saved in Christ no future destruction is possible. They are for ever secure from the floods of wrath.

12 And God said, This *is* the token of the covenant which I make between me and you and every living creature that *is* with you, for perpetual generations:

13 I do set my bow in the cloud, and it shall be for a token of a covenant between me and the earth.

14 And it shall come to pass, when I bring a cloud over the earth, that the bow shall be seen in the cloud: (*The covenant sign is seen in cloudy times when faith most requires a seal of the Lord's faithfulness. No cloud, no bow. It is worth while to have a cloud to have a rainbow painted upon it.*)

15 And I will remember my covenant, which *is* between me and you and every living creature of all flesh; and the waters shall no more become a flood to destroy all flesh..

16 And the bow shall be in the cloud; and I will look upon it, (*This is better than man's looking upon it, for He will never gaze with forgetful eye.*) that I may remember the everlasting covenant between God and every living creature of all flesh that *is* upon the earth. (*The word* everlasting *has heavenly music in it. A temporary covenant is of small value, but an everlasting covenant is a wellspring of delight.*)

17 And God said unto Noah, This *is* the token of the covenant, which I have established between me and all flesh that *is* upon the earth.

The rainbow is thus made the lovely symbol of God's truth. A bow unstrung, for war is over;

a bow without a string never to be used against us; a bow turned upward, that we may direct our thoughts and prayers thither; a bow of bright colours, for joy and peace are signified by it. Blessed arch of beauty, be thou to us ever the Lord's preacher.

We will now turn to a passage in the prophets where the covenant of divine grace is linked with this bow.

ISAIAH LIV. 4—10.

4 Fear not; for thou shalt not be ashamed: neither be thou confounded; for thou shalt not be put to shame: for thou shalt forget the shame of thy youth, and shalt not remember the reproach of thy widowhood any more.

5 For thy Maker *is* thine husband; the LORD of hosts *is* his name; and thy Redeemer the Holy One of Israel; The God of the whole earth shall he be called.

6 For the LORD hath called thee as a woman forsaken and grieved in spirit, and a wife of youth, when thou wast refused, saith thy God.

7 For a small moment have I forsaken thee; but with great mercies will I gather thee.

8 In a little wrath I hid my face from thee for a moment; but with everlasting kindness will I have mercy on thee, saith the LORD thy Redeemer.

9 For this *is as* the waters of Noah unto me: for *as* I have sworn that the waters of Noah should no more go over the earth; so have I sworn that I would not be wroth with thee, nor rebuke thee.

10 For the mountains shall depart, and the hills be removed; but my kindness shall not depart from thee, neither shall the covenant of my peace be removed, saith the LORD that hath mercy on thee. (*Let us henceforth be ashamed to doubt the Lord. These steadfast signs should create in us unstaggering confidence in the faithfulness of our immutable God. Only let us make sure that we are exercising true faith in* HIM.)

> The warm affections of his breast
>   Towards his chosen burn;
> And in his love he'll ever rest,
>   Nor from his oath return.
>
> Still to confirm his oath of old,
>   See in the heavens his bow;
> No fierce rebukes, but joys untold
>   Await his children now.

GENESIS XI. 1—9.

AND the whole earth was of one language, and of one speech.

2, 3 And it came to pass, as they journeyed from the east, that they found a plain in the land of Shinar; and they dwelt there. And they said one to another, Go to, let us make brick, and burn them throughly. And they had brick for stone, and slime had they for morter.

4 And they said, Go to, let us build us a city and a tower, whose top *may reach* unto heaven; and let us make us a name, lest we be scattered abroad upon the face of the whole earth. *(They would found a universal monarchy of which this tower should be the centre. They planned the tower that they might not be scattered, and they thus forgot the command to replenish the earth. Ambition was at the bottom of the plan; by centralising all mankind they hoped to build up an empire, which, like their tower, should defy heaven itself.)*

5 And the LORD came down to see the city and the tower, which the children of men builded.

To him their huge tower was a mere nothing; he is said, after the manner of men, to come down from heaven in order to see such a trifle.

6, 7 And the LORD said, Behold, the people *is* one, and they have all one language; and this they begin to do: and now nothing will be restrained from them, which they have imagined to do. Go to, let us go down, and there confound their language, that they may not understand one another's speech.

8 So the LORD scattered them abroad from thence upon the face of all the earth: and they left off to build the city. *(How easily can God thwart our plans, and bring to pass his own purposes, despite all opposition. The scene has been very graphically sketched by* Bishop Hall. " *One calls for brick, the other looks him in the face, and wonders what he commands, and how and why he speaks such words as were never heard, and instead thereof brings him mortar, returning him an answer as little understood; each chides with other, expressing his choler, so as he only can understand himself. From heat they fall to quiet entreaties, but still with the same success. At first every man thinks his fellow mocks him; but now perceiving this serious confusion, their only answer was silence, and ceasing: they could not come together, for no man*

could call them to be understood; and if they had assembled, nothing could be determined, because one could never attain to the other's purpose.")

9 Therefore is the name of it called Babel; because the LORD did there confound the language of all the earth: and from thence did the LORD scatter them abroad upon the face of all the earth.

AS *a fit comment on the transaction at Babel we will read a part of*

PSALM XXXIII. 10—22.

10 The LORD bringeth the counsel of the heathen to nought: he maketh the devices of the people of none effect.

11 The counsel of the LORD standeth for ever, the thoughts of his heart to all generations.

12 Blessed *is* the nation whose God *is* the LORD; *and* the people *whom* he hath chosen for his own inheritance.

13, 14, 15 The LORD looketh from heaven; he beholdeth all the sons of men. From the place of his habitation he looketh upon all the inhabitants of the earth. He fashioneth their hearts alike; he considereth all their works.

16 There is no king saved by the multitude of an host: a mighty man is not delivered by much strength.

17 An horse *is* a vain thing for safety: neither shall he deliver *any* by his great strength.

18 Behold, the eye of the LORD *is* upon them that fear him, upon them that hope in his mercy;

19 To deliver their soul from death, and to keep them alive in famine.

20, 21 Our soul waiteth for the LORD: he *is* our help and our shield. For our heart shall rejoice in him, because we have trusted in his holy name.

22 Let thy mercy, O LORD, be upon us, according as we hope in thee. *(We have done with self-confidence which is but a vain tower of Babel, and we fly unto the Lord our God who is a tower of defence to save us.)*

In his providential reign,
Oh, what various wisdom shines!
He confounds the pride of man,
Blasts the people's vain designs;

Brings their counsels all to nought;
Only his abideth sure;
What the gracious Lord has thought
Shall from age to age endure.

GENESIS XII. 1—8.

NOW the LORD had said unto Abram, Get thee out of thy country, and from thy kindred, and from thy father's house, unto a land that I will shew thee:

2 And I will make of thee a great nation, and I will bless thee, and make thy name great; and thou shalt be a blessing:

3 And I will bless them that bless thee, and curse him that curseth thee: and in thee shall all families of the earth be blessed.

God had elected Abram, and therefore in due time he called him, and so separated him unto himself. All the chosen seed must in this be conformed to the father of the faithful.

4 So Abram departed, as the LORD had spoken unto him; and Lot went with him: and Abram *was* seventy and five years old when he departed out of Haran. *(The grace which chose him made him obedient, and he left all at the divine command. Only in the separated life could he inherit the blessing, and therefore he cheerfully forsook all to follow his Lord.)*

5 And Abram took Sarai his wife, and Lot his brother's son, and all their substance that they had gathered, and the souls that they had gotten in Haran; and they went forth to go into the land of Canaan; and into the land of Canaan they came. *(It is not enough to set out, we must persevere to the end.)*

6 ¶ And Abram passed through the land unto the place of Sichem, unto the plain of Moreh. And the Canaanite *was* then in the land. *(Though the land was given to the patriarch by promise, yet he did not actually possess a single foot of it. Unbelief would have reckoned this to be a very shadowy inheritance; but faith is the substance of things hoped for, and makes us content to wait. The Canaanite is still in the land, yet we rightly reckon that all things are ours.)*

7 And the LORD appeared unto Abram, and said, Unto thy seed will I give this land: and there builded he an altar unto the LORD, who appeared unto him.

8 And he removed from thence unto a mountain on the east of Beth-el: and there he builded an altar unto the LORD, and called upon the name of the LORD. *(The patriarch was careful to maintain the worship of God wherever he might be placed. Go where we may, let us not forget to render devotion and obedience to God.)*

THE *secret of Abram's prompt action may be seen in—*

HEBREWS XI. 8—10.

8 By faith Abraham, when he was called to go out into a place which he should after receive for an inheritance, obeyed; and he went out, not knowing whither he went.

9 By faith he sojourned in the land of promise, as *in* a strange country, dwelling in tabernacles with Isaac and Jacob, the heirs with him of the same promise:

10 For he looked for a city which hath foundations, whose builder and maker *is* God.

Abram had to come out from idolatrous Chaldea, and so must we be separate from the world which lieth in the wicked one. He became a pilgrim and a sojourner, and so must we. This is not our rest, ours is a pilgrim's life, we are wanderers till we reach the city which hath foundations. He pitched his tent and wandered up and down in the land as a stranger, but he was no Canaanite: here we have no continuing city, but we seek one to come. He who finds a rest here has none in heaven.

II CORINTHIANS VI. 14—18.

14, 15 Be ye not unequally yoked together with unbelievers: for what fellowship hath righteousness with unrighteousness? and what communion hath light with darkness? And what concord hath Christ with Belial? or what part hath he that believeth with an infidel?

16 And what agreement hath the temple of God with idols? for ye are the temple of the living God; as God hath said, I will dwell in them, and walk in *them;* and I will be their God, and they shall be my people.

17 Wherefore come out from among them, and be ye separate, saith the Lord, and touch not the unclean *thing;* and I will receive you,

18 And will be a Father unto you, and ye shall be my sons and daughters, saith the Lord Almighty. *(Oh, that the Lord may make us, as a family, separated unto himself.)*

We've no abiding city here;
Then let us live as pilgrims do:
Let not the world our rest appear,
But let us haste from all below.

We've no abiding city here;
We seek a city out of sight:
Zion's its name—the Lord is there;
It shines with everlasting light.

GENESIS XII. 10—20.

AND there was a famine in the land : and Abram went down into Egypt to sojourn there ; for the famine *was* grievous in the land.

11, 12 And it came to pass, when he was come near to enter into Egypt, that he said unto Sarai his wife, Behold now, I know that thou *art* a fair woman to look upon : therefore it shall come to pass, when the Egyptians shall see thee, that they shall say, This *is* his wife : and, they will kill me, but they will save thee alive.

13 Say, I pray thee, thou *art* my sister : that it may be well with me for thy sake ; and my soul shall live because of thee. *(To say that she was his sister was part of the truth, but the intention was to deceive. Whether what we say be true or not, if our object be to mislead others, we are guilty of falsehood. Let us pray for grace to be strictly truthful.)*

14 ¶ And it came to pass, that, when Abram was come into Egypt, the Egyptians beheld the woman that she *was* very fair.

15 The princes also of Pharaoh saw her, and commended her before Pharaoh : and the woman was taken into Pharaoh's house.

16 And he entreated Abram well for her sake : and he had sheep, and oxen, and he asses, and menservants, and maidservants, and she asses, and camels. *(Yet surely these gifts must have given Abram but little pleasure ; he must have felt mean in spirit and sick at heart.)*

17 And the LORD plagued Pharaoh and his house with great plagues because of Sarai Abram's wife.

18 And Pharaoh called Abram, and said, What *is* this *that* thou hast done unto me ? why didst thou not tell me that she *was* thy wife ?

19 Why saidst thou, She *is* my sister ? so I might have taken her to me to wife : now therefore behold thy wife, take *her*, and go thy way. *(It must have been very humbling to the man of God to be rebuked by a heathen. It is sad indeed when the worldling shames the believer ; yet it is too often the case.)*

20 And Pharaoh commanded *his* men concerning him : and they sent him away, and his wife, and all that he had.

From this Scripture we learn that the best of men, though in the path of duty, will nevertheless have their trials. It is Abram, he is a pilgrim according to God's command, and yet he is afflicted by the famine which falls upon the land in which he dwells. Trials find out the weak places in good men, and even the holy patriarch had some blemishes. He went into Egypt, into a land where he had no right to be : he was out of the path of duty, and therefore out of the place of safety. On the devil's ground he was in slippery places, and found it hard to maintain his uprightness. He equivocated, in order to save himself and Sarai ; he deceived Pharaoh by telling him only half the truth, and he exposed his wife to great peril : all this arose out of the unbelief which marred even the mighty faith of the father of the faithful. The best of men are but men at the best, and this record suffices to show us that even the chief of the patriarchs was a man of like passions with ourselves. Why can we not have Abram's faith, since Abram had our infirmities ? The same Spirit can work in us also a majestic faith, and lead us to triumph by its power.

GENESIS XIII. 1—4.

AND Abram went up out of Egypt, he, and his wife, and all that he had, and Lot with him, into the south. *(He did not feel safe till he had returned to his separated condition. Association with the world is not good for the believer's soul. The more he is a sojourner with his God, and a separatist from sinners, the better.)*

2, 3, 4 And Abram *was* very rich in cattle, in silver, and in gold. And he went on his journeys from the south even to Beth-el, unto the place where his tent had been at the beginning, between Beth-el and Hai ; unto the place of the altar, which he had made there at the first : and there Abram called on the name of the LORD. *(Doubtless he confessed his sinful weakness, and renewed the allegiance of his faith in God. If we have erred or backslidden, let us also return to our first love, to that Bethel where first we set up an altar unto the Lord.)*

Oh send thy Spirit down, to write
Thy law upon my heart !
Nor let my tongue indulge deceit,
Nor act the liar's part.

Order my footsteps by thy word,
And make my heart sincere ;
Let sin have no dominion, Lord,
But keep my conscience clear.

20   " All things are yours."   JANUARY 10.—EVENING

[*Or January* 20.]

GENESIS XIII. 5—18.

AND Lot also, which went with Abram, had flocks, and herds, and tents. And the land was not able to bear them, that they might dwell together: for their substance was great, so that they could not dwell together.

7 And there was a strife between the herdmen of Abram's cattle and the herdmen of Lot's cattle. *(Rich men may be godly, and godly men may be rich, but riches are the sure source of trial. In this case abundance did not bring peace, but became the source of discomfort. Good men cannot rule their servants' tempers, even though they control their own. When relatives dwell together they must be very careful, lest they be made to disagree through their servants. It is a rare thing for relations in the second degree to live in the same house without strife; and it becomes every inmate of such a household to watch against suspicions, envies, and bickerings.)* And the Canaanite and the Perizzite dwelled then in the land. *(The presence of such powerful enemies ought to have made these good men cautious how they disagreed. Since the eyes of the world are upon us we must be careful how we act. Let not a Christian household make sport for worldlings by internal disagreements.)*

8 And Abram said unto Lot, Let there be no strife, I pray thee, between me and thee, and between my herdmen and thy herdmen; for we *be* brethren.

9 *Is* not the whole land before thee ? separate thyself, I pray thee, from me : if *thou wilt take* the left hand, then I will go to the right; or if *thou depart* to the right hand, then I will go to the left. *(Abram was the older, the greater, the richer, and the better man, yet he gave way to his nephew. In all differences it becomes the more powerful to be the first to yield. By so doing he will prove himself to be of the nobler disposition. Abram's faith brought forth in this case the fruit of a noble, generous, yielding spirit. All true faith is thus fruitful.)*

10, 11 And Lot lifted up his eyes, and beheld all the plain of Jordan, that it *was* well watered every where, before the LORD destroyed Sodom and Gomorrah, *even* as the garden of the LORD, like the land of Egypt, as thou comest unto Zoar. Then Lot chose him all the plain of Jordan; and Lot journeyed east : and they separated themselves the one from the other.

12 Abram dwelled in the land of Canaan, and Lot dwelled in the cities of the plain, and pitched *his* tent toward Sodom.

13 But the men of Sodom *were* wicked and sinners before the LORD exceedingly.

This was a grave fault on Lot's part. He looked only to the richness of the country, and not to the character of the people. He walked by sight not. by faith ; he looked at temporal advantage, and did not seek first the kingdom of God. Hence he became worldly himself, and gave up the separated life of faith to go and dwell in a city ; thus he forfeited all claim to the promised inheritance, and pierced himself through with many sorrows. In the end, he who sought this world lost it, and he who was willing to give up anything for the honour of God found it.

When friends leave us we may look for renewed visits from the Lord to sustain and console us, for when Lot was gone the Lord appeared again to Abram.

14 ¶ And the LORD said unto Abram, after that Lot was separated from him, Lift up now thine eyes, and look from the place where thou art northward, and southward, and eastward, and westward :

15 For all the land which thou seest, to thee will I give it, and to thy seed for ever.

16 And I will make thy seed as the dust of the earth : so that if a man can number the dust of the earth, *then* shall thy seed also be numbered.

17 Arise, walk through the land in the length of it and in the breadth of it; for I will give it unto thee. *(He was bidden to survey his possessions and walk abroad like an owner in his own grounds : even thus may our faith behold the covenant blessings which are ours in Christ Jesus, and we may rejoice in them with joy unspeakable.)*

18 Then Abram removed *his* tent, and came and dwelt in the plain of Mamre, which *is* in Hebron, and built there an altar unto the LORD.

So let our lips and lives express
The holy gospel we profess ;
So let our works and virtues shine,
To prove the doctrine all divine.

Thus shall we best proclaim abroad
The honours of our Saviour God,
When his salvation reigns within,
And grace subdues the power of sin.

GENESIS XIV. 1—3; 10—24.

AND it came to pass in the days of Amraphel king of Shinar, Arioch king of Ellasar, Chedorlaomer king of Elam, and Tidal king of nations; *that these* made war with Bera king of Sodom, and with Birsha king of Gomorrah, Shinab king of Admah, and Shemeber king of Zeboiim and the king of Bela, which is Zoar.

3 All these were joined together in the vale of Siddim, which is the salt sea.

10, 11, 12 And the vale of Siddim *was full of* slimepits; and the kings of Sodom and Gomorrah fled, and fell there; and they that remained fled to the mountain. And they took all the goods of Sodom and Gomorrah, and all their victuals, and went their way. And they took Lot, Abram's brother's son, who dwelt in Sodom, and his goods, and departed. *(All is not gold that glitters. Lot had made a poor choice after all. Those believers who conform to the world must expect to suffer for it. For the sake of gain Lot went to Sodom, and now he loses all at a blow: if we are too careful to grow rich, the Lord can soon impoverish us.)*

14 And when Abram heard that his brother was taken captive, he armed his trained *servants*, born in his own house, three hundred and eighteen, and pursued *them* unto Dan. *(If our relatives desert us we must not desert them. Lot left Abram but Abram did not forget Lot.)*

15 And he divided himself against them, he and his servants, by night, and smote them, and pursued them unto Hobah, which *is* on the left hand of Damascus.

16 And he brought back all the goods, and also brought again his brother Lot, and his goods, and the women also, and the people. *Thus whether in peace or war faith made Abram the victor; but, alas for poor Lot, his worldly conformity was not cured by his trouble, for he went back again to Sodom to reside in it. He was vexed by the sins of the city, but he loved the ease of its settled life.*

¶ 17, 18 And the king of Sodom went out to meet him after his return from the slaughter of Chedorlaomer, and of the kings that *were* with him, at the valley of Shaveh, which *is* the king's dale. And Melchizedek king of Salem brought forth bread and wine: and he *was* the priest of the most high God. *(When we are weary with fighting the Lord's battles, we may expect that Jesus will appear to our refreshment.)*

19 And he blessed him, and said, Blessed *be* Abram of the most high God, possessor of heaven and earth: *(The Lord Jesus never meets his people without blessing them: his lips are like lilies dropping sweet-smelling myrrh.)*

20 And blessed be the most high God, which hath delivered thine enemies into thy hand. And he gave him tithes of all. *(To our great Melchizedek we cheerfully offer of our substance. Melchizedek was rightly a receiver of Abram's temporals, since Abram had received of his spirituals.)*

21 And the king of Sodom said unto Abram, Give me the persons, and take the goods to thyself. *(He felt no interest in what was passing between Abram and Melchizedek, but broke in upon their holy intercourse with his secular business.)*

22, 23, 24 And Abram said to the king of Sodom, I have lift up mine hand unto the LORD, the most high God, the possessor of heaven and earth, that I will not *take* from a thread even to a shoelatchet, and that I will not take any thing that *is* thine, lest thou shouldest say, I have made Abram rich: Save only that which the young men have eaten, and the portion of the men which went with me, Aner, Eshcol, and Mamre; let them take their portion. *(What the king of Sodom offered was Abram's due by the laws of war, but he would not take it. Sometimes it is right to waive our rights. Abram felt that God could give him all he needed without his being beholden to the king of Sodom. Faith is royally independent of man. She will not give the world an opportunity to stop her glorying in the Lord. Jehovah All-sufficient is enough for us without our leaning upon an arm of flesh.)*

King of Salem, bless my soul!
Make a wounded sinner whole!
King of righteousness and peace,
Let not thy sweet visits cease!

Come, refresh this soul of mine
With thy sacred bread and wine!
All thy love to me unfold,
Half of which can not be told.

Hail, Melchizedek divine;
Great High-Priest, thou shalt be mine;
All my powers before thee fall;
Take not tithe, but take them all.

I T *would be unwise to pass by the story of Melchizedek without noticing its typical meaning. This is fully expounded to us in—*

HEBREWS VII. 1—25.

1, 2, 3 For this Melchisedec, king of Salem, priest of the most high God, who met Abram returning from the slaughter of the kings, and blessed him ; To whom also Abraham gave a tenth part of all; first being by interpretation King of righteousness, and after that also King of Salem, which is, King of peace; Without father, without mother, without descent, having neither beginning of days, nor end of life ; but made like unto the Son of God; abideth a priest continually. *(No ancestors, or predecessors, or successors to Melchisedec are mentioned, and the apostle finds a meaning in the silence of Scripture. Some will not learn from what the Bible plainly says ; but the apostle could learn even from what it does not say. In Melchisedec the regal and priestly offices were united, and he received his priesthood not by inheritance, but by an immediate divine ordination. In these things he was eminently a type of our Lord Jesus.)*

4 Now consider how great this man *was*, unto whom even the patriarch Abraham gave the tenth of the spoils.

5 And verily they that are of the sons of Levi, who receive the office of the priesthood, have a commandment to take tithes of the people according to the law, that is, of their brethren, though they come out of the loins of Abraham :

6, 7 But he whose descent is not counted from them received tithes of Abraham, and blessed him that had the promises. And without all contradiction the less is blessed of the better.

8, 9, 10 And here men that die receive tithes ; but there he *receiveth them*, of whom it is witnessed that he liveth. And as I may so say, Levi also, who receiveth tithes, payed tithes in Abraham. For he was yet in the loins of his father, when Melchisedec met him.

11 If therefore perfection were by the Levitical priesthood, (for under it the people received the law,) what further need *was there* that another priest should rise after the order of Melchisedec, and not be called after the order of Aaron ?

12 For the priesthood being changed, there is made of necessity a change also of the law.

13, 14 For he of whom these things are spoken pertaineth to another tribe, of which no man gave attendance at the altar. For *it is* evident that our Lord sprang out of Juda; of which tribe Moses spake nothing concerning priesthood. *(Therefore our Lord did not receive the priesthood by descent, but, like Melchisedec, his ordination was direct from God.)*

15, 16, 17 And it is yet far more evident: for that after the similitude of Melchisedec there ariseth another priest, Who is made, not after the law of a carnal commandment, but after the power of an endless life. For he testifieth, Thou *art* a priest for ever after the order of Melchisedec. *(This is the inspired testimony of David in Psalm cx., where he speaks of the Lord Jesus as his Lord, and salutes him as king and priest.)*

20, 21, 22 And inasmuch as not without an oath *he was made priest*: (For those priests were made without an oath; but this with an oath by him that said unto him, The Lord sware and will not repent, Thou *art* a priest for ever after the order of Melchisedec :) By so much was Jesus made a surety of a better testament. *(The priesthood of Jesus therefore deals with sure things which cannot pass away or change, since the oath of God confirms them.)*

23, 24, 25 And they truly were many priests, because they were not suffered to continue by reason of death : But this *man*, because he continueth ever, hath an unchangeable priesthood. Wherefore he is able also to save them to the uttermost that come unto God by him, seeing he ever liveth to make intercession for them.

Jesus resembles Melchisedec in being both king and priest, in having no predecessor or successor in office, and in being greater than the Levitical Priesthood. He is a priest for ever by the oath of God, and we who trust in him have this sweet consolation that our Great High Priest ever lives, is always in power, is always accessible, and always ready to perform his office on our behalf.

Thou dear Redeemer, dying Lamb,
  We love to hear of thee ;
No music's like thy charming name,
  Nor half so sweet can be.

Oh may we ever hear thy voice,
  In mercy to us speak ;
And in our Priest we will rejoice,
  Thou great Melchizedek.

GENESIS XV. 1—18.

AFTER these things the word of the LORD came unto Abram in a vision, saying, Fear not, Abram , I *am* thy shield, *and* thy exceeding great reward. (*Let those fear who touch the Lord's anointed, but as for those who trust in the living God they have no cause for alarm. Five kings or fifty kings may come against them, but while Jehovah defends them they are secure. Perhaps the Lord saw a rising fear in Abram's mind, and therefore came to him with this word of comfort: God is not willing that his servants should be in bondage to fear.*)

2, 3 And Abram said, Lord GOD, what wilt thou give me, seeing I go childless, and the steward of my house *is* this Eliezer of Damascus? And Abram said, Behold, to me thou hast given no seed: and, lo, one born in my house is mine heir.

4 And, behold, the word of the LORD *came* unto him, saying, This shall not be thine heir; but he that shall come forth out of thine own bowels shall be thine heir. (*The strongest faith has its conflicts. Abram's heart was set upon being the progenitor of the Messiah, and he believed in the promise of God that he should be so, but still it appeared impossible, for he had no son, nor did it appear likely that he would ever have one. It is wise always to spread our doubts before the Lord, for he can meet them for us.*)

5 And he brought him forth abroad, and said, Look now toward heaven, and tell the stars, if thou be able to number them: and he said unto him, So shall thy seed be.

6 And he believed in the LORD; and he counted it to him for righteousness. (*Over the head of every difficulty and physical impossibility he believed in God; and therefore he stood accepted as righteous before the Lord.*)

7, 8, 9, 10, 11 And he said unto him, I *am* the LORD that brought thee out of Ur of the Chaldees, to give thee this land to inherit it. And he said, Lord GOD, whereby shall I know that I shall inherit it? And he said unto him, Take me an heifer of three years old, and a she goat of three years old, and a ram of three years old, and a turtle dove, and a young pigeon. And he took unto him all these, and divided them in the midst, and laid each piece one against another: but the birds divided he not. And when the fowls came down upon the carcases, Abram drove them away. (*The sacrifice ratifying the covenant is the most satisfying food for faith. Let us see Jesus confirming the promises and we are content. True, a few distracting questions like these ravenous birds will molest us, but by faith we chase them away. When the Lord covenanted with his servant over the bodies of the beasts slain in sacrifice, he gave him the strongest possible confirmation; and in the death of Jesus we have solid assurance that the promises shall all be fulfilled.*)

12 And when the sun was going down, a deep sleep fell upon Abram; and, lo, an horror of great darkness fell upon him.

13, 14, 15, 16 And he said unto Abram, Know of a surety that thy seed shall be a stranger in a land *that is* not their's, and shall serve them; and they shall afflict them four hundred years; And also that nation, whom they shall serve, will I judge: and afterward shall they come out with great substance. And thou shalt go to thy fathers in peace; thou shalt be buried in a good old age. But in the fourth generation they shall come hither again: for the iniquity of the Amorites *is* not yet full.

17 And it came to pass, that, when the sun went down, and it was dark, behold a smoking furnace, and a burning lamp that passed between those pieces. (*This symbolised the history of the chosen seed: the furnace of affliction with its darkening smoke is often theirs, but the lamp of God's salvation is never removed from them.*)

18 In the same day the LORD made a covenant with Abram, saying, Unto thy seed have I given this land, from the river of Egypt unto the great river, the river Euphrates. (*Thus was the fear of Abram cured by the covenant: let us ever resort to the same remedy.*)

'Tis mine the covenant of grace,
    And every promise mine;
All flowing from eternal love,
    And sealed by blood divine.

On my unworthy, favour'd head,
    Its blessings all unite;
Blessings more numerous than the stars,
    More lasting and more bright.

That covenant the last accent claims
    Of this poor faltering tongue;
And that shall the first notes employ
    Of my celestial song.

ROMANS IV. 1—25.

PAUL *was moved by the Spirit to explain to us the bearings of the solemn transaction which we considered in our last reading. Let us hear his exposition.*

1 What shall we say then that Abraham our father, as pertaining to the flesh, hath found?

2 For if Abraham were justified by works, he hath *whereof* to glory; but not before God.

3, 4, 5 For what saith the scripture? Abraham believed God, and it was counted unto him for righteousness. Now to him that worketh is the reward not reckoned of grace, but of debt. But to him that worketh not, but believeth on him that justifieth the ungodly, his faith is counted for righteousness.

6, 7, 8 Even as David also describeth the blessedness of the man, unto whom God imputeth righteousness without works, *Saying,* Blessed *are* they whose iniquities are forgiven, and whose sins are covered. Blessed *is* the man to whom the Lord will not impute sin.

9, 10 *Cometh* this blessedness then upon the circumcision *only,* or upon the uncircumcision also? for we say that faith was reckoned to Abraham for righteousness. How was it then reckoned? when he was in circumcision, or in uncircumcision? Not in circumcision, but in uncircumcision.

11 And he received the sign of circumcision, a seal of the righteousness of the faith which *he had yet* being uncircumcised: that he might be the father of all them that believe, though they be not circumcised; that righteousness might be imputed unto them also:

12 And the father of circumcision to them who are not of the circumcision only, but who also walk in the steps of that faith of our father Abraham, which *he had* being *yet* uncircumcised.

13 For the promise, that he should be the heir of the world, *was* not to Abraham, or to his seed, through the law, but through the righteousness of faith.

14, 15 For if they which are of the law *be* heirs, faith is made void, and the promise made of none effect: Because the law worketh wrath: for where no law is, *there is* no transgression.

16 Therefore *it is* of faith, that *it might be* by grace; to the end the promise might be sure to all the seed; not to that only which is of the law, but to that also which is of the faith of Abraham; who is the father of us all,

17 (As it is written, I have made thee a father of many nations,) before him whom he believed, *even* God, who quickeneth the dead, and calleth those things which be not as though they were.

18, 19, 20, 21, 22 Who against hope believed in hope, that he might become the father of many nations, according to that which was spoken, So shall thy seed be. And being not weak in faith, he considered not his own body now dead, when he was about an hundred years old, neither yet the deadness of Sarah's womb: He staggered not at the promise of God through unbelief; but was strong in faith, giving glory to God; And being fully persuaded that, what he had promised, he was able also to perform. And therefore it was imputed to him for righteousness.

23, 24, 25 Now it was not written for his sake alone, that it was imputed to him; But for us also, to whom it shall be imputed, if we believe on him that raised up Jesus our Lord from the dead; Who was delivered for our offences, and was raised again for our justification. *(The argument is very clear and conclusive. Abraham was justified by faith, therefore by grace; and this justification was not given to him as a circumcised man, for he was not circumcised till years after; therefore the covenant blessings are not given in connection with the law and its work, but in connection with faith and grace. The covenant promise was made to a seed to be born not after the flesh but according to promise, and in that promise all nations had an interest, for out of them would come a blessed people whose badge should be faith, and not the deeds of the law. Jesus is the promised seed, and those believing in him are Abraham's seed. Are we all in this family believers in Jesus? Who is there among us unsaved? Pass the solemn question round.)*

No more, my God, I boast no more
Of all the duties I have done;
I quit the hopes I held before,
To trust the merits of thy Son.

The best obedience of my hands
Dares not appear before thy throne;
But faith can answer thy demands,
By pleading what my Lord has done.

GENESIS XVI.

NOW Sarai Abram's wife bare him no children : and she had an handmaid, an Egyptian, whose name *was* Hagar. *(Sarai therefore proposed to Abram that Hagar should become his secondary wife. This was a very usual custom in those days, but it was not a commendable one, and it was an unbelieving act on Sarai's part to propose it.*

It is not always easy to patiently wait the Lord's time. We are all too apt to run to expedients of our own ; as if the Lord needed our help to fulfil his promises.)

2 And Abram hearkened to the voice of Sarai. *(Thus those we love best may be the means of leading us astray. The father of mankind sinned by hearkening to his wife, and now the father of the faithful follows his example.)*

3 And Sarai Abram's wife took Hagar her maid the Egyptian, after Abram had dwelt ten years in the land of Canaan, and gave her to her husband Abram to be his wife.

4 ¶ And when Hagar saw that she had conceived, her mistress was despised in her eyes.

5 And Sarai said unto Abram, My wrong *be* upon thee : I have given my maid into thy bosom ; and when she saw that she had conceived, I was despised in her eyes : the LORD judge between me and thee. *(It was Sarai who proposed the arrangement, and now she upbraids her husband for it. It is of no use to lay the blame of our faults upon others, for if we step out of the straight path we shall be sure personally to smart for it.)*

6 But Abram said unto Sarai, Behold, thy maid *is* in thy hand ; do to her as it pleaseth thee. And when Sarai dealt hardly with her, she fled from her face.

Thus Sarai was first unbelieving to God, next unkind to her husband, and then cruel to her servant ; so one wrong step leads to others. Unbelief sins, and produces other sins. Even this holy woman was not without infirmity. " There is none good, save one, that is God."

7 ¶ And the angel of the LORD found her by a fountain of water in the wilderness, by the fountain in the way to Shur.

8 And he said, Hagar, Sarai's maid, whence camest thou ? and whither wilt thou go ? And she said, I flee from the face of my mistress

Sarai. *(She did not say where she was going, for she did not know. Let each of us ask himself. " Whither am I going?")*

9 And the angel of the LORD said unto her, Return to thy mistress, and submit thyself under her hands.

10 And the angel of the LORD said unto her, I will multiply thy seed exceedingly, that it shall not be numbered for multitude. *(No one could use such language as this but the Angel of the Covenant. Here is a proof of the inspired declaration, " My delights were with the sons of men.")*

11 And the angel of the LORD said unto her, Behold, thou *art* with child, and shalt bear a son, and shalt call his name Ishmael ; because the LORD hath heard thy affliction.

12 And he will be a wild man ; his hand *will be* against every man, and every man's hand against him ; and he shall dwell in the presence of all his brethren.

13 And she called the name of the LORD that spake unto her, Thou God seest me : for she said, Have I also here looked after him that seeth me ? *(First, God sees us ; and then, by his gracious visitations, he leads us to look after himself.)*

14 Wherefore the well was called Beer-lahairoi ; *(The well of the living One, my Seer ;)* behold, *it is* between Kadesh and Bered.

15 ¶ And Hagar bare Abram a son : and Abram called his son's name, which Hagar bare, Ishmael. *(But this was not, as he had hoped, the promised heir ; on the contrary, he became the occasion of much trial to the family. When we call in legality to help grace, or sight to assist faith, we miss our object, and ensure for ourselves no little sorrow. The whole scene is a painful one, and should warn us that even in a gracious household sin may sow dissension, and cause heartburnings and distress.)*

Quick as the apple of an eye,
O God, my conscience make !
Awake my soul, when sin is nigh,
And keep it still awake.

Oh may the least omission pain
My well-instructed soul ;
And drive me to the blood again,
Which makes the wounded whole !

HAGAR *in the desert learned the omniscience of God, and exclaimed, " Thou God seest me:" it will profit us if we meditate at this time upon that solemn truth, as we find it written out at large in—*

PSALM CXXXIX.

1, 2, 3 O LORD, thou hast searched me, and known *me.* Thou knowest my downsitting and mine uprising, thou understandest my thought afar off. Thou compassest my path and my lying down, and art acquainted *with* all my ways. *Rising or resting, God beholds me. Awake or asleep, his eye is upon me!*

4 For *there is* not a word in my tongue, *but,* lo, O LORD, thou knowest it altogether. *(Not only the words* on *my tongue which have been uttered, but those* in *my tongue which as yet have not been sounded. The words I mean to speak he knows.)*

5 Thou hast beset me behind and before, and laid thine hand upon me.

6 *Such* knowledge *is* too wonderful for me; it is high, I cannot *attain* unto it.

7 Whither shall I go from thy spirit? or whither shall I flee from thy presence?

8 If I ascend up into heaven, thou *art* there : if I make my bed in hell, behold, thou *art there.*

9 *If* I take the wings of the morning, *and* dwell in the uttermost parts of the sea;

10 Even there shall thy hand lead me, and thy right hand shall hold me.

11 If I say, Surely the darkness shall cover me; even the night shall be light about me.

12 Yea, the darkness hideth not from thee; but the night shineth as the day : the darkness and the light *are* both alike *to thee.*

13 For thou hast possessed my reins: *(The most secret parts of my being thou dost penetrate with a glance:)* thou hast covered me in my mother's womb.

14 I will praise thee; for I am fearfully *and* wonderfully made : marvellous *are* thy works; and *that* my soul knoweth right well.

15 My substance was not hid from thee, when I was made in secret, *and* curiously wrought in the lowest parts of the earth. *(Our bodily frame is like a very skilful piece of embroidery, " curiously wrought;" its nerves, veins, and muscles are fashioned with divine art. At our first formation the wisdom of the Lord was present, working all things with benevolent design. He* who made the watch understands *it, and even thus the Creator knows all the secret workings of our souls.)*

16 Thine eyes did see my substance, yet being unperfect; and in thy book all *my members* were written, *which* in continuance were fashioned, when *as yet there was* none of them.

17 How precious also are thy thoughts unto me, O God! how great is the sum of them!

18 *If* I should count them, they are more in number than the sand : when I awake, I am still with thee. *(The omniscient eye is not that of an enemy, but an eye which watches over us to do us good. The Lord's heart is never removed from his people: he thinks upon them to bless them.)*

19 Surely thou wilt slay the wicked, O God: depart from me therefore, ye bloody men. *Since the Lord sees and punishes the wicked, we should not be found in their company, lest we share in their doom.*

20 For they speak against thee wickedly, *and* thine enemies take *thy name* in vain. *(And this they do in the Lord's own presence, thus provoking him to his face.)*

21 Do not I hate them, O LORD, that hate thee? and am not I grieved with those that rise up against thee?

22 I hate them with perfect hatred : I count them mine enemies. *(A faithful servant of God has the same interests, the same friends, and the same enemies as his Master.)*

23 Search me, O God, and know my heart : try me, and know my thoughts :

24 And see if *there be any* wicked way in me, and lead me in the way everlasting. *This is the way in which to derive gracious advantage from that attribute of God which to the sinner is full of terror. Since the Lord will pardon all the sins of believers in Jesus, we are glad that he should see them all, so that he may completely and effectually remove them.*

Lord, thou hast search'd and seen me through;
Thine eye commands with piercing view
My rising and my resting hours,
My heart and flesh, with all their powers.

Within thy circling power I stand;
On every side I find thy hand;
Awake, asleep, at home, abroad,
I am surrounded still with God.

GENESIS XVIII. 1—15.

A ND the LORD appeared unto Abraham in the plains of Mamre : and he sat in the tent door in the heat of the day ;

2 And he lift up his eyes and looked, and, lo, three men stood by him : and when he saw *them*, he ran to meet them from the tent door, and bowed himself toward the ground,

3, 4, 5 And said, My Lord, if now I have found favour in thy sight, pass not away, I pray thee, from thy servant : Let a little water, I pray you, be fetched, and wash your feet, and rest yourselves under the tree : And I will fetch a morsel of bread, and comfort ye your hearts ; after that ye shall pass on : for therefore are. ye come to your servant. And they said, So do, as thou hast said.

Abraham here became an example of hospitality, and thereby entertained angels unawares He ran to meet the strangers, he saluted them respectfully, welcomed them heartily, and even made a favour to himself of their resting near his tent. Ungenerous spirits who never entertain either God's servants or the poor, miss many a blessing. May we never be a churlish household.

6 And Abraham hastened into the tent unto Sarah, and said, Make ready quickly three measures of fine meal, knead *it*, and make cakes upon the hearth.

7 And Abraham ran unto the herd, and fetch a calf tender and good, and gave *it* unto a young man ; and he hasted to dress it.

8 And he took butter, and milk, and the calf which he had dressed, and set *it* before them ; and he stood by them under the tree, and they did eat. *(The noble old man waited with pleasure upon the strangers. He spoke of a morsel of bread, but he made a feast. He was all kindness, goodness, and humbleness of mind : at once a true nobleman and a believer in God. Such are the fruits of elevated piety. Would to God we saw them in all professors.)*

9 ¶ And they said unto him, Where *is* Sarah thy wife ? And he said, Behold, in the tent.

Where she should be. She was a worthy wife of her worthy husband, and therefore cheerfully aided him in providing for the guests. She was at that moment busy with household duties. We are in the way of blessing when we are in the way of duty. Abraham must have wondered how the chief one of the three strangers knew the name of his wife.

10 And he said, I will certainly return unto thee according to the time of life ; and, lo, Sarah thy wife shall have a son. And Sarah heard *it* in the tent door, which *was* behind him.

11 Now Abraham and Sarah *were* old *and* well stricken in age.

12 Therefore Sarah laughed within herself, saying, After I am waxed old shall I have pleasure, my lord being old also ? *(Here was unbelief, which can express itself as much in a laugh as in a cry.)*

13 And the LORD said unto Abraham, Wherefore did Sarah laugh, saying, Shall I of a surety bear a child, which am old?

14 Is any thing too hard for the LORD? At the time appointed I will return unto thee, according to the time of life, and Sarah shall have a son *(What an encouraging question is that. " Is anything too hard for the Lord ?" Our family troubles, cares, and needs are not beyond the power and wisdom of our heavenly Father. Let us not despair, but in faith cast our burden upon him.)*

15 Then Sarah denied, saying, I laughed not; for she was afraid. And he said, Nay; but thou didst laugh.

He who discerns all hearts could not be deceived. See how honest Holy Scripture is, for it records the faults even of the best of the saints; and yet how tender is the Spirit of God, for in the New Testament Sarah's fault is not mentioned, for it had been forgiven and blotted out, but the fact that she called her husband " lord " is recorded to her honour. We serve a gracious God who, when our hearts are right, commends our good fruit, and leaves the untimely figs to drop out of notice. Let us be careful not to mar the joy of his promises and his grace by any unseemly expressions or actions. It would be a sad remembrance for us amid the recollections of divine love, to have to confess that we laughed at the promise.

The thing surpasses all my thought ;
But faithful is my Lord ;
Through unbelief I stagger not,
For God hath spoke the word.

Faith, mighty faith, the promise sees,
And looks to that alone ;
Laughs at impossibilities,
And cries, " It shall be done !"

GENESIS XVIII. 16, 17; 22—33.

A ND the men rose up from thence, and looked toward Sodom: and Abraham went with them to bring them on the way.

17 And the LORD said, Shall I hide from Abraham that thing which I do? *(One of the three was the Lord himself, who for the time had taken upon him a human form. It may be that Jesus, who was one day to be born a man, thus anticipated his incarnation. Truly, " his goings forth were of old." What condescension was this on Jehovah's part that he would make Abraham his confidential friend! He is willing to do the same with us, for even now " the secret of the Lord is with them that fear him.")*

22 And the men turned their faces from thence, and went toward Sodom: but Abraham stood yet before the LORD.

Two angels went to Sodom, but the third, the Lord of angels, staid to commune with Abraham, his friend.

23 ¶ And Abraham drew near, and said, Wilt thou also destroy the righteous with the wicked?

24 Peradventure there be fifty righteous within the city: wilt thou also destroy and not spare the place for the fifty righteous that *are* therein ?

25 That be far from thee to do after this manner, to slay the righteous with the wicked: and that the righteous should be as the wicked, that be far from thee: Shall not the Judge of all the earth do right? *(When we are favoured with close access to God we should use it for intercession on the behalf of others. Note the arguments the patriarch used. We also should bring forth our strong reasons when we plead. The Lord is moved with pleas like those of Abraham. Undoubtedly he saves wicked nations for the sake of the saints who dwell among them, and, indeed, all the saved are forgiven not for their own sakes but for Jesus' sake.)*

26 And the LORD said, If I find in Sodom fifty righteous within the city, then I will spare all the place for their sakes.

27 And Abraham answered and said, Behold now, I have taken upon me to speak unto the Lord, which *am but* dust and ashes.

In our boldest pleadings we must not forget what poor creatures we are, and how condescending it is on the Lord's part to let us plead with him.

28 Peradventure there shall lack five of the fifty righteous: wilt thou destroy all the city for *lack of* five? And he said, If I find there forty and five, I will not destroy *it*. *(The Lord kept pace with his servant, being quite as willing to answer as he was to ask.)*

29 And he spake unto him yet again, and said, Peradventure there shall be forty found there. And he said, I will not do *it* for forty's sake.

30 And he said *unto him*, Oh let not the Lord be angry, and I will speak : Peradventure there shall thirty be found there. And he said, I will not do *it*, if I find thirty there.

31 And he said, Behold now, I have taken upon me to speak unto the Lord : Peradventure there shall be twenty found there. And he said, I will not destroy *it* for twenty's sake.

32 And he said, Oh let not the Lord be angry, and I will speak yet but this once : Peradventure ten shall be found there. And he said, I will not destroy *it* for ten's sake.

There is a time to keep silent as well as a time to speak. Abraham had gone as far as the Spirit of the Lord guided him, and he did not attempt to go further.

33 And the LORD went his way, as soon as he had left communing with Abraham : and Abraham returned unto his place.

Had there been but the small remnant of ten, Sodom and Gomorrah would have escaped. See then how precious the saints are to a nation. They may be unknown or despised, but they are the salt which preserves the whole. May our family be a part of that good salt; parents, children, and servants, all being through divine grace numbered with the righteous. But we must first have salt in ourselves by possessing a living faith in the Lord Jesus ; otherwise we cannot benefit others, for we are not even saved ourselves.

Our guilt might draw thy vengeance down
On every shore, on every town :
But view us, Lord, with pitying eye,
And lay thy lifted thunder by.

Forgive the follies of our times,
And purge our land from all its crimes :
Reform'd and deck'd with grace divine,
Let Britain yet arise and shine.

WE *must not suffer the intercession of Abraham to pass away from our thoughts till it has reminded us of the yet more powerful advocacy of our Blessed Lord Jesus. We see him in one of his own parables describing himself as preserving the sinful by his pleadings, and the passage is a fit sequel to our yesterday's reading.*

LUKE XIII. 1—9.

1 There were present at that season some that told him of the Galilæans, whose blood Pilate had mingled with their sacrifices.

2 And Jesus answering said unto them, Suppose ye that these Galilæans were sinners above all the Galilæans, because they suffered such things?

3 I tell you, Nay: but, except ye repent, ye shall all likewise perish. (*See the need of repentance. Philip Henry once said, " Some people do not like to hear much of repentance ; but I think it so necessary that if I were to die in the pulpit, I should desire to die preaching repentance, and if I should die out of the pulpit I hope to die practising it.")*

4 Or those eighteen, upon whom the tower in Siloam fell, and slew them, think ye that they were sinners above all men that dwelt in Jerusalem?

5 I tell you, Nay: but, except ye repent, ye shall all likewise perish.

When we hear or read of terrible judgments upon sinners, such as these here recorded, and that which befell Sodom of old, we ought not to congratulate ourselves as though we were exempted because of our innocence, but rather we should regard these events as warnings to ourselves; since, if we fall into the same sins, sooner or later a doom equally overwhelming will come upon us. If any enquire why it has not come already, let them pay special attention to the parable which follows. There has been an intercessor at work, or we should have perished long ere this.

6 ¶ He spake also this parable; A certain *man* had a fig tree planted in his vineyard; and he came and sought fruit thereon, and found none. (*It was in good soil, and under the gardener's care; it would therefore yield fruit, or prove itself to be good for nothing.*)

7 Then said he unto the dresser of his vineyard, Behold, these three years I come seeking fruit on this fig tree, and find none: cut it down; why cumbereth it the ground?

Three years was long enough for a test: there might have been two bad seasons to account for the absence of fruit, but when a third time the tree was fruitless the fault must be in the tree itself. God gives us time enough for trial. All of us have been borne with quite long enough to prove us, and perhaps at this moment the Lord is saying, " Cut it down." How very like are some of us to the barren tree! In itself it is of no use, it fills the place of a good tree, it draws the goodness from the soil, and hurts others near it. It is thus that men live useless lives, and meanwhile are occupying wastefully positions in which others would bring glory to God.

8 And he answering said unto him, Lord, let it alone this year also, till I shall dig about it, and dung *it*. (*It is the voice of Jesus the Intercessor. He is unwilling to see the axe uplifted, for he is full of compassion. See how unconverted men owe their lives to Jesus. They are not preserved by their own worth or worthiness, but they live upon sufferance, and will die as soon as the voice of Jesus ceases to plead for them.*)

9 And if it bear fruit, *well*: and if not, *then* after that thou shalt cut it down.

May we who have been without grace till now hear the word of God at this hour and live; for this may be our last year of grace, and when it is over we may be cast into the fire of hell. Jesus has pleaded that we may be tried once more; but there is a limit to his pleadings. Note the two ifs, " And if," " and if not." Upon these two ifs hang eternity. The Lord grant that none of us may be cut down and cast into the eternal burnings.

See how the fruitless fig-tree stands,
  Beneath its owner's frown:
The axe is lifted in his hands,
  To cut the cumberer down.

"Year after year, I come," he cries,
  "And still no fruit is shown ;
Nothing but empty leaves arise,
  Then cut the cumberer down."

Sinner, beware ! the axe of death
  Is rais'd and aimed at thee:
Awhile thy Maker spares thy breath,
  Beware, O barren tree !

GENESIS XIX. 1—3; 15—26.

AND there came two angels to Sodom at even; and Lot sat in the gate of Sodom: and Lot seeing *them* rose up to meet them; and he bowed himself with his face toward the ground;

2 And he said, Behold now, my lords, turn in, I pray you, into your servant's house, and tarry all night, and wash your feet, and ye shall rise up early, and go on your ways. *(Bad as his neighbours were, Lot had not forgotten to be hospitable. Grace does not flourish in bad companionship, but still it lives.)* And they said, Nay; but we will abide in the street all night.

3 And he pressed upon them greatly; and they turned in unto him, and entered into his house; and he made them a feast, and did bake unleavened bread, and they did eat.

Then at nightfall followed a horrible scene in which the angels saw for themselves that Sodom was filthy, cruel, malicious, and abominable. Those holy beings, therefore, shut to the door, and waited till the morning to execute the sentence of God upon the city. It was time that such a den of abominations should be swept away. Meanwhile, Lot went to his sons-in-law, and urged them to fly with him, but they thought him mad, and refused.

15 ¶ And when the morning arose, then the angels hastened Lot, saying, Arise, take thy wife, and thy two daughters, which are here; lest thou be consumed in the iniquity of the city.

It is true kindness to men to warn them earnestly of their danger; and we cannot be too pressing in urging them to escape.

16 And while he lingered, the men laid hold upon his hand, and upon the hand of his wife, and upon the hand of his two daughters; the LORD being merciful unto him: and they brought him forth, and set him without the city.

We must repeat our warnings, and use holy violence with sinners. At the same time let us beware of lingering ourselves. We are never safe a single moment till we have fled to Jesus.

17 ¶ And it came to pass, when they had brought them forth abroad, that he said, Escape for thy life; look not behind thee, neither stay thou in all the plain; escape to the mountain, lest thou be consumed.

18, 19 And Lot said unto them, Oh, not so, my Lord: Behold now, thy servant hath found grace in thy sight, and thou hast magnified thy mercy, which thou hast· shewed unto me in saving my life; and I cannot escape to the mountain, lest some evil take me, and I die:

20 Behold now, this city *is* near to flee unto, and it *is* a little one: Oh, let me escape thither, (*is* it not a little one?) and my soul shall live.

21 And he said unto him, See, I have accepted thee concerning this thing also, that I will not overthrow this city, for the which thou hast spoken.

22 Haste thee, escape thither; for I cannot do any thing till thou be come thither. Therefore the name of the city was called Zoar.

Though Lot was not such a believer as Abraham, yet being a good man his prayer was heard, and at his request a little city was saved. Was not this also an answer to Abraham's prayer?

23 ¶ The sun was risen upon the earth when Lot entered into Zoar.

24 Then the LORD rained upon Sodom and upon Gomorrah brimstone and fire from the LORD out of heaven;

25 And he overthrew those cities, and all the plain, and all the inhabitants of the cities, and that which grew upon the ground.

26 ¶ But his wife looked back from behind him, and she became a pillar of salt. *(Lot's prayer saved Zoar, but could not save his wife. A minister may bring thousands to Jesus, and yet his own household may perish. The Scripture says, "Remember Lot's wife." Remember that she was Lot's wife, and yet was destroyed. She was half way to Zoar and out of Sodom, and yet escaped not, and all because her heart was still with sinners, and she could not leave them. She started to escape, but she started aside. O for grace to persevere.*

Remember Lot's wife, and beware of even a desire to return to old sins, lest we prove ourselves unworthy of eternal life. This terrible chapter should make us tremble if we have not reached the mountain of atoning love. Let us not delay, but flee to Jesus now, and put our trust in him.

Hasten, sinner, to be blest,
Stay not for the morrow's sun,
Lest perdition thee arrest
Ere the morrow is begun.
Lord, do thou the sinner turn!
Rouse him from his senseless state;
Let him not thy counsel spurn,
Rue his fatal choice too late!

GENESIS XXI. 1—21.

AND the LORD visited Sarah as he had said, and the LORD did unto Sarah as he had spoken.

2 For Sarah conceived, and bare Abraham a son in his old age, at the set time of which God had spoken to him. *(The Lord's promises are always fulfilled to the hour.)*

3 And Abraham called the name of his son that was born unto him, whom Sarah bare to him, Isaac. *(Or laughter, for both parents had laughed for joy. The best laughing in all the world is that which arises from fulfilled promises; then is our mouth filled with laughter, and our tongue with singing.)*

4 And Abraham circumcised his son Isaac, being eight days old, as God had commanded him. *(Abraham's laughter was no worldly merriment, but a joy which led him to be obedient to the Lord's will. This is solid pleasure.)*

5 And Abraham was an hundred years old, when his son Isaac was born unto him.

6 ¶ And Sarah said, God hath made me to laugh, *so that* all that hear will laugh with me. *When the promise is realised by any of us, others ought to share our joy. Let us tell the saints what the Lord has done for us, that they may rejoice also.*

7 And she said, Who would have said unto Abraham, that Sarah should have given children suck? for I have born *him* a son in his old age.

8 And the child grew, and was weaned: and Abraham made a great feast the *same* day that Isaac was weaned.

9 ¶ And Sarah saw the son of Hagar the Egyptian, which she had born unto Abraham, mocking. *(Children are too apt·to do this; but how wrong it is for the elder to tease and grieve the younger. God notices it and is displeased.)*

10 Wherefore she said unto Abraham, Cast out this bondwoman and her son: for the son of this bondwoman shall not be heir with my son, *even* with Isaac.

11 And the thing was very grievous in Abraham's sight because of his son.

12 ¶ And God said unto Abraham, Let it not be grievous in thy sight because of the lad, and because of thy bondwoman; in all that Sarah hath said unto thee, hearken unto her voice; for in Isaac shall thy seed be called.

13 And also of the son of the bondwoman will I make a nation, because he *is* thy seed. *It was hard for Ishmael to be sent from home, but God ordered it for the best, even for him.*

14 And Abraham rose up early in the morning, and took bread, and a bottle of water, and gave *it* unto Hagar, putting *it* on her shoulder, and the child, and sent her away: and she departed, and wandered in the wilderness of Beer-sheba.

15 And the water was spent in the bottle, and she cast the child under one of the shrubs.

16 And she went, and sat her down over against *him* a good way off, as it were a bowshot: for she said, Let me not see the death of the child. And she sat over against *him*, and lift up her voice, and wept. *(Had she forgotten the Lord who appeared to her before? So it seems. Our forgetfulness of former mercy is the root of present despair.)*

17 And God heard the voice of the lad; and the angel of God called to Hagar out of heaven, and said unto her, What aileth thee, Hagar? fear not; for God hath heard the voice of the lad where he *is*. *God takes pity on boys and girls, and hears their little prayers as well as those of their fathers and mothers. Dear children, do you pray?*

18 Arise, lift up the lad, and hold him in thine hand; for I will make him a great nation.

19 And God opened her eyes, and she saw a well of water; and she went, and filled the bottle with water, and gave the lad drink.

20 And God was with the lad ; and he grew, and dwelt in the wilderness, and became an archer.

21 And he dwelt in the wilderness of Paran: and his mother took him a wife out of the land of Egypt. *(Thus God who ordered Hagar and her son to be sent away, took good care of them in the desert: he will therefore watch over us if we commit ourselves to his care.)*

Our Lord is rich and merciful,
　Our God is very kind ;
O come to him, come now to him,
　With a believing mind.

The Lord is great and full of might,
　Our God is ever nigh :
O trust in him, trust now in him,
　And have security.

PAUL *teaches us how to gather instruction from the ancient story of Ishmael and Isaac. Writing to those who were anxious to introduce Jewish ceremonialism into the Christian church, he says in—*

GALATIANS IV. 21—31.

21 Tell me, ye that desire to be under the law, do ye not hear the law?

Are ye not able to see a meaning in the incidents it records? Will ye only learn one part of its teaching, and shut your ears to the rest?

22 For it is written, that Abraham had two sons, the one by a bondmaid, the other by a freewoman.

23 But he *who was* of the bondwoman was born after the flesh; but he of the freewoman *was* by promise.

24 Which things are an allegory: for these are the two covenants; the one from the mount Sinai, which gendereth to bondage, which is Agar.

25 For this Agar is mount Sinai in Arabia, and answereth to Jerusalem which now is, and is in bondage with her children.

26 But Jerusalem which is above is free, which is the mother of us all.

27 For it is written, Rejoice, *thou* barren that bearest not; break forth and cry, thou that travailest not: for the desolate hath many more children than she which hath an husband.

28 Now we, brethren, as Isaac was, are the children of promise. *(We were not made sons of God by the energy of nature, but by the power of divine grace.)*

29 But as then he that was born after the flesh persecuted him *that was born* after the Spirit, even so *it is* now. *(Pharisees and self-righteous persons display great enmity towards those who depend upon the grace of God in Christ Jesus. They call them presumptuous, and revile their doctrine as tending to licentiousness.)*

30 Nevertheless what saith the scripture? Cast out the bondwoman and her son: for the son of the bondwoman shall not be heir with the son of the freewoman.

The system of salvation by works must be banished if grace is to reign; you cannot mix the two systems. The power and energy of self must also be no longer our trust if we desire to be saved through the promise. Human merit, the

child of the flesh, will never agree with faith, the offspring of the promise.

31 So then, brethren, we are not children of the bondwoman, but of the free.

GALATIANS V. 1—6.

1 Stand fast therefore in the liberty wherewith Christ hath made us free, and be not entangled again with the yoke of bondage.

Do not go back to legal hopes, and ceremonial observances. You are free-born; do not submit to the yoke of bondage.

2 Behold, I Paul say unto you, that if ye be circumcised, Christ shall profit you nothing.

3 For I testify again to every man that is circumcised, that he is a debtor to do the whole law.

4 Christ is become of no effect unto you, whosoever of you are justified by the law; ye are fallen from grace. *(If a man could be justified by the law he would have left the system of grace altogether, for the two are diametrically opposed. Thanks be to God, we dare not even hope for a legal righteousness, and if we never fall from grace till we have become justified by the law, that evil will never befall us.)*

5 For we through the Spirit wait for the hope of righteousness by faith. *(Our confidence is in the promise and grace of God; thus we are true Isaacs, born of the promise of God.)*

6 For in Jesus Christ neither circumcision availeth any thing, nor uncircumcision; but faith which worketh by love. *(The outward is disregarded and the inward becomes all-important. The flesh, like Ishmael, is sent away, and the newborn nature abides with the father, and inherits the covenant promises. All believers understand this riddle: can all of us in this household interpret it?)*

Once all my servile works were done
  A righteousness to raise;
Now, freely chosen in the Son,
  I freely choose his ways.

"What shall I do," was then the word,
  "That I may worthier grow?"
"What shall I render to the Lord?"
  Is my enquiry now.

GENESIS XXII. 1—19.

AND it came to pass after these things, that God did tempt Abraham, and said unto him, Abraham: and he said, Behold, *here I am. (This was at once the patriarch's crowning trial and grandest victory, and it came after he had obtained the choicest blessing of his life. Great privileges involve great trial.)*

2 And he said, Take now thy son, thine only *son* Isaac, whom thou lovest, and get thee into the land of Moriah; and offer him there for a burnt offering upon one of the mountains which I will tell thee of.

3 ¶ And Abraham rose up early in the morning, and saddled his ass, and took two of his young men with him, and Isaac his son, and clave the wood for the burnt offering, and rose up, and went unto the place of which God had told him. *(His obedience was speedy, unhesitating, and complete. Think of that early hour, and the task of cleaving the wood for such a sacrifice. Could we thus obey the Lord?)*

4 Then on the third day Abraham lifted up his eyes, and saw the place afar off. *(Those days of deliberation must have severely tried him. We can do in a hurry what we should shrink from if we weighed it calmly.)*

5 And Abraham said unto his young men, Abide ye here with the ass; and I and the lad will go yonder and worship, and come again to you. *(Perhaps he feared lest the servants should interpose to prevent his obedient act.)*

6 And Abraham took the wood of the burnt offering, and laid *it* upon Isaac his son; and he took the fire in his hand, and a knife; and they went both of them together.

7 And Isaac spake unto Abraham his father, and said, My father: and he said, Here *am* I, my son. And he said, Behold the fire and the wood: but where *is* the lamb for a burnt offering?

A touching question, but Abraham would not allow his feelings to master his faith.

8 And Abraham said, My son, God will provide himself a lamb for a burnt offering: *(These were grandly prophetic words, and have been divinely fulfilled;)* so they went both of them together.

9 And they came to the place which God had told him of; and Abraham built an altar there, and laid the wood in order, and bound Isaac his son, and laid him on the altar upon the wood.

10 And Abraham stretched forth his hand, and took the knife to slay his son.

11 And the angel of the LORD called unto him out of heaven, and said, Abraham, Abraham: and he said, Here *am* I.

12 And he said, Lay not thine hand upon the lad, neither do thou any thing unto him: for now I know that thou fearest God, seeing thou hast not withheld thy son, thine only *son* from me.

13 And Abraham lifted up his eyes, and looked, and behold behind *him* a ram caught in a thicket by his horns: and Abraham went and took the ram, and offered him up for a burnt offering in the stead of his son.

14 And Abraham called the name of that place Jehovah-jireh *(or the Lord will provide);* as it is said *to* this day, In the mount of the LORD it shall be seen.

15 ¶ And the angel of the LORD called unto Abraham out of heaven the second time,

16 And said, By myself have I sworn, saith the LORD, for because thou hast done this thing, and hast not withheld thy son, thine only *son:*

17 That in blessing I will bless thee, and in multiplying I will multiply thy seed as the stars of the heaven, and as the sand which *is* upon the sea shore; and thy seed shall possess the gate of his enemies;

18 And in thy seed shall all the nations of the earth be blessed; because thou hast obeyed my voice. *(Thus was the covenant renewed in full, in connection with this great intended act of sacrifice: it is sweet to see the covenant of grace confirmed in the actual offering up of Jesus, the Only Begotten of the Father. O for grace to be in covenant with God in Christ Jesus.)*

19 So Abraham returned unto his young men, and they rose up and went together to Beer-sheba; and Abraham dwelt at Beer-sheba.

My God and Father! while I stray
Far from my home, in life's rough way,
Oh! teach me from my heart to say,
   "Thy will be done!" "Thy will be done!"

If thou shouldst call me to resign
What most I prize—it ne'er was mine;
I only yield thee what was thine:
   "Thy will be done!"

THE *sacrifice of Isaac reminds us of the Divine Father, who spared not his own Son, but freely delivered him up for us al!. Let us read Isaiah's account of the sufferings of the Great Son of God.*

ISAIAH LIII.

1 Who hath believed our report? and to whom is the arm of the LORD revealed?

None believe the gospel, but those who are wrought upon by the power of God.

2 For he shall grow up before him as a tender plant, and as a root out of a dry ground: he hath no form nor comeliness; and when we shall see him, *there is* no beauty that we should desire him.

3 He is despised and rejected of men; a man of sorrows, and acquainted with grief: and we hid as it were *our* faces from him; he was despised, and we esteemed him not. *(The Eternal Father out of love to man sent forth his Son to be thus dishonoured, and shamefully entreated among men. Herein is love!)*

4 ¶ Surely he hath borne our griefs, and carried our sorrows: yet we did esteem him stricken, smitten of God, and afflicted.

5 But he *was* wounded for our transgressions, *he was* bruised for our iniquities: the chastisement of our peace *was* upon him; and with his stripes we are healed. *(Four words are used to describe the pains of the Lord Jesus—" wounded," " bruised," "chastisement," " stripes." How many, how varied, and how acute were his pains none of us can tell.)*

6 All we like sheep have gone astray; we have turned every one to his own way; and the LORD hath laid on him the iniquity of us all.

Here is the essence of the gospel—sin was laid on Jesus, and lies no longer on his people. Jehovah himself made the transfer, and therefore none dare question the lawfulness of it.

7 He was oppressed, and he was afflicted, yet he opened not his mouth: he is brought as a lamb to the slaughter, and as a sheep before her shearers is dumb, so he openeth not his mouth.

8 He was taken from prison and from judgment: and who shall declare his generation? for he was cut off out of the land of the living: for the transgression of my people was he stricken.

9 And he made his grave with the wicked, and with the rich in his death; because he had done no violence, neither *was any* deceit in his mouth.

10 Yet it pleased the LORD to bruise him; *(Jehovah took pleasure in the atoning sacrifice. So great was his love that he bruised the Son of his love to save rebellious sinners;)* he hath put *him* to grief: *(Yes, Jehovah himself put his own Son to grief. In this God commendeth his love towards us, and we ought to give our whole souls to him in return.)* when thou shalt make his soul an offering for sin, he shall see *his* seed, he shall prolong *his* days, and the pleasure of the LORD shall prosper in his hand.

11 He shall see of the travail of his soul, *and* shall be satisfied: by his knowledge shall my righteous servant justify many; for he shall bear their iniquities.

12 Therefore will I divide him *a portion* with the great, and he shall divide the spoil with the strong; because he hath poured out his soul unto death: and he was numbered with the transgressors; and he bare the sin of many, and made intercession for the transgressors.

Those who unfeignedly trust in the Lord Jesus may rest assured that their sins have ceased to be, for Jesus has fully discharged their debt: they may also rejoice that the prevalent plea of the exalted Intercessor secures them from all harm. Let us draw near to the cross of Jesus, and rest our souls beneath the shadow of the Crucified. God has provided himself a Lamb for a burnt-offering, the victim is slain, the covenant is established, believers are secure. For this let the Eternal Father be evermore adored.

Nature with open volume stands,
To spread her Maker's praise abroad;
And every labour of his hands
Shows something worthy of a God.

But in the grace that rescued man
His brightest form of glory shines;
Here, on the cross, 'tis fairest drawn
In precious blood and crimson lines.

Here I behold his inmost heart,
Where grace and vengeance strangely join,
Piercing his Son with sharpest smart,
To make the purchased pleasures mine.

GALATIANS III. 6—18.

IN *this passage the apostle shows that Abraham's righteousness was gained by his faith; that the covenant made with him was upon the tenure of faith; and that by the way of faith alone we who are sinners of the Gentiles are made partakers of covenant blessings.*

6 Abraham believed God, and it was accounted to him for righteousness.

7 Know ye therefore that they which are of faith, the same are the children of Abraham.

Not the trusters in works and boasters in circumcision; these, even among the Jews, are but his children by the power of nature, to whom no more belongs than to Ishmael. Abraham was the father of the faithful, or believing. In his grandest aspect he is not the sire of a rebellious nation, but of the believing seed.

8 And the scripture, foreseeing that God would justify the heathen through faith, preached before the gospel unto Abraham, *saying,* In thee shall all nations be blessed.

9 So then they which be of faith are blessed with faithful Abraham.

For in no other way can all nations share in the blessing, since they neither inherit it by descent, nor obtain it by circumcision, nor earn it by merit.

10 For as many as are of the works of the law are under the curse: for it is written, Cursed *is* every one that continueth not in all things which are written in the book of the law to do them. *(Let us learn this verse well, and may it ring the death knell of all legal hopes. All that the law can do for sinners is to judge them, condemn them, and curse them. Let us flee from the vain hope of ignorant and proud men, and look to another way of salvation; which, indeed, is the only one.)*

11 But that no man is justified by the law in the sight of God, *it is* evident: for, The just shall live by faith. *(The only just men before God are the men of faith, and these do not live by their works, but by believing; hence it is clear that the law has nothing to do with their righteousness.)*

12 And the law is not of faith: but, The man that doeth them shall live in them. *(Hence we cannot be saved partly by faith and partly by works. The roads are distinct. We must keep* the whole law if we would be saved by it. Our only hope is in the righteousness of the Lord Jesus Christ received by faith.)

13, 14 Christ hath redeemed us from the curse of the law, being made a curse for us: for it is written, Cursed *is* every one that hangeth on a tree: That the blessing of Abraham might come on the Gentiles through Jesus Christ; that we might receive the promise of the Spirit through faith. *(His the curse, that ours might be the blessing. By the gate of Substitution all blessings come to us, and even that best of blessings—the Holy Spirit.)*

15 Brethren, I speak after the manner of men; Though *it be* but a man's covenant, yet *if it be* confirmed, no man disannulleth, or addeth thereto.

Once made, a covenant cannot be justly altered by an afterthought, or affected by an unforeseen event. What consolation is here!

16 Now to Abraham and his seed were the promises made. He saith not, And to seeds, as of many; but as of one, And to thy seed, which is Christ. *(Mark how the apostle believed in verbal inspiration, for he finds a meaning in so small a matter as the use of a singular word instead of a plural.)*

17 And this I say, *that* the covenant, that was confirmed before of God in Christ, the law, which was four hundred and thirty years after, cannot disannul, that it should make the promise of none effect. *(Sinai and Leviticus cannot supersede the covenant of grace. Notwithstanding the law, the believer is secure in faith.)*

18 For if the inheritance *be* of the law, *it is* no more of promise: but God gave *it* to Abraham by promise. *(And we by faith grasping the promise are made partakers of it, not at all by our doings, but by the simple act of reliance upon the Lord Jesus Christ.)*

In vain we ask God's righteous law
    To justify us now;
Since to convince and to condemn,
    Is all the law can do.

Jesus, how glorious is thy grace!
    When in thy name we trust,
Our faith receives a righteousness
    That makes the sinner just.

GENESIS XXIII.

A ND Sarah was an hundred and seven and twenty years old : *these were* the years of the life of Sarah.

2 And Sarah died in Kirjath-arba; the same *is* Hebron in the land of Canaan : and Abraham came to mourn for Sarah, and to weep for her.

Into the holiest and happiest households death will come, but faith learns how to make him welcome.

3 ¶ And Abraham stood up from before his dead, and spake unto the sons of Heth, saying,

4 I *am* a stranger and a sojourner with you : give me a possession of a burying-place with you, that I may bury my dead out of my sight.

Dear as our beloved ones may be in life, we cannot endure to look upon their dead bodies, but affection itself demands that we hide them in the dust. What an instructive expression is that,—" the possession of a burial place;" it is often the only landed estate the godly possess.

5 And the children of Heth answered Abraham, saying unto him,

6 Hear us, my lord : thou *art* a mighty prince among us : in the choice of our sepulchres bury thy dead; none of us shall withhold from thee his sepulchre, but that thou mayest bury thy dead. *(But this would not be after Abraham's mind. He would not wish to sleep in the same grave with those from whom he was separated in life. He would maintain his separateness unto God even to the end.)*

7 And Abraham stood up, and bowed himself to the people of the land, *even* to the children of Heth. *(Courtesy is due even to the ungodly. A believer should not be any the less gentle in manners because gracious in heart.)*

8, 9 And he communed with them saying, If it be your mind that I should bury my dead out of my sight; hear me, and intreat for me to Ephron the son of Zohar, That he may give me the cave of Machpelah, which he hath, which *is* in the end of his field; for as much money as it is worth he shall give it me for a possession of a buryingplace amongst you.

10, 11 And Ephron dwelt among the children of Heth : and Ephron the Hittite answered Abraham in the audience of the children of Heth, *even* of all that went in at the gate of his city, saying, Nay, my lord, hear me : the field give I

thee, and the cave that *is* therein, I give it thee; in the presence of the sons of my people give I it thee : bury thy dead.

12 And Abraham bowed down himself before the people of the land. *(This is a second time mentioned. The truly noble are conciliatory and courteous. A believer is not a bear.)*

13 And he spake unto Ephron in the audience of the people of the land, saying, But if thou *wilt give it,* I pray thee, hear me : I will give thee money for the field; take *it* of me, and I will bury my dead there.

14, 15, 16 And Ephron answered Abraham, saying unto him, My lord, hearken unto me: the land *is worth* four hundred shekels of silver; what *is* that betwixt me and thee? bury therefore thy dead. And Abraham hearkened unto Ephron; and Abraham weighed to Ephron the silver, which he had named in the audience of the sons of Heth, four hundred shekels of silver, current *money* with the merchant. *(Abraham would not put himself under obligation to idolaters. True faith produces an independent spirit.)*

17 ¶ And the field of Ephron, which *was* in Machpelah, which *was* before Mamre, the field, and the cave which *was* therein, and all the trees that *were* in the field, that *were* in all the borders round about, were made sure

18 Unto Abraham for a possession in the presence of the children of Heth, before all that went in at the gate of his city. *(This is as precise as a legal document. Faith does not make a man less business-like in his transactions.)*

19 And after this, Abraham buried Sarah his wife in the cave of the field of Machpelah before Mamre : the same *is* Hebron in the land of Canaan. *(In firm faith that the land would one day be all his own he laid down the bones of his beloved spouse in the promised soil, and so, as it were, took possession of the country till the set time should come for entering upon it.)*

What though this goodly mortal frame
Sink to the dust, from whence it came ;
Though buried in the silent tomb,
Worms shall my skin and flesh consume ;

Yet on that happy rising morn,
New life this body shall adorn ;
These active powers refined shall be,
And God my Saviour, I shall see.

A S *the last lesson brought us to Machpelah with the weeping train who buried Sarah, it may be a fitting season for a "meditation among the tombs."*

JOB XIV. 1—15.

1 Man *that is* born of a woman *is* of few days, and full of trouble. (*Our life is not short and sweet, but brief and bitter. Its only fulness is fulness of trouble. Sin has done all this.*)

2 He cometh forth like a flower, and is cut down: he fleeth also as a shadow, and continueth not. (*The flower is not always allowed to flourish till it withers, but is cut down by the scythe while yet in its glory; and so is man full often taken away in the midst of his days.*)

3 And dost thou open thine eyes upon such an one, and bringest me into judgment with thee? (*Job wonders that the Lord should think upon so frail a creature as mortal man.*)

4 Who can bring a clean *thing* out of an unclean? not one. (*The length of our troubles and the shortness of our lives are both caused by the impurity of our nature; and that is a matter of inheritance, for from unclean flesh there cannot come a pure posterity. A poisonous plant bears poisonous seed. A fallen man becomes the father of fallen children.*)

5 Seeing his days *are* determined, the number of his months *are* with thee, thou hast appointed his bounds that he cannot pass;

6 Turn from him, that he may rest, till he shall accomplish, as an hireling, his day. *We have a day and a work appointed us, and we are immortal till these are ended.*

7 For there is hope of a tree, if it be cut down, that it will sprout again, and that the tender branch thereof will not cease.

8 Though the root thereof wax old in the earth, and the stock thereof die in the ground;

9 *Yet* through the scent of water it will bud, and bring forth boughs like a plant.

10 But man dieth, and wasteth away: yea, man giveth up the ghost, and where *is* he? *So far as this visible world is concerned, man at death is gone never to return. For him there is no second budding and sprouting into another mortal life. The ancients chose the cypress as the symbol of death, because when once cut down it puts forth no shoots, but dies altogether. As regards this earthly existence their choice was wise and instructive. Let us then live while we live.*

11 *As* the waters fail from the sea, and the flood decayeth and drieth up:

12 So man lieth down, and riseth not: till the heavens *be* no more, they shall not awake, nor be raised out of their sleep. (*Job had seen lakes or inland seas evaporated, and torrent-beds left dry, and he compares them to man's decay. But as rain from heaven can refill the pools and cause the torrents to rush with boundless strength, so will the Lord restore life to the dead. When the heavens are no more, but shall have passed away with a great noise, the graves shall yield up their charge, and men shall rise again.*)

13 O that thou wouldest hide me in the grave, (*Hide me as a treasure, kept by its possessor*), that thou wouldest keep me secret, until thy wrath be past, that thou wouldest appoint me a set time, and remember me! (*The sufferer begged for rest, he petitioned for pity, he prayed the Lord to remember him; but, indeed, the Lord never forgets his servants.*)

14 If a man die, shall he live *again?* all the days of my appointed time will I wait, till my change come.

15 Thou shalt call, and I will answer thee: thou wilt have a desire to the work of thine hands. (*When the waking morn shall come, the saints shall answer to their Creator's resurrection-call, and rise to eternal life. In order to share in this blessedness we must have personal faith in the risen Saviour. Is this the case with all in our family? Is there an unsaved one among us? If so, since we may die to-day, may God arouse us that we may at once seek salvation through faith in the Lord Jesus, who is always ready to save.*)

God my Redeemer lives,
And often from the skies
Looks down, and watches all my dust,
Till he shall bid it rise.

Array'd in glorious grace
Shall these vile bodies shine:
And every shape and every face,
Look heavenly and divine.

These lively hopes we owe
To Jesus' dying love:
We would adore his grace below,
And sing his power above.

38   "The Lord shall guide thee continually."   JANUARY 19.—EVENING.

[*Or February 7.*]

GENESIS XXIV. 1—4; 10—31.

AND Abraham was old, *and* well stricken in age: and the LORD had blessed Abraham in all things. *(This is the summing-up of his life. Yet the former chapters record many and painful afflictions; and, doubtless, the Lord had made these also to be blessings.)*

2, 3, 4 And Abraham said unto his eldest servant of his house, that ruled over all that he had, Put, I pray thee, thy hand under my thigh: And I will make thee swear by the LORD, the God of heaven, and the God of the earth, that thou shalt not take a wife unto my son of the daughters of the Canaanites, among whom I dwell: But thou shalt go unto my country, and to my kindred, and take a wife unto my son Isaac. *(The godly seed must be kept separate. It is not fit for believers to be joined in marriage with the unregenerate.)*

10, 11, 12, 13, 14 And the servant took ten camels of the camels of his master, and departed; for all the goods of his master *were* in his hand: and he arose, and went to Mesopotamia, unto the city of Nahor. And he made his camels to kneel down without the city by a well of water at the time of the evening, *even* the time that women go out to draw *water*. And he said, O LORD God of my master Abraham, I pray thee, send me good speed this day, and shew kindness unto my master Abraham. Behold, I stand *here* by the well of water; and the daughters of the men of the city come out to draw water: And let it come to pass, that the damsel to whom I shall say, Let down thy pitcher, I pray thee, that I may drink; and she shall say, Drink, and I will give thy camels drink also: *let the same be* she *that* thou hast appointed for thy servant Isaac; and thereby shall I know that thou hast shewed kindness unto my master. *(That business will be sure to speed which is carried on in the spirit of prayer. All matters concerning marriage should especially be prayed over.)*

15 ¶ And it came to pass, before he had done speaking, that, behold, Rebekah came out, who was born to Bethuel, son of Milcah, the wife of Nahor, Abraham's brother, with her pitcher upon her shoulder. *(Here was the hand of Providence. Observe it in your own lives also.)*

16, 17 And the damsel *was* very fair to look upon, a virgin, neither had any man known her:

and she went down to the well, and filled her pitcher, and came up. And the servant ran to meet her, and said, Let me, I pray thee, drink a little water of thy pitcher.

18, 19 And she said, Drink, my lord: and she hasted, and let down her pitcher upon her hand, and gave him drink. And when she had done giving him drink, she said, I will draw *water* for thy camels also, until they have done drinking.

21 And the man wondering at her held his peace, to wit *(or know)* whether the LORD had made his journey prosperous or not.

22 And it came to pass, as the camels had done drinking, that the man took a golden earring of half a shekel weight, and two bracelets for her hands of ten *shekels* weight of gold;

23 And said, Whose daughter *art* thou? tell me, I pray thee: is there room *in* thy father's house for us to lodge in?

24, 25 And she said unto him, I *am* the daughter of Bethuel the son of Milcah, which she bare unto Nahor. She said moreover unto him, We have both straw and provender enough, and room to lodge in.

26 And the man bowed down his head, and worshipped the LORD.

27 And he said, Blessed *be* the LORD God of my master Abraham, who hath not left destitute my master of his mercy and his truth: I *being* in the way, the LORD led me to the house of my master's brethren. *(Answered prayer should be thankfully acknowledged unto God.)*

28 And the damsel ran, and told *them* of her mother's house these things.

29 ¶ And Rebekah had a brother, and his name *was* Laban: and Laban ran out unto the man, unto the well.

30 And it came to pass, when he saw the earring and bracelets upon his sister's hands, and when he heard the words of Rebekah his sister, saying, Thus spake the man unto me; that he came unto the man; and, behold, he stood by the camels at the well.

31 And he said, Come in, thou blessed of the LORD; wherefore standest thou without? for I have prepared the house, and room for the camels. *(All difficulties vanished, everything was as he could wish it. It may not be thus with us; but if any course of conduct can make it so, it is that which begins and ends with prayer.)*

GENESIS XXIV. 50—67.

LABAN, *having heard Eliezer's story and seen the jewels, which were no doubt great arguments with his mercenary mind, consented that Rebekah should go with him to Isaac.*

50 Then Laban and Bethuel answered and said, The thing proceedeth from the LORD: we cannot speak unto thee bad or good.

51 Behold, Rebekah *is* before thee, take *her,* and go, and let her be thy master's son's wife, as the LORD hath spoken. *(It is always right for young people to seek the consent of parents and natural guardians in such an important business.)*

52 And it came to pass, that, when Abraham's servant heard their words, he worshipped the LORD, *bowing himself* to the earth. *(He was too devout a man to fail to adore in gratitude; too many, however, only pray in need, but forget to worship in thanksgiving.)*

53 And the servant brought forth jewels of silver, and jewels of gold, and raiment, and gave *them* to Rebekah: he gave also to her brother and to her mother precious things. *(He was a wise steward, and knew what arguments weighed most with Laban.)*

54 And they did eat and drink, he and the men that *were* with him, and tarried all night; and they rose up in the morning, and he said, Send me away unto my master. *(God's servants should imitate this steward, and never be loiterers.)*

55 And her brother and her mother said, Let the damsel abide with us *a few* days, at the least ten; after that she shall go.

56 And he said unto them, Hinder me not, seeing the LORD hath prospered my way; send me away that I may go to my master. *(We ought not easily to be delayed from duty. To loiter is to disobey. When God speeds us we should speed indeed.)*

57 And they said, We will call the damsel, and enquire at her mouth.

58 And they called Rebekah, and said unto her, Wilt thou go with this man? And she said, I will go. *(How happy would ministers be if all young people could be as readily led to the great Bridegroom, the Lord Jesus. He accepts the willing mind. He asks for the heart. Alas, how many deny their consent to his loving claims.)*

59 And they sent away Rebekah their sister, and her nurse, and Abraham's servant, and his men.

60 And they blessed Rebekah, and said unto her, Thou *art* our sister, be thou *the mother* of thousands of millions, and let thy seed possess the gate of those which hate them. *(The blessing of parents is a precious dowry.)*

61 ¶ And Rebekah arose, and her damsels, and they rode upon the camels, and followed the man: and the servant took Rebekah, and went his way.

62 And Isaac came from the way of the well Lahai-roi; for he dwelt in the south country.

63 And Isaac went out to meditate in the field at the eventide; *(This good man, in his choice of a suitable place and time for one of the most heavenly of occupations, is an example to us all. If we meditated more we should be far more gracious than we are;)* and he lifted up his eyes, and saw, and behold, the camels *were* coming.

64 And Rebekah lifted up her eyes, and when she saw Isaac, she lighted off the camel.

65 For she *had* said unto the servant, What man *is* this that walketh in the field to meet us? And the servant *had* said, It *is* my master: therefore she took a vail, and covered herself.

66 And the servant told Isaac all things that he had done. *(Happy is that servant of God who dare tell his Master in heaven all that he has done. What a sad account would some have to render; for, "who hath believed our report, and to whom is the arm of the Lord revealed?")*

67 And Isaac brought her into his mother Sarah's tent, and took Rebekah, and she became his wife; and he loved her: and Isaac was comforted after his mother's *death.*

In all my Lord's appointed ways,
　My journey I'll pursue;
" Hinder me not," ye much-loved saints,
　For I must go with you.

Through floods and flames, if Jesus lead,
　I'll follow where he goes;
" Hinder me not," shall be my cry,
　Though earth and hell oppose.

My spirit looks to God alone;
My rock and refuge is his throne;
In all my fears, in all my straits,
My soul on his salvation waits.

Trust him, ye saints, in all your ways,
Pour out your hearts before his face;
When helpers fail, and foes invade,
God is our all-sufficient aid.

HEBREWS XI. 8—19.

T HE *portion of Scripture we shall now read gives us a retrospect of our former reading, and shows us what it was which sustained the patriarchs in their wandering and separated life.*

8 By faith Abraham, when he was called to go out into a place which he should after receive for an inheritance, obeyed; and he went out, not knowing whither he went. *(Faith is a better guide than mere reason, if it be faith in God. Our knowledge is partial and may mislead us, but trust in the omniscient Lord gives us an infallible guide.)*

9 By faith he sojourned in the land of promise, as *in* a strange country, dwelling in tabernacles with Isaac and Jacob, the heirs with him of the same promise :

10 For he looked for a city which hath foundations, whose builder and maker *is* God.

His eye saw into the far off future, and his hope was set upon eternal things. Are we also looking beyond this world for our portion? Shame will one day cover our faces if it be not so, for all the things which are seen will melt away like the mist of the morning. Heaven has a foundation, earth has none, for Job tells us concerning the Great Creator, "he hangeth the world upon nothing."

11 Through faith also Sara herself received strength to conceive seed, and was delivered of a child when she was past age, because she judged him faithful who had promised.

12 Therefore sprang there even of one, and him as good as dead, *so many* as the stars of the sky in multitude, and as the sand which is by the sea shore innumerable. *(Abraham himself was so aged as to be long past the years in which children could naturally be born to him; and therefore his body was as dead. Yet the father of the faithful staggered not at the promise of the Almighty God.*

There is no exaggeration in the description of the patriarch's descendants, for not only the Jews, but all believers, are reckoned as the seed of Abraham. The spiritual seed are countless and glorious as the stars; and the natural or earthly seed are a great host like the sand of the sea shore.)

13 These all died in faith, not having received the promises, but having seen them afar off, and were persuaded of *them,* and embraced *them,* and confessed that they were strangers and pilgrims on the earth.

14 For they that say such things declare plainly that they seek a country. *(Even thus at this day we are here as strangers and foreigners, and we seek a city out of sight. "Jerusalem the golden" is the desire of our hearts, but here we have no continuing city. This is to walk by faith.)*

15 And truly, if they had been mindful of that *country* from whence they came out, they might have had opportunity to have returned.

Correspondence with the old country was easy, and the temptation to seek their fatherland was a strong one, but they persevered in the pilgrim life, and so must we. Opportunities to return to sin are legion, but we must by the power of the Holy Spirit continue to walk with God.

16 But now they desire a better *country,* that is, an heavenly : wherefore God is not ashamed to be called their God : for he hath prepared for them a city.

17 By faith Abraham, when he was tried, offered up Isaac : and he that had received the promises offered up his only begotten *son,*

18 Of whom it was said, That in Isaac shall thy seed be called :

19 Accounting that God *was* able to raise *him* up, even from the dead; from whence also he received him in a figure. *(Isaac lived as if he had been raised from the dead, for he was dead in Abraham's intent and expectation. In this way he became to the patriarch a living type of the resurrection.*

The faith of Abraham was tried in many fires, and so must ours be. Will it stand the test? Are we resting upon the faithfulness and omnipotence of God? Any pillars less strong than these will give way beneath us. The faith of God's elect, which is the gift of God, and the work of the Holy Spirit, will endure and overcome and land us safely in the promised inheritance. Have we this faith or no? May the Lord grant us this most precious grace.)

My rest is in heaven, my rest is not here,
Then why should I tremble when trials are near?
Be hush'd my dark spirit, the worst that can come
But shortens thy journey, and hastens thee home.

It is not for me to be seeking my bliss,
Or building my hopes in a region like this;
I look for a city that hands have not piled,
I pant for a country by sin undefiled.

WE omit some of the minor details of the history as contained in Genesis, and pass on to the birth of Isaac's twin sons, Esau and Jacob. Let us see how the New Testament explains the Old. We shall read

ROMANS IX. 1—13.

In this chapter the apostle illustrates the doctrine of election by the history of the households of Abraham and Isaac, in which the will of the Lord made differences irrespective of merit. Here he brings us into a great deep; but if we only wish to know what God reveals and no more, we may safely follow where Scripture leads. Election is not a fit subject for idle curiosity, neither is it to be passed over in neglect, for whatever is taught us in the Word is profitable for some gracious purpose.

1, 2, 3 I say the truth in Christ, I lie not, my conscience also bearing me witness in the Holy Ghost, That I have great heaviness and continual sorrow in my heart. For I could wish that myself were accursed from Christ for my brethren, my kinsmen according to the flesh :

Paul did not write as he did because he hated the nation to which he belonged. Far from it. He would have sacrificed everything for their good; and he felt almost ready to be cast away himself, if by such a fate he could have rescued the Jewish people. Passionate love speaks a language which must not be weighed in the balances of cold reasoning. View the words as the outburst of a loving heart, and they are clear enough. O that all Christians had a like love for perishing sinners.

4, 5 Who are Israelites; to whom *pertaineth* the adoption, and the glory, and the covenants, and the giving of the law, and the service *of God*, and the promises ; Whose *are* the fathers, and of whom as concerning the flesh Christ *came*, who is over all, God blessed for ever. Amen.

Paul pauses to adore the Lord whom he loved. Let us bow our heads and worship also.

6, 7 Not as though the word of God hath taken none effect. For they *are* not all Israel, which are of Israel : Neither, because they are the seed of Abraham, *are they* all children : but, In Isaac shall thy seed be called.

Here was a difference made according to the divine will. God has a right to dispense his favours as he pleases, and it is not for us either to censure his actions or ask an account of them.

8 That is, They which are the children of the flesh, these *are* not the children of God : but the children of the promise are counted for the seed.

9 For this *is* the word of promise, At this time will I come, and Sarah shall have a son.

10 And not only *this ;* but when Rebekah also had conceived by one, *even* by our father Isaac ;

11 (For *the children* being not yet born, neither having done any good or evil, that the purpose of God according to election might stand, not of works, but of him that calleth ;)

12 It was said unto her, The elder shall serve the younger.

13 As it is written, Jacob have I loved, but Esau have I hated.

God passed by Esau, and gave Jacob the covenant blessing. This is a fact to be believed, and not to be made a matter for human judgment. Who are we that we should summon Jehovah to our bar? God is righteous in all his ways. We find that Esau despised his birthright, and sold it for a mess of pottage, and so by his actions abundantly justified, as well as fulfilled, the purpose of God.

How it ought to humble us when we remember that we have no claims upon God. If he should leave us to go on in sin and perish, we have no right to complain, for we deserve it. How earnestly and humbly should we implore him to look upon us in mercy, and save us with his great salvation. "Whosoever cometh unto me I will in no wise cast out," is the voice of Jesus, and whether we see it or not, it is quite consistent with the predestination taught in this chapter. The Lord has a chosen people, and yet his gospel is to be preached to every creature. Believe, but do not cavil. When we believe on the Lord Jesus, we are in the way to make our calling and election sure. Only by faith can we be assured that the Lord has called and chosen us.

'Tis not that I did choose thee,
  For, Lord, that could not be ;
This heart would still refuse thee,
  But thou hast chosen me :

Thou from the sin that stain'd me
  Wash'd me and set me free,
And to this end ordain'd me,
  That I should live to thee.

GENESIS XXV. 27—34.

H AVING *read of the purpose of God concerning Esau and Jacob, we will now follow their history.*

27 And the boys grew: and Esau was a cunning hunter, a man of the field; and Jacob was a plain man, dwelling in tents.

Children of the same parents may differ greatly in disposition, in conduct, and in character. The sovereign grace of God creates grave distinctions when it begins to operate, and every year makes the differences more apparent. Esau was wild and Jacob gentle. The one was roving, unsteady, and proud, and the other domesticated, thoughtful, and sedate.

28 And Isaac loved Esau, because he did eat of *his* venison: but Rebekah loved Jacob.

This was bad on the part of both parents. Favouritism ought to be avoided, for nothing but discontent and ill feeling can come of it. Yet if Rebekah loved Jacob because of his quiet, pious disposition, she had good reason for it, which is more than can be said of Isaac's love of the rough huntsman Esau, only because "he did eat of his venison."

29 ¶ And Jacob sod pottage: and Esau came from the field, and he *was* faint:

30 And Esau said to Jacob, Feed me, I pray thee, with that same red *pottage*; for I *am* faint: therefore was his name called Edom *(or Red).*

31 And Jacob said, Sell me this day thy birthright. *(This was unbrotherly and ungenerous of Jacob; the only good point about it is that he set a high value upon the birthright, and so showed his spiritual understanding. It is plain from this that Jacob's salvation was due to the mercy of God, for his natural character was by no means commendable. The good points in him were of the Lord, the bargaining propensity was inherited from his mother's family.)*

32 And Esau said, Behold, I *am* at the point to die: and what profit shall this birthright do to me?

33, 34 And Jacob said, Swear to me this day; and he sware unto him: and he sold his birthright unto Jacob. Then Jacob gave Esau bread and pottage of lentiles; and he did eat and drink, and rose up, and went his way: thus Esau despised *his* birthright.

He valued it so little that a sorry mess of lentiles could buy it of him. Surely it was the dearest dish of meat man ever bought, though we remember a little fruit which cost us more. Many a worldling barters his soul for the pleasures of an hour, crying, "Let us eat and drink, for to-morrow we die." In order to be rich, to indulge in pleasure, or to have their own way, men have thrown aside all hope of heaven. This is to exchange pearls for pebbles, realities for shams, lasting bliss for fleeting mirth. May those who are just growing up into life take warning from this sad act of Esau, and choose earnestly the good part which shall not be taken from them. The apostle turns Esau's story to good account in

HEBREWS XII. 15—17.

L OOKING diligently lest any man fail of the grace of God; *(We are to watch lest any of us who profess to be children of God should fall short of grace, like an arrow which does not quite reach the target. To fail to possess grace in the heart is a fatal thing.)* lest any root of bitterness springing up trouble *you*, and thereby many be defiled; *(Sin is a bitter root, and brings forth sorrow and shame.)*

16 Lest there *be* any fornicator, or profane person, as Esau, who for one morsel of meat sold his birthright. *(It is a profane thing to compare the priceless blessing of God to a merely sensual enjoyment. It is an acted blasphemy.)*

17 For ye know how that afterward, when he would have inherited the blessing, he was rejected; for he found no place of repentance, though he sought it carefully with tears.

The deed was done, the blessing had been given to Jacob, and Isaac could not withdraw it from him. If men sell their hope of heaven for the joys of earth they will in the world to come repent of their bargain, but there will be no repentance with God. He that is filthy must be filthy still.

Should I to gain the world's applause,
Or to escape its harmless frown,
Refuse to countenance thy cause,
And make thy people's lot my own;
I sell my birthright in that day,
And throw my precious soul away.

No! let the world cast out my name,
And vile account me if they will;
If to confess the Lord be shame,
I purpose to be viler still.
For thee, my God, I all resign,
Content if I can call thee mine.

GENESIS XXVII. 1—5; 17—29.

AND it came to pass, that when Isaac was old, and his eyes were dim, so that he could not see, he called Esau his eldest son, and said unto him, My son : and he said unto him, Behold, *here am* I.

2, 3, 4 And he said, Behold now, I am old, I know not the day of my death : Now therefore take, I pray thee, thy weapons, thy quiver and thy bow, and go out to the field, and take me *some* venison ; And make me savoury meat, such as I love, and bring *it* to me, that I may eat ; that my soul may bless thee before I die.

5 And Rebekah heard when Isaac spake to Esau his son. And Esau went to the field to hunt *for* venison, *and* to bring *it.*

When Rebekah heard this she determined to obtain the blessing for her favourite son Jacob by a crafty stratagem. She prepared two kids of goats in a savoury manner, dressed Jacob in Esau's clothes, put skins upon his hands and neck that he might appear to be hairy like his brother, and sent him in to deceive his father.

17, 18 And she gave the savoury meat and the bread, which she had prepared, into the hand of her son Jacob. And he came unto his father, and said, My father : and he said, Here *am* I ; who *art* thou, my son ?

19 And Jacob said unto his father, I *am* Esau thy first-born ; I have done according as thou badest me : arise, I pray thee, sit and eat of my venison, that thy soul may bless me.

20 And Isaac said unto his son, How *is it* that thou hast found *it* so quickly, my son ? And he said, Because the LORD thy God brought *it* to me. *(When we begin to sin we go from bad to worse. It was base enough of Jacob to utter so many falsehoods, but to bring in the Lord God of his father to give them the appearance of truth, was much worse.)*

21 And Isaac said unto Jacob, Come near, I pray thee, that I may feel thee, my son, whether thou *be* my very son Esau or not.

22 And Jacob went near unto Isaac his father ; and he felt him, and said, The voice *is* Jacob's voice, but the hands *are* the hands of Esau.

23 And he discerned him not, because his hands were hairy, as his brother Esau's hands : so he blessed him.

24 And he said, *Art* thou my very son Esau ? and he said, I *am. (Thus Jacob persisted in his falsehood. This narrative shows us the* *truthfulness of God's word, since it does not conceal the faults of its most eminent saints. Had the Old Testament been a cunningly devised fable, it would never have exhibited the great progenitor of the twelve tribes in so sorry a light.)*

25 And he said, Bring *it* near to me, and I will eat of my son's venison, that my soul may bless thee. And he brought *it* near to him, and he did eat : and he brought him wine, and he drank. *(Isaac did not seek counsel of the Lord, hence his mistake. By this he was punished for his ill-placed partiality to Esau, for it was very unworthy of the patriarch to prefer his profane son " because he did eat of his venison.")*

26 And his father Isaac said unto him, Come near now, and kiss me, my son.

27 And he came near, and kissed him : and he smelled the smell of his raiment, and blessed him, and said, See, the smell of my son *is* as the smell of a field which the LORD hath blessed :

28 Therefore God give thee of the dew of heaven, and the fatness of the earth, and plenty of corn and wine :

29 Let people serve thee, and nations bow down to thee : be lord over thy brethren, and let thy mother's sons bow down to thee : cursed *be* every one that curseth thee, and blessed *be* he that blesseth thee.

Thus the prophecy concerning Esau and Jacob was repeated with enlargements, " the elder shall serve the younger." God's purpose was accomplished, but this did not excuse Rebekah and Jacob, or screen them from the chastisements of God, which commenced at once. We ought never to do evil that good may come.

Father, to that first-born of thine
  Thou hast the blessing given,
The power, and dignity divine,
  Th' inheritance of heaven.

O how shall I the younger son,
  The Elder's right obtain ?
I'll put my Brother's raiment on,
  And thus the blessing gain.

Father, I joyfully believe
  Thou art well pleased with me ;
Thou dost at my approach perceive
  A heavenly fragrancy.

Thou dost thy gracious will declare,
  Thou dost delight to bless ;
And why ? My Brother's garb I wear,
  My Saviour's righteousness.

ESAU *vowed to kill Jacob, and therefore Rebekah was obliged to send her favourite son away. This she little expected when she travelled a crooked way to earn him promotion.*

GENESIS XXVIII. 10—22.

10 ¶ And Jacob went out from Beer-sheba, and went toward Haran. (*Alone, without a servant to attend him, or a beast to carry him, with only his staff to lean upon, the heir of the promises set out upon his long journey of about five hundred miles.*)

11 And he lighted upon a certain place, and tarried there all night, because the sun was set; and he took of the stones of that place, and put *them for* his pillows, and lay down in that place to sleep. (*He had a hard bed and a cold bolster, but he had a sweet sleep, and a sweeter dream. Often when the head lies hardest the heart is lightest. Our times of great trial are times of heavenly visitation.*)

12 And he dreamed, and behold a ladder set up on the earth, and the top of it reached to heaven: and behold the angels of God ascending and descending on it. (*Note the many "beholds" in the passage. They call for our special attention. The patriarch dreamed of Jesus— sweetest of all dreams. He saw how heaven and earth are joined by the Messiah, and how free is the intercourse between God and man by the way of the Mediator.*)

13 And, behold, the LORD stood above it, and said, I *am* the LORD God of Abraham thy father, and the God of Isaac: the land whereon thou liest, to thee will I give it, and to thy seed;

14 And thy seed shall be as the dust of the earth, and thou shalt spread abroad to the west, and to the east, and to the north, and to the south: and in thee and in thy seed shall all the families of the earth be blessed.

15 And, behold, I *am* with thee, and will keep thee in all *places* whither thou goest, and will bring thee again into this land; for I will not leave thee, until I have done *that* which I have spoken to thee of. (*Having seen the Messiah as the ladder, he beheld the glory of Jehovah the covenant God, and received the covenant blessing. Every syllable must have sounded as sweetest music in his ears. Note that choice word, "I will not leave thee." Whom God loves he never leaves. "Till I have done that which I have spoken to thee of;"—saying*

and doing are two very different things with men, but not with God.)

16 ¶ And Jacob awaked out of his sleep, and he said, Surely the LORD is in this place; and I knew *it* not.

17 And he was afraid, and said, How dreadful *is* this place! this *is* none other but the house of God, and this *is* the gate of heaven. *He was full of awe, even to trembling. He felt as if he had slept in the temple of Jehovah, and therefore as a sinner he was moved with fear. He had not been afraid of wild beasts or heathen men, but now though filled with holy confidence he is equally filled with sacred awe.*

18 And Jacob rose up early in the morning, and took the stone that he had put *for* his pillows, and set it up *for* a pillar, and poured oil upon the top of it. (*We must honour God with our substance. Some set up a stone of remembrance, but they pour no oil on the top of it, for they offer nothing unto the Lord.*)

19 And he called the name of that place Beth-el (*the house of God*): but the name of that city *was called* Luz at the first.

20 And Jacob vowed a vow, saying, If God will be with me, and will keep me in this way that I go, and will give me bread to eat, and raiment to put on,

21 So that I come again to my father's house in peace; then shall the LORD be my God:

22 And this stone, which I have set *for* a pillar, shall be God's house: and of all that thou shalt give me I will surely give the tenth unto thee. (*Here was a little of the bargaining spirit in covenanting for bread to eat and raiment to put on, but still there was genuine faith. He renounces all other trusts, casts himself upon the divine care, and dedicates a tithe unto the Lord. God has dealt so well with each of us, that we ought never to stint his cause. Can we not do something even now to honour the Lord with our substance and with the first-fruits of our increase?*)

Jesus that ladder is
Th' incarnate Deity,
Partaker of celestial bliss
And human misery;

Lo! up and down the scale
The angels move! with love!
And God, the Great Invisible,
Himself appears above.

JACOB *reached the house of Laban, and there married his two wives, Leah and Rachel. After toiling hard for Laban for years, he felt a longing to see his father's face again. Besides, he felt that Laban had treated him badly, and that it was time to separate and become his own master. He therefore stole away with his family and his goods, but was hotly pursued by Laban, who evidently intended him no good. The night before Laban overtook Jacob the Lord visited him in a dream, and warned him against doing Jacob any violence, or attempting to entice him back to Haran. This was a very gracious interposition, and the patriarch had abundant cause to bless the Lord for it. Laban was thus providentially restrained from doing mischief. However, he accused Jacob of having stolen his images: Jacob did not know that Rachel had concealed them, and when Laban could not find them, the patriarch upbraided him for bringing such a groundless charge against him.*

GENESIS XXXI. 36—44.

36, 37, 38, 39, 40, 41, 42 And Jacob was wroth, and chode with Laban: and Jacob answered and said to Laban, What *is* my trespass? what *is* my sin, that thou hast so hotly pursued after me? Whereas thou hast searched all my stuff, what hast thou found of all thy household stuff? set *it* here before my brethren and thy brethren, that they may judge betwixt us both. This twenty years *have* I *been* with thee; thy ewes and thy she goats have not cast their young, and the rams of thy flock have I not eaten. That which was torn *of beasts* I brought not unto thee; I bare the loss of it; of my hand didst thou require it, *whether* stolen by day, or stolen by night. *Thus* I was; in the day the drought consumed me, and the frost by night; and my sleep departed from mine eyes. Thus have I been twenty years in thy house; I served thee fourteen years for thy two daughters, and six years for thy cattle: and thou hast changed my wages ten times. Except the God of my father, the God of Abraham, and the fear of Isaac, had been with me, surely thou hadst sent me away now empty. God hath seen mine affliction and the labour of my hands, and rebuked *thee* yesternight.

Laban was a great boaster, but a miserable churl. He claimed credit for leaving Jacob unharmed, but the patriarch saw through his pretences, and knew that he had only been harmless because the Lord had laid an embargo upon him.

43 ¶ And Laban answered and said unto Jacob, These daughters *are* my daughters, and *these* children *are* my children, and *these* cattle *are* my cattle, and all that thou seest *is* mine: and what can I do this day unto these my daughters, or unto their children which they have born?

44 Now therefore come thou, let us make a covenant, I and thou; and let it be for a witness between me and thee. *(He made a merit of necessity, and so, by the good hand of the Lord, what might have been a fearful slaughter ended in a friendly compact. The Lord can make the wrath of men to praise him, and restrain it when he pleases. This event reminds us of one of David's grateful songs.)*

PSALM CXXIV.

IF *it had not been* the LORD who was on our side, now may Israel say:

2 If *it had not been* the LORD who was on our side, when men rose up against us:

3 Then they had swallowed us up quick, when their wrath was kindled against us:

4 Then the waters had overwhelmed us, the stream had gone over our soul:

5 Then the proud waters had gone over our soul.

6 Blessed *be* the LORD, who hath not given us *as* a prey to their teeth.

7 Our soul is escaped as a bird out of the snare of the fowlers: the snare is broken, and we are escaped.

8 Our help *is* in the name of the LORD, who made heaven and earth.

In all times of danger from men our wisest course is to fly to the Lord our helper. He has ways and means for delivering us which we know not of. He can either turn our enemies into friends, or else so check all their efforts that they shall do us no real injury. Blessed are those men whose trust in the Lord never wavers.

Israel, a name divinely blest,
May rise secure, securely rest;
Thy holy Guardian's wakeful eyes
Admit no slumber, nor surprise.

Should earth and hell with malice burn,
Still thou shalt go, and still return,
Safe in the Lord; his heavenly care
Defends thy life from every snare.

N O *sooner had Jacob escaped from Laban than he was plunged into another trial, for he had to face his injured brother Esau. We shall see how the Lord again preserved his servant.*

GENESIS XXXII. 6—13; 21—31.

6 ¶ And the messengers returned to Jacob, saying, We came to thy brother Esau, and also he cometh to meet thee, and four hundred men with him.

7, 8, 9, 10, 11, 12 Then Jacob was greatly afraid and distressed: and he divided the people that *was* with him, and the flocks, and herds, and the camels, into two bands; And said, If Esau come to the one company, and smite it, then the other company which is left shall escape. (*Men of faith are yet men of common sense. We are to use our wits as well as our prayers. Grace does not make men stupid.*) And Jacob said, O God of my father Abraham, and God of my father Isaac, the LORD which saidst unto me, Return unto thy country, and to thy kindred, and I will deal well with thee: I am not worthy of the least of all thy mercies, and of all the truth, which thou hast shewed unto thy servant; for with my staff I passed over this Jordan; and now I am become two bands. Deliver me, I pray thee, from the hand of my brother, from the hand of Esau: for I fear him, lest he will come and smite me, *and* the mother with the children. And thou saidst, I will surely do thee good, and make thy seed as the sand of the sea, which cannot be numbered for multitude. (*This is a master argument, " and thou saidst." It is real prayer when we plead the promise, and hold the Lord to his word.*)

13 ¶ And he lodged there that same night; and took of that which came to his hand a present for Esau his brother;

21 So went the present over before him: and himself lodged that night in the company.

22 And he rose up that night, and took his two wives, and his two womenservants, and his eleven sons, and passed over the ford Jabbok.

23 And he took them, and sent them over the brook, and sent over that he had.

24 ¶ And Jacob was left alone; (*Solitude is the fit helper of devotion. . Company distracts*

us, but alone we enter into the very soul of prayer); and there wrestled a man with him until the breaking of the day. (*Prayer must become an agony, a wrestling, if we mean to prevail.*)

25 And when he saw that he prevailed not against him, he touched the hollow of his thigh; and the hollow of Jacob's thigh was out of joint, as he wrestled with him. (*He who shrank one sinew could have crushed Jacob's whole body: if we overcome the Lord in prayer, it is because he lends us strength, and condescends to be conquered.*)

26 And he said, Let me go, for the day breaketh. And he said, I will not let thee go, except thou bless me. (*This was bravely spoken. Those who thus plead must win the day.*)

27 And he said unto him, What *is* thy name? And he said, Jacob.

28 And he said, Thy name shall be called no more Jacob, but Israel: for as a prince hast thou power with God and with men, and hast prevailed. (*One night spent in prayer ennobled Jacob. How few of us have ever tried to win a prince's rank in this way. How much might we gain if we would wrestle for it. When Jacob overcame the angel he virtually disarmed Esau. He who has power with God will surely prevail with men.*)

29 And Jacob asked *him*, and said, Tell *me*, I pray thee, thy name. And he said, Wherefore *is* it *that* thou dost ask after my name? And he blessed him there. (*He did not gratify his curiosity, but he did better, he enriched him with a divine blessing.*)

30 And Jacob called the name of the place Peniel (*or the face of God*): for I have seen God face to face, and my life is preserved.

31 And as he passed over Penuel the sun rose upon him, and he halted upon his thigh.

And who would not be content to halt if he might win what Israel won ?

Lord, I cannot let thee go,
Till a blessing thou bestow;
Do not turn away thy face,
Mine's an urgent pressing case.

No—I must maintain my hold,
'Tis thy goodness makes me bold;
I can no denial take,
When I plead for Jesu's sake.

JOSEPH *was Jacob's best loved and most tried son. Whom the Lord loveth he chasteneth. This chapter opens a long scene of suffering.*

GENESIS XXXVII. 2—14; 18—24; 28; 31—35.

2 Joseph *being* seventeen years old, was feeding the flock with his brethren ; and the lad *was* with the sons of Bilhah, and with the sons of Zilpah, his father's wives : and Joseph brought unto his father their evil report.

3 Now Israel loved Joseph more than all his children, because he *was* the son of his old age : and he made him a coat of *many* colours.

4 And when his brethren saw that their father loved him more than all his brethren, they hated him, and could not speak peaceably unto him.

His piety led him to protest against the wrong-doing of his brethren. He would not join them in evil, nor aid them by concealing their evil deeds.

5 ¶ And Joseph dreamed a dream, and he told *it* his brethren : and they hated him yet the more.

6 And he said unto them, Hear, I pray you, this dream which I have dreamed :

7 For, behold, we *were* binding sheaves in the field, and, lo, my sheaf arose, and also stood upright ; and, behold, your sheaves stood round about, and made obeisance to my sheaf.

8 And his brethren said to him, Shalt thou indeed reign over us ? or shalt thou indeed have dominion over us ? And they hated him yet the more for his dreams, and for his words.

9, 10, 11 And he dreamed yet another dream, and told it his brethren, and said, Behold, I have dreamed a dream more ; and, behold, the sun and the moon and the eleven stars made obeisance to me. And he told *it* to his father, and to his brethren : and his father rebuked him, and said unto him, What *is* this dream that thou hast dreamed ? Shall I and thy mother and thy brethren indeed come to bow down ourselves to thee to the earth ? And his brethren envied him ; but his father observed the saying. *(Whom God favours the ungodly are sure to dislike. The evil hate the righteous.)*

12, 13, 14 And his brethren went to feed their father's flock in Shechem. And Israel said unto Joseph, Do not thy brethren feed *the flock* in Shechem ? come, and I will send thee unto them. . . . . So he sent him out of the vale of Hebron, and he came to Shechem.

18, 19, 20 And when they saw him afar off, even before he came near unto them, they conspired against him to slay him. And they said one to another, Behold, this dreamer cometh. Come now therefore, and let us slay him, and cast him into some pit, and we will say, Some evil beast hath devoured him : and we shall see what will become of his dreams.

21, 22 And Reuben heard *it*, and he delivered him out of their hands ; and said, Let us not kill him. And Reuben said unto them, Shed no blood, *but* cast him into this pit that *is* in the wilderness, and lay no hand upon him ; that he might rid him out of their hands, to deliver him to his father again.

23 And it came to pass, when Joseph was come unto his brethren, that they stript Joseph out of his coat, *his* coat of *many* colours that *was* on him.

24 And they took him, and cast him into a pit : and the pit *was* empty, *there was* no water in it.

28 Then there passed by Midianites merchantmen ; and they drew and lifted up Joseph out of the pit, and sold Joseph to the Ishmeelites for twenty *pieces* of silver : and they brought Joseph into Egypt.

31, 32 And they took Joseph's coat, and killed a kid of the goats, and dipped the coat in the blood : And they sent the coat of *many* colours, and they brought *it* to their father, and said, This have we found : know now whether it *be* thy son's coat or no.

33 And he knew it, and said, *It is* my son's coat ; an evil beast hath devoured him ; Joseph is without doubt rent in pieces.

34, 35 And Jacob rent his clothes, and put sack-cloth upon his loins, and mourned for his son many days. And all his sons and all his daughters rose up to comfort him ; but he refused to be comforted ; and he said, For I will go down into the grave unto my son mourning. Thus his father wept for him. *(This was a very painful transaction, but let us not forget that the Lord overruled it for the highest good.)*

Crosses and changes are their lot,
Long as they sojourn here ;
But since their Saviour changes not,
What have his saints to fear ?

GENESIS XXXIX. 1—6 ; 16—23.

AND Joseph was brought down to Egypt ; and Potiphar, an officer of Pharaoh, captain of the guard, an Egyptian, bought him of the hands of the Ishmeelites, which had brought him down thither.

2 And the LORD was with Joseph, and he was a prosperous man ; and he was in the house of his master the Egyptian.

Grace enabled Joseph to make the best of his position, and to be amiable, industrious, and useful. This was as it should be. A child of God, even as a slave, should honour his religion, and God will bless him in so doing.

3 And his master saw that the LORD *was* with him, and that the LORD made all that he did to prosper in his hand.

This shews that Joseph did not fall into Egyptian idolatry, but avowed his faith in Jehovah, so that his master saw that Jehovah was with him.

4 And Joseph found grace in his sight, and he served him : and he made him overseer over his house, and all *that* he had he put into his hand. (*The fear of God leads to honesty and faithfulness, and this is often the road to promotion even among men. Godliness hath the promise of the life that now is.*)

5 And it came to pass from the time *that* he had made him overseer in his house, and over all that he had, that the LORD blessed the Egyptian's house for Joseph's sake ; and the blessing of the LORD was upon all that he had in the house, and in the field.

6 And he left all that he had in Joseph's hand ; and he knew not aught he had, save the bread which he did eat. And Joseph was *a* goodly *person,* and well favoured. (*This became a trial to him. Personal beauty is a dangerous gift: we must not be proud of it, but be the more guarded in our conduct if we possess it.*)

Joseph found a tempter in his master's wife, who would have led him into great sin. He refused to listen to her disgraceful request, and said, " How can I do this great wickedness, and sin against God?" The wicked woman again and again sought to lead him astray, and at last seized him, and held him, so that, to escape from her, he had to leave his garment in her hand. Then her wicked heart turned to malice, and she charged Joseph with being guilty of that unclean action which he had so earnestly refused.

16, 17, 18 And she laid up his garment by her, until his lord came home. And she spake unto him according to these words, saying, The Hebrew servant, which thou hast brought unto us, came in unto me to mock me. And it came to pass as I lifted up my voice and cried, that he left his garment with me, and fled out.

Thus she convinced her husband by showing the garment, which, could it have spoken, would have declared his innocence. A great deal of evidence may be brought against a perfectly innocent man. Let us, therefore, be slow to condemn persons of unblemished character.

19, 20 And it came to pass, when his master heard the words of his wife, which she spake unto him, saying, After this manner did thy servant to me ; that his wrath was kindled. And Joseph's master took him, and put him into the prison, a place where the king's prisoners *were* bound : and he was there in the prison.

Here his feet were hurt with fetters, and the iron entered into his soul.

21 ¶ But the LORD was with Joseph, and shewed him mercy, and gave him favour in the sight of the keeper of the prison. (*God is as much with his servants in a prison as in a palace; he does not desert us however low we may be brought.*)

22 And the keeper of the prison committed to Joseph's hand all the prisoners that *were* in the prison ; and whatsoever they did there, he was the doer *of it.*

When a good man is thrown down he is soon up again. Truth ever floats where sin is drowned.

23 The keeper of the prison looked not to anything *that was* under his hand ; because the LORD was with him, and *that* which he did, the LORD made *it* to prosper.

May each youthful descendant of godly parents be so kept by God's grace that the Lord may always be with him. Keep God's favour, and nothing is lost. Lose that, and all is gone.

Endow me, Lord, with godly fear,
　　A quick discerning eye,
To look to thee when sin is near,
　　And from the tempter fly.

Create in me a holy mind,
　　A sin-abhorring will,
That tramples down, and casts behind
　　The baits of pleasing ill.

GENESIS XL. 1; 3—23.

AND it came to pass after these things, *that* the butler of the king of Egypt and *his* baker had offended their lord the king of Egypt.

3, 4 And he put them in ward in the house of the captain of the guard, into the prison, the place where Joseph *was* bound. And the captain of the guard charged Joseph with them, and he served them: and they continued a season in ward. (*Thus providence regulated the royal household with an eye to Joseph, who was even in prison favoured of the Lord.*)

5 ¶ And they dreamed a dream both of them, each man his dream in one night.

Not only men awake but asleep also shall be made to serve Joseph's interests.

6, 7 And Joseph came in unto them in the morning, and looked upon them, and, behold, they *were* sad. And he asked Pharaoh's officers that *were* with him in the ward of his lord's house, saying, Wherefore look ye *so* sadly to day? (*Thus should we show kindly sympathy, and seek each other's welfare. What was fitting in a prison is even more so in a family.*)

8, 9, 10, 11 And they said unto him, We have dreamed a dream, and *there is* no interpreter of it. And Joseph said unto them, *Do* not interpretations *belong* to God? tell me *them*, I pray you. (*Joseph bore brave witness to the living God; every believer should do so.*) And the chief butler told his dream to Joseph, and said to him, In my dream, behold, a vine *was* before me; And in the vine *were* three branches: and it *was* as though it budded, *and* her blossoms shot forth; and the clusters thereof brought forth ripe grapes: And Pharaoh's cup *was* in my hand: and I took the grapes, and pressed them into Pharaoh's cup, and I gave the cup into Pharaoh's hand.

12, 13, 14, 15 And Joseph said unto him, This *is* the interpretation of it: The three branches *are* three days: Yet within three days shall Pharaoh lift up thine head, and restore thee unto thy place: and thou shalt deliver Pharaoh's cup into his hand, after the former manner when thou wast his butler. But think on me when it shall be well with thee, and shew kindness, I pray thee, unto me, and make mention of me unto Pharaoh, and bring me out of this house: For indeed I was stolen away out

of the land of the Hebrews: and here also have I done nothing that they should put me into the dungeon. (*How lovingly does Joseph hide his brethren's fault, and speak not of his being sold but "stolen." He was stolen, for the Ishmeelites bought what the sellers had no right to sell. Let us use the gentlest word when called to speak of the wrong doing of others.*)

16, 17, 18, 19 When the chief baker saw that the interpretation was good, he said unto Joseph, I also *was* in my dream, and, behold, *I had* three white baskets on my head: And in the uppermost basket *there was* of all manner of bakemeats for Pharaoh; and the birds did eat them out of the basket upon my head. And Joseph answered and said, This *is* the interpretation thereof: The three baskets *are* three days: Yet within three days shall Pharaoh lift up thy head from off thee, and shall hang thee on a tree; and the birds shall eat thy flesh from off thee.

20, 21, 22 And it came to pass the third day, *which was* Pharaoh's birthday, that he made a feast unto all his servants: and he lifted up the head of the chief butler and of the chief baker among his servants. And he restored the chief butler unto his butlership again; and he gave the cup into Pharaoh's hand: But he hanged the chief baker: as Joseph had interpreted to them. (*Whether for good or evil, the word of the Lord will be accomplished. Be it ours to have it in reverence.*)

23 Yet did not the chief butler remember Joseph, but forgat him. (*Sad would it have been for Joseph had he put his trust in man; but though the butler forgot him his God did not. The Lord was reserving Joseph for a more timely deliverance; he was to come out of prison to a throne, and that was best secured by his waiting a little longer. It is good for a man to hope, and quietly wait for the salvation of God.*)

Put thou thy trust in God;
In duty's path go on;
Fix on himself thy steadfast eye,
So shall thy work be done.

Though years on years roll on
His mercy shall endure;
Though clouds and darkness hide his path,
His promised grace is sure.

" The secret of the Lord is with them that fear Him."

TWO *years rolled away and Joseph was still in prison, for the right time had not come. If the vision tarry let us wait for it.*

GENESIS XLI. 1; 8—16; 25—36.

1 And it came to pass at the end of two full years that Pharaoh dreamed:

8 And in the morning his spirit was troubled; and he sent and called for all the magicians of Egypt, and all the wise men thereof: and Pharaoh told them his dream; but *there was* none that could interpret them unto Pharaoh.

9, 10, 11, 12, 13 ¶ Then spake the chief butler unto Pharaoh, saying, I do remember my faults this day: Pharaoh was wroth with his servants, and put me in ward in the captain of the guard's house, *both* me and the chief baker: And we dreamed a dream in one night, I and he; we dreamed each man according to the interpretation of his dream. And *there was* there with us a young man, an Hebrew, servant to the captain of the guard; and we told him, and he interpreted to us our dreams; to each man according to his dream he did interpret. And it came to pass, as he interpreted to us, so it was; me he restored unto mine office, and him he hanged.

14 ¶ Then Pharaoh sent and called Joseph, and they brought him hastily out of the dungeon: and he shaved *himself*, and changed his raiment, and came in unto Pharaoh. *(Joseph was under no obligation to any one for his release; he was fetched out of prison because the king needed him. Like his ancestor Abraham he owed not a thread or a shoe latchet to any man. God's people shall thus be made the head and not the tail. The king of Egypt could not say, " I have made Joseph rich." The Lord will exalt his servants in the best time, and in the best manner.)*

15 And Pharaoh said unto Joseph, I have dreamed a dream, and *there is* none that can interpret it: and I have heard say of thee, *that* thou canst understand a dream to interpret it.

16 And Joseph answered Pharaoh, saying, *It is* not in me: God shall give Pharaoh an answer of peace. *(Then the king detailed his double dream to Joseph, which was at once interpreted by divine illumination, Joseph humbly and plainly ascribing all his knowledge to the true God. Pharaoh had complimented him, but he*

was not a man of vain mind, and therefore disclaimed all honour for himself.)

25, 26, 27, 28 ¶ And Joseph said unto Pharaoh. The dream of Pharaoh *is* one: God hath shewed Pharaoh what he *is* about to do. The seven good kine *are* seven years; and the seven good ears *are* seven years: the dream *is* one. And the seven thin and ill favoured kine that came up after them *are* seven years; and the seven empty ears blasted with the east wind shall be seven years of famine. This *is* the thing which I have spoken unto Pharaoh: What God *is* about to do he sheweth unto Pharaoh.

29, 30, 31, 32 Behold, there come seven years of great plenty throughout all the land of Egypt: And there shall arise after them seven years of famine; and all the plenty shall be forgotten in the land of Egypt; and the famine shall consume the land; And the plenty shall not be known in the land by reason of that famine following; for it *shall be* very grievous. And for that the dream was doubled unto Pharaoh twice; *it is* because the thing *is* established by God, and God will shortly bring it to pass.

33, 34, 35, 36 Now therefore let Pharaoh look out a man discreet and wise, and set him over the land of Egypt. Let Pharaoh do *this*, and let him appoint officers over the land, and take up the fifth part of the land of Egypt in the seven plenteous years. And let them gather all the food of those good years that come, and lay up corn under the hand of Pharaoh, and let them keep food in the cities. And that food shall be for store to the land against the seven years of famine, which shall be in the land of Egypt; that the land perish not through the famine. *(Here was practical wisdom. This is what we should seek of God. Knowledge is of little service unless it be prudently utilised. To be anxiously careful for the future is wrong, but provident prudence is so evidently a virtue, that we wonder any should question it.)*

Ill that God blesses is our good,
    And unblest good is ill,
And all is right that seems most wrong,
    If it be his dear will.

I have no cares, O blessed Lord!
    For all my cares are thine;
I live in triumph, Lord, for thou
    Hast made thy triumphs mine.

WE left *Joseph before Pharaoh, whose dream he had interpreted, and to whom he had given sage advice.*

GENESIS XLI. 37—43; 46—57.

37 ¶ And the thing was good in the eyes of Pharaoh, and in the eyes of all his servants.

38 And Pharaoh said unto his servants, Can we find *such a one* as this *is*, a man in whom the Spirit of God *is*? (*Joseph's words concerning the Lord had a manifest effect on idolatrous Pharaoh, and he spoke with reverence. We need never be ashamed to avow our faith. Good will come of holy speech.*)

39, 40 And Pharaoh said unto Joseph, Forasmuch as God hath shewed thee all this, *there is* none so discreet and wise as thou *art:* Thou shalt be over my house, and according unto thy word shall all my people be ruled: only in the throne will I be greater than thou.

41 And Pharaoh said unto Joseph, See, I have set thee over all the land of Egypt.

42, 43 And Pharaoh took off his ring from his hand, and put it upon Joseph's hand, and arrayed him in vestures of fine linen, and put a gold chain about his neck; And he made him to ride in the second chariot which he had; and they cried before him, Bow the knee: and he made him *ruler* over all the land of Egypt.

What a change from the prison to the chariot. Thus was the Lord Jesus uplifted from the grave, that at the name of Jesus every knee should bow. Such honours in their degree shall all persecuted saints obtain either here or hereafter.

46 ¶ And Joseph *was* thirty years old when he stood before Pharaoh king of Egypt. And Joseph went out from the presence of Pharaoh, and went throughout all the land of Egypt.

Prosperity did not spoil him. He set about his business, and discharged the duties of his office with great diligence.

47, 48, 49 And in the seven plenteous years the earth brought forth by handfuls. And he gathered up all the food of the seven years, which were in the land of Egypt, and laid up the food in the cities: the food of the field, which *was* round about every city, laid he up in the same. And Joseph gathered corn as the sand of the sea, very much, until he left numbering; for *it was* without number.

50 And unto Joseph were born two sons before the years of famine came, which Asenath the daughter of Poti-pherah priest of On bare unto him.

51 And Joseph called the name of the firstborn Manasseh: For God, *said he*, hath made me forget all my toil, and all my father's house.

Our afflictions leave no sting behind. The Lord's love so rinses out our cup of sorrow that no bitterness remains. Such forgetfulness is sweet.

52 And the name of the second called he Ephraim: For God hath caused me to be fruitful in the land of my affliction. (*Here again he ascribes his happiness to his God, and blesses him for his double gift. To forget the past, and bear fruit in the present is a precious boon.*)

53 ¶ And the seven years of plenteousness, that was in the land of Egypt, were ended.

54 And the seven years of dearth began to come, according as Joseph had said : and the dearth was in all lands; but in all the land of Egypt there was bread.

55 And when all the land of Egypt was famished, the people cried to Pharaoh for bread: and Pharaoh said unto all the Egyptians, Go unto Joseph; what he saith to you, do.

We may call this a typical gospel, for poor hungry sinners are now bidden to go unto Jesus, and what he saith unto them do. May we be every one of us led of the Spirit of God to seek unto him who alone can open the well-stored granaries of grace.

56 And the famine was over all the face of the earth : And Joseph opened all the storehouses, and sold unto the Egyptians; and the famine waxed sore in the land of Egypt.

57 And all countries came into Egypt to Joseph for to buy *corn;* because that the famine was *so* sore in all lands. (*To whom else can men go for salvation but to Jesus, the Saviour? Have all who join in this reading gone unto the Redeemer for heavenly bread? If not—why not?*)

Hail to the Prince of life and peace
Who holds the keys of death and hell !
The kingdoms of the earth are his,
And sovereign power becomes him well.

In shame and sorrow once he died,
But now he reigns for evermore ;
Bow down ye saints before his feet,
And all ye angel-bands adore.

GENESIS XLII. 1—4; 6—10; 13—24.

NOW when Jacob saw that there was corn in Egypt, Jacob said unto his sons, Why do ye look one upon another?

2 And he said, Behold, I have heard that there is corn in Egypt: get you down thither, and buy for us from thence; that we may live, and not die. *(It is wise to seek relief, and not sit down in despair. If we need heavenly bread we must bestir ourselves and go to Jesus for it.)*

3, 4 ¶ And Joseph's ten brethren went down to buy corn in Egypt. But Benjamin, Joseph's brother, Jacob sent not with his brethren; for he said, Lest peradventure mischief befall him.

6 And Joseph *was* the governor over the land, *and* he *it was* that sold to all the people of the land: and Joseph's brethren came, and bowed down themselves before him *with* their faces to the earth. *(Now was his dream fulfilled, though two-and-twenty years had intervened, and he had passed through slavery and prison.)*

7 And Joseph saw his brethren, and he knew them, but made himself strange unto them, and spake roughly unto them: and he said unto them, Whence come ye? And they said, From the land of Canaan to buy food.

8, 9, 10 And Joseph knew his brethren, but they knew not him. And Joseph remembered the dreams which he dreamed of them, and said unto them, Ye *are* spies; to see the nakedness of the land ye are come. And they said unto him, Nay, my lord, but to buy food are thy servants come.

13 And they said, Thy servants *are* twelve brethren, the sons of one man in the land of Canaan; and, behold, the youngest *is* this day with our father, and one *is* not.

14 And Joseph said unto them, That *is it* that I spake unto you, saying, Ye *are* spies:

15 Hereby ye shall be proved: By the life of Pharaoh ye shall not go forth hence, except your youngest brother come hither.

16 Send one of you, and let him fetch your brother, and ye shall be kept in prison, that your words may be proved, whether *there be any* truth in you: or else by the life of Pharaoh surely ye *are* spies. *(Evil communications corrupt good manners. Joseph swears by the life of Pharaoh. He did it to conceal his true character, for they would assuredly judge that such was not the language of the seed of Israel.)*

17 And he put them all together into ward three days. *(He awakened their reflections by exciting their fears, dealing with them in the same manner as the Lord does with sinners whom he intends to reconcile unto himself. Divine severity brings the chosen to repentance.)*

18 And Joseph said unto them the third day, This do, and live; *for* I fear God:
This assurance must have been alike surprising and consoling to them. He who fears God will do his fellow men no wrong.

19 If ye *be* true *men*, let one of your brethren be bound in the house of your prison: go ye, carry corn for the famine of your houses:

20 But bring your youngest brother unto me; so shall your words be verified, and ye shall not die. And they did so.

21 And they said one to another, We *are* verily guilty concerning our brother, in that we saw the anguish of his soul, when he besought us, and we would not hear; therefore is this distress come upon us. *(Their sin found them out, as ours will do sooner or later. When we sow wild oats we ought to remember that we shall have to reap them.)*

22 And Reuben answered them, saying, Spake I not unto you, saying, Do not sin against the child; and ye would not hear? therefore, behold, also his blood is required. *(He who has a clear conscience is buoyed up in times of calamity.)*

23, 24 And they knew not that Joseph understood *them;* for he spake unto them by an interpreter. And he turned himself about from them, and wept. *(This is a touching picture. Joseph in his great wisdom felt bound not to reveal himself at once, but his love was so great that he could not restrain his tears. When the Lord deals roughly with sinners to make them more deeply conscious of sin, he loves them notwithstanding all. Jesus has an eye of sympathy for weeping penitents.)*

Oh that I could repent,
With all my idols part,
And to thy gracious eyes present
A humble, contrite heart.

Jesus on me bestow
The penitent desire;
With true sincerity of woe
My aching breast inspire.

JOSEPH'S *brethren returned to their father with abundant provisions, but these were before long exhausted, and the same distress filled Jacob's household. Bread that perisheth does not endure like the bread of heaven.*

GENESIS XLIII. 1—14.

1 And the famine *was* sore in the land.

2 And it came to pass, when they had eaten up the corn which they had brought out of Egypt, their father said unto them, Go again, buy us a little food.

3 And Judah spake unto him, saying, The man did solemnly protest unto us, saying, Ye shall not see my face, except your brother *be* with you.

4 If thou wilt send our brother with us, we will go down and buy thee food :

5 But if thou wilt not send *him*, we will not go down : for the man said unto us, Ye shall not see my face, except your brother *be* with you.

Israel had said positively " My son shall not go down," and yet it was needful that he should do so. We had better not be too positive in our determinations, or we may have to eat our words.

6 And Israel said, Wherefore dealt ye *so* ill with me, *as* to tell the man whether ye had yet a brother ? (*Poor Jacob, out of fear for his darling son, thinks his sons unkind. We should not do injustice to others because of our partiality to one, but we are very apt to do so.*)

7 And they said, The man asked us straitly of our state, and of our kindred, saying, *Is* your father yet alive ? have ye *another* brother ? and we told him according to the tenor of these words : could we certainly know that he would say, Bring your brother down ?

8, 9, 10 And Judah said unto Israel his father, Send the lad with me, and we will arise and go; that we may live, and not die, both we, and thou, *and* also our little ones. I will be surety for him ; of my hand shalt thou require him : if I bring him not unto thee, and set him before thee, then let me bear the blame for ever : for except we had lingered, surely now we had returned this second time.

Judah in becoming surety for Benjamin is a delightful type of our Lord Jesus, who is the surety of the New Covenant. He will assuredly fulfil his obligations and say at the last, " Of all those whom thou hast given me I have lost none."

11 And their father Israel said unto them, If *it must be* so now, do this; take of the best fruits in the land in your vessels, and carry down the man a present, a little balm, and a little honey, spices, and myrrh, nuts, and almonds :

This was prudence. Faith in God is not above using the means. It was well to conciliate those upon whom they were so dependent.

12 And take double money in your hand; and the money that was brought again in the mouth of your sacks, carry *it* again in your hand; peradventure it *was* an oversight :

The money had been put into their sacks by Joseph's order, but they were not aware of that fact ; therefore they were to restore it. This was scrupulous honesty, but not too scrupulous. We are not permitted to take advantage of the oversights of others. Every honest man will rectify mistakes by which another is the loser, even though he had no share in the error. Note what a good calculator Jacob was, and how he knew that the corn would rise in price, " Take double money," says he. Men of faith are not simpletons.

13 Take also your brother, and arise, go again unto the man :

14 And God Almighty give you mercy before the man, that he may send away your other brother, and Benjamin. If I be bereaved *of my children,* I am bereaved.

Jacob's faith now came to the front. He left the issues of his case with the all-sufficient God, and in holy resignation accepted the trial, if the Lord willed to lay it upon him. When we resign our mercies cheerfully, we are most likely to have them back again. Abraham was allowed to keep Isaac because he was willing to part with him at the divine bidding, and so Israel received Benjamin again because, after some struggling, he at last acquiesced in the Lord's will. When we are at the end of our self-will we are not far off the close of our trials.

> Our times are in thy hand,
> Why should we doubt or fear ?
> A Father's hand will never cause
> His child a needless tear.
>
> Our times are in thy hand,
> Jesus, the Crucified !
> The hand our many sins had pierced
> Is now our guard and guide.

S O *deeply interesting is this story of Joseph, that we must needs linger over it. The Holy Spirit indulges us with details, and we may be sure that he intended our profit thereby.*

GENESIS XLIII. 15, 16; 18—23; 26—34.

15 ¶ And the men took that present, and they took double money in their hand, and Benjamin; and rose up, and went down to Egypt, and stood before Joseph.

16 And when Joseph saw Benjamin with them, he said to the ruler of his house, Bring *these* men home, and slay, and make ready; for *these* men shall dine with me at noon.

Thus Joseph's love sought an opportunity for closer personal intercourse with them.

18 And the men were afraid, because they were brought into Joseph's house; and they said, Because of the money that was returned in our sacks at the first time are we brought in; that he may seek occasion against us, and fall upon us, and take us for bondmen, and our asses. *(Love intended pleasure, but fear turned it into dread. Beware of doubts and mistrusts of the Lord Jesus, lest even his goodness should make us afraid.)*

19, 20, 21, 22 And they came near to the steward of Joseph's house, and they communed with him at the door of the house, And said, O sir, we came indeed down at the first time to buy food: And it came to pass, when we came to the inn, that we opened our sacks, and, behold, *every* man's money *was* in the mouth of his sack, our money in full weight: and we have brought it again in our hand. And other money have we brought down in our hands to buy food: we cannot tell who put our money in our sacks.

Open confession was natural to honest men when in fear; it is also the ready way to peace with God.

23 And he said, Peace *be* to you, fear not: your God, and the God of your father, hath given you treasure in your sacks: I had your money. And he brought Simeon out unto them. *(The hostage being delivered all was well. The bringing of our Lord Jesus from the dead was a token for good to all his brethren.)*

26, 27 And when Joseph came home, they brought him the present which *was* in their hand into the house, and bowed themselves to him to the earth. And he asked them of *their*

welfare, and said, *Is* your father well, the old man of whom ye spake? *Is* he yet alive?'

28 And they answered, Thy servant our father *is* in good health, he *is* yet alive. And they bowed down their heads, and made obeisance. *(By calling their father " thy servant," and making obeisance for themselves and him, they fulfilled his second dream. The sun and the moon and the eleven stars did him homage.)*

29, 30 And he lifted up his eyes, and saw his brother Benjamin, his mother's son, and said, *Is* this your younger brother, of whom ye spake unto me? And he said, God be gracious unto thee, my son. And Joseph made haste; for his bowels did yearn upon his brother: and he sought *where* to weep; and he entered into *his* chamber, and wept there. *(Love longs to express itself, but there is a time for everything. Jesus loves his brethren always, but he prudently conceals himself at times for their good.)*

31 And he washed his face, and went out, and refrained himself, and said, Set on bread.

32 And they set on for him by himself, and for them by themselves, and for the Egyptians, which did eat with him, by themselves: because the Egyptians might not eat bread with the Hebrews; for that *is* an abomination unto the Egyptians.

33 And they sat before him, the firstborn according to his birthright, and the youngest according to his youth: and the men marvelled one at another.

34 And he took *and sent* messes unto them from before him: but Benjamin's mess was five times so much as any of theirs. And they drank, and were merry with him.

How they must have wondered while they feasted to see the order in which he placed them, and the favour shown to Benjamin. How plainly everything said, " I am Joseph," yet they perceived him not; and just so, despite all the loving deeds of Jesus, none ever discover him till he reveals himself by his Spirit.

Speak to us, Lord, thyself reveal,
   While here on earth we rove;
Speak to our hearts and let us feel
   The kindlings of thy love.

With thee conversing, we forget
   All time, and toil, and care;
Labour is rest, and pain is sweet,
   If thou, our God, art there.

JOSEPH *ordered a silver cup to be placed in Benjamin's sack, and when his brethren had set out upon their journey he sent his steward after them to bring them back. By this means Joseph tried his brethren, and brought them into a fit condition to be informed of their relationship. Our reading commences with the scene when the brothers had been brought back into Joseph's court-house.*

GENESIS XLIV. 14—34.

14 ¶ And Judah and his brethren came to Joseph's house; for he *was* yet there : and they fell before him on the ground.

15 And Joseph said unto them, What deed *is* this that ye have done? wot ye not that such a man as I can certainly divine? *(This he said to help himself in acting the part he had assumed.)*

16 And Judah said, What shall we say unto my lord? what shall we speak? or how shall we clear ourselves? God hath found out the iniquity of thy servants: behold, we *are* my lord's servants, both we, and *he* also with whom the cup is found. *(Though innocent of the present charge, Judah confesses that their sad plight was well deserved by other sins.)*

17 And he said, God forbid that I should do so: *but* the man in whose hand the cup is found, he shall be my servant; and as for you, get you up in peace unto your father. *(To this Judah, the surety, could not yield; but pleaded in a marvellously touching manner. Note how eloquent he was. Our surety is our advocate, and his pleadings are mighty.)*

18, 19 ¶ Then Judah came near unto him, and said, Oh my lord, let thy servant, I pray thee, speak a word in my lord's ears, and let not thine anger burn against thy servant: for thou *art* even as Pharaoh. My lord asked his servants, saying, Have ye a father, or a brother?

20 And we said unto my lord, We have a father, an old man, and a child of his old age, a little one; and his brother is dead, and he alone is left of his mother, and his father loveth him.

21, 22, 23 And thou saidst unto thy servants, Bring him down unto me, that I may set mine eyes upon him. And we said unto my lord, The lad cannot leave his father: for *if* he should leave his father, *his father* would die. And

thou saidst unto thy servants, Except your youngest brother come down with you, ye shall see my face no more.

24 And it came to pass when we came up unto thy servant my father, we told him the words of my lord.

25, 26 And our father said, Go again, *and* buy us a little food. And we said, We cannot go down : if our youngest brother be with us, then will we go down: for we may not see the man's face, except our youngest brother *be* with us.

27, 28, 29 And thy servant my father said unto us, Ye know that my wife bare me two *sons:* And the one went out from me, and I said, Surely he is torn in pieces; and I saw him not since: And if ye take this also from me, and mischief befall him, ye shall bring down my gray hairs with sorrow to the grave.

30, 31, 32, 33, 34 Now therefore when I come to thy servant my father, and the lad *be* not with us; seeing that his life is bound up in the lad's life; It shall come to pass, when he seeth that the lad *is* not *with us,* that he will die: and thy servant shall bring down the gray hairs of thy servant our father with sorrow to the grave. For thy servant became surety for the lad unto my father, saying, If I bring him not unto thee, then I shall bear the blame to my father for ever. Now therefore, I pray thee, let thy servant abide instead of the lad a bondman to my lord; and let the lad go up with his brethren. For how shall I go up to my father, and the lad *be* not with me? lest peradventure I see the evil that shall come on my father.

The power of Judah's advocacy lay very much in its truth. It is a simple unvarnished narrative of facts. But its master weapon is found in the proposed substitution of himself for Benjamin. He is ready to smart for his suretyship. Do we not remember how Judah's great antitype not only proferred to be our substitute but actually was so: in this lies the power of his intercession.

Where high the heavenly temple stands,
The house of God not made with hands,
Jesus, our Judah, stands to plead,
A brother born for time of need.

He, who for men their surety stood,
And pour'd on earth his precious blood,
Pursues in heaven his mighty plan,
The advocate and friend of man.

AFTER *Judah's thrilling speech a solemn pause would follow. All hearts were full, but all tongues were silent.*

GENESIS XLV. 1—15.

1 Then Joseph could not refrain himself before all them that stood by him; and he cried, Cause every man to go out from me. And there stood no man with him, while Joseph made himself known unto his brethren. *It was not meet that strangers should view that tender scene.. When Jesus reveals himself to his chosen, it is " not unto the world."*

2 And he wept aloud: and the Egyptians and the house of Pharaoh heard. *(His heart long pent up burst forth at last uncontrollably.)*

3 And Joseph said unto his brethren, I *am* Joseph; doth my father yet live? *(How amazed they must have been to see before them the brother whom they sold for a slave, and themselves in his power. What a discovery the soul makes when it perceives that Jesus whom it crucified is Lord and God.)* And his brethren could not answer him; for they were troubled at his presence.

4 And Joseph said unto his brethren, Come near to me, I pray you. And they came near. *(Tenderness courts communion and seeks to cast out fear. The words before us are such as Jesus uses to his troubled brethren; let us not be slow to draw near.)* And he said, I *am* Joseph your brother, whom ye sold into Egypt.

5 Now therefore be not grieved, nor angry with yourselves, that ye sold me hither: for God did send me before you to preserve life.

6 For these two years *hath* the famine *been* in the land : and yet *there are* five years, in the which *there shall* neither *be* earing nor harvest.

7 And God sent me before you to preserve you a posterity in the earth, and to save your lives by a great deliverance.

8 So now *it was* not you *that* sent me hither, but God: and he hath made me a father to Pharaoh, and lord of all his house, and a ruler throughout all the land of Egypt. *He has so completely pardoned them, that he does not speak of forgiving them himself, but urges them to forgive themselves. He labours to expel from them the sorrow of the world which worketh death, for he knew that there would then be more room for godly sorrow.*

9, 10 Haste ye, and go up to my father, and say unto him, Thus saith thy son Joseph, God hath made me lord of all Egypt: come down unto me, tarry not: And thou shalt dwell in the land of Goshen, and thou shalt be near unto me, thou, and thy children, and thy children's children, and thy flocks, and thy herds, and all that thou hast: *(To be near to Joseph would be the choicest joy to Jacob. To be in fellowship with Jesus is the believer's heaven.)*

11 And there will I nourish thee; for yet *there are* five years of famine; lest thou, and thy household, and all that thou hast, come to poverty. *(He who forgives provides bountifully for the pardoned ones. Those whom Jesus cleanses from sin shall have all their wants supplied.)*

12 And, behold, your eyes see, and the eyes of my brother Benjamin, that *it is* my mouth that speaketh unto you.

13 And ye shall tell my father of all my glory in Egypt, and of all that ye have seen ; and ye shall haste and bring down my father hither.

14 And he fell upon his brother Benjamin's neck, and wept; and Benjamin wept upon his neck. *(The loves of Jesus and his favoured ones are mutual. What one feels the other feels.)*

15 Moreover he kissed all his brethren, and wept upon them: and after that his brethren talked with him. *(These kisses were seals of love, comparable to the witness of the Spirit in believing men. Such tokens unloose the tongue, and enable us to talk with Jesus in the holy familiarities of sacred fellowship. " Let him kiss me with the kisses of his mouth," saith the spouse in the song.. Amen. The Lord do so unto each one of us.)*

Oh see how Jesus trusts himself
  Unto our childish love,
As though by his free ways with us
  Our earnestness to prove!

His sacred name a common word
  On earth he loves to hear ;
There is no majesty in him
  Which love may not come near.

The light of love is round his feet,
  His paths are never dim ;
And he comes nigh to us when we
  Dare not come nigh to him.

GENESIS XLV. 16—28.

JOSEPH'S *meeting with his family could not be long concealed; the happy fact oozed out, and the news was carried to the King himself.*

16 And the fame thereof was heard in Pharaoh's house, saying, Joseph's brethren are come: and it pleased Pharaoh well, and his servants. (*They were glad because so great a benefactor of their nation was made happy.*)

17, 18, 19 And Pharaoh said unto Joseph, Say unto thy brethren, This do ye; lade your beasts, and go, get you unto the land of Canaan; And take your father and your households, and come unto me : and I will give you the good of the land of Egypt, and ye shall eat the fat of the land. Now thou art commanded, this do ye; take you wagons (*or chariots*) out of the land of Egypt for your little ones, and for your wives, and bring your father, and come.

20 Also regard not your stuff; for the good of all the land of Egypt *is* your's. (*Pharaoh thus delicately and with lordly generosity, spared Joseph any scruples about inviting his kinsmen to dwell in the land; they were to come into the country as the king's own guests. Observe how he bids them leave all their " stuff" behind, as if he meant to give them so much that would be better that they need not bring their tents or their furniture with them. Certainly, when we come to Jesus, and receive his treasures of grace, all earthly things become mere " stuff" to us.*)

21 And the children of Israel did so : and Joseph gave them wagons, according to the commandment of Pharaoh, and gave them provision for the way.

22 To all of them he gave each man changes of raiment; but to Benjamin he gave three hundred *pieces* of silver, and five changes of raiment. (*How Joseph's goodness contrasted with their former cruelty. " They sent him naked to strangers, he sends them in new and rich liveries; they took a small sum of money for him, he gives them large treasures; they sent his torn coat to his father, he sends variety of costly garments; they sold him to be the load of camels, he sends them home in chariots." Far greater still is the contrast between our ungenerous treatment of the Lord Jesus and his bountiful returns of grace to us.*)

23 And to his father he sent after this manner; ten asses laden with the good things of Egypt, and ten she asses laden with corn and bread and meat for his father by the way.

24 So he sent his brethren away, and they departed : and he said unto them, See that ye fall not out by the way. (*He knew them well, and feared that they might begin accusing each other, or might even become envious of Benjamin, as they had formerly been of himself.*)

25, 26 ¶ And they went up out of Egypt, and came into the land of Canaan unto Jacob their father. And told him, saying, Joseph *is* yet alive, and he *is* governor over all the land of Egypt. And Jacob's heart fainted, for he believed them not. (*A sad heart is far more ready to believe a mournful falsehood than a joyful truth. When his sons wickedly shewed him Joseph's coat he said, " Joseph is without doubt rent in pieces," but when they tell him a true story, he believes them not. It is a pity when despondency makes our judgment lose its balance.*)

27 And they told him all the words of Joseph, which he had said unto them : and when he saw the wagons which Joseph had sent to carry him, the spirit of Jacob their father revived :

28 And Israel said, *It is* enough; Joseph my son *is* yet alive : I will go and see him before I die. (*First the words, and then the wagons aided Jacob's faith, even as the words of Jesus and the gifts of Jesus enable us to believe on him. The venerable patriarch was more glad to hear that his son was " alive," than that he was " governor over all the land of Egypt." This was enough for him, and he resolved to have a sight of his beloved one. Where there is true love there will be a desire for communion. Those who love the Son of God will not be willing to live without heavenly fellowship. O may all united here in family worship, see Jesus by faith before they die, when they die, and then for ever.*)

> Jesus, these eyes have never seen
> That radiant form of Thine !
> The veil of sense hangs dark between
> Thy blessed face and mine !
> Yet though I have not seen, and still,
> Must rest in faith alone ;
> I love thee, dearest Lord ! and will,
> Unseen, but not unknown.
> When death these mortal eyes shall seal,
> And still this throbbing heart,
> The rending veil shall thee reveal,
> All glorious as thou art.

GENESIS XLVI. 29—34.

AND Joseph made ready his chariot, and went up to meet Israel his father, to Goshen, and presented himself unto him; and he fell on his neck, and wept on his neck a good while.

30 And Israel said unto Joseph, Now let me die, since I have seen thy face, because thou *art* yet alive. *(As if now he could lie down and sleep, for his last desire was fulfilled. Bishop Hall says, "And if the meeting of earthly friends be so unspeakably comfortable, how happy shall we be in the light of the glorious face of God our Father! of that of our blessed Redeemer, whom we sold to death for our sins, and who now, after his noble triumph, hath all power given him in heaven and earth")*

31, 32 And Joseph said unto his brethren, and unto his father's house, I will go up, and shew Pharaoh, and say unto him, My brethren, and my father's house, which *were* in the land of Canaan, are come unto me; And the men *are* shepherds, for their trade hath been to feed cattle; and they have brought their flocks, and their herds, and all that they have.

33, 34 And it shall come to pass, when Pharaoh shall call you, and shall say, What *is* your occupation? That ye shall say, Thy servants' trade hath been about cattle from our youth even until now, both we, *and* also our fathers: that ye may dwell in the land of Goshen; for every shepherd *is* an abomination unto the Egyptians. *(To speak the honest truth is always the best policy, and to follow an honest calling the best condition. Joseph might have bid them ask to be made nobles, but he knew that they would prosper better as shepherds. "Seekest thou great things for thyself, seek them not.")*

GENESIS XLVII. 2—10; 12.

AND Joseph took some of his brethren, *even* five men, and presented them unto Pharaoh.

3 And Pharaoh said unto his brethren, What *is* your occupation? And they said unto Pharaoh, Thy servants *are* shepherds, both we, *and* also our fathers.

4 They said moreover unto Pharaoh, For to sojourn in the land are we come; for thy servants have no pasture for their flocks; for the famine *is* sore in the land of Canaan; now therefore, we pray thee, let thy servants dwell in the land of Goshen.

5, 6 And Pharaoh. spake unto Joseph, saying, Thy father and thy brethren are come unto thee: The land of Egypt *is* before thee; in the best of the land make thy father and brethren to dwell; in the land of Goshen let them dwell: and if thou knowest *any* men of activity among them, then make them rulers over my cattle.

7 And Joseph brought in Jacob his father, and set him before Pharaoh: and Jacob blessed Pharaoh.

8 And Pharaoh said unto Jacob, How old *art* thou?

9 And Jacob said unto Pharaoh, The days of the years of my pilgrimage *are* an hundred and thirty years: few and evil have the days of the years of my life been, and have not attained unto the days of the years of the life of my fathers in the days of their pilgrimage.

He avowed himself a pilgrim, thus bearing witness to the hope which sustained him, but he gave to Pharaoh a more gloomy view of pilgrim life than Abraham or Isaac would have done. However, since this man of many trials yet reached the promised rest, even so shall every afflicted believer.

10 And Jacob blessed Pharaoh, and went out from before Pharaoh. *(The reverend age of Jacob gave him liberty to bless even the monarch of the land. An old man's blessing is precious. Let us so act towards the aged, that they may invoke blessings upon us.)*

12 And Joseph nourished his father, and his brethren, and all his father's household, with bread, according to *their* families. *(Thus our elder brother Jesus, who is Lord over the whole earth for the good of his church, takes care to nourish all his Father's household " according to their families." Be pleased, O Jesus, to let this family share in thy great love.)*

When famine frowns and fields are bare
God shall for saints provide;
He has a land of Goshen where
He makes their souls abide.

In darkest times they need not fear,
Their wants are all foreknown;
Jesus their Lord shall now appear
As Joseph on the throne.

THE *Psalmist commemorates the providential care of the Lord towards the chosen family in the delightful verses of—*

PSALM CV.

1 O give thanks unto the LORD; call upon his name: make known his deeds among the people. *(Thankfulness should sweeten our spirit, worship should be our delight, and to make known the goodness of the Lord our constant employment.)*

2 Sing unto him, sing psalms unto him: talk ye of all his wondrous works. *(Both singing and talking ought to be consecrated to the Lord's honour, though, alas! they are too often desecrated to the most unworthy purposes.)*

3 Glory ye in his holy name: let the heart of them rejoice that seek the LORD. *We are very prone to glory in something; wise are they who glory only in the Lord.*

4 Seek the LORD, and his strength: seek his face evermore. *(Even when we have found him and know his love, let us press onward and seek him more and more.)*

5, 6 Remember his marvellous works that he hath done; his wonders, and the judgments of his mouth; O ye seed of Abraham his servant, ye children of Jacob his chosen. *Those who receive special favours should consider themselves under peculiar obligations to glorify God by publishing abroad his goodness and power.*

7 He *is* the LORD our God: his judgments *are* in all the earth.

8 He hath remembered his covenant for ever, the word *which* he commanded to a thousand generations. *(Glory be to God, he has never ceased to be faithful to the covenant of grace. It is ordered in all things and sure, and not one word of it has ever fallen to the ground. His promises stand fast for ever, firm as the throne of the I AM.)*

9 Which *covenant* he made with Abraham, and his oath unto Isaac;

10 And confirmed the same unto Jacob for a law, *and* to Israel *for* an everlasting covenant:

11 Saying, Unto thee will I give the land of Canaan, the lot of your inheritance:

12 When they were *but* a few men in number; yea, very few, and strangers in it.

13 When they went from one nation to another; from *one* kingdom to another people;

14 He suffered no man to do them wrong: yea, he reproved kings for their sakes;

15 *Saying,* Touch not mine anointed, and do my prophets no harm. *(With ease the surrounding potentates might have crushed the chosen race while one single tent could hold them; but the Preserver of men mysteriously guarded them, as evermore he keeps the little flock of his people. The persons of the saints are sacred, and sanctified unto God, they cannot be touched with impunity.)*

16 Moreover he called for a famine upon the land: he brake the whole staff of bread. *Before the famine came, arrangements had been made for the housing of Jacob and his family. Before our trials befall us the way out of them has been prepared. There was a Joseph before there was a famine.*

17, 18 He sent a man before them, *even* Joseph, *who* was sold for a servant: Whose feet they hurt with fetters: he was laid in iron:

19 Until the time that his word came: the word of the LORD tried him. *God's word caused the trial, and the same word ended it. There is as much a divine fiat concerning our daily trials as there was in the creation of the world. One word from God can bring us down, but, blessed be his name, another can raise us up.*

20 The king sent and loosed him; *even* the ruler of the people, and let him go free.

21, 22 He made him lord of his house, and ruler of all his substance: To bind his princes at his pleasure; and teach his senators wisdom.

23 Israel also came into Egypt; and Jacob sojourned in the land of Ham. *(Even favoured Israel must go into Egypt where trouble awaited his household; but it was needful for the preservation of the race, and therefore a matter for praise. Let us bless God also when we go down into Egypt, for the hand of the Lord is in it.)*

To God, the great, the ever bless'd,
Let songs of honour be address'd;
His mercy firm for ever stands;
Give him the thanks his love demands.

Remember what thy mercy did
For Jacob's race thy chosen seed;
And with the same salvation bless
The meanest suppliant of thy grace.

60　　　　　　　　　　"God shall be with you."　　　　JANUARY 30.—EVENING.

[*Or February* 29.]

GENESIS XLVIII. 1—5; 8—21. /

AND it came to pass after these things, that *one* told Joseph, Behold, thy father is sick: and he took with him his two sons, Manasseh and Ephraim.

2 And *one* told Jacob, and said, Behold, thy son Joseph cometh unto thee: and Israel strengthened himself, and sat upon the bed.

3 And Jacob said unto Joseph, God Almighty appeared unto me at Luz in the land of Canaan, and blessed me,

4 And said unto me, Behold, I will make thee fruitful, and multiply thee, and I will make of thee a multitude of people; and will give this land to thy seed after thee *for* an everlasting possession. (*Jacob would not have Joseph fix his heart upon Egypt, but have a believing eye towards Canaan, therefore he speaks to him concerning it. We must ever guard against loving the world because things go smoothly with us.*)

5 And now thy two sons, Ephraim and Manasseh, which were born unto thee in the land of Egypt before I came unto thee into Egypt, *are* mine; as Reuben and Simeon, they shall be mine. (*Thus they were to be regarded as founders of distinct tribes, and to have each of them a portion among the sons of Jacob.*)

8 And Israel beheld Joseph's sons, and said, Who *are* these?

9 And Joseph said unto his father, They *are* my sons, whom God hath given me in this *place*. And he said, Bring them, I pray thee, unto me, and I will bless them.

10 Now the eyes of Israel were dim for age, *so that* he could not see. And he brought them near unto him; and he kissed them, and embraced them.

11 And Israel said unto Joseph, I had not thought to see thy face: and, lo, God hath shewed me also thy seed. (*God is much better to us than our fears; yea, far better than our hopes.*)

12 And Joseph brought them out from between his knees, and he bowed himself with his face to the earth.

13 And Joseph took them both, Ephraim in his right hand towards Israel's left hand, and Manasseh in his left hand toward Israel's right hand, and brought *them* near unto him.

14 And Israel stretched out his right hand, and laid *it* upon Ephraim's head, who *was* the younger, and his left hand upon Manasseh's head, guiding his hands wittingly; for Manasseh *was* the firstborn.

15 And he blessed Joseph, and said, God, before whom my fathers Abraham and Isaac did walk, the God which fed me all my life long unto this day,

16 The Angel which redeemed me from all evil, bless the lads; and let my name be named on them, and the name of my fathers Abraham and Isaac; and let them grow into a multitude in the midst of the earth.

17 And when Joseph saw that his father laid his right hand upon the head of Ephraim, it displeased him: and he held up his father's hand, to remove it from Ephraim's head unto Manasseh's head.

18 And Joseph said unto his father, Not so, my father: for this *is* the first-born; put thy right hand upon his head.

19 And his father refused, and said I know *it*, my son, I know *it*: he also shall become a people, and he also shall be great: but truly his younger brother shall be greater than he, and his seed shall become a multitude of nations.

The order of nature is not the order of grace. Jacob well knew this, for in his own case it was written, " the elder shall serve the younger." The Lord's purposes must stand.

20 And he blessed them that day, saying, In thee shall Israel bless, saying, God make thee as Ephraim and as Manasseh: and he set Ephraim before Manasseh.

21 And Israel said unto Joseph, Behold, I die: but God shall be with you, and bring you again unto the land of your fathers.

Whoever dies, the Lord remains with his people. Let us not be in despair, though the best of our friends or the ablest of our ministers be taken from us.

> When good old Jacob blest the seed,
> 　From Joseph's loins that came,
> He cross'd his withered hands, 'tis said,
> 　And God has done the same.
> Crosses each day with trials hot,
> 　The Christian's path has been;
> And who has found a happy lot
> 　Without a cross between?
> "Not so, my father," oft we say,
> 　This pain, this grief remove;
> Too blind to fathom wisdom's way,
> 　Or think 'tis sent in love.

GENESIS XLIX. 1—15.

AND Jacob called unto his sons, and said, Gather yourselves together, that I may tell you *that* which shall befall you in the last days.

2 Gather yourselves together, and hear, ye sons of Jacob; and hearken unto Israel your father. *(Jacob was about to speak by inspiration. The blessing of a parent whose tongue is taught of God is priceless beyond conception.)*

3 ¶ Reuben, thou *art* my firstborn, my might, and the beginning of my strength, the excellency of dignity, and the excellency of power :

4 Unstable as water, thou shalt not excel; because thou wentest up to thy father's bed; then defiledst thou *it:* he went up to my couch.

Though he was the firstborn Reuben missed the birth-right, because he was light and loose. Whatever good points may be in a man, if he be not sober, steady, and substantial, he will come to nothing. To be unstable as the waves of the sea is one of the worst of faults and mars the whole character.

5 ¶ Simeon and Levi *are* brethren; instruments of cruelty *are in* their habitations.

6 O my soul, come not thou into their secret; unto their assembly, mine honour, be not thou united : for in their anger they slew a man, and in their selfwill they digged down a wall.

7 Cursed *be* their anger, for *it was* fierce ; and their wrath, for it was cruel : I will divide them in Jacob, and scatter them in Israel.

A great wrong was here disavowed by Jacob. He could not prevent it, for his sons acted hastily in selfwill, and he knew nothing of their murderous deed till it was over, but he takes care to bear his witness against it in the most solemn manner. The follies of youth will come home to men in their riper years. It is a great mercy when from our childhood, we walk uprightly.

8 ¶ Judah, thou *art he* whom thy brethren shall praise : thy hand *shall be* in the neck of thine enemies ; thy father's children shall bow down before thee. *(When the dying patriarch reached that name which is a type of Christ, he rose to a higher key, he had no more faults to mention, but fell to blessing.)*

9 Judah *is* a lion's whelp : from the prey, my son, thou art gone up : he stooped down, he couched as a lion, and as an old lion ; who shall rouse him up ? *(Who dare defy the Lion of the tribe of Judah ? Jesus the Lord is terrible to his enemies.)*

10 The sceptre shall not depart from Judah, nor a lawgiver from between his feet, until Shiloh come ; and unto him *shall* the gathering of the people *be*. *(When our Lord came his enemies said, "Behold, the world is gone after him." To this day he is the greatest of loadstones to attract mens' hearts. He came just when the kingdom had gone from Judah, and now he reigns as our Shiloh, the Prince of Peace.)*

11, 12 Binding his foal unto the vine, and his ass's colt unto the choice vine ; he washed his garments in wine, and his clothes in the blood of grapes : His eyes *shall be* red with wine, and his teeth white with milk. *(Truly in our Immanuel's land the wine and milk flow in rivers. Come ye and buy without money and without price.)*

13 ¶ Zebulun shall dwell at the haven of the sea ; and he *shall be* for an haven of ships ; and his border *shall be* unto Zidon. *(May our seafaring people be favoured of the Lord, and never sit in darkness as Zebulun came to do.)*

14, 15 Issachar *is* a strong ass couching down between two burdens : And he saw that rest *was* good, and the land that *it was* pleasant; and bowed his shoulder to bear, and became a servant unto tribute. *(Though quiet and industrious, it may be Issachar was somewhat deficient in courage and energy. There are no perfect characters ; but it were greatly to be wished that our contented brethren were also more energetic. Yet as Issachar was a true son of Jacob, we trust our slow-moving brethren are the same. It were well, however, for each of us to be more in earnest than ever, for we serve an earnest God.)*

We leave the rest of the blessing for our next reading.

God of mercy, hear our prayer
For the children Thou hast given ;
Let them all Thy blessings share,
Grace on earth, and bliss in heaven !

Cleanse their souls from every stain,
Through the Saviour's precious blood ;
Let them all be born again,
And be reconciled to God.

WE *will now read the rest of the benedictions pronounced by Jacob upon his sons.*

GENESIS XLIX. 16—33.

16 ¶ Dan shall judge his people, as one of the tribes of Israel. *(Dan signifies judge; the patriarch declared that he would verify his name.)*

17 Dan shall be a serpent by the way, an adder in the path, that biteth the horse heels, so that his rider shall fall backward.

18 I have waited for thy salvation, O LORD. *Here Jacob made a pause. His utterance of weakness has neither petulance nor complaining in it, but is expressive of hope growing out of long confidence. Soon he hoped to enjoy the fulness of salvation in the presence of the Lord.*

19 ¶ Gad, a troop shall overcome him: but he shall overcome at the last. *(This is often exemplified in the believer's life. Many trials press him down, but he rises up again.)*

20 ¶ Out of Asher his bread *shall be* fat, and he shall yield royal dainties.

21 ¶ Naphtali *is* a hind let loose: he giveth goodly words. *(Vivacity of spirit was linked with readiness of speech, a good combination for a minister of the gospel.)*

22 ¶ Joseph *is* a fruitful bough, *even* a fruitful bough by a well; *whose* branches run over the wall:

23 The archers have sorely grieved him, and shot *at him*, and hated him:

24 But his bow abode in strength, and the arms of his hands were made strong by the hands of the mighty *God* of Jacob; (from thence *is* the shepherd, the stone of Israel:)

25 *Even* by the God of thy father, who shall help thee; and by the Almighty, who shall bless thee with blessings of heaven above, blessings of the deep that lieth under, blessings of the breasts, and of the womb;

26 The blessings of thy father have prevailed above the blessings of my progenitors unto the utmost bound of the everlasting hills: they shall be on the head of Joseph, and on the crown of the head of him that was separate from his brethren. *(The heart of the venerable patriarch was enlarged concerning Joseph; he evidently felt that he could not pour out a benediction copious enough. And truly, if we turn our thoughts to Jesus, the greater Joseph, no language can ever*

express our desires for his exaltation. Watts has well put it—

"Blessings more than we can give,
Be, Lord, for ever thine."

27 ¶ Benjamin shall ravin *as* a wolf: in the morning he shall devour the prey, and at night, he shall divide the spoil. *This was to be a contentious tribe. Though Benjamin stood high in his father's natural affection, he did not dare for that reason to invent a blessing for him, but speaks the word of the Lord neither less nor more. To fight from morning to night is a sorry business, unless it be against sin.*

28 ¶ All these *are* the twelve tribes of Israel: and this *is it* that their father spake unto them, and blessed them; every one according to his blessing he blessed them.

29, 30 And he charged them, and said unto them, I am to be gathered unto my people: bury me with my fathers in the cave that *is* in the field of Ephron the Hittite, In the cave that *is* in the field of Machpelah, which *is* before Mamre, in the land of Canaan, which Abraham bought with the field of Ephron the Hittite for a possession of a buryingplace.

31 There they buried Abraham and Sarah his wife; there they buried Isaac and Rebekah his wife; and there I buried Leah.

32 The purchase of the field and of the cave that *is* therein *was* from the children of Heth.

33 And when Jacob had made an end of commanding his sons, he gathered up his feet into the bed, and yielded up the ghost, and was gathered unto his people.

He was not left even after death among the Egyptians, but slept in the family tomb of the pilgrim band, to awake with them at the resurrection. In all things he maintained his character as a sojourner with God, looking for a city yet to be revealed.

Shrinking from the cold hand of death,
I soon must gather up my feet;
Must swift resign this fleeting breath,
And die, my father's God to meet.

Number'd among thy people, I
Expect with joy thy face to see;
Because thou didst for sinners, die,
Jesus, in death, remember me!

JOB I. 1—12.

IT is the general opinion that *Job flourished at some time between the age of Abraham and the time of Moses. It is probable that Moses wrote the sacred poem which records the discussion between Job and his friends. We shall therefore, in this place, consider his history, and gather a few gems from the remarkable book which bears his name.*

1 There was a man in the land of Uz, whose name *was* Job; *(he was but a plain " man" and not a noble, yet was he more noble than the nobles of his time.)* And that man was perfect and upright, and one that feared God, and eschewed evil. *(His character is given him by infallible inspiration, and surely no man could win a better. His life was well balanced and displayed all the virtues, both towards God and towards man.)*

2 And there were born unto him seven sons and three daughters.

3 His substance also was seven thousand sheep, and three thousand camels, and five hundred yoke of oxen, and five hundred she asses, and a very great household; so that this man was the greatest of all the men of the east. *So that a rich man may be a good man, and though " gold and the gospel seldom do agree," yet it may happen that a man of substance may also have substance in heaven. Job was gracious in prosperity, and therefore was sustained in adversity.*

4 And his sons went and feasted *in their* houses, every one his day; and sent and called for their three sisters to eat and to drink with them. *(Probably they celebrated their birthdays in this happy and united manner. It is a great happiness to see brothers and sisters knit together in love.)*

5 And it was so, when the days of *their* feasting were gone about, that Job sent and sanctified them, and rose up early in the morning, and offered burnt offerings *according* to the number of them all: for Job said, It may be that my sons have sinned, and cursed God in their hearts. Thus did Job continually. *(He did not forbid their festivals, for they were not in themselves sinful, but knowing how prone men are to forget their God, if not themselves, when in the house of feasting, he was anxious to remove any spot which might remain. It is to be feared that few parents are as careful as Job was in this matter.)*

6 ¶ Now there was a day when the sons of God came to present themselves before the LORD, and Satan came also among them. *To do this he need not be in heaven. God's assembly room includes all space. What impudence it was on Satan's part to come before God! What equal impudence when hypocrites pretend to worship the Most High.*

7 And the LORD said unto Satan, Whence comest thou? Then Satan answered the LORD, and said, From going to and fro in the earth, and from walking up and down in it. *He is a busy itinerant. He is never idle.*

8 And the LORD said unto Satan, Hast thou considered my servant Job, that *there is* none like him in the earth, a perfect and an upright man, one that feareth God, and escheweth evil? *Satan reflects carefully and acts craftily. He had "considered" Job, and watched him narrowly.*

9 Then Satan answered the LORD, and said, Doth Job fear God for nought?

10 Hast not thou made an hedge about him, and about his house, and about all that he hath on every side? thou hast blessed the work of his hands, and his substance is increased in the land. *(And why not? If Job had been poor and wretched, Satan would have said that the Lord paid his servants wretched wages.)*

11 But put forth thine hand now, and touch all that he hath, and he will curse thee to thy face. *(A cruel insinuation, but Satan was measuring Job's corn with his own bushel.)*

12 And the LORD said unto Satan, Behold, all that he hath *is* in thy power; only upon himself put not forth thine hand. So Satan went forth from the presence of the LORD. *The Lord intended to glorify himself, to further perfect the character of Job, and to furnish his church with a grand example. Hence his challenge to the arch-enemy. Satan went off upon his errand willingly enough, but he little dreamed of the defeat which awaited him.*

Hast Thou protected me thus far,
To leave me in this dangerous hour?
Shall Satan be allow'd to mar
Thy work, or to resist Thy power?

Oh never wilt Thou leave the soul
That flies for refuge to Thy breast!
Thy love, which once hath made me whole,
Shall guide me to eternal rest.

JOB I. 13—22.

AND there was a day when his sons and his daughters *were* eating and drinking wine in their eldest brother's house :

Satan was crafty in his selection of the time. When troubles come upon us at seasons of rejoicing they have a double bitterness. The brightness of the morning of that memorable day made the darkness of the night all the darker.

14 And there came a messenger unto Job, and said, The oxen were plowing, and the asses feeding beside them :

15 And the Sabeans fell *upon them*, and took them away ; yea, they have slain the servants with the edge of the sword ; and I only am escaped alone to tell thee.

Job did not lose his property through neglect of business, the oxen were plowing, and the asses were not left to go astray : this proves that all our care and diligence cannot preserve our substance to us unless the Lord is the keeper thereof. To lose the oxen which plowed his fields, and the asses which carried his burdens was no small calamity, yet we do not find the man of God uttering one word of complaint. Some would have been in a sad way if but one ox had died.

16 While he *was* yet speaking, there came also another, and said, The fire of God is fallen from heaven, and hath burned up the sheep, and the servants, and consumed them ; and I only am escaped alone to tell thee.

The trial increased in intensity, for the hand of God was more directly to be seen in it, and this would keenly wound the holy soul of Job. Moreover, an eastern's wealth lies mainly in his flocks, and therefore the bulk of Job's property was gone at a blow ; yet he murmured not. Some professors of religion would have grievously fretted, if but one lamb had perished.

17 While he *was* yet speaking, there came also another, and said, The Chaldeans made out three bands, and fell upon the camels, and have carried them away, yea, and slain the servants with the edge of the sword ; and I only am escaped alone to tell thee.

How dolefully each messenger finishes his tidings. Satan knows how to drum a mournful truth into a man's ears, and weary his heart with the reiteration. Three companies of servants had

thus been destroyed, and the last relics of his live stock, yet not a word did he say. His heart was so fixed in God, that he was not afraid of evil tidings. What an example for us!

18 While he *was* yet speaking, there came also another, and said, Thy sons and thy daughters *were* eating and drinking wine in their eldest brother's house :

19 And, behold, there came a great wind from the wilderness, and smote the four corners of the house, and it fell upon the young men, and they are dead ; and I only am escaped alone to tell thee. (*This was a home-thrust indeed. This would stir the man if anything would. Great reasoners make the lesser arguments lead up to the greater, so here the arch-enemy weakens Job with the lesser afflictions, and then comes to his heaviest assaults. To lose his whole family at once, was heart-breaking work, yet did not his faith fail.*)

20, 21 Then Job arose, and rent his mantle, and shaved his head, and fell down upon the ground, and worshipped, And said, Naked came I out of my mother's womb, and naked shall I return thither : the LORD gave, and the LORD hath taken away ; blessed be the name of the LORD. (*Now indeed was Job great. Surely no man, besides the Son of Man in Gethsemane, ever rose to a greater height of resignation. Instead of cursing God, as Satan said he would, he blesses the Lord with all his heart. How thoroughly beaten the evil spirit must have felt. May the Holy Spirit help each one of us to triumph over him in like manner. Neither in his heart, nor in his speech did he offend. He was taught the sacred wisdom of resignation, and in nothing was he displeased with his God.*)

22 In all this Job sinned not, nor charged God foolishly. (*Grace made him more than a conqueror over Satan.*)

'Tis God that lifts our comforts high,
Or sinks them in the grave,
He gives, and (blessed be his name!)
He takes but what he gave.

Peace, all our angry passions then,
Let each rebellious sigh
Be silent at his sov'reign will,
And every murmur die.

JOB II. 1—13.

AGAIN there was a day when the sons of God came to present themselves before the LORD, and Satan came also among them to present himself before the LORD.

Even the devil will attend divine worship to serve his own ends. It is, therefore, a poor confidence which looks for salvation because church or chapel have been regularly attended. We ought also to watch and pray even when we are in the assemblies of the saints, for Satan enters there, and is busy with his temptations.

2 And the LORD said unto Satan, From whence comest thou? And Satan answered the LORD, and said, From going to and fro in the earth, and from walking up and down in it.

Full of evil as Satan is, he is not idle. A lazy man commits one more sin than the devil himself.

3 And the LORD said unto Satan, Hast thou considered my servant Job, that *there is* none like him in the earth, a perfect and an upright man, one that feareth God, and escheweth evil? and still he holdeth fast his integrity, although thou movedst me against him, to destroy him without cause. *(The glory of Job's character was his sincerity and uprightness, and this like an impregnable fortress defied the attacks of hell, though the prince of darkness himself personally assailed him, with permission from God to take from him all that he possessed.)*

4 And Satan answered the LORD, and said, Skin for skin, yea all that a man hath will he give for his life.

5 But put forth thine hand now, and touch his bone and his flesh, and he will curse thee to thy face. *(Satan suggested that bodily pain would be the weapon to wound Job's faith; yea, and turn it into rebellion. There was much malicious cunning in this, for many a man has yielded before the miseries of physical pain though he had been proof against every other trial. Yet the Lord can make his people more than conquerors even there.)*

6 And the LORD said unto Satan, Behold, he *is* in thine hand; but save his life.

7 ¶ So went Satan forth from the presence of the LORD, and smote Job with sore boils from the sole of his foot unto his crown.

8 And he took him a potsherd to scrape himself withal; and he sat down among the ashes.

In this wretched state he had no soft bed, but lay upon the hard ashes; nor does it seem that he had either surgeon or nurse. There he sat, the prince of misery; but there was worse to come.

9 ¶ Then said his wife unto him, Dost thou still retain thine integrity? curse God, and die.

10 But he said unto her, Thou speakest as one of the foolish women speaketh. What? shall we receive good at the hand of God, and shall we not receive evil? In all this did not Job sin with his lips. *(Satan tried to ruin Job through her who should have been his best comforter, but he was defeated, for he only led Job to utter another of those notable speeches which are now the treasures of the church.)*

11 ¶ Now when Job's three friends heard of all this evil that was come upon him, they came every one from his own place; Eliphaz the Temanite, and Bildad the Shuhite, and Zophar the Naamathite: for they had made an appointment together to come to mourn with him, and to comfort him.

12 And when they lifted up their eyes afar off, and knew him not, they lifted up their voice, and wept; and they rent every one his mantle, and sprinkled dust upon their heads toward heaven.

13 So they sat down with him upon the ground seven days and seven nights, and none spake a word unto him: for they saw that *his* grief was very great. *(This showed sympathy, but even this was not permitted to continue lest it should comfort the afflicted one. Soon these three friends judged Job's condition, and came to the conclusion that such unusual sorrow could only have been brought about by unusual sin. Under this impression, they added the last drop of gall to Job's cup by accusing him of hypocrisy and secret sin.)*

I am a sinner—shall I dare
To murmur at the strokes I bear?
Strokes, not in wrath, but mercy sent,
A wise and needful chastisement.

Saviour! I breathe the prayer once thine,
"Father! *thy* will be done, not mine!"
One only blessing would I claim;
In me, O glorify thy name!

ELIPHAZ, *the Temanite, though he took a wrong and cruel line of argument with Job, nevertheless, in the course of his reasoning, uttered some grand things: we will read two passages of his first speech. In the first, he shows that weak and erring man must not question the wisdom and justice of God's actions.*

JOB IV. 12—21.

12 Now a thing was secretly brought to me, and mine ear received a little thereof.

13 In thoughts from the visions of the night, when deep sleep falleth on men,

14 Fear came upon me, and trembling, which made all my bones to shake.

15 Then a spirit passed before my face; the hair of my flesh stood up:

16 It stood still, but I could not discern the form thereof: an image *was* before mine eyes, *there was* silence, and I heard a voice, *saying,*

17 Shall mortal man be more just than God? shall a man be more pure than his maker?

18 Behold, he put no trust in his servants; and his angels he charged with folly:

19 How much less *in* them that dwell in houses of clay, whose foundation *is* in the dust, *which* are crushed before the moth?

20 They are destroyed from morning to evening: they perish for ever without any regarding *it.*

21 Doth not their excellency *which is* in them go away? they die, even without wisdom.

In comparison with God what are men or even angels? Angels have but finite wisdom, and where their wisdom ends folly begins; theirs is not sinful folly, but such as ever must be in creatures when compared with the Omniscient One. Even angels know but little in comparison with God. How then can we think highly of frail beings, who from day to day are dying, and are so accustomed to see each other turn to dust that they think nothing of it? How can a mere insect like man, who is moreover foolish and sinful, dare to call in question the doings of the Eternal God?

CHAPTER V. 17—27.

IN *our second extract Eliphaz teaches us not to repine under divine chastisements, for they will be blessed to our highest good.*

17 Behold, happy *is* the man whom God

correcteth: therefore despise not thou the chastening of the Almighty:

Be not averse to it, rebel not against it, ascribe it not to anger, and do not disregard it as if it were a trifle.

18 For he maketh sore, and bindeth up: he woundeth, and his hands make whole.

The same Lord is in both our afflictions and our consolations, and he arranges that the one shall be surely followed by the other.

19 He shall deliver thee in six troubles: yea, in seven there shall no evil touch thee. (*Trouble may roar upon us, but it cannot devour us. It may vex us, but it shall not do us real harm. If we suffer a perfect number of trials we shall also have an all-sufficient degree of grace.*)

20 In famine he shall redeem thee from death: and in war from the power of the sword.

21 Thou shalt be hid from the scourge of the tongue: (*a mercy indeed*) neither shalt thou be afraid of destruction when it cometh.

22 At destruction and famine thou shalt laugh: neither shalt thou be afraid of the beasts of the earth.

23 For thou shalt be in league with the stones of the field: and the beasts of the field shall be at peace with thee. (*The Great Master's dogs will not bite his friends.*)

24 And thou shalt know that thy tabernacle *shall be* in peace; and thou shalt visit thy habitation, and shalt not sin.

25 Thou shalt know also that thy seed *shall be* great, and thine offspring as the grass of the earth. (*The Friend of the father will be gracious to the children.*)

26 Thou shalt come to *thy* grave in a full age, like as a shock of corn cometh in in his season.

27 Lo this, we have searched it, so it *is;* hear it, and know thou *it* for thy good.

We have not only been told this, but we have assured ourselves of it—" We know that all things work together for good to them that love God."

Why should I doubt his love at last,
    With anxious thoughts perplex'd?
Who saved me in the troubles pass'd,
    Will save me in the next.

Will save, till at my latest hour,
    With more than conquest bless'd,
I soar beyond temptation's power,
    To my Redeemer's breast.

OUR *space will not allow us to give much of this wonderful book of Job, but the following is an instance of the patriarch's expressions of distress.*

JOB XXIII. 1—17.

1 Then Job answered and said,

2 Even to day *is* my complaint bitter : my stroke is heavier than my groaning.

Most men cry before they are hurt, or more than they are hurt; but such was not Job's case: he had good reason for every groan, and when he groaned most he fell short of expressing what he felt within.

3 Oh that I knew where I might find him! *that* I might come *even* to his seat!

Even at his worst estate the good man knows his true refuge. When sinners turn from God in anger the saints fly to him with hope. Yet sometimes the Lord is a God that hideth himself. In this he has wise ends to answer, and he will continue it no longer than is absolutely needful.

4 I would order *my* cause before him, and fill my mouth with arguments.

5 I would know the words *which* he would answer me, and understand what he would say unto me. *(Job wished to have the question, which his three friends had raised, fairly tried in the highest court. He felt that he could with freedom plead with so righteous a judge. It is only the pure heart which can court such an investigation. He who knows that he is clear through Jesu's blood is not afraid to appear in the courts of heaven.)*

6 Will he plead against me with *his* great power? No; but he would put *strength* in me.

Innocence fears not power, but like Una rides on the lion. The Lord never crushes a man because he is down, but rather he delights to lift up the prostrate.

7 There the righteous might dispute with him ; so should I be delivered for ever from my judge.

8 Behold, I go forward, but he *is* not *there;* and backward, but I cannot perceive him :

9 On the left hand, where he doth work, but I cannot behold *him:* he hideth himself on the right hand, that I cannot see *him:*

10 But he knoweth the way that I take : *when* he hath tried me, I shall come forth as

gold. *(He comforts himself with the assurance that if he could not find the Lord, and speak in his own defence, yet the case was already known to him, and would in due time be decided in his favour. How blessedly his faith held its anchorage though the storm raged terribly.)*

11 My foot hath held his steps, his way have I kept, and not declined.

12 Neither have I gone back from the commandment of his lips; I have esteemed the words of his mouth more than my necessary food. *(Again in answer to the accusations of his three unfriendly friends, he protests his innocence of their charges, and scouts the idea that he is suffering for some secret apostacy.)*

13 But he *is* in one *mind,* and who can turn him? and *what* his soul desireth, even *that* he doeth.

14 For he performeth *the thing that is* appointed for me : and many such *things are* with him. *(He accounts for his trials by considering the immutable and inscrutable decrees of God, and suggests that many more troubles might yet befall him, for which he might be unable to find a reason.)*

15 Therefore am I troubled at his presence : when I consider, I am afraid of him.

Great suffering could not kill his faith, but it damped his joy. He had also come to think of an absolute God doing as he willed, and it is no wonder that he trembled at the contemplation. Only when we see Jesus do we see that God is love.

16 For God maketh my heart soft, and the Almighty troubleth me :

17 Because I was not cut off before the darkness, *neither* hath he covered the darkness from my face. *(He wished that by an early death he had escaped suffering, but all such wishes are vain. We cannot go back: let us therefore by faith press onward.)*

God is a King of power unknown ;
Firm are the orders of his throne ;
If he resolves, who dare oppose,
Or ask him why, or what he does?

He wounds the heart, and he makes whole ;
He calms the tempest of the soul ;
He rescues souls from long despair,
And snaps in twain the iron bar.

68   " The fear of the Lord is the beginning of wisdom."   FEBRUARY 3.— EVENING.

[*Or March 8.*]

LET *us read Job's famous passage upon the search after wisdom, and in order that we may see its beauties we will read it in an accurate translation; arranged as it should be in parallel lines.*

JOB XXVIII.

1 For there is a vein for the silver,
  and a place for the gold, which they refine.
2 Iron is taken out of the dust,
  and stone is fused into copper.

The following verses describe the operations of mining, and the hazards of the miner.

3 He puts an end to the darkness;
  and he searches out, to the very end,
  stones of thick darkness and of death-shade.
4 He drives a shaft away from man's abode;
  forgotten of the foot,
  they swing suspended, far from men!

That is to say, having no use for their feet in descending the shaft, they swing in mid air.

5 The earth, out of it goes forth bread;
  and under it, is destroyed as with fire.
6 A place of sapphires, are its stones;
  and it has clods of gold.
7 The path, no bird of prey has known it,
  nor the falcon's eye glanced on it:
8 Nor proud beasts trodden it,
  nor roaring lion passed over it.
9 Against the flinty rock he puts forth his hand;
  he overturns mountains from the base.

The solid rock is broken, and the hills are undermined by those who search for precious metals. Their tunnels pierce the centre of the Alps, and tear out the bowels of the hills.

10 In the rocks he cleaves out rivers;
  and his eye sees every precious thing.
11 He binds up streams, that they drip not:
  and the hidden he brings out to light.

Miners take great care to prevent the water from breaking in upon them so as to flood the mines, and by such care they are able to penetrate into earth's deep places, and reveal her secrets.

12 But wisdom, whence shall it be found?
  and where is the place of understanding?
13 Man knows not its price;
  nor is it found in the land of the living.
14 The deep saith, It is not in me;
  and the sea saith, It is not with me.
15 Choice gold shall not be given in exchange for it;
  nor shall silver be weighed for its price.

16 It cannot be weighed with gold of Ophir,
  with the precious onyx and sapphire.
17 Gold and glass shall not be compared with it,
  nor vessels of fine gold be an exchange for it.

Glass in ancient times was a costly article, used only for splendour and luxury, but however precious it might be, wisdom far excels it.

18 Corals and crystals shall not be named;
  and the possession of wisdom is more than pearls.
19 The topaz of Ethiopia shall not be compared with it;
  it shall not be weighed with pure gold.
20 But wisdom, whence comes it?
  and where is the place of understanding?
21 Since it is hidden from the eyes of all living,
  and covered from the fowls of heaven.
22 Destruction and death say:
  with our ears have we heard the fame of it.
23 God understands the way to it,
  and he knows the place of it.
24 For he, to the ends of the earth he looks;
  and he sees under the whole heaven:
25 To make the weight for the wind;
  and he meted out the waters by measure.
26 When he made a decree for the rain,
  and a track for the thunder's flash:
27 Then he saw it, and he declared it;
  he established it, yea, and searched it out.
28 And to man he said:
  Behold, the fear of the Lord, that is wisdom;
  and to depart from evil is understanding.

Job comes to the same conclusion as Solomon, who said, "The fear of the Lord is the beginning of wisdom." True religion is priceless beyond all the treasures of earth. Seek it first, ye children and young men; for then shall you be truly rich.

Jesus is the Captain of the mine of wisdom, and he will show you the lodes of precious knowledge.

In vain we search; in vain we try;
Till Jesus brings his gospel nigh;
'Tis there such power and glory dwell
As save rebellious souls from hell.

Let men or angels dig the mines,
Where nature's golden treasure shines;
Brought near the doctrine of the cross,
All nature's gold appears but dross.

JOB XXXVIII. 1—11 ; 16, 17 ; 22, 23 ; 31—41.

WHEN *the three accusers were silent, when Elihu had concluded his eloquent address, and Job had no more to say, the Lord himself interposed, and as with a long succession of thunder-claps hushed every heart and voice into awe.*

1 Then the LORD answered Job out of the whirlwind, and said,

2 Who *is* this that darkeneth counsel by words without knowledge ? *(How solemn is that word "Who is this?" Is it a poor, weak, foolish man? Is it Job? My servant Job! Does he speak of that which he cannot understand and venture to complain of his God? Our wisdom is only wisdom when it admits its own folly.)*

3 Gird up now thy loins like a man ; for I will demand of thee, and answer thou me.

4 Where wast thou when I laid the foundations of the earth ? declare, if thou hast understanding.

5 Who hath laid the measures thereof, if thou knowest ? or who hath stretched the line upon it ?

6 Whereupon are the foundations thereof fastened ? or who laid the corner stone thereof;

7 When the morning stars sang together, and all the sons of God shouted for joy ?
We know nothing of the common things of God, how foolish we are to think that we can pry into his arcana, and lay bare his mysterious secrets. We had better sing with angels, than doubt with devils. The angels all sang, sang together, and sang with one common joy. O for such unanimous joyful praise among men.

8 Or *who* shut up the sea with doors, when it brake forth, *as if* it had issued out of the womb ?

9 When I made the cloud the garment thereof, and thick darkness a swaddling-band for it,

10 And brake up for it my decreed *place*, and set bars and doors,

11 And said, Hitherto shalt thou come, but no further : and here shall thy proud waves be stayed ?

16 Hast thou entered into the springs of the sea ? or hast thou walked in the search of the depth ?

17 Have the gates of death been opened unto thee ? or hast thou seen the doors of the shadow of death ? *(The secrets of earth are too deep for us, how much more the mysteries of eternity. One thing, however, is consoling; if we do not see the gates of death open, we know who it is that has opened for us the door of heaven.)*

22 Hast thou entered into the treasures of the snow ? or hast thou seen the treasures of the hail,

23 Which I have reserved against the time of trouble, against the day of battle and war ?

31 Canst thou bind the sweet influences of Pleiades, or loose the bands of Orion ?

32 Canst thou bring forth Mazzaroth in his season ? or canst thou guide Arcturus with his sons ? *(Who among us can control the stars or change the seasons?)*

33 Knowest thou the ordinances of heaven ? canst thou set the dominion thereof in the earth ?

34 Canst thou lift up thy voice to the clouds, that abundance of waters may cover thee ?

35 Canst thou send lightnings, that they may go, and say unto thee, Here we *are* ?

36 Who hath put wisdom in the inward parts; or who hath given understanding to the heart?

37 Who can number the clouds in wisdom ? or who can stay the bottles of heaven,

38 When the dust groweth into hardness, and the clods cleave fast together ?

39 Wilt thou hunt the prey for the lion ? or fill the appetite of the young lions,

40 When they couch in *their* dens, *and* abide in the covert to lie in wait ?

41 Who provideth for the raven his food ? when his young ones cry unto God, they wander for lack of meat.
In all these things the greatness of the Lord, and the nothingness of man are alike apparent. God forbid that a thought of pride should defile our spirit.

Great God ! how infinite art thou !
  What worthless worms are we !
Let the whole race of creatures bow,
  And pay their praise to Thee.

Eternity, with all its years,
  Stands present in Thy view ;
To Thee there's nothing old appears ;
  Great God ! there's nothing new.

JOB XXXIX. 19—30.

THE *sublime language of Jehovah in his address to Job is far above all human eloquence. Let us take a second lesson from that divine discourse. First, let us read the unrivalled description of a war-horse.*

19 Hast thou given the horse strength? hast thou clothed his neck with thunder?

20 Canst thou make him afraid as a grasshopper? the glory of his nostrils *is* terrible.

21 He paweth in the valley, and rejoiceth in *his* strength: he goeth on to meet the armed men.

22 He mocketh at fear, and is not affrighted; neither turneth he back from the sword.

23 The quiver rattleth against him, the glittering spear and the shield.

24 He swalloweth the ground with fierceness and rage: neither believeth he that *it is* the sound of the trumpet.

25 He saith among the trumpets, Ha, ha; and he smelleth the battle afar off, the thunder of the captains, and the shouting.

He who created a creature so noble, powerful, and courageous, is not to be summoned to our bar, or questioned as to what he does.

26 Doth the hawk fly by thy wisdom, *and* stretch her wings toward the south?

We commonly speak of instinct. What is it but the teaching of God? He who has given so much wisdom to birds and beasts is full of wisdom himself. Let us bow before him, and rest assured that what he does is ever best.

27 Doth the eagle mount up at thy command, and make her nest on high?

28 She dwelleth and abideth on the rock, upon the crag of the rock, and the strong place.

29 From thence she seeketh the prey, *and* her eyes behold afar off.

30 Her young ones also suck up blood: and where the slain *are*, there *is* she. *(Far-seeing and terrible, the royal bird belongs not to the kings of the earth though they figure it upon their banners: it is but another incarnation of the sublime thoughts of God, a further illustration of his greatness.)*

JOB XL. 1—14.

1 Moreover the LORD answered Job, and said,

2 Shall he that contendeth with the Almighty instruct *him?* he that reproveth God, let him answer it.

3 ¶ Then Job answered the LORD, and said,

4 Behold, I am vile; what shall I answer thee? I will lay mine hand upon my mouth.

5 Once have I spoken; but I will not answer: yea, twice; but I will proceed no further.

6 ¶ Then answered the LORD unto Job out of the whirlwind, and said,

7 Gird up thy loins now like a man: I will demand of thee, and declare thou unto me.

8 Wilt thou also disannul my judgment? wilt thou condemn me, that thou mayest be righteous?

9 Hast thou an arm like God? or canst thou thunder with a voice like him? *(If we fancy that we can vie with God in justice, we are challenged first to compete with him in power. All the attributes of God are equally great, and if we cannot rival one, it will be wise not to impugn another.)*

10 Deck thyself now *with* majesty and excellency; and array thyself with glory and beauty. *(Come thou poor glow-worm, put forth thy light, and see if thou art comparable to the sun.)*

11 Cast abroad the rage of thy wrath: and behold every one *that is* proud, and abase him.

12 Look on every one *that is* proud, *and* bring him low; and tread down the wicked in their place.

13 Hide them in the dust together: *and* bind their faces in secret.

14 Then will I also confess unto thee that thine own right hand can save thee.

Until we can manage providence as the Lord has done, so as to abase tyrants and deliver the oppressed, we had better learn submission to the divine will, and cease for ever from all rebellious questionings.

In heaven and earth, in air and seas,
He executes His wise decrees:
And by His saints it stands confest,
That what He does is ever best.

Wait, then, my soul, submissive wait,
With reverence bow before His seat;
And, midst the terrors of His rod,
Trust in a wise and gracious God.

JOB XLII. 1—13.

THEN Job answered the LORD, and said,
2 I know that thou canst do every *thing*,
and *that* no thought can be withholden from
thee. (*The patriarch made an unreserved submission. He felt that the very idea of judging
the conduct of the Almighty was preposterous.
Omnipotence and Omniscience render the thought
of calling the Eternal into question superlatively
ridiculous.*)

3 Who *is* he that hideth counsel without
knowledge? therefore have I uttered that I
understood not; things too wonderful for me,
which I knew not. (*That first question of the
Lord abides in his memory, and now in humble
wonder at his own temerity he asks it of himself.
It is tantamount to that apostolic question, " Nay,
but O man, who art thou that repliest against
God?" The patriarch illuminated with new
light sees his own folly, and humbly confesses it
before the Lord. A very great part of our
religious talk consists of utterances which we ourselves do not understand, and all our complaining
is based upon ignorance.*)

4 Hear, I beseech thee, and I will speak: I
will demand of thee, and declare thou unto me.
*Job desired to enter God's school, and to be
taught of him. He will no longer be a pleader
but a humble enquirer.*

5 I have heard of thee by the hearing of the
ear: but now mine eye seeth thee.

6 Wherefore I abhor *myself*, and repent in
dust and ashes. (*Hearing goes for little till the
Lord's arm is revealed in a man's heart. Caryl
well observes, " No man knoweth what a nothing
he is in knowledge, grace, and goodness till the
Lord is pleased to reveal himself to him." While
we compare ourselves with ourselves, or with
others who are below us, we fancy ourselves important personages, but when the Lord unveils
himself we become as nothing in our own eyes.
The more we see of God the less shall we think of
ourselves. Sound knowledge is the death of conceit.*)

7 ¶ And it was *so*, that after the LORD had
spoken these words unto Job, the LORD said to
Eliphaz the Temanite, My wrath is kindled
against thee, and against thy two friends: for ye
have not spoken of me *the thing that is* right,
as my servant Job *hath*. (*Out of zeal to defend
God's providence they were not fair in argument.
We have no business to defend truth with lies or
suppressions. God will have honest defenders or*

none. *He is displeased with untruthful advocates
even though they fancy that they are upon the
Lord's side, and at any rate desire to be so.*)

8 Therefore take unto you now seven bullocks
and seven rams, and go to my servant Job, and
offer up for yourselves a burnt offering; and my
servant Job shall pray for you: for him will I
accept: lest I deal with you *after your* folly, in
that ye have not spoken of me *the thing which is*
right, like my servant Job. (*Let us never judge
others, for it may be we may come to be indebted
to them for their prayers. We may have to crave
their intercession, therefore let us not now judge
them harshly.*)

9 So Eliphaz the Temanite and Bildad the
Shuhite *and* Zophar the Naamathite went, and
did according as the LORD commanded them: the
LORD also accepted Job. (*If the Lord accepted
Job and blessed his friends for his sake, how much
more doth he accept the Lord Jesus Christ who
offered himself a sacrifice for sin, and how safe
we, his poor offending friends, are in him.*)

10 And the LORD turned the captivity of
Job, when he prayed for his friends: also the
LORD gave Job twice as much as he had before.
*When in a forgiving spirit we pray for those
who have behaved harshly to us some blessing is
in store for us.*

11, 12 Then came there unto him all his
brethren, and all his sisters, and all they that had
been of his acquaintance before, and did eat bread
with him in his house: and they bemoaned him,
and comforted him over all the evil that the LORD
had brought upon him: every man also gave
him a piece of money, and every one an earring
of gold. So the LORD blessed the latter end of
Job more than his beginning: for he had fourteen
thousand sheep, and six thousand camels, and a
thousand yoke of oxen, and a thousand she asses.

13 He had also seven sons and three daughters.
*Thus shall the Lord's procedures vindicate
themselves, and his people shall be no losers by
their afflictions.*

If peace and plenty crown my days,
They help me, Lord, to speak thy praise;
If bread of sorrows be my food,
Those sorrows work my real good.

I would not change my blest estate
For all that earth calls good or great;
And while my faith can keep her hold,
I envy not the sinner's gold.

EXODUS I. 1—14; 22.

OUR *reading will now take us back from the land of Uz to the land of Egypt, where we left the chosen family in Goshen.*

1 Now these *are* the names of the children of Israel, which came into Egypt; every man and his household came with Jacob. *(The Lord knoweth them that are his. The names of the godly seed are precious to his heart.)*

2 Reuben, Simeon, Levi, and Judah,

3 Issachar, Zebulun, and Benjamin,

4 Dan, and Naphtali, Gad, and Asher.

5 And all the souls that came out of the loins of Jacob were seventy souls: for Joseph was in Egypt *already.*

6 And Joseph died, and all his brethren, and all that generation.

7 And the children of Israel were fruitful, and increased abundantly, and multiplied, and waxed exceeding mighty; and the land was filled with them. *(Thus the ancient covenant that Abraham's seed should be many received its first fulfilment. God is not unmindful of his promises.)*

8 Now there arose up a new king over Egypt, which knew not Joseph. *(Out of sight out of mind; a man may confer on a nation permanent advantages, but he cannot hope for permanent gratitude. Those who serve man are generally rewarded with forgetfulness.)*

9 And he said unto his people, Behold, the people of the children of Israel *are* more and mightier than we :

10 Come on, let us deal wisely with them; lest they multiply, and it come to pass, that, when there falleth out any war, they join also unto our enemies, and fight against us, and *so* get them up out of the land. *(The ungodly always try to make out that God's people are a dangerous set, but indeed, if they would treat them kindly they would find them the best of neighbours. It is only when they wilfully stumble at this stone that it breaks them. The Egyptians tried to prevent the increase of Israel. Vain was this attempt. Pharaoh might as well have tried to stem the sea, or prevent the rising of the Nile. Jehovah had determined that the people should be multiplied, and no policy of kings and princes could prevent it. Great was the monarch's worldly*

wisdom, his plan had in it both the subtlety and cruelty of Satan, and yet he was but a fool, and his schemes failed at every point.)

11 Therefore they did set over them taskmasters to afflict them with their burdens. And they built for Pharaoh treasure cities, Pithom and Raamses.

12 But the more they afflicted them, the more they multiplied and grew. And they were grieved because of the children of Israel.

Unscrupulous and determined as the enemies of God's people have been, they have nevertheless been unable to achieve their design. The church must spread, and spread too by the very means made use of to destroy her. There are herbs which increase rapidly when they are trodden upon, and true religion is one of them.

13 And the Egyptians made the children of Israel to serve with rigour :

14 And they made their lives bitter with hard bondage, in mortar, and in brick, and in all manner of service in the field: all their service, wherein they made them serve, *was* with rigour.

This was with the view of degrading them, crushing their spirit, and lessening their vigour, but the cruel device succeeded not. No weapon can prosper against the Lord's chosen. Hard labour is after all less injurious than pampered indolence. Better slave in a brick-kiln than canker in laziness.

After a futile attempt to procure the murder of all the male children by those who attended at their birth, Pharaoh passed a tyrannical decree which is thus recorded.

22 And Pharaoh charged all his people, saying, Every son that is born ye shall cast into the river, and every daughter ye shall save alive.

Murder was thus called in to make an end of the elect people, but it was in vain. The Lord of Israel was greater than the King of Egypt, and proved more than a match for all his plots and plans.

What though to make our numbers less
  Our foes their wisdom try,
The more our enemies oppress,
  The more we multiply.

Then let the world forbear its rage,
  Nor put the church in fear,
Israel must live through every age
  And be th' Almighty's care.

EXODUS II. 1—10.

AND there went a man of the house of Levi, and took *to wife* a daughter of Levi. And the woman conceived, and bare a son: and when she saw him that he *was a* goodly *child,* she hid him three months. And when she could not longer hide him, she took for him an ark of bulrushes, and daubed it with slime and with pitch, and put the child therein; and she laid *it* in the flags by the river's brink.

4 And his sister stood afar off, to wit *(or know)* what would be done to him. *(Faith watches to see what God will do.)*

5 ¶ And the daughter of Pharaoh came down to wash *herself* at the river; and her maidens walked along by the river's side; and when she saw the ark among the flags, she sent her maid to fetch it. *(Providence is manifest here. How was the ark kept from the crocodiles? Why did the princess come to that particular spot? How came her eye to light upon that little floating coffer hidden among the bulrushes? Why should she desire to look within it? Surely the Lord's hand was in it all.)*

6 And when she had opened *it,* she saw the child: and, behold, the babe wept. *(The providence which brought the princess to the spot, brought the tears into the babe's eyes at the very moment when they would be seen, and aid in touching the beholder's pity.)* And she had compassion on him, and said, This *is* one of the Hebrews' children.

7, 8 Then said his sister to Pharaoh's daughter, Shall I go and call to thee a nurse of the Hebrew women, that she may nurse the child for thee? And Pharaoh's daughter said to her, Go. And the maid went and called the child's mother. *(How graciously the Lord arranges for us.)*

9 And Pharaoh's daughter said unto her, Take this child away, and nurse it for me, and I will give *thee* thy wages. *(Thus speaks the Lord to every godly mother. No service upon earth is so well repaid to a parent as the pious nurture of her children.)* And the woman took the child, and nursed it.

10 And the child grew, and she brought him unto Pharaoh's daughter, and he became her son. And she called his name Moses: and she said, Because I drew him out of the water.

HEBREWS XI. 24—26.

24 By faith Moses, when he was come to years, refused to be called the son of Pharaoh's daughter; *(He had been so called in his youthful days, but when he could choose for himself he declined the highest rank as an Egyptian, and took his place with persecuted Israel.)*

25, 26 Choosing rather to suffer affliction with the people of God, than to enjoy the pleasures of sin for a season: Esteeming the reproach of Christ greater riches than the treasures in Egypt: for he had respect unto the recompence of the reward.

ACTS VII. 22—29.

22 And Moses was learned in all the wisdom of the Egyptians, and was mighty in words and in deeds. *(His education, when sanctified by God's Spirit, helped to prepare him for his eminent position as the leader and lawgiver of the tribes. No other prophet until our Lord came was mighty both in words and deeds.)*

23 And when he was full forty years old, it came into his heart to visit his brethren the children of Israel. *(The life of Moses divides itself into three forties—forty at court, forty with Jethro, and forty in the wilderness.)*

24 And seeing one *of them* suffer wrong, he defended *him,* and avenged him that was oppressed, and smote the Egyptian:

25 For he supposed his brethren would have understood how that God by his hand would deliver them: but they understood not.

26 And the next day he shewed himself unto them as they strove, and would have set them at one again, saying, Sirs, ye are brethren; why do ye wrong one to another?

27, 28 But he that did his neighbour wrong thrust him away, saying, Who made thee a ruler and a judge over us? Wilt thou kill me, as thou diddest the Egyptian yesterday?

The mission of the greatest and best of men is not at once perceived.

29 Then fled Moses at this saying, and was a stranger in the land of Midian, where he begat two sons.

Now for the love I bear His name,
What was my gain I count my loss;
My former pride I call my shame,
And nail my glory to His cross.

Yes, and I must and will esteem
All things but loss for Jesus' sake:
Oh may my soul be found in Him,
And of His righteousness partake!

EXODUS III. 1—8; 10—20.

NOW Moses kept the flock of Jethro his father in law, the priest of Midian: *(Though a man of deep learning he did not disdain the shepherd's calling. There is no disgrace in work, but great shame in idleness,)* and he led the flock to the backside of the desert, and came to the mountain of God, *even* to Horeb.

2 And the angel of the LORD appeared unto him in a flame of fire out of the midst of a bush : and he looked, and, behold, the bush burned with fire, and the bush *was* not consumed.

3 And Moses said, I will now turn aside, and see this great sight, why the bush is not burnt. *This is a standing emblem of the church, and often both friend and foe, like Moses, are puzzled to understand the marvel. It is wonderful that so poor and powerless a thing as a bush should survive the fires which try it so severely.*

4 And when the LORD saw that he turned aside to see, God called unto him out of the midst of the bush, and said, Moses, Moses. And he said, Here *am* I.

5 And he said, Draw not nigh hither : put off thy shoes from off thy feet, for the place whereon thou standest *is* holy ground.

6 Moreover he said, I *am* the God of thy father, the God of Abraham, the God of Isaac, and the God of Jacob. And Moses hid his face; for he was afraid to look upon God. *(Like his ancestor Jacob, he felt "how dreadful is this place." Fear rather than joy prevailed.)*

7, 8 And the LORD said, I have surely seen the affliction of my people which *are* in Egypt, and have heard their cry by reason of their taskmasters ; for I know their sorrows ; And I am come down to deliver them out of the hand of the Egyptians, and to bring them up out of that land unto a good land and a large, unto a land flowing with milk and honey; unto the place of the Canaanites, and the Hittites, and the Amorites, and the Perizzites, and the Hivites, and the Jebusites. Come now therefore, and I will send thee unto Pharaoh, that thou mayest bring forth my people the children of Israel out of Egypt.

11 ¶ And Moses said unto God, Who *am* I, that I should go unto Pharaoh, and that I should bring forth the children of Israel out of Egypt ? *(The more fit a man is for God's work the lower is his esteem of himself.)*

12 And he said, Certainly I will be with thee ; and this *shall be* a token unto thee, that I have sent thee : When thou hast brought forth the people out of Egypt, ye shall serve God upon this mountain. *(What an answer to all fears is that sweet word "Certainly I will be with thee.")*

13 And Moses said unto God, Behold, *when* I come unto the children of Israel, and shall say unto them, The God of your fathers hath sent me unto you; and they shall say to me, What *is* his name ? what shall I say unto them ?

14 And God said unto Moses, I AM THAT I AM : and he said, Thus shalt thou say unto the children of Israel, I AM hath sent me unto you. *(By these two names the immutability and self-existence of God are set forth. Our God for ever exists and is for ever the same.)*

15, 16, 17 And God said moreover unto Moses, Thus shalt thou say unto the children of Israel, The LORD God of your fathers, the God of Abraham, the God of Isaac, and the God of Jacob, hath sent me unto you : this *is* my name for ever, and this *is* my memorial unto all generations. Go, and gather the elders of Israel together, and say unto them, The LORD God of your fathers, the God of Abraham, of Isaac, and of Jacob, appeared unto me, saying, I have surely visited you, and *seen* that which is done to you in Egypt : And I have said, I will bring you up out of the affliction of Egypt unto a land flowing with milk and honey. *(Sooner or later the Lord will bless his people and deliver them. He may for awhile leave them under severe trial, but he is mindful of his covenant and will visit them at the set time.)*

18 And they shall hearken to thy voice : and thou shalt come, thou and the elders of Israel, unto the king of Egypt, and ye shall say unto him, The LORD God of the Hebrews hath met with us : and now let us go, we beseech thee, three days' journey into the wilderness, that we may sacrifice to the LORD our God.

19, 20 And I am sure that the king of Egypt will not let you go, no, not by a mighty hand. And I will stretch out my hand, and smite Egypt with all my wonders which I will do in the midst thereof: and after that he will let you go.

Love's presence keeps the bush alive,
Grace 'mid the flames can make us thrive ;
Nor need th' afflicted saint despair,
Though in the fire, the Lord is there.

EXODUS IV. 1—16.

AND Moses answered and said, But, behold, they will not believe me, nor hearken unto my voice: for they will say, the LORD hath not appeared unto thee. *(Those whom God sends are often slow to go, and yet men whom the Lord never sent push themselves into office eagerly.)*

2, 3 And the LORD said unto him, What *is* that in thine hand? And he said, A rod. And he said, Cast it on the ground. And he cast it on the ground, and it became a serpent; and Moses fled from before it. *(This was a sign to him that though now a humble shepherd he would become so powerful as to terrify Pharaoh. The pastoral staff should be dreadful as a serpent.)*

4 And the LORD said unto Moses, Put forth thine hand, and take it by the tail. And he put forth his hand, and caught it, and it became a rod in his hand:

5 That they may believe that the LORD God of their fathers, the God of Abraham, the God of Isaac, and the God of Jacob, hath appeared unto thee. *(Here he learned that the power with which he was endowed while it would be as a terrible serpent towards Egypt, would be for himself and for Israel a harmless shepherd's crook. Both the signs would encourage Moses.)*

6 ¶ And the LORD said furthermore unto him, Put now thine hand into thy bosom. And he put his hand into his bosom : and when he took it out, behold, his hand *was* leprous as snow.

7, 8 And he said, Put thine hand into thy bosom again. And he put his hand into his bosom again; and plucked it out of his bosom, and, behold, it was turned again as his *other* flesh. And it shall come to pass, if they will not believe thee, neither hearken to the voice of the first sign, that they will believe the voice of the latter sign. *(Thus he saw that the Lord can both wither and restore. All who work for the Lord should remember this.)*

9 And it shall come to pass, if they will not believe also these two signs, neither hearken unto thy voice, that thou shalt take of the water of the river, and pour *it* upon the dry *land:* and the water which thou takest out of the river shall become blood upon the dry *land.*

10 ¶ And Moses said unto the LORD, O my Lord, I *am* not eloquent, neither heretofore, nor since thou hast spoken unto thy servant: but I *am* slow of speech, and of a slow tongue.

11, 12 And the LORD said unto him, Who hath made man's mouth? or who maketh the dumb, or deaf, or the seeing, or the blind? have not I the LORD? Now therefore go, and I will be with thy mouth, and teach thee what thou shalt say.

13 And he said, O my Lord, send, I pray thee, by the hand *of him whom* thou wilt send.

By this reluctance Moses lost much honour, for Aaron became the high priest, and he obtained a helper who also proved to be a hindrance.

14, 15, 16, And the anger of the LORD was kindled against Moses, and he said, *Is* not Aaron the Levite thy brother? I know that he can speak well. And also, behold, he cometh forth to meet thee: and when he seeth thee, he will be glad in his heart. And thou shalt speak unto him, and put words in his mouth: and I will be with thy mouth, and with his mouth, and will teach you what ye shall do. And he shall be thy spokesman unto the people: and he shall be, *even* he shall be to thee instead of a mouth, and thou shalt be to him instead of God.

IT *is interesting to note that other eminent prophets besides Moses have shrunk at first from their commission. We will read how Jeremiah did so.*

JEREMIAH I. 6—9.

6 Then said I, Ah, Lord GOD! behold, I cannot speak : for I *am* a child.

7, 8 But the LORD said unto me, Say not, I *am* a child : for thou shalt go to all that I shall send thee, and whatsoever I command thee thou shalt speak. Be not afraid of their faces : for I *am* with thee to deliver thee, saith the LORD.

9 Then the LORD put forth his hand, and touched my mouth. And the LORD said unto me, Behold, I have put my words in thy mouth.

O Lord, grant that all thy ministers may have their mouths touched in the same manner.

Father of mercies, bow thine ear,
Attentive to our earnest prayer ;
We plead for those who plead for thee,
Successful pleaders may they be !

Lord, how can sinful lips proclaim
The honours of so great a name !
O for thine altar's glowing coal,
To touch their lips, and fire their soul.

76   "𝕮𝖍𝖔𝖚𝖌𝖍 𝕳𝖊 𝖈𝖆𝖚𝖘𝖊 𝖌𝖗𝖎𝖊𝖋, 𝖞𝖊𝖙 𝖜𝖎𝖑𝖑 𝕳𝖊 𝖍𝖆𝖇𝖊 𝖈𝖔𝖒𝖕𝖆𝖘𝖘𝖎𝖔𝖓."   FEBRUARY 7.—EVENING.

[*Or March 16.*]

EXODUS V. 1—4; 6—23.

AND Moses and Aaron went in, and told Pharaoh, Thus saith the LORD God of Israel, Let my people go, that they may hold a feast unto me in the wilderness.

2 And Pharaoh said, Who *is* the LORD, that I should obey his voice to let Israel go ? I know not the LORD, neither will I let Israel go. *(Though his proud spirit defied Jehovah, he had before long good reason to know who Jehovah was.)*

3 And they said, The God of the Hebrews hath met with us : let us go, we pray thee, three days' journey into the desert, and sacrifice unto the LORD our God; lest he fall upon us with pestilence, or with the sword. *(This was by no means a large demand, and was doubtless meant to be a test question. He who would not yield the less would be sure to refuse the greater.)*

4 And the king of Egypt said unto them, Wherefore do ye, Moses and Aaron, let *(or hinder)* the people from their works ? get you unto your burdens. *(With what impudent scorn he defied the messengers of the Lord, haughtily treating them as slaves, who had better go back to their labour at once.)*

6, 7, 8, 9 And Pharaoh commanded the same day the taskmasters of the people, and their officers, saying, Ye shall no more give the people straw to make brick, as heretofore, let them go and gather straw for themselves. And the tale of the bricks, which they did make heretofore, ye shall lay upon them ; ye shall not diminish *ought* thereof : for they *be* idle ; therefore they cry, saying, Let us go *and* sacrifice to our God. Let there more work be laid upon the men, that they may labour therein ; and let them not regard vain words. *(As the bricks were made of mud mixed with straw, and the straw had hitherto been supplied to them in the brickfields, it was a heavy addition to their toils when they had to collect straw themselves.)*

10, 11 ¶ And the taskmasters of the people went out, and their officers, and they spake to the people, saying, Thus saith Pharaoh, I will not give you straw. Go ye, get you straw where ye can find it : yet not ought of your work shall be diminished.

12, 13 So the people were scattered abroad throughout all the land of Egypt to gather stubble instead of straw. And the taskmasters hasted *them*, saying, Fulfil your works, *your* daily tasks, as when there was straw.

14 And the officers of the children of Israel, which Pharaoh's taskmasters had set over them, were beaten, *and* demanded, Wherefore have ye not fulfilled your task in making brick both yesterday and to day, as heretofore ?

15, 16 Then the officers of the children of Israel came and cried unto Pharaoh, saying, Wherefore dealest thou thus with thy servants ? There is no straw given unto thy servants, and they say to us, Make brick : and, behold, thy servants *are* beaten ; but the fault *is* in thine own people. *(These poor Israelitish officers thought that the Egyptian taskmasters were unwarrantably keeping back the straw, but indeed they were acting under the King's own orders.)*

17, 18, 19 But he said, Ye *are* idle, *ye are* idle : therefore ye say, Let us go *and* do sacrifice to the LORD. Go therefore now, *and* work ; for there shall no straw be given you, yet shall ye deliver the tale of bricks. And the officers of the children of Israel did see *that* they *were* in evil *case*, after it was said, Ye shall not minish *ought* from your bricks of your daily task.

20, 21 And they met Moses and Aaron, who stood in the way, as they came forth from Pharaoh : And they said unto them, The LORD look upon you, and judge : because ye have made our savour to be abhorred in the eyes of Pharaoh, and in the eyes of his servants, to put a sword in their hand to slay us.

Things are always worst when they are about to mend, but these downcast spirits could not see far before them.

22 And Moses returned unto the LORD, and said, Lord, wherefore hast thou *so* evil entreated this people ? why *is* it *that* thou hast sent me ?

23 For since I came to Pharaoh to speak in thy name, he hath done evil to this people ; neither hast thou delivered thy people at all.

Moses did well thus to refer the case to the Lord. Let us bring all our troubles to our heavenly Father.

Mighty Redeemer set me free
From my old state of sin,
O break these bonds of slavery,
This iron worn within.

From daily load and daily smart
Thy pleading captive free,
Then shall my liberated heart
Thy willing servant be.

EXODUS VII. 1—5; 10—22.

AND the Lord said unto Moses, See, I have made thee a god to Pharaoh: and Aaron thy brother shall be thy prophet. Thou shalt speak all that I command thee: and Aaron thy brother shall speak unto Pharaoh, that he send the children of Israel out of his land. And I will harden Pharaoh's heart, and multiply my signs and my wonders in the land of Egypt. But Pharaoh shall not hearken unto you, that I may lay my hand upon Egypt, and bring forth mine armies, *and* my people the children of Israel, out of the land of Egypt by great judgments. And the Egyptians shall know that I *am* the Lord, when I stretch forth mine hand upon Egypt, and bring out the children of Israel from among them. *(God's judgments hardened Pharaoh's heart. They are sure to harden if they do not soften. The monarch was of such a nature that terrors and plagues only made his spirit more unbending.)*

10 ¶ And Moses and Aaron went in unto Pharaoh, and they did so as the Lord had commanded: and Aaron cast down his rod before Pharaoh, and before his servants, and it became a serpent. *(They had delivered their message, they here show their credentials.)*

11, 12 Then Pharaoh also called the wise men and the sorcerers: now the magicians of Egypt, they also did in like manner with their enchantments. For they cast down every man his rod, and they became serpents: but Aaron's rod swallowed up their rods.

13 And he hardened Pharaoh's heart, that he hearkened not unto them; as the Lord had said.

He concluded that Moses was only a magician, like those in his own pay, and he therefore again defied the power of Jehovah.

14, 15 And the Lord said unto Moses, Pharaoh's heart *is* hardened, he refuseth to let the people go. Get thee unto Pharaoh in the morning; lo, he goeth out unto the water; and thou shalt stand by the river's brink against he come; and the rod which was turned to a serpent shalt thou take in thine hand.

16, 17, 18 And thou shalt say unto him, the Lord God of the Hebrews hath sent me unto thee saying, Let my people go, that they may serve me in the wilderness: and, behold, hitherto thou wouldest not hear. Thus saith the Lord, In this thou shalt know that I *am* the

Lord: behold, I will smite with the rod that *is* in mine hand upon the waters which *are* in the river, and they shall be turned to blood. And the fish that *is* in the river shall die, and the river shall stink; and the Egyptians shall lothe to drink of the water of the river.

They had before defiled the river with the blood of innocents, and now it appears to them in blood-red colours; as if it published aloud their murderous deeds.

19 ¶ And the Lord spake unto Moses, Say unto Aaron, Take thy rod, and stretch out thine hand upon the waters of Egypt, upon their streams, upon their rivers, and upon their ponds, and upon all their pools of water, that they may become blood; and *that* there may be blood throughout all the land of Egypt, both in *vessels of* wood, and in *vessels of* stone.

20 And Moses and Aaron did so, as the Lord commanded; and he lifted up the rod, and smote the waters that *were* in the river, in the sight of Pharaoh, and in the sight of his servants; and all the waters that *were* in the river were turned to blood.

21 And the fish that *was* in the river died; and the river stank, and the Egyptians could not drink of the water of the river; and there was blood throughout all the land of Egypt.

Horrible! A crowd of horrors! Their drink becomes blood; the river which they accounted sacred pours forth an intolerable stench; the delicious water grows worse than putrid; and the fish which were a great part of their food float dead upon the abominable stream! This was a plague indeed.

22 And the magicians of Egypt did so with their enchantments: and Pharaoh's heart was hardened, neither did he hearken unto them; as the Lord had said. *(Proud Pharaoh cares not. His magicians ingeniously imitate the miracle by sleight of hand, and the heartless king cares nothing for the sufferings of his people.)*

Lo, Moses scatters plagues of wrath,
A ministry of fire and death,
But our Immanuel cometh forth,
With life and love in every breath.

He turn'd their water into blood,
For vengeance was his dread design:
But, thanks to our incarnate God,
He turn'd our water into wine.

78   " 𝕿𝖍𝖊 𝕷𝖔𝖗𝖉 𝖜𝖎𝖑𝖑 𝖉𝖊𝖘𝖙𝖗𝖔𝖞 𝖙𝖍𝖊 𝖍𝖔𝖚𝖘𝖊 𝖔𝖋 𝖙𝖍𝖊 𝖕𝖗𝖔𝖚𝖉."   FEBRUARY 8.—EVENING.

[Or March 18.]

A S *our endeavour is to gather up the substance of the Scriptures during the reading of one year, we are unable to pause over each of the ten great plagues. We ought, each one of us, to read them for our own instruction. We have them for our family reading summed up in*

PSALM CV. 24—38.

24 And he increased his people greatly; and made them stronger than their enemies. *(The Lord is just as able to increase his church at this time, and he will do so in answer to prayer.)*

25 He turned their heart to hate his people, to deal subtilly with his servants. *(Persecution generally attends the prosperity of the church. Where God blesses, Satan is sure to stir up all his wrath to vex the church.)*

26 He sent Moses his servant; *and* Aaron whom he had chosen. *(When evil days come, the Lord has deliverers provided, who shall appear at the exact moment when they are most required. Let us pray the Lord to raise up eminent ministers and evangelists at this time, for they are greatly needed.)*

27 They shewed his signs among them, and wonders in the land of Ham.

28 He sent darkness, and made it dark; and they rebelled not against his word. *(This unusual darkness filled all hearts with horror, and the Egyptians were so cowed that they yielded for the time, but were hardened again when the plague was over.)*

29 He turned their waters into blood, and slew their fish.

30 Their land brought forth frogs in abundance, in the chambers of their kings.

Fish died, but frogs lived. God can with one hand kill our comforts, and with the other multiply our miseries. This time Pharaoh himself had to endure personal annoyance, for frogs swarmed upon the royal bed.

31 He spake, and there came divers sorts of flies, *and* lice in all their coasts.

Here filthiness and venom were united; these little tormentors made the Egyptians feel the power of the great God. Often little plagues are the worst of plagues. From this visitation Pharaoh's bodyguards could not defend his royal person. Such enemies laughed at sword and spear.

32 He gave them hail for rain, *and* flaming fire in their land.

It is a judgment indeed when the fountains of

blessing become the channels of wrath, and the very rain is fire. Let the enemies of God beware.

33 He smote their vines also and their fig trees; and brake the trees of their coasts.

God's blows are heavy, and they leave no place unbruised. Egypt must miss its wine and its pleasant fruits if it will not obey the Lord.

34 He spake, and the locusts came, and caterpillers, and that without number,

35 And did eat up all the herbs in their land, and devoured the fruit of their ground.

Locusts literally eat up every green thing, and there is no preserving anything from them. God has many ways of punishing men. In this case we wonder at the hardness of heart of those who stood out against such humbling judgments. He who can with a word bring up countless hosts of devourers is not a God to be trifled with.

36 He smote also all the firstborn in their land, the chief of all their strength. *(This was the last and heaviest blow, and the proud king and nation staggered under it. When one arrow does not suffice, the Lord has others in his quiver, and one way or another he will hit the mark.)*

37 He brought them forth also with silver and gold: and *there was* not one feeble *person* among their tribes.

What a miracle that after all their toil and bondage they should all be in health. They were all called to go upon a long journey, and therefore the Lord prepared them for it.

38 Egypt was glad when they departed: for the fear of them fell upon them.

Thus can providence so work that the stoutest opponents shall only be too glad to yield.

Let us beware of provoking this terrible God. Let us by faith enlist him upon our side: then we shall have no ground for fear, for all the creatures he has made will be our friends. Fire and water, locusts and flies, darkness and death, were all the allies of Israel. He who is at peace with God has the whole creation enlisted upon his side.

Thus shall the nations be destroy'd
  That dare insult the saints;
God hath an arm t'avenge their wrongs,
  An ear for their complaints.

Thine honours, O victorious king,
  Thine own right hand shall raise,
While we thine awful vengeance sing,
  And our Deliverer praise.

ISRAEL'S *deliverance from Egypt was a redemption both by blood and by power. In the following chapter we read of the redemption by blood.*

EXODUS XII. 1—15.

1, 2 And the LORD spake unto Moses and Aaron in the land of Egypt, saying, This month *shall be* unto you the beginning of months : it *shall be* the first month of the year to you. *(To be redeemed is the greatest event in a man's history. The day in which we realise redemption must be the pearl of days to us for ever.)*

3, 4 Speak ye unto all the congregation of Israel, saying, In the tenth *day* of this month they shall take to them every man a lamb, according to the house of *their* fathers, a lamb for an house : And if the household be too little for the lamb, let him and his neighbour next unto his house take *it* according to the number of the souls ; every man according to his eating shall make your count for the lamb.

5 Your lamb shall be without blemish, a male of the first year : ye shall take *it* out from the sheep, or from the goats : *(Jesus was perfect, and in the fulness of his strength when he became the lamb of our passover.)*

6 And ye shall keep it up until the fourteenth day of the same month : and the whole assembly of the congregation of Israel shall kill it in the evening. *(It was both in the evening of the day and in the evening of time, that by the general voice of the nation, Jesus was put to death.)*

7 And they shall take of the blood, and strike *it* on the two side posts and on the upper door post of the houses, wherein they shall eat it. *(Not on the threshold, for woe unto the man who tramples on the blood of Christ.)*

8 And they shall eat the flesh in that night, roast with fire, and unleavened bread ; *and* with bitter *herbs* they shall eat it. *(Do these bitter herbs signify our repentance or the Redeemer's woes ? Perhaps both.)*

9 Eat not of it raw, nor sodden at all with water, but roast *with* fire ; his head with his legs, and with the purtenance thereof. *Our Lord's sufferings are well symbolised by the fire before which the lamb was roasted.*

10 And ye shall let nothing of it remain until the morning ; and that which remaineth of it until the morning ye shall burn with fire. *(We must feed upon Christ and upon a whole Christ.)*

11, 12 And thus shall ye eat it ; *with* your loins girded, your shoes on your feet, and your staff in your hand ; and ye shall eat it in haste : it *is* the LORD's passover. For I will pass through the land of Egypt this night, and will smite all the firstborn in the land of Egypt both man and beast ; and against all the gods of Egypt I will execute judgment : I *am* the LORD.

13 And the blood shall be to you for a token upon the houses where ye *are :* and when I see the blood, I will pass over you, and the plague shall not be upon you to destroy *you,* when I smite the land of Egypt. *(Mark that word,* " when I see the blood." *Our sight of the atonement brings us comfort, but the Lord's own sight of it is the true reason of our salvation.)*

14 And this day shall be unto you for a memorial ; and ye shall keep it a feast to the LORD throughout your generations ; ye shall keep it a feast by an ordinance for ever.

15 Seven days shall ye eat unleavened bread ; even the first day ye shall put away leaven out of your houses : for whosoever eateth leavened bread from the first day until the seventh day, that soul shall be cut off from Israel.

SIN *is that sour leaven which must go from the heart where Jesus is the Saviour. The apostle Paul puts this more at length in*

I COR V. 6—8.

6 Know ye not that a little leaven leaveneth the whole lump ? *(It is a spreading thing, and if any be left it will speedily multiply itself.)*

7 Purge out therefore the old leaven, that ye may be a new lump, as ye are unleavened. For even Christ our passover is sacrificed for us :

8 Therefore let us keep the feast, not with old leaven, neither with the leaven of malice and wickedness ; but with the unleavened *bread* of sincerity and truth. *(May the Holy Spirit grant us grace to accomplish this sweeping of the house. Where the precious blood is sprinkled, no sin can be tolerated.)*

Saints behold your Paschal lamb,
Trust his blood, and praise his name ;
Keep the sacred feast and be
Now from guile and malice free.

Stand as pilgrims, staff in hand,
Quitting soon this servile land,
Follow on where Christ has trod,
Till he brings you home to God.

OUR *last reading set forth the Lord's com- mand as to the passover, we shall now see it obeyed.*

EXODUS XII. 21—36.

21, 22 Then Moses called for all the elders of Israel, and said unto them, Draw out and take you a lamb according to your families, and kill the passover. And ye shall take a bunch of hyssop, and dip *it* in the blood that *is* in the bason, and strike the lintel and the two side posts with the blood that *is* in the bason ; and none of you shall go out at the door of his house until the morning. *(They must abide under the shelter of the blood or perish.)*

23 For the LORD will pass through to smite the Egyptians; and when he seeth the blood upon the lintel, and on the two side posts, the LORD will pass over the door, and will not suffer the destroyer to come in unto your houses to smite *you. (Else had Israel died as well as Egypt. It was not character or position, but the sprinkled blood which made the difference. The sacrifice of Jesus is the true reason of our salvation.)*

24 And ye shall observe this thing for an ordinance to thee and to thy sons for ever. *Whatever else we forget we must hold by the substitutionary atonement as long as time endures.*

25 And it shall come to pass, when ye be come to the land which the LORD will give you, according as he hath promised, that ye shall keep this service.

26 And it shall come to pass, when your children shall say unto you, What mean ye by this service ?

27 That ye shall say, It *is* the sacrifice of the LORD's passover, who passed over the houses of the children of Israel in Egypt, when he smote the Egyptians, and delivered our houses. And the people bowed the head and worshipped. *The youngest ought to be instructed in the doctrine of atonement by blood : it is the most vital truth of our most holy faith.*

28 And the children of Israel went away, and did as the LORD had commanded Moses and Aaron, so did they.

29 ¶ And it came to pass, that at midnight the LORD smote all the firstborn in the land of Egypt, from the firstborn of Pharaoh that sat on his throne unto the firstborn of the captive that *was* in the dungeon ; and all the firstborn of cattle.

30 And Pharaoh rose up in the night, he, and all his servants, and all the Egyptians ; and there was a great cry in Egypt ; for *there was* not a house where *there was* not one dead. *Death reigned where the blood was not sprinkled, and so must it be. Are we all marked with the blood of our Great Substitute ?*

31, 32 And he called for Moses and Aaron by night, and said, Rise up, *and* get you forth from among my people, both ye and the children of Israel ; and go, serve the LORD, as ye have said. Also take your flocks and your herds, as ye have said, and be gone ; and bless me also. *(Here was the overthrow of pride. The haughty tyrant surrenders, and becomes himself a suppliant. God's sword can reach the heart of leviathan himself, though he thinks himself invulnerable and invincible.)*

33 And the Egyptians were urgent upon the people, that they might send them out of the land in haste ; for they said, We *be* all dead *men.*

34 And the people took their dough before it was leavened, their kneading-troughs being bound up in their clothes upon their shoulders.

35 And the children of Israel did according to the word of Moses ; and they borrowed of the Egyptians jewels of silver, and jewels of gold, and raiment. *(These were not borrowed as we understand the word, but asked for, and freely given, because the people honoured the Israelites, and were afraid to incur their anger.)*

36 And the LORD gave the people favour in the sight of the Egyptians, so that they lent unto them *such things as they required.* And they spoiled the Egyptians. *Their long and unpaid services were thus, in a measure, requited by the gifts of the Egyptians.*

When souls are spiritually set free from sin, the Lord is pleased to adorn them with many precious things ; for he is abundant in loving- kindness towards his people.

Paschal Lamb, by God appointed,
    All our sins on Thee were laid :
By almighty love anointed,
    Thou hast full atonement made :
All Thy people are forgiven
    Through the virtue of Thy blood :
Open'd is the gate of heaven ;
    Peace is made 'twixt man and God.

EXODUS XIII. 17, 18; 20—22.

AND it came to pass, when Pharaoh had let the people go, that God led them not *through* the way of the land of the Philistines, although that *was* near; for God said, Lest peradventure the people repent when they see war, and they return to Egypt:

18 But God led the people about, *through* the way of the wilderness of the Red sea: and the children of Israel went up harnessed out of the land of Egypt: (*The Lord is mindful of the infirmities of his people. He meant them to see many wars hereafter, but as yet they were all unused to fighting, and therefore were to be led by a quieter though a longer road. Blessed be God, our troubles shall not be ready for us till we are ready for them.*)

20, 21, 22 And they took their journey from Succoth, and encamped in Etham, in the edge of the wilderness. And the LORD went before them by day in a pillar of a cloud, to lead them the way; and by night in a pillar of fire, to give them light; to go by day and night: He took not away the pillar of the cloud by day, nor the pillar of fire by night, *from* before the people. (*The pillar was their infallible conductor; it also screened them by day and lit up the camp by night. God's mercies are many-sided. We can only do one thing well at a time, but the Lord accomplishes many devices at one stroke.*)

EXODUS XIV. 1—5; 8—14.

AND the LORD spake unto Moses, saying, 2 Speak unto the children of Israel, that they turn and encamp before Pi-hahiroth, between Migdol and the sea, over against Baal-zephon: before it shall ye encamp by the sea. *This seemed a strange direction, but Moses obeyed it without question. Let us go where the Lord bids us though the way be perilous.*

3, 4 For Pharaoh will say of the children of Israel, They *are* entangled in the land, the wilderness hath shut them in. And I will harden Pharaoh's heart, that he shall follow after them; and I will be honoured upon Pharaoh, and upon all his host; that the Egyptians may know that I *am* the Lord. And they did so.

5 ¶ And it was told the king of Egypt that the people fled: and the heart of Pharaoh and of his servants was turned against the people, and they said, Why have we done this, that we have let Israel go from serving us?

8 And the LORD hardened the heart of Pharaoh king of Egypt, and he pursued after the children of Israel: and the children of Israel went out with an high hand. (*God's plagues had not changed the King's rebellious nature. When he saw that he had lost his valuable slaves, his greed made him rush after them.*)

9 But the Egyptians pursued after them, all the horses *and* chariots of Pharaoh, and his horsemen, and his army, and overtook them encamping by the sea, beside Pi-hahiroth, before Baal-zephon.

10, 11 And when Pharaoh drew nigh, the children of Israel lifted up their eyes, and, behold, the Egyptians marched after them; and they were sore afraid: and the children of Israel cried out unto the LORD. And they said unto Moses, Because *there were* no graves in Egypt, hast thou taken us away to die in the wilderness? wherefore hast thou dealt thus with us, to carry us forth out of Egypt?

12 *Is* not this the word that we did tell thee in Egypt, saying, Let us alone, that we may serve the Egyptians? For *it had been* better for us to serve the Egyptians, than that we should die in the wilderness. (*This unbelief was both unjust and cruel. Had they not seen the Lord's works in the great plagues? Could they not believe that he who had wrought such marvels could and would deliver them? They were smitten with panic, and were willing to return to bondage; whereas true freemen never debate which of the two to choose, slavery or death.*)

13, 14 And Moses said unto the people, Fear ye not, stand still, and see the salvation of the LORD, which he will shew to you to day: for the Egyptians whom ye have seen to day, ye shall see them again no more for ever. The LORD shall fight for you, and ye shall hold your peace. (*This meekest of men answered the people meekly and believingly, for prayer enabled him to conquer his own spirit.*)

Forward! but whither shall we go?
The desert is on either side,
Behind us the Egyptian foe,
Before, the interposing tide!

Yet while we thy command obey,
Our road impassable pursue,
The ocean yields an open way,
And lets thy ransomed people through.

EXODUS XIV. 15—31.

AND the LORD said unto Moses, Wherefore criest thou unto me? speak unto the children of Israel, that they go forward:

*We read not that Moses had spoken a word; but his heart cried unto the Lord. The Lord bade him no longer hesitate, but cry, "*FORWARD,*" and advance through the sea.*

16, 17, 18 But lift thou up thy rod, and stretch out thine hand over the sea, and divide it : and the children of Israel shall go on dry *ground* through the midst of the sea. And I, behold, I will harden the hearts of the Egyptians, and they shall follow them : and I will get me honour upon Pharaoh, and upon all his host, upon his chariots, and upon his horsemen. And the Egyptians shall know that I *am* the LORD, when I have gotten me honour upon Pharaoh, upon his chariots, and upon his horsemen.

19 ¶ And the angel of God, which went before the camp of Israel, removed and went behind them ; and the pillar of the cloud went from before their face, and stood behind them :

The glory of the Lord was their rereward.

20 And it came between the camp of the Egyptians and the camp of Israel; and it was a cloud and darkness *to them*, but it gave light by night *to these :* so that the one came not near the other all the night. *(Both God's word and providence have a twofold aspect, they frown on sinners while they smile on saints. Thus God still sets a difference between Israel and Egypt.)*

21 And Moses stretched out his hand over the sea ; and the LORD caused the sea to go *back* by a strong east wind all that night, and made the sea dry *land*, and the waters were divided.

22 And the children of Israel went into the midst of the sea upon the dry *ground :* and the waters *were* a wall unto them on their right hand, and on their left. *(Calmly the historian records it, but what a wonder is here ! Water erect like solid ice, and a damp sea bed made dry and fit to be a highway for a marching army.)*

23 ¶ And the Egyptians pursued, and went in after them to the midst of the sea, *even* all Pharaoh's horses, his chariots, and his horsemen.

What infatuation ! Were they beguiled by the darkness around them or that within them ?

24 And it came to pass, that in the morning watch the LORD looked unto the host of the Egyptians through the pillar of fire and of the cloud, and troubled the host of the Egyptians,

25 And took off their chariot wheels, that they drave them heavily : so that the Egyptians said, Let us flee from the face of Israel ; for the LORD fighteth for them against the Egyptians.

One look from Jehovah was enough, one flash from his eye of fire, struck the host with panic.

26 ¶ And the LORD said unto Moses, Stretch out thine hand over the sea, that the waters may come again upon the Egyptians, upon their chariots, and upon their horsemen.

27 And Moses stretched forth his hand over the sea, and the sea returned to his strength when the morning appeared ; and the Egyptians fled against it; and the LORD overthrew the Egyptians in the midst of the sea.

28 And the waters returned, and covered the chariots, and the horsemen, *and* all the host of Pharaoh that came into the sea after them ; there remained not so much as one of them.

Even thus "our tyrannous sins are buried and drowned, and though they be sought for they shall not be found."

29, 30 But the children of Israel walked upon dry *land* in the midst of the sea ; and the waters *were* a wall unto them on their right hand, and on their left. Thus the LORD saved Israel that day out of the hand of the Egyptians; and Israel saw the Egyptians dead upon the sea shore. *(So completely was Egypt shattered, that though the Israelites were for forty years close to the Egyptian borders, they were never molested by their former oppressors.)*

31 And Israel saw that great work which the LORD did upon the Egyptians : and the people feared the LORD, and believed the LORD, and his servant Moses. *(And well they might, but, alas, this good state of mind did not last long.)*

Awake, awake, thou mighty Arm,
  Which has such wonders wrought !
Which captive Israel freed from harm,
  And out of Egypt brought.

Art thou not it which Rahab slew ?
  And crush'd the dragon's head ?
Constrain'd by thee the waves withdrew
  From their accustom'd bed.

Again thy wonted prowess show,
  Be thou made bare again :
And let thine adversaries know
  That they resist in vain.

EXODUS XV. 1—21.

WE will now read the song of Moses, which is prophetically typical of the ultimate victory of the Lord Jesus.

1 Then sang Moses and the children of Israel this song unto the Lord, and spake, saying, I will sing unto the Lord, for he hath triumphed gloriously: the horse and his rider hath he thrown into the sea.

2 The Lord is my strength and song, and he is become my salvation: he is my God, and I will prepare him an habitation; my father's God, and I will exalt him.

3, 4 The Lord is a man of war: the Lord is his name. Pharaoh's chariots and his host hath he cast into the sea: his chosen captains also are drowned in the Red sea.

5 The depths have covered them: they sank into the bottom as a stone.

6, 7 Thy right hand, O Lord, is become glorious in power: thy right hand, O Lord, hath dashed in pieces the enemy. And in the greatness of thine excellency thou hast overthrown them that rose up against thee: thou sentest forth thy wrath, which consumed them as stubble.

8 And with the blast of thy nostrils the waters were gathered together, the floods stood upright as an heap, and the depths were congealed in the heart of the sea.

9 The enemy said, I will pursue, I will overtake, I will divide the spoil; my lust shall be satisfied upon them; I will draw my sword, my hand shall destroy them.

10 Thou didst blow with thy wind, the sea covered them: they sank as lead in the mighty waters.

11 Who is like unto thee, O Lord, among the gods? who is like thee, glorious in holiness, fearful in praises, doing wonders?

12 Thou stretchedst out thy right hand, the earth swallowed them.

13 Thou in thy mercy hast led forth the people which thou hast redeemed: thou hast guided them in thy strength unto thy holy habitation.

14, 15, 16 The people shall hear, and be afraid: sorrow shall take hold on the inhabitants of Palestina. Then the dukes of Edom shall be amazed; the mighty men of Moab, trembling shall take hold upon them; all the inhabitants of Canaan shall melt away. Fear and dread shall fall upon them; by the greatness of thine arm they shall be as still as a stone; till thy people pass over, O Lord, till the people pass over, which thou hast purchased.

17 Thou shalt bring them in, and plant them in the mountain of thine inheritance, in the place, O Lord, which thou hast made for thee to dwell in, in the Sanctuary, O Lord, which thy hands have established.

18 The Lord shall reign for ever and ever.

19 For the horse of Pharaoh went in with his chariots and with his horsemen into the sea, and the Lord brought again the waters of the sea upon them; but the children of Israel went on dry land in the midst of the sea.

20, 21 And Miriam the prophetess, the sister of Aaron, took a timbrel in her hand; and all the women went out after her with timbrels and with dances. And Miriam answered them, Sing ye to the Lord, for he hath triumphed gloriously; the horse and his rider hath he thrown into the sea.

In order to leave the song unbroken, we have reserved our few notes for the end of it.

Observe the sublimity and simplicity of the composition. Fine, florid language suits the little elegancies of man but not the glories of the Lord. Note how all the song is to the praise of the Lord alone, there is not a note for Moses or for Aaron; no hint of secondary agents, but Jehovah alone is exalted. Remark the noise, hurry, and violence of the foe, in verse 9, and the calmness of the Lord, in verse 10. It will be well to read them both again. Man is raving and threatening, and the Lord in placid omnipotence defeats his rage. Consider also, how the poet infers the future from the present. God who brought his people through the sea, would surely bring them into their heritage. He who has wrought marvels of grace already, will not leave us till grace is turned into glory.

What a noble hallelujah is that of verse 18, "Jehovah shall reign for ever and ever." It is a plain inference from his overthrow of his enemies. Let us triumph in our reigning God. He has overcome sin, death, and hell for us; let us therefore, like Miriam, rejoice with all the saints. Let our heart dance, and our hand make music unto our Redeemer, who has cast our enemies into the depths of the sea.

84   "𝕿𝖍𝖔𝖚 𝖆𝖗𝖙 𝖙𝖍𝖊 𝕷𝖔𝖗𝖉 𝖙𝖍𝖆𝖙 𝖉𝖔𝖊𝖘𝖙 𝖜𝖔𝖓𝖉𝖊𝖗𝖘."   FEBRUARY 11.—EVENING.

[Or March 24.]

O N *this occasion we shall read*

PSALM LXXVII.

This will show us the way in which holy men of old derived comfort from the great miracle of the Red Sea. Here is Asaph, almost in despair, encouraged by remembering the Lord's wonders of old.

1 I cried unto God with my voice, *even* unto God with my voice ; and he gave ear unto me.

2 In the day of my trouble I sought the LORD : my sore ran in the night, and ceased not: my soul refused to be comforted.

His spirits sank so low that like a sick man who cannot eat what is good for him, he was unable to believe cheering truths.

3 I remembered God, and was troubled : I complained, and my spirit was overwhelmed. *(God's people know by experience the lonely glens of soul trouble.)* Selah. *(This is a musical pause, or perhaps it means " lift up the tune." Let us lift up our hearts.)*

4 Thou holdest mine eyes waking : I am so troubled that I cannot speak.

5 I have considered the days of old, the years of ancient times.

6 I call to remembrance my song in the night: I commune with mine own heart : and my spirit made diligent search.

7 Will the Lord cast off for ever ? and will he be favourable no more ? *(These questions are suggested by fear, but they may serve as the cure of fear. Their answers are both self-evident and heart-cheering.)*

8 Is his mercy clean gone for ever ? doth *his* promise fail for evermore ?

9 Hath God forgotten to be gracious ? hath he in anger shut up his tender mercies ? Selah.

10 And I said, This *is* my infirmity: *(This accounts for most of our fears. They have no real ground, but are based upon our weakness of faith. The evil is in us, not in providence ; the change in our hearts, not in the immutable God:)* but *I will remember* the years of the right hand of the most High.

11 I will remember the works of the LORD : surely I will remember thy wonders of old.

12 I will meditate also of all thy work, and talk of thy doings. *(" Remember," " meditate," " talk,"—this is a wise order. Imitate it.)*

13 Thy way, O God, *is* in the sanctuary : who *is so* great a God as *our* God ?

14, 15 Thou *art* the God that doest wonders : thou hast declared thy strength among the people. Thou hast with *thine* arm redeemed thy people, the sons of Jacob and Joseph. Selah.

16 The waters saw thee, O God, the waters saw thee ; they were afraid : the depths also were troubled. *(Quiet caves of the sea, far down in the abyss, were stirred with fright ; and the waters fled as if they feared the face of the Lord.)*

17 The clouds poured out water : the skies sent out a sound : thine arrows also went abroad.

Lightnings flew like bolts from the bow of God, and the rain dashed down in torrents.

18 The voice of thy thunder *was* in the heaven : the lightnings lightened the world : the earth trembled and shook. *(According to Josephus there was a terrible storm when the Egyptians were in the midst of the sea ; there would seem from the text to have been rain, tempest, and earthquake combined. All the elements are the allies of Israel, and the enemies of the ungodly.)*

19 Thy way *is* in the sea, and thy path in the great waters, and thy footsteps are not known.

Our God has mysterious ways of delivering his people, but deliver them he will.

20 Thou leddest thy people like a flock by the hand of Moses and Aaron.

They felt no storm and feared no ill, but were as quiet and safe as sheep protected by their shepherd. Even thus shall all the saints be secure, while their enemies are utterly overwhelmed.

I'll call to mind thy works of old,
   The wonders of thy might ;
On them my heart shall meditate,
   Them shall my tongue recite.

Thy people, Lord, long since have thee
   A God of wonders found :
Long since hast thou thy chosen seed
   With strong deliv'rance crown'd.

Sound the loud timbrel o'er Egypt's dark sea !
Jehovah hath triumph'd : his people are free.
Sing, for the pride of the tyrant is broken,
His chariots and horsemen all splendid and brave,
How vain was their boasting ! the Lord hath but
   spoken,
And chariots and horsemen are sunk in the wave.
Sound the loud timbrel o'er Egypt's dark sea !
Jehovah hath triumph'd : his people are free.

EXODUS XV. 22—27.

SO Moses brought Israel from the Red sea, and they went out into the wilderness of Shur; and they went three days in the wilderness, and found no water.

Their first trouble was too much water, the second is too little; our trials are of all kinds.

23 ¶ And when they came to Marah, they could not drink of the waters of Marah, for they *were* bitter: therefore the name of it was called Marah. (*This was tantalizing, they had water, but could not drink it*).

24 And the people murmured against Moses, saying, What shall we drink?

25, 26 And he cried unto the LORD; and the LORD shewed him a tree, *which* when he had cast into the waters, the waters were made sweet: there he made for them a statute and an ordinance, and there he proved them, And said, If thou wilt diligently hearken to the voice of the LORD thy God, and wilt do that which is right in his sight, and wilt give ear to his commandments, and keep all his statutes, I will put none of these diseases upon thee, which I have brought upon the Egyptians: for I *am* the LORD that healeth thee. (*God has provided remedies for all ills, sweetening trees for bitter waters, and the cross to sweeten all.*)

27 ¶ And they came to Elim, where *were* twelve wells of water, and threescore and ten palm trees: and they encamped there by the waters. (*It is not all rough work with pilgrims to Canaan, they have their pleasant seasons. Let them thank God for them.*)

EXODUS XVI. 1—10.

AND they took their journey from Elim, and all the congregation of the children of Israel came unto the wilderness of Sin. (*It was strange that God should lead two millions of people into a desert, but wisdom directed his course. Strange providences are gracious providences.*)

2 And the whole congregation of the children of Israel murmured against Moses and Aaron in the wilderness: and said unto them, Would to God we had died by the hand of the LORD in the land of Egypt, when we sat by the flesh pots, *and* when we did eat bread to the full; for ye have brought us forth into this wilderness, to kill this whole assembly with hunger. (*With shameful readiness they ran to a low-minded form of complaining. There was no spirit in them. The flesh pots and the bread were all they thought of; the brick-making and the whips they overlooked. It is easy to make out the past to have been bright when we wish to find fault with the present.*)

4, 5 Then·said the LORD unto Moses, Behold, I will rain bread from heaven for you; and the people shall go out and gather a certain rate every day, that I may prove them, whether they will walk in my law, or no. And it shall come to pass, that on the sixth day they shall prepare *that* which they bring in; and it shall be twice as much as they gather daily. (*Our mercies are tests; let us eat and drink to God's glory.*)

6, 7 And Moses and Aaron said unto all the children of Israel, At even, then ye shall know that the LORD hath brought you out from the land of Egypt: And in the morning, then ye shall see the glory of the LORD; for that he heareth your murmurings against the LORD: and what *are* we, that ye murmur against us?

8 And Moses said, *This shall be*, when the LORD shall give you in the evening flesh to eat, and in the morning bread to the full; for that the LORD heareth your murmurings which ye murmur against him: and what *are* we? your murmurings *are* not against us, but against the LORD. (*We think it a small thing to murmur against parents and friends, but this sheds a new light upon the matter. It is clear that a discontented heart really murmurs against God himself.*)

9, 10 ¶ And Moses spake unto Aaron, Say unto all the congregation of the children of Israel, Come near before the LORD: for he hath heard your murmurings. (*This is a solemn truth; let all grumblers remember it.*) And it came to pass, as Aaron spake unto the whole congregation of the children of Israel, that they looked toward the wilderness, and, behold, the glory of the LORD appeared in the cloud.

> The cross on which the Saviour died,
> And conquer'd for his saints;
> This is the tree by faith applied
> To sweeten all complaints.
>
> When we by faith behold the cross,
> Though many griefs we meet;
> We draw a gain from every loss,
> And make our Marahs sweet.

EXODUS XVI. 11—31.

AND the LORD spake unto Moses, saying, I have heard the murmurings of the children of Israel: speak unto them, saying, At even ye shall eat flesh, and in the morning ye shall be filled with bread; and ye shall know that I am the Lord your God.

One would have expected a far severer rebuke than this, but the Lord was very pitiful towards them, as he is also towards us. These first murmurings were not visited so severely as those further on. The Lord is loath to use his rod.

13, 14 And it came to pass, that at even the quails came up, and covered the camp: and in the morning the dew lay round about the host. And when the dew that lay was gone up, behold, upon the face of the wilderness *there lay* a small round thing, *as* small as the hoar frost on the ground.

15 And when the children of Israel saw *it*, they said one to another, It *is* manna: for they wist not what it *was*. And Moses said unto them, This *is* the bread which the LORD hath given you to eat. (*They had the best of flesh and better than the best of bread. No king's table was better spread than theirs. Rest assured he who fed murmurers will not desert believers.*)

16 ¶ This *is* the thing which the LORD hath commanded, Gather of it every man according to his eating, an omer for every man, *according to* the number of your persons; take ye every man for *them* which *are* in his tents. (*Heaven's bread must be gathered. We must hear the word, and retain it, or it cannot profit us.*)

17 And the children of Israel did so, and gathered, some more, some less.

18 And when they did mete *it* with an omer, he that gathered much had nothing over, and he that gathered little had no lack; they gathered every man according to his eating.

19, 20 And Moses said, Let no man leave of it till the morning. Notwithstanding they hearkened not unto Moses: but some of them left of it until the morning, and it bred worms, and stank: and Moses was wroth with them.

There were misers in the wilderness, and their hoardings stank; there are other misers now upon the earth, whose scrapings are cankered and corrupt. Covetousness is loathsome.

21 And they gathered it every morning, every man according to his eating: and when the sun waxed hot, it melted. (*Yet it could be cooked! Strange that it could bear one heat and not another.*)

22 ¶ And it came to pass, *that* on the sixth day they gathered twice as much bread, two omers for one *man*: and all the rulers of the congregation came and told Moses.

23, 24 And he said unto them, This *is that* which the Lord hath said, To morrow *is* the rest of the holy sabbath unto the Lord: bake *that* which ye will bake *to day*, and seethe that ye will seethe; and that which remaineth over lay up for you to be kept until the morning. And they laid it up till the morning, as Moses bade: and it did not stink, neither was there any worm therein.

25, 26 And Moses said, Eat that to day; for to day *is* a sabbath unto the LORD: to day ye shall not find it in the field. Six days ye shall gather it; but on the seventh day, *which is* the sabbath, in it there shall be none. (*Thus the seventh day was honoured by the ceasing of the visible manna, but our first-day Sabbath has a double fall of spiritual manna, and we ought to gather in good store for all the week-days.*)

27 ¶ And it came to pass, *that* there went out *some* of the people on the seventh day for to gather, and they found none. (*This was the surest way of stopping the sin, but it was very grievous that a people so marvellously favoured should be guilty of such a superfluous provocation.*)

28, 29, 30 And the LORD said unto Moses, How long refuse ye to keep my commandments and my laws? See, for that the LORD hath given you the sabbath, therefore he giveth you on the sixth day the bread of two days; abide ye every man in his place, let no man go out of his place on the seventh day. So the people rested on the seventh day.

31 And the house of Israel called the name thereof Manna: and it *was* like coriander seed, white; and the taste of it *was* like wafers *made* with honey. (*God might have made it bitter, but he delights to see his creatures happy. What a blessed God he is!*)

Day by day the manna fell;
Oh! to learn this lesson well:
Still by constant mercy fed,
Give me, Lord, my daily bread.

"Day by day," the promise reads;
Daily strength for daily needs;
Cast foreboding fears away;
Take the manna of to-day.

EXODUS XVI. 32—35.

AND Moses said, This *is* the thing which the LORD commandeth, Fill an omer of it to be kept for your generations; that they may see the bread wherewith I have fed you in the wilderness, when I brought you forth from the land of Egypt. *(The education of future generations should be the earnest care of the people of God, since the Lord himself so constantly ordained means for perpetuating the memory of his deeds of grace. The Lord knows that the race is apt to forget even his greatest wonders, and therefore he puts them in remembrance.)*

33, 34 And Moses said unto Aaron, Take a pot, and put an omer full of manna therein, and lay it up before the LORD, to be kept for your generations. As the LORD commanded Moses, so Aaron laid it up before the Testimony, to be kept. *(Even thus should we treasure the memory of the Lord's great goodness to us. In the ark of our memory, the golden pot should be kept in store.)*

35 And the children of Israel did eat manna forty years, until they came to a land inhabited; they did eat manna, until they came unto the borders of the land of Canaan. *(The storehouses of Jehovah are never exhausted. All the while the Lord's people are in the wilderness, whether it be forty years or eighty years, their bread shall be given them, their waters shall be sure. Trust ye in the Lord for ever.)*

THE manna was a very full and instructive type of our Lord Jesus, who is the spiritual bread of his people. In order to understand this, let us read his own words in

JOHN VI. 47—58,

47 Verily, verily, I say unto you, He that believeth on me hath everlasting life.

48 I am that bread of life. *(He is life to believers and the support of their life.)*

49 Your fathers did eat manna in the wilderness, and are dead. *(Though the manna came from heaven, yet it brought not immortality with it as Jesus does. The Jews died, and died very terribly too, many of them; but those who feed on Jesus live for ever.)*

50 This is the bread which cometh down from heaven, that a man may eat thereof, and not die. *(This spiritual bread confers, supports, and preserves spiritual life.)*

51 I am the living bread which came down from heaven: if any man eat of this bread, he shall live for ever: and the bread that I will give is my flesh, which I will give for the life of the world.

52 The Jews therefore strove among themselves, saying, How can this man give us *his* flesh to eat? *(They looked at the words and did not discern the sense, and hence they asked this very natural question.)*

53 Then Jesus said unto them, Verily, verily, I say unto you, Except ye eat the flesh of the Son of man, and drink his blood, ye have no life in you. *(Our Lord would not explain his parabolic speech to them. It was not given to them to understand.)*

54 Whoso eateth my flesh, and drinketh my blood, hath eternal life; and I will raise him up at the last day.

55 For my flesh is meat indeed, and my blood is drink indeed. *(Some persons dream that this applies to the Lord's supper, which was not even instituted at the time. It refers neither to the supper, nor to the mass, nor to any sacrificial bread, but to our Lord himself, who must be fed upon spiritually and not in symbol only. Too many even now are like the Jews, and cannot understand spiritual truth, but stumble over the literal meaning.)*

56 He that eateth my flesh, and drinketh my blood, dwelleth in me, and I in him. *(The nearest possible union is established between Jesus and the believer.)*

57, 58 As the living Father hath sent me, and I live by the Father: so he that eateth me, even he shall live by me. This is that bread which came down from heaven: not as your fathers did eat manna, and are dead: he that eateth of this bread shall live for ever. *(Have we all in our hearts received Jesus? Are we trusting in Him alone? Do we commune with him? For this is to feed upon him, and enter into living union with him.)*

Bread of heaven! on thee I feed,
For thy flesh is meat indeed;
Ever may my soul be fed
With this true and living bread.

Those who feed on thee are blest,
Never more by hunger pressed;
Day by day with strength supplied,
Through the life of Him who died.

THE *way in which the Lord supplied the needs of his people in the desert, suggests to us a meditation upon the divine care and faithfulness as to the temporal wants of his people. It is our privilege to depend upon the Lord for everything as much as Israel did in the wilderness. It is still true that our God will supply all our needs. Hence our Lord Jesus has taught us to keep clear of all carking care and to walk by faith. Let us read his words in*

MATTHEW VI. 25—34.

25 Therefore I say unto you, Take no thought for your life, what ye shall eat, or what ye shall drink ; nor yet for your body, what ye shall put on. Is not the life more than meat, and the body than raiment? *(Do not fret and worry about such secondary things. God who gives us lives and bodies will give us food and clothing).*

26 Behold the fowls of the air : for they sow not, neither do they reap, nor gather into barns; yet your heavenly Father feedeth them. Are ye not much better than they ? *(Martin Luther was one day walking in the fields when in great straits, with his Bible in his hands, and reading the Sermon on the Mount, was much comforted by* Matt. vi. 26, *" Behold the fowls of the air, they toil not neither do they reap, nor gather into barns; yet your heavenly Father feedeth them." Just then a little bird was hopping from sprig to spray, with its sweet chirping note, seeming to say,*

"Mortals, cease from toil and sorrow,
  God provideth for the morrow."

It then came to the ground to pick up a crumb, and rising merrily, again seemed to repeat its simple song—

"Mortals, cease from toil and sorrow,
  God provideth for the morrow."

This greatly comforted the Reformer's heart.)

27 Which of you by taking thought can add one cubit unto his stature ? *(All the thought in the world cannot lengthen our stature or our life.)*

28, 29, 30 And why take ye thought for raiment ? Consider the lilies of the field, how they grow ; they toil not, neither do they spin : And yet I say unto you, That even Solomon in all his glory was not arrayed like one of these. Wherefore, if God so clothe the grass of the field, which to day is, and to morrow is cast into the oven, *shall he* not much more *clothe* you, O ye

of little faith ? *(This is good reasoning : he who cares for poor fading lilies and robes them so sumptuously, will not let his own immortal sons go bare. Surely we can trust our own Father.)*

31, 32 Therefore take no thought, saying, What shall we eat ? or, What shall we drink ? or, Wherewithal shall we be clothed ? (For after all these things do the Gentiles seek :) for your heavenly Father knoweth that ye have need of all these things. *(All anxious care is forbidden. We have a Father in heaven, shall we fret as if we had none? Doubt not till you have cause to doubt.)*

33 But seek ye first the kingdom of God, and his righteousness; and all these things shall be added unto you.

34 Take therefore no thought for the morrow : for the morrow shall take thought for the things of itself. Sufficient unto the day *is* the evil thereof. *(Never anticipate troubles, each day has its own, and enough of them; yes, and enough grace comes daily to bear us through them.)*

LET *us cheer our hearts by reading that delicious song of contentment,*

PSALM XXIII.

The LORD is my shepherd ; I shall not want.

2 He maketh me to lie down in green pastures : he leadeth me beside the still waters.

3 He restoreth my soul : he leadeth me in the paths of righteousness for his name's sake.

4 Yea, though I walk through the valley of the shadow of death, I will fear no evil : for thou *art* with me ; thy rod and thy staff they comfort me.

5 Thou preparest a table before me in the presence of mine enemies : thou anointest my head with oil ; my cup runneth over.

6 Surely goodness and mercy shall follow me all the days of my life : and I will dwell in the house of the LORD for ever.

He leads me to the place
  Where heavenly pasture grows,
Where living waters gently pass,
  And full salvation flows.

If e'er I go astray,
  He doth my soul reclaim ;
And guides me in his own right way,
  For his most holy name.

EXODUS XVII. 1—7.

AND all the congregation of the children of Israel journeyed from the wilderness of Sin, after their journeys, according to the commandment of the Lord, and pitched in Rephidim : and *there was* no water for the people to drink. *(God's people are never long untried.)*

2 Wherefore the people did chide with Moses, and said, Give us water that we may drink. And Moses said unto them, Why chide ye with me ? wherefore do ye tempt the Lord ? *Complaining of second causes is really complaining of the Lord, let us disguise it as we may. What, after all, had Moses to do with it ? The root of this sin of murmuring was unbelief. Could they not trust Jehovah ? Would he not be sure to supply their wants ? Had he ever been unmindful of them ? Alas, notwithstanding all our experience of his faithfulness we ourselves are not clear from unbelief. He that is without fault among us, let him throw the first stone at Israel.*

3 And the people thirsted there for water ; and the people murmured against Moses, and said, Wherefore *is* this *that* thou hast brought us up out of Egypt, to kill us and our children and our cattle with thirst ?

4 And Moses cried unto the Lord, saying, What shall I do unto this people ? they be almost ready to stone me. *(Moses took the case into the right court. The people cried against him, but he cried unto the Lord. Here is our best resource. We may cry to God now.)*

5 And the Lord said unto Moses, Go on before the people, and take with thee of the elders of Israel ; and thy rod, wherewith thou smotest the river, take in thine hand, and go.

6 Behold, I will stand before thee there upon the rock in Horeb ; and thou shalt smite the rock, and there shall come water out of it, that the people may drink. And Moses did so in the sight of the elders of Israel. *(See how the Lord answers their murmurings ; not by fulfilling their bitter speeches and leaving them to die of thirst, but by fetching living streams from a rock. Surely the Lord, who thus recompenses good for evil, deserves our heart's unwavering confidence from this day forward. It is wanton insult to doubt one who is so overflowing with kindness. Render not evil for good.)*

7 And he called the name of the place Massah, and Meribah, because of the chiding of the children of Israel, and because they tempted the Lord, saying, Is the Lord among us, or not ? *(The Lord takes note of his people's chidings and commemorates them. We must not think a grumbling spirit to be a small evil. The Lord has here set a mark and a brand upon it.)*

THE God who supplied Israel with natural water is ready to grant us the living water of his grace. Hear what his words are in

ISAIAH XLI. 17, 18.

17 When the poor and needy seek water, and *there is* none, *and* their tongue faileth for thirst, I the Lord will hear them, *I* the God of Israel will not forsake them.

18 I will open rivers in high places, and fountains in the midst of the valleys : I will make the wilderness a pool of water, and the dry land springs of water.

TO strengthen our faith in this promise we are bidden to look back upon the Lord's wonders of old and to expect yet greater things, for God has not changed, nor are the fountains of his power and grace exhausted.

ISAIAH XLIII. 18—21.

18 Remember ye not the former things, neither consider the things of old.

19 Behold, I will do a new thing ; now it shall spring forth ; shall ye not know it ? I will even make a way in the wilderness, *and* rivers in the desert.

20 The beast of the field shall honour me, the dragons and the owls : because I give waters in the wilderness, *and* rivers in the desert, to give drink to my people, my chosen.

21 This people have I formed for myself ; they shall shew forth my praise. *(Glory be unto the Lord, we can bear witness that we daily and hourly receive fresh supplies of grace from him. No good thing hath he withheld from us. His praise shall continually be in our mouths.)*

Poor needy souls athirst and faint,
Who gasp for my redeeming love ;
I will attend to their complaint,
And pour them rivers from above.

Water'd by me, the desert-soul,
The garden of the Lord shall prove,
Replenished as a wide-spread pool,
By springs of everlasting love.

EXODUS XVII. 8—16.

THEN came Amalek, and fought with Israel in Rephidim. (*These ferocious wanderers attacked Israel unawares in a cowardly and unprovoked manner, when they were least able to defend themselves. They seem to have been of all Israel's foes the most wantonly malicious, and hence they are instructive emblems of sin and Satan.*)

9 And Moses said unto Joshua, Choose us out men, and go out, fight with Amalek: to morrow I will stand on the top of the hill with the rod of God in mine hand. (*We must fight as well as pray. Though effort without prayer would be presumption, prayer without effort is mockery. Joshua must go to battle as well as Moses to the hill. Jesus said, " Watch and pray."*)

10 So Joshua did as Moses had said to him, and fought with Amalek: and Moses, Aaron, and Hur went up to the top of the hill.

11 And it came to pass, when Moses held up his hand, that Israel prevailed: and when he let down his hand, Amalek prevailed.

12 But Moses' hands *were* heavy; and they took a stone, and put *it* under him, and he sat thereon; and Aaron and Hur stayed up his hands, the one on the one side, and the other on the other side; and his hands were steady until the going down of the sun. (*Let all of us labour to uphold the prayerfulness of the church, for if that flags all flags. " Lift up the hands that hang down, and confirm the feeble knees." Spiritual evil can only be overcome by the energy of prayer, and when we fail in devotion, the enemy easily overcomes us.*)

13 And Joshua discomfited Amalek and his people with the edge of the sword.

14 And the LORD said unto Moses, Write this *for* a memorial in a book, and rehearse *it* in the ears of Joshua: for I will utterly put out the remembrance of Amalek from under heaven.

It has been suggested by a quaint author, that the Lord's reason for specially commanding this event to be recorded is, that his people may imitate it. We are to fight against sin, and to expect victory over it by God's help, afforded us in answer to supplication. Our Lord Jesus is both our Joshua to slay our sins, and our Moses to intercede for us against them, and his hands never need upholding. " He shall not fail nor be

discouraged." *Amalek shall be utterly destroyed, and we shall be for ever freed from sin.*

15 And Moses built an altar, and called the name of it Jehovah-nissi: (*or, the Lord my banner, for the uplifted rod had been as a sacred banner to Israel. Whenever we win victories we ought to bring thank-offerings, and ascribe the glory unto the Lord alone.*)

16 For he said, Because the LORD hath sworn *that* the LORD *will have* war with Amalek from generation to generation. (*We find this war carried on in Saul's day, and he was bidden to root out the nation.*)

ON account of the sinfulness of Amalek, as well as its unprovoked hostility to the tribes, the nation was doomed by divine justice to utter extirpation, even as our sins are by divine grace doomed to be crucified with Christ, that henceforth we should not serve sin. *Let us read*

DEUTERONOMY XXV. 17—19.

17, 18 Remember what Amalek did unto thee by the way, when ye were come forth out of Egypt; How he met thee by the way, and smote the hindmost of thee, *even* all *that were* feeble behind thee, when thou *wast* faint and weary; and he feared not God. (*God will not endure it that his people should be assailed. He counts their injuries as done to himself.*)

19 Therefore it shall be, when the LORD thy God hath given thee rest from all thine enemies round about, in the land which the LORD thy God giveth thee *for* an inheritance to possess it, *that* thou shalt blot out the remembrance of Amalek from under heaven; thou shalt not forget *it*. (*By the aid of the Eternal Spirit let us carry on war to the knife against all sin, whether in ourselves or others. All sins are our deadly foes, with whom we must hold neither truce nor parley. Death to them all, for they all aim at our death, and they were the crucifiers of our Lord Jesus.*)

While Moses stood with arms spread wide,
Success was found on Israel's side;
But when through weariness they fail'd,
That moment Amalek prevail'd.

O thou whose hand is stretch'd out still,
Our sinking hands confirm and stay;
While praying *for* us on the hill,
Fight *with* us in the plain to-day.

U PON *this occasion we shall read a part of the outline of Israel's history contained in*

PSALM LXXVIII. 13—32.

13 He divided the sea, and caused them to pass through ; and he made the waters to stand as an heap.

This recapitulation begins at the Red Sea even as our spiritual liberty begins at the drowning of all our sins in Jesus' blood.

14 In the daytime also he led them with a cloud, and all the night with a light of fire.

Thanks be to God for providential guidance. We are not wanderers who have lost their way amid a trackless waste, but we follow where the unerring wisdom of Jehovah leads.

15 He clave the rocks in the wilderness, and gave them drink as out of the great depths.

16 He brought streams also out of the rock, and caused waters to run down like rivers.

Here were abounding and extraordinary supplies; apt symbols of the streams of grace which flow to us from the great deeps of electing love and covenant faithfulness.

17 And they sinned yet more against him by provoking the most High in the wilderness.

What a change from grace to sin! It is enough to make us weep to see how good God is, and how base a return man makes. It would seem as if the more the Lord blessed man the less man blessed his God.

18 And they tempted God in their heart by asking meat for their lust. *(To desire God to aid us in gratifying unholy appetites, is to tempt the Lord; but his holiness will not yield to our solicitations, for God cannot be tempted.)*

19 Yea, they spake against God ; they said, Can God furnish a table in the wilderness ?

20 Behold, he smote the rock, that the waters gushed out, and the streams overflowed ; can he give bread also ? can he provide flesh for his people ? *(To question the Lord's power is to speak against him. Unbelief is essentially a slandering of the Omnipotent and gracious God.)*

21, 22 Therefore the LORD heard *this*, and was wroth : so a fire was kindled against Jacob, and anger also came up against Israel; Because they believed not in God, and trusted not in his salvation : *(Nothing so angers God as unbelief. O for grace to be kept from it.)*

23 Though he had commanded the clouds from above, and opened the doors of heaven,

24 And had rained down manna upon them to eat, and had given them of the corn of heaven.

This made unbelief so much the worse. Mercies received aggravate the criminality of distrust. It is so much the worse to doubt when we have received already such great favours from our gracious Father.

25, 26, 27, 28 Man did eat angels' food : he sent them meat to the full. He caused an east wind to blow in the heaven : and by his power he brought in the south wind. He rained flesh also upon them as dust, and feathered fowls like as the sand of the sea : And he let *it* fall in the midst of their camp, round about their habitations. *(God gives plenteously when he gives.)*

29 So they did eat, and were well filled : for he gave them their own desire ;

30, 31 They were not estranged from their lust. *(No. Gratification does not kill the passion. Man can be satiated with evil, but he is not nauseated with it. He changes the form of the sin, but sins on. Note here that God's bounties in this case were not pledges of love, but rather tokens of anger.)* But while their meat *was* yet in their mouths, The wrath of God came upon them, and slew the fattest of them, and smote down the chosen *men* of Israel. *(God often smites the mighty when he has pity on the poor and weak.)*

32 For all this they sinned still, and believed not for his wondrous works.

As mercy did not soften, so chastisement did not humble them. Lord, what is man!

> God of eternal love,
>   How fickle are our ways !
> And yet how oft did Israel prove
>   Thy constancy of grace !
>
> Now they believe his word,
>   While rocks with rivers flow ;
> Now with their lusts provoke the Lord,
>   And he reduced them low.
>
> Yet when they mourn'd their faults,
>   He hearken'd to their groans ;
> Brought his own covenant to his thoughts,
>   And call'd them still his sons.

EXODUS XIX.

IN the third month, when the children of Israel were gone forth out of the land of Egypt, the same day came they *into* the wilderness of Sinai. And Moses went up unto God, and the LORD called unto him out of the mountain, saying, Thus shalt thou say to the house of Jacob, and tell the children of Israel; Ye have seen what I did unto the Egyptians, and *how* I bare you on eagles' wings, and brought you unto myself. Now therefore, if ye will obey my voice indeed, and keep my covenant, then ye shall be a peculiar treasure unto me above all people: for all the earth *is* mine: And ye shall be unto me a kingdom of priests, and an holy nation. *(What a loving preface to the law! If anything could have engaged rebellious man to obedience, this would have done it, but, alas, the Lord has nourished and brought up children, and they have rebelled against him.)*

10 ¶ And the LORD said unto Moses, Go unto the people, and sanctify them to-day and to-morrow, and let them wash their clothes,

11 And be ready against the third day: for the third day the LORD will come down in the sight of all the people upon Mount Sinai. *Their garments smell of Egypt, and must be washed, to show them that man is unholy and all about him, and even when God meets him in love he must be cleansed from impurity.*

16 ¶ And it came to pass on the third day in the morning, that there were thunders and lightnings, and a thick cloud upon the mount, and the voice of the trumpet exceeding loud; so that all the people that *was* in the camp trembled. *(He who has ears to hear the law must tremble, for it condemns all who are under it.)*

17, 18 And Moses brought forth the people out of the camp to meet with God; and they stood at the nether part of the mount. And Mount Sinai was altogether on a smoke, because the LORD descended upon it in fire: and the smoke thereof ascended as the smoke of a furnace, and the whole mount quaked greatly.

20 And the LORD came down upon Mount Sinai, on the top of the mount: and the LORD called Moses *up* to the top of the mount; and Moses went up.

21, 22, 23 And the LORD said unto Moses, Go down, charge the people, lest they break through unto the LORD to gaze, and many of them perish. And let the priests also, which come near to the LORD, sanctify themselves, lest the LORD break forth upon them. And Moses said unto the LORD, The people cannot come up to Mount Sinai; for thou chargedst us, saying, Set bounds about the mount, and sanctify it. *Such is the spirit of the law. It shows us our sinfulness, and so sets us at a distance from God, but the gospel removes our sin and brings us nigh. Hear how the Holy Ghost speaks concerning it, by his servant Paul, in*

HEBREWS XII. 18—26.

FOR ye are not come unto the mount that might be touched, and that burned with fire, nor unto blackness, and darkness, and tempest, And the sound of a trumpet, and the voice of words; which *voice* they that heard intreated that the word should not be spoken to them any more:

20, 21 (For they could not endure that which was commanded, And if so much as a beast touch the mountain, it shall be stoned or thrust through with a dart: And so terrible was the sight, *that* Moses said, I exceedingly fear and quake :)

22, 23, 24 But ye are come unto Mount Sion, and unto the city of the living God, the heavenly Jerusalem, and to an innumerable company of angels, To the general assembly and church of the firstborn, which are written in heaven, and to God the Judge of all, and to the spirits of just men made perfect, And to Jesus the mediator of the new covenant, and to the blood of sprinkling, that speaketh better things than *that of* Abel.

25, 26 See that ye refuse not him that speaketh. For if they escaped not who refused him that spake on earth, much more *shall not* we *escape*, if we turn away from him that *speaketh* from heaven: Whose voice then shook the earth : but now he hath promised, saying, Yet once more I shake not the earth only, but also heaven. *(Dear members of this family, let these solemn words sink deep into your souls. Despise not the Lord Jesus, but believe in him now.)*

Not to the terrors of the Lord,
The tempest, fire, and smoke;
Not to the thunder of that word
Which God on Sinai spoke:
But we are come to Sion's hill,
The city of our God,
Where milder words declare his will,
And spread his love abroad.

WE *are now about to read that solemn epitome of the law of God, which is contained in*

EXODUS XX. 1—17;

but, before we read a line, let us beseech the Lord to forgive our offences against his holy name, and to accept us in the Son of his love, by whom this law has been magnified and made honourable. We are now to read a code of law in which there is no omission and no redundancy. It is the only perfect law in the universe. None of us have kept it, and therefore it were folly to look for salvation by it, since nothing but perfect obedience can be accepted by the justice of God.

1 And God spake all these words, saying,

2 I *am* the LORD thy God, which have brought thee out of the land of Egypt, out of the house of bondage.

3 Thou shalt have no other gods before me.

There is but one God, and we must not dare to worship or obey another. Beware of making gold or your self, or your dearest relation into a god. "Little children keep yourselves from idols."

4 Thou shalt not make unto thee any graven image, or any likeness *of any thing* that *is* in heaven above, or that *is* in the earth beneath, or that *is* in the water under the earth :'

5 Thou shalt not bow down thyself to them, nor serve them ; for I the LORD thy God *am* a jealous God, visiting the iniquity of the fathers upon the children unto the third and fourth *generation* of them that hate me ;

6 And shewing mercy unto thousands of them that love me, and keep my commandments.

We are in the second commandment forbidden to worship God under any visible symbol, or after any other fashion than he has commanded. How great are the crimes of those who worship crosses, pictures, and bread, and even attach the idea of holiness to enclosures and buildings.

7 Thou shalt not take the name of the LORD thy God in vain; for the LORD will not hold him guiltless that taketh his name in vain.

Any unhallowed use of the divine name is exceedingly sinful. Beware of flippantly saying, " O Lord," and such like irreverent speeches.

8 Remember the sabbath day, to keep it holy.

9, 10 Six days shalt thou labour, and do all thy work: But the seventh day *is* the sabbath of the LORD thy God : *in it* thou shalt not do any

work, thou, nor thy son, nor thy daughter, thy manservant, nor thy maidservant, nor thy cattle, nor thy stranger that *is* within thy gates :

11 For *in* six days the LORD made heaven and earth, the sea, and all that in them *is*, and rested the seventh day : wherefore the LORD blessed the sabbath day, and hallowed it.

One day in seven is the Lord's, and to rob him of it is to injure ourselves as well as to disobey our Maker. Rest and worship are two of our sweetest blessings, and to them the day should be sacredly given.

12 Honour thy father and thy mother: that thy days may be long upon the land which the LORD thy God giveth thee. *(Respect, love, and obedience are our parents' due. This is the first commandment with promise.)*

13 Thou shalt not kill.

Anger, and the doing of anything injurious to the health of ourselves or others, are here forbidden.

14 Thou shalt not commit adultery.

This forbids lust of heart, thought, and look, as well as actual uncleanness.

15 Thou shalt not steal. *(This forbids pilfering, cheating, and every kind of wrong.)*

16 Thou shalt not bear false witness against thy neighbour. *(All lying is herein condemned.)*

17 Thou shalt not covet thy neighbour's house, thou shalt not covet thy neighbour's wife, nor his manservant, nor his maidservant, nor his ox, nor his ass, nor any thing that *is* thy neighbour's. *(This touches a heart sin, and shews that the precept is exceeding broad, and reaches thoughts and imaginations. Who can read it and then hope to be saved by his own doings? Lord have mercy upon us, and forgive us our transgressions of this thy holy law.)*

Lord, make me understand thy law ;
Show what my faults have been ;
And from thy gospel let me draw
The pardon of my sin.

Not one can e'er be just with God
By works his hands have wrought ;
For thy command's exceeding broad,
And reaches every thought.

My God, 'tis through thy Son I wait
For thy salvation still ;
While thy whole law is my delight,
And I revere thy will.

WE have selected for our present reading a chapter which illustrates the difference between the law and the gospel.

ROMANS X. 1—21.

1 Brethren, my heart's desire and prayer to God for Israel is, that they might be saved.

The true spirit of Christianity is that of love and sympathy, it leads to prayer even for persecutors, and to hope for the most obdurate of men. Paul pleaded for the Jews.

2 For I bear them record that they have a zeal of God, but not according to knowledge.

Do not deny the good points in others, even if they are not all we could wish them to be.

3 For they being ignorant of God's righteousness, and going about to establish their own righteousness, have not submitted themselves unto the righteousness of God.

4 For Christ *is* the end of the law for righteousness to every one that believeth.

He fulfils the law's purpose for us, and when we have HIM *we have all the law requires.*

5 For Moses describeth the righteousness which is of the law, That the man which doeth those things shall live by them.

6, 7, 8, 9 But the righteousness which is of faith speaketh on this wise, Say not in thine heart, Who shall ascend into heaven? (that is, to bring Christ down *from above:*) Or, who shall descend into the deep? (that is, to bring up Christ again from the dead.) But what saith it? The word is nigh thee, *even* in thy mouth, and in thy heart: that is, the word of faith, which we preach; That if thou shalt confess with thy mouth the Lord Jesus, and shalt believe in thine heart that God hath raised him from the dead, thou shalt be saved. *(Precious gospel. Not doing, but believing, saves us. We have not to do or feel great things but simply to trust.)*

10 For with the heart man believeth unto righteousness; and with the mouth confession is made unto salvation.

11 For the scripture saith, Whosoever believeth on him shall not be ashamed.

12 For there is no difference between the Jew and the Greek: for the same Lord over all is rich unto all that call upon him.

13 For whosoever shall call upon the name of the Lord shall be saved. *(Think over this*

verse, for it ought to comfort even the most depressed seeker. Real prayer will be heard sooner or later.)*

14 How then shall they call on him in whom they have not believed? and how shall they believe in him of whom they have not heard? and how shall they hear without a preacher?

15 And how shall they preach, except they be sent? as it is written, How beautiful are the feet of them that preach the gospel of peace, and bring glad tidings of good things!

16 But they have not all obeyed the gospel. For Esaias saith, Lord, who hath believed our report?

17 So then faith *cometh* by hearing, and hearing by the word of God. *(Be constant in attendance upon the gospel ministry, and be devoutly attentive while hearing, for it is the way by which faith comes.)*

18 But I say, Have they not heard? Yes verily, their sound went into all the earth, and their words unto the ends of the world. *(Alas, all hearers do not become believers. The many hear with deaf ears, and obey not the truth.)*

19 But I say, Did not Israel know? First Moses saith, I will provoke you to jealousy by *them* that are no people, *and* by a foolish nation I will anger you.

20 But Esaias is very bold, and saith, I was found of them that sought me not; I was made manifest unto them that asked not after me.

Sovereign grace sometimes saves the most unlikely, while those who sit under the gospel harden their hearts and perish. Beware of resting in outward privileges: ye must possess real faith in Jesus.

21 But to Israel he saith, All day long I have stretched forth my hands unto a disobedient and gainsaying people. *(So that they were sincerely warned, and lovingly invited, yet it was all in vain. Shall it be so with any of this household? God forbid.)*

All the *doing* is completed,
  Now 'tis "look, believe, and live;"
None can purchase His salvation,
  Life's a gift, that God must *give;*
Grace, through righteousness, is reigning,
  Not of works, lest man should boast;
Man must take the mercy freely,
  Or eternally be lost.

AFTER *the giving of the law upon Sinai, Moses received instructions as to the institution of public worship and sacrifice. As all that which was then appointed was typical of spiritual things, we will read the New Testament summary of it, contained in*

HEBREWS IX. 1—14.

1 Then verily the first *covenant* had also ordinances of divine service, and a worldly *(or material)* sanctuary.

2 For there was a tabernacle made; the first *(or outer tabernacle)*, wherein *was* the candlestick, and the table, and the shewbread; which is called the sanctuary *(or holy place.)*

3, 4, 5 And after the second veil, the tabernacle which is called the Holiest of all; *(or Holy of Holies;)* Which had the golden censer, and the ark of the covenant overlaid round about with gold, wherein *was* the golden pot that had manna, and Aaron's rod that budded, and the tables of the covenant; And over it the cherubims of glory shadowing the mercyseat; of which we cannot now speak particularly.

6 Now when these things were thus ordained, the priests went always into the first tabernacle, accomplishing the service *of God.*

7 But into the second *went* the high priest alone once every year, not without blood, which he offered for himself, and *for* the errors of the people: *(The greatest of the Jewish high priests had to admit that they were sinners themselves, for they had to present sin-offerings on their own account, but our Lord Jesus has no sin of his own; hence in part his ability to bear our sin.)*

8 The Holy Ghost this signifying, that the way into the holiest of all was not yet made manifest, while as the first tabernacle was yet standing: *(The Holy of Holies was not open to all men, but only to Jews; and not to all Jews, but only to priests; and not to all priests, but to the high priest alone; and not even to him at all times, or indeed at any time, except upon one solitary day in the year:)*

9 Which *was* a figure for the time then present, in which were offered both gifts and sacrifices, that could not make him that did the service perfect, as pertaining to the conscience; *They could not expiate sin, and consequently could not give the conscience peace.*

10 *Which stood* only in meats and drinks, and divers washings, and carnal ordinances, imposed *on them* until the time of reformation.

The appearance of the substance and the putting away of the shadows, was a reformation, or emendation. Is it not wonderful that any should wish to undo this reformation, and go back to the beggarly elements of the law? Nay, worse, they would even revive the follies of old Rome.

11 But Christ being come an high priest of good things to come, by a greater and more perfect tabernacle, not made with hands, that is to say, not of this building;

12 Neither by the blood of goats and calves, but by his own blood he entered in once into the holy place, having obtained eternal redemption *for us.* *(Our Lord's offering is never to be repeated. It has been presented once, and has effectually secured the eternal redemption of all for whom he bled as a substitute. O what joy to see Jesus within the veil with a perfect offering, and to know that the one sacrifice has saved us.)*

13 For if the blood of bulls and of goats, and the ashes of an heifer sprinkling the unclean, sanctifieth to the purifying of the flesh:

14 How much more shall the blood of Christ, who through the eternal Spirit offered himself without spot to God, purge your conscience from dead works to serve the living God?

Who can answer this question, "How much more?" It amounts to a solemn affirmation. Jesus can most assuredly remove our sins. Beloved, has he removed yours? Answer as before the living God!

Jesus, in Thee our eyes behold
  A thousand glories more
Than the rich gems, and polish'd gold,
  The sons of Aaron wore.

They first their own burnt-offerings brought
  To purge themselves from sin:
Thy life was pure, without a spot;
  And all Thy nature clean.

Once in the circuit of a year,
  With blood, but not his own,
Aaron within the veil appears,
  Before the golden throne.

But Christ by His own powerful blood
  Ascends above the skies,
And in the presence of our God
  Shows His own sacrifice.

EXODUS XXIV. 1—15; 18.

AND he said unto Moses, Come up unto the LORD, thou, and Aaron, Nadab, and Abihu, and seventy of the elders of Israel ; and worship ye afar off.

2 And Moses alone shall come near the LORD : but they shall not come nigh ; neither shall the people go up with him.

Even the most favoured under the law came not very near to God. Even when he said "Come up unto Jehovah," it was added, "but they shall not come nigh." How different the gospel, for now, in Christ Jesus, we, who sometimes were afar off, are made nigh by the blood of Jesus.

3 ¶ And Moses came and told the people all the words of the LORD, and all the judgments : and all the people answered with one voice, and said, All the words which the LORD hath said will we do. *(Their tongues went faster than their lives. Man is swift at promising, but lame in performing.)*

4 And Moses wrote all the words of the LORD, and rose up early in the morning, and builded an altar under the hill, and twelve pillars, according to the twelve tribes of Israel.

5 And he sent young men of the children of Israel, which offered burnt offerings, and sacrificed peace offerings of oxen unto the LORD.

6, 7 And Moses took half of the blood, and put *it* in basons ; and half of the blood he sprinkled on the altar. And he took the book of the covenant, and read in the audience of the people : and they said, All that the LORD hath said will we do, and be obedient.

8 And Moses took the blood, and sprinkled *it* on the people, and said, Behold the blood of the covenant, which the LORD hath made with you concerning all these words. *(The blood is the main thing in all communion with God. No road is open to us but the crimson one. Where the blood of Jesus falls peace comes, but apart from that we are unclean, and, consequently, unfit for communion with God. Dear friends, has the blood of Jesus ever been sprinkled upon you? Faith, like the bunch of hyssop, applies the blood : have you that faith ?)*

9, 10 Then went up Moses, and Aaron, Nadab, and Abihu, and seventy of the elders of Israel : And they saw the God of Israel : and *there was* under his feet as it were a paved work of a sapphire stone, and as it were the body of heaven in *his* clearness.

11 And upon the nobles of the children of Israel he laid not his hand : also they saw God, and did eat and drink. *(When the blood was on them, they could come near, and enjoy quiet fellowship, even to eating and drinking. What they saw is not described to us except in one point, they saw the azure pavement beneath the sacred feet. All our conceptions fall below the glory of our God, we see only the place of his footstool.)*

12 ¶ And the LORD said unto Moses, Come up to me into the mount, and be there : and I will give thee tables of stone, and a law, and commandments which I have written; that thou mayest teach them.

13 And Moses rose up, and his minister Joshua : and Moses went up into the mount of God. *(Moses enjoyed a higher degree of communion than any other man, and went up alone into the cloud. There are elect ones out of the elect to whom it is given to lie in their Master's bosom, and to walk in the light as he is in the light. To be highly favoured in this respect is honour and joy indeed.)*

14, 15 And he said unto the elders, Tarry ye here for us, until we come again unto you : and, behold, Aaron and Hur *are* with you : if any man have any matters to do, let him come unto them. And Moses went up into the mount, and a cloud covered the mount. *(This was a sweet retreat for Moses, who would now for awhile forget the burden of the people.)*

18 And Moses went into the midst of the cloud, and gat him up into the mount : and Moses was in the mount forty days and forty nights. *(O sweet stretch of intercourse with heaven. Six weeks with God! What a rest! Alas, Moses needed it, for the people were rebelling down below, and making trouble for their leader's heart.)*

Through the sacrificial blood,
Shed in honour of his law,
Chosen men drew near to God,
And his gracious glory saw.

Underneath his feet serene,
Sapphires, like a pavement, lay,
Bright as heaven itself is seen,
On a clear and cloudless day.

Heaven no frowning aspect wears;
Boldly we approach the throne :
Brighter grace to us appears
Than on Sinai's Mount was shown.

EXODUS XXX. 11—16. ✓

AND the LORD spake unto Moses, saying, 12 When thou takest the sum of the children of Israel after their number, then shall they give every man a ransom for his soul unto the LORD, when thou numberest them; that there be no plague among them, when *thou* numberest them. *(Each census was to be attended with a redemption. Every one of the Lord's people was thus to be redeemed as a testimony to all generations that redemption is essential to acceptance with God. Had we not been bought with a price, the fierce plagues of divine punishment would have followed us even to the lowest hell.)*

13 This they shall give, every one that passeth among them that are numbered, half a shekel after the shekel of the sanctuary: (a shekel *is* twenty gerahs:) an half shekel *shall be* the offering of the LORD. *God sets his own estimate upon men, for he best knows their value. The standard of our indebtedness is not left to be fixed by our own feelings; the Lord's own will is the law of our condition. Duty is duty, because HE requires it.*

14 Every one that passeth among them that are numbered, from twenty years old and above, shall give an offering unto the LORD.

15 The rich shall not give more, and the poor shall not give less than half a shekel, when *they* give an offering unto the LORD, to make an atonement for your souls. *Believers vary in knowledge, gifts, and graces, but they are all redeemed with the same price. The meanest believer was bought with the same blood as the chief of the apostles. The poor, the obscure, the faulty, the illiterate, are as dear to the heart of Jesus as the richest and most gifted saint. What a sweet thought! Here is the true equality. " His righteousness is unto all and upon all them that believe, for there is no difference." Let us all equally bless and love the Lord by whose blood we are equally redeemed.*

16 And thou shalt take the atonement money of the children of Israel, and shalt appoint it for the service of the tabernacle of the congregation; that it may be a memorial unto the children of Israel before the LORD, to make an atonement for your souls. *(A memorial of them testifying that the price was paid, and a memorial to them of their great indebtedness to the Redeemer.)*

THE *obligations arising out of our redemption by the Lord Jesus are set forth in*

I. PETER I. 15—21.

15 As he which hath called you is holy, so be ye holy in all manner of conversation;

16 Because it is written, Be ye holy; for I am holy. *(The essence of religion consists in the imitation of him whom we worship.)*

17 And if ye call on the Father, who without respect of persons judgeth according to every man's work, pass the time of your sojourning here in fear: *(Let a childlike fear of offending your Great Father ever restrain you from sin. "Blessed is the man who feareth always.")*

18 Forasmuch as ye know that ye were not redeemed with corruptible things, *as* silver and gold, from your vain conversation *received* by tradition from your fathers;

19 But with the precious blood of Christ, as of a lamb without blemish and without spot. *The same price which redeems us from destruction also redeems us from our vain conversation; and this is no less than the heart's blood of the Son of God. Until the world can offer us something more precious than the blood of Jesus, we shall feel ourselves bound by bonds of love to walk in holiness, to Jesus' praise.*

20 Who verily was foreordained before the foundation of the world, but was manifest in these last times for you,

21 Who by him do believe in God, that raised him up from the dead, and gave him glory; that your faith and hope might be in God. *The love of Jesus to us is no novelty; he was ordained to redeem us ere worlds began; let none of the trifles of earth charm us with their new pretensions. It was truly practical love which brought him to earth to be our suffering substitute; let our love be practical too; not in word only, but in deed and in truth. O to be a redeemed family, and to live as such. The Lord grant it for Jesus' sake. Amen.*

Lord, I desire to live as one
Who bears a blood-bought name,
As one who fears but grieving Thee,
And knows no other shame.

As one by whom Thy walk below
Should never be forgot;
As one who fain would keep apart
From all Thou lovest not.

EXODUS XXXII. 1—14.

AND when the people saw that Moses delayed to come down out of the mount, the people gathered themselves together unto Aaron, and said unto him, Up, make us gods, which shall go before us; for *as for* this Moses, the man that brought us up out of the land of Egypt, we wot not what is become of him.

They were so fickle that they could not be trusted alone; and worse than this, they were basely ungrateful to forget their God, and ascribe their deliverance to Moses; and even to him they were foully thankless, for they called him " this Moses," as if in contempt, and that to the face of his own brother. They must have been in a state of wild rebellion, thus to insult both their great leader and his brother. The fact was, that they were so utterly unspiritual that without something to see they could not abide in peace: the faith which seeth him who is invisible they had not learned.

2, 3, 4 And Aaron said unto them, Break off the golden earrings, which *are* in the ears of your wives, of your sons, and of your daughters, and bring *them* unto me. And all the people brake off the golden earrings which *were* in their ears, and brought *them* unto Aaron. And he received *them* at their hand, and fashioned it with a graving tool, after he had made it a molten calf : and they said, These *be* thy gods, O Israel, which brought thee up out of the land of Egypt.

Shame upon Aaron to pander to them! What idolatry to think that the infinite Jehovah can be likened unto a bullock which hath horns and hoofs. They went back to old Egyptian idolatry, and set up an ox as the symbol of the God of power.

5 And when Aaron saw *it*, he built an altar before it ; and Aaron made proclamation, and said, To morrow *is* a feast to the LORD. (*Or to Jehovah; so that they did not leave off worshipping Jehovah, but transgressed the second commandment by likening him to an ox.*)

6 And they rose up early on the morrow, and offered burnt offerings, and brought peace offerings ; and the people sat down to eat and to drink, and rose up to play.

7, 8 ¶ And the LORD said unto Moses, Go, get thee down : for thy people, which thou broughtest out of the land of Egypt, have corrupted *themselves*: They have turned aside quickly out of the way which I commanded them : they have made them a molten calf, and

have worshipped it, and have sacrificed thereunto, and said, These *be* thy gods, O Israel, which have brought thee up out of the land of Egypt. (*Who wonders that the Lord resented the insult offered to him by the people who owed him so much ?*)

9, 10 And the LORD said unto Moses, I have seen this people, and, behold, it *is* a stiffnecked people : Now therefore let me alone, that my wrath may wax hot against them, and that I may consume them : and I will make of thee a great nation. (*Here was a great opportunity for Moses if he had been an ambitious or selfish man; but he loved the people better than himself.*)

11 And Moses besought the LORD his God, and said, LORD, why doth thy wrath wax hot against thy people, which thou hast brought forth out of the land of Egypt with great power, and with a mighty hand ? (*See the point of his plea: God had called them Moses' people, but he will not have it so, he calls them, " thy people," and beseeches the Lord not to be angry with them.*)

12 Wherefore should the Egyptians speak, and say, For mischief did he bring them out, to slay them in the mountains, and to consume them from the face of the earth ? Turn from thy fierce wrath, and repent of this evil against thy people. (*Here he urges the name and honour of God. Forcible pleading this!*)

13, 14 Remember Abraham, Isaac, and Israel, thy servants, to whom thou swarest by thine own self, and saidst unto them, I will multiply your seed as the stars of heaven, and all this land that I have spoken of will I give unto your seed, and they shall inherit *it* for ever. (*His third master plea is " the covenant" confirmed by oath : he who can plead this cannot but succeed.*) And the LORD repented of the evil which he thought to do unto his people. (*If Moses succeeded as Mediator, how much more shall the Lord Jesus, who makes intercession for the transgressors.*)

From Sinai we have heard thee speak
  And from Mount Calv'ry too ;
And yet to idols oft we seek
  While thou art in our view.

Lord, save us from our golden calves;
  Our sin with grief we own ;
We would no more be thine by halves,
  But live to thee alone.

EXODUS XXXII. 15—20; 30—35.

AND Moses turned, and went down from the mount, and the two tables of the testimony *were* in his hand: the tables *were* written on both their sides; on the one side and on the other *were* they written.

16 And the tables *were* the work of God, and the writing *was* the writing of God, graven upon the tables. *(It is no small trial to come down from communion with God to battle with other men's sins. This may fall to our lot this day. The Lord prepare us for it.)*

17 And when Joshua heard the noise of the people as they shouted, he said unto Moses, There *is* a noise of war in the camp.

Joshua was a soldier, and therefore his thoughts ran that way, but Moses knew better. It would be far better to hear the noise of war with spiritual enemies, than the sound of rebellion against the Lord.

18 And he said, *It is* not the voice of *them that* shout for mastery, neither *is it* the voice of *them that* cry for being overcome: *but* the noise of *them that* sing do I hear.

19 ¶ And it came to pass, as soon as he came nigh unto the camp, that he saw the calf, and the dancing: and Moses' anger waxed hot, and he cast the tables out of his hands, and brake them beneath the mount.

Moses is nowhere blamed for this. It was a symbolical action testifying his great abhorrence of sin, and his zeal for the Lord of hosts. He felt that tables written with God's finger would be polluted by being brought among such a people.

20 And he took the calf which they had made, and burnt *it* in the fire, and ground *it* to powder, and strawed *it* upon the water, and made the children of Israel drink *of it*.

Thus he put the utmost scorn upon their idol by making them drink it. Is it not beyond measure strange that popish idolaters of our day actually worship the wafer which they afterwards eat, and imagine that it is a religious homage to devour what they declare to be divine?

It is a wonderful instance of the influence of one man, that Moses was able in the midst of thousands of idolaters to tear down their idol, to deface it, grind it to powder, mix it with water, and compel the people to drink. God was with him, or he would have been resisted by the stiffnecked throng. He was very decided in his behaviour,

and did not tolerate idol worship for a moment: this decision, no doubt, gave him great moral power.

30 ¶ And it came to pass on the morrow, that Moses said unto the people, Ye have sinned a great sin: and now I will go up unto the LORD; peradventure I shall make an atonement for your sin. *(His one thought was to do them good. He was like our Lord Jesus, a faithful Intercessor.)*

31, 32 And Moses returned unto the LORD, and said, Oh, this people have sinned a great sin, and have made them gods of gold. Yet now, if thou wilt forgive their sin—; and if not, blot me, I pray thee, out of thy book which thou hast written. *(This was splendid self-sacrifice, of which we find a parallel case in the apostle Paul. Moses meant what he said, but we must not judge his expressions by cold-blooded logic: they were the warm outgushing of a tender heart.)*

33 And the LORD said unto Moses, Whosoever hath sinned against me, him will I blot out of my book. *(This is the voice of the law threatening to blot out the sinner, but the gospel freely blots out the sin.)*

34 Therefore now go, lead the people unto the place of which I have spoken unto thee: behold, mine Angel shall go before thee: nevertheless in the day when I visit I will visit their sin upon them. *(The Lord refused to be personally present with the tribes, but graciously promised to direct them by an angelic deputy. This was a sad threatening for Moses, who knew the value of the divine presence; and to the people themselves it was grievous news, especially the sentence that the Lord would visit them for sin.)*

35 And the LORD plagued the people, because they made the calf, which Aaron made.

They were the real makers—Aaron was but their agent: they are neither of them excused, but the guilt of each is clearly stated. It was sad to see such a man as Aaron so far astray. Lord, keep thou each one of us by thy Holy Spirit.

Though our sins, our hearts confounding,
  Long and loud for vengeance call,
Thou hast mercy more abounding,
  Jesus' blood can cleanse them all.

Let that love veil our transgression,
  Let that blood our guilt efface,
Save thy people from oppression,
  Save from death thy chosen race.

100   " 𝕸𝖞 𝖕𝖗𝖊𝖘𝖊𝖓𝖈𝖊 𝖘𝖍𝖆𝖑𝖑 𝖌𝖔 𝖜𝖎𝖙𝖍 𝖙𝖍𝖊𝖊."   FEBRUARY 19 —EVENING.

[*Or April* 9.]

EXODUS XXXIII. 1—7; 12—23.

AND the LORD said unto Moses, Depart, *and* go up hence, thou and the people which thou hast brought up out of the land of Egypt, unto the land which I sware unto Abraham, to Isaac, and to Jacob, saying, Unto thy seed will I give it: And I will send an angel before thee; and I will drive out the Canaanite, the Amorite, and the Hittite, and the Perizzite, the Hivite, and the Jebusite: Unto a land flowing with milk and honey: for I will not go up in the midst of thee; for thou *art* a stiffnecked people: lest I consume thee in the way.

4 ¶ And when the people heard these evil tidings, they mourned: and no man did put on him his ornaments. *(There was some right feeling left, and while Moses spoke to them it came to the front; but, alas, it was as fleeting as the early dew.)*

5 For the LORD had said unto Moses, Say unto the children of Israel, Ye *are* a stiffnecked people: I will come up into the midst of thee in a moment, and consume thee: therefore now put off thy ornaments from thee, that I may know what to do unto thee. *(As if the Lord knew not how to shew mercy to impenitent sinners.)*

6 And the children of Israel stripped themselves of their ornaments by the mount Horeb. *This is always a preliminary to mercy. Pride must strip, self-righteousness must throw off her mantle, and carnal security pull off its tinkling jewellery.*

7 And Moses took the tabernacle, and pitched it without the camp, afar off from the camp, and called it the Tabernacle of the congregation. And it came to pass, *that* every one which sought the LORD went out unto the tabernacle of the congregation, which *was* without the camp. *They were not worthy to have the residence of the Lord in the centre of the encampment. The Lord did not utterly leave them, but he went into the outer circle, and all who would seek the Lord must go without the camp. The lesson is plain, and holds good even now.*

12 ¶ And Moses said unto the LORD, See, thou sayest unto me, Bring up this people: and thou hast not let me know whom thou wilt send with me. Yet thou hast said, I know thee by name, and thou hast also found grace in my sight.

13, 14 Now therefore, I pray thee, if I have found grace in thy sight, shew me now thy way, that I may know thee, that I may find grace in thy sight: and consider that this nation *is* thy people. And he said, My presence shall go *with thee*, and I will give thee rest. *(Thus the Lord gives us his presence now and rest at the end. What a precious promise!)*

15 And he said unto him, If thy presence go not *with me*, carry us not up hence.

16 For wherein shall it be known here that I and thy people have found grace in thy sight? *is it* not in that thou goest with us? so shall we be separated, I and thy people, from all the people that *are* upon the face of the earth.

17 And the LORD said unto Moses, I will do this thing also that thou hast spoken: for thou hast found grace in my sight, and I know thee by name. *(Grace received is the guarantee of answers to prayer.)*

18 And he said, I beseech thee, shew me thy glory.

19 And he said, I will make all my goodness pass before thee, and I will proclaim the name of the LORD before thee; and will be gracious to whom I will be gracious, and will shew mercy on whom I will shew mercy. *(Thus we see that the sovereignty of his grace is the very glory of God. Why do men quarrel with it?)*

20 And he said, Thou canst not see my face: for there shall no man see me and live.

21 And the LORD said, Behold, *there is* a place by me, and thou shalt stand upon a rock:

22, 23 And it shall come to pass, while my glory passeth by, that I will put thee in a clift of the rock, and will cover thee with my hand while I pass by: And I will take away mine hand, and thou shalt see my back parts: but my face shall not be seen. *(Nowhere else can God be spiritually seen, save in the Rock of ages cleft for us. As yet we see but the skirts of his garments, but even this glimpse delights us. How sweet to know that however little we see of God, yet it is God, our Father.)*

I need thy presence every passing hour,—
What but thy grace can foil the tempter's power?
Who like thyself my guide and stay can be?
Through cloud and sunshine, O abide with me.

I fear no foe with thee at hand to bless:
Ills have no weight and tears no bitterness;
Where is death's sting? Where, grave, thy victory?
I triumph still if thou abide with me.

I. CORINTHIANS X. 1—12. ✓

MOREOVER, brethren, I would not that ye should be ignorant, how that all our fathers were under the cloud, and all passed through the sea;

2 And were all baptized unto Moses in the cloud and in the sea. *(Ignorance about Old Testament history is very undesirable, for thereby much of spiritual instruction is lost. The Israelites were intended to be practical lessons to us. They had all the outward ordinances and privileges of religion, and yet they perished, and we ought to take heed lest we do the same. Were we baptized with an outward baptism at the outset of our religious history? So were they, with the cloud above them and the sea on either side, buried in baptism with their leader.)*

3 And did all eat the same spiritual meat;

4 And did all drink the same spiritual drink: for they drank of that spiritual Rock that followed them; and that Rock was Christ. *Thus they had the analogy of the Lord's Supper; they ate manna, and drank from the riven rock; the bread and wine of the Communion are similar types of him whose flesh is meat indeed, and whose blood is drink indeed.*

5 But with many of them God was not well pleased : for they were overthrown in the wilderness. *(They died, notwithstanding their participation in divine ordinances, and so shall we, unless by faith we avoid their faults.)*

6, 7, 8, 9 Now these things were our examples, to the intent we should not lust after evil things, as they also lusted. Neither be ye idolaters, as *were* some of them ; as it is written, The people sat down to eat and drink, and rose up to play. Neither let us commit fornication, as some of them committed, and fell in one day three and twenty thousand. Neither let us tempt Christ, as some of them also tempted, and were destroyed of serpents.

10 Neither murmur ye, as some of them also murmured, and were destroyed of the destroyer.

11 Now all these things happened unto them for ensamples ; and they are written for our admonition, upon whom the ends of the world are come.

12 Wherefore let him that thinketh he standeth take heed lest he fall. *(Our baptism, participation in the Lord's Supper, and other privileges, may make us think ourselves secure, but we must take heed, for far more is needed.)*

In the Psalms we find the same lesson set to music.

PSALM XCV.

O COME, let us sing unto the LORD: let us make a joyful noise to the rock of our salvation. Let us come before his presence with thanksgiving, and make a joyful noise unto him with psalms.

3 For the LORD *is* a great God, and a great King above all gods.

4 In his hand *are* the deep places of the earth : the strength of the hills *is* his also.

5 The sea *is* his, and he made it : and his hands formed the dry *land.*

6 O come, let us worship and bow down : let us kneel before the LORD our maker.

7, 8, 9 For he *is* our God : and we *are* the people of his pasture, and the sheep of his hand. To day if ye will hear his voice, Harden not your heart, as in the provocation, *and* as *in* the day of temptation in the wilderness : When your fathers tempted me, proved me, and saw my work.

10 Forty years long was I grieved with *this* generation, and said, It *is* a people that do err in their heart, and they have not known my ways :

11 Unto whom I sware in my wrath that they should not enter into my rest. *(They were outwardly his people, and had every means used upon them to make them worthy of their calling, but as they never became a spiritual people, their privileges were of no avail, and they died in the wilderness. Let us beware of resting in anything short of saving faith, and a real change of heart. " Ye must be born again.")*

Come, sound his praise abroad,
And hymns of glory sing ;
Jehovah is the sovereign God,
The universal King.

Come, worship at his throne,
Come, bow before the Lord :
We are his works, and not our own ;
He form'd us by his word.

To-day attend his voice,
Nor dare provoke his rod ;
Come, like the people of his choice,
And own your gracious God.

102   "𝕸𝖆𝖐𝖊 𝖙𝖍𝖞 𝖋𝖆𝖈𝖊 𝖙𝖔 𝖘𝖍𝖎𝖓𝖊 𝖚𝖕𝖔𝖓 𝖙𝖍𝖞 𝖘𝖊𝖗𝖛𝖆𝖓𝖙."   FEBRUARY 20.—EVENING.

[*Or April* 11.]

IN our present reading we shall see how the Lord reopened his communications with Israel, though their sin had abruptly broken up all the treaty engagements almost before they were ratified.

EXODUS XXXIV. 1—5; 28—35.

1 And the LORD said unto Moses, Hew thee two tables of stone like unto the first : and I will write upon *these* tables the words that were in the first tables, which thou brakest.

Here let us learn that although man has broken the law of God, yet the Lord in infinite mercy to his people visits them again, causes their hearts to be hewn and prepared by his prophets and ministers, and then writes the law upon those fleshy tablets. The law in the heart is better than the law on stone.

2 And be ready in the morning, and come up in the morning unto mount Sinai, and present thyself there to me in the top of the mount.

Moses must go up a second time and sojourn with the Lord, and the people must thus be tried to see if they can wait upon God in their leader's absence.

3 And no man shall come up with thee, neither let any man be seen throughout all the mount; neither let the flocks nor herds feed before that mount. *(Distance was always the rule of the law. Moses went up to God alone, but Jesus takes all his people with him.)*

4 ¶ And he hewed two tables of stone like unto the first ; and Moses rose up early in the morning, and went up unto mount Sinai, as the LORD had commanded him, and took in his hand the two tables of stone. *(Note, that Moses, like other good men, was up betimes in the morning. Matthew Henry says, "the morning is as good a friend to the graces as it is to the muses." God loves punctual servants.)*

5 And the LORD descended in the cloud, and stood with him there, and proclaimed the name of the LORD. *(He declared the nature and the attributes of Jehovah.)*

28 And he was there with the LORD forty days and forty nights; he did neither eat bread, nor drink water. And he wrote upon the tables the words of the covenant, the ten commandments. *(In being miraculously supported for forty days without food, Moses, as the law, is followed by*

Elijah, the chief of the prophets, and our Lord Jesus, in whom the gospel is revealed.)

29 ¶ And it came to pass, when Moses came down from mount Sinai with the two tables of testimony in Moses' hand, when he came down from the mount, that Moses wist not that the skin of his face shone while he talked with him.

After such long communion Moses came down enriched with the best treasure, and adorned with the best beauty. What he had seen was unconsciously reflected from him, as it always is from those who have had fellowship with God.

30 And when Aaron and all the children of Israel saw Moses, behold, the skin of his face shone ; and they were afraid to come nigh him.

Everybody could see the brightness of Moses' face except himself ; and the same may be said of the man who communes with God.

31, 32 And Moses called unto them; and Aaron and all the rulers of the congregation returned unto him : and Moses talked with them. And afterward all the children of Israel came nigh : and he gave them in commandment all that the LORD had spoken with him in mount Sinai.

33 And *till* Moses had done speaking with them, he put a vail on his face. *(In this he was unlike most men, for they are usually far too ready to show their brightness to everybody, coveting admiration. Modesty dwells with true excellence.)*

34 But when Moses went in before the LORD to speak with him, he took the vail off, until he came out. *(Before God we must be all unveiled. All things are open before him.)* And he came out, and spake unto the children of Israel *that* which he was commanded. *(God's ministers may learn here their only theme.)*

35 And the children of Israel saw the face of Moses, that the skin of Moses' face shone : and Moses put the vail upon his face again, until he went in to speak with him.

Lord, from thy burning throne on high,
Thy law comes forth in majesty ;
Its glory shines with beams so bright,
No mortal can sustain the sight.

But through thy Son, th' incarnate God,
Thy milder radiance shines abroad ;
His flesh becomes the Godhead's veil,
And beams of grace and love prevail.

THE *apostle Paul gathers instruction from the veiled face of Moses, and presents it to us in*

II. CORINTHIANS III. 7—18.

7 But if the ministration of death, written *and* engraven in stones, was glorious, so that the children of Israel could not stedfastly behold the face of Moses for the glory of his countenance; which *glory* was to be done away :

8 How shall not the ministration of the spirit be rather glorious ? *(Moses taught the letter— the outward signs and details of rule and order— but the gospel reveals the inner secret, the essence, the spirit of truth; surely this is more glorious than forms. Babes in knowledge may be most impressed with the glory which blazes before the eye, but men esteem most that inner light of spiritual beauty which irradiates the soul.)*

9 For if the ministration of condemnation *be* glory, much more doth the ministration of righteousness exceed in glory. *(The law only reveals condemnation and death, how much more glorious is the gospel, which reveals righteousness and life! If the halberts and trumpets of a judge, when he opens an assize, are held in esteem, how much more the chariots of love and the banners of grace which adorn the procession of a beloved Prince!)*

10 For even that which was made glorious had no glory in this respect, by reason of the glory that excelleth. *(As the moon's light is no more bright when the sun appears, so is Moses eclipsed by our Lord.)*

11 For if that which is done away *was* glorious, much more that which remaineth *is* glorious.

Transient things can never, to the eyes of wisdom, shine with the same lustre as eternal realities. Sparks can never rival stars. It is the crowning excellence of the gospel that it shall never pass away. It is " the everlasting gospel". Blessed be God for this.

Our Lord's transfiguration was a visible token of the superior glory of the gospel, for not his face alone but his whole body glowed with a light excessive, which quite overpowered the three disciples. The glory of the gospel of grace astounds the angels, delights the perfect spirits, and deserves to be the constant theme of our reverent wonder. God in the gospel has laid

open more of the glory of his nature and character than in all the world besides.

12, 13, 14 Seeing then that we have such hope, we use great plainness of speech : and not as Moses, *which* put a vail over his face, that the children of Israel could not stedfastly look to the end of that which is abolished : but their minds were blinded : for until this day remaineth the same vail untaken away in the reading of the old testament; which *vail* is done away in Christ. *(The glory of the gospel, in the types, was too great for the Jews, and a veil was needed; and now, alas, the glory of the unveiled truth has quite confounded them; but it is not so with us, we delight in a plain, unveiled gospel.)*

15 But even unto this day, when Moses is read, the vail is upon their heart. *(Or else they would clearly see Jesus revealed in their law, and would at once accept Him as Messiah. A veil over the intellect is bad, but a veil upon the heart is worst of all.)*

16 Nevertheless when it shall turn to the Lord, the vail shall be taken away. *(Poor Israel shall yet see her Messiah. The heart-veil shall be removed by His Spirit.)*

17 Now the Lord is that Spirit : and where the Spirit of the Lord *is*, there *is* liberty. *(The Spirit of God forbids our standing afar off because of the terrible presence of the Lord, and gives us in lieu thereof liberty to draw near to our heavenly Father in the sweet familiarity of reverent love.)*

18 But we all, with open face beholding as in a glass the glory of the Lord, are changed into the same image from glory to glory, *even* as by the Spirit of the Lord. *(Ours it is to possess a spiritual faith which looks into the inner truth, whose brightness is too great for unregenerate eyes. The Spirit of the Lord has brought us near to God, opened our purblind eyes, and given us to see the character of the Invisible God, and to become partakers of it.)*

Thou glorious Bridegroom of our hearts,
Thy radiant smile a heaven imparts ;
Oh lift the veil, if veil there be.
Let thy redeem'd thy beauties see.

Then on our faces shall the sight
Kindle a blaze of holy light,
And men with awe-struck wonder see
The glory we derive from thee.

EXODUS XXXV. 4, 5; 20—29.

AND Moses spake unto all the congregation of the children of Israel, saying, This is the thing which the Lord commanded, saying,

5 Take ye from among you an offering unto the Lord : whosoever is of a willing heart, let him bring it, an offering of the LORD.

The Lord loveth a cheerful giver. His revenues are his due, yet they are not levied as a tax, but given spontaneously by willing minds. Every Israelite should be a giver, for he is a receiver.

20 ¶ And all the congregation of the children of Israel departed from the presence of Moses.

They went off at once to fetch their offering; promptness is a sign of willingness.

21 And they came, every one whose heart stirred him up, and every one whom his spirit made willing, and they brought the LORD's offering to the work of the tabernacle of the congregation, and for all his service, and for the holy garments. *(Some there were who loved their gold better than their God, but the majority were free hearted, and gave not of constraint but joyfully.)*

22 And they came, both men and women, as many as were willing hearted, and brought bracelets, and earrings, and rings, and tablets, all jewels of gold : and every man that offered offered an offering of gold unto the LORD.

This is a good example. If Christian women would cast their ornaments into God's treasury, and if godly men would present their superfluity of gold, there would be enough and to spare.

23 And every man, with whom was found blue, and purple, and scarlet, and fine linen, and goats' hair, and red skins of rams, and badgers' skins, brought them. *(The gifts varied in value but not in acceptance; where they were willingly given they were graciously accepted.)*

24. Every one that did offer an offering of silver and brass brought the LORD's offering : and every man, with whom was found shittim wood for any work of the service, brought it.

25, 26 And all the women that were wise hearted did spin with their hands, and brought that which they had spun, both of blue, and of purple, and of scarlet, and of fine linen. And all the women whose heart stirred them up in wisdom spun goats' hair. *(Work is as good as material. The women worked with their best skill. When the needle is used for the Lord it ought to be the best needlework in the world.)*

27 And the rulers brought onyx stones, and stones to be set, for the ephod, and for the breastplate ;

28 And spice, and oil for the light, and for the anointing oil, and for the sweet incense.

29 The children of Israel brought a willing offering unto the LORD, every man and woman, whose heart made them willing to bring for all manner of work, which the LORD had commanded to be made by the hand of Moses. *(Shall we allow those who were under the law to outstrip us who are under the gospel? Nay, rather let us far exceed them in gifts unto the Lord our God.)*

Paul gives admirable directions for contributing to the cause of God in

II CORINTHIANS IX. 6—8.

6 This I say, He which soweth sparingly shall reap also sparingly ; and he which soweth bountifully shall reap also bountifully.

Both in temporals and spirituals men will find that this rule holds good. Those who stint the Lord stint themselves. Little give, little have.

7 Every man according as he purposeth in his heart, so let him give; not grudgingly, or of necessity : for God loveth a cheerful giver.

8 And God is able to make all grace abound toward you; that ye, always having all sufficiency in all things, may abound to every good work. *(Notice the many "alls" here, may we have them all, and then abound in giving.)*

I CORINTHIANS XVI. 2.

2 Upon the first day of the week let every one of you lay by him in store, as God hath prospered him, that there be no gatherings when I come. *(This is the true Christian custom to lay by the Lord's portion weekly and then give from the Lord's purse to the various works which need our help. From the oldest to the youngest let us all be cheerful givers.)*

The mite my willing hands can give,
  At Jesus' feet I lay ;
Grace shall the humble gift receive,
  And heaven at last repay.

Ne'er shall thy service stand in need
  While substance, Lord, is mine ;
To give to thee is bliss indeed,
  For all I have is thine.

THE *laws which the Lord gave to Moses in reference to sacrifices are all deeply instructive, and every detail deserves earnest study :* we select for present reading the law of the sin-offering in

LEVITICUS IV. 1—12.

1 And the LORD spake unto Moses, saying,

2 Speak unto the children of Israel, saying, If a soul shall sin through ignorance against any of the commandments of the LORD *concerning things* which ought not to be done, and shall do against any of them :

3 If the priest that is anointed do sin according to the sin of the people ; then let him bring for his sin, which he hath sinned, a young bullock, without blemish unto the LORD for a sin offering. *(The case is put with an " if,"—if a soul shall sin, and if the priest do sin ; but indeed, it is all too certain that they do sin, and it is most gracious on the Lord's part to ordain a sacrifice to meet the case. The victim must itself be without blemish, or it cannot be an accepted substitute. How well the Lord Jesus answers to this type.)*

4 And he shall bring the bullock unto the door of the tabernacle of the congregation before the LORD ; and shall lay his hand upon the bullock's head, and kill the bullock before the LORD. *(By an act of penitential faith we must accept the atoning sacrifice as available for us. But the victim must die, and pour out its blood, for the blood is the very life of the expiation.)*

5 And the priest that is anointed shall take of the bullock's blood, and bring it to the tabernacle of the congregation : *(Everywhere the blood was conspicuous, for it is the essence of atonement.)*

6 And the priest shall dip his finger in the blood, and sprinkle of the blood seven times before the LORD, before the vail of the sanctuary.

7 And the priest shall put *some* of the blood upon the horns of the altar of sweet incense before the LORD, which *is* in the tabernacle of the congregation ; and shall pour all the blood of the bullock at the bottom of the altar of the burnt offering, which *is at* the door of the tabernacle of the congregation.

8, 9, 10 And he shall take off from it all the fat of the bullock for the sin offering ; the fat that covereth the inwards, and all the fat that *is* upon the inwards, And the two kidneys, and the fat that *is* upon them, which *is* by the flanks, and the caul above the liver, with the kidneys, it shall he take away, As it was taken off from the bullock of the sacrifice of peace offerings : and the priest shall burn them upon the altar of the burnt offering. *(When our Lord Jesus was made sin for us, and so became forsaken of God, he was nevertheless dear unto God—hence some part of the sin offering was laid upon the altar of acceptance.)*

11, 12, And the skin of the bullock, and all his flesh, with his head, and with his legs, and his inwards, and his dung, Even the whole bullock shall he carry forth without the camp unto a clean place, where the ashes are poured out, and burn him on the wood with fire : where the ashes are poured out shall he be burnt. *(As a thing unclean the sin-offering was put away, and even thus Jesus was made sin for us, and in token thereof he was made to suffer outside Jerusalem.)*

HEBREWS XIII. 10—14.

10 We have an altar, whereof they have no right to eat which serve the tabernacle. *(Of our spiritual altar formalists cannot partake.)*

11 For the bodies of those beasts, whose blood is brought into the sanctuary by the high priest for sin, are burned without the camp.

12, 13, Wherefore Jesus also, that he might sanctify the people with his own blood, suffered without the gate. *(Calvary was outside Jerusalem.)* Let us go forth therefore unto him without the camp, bearing his reproach.

14 For here have we no continuing city, but we seek one to come. *(Our holy faith makes us a separated people, because our Lord in whom we trust was separated, and covered with reproach for our sakes. Mere going out from society is nothing, going forth unto him is the great matter. With joy do we follow him into the place of separation, expecting soon to dwell with him for ever.)*

My faith would lay her hand
On that dear head of thine,
While like a penitent I stand,
And there confess my sin.

My soul looks back to see
The burdens thou didst bear,
When hanging on the cursed tree,
And hopes her guilt was there.

LEVITICUS X. 1—11. ✓

AND Nadab and Abihu, the sons of Aaron, took either of them his censer, and put fire therein, and put incense thereon, and offered strange fire before the LORD, which he commanded them not. *(These young men were self-willed, and perhaps also excited by strong drink, and therefore daringly violated the Lord's commands in his own immediate presence. They followed their own wills as to time, place, and manner of offering the incense, no doubt considering these to be small matters, but indeed nothing is small in the service of God. He will be worshipped in his own way, and not in ours. There is more sin than they suppose in altering the ordinances as some do in our day. Moreover, there is one fire in the church, namely the Holy Spirit, and one incense, namely the merit of Jesus, and it is a daring impiety to seek other excitement, or offer any other righteousness to God.)*

2 And there went out fire from the LORD, and devoured them, and they died before the LORD. *(The devouring flame flashed right across the mercy seat and slew them. Think of that, and remember that they were minister's sons and ministers themselves. Even our God is a consuming fire. They died while offering a vain will-worship, and it is to be feared that thousands will perish in like manner. Let us be careful and prayerful, and walk jealously before the jealous God; seeking even to worship him as his own Word directs.)*

3 Then Moses said unto Aaron, This *is it* that the LORD spake, saying, I will be sanctified in them that come nigh me, and before all the people I will be glorified. And Aaron held his peace. *(Even as all godly parents must when they see their graceless children perish before the Lord. God is most strict with those nearest to him. Let such be very jealous over themselves.)*

4 And Moses called Mishael and Elzaphan, the sons of Uzziel the uncle of Aaron, and said unto them, Come near, carry your brethren from before the sanctuary out of the camp.

5 So they went near, and carried them in their coats out of the camp; as Moses had said. *Thus all saw them and were warned. Sad indeed that these who should have taught holiness by their lives, could only teach it by becoming warnings of divine wrath in their deaths.*

6 And Moses said unto Aaron, and unto Eleazar and unto Ithamar, his sons, Uncover not your heads, neither rend your clothes; lest ye die, and lest wrath come upon all the people: but let your brethren, the whole house of Israel, bewail the burning which the LORD hath kindled.

7 And ye shall not go out from the door of the tabernacle of the congregation, lest ye die: for the anointing oil of the LORD *is* upon you. And they did according to the word of Moses. *The nearest friends were called upon to approve the divine justice. Others might mourn the sin and doom of the offenders, but their brethren were bidden to make no sign of mourning.*

8 ¶ And the LORD spake unto Aaron, saying,

9 Do not drink wine nor strong drink, thou, nor thy sons with thee, when ye go into the tabernacle of the congregation, lest ye die: *it shall be* a statute for ever throughout your generations:

10 And that ye may put difference between holy and unholy, and between unclean and clean;

11 And that ye may teach the children of Israel all the statutes which the LORD hath spoken unto them by the hand of Moses. *Probably because Nadab and Abihu had been drinking, all priests were for the future forbidden to drink wine at times of service. It is a foul sin when the Christian minister seeks to stimulate his eloquence by wine; it is offering strange fire before the Lord, and will surely be visited upon him. He who serves God must be calm, sober, and not excited with any fleshly passion. O for a baptism of the Holy Ghost, to free the Lord's ministers from every false excitement, and make them wait upon the Lord in quiet holiness.*

Holy and reverend is the name
  Of our eternal King!
"Thrice holy Lord," the angels cry,
  "Thrice holy," let us sing.

With sacred awe pronounce His name,
  Whom words nor thoughts can reach,
A contrite heart shall please Him more
  Than noblest forms of speech.

Thou holy God, preserve my soul
  From all pollution free;
The pure in heart are Thy delight,
  And they Thy face shall see.

THE *fearful disease of leprosy was so common among the Israelites that laws were
made for its regulation, and ordinances by which
cleansed persons were restored to the society of
Israel, from which their leprosy had excluded
them. Among the laws was one singular one
which we will read because it is full of teaching.*

LEVITICUS XIII. 12—17 ; 45, 46.

12 And if a leprosy break out abroad in the
skin, and the leprosy cover all the skin of *him
that hath* the plague from his head even to his
foot, wheresoever the priest looketh ;

13 Then the priest shall consider : and,
behold, *if* the leprosy have covered all his flesh,
he shall pronounce *him* clean *that hath* the
plague : it is all turned white : he *is* clean.

*This seems very strange, and we cannot stay to
account for it ; but assuredly when a soul appears
to itself to be nothing else but sin it is very near
to salvation. Corruption hidden within is far
more dangerous than that which the eye sees and
laments. When the sinner's iniquity comes out
to view, he will fly for cleansing to the Lord
Jesus. As long as we think there is some
soundness in us, we boast ourselves proudly and
are in a sorry case; but when we see that, from
the sole of the foot even to the head, we are only
wounds and bruises and putrifying sores, then are
we humbled and our cure begins.*

14, 15 But when raw flesh appeareth in him,
he shall be unclean. And the priest shall see
the raw flesh, and pronounce him to be unclean :
for the raw flesh *is* unclean : it *is* a leprosy.

*Just what our ignorance values most in our
nature the Lord considers to be our deadliest mark.*

16, 17 Or if the raw flesh turn again, and
be changed unto white, he shall come unto the
priest ; and the priest shall see him : and, behold,
if the plague be turned into white; then the
priest shall pronounce *him* clean *that hath* the
plague : he *is* clean. *(When to the eye he
seemed worst he was really better. The Lord
seeth not as man seeth. When the disease is
all upon the surface, all beneath the man's own
view, he is clean. When self-righteousness is
gone, when we have no soundness in us, then is the
hour of grace. If the priest found the man to
be unclean, the law shut him out from the camp.)*

45 And the leper in whom the plague *is*, his
clothes shall be rent, and his head bare, and he
shall put a covering upon his upper lip, and
shall cry, Unclean, unclean.

*He was made to wear the rent garments of woe,
his head was laid bare as though he mourned for
himself as dead, and his lip was covered as though
for ever closed from all intercourse with men.
To prevent others from coming near him, and
catching the dreadful infection, he had to utter the
warning cry, " Unclean, unclean."*

46 All the days wherein the plague *shall be*
in him he shall be defiled; he *is* unclean : he
shall dwell alone; without the camp *shall* his
habitation *be. (He sat without, and none dare
approach him, neither was he permitted to come
near to any man. His disease was foul, painful,
wasting, and deadly. Such too is sin, and such
is the sinner's condition before the Lord. He is
excluded from the divine presence, and dead in
trespasses and sins. The principle of health or
holiness is gone from him; his spiritual powers are
withered, and every sinew shrunk. Streams of
impurity burst forth in his soul, and render him
utterly loathsome to God. Upon him has fallen
the shadow of death. No human hand can heal
him, there is no balm in Gilead, there is no physician
there. The sinner is sick unto death, and is far
past all earthly help. Yet one there is who can
heal with a word, and he is present here, saying
to each one of us, " Look unto me and be saved,
for I am God, and beside me there is none else."
He who refuses this Physician deserves to die;
and die he must. Will it be so with any one of
us ? Rather let each one of us put our trust in
Jesus from this hour.)*

Physician of my sin-sick soul,
  To thee I bring my case ;
My raging malady control,
  And heal me by thy grace.

It lies not in a single part,
  But through my frame is spread **;**
A burning fever in my heart,
  A palsy in my head.

Lord, I am sick, regard my cry,
  And set my spirit free :
Say, canst thou let a sinner die,
  Who longs to live to thee ?

LEVITICUS XIV. 1—7.

AND the LORD spake unto Moses, saying,
2 This shall be the law of the leper in the day of his cleansing : He shall be brought unto the priest :

3 And the priest shall go forth out of the camp; *(perhaps the priest was otherwise occupied, and then the leper must wait until he could leave the camp and come to him, but Jesus is always ready to hear the sinner's cry. Moreover all that the priest could do was to pronounce a man ceremonially clean who was already healed, but Jesus actually heals the sin-sick soul)* and the priest shall look, and, behold, *if* the plague of leprosy be healed in the leper ;

4 Then shall the priest command to take for him that is to be cleansed two birds alive *and* clean, and cedar wood, and scarlet, and hyssop :

5 And the priest shall command that one of the birds be killed in an earthen vessel over running water :

6 As for the living bird, he shall take it, and the cedar wood, and the scarlet, and the hyssop, and shall dip them and the living bird in the blood of the bird *that was* killed over the running water :

7 And he shall sprinkle upon him that is to be cleansed from the leprosy seven times, and shall pronounce him clean, and shall let the living bird loose into the open field. *(See how the two streams of blood and water meet in the type as they do yet more fully in Jesus. He, as slain for us, purges away our guilt; and, as living for us, he is our righteousness. "He was delivered for our offences, and was raised again for our justification." He came not by water only, but by water and blood, and we also are now born of water and of the Spirit. Now also we fly in the open field, and a new song is in our mouth, even praise unto our God.)*

IN the Evangelists we meet with the cure of a leper by our Lord, in which the Jewish rites and ceremonies are alluded to.

MARK I. 40—45.

40 And there came a leper to him, beseeching him, and kneeling down to him, and saying unto him, If thou wilt, thou canst make me clean. *Here was faith enough to believe that Jesus*

could remove an incurable disease, but there lingered a sad "if" in his faith, like a dead fly in the pot of ointment. Nevertheless, the Lord Jesus accepted the imperfect faith, and gave in return a perfect cure.

41 And Jesus, moved with compassion, put forth *his* hand, and touched him, and saith unto him, I will ; be thou clean. *(What a blessed "I will." Christ's will is omnipotent. He can save us even with his wish. He can save us at this present moment.)*

42 And as soon as he had spoken, immediately the leprosy departed from him, and he was cleansed. *(Salvation is instantaneous. The moment we believe in Jesus we have eternal life.)*

43 And he straitly charged him, and forthwith sent him away;

44 And saith unto him, See thou say nothing to any man : but go thy way, shew thyself to the priest, and offer for thy cleansing those things which Moses commanded, for a testimony unto them. *(While the law stood our Lord observed it; how much more should we obey the gospel in every point of precept and ordinance.)*

45 But he went out, and began to publish *it* much, and to blaze abroad the matter, insomuch that Jesus could no more openly enter into the city, but was without in desert places : and they came to him from every quarter. *(Jesus was modest and retiring, and sought not honour of men. But the man's gratitude would not let him be silent. He told his story, and the news ran along like fire over a prairie—it blazed abroad, to the praise of the Good Physician.)*

Lord, I am vile, conceived in sin,
And born unholy and unclean ;
Sprung from the man whose guilty fall
Corrupts the race, and taints us all.

Behold I fall before Thy face,
My only refuge is Thy grace ;
No outward forms can make me clean;
The leprosy lies deep within.

No bleeding bird, nor bleeding beast,
Nor hyssop branch, nor sprinkling priest,
Nor running brook, nor flood, nor sea,
Can wash the dismal stain away.

Jesus, my God ! Thy blood alone
Hath power sufficient to atone ;
Thy blood can make me white as snow;
No Jewish types could cleanse me so.

LEVITICUS XVI. 1—10; 15—22.

AND the LORD spake unto Moses after the death of the two sons of Aaron, when they offered before the LORD, and died; And the LORD said unto Moses, Speak unto Aaron thy brother, that he come not at all times into the holy *place* within the vail before the mercy seat, which *is* upon the ark; that he die not: for I will appear in the cloud upon the mercy seat. *The death of Nadab and Abihu became the occasion of fresh instruction to Israel. We should always learn from the Lord's judgments upon others. Aaron was taught that even he could only come to God as the Lord led him into nearness of access.*

3, 4 Thus shall Aaron come into the holy *place:* with a young bullock for a sin offering, and a ram for a burnt offering. He shall put on the holy linen coat, and he shall have the linen breeches upon his flesh, and shall be girded with a linen girdle, and with the linen mitre shall he be attired: these *are* holy garments; therefore shall he wash his flesh in water, and *so* put them on. *(He was to wear his plain ordinary garments, and his washing was meant to show his purity: even thus, in making atonement for us, our Lord Jesus laid aside his glory and became like unto his brethren, yet without sin.)*

5 And he shall take of the congregation of the children of Israel two kids of the goats for a sin offering, and one ram for a burnt offering.

6 And Aaron shall offer his bullock of the sin offering, which *is* for himself, and make an atonement for himself, and for his house.

See how superior is our Lord, for he had no need to offer for himself.

7, 8, 9, 10 And he shall take the two goats, and present them before the LORD *at* the door of the tabernacle of the congregation. And Aaron shall cast lots upon the two goats; one lot for the LORD, and the other lot for the scapegoat. And Aaron shall bring the goat upon which the LORD's lot fell, and offer him *for* a sin offering. *(Atonement is by substitutionary death.)* But the goat, on which the lot fell to be the scapegoat, shall be presented alive before the LORD, to make an atonement with him, *and* to let him go for a scapegoat into the wilderness.

Thus our great substitute bears away the sins of his people into oblivion.

15, 16 Then shall he kill the goat of the sin offering, that *is* for the people, and bring his blood within the vail, and sprinkle it upon the mercy seat, and before the mercy seat: And he shall make an atonement for the holy *place*, because of the uncleanness of the children of Israel, and because of their transgressions in all their sins: and so shall he do for the tabernacle of the congregation, that remaineth among them in the midst of their uncleanness.

17, 18, 19 And there shall be no man in the tabernacle of the congregation when he goeth in to make an atonement in the holy *place*, until he come out, and have made an atonement for himself, and for his household, and for all the congregation of Israel. And he shall go out unto the altar that *is* before the LORD, and make an atonement for it; and he shall sprinkle of the blood upon it with his finger seven times, and cleanse it, and hallow it from the uncleanness of the children of Israel. *(Do we not see here our Great High Priest, alone, without a helper, making atonement for us.)*

20, 21, 22 And when he hath made an end of reconciling the holy *place*, and the tabernacle of the congregation, and the altar, he shall bring the live goat: And Aaron shall lay both his hands upon the head of the live goat, and confess over him all the iniquities of the children of Israel, and all their transgressions in all their sins, putting them upon the head of the goat, and shall send *him* away by the hand of a fit man into the wilderness: *(The laying of the hand is very important, it represents faith which accepts the substitute. Have we this faith?)* And the goat shall bear upon him all their iniquities unto a land not inhabited: and he shall let go the goat in the wilderness. *(The first goat showed the Saviour suffering, and the second typified the effect of that suffering in the complete removal of Israel's sin. Sin is gone, gone for ever, from the man who rests in Jesus.)*

I lay my sins on Jesus,
  The spotless Lamb of God:
He bears them all and frees us
  From the accursed load.
I bring my guilt to Jesus,
  To wash my crimson stains
White in his blood most precious,
  Till not a spot remains.

110   " Let us keep the feast."   FEBRUARY 24.—EVENING.

[Or April 19.]

LEVITICUS XXIII. 26—32 ; 37—43.

TO-DAY *let us consider two of the sacred seasons appointed by God, namely, the day of atonement and the feast of Tabernacles.*

And the LORD spake unto Moses, saying,

27 Also on the tenth *day* of this seventh month *there shall be* a day of atonement: it shall be an holy convocation unto you ; and ye shall afflict your souls, and offer an offering made by fire unto the LORD. *(Sorrow for sin is a blessed thing. It cannot make an atonement, but it always goes with the reception of the atonement. If sin be sweet to us it will destroy us, but when we are afflicted in soul concerning it, the day of atonement has come.)*

28 And ye shall do no work in that same day: for it *is* a day of atonement, to make an atonement for you before the LORD your God.

Sin is not put away by works, for on the day of atonement, the sinner ceases to work with the idea of self-salvation.

29 For whatsoever soul *it be* that shall not be afflicted in that same day, he shall be cut off from among his people. *(No surer sign of destruction, than to have no soul affliction for sin. True sorrow for sin is deep. The Jews said that " a man had never seen sorrow who had not seen the sorrow of the day of atonement.")*

30 And whatsoever soul *it be* that doeth any work in that same day, the same soul will I destroy from among his people.

31 Ye shall do no manner of work : *it shall be* a statute for ever throughout your generations in all your dwellings.

32 It *shall be* unto you a sabbath of rest, and ye shall afflict your souls : in the ninth *day* of the month at even, from even unto even, shall ye celebrate your sabbath. *(This day of mourning led on to the gladsome feast of tabernacles. Sacred sorrow prepares the heart for holy joy. We must receive the atonement before we can enter into the joy of the Lord.)*

37 These *are* the feasts of the LORD, which ye shall proclaim *to be* holy convocations, to offer an offering made by fire unto the LORD, a burnt offering, and a meat offering, a sacrifice, and drink offerings, every thing upon his day :

38 Beside the sabbaths of the LORD, and beside your gifts, and beside all your vows, and beside all your freewill offerings, which ye give unto the LORD. *(The Spirit of God lays great stress upon the joyful things, and recapitulates them carefully ; the fruit of the Spirit is joy.)*

39 Also in the fifteenth day of the seventh month, when ye have gathered in the fruit of the land, ye shall keep a feast unto the LORD seven days : on the first day *shall be* a sabbath, and on the eighth day *shall be* a sabbath.

This was a very joyful season, so that the Jews said, " he who never saw the rejoicing of the feast of tabernacles, had never seen rejoicing in his life."

40 And ye shall take you on the first day the boughs of goodly trees, branches of palm trees, and the boughs of thick trees, and willows of the brook ; and ye shall rejoice before the LORD your God seven days. *(Andrew Bonar says, " Imagine the scene thus presented to the view. It is an image of paradise restored—the New Earth in its luxuriance during the reign of righteousness and peace and joy. ' Every goodly tree' furnishes its boughs for the occasion. The palm is first mentioned because it was the tree which had oftenest sheltered them in the wilderness, as at Elim." Thus reminded of what divine love had done for them, the people spent a happy season beneath the boughs, no doubt feeling and saying, " it is good to be here.")*

41 And ye shall keep it a feast unto the LORD seven days in the year. *It shall be* a statute for ever in your generations : ye shall celebrate it in the seventh month.

42 Ye shall dwell in booths seven days ; all that are Israelites born shall dwell in booths :

43 That your generations may know that I made the children of Israel to dwell in booths, when I brought them out of the land of Egypt : I *am* the LORD your God. *(Sunny memories were refreshed in men's hearts by so delightful an observance, and the whole matter illustrated the loving-kindness of the Lord, who when his people have sorrowed for sin would have their sorrow turned into joy.)*

The hill of Sion yields
A thousand sacred sweets,
Before we reach the heavenly fields,
Or walk the golden streets.

Then let our songs abound,
And every tear be dry :
We're marching thro' Immanuel's ground
To fairer worlds on high.

WE shall now read a brief incident, very terrible to think upon, and full of solemn teaching to us all. May the Holy Spirit enable us to profit by it.

LEVITICUS XXIV. 10—16; 23.

10 ¶ And the son of an Israelitish woman, whose father *was* an Egyptian, went out among the children of Israel: and this son of the Israelitish *woman* and a man of Israel strove together in the camp. *(Among the people of God there are some who are not altogether of Israel, they are in heart Egyptians or lovers of sin, and yet they are near of kin to true believers, and mingle freely in their gatherings.)*

11 And the Israelitish woman's son blasphemed the name *of the* LORD, and cursed. *(Observe that the words—" of the* LORD*" are not in the original. He blasphemed* THE NAME. *Now there is given among us a name which is above every name, a name at which every knee shall bow, and woe shall be unto the man who shall lightly esteem the name of Jesus.)* And they brought him unto Moses: (and his mother's name *was* Shelomith, the daughter of Dibri, of the tribe of Dan:) *(Bad men shame their mothers. May we never do that.)*

12 And they put him in ward, that the mind of the LORD might be shewed them.

It is not for us to judge unbelievers except as we have the Lord's warrant for it from his own mouth. Utterances against the name and glory of the Lord Jesus should, however, strike us with horror, and lead us to consider what will be the doom of those who utter them.

13 And the LORD spake unto Moses, saying,

14 Bring forth him that hath cursed without the camp; and let all that heard *him* lay their hands upon his head, and let all the congregation stone him. *(No ordinary punishment could meet the despiser's case: he must die. There is none other name under heaven given among men whereby we must be saved, and as the offender had done despite to that blessed name, he must be suddenly destroyed, and that without remedy. We should be unfaithful if we held out even the slightest hope of eternal life to those who despise the name of Jesus. Rather must all the faithful lay their hands upon the unbeliever's head, as assenting and*

consenting to his just punishment. Mercy there is in Jesus, but those who put him away from them bring down their blood upon their own heads.)

15 And thou shalt speak unto the children of Israel, saying, Whosoever curseth his God shall bear his sin.

16 And he that blasphemeth the name of the LORD, he shall surely be put to death, *and* all the congregation shall certainly stone him: as well the stranger, as he that is born in the land, when he blasphemeth the name *of the* LORD, shall be put to death.

23 And Moses spake to the children of Israel, that they should bring forth him that had cursed out of the camp, and stone him with stones. And the children of Israel did as the LORD commanded Moses. *(No other end is decreed for a blasphemer of "the name" than death, swift and terrible. Those awful words of the apostle which we will now quote, ought to sink down into every heart, and move us to reverent obedience to the name of Jesus.)*

HEBREWS X. 28—31.

28 He that despised Moses' law died without mercy under two or three witnesses:

29 Of how much sorer punishment, suppose ye, shall he be thought worthy, who hath trodden under foot the Son of God, and hath counted the blood of the covenant, wherewith he was sanctified, an unholy thing, and hath done despite unto the Spirit of grace?

30 For we know him that hath said, Vengeance *belongeth* unto me, I will recompense, saith the Lord. And again, the Lord shall judge his people.

31 *It is* a fearful thing to fall into the hands of the living God.

Jesus, the name high over all,
  In hell, or earth, or sky;
Angels and men before it fall,
  And devils fear and fly.

Jesus, the name to sinners dear,
  The name to sinners given,
Woe to the man who will not hear
  Th' ambassador from heaven.

LEVITICUS XXV. 8—17 ; 25—28 ; 39—42. ✓

AND thou shalt number seven sabbaths of years unto thee, seven times seven years : and the space of the seven sabbaths of years shall be unto thee forty and nine years.

9 Then shalt thou cause the trumpet of the jubile to sound on the tenth *day* of the seventh month, in the day of atonement shall ye make the trumpet sound throughout all your land.

10 And ye shall hallow the fiftieth year, and proclaim liberty throughout *all* the land unto all the inhabitants thereof : it shall be a jubile unto you : and ye shall return every man unto his possession, and ye shall return every man unto his family. *(The preaching of the Gospel is a proclamation of a spiritual jubilee. Jesus our great High-priest has preached deliverance to the captive, and the opening of the prison to them that are bound. Now, even now, each believer keeps his jubilee. Note that the jubilee began on the evening of the day of atonement; our Lord's atoning work is the fountain-head of our holy joy.)*

11, 12 A jubile shall that fiftieth year be unto you : ye shall not sow, neither reap that which groweth of itself in it, nor gather *the grapes* in it of thy vine undressed. For it *is* the jubile ; it shall be holy unto you : ye shall eat the increase thereof out of the field.

13 In the year of this jubile ye shall return every man unto his possession.

14, 15 And if thou sell ought unto thy neighbour, or buyest *ought* of thy neighbour's hand, ye shall not oppress one another : According to the number of years after the jubile, thou shalt buy of thy neighbour, *and* according unto the number of years of the fruits he shall sell unto thee :

16 According to the multitude of years thou shalt increase the price thereof, and according to the fewness of years thou shalt diminish the price of it : for *according* to the number *of the years* of the fruits doth he sell unto thee.

17 Ye shall not therefore oppress one another ; but thou shalt fear thy God : for I *am* the LORD your God. *(The Jews could overreach each other by selling the lease of their lands for forty-nine years, whereas the seven seventh years were not "years of the fruits," but sabbatic years, and therefore the Lord enacts that the sabbatic years shall not count in the estimate. In our buying and selling let us be scrupulously just, lest we provoke the Lord.)*

25 ¶ If thy brother be waxen poor, and hath sold away *some* of his possession, and if any of his kin come to redeem it, then shall he redeem that which his brother sold. *(Blessed be God, we have a near "kinsman" who has redeemed our lost inheritance for us.)*

26, 27 And if the man have none to redeem it, and himself be able to redeem it ; Then let him count the years of the sale thereof, and restore the overplus unto the man to whom he sold it ; that he may return unto his possession.

28 But if he be not able to restore *it* to him, then that which is sold shall remain in the hand of him that hath bought it until the year of jubile : and in the jubile it shall go out, and he shall return unto his possession. *(Our lost possession is now restored to us, and we have obtained even more than Adam forfeited.)*

39 ¶ And if thy brother *that dwelleth* by thee be waxen poor, and be sold unto thee ; thou shalt not compel him to serve as a bondservant :

40, 41, 42 *But* as an hired servant, *and* as a sojourner, he shall be with thee, *and* shall serve thee unto the year of jubile : And *then* shall he depart from thee, *both* he and his children with him, and shall return unto his own family, and unto the possession of his fathers shall he return. For they *are* my servants, which I brought forth out of the land of Egypt : they shall not be sold as bondmen. *(Thus by the gospel jubilee we are set free, with the true liberty. Now know we the meaning of the Lord's words, "the year of my redeemed is come." Have all in this house kept the jubilee ? If not, the Lord grant that we may.)*

Jesus our great High Priest,
    Hath full atonement made ;
Ye weary spirits, rest ;
    Ye mournful souls, be glad !
The year of jubilee is come :
Return, ye ransom'd sinners, home.

Ye who have sold for nought
    The heritage above,
Receive it back unbought,
    The gift of Jesus' love ;
       The year, &c.

Ye slaves of sin and hell,
    Your liberty receive ;
And safe in Jesus dwell,
    And blest in Jesus live ;
       The year, &c.

NUMBERS X. 29—36.

AND Moses said unto Hobab, the son of Raguel the Midianite, Moses' father in law, We are journeying unto the place of which the LORD said, I will give it you : come thou with us, and we will do thee good : for the LORD hath spoken good concerning Israel. *(We should talk to our friends and kinsfolk of the advantages which arise out of connection with the people of God; it may be they will be led to cast in their lot with us.)*

30, 31 And he said unto him, I will not go; but I will depart to mine own land, and to my kindred. And he said, Leave us not, I pray thee; forasmuch as thou knowest how we are to encamp in the wilderness, and thou mayest be to us instead of eyes. *(Those who are converted to the faith often become of great service to the church, and this should urge us the more eagerly to seek their conversion.)*

32 And it shall be, if thou go with us, yea, it shall be, that what goodness the LORD shall do unto us, the same will we do unto thee.

Thus the compact was made to share and share alike. This was true brotherhood. Believers know that the Lord dealeth with all his servants as he is wont to do unto those who fear his name. He feeds them with the same bread of life, clothes them with the same righteousness, shelters them beneath the same providential care, and brings them by the same grace to the same glory. Those who truly join with us in Christ's church shall enjoy all the privileges with which we are enriched.

33 ¶ And they departed from the mount of the LORD three days' journey : and the ark of the covenant of the LORD went before them in the three days' journey, to search out a resting place for them.

34 And the cloud of the LORD *was* upon them by day, when they went out of the camp.

35 And it came to pass, when the ark set forward, that Moses said, Rise up, LORD, and let thine enemies be scattered; and let them that hate thee flee before thee. *(This is the Rising Prayer. It confesses that Israel's path is beset with foes, and it looks away from all human help to the Lord alone. The Lord has but to rise, and his foes and ours are gone. O Lord, now arise!)*

36 And when it rested, he said, Return, O LORD, unto the many thousands of Israel.

This was the Resting Prayer. It pleads for the divine presence. Fearing that the Lord may have been grieved during the day, it beseeches him to return. It is of the same tenor as our sweet evening hymn, "Abide with us."

LET us read a few verses of David's psalm, in which he sings of the Lord's glorious marching through the wilderness.

PSALM LXVIII. 1—8.

1 Let God arise, let his enemies be scattered : let them also that hate him flee before him.

2 As smoke is driven away, *so* drive *them* away : as wax melteth before the fire, *so* let the wicked perish at the presence of God.

3 But let the righteous be glad; let them rejoice before God : yea, let them exceedingly rejoice. *(Such a God is not to be worshipped with sadness or half-heartedness. Let us be very joyful in him.)*

4 Sing unto God, sing praises to his name : extol him that rideth upon the heavens by his name JAH, and rejoice before him. *He is as much with us as he was with the Jews, let us equally sing his praises.*

5 A father of the fatherless, and a judge of the widows, *is* God in his holy habitation. *Therefore let his people remember the orphan, and aid those institutions which are for their benefit. Let them also be very pitiful towards poor widows who are God's peculiar charge.*

6 God setteth the solitary in families : he bringeth out those which are bound with chains: but the rebellious dwell in a dry *land*. *(Gracious as God is he cannot bless those who persist in rebellion. Sin is and ever must be the source of misery.)*

7 O God, when thou wentest forth before thy people, when thou didst march through the wilderness; Selah :

8 The earth shook, the heavens also dropped at the presence of God : *even* Sinai itself *was moved* at the presence of God, the God of Israel. *Eternal honour be unto the God of Israel, whose presence is still our succour and solace. Our inmost hearts adore him. Lord throughout this day go before us, and bless us with thy presence.*

NUMBERS XI. 4—5; 10—23.

AND the mixt multitude that *was* among them fell a lusting : and the children of Israel also wept again, and said, Who shall give us flesh to eat ? *(The mischief in the camp usually commenced with the mixed multitude, and it is the same with the church of God now : the merely nominal Christians in her are the tinder for Satan's sparks. It is sad, however, to note that the Israelites were ready enough to follow the bad example of the mixed company. They murmured wantonly. They did not want for either bread or water, but pined for luxuries. Such complaining is sure to be punished.)*

5 We remember the fish, which we did eat in Egypt freely ; the cucumbers, and the melons, and the leeks, and the onions, and the garlick.

10 ¶ Then Moses heard the people weep throughout their families, every man in the door of his tent : and the anger of the LORD was kindled greatly ; Moses also was displeased.

11—15 And Moses said unto the LORD, Wherefore hast thou afflicted thy servant ? and wherefore have I not found favour in thy sight, that thou layest the burden of all this people upon me ? Have I conceived all this people ? have I begotten them, that thou shouldest say unto me, Carry them in thy bosom, as a nursing father beareth the sucking child, unto the land which thou swarest unto their fathers ? Whence should I have flesh to give unto all this people ? for they weep unto me, saying, Give us flesh, that we may eat. I am not able to bear all this people alone, because *it is* too heavy for me. And if thou deal thus with me, kill me, I pray thee, out of hand, if I have found favour in thy sight ; and let me not see my wretchedness. *The meekest man failed in his meekness. He was so provoked by the senseless clamours of the people that he spake unadvisedly with his lips unto God. The best of men are subject to infirmities. The Lord in Moses' case was very pitiful towards his servant, and sent him help that he might the better bear the burden of so great a charge.*

16 ¶ And the LORD said unto Moses, Gather unto me seventy men of the elders of Israel, whom thou knowest to be the elders of the people, and officers over them ; and bring them unto the tabernacle of the congregation, that they may stand there with thee.

17 And I will come down and talk with thee there : and I will take of the spirit which *is* upon thee, and will put *it* upon them ; and they shall bear the burden of the people with thee, that thou bear *it* not thyself alone. *The Lord overlooked the petulance of Moses' language, and met the real burden of his case. The seventy men would have been of no use without the Spirit, but with it they became valuable helpers. O Lord, give thy Spirit to all the elders and deacons of our churches, as well as to all pastors and evangelists.*

18 And say thou unto the people, Sanctify yourselves against to morrow, and ye shall eat flesh : for ye have wept in the ears of the LORD, saying, Who shall give us flesh to eat ? for *it was* well with us in Egypt : therefore the LORD will give you flesh, and ye shall eat.

19, 20 Ye shall not eat one day, nor two days, nor five days, neither ten days, nor twenty days ; *But* even a whole month, until it come out at your nostrils, and it be loathsome unto you : because that ye have despised the LORD which *is* among you, and have wept before him, saying, Why came we forth out of Egypt ? *Too much becomes nauseous. It is a most just method of punishment to make those things loathsome which have been the cause of lusting. The Lord often wearies men with their darling sins.*

21 And Moses said, The people, among whom I *am, are* six hundred thousand footmen ; and thou hast said, I will give them flesh, that they may eat a whole month.

22 Shall the flocks and the herds be slain for them, to suffice them ? or shall all the fish of the sea be gathered together for them, to suffice them ? *(Moses began reckoning second causes, and then saw much ground for doubt ; yet even then he left out a part of the calculation, for he forgot the fowls of heaven from which the Lord gathered meat for the people.)*

23 And the LORD said unto Moses, Is the LORD's hand waxed short ? thou shalt see now whether my word shall come to pass unto thee or not. *(Unbelief is very grievous to the Lord : perhaps some of us are guilty of it. Is it so? Then let us humbly bow before the rebuke of this verse, and then hopefully expect to see every promise of the Lord fulfilled, for so it shall be.)*

NUMBERS XI. 24—34. ✓

A ND Moses went out, and told the people the words of the LORD, and gathered the seventy men of the elders of the people, and set them round about the tabernacle.

25 And the LORD came down in a cloud, and spake unto him, and took of the spirit that *was* upon him, and gave *it* unto the seventy elders : and it came to pass, *that*, when the spirit rested upon them, they prophesied, and did not cease.

See what the Lord can do, and let it encourage us to pray the Lord of the harvest to send forth labourers into his harvest. Many a Moses is burdened for want of helpers, but the Lord can send him all the assistance he needs.

26 But there remained two *of the* men in the camp, the name of the one *was* Eldad, and the name of the other Medad : and the spirit rested upon them ; and they *were* of them that were written, but went not out unto the tabernacle : and they prophesied in the camp. *(Perhaps Moses and the people had not looked for prophetic gifts to follow the gift of the Spirit, but only the power to govern ; hence the excitement when two of the elders began to preach in parts of the camp where the prophesying at the tabernacle had not yet been made known.)*

27 And there ran a young man, and told Moses, and said, Eldad and Medad do prophesy in the camp.

28 And Joshua the son of Nun, the servant of Moses, *one* of his young men, answered and said, My lord Moses, forbid them.

Jealousy for his master's honour moved Joshua to stay the irregular ministry of Eldad and Medad ; and still there are many who are zealous to put down those who presume to prophesy, because they are " men authorised by God alone," as if that were not authority enough.

29 And Moses said unto him, Enviest thou for my sake ? would God that all the LORD's people were prophets, *and* that the LORD would put his spirit upon them ! *(Moses was of a noble spirit. If the men were really moved by the Spirit of God, he had no desire to restrain their unusual procedure ; but far otherwise, he wished that all the Lord's servants had the same gifts and graces. Irregular ministries have been the means of the salvation of thousands, and therein we rejoice, yea, and will rejoice.)*

30 And Moses gat him into the camp, he and the elders of Israel.

31 ¶ And there went forth a wind from the LORD, and brought quails from the sea, and let *them* fall by the camp, as it were a day's journey on this side, and as it were a day's journey on the other side, round about the camp, and as it were two cubits *high* upon the face of the earth.

32 And the people stood up all that day, and all *that* night, and all the next day, and they gathered the quails : he that gathered least gathered ten homers : and they spread *them* all abroad for themselves round about the camp.

They feasted themselves without fear, though they had been told that evil would come of it. No doubt they fed ravenously, and then gave their whole minds to the curing of what remained, as if they thought they should never have such provision again. Greediness is, in itself, a plague, and brings other evils with it.

33 And while the flesh *was* yet between their teeth, ere it was chewed, the wrath of the LORD was kindled against the people, and the LORD smote the people with a very great plague.

These gluttons digged their graves with their teeth. Many die through sins of the table ; drunkenness and gluttony devour their thousands. Thus by one sin God punished another. Those who murmured for flesh, received, as a penalty, death while eating the flesh for which they murmured.

34 And he called the name of that place Kibroth-hattaavah : because there they buried the people that lusted. *(Scandalous sins have their memorials ; may they act as warnings to us, that we do not become discontented and greedy. The Lord make us thankful for His mercies, and save us from fleshly lusts.)*

O Lord, Thy messengers ordain,
    And whom Thou wilt inspire ;
We will not of Thy course complain,
    But hail the sacred fire.

Blow as He list, the Spirit's choice
    Of instruments we bless ;
We will, if Christ be preached, rejoice.
    And wish the Word success.

NUMBERS XII. 1—15.

AND Miriam and Aaron spake against Moses because of the Ethiopian woman whom he had married : for he had married an Ethiopian woman. *(Jealousy of his power was at the bottom of their complaining. How good a man Moses must have been when even those who knew him best could find no fault with him except that he had married a foreign lady, against whom they had nothing to allege but that she was an Ethiopian.)*

2 And they said, Hath the LORD indeed spoken only by Moses ? hath he not spoken also by us ? And the LORD heard *it. (Moses must have felt the jealousy of his brother and sister very keenly, but he did not fight his own battle, he left the matter to God, who observed with indignation the wanton envy of the ungenerous pair.)*

3 (Now the man Moses *was* very meek, above all the men which *were* upon the face of the earth.) *(Some other hand has inserted this verse under divine direction. Moses would not have said it of himself, but the Lord took care that somebody else should record it, for he honours those who honour him. As Moses was meek he did not strive for himself, and therefore the Lord became his champion.)*

4 And the LORD spake suddenly unto Moses, and unto Aaron, and unto Miriam, Come out ye three unto the tabernacle of the congregation. And they three came out. *(The suddenness of the interference marks the importance of the matter, and the Lord's anger concerning it.)*

5 And the LORD came down in the pillar of the cloud, and stood *in* the door of the tabernacle, and called Aaron and Miriam : and they both came forth.

6 And he said, Hear now my words : If there be a prophet among you, *I* the LORD will make myself known unto him in a vision, *and* will speak unto him in a dream.

7 My servant Moses *is* not so, who *is* faithful in all mine house.

8 With him will I speak mouth to mouth, even apparently, and not in dark speeches ; and the similitude of the LORD shall he behold : wherefore then were ye not afraid to speak against my servant Moses ? *(Aaron had been faulty in the matter of the golden calf, and therefore he ought to have been very quiet, and*

Miriam's sex should have sufficed to make her modest ; yet, envy thrust both these good persons into a bad spirit, and then into a false and sinful position. Above all things, let us shun envy, for it is cruel as the grave. If God chooses to make other men greater and more honourable than ourselves, what right have we to question his prerogative?)

9 And the anger of the LORD was kindled against them ; and he departed. *(This was the surest token of his anger. His presence is heaven, his absence misery to his children.)*

10 And the cloud departed from off the tabernacle ; and, behold, Miriam *became* leprous, *white* as snow : and Aaron looked upon Miriam, and, behold, *she was* leprous.

If Aaron had been made a leper he could not have executed his office ; but Miriam's disease was a punishment to both, and possibly she had also been the chief offender.

11 And Aaron said unto Moses, Alas, my lord, I beseech thee, lay not the sin upon us, wherein we have done foolishly, and wherein we have sinned.

12 Let her not be as one dead, of whom the flesh is half consumed when he cometh out of his mother's womb.

13 And Moses cried unto the LORD, saying, Heal her now, O God, I beseech thee.

Miriam wounded Moses with her tongue, and now Moses uses his tongue to cry, " Heal her now, O God." This is the true way to heap coals of fire on the heads of those who injure us. We must pray for those who despitefully use us.

14 ¶ And the LORD said unto Moses, If her father had but spit in her face, should she not be ashamed seven days ? let her be shut out from the camp seven days, and after that let her be received in *again. (In cases of extreme provocation an eastern father would spit in his child's face, and then the child was banished from the father's presence for seven days : how much more then should Miriam be shut out of the camp for a while when she had so grossly offended, and against the Lord, and had received so terrible a mark of the divine displeasure.)*

15 And Miriam was shut out from the camp seven days : and the people journeyed not till Miriam was brought in *again. (This shewed their respect for her, and their grief at her sickness.)*

NUMBERS XIII. 1, 2 ; 17—21 ; 23—33.

AND the LORD spake unto Moses, saying,
2 Send thou men, that they may search the land of Canaan, which I give unto the children of Israel. (*Because of the hardness of the people's hearts, the Lord permitted Moses to send spies. It had been far better for them to have believed the Word of the Lord, and to have followed the pillar of cloud. How foolish for them to have the land spied out which the Lord had long before spied out for them*); of every tribe of their fathers shall ye send a man, every one a ruler among them. (*The best men should always be the most ready for works of daring and self-sacrifice. He is noblest in the church who is readiest to be the servant of all.*)

17, 18 And Moses sent them to spy out the land of Canaan, and said unto them, Get you up this *way* southward, and go up into the mountain : And see the land, what it *is ;* and the people that dwelleth therein, whether they *be* strong or weak, few or many;

19 And what the land *is* that they dwell in, whether it *be* good or bad : and what cities *they be* that they dwell in, whether in tents, or in strong holds ;

20 And what the land *is,* whether it *be* fat or lean, whether there be wood therein, or not. And be ye of good courage, and bring of the fruit of the land. Now the time *was* the time of the first ripe grapes.

21 ¶ So they went up, and searched the land from the wilderness of Zin unto Rehob, as men come to Hamath.

23 And they came unto the brook of Eshcol, and cut down from thence a branch with one cluster of grapes, and they bare it between two upon a staff; and *they brought* of the pomegranates, and of the figs. *They brought home conclusive evidence of the fertility of the country. This cluster of Eshcol is typical of those holy comforts which saints enjoy even in this world, which are earnests of the joys hereafter.*

24 The place was called the brook Eshcol, because of the cluster of grapes which the children of Israel cut down from thence.

25 And they returned from searching of the land after forty days. (*Every day of spying cost Israel a year of wandering. Walking by sight is expensive work.*)

26 ¶ And they went and came to Moses, and to Aaron, and to all the congregation of the children of Israel, unto the wilderness of Paran, to Kadesh ; and brought back word unto them, and unto all the congregation, and shewed them the fruit of the land.

27 And they told him, and said, We came unto the land whither thou sentest us, and surely it floweth with milk and honey; and this *is* the fruit of it.

28 Nevertheless the people *be* strong that dwell in the land, and the cities *are* walled, *and* very great : and moreover we saw the children of Anak there.

29 The Amalekites dwell in the land of the south: and the Hittites, and the Jebusites, and the Amorites, dwell in the mountains : and the Canaanites dwell by the sea, and by the coast of Jordan. (*Thus, the report of sight was altogether discouraging. How much better would it have been for Israel had they walked by faith ! Every circumstance which could discourage the heart these spies took careful note of, but they omitted, or misinterpreted many hopeful tokens. If we will leave the line of faith, we are sure to be sorely put to it.*)

30 And Caleb stilled the people before Moses, and said, Let us go up at once, and possess it; for we are well able to overcome it.

31 But the men that went up with him said, We be not able to go up against the people; for they *are* stronger than we.

32 And they brought up an evil report of the land which they had searched unto the children of Israel, saying, The land, through which we have gone to search it, *is* a land that eateth up the inhabitants thereof; and all the people that we saw in it *are* men of a great stature.

33 And there we saw the giants, the sons of Anak, *which come* of the giants : and we were in our own sight as grasshoppers, and so we were in their sight. (*But what of all this if they had but believed their God. Had he not smitten the Egyptians? Caleb and Joshua had faith, and hence they had courage, but unbelief is cowardly. O, for grace to trust in the Lord, and cease from all confidence in man, then shall our lives grow great and good before the Lord.*)

NUMBERS XIV. 1—21.

AND all the congregation lifted up their voice, and cried; and the people wept that night. *(When children cry for nothing, they soon have good cause for crying, and such was the case in this instance; but do we never fall into the same sin ourselves?)*

2 And all the children of Israel murmured against Moses and against Aaron: and the whole congregation said unto them, Would God that we had died in the land of Egypt: or would God we had died in this wilderness!

3 And wherefore hath the LORD brought us unto this land, to fall by the sword, that our wives and our children should be a prey? were it not better for us to return into Egypt?

What a shameful slur they cast upon Jehovah when they asked whether he had brought them out to slay them, and truly we are equally guilty when we imagine that after leading us so far on the road to heaven, he will leave us to our enemies.

4 And they said one to another, Let us make a captain, and let us return into Egypt.

To avoid one evil they would rush into a worse. Without the cloud to guide them, or the manna to feed them, they talk of going back to Egypt. Unbelief is insanity.

5 Then Moses and Aaron fell on their faces before all the assembly of the congregation of the children of Israel.

The people ought far rather to have fallen on their faces before them; so is it often that the best men are worst spoken of.

6 ¶ And Joshua the son of Nun, and Caleb the son of Jephunneh, *which were* of them that searched the land, rent their clothes:

7 And they spake unto all the company of the children of Israel, saying, The land, which we passed through to search it, *is* an exceeding good land.

8 If the LORD delight in us, then he will bring us into this land, and give it us; a land which floweth with milk and honey.

9 Only rebel not ye against the LORD, neither fear ye the people of the land; for they *are* bread for us: their defence is departed from them, and the LORD *is* with us: fear them not.

10 But all the congregation bade stone them with stones. *(The case had been well put, but stones were the reward of faithfulness.)* And

the glory of the LORD appeared in the tabernacle of the congregation before all the children of Israel. *(God appeared for the defence of his servants. He who touches them, touches the apple of his eye.)*

11 ¶ And the LORD said unto Moses, How long will this people provoke me? and how long will it be ere they believe me, for all the signs which I have shewed among them?

12 I will smite them with the pestilence, and disinherit them, and will make of thee a greater nation and mightier than they. *(This was a great offer, but how lovingly Moses declined it, thinking more of Israel's good and of God's glory than of his own honour.)*

13 ¶ And Moses said unto the LORD, Then the Egyptians shall hear *it,* (for thou broughtest up this people in thy might from among them;)

14 And they will tell *it* to the inhabitants of this land: *for* they have heard that thou LORD *art* among this people, that thou LORD art seen face to face, and *that* thy cloud standeth over them, and *that* thou goest before them, by day time in a pillar of a cloud, and in a pillar of fire by night..

15 ¶ Now *if* thou shalt kill *all* this people as one man, then the nations which have heard the fame of thee will speak, saying,

16 Because the LORD was not able to bring this people into the land which he sware unto them, therefore he hath slain them in the wilderness.

17 And now, I beseech thee, let the power of my LORD be great, according as thou hast spoken, saying,

18 The LORD *is* longsuffering, and of great mercy, forgiving iniquity and transgression, and by no means clearing *the guilty,* visiting the iniquity of the fathers upon the children unto the third and fourth *generation.*

19 Pardon, I beseech thee, the iniquity of this people according unto the greatness of thy mercy, and as thou hast forgiven this people, from Egypt even until now.

20, 21 And the LORD said, I have pardoned according to thy word: But *as* truly *as* I live, all the earth shall be filled with the glory of the LORD. *(See the value of an Intercessor to stand in the gap. Blessed be God; if any man sin, we have an advocate.)*

A S *this day comes but once in four years, we would pray God to give us a fourfold blessing. May we take a leap in grace, and advance an unusual day's journey in the divine pilgrimage. As a change in our reading, let us turn to*

PHILIPPIANS III. 1—14.

1 Finally, my brethren, rejoice in the Lord. *(This is never out of season, and by grace it is always possible. Let grumblers take note of this.)* To write the same things to you, to me indeed *is* not grievous, but for you *it is* safe.

Repetitions of holy precepts neither weary the preacher nor his hearers. God's word does not grow stale.

2 Beware of dogs, beware of evil workers, beware of the concision.

3 For we are the circumcision, which worship God in the spirit, and rejoice in Christ Jesus, and have no confidence in the flesh. *(There were some in Paul's days who made a Jewish party and gloried in their being circumcised ; Paul calls them the cutters off, and claims for spiritual worshippers all the privileges which the Judaizers sought to monopolize.)*

4, 5, 6, 7 Though I might also have confidence in the flesh. If any other man thinketh that he hath whereof he might trust in the flesh, I more : Circumcised the eighth day, of the stock of Israel, *of* the tribe of Benjamin, an Hebrew of the Hebrews ; as touching the law, a Pharisee ; Concerning zeal, persecuting the church ; touching the righteousness which is in the law, blameless. But what things were gain to me, those I counted loss for Christ. *(Grace leads a man to renounce his most prized and boasted privileges for Jesus' sake. This is a test to which many cannot submit.)*

8 Yea doubtless, and I count all things *but* loss for the excellency of the knowledge of Christ Jesus my Lord : for whom I have suffered the loss of all things, and do count them *but* dung, that I may win Christ,

9 And be found in him, not having mine own righteousness, which is of the law, but that which is through the faith of Christ, the righteousness which is of God by faith :

10 That I may know him, *(This is a knowledge not gained at college,)* and the power of his resurrection, and the fellowship of his sufferings,

being made conformable unto his death ; *(To be ready to die as Jesus did, and so to have fellowship with him in death, is a glorious lesson in the learning of grace.)*

11 If by any means I might attain unto the resurrection of the dead. *(The resurrection of the blessed was the prize towards which the Apostle pressed forward. This he sought for in God's fashion, not by his own works, but by the righteousness which is of God by faith.)*

12 Not as though I had already attained, either were already perfect : but I follow after, if that I may apprehend that for which also I am apprehended of Christ Jesus. *(He claimed no perfection in the flesh, but he sought after perfect holiness in Christ Jesus. He had laid hold of Jesus because Jesus had laid hold of him, and Jesus was to him his all in all.)*

13 Brethren, I count not myself to have apprehended : but *this* one thing *I do*, forgetting those things which are behind, and reaching forth unto those things which are before,

14 I press toward the mark for the prize of the high calling of God in Christ Jesus.

"Onward" is our marching order. We never think ourselves good enough. What we have done, through divine grace, we are far from being content with. Our ideal is far above our attainments, we have but begun as yet on the lower forms of the Lord's school of grace, and we aspire to far higher things. We must be diligent in spiritual things. To be early in the shop and late in the closet is ill. How dare we be busy in our own farm and slack in God's vineyard, awake on the market and asleep in the congregation. So run that ye may obtain. He who would have holiness, happiness, and heaven, must run for them.

Soldiers of the Lord below,
Strong in faith resist the foe :
Boundless is the pledged reward
Unto them who serve the Lord.

'Tis no palm of fading leaves,
Which the conqueror's hand receives ;
Joys are his serene and pure,
Light that ever shall endure.

For the souls that overcome
Waits the beauteous heavenly Home,
Where the blessed evermore
Tread, on high, the starry floor.

LET *us read a passage in the book of Revelation, which will keep us in mind of the twelve tribes whose story has occupied us so long—*

REVELATION VII. 1—10.

1 And after these things I saw four angels standing on the four corners of the earth, holding the four winds of the earth, that the wind should not blow on the earth, nor on the sea, nor on any tree. *(The most volatile powers of nature are under God's control, and though they are also the most powerful and destructive, yet his angelic messengers have them as thoroughly under control as though they were horses restrained by bit and bridle. God has many servants, and therefore no quarter of the universe shall suffer because there are no agents to protect it. Go where we may, the sacred body-guard shall attend us.)*

2, 3 And I saw another angel ascending from the east, having the seal of the living God: and he cried with a loud voice to the four angels, to whom it was given to hurt the earth and the sea, Saying, Hurt not the earth, neither the sea, nor the trees, till we have sealed the servants of our God in their foreheads. *(Not a ripple ruffled the waters, not a leaf stirred on the trees, till leave was given to the winds to blow. Evils are impotent till the Lord lets them loose. No child of God need fear the terrible years to come, for until all the Lord's Noahs are safely housed, no destruction can come.)*

4 And I heard the number of them which were sealed: *and there were* sealed an hundred *and* forty *and* four thousand of all the tribes of the children of Israel. *(A large number to indicate a great multitude, a certain and complete number to represent a company known to God, and fixed by his decree.)*

5 Of the tribe of Juda *were* sealed twelve thousand. *(The royal tribe takes its part, else were its royalty wretched preferment.)* Of the tribe of Reuben *were* sealed twelve thousand. *(Unstable, but yet preserved. It is not our faithfulness to God, but his faithfulness to us which saves us.)* Of the tribe of Gad *were* sealed twelve thousand. *(Overcome by troops of trials, they overcome at the last.)*

6 Of the tribe of Aser *were* sealed twelve thousand. *(He dipped his foot in oil, having a rich anointing here, and glory hereafter.)* Of

the tribe of Nepthalim *were* sealed twelve thousand. *(He gave goodly words, and now enjoys a goodly heritage.)* Of the tribe of Manasses *were* sealed twelve thousand. *(He received a double portion on earth, and yet has his lot in heaven.)*

7 Of the tribe of Simeon *were* sealed twelve thousand. *(Cursed by their father for their sin, yet the tribe yielded an elect remnant.)* Of the tribe of Levi *were* sealed twelve thousand. *(Now in very deed made priests unto God.)* Of the tribe of Issachar *were* sealed twelve thousand. *(Too fond of ease, yet redeemed.)*

8 Of the tribe of Zabulon *were* sealed twelve thousand. *(The sea-dwelling people. Thank God for converted sailors.)* Of the tribe of Joseph *were* sealed twelve thousand. *(Archers shot at him, but his full number is saved.)* Of the tribe of Benjamin *were* sealed twelve thousand. *(Last and least in Israel, yet not forgotten by electing love.)*

These make up the Jewish believers, and the elect among the Gentiles are mentioned next.

9 After this I beheld, and, lo, a great multitude, which no man could number, of all nations, and kindreds, and people, and tongues, stood before the throne, and before the Lamb, clothed with white robes, and palms in their hands;

10 And cried with a loud voice, saying, Salvation to our God which sitteth upon the throne, and unto the Lamb. *(In this heavenly song we join with heart and voice. All glory be to Jesus, our Lord. Happy were John's ears to hear the eternal harmonies; we listen not to them as yet, but even now we send up our joy notes to swell their volume.)*

For thee, O dear, dear country,
   Mine eyes their vigils keep;
For very love, beholding
   Thy happy name—they weep.
The mention of thy glory
   Is unction to the breast,
And medicine in sickness,
   And love, and life, and rest.

O one, O only mansion!
   O paradise of joy!
Where tears are ever banished,
   And smiles have no alloy;
The Lamb is all thy splendour;
   The Crucified thy praise;
His laud and benediction,
   Thy ransomed people raise.

Let God arise, and scatteréd
Let all his enemies be ;
And let all those that do him hate
Before his presence flee.

As smoke is driv'n so drive thou them ;
As fire melts wax away,
Before God's face let wicked men
So perish and decay.

But let the righteous all be glad :
Let them before God's sight
Be very joyful ; yea, let them
Rejoice with all their might.

How strange that souls, whom Jesus feeds,
With manna from above,
Should grieve him by their evil deeds,
And sin against his love !

But 'tis a greater marvel still,
That he, from whom they stray,
Should bear with their rebellious will,
And wash their sins away.

Jesus ! who in the form of God
Didst equal honour claim,
Yet, to redeem our guilty souls,
Didst stoop to death and shame.

Oh may that mind in us be form'd,
Which shone so bright in thee ;
May we be humble, lowly, meek,
From pride and envy free.

May we to others stoop, and learn
To emulate thy love ;
So shall we bear thine image here,
And share thy throne above.

Since I have tasted of the grapes,
I sometimes long to go
Where my dear Lord, the vineyard keeps,
And all the clusters grow.

Weak as I am, yet through his grace,
I can the land subdue ;
Tread down the Canaanitish race,
And force a passage through.

Is anything too hard for God ?
Through Jesus we can all things do ;
Who Satan and his works destroyed,
Shall make us more than conquerors, too.

Let us at once the land possess,
And taste the blessings from above,
The milk sincere of pardoning grace,
The honey of his perfect love.

The rising morning can't assure
That we shall end the day ;
For death stands ready at the door,
To seize our lives away.

Our breath is forfeited by sin,
To God's avenging law ;
We own thy grace, immortal king,
In every gasp we draw.

Are we not set apart
To live for Christ alone ?
If we are sanctified in heart,
Our life must make it known.

Oh ! be ye pure that bear
The vessels of the Lord ;
Be separate from sin, who share
Communion at his board.

Should bounteous nature kindly pour
Her richest gifts on me,
Still, O my God, I should be poor
If void of love to thee,

Though thou shouldst give prophetic skill
Each mystery to explain,
If I'd no heart to do thy will,
Such knowledge would be vain.

O grant me then this one request,
And I'll be satisfied,
That love divine may rule my breast
And all my actions guide.

The object of his gracious care
He never yet forsook,
But did himself my weakness bear,
And all my burden took.

He bore me up, from earth he bore
On wings of heavenly love,
And taught my callow soul to soar
To those bright realms above.

"Sin when it is finished bringeth forth death."

NUMBERS XIV. 26—32; 36—45.

AND the LORD spake unto Moses and unto Aaron, saying,

27 How long *shall I bear with* this evil congregation, which murmur against me? I have heard the murmurings of the children of Israel, which they murmur against me.

28 Say unto them, *As truly as* I live, saith the LORD, as ye have spoken in mine ears, so will I do to you: (*It is an awful thing when the Lord takes men at their word, and says Amen to their wicked speeches. They said that they were brought out to die in the wilderness, and the Lord tells them that die they shall. It was at this time that the Lord sware in his wrath, that they should not enter into his rest.*)

29 Your carcases shall fall in this wilderness; and all that were numbered of you, according to your whole number, from twenty years old and upward, which have murmured against me,

30 Doubtless ye shall not come into the land, *concerning* which I sware to make you dwell therein, save Caleb the son of Jephunneh, and Joshua the son of Nun. (*God will not forget the innocent: though there be but two of them there shall be a clause of exemption in the act of judgment.*)

31 But your little ones, which ye said should be a prey, them will I bring in, and they shall know the land which ye have despised.

32 But *as for* you, your carcases, they shall fall in this wilderness. (*With what contempt are they spoken of! Again and again their bodies are called* "carcases," *as if they were no better than beasts. Sin makes men contemptible.*)

36 And the men, which Moses sent to search the land, who returned, and made all the congregation to murmur against him, by bringing up a slander upon the land,

37 Even those men that did bring up the evil report upon the land, died by the plague before the LORD.

38 But Joshua the son of Nun, and Caleb the son of Jephunneh, *which were* of the men that went to search the land, lived *still.* (*The ten spies had been the cause of all this evil, and they were justly cut off at once, as a pledge that the Lord would be as good as his word to the rest of that evil generation.*)

39 And Moses told these sayings unto all the children of Israel: and the people mourned greatly.

40 ¶ And they rose up early in the morning, and gat them up into the top of the mountain, saying, Lo, we *be here*, and will go up unto the place which the LORD hath promised: for we have sinned. (*Like the pendulum which swings from one side to the other, they went from one form of sin to its opposite.*)

41 And Moses said, Wherefore now do ye transgress the commandment of the LORD? but it shall not prosper.

42 Go not up, for the LORD is not among you; that ye be not smitten before your enemies.

43 For the Amalekites and the Canaanites *are* there before you, and ye shall fall by the sword: because ye are turned away from the LORD, therefore the LORD will not be with you. *It is dangerous, yea, deadly, to go where God will not go with us.*

44 But they presumed to go up unto the hill top: nevertheless the ark of the covenant of the LORD, and Moses, departed not out of the camp.

45 Then the Amalekites came down, and the Canaanites which dwelt in that hill, and smote them, and discomfited them, *even* unto Hormah. (*Nothing is difficult when the Lord's power goes forth with us, but to enter upon any service without the help of God is folly, and can only end in defeat. Those who try to fight their own way to heaven, will, like these Jews, find the enemies of their souls too many for them. Presumption is as dangerous as unbelief: they are often companions, and seem to alternate in the souls of the unregenerate like the heat of summer, and the cold of winter: may the Lord deliver us from both.*)

We live estranged and far from God,
  And love the distance well;
With haste we run the dangerous road
  That leads to death and hell.

And can such rebels be restored?
  Such natures made divine?
Let sinners see thy glory, Lord,
  And feel this power of thine.

We raise our Father's name on high,
  Who his own Spirit sends
To bring rebellious strangers nigh,
  And turn his foes to friends.

PSALM XC. ✓

THIS *Psalm is the record of Moses' feelings when he saw the people dying in the wilderness, and it ought not to be read as exactly descriptive of the feelings of godly men, whose death is not a judgment of God's wrath, but a falling asleep in God's arms, that they may depart out of this present evil world to be where Jesus is.*

A Prayer of Moses the man of God.

1 LORD, thou hast been our dwelling place in all generations. (*We wander in tents, but, like our fathers, we dwell in thee. Sweet thought, in every age God is the home of his people.*)

2 Before the mountains were brought forth, or ever thou hadst formed the earth and the world, even from everlasting to everlasting, thou *art* God. (*Though men die, Thou ever livest; though nature itself expire, Thou art the same.*)

3 Thou turnest man to destruction; and sayest, Return, ye children of men. (*One word from thee is enough. When thy fiat has gone forth, the spirits of men return to thee.*)

4 For a thousand years in thy sight *are but* as yesterday when it is past, and *as* a watch in the night. (*What are ages to eternity? The drop is more in relation to the sea than time to the life of the Eternal One.*)

5 Thou carriest them away as with a flood; they are *as* a sleep: in the morning *they are* like grass *which* groweth up.

6 In the morning it flourisheth, and groweth up; in the evening it is cut down, and withereth. *Men flourish and decay: the meadow grass is not more frail than they. Where are all the ancient generations? Are they not as undiscoverable as the generations yet unborn? Like the grass which grew when Jacob fed his flocks, the people of the past have disappeared.*

7 For we are consumed by thine anger, and by thy wrath are we troubled. (*Not we at this time, but that generation of Israel. We enjoy Jehovah's love, but Israel in the wilderness melted away before the Lord's hot displeasure.*)

8 Thou hast set our iniquities before thee, our secret *sins* in the light of thy countenance. *Glory be to God, as believers, our sins are pardoned, and put behind the Lord's back, but it was not so with that generation. This verse can now only be applied to the ungodly. Are there any such in this household?*

9 For all our days are passed away in thy wrath: we spend our years as' a tale *that is* told. (*Our days are passed in peace, for the Lord has given us rest, but as for Israel in the desert it was sadly the reverse; and upon the ungodly at this day the curse is resting.*)

10 The days of our years *are* threescore years and ten; and if by reason of strength *they be* fourscore years, yet *is* their strength labour and sorrow; for it is soon cut off, and we fly away. (*The very strength of age is sorrow. What then is its weakness? Covet not extreme old age; but know that if it comes God must be our portion, or else life will be a burden.*)

11 Who knoweth the power of thine anger? even according to thy fear, *so is* thy wrath. *May we never know the power of God's anger. The dread of it is awful, but the reality is beyond conception.*

12 So teach *us* to number our days, that we may apply *our* hearts unto wisdom.

13 Return, O LORD, how long? and let it repent thee concerning thy servants? (*Be gracious to those whom thou hast doomed to die.*)

14 O satisfy us early with thy mercy; that we may rejoice and be glad all our days.

15 Make us glad according to the days *wherein* thou hast afflicted us, *and* the years *wherein* we have seen evil. (*Balance our woes with a weight of mercy. Give a joy for every sorrow.*)

16 Let thy work appear unto thy servants, and thy glory unto their children. (*They would accept the toil of the wilderness with cheerfulness because their children would obtain the joys of the promised land. So long as God's church is continued in the world, we who now bear the burden and heat of the day are content to die.*)

17 And let the beauty of the LORD our God be upon us: and establish thou the work of our hands upon us; yea, the work of our hands establish thou it. (*The labour of Moses' lifetime had been very great in building up the Jewish commonwealth, and therefore he is prayerfully anxious that he may not have laboured in vain. Nor was it so, for a great nation was formed, and its mission has been fulfilled, unto this day. Fear not, servants of God, though death should seem to sweep away your life-work: true service for the Lord will outlast the pyramids.*)

124   **"Abstain from all Appearance of Evil."**   MARCH 2.—MORNING.

[*Or May* 1.]

DEUTERONOMY XIV. 1—21.

YE *are* the children of the LORD your God: ye shall not cut yourselves, nor make any baldness between your eyes for the dead.

2 For thou *art* an holy people unto the LORD thy God, and the LORD hath chosen thee to be a peculiar people unto himself, above all the nations that *are* upon the earth.

See how the Lord honoured Israel, he spoke of their election —" *the Lord hath chosen thee;*" *of their* adoption—" *ye are the children of the Lord your God;*" *and of their* sanctification,"—"*thou art an holy people unto the Lord.*" *These honours entailed duties, and among them that of maintaining a distinction from the heathen around them. They were not to imitate the superstition of their neighbours, by disfiguring themselves, or by any act indicative of excessive grief.*

3 ¶ Thou shalt not eat any abominable thing. (*Manifestly disgusting and loathsome.*)

4 These *are* the beasts which ye shall eat: the ox, the sheep, and the goat,

5 The hart, and the roebuck, and the fallow deer, and the wild goat, and the pygarg, *(or antelope,)* and the wild ox, and the chamois.

6 And every beast that parteth the hoof, and cleaveth the cleft into two claws, *and* cheweth the cud among the beasts, that ye shall eat.

7 Nevertheless these ye shall not eat of them that chew the cud, or of them that divide the cloven hoof; *as* the camel, and the hare, and the coney: for they chew the cud, but divide not the hoof; *therefore* they *are* unclean unto you.

Minute distinctions—God takes note of littles.

8 And the swine, because it divideth the hoof, yet cheweth not the cud, it *is* unclean unto you: ye shall not eat of their flesh, nor touch their dead carcase. *(By these regulations the Jews were kept a separate people, for they could not partake in the feasts of the heathen because some one or other of these unclean creatures would be brought to table. Moreover, the thoughtful Israelite would be daily reminded of sin by the presence of unclean creatures. Neither in his labours, his walks, or his rest, could he be long observant without seeing the representatives of uncleanness, and so being reminded of his need to watch against sin.)*

9, 10 These ye shall eat of all that *are* in the waters: all that have fins and scales shall ye eat: And whatsoever hath not fins and scales ye may not eat; it *is* unclean unto you.

Hence, even in their recreations by the river, or voyages at sea, there were tests for their obedience, trials of their faith, and reminders that sin was in the world.

11, 12, 13, 14, 15, 16, 17, 18, 19, 20 Of all clean birds ye shall eat. But these *are they* of which ye shall not eat: the eagle, and the ossifrage, and the ospray, And the glede, and the kite, and the vulture after his kind, And every raven after his kind, And the owl, and the night hawk, and the cuckow, and the hawk after his kind, The little owl, and the great owl, and the swan, And the pelican, and the gier eagle, and the cormorant, And the stork, and the heron after her kind, and the lapwing, and the bat. And every creeping thing that flieth *is* unclean unto you: they shall not be eaten. *But of* all clean fowls ye may eat.

The air too, had its warnings, its things to be avoided. Even thus, in all places we are in danger of defilement. On the land, on the sea, and in the air, there are evils all around. There are snares everywhere.

" Snares tuck thy bed, and snares attend thy board;
" Snares watch thy thoughts, and snares attach thy word;
" Snares in thy quiet, snares in thy commotion;
" Snares in thy diet, snares in thy devotion."

21 ¶ Ye shall not eat *of* any thing that dieth of itself: thou shalt give it unto the stranger that *is* in thy gates, that he may eat it; or thou mayest sell it unto an alien: for thou *art* an holy people unto the LORD thy God. *(Because the blood had not been thoroughly separated from it, and it was ceremonially unclean. They might, however, sell it if foreigners cared to eat it. God requires his people to be more strict than others. Amusements and habits which might be tolerated in worldlings, would be abominable in Christians.)* Thou shalt not seethe a kid in his mother's milk. *(It is unnatural to make the mother yield her milk for the seething of her own young, and God's people are to do nothing which would mar the delicacy and tenderness of their moral feelings. We are to be too sensitive to do anything coarse, brutish, and indelicate. Let young people be mindful of this.)*

NUMBERS XVI. 1—4; 16—24; 26—34.

NOW Korah, the son of Izhar, the son of Kohath, the son of Levi, and Dathan and Abiram, the sons of Eliab, and On, the son of Peleth, sons of Reuben, took *men:*

2 And they rose up before Moses, with certain of the children of Israel, two hundred and fifty princes of the assembly, famous in the congregation, men of renown :

3 And they gathered themselves together against Moses and against Aaron, and said unto them, *Ye take* too much upon you, seeing all the congregation *are* holy, every one of them, and the Lord *is* among them : wherefore then lift ye up yourselves above the congregation of the LORD ? *(Moses gained nothing but trial and trouble by his leadership, and yet there were traitors in the camp who would have raised a rebellion against him.)*

4 And when Moses heard *it,* he fell upon his face :

16 And Moses said unto Korah, Be thou and all thy company before the LORD, thou, and they, and Aaron, to morrow :

17 And take every man his censer, and put incense in them, and bring ye before the LORD every man his censer, two hundred and fifty censers ; thou also, and Aaron, each *of you* his censer. *(This was an appeal to God that he might himself decide who were the authorised priests and leaders.)*

18 And they took every man his censer, and put fire in them, and laid incense thereon, and stood in the door of the tabernacle of the congregation with Moses and Aaron.

19 And Korah gathered all the congregation against them unto the door of the tabernacle of the congregation : and the glory of the LORD appeared unto all the congregation.

20, 21 And the LORD spake unto Moses and unto Aaron, saying, Separate yourselves from among this congregation, that I may consume them in a moment.

22 And they fell upon their faces, and said, O God, the God of the spirits of all flesh, shall one man sin, and wilt thou be wroth with all the congregation ? *(How ready they were to intercede ! How free from any trace of a revengeful spirit !)*

23, 24, 26 ¶ And the LORD spake unto Moses, saying, Speak unto the congregation, saying, Get you up from about the tabernacle of Korah, Dathan, and Abiram. *(If we would escape from the doom of the wicked, we must flee from their company.)* And he spake unto the congregation, saying, Depart, I pray you, from the tents of these wicked men, and touch nothing of their's, lest ye be consumed in all their sins.

27 So they gat· up from the tabernacle of Korah, Dathan, and Abiram, on every side : and Dathan and Abiram came out, and stood in the door of their tents, and their wives, and their sons, and their little children.

28, 29, 30 And Moses said, Hereby ye shall know that the LORD hath sent me to do all these works ; for *I have* not *done them* of mine own mind. · If these men die the common death of all men, or if they be visited after the visitation of all men ; *then* the LORD hath not sent me. But if the LORD make a new thing, and the earth open her mouth, and swallow them up, with all that *appertain* unto them, and they go down quick into the pit ; then ye shall understand that these men have provoked the LORD.

31, 32 ¶ And it came to pass, as he had made an end of speaking all these words, that the ground clave asunder that *was* under them : And the earth opened her mouth, and swallowed them up, and their houses, and all the men that *appertained* unto Korah, and all *their* goods.

33 They, and all that *appertained* to them, went down alive into the pit, and the earth closed upon them : and they perished from among the congregation.

34 And all Israel that *were* round about them fled at the cry of them : for they said, Lest the earth swallow us up *also.*

Thus, by terrible things in righteousness, did the Lord uphold the power of his servants ; how much more will he maintain the throne of his Son. " Kiss the Son, lest he be angry, and ye perish from the way, when his wrath is kindled but a little."

With humble love address the Son,
Lest he grow angry, and ye die ;
His wrath will burn to worlds unknown,
If ye provoke his jealousy.

His storms shall drive you quick to hell ;
He is a God, and ye but dust;
Happy the souls that know him well,
And make his grace their only trust.

126   "𝕺 keep my Soul and deliver me."   MARCH 3.—MORNING.

[Or May 3.]

NUMBERS XVI. 41—50.

BUT on the morrow all the congregation of the children of Israel murmured against Moses and against Aaron, saying, Ye have killed the people of the LORD.

Wonderful audacity! Yesterday they fled in terror while they saw the earth open and swallow up the rebels, and now they, themselves, break out into revolt, and charge Moses with murdering those whom the Lord, himself, so justly executed. Is there any bound to human sin? Lions and tigers may be tamed, but man breaks off from all restraint, and follows his own devices, despite every warning and instruction.

42 And it came to pass, when the congregation was gathered against Moses and against Aaron, that they looked toward the tabernacle of the congregation : and behold, the cloud covered it, and the glory of the LORD appeared.

43 And Moses and Aaron came before the tabernacle of the congregation.

44, 45 And the LORD spake unto Moses, saying, Get you up from among this congregation, that I may consume them as in a moment. And they fell upon their faces. *(This was the second time in which the Lord had spoken thus to his servants, and a second time they fall upon their faces in reverent but earnest intercession. They pleaded for those very people who were up in arms against them ; such is the true love of God's ministers. Never will they give sinners up while they have breath in their bodies.)*

46 ¶ And Moses said unto Aaron, Take a censer, and put fire therein from off the altar, and put on incense, and go quickly unto the congregation, and make an atonement for them : for there is wrath gone out from the LORD ; the plague is begun. *(His spiritual soul could see what others could not, for he perceived that danger was near. Those who have had communion with God possess a sensitiveness unknown to others. Moses bade Aaron hasten, and, indeed when men are dying, we must make no delay in our efforts to save them. Lord, help us to fly on the wings of love.)*

47 And Aaron took as Moses commanded, and ran into the midst of the congregation ; and, behold, the plague was begun among the people : and he put on incense, and made an atonement for the people.

48 And he stood between the dead and the living ; and the plague was stayed. *(He stood as a champion, blocking the pathway of the destroyer. He came to the front of the danger, as though he would either die with the people, or else if he lived, they should live. Was it not bravely and kindly done of Aaron thus to stand in the gap for his enemies? What a noble type he was of the Lord Jesus, who interposed on our behalf!)*

49 Now they that died in the plague were fourteen thousand and seven hundred, beside them that died about the matter of Korah.

Who slew all these? Or rather, what slew them? Was it not sin which is a murderer from the beginning? Sin will slay us also unless we are sheltered behind our great High Priest.

50 And Aaron returned unto Moses unto the door of the tabernacle of the congregation : and the plague was stayed. *(By such a terrible event of judgment, and such a wonderful miracle of mercy connected with Aaron's priesthood, one would think that the question of his right to the sacred office would be settled for ever beyond all dispute, and yet it was not so. How set on mischief sinners are! Sin is ingrained in our very nature. Alas! alas!*

Let us, by faith, see our Lord Jesus standing between his living people and dead souls, waving his censer, and keeping off death from all his believing ones. He is our shield from the destroying plague of sin and all the powers of evil. His sacred person bars the way. Vengeance cannot smite those to whom the Lord's Anointed is a shield. Happy they who have Jesus to stand before them. On one side all is ruin, on the other all is safety. On which side of Jesus are we at this hour? Are we with the living in him, or are we numbered with those who are without him, and consequently are condemned already? Lord save us, or we perish.)

Jesus the merciful and true,
Between the dead and living stand ;
The numerous dead, the living few,
Who now divide this sinful land.

Now in our midst, great Priest, appear,
For sin thou hast atonement made,
Present the incense of thy prayer,
And let the plague of sin be stayed.

TO settle for ever the vexed question as to the priesthood, the Lord arranged a solemn ordeal to which none could object, and which all would admit to be decisive.

NUMBERS XVII. 1—13.

1 And the LORD spake unto Moses, saying,

2 Speak unto the children of Israel, and take of every one of them a rod according to the house of *their* fathers, of all their princes according to the house of their fathers twelve rods : write thou every man's name upon his rod. *(Rods were the ensigns of government, the sceptres of the rulers. To submit the sceptre of each tribe to the Lord was a symbolical presentation of all their claims to him. All the rods were alike dead and dry, and it remained with the Lord to choose which he pleased, and quicken it into life and verdure.)*

3 And thou shalt write Aaron's name upon the rod of Levi : for one rod *shall be* for the head of the house of their fathers.

Owing to the destruction of Korah, the Levites were not divided as to who should be their claimant for office, but unanimous that Aaron should stand for them.

4 And thou shalt lay them up in the tabernacle of the congregation before the testimony, where I will meet with you.

5 And it shall come to pass, *that* the man's rod, whom I shall choose, shall blossom : and I will make to cease from me the murmurings of the children of Israel, whereby they murmur against you. *(God has a right to choose his own servants, and he will do so whether we will agree therewith or not. He gives life and fruitfulness to his chosen servants, and either silences the jealousies and fault-findings of the people, or else visits the murmurers for their offence.)*

6 ¶ And Moses spake unto the children of Israel, and every one of their princes gave him a rod apiece, for each prince one, according to their fathers' houses, *even* twelve rods : and the rod of Aaron *was* among their rods.

7 And Moses laid up the rods before the LORD in the tabernacle of witness.

8 And it came to pass, that on the morrow Moses went into the tabernacle of witness ; and, behold, the rod of Aaron for the house of Levi was budded, and brought forth buds, and bloomed blossoms, and yielded almonds. *(A miracle indeed! Here was not only life, but an instant*

and perfect fruitfulness, not caused by the season, but suddenly brought forth by the divine power! Surely this is the best proof of a divine call to the Lord's work. Naturally barren, as men are, the grace of God makes his ministers fruitful unto God, through abiding in his secret presence, and thus they are known among the Lord's people as the ordained servants of the Lord.)

9 And Moses brought out all the rods from before the LORD unto all the children of Israel : and they looked, and took every man his rod.

10 ¶ And the LORD said unto Moses, Bring Aaron's rod again before the testimony, to be kept for a token against the rebels : and thou shalt quite take away their murmurings from me, that they die not. *(This miraculous proof was meant to prevent future disputes, lest they should provoke God beyond all bearing.)*

11 And Moses did *so :* as the LORD commanded him, so did he. *(Moses was a wise man, but he did not follow his own opinion. His wisdom lay in complete obedience to God.)*

12, 13 And the children of Israel spake unto Moses, saying, Behold, we die, we perish, we all perish. Whosoever cometh any thing near unto the tabernacle of the LORD shall die : shall we be consumed with dying ? *(Not long could they be without some wicked complaint or another. This time they make light of their sin, and cry out against the severity with which their insolence had been repressed. It was time they had found fault with themselves rather than with the just judgments of God ; but, indeed, it is very hard to bring Israel, or any of us, to true repentance.)*

From this whole passage let us learn that Jesus, our great High Priest, has life in himself, and brings forth soul-saving fruit, which neither the law nor the prophets could do—hence he is proved to be the true priest of God. If we also would have life and fruit, we must be vitally united to him, for apart from him we are withered branches only fit for the fire.

Jesus, we own thee priest alone,
Thou only canst for sin atone ;
Thy sacred rod ends all the strife
Thou only hast eternal life.

Nor life nor fruit elsewhere is found,
Death sways his barren sceptre round ;
But thou hast come new life to give,
And, joined to thee, our spirits live.

NUMBERS XX. 1—13.

THEN came the children of Israel, *even* the whole congregation, into the desert of Zin in the first month : and the people abode in Kadesh ; and Miriam died there, and was buried there. *(Here was a great sorrow for Moses. Excepting her one fault in once being jealous of her brother, she was a noble woman—a true princess and prophetess. Moses, no doubt, sorrowed greatly under the bereavement.)*

2 And there was no water for the congregation : and they gathered themselves together against Moses and against Aaron.

3 And the people chode with Moses, and spake, saying, Would God that we had died when our brethren died before the LORD. *They evidently laid the destruction of Korah and his company to heart, and resented it upon Moses, instead of being held in awe by it. While the two holy brothers were yet sorrowing over their departed sister, the unfeeling crowd raised a clamour against them, and laid the deficiency of water at their door ; as if they could be expected to dig rivers in the desert.*

4 And why have ye brought up the congregation of the LORD into this wilderness, that we and our cattle should die there ?

5 And wherefore have ye made us to come up out of Egypt, to bring us in unto this evil place ? it *is* no place of seed, or of figs, or of vines, or of pomegranates ; neither *is* there any water to drink. *(They taunted Moses with the old, worn-out cry that he brought them out to die in the wilderness, and added the new sting—that he had not brought them into the goodly land of promise; though, indeed, it was only their own sin which kept them out of it. Those who want to murmur are never very long without a peg to hang their complaints upon.)*

6 And Moses and Aaron went from the presence of the assembly unto the door of the tabernacle of the congregation, and they fell upon their faces : and the glory of the LORD appeared unto them. *(These holy men knew where their great strength was, they fell down in prayer and adoration, leaving the matter with the Lord, who was not slow in appearing for them.)*

7, 8 And the LORD spake unto Moses, saying, Take the rod, and gather thou the assembly together, thou, and Aaron thy brother, and speak ye unto the rock before their eyes ; and it shall give forth his water, and thou shalt bring forth to them water out of the rock : so thou shalt give the congregation and their beasts drink. *(To show that the Lord is not tied to any one mode of action, the rock is not to be smitten this time, but only spoken to.)*

9 And Moses took the rod from before the LORD, as he commanded him.

10 And Moses and Aaron gathered the congregation together before the rock, and he said unto them, Hear now, ye rebels ; must we fetch you water out of this rock ?

11 And Moses lifted up his hand, and with his rod he smote the rock twice : and the water came out abundantly, and the congregation drank, and their beasts *also*. *Were they not wrong in calling the people rebels, and in saying "must we fetch you water ?" Certainly Moses erred in smiting the rock, for he was bidden to speak to it. The best of men are men at the best.*

12 ¶ And the LORD spake unto Moses and Aaron, Because ye believed me not, to sanctify me in the eyes of the children of Israel, therefore ye shall not bring this congregation into the land which I have given them. *See how jealous the Lord is of those whom he most loves. He will have them obey him in every particular, or else he will chasten them. A whole life of service shall not excuse us for one glaring offence. What manner of persons ought we to be ? How careful should we be in thought, and word, and deed ; and how doubly anxious lest we transgress by unbelief !*

13 This *is* the water of Meribah ; because the children of Israel strove with the LORD, and he was sanctified in them. *(This was one of the most memorable of Israel's sins, because it was a repetition of an old crime, in the face of former mercies and judgments. May the Lord save us from repeating our sins, lest we be made bitterly to smart for them ! Keep us, dear Saviour, that we rebel not against thee.)*

> Rock of Ages, cleft for me,
> Let me hide myself in Thee !
> Let the water and the blood,
> From thy riven side which flow'd,
> Be of sin the double cure,
> Cleanse me from its guilt and power.

LET us read at this time—

PSALM LXXXI.

This song exhorts men to praise the Lord, tells of his goodness to Israel, and bewails the sins and consequent sorrows of that erring people.

1 Sing aloud unto God our strength : make a joyful noise unto the God of Jacob. *(Singing should be hearty and joyful: we should all take our share in the public thanksgiving.)*

2 Take a psalm, and bring hither the timbrel, the pleasant harp with the psaltery.

3 Blow up the trumpet in the new moon, in the time appointed, on our solemn feast day. *By which the passover is intended.*

4 For this *was* a statute for Israel, *and* a law of the God of Jacob.

5 This he ordained in Joseph *for* a testimony, when he went out through the land of Egypt: *where* I heard a language *that* I understood not. *The Egyptian tongue was unknown to the Lord in the sense of having no fellowship with it ; just as we read in the New Testament that the Lord will say to the hypocrite, " I never knew you." In Egypt the Passover was established as a memorial of Israel's redemption, and the freeborn sons of Israel delighted to maintain the commemoration.*

6 I removed his shoulder from the burden : his hands were delivered from the pots. *Or from the earth baskets. God set his people free from the slavish business of brick-making, as he has also redeemed all his people from the accursed bondage of their sins.*

7 Thou calledst in trouble, and I delivered thee ; I answered thee in the secret place of thunder : I proved thee at the waters of Meribah. Selah. *(Poorly did they bear that test. Their murmurings were both deep and loud, and their inconstancy was self-evident. Yet see how, when the Lord was tested by the people, he proved himself to be ready to hear and swift to bless.)*

8 Hear, O my people, and I will testify unto thee : O Israel, if thou wilt hearken unto me ;

9 There shall no strange god be in thee ; neither shalt thou worship any strange god.

10 I *am* the LORD thy God, which brought thee out of the land of Egypt : open thy mouth wide, and I will fill it. *(Have large expectations of God, and offer large prayers to him, then shall great things be your joyful portion. Who would* not ask largely if he believed that his requests would be granted? In the matter of prayer to God if we be stinted, it is by ourselves, for God has not straitened us in his promise. Come then, let those of us who are believers, plead for the salvation of the whole family, the servants, and the neighbours. Let our prayer, during this day, be on a great scale. Men sin hugely—let us pray abundantly.)*

11 But my people would not hearken to my voice ; and Israel would none of me.

12 So I gave them up unto their own hearts' lust : *and* they walked in their own counsels.

13 Oh that my people had hearkened unto me, *and* Israel had walked in my ways ! *See the loving tenderness of the Lord, he laments our sins because he sees what they cost us. He knows what we lose by our folly, and he is sorry for us. Not as a judge does he condemn with tearless eye, but as a father he censures with loving regret in his heart.*

14 I should soon have subdued their enemies, and turned my hand against their adversaries. *God either turns our enemies' hearts, or makes them turn their backs, when he sees his people walking carefully in the " way of obedience." " When a man's ways please the Lord, he maketh even his enemies to be at peace with him."*

15 The haters of the LORD should have submitted themselves unto him : but their time should have endured for ever.

16 He should have fed them also with the finest of the wheat : and with honey out of the rock should I have satisfied thee. *(May we, as a family, walk in continual obedience to the Lord that we may be fed upon the precious promises which are " the finest of the wheat," and may enjoy in close fellowship with Jesus that honey of sweet peace which drops from no other rock but that which was smitten for us. Holiness is happiness—hence obedience to God is true wisdom. Enemies we shall have none to fear, if we dwell in the bosom of Jesus our friend.)*

> Oh how I love thy holy law !
> 'Tis daily my delight ;
> And thence my meditations draw
> Divine advice by night.
>
> Am I a stranger, or at home,
> 'Tis my perpetual feast ;
> Not honey dropping from the comb
> So much allures the taste.

NUMBERS XXI. 4—8.

AND they journeyed from mount Hor by the way of the Red sea, to compass the land of Edom: and the soul of the people was much discouraged because of the way.

At mount Hor, Moses had seen his brother Aaron die, and now, all alone, he has to bear anew the contentions of the people; yet he was not alone, his God was with him. The people were getting weary of tent life, and of the inconveniences of perpetually moving, but they forgot their many mercies, and the great deliverances which the Lord had wrought for them. Fretting, groaning, and complaining are very easy, but they are ungrateful, unholy, and useless habits.

5 And the people spake against God, and against Moses, Wherefore have ye brought us up out of Egypt to die in the wilderness? for *there is* no bread, neither *is there any* water; and our soul loatheth this light bread.

What a weariness it is to read this repetition of the stale complaint! It is always the same old and cruel slander; but each time there is more sin in it, because it is committed against a longer experience of the divine faithfulness. How wretched a thing is discontent—it rails at the bread of heaven, and despises the clear crystal leaping from the rock.

6 And the Lord sent fiery serpents among the people, and they bit the people; and much people of Israel died. *(They acted like serpents in hissing at Moses, and now serpents are sent to punish them. God has many ways of chastising sinners. He who made Moses' rod a serpent, can also use a serpent as his rod to smite Israel. He will sting those who sting his servants.)*

7 ¶ Therefore the people came to Moses, and said, We have sinned, for we have spoken against the LORD, and against thee; pray unto the LORD, that he take away the serpents from us. And Moses prayed for the people.

Admirable meekness. He prays at once for the aggravating people who had been so basely libelling him. They had but to say "pray," and Moses prayed. O! for the like holy readiness to return good for evil.

8 And the LORD said unto Moses, Make thee a fiery serpent, and set it upon a pole: and it shall come to pass, that every one that is bitten, when he looketh upon it shall live.

It was "like curing like," an uplifted serpent heals the mischief wrought by a serpent: by man came death, by man came also the resurrection from the dead. The serpent on the pole was, as it were, executed by hanging on a tree, and so was the more lively type of the Crucified One, who was made a curse for us. A look was demanded of all who were bitten; there was one command for princes and paupers; they must all look, and look in one direction, for no other remedy was provided. It was the duty of Moses to lift up the serpent, but he could do no more, he had no mystic power in his own person to heal the wounded: even thus, ministers are to preach Christ Jesus to us, but they cannot save us, they are as weak as other men in such matters. Our Lord applied to himself the incident before us, we will read his words in—

JOHN III. 14—17.

AND as Moses lifted up the serpent in the wilderness, even so must the Son of man be lifted up:

15 That whosoever believeth in him should not perish, but have eternal life.

16, 17 For God so loved the world, that he gave his only begotten Son, that whosoever believeth in him should not perish, but have everlasting life. For God sent not his Son into the world to condemn the world; but that the world through him might be saved.

We have but to look to Jesus, and whoever we may be, we shall find immediate deliverance from all our sins. One glance of faith brings a present salvation. This gospel is for all mankind, and no man of woman born need hesitate to trust his soul's eternal interests in the hands of the Son of God. Whoever trusts him is and shall be saved.

So did the Hebrew prophet raise
   The brazen serpent high;
The wounded felt immediate ease,
   The camp forbore to die.

"Look upward in the dying hour,
   And live," the prophet cries:
But Christ performs a nobler cure
   When faith lifts up her eyes.

ABOUT *this time happened the defeat of Sihon and Og. Moses thus narrated the matter to the people in his discourse.*

DEUTERONOMY II. 26—37.

26 ¶ And I sent messengers out of the wilderness of Kedemoth unto Sihon king of Heshbon with words of peace, saying,

27, 28 Let me pass through thy land : I will go along by the high way, I will neither turn unto the right hand nor to the left. Thou shalt sell me meat for money, that I may eat; and give me water for money, that I may drink : only I will pass through on my feet;

29 (As the children of Esau which dwell in Seir, and the Moabites which dwell in Ar, did unto me;) until I shall pass over Jordan into the land which the LORD our God giveth us.

Nothing could be more fair or friendly than this request, and Sihon had good evidence that Israel would act in good faith, for though some of the Edomites and Moabites had refused the nation a passage, yet others had granted it, and had suffered no injury, therefore Sihon might have rested sure that Israel would do him no harm.

30 But Sihon king of Heshbon would not let us pass by him : for the LORD thy God hardened his spirit, and made his heart obstinate, that he might deliver him into thy hand, as *appeareth* this day. *(When men are mad with sin they only need leaving to themselves, and they are hardened at once, and being hardened they become their own executioners.)*

31 And the LORD said unto me, Behold, I have begun to give Sihon and his land before thee : begin to possess, that thou mayest inherit his land.

32 Then Sihon came out against us, he and all his people, to fight at Jahaz.

33, 34 And the LORD our God delivered him before us; and we smote him, and his sons, and all his people. And we took all his cities at that time, and utterly destroyed the men, and the women, and the litttle ones, of every city, we left none to remain :

35 Only the cattle we took for a prey unto ourselves, and the spoil of the cities which we took. *(God thus swept away guilty nations, whose sins he could no longer endure. How gracious is he to our sinful isle!)*

36, 37 From Aroer, which *is* by the brink of the river of Arnon, and *from* the city that *is* by the river, even unto Gilead, there was not one city too strong for us : the LORD our God delivered all unto us : Only unto the land of the children of Ammon thou camest not, *nor* unto any place of the river Jabbok, nor unto the cities in the mountains, nor unto whatsoever the LORD our God forbad us. *(If we advance only where God bids us, and forbear where he gives us no leave, our course will be full of prosperity.)*

CHAPTER III. 1—5.

THEN we turned, and went up the way to Bashan : and Og the king of Bashan came out against us, he and all his people, to battle at Edrei. *(One battle over, another begins. Blessed be God, the power which overthrew Sihon, is quite able to cope with Og also.)*

2 And the LORD said unto me, Fear him not : for I will deliver him, and all his people, and his land, into thy hand; and thou shalt do unto him as thou didst unto Sihon king of the Amorites, which dwelt at Heshbon. *(Former mercies are types of coming favours. He who helped us yesterday is the same to-day and for ever.)*

3, 4 So the LORD our God delivered into our hands Og also, the king of Bashan, and all his people : and we smote him until none was left to him remaining. And we took all his cities at that time, there was not a city which we took not from them, threescore cities, all the region of Argob, the kingdom of Og in Bashan.

5 All these cities *were* fenced with high walls, gates, and bars; beside unwalled towns a great many. *(Thus shall God's chosen go from victory to victory. Sin, death, and hell, shall fly before us. None shall be able to resist the divine power which girds us for the battle. Where the Lord leads the van, the enemy's rout is certain and complete.)*

Jesu's tremendous name
Puts all our foes to flight :
Jesus, the meek, the angry Lamb,
A Lion is in fight.

By all hell's host withstood;
We all hell's host o'erthrow;
And conquering them, through Jesu's blood
We still to conquer go.

"No weapon that is formed against thee shall prosper."

NUMBERS XXII. 1—20.

AND the children of Israel set forward, and pitched in the plains of Moab on this side Jordan, *by* Jericho.

2 ¶ And Balak the son of Zippor saw all that Israel had done to the Amorites.

3 And Moab was sore afraid of the people, because they *were* many: and Moab was distressed because of the children of Israel.

Yet they ought to have rejoiced, for the Amorites had been their great enemies, and Israel had put them down: but men who are bent on opposing God's servants are under such an infatuation that they know not their own mercies.

4 And Moab said unto the elders of Midian, Now shall this company lick up all *that are* round about us, as the ox licketh up the grass of the field. And Balak the son of Zippor *was* king of the Moabites at that time.

5 He sent messengers therefore unto Balaam the son of Beor to Pethor, which *is* by the river of the land of the children of his people, to call him, saying, Behold, there is a people come out from Egypt: behold, they cover the face of the earth, and they abide over against me:

6 Come now therefore, I pray thee, curse me this people; for they *are* too mighty for me: peradventure I shall prevail, *that* we may smite them, and *that* I may drive them out of the land: for I wot that he whom thou blessest *is* blessed, and he whom thou cursest is cursed.

Moab hated Israel, but did not come to open fighting at first. Many are the underhanded enemies of Israel, but God will defeat their devices.

7 And the elders of Moab and the elders of Midian departed with the rewards of divination in their hand; and they came unto Balaam, and spake unto him the words of Balak.

8 And he said unto them, Lodge here this night, and I will bring you word again, as the LORD shall speak unto me: and the princes of Moab abode with Balaam.

9 And God came unto Balaam, and said, What men *are* these with thee? *(Probably Balaam was surprised beyond measure that God should actually come to him. He had been a mere magician, but now for awhile the true prophetic spirit filled him.)*

10 And Balaam said unto God, Balak the son of Zippor, king of Moab, hath sent unto me, *saying,*

11 Behold, *there is* a people come out of Egypt, which covereth the face of the earth: come now, curse me them; peradventure I shall be able to overcome them, and drive them out.

12 And God said unto Balaam, Thou shalt not go with them; thou shalt not curse the people: for they *are* blessed. *(What an opportunity for Balaam, if he had but been blessed with grace as well as with the prophetic gift. Here the Lord told him of a blessed people; why did he not cast in his lot with them?)*

13, 14 And Balaam rose up in the morning, and said unto the princes of Balak, Get you into your land: for the LORD refuseth to give me leave to go with you. *(So far so good. Under the pressure of fear Balaam is obedient, but will he hold on?)* And the princes of Moab rose up, and they went unto Balak, and said, Balaam refuseth to come with us.

15, 16, 17 ¶ And Balak sent yet again princes, more, and more honourable than they. And they came to Balaam, and said to him, Thus saith Balak the son of Zippor, Let nothing, I pray thee, hinder thee from coming unto me: For I will promote thee unto very great honour, and I will do whatsoever thou sayest unto me: come therefore, I pray thee, curse me this people. *(Here are larger bribes—how will the prophet act now?)*

18 And Balaam answered and said unto the servants of Balak, If Balak would give me his house full of silver and gold, I cannot go beyond the word of the LORD my God, to do less or more.

19 Now therefore, I pray you, tarry ye also here this night, that I may know what the LORD will say unto me more.

20 And God came unto Balaam at night, and said unto him, If the men come to call thee, rise up, *and* go with them; but yet the word which I shall say unto thee, that shalt thou do.

He wanted to go, for he loved the wages of unrighteousness, and to try him he has a conditional permit to go if the princes come again and press him, but not else. We shall see in our next reading how his evil heart broke this gentle bond. He was a great man, an enlightened man, and for a while a supernaturally endowed man, but a grain of grace would have been of more value to him than all this, and for lack of it he perished miserably. O Lord, give us grace rather than the rarest endowments.

NUMBERS XXII. 21—35.

AND Balaam rose up in the morning, and saddled his ass, and went with the princes of Moab. *(It does not seem that the princes pressed him to go, it would rather appear that they started off before him; they were evidently on before when the angel met him. A covetous man needs no tempting, he is ready for anything.)*

22, 23 And God's anger was kindled because he went: and the angel of the LORD stood in the way for an adversary against him. *(Balaam knew he could not curse Israel, but he shewed his will to do so by going with the men. God was justly angry with such an evil intent.)* Now he was riding upon his ass, and his two servants *were* with him. And the ass saw the angel of the LORD standing in the way, and his sword drawn in his hand: *(Who can be proud of seeing visions since this poor beast saw an angel, and saw it sooner than a prophet?)* and the ass turned aside out of the way, and went into the field: and Balaam smote the ass, to turn her into the way. *(Even an ass pays reverence to the angel of God. What are those who sneer at all divine things?)*

24, 25 But the angel of the LORD stood in a path of the vineyards, a wall *being* on this side, and a wall on that side. And when the ass saw the angel of the LORD, she thrust herself unto the wall, and crushed Balaam's foot against the wall: and he smote her again.

26 And the angel of the LORD went further, and stood in a narrow place, where *was* no way to turn either to the right hand or to the left.

27 And when the ass saw the angel of the LORD, she fell down under Balaam: and Balaam's anger was kindled, and he smote the ass with a staff.

28 And the LORD opened the mouth of the ass, and she said unto Balaam, What have I done unto thee, that thou hast smitten me these three times?

29 And Balaam said unto the ass, Because thou hast mocked me: would I there were a sword in mine hand, for now would I kill thee.

Balaam did not seem to be either surprised or alarmed. He was familiar with supernatural wonders, and was moreover so taken up with the one idea of gaining Balak's reward that he neither feared nor cared. Greed for gold hardens men's

hearts beyond measure; this passion created the monster Judas and others of his class.

30 And the ass said unto Balaam, Am not I thine ass, upon which thou hast ridden ever since *I was* thine unto this day? was I ever wont to do so unto thee? And he said, Nay.

The best comment upon this is to be found in Peter's Second Epistle; "He was rebuked for his iniquity, the dumb ass speaking with man's voice forbad the madness of the prophet." To go with the Moabites to obtain rewards by trying to do what he knew was contrary to God, was utter madness; even a beast was more wise than he, and it was meet that he should be so rebuked.

31 Then the LORD opened the eyes of Balaam, and he saw the angel of the LORD standing in the way, and his sword drawn in his hand: and he bowed down his head, and fell flat on his face.

32 And the angel of the LORD said unto him, Wherefore hast thou smitten thine ass these three times? behold, I went out to withstand thee, because *thy* way is perverse before me:

33 And the ass saw me, and turned from me these three times: unless she had turned from me, surely now also I had slain thee, and saved her alive. *(God takes notice of cruelty to animals, the angel expostulates with Balaam for cruelty to his ass.)*

34 And Balaam said unto the angel of the LORD, I have sinned; for I knew not that thou stoodest in the way against me: now therefore, if it displease thee, I will get me back again.

He yields under pressure, but his heart goes after gain.

35 And the angel of the LORD said unto Balaam, Go with the men: but only the word that I shall speak unto thee, that thou shalt speak. So Balaam went with the princes of Balak. *(Knowing the right, he yet desired to win the rewards of wrong doing, and went as far into opposition of God's will as he dare.)*

From vanity turn off my eyes;
Let no corrupt design,
Nor covetous desires arise
Within this soul of mine.

Make me to walk in Thy commands,
'Tis a delightful road;
Nor let my head, or heart, or hands,
Offend against my God.

BALAK, *anxious to induce Balaam to curse Israel, took him from place to place, and offered one sacrifice after another, but all in vain; the Lord stood between his people and the machinations of their enemies. We will read the inspired record of one of Balaam's oracular speeches—it may serve for all.*

NUMBERS XXIII. 13—24.

13 And Balak said unto him, Come, I pray thee, with me unto another place, from whence thou mayest see them : thou shalt see but the utmost part of them, and shalt not see them all: and curse me them from thence.

The king thought that the number, beauty, and order of Israel might have influenced the prophet, and therefore he would only let him see a part of them. The trick was in vain. God does not love his people because of their number. If there were but two or three he would be quite as sure to bless them.

14 ¶ And he brought him into the field of Zophim, to the top of Pisgah, and built seven altars, and offered a bullock and a ram on *every* altar. *(Moses and Balaam both stood on the same hill, but with very different objects. Places cannot change character.)*

15 And he said unto Balak, Stand here by thy burnt offering, while I meet *the LORD* yonder.

16 And the LORD met Balaam, and put a word in his mouth, and said, Go again unto Balak, and say thus.

17 And when he came to him, behold, he stood by his burnt offering, and the princes of Moab with him. And Balak said unto him, What hath the LORD spoken ? *(An enquiry which we all should raise, and search the Scriptures to find the reply.)*

18 And he took up his parable, and said, Rise up, Balak, and hear; hearken unto me, thou son of Zippor :

19 God *is* not a man, that he should lie ; neither the son of man, that he should repent : hath he said, and shall he not do *it ?* or hath he spoken, and shall he not make it good ?

The immutability of the divine counsel is the safety of the saints. No entreaties of our foes can move the heart of God away from us : we are his chosen, and we shall be so evermore. Every promise is yea and amen in Christ Jesus, and not one single word of the Lord shall ever fall to the ground. Men shift like quicksand, but the Lord is firm as a rock.

20 Behold, I have received *commandment* to bless : and he hath blessed; and I cannot reverse it. *(No, nor all the devils in hell. The promise is not yea and nay, but yea, yea.)*

21 He hath not beheld iniquity in Jacob, neither hath he seen perverseness in Israel : the LORD his God *is* with him, and the shout of a king *is* among them. *(Not such iniquity as to lead him to put them away. Balaam knew that nothing but sin could separate God from Israel, and he saw that by some means or other the Lord had not seen iniquity in his people. We know, what he did not, that a Mediator came between, otherwise Israel's sins had long before been her destruction. No doubt compared with the Moabites and especially the filthy Canaanites, the people in the wilderness were remarkably pure to Balaam's judgment; but it would have fared very ill with them if this had been their only righteousness.)*

22 God brought them out of Egypt; he hath as it were the strength of an unicorn. *(God makes his saints so strong that they astound their adversaries.)*

23 Surely *there is* no enchantment against Jacob, neither *is there* any divination against Israel: *(No plan of men or devils can succeed against the elect of God. We have no cause to fear evil omens, in fact, it would be sinful to do so. It is wicked to feel the superstitious fear of the old heathen. No magical arts, Satanic devices, or malicious plottings can really injure the beloved of the Lord)* according to this time it shall be said of Jacob and of Israel, What hath God wrought!

God's work shall baffle man's, and excite wonder when human malice is forgotten.

24 Behold, the people shall rise up as a great lion, and lift up himself as a young lion: he shall not lie down until he eat *of* the prey, and drink the blood of the slain. *(He foresaw the military prowess of the nation, and foretold the destruction of the Canaanites by Israel, thus in reality blessing the people whom he was invited to curse.)*

Vain were the heathen altars
  The tide of love to stem;
That tongue for ever falters
  That would the saints condemn.

In vain the wrath it mutters,
  For God will never curse;
When he the blessing utters,
  There's no man can reverse.

WE *find a recapitulation of the history of the tribes up to this date in—*

PSALM CVI. 13—33.

13 They soon forgat his works; they waited not for his counsel: (*After seeing the wonders of the Red sea and other displays of divine power, they speedily forget them all. Sinners have short memories.*)

14 But lusted exceedingly in the wilderness, and tempted God in the desert.

15 And he gave them their request; but sent leanness into their soul.

16 They envied Moses also in the camp, *and* Aaron the saint of the LORD.

17 The earth opened and swallowed up Dathan, and covered the company of Abiram.

18 And a fire was kindled in their company; the flame burned up the wicked.

19 They made a calf in Horeb, and worshipped the molten image.

20 Thus they changed their glory into the similitude of an ox that eateth grass.

21 They forgat God their saviour, which had done great things in Egypt;

22 Wondrous works in the land of Ham, *and* terrible things by the Red sea.

23 Therefore he said that he would destroy them, had not Moses his chosen stood before him in the breach, to turn away his wrath, lest he should destroy *them.*

24 Yea, they despised the pleasant land, they believed not his word:

25 But murmured in their tents, *and* hearkened not unto the voice of the LORD.

It was a great sin on their part that they spoke of the heritage which the Lord promised them as either not existing, or not to be won, or as unworthy of all the toils they endured in reaching it. We must not think lightly of our eternal rest, lest we become slack in our efforts to reach the promised inheritance.

26 Therefore he lifted up his hand against them, to overthrow them in the wilderness:

27 To overthrow their seed also among the nations, and to scatter them in the lands.

28 They joined themselves also unto Baalpeor, and ate the sacrifices of the dead.

Although Balaam was unable to curse Israel, he did his worst to injure the nation. Believing that nothing but sin could deprive Israel of the protection *of Jehovah, he advised Balak to seduce the people to mingle in the licentious festivals held in honour of Baal-peor. This horribly cunning advice was followed, the Moabites exhibited great friendliness, their women fascinated the men of Israel, and the people were led to unite in the dances and other orgies associated with the worship of the Moabitish idol. By this foul plot Balaam did the nation the most serious mischief, by bringing upon them the righteous indignation of the Lord.*

29 Thus they provoked *him* to anger with their inventions: and the plague brake in upon them. (*Twenty-four thousand persons perished by this plague, which ceased not until summary vengeance had been executed upon those who had turned aside to the Moabitish idols.*)

30 Then stood up Phinehas, and executed judgment: and *so* the plague was stayed.

Phinehas showed a holy zeal for God, and slew a bold blasphemer, who dared pollute the camp of Israel. Zeal for God, and indignation against sin are highly acceptable to the Lord. On account of the thorough decision of one single individual the plague was withdrawn; this teaches us the great value of holy and fervent spirits in the church.

31 And that was counted unto him for righteousness unto all generations for evermore.

32 They angered *him* also at the waters of strife, so that it went ill with Moses for their sakes:

33 Because they provoked his spirit, so that he spake unadvisedly with his lips. (*He who was the meekest of men spake in anger. We have no perfect example save our Lord Jesus. He was never provoked, and never spake unadvisedly. May the same mind be in us which was in him. The wrath of man worketh not the righteousness of God; may we be delivered from falling into it, however much we may be irritated.*)

Great Shepherd of Thine Israel,
Who didst between the cherubs dwell,
And ledd'st the tribes, thy chosen sheep,
Safe through the desert and the deep:

Thy church is in the desert now;
Shine from on high, and guide us through;
Turn us to thee, thy love restore;
We shall be saved, and sigh no more.

LET *us attentively read a part of Moses'*
last discourse to the people whom he had
so lovingly ruled.

DEUTERONOMY IV. 9—20, 23, 24.

9 Take heed to thyself, and keep thy soul
diligently, lest thou forget the things which
thine eyes have seen, and lest they depart from
thy heart all the days of thy life : but teach
them thy sons, and thy sons' sons; *(If the
Lord condescend to teach, let us not be forgetful
hearers, neither let us neglect to transmit his
teachings to our children.)*

10, 11 *Specially* the day that thou stoodest
before the LORD thy God in Horeb, when the
LORD said unto me, Gather me the people
together, and I will make them hear my words,
that they may learn to fear me all the days that
they shall live upon the earth, and *that* they
may teach their children. And ye came near
and stood under the mountain ; and the mountain burned with fire unto the midst of heaven,
with darkness, clouds, and thick darkness.

12 And the LORD spake unto you out of the
midst of the fire : ye heard the voice of the
words, but saw no similitude ; only *ye heard* a
voice. *(He dwells much upon this because there
was, and is, great need for reminding all men of
it. Symbol worship is the crying sin of the
present age. It were well if all godly persons
gave up wearing crosses, for this reason.)*

13, 14 And he declared unto you his covenant,
which he commanded you to perform, *even* ten
commandments ; and he wrote them upon two
tables of stone. And the LORD commanded
me at that time to teach you statutes and judgments, that ye might do them in the land
whither ye go over to possess it.

15 Take ye therefore good heed unto yourselves ; for ye saw no manner of similitude on
the day *that* the Lord spake unto you in Horeb
out of the midst of the fire :

16 Lest ye corrupt *yourselves*, and make you
a graven image, the similitude of any figure, the
likeness of male or female, *(Men not only dishonour God by worshipping similitudes, but they
also corrupt themselves.)*

17, 18 The likeness of any beast that *is* on
the earth, the likeness of any winged fowl that
flieth in the air, The likeness of any thing that

creepeth on the ground, the likeness of any
fish that *is* in the waters beneath the earth :

19 And lest thou lift up thine eyes unto
heaven, and when thou seest the sun, and the
moon, and the stars, *even* all the host of heaven,
shouldest be driven to worship them, and serve
them, which the LORD thy God hath divided
unto all nations under the whole heaven.

*The list is very comprehensive, and is intended
to embrace every possible similitude, whether it be
the clumsy device of the savage, the artistic gem
of the Papist, or the sublimities of the worshipper
of nature. God alone is to be worshipped, and
as he is pure spirit we ought sacredly to guard
the spirituality of his worship. Away with all
material signs, however venerable, the Lord
abhors them.*

20 But the LORD hath taken you, and brought
you forth out of the iron furnace, *even* out of
Egypt, to be unto him a people of inheritance,
as *ye are* this day. *(Peculiar privileges involve
special responsibilities. He who has done so
much for us must be reverently adored.)*

23 Take heed **unto** yourselves, lest ye forget
the covenant of the LORD your God, which he
made with you, and make you a graven image,
or the likeness of any *thing*, which the LORD
thy God hath forbidden thee. *(Again and
again is the command repeated, and a ban put for
ever upon any attempt to worship God through
any image or likeness.)*

24 For the LORD thy God *is* a consuming
fire, *even* a jealous God. *(He cannot endure sin.
He does not treat it as a trifle, but his holy
anger rises when he sees hearts going aside from
him. He will have all our love or none. Has
he cause to be jealous of us ?*

Unto the Lord, unto the Lord,
Oh, sing a new and joyful song !
Declare His glory, tell abroad
The wonders that to Him belong.

For He is great, for He is great ;
Above all gods His throne is raised ;
He reigns in majesty and state,
In strength and beauty He is praised.

WE *will take another passage from the discourse of Moses*—

DEUTERONOMY VIII. ✓

1 All the commandments which I command thee this day shall ye observe to do, that ye may live, and multiply, and go in and possess the land which the LORD sware unto your fathers. *(Obedience must be given to "all" the commands of God.)*

2, 3 And thou shalt remember all the way which the LORD thy God led thee these forty years in the wilderness, to humble thee, *and* to prove thee, to know what *was* in thine heart, whether thou wouldest keep his commandments, or no. And he humbled thee, and suffered thee to hunger, and fed thee with manna, which thou knewest not, neither did thy fathers know; that he might make thee know that man doth not live by bread only, but by every *word* that proceedeth out of the mouth of the LORD doth man live. *(The end of the Lord's providence is to school us to faith. All too slowly do we learn the lesson. What a sweet series of sentences are those—" humbled thee,and suffered thee to hunger, and fed thee with manna.")*

4 Thy raiment waxed not old upon thee, neither did thy foot swell, these forty years. *How much grace have we received in forty years! What wonders have we seen!*

5, 6 Thou shalt also consider in thine heart, that, as a man chasteneth his son, *so* the LORD thy God chasteneth thee. Therefore thou shalt keep the commandments of the LORD thy God, to walk in his ways, and to fear him.

7, 8, 9 For the LORD thy God bringeth thee into a good land, a land of brooks of water, of fountains and depths that spring out of valleys and hills; A land of wheat, and barley, and vines, and fig trees, and pomegranates; a land of oil olive, and honey; A land wherein thou shalt eat bread without scarceness, thou shalt not lack any *thing* in it; a land whose stones *are* iron, and out of whose hills thou mayest dig brass *(or copper.)*

10, 11, 12, 13, 14 When thou hast eaten and art full, then thou shalt bless the LORD thy God for the good land which he hath given thee. Beware that thou forget not the LORD thy God, in not keeping his commandments, and his judgments, and his statutes, which I command thee this day: Lest *when* thou hast eaten and

art full, and hast built goodly houses, and dwelt *therein;* And *when* thy herds and thy flocks multiply, and thy silver and thy gold is multiplied, and all that thou hast is multiplied; Then thine heart be lifted up, and thou forget the LORD thy God, which brought thee forth out of the land of Egypt, from the house of bondage. *Temptations grow out of prosperity. Has the Lord been very good to this household? let us not be lifted up so as to despise his poor people, or forsake his lowly worship, but the rather let us love our Lord the more.*

15 Who led thee through that great and terrible wilderness, *wherein were* fiery serpents, and scorpions, and drought, where *there was* no water; .who brought thee forth water out of the rock of flint;

16 Who fed thee in the wilderness with manna, which thy fathers knew not, that he might humble thee, and that he might prove thee, to do thee good at thy latter end;

17 And thou say in thine heart, My power and the might of *mine* hand hath gotten me this wealth. *(O for grace to banish far from us all boasting. It is hateful both to God and man.)*

18 But thou shalt remember the LORD thy God: for *it is* he that giveth thee power to get wealth, that he may establish his covenant which he sware unto thy fathers, as *it is* this day.

19 And it shall be, if thou do at all forget the LORD thy God, and walk after other gods, and serve them, and worship them, I testify against you this day that ye shall surely perish.

20 As the nations which the LORD destroyeth before your face, so shall ye perish; because ye would not be obedient unto the voice of the LORD your God. *(Yet were the Lord's grace to be withdrawn, we should surely be disobedient and perish in our sins. Keep us,good Lord; keep us evermore.)*

I knew thee in the land of drought,
    Thy comfort and control,
Thy truth encompass'd me about,
    Thy love refresh'd my soul.

And if thine alter'd hand doth now
    My sky with sunshine fill,
Who amid all so fair as thou?
    Oh let me know thee still:

Still turn to thee in days of light,
    As well as nights of care,
Thou brightest amid all that's bright!
    Thou fairest of the fair!

WE select from the bulk a few of the special laws which the Lord gave to his people. They were all full of instruction, and should be carefully studied.

DEUTERONOMY XXI. 22, 23.

22 ¶ And if a man have committed a sin worthy of death, and he be to be put to death, and thou hang him on a tree:

23 His body shall not remain all night upon the tree, but thou shalt in any wise bury him that day; (for he that is hanged *is* accursed of God;) that thy land be not defiled, which the LORD thy God giveth thee *for* an inheritance.

Pause here, and lovingly adore the Lord Jesus, who submitted for our sakes to the accursed death of the cross. Sin brought a curse upon us, and our blessed Substitute took that curse upon him and bore it in our stead. " He was made a curse for us "—blessed miracle of condescending love !

CHAPTER XXII. 1—12.

THOU shalt not see thy brother's ox or his sheep go astray, and hide thyself from them : thou shalt in any case bring them again unto thy brother.

2 And if thy brother *be* not nigh unto thee, or if thou know him not, then thou shalt bring it unto thine own house, and it shall be with thee until thy brother seek after it, and thou shalt restore it to him again.

3 In like manner shalt thou do with his ass ; and so shalt thou do with his raiment; and with all lost thing of thy brother's, which he hath lost, and thou hast found, shalt thou do likewise : thou mayest not hide thyself.

4 ¶ Thou shalt not see thy brother's ass or his ox fall down by the way, and hide thyself from them : thou shalt surely help him to lift *them* up again. *(All these precepts are involved in loving our neighbour as ourself, but it is very gracious on the Lord's part to point out particulars ; let us be particular in regarding them, and in every way act kindly towards others.)*

5 ¶ The woman shall not wear that which pertaineth unto a man, neither shall a man put on a woman's garment : for all that do so *are* abomination unto the LORD thy God. *(All*

indelicacy is to be shunned. No idea of merriment can excuse that which has a lewd appearance.)

6 ¶ If a bird's nest chance to be before thee in the way in any tree, or on the ground, *whether they be* young ones, or eggs, and the dam sitting upon the young, or upon the eggs, thou shalt not take the dam with the young :

7 *But* thou shalt in any wise let the dam go, and take the young to thee ; that it may be well with thee, and *that* thou mayest prolong *thy* days. *(We must not be devoid of feeling, but act considerately towards the least of God's creatures.)*

8 ¶ When thou buildest a new house, then thou shalt make a battlement for thy roof, that thou bring not blood upon thine house, if any man fall from thence. *(Care of life is a duty, hence cleanliness in person and abode is to be carefully maintained ; and we must not expose ourselves, or others to needless risks.)*

9 ¶ Thou shalt not sow thy vineyard with divers seeds : lest the fruit of thy seed which thou hast sown, and the fruit of thy vineyard, be defiled.

10 ¶ Thou shalt not plow with an ox and an ass together.

11 ¶ Thou shalt not wear a garment of divers sorts, *as* of woollen and linen together.

God would have his people distinct and separate, and therefore he forbids mixtures in sowing, working, and clothing, to remind them of this. We must sow only the pure gospel, work only with gracious motives, and be adorned only in Christ's righteousness. Mixtures are an abomination in religion.

12 ¶ Thou shalt make thee fringes upon the four quarters of thy vesture, wherewith thou coverest *thyself. (This was one of Israel's distinguishing marks : Christians also should be known by their robes of holiness.)*

Through day and darkness, Saviour dear,
Abide with us more nearly near ;
Till on thy face we lift our eyes,
The sun of God's own paradise.

Praise God, our Maker and our Friend ;
Praise him through time, till time shall end ;
Till psalm and song his name adore,
Through heaven's great day of evermore.

WE *shall now read some verses of Moses'
dying song. Like the fabled swan, he
sang himself away—*

DEUTERONOMY XXXII.

1, 2 Give ear, O ye heavens, and I will speak;
and hear, O earth, the words of my mouth.
My doctrine shall drop as the rain, my speech
shall distil as the dew, as the small rain upon
the tender herb, and as the showers upon
the grass. (*Though the law is as a tempest,
yet Moses as the mediator was as the soft,
refreshing, insinuating dew; and far more so is
the Lord Jesus as the dew unto Israel.*)

3, 4 Because I will publish the name of the
LORD: ascribe ye greatness unto our God. *He
is* the Rock, his work *is* perfect: for all his
ways *are* judgment: a God of truth and without iniquity, just and right *is* he.

5, 6 They have corrupted themselves, their
spot *is* not *the spot* of his children: *they are* a
perverse and crooked generation. (*They have
not the marks of saints, the secret, sacred marks
of inward grace by which the heavenly Father
distinguishes his own children.*) Do ye thus
requite the LORD, O foolish people and unwise?
is not he thy father *that* hath bought thee?
hath he not made thee, and established thee?

7, 8, 9 Remember the days of old, consider
the years of many generations: ask thy father,
and he will shew thee; thy elders, and they will
tell thee. When the Most High divided to the
nations their inheritance, when he separated the
sons of Adam, he set the bounds of the people
according to the number of the children of
Israel. For the LORD's portion *is* his people;
Jacob is the lot of his inheritance. (*God is
their portion, and they are* his *portion.*)

10 He found him in a desert land, and in
the waste howling wilderness; (*This is where
the Lord finds us all by nature, but mark his
wise and tender dealings with us;*) he led him
about, he instructed him, he kept him as the
apple of his eye.

11, 12 As an eagle stirreth up her nest, flut-
tereth over her young, spreadeth abroad her
wings, taketh them, beareth them on her wings:
So the LORD alone did lead him, and *there was*
no strange god with him. (*The eagle, when its
young are fit to leave the nest, will not let them*

*remain idle, but disturbs them, entices them to try
their pinions, and even carries them up to teach
them to fly; thus graciously does the Lord train
his people.*)

13, 14, 15 He made him ride on the high
places of the earth, that he might eat the increase
of the fields; and he made him to suck honey
out of the rock, and oil out of the flinty rock;
Butter of kine, and milk of sheep, with fat of
lambs, and rams of the breed of Bashan, and
goats, with the fat of kidneys of wheat; and
thou didst drink the pure blood of the grape.
But Jeshurun waxed fat, and kicked: thou art
waxen fat, thou art grown thick, thou art
covered *with fatness;* then he forsook God
which made him, and lightly esteemed the Rock
of his salvation. (*A sad picture of many professors. They are like lean horses, which at last
come under the care of a kind master, they grow
fat and then they kick, and leap away from the
pasturage. Men increase in riches, and forget
the God who gave them all they have.*)

16 They provoked him to jealousy with
strange *gods*, with abominations provoked they
him to anger.

17 They sacrificed unto devils, not to God;
to gods whom they knew not, to new *gods that*
came newly up, whom your fathers feared not.

18 Of the Rock *that* begat thee thou art
unmindful, and hast forgotten God that formed
thee. (*Never let us forget our God from whom
we derive our being, as the stream finds its fountain in the rock.*)

19 And when the LORD saw *it*, he abhorred
them, because of the provoking of his sons, and
of his daughters. (*The sins of God's own
children are peculiarly provoking to him. He
might endure from strangers what he cannot
tolerate in his own beloved.*)

20 And he said, I will hide my face from
them, I will see what their end *shall be:* for
they *are* a very froward generation, children in
whom *is* no faith. (*Or no steadfastness. The
hiding of God's face is never sent arbitrarily, but
is ever meant to shew us that there is some evil
thing in us which grieves the Lord. How can
he, as our Father, continue to smile upon us if
we do the things which he hates. May we all of
us be very careful to please God in all things.*)

NUMBERS XXXV. 9—16; 19; 22—28.

AND the LORD spake unto Moses, saying, Speak unto the children of Israel, and say unto them, When ye be come over Jordan into the land of Canaan;

11 Then ye shall appoint you cities to be cities of refuge for you; that the slayer may fleę thither, which killeth any person at unawares.

The Israelites, in common with other nations, had among them the institution of blood-revenge, by which the nearest relative was bound to revenge a man's death. To meet the evils connected with this deep-seated custom, places were appointed to which the man-slayer might flee, and be secure till the time came for a fair trial.

12 And they shall be unto you cities for refuge from the avenger; that the manslayer die not, until he stand before the congregation in judgment.

14 Ye shall give three cities on this side Jordan, and three cities shall ye give in the land of Canaan, *which* shall be cities of refuge.

These were chosen on each side of the river, that a refuge might be accessible to every man; even so is Jesus a Saviour freely presented to all who desire him. The roads were repaired, and hand-posts set up to direct fugitives, and thus the gospel is made plain, so that he who runs may read.

15 These six cities shall be a refuge, *both* for the children of Israel, and for the stranger, and for the sojourner among them: that every one that killeth any person unawares may flee thither. *(No sooner had the fearful deed been done than the unhappy manslayer hastened at full speed to the nearest refuge, for the blood-avenger was sure to pursue him and demand life for life. Oh! that sinners would up and away to Jesus, their sole and sure salvation.)*

16 And if he smite him with an instrument of iron, so that he die, he *is* a murderer: the murderer shall surely be put to death.

19 The revenger of blood himself shall slay the murderer: when he meeteth him, he shall slay him. *(God provided no sanctuary for real guilt, murder was not winked at, else had the land become both polluted and unsafe. Mercy to murderers would be cruelty to the innocent. It was accidental or unpremeditated killing which here found shelter. The spiritual fact, however,*

far excels the type, for in Jesus, the real sinner finds pardon and safety.)

22, 23, 24 But if he thrust him suddenly without enmity, or have cast upon him any thing without laying of wait, Or with any stone, wherewith a man may die, seeing *him* not, and cast *it* upon him, that he die, and *was* not his enemy, neither sought his harm: Then the congregation shall judge between the slayer and the revenger of blood according to these judgments:

25 And the congregation shall deliver the slayer out of the hand of the revenger of blood, and the congregation shall restore him to the city of his refuge, whither he was fled: *(There he was safe, no avenging hand could touch him—Fair picture of the security of those who rest in Jesus, the refuge of guilty souls:)* And he shall abide in it unto the death of the high priest, which was anointed with the holy oil.

The death of the high priest brought freedom to the man who had fled for refuge. The instruction here lies upon the surface.

26, 27 But if the slayer shall at any time come without the border of the city of his refuge, whither he was fled; And the revenger of blood find him without the borders of the city of his refuge, and the revenger of blood kill the slayer; he shall not be guilty of blood:

28 Because he should have remained in the city of his refuge until the death of the high priest; but after the death of the high priest the slayer shall return into the land of his possession. *(We are not now under the restraints and conditions which were imposed upon a dweller in a refuge city; for our Great High Priest is dead, we are liberated unconditionally, we have no avenger to fear, but may possess our inheritance in peace. This, however, is only true of believers—are we all such?)*

When God's right arm is bared for war,
And thunders clothe his cloudy car,
Where? Where? Oh where shall man retire
To escape the horror of his ire?

'Tis he, the Lamb, to him we fly,
While the dread tempest passes by:
God sees His Well-Beloved's face,
And spares us in our hiding-place.

DEUTERONOMY XXXIII. 1—3; 6—17.

AND this *is* the blessing, wherewith Moses the man of God blessed the children of Israel before his death. *(They had worried but they had not wearied him. Evil was their recompense, but ardent was his love. He died with a blessing on his lips.)*

2 And he said, The LORD came from Sinai, and rose up from Seir unto them; he shined forth from mount Paran, and he came with ten thousands of saints *(or holy ones)*: from his right hand *went* a fiery law for them.

3 Yea, he loved the people; all his saints *are* in thy hand: and they sat down at thy feet; *every one* shall receive of thy words. *(Love made the Lord reveal himself through Moses; but what shall we say of the divine manifestation in Christ Jesus? Herein is love made perfect!)*

6 ¶ Let Reuben live, and not die; and let *not* his men be few. *(God grant that our little churches may live and become strong.)*

7 ¶ And this *is the blessing* of Judah: and he said, Hear, LORD, the voice of Judah, and bring him unto his people: let his hands be sufficient for him; and be thou an help *to him* from his enemies. *(May the like blessing be upon each believer. Strength sufficient is what we need and all we need; strength to waste would be no blessing.)*

8 ¶ And of Levi he said, *Let* thy Thummim and thy Urim *be* with thy holy one, whom thou didst prove at Massah, *and with* whom thou didst strive at the waters of Meribah; .

9 Who said unto his father and to his mother, I have not seen him; neither did he acknowledge his brethren, nor knew his own children: for they have observed thy word, and kept thy covenant. *(This alludes to the fidelity of the tribe of Levi upon several trying occasions, when they not only held fast to the Lord, but became the executioners of divine vengeance upon their own brethren. Being found faithful, they were entrusted with the sacred ministry.)*

10 They shall teach Jacob thy judgments, and Israel thy law: they shall put incense before thee, and whole burnt sacrifice upon thine altar.

11 Bless, LORD, his substance, and accept the work of his hands: smite through the loins of them that rise against him, and of them that hate him, that they rise not again.

12 *And* of Benjamin he said, The beloved of the LORD shall dwell in safety by him; *and the Lord* shall cover him all the day long, and he shall dwell between his shoulders. *(The Lord was the strength of Benjamin, and graciously placed his power where Benjamin carried his burden—between his shoulders.)*

13 ¶ And of Joseph he said, Blessed of the LORD *be* his land, for the precious things of heaven, for the dew, and for the deep that coucheth beneath, *(that is, for the fountains and springs which arise from the bowels of the earth,)*

14 And for the precious fruits *brought forth* by the sun, and for the precious things put forth by the moon. *(The sun of prosperity and the moon of adversity each produces its choice graces.)*

15 And for the chief things of the ancient mountains, and for the precious things of the lasting hills,

16 And for the precious things of the earth and fulness thereof, and *for* the good will of him that dwelt in the bush: *(This was the crowning mercy. Lord, give us this, and we are well content;)* let the *blessing* come upon the head of Joseph, and upon the top of the head of him *that was* separated from his brethren.

17 His glory *is like* the firstling of his bullock, and his horns *are like* the horns of unicorns: with them he shall push the people together to the ends of the earth: and they *are* the ten thousands of Ephraim, and they *are* the thousands of Manasseh. *(The separated one, though persecuted by his brethren, received the richest blessing and the double inheritance. The more we are set apart for the Lord, the more of blessing shall we receive; and as to the persecution brought on us thereby, we may cheerfully bear it as a light and momentary affliction.)*

The people whom the Lord hath brought
  From Egypt's cruel land,
For whom with wondrous deeds he fought
  Are ever in his hand.

Stronger than death his love is shown;
  Right well he doth defend;
And having freely loved his own
  He'll love them to the end.

DEUTERONOMY XXXIII. 18—29.

AND of Zebulun he said, Rejoice, Zebulun, in thy going out; and, Issachar, in thy tents. *(Here is a blessing for the traveller, and a blessing for the stayer at home. In both cases it is given to the children of God to rejoice, for the Lord is with them. If we go only where we ought, and dwell only where we should, we have the Lord for our companion, and, therefore, may constantly rejoice.)*

19 They shall call the people unto the mountain; there they shall offer sacrifices of righteousness : for they shall suck *of* the abundance of the seas, and *of* treasures hid in the sand.

It is a happy office to call others to worship the Lord, and a happy providence which makes the salt sea and the sandy waste minister to the supply of our needs.

20 ¶ And of Gad he said, Blessed *be* he that enlargeth Gad : he dwelleth as a lion, and teareth the arm with the crown of the head.

21 And he provided the first part for himself, because there, *in* a portion of the lawgiver, *was he* seated ; and he came with the heads of the people, he executed the justice of the LORD, and his judgments with Israel. *(It is a blessing from God to be decided and vigorous in executing the will of the Lord. Too many are weak and undecided.)*

22 ¶ And of Dan he said, Dan *is* a lion's whelp : he shall leap from Bashan.

Strength and courage show themselves in bold enterprises. Dan leaped and increased his territory. We ought to be bold for the Lord Jesus, and enlarge the boundaries of his kingdom.

23 ¶ And of Naphtali he said, O Naphtali, satisfied with favour, and full with the blessing of the LORD : possess thou the west and the south. *(What richer words were ever spoken of mortal men. He has a fulness indeed who is full with the blessing of Jehovah.)*

24 ¶ And of Asher he said, *Let* Asher *be* blessed with children ; let him be acceptable to his brethren, and let him dip his foot in oil.

A sweet prayer for our minister. Let him have thousands of spiritual children, let him furnish the saints with acceptable teaching and edification, and may he practically manifest that he is abundantly anointed of the Lord.

25 Thy shoes *shall be* iron and brass; and as thy days, *so shall* thy strength *be.*

Blessed promise. A rough road needs strong shoes, and they shall be given us ; weary days need plenteous grace, and it shall be afforded us. Our strength shall always be equal to every emergency. Hitherto, the saints of God have proved the promise to be true, and they need not fear that it shall ever fail them. Moses now turns his thoughts to his God, whom he magnifies in glowing language.

26 ¶ *There is* none like unto the God of Jeshurun, *who* rideth upon the heaven in thy help, and in his excellency on the sky.

None in earth or heaven is so good, so ready, and so able to bless his people.

27 The eternal God *is thy* refuge, and underneath *are* the everlasting arms : and he shall thrust out the enemy from before thee ; and shall say, Destroy *them. (Very sweet is that word, "underneath are the everlasting arms,"— they will break our fall, or prevent us from falling ; they will embrace us, give us repose, and finally lift us up to everlasting glory.)*

28 Israel then shall dwell in safety alone. *(God's people must maintain the separated condition if they would be safe:)* the fountain of Jacob *shall be* upon a land of corn and wine ; also his heavens shall drop down dew.

Earth's fountains and heaven's dews both bless the chosen. All things are full of benediction to those whom the Lord sets apart for himself.

29 Happy *art* thou, O Israel : who *is* like unto thee, O people saved by the LORD, the shield of thy help, and who *is* the sword of thy excellency! and thine enemies shall be found liars unto thee ; and thou shalt tread upon their high places. *(As there is none like the Lord, so there are none like his people. They are happy in the present, and secure for the future—since this God is their God for ever and ever.)*

Afflicted soul, to Jesus dear,
Thy Saviour's gracious promise hear ;
His faithful word declares to thee
That, "as thy day, thy strength shall be."

Let not thy heart despond, and say,
How shall I stand the trying day ?
He has engaged, by firm decree,
That, "as thy day, thy strength shall be."

M OSES *was not permitted to cross the Jordan and take possession of the promised land; we will, on this occasion, hear from his own lips the reason of his exclusion. It does not appear to have been announced to him at the time when the sentence was passed upon all those who came out of Egypt, but thirty-eight years after, at the second smiting of the rock.*

DEUTERONOMY I. 34—38.

34 And the LORD heard the voice of your words, *(Not merely the words themselves, but the inner speech of their hearts, which the words did not fully express; the Lord heard the voice of their words,)* and was wroth, and sware, saying,

35 Surely there shall not one of these men of this evil generation see that good land, which I sware to give unto your fathers,

36 Save Caleb the son of Jephunneh; he shall see it, and to him will I give the land that he hath trodden upon, and to his children, because he hath wholly followed the LORD. *God's oath was steadfast, and not one of that generation crossed the Jordan save Caleb and Joshua. The Lord notes and rewards the fidelity of individuals, and screens his faithful ones from many of the judgments which fall upon his erring church. Blessed are they who in all things endeavour to follow their Lord's tracks.*

37 Also the LORD was angry with me for your sakes, saying, Thou also shalt not go in thither. *(Because his example had not, in the case of the smitten rock, tended to sanctify the Lord's name among the people. If we are placed in eminent office, God will not only judge the fault itself, but he will consider the ill effect it may have upon his people.)*

38 *But* Joshua the son of Nun, which standeth before thee, he shall go in thither: encourage him: for he shall cause Israel to inherit it. *Who but a meek man could obey the command? To encourage the man who is to supersede us is hard for flesh and blood, and the more so if that man has for years been our servant.*

DEUTERONOMY III. 23—28.

23, 24 And I besought the LORD at that time, saying, O LORD God, thou hast begun to shew thy servant thy greatness, and thy mighty hand: for what God *is there* in heaven or in earth,

that can do according to thy works, and according to thy might?

25 I pray thee, let me go over, and see the good land that *is* beyond Jordan, that goodly mountain, and Lebanon. *(Moses prayed humbly for a reversal of the sentence which excluded him from Canaan, and he may have felt encouraged to do so because there was no oath against him as against the people. But he who prevailed for others pleaded in vain for himself. His prayer was powerful in argument, and humbly presented, and yet it was denied. It is not everything that a good man asks that God will give, for there are some points in which he shews himself supreme, and bids us cry, " Nevertheless, not as I will, but as thou wilt.")*

26 But the LORD was wroth with me for your sakes, and would not hear me : *(To Jesus only it belongs to be always heard without limit. A Moses may plead in vain—can we wonder if sometimes we are denied?)* and the LORD said unto me, Let it suffice thee; speak no more unto me of this matter.

27 Get thee up into the top of Pisgah, and lift up thine eyes westward, and northward, and southward, and eastward, and behold *it* with thine eyes : for thou shalt not go over this Jordan. *(If we do not have such an issue to our prayers as we expected, we shall nevertheless have an answer of peace. Moses saw Canaan on earth, and as the vision melted away he saw the better land above. He was a great gainer by not having his petition granted him.)*

28 But charge Joshua, and encourage him, and strengthen him: for he shall go over before this people, and he shall cause them to inherit the land which thou shalt see. *(It is very comforting to know that when one good man dies another is ready to take his place. God is never at a loss for a man. His people shall not fail for lack of a leader.)*

Moses beheld the promised land,
    Yet never reach'd the place ;
But Christ shall bring his followers home,
    To see his Father's face.

Of Canaan's land, from Pisgah's top,
    Grant me, my Lord, a view ;
Though Jordan should o'erflow its banks,
    With thee I'll venture through.

144   " 𝔗𝔥𝔦𝔫𝔢 𝔢𝔶𝔢𝔰 𝔰𝔥𝔞𝔩𝔩 𝔟𝔢𝔥𝔬𝔩𝔡 𝔱𝔥𝔢 𝔩𝔞𝔫𝔡 𝔱𝔥𝔞𝔱 𝔦𝔰 𝔟𝔢𝔯𝔶 𝔣𝔞𝔯 𝔬𝔣𝔣."   MARCH 12.—MORNING.

[*Or May* 21.]

DEUTERONOMY XXXIV.

AND Moses went up from the plains of Moab unto the mountain of Nebo, to the top of Pisgah, that *is* over against Jericho. *(Having finished his work and pronounced his last blessing, the prophet cheerfully climbs towards heaven. Death to the saints is an ascent. Alone he pursued his upward pathway, but the Lord was at his side, and thus when earthly companions shall bid us adieu, we shall find the Lord at our right hand.)* And the LORD shewed him all the land of Gilead, unto Dan.

2 And all Naphtali, and the land of Ephraim, and Manasseh, and all the land of Judah, unto the utmost sea,

3 And the south, and the plain of the valley of Jericho, the city of palm trees, unto Zoar. *(No doubt that eagle eye was supernaturally strengthened for its last earthly gaze; and even so have we seen the faculties of dying saints greatly enlarged just as they were departing. They have appeared to see and know more than unaided minds could have perceived. Heaven lay unveiled before them, and the land so far off to us, was very near to the eye of their faith.)*

4 And the LORD said unto him, This is the land which I sware unto Abraham, unto Isaac, and unto Jacob, saying, I will give it unto thy seed: I have caused thee to see *it* with thine eyes, but thou shalt not go over thither.

And truly there was no need that he should cross into the land, for it was full of Canaanites, and it was better for the grand old man to go to the land where the wicked cease from troubling, than to endure the toils of war in his old age.

5 ¶ So Moses the servant of the LORD died there in the land of Moab, according to the word of the LORD. *(Or "at the mouth of the Lord." The Jews say, "with a kiss from the mouth of God.")*

6 And he buried him in a valley in the land of Moab, over against Beth-peor: but no man knoweth of his sepulchre unto this day.

Or else, perhaps, they would have idolised his bones. We need not care to have our burial-place known, for Moses sleeps in forgotten soil.

7 ¶ And Moses *was* an hundred and twenty years old when he died: his eye was not dim, nor his natural force abated. *(When the law is sweetly laid asleep to make room for Jesus, our*

true Joshua, it is not because its eye cannot see sin, or its arm avenge it, but because the Lord, himself, lays it in its honourable repose.)

8 ¶ And the children of Israel wept for Moses in the plains of Moab thirty days: so the days of weeping *and* mourning for Moses were ended. *(The mourning was long, for Moses was a great man, but it was not too long, for there was other work for living men to do.)*

9 ¶ And Joshua the son of Nun was full of the spirit of wisdom; for Moses had laid his hands upon him: and the children of Israel hearkened unto him, and did as the LORD commanded Moses. *(God fitted him for the work, Moses ordained him, and the people chose him, thus Joshua was fully equipped. Men may die, but God's work goes on. When those who seem the most necessary pillars are removed, the temple still stands.)*

10, 11, 12 And there arose not a prophet since in Israel like unto Moses, whom the LORD knew face to face, In all the signs and the wonders, which the LORD sent him to do in the land of Egypt to Pharaoh, and to all his servants, and to all his land, And in all that mighty hand, and in all the great terror which Moses shewed in the sight of all Israel.

All other prophets fall almost as much short of Moses as Jesus goes beyond him. Taking his whole life into consideration, we may pronounce him peerless,—an incomparable man in whom the grace of God brought human nature as near to perfection as we can expect it to be this side eternity. He fell asleep after having been faithful unto death. In this manner, in our own humble sphere, may we be enabled to persevere till we lay down our body and our charge, and cease at once to work and live.

Sweet was the journey to the sky
   The wondrous prophet tried ;
" Climb up the mount," says God, "and die."
   The prophet climb'd and died.

Softly his fainting head he lay
   Upon his Maker's breast ;
His Maker kiss'd his soul away,
   And laid his flesh to rest.

Shew me thy face, and I'll away
   From all inferior things ;
Speak, Lord, and here I quit my clay,
   And stretch my spirit's wings.

HEBREWS III. 1—6. ✓

WHEREFORE, holy brethren, partakers of the heavenly calling, consider the Apostle and High Priest of our profession, Christ Jesus. *(This will be the most profitable subject upon which the mind can fix itself; profitable for instruction, consolation, and example. Our Lord combined in his own person the official characters of Moses and Aaron, and discharged both offices most fully.)*

2 Who was faithful to him that appointed him, as also Moses *was faithful* in all his house. *Having taken the servant's place, he was as faithful as the best of servants could be; nay, he excelled them all.*

3, 4 For this *man* was counted worthy of more glory than Moses, inasmuch as he who hath builded the house hath more honour than the house. For every house is builded by some *man;* but he that built all things *is* God. *Jesus is the builder of the church, Moses was but a pillar in it. Jesus is God, Moses was but man. Yet the Jews greatly reverence Moses; shall we not much more honour and reverence our Lord?*

5 And Moses verily *was* faithful in all his house, as a servant, for a testimony of those things which were to be spoken after;

6 But Christ as a son over his own house; whose house are we, if we hold fast the confidence and the rejoicing of the hope firm unto the end. *The superior relation of Christ to God as a Son, places him far above Moses, and also raises believers far above those who are under the law! We should walk in faith, and rejoice in hope; for only in holding fast both of these can we realize our honourable position as the household of the Son of God. So shall we experimentally know how far the Lord Jesus excels Moses.*

STEPHEN, *in his discourse before his enemies, gives us a few more words concerning Moses, with which we will conclude our consideration of his history.*

ACTS VII. 37—41; 44, 45.

37 This is that Moses, which said unto the children of Israel, A prophet shall the LORD your God raise up unto you of your brethren, like unto me; him shall ye hear.

Like Moses, our Lord was the revealer of a system, a ruler, a deliverer, a mediator, and a teacher. He was mighty both in deeds and words, which combination we find nowhere else. He was rejected by his own people, but accredited by God, and to this day he leads his people through the wilderness towards the promised rest.

38 This is he, that was in the church in the wilderness with the angel which spake to him in the mount Sina, and *with* our fathers : who received the lively oracles to give unto us :

Coming from the living God, the law was a living oracle, though now, through man's sins, it has become a death-dealing word. How honoured was Moses to be the channel of communication between God and his people, and to be the associate of the great covenant angel, who spake the law.

39, 40 To whom our fathers would not obey, but thrust *him* from them, and in their hearts turned back again into Egypt, Saying unto Aaron, Make us gods to go before us : for *as for* this Moses, which brought us out of the land of Egypt, we wot not what is become of him.

41 And they made a calf in those days, and offered sacrifice unto the idol, and rejoiced in the works of their own hands. *(All this we have read before. Shall* we *thus treat the Lord Jesus? Shall we rebel against him and set up other gods? The Lord forbid!)*

44 Our fathers had the tabernacle of witness in the wilderness, as he had appointed, speaking unto Moses, that he should make it according to the fashion that he had seen.

45 Which also our fathers that came after brought in with Jesus *(or rather Joshua),* into the possession of the Gentiles, whom God drave out before the face of our fathers, unto the days of David. *(But though they had all the outward signs, they missed the inward spiritual grace. May the Lord prevent our falling into the same condemnation.)*

Amidst the house of God,
Their different works were done,—
Moses, a faithful servant, stood,
But Christ a faithful Son.

Then to his new commands,
Be strict obedience paid;
O'er all his Father's house he stands
The sovereign and the head.

146   " There shall be a resurrection of the dead."   MARCH 13.—MORNING.

[Or May 23.]

HAVING *seen the great law-giver resign his breath, it may be fitting to note those passages of the Old Testament which declare a belief in the resurrection. The first is the memorable passage from the ancient book of Job—*

JOB XIX. 21—27.

21 Have pity upon me, have pity upon me, O ye my friends ; for the hand of God hath touched me. *(The patriarch was in a very sad condition, and he implored his cruel friends to spare him, seeing he was already sufficiently pressed down by the hand of God. Let us be very gentle with those upon whom God has laid his afflicting hand, and even should they seem to be a little petulant and fretful, let us bear with them, knowing that pain is very hard to suffer.)*

22 Why do ye persecute me as God, and are not satisfied with my flesh ? *(His poor flesh was all a mass of anguish, and yet they annoyed his mind with upbraidings. This mention of his flesh led him to speak of the better lot which he expected for his body, and caused him to utter the following famous confession of faith.)*

23 Oh that my words were now written ! oh that they were printed in a book !

24 That they were graven with an iron pen and lead in the rock for ever !

25 For I know *that* my redeemer liveth, *(Job knew it, and was certain of it—that he had "a kinsman" who still lived, who would redeem his body from its captivity, whatever might come of it),* and *that* he shall stand at the latter *day* upon the earth. *(He foresaw the victorious second advent of Christ as standing in his own proper person upon the earth: his hope of resurrection was based upon that advent.)*

26 And *though* after my skin *worms* destroy this *body*, yet in my flesh shall I see God.

He expected the worms to pierce his skin and devour his flesh, but he believed that it would rise again, that in his flesh he might behold the Lord.

27 Whom I shall see for myself, and mine eyes shall behold, and not another ; *though* my reins be consumed within me. *(He, himself, in his own personality, would look upon the Lord, out of his own eyes, although the most vital parts of his frame and all his flesh would long before have rotted in the tomb. Job is clear as the sun in his testimony.)* *Let us now look to Isaiah—*

ISAIAH XXVI. 19—21.

THY dead *men* shall live, *together with* my dead body shall they arise. *(With Jesus shall we rise.)* Awake and sing, ye that dwell in dust : for thy dew *is as* the dew of herbs, and the earth shall cast out the dead.

20 Come, my people, enter thou into thy chambers, and shut thy doors about thee : hide thyself as it were for a little moment, until the indignation be overpast. *(The grave shall only be a withdrawing-room for the saints' bodies during the tribulations to come.)*

21 For, behold, the LORD cometh out of his place to punish the inhabitants of the earth for their iniquity : the earth also shall disclose her blood, and shall no more cover her slain.

Great troubles have been and yet must be among men. God will punish oppressors, and at the last the dead shall rise from the dust, and convict all tyrants of their murderous crimes. Till then the saints sleep in Jesus, so far as their bodies are concerned. Let us now hear Daniel—

DANIEL XII. 2, 3 ; 13.

AND many of them that sleep in the dust of the earth shall awake, *(This does not refer to the soul which is in heaven, but to the body which alone is in the dust of the earth,)* some to everlasting life, and some to shame *and* everlasting contempt. *(So that both the righteous and the wicked will rise from the grave.)*

3 And they that be wise shall shine as the brightness of the firmament ; and they that turn many to righteousness as the stars for ever and ever. *(May every one of us labour to be of that brilliant company.)*

13 But go thou thy way till the end *be :* for thou shalt rest, and stand in thy lot at the end of the days. *(Cheerfully we will go to our tombs and rest, for our portion is secured till Jesus comes in his Father's glory.)*

Soon, too, my slumbering dust shall hear,
  The trumpet's quickening sound ;
And, by my Saviour's power rebuilt,
  At his right hand be found.

These eyes shall see him in that day,
  The God that died for me ;
And all my rising bones shall say,
  Lord, who is like to thee ?

HAVING *followed the Bible history to the death of Moses, we will make a break, and consider for a day or two a number of passages from various parts of the Holy Scriptures, that our reading may be varied. First, let us solemnly read the narrative of our Lord's crucifixion,—the best comment upon it will be our repentance, faith, and love.*

MARK XV. 16—38.

16 And the soldiers led Jesus away into the hall, called Prætorium ; and they call together the whole band. (*That he might suffer the full chorus of their ridicule. Men were unanimous and hearty in mocking their Redeemer; when will his people be as zealous in his praises? Should not the " whole band" of believers adore him.*)

17, 18, 19 And they clothed him with purple, and platted a crown of thorns, and put it about his *head,* And began to salute him, Hail, King of the Jews ! And they smote him on the head with a reed, and did spit upon him, and bowing *their* knees worshipped him. (*Here was Majesty in misery ! Our Lord who is the angels' king, was spit upon by rude fellows! How we ought to love him for enduring this shame.*)

20 And when they had mocked him, they took off the purple from him, and put his own clothes on him, and led him out to crucify him.

21 And they compel one Simon a Cyrenian, who passed by, coming out of the country, the father of Alexander and Rufus, to bear his cross. *How honoured was this Simon: but let us not envy him ; we shall have a cross to carry too.*

22, 23 And they bring him unto the place Golgotha, which is, being interpreted, The place of a skull. And they gave him to drink wine mingled with myrrh : but he received *it* not. *He did not wish to be stupefied. He came to suffer in our stead, and he intended to go through with it, enduring to the uttermost.*

24 And when they had crucified him, they parted his garments, casting lots upon them, what every man should take.

25 And it was the third hour, and they crucified him. (*Or nine o'clock of our time.*)

26 And the superscription of his accusation was written over, THE KING OF THE JEWS.

> " *A king my title is, prefix'd on high,*
> *Yet by my subjects I'm condemned to die*
> *A servile death, in servile company.*
> *Was ever grief like mine !*"

27, 28 And with him they crucify two thieves ; the one on his right hand, and the other on his left. And the scripture was fulfilled, which saith, And he was numbered with the transgressors. (*He died a felon's death with felons, and men wrote his guiltless name on the roll of transgressors.*)

29, 30, 31, 32 And they that passed by railed on him, wagging their heads, and saying, Ah, thou that destroyest the temple, and buildest *it* in three days, Save thyself, and come down from the cross. Likewise also the chief priests mocking said among themselves with the scribes, He saved others ; himself he cannot save. Let Christ the King of Israel descend now from the cross, that we may see and believe. And they that were crucified with him reviled him. (*O the patience, the omnipotent patience which bore all this !*)

33 And when the sixth hour was come, there was darkness over the whole land until the ninth hour. (*From noon till three in the afternoon night brooded over all.*)

34 And at the ninth hour (*or three o'clock*) Jesus cried with a loud voice, saying, Eloi, Eloi, lama sabachthani? which is, being interpreted, My God, my God, why hast thou forsaken me ?

35, 36 And some of them that stood by, when they heard *it,* said, Behold, he calleth Elias. And one ran and filled a spunge full of vinegar, and put *it* on a reed, and gave him to drink, saying, Let alone ; let us see whether Elias will come to take him down.

37 And Jesus cried with a loud voice, and gave up the ghost. (*He died in full strength, laying down his life voluntarily for our sakes.*)

38 And the veil of the temple was rent in twain from the top to the bottom. (*Thus were the inner mysteries laid bare, and the ceremonials of the law brought to an end. Glory to Thee, thou Dear Redeemer of the souls of men.*)

> To him who suffer'd on the tree,
> Our souls at his soul's price to gain ;
> Blessing and praise and glory be :
> Worthy the Lamb for he was slain.
>
> To him enthroned by filial right,
> All power in heaven and earth proclaim,
> Honour, and majesty, and might :
> Worthy the Lamb, for he was slain.

148   " Unto you that believe He is precious."   MARCH 14.—MORNING

[Or May 25.]

I PETER II. 1—10.

WHEREFORE laying aside all malice, and all guile, and hypocrisies, and envies, and all evil speakings,

2, 3 As newborn babes, desire the sincere *(or unadulterated)* milk of the word, that ye may grow thereby : If so be ye have tasted that the Lord *is* gracious.

That is to say, if we be indeed believers, God has bestowed upon us a spiritual and incorruptible life; therefore, let us have done with the evil fruits of the old nature. We are born into a new world, let us cast aside the defiled and leprous garments of our former condition. Anger, deceit, and slander, are as unbecoming in a Christian as the cerements of the grave would be unfit for a living man. It is ours, henceforth, to live upon the truth and to practise it, to rejoice in a gracious God, and act graciously ourselves. We desire to know the word of God, that by its sustaining power the life within us may be nurtured and made to advance to perfection.

4, 5 To whom coming, *as unto* a living stone, disallowed indeed of men, but chosen of God, *and* precious, Ye also, as lively stones, are built up a spiritual house, an holy priesthood, to offer up spiritual sacrifices, acceptable to God by Jesus Christ.

We desire to be holy because we are so near akin to our Lord Jesus. He is the foundation, and we are the stones of the spiritual building. Men may rail at us, as they did at him, but God has chosen us, and we are precious in his sight, even as Jesus is; hence we desire to live as consecrated persons, in whom God dwells, whose whole business is to present sacrifices unto the Lord. As is the foundation, such should all the building be: upon the living, chosen, precious foundation, there ought to be built up a church of lively, choice, and holy spirits.

6 Wherefore also it is contained in the scripture, Behold, I lay in Sion a chief corner stone, elect, precious: and he that believeth on him shall not be confounded. *(This is good cheer for us who believe in him : let us be bold because of it, and never for a moment hesitate to confess Christ before men.)*

7, 8 Unto you therefore which believe *he is* precious : *(But he does not say how precious.*

This is more than tongue or pen could tell. Verily, the Lord Jesus is all in all, and more than all to his people) but unto them which be disobedient, the stone which the builders disallowed, the same is made the head of the corner, And a stone of stumbling, and a rock of offence, *even to them* which stumble at the word, being disobedient : whereunto also they were appointed. *(It is clear that none can be neutral, we must either feel Jesus to be precious or else we shall stumble at him : and, if we are so disobedient as to be offended at the Lord, our unbelief will not injure him, for God has ordained him to be the headstone of the corner; nor will it disarrange the purposes of God, for in them there is a dark place for the rebel as well as a bright spot for the believer.)*

9 But ye *are* a chosen generation, a royal priesthood, an holy nation, a peculiar people ; that ye should shew forth the praises of him who hath called you out of darkness into his marvellous light : *(As a family, let us remember how the Lord has favoured us in his grace, and let each saved one among us remember whereunto he is called. Chosen, royal, priestly, peculiar, and beloved of heaven,—what manner of persons ought we to be? We ought to be far better than others, for the Lord has dealt so much better with us. May rich grace rest upon us, and cause us to show forth the praises of our God.)*

10 Which in time past *were* not a people, but *are* now the people of God : which had not obtained mercy, but now have obtained mercy.

We were outcast Gentiles, who were counted as little better than dogs: how grateful ought we to be that we now enjoy the same portion as the favoured people of old. Lord, cleanse us from all sin, and make us a family separated to thy service.

Oh might this worthless heart of mine,
  The Saviour's temple be !
Emptied of every love but thine,
  And shut to all but thee !

I long to find thy presence there,
  I long to see thy face ;
Almighty Lord, my heart prepare
  The Saviour to embrace.

EPHESIANS VI. 1—10.

CHILDREN, obey your parents in the Lord: for this is right. *(It is right according to nature, that those who have so long cared for children and nourished them, should be obeyed by them, and it is right also according to the will of God. It is right for the house, which cannot else be kept in order; and right for the children themselves, who will never be happy till they have learned to obey. Yet observe there is a limit—children are to obey "in the Lord," that is to say, so far as the commands of parents are not opposed to the laws of God.)*

2 Honour thy father and mother; which is the first commandment with promise;

3 That it may be well with thee, and thou mayest live long on the earth. *(It has been observed that God frequently prospers those who have shewn a dutiful attention to their parents; at any rate, such children are in the right way, and we all know that the way of duty is the way of safety and happiness. On the other hand, unkindness to parents has often been remarkably punished in this life. Nothing shortens life like rebellion against parents. Absalom is a prominent instance of this general rule. Moreover, this sin is a dreadful sign of a graceless nature. He who does not love and honour his father and mother whom he hath seen, certainly does not love the Lord whom he hath not seen.)*

4 And, ye fathers, provoke not your children to wrath: but bring them up in the nurture and admonition of the Lord. *(Undue harshness, and irritating severity are here forbidden, but holy discipline and religious training are commanded. Wise fathers will take note of this verse; it is not addressed to mothers, because they seldom, if ever, err on the side of severity. Fathers must not be ill-humoured and morose to their sons and daughters, nor must they exact from them more service than they can render, nor ridicule them, nor shew partiality to one above another, nor stint them in necessaries, for this is to provoke them to anger.)*

5 Servants, be obedient to them that are *your* masters according to the flesh, with fear and trembling, *(or with diffident anxiety and self-distrust)* in singleness of your heart, as unto Christ;

6 Not with eyeservice, as menpleasers; but as the servants of Christ, doing the will of God from the heart. *(Those who need looking after are but poor servants. True Christians care more for God's eye than their master's or mistress's observation, and they do their duty as well alone as they would with all eyes upon them. It is a mean thing to be diligent only when one is watched; it is a vice only fit for slaves.)*

7, 8 With good will doing service, as to the Lord, and not to men: Knowing that whatsoever good thing any man doeth, the same shall he receive of the Lord, whether *he be* bond or free.

Beautifully does George Herbert put it—

> " All may of thee partake:
> Nothing can be so mean,
> Which with this tincture (for thy sake),
> Will not grow bright and clean.
>
> A servant with this cause,
> Makes drudgery divine:
> Who sweeps a room, as for thy laws,
> Makes that and th' action fine."

9 And, ye masters, do the same things unto them, forbearing threatening; knowing that your Master also is in heaven; neither is there respect of persons with him.

Masters are not to use a continual fault-finding and threatening tone, but to act towards servants as Jesus, their Master, has acted towards them. The Apostle does not speak against the various distinctions of society, but he would have us act rightly in them. May our household always be a happy one, because each one seeks the happiness of the rest, and does so by keeping his own place, and behaving towards others in the spirit of love.

10 Finally, my brethren, be strong in the Lord, and in the power of his might.

Happy the home where Jesus' name
Is sweet to every ear;
Where children early lisp his fame,
And parents hold him dear.

Lord, let us in this home agree,
That thou alone shalt reign,
For those who love and worship thee,
In joyous peace remain.

WE *will now read a part of Psalm cxix, that longest of the Psalms, which Luther professed to prize so highly that he would not take the whole world in exchange for one leaf of it. Bishop Cowper called it "a Holy Alphabet." Philip Henry recommended his children to take a verse of it every morning "and meditate upon it, and so go over the Psalm twice in a year, and that will bring you to be in love with all the rest of Scripture." May such an excellent result follow our reading.*

PSALM CXIX. 1—16.

1 Blessed *are* the undefiled in the way, who walk in the law of the LORD.

Men defile themselves with sin: the only clean walking is in the path of obedience. Such holy walkers enjoy a blessedness which neither wealth nor rank could bestow upon them. This Psalm, like the Sermon on the Mount, begins with benedictions. Our holy religion teems with blessings.

2 Blessed *are* they that keep his testimonies, *and that* seek him with the whole heart.

3 They also do no iniquity: they walk in his ways. *(Where the whole heart loves the testimonies of God, the whole life will be sanctified, and no habit of evil will be tolerated. Yet even those who keep his testimonies, have still need to seek him more and more. They are perfect in intention, but absolute perfection they have not attained.)*

4 Thou hast commanded *us* to keep thy precepts diligently.

5 O that my ways were directed to keep thy statutes! *(What a mercy when God's precept and our prayer tally so well. These two verses show us that what God would have his people to be, they also desire to be. He works in them to will, and then they will do his will.)*

6 Then shall I not be ashamed, when I have respect unto all thy commandments.

True obedience does not pick and choose, but delights in all the statutes of the Lord. If we begin to set aside one of the precepts, where shall we stop? The only way by which a man can fearlessly defend his profession against all accusers, is by rendering a sincere obedience to all the commands of God. What need there is of grace for all this.

7 I will praise thee with uprightness of heart, when I shall have learned thy righteous judgments. *(God's worship should be the product of*

all our learning. Prayer is the helper of study, but praise should be the object and result of it.)

8 I will keep thy statutes: O forsake me not utterly. *(The resolve is good, but it needs the prayer to accompany it. The last sentence should be on our lips every day. What a calamity it would be to be deserted of the Lord!)*

9 Wherewithal shall a young man cleanse his way? by taking heed *thereto* according to thy word. *(This verse contains a weighty question and a satisfactory answer: let all young people lay both of them to heart. Grace in the heart is the young man's best life insurance.)*

10 With my whole heart have I sought thee: O let me not wander from thy commandments.

Those who are most fervent in religion are the most afraid of failing in it. Their anxiety is wise. However good our intentions may be, we cannot preserve ourselves from sin. The most ardent seeker will soon become a wanton wanderer unless the grace of God prevent.

11 Thy word have I hid in mine heart, that I might not sin against thee. *(The best thing in the best place, for the best of purposes. Can all in this family say what David here declares.)*

12 Blessed *art* thou, O LORD: teach me thy statutes. *(He gives God glory, and asks God to give him grace. Prayers and praises make a sweet mixture.)*

13 With my lips have I declared all the judgments of thy mouth. *(Those who can speak should speak. Eloquent tongues should never be idle.)*

14 I have rejoiced in the way of thy testimonies, as *much as* in all riches. *(In the last verse he says that he had edified others, and in this he rejoices that he had entertained himself.)*

15, 16 I will meditate in thy precepts, and have respect unto thy ways. I will delight myself in thy statutes: I will not forget thy word. *(What the heart delights in, the memory retains. A warm heart forgets not the Lord's word. Is our heart warm?)*

Charged we are, with earnest care,
To observe thy precepts, Lord;
O that all my actions were
Ruled and guided by thy word!

Then shall I from shame be freed,
Joy and peace my heart shall fill,
When I mark with reverent heed,
Every dictate of thy will.

PROVERBS XXVI. 1—16. ✓

A S snow in summer, and as rain in harvest,
so honour is not seemly for a fool.
*It is out of place, and does mischief. If then
we would be honoured, we must pray against
being foolish or wicked.*

2 As the bird by wandering, as the swallow
by flying, so the curse causeless shall not come.
*It flies about harmlessly and does nobody any
hurt, except the man who uttered it. If we are
evil spoken of for doing our duty, we need not
mind, it will not harm us any more than the
flying of a swallow over our head.*

3 A whip for the horse, a bridle for the ass,
and a rod for the fool's back. *(Follies bring us
smarts. If we would be happy, God must make
us wise: but if we will be foolish, the rod must
be our portion.)*

4 Answer not a fool according to his folly,
lest thou also be like unto him.

5 Answer a fool according to his folly, lest
he be wise in his own conceit. *(The two texts
are for two different occasions and persons. One
will be best at one time, and one at another.
Some men it is best to ridicule that they may see
their folly and amend, but others would only be
provoked by our speech, and therefore it is better
to remain silent. Wisdom will direct us which
course to pursue.)*

6 He that sendeth a message by the hand of
a fool cutteth off the feet, *and* drinketh damage.
*Nothing but loss comes from trusting vain
persons.*

7 The legs of the lame are not equal : so *is*
a parable in the mouth of fools. *(He shows his
folly when he endeavours to talk wisely, just as
the cripple displays his deformity when. he tries
to dance. His speech is not consistent, and his
discourse limps like a cripple in walking. May
true religion make all of us wise.)*

8 As he that bindeth a stone in a sling, so *is*
he that giveth honour to a fool. *(He puts a
a worthless person into a place where he can do
great damage, and where he is not likely long to
remain. Every sinner is like a stone in a sling,
and his soul will be slung out by the hand of
God, far off from his present rest and comfort.)*

9 *As* a thorn goeth up into the hand of a
drunkard, so *is* a parable in the mouth of fools.

*They had better let it alone—they only hurt
themselves, like drunken men playing with thorn
bushes. Foolish persons are sure to expose themselves if they attempt a parable, if there be any
point in it they run it into themselves before long.
Out of their own mouths are they condemned.*

10 The great *God* that formed all *things* both
rewardeth the fool, and rewardeth transgressors.
*But what terrible rewards he gives them. Lord,
save us from such.*

11 As a dog returneth to his vomit, *so* a fool
returneth to his folly. *(Sin is ingrained in
human nature, and if you draw a man aside
from it for a time, yet he naturally flies back to
it. The dog must be changed into a lamb, and
then he will not return to his former delight;
and if fools be born again from above, they will
love sin no longer.)*

12 Seest thou a man wise in his own conceit ?
there is more hope of a fool than of him. *(The
fool may learn, but the conceited man will not.
There is more hope of a sinful Publican than of
a self-righteous Pharisee.)*

13 The slothful *man* saith, There *is* a lion in
the way ; a lion *is* in the streets. *(He invents
bugbears to excuse his idleness. Any falsehood
will serve as an apology for his laziness. How
doubly wicked this is ; but a lazy person is capable
of anything.)*

14 *As* the door turneth upon his hinges, so
doth the slothful upon his bed.

15 The slothful hideth his hand in *his* bosom ;
it grieveth him to bring it again to his mouth.

16 The sluggard *is* wiser in his own conceit
than seven men that can render a reason.
*He does nothing, but considers himself a great
genius. Being always half asleep he dreams that
he is wise, but it is only a dream. Above all
things, let us avoid conceited idleness. Let us
labour with all our might, and ever cultivate a
humble spirit.*

We for whom God the Son came down,
And laboured for our good,
How careless to secure the crown
He purchased with his blood.

Lord, shall we lie so sluggish still
And never act our parts ?
Come Holy Dove with sacred fire,
Inflame our frozen hearts.

WE *will continue to read from the wise sayings of Solomon, and complete the chapter which we commenced.*

PROVERBS XXVI. 17—28.

17 He that passeth by, *and* meddleth with strife *belonging* not to him, *is like* one that taketh a dog by the ears. *(He may expect to be bitten and he is not likely to get any good. He has done a very needless and absurd thing, and he will get nobody's thanks for his pains. It is honourable to suffer as a Christian, but disgraceful to smart for being a busy-body. Blessed are the peace makers, but very far from blessed are the meddlers.)*

18 As a mad *man* who casteth firebrands, arrows, and death,

19 So *is* the man *that* deceiveth his neighbour, and saith, Am not I in sport? *(To sin in jest is often to do mischief in earnest, and it will be punished in earnest at the last great day.)*

20 Where no wood is, *there* the fire goeth out: so where *there is* no talebearer, the strife ceaseth. *(Do not talk about it and it will die out. No hurt ever comes from holding our tongues; silly tattling causes much sorrow. If we will not reply, those who slander us will 'tire of their dirty work, or will be powerless for mischief. Evil speaking seldom injures those who take no notice of it. Do not find fagots for your own burning. Let the talebearers alone, and their fire will go out for want of fuel.)*

21 As coals are to burning coals, and wood to fire; so is a contentious man to kindle strife. *Wherever he is, quarrelling begins, or being already commenced, it is fanned to a fiercer flame. He is a stoker for Satan's fires. Let us never grow like him.*

22 The words of a talebearer *are* as wounds, and they go down into the innermost parts of the belly. *(They are deadly stabs, which have sent many to their graves with broken hearts.)*

23 Burning lips and a wicked heart *are like* a potsherd covered with silver dross. *There is a film of fair speech like a coating of silver, but underneath is deceit. They appear to glow with love, but in very truth malice is smouldering in their souls. Lord, save us from lying lips and malicious hearts.*

24 He that hateth dissembleth with his lips, and layeth up deceit within him. *(He is brooding mischief, and storing up revenge, yet he speaks fairly. He hangs out the sign of the angel, but the devil keeps his house.)*

25 When he speaketh fair, believe him not: for *there are* seven abominations in his heart. *All kinds of evils lurk in a dissembler's soul. The man's heart is a hell, full of evil spirits, the forge of Satan, the workshop of all mischief. Whenever any one flatters us, let us fly from him at once, and avoid him for the future. He would not spin so fine a web if he did not wish to catch a fly.*

26 *Whose* hatred is covered by deceit, his wickedness shall be shewed before the *whole* congregation. *(If not in this world, yet certainly in the next, all secrets will be revealed to the shame of those who acted the part of the hypocrite. Even in this life masks are very apt to drop off. Clever counterfeits fail in some point or other, and are found out: dissembling is a difficult game, and the players are sure to be the losers, sooner or later.)*

27 Whoso diggeth a pit shall fall therein: and he that rolleth a stone, it will return upon him. *(Often do we observe the law of providential retaliation at work. If any of us try to injure another, we only hurt ourselves: God will make all our ill thoughts to return to us, like birds which come home to roost. O for a loving spirit which seeks the good of all.)*

28 A lying tongue hateth *those that are* afflicted by it; and a flattering mouth worketh ruin. *(It is the nature of ill will to hate those whom it injures. Hurt another and you will dislike him, benefit him and you will love him. Above all things abhor flattery, for he who uses this detestable art is surely plotting your overthrow. Young people should learn this lesson early, or their ignorance may cost them dear.)*

Oh, tame my tongue to peace,
And tune my heart to love;
From all reproaches may I cease,
Made harmless as a dove.

Faithful, but meekly kind;
Gentle, yet boldly true;
I would possess the perfect mind
Which in my Lord I view.

ISAIAH LV.

HO, every one that thirsteth, come ye to the waters, and he that hath no money; come ye, buy, and eat; yea, come, buy wine and milk without money and without price.

With matchless condescension the Lord invites us to come to himself. He presses upon us the calls of his mercy. The gospel provides for all our spiritual needs in the amplest manner, and it gives us everything for nothing. We have but to receive freely what God gives gratis.

2 Wherefore do ye spend money for *that which is* not bread? and your labour for *that which* satisfieth not? hearken diligently unto me, and eat ye *that which is* good, and let your soul delight itself in fatness. *(Why do men labour after salvation by their own efforts, when Jesus has finished the work? Why do they try to find a heaven in things below when Christ is all? They gather smoke, and hunt after shadows. Why are they so foolish?)*

3 Incline your ear, and come unto me : hear, and your soul shall live; and I will make an everlasting covenant with you, *even* the sure mercies of David. *(By hearing we receive grace, for by it faith comes. A willing ear leads to a converted mind. Salvation is by covenant—God enters into covenant with sinners through Christ Jesus; and that covenant is everlasting and sure. What an honour and a favour to be in covenant with God.)*

4 Behold, I have given him *for* a witness to the people, a leader and commander to the people. *(Jesus is here set forth as the great witness of divine love, who is able and willing to lead men back to God.)*

5 Behold, thou shalt call a nation *that* thou knowest not, and nations *that* knew not thee shall run unto thee because of the Lord thy God, and for the Holy One of Israel; for he hath glorified thee. *(This is doubtless a promise to Jesus, the Messiah. Tens of thousands shall gladly accept him as their Lord.)*

6 ¶ Seek ye the Lord while he may be found, call ye upon him while he is near :

While mercy may be had, seek for it in prayer.

7 Let the wicked forsake his way, and the unrighteous man his thoughts : and let him return unto the Lord, and he will have mercy upon him; and to our God, for he will abundantly pardon.

8 ¶ For my thoughts *are* not your thoughts, neither *are* your ways my ways, saith the Lord.

9 For *as* the heavens are higher than the earth, so are my ways higher than your ways, and my thoughts than your thoughts. *(What a large and free promise! Can any man desire more? Mercy is freely proclaimed for the guilty, and that for the worst and most glaring of transgressions. Do not let us miss the gracious opportunity, but come at once, and receive pardon as the free gift of God. He speaks to each one of us as much as he did to Israel of old.)*

10 For as the rain cometh down, and the snow from heaven, and returneth not thither, but watereth the earth, and maketh it bring forth and bud, that it may give seed to the sower, and bread to the eater :

11 So shall my word be that goeth forth out of my mouth : it shall not return unto me void, but it shall accomplish that which I please, and it shall prosper *in the thing* whereto I sent it.

So we are invited to trust in an effectual gospel which can by no means fall to the ground. We have no cunningly devised fable put before us, but the infallible truth of God who cannot lie. All things else may fail, but the promise of God will be fulfilled as surely as God is God.

12 For ye shall go out with joy, and be led forth with peace : the mountains and the hills shall break forth before you into singing, and all the trees of the field shall clap *their* hands.

13 Instead of the thorn shall come up the fir tree, and instead of the brier shall come up the myrtle tree : and it shall be to the Lord for a name, for an everlasting sign *that* shall not be cut off. *(All joy belongs to the pardoned, and all nature is in sympathy with that joy. The outward echoes the inward. When the soul is eased of its burden, and drinks in the bliss of divine love, earth seems a paradise of sweets, and a temple of rich music. To the wretched the universe is hung in sable, but to the joyous the day is clear and bright, " the bridal of the earth and sky." Who would not be forgiven? Who would not live by the covenant of grace when such are the joy and peace which he will inherit? The joy is no transient emotion, it is based upon "everlasting" love and faithfulness, and this renders it infinitely precious and desirable.)*

154   "𝕷𝖔𝖇𝖊 𝖔𝖓𝖊 𝖆𝖓𝖔𝖙𝖍𝖊𝖗, 𝖆𝖘 𝕴 𝖍𝖆𝖇𝖊 𝖑𝖔𝖇𝖊𝖉 𝖞𝖔𝖚."   MARCH 17.—MORNING.

[*Or* May 31.]

JOHN XV. 1—15. ✓

I AM the true vine, and my Father is the husbandman. *(See how the question is solved as to which is the true Church, and who has care of it. In Jesus, and all who are vitally joined to him, we find the only true Church, and in our heavenly Father, the great overseer and purifier of it.)*

2 Every branch in me that beareth not fruit he taketh away : and every *branch* that beareth fruit, he purgeth it, that it may bring forth more fruit. *(Fruitless branches must come away, for the very mark of a living branch is fruit. The dead wood of mere profession, being worthless and pernicious, must be pruned out.)*

3 Now ye are clean *(or purged)* through the word which I have spoken unto you.

4 Abide in me, and I in you. As the branch cannot bear fruit of itself, except it abide in the vine ; no more can ye, except ye abide in me. *(Do what we may, we can bring forth no truly good thing except in union with our Lord : our strength, our fruitfulness, yea, and our very life, all lie in Him.)*

5 I am the vine, ye *are* the branches ; He that abideth in me, and I in him, the same bringeth forth much fruit : for without me ye can do nothing. *(Nothing! mark the word. He does not say "only a little," but nothing.)*

6 If a man abide not in me, he is cast forth as a branch, and is withered ; and men gather them, and cast *them* into the fire, and they are burned. *(There is the end of the man who is fruitless ; because not vitally united to Jesus, he utterly perishes. What a change,—numbered one day with the branches of the true vine, and the next, burning in the fire.)*

7 If ye abide in me, and my words abide in you, ye shall ask what ye will, and it shall be done unto you. *(Power in prayer depends upon union with Jesus, and obedience to his will.)*

8 Herein is my Father glorified, that ye bear much fruit ; so shall ye be my disciples.

9 As the Father hath loved me, so have I loved you : continue ye in my love.
One of the most sublime verses in Holy Scripture. The Father loves the Son without beginning, without change, without measure, and without end—and even thus does Jesus love us.

10 If ye keep my commandments, ye shall abide in my love ; even as I have kept my Father's commandments, and abide in his love.

11 These things have I spoken unto you, that my joy might remain in you, and *that* your joy might be full. *(Christ's own joy in us ! Think of that. Here is enough to fill us with joy to running over.)*

12 This is my commandment, That ye love one another, as I have loved you. *(Here is love's law—her diamond rule.)*

13 Greater love hath no man than this, that a man lay down his life for his friends. *(Here is love's fairest model. Note it well.)*

14 Ye are my friends, if ye do whatsoever I command you. *(Here is love's life, and love's reward. Obedience to Jesus leads to a sense of the love of Jesus. If we walk after his rule he will walk with us.)*

15 Henceforth I call you not servants ; for the servant knoweth not what his lord doeth : but I have called you friends ; for all things that I have heard of my Father I have made known unto you. *(We are made his table-companions, for we sit at the Communion feast, and there are no secrets between us, for he tells us all that is in his heart. This is love indeed, which lifts poor worms of the dust into friendship with " the Prince of the kings of the earth.")*

Quicken'd by thee, and kept alive,
   I flourish and bear fruit ;
My life I from thy sap derive,
   My vigour from thy root.

I can do nothing without thee ;
   My strength is wholly thine :
Wither'd and barren should I be,
   If sever'd from the vine.

Come just as ye are, for Jesus invites
Poor sinners to share substantial delights :
Ye weary and burden'd who happy would be,
And wish to be pardon'd, come listen to me.

The ear of your heart if you will incline
To you I'll impart my fulness divine,
Your souls by my Spirit made meet for the sky,
The life shall inherit which never shall die.

JOHN XV. 16—27.

YE have not chosen me, but I have chosen you, and ordained you, that ye should go and bring forth fruit, and *that* your fruit should remain : that whatsoever ye shall ask of the Father in my name, he may give it you. *The great first cause of our salvation is not our choice of the Lord Jesus, but his choice of us. The election of his people is with him. He takes the first step towards us. He has, however, chosen us not to be idlers, but fruit-bearers, not to be occasional workers, but persevering labourers. He has also chosen us to be men of prayer ; and he would not have us formal worshippers but prevalent pleaders. Have the objects of the Lord's choice been realised in us ? How can we know our election except by fruits of holiness, and answers to prayer ?*

17 These things I command you, that ye love one another. *(This command comes often, but never too often. We need to hear it again and again.)*

18 If the world hate you, ye know that it hated me before *it hated* you. *(Therefore there is nothing to wonder at when men slander and abuse us; it is their ordinary manner of saluting every vessel which bears our great Captain's flag.)*

19 If ye were of the world, the world would love his own : but because ye are not of the world, but I have chosen you out of the world, therefore the world hateth you. *(Election secures us human hatred as well as divine love, but for the sake of the sweet, we joyfully accept the bitter. What we have most to dread is the smile of the world, for many have been fascinated by it and fallen into destruction.)*

20 Remember the word that I said unto you, The servant is not greater than his lord. If they have persecuted me, they will also persecute you ; if they have kept my saying, they will keep your's also.

21 But all these things will they do unto you for my name's sake, because they know not him that sent me. *(Let us not reckon upon easy times. We are servants of a Master who lived amid reproach and died upon a cross. How can we expect those who crowned Him with thorns to crown us with roses ?)*

22 If I had not come and spoken unto them, they had not had sin : but now they have no cloke for their sin. *(Light when rejected increases sin. No apology remains for a man when his ignorance is removed. He who has had Jesus for his teacher and yet refuses to learn, is guilty of wilful ignorance, and deserves the severest judgment.)*

23 He that hateth me hateth my Father also. *An opponent of Christianity cannot, therefore, be a sincere worshipper of God. A pure Theist in a country where the Gospel is preached, is an impossibility.*

24 If I had not done among them the works which none other man did, they had not had sin : but now have they both seen and hated both me and my Father. *(Our Lord's miracles proved his mission, and rendered Israel's rejection of him a most wanton rebellion against the light. So greatly did their sinning against the light add to their sin, that comparatively speaking, their sins were nothing till their conscience being enlightened, they were able to sin with an emphasis.)*

25 But *this cometh to pass*, that the word might be fulfilled that is written in their law, They hated me without a cause.

26 But when the Comforter is come, whom I will send unto you from the Father, *even* the Spirit of truth, which proceedeth from the Father, he shall testify of me : *(This is the Holy Spirit's great work. What sweet witness does he bear in his people's hearts ! Do we know the power of that inward testimony ? Let us examine ourselves upon this matter, as in the sight of God.)*

27 And ye also shall bear witness, because ye have been with me from the beginning. *Yes, and we too, when the Holy Spirit has witnessed in us, may become witnesses to others concerning the Lord Jesus. But we must be with him to know him, and we must know him before we can witness concerning him.*

My precious Lord, for thy dear name
I bear the cross, despise the shame ;
Nor do I faint while thou art near ;
I lean on thee ; how can I fear ?

No other name but thine is given
To cheer my soul in earth or heaven ;
No other wealth will I require ;
No other friend can I desire.

Yea, into nothing would I fall
For thee alone, my All in All ;
To feel thy love, my only joy ;
To tell thy love, my sole employ.

JOSHUA I. 1—9.

NOW after the death of Moses the servant of the LORD it came to pass, that the LORD spake unto Joshua the son of Nun, Moses' minister, saying, Moses my servant is dead. *(This he knew, but the impressive circumstance was mentioned to awaken his mind to a sense of his own responsibility and the need of his at once proceeding to act. The deaths of good men are calls to others to bestir themselves.)* Now therefore arise, go over this Jordan, thou, and all this people, unto the land which I do give to them, *even* to the children of Israel.

This was easier said than done; but Joshua's faith staggered not. He knew that the Lord was master of the river as he had been of the sea.

3 Every place that the sole of your foot shall tread upon, that have I given unto you, as I said unto Moses.

4 From the wilderness and this Lebanon even unto the great river, the river Euphrates, all the land of the Hittites, and unto the great sea toward the going down of the sun, shall be your coast.

5 There shall not any man be able to stand before thee all the days of thy life: as I was with Moses, *so* I will be with thee : I will not fail thee, nor forsake thee. *(Here were exceeding great and precious promises to cheer him. A promise of conquest in war, guidance upon the judgment seat, and of blessing for himself personally. The Lord abounds in tender promises. May he, by the Holy Spirit, speak home some gracious word to our hearts. It would be a joy, indeed, to hear him say, "I will not fail thee, nor forsake thee."*)

6 Be strong and of a good courage : for unto this people shalt thou divide for an inheritance the land, which I sware unto their fathers to give them. *(The oath and covenant of God are a mainstay to faith, hence the Lord mentions them to his servant. There is no better rock of confidence than the immutable promise of a faithful God.)*

7 Only be thou strong and very courageous, that thou mayest observe to do according to all the law, which Moses my servant commanded thee : turn not from it *to* the right hand or *to* the left, that thou mayest prosper whithersoever thou goest. *(It seems, then, that it needs strength and courage to be obedient to God. Some count*

the godly cowards, but the Holy Spirit thinketh not so. He is a brave man who is afraid to sin, and he is a hero who flees youthful lusts which war against the soul. Note that Joshua was to avoid a turn to the right hand as much as a turn to the left: we are no more permitted to offend with the view of doing more good, than with the idea of doing mischief.)

8 This book of the law shall not depart out of thy mouth, *(talk about it:)* but thou shalt meditate therein day and night, *(think about it:)* that thou mayest observe to do according to all that is written therein, *(practise it:)* for then thou shalt make thy way prosperous, and then thou shalt have good success,*(rejoice in it.)*

Before the Lord obedience is prosperity, and transgression is a root of bitterness. In order to practical obedience, however, there must be a delight in the Lord's law. Those who forget to meditate soon cease to obey, in fact their heart has never been truly in accord with the divine statutes.

9 Have not I commanded thee? Be strong and of a good courage; be not afraid, neither be thou dismayed : for the LORD thy God *is* with thee whithersoever thou goest.

Where God's command is our authority we can afford to be bold. Who shall gainsay us when the Lord of Hosts gives us leave? Fear, in such a case, is dishonour to our Invincible Commander. When the Lord is on his side, confidence is but the reasonable condition of a believing man.

> By faith I on thy strength lay hold,
> And walk in Christ my way,
> Divinely confident and bold
> Thy precepts to obey.
>
> I would perform thy utmost will,
> With heart most fixed and true;
> And dare to follow onward still
> Where Jesus bids me go.

> We of Jehovah's wrath have heard
> The thunders from above ;
> And trusting his prophetic word,
> Take refuge in his love.
>
> Now in the window of our soul
> The scarlet line we tie ;
> When judgment o'er the earth shall roll,
> Its sword shall pass us by.

A S *it is not possible to divide this narrative at an appropriate place, we must take, on this occasion, a little extra time for our reading.*

JOSHUA II. 1—21.

1 And Joshua the son of Nun sent out of Shittim two men to spy secretly, saying, Go view the land, even Jericho. And they went, and came into an harlot's house, named Rahab, and lodged there. (*There is no pretence for believing that Rahab was, originally, better than her name implies. She had been a sinful woman, but God's grace had appeared to her and enabled her to believe in Jehovah, the only living and true God. Perhaps, on this account, she began to practise hospitality, and therefore, when the two men came to the city gates she was waiting to give them shelter. At any rate, providence co-operated with grace, and brought the believing woman into communication with those who could secure her safety. It was a work of faith on her part to receive the spies.*)

2 And it was told the king of Jericho, saying, Behold, there came men in hither to night of the children of Israel to search out the country. *Israel's enemies do not sleep, but keep good watch, and we also may rest assured that Satan and his legions will soon find us out if we go to war with his kingdom.*

3 And the king of Jericho sent unto Rahab, saying, Bring forth the men that are come to thee, which are entered into thine house : for they be come to search out all the country. *This must have been a trying moment for Rahab, and she had at once to decide whether she would give up her country or her God : whatever error she committed in her mode of action, her decision for the living God had no flaw in it.*

4 And the woman took the two men, and hid them, and said thus, There came men unto me, but I wist not whence they were :

5 And it came to pass *about the time* of shutting of the gate, when it was dark, that the men went out : whither the men went, I wot not : pursue after them quickly; for ye shall overtake them. (*This was a gross falsehood, and is not to be regarded in any other light. Her faith was weak, and therefore she adopted a wrong plan for accomplishing a right thing.*

We may not lie under any circumstances; but Rahab was very imperfectly aware of this. Orientals do not condemn, but rather admire clever deceit, and therefore her conscience did not condemn her upon this point. This fact shows that although faith may be marred by failings, it will save the soul if it be sincere.)

6 But she had brought them up to the roof of the house, and hid them with the stalks of flax, which she had laid in order upon the roof. *Does not this look as if she had already, through her faith, become a virtuous and industrious woman, diligent in business proper to her sex? Vice is very seldom industrious.*

7 And the men pursued after them the way to Jordan unto the fords : and as soon as they which pursued after them were gone out, they shut the gate. (*Rahab had effectually misdirected the pursuers, and lulled to sleep all suspicion against herself. Her success does not, however, justify her deceit. Whether it succeed or fail, falsehood is always wrong.*)

8 ¶ And before they were laid down, she came up unto them upon the roof;

9 And she said unto the men, I know that the LORD hath given you the land, and that your terror is fallen upon us, and that all the inhabitants of the land faint because of you.

10 For we have heard how the LORD dried up the water of the Red sea for you, when ye came out of Egypt; and what ye did unto the two kings of the Amorites, that *were* on the other side Jordan, Sihon and Og, whom ye utterly destroyed.

11 And as soon as we had heard *these things*, our hearts did melt, neither did there remain any more courage in any man, because of you : for the LORD your God, he *is* God in heaven above, and in earth beneath. (*She avowed her faith and gave her reasons for it, reasons which show that she had diligently gathered all information, had been a shrewd observer, and was fully convinced that Jehovah alone was the true God, ruling both in heaven and earth. She had heard no sermons, and seen neither Moses nor the prophets, and yet she believed. She will surely rise up in judgment against those, who, living in the midst of the means of grace, remain unbelievers still.*)

12 Now therefore, I pray you, swear unto me by the LORD, since I have shewed you

kindness, that ye will also shew kindness unto my father's house, and give me a true token :

13 And *that* ye will save alive my father, and my mother, and my brethren, and my sisters, and all that they have, and deliver our lives from death. *(She sued for her own life, but like a true child of God she did not forget her kindred. One of the certain results of grace in the heart is a holy care for others. Grace and selfishness are as opposite as light and darkness. O may none of us forget to pray for our fathers, and mothers, and brethren, and sisters. May we live to see the whole family saved in the Lord with an everlasting salvation.)*

14 And the men answered her, Our life for yours, if ye utter not this our business. And it shall be, when the LORD hath given us the land, that we will deal kindly and truly with thee. *Thus she obtained a promise of safety at once, and it was couched in very cheering words. "We will deal kindly and truly with thee." This is the manner in which the Lord Jesus deals with all who put their trust in him.*

15 Then she let them down by a cord through the window: for her house *was* upon the town wall, and she dwelt upon the wall.

16 And she said unto them, Get you to the mountain, lest the pursuers meet you ; and hide yourselves there three days, until the pursuers be returned : and afterward may ye go your way.

17, 18 And the men said unto her, We *will be* blameless of this thine oath which thou hast made us swear. Behold, *when* we come into the land, thou shalt bind this line of scarlet thread in the window which thou didst let us down by : and thou shalt bring thy father, and thy mother, and thy brethren, and all thy father's household, home unto thee.

19 And it shall be, *that* whosoever shall go out of the doors of thy house into the street, his blood *shall be* upon his head, and we *will be* guiltless : and whosoever shall be with thee in the house, his blood *shall be* on our head, if *any* hand be upon him. *(When the men were leaving her they gave her a token, and made with her an agreement which is full of instruction. The scarlet line was to her house what the blood upon the lintel was to Israel in Egypt: the blood-red standard is the national flag of believers. Those who would share with God's people must enlist under their banner, and therefore Rahab was*

instructed to hoist the sacred ensign. Safety was promised to all beneath the scarlet line, but to none else, however near and dear to her they might be. The like benefits belong to Christian households. Those of us who believe in Jesus, and rest in his precious blood, will be saved, but none besides. O let us see to it that we do not rest content until we lodge where the blood-red standard is displayed, for that house alone will stand when all others fall with a crash. In Jesus we must dwell, if we would escape the general doom. The sole token by which our faith realises her security is the blood of the covenant.)

20 And if thou utter this our business, then we will be quit of thine oath which thou hast made us to swear.

21 And she said, According unto your words, so *be* it. And she sent them away, and they departed : and she bound the scarlet line in the window. *(She complied with the stipulation. We must neglect no gospel command, however trifling it may seem to those who understand it not. By a public profession of faith we must bind the scarlet cord in the window. Neither Baptism, nor the Lord's Supper, nor any other Gospel statute must be neglected, and we must note well that the gospel runs thus—He that believeth and is baptized shall be saved.*

IN *Rahab's case faith was most prominent, as Paul reminds us in—*

HEBREWS XI. 31.

31 By faith the harlot Rahab perished not with them that believed not, when she had received the spies with peace.

BUT *at the same time good works were not wanting, for we are reminded of the practical nature of her faith in—*

JAMES II. 25, 26.

25 Likewise also was not Rahab the harlot justified by works, when she had received the messengers, and had sent *them* out another way?

26 For as the body without the spirit is dead, so faith without works is dead also.

JOSHUA III. 1—13.

AND Joshua rose early in the morning; *(He did not serve God and his people in a dilatory manner. He who would accomplish great things, will never do them by lying in bed.)* and they removed from Shittim, and came to Jordan, he and all the children of Israel, and lodged there before they passed over. *They had a promise that they should pass over, but they knew not how : nevertheless they went forward in faith. If we only know our duty up to a certain point, let us advance, even if we cannot see another inch beyond us. Let us do as we are bidden, and leave events with God.*

2 And it came to pass after three days, that the officers went through the host;

3 And they commanded the people, saying, When ye see the ark of the covenant of the Lord your God, and the priests the Levites bearing it, then ye shall remove from your place, and go after it. *(In former times the ark was in the centre of the host, but now it leads the van, as though the Lord defied his enemies, and went on before, alone and unattended to give them battle.)*

4 Yet there shall be a space between you and it, about two thousand cubits by measure : come not near unto it, that ye may know the way by which ye must go: for ye have not passed *this* way heretofore. *(The distance set was intended to enable the people to see the ark, and also as it were to shew that the Lord met his foes alone, keeping the armed ranks behind, and advancing unarmed against his foes. This day let us reflect that we shall tread a new road, but let us rejoice that our gracious covenant God goes before.)*

5 And Joshua said unto the people, Sanctify yourselves : for to morrow the Lord will do wonders among you. *(God always does wonders among a sanctified people. Our sins may put a restraint upon him, but we are not straitened in him.)*

6 And Joshua spake unto the priests, saying, Take up the ark of the covenant, and pass over before the people. And they took up the ark of the covenant, and went before the people.

7 ¶ And the Lord said unto Joshua, This day will I begin to magnify thee in the sight of all Israel, that they may know that, as I was with Moses, *so* I will be with thee.

God would have his ministers honoured, and therefore works by them.

8 And thou shalt command the priests that bear the ark of the covenant, saying, When ye are come to the brink of the water of Jordan, ye shall stand still in Jordan.

9 ¶ And Joshua said unto the children of Israel, Come hither, and hear the words of the Lord your God.

10 And Joshua said, Hereby ye shall know that the living God *is* among you, and *that* he will without fail drive out from before you the Canaanites, and the Hittites, and the Hivites, and the Perizzites, and the Girgashites, and the Amorites, and the Jebusites.

11 Behold, the ark of the covenant of the Lord of all the earth passeth over before you into Jordan. *(Thus the ark's passage of the Jordan was both a token of the Lord's presence, and a pledge of the conquest of Canaan. Every display of grace to us is a fresh assurance of our ultimate victory over all sin, and our entrance into the promised rest.)*

12 Now therefore take you twelve men out of the tribes of Israel, out of every tribe a man.

13 And it shall come to pass, as soon as the soles of the feet of the priests that bear the ark of the Lord, the Lord of all the earth, shall rest in the waters of Jordan, *that* the waters of Jordan shall be cut off *from* the waters that come down from above ; and they shall stand upon an heap. *(Thus the Lord who was the Alpha of his people's deliverance at the Red Sea, became the Omega of it, by a repetition of the miracle at Jordan. Fear not, for the Lord will also for us do as great things at the close of our days, as he did when he brought us out of the Egyptian bondage of our sins.)*

One army of the living God,
 To His command we bow ;
Part of His host have cross'd the flood,
 And part are crossing now.

Ten thousand to their endless home
 This solemn moment fly ;
And we are to the margin come,
 And soon expect to die.

JOSHUA III. 14—17.

AND it came to pass, when the people removed from their tents, to pass over Jordan, and the priests bearing the ark of the covenant before the people ; And as they that bare the ark were come unto Jordan, and the feet of the priests that bare the ark were dipped in the brim of the water, (for Jordan overfloweth all his banks all the time of harvest,) *(But that was no difficulty with God, who can as well dry up an overflowing river as a shallow one,)* That the waters which came down from above stood *and* rose up upon an heap very far from the city Adam, that *is* beside Zaretan : and those that came down toward the sea of the plain, *even* the salt sea, failed, *and* were cut off : *(At the division of the Red sea the waters stood as a wall on both sides, but on this occasion the floods arose on one side only, and on the left hand the water quite disappeared, flowing at once into the Dead sea. The Lord has many ways of effecting the same end. Variety in the divine operations is a clear proof that the Lord is never at a loss for ways and means :)* and the people passed over right against Jericho. *(Under the eyes of their enemies the miracle was wrought, and in the face of the arch-enemy God will grant his people safe passage through death's cold flood.)*

17 And the priests that bare the ark of the covenant of the LORD stood firm on dry ground in the midst of Jordan, and all the Israelites passed over on dry ground, until all the people were passed clean over Jordan. *(The ark of the covenant first led the way, and then kept the road open. The priesthood of Jesus and the ark of his redemption make for all believers a passage into the better land.)*

CHAPTER IV. 4—11 ; 18.

THEN Joshua called the twelve men, whom he had prepared of the children of Israel, out of every tribe a man : And Joshua said unto them, Pass over before the ark of the LORD your God into the midst of Jordan, and take you up every man of you a stone upon his shoulder, according unto the number of the tribes of the children of Israel : That this may be a sign among you, *that* when your children ask *their fathers* in time to come, saying, What *mean* ye by these stones ? Then ye shall answer them, That the waters of Jordan were cut off before the ark of the covenant of the LORD : when it passed over Jordan, the waters of Jordan were cut off : and these stones shall be for a memorial unto the children of Israel for ever. *Care must be taken by the best possible means to keep the Lord's wonders of grace in remembrance in coming generations. This is a principal use of the two sacred ordinances of our holy faith, and it should be a main object of care with all good men.*

8 And the children of Israel did so as Joshua commanded, and took up twelve stones out of the midst of Jordan, as the LORD spake unto Joshua, according to the number of the tribes of the children of Israel, and carried them over with them unto the place where they lodged, and laid them down there.

9 And Joshua set up twelve stones in the midst of Jordan, in the place where the feet of the priests which bare the ark of the covenant stood : and they are there unto this day.

10 ¶ For the priests which bare the ark stood in the midst of Jordan, until every thing was finished that the LORD commanded Joshua to speak unto the people, according to all that Moses commanded Joshua : and the people hasted and passed over. *(Christ will never cease his mediatorial work, till all his redeemed are safely landed. Ministers ought to be brave men, the first to risk all for God's sake, and the last to leave their post. Note how the Israelites were both trembling and believing; they "hasted,"—here was fear, and "passed over"—here was faith.)*

11 And it came to pass, when all the people were clean passed over, that the ark of the LORD passed over, and the priests, in the presence of the people.

18 And it came to pass, when the priests that bare the ark of the covenant of the LORD were come up out of the midst of Jordan, *and* the soles of the priests' feet were lifted up unto the dry land, that the waters of Jordan returned unto their place, and flowed over all his banks, as they did before. *(This proved that the whole transaction was a miracle, not to be accounted for by referring it to natural causes. Let the Lord be praised for it.)*

> When I tread the verge of Jordan,
>   Bid my anxious fears subside ;
> Death of deaths, and hell's destruction,
>   Land me safe on Canaan's side :
>   Songs of praises
>   I will ever give to Thee.

JOSHUA V. 1; 10—15.

AND it came to pass, when all the kings of the Amorites, which *were* on the side of Jordan westward, and all the kings of the Canaanites, which *were* by the sea, heard that the LORD had dried up the waters of Jordan from before the children of Israel, until we were passed over, that their heart melted, neither was there spirit in them any more, because of the children of Israel.

Matthew Henry says upon this verse, " How dreadful is their case who see the wrath of God and his deserved vengeance advancing towards them with steady pace, without any possibility of averting or escaping it. Such will be the horrible situation of the wicked when summoned to appear before the tribunal of an offended God; nor can words express the anguish of their feelings, or the greatness of their terror. O that they would now take warning, and before it be too late, would flee for refuge to lay hold upon that hope which is set before them in the salvation of the gospel."

10 ¶ And the children of Israel encamped in Gilgal, and kept the passover on the fourteenth day of the month at even in the plains of Jericho. *(Before they entered upon the conquest of Canaan the people gave attention to circumcision and the passover. We cannot expect God to help us if we are negligent of his commands. Before entering upon any Christian enterprise it is well to look to home duties. When all is right within ourselves, we shall be in a fit condition to do battle with the evils around us.)*

11 And they did eat of the old corn of the land on the morrow after the passover, unleavened cakes, and parched *corn* in the selfsame day.

12 And the manna ceased on the morrow after they had eaten of the old corn of the land; neither had the children of Israel manna any more; but they did eat of the fruit of the land of Canaan that year. *(We must not expect miracles when ordinary providences will suffice. There is, if we would but see it, as much wisdom and grace in supplying our daily wants in the common methods as there would be in the Lord's raining bread from heaven upon us. We may here also remark that means and ordinances will last us until we reach the heritage above. We must gather the manna of the wilderness till we feast upon the harvests of Immanuel's land. Grace will be our daily portion till we enter glory.)*

13 ¶ And it came to pass, when Joshua was by Jericho, that he lifted up his eyes and looked, and, behold, there stood a man over against him with his sword drawn in his hand : *(The Lord Jesus usually appears to his people in a manner which proves his communion with them. He shows himself to be like his brethren. To Abraham the pilgrim he appeared as a pilgrim, with Jacob the wrestler he wrestled, to the holy children he appeared as one in the furnace, and to Joshua the soldier he showed himself as a warrior. Our Lord is the defender of his chosen, and will show himself strong on their behalf:)* and Joshua went unto him, and said unto him, Art thou for us, or for our adversaries ? *(Like a brave man Joshua spake, and like a resolute friend of Israel, who would know each man's mind about the coming fight, and act towards him accordingly.)*

14 And he said, Nay; but *as* captain of the host of the LORD am I now come. *(Jesus is Commander-in-Chief; he is not only, as one was wont to call him, " our august ally," but the Captain over all.)* And Joshua fell on his face to the earth, and did worship, and said unto him, What saith my lord unto his servant ?

True adoration bows its heart to hear as well as its knee to worship.

15 And the captain of the LORD's host said unto Joshua, Loose thy shoe from off thy foot ; for the place whereon thou standest *is* holy. And Joshua did so. *(He must first worship, and then go to war. God will not honour irreverent spirits. It is not enough to ask instructions from the Lord Jesus; we must adore him, and maintain a devout spirit. Great Captain of the sacred host, we adore thee at this hour ! Give us thy commands, and go with us to the conflict, and we will not fear our adversaries, however great or many they be.)*

Thee we acknowledge, God and Lord,
   Jesus for sinners slain ;
Who art by heaven and earth adored,
   Worthy o'er both to reign.

Great Captain of the hosts of God,
   Low at thy feet we bow ;
'Tis holy ground where thou hast trod,
   We loose our sandals now.

162   *" My strength is made perfect in weakness."*   MARCH 20.—EVENING.

[*Or June 7.*]

JOSHUA VI. 1—5; 12—21; 23, 25.

NOW Jericho was straitly shut up because of the children of Israel : none went out, and none came in.

2 And the LORD said unto Joshua, See, I have given into thine hand Jericho, and the king thereof, *and* the mighty men of valour.

God had given the city to them, but they were to use the appointed means. God's election fulfils itself through earnest seeking on our part.

3 And ye shall compass the city, all *ye* men of war, *and* go round about the city once. Thus shalt thou do six days.

4, 5 And seven priests shall bear before the ark seven trumpets of rams' horns : (*Mean instruments were chosen to work wonders,*) and the seventh day ye shall compass the city seven times, and the priests shall blow with the trumpets. And it shall come to pass, that when they make a long *blast* with the ram's horn, *and* when ye hear the sound of the trumpet, all the people shall shout with a great shout; and the wall of the city shall fall down flat, and the people shall ascend up every man straight before him.

Little connection was apparent between the means and the desired result, yet it was not for the people to reason why; it was theirs to follow the prescribed rule.

12 ¶ And Joshua rose early in the morning, and the priests took up the ark of the LORD.

13 And seven priests bearing seven trumpets of rams' horns before the ark of the LORD went on continually, and blew with the trumpets : and the armed men went before them; but the rereward came after the ark of the LORD, *the priests* going on, and blowing with the trumpets.

They did precisely as they were bidden, no doubt greatly to the amusement of the sons of Belial, who thought the procedure a very unphilosophical one, and quite unfit for men of common sense to spend their time upon.

14 And the second day they compassed the city once, and returned into the camp : so they did six days.

15 And it came to pass on the seventh day, that they rose early about the dawning of the day, and compassed the city seven times.

16 And it came to pass at the seventh time, when the priests blew with the trumpets, Joshua said unto the people, Shout ; for the LORD hath given you the city. (*Their former silence had proved their patience, and this commanded shout was a token of the expectancy of their faith.*)

17—19 And the city shall be accursed, *even it,* and all that *are* therein, to the LORD : only Rahab the harlot shall live, she and all that *are* with her in the house, because she hid the messengers that we sent. And ye, in anywise keep *yourselves* from the accursed thing, lest ye make *yourselves* accursed, when ye take of the accursed thing, and make the camp of Israel a curse, and trouble it. But all the silver, and gold, and vessels of brass and iron, *are* consecrated unto the LORD : they shall come into the treasury of the LORD. (*It was meet that the firstfruits of Canaan should be the Lord's.*)

20 So the people shouted when *the priests* blew with the trumpets : and it came to pass, when the people heard the sound of the trumpet, and the people shouted with a great shout, that the wall fell down flat, so that the people went up into the city, every man straight before him, and they took the city. (*A strange method of overturning strongholds, and yet when God so ordained, it was as effectual as the best constructed battering-ram. How strangely must Rahab's house have towered aloft, when all others fell in heaps. Faith pulls down, but faith also upholds.*)

21 And they utterly destroyed all that *was* in the city, both man and woman, young and old, and ox, and sheep, and ass, with the edge of the sword.

23 And the young men that were spies went in, and brought out Rahab, and her father, and her mother, and her brethren, and all that she had ; and they brought out all her kindred, and left them without the camp of Israel.

In the day of judgment the house with the scarlet line in the window is not left to perish in the general wreck. Perish who may, believers are secured by the promise of one who cannot lie, and they have nothing to fear.

25 And Joshua saved Rahab the harlot alive, and her father's household, and all that she had.

> Make bare thine own resistless arm,
>   Through all the earth abroad ;
> Let every nation now behold
>   Their Saviour and their God.

THE *history of the fall of Jericho through the blast of rams'-horns reminds us of* Paul's *expression in the Corinthians, "The weapons of our warfare are not carnal, but mighty through God to the pulling down of strongholds." Let us read a passage in which the reputed weakness of the gospel is gloried in because the Lord, nevertheless, works by it—*

I CORINTHIANS I. 18—31.

18 For the preaching of the cross is to them that perish foolishness; but unto us which are saved it is the power of God. *(The same thing is different to differing persons. One sees in the gospel folly, and another omnipotence. These last have felt its gracious power, and therefore are well assured of what they believe.)*

19 For it is written, I will destroy the wisdom of the wise, and will bring to nothing the understanding of the prudent.

20 Where *is* the wise? where *is* the scribe? where *is* the disputer of this world? hath not God made foolish the wisdom of this world?

Let this be remembered still, and it will help to cure the craving after learned and intellectual preaching. What have we to do with setting up what God means to destroy? The plain gospel of Jesus, simply preached, is infinitely superior to all the "deep thinking" and "exact criticism" of modern times.

21 For after that in the wisdom of God the world by wisdom knew not God, it pleased God by the foolishness of preaching to save them that believe. *(Philosophy left the world in the foulest mire of lasciviousness and unbelief, but the unlettered men who delivered the Lord's message of love just as they received it, became the salvation of myriads.)*

22, 23, 24 For the Jews require a sign, and the Greeks seek after wisdom: But we preach Christ crucified, unto the Jews· a stumbling-block, and unto the Greeks foolishness; But unto them which are called, both Jews and Greeks, Christ the power of God, and the wisdom of God. *(Tastes are not to regulate the gospel. What men desire is one thing, but what the gospel gives them is another. Instead of signs and wisdom, God's ministers show unto men the crucified Saviour, and nothing else.)*

25 Because the foolishness of God is wiser than men; and the weakness of God is stronger

than men. *(It will be seen in the end that what men think foolish and weak in God's gospel, will be more than a match for human power and learning.)*

26 For ye see your calling, brethren, how that not many wise men after the flesh, not many mighty, not many noble, *are called:*

27 But God hath chosen the foolish things of the world to confound the wise; and God hath chosen the weak things of the world to confound the things which are mighty;

28 And base things of the world, and things which are despised, hath God chosen, *yea,* and things which are not, to bring to nought things that are:

29 That no flesh should glory in his presence.

As election thus makes no account of human greatness, the preacher must pay no deference to it in his ministry. He is to proclaim his message to the common people, and to be content if his converts are despised as belonging to the base things of this world. If God's election ran among the grandees, he might have sent to them a philosophical gospel to be delivered with all the graces of classic oratory: but such is not the mind of the Lord. Let us, as a family, hold fast to the old gospel, and love the honest ministers of it who care more about winning souls than about being considered fine orators. The gospel which saved the apostles, the martyrs, the reformers, and our godly ancestors, is quite good enough for us. Let those who please seek after the wisdom of man, we will abide by the teaching of the Lord.

30 But of him are ye in Christ Jesus, who of God is made unto us wisdom, and righteousness, and sanctification, and redemption:

31 That, according as it is written, He that glorieth, let him glory in the Lord.

All is of Jesus, from first to last, and so all the glory is unto him who deserves it. Blessed be the name of the Lord, from the rising of the sun to the going down of the same.

Nor voice can sing, nor heart can frame,
   Nor can the memory find,
A sweeter sound than thy blest name,
   O Saviour of mankind!

Jesus, our only joy be thou,
   As thou our crown wilt be;
Jesus, be thou our glory now,
   And through eternity.

JOSHUA VII. 1—13; 15.

BUT the children of Israel committed a trespass in the accursed thing: for Achan, the son of Carmi, the son of Zabdi, the son of Zerah, of the tribe of Judah, took of the accursed thing: and the anger of the LORD was kindled against the children of Israel.

The chapter opens with a "but," and a very serious "but" it was. One man in Israel had presumed to violate the express command of Jehovah, and had taken of the spoil of Jericho for himself, and had thus defied the curse which had been pronounced upon any who so acted. That one man's sin, like a single drop of a potent poison, was sufficient to do damage to the whole body of Israel. Sin is so deadly an evil that the smallest measure of it may do more injury than we can reckon or imagine.

2, 3 And Joshua sent men from Jericho to Ai, and spake unto them, saying, Go up and view the country. And the men went up and viewed Ai. And they returned to Joshua, and said unto him, Let not all the people go up; but let about two or three thousand men go up and smite Ai; *and* make not all the people to labour thither; for they *are but* few. *(Israel had become confident of an easy victory, and a disposition to spare themselves was evidently growing up among them. The Lord would fight for them, and therefore they might ground their weapons. In this way, in all ages, the grace of God has been abused by the self-indulgence of men.)*

4, 5 So there went up thither of the people about three thousand men: and they fled before the men of Ai. And the men of Ai smote of them about thirty and six men: wherefore the hearts of the people melted, and became as water. *(Defeat is the sure result of an indolent carnal security, and it is well when it drives the believer to his God again, and leads him with holy earnestness to put forth all his strength. God worketh in us to make us work ourselves; he never works indolence in us.)*

6 ¶ And Joshua rent his clothes, and fell to the earth upon his face before the ark of the LORD until the eventide, he and the elders of Israel, and put dust upon their heads.

7 And Joshua said, Alas, O Lord GOD, wherefore hast thou at all brought this people over Jordan, to deliver us into the hand of the Amorites, to destroy us? would to God we had been content, and dwelt on the other side Jordan! *(This was a faulty expression, and savoured of distrust. It was not the position of the people, but their sin which had destroyed them.)*

8 O Lord, what shall I say, when Israel turneth their backs before their enemies!

The grand old warrior felt his blood boil at the thought of his nation put to the rout.

9 For the Canaanites and all the inhabitants of the land shall hear *of it*, and shall environ us round, and cut off our name from the earth: and what wilt thou do unto thy great name?

Here was the master plea of Moses; and when Joshua came to plead that, he was sure of success. We ought to be more concerned for the honour of God, than for anything else in the world.

10—13 ¶ And the LORD said unto Joshua, Get thee up; wherefore liest thou thus upon thy face? Israel hath sinned, and they have also transgressed my covenant which I commanded them: for they have even taken of the accursed thing, and have also stolen, and dissembled also, and they have put *it* even among their own stuff. Therefore the children of Israel could not stand before their enemies, *but* turned *their* backs before their enemies, because they were accursed: neither will I be with you any more, except ye destroy the accursed from among you. Up, sanctify the people, and say, Sanctify yourselves against to morrow: for thus saith the LORD God of Israel, *There is* an accursed thing in the midst of thee, O Israel: thou canst not stand before thine enemies, until ye take away the accursed thing from among you. *(Sin will deprive a church of all power to do good. Though it may be an unknown sin, its effects will soon be visible enough. It is a blessed thing when affliction leads to humbling, and humbling to heartsearching. Lord, grant that no sin may be in this family either open or concealed, but make and keep us obedient to thy will evermore.)*

15 And it shall be, *that* he that is taken with the accursed thing shall be burnt with fire, he and all that he hath: because he hath transgressed the covenant of the LORD, and because he hath wrought folly in Israel.

JOSHUA VII. 16—26.

SO Joshua rose up early in the morning, *(It was a business not to be delayed. The sooner sin is found out and put away the better. Nobody would rest long if he knew his house to be on fire, but sin is a far worse evil than the devouring flame,)* and brought Israel by their tribes; and the tribe of Judah was taken:

17, 18 And he brought the family of Judah; and he took the family of the Zarhites: and he brought the family of the Zarhites man by man; and Zabdi was taken: And he brought his household man by man; and Achan, the son of Carmi, the son of Zabdi, the son of Zerah, of the tribe of Judah, was taken. *(Achan may at first have laughed at the idea of his being detected, but when the tribe of Judah was taken, he must have felt ill at ease; when the Zarhites were taken, fear must have seized him, and his terror must have been extreme when at last the lot fell on his father's family. By some means sin will be brought home to the guilty individual, and what will be his horror when the finger of God points directly at him with a "thou art the man.")*

19 And Joshua said unto Achan, My son, give, I pray thee, glory to the LORD God of Israel, and make confession unto him; and tell me now what thou hast done; hide it not from me. *(Joshua urged the criminal to confess. His detection was certain, and he gave him the wisest counsel a judge can give to a condemned man, namely, to do his best to justify God in punishing him by acknowledging his fault.)*

20 And Achan answered Joshua, and said, Indeed I have sinned against the LORD God of Israel, and thus and thus have I done;

21 When I saw among the spoils a goodly Babylonish garment, and two hundred shekels of silver, and a wedge of gold of fifty shekels weight, then I coveted them and took them; and, behold, they are hid in the earth in the midst of my tent, and the silver under it. *(He saw, he coveted, he took, he hid, he was detected, convicted, and condemned. See here in brief "the Sinner's Progress.")*

22 ¶ So Joshua sent messengers, and they ran unto the tent; and, behold, it was hid in his tent, and the silver under it. *(What use could buried gold and garments be? The man was foolish as well as wicked. Illgotten goods are not true riches.)*

23 And they took them out of the midst of the tent, and brought them unto Joshua, and unto all the children of Israel, and laid them out before the LORD.

24 And Joshua, and all Israel with him, took Achan the son of Zerah, and the silver, and the garment, and the wedge of gold, and his sons, and his daughters, and his oxen, and his asses, and his sheep, and his tent, and all that he had: and they brought them unto the valley of Achor.

25 And Joshua said, Why hast thou troubled us? the LORD shall trouble thee this day. And all Israel stoned him with stones, and burned them with fire, after they had stoned them with stones. *(This terrible punishment may have been the more needful, because at the outset of their history in Canaan it was necessary to impress the people with the fact that God would not be trifled with, but would have his laws respected.)*

26 And they raised over him a great heap of stones unto this day. So the LORD turned from the fierceness of his anger. Wherefore the name of that place was called, The valley of Achor, unto this day. *(Let this heap of stones be a monumental warning to us. Have we any hidden sin within our hearts? Are any of this household indulging evil passions or following wrong courses in secret? If so, be sure your sin will find you out. The only way of escape is a penitent confession to God, and a believing cry to the Lord Jesus for pardon.)*

Sins and follies unforsaken,
All will end in deep despair;
Formal prayers are unavailing,
Fruitless is the worldling's tear;
Small the number
Who to wisdom's path repair.

If, lurking in its inmost folds,
I any sin conceal,
Oh let a ray of light divine
That secret guile reveal.

If, tinctured with that odious gall,
Unknowing I remain,
Let grace, like a pure silver stream,
Wash out the accursed stain.

166   " Speak ye every man the truth to his neighbour."   MARCH 22.—EVENING.

[*Or June* 11.]

A FTER *the destruction of Achan the conquest of Ai was readily accomplished, and then followed the singular event recorded in the following chapter.*

JOSHUA IX. 3—21.

3 ¶ And when the inhabitants of Gibeon heard what Joshua had done unto Jericho and to Ai,

4, 5 They did work wilily, and went and made as if they had been ambassadors, and took old sacks upon their asses, and wine bottles, old, and rent, and bound up ; And old shoes and clouted *(or patched)* upon their feet, and old garments upon them ; and all the bread of their provision was dry *and* mouldy.

6 And they went to Joshua unto the camp at Gilgal, and said unto him, and to the men of Israel, We be come from a far country : now therefore make ye a league with us.

7 And the men of Israel said unto the Hivites, Peradventure ye dwell among us ; and how shall we make a league with you ?

8 And they said unto Joshua, We *are* thy servants. And Joshua said unto them, Who *are* ye ? and from whence come ye ?

9—13 And they said unto him, from a very far country thy servants are come because of the name of the LORD thy God : for we have heard the fame of him, and all that he did in Egypt, And all that he did to the two kings of the Amorites, that *were* beyond Jordan, to Sihon king of Heshbon, and to Og king of Bashan, which was at Ashtaroth. Wherefore our elders and all the inhabitants of our country spake to us, saying, Take victuals with you for the journey, and go to meet them, and say unto them, We *are* your servants : therefore now make ye a league with us. This our bread we took hot *for* our provision out of our houses on the day we came forth to go unto you ; but now, behold, it is dry, and it is mouldy : And these bottles of wine *(skin bottles)* which we filled, *were* new ; and, behold, they be rent ; and these our garments and our shoes are become old by reason of the very long journey. *(Their wish to be spared was natural, their submission to Israel was commendable, but their crafty deception was unjustifiable. When we yield ourselves to Jesus we have only to speak the truth, and there is no need for us to*

put on old and tattered clothing, for a sinner's spiritual wardrobe contains nothing else.)

14, 15 And the men took of their victuals, and asked not *counsel* at the mouth of the LORD. And Joshua made peace with them, and made a league with them, to let them live : and the princes of the congregation sware unto them. *Joshua thought the matter so clear that he had no need to seek divine direction. It is usually in such cases that we err.*

16 ¶ And it came to pass at the end of three days after they had made a league with them, that they heard that they *were* their neighbours, and *that* they dwelt among them.

17 And the children of Israel journeyed, and came unto their cities on the third day. Now their cities *were* Gibeon, and Chephirah, and Beeroth, and Kirjath-jearim.

18 And the children of Israel smote them not, because the princes of the congregation had sworn unto them by the LORD God of Israel. And all the congregation murmured against the princes. *Some probably because they wanted to take the spoil of the Gibeonites, and others because they conscientiously thought that they ought not to be spared.*

19 But all the princes said unto all the congregation, We have sworn unto them by the LORD God of Israel : now therefore we may not touch them. *(An oath is never to be lightly treated, nor a promise either, indeed the Christian man's word is his bond, and is everyway as binding as an oath.)*

20 This we will do to them ; we will even let them live, lest wrath be upon us, because of the oath which we sware unto them.

21 And the princes said unto them, Let them live ; but let them be hewers of wood and drawers of water unto all the congregation, as the princes had promised them. *(The poor Gibeonites were glad to escape even on these terms. If the Lord Jesus will but spare us, we also shall be only too glad to hew wood or draw water for him, and for his people.)*

The passage shews us that the desire of self-preservation makes men use their wits, and it leads us to wonder how it is that so few persons appear to use common judgment and ordinary care as to the salvation of their souls.

T HE *commendable manner in which Joshua and the princes of Israel kept their promise to the Gibeonites, even though that promise had been drawn out of them by deceit, reminds us of that portrait of an upright man, which was sketched by the master hand of David, in—*

PSALM XV.

1 LORD, who shall abide in thy tabernacle? who shall dwell in thy holy hill? *(Who shall be owned as thy friend, admitted as thine honoured guest, and allowed to take up a perpetual lodging place with thee? What must be his character who is allowed to abide with thee, O thrice Holy God? Like fire thy nature burns against all sin, who then is he that can dwell with such a devouring flame?)*

2 He that walketh uprightly *(Here is the first line of the good man's portrait—he must be honest, genuine, sincere, just, both towards God and man; and this habitually, for this is implied in the word, "walketh,")* and worketh righteousness, *(His practice must be right. He must not only be negatively but positively good),* and speaketh the truth in his heart. *(His tongue must reflect his soul. He must speak truth, love truth, and live truth. God will not allow liars to tarry in his sight. Who can make us thus righteous, but the Holy Spirit?)*

3 He that backbiteth not with his tongue nor doeth evil to his neighbour, nor taketh up a reproach against his neighbour. *(He is too brave to say behind a man's back that which he would not say to his face, and he is too good to wish or do his neighbour any ill. God will have no gossips at his board, revilers are none of his company. Readiness to take up a reproach shows a gross want of love. God is just, and therefore does not listen to slander, nor should we. If honoured by being taken into the family of God, let us do nothing inconsistent with love, for God is love.)*

4 In whose eyes a vile person is contemned; but he honoureth them that fear the LORD. *(Upright men are not swayed in their judgment by a man's position and rank: they honour grace when they see it in poverty, but they loathe vice though half the stars and garters of nobility should decorate it.)* He that sweareth to *his own* hurt, and changeth not. *(Here is the point, which shone in the case of Joshua. Let us re-*member that nothing can excuse us from a promise made, unless it be positive inability to perform it or the unlawfulness of the thing promised. If there be no other men of honour in the world, let the saints be such.)*

5 He that putteth not out his money to usury, nor taketh reward against the innocent. *(The true believer does not extort from the needy. He never makes other men's necessities an opportunity for eating up their estates, by lending them money at heavy premiums, and crushing interest. As for anything like a bribe he loathes it with his whole heart.)* He that doeth these *things* shall never be moved.

Good men will have troubles as others have, but they shall abide the hour of trial. He whom God makes to be one of the excellent of the earth, he will surely preserve: such pieces of work are too rare and too choice to be left unguarded.

As a family, let us aim at a high standard of character. If we be not believers in Jesus as yet, may the Lord grant us faith, for that is the foundation grace; but if we are already believers, let us, by our consistent lives, prove to others the elevating and purifying power of the religion of the Most Holy God.

Lord, I would dwell with thee,
On thy most holy hill:
Oh shed thy grace abroad in me,
To mould me to thy will.

Faithful, but meekly kind:
Gentle, yet boldly true;
I would possess the perfect mind
Which in my Lord I view.

But, Lord, these graces all
Thy Spirit's work must be;
To thee, through Jesus' blood I call,
Create them all in me.

Oh! teach me at thy feet to fall,
And yield thee up myself, my all;
Before thy saints my debt to own,
And live and die to thee alone!

Thy Spirit, Lord, at large impart;
Expand, and raise, and fill my heart;
So may I hope my life shall be
Some faint return, O Lord, to thee.

168   "𝕿𝖍𝖊 𝕷𝖔𝖗𝖉 most high is terrible."   MARCH 23.—EVENING.

[*Or June* 13.]

JOSHUA X. 1—6; 8—14.

NOW it came to pass, when Adoni-zedec king of Jerusalem had heard how Joshua had taken Ai, and had utterly destroyed it ; as he had done to Jericho and her king; so he had done to Ai and her king ; and how the inhabitants of Gibeon had made peace with Israel, and were among them ; *(The name Adoni-zedec ·signifies* Lord of righteousness, *and is very similar to that of Melchizedec, who ages before was the king of Salem or Jerusalem. Adoni-zedec was therefore the successor if not the descendant of Melchizedec, and bore his name; but how frequently those who succeed to the name and position of the best of men, are themselves among the worst of characters. Grace is not inheritable. A man may entail his estate but not his piety.)*

2 That they feared greatly, because Gibeon *was* a great city, as one of the royal cities, and because it *was* greater than Ai, and all the men thereof *were* mighty.

3 Wherefore Adoni-zedec king of Jerusalem sent unto Hoham king of Hebron, and unto Piram king of Jarmuth, and unto Japhia king of Lachish, and unto Debir king of Eglon, saying,

4 Come up unto me, and help me, that we may smite Gibeon : for it hath made peace with Joshua and with the children of Israel.

5 Therefore the five kings of the Amorites, the king of Jerusalem, the king of Hebron, the king of Jarmuth, the king of Lachish, the king of Eglon, gathered themselves together, and went up, they and all their hosts, and encamped before Gibeon, and made war against it.

6 ¶ And the men of Gibeon sent unto Joshua to the camp to Gilgal, saying, Slack not thy hand from thy servants ; come up to us quickly and save us, and help us : for all the kings of the Amorites that dwell in the mountains are gathered together against us. *(Those who join the Lord's side are sure to have enemies, but they may rest assured that the Lord will come to the rescue.)*

8 And the LORD said unto Joshua, Fear them not : for I have delivered them into thine hand; there shall not a man of them stand before thee.

9 Joshua therefore came unto them suddenly, *and* went up from Gilgal all night. *(Joshua made a hasty forced march by night, thus shewing his resolve to defend all who were connected with Israel.)*

10 And the LORD discomfited them before Israel, and slew them with a great slaughter.

11 And it came to pass, as they fled from before Israel, *and* were in the going down to Beth-horon, that the LORD cast down great stones from heaven upon them unto Azekah, and they died : *they were* more which died with hailstones than *they* whom the children of Israel slew with the sword. *(Though the Lord fought for his people, he would only give them success when they put forth all their energies. When however they came up to their work zealously, he put forth his power in such a manner, that all the glory of the victory was manifestly seen to belong to him only. Where we do most, God does more ; yea, he does all.)*

12 ¶ Then spake Joshua to the LORD in the day when the LORD delivered up the Amorites before the children of Israel, and he said in the sight of Israel, Sun, stand thou still upon Gibeon ; and thou, Moon, in the valley of Ajalon.

13 And the sun stood still, and the moon stayed, until the people had avenged themselves upon their enemies. *Is* not this written in the book of Jasher ? So the sun stood still in the midst of heaven, and hasted not to go down about a whole day. *(The book of Jasher is lost, but the book of God is not, nor a single line of it. See how inspiration embalms all things which are recorded in it. We should never have heard the name of this book if it had not been preserved like a fly in the amber of Scripture.)*

14 And there was no day like that before it or after it, that the LORD hearkened unto the voice of a man : for the LORD fought for Israel.

To please sceptical minds, scores of explanations of this wonderful occurrence have been laboriously elaborated, but there is no need for them and no use in them. The Almighty God can as easily stop the sun and moon as a watchmaker can alter a watch ; he did do so, and how he did it is no question for us : we may rest assured he prolonged the daylight by the very wisest means. It is not ours to try and soften down miracles, but to glorify God in them. At the appearing of our greater Joshua, the sun and moon shall be confounded while he shall be revealed in flaming fire, taking vengeance on his enemies.

PSALM CXXXVI.

THIS *psalm may be very fittingly read at this time, for it celebrates the Lord's dealings with Israel until he had settled them in the land which he had promised to them as a heritage.*

1 O give thanks unto the LORD ; for *he is* good : for his mercy *endureth* for ever.
Praise the Lord for what he is by nature, for his own personal goodness deserves our adoration.

2 O give thanks unto the God of gods : for his mercy *endureth* for ever.

3 O give thanks to the Lord of lords : for his mercy *endureth* for ever. *(His sovereignty over all, and his transcendant superiority above all other existences should command our reverent praise at all times. All his power and majesty are sweetened with mercy.)*

4 To him who alone doeth great wonders : for his mercy *endureth* for ever. *(How sweet is the chorus. It comes over and over again, but it never degenerates into a vain repetition. God is to be praised not only for his nature and dignity, but also for his works.)*

5 To him that by wisdom made the heavens : for his mercy *endureth* for ever.

6 To him that stretched out the earth above the waters : for his mercy *endureth* for ever.
O thou Creator of all things, we magnify the mercy which shines in all thy handiworks.

7 To him that made great lights : for his mercy *endureth* for ever. *(What should we do without the sun ? Could life itself hold out ? And how cheerless would night be if the moon were quenched ! Herein is mercy.)*

8 The sun to rule by day : for his mercy *endureth* for ever :

9 The moon and stars to rule by night : for his mercy *endureth* for ever. *(Each distinct blessing deserves a verse of praise to itself.)*

10 To him that smote Egypt in their firstborn : for his mercy *endureth* for ever :
From nature, the psalmist turns to providence and sees mercy all around. Mercy is everywhere around us, like the air we breathe. Judgment to Egypt was mercy to Israel.

11 And brought out Israel from among them : for his mercy *endureth* for ever :

12 With a strong hand, and with a stretched out arm : for his mercy *endureth* for ever :

13 To him which divided the Red sea into parts : for his mercy *endureth* for ever :

14 And made Israel to pass through the midst of it : for his mercy *endureth* for ever :

15 But overthrew Pharaoh and his host in the Red sea : for his mercy *endureth* for ever.
Destruction it was to Pharaoh, but that destruction was needful for the escape of the Israelites, and for their safety while in the wilderness, and therefore mercy was in it all.

16 To him which led his people through the wilderness : for his mercy *endureth* for ever.
Notwithstanding all their provocations, the Lord continued to lead them on; and in their case, as in ours, proved the eternity of his mercy. Time cannot rust it, sin cannot conquer it; throughout eternity it must and shall endure.

17 To him which smote great kings : for his mercy *endureth* for ever :

18 And slew famous kings : for his mercy *endureth* for ever :

19 Sihon king of the Amorites : for his mercy *endureth* for ever :

20 And Og the king of Bashan : for his mercy *endureth* for ever :

21 And gave their land for an heritage : for his mercy *endureth* for ever :

22 *Even* an heritage unto Israel his servant : for his mercy *endureth* for ever. *(He makes the just punishment of some to redound to the gain of others, and thus in his judgments magnifies his grace.)*

23 Who remembered us in our low estate : for his mercy *endureth* for ever :

24 And hath redeemed us from our enemies : for his mercy *endureth* for ever. *(Our personal experience is one of the sweetest notes of the song which celebrates infinite mercy. Our redemption is the joy of all our joy.)*

25 Who giveth food to all flesh : for his mercy *endureth* for ever. *(Daily providence which feeds the countless fish of the sea, and birds of the air, and beasts of the field, deserves our reverent gratitude.)*

26 O give thanks unto the God of heaven : for his mercy *endureth* for ever. *(The Lord reigneth in the highest above all, making heaven the throne of his glory. Our Father which art in heaven, hallowed be thy name.)*

170   "I will run in the way of Thy commandments."   MARCH 24.—EVENING.

[*Or June* 15.]

JOSHUA XIV. 6—14.

THEN the children of Judah came unto Joshua in Gilgal : and Caleb the son of Jephunneh the Kenezite said unto him, Thou knowest the thing that the LORD said unto Moses the man of God concerning me and thee in Kadesh-barnea. *(We are glad to meet with this old hero, Joshua's compatriot. Note how he dwells upon the promise, " Thou knowest the thing that the Lord said concerning me and thee." Faithful hearts treasure up the divine word and prize it more than gold.)*

7 Forty years old *was* I when Moses the servant of the LORD sent me from Kadesh-barnea to espy out the land ; and I brought him word again as *it was* in mine heart. *(He was a man of true heart, and spake as his heart bade him, and not as the majority of the spies would have had him. Only a true-souled man has courage to go against the stream, and speak the truth in the teeth of a false public opinion. Oh, that we had more such men now-a-days ! The old man looks back with gratitude to this fact which had happened so many years ago. It is well to sow seed in our youth, which we shall not be afraid to harvest in our old age.)*

8 Nevertheless my brethren that went up with me made the heart of the people melt : but I wholly followed the LORD my God.

9 And Moses sware on that day, saying, Surely the land whereon thy feet have trodden shall be thine inheritance, and thy children's for ever, because thou hast wholly followed the LORD my God. *(What his own conscience had told him, Moses also had admitted. It is well when our own consciousness tallies with the encomiums which others may give to us, otherwise their praises may make us blush rather than smile. Caleb now claims what had been promised him ; things are very sweet when they come to us by the way of the promise.)*

10 And now, behold, the LORD hath kept me alive, as he said, these forty and five years, even since the LORD spake this word unto Moses, while *the children of* Israel wandered in the wilderness : and now, lo, I *am* this day fourscore and five years old.

11 As yet I *am as* strong this day as *I was* in the day that Moses sent me : as my strength *was* then, even so *is* my strength now, for war, both to go out, and to come in.

This was a rare privilege, and Caleb was thankful for it, and ready to use all the strength which God had given him against the enemies of Israel. He might have claimed his retiring pension, but instead thereof, he sues for fresh work, with all the ardour of a young man.

12 Now therefore give me this mountain, whereof the LORD spake in that day ; for thou heardest in that day how the Anakims *were* there, and *that* the cities *were* great *and* fenced : if so be the LORD *will be* with me, then I shall be able to drive them out, as the LORD said.

He probably reminded Joshua of a brave conversation he had held with him under the walls of the city of Hebron, when they had seen the giants, and marked the stupendous strength of the fortifications. He then spoke like a bold believer, and now he desired to prove that his words were not mere vapouring, but could be backed up by valiant deeds. Hebron it seems had once been captured by Israel, but the Anakims had returned to their strongholds, and Caleb felt that with God's help, he would hunt them out again, once for all.

13 And Joshua blessed him, and gave unto Caleb the son of Jephunneh Hebron for an inheritance.

14 Hebron therefore became the inheritance of Caleb the son of Jephunneh the Kenezite unto this day, because that he wholly followed the LORD God of Israel. *(The good old soldier had his desire, and in due time he took possession of the territory allotted to him. Whole-hearted loyalty to the Lord will have its reward. The Lord never allowed a man to be confounded, whose sole trust was in him, and whose entire heart followed him. In this family may there be many a Caleb ; yea, may we all be whole-hearted for the Lord.)*

Up comrades up ! undaunted be,
  And valiant in the fight,
For him who died upon the tree,
  For him who reigns in light.

Jesus himself leads on the strife :
  Stand to his banner true ;
Be steadfast now and all through life,
  For he will strengthen you.

WE shall now see what Caleb did with his inheritance in the land of promise.

JOSHUA XV. 13—19.

13 ¶ And unto Caleb the son of Jephunneh, he gave a part among the children of Judah, according to the commandment of the Lord to Joshua, *even* the city of Arba the father of Anak, which *city is* Hebron.

14 And Caleb drove thence the three sons of Anak, Sheshai, and Ahiman, and Talmai, the children of Anak. *(These were giants, but their gigantic stature did not frighten Caleb from attacking them. He who fears God is not the man to fear anyone else.)*

15 And he went up thence to the inhabitants of Debir : and the name of Debir before *was* Kirjath-sepher. *(This Debir appears to have been mastered before, but the Canaanites had re-occupied it. Our sins are very apt to return upon us, and when they do so we must drive them out a second time. The ancient name of Debir is here given, but why it would be hard to say. Kirjath-sepher signifies the city of the book. Since learning was scarce in those days, it may be that this place was famed for its records. Anyhow it was a Canaanitish city, and it was to be captured. Ungodliness is none the better for being associated with education.)*

16 ¶ And Caleb said, He that smiteth Kirjath-sepher, and taketh it, to him will I give Achsah my daughter to wife.

17 And Othniel the son of Kenaz, the brother of Caleb, took it : and he gave him Achsah his daughter to wife. *(This exploit is recorded again in the book of Judges ; probably because the hero of it, in after years was moved by the Spirit of God to become a judge and deliverer of Israel. He was a worthy nephew of a noble man. The younger members of a family should never allow their elders to engross all the zeal and faith. If there be one earnest Christian of our kin, let us endeavour to equal him.)*

18 And it came to pass, as she came *unto him,* that she moved him to ask of her father a field : and she lighted off *her* ass : and Caleb said unto her, What wouldest thou ?

19 Who answered, Give me a blessing ; for thou hast given me a south land ; give me also springs of water. And he gave her the upper springs and the nether springs. *(If earthly parents thus give to their children what they desire, how much more will our heavenly Father bestow upon us more of his Holy Spirit. Some blessings we must fight for, as Othniel fought for Kirjath-sepher ; others may be won by prayer, as Achsah gained the field of the abounding springs.)*

CALEB *having gained his promised inheritance appears to have shown a noble spirit by generously resigning the city of Hebron to the Levites. He was brave to win, but not greedy to hold.*

JOSHUA XXI. 3 ; 10—13.

3 And the children of Israel gave unto the Levites out of their inheritance, at the commandment of the LORD, these cities and their suburbs.

10 The children of Aaron, *being* of the families of the Kohathites, *who were* of the children of Levi, had the first lot.

11 And they gave them the city of Arba the father of Anak, which *city is* Hebron, in the hill country of Judah, with the suburbs thereof round about it.

12 But the fields of the city, and the villages thereof, gave they to Caleb the son of Jephunneh for his possession. *(Thus Caleb had the Lord's servants for near neighbours, and the very chief of them lived at his doors. It was well for them to have so valiant a defender, and well for him and his household to have such excellent instructors. God's ministers are our best friends.)*

13 ¶ Thus they gave to the children of Aaron the priest Hebron with her suburbs, *to be* a city of refuge for the slayer ; and Libnah with her suburbs. *(A double honour was thus put upon Caleb's city. If the Lord will but use our property for his service we will cheerfully give him the best that we have.)*

O happy soldiers they who serve
    Beneath thy banner, Lord !
And glad the task if thou but nerve
    Their arm to wield the sword.

Though Satan fiercely rage without,
    And fears o'erwhelm within,
Rings in the air Faith's victor note
    "Against the world I'll win."

172   " Thou shalt stand in thy lot at the end of the days."   MARCH 25.—EVENING.

[*Or June* 17.]

JOSHUA XVIII. 1—10.

AND the whole congregation of the children of Israel assembled together at Shiloh, and set up the tabernacle of the congregation there. And the land was subdued before them. *(Shiloh was a fit name for the dwelling of the God who is Israel's rest, and as a place for those sacred institutions which typified Jesus, our peace. Yet it was in the city of peace that Joshua stirred up the people to war. True peace wages a determined war against all the enemies of the Lord. Even The Great Peace-maker came to make war in the earth, war with evil, war with Satan, for there can be no peace for holiness till sin is exterminated.)*

2 And there remained among the children of Israel seven tribes, which had not yet received their inheritance.

3 And Joshua said unto the children of Israel, How long *are* ye slack to go to possess the land, which the LORD God of your fathers hath given you? *(Enriched with the spoil already taken, the people declined the toils of further conquest. Too often this is the sin of believers; they rejoice in the things whereunto they have already attained, and no longer press forward to that which is beyond. Self-satisfaction is the end of progress; the Lord deliver us from it. Joshua rebuked the people for their slackness.)*

4 Give out from among you three men for *each* tribe : and I will send them, and they shall rise, and go through the land, and describe it according to the inheritance of them; and they shall come *again* to me.

5 And they shall divide it into seven parts : Judah shall abide in their coast on the south, and the house of Joseph shall abide in their coasts on the north.

6 Ye shall therefore describe the land *into* seven parts, and bring *the description* hither to me, that I may cast lots for you here before the LORD our God. *(Surveyors were to go forth to take a prospect of all the land : it is good for us to consider what graces are attainable by us, for this will aid in stirring us to action. The division of the land among the tribes would also secure more ardent service on the part of each tribe. Division of labour, so long as it does not lead to envying and jealousy, is a wise arrange-*

ment in the service of God. All the land will be conquered when each tribe fights for its own portion : all church work will be done when each worker diligently performs the peculiar duty allotted to him.)

7 But the Levites have no part among you; for the priesthood of the LORD *is* their inheritance : *(God's ministers, now-a-days, ought to be cared for by the people, since they are shut out from the profits of trade, and the emoluments of secular offices. God will take care of those whose lives are freely given to his service:)* and Gad, and Reuben, and half the tribe of Manasseh, have received their inheritance beyond Jordan on the east, which Moses the servant of the LORD gave them.

8 ¶ And the men arose, and went away: and Joshua charged them that went to describe the land, saying, Go and walk through the land, and describe it, and come again to me, that I may here cast lots for you before the LORD in Shiloh. *(He who was once a spy himself is now the sender forth of others: those who serve God well in a lower position are the most likely to be promoted to a higher office.)*

9 And the men went and passed through the land, and described it by cities into seven parts in a book, and came *again* to Joshua to the host at Shiloh. *(They were brave and pushing men who performed this service. The church has need at this time both of enterprising spirits who will survey and describe the state of the unconverted world, and of diligent and brave soldiers who will go forth to the conquest of it. At present we are slack to go up and possess the land, and need to be aroused to our duty. O that zeal might revive among us, till the Lord's host should again press forward in the holy war.)*

10 ¶ And Joshua cast lots for them in Shiloh before the LORD : and there Joshua divided the land unto the children of Israel according to their divisions. *(God chose to appoint the casting of lots as his way of revealing his mind, but this by no means teaches us to follow the superstitious method of judgment by lot. That is little better than tempting the Lord our God. We have no precept for using the lot, and consequently no promise is connected with it. It would be in our case a heathenish custom, which as Christians we must not follow.)*

JOSHUA XXII. 1—6; 10—20.

THEN Joshua called the Reubenites, and the Gadites, and the half tribe of Manasseh, And said unto them, Ye have kept all that Moses the servant of the LORD commanded you, and have obeyed my voice in all that I commanded you : Ye have not left your brethren these many days unto this day, but have kept the charge of the commandment of the LORD your God. *(It is simple justice to give praise wherever it is deserved. There is a notion abroad, that to commend is dangerous, but wise men of old did not think so. While fault-finding is so abundant, it is refreshing to meet with a man who can speak in praise of his fellows. It is not so very common for men to be thoroughly true to their engagements, and when they are so, they ought to have it mentioned to their honour.)*

4, 5 And now the LORD your God hath given rest unto your brethren, as he promised them : therefore now return ye, and get you unto your tents, *and* unto the land of your possession, which Moses the servant of the LORD gave you on the other side Jordan. But take diligent heed to do the commandment and the law, which Moses the servant of the LORD charged you, to love the LORD your God, and to walk in all his ways, and to keep his commandments, and to cleave unto him, and to serve him with all your heart and with all your soul. *Having praised them, Joshua now directs them to their further duty. The terms of his exhortation deserve careful notice. They were to do the commandment—their religion must be practical; they were to love the Lord—their service must be hearty and sincere; they were to walk in all his ways—their obedience must be universal; they were to cleave to him—it must be persevering. Many excellent graces make up a believer's obedience, and the lack of any one will grievously mar it. Who but the Spirit of God can produce all these good things in fallen man?*

6 So Joshua blessed them, and sent them away : and they went unto their tents.

10 ¶ And when they came unto the borders of Jordan, that *are* in the land of Canaan, the children of Reuben and the children of Gad and the half tribe of Manasseh built there an altar by Jordan, a great altar to see to. *Not a wise thing, because not commanded of*

God, and very liable both to be misunderstood by others, and misused by themselves.

11 ¶ And the children of Israel heard say, Behold, the children of Reuben and the children of Gad and the half tribe of Manasseh have built an altar over against the land of Canaan, in the borders of Jordan, at the passage of the children of Israel.

12 And when the children of Israel heard *of it*, the whole congregation of the children of Israel gathered themselves together at Shiloh, to go up to war against them. *(A departure from God by setting up another altar in opposition to that of the tabernacle was apprehended, and right zealously the loyal spirit of Israel resolved to nip the evil in the bud. Was there not, however, rather too great sharpness of temper in talking so speedily of civil war ?)*

13 And the children of Israel sent unto the children of Reuben, and to the children of Gad, and to the half tribe of Manasseh, into the land of Gilead, Phinehas the son of Eleazar the priest,

14 And with him ten princes, of each chief house a prince throughout all the tribes of Israel ; and each one *was* an head of the house of their fathers among the thousands of Israel. *We should hear before we judge. Israel did not rush into strife, but sent prudent men to see how the case really stood, and what their brethren had to say.*

15 ¶ And they came unto the children of Reuben, and to the children of Gad, and to the half tribe of Manasseh, unto the land of Gilead, and they spake with them, saying,

16 Thus saith the whole congregation of the LORD, What trepass *is* this that ye have committed against the God of Israel, to turn away this day from following the LORD, in that ye have builded you an altar, that ye might rebel this day against the LORD? *(Here they stated the case and the cause of their anger. Had their suspicions been correct their anger would have needed no further justification.)*

17, 18 *Is* the iniquity of Peor too little for us, from which we are not cleansed until this day, although there was a plague in the congregation of the LORD, But that ye must turn away this day from following the LORD ? and it will be, *seeing* ye rebel to day against the LORD, that to morrow he will be wroth with the whole congregation of Israel. *(They here shew that the sin of a part might bring evil upon the whole community, and therefore they meant to stamp out the evil before it spread further.)*

19 Notwithstanding, if the land of your possession *be* unclean, *then* pass ye over unto the land of the possession of the LORD, wherein the LORD's tabernacle dwelleth, and take possession among us : but rebel not against the LORD, nor rebel against us, in building you an altar beside the altar of the LORD our God.

With true generosity they offer them a possession on their own side of Jordan, if their position across the river had driven them into setting up another altar. To enable a man to correct an error without great loss to himself is a great help towards getting him right. The pleading of the tribes with their brethren was very practical, earnest, decided, and generous.

20 Did not Achan the son of Zerah commit

a trespass in the accursed thing, and wrath fell on all the congregation of Israel ? and that man perished not alone in his iniquity. *(This judgment was fresh in their memories, and therefore, they finished their argument with it. They feared that their brethren were about to do very wrong, and to bring upon all Israel much mischief, and therefore they spoke warmly. O that we were all zealous to prevent sin in the family, and in ourselves. God still chastens those he has chosen, and though in this life the wicked may go unpunished, his own children shall not be left without chastisement. Let us walk humbly and jealously before the Lord.)*

To God the Father, God the Son,
And God the Spirit, three in one,
Be honour, praise, and glory given
By all on earth, and all in heaven.

Our ears have heard, O glorious God,
What work thou did'st of old ;
And how the heathen felt thy rod
Our fathers oft have told.

'Twas not thy people's arm or sword,
But only thy right hand,
Which scatter'd all the race abhorr'd,
And gave thy tribes their land.

In thee alone we make our boasts,
And glory all day long,
Arise at once, thou Lord of hosts,
And fill our mouth with song.

Let us, with a gladsome mind,
Praise the Lord, for he is kind :
For his mercies shall endure,
Ever faithful, ever sure.

He his chosen race did bless
In the wasteful wilderness :
For his mercies shall endure,
Ever faithful, ever sure.

He hath, with a piteous eye,
Look'd upon our misery :
For his mercies shall endure,
Ever faithful, ever sure.

My name is entered on the list,
I've plighted hand and word,
To fight to death for Jesus Christ,
And conquer for my Lord.

And I will prove my vow sincere,
If he my helper be ;
Nor all his foemen will I fear,
Since he upholdeth me.

May the grace of Christ our Saviour,
And the Father's boundless love,
With the Holy Spirit's favour,
Rest upon us from above ;

Thus may we abide in union
With each other and the Lord ;
And possess, in sweet communion,
Joys which earth cannot afford.

Jesus thy perfect love reveal,
My Alpha and Omega be,
And I thy blessed words shall feel
And witness them fulfill'd in me :
"Nothing hath fail'd of all the good,
My Saviour hath performed the whole,"
Firm to his promise he hath stood
I witness this with all my soul.

THE *tribes on the other side of Jordan received the deputation with courtesy, and* answered for themselves without anger.

JOSHUA XXII. 21—34.

21, 22 Then the children of Reuben and the children of Gad and the half tribe of Manasseh answered, and said unto the heads of the thousands of Israel, The Lord God of gods, the Lord God of gods, he knoweth, and Israel he shall know ; if *it be* in rebellion, or if in transgression against the Lord, (save us not this day),

23 That we have built us an altar to turn from following the Lord, or if to offer thereon burnt offering or meat offering, or if to offer peace offerings thereon, let the Lord himself require *it ; (In the sincerity of their hearts they appealed to God that they had no idea of offering sacrifice anywhere but at the one appointed altar. Appeals to God must never be lightly made, nor in any case where anything less than the highest interests are concerned. It is consoling to feel that God knows our motives, but we must do our best so to act that God's people shall also know what we aim at.)*

24, 25, 26, 27 And if we have not *rather* done it for fear of *this* thing, saying, In time to come your children might speak unto our children, saying, What have ye to do with the Lord God of Israel ? For the Lord hath made Jordan a border between us and you, ye children of Reuben and children of Gad ; ye have no part in the Lord : so shall your children make our children cease from fearing the Lord. Therefore we said, Let us now prepare to build us an altar, not for burnt offering, nor for sacrifice : But *that* it *may be* a witness between us, and you, and our generations after us, that we might do the service of the Lord before him with our burnt offerings, and with our sacrifices, and with our peace offerings ; that your children may not say to our children in time to come, Ye have no part in the Lord. *They feared lest they should lose the means of grace, and lest the Jordan should become a line of division between them and their brethren at some future time.*

28, 29 Therefore said we, that it shall be, when they should *so* say to us or to our generations in time to come, that we may say *again,*

Behold the pattern of the altar of the Lord, which our fathers made, not for burnt offerings, nor for sacrifices ; but it *is* a witness between us and you. God forbid that we should rebel against the Lord, and turn this day from following the Lord, to build an altar for burnt offerings, for meat offerings, or for sacrifices, beside the altar of the Lord our God that *is* before his tabernacle. *(Their intention was thus shown to be honest, though the action had a very doubtful appearance. We are bound, however, never to put a worse construction than we can help upon other peoples' conduct.)*

30 ¶ And when Phinehas the priest, and the princes of the congregation and heads of the thousands of Israel which *were* with him, heard these words, it pleased them.

31 And Phinehas the son of Eleazar the priest said unto them, This day we perceive that the Lord *is* among us, because ye have not committed this trespass against the Lord : now ye have delivered the children of Israel out of the hand of the Lord. *(Religious quarrels are usually very fierce, but in this case true wisdom ended the strife. When one is ready to explain, and the other willing to receive the explanation, difficulties will soon be got over. May all differences in this family be handled wisely and tenderly, and peace and love ever rule among us.)*

32, 33 And Phinehas the son of Eleazar the priest, and the princes, returned to the children of Israel, and brought them word again. And the thing pleased the children of Israel ; and the children of Israel blessed God, and did not intend to go up against them in battle, to destroy the land wherein the children of Reuben and Gad dwelt. *(Zeal for the truth made Israel prepare for war, but they were not hot-headed as some are in these days. Once enabled to believe well of their brethren, they were glad of it, and gave God thanks that doubtful matters were cleared up. It is well to watch over others with holy jealousy, but not to be rancorous and bitter.)*

34 And the children of Reuben and the children of Gad called the altar *Ed, (or witness :)* for it *shall be* a witness between us that the Lord *is* God. *(Thus all ended well, and true religion ruled on both sides the Jordan. When shall our land become one again,—knowing only one Lord. one faith, and one baptism ?)*

HAVING *served his nation faithfully, Joshua at the close of his life delivered his soul to the people in an earnest exhortation, the spirit of which as much needs pressing home upon believers now as in his day—*

JOSHUA XXIII. 1—15.

1 And it came to pass a long time after that the LORD had given rest unto Israel from all their enemies round about, that Joshua waxed old *and* stricken in age.

2 And Joshua called for all Israel, *and* for their elders, and for their heads, and for their judges, and for their officers, and said unto them, I am old *and* stricken in age :

3 And ye have seen all that the LORD your God hath done unto all these nations because of you ; for the LORD your God *is* he that hath fought for you. *(The sight of the judgments of God upon the ungodly should have a salutary influence upon us, and the remembrance of the Lord's mercy to us should bind us for ever to him.)*

4 Behold, I have divided unto you by lot these nations that remain, to be an inheritance for your tribes, from Jordan, with all the nations that I have cut off, even unto the great sea westward.

5 And the LORD your God, he shall expel them from before you, and drive them from out of your sight ; and ye shall possess their land, as the LORD your God hath promised unto you.

6 Be ye therefore very courageous to keep and to do all that is written in the book of the law of Moses, that ye turn not aside therefrom *to* the right hand or *to* the left ; *(This had been the command of the Lord to himself, the music of it was not out of his ears, and therefore he used the selfsame words to the people. Language which has acted powerfully upon our own hearts we fondly hope will have the like effect upon others.)*

7 That ye come not among these nations, these that remain among you ; neither make mention of the name of their gods, nor cause to swear *by them*, neither serve them, nor bow yourselves unto them :

8 But cleave unto the LORD your God, as ye have done unto this day. *(He commends them as well as commands them. A little judicious praise makes men all the readier to hear. Separation from sinners was Joshua's lesson, and it is one which is not stale or needless at this time.)*

9, 10, 11 For the LORD hath driven out from before you great nations and strong : but *as for* you, no man hath been able to stand before you unto this day. One man of you shall chase a thousand : for the LORD your God, he *it is* that fighteth for you, as he hath promised you. Take good heed therefore unto yourselves, that ye love the LORD your God. *(Sin is weakness. Love to God gives us the strength of God.)*

12 Else if ye do in any wise go back, and cleave unto the remnant of these nations, *even* these that remain among you, and shall make marriages with them :

13 Know for a certainty that the LORD your God will no more drive out *any of* these nations from before you ; but they shall be snares and traps unto you, and scourges in your sides, and thorns in your eyes, until ye perish from off this good land which the LORD your God hath given you. *(Marriage with the ungodly is expressly mentioned, because it is a frequent and deadly snare. It has done more mischief in the church of God than tongue can tell. It is the wolf which devours the lambs.)*

Note from this verse that any sins in our own hearts which we do not resolutely drive out will become our plague and scourge. Think of " thorns in the eyes." No man can have peace while he is at peace with any sin. Can a man carry coals in his bosom and not be burned ?

14 And, behold, this day I *am* going the way of all the earth : and ye know in all your hearts and in all your souls, that not one thing hath failed of all the good things which the LORD your God spake concerning you ; all are come to pass unto you, *and* not one thing hath failed thereof.

15 Therefore it shall come to pass, *that* as all good things are come upon you, which the LORD your God promised you ; so shall the LORD bring upon you all evil things, until he have destroyed you from off this good land which the LORD your God hath given you.

God's faithfulness to his promises leaves us no room to doubt his equal faithfulness to his threatenings. He is a true God, both in mercy and in justice. We had need be carefully obedient, for the Lord is in earnest in every word he utters.

JOSHUA *was moved to speak in the name of the Lord, and remind the people of what had been done for them. Having recapitulated the wonders of Egypt and the wilderness, he mentions the Lord's goodness to them in Canaan.*

JOSHUA XXIV. 11–26.

11 Ye went over Jordan, and came unto Jericho: and the men of Jericho fought against you, the Amorites, and the Perizzites, and the Canaanites, and the Hittites, and the Girgashites, the Hivites, and the Jebusites; and I delivered them into your hand.

12 And I sent the hornet before you, which drave them out from before you, *even* the two kings of the Amorites; *but* not with thy sword, nor with thy bow. *(God can make insects to be more terrible than men-at-arms, and he did so in this case. Israel fought, but her victories were due to a higher arm. After all we can do, our salvation is still of the Lord alone.)*

13 And I have given you a land for which ye did not labour, and cities which ye built not, and ye dwell in them; of the vineyards and oliveyards which ye planted not do ye eat.

Everything which we *possess is as much given to us of God as Canaan was to the tribes.*

14, 15 Now therefore fear the LORD, and serve him in sincerity and in truth: and put away the gods which your fathers served on the other side of the flood, and in Egypt; and serve ye the LORD. And if it seem evil unto you to serve the LORD, choose you this day whom ye will serve; whether the gods which your fathers served that *were* on the other side of the flood, or the gods of the Amorites, in whose land ye dwell: but as for me and my house, we will serve the LORD. *(Every man must have a god, the question was, who should be their god? Joshua declares that Jehovah alone should be God to him and to his household. We cannot serve two gods, and it will be a happy thing if in our house we never attempt it, but once for all choose the Lord alone to be our God. May divine grace so direct us.)*

16, 17, 18 And the people answered and said, God forbid that we should forsake the LORD, to serve other gods; For the LORD our God, he *it is* that brought us up and our fathers out of the land of Egypt, from the house of bondage, and which did those great signs in our sight, and preserved us in all the way wherein we

went, and among all the people through whom we passed: And the LORD drave out from before us all the people, even the Amorites which dwelt in the land: *therefore* will we also serve the LORD; for he *is* our God. *(They spoke well, yet not well enough, for they were much too confident in their own resolves. Having so often turned aside, it had been wiser to pray, "Lord, keep us," than to cry so confidently, "we will" and "we will.")*

19 And Joshua said unto the people, Ye cannot serve the LORD: for he *is* an holy God; he *is* a jealous God; he will not forgive your transgressions nor your sins.

20 If ye forsake the LORD, and serve strange gods, then he will turn and do you hurt, and consume you, after that he hath done you good.

Joshua reminded them that their promise would not be so easy to keep as they imagined. It is one thing to promise, but quite another to perform. How solemn are the thoughts suggested by the words—" he is a jealous God." He will not endure a rival, nor tolerate half-hearted service.

21 And the people said unto Joshua, Nay; but we will serve the LORD.

22 And Joshua said unto the people, Ye *are* witnesses against yourselves that ye have chosen you the LORD, to serve him. And they said, We are witnesses. *(With good intent, but far too little self-knowledge, they entered into a covenant which they soon violated. Beware of trusting self in its best mood. It is fickle as the wind.)*

23, 24, 25, 26 Now therefore put away, *said he,* the strange gods which *are* among you, and incline your heart unto the LORD God of Israel. And the people said unto Joshua, The LORD our God will we serve, and his voice will we obey. So Joshua made a covenant with the people that day, and set them a statute and an ordinance in Shechem. And Joshua wrote these words in the book of the law of God, and took a great stone, and set it up there under an oak, that *was* by the sanctuary of the LORD.

O Lord, we in this house desire to serve thee for ever. Help us by thy grace to be thy beloved children and thy faithful servants.

Lord, I long thy will t'obey
Fain I'd put all sin away;
But that I may serve aright,
Let thy Spirit be my might.

AS we have now ended the book of *Joshua,*
we will select a few passages from other
portions of the Bible before we continue the
history. We will again read a part of David's
wonderful panegyric upon the book of God in—

PSALM CXIX. 17–32.

17 Deal bountifully with thy servant, *that I*
may live, and keep thy word. (*Our lives are*
preserved by God's bounty, and should be devoted
to his service. True life is the product of rich
grace, and always reveals itself by holy obedience
to the divine will.)

18 Open thou mine eyes, that I may behold
wondrous things out of thy law. (*The Scrip-*
tures are full of wonders, and especially they
reveal him whose name is "Wonderful," but we
need to have our eyes opened by the Holy Spirit, or
we shall see nothing aright. Far enough are we
by nature from being able to keep the law, for
we cannot even understand it without divine
teaching.)

19 I *am* a stranger in the earth : hide not thy
commandments from me. (*Stranger as I am*
to the world, let me not be a stranger to thy will.
With thy precepts as my map I shall find my
road, even in this foreign country ; without them
I shall be as a traveller lost in the desert.)

20 My soul breaketh for the longing *that it*
hath unto thy judgments at all times. (*His*
desire was importunate even to heartbreak, and
it was constant "at all times." Such a desire is
a sure token that the Spirit of God dwells within.)

21 Thou hast rebuked the proud *that are*
cursed, which do err from thy commandments.
Pride brings forth error, and error provokes
God to inflict the curse, of which his rebukes are
but the fore-runners.

22 Remove from me reproach and contempt ;
for I have kept thy testimonies. (*The best of*
men are slandered, their appeal is to God, their
comfort is the testimony of their conscience.)

23 Princes also did sit *and* speak against me :
but thy servant did meditate in thy statutes.
He was not so disturbed or disheartened as to
give up his faith, but he was in earnest to sustain
it with the best spiritual food.

24 Thy testimonies also *are* my delight *and*
my counsellors. (*In consequence of his medita-*
ting in the word, David was kept both from
sadness and perplexity. We can only gain com-
fort from the Bible by following its directions,
and living upon its doctrines.)

25 My soul cleaveth unto the dust : quicken
thou me according to thy word. (*Here we find*
nature's disease confessed, and a cry directed to the
Lord for the only remedy. Dust will cleave to
dust ; only the divinely regenerated rises to God,
and even that needs daily renewal. The Lord
has promised us quickening, let us seek it.)

26 I have declared my ways, and thou heardest
me : teach me thy statutes. (*Confession into the*
ear of God is good for the soul, and divine in-
struction is the best preservative for the life. If
we confess past failure, we can only avoid future
sin by seeking heavenly teaching.)

27 Make me to understand the way of thy
precepts : so shall I talk of thy wondrous works.
It were well if all talk were upon such themes.
When there is gold in the understanding, our
speech will be golden, but how seldom is it so. When
God instructs us we talk to profit, but not else.

28 My soul melteth for heaviness : strengthen
thou me according unto thy word. (*Lord, when*
we dissolve with weakness, make thy word to be
the bread of heaven to strengthen us.)

29 Remove from me the way of lying : (*Take*
it from me as well as me from it ; for its
presence is grievous to me :) and grant me thy
law graciously.

30 I have chosen the way of truth : thy
judgments have I laid *before me.* (*Like a boy's*
copy, or an artist's model. We cannot learn
unless we have our great class-book open before us.)

31 I have stuck unto thy testimonies : O
LORD, put me not to shame.

32 I will run the way of thy commandments,
when thou shalt enlarge my heart. (*The more*
God gives us of comfort and knowledge, the more
will we serve him. The weight of his grace shall
lead us to put off " every weight " of sin. May
the Lord make more room in our hearts for
himself and his love.)

Smile on thy servant, bounteous Lord !
Grant me to live, and keep thy word :
Grant me to view, with eyes unsealed,
The wonders by thy law revealed.

Shine on me still, while far from home,
A stranger here on earth I roam ;
While pines my soul with restless love,
Thy righteous judgments, Lord, to prove.

PSALM CXIX. 33—48.

TEACH me, O LORD, the way of thy statutes; and I shall keep it *unto* the end. *(Bernard says, "He who is his own teacher has a fool for his master." We cannot teach ourselves what we do not know, and to know anything aright we must be taught of God. Those whom the Lord himself instructs, become practical scholars and persevering disciples. Lessons divinely learned are never forgotten.)*

34 Give me understanding, and I shall keep thy law; yea, I shall observe it with *my* whole heart. *(Where the Spirit of God gives a spiritual understanding of the Word, the whole nature is sanctified and set upon keeping the Lord's commands. This prayer is suitable for each one in the family; let us stop a moment, while we breathe it from our hearts.)*

35 Make me to go in the path of thy commandments; for therein do I delight. *(I am like the poor impotent man who could not move; therefore, Lord, make me to go. Where my heart already runs, there let all my faculties follow.)*

36 Incline my heart unto thy testimonies, and not to covetousness. *(Covetousness is the rival of religion. Those who love not God, frequently make a god of their gold. This sin is sure to bring ruin upon those who fall into it. It made Judas a traitor, and dragged him down to hell.)*

37 Turn away mine eyes from beholding vanity; *and* quicken thou me in thy way. *Looking brings longing, and longing leads to sin, therefore let not the eye gaze on evil.*

38 Stablish thy word unto thy servant, who is devoted to thy fear. *(My whole nature is set upon honouring thee; therefore, O Lord, make all thy promises to stand firm for me.)*

39 Turn away my reproach which I fear: for thy judgments *are* good. *(The reproach of Christ we rejoice in, but from the reproach of inconsistency we should daily pray to be delivered.)*

40 Behold, I have longed after thy precepts: quicken me in thy righteousness. *(Mere professors long after the promises, but genuine saints long after the precepts also. He who does not desire holiness will be shut out of heaven. Lord, send us more grace that we may be more holy.)*

41 Let thy mercies come also unto me, O LORD, *even* thy salvation, according to thy word.

Mercy, yea, many mercies, we need, and we cannot be saved without them, but then they are promised in the Word, and here is our ground of comfort. Let us plead the promise in prayer.

42 So shall I have wherewith to answer him that reproacheth me : for I trust in thy word. *Faith, by the help of realised joy and manifested holiness, shuts the mouths of gainsayers.*

43 And take not the word of truth utterly out of my mouth; for I have hoped in thy judgments. *(If we are somewhat straitened in spiritual enjoyments, yet do not quite prevent our praising Thee. Let us rather stammer out Thy praises, than be entirely silent.)*

44 So shall I keep thy law continually for ever and ever. *(This would be heaven upon earth; it is heaven in heaven.)*

45 And I will walk at liberty: for I seek thy precepts. *(Holiness is the truest liberty.)*

46 I will speak of thy testimonies also before kings, and will not be ashamed. *(What is there to be ashamed of? God grant us the boldness of true faith in all companies.)*

47 And I will delight myself in thy commandments, which I have loved.

"I live a voluptuous life," said holy Joseph Alleine; "but it is upon spiritual dainties, such as men of the world know not and taste not of."

48 My hands also will I lift up unto thy commandments, which I have loved; and I will meditate in thy statutes.

He longed to embrace the truth, and therefore held up his hands to receive it with inward delight. He felt encouraged to practise diligently the law of his God, because he loved the Lord's Word, and daily meditated therein. It should be our daily habit to search the Scriptures. We must not be content with this family reading, but must each, in private, feed upon the precious Word. Are we all mindful of this?

In thee I live, and move and am ;
  Thou dealest out my days :
Lord, as thou dost my life renew,
  Let me renew thy praise.

To thee I come, from thee I am ;
  For thee I still would be ;
'Tis better for me not to live,
  Than not to live to thee.

OUR *time will be well spent if we study one of our Lord's discourses upon prayer. It consists of two parables.*

LUKE XVIII. 1—14.

1 And he spake a parable unto them *to this end, that men ought always to pray,* and not to faint. *(To commence prayer is easy, but to continue in it is another thing. We too often flag and grow remiss, and so we lose the blessing.)*

2 Saying, There was in a city a judge, which feared not God, neither regarded man :

3 And there was a widow in that city ; and she came unto him, saying, Avenge me of mine adversary.

4 And he would not for a while : but afterward he said within himself, Though I fear not God, nor regard man ;

5 Yet because this widow troubleth me, I will avenge her, lest by her continual coming she weary me. *(He was a wicked, unfeeling man, ready enough to pervert justice and grant the suit to the oppressor; his petitioner was a poor woman, bereft of her natural protector, and quite unable to affect his hard heart by her sad tale; yet her importunity won her suit, he was afraid of being tired to death, and therefore he attended to her cry. Every part of the parable strengthens our case, for we deal with a faithful and gracious God, who is ready to hear us; we are poor and feeble, it is true, but we have a powerful Advocate in the great Husband of the church; therefore if we do not obtain our request the first time, we should pray again and again, and never cease till our importunity obtains its end.)*

6 And the Lord said, Hear what the unjust judge saith.

7 And shall not God avenge his own elect, which cry day and night unto him, though he bear long with them ? *(They are no strangers, but "his own elect;" surely he will hear them.)*

8 I tell you that he will avenge them speedily. *(The prayers of the suffering church will not have long to wait. God's time comes on.)* Nevertheless when the Son of man cometh, shall he find faith on the earth ? *(It is so scarce that even He who best can discover faith will hardly find any of it. Shame upon our unbelief.)*

9 And he spake this parable unto certain which trusted in themselves that they were righteous, and despised others :

10 Two men went up into the temple to pray ; the one a Pharisee, and the other a publican.

11 The Pharisee stood and prayed thus with himself, *(He stood by himself as if too holy to be touched by others, and his prayer was indeed, no prayer, but a self-glorification),* God, I thank thee, that I am not as other men *are,* extortioners, unjust, adulterers, or even as this publican.

12 I fast twice in the week, I give tithes of all that I possess. *(Under the pretence of praising God, he praised himself. It is all "I," "I fast," "I give," and so on. Nor was this enough, he indulged in uncharitable reflections upon others, making at the same time a list of his own virtues and a catalogue of other men's failings, and crowning all with a sneer at his neighbour.)*

13 And the publican, standing afar off, would not lift up so much as *his* eyes unto heaven, but smote upon his breast, saying, God be merciful to me a sinner. *(He confessed his sin, he smote upon his heart as the cause of it, he pleaded for mercy, and he had an eye to the atonement, for his prayer really meant, "Be propitious towards me through sacrifice.")*

14 I tell you, this man went down to his house justified *rather* than the other : *(He had a sweet sense of pardon in his breast, and the other had it not, for indeed he had not even asked for it:)* for every one that exalteth himself shall be abased ; and he that humbleth himself shall be exalted. *(From all this let us learn to pray importunately, but not proudly. We must be earnest, but yet humble. We may be bold, but not arrogant. Lord teach us to pray.)*

The Lord their different language knows,
And different answers he bestows ;
The humble soul with grace he crowns,
Whilst on the proud his anger frowns.

Dear Father ! let me never be
Join'd with the boasting Pharisee ;
I have no merits of my own,
But plead the sufferings of thy Son.

LET us learn a little of the wisdom of Solomon, from

PROVERBS XVI. 1—16.

1 The preparations of the heart in man, and the answer of the tongue, *is* from the LORD.

We are neither able to think nor speak anything aright without divine aid. Especially in prayer, we require to have the heart prepared, and the mouth opened by the Spirit of all grace.

2 All the ways of a man *are* clean in his own eyes; but the LORD weigheth the spirits.

We judge by the eye, superficially, but the Lord uses surer tests, and puts everything into his unerring balances; hence he arrives at a very different conclusion from ours.

3 Commit thy works unto the LORD, and thy thoughts shall be established. *(Both our bodily and spiritual interests will be safe when we place them in the Lord's hands, and, through the peace which will result from our faith, our thoughts will become steady, calm, resolute, and joyful.)*

4 The LORD hath made all *things* for himself: yea, even the wicked for the day of evil. *(Let them rebel as they may, he will make them fulfil some purpose in his providential arrangements.)*

5 Every one *that is* proud in heart *is* an abomination to the Lord: *though* hand *join* in hand, he shall not be unpunished. *(The pride of the wicked makes them abominable, but their power cannot protect them. God will break up all godless societies, however strong they may be.)*

6 By mercy and truth iniquity is purged: and by the fear of the LORD men depart from evil.

7 When a man's ways please the LORD, he maketh even his enemies to be at peace with him. *(This the Lord often does, as in the cases of Isaac and Abimelech, Jacob and Esau; but this truth must be qualified by another—the Lord's enemies will not be at peace with us, let us live as graciously as we may.)*

8 Better *is* a little with righteousness than great revenues without right.

9 A man's heart deviseth his way: but the LORD directeth his steps. *(Man proposes, but God disposes. Napoleon sneered at this saying, and vowed that he would propose and dispose too, but his end was not far off.)*

10 A divine sentence *is* in the lips of the king: his mouth transgresseth not in judgment.

This should be true, and of Solomon it was true, but of many a king the reverse might be spoken. There is one King, the Lord of all, concerning whom this is divinely certain.

11 A just weight and balance *are* the LORD's: all the weights of the bag *are* his work.

Justice should rule everywhere, both on the bench and over the counter. Let us be very exact in all our dealings, lest we grieve the Lord.

12 *It is* an abomination to kings to commit wickedness: for the throne is established by righteousness.

13 Righteous lips *are* the delight of kings; and they love him that speaketh right.

14 The wrath of a king *is as* messengers of death: but a wise man will pacify it.

15 In the light of the king's countenance *is* life; and his favour *is* as a cloud of the latter rain. *(This is most true of the King of kings, his wrath is death, his love is life. Those who enjoy the conscious favour of the Lord, know by experience the refreshing and comforting influence of his presence. To walk in the light of God's countenance is perfect bliss, to lose fellowship with him, is to his chosen the bitterest sorrow.)*

16 How much better *is it* to get wisdom than gold! and to get understanding rather to be chosen than silver! *(It is better, much better, none can say how much better. Gold comes from common providence, but grace is the token of electing love. Gold is but a nobler form of earth, but grace is the essence of heaven. Gold is soon spent, but grace abides to enrich us. Gold may be stolen from us, but grace none can take away. Gold and silver cannot comfort us in death, but the true wisdom can. Wealth of precious metals will be useless in eternity, but grace will make us glorious there. Lord, evermore give us understanding through thy Holy Spirit!)*

Thine for ever! Lord of life,
Shield us through our earthly strife;
Thou the Life, the Truth, the Way,
Guide us to the realms of day.

Thine for ever! O how blest
They who find in thee their rest;
Saviour, guardian, heavenly friend,
O defend us to the end.

PROVERBS XVI. 17—33.

THE highway of the upright *is* to depart from evil : he that keepeth his way preserveth his soul. *(Keep thy way and God will keep thee; but let it be the King's highway, the ancient, well-trodden way, marked out by authority, and traversed by the Prince of pilgrims himself.)*

18 Pride *goeth* before destruction, and an haughty spirit before a fall. *(Pride must have a fall. As the mercury in the barometer foretells the weather, so does pride warn us that a humbling time is near.)*

19 Better *it is to be* of an humble spirit with the lowly, than to divide the spoil with the proud. *(It does not seem so, and few would choose it, but the Word of God knows best. The sharer of the spoil is afraid that he may lose it again, and probably is even now discontented and greedy for more, but the lowly mind is satisfied, and so possesses happiness.)*

20 He that handleth a matter wisely shall find good : and whoso trusteth in the LORD, happy *is* he. *(To trust God in all our matters is the wise way of handling them. Let us trust him in all things this day.)*

21 The wise in heart shall be called prudent: and the sweetness of the lips increaseth learning. *The really wise will be discovered, and shall have the credit they deserve ; and those who can speak attractively increase the knowledge of the people if their own hearts are rightly instructed.*

22 Understanding *is* a wellspring of life unto him that hath it : but the instruction of fools *is* folly. *(Even his wisdom is ridiculous. When he does his best it is but folly.)*

23 The heart of the wise teacheth his mouth, and addeth learning to his lips.

24 Pleasant words *are as* an honeycomb, sweet to the soul, and health to the bones. *Since pleasant words are both sweet and wholesome, let us use many of them. Words out of God's Word, kind words—words which cause pleasure to others—let us use them from morning to night, and so though we keep no bees, we shall never be without honeycombs.*

25 There is a way that seemeth right unto a man, but the end thereof *are* the ways of death.

26 He that laboureth laboureth for himself ; for his mouth craveth it of him. *(Our mouth calls daily for bread, and therefore we must work for it. And spiritual bread is to be laboured for, for so the Saviour has told us.)*

27 An ungodly man diggeth up evil : *(He searches it out, he dives into secrets, he works hard to unearth it. How men will labour for Satan.)* And in his lips *there is* as a burning fire. *(Ready to break forth at any moment, and do infinite mischief.)*

28 A froward man soweth strife : and a whisperer separateth chief friends. *(If you have anything to say which you dare not speak out, never say it at all. Whispering against persons is mean to the last degree, and those who listen to it are mean too.)*

29 A violent man enticeth his neighbour, and leadeth him into the way *that is* not good.

30 He shutteth his eyes to devise froward things: moving his lips he bringeth evil to pass. *Some shut their eyes and move their lips in prayer, but revengeful men make malice their devotion, they are always thinking of it, and muttering about it to themselves.*

31 The hoary head *is* a crown of glory, *if* it be found in the way of righteousness. *Honour, then, all aged saints. Regard them as crowned heads, and treat them with double respect. Old age is honourable by itself, but associated with piety it is venerable.*

32 He that is slow to anger is better than the mighty ; and he that ruleth his spirit than he that taketh a city. *(He conquers himself, he crushes an inward insurrection, and these are the noblest of achievements. The Lord make each one of us gentle and forbearing. Are we of a hot and angry spirit, let us pray for the waters of grace to quench the flames of nature.)*

33 The lot is cast into the lap; but the whole disposing thereof *is* of the LORD. *(Even in trivial matters and matters contingent and accidental, the Lord rules. This is a sweet comfort.)*

Thine for ever ! Saviour keep
These thy frail and trembling sheep ;
Safe enclosed beneath thy care,
Let us all thy goodness share.

Thine for ever ! thou our Guide,
All our wants by thee supplied,
All our sins by thee forgiven,
Led by thee from earth to heaven.

LET us for our instruction read Paul's description of holy love, which is so excellent a grace as to be absolutely essential to the Christian character.

I. CORINTHIANS XIII.

1 Though I speak with the tongues of men and of angels, and have not charity, I am become *as* sounding brass, or a tinkling cymbal. *Eloquence of the most lofty kind is mere sound, unless there be love in the speaker's heart to give weight to his words. Better to have a loving heart than to speak twenty languages.*

2 And though I have *the gift* of prophecy, and understand all mysteries, and all knowledge; and though I have all faith, so that I could remove mountains, and have not charity, I am nothing. *(Gifts may be plentiful, and those of the highest order, and yet we may perish; grace in the heart is the only sure evidence of salvation. A man may prophesy and be a Balaam, he may understand mysteries and be a Simon Magus, he may have all knowledge and perish like Ahithophel, and he may have a mountain-moving faith, and be a son of perdition like Judas. Love to God and man there must be, or we have nothing good in us.)*

3 And though I bestow all my goods to feed *the poor*, and though I give my body to be burned, and have not charity, it profiteth me nothing. *(Men may endow the poor with all their substance out of mere ostentation, or die as martyrs out of sheer obstinacy, but if they have no love to God they have suffered in vain. Love is an essential grace, it is the soul of godliness, and without it religion is but a dead carcase.)*

4 Charity suffereth long, *and* is kind; charity envieth not. *(It is glad of another's good.)* Charity vaunteth not itself. *(It never glorifies itself.)* Is not puffed up. *(It hates flattery.)*

5 Doth not behave itself unseemly. *(Christian love conducts itself properly. Love to others will not allow us to act in a manner unbecoming our position and the decencies of society.)* Seeketh not her own, is not easily provoked, thinketh no evil. *(Is not suspicious and captious.)*

6, 7 Rejoiceth not in iniquity, but rejoiceth in the truth; Beareth all things. *(Covers many things with its mantle, and as Old Master Trapp says, "swallows down whole many pills which*

would be very bitter in her mouth if she were so foolish as to chew them.")* Believeth all things. *(That is to say, all things which are for a neighbour's credit; trying to put a good construction upon everything, even where it needs great faith to be able to do so.)* Hopeth all things, endureth all things.

8, 9 Charity never faileth. *(It is an unwithering flower.)* But whether *there be* prophecies, they shall fail; whether *there be* tongues, they shall cease; whether *there be* knowledge, it shall vanish away. For we know in part, and we prophesy in part. *(Our greatest knowledge is to know that we know nothing. We are but scholars in the lower forms of Christ's College.)*

10 But when that which is perfect is come, then that which is in part shall be done away.

11 When I was a child, I spake as a child, I understood as a child, I thought as a child: but when I became a man, I put away childish things.

12 For now we see through a glass, darkly; but then face to face: now I know in part; but then shall I know even as also I am known. *He shews that our best intellectual attainments here below, even in heavenly things, must be necessarily temporary, and thus he leads us to prize those choice graces of the heart which will outlast time, and be perfected in eternity.*

13 And now abideth faith, hope, charity, these three; but the greatest of these *is* charity. *It is not true that faith and hope will cease any more than love. The three divine sisters are each immortal. We shall trust the Lord all the more when we meet him face to face, and we shall hope all the more ardently for the continued enjoyment of his glory when we enter into it. Still love bears the palm, may we be made perfect in it.*

Had I the tongues of Greeks and Jews,
And nobler speech than angels use,
If love be absent, I am found
Like tinkling brass, an empty sound.

Should I distribute all my store,
To feed the bowels of the poor,
Or give my body to the flame,
To gain a martyr's glorious name:

If love to God and love to men
Be absent, all my hopes are vain;
Nor tongues, nor gifts, nor fiery zeal,
The work of love can e'er fulfil.

I. PETER II. 13—25.

SUBMIT yourselves to every ordinance of man for the Lord's sake : (*True religion is always the friend of order, as well as of liberty. The gospel is no doctrine of anarchy, and the Christian is no fomenter of strife,*) whether it be to the king, as supreme ; Or unto governors, as unto them that are sent by him for the punishment of evildoers, and for the praise of them that do well. (*Civil government is necessary for the well-being of mankind, and those who delight in the law of the Lord are among the last to wish to see its power weakened, or its executive despised. We had sooner suffer wrong, than see our country the prey of lawless mobs.*)

15 For so is the will of God, that with well doing ye may put to silence the ignorance of foolish men : (*Men are ready enough to speak against our holy faith, and in Peter's day the charge was laid against Christians that they were the enemies of social order; the habitual obedience of Christians to the laws of the countries in which they were scattered was the most conclusive answer to the calumny.*)

16 As free, and not using *your* liberty for a cloke of maliciousness, but as the servants of God. (*Believers are the freest of men, but they know the difference between liberty and license. As servants of the Lord, they submit for peace sake to man's laws, because their Great Lawgiver so commands.*)

17 Honour all men. (*This is quite as much our duty as to honour the king. Manhood deserves honour,—not wealth, dress, rank, and so on, but man, as our own flesh and blood; for however poor or obscure a man may be, he is a man for all that, and as such must not be treated as if he were a beast.*) Love the brotherhood. Fear God. Honour the king. (*Four precepts which are meant to balance one another. There should be a blending of them all in our lives.*)

18 Servants, *be* subject to *your* masters with all fear (*or respect*) : not only to the good and gentle, but also to the froward.

19 For this *is* thankworthy, if a man for conscience toward God endure grief, suffering wrongfully.

20 For what glory *is it*, if when ye be buffeted for your faults, ye shall take it patiently? (*Ordinary people can do that, but Christians are extraordinary men, and must rise to the highest style of virtue;*) but if, when ye do well, and suffer *for it*, ye take it patiently, this *is* acceptable with God. (*Many will say, "If I had deserved it, I should not have cared about it." But it is evident that were we guilty we ought to care all the more. If we are wise, we shall feel that if we do not deserve a rebuke, we can bear it patiently, and thank God for the grace which enables us to rejoice amidst it all.*)

21 For even hereunto were ye called : because Christ also suffered for us, leaving us an example, that ye should follow his steps :

22 Who did no sin, neither was guile found in his mouth :

23 Who, when he was reviled, reviled not again ; when he suffered, he threatened not ; but committed *himself* to him that judgeth righteously : (*What an example! May the Holy Spirit enable us to imitate it. He was the paragon of patience, the mirror of endurance. He was absolutely perfect, and yet was infinitely a sufferer, but he never complained, or resented wrong. Master of Patience, teach thy disciples.*)

24 Who his own self bare our sins in his own body on the tree, that we, being dead to sins, should live unto righteousness : by whose stripes ye were healed.

25 For ye were as sheep going astray ; but are now returned unto the Shepherd and Bishop of your souls. (*Let us then follow our Shepherd wherever he leads the way. Especially in the paths of sacred patience and forbearance, let us walk in close attendance upon him. For this we need thy grace, O Spirit of love!*)

My dear Redeemer and my Lord,
I read my duty in thy word ;
But in thy life the law appears
Drawn out in living characters.

Such was thy truth, and such thy zeal,
Such deference to thy Father's will,
Such love, and meekness so divine,
I would transcribe and make them mine.

Be thou my pattern ; make me bear
More of thy gracious image here ;
Then God, the Judge, shall own my name
Amongst the followers of the Lamb.

I. THESSALONIANS, IV. 13—18; V. 1—10.

BUT I would not have you to be ignorant, brethren, concerning them which are asleep, that ye sorrow not, even as others which have no hope. *(We may sorrow, but with measure and limit. We know that the souls of departed believers are safe, and that their bodies will rise from the grave: wherefore, then, should we weep and lament as the heathen and the unbelieving do?)*

14 For if we believe that Jesus died and rose again, even so them also which sleep in Jesus will God bring with him. *(Note the words, "sleep in Jesus." Death does not break the union between Jesus and his saints. We are one with him eternally; and therefore as surely as Jesus rose, so surely must all the members of his mystical body rise also.)*

15 For this we say unto you by the word of the Lord, that we which are alive *and* remain unto the coming of the Lord shall not prevent *(anticipate or take precedence of)* them which are asleep. *(We shall in no respect fare better. To sleep in Jesus is no dishonour to saints, and it shall not place them in a second class. They shall be in all things equal to those who survive till the Lord comes. We need not therefore dread death, nor feel any over-weening desire to live till the second advent. That the Lord shall come is our confidence; that we shall escape death by his coming is but a poor subject for congratulation. It will give us no gain over the sacred dead.)*

16 For the Lord himself shall descend from heaven with a shout, with the voice of the archangel, and with the trump of God: and the dead in Christ shall rise first: *(So that, in order, those who have died will have the preference. Their glory is reached first:)*

17 Then we which are alive *and* remain shall be caught up together with them in the clouds, to meet the Lord in the air: and so shall we ever be with the Lord. *(The resurrection first, then the rapture, and the eternal abode with Jesus. Fairest of hopes, art thou ours?)*

18 Wherefore comfort one another with these words.

CHAPTER V. 1—10.

BUT of the times and the seasons, brethren, ye have no need that I write unto you.

2 For yourselves know perfectly that the day of the Lord so cometh as a thief in the night. *(Unexpectedly to those who have slighted the warnings of prophecy.)*

3 For when they shall say, Peace and safety; then sudden destruction cometh upon them, as travail upon a woman with child; and they shall not escape. *(Certainly, suddenly, irresistibly. Turn which way they will they shall find no safety,—no deliverance.)*

4 But ye, brethren, are not in darkness, that that day should overtake you as a thief. *Unrevealed though the time be, your faith stands on the watch, and you are prepared.*

5, 6 Ye are all the children of light, and the children of the day: we are not of the night, nor of darkness. Therefore let us not sleep, as *do* others; but let us watch and be sober. *Privilege involves responsibility. Are we children of the light? Then we are bound to be awake. The sons of darkness may legitimately slumber, but we must not, or we shall be unpardonably inconsistent.*

7 For they that sleep sleep in the night; and they that be drunken are drunken in the night. *Drunkenness in those days had not grown so brazen-faced as now,—men who were given to intoxication reserved their revels for the darkness which would veil them. It would ill become us who have heavenly light to fall into the vices of nature's midnight.*

8 But let us, who are of the day, be sober, putting on the breastplate of faith and love; and for an helmet, the hope of salvation.

9 For God hath not appointed us to wrath, but to obtain salvation by our Lord Jesus Christ,

10 Who died for us, that, whether we wake or sleep, we should live together with him. *Jesus' great love can only fitly be acknowledged by the entire consecration of our redeemed manhood to him, at all times and in all places. Spirit of holiness, work in us communion with Jesus and conformity to him. Amen.*

Hear what the voice from heaven proclaims
    For all the pious dead,
Sweet is the savour of their names,
    And soft their sleeping bed.

They die in Jesus, and are bless'd;
    How kind their slumbers are!
From sufferings and from sins released,
    And freed from every snare.

186   "𝕭ring forth fruits meet for repentance."   APRIL 1.—MORNING.

[*Or June* 30.]

W E *will now return to the Bible narrative.*

JUDGES II. 6—16.

6 ¶ And when Joshua had let the people go, the children of Israel went every man unto his inheritance to possess the land. *(After a good sermon, the fittest thing is diligent practice.)*

7 And the people served the LORD all the days of Joshua, and all the days of the elders that outlived Joshua, who had seen all the great works of the LORD, that he did for Israel. *Mighty is the influence of good men. Pray that God may preserve to us useful ministers and holy men in the church. They act as anchors to the church, which else might drift into error. How well is it for the good cause that our great Joshua never dies.*

8, 9 And Joshua the son of Nun, the servant of the LORD, died, *being* an hundred and ten years old. And they buried him in the border of his inheritance in Timnath-heres, in the mount of Ephraim, on the north side of the hill Gaash. *The best of men must finish their course in due season: even those who live longest die at last, and so must we.*

10 And also all that generation were gathered unto their fathers: and there arose another generation after them, which knew not the LORD, nor yet the works which he had done for Israel.

11 ¶ And the children of Israel did evil in the sight of the LORD, and served Baalim:

12, 13 And they forsook the LORD God of their fathers, which brought them out of the land of Egypt, and followed other gods, of the gods of the people that *were* round about them, and bowed themselves unto them, and provoked the LORD to anger. And they forsook the LORD, and served Baal and Ashtaroth. *(Gross infatuation, to leave the true God for idols, the work of men's hands.)*

14 ¶ And the anger of the LORD was hot against Israel, and he delivered them into the hands of spoilers that spoiled them, and he sold them into the hands of their enemies round about, so that they could not any longer stand before their enemies.

15 Whithersoever they went out, the hand of the LORD was against them for evil, as the LORD had said, and as the LORD had sworn unto them: and they were greatly distressed.

Sin must be chastened in God's people. Even though others transgress with impunity, the Lord's chosen shall not. Alas! what misery comes of departing from the Lord.

16 ¶ Nevertheless the LORD raised up judges, which delivered them out of the hand of those that spoiled them. *(He was far more ready to deliver them than to smite them. He delighteth in mercy.)*

CHAPTER II. 1—5.

A ND an angel of the LORD came up from Gilgal to Bochim, and said, I made you to go up out of Egypt, and have brought you unto the land which I sware unto your fathers; and I said, I will never break my covenant with you. *(Was not this the great angel of the covenant, even the Lord Jesus? Who could use such language but one who is equal with God?)*

2, 3 And ye shall make no league with the inhabitants of this land; ye shall throw down their altars: but ye have not obeyed my voice: why have ye done this? Wherefore I also said, I will not drive them out from before you; but they shall be as *thorns* in your sides, and their gods shall be a snare unto you. *(Their sin was to be their punishment. If we will not smite our sins, our sins will smite us.)*

4, 5 And it came to pass, when the angel of the LORD spake these words unto all the children of Israel, that the people lifted up their voice, and wept. And they called the name of that place Bochim *(or weepers)*; and they sacrificed there unto the LORD. *(Tears will not serve, there must be sacrifice also. Blessed are they who with broken heart compass the altar of the Lord. May the Holy Spirit work in each of us a sacred sorrow for all sin. Amen.)*

Why, O my soul! why weepest thou?
    Tell me from whence arise
Those briny tears that often flow,
    Those groans that pierce the skies?

Is sin the cause of thy complaint,
    Or the chastising rod?
Dost thou an evil heart lament,
    And mourn an absent God?

Lord, let me weep for naught but sin!
    And after none but thee!
And then I would—O that I might,
    A constant weeper be!

JUDGES III. 1—15; 31.

NOW these *are* the nations which the Lord left, to prove Israel by them, *even* as many *of Israel* as had not known all the wars of Canaan ;

2 Only that the generations of the children of Israel might know, to teach them war, at the least such as before knew nothing thereof ;

Surrounded as they were by warlike nations, the Lord meant his people to be expert in war, and therefore kept them in marching order, by leaving certain nations near at home to be a trouble to them. The church also is meant to be a militant army, and therefore the Lord will not allow everything to go smoothly with us.

3 *Namely,* five lords of the Philistines, and all the Canaanites, and the Sidonians, and the Hivites that dwelt in mount Lebanon, from mount Baal-hermon unto the entering in of Hamath.

4 And they were to prove Israel by them, to know whether they would hearken unto the commandments of the Lord, which he commanded their fathers by the hand of Moses.

5 ¶ And the children of Israel dwelt among the Canaanites, Hittites, and Amorites, and Perizzites, and Hivites, and Jebusites :

6 And they took their daughters to be their wives, and gave their daughters to their sons, and served their gods. *(Ungodly marriages are the source of abounding evil. We must maintain the separated condition of the people of God, or else we shall fall into sin and pierce ourselves through with many sorrows. We are not of the world, and we must not act as if we were.)*

7 And the children of Israel did evil in the sight of the Lord, and forgat the Lord their God, and served Baalim and the groves.

They grew accustomed to talk of Baal and the thick trees in which he was worshipped; by and by they reverenced the lying vanities of the idolaters, and at last their treacherous memories forgot their God. Beware of sin's sliding-scale.

8 ¶ Therefore the anger of the Lord was hot against Israel, and he sold them into the hand of Chushan-rishathaim king of Mesopotamia : and the children of Israel served Chushan-rishathaim eight years.

This king reigned at a great distance, but God will find a rod for rebels, even if he sends hundreds of miles for it.

9, 10, 11 And when the children of Israel cried unto the Lord, the Lord raised up a deliverer to the children of Israel, who delivered them, *even* Othniel the son of Kenaz, Caleb's younger brother. And the Spirit of the Lord came upon him, and he judged Israel, and went out to war : and the Lord delivered Chushan-rishathaim king of Mesopotamia into his hand. And the land had rest forty years. And Othniel the son of Kenaz died. *(Othniel had been brave in his youth, and it is pleasant to hear of him in his old age. If we serve God well in the morning of life, we may be sure that he will honour us before the day is over.)*

12 ¶ And the children of Israel did evil again in the sight of the Lord : *(Repetition of sin greatly increases guilt.)* and the Lord strengthened Eglon the king of Moab against Israel, because they had done evil in the sight of the Lord. *(This time the oppressor was nearer home, and the punishment more severe.)*

13 And he gathered unto him the children of Ammon and Amalek, and went and smote Israel, and possessed the city of palm trees.

14 So the children of Israel served Eglon the king of Moab eighteen years.

15 But when the children of Israel cried unto the Lord, the Lord raised them up a deliverer, Ehud the son of Gera, a Benjamite, a man lefthanded. *(This man struck a deadly blow at Eglon, and so delivered his country. God will use men of any kind for his work sooner than allow the cries of his people to remain unheard.)*

31 ¶ And after him was Shamgar the son of Anath, which slew of the Philistines six hundred men with an ox goad : and he also delivered Israel. *(Rough as he was, Shamgar was honoured of God, and his humble weapon is laid up among the most renowned treasures of the Lord's armoury. God can use us for great purposes, and he will do so, if we have real faith in him, and full submission to his will.)*

Beset with darkness, pressed with cares,
  To God, in grief, I cried ;
His mercy listened to my prayers,
  His hand my wants supplied.

Oh, magnify the Lord with me !
  His might, his mercies, prove !
How blest his sway ! oh, taste and see
  How vast, how kind, his love !

JUDGES IV. 1—23.

AND the children of Israel again did evil in the sight of the LORD, when Ehud was dead. *(That sentence, "the children of Israel again did evil in the sight of the Lord," comes over and over again so often that it seems to be the only invariable fact in their history. Would not such words frequently occur in our biographies if they could be fully written?)*

2 And the LORD sold them into the hand of Jabin king of Canaan, that reigned in Hazor; the captain of whose host *was* Sisera, which dwelt in Harosheth of the Gentiles.

3 And the children of Israel cried unto the LORD; for he had nine hundred chariots of iron; and twenty years he mightily oppressed the children of Israel. *(When we read of Israel crying, we know that deliverance will come. Prayer has mercy at its heels.)*

4 ¶ And Deborah, a prophetess, the wife of Lapidoth, she judged Israel at that time. *God uses all classes and both sexes for his work. In this case a man plays a very secondary part, and two women share the honour. One strikes the first blow, and the other the last. Although women do not go out into public preaching, or to fight in the open field like Barak, they can do much at home with the tent-pin of personal address, and in society by encouraging the soldiers of the Lord.*

5 And she dwelt under the palm tree of Deborah between Ramah and Beth-el in mount Ephraim: and the children of Israel came up to her for judgment.

6, 7 And she sent and called Barak the son of Abinoam out of Kedesh-naphtali, and said unto him, Hath not the LORD God of Israel commanded, *saying,* Go and draw toward mount Tabor, and take with thee ten thousand men of the children of Naphtali and of the children of Zebulun? And I will draw unto thee to the river Kishon Sisera, the captain of Jabin's army, with his chariots and his multitude; and I will deliver him into thine hand. *The Lord has not only leading strings to draw his people, but fatal cords with which to draw his foes whithersoever he wills.*

8 And Barak said unto her, If thou wilt go with me, then I will go: but if thou wilt not go with me, *then* I will not go.

9 And she said, I will surely go with thee: notwithstanding the journey that thou takest shall not be for thine honour; for the LORD shall sell Sisera into the hand of a woman. And Deborah arose, and went with Barak to Kedesh. *(He had not faith enough to go alone, and therefore, though he won the battle, he had not the honour of the victory. We lose much when we lean upon an arm of flesh. At the same time he showed a noble spirit in entering upon a conflict in which another was to receive the chief honour.)*

10 ¶ And Barak called Zebulun and Naphtali to Kedesh; and he went up with ten thousand men at his feet: and Deborah went up with him. *(Many good men only need a call from some brave leader, and they will rally to the standard. God has his ten thousands in our Israel yet. O for the man and the hour! Rather, O for the Lord's own Spirit to call us to the combat!)*

11 Now Heber the Kenite, *which was* of the children of Hobab the father in law of Moses, had severed himself from the Kenites, and pitched his tent unto the plain of Zaanaim, which *is* by Kedesh.

12 And they shewed Sisera that Barak the son of Abinoam was gone up to mount Tabor.

13 And Sisera gathered together all his chariots, *even* nine hundred chariots of iron, and all the people that *were* with him, from Harosheth of the Gentiles unto the river of Kishon. *Little dreamed he when he sallied forth in his pride that he was being lured to his destruction. Some trust in horses, and some in chariots, but vain are such defences against the Lord of hosts.*

14 And Deborah said unto Barak, Up; for this *is* the day in which the LORD hath delivered Sisera into thine hand: is not the LORD gone out before thee? So Barak went down from mount Tabor, and ten thousand men after him. *The word of Deborah sharpened the sword of Barak. Holy women often encourage the Lord's ministers.*

15 And the LORD discomfited Sisera, and all *his* chariots, and all *his* host, with the edge of the sword before Barak; *(The Lord did it, Barak was but the sword in his hand.)*

16 But Barak pursued after the chariots, and after the host, unto Harosheth of the Gentiles:

and all the host of Sisera fell upon the edge of the sword; *and* there was not a man left.

God's sword never misses one whom he means to smite. This is fatal news for the impenitent.

17 Howbeit Sisera fled away on his feet to the tent of Jael the wife of Heber the Kenite: for *there was* peace between Jabin the king of Hazor and the house of Heber the Kenite.

18 ¶ And Jael went out to meet Sisera, and said unto him, Turn in, my lord, turn in to me; fear not. And when he had turned in unto her into the tent, she covered him with a mantle.

19 And he said unto her, Give me, I pray thee, a little water to drink; for I am thirsty. And she opened a bottle of milk, and gave him drink, and covered him.

20 Again he said unto her, Stand in the door of the tent, and it shall be, when any man doth come and enquire of thee, and say, Is there any man here? that thou shalt say, No.

This instruction was very like the shameful custom which is so common, for servants to be ordered to say, " my mistress is not at home," when she is in the house all the time. Let not Christians borrow lying habits from heathens.

21 Then Jael Heber's wife took a nail of the tent, and took an hammer in her hand, and went softly unto him, and smote the nail into his temples, and fastened it into the ground: for he was fast asleep and weary. So he died.

This would have been a dastardly action had she been moved by motives of gain, but as an act in which she became the executioner of a man condemned of God, and the slayer of the great enemy of her adopted country, her conduct is rightly praised. The patriotic heroine recognized in the fugitive the enemy of her God and of his people, and her eye had no pity, neither did her hand spare him.

22 And, behold, as Barak pursued Sisera, Jael came out to meet him, and said unto him, Come, and I will shew thee the man whom thou seekest. And when he came into her *tent*, behold, Sisera lay dead, and the nail *was* in his temples. *(So the proud tyrant was disgraced as well as killed. Somewhere or other God has feeble instruments who will be made wise to put down error, and drive a nail through the head of false doctrine. O Lord, arise and plead thine own cause.)*

23 So God subdued on that day Jabin the king of Canaan before the children of Israel.

O God, be thou no longer still,
Thy foes are leagued against thy law;
Make bare thine arm on Zion's hill,
Great Captain of our Holy War.

As Amalek and Ishmael
Had war for ever with thy seed,
So all the hosts of Rome and hell
Against thy Son their armies lead.

By Kishon's brook all Jabin's band
At thy rebuke were swept away;
O Lord, display thy mighty hand,
A single stroke shall win the day.

O glorious hour! O blest abode!
I shall be near and like my God;
And flesh and sin no more control
The sacred pleasures of my soul.

My flesh shall slumber in the ground,
'Till the last trumpet's joyful sound;
Then burst the chains with sweet surprise,
And in my Saviour's image rise.

Sleep not, soldier of the Cross!
Foes are lurking all around;
Look not here to find repose:
This is but thy battle ground.

Up! and take thy shield and sword;
Up! it is the call of heaven:
Shrink not faithless from thy Lord;
Nobly strive as he hath striven.

To the God of all creation
    Let us sing with cheerful voice
In the Rock of our salvation
    Let us heartily rejoice.

In his presence let us gather
    With glad hearts and thankful lays,
And to God, our heavenly Father,
    Show our joy with psalms of praise.

He is King among all nations,
    God above all gods is he;
In his hand are earth's foundations,
    The strong hills and rolling sea.

He created land and ocean,
    He with beauty clothes the sod;
Let us kneel in deep devotion,
    Bless our Maker and our God.

190   "Lead thy captivity captive."   APRIL 2.—EVENING.

[Or July 3.]

WE shall now hear Deborah sing her right noble poem of victory. She was both prophetess and poetess. All powers of poetry should be consecrated to the honour of God who bestows them.

JUDGES V. 1—18.

1, 2 Then sang Deborah and Barak the son of Abinoam on that day, saying, Praise ye the LORD for the avenging of Israel, when the people willingly offered themselves. (Unto God all the praise is given. The people were willing, but God made their zealous valour to be successful.)

3 Hear, O ye kings; give ear, O ye princes; I, even I, will sing unto the LORD; I will sing praise to the LORD God of Israel. (To such a woman, upon such a theme, the loftiest monarchs might wisely listen.)

4, 5 LORD, when thou wentest out of Seir, when thou marchedst out of the field of Edom, the earth trembled, and the heavens dropped, the clouds also dropped water. The mountains melted from before the LORD, even that Sinai from before the LORD God of Israel. (All the kings around are bidden to remember the glorious marching of Jehovah, when he led his people from Egypt to Canaan; even on the road to battle the Lord displayed the glory of his majesty.)

6, 7 In the days of Shamgar the son of Anath, in the days of Jael, the highways were unoccupied, and the travellers walked through byways. (Trade and travelling were at an end, for the country was unsafe.) The inhabitants of the villages ceased, they ceased in Israel, until that I Deborah arose, that I arose a mother in Israel. (Husbandry could not be carried on, the people fled to the walled towns for fear.)

8 They chose new gods; then was war in the gates: was there a shield or spear seen among forty thousand in Israel? (On account of Israel's idolatry, they had become so reduced, and their oppressors had so completely disarmed them, that they had no fit weapons for war.)

9 My heart is toward the governors of Israel, that offered themselves willingly among the people. Bless ye the Lord. (It is indeed a blessing when the governors lead the way in good things.)

10 Speak, ye that ride on white asses, ye that sit in judgment, and walk by the way. Justice could not be dispensed, civil affairs were all unhinged, no one was safe, but Deborah and Barak changed the scene.

11 They that are delivered from the noise of archers in the places of drawing water, there shall they rehearse the righteous acts of the LORD, even the righteous acts toward the inhabitants of his villages in Israel: then shall the people of the LORD go down to the gates. In times of peace, when no robber was to be feared at the well, this song of gratitude would be sung, and the Lord would be praised.

12 Awake, awake, Deborah: awake, awake, utter a song: arise, Barak, and lead thy captivity captive, thou son of Abinoam. Mark how the poet glows and burns.

13 Then he made him that remaineth have dominion over the nobles among the people: the LORD made me have dominion over the mighty. (God put Deborah first as ruler, but she did not fail to make honourable mention of all who shared in the fight, nor afterwards to rebuke those who shunned it.)

14, 15 Out of Ephraim was there a root of them against Amalek; after thee, Benjamin, among thy people; out of Machir came down governors, and out of Zebulun they that handle the pen of the writer. And the princes of Issachar were with Deborah; even Issachar, and also Barak: he was sent on foot into the valley. For the divisions of Reuben there were great thoughts of heart.

16 Why abodest thou among the sheepfolds, to hear the bleatings of the flocks? For the divisions of Reuben there were great searchings of heart. (Divided in council and indolent in spirit, Reuben lent no assistance. This was a sad business.)

17 Gilead abode beyond Jordan: and why did Dan remain in ships? Asher continued on the sea shore, and abode in his breaches. Some with no excuse, and others with a bad excuse, refrained from the patriotic war, and missed its glories. How disgraceful not to do their utmost in such a cause. Lord, save us from cowardice and slothfulness, and let us rather be such bold, self-sacrificing spirits as those the poet sings of in the next verse.

18 Zebulun and Naphtali were a people that jeoparded their lives unto the death in the high places of the field. (Here we are compelled to make a break, until our next reading.)

LET *us now take the remainder of Deborah's noble song—*

JUDGES V. 19—31.

19 The kings came *and* fought, then fought the kings of Canaan in Taanach by the waters of Megiddo; they took no gain of money.

They were ready volunteers. Their hatred of Israel made them eager for the battle. They sought no other reward than that which they found in oppressing the nation they so much abhorred. Satan has his volunteers—shall any of us need pressing to serve the Lord?

20 They fought from heaven; the stars in their courses fought against Sisera. (*The heavenly hosts entered the lists. The elements took Israel's side. The rainy constellations were in the ascendant. The clouds blazed with lightning, and tremendous water-floods poured from them.*)

21 The river of Kishon swept them away, that ancient river, the river Kishon. (*The torrent-bed being suddenly swollen, washed away whole armies of men.*) O my soul, thou hast trodden down strength.

22 Then were the horsehoofs broken by the means of the pransings, the pransings of their mighty ones. (*The frighted horses pranced till their unshod hoofs failed them. Sisera's boasted cavalry became useless, and his chariots of iron an encumbrance to his army.*)

23 Curse ye Meroz, said the angel of the LORD, curse ye bitterly the inhabitants thereof; because they came not to the help of the LORD, to the help of the LORD against the mighty.

The laggards of Meroz are cursed, not for what they did, but for what they failed to do. Fear made them neutral, and neutrals in a patriotic war are detestable. "I would thou wert either cold or hot." Earnest spirits feel great indignation against good-for-nothing indifferents.

24 Blessed above women shall Jael the wife of Heber the Kenite be, blessed shall she be above women in the tent.

25 He asked water, *and* she gave *him* milk; she brought forth butter in a lordly dish.

Sisera saw the milk, but not the nail, and many tempted ones are in the same case.

26, 27 She put her hand to the nail, and her right hand to the workman's hammer; and with the hammer she smote Sisera, she smote off his head, when she had pierced and stricken through his temples. At her feet he bowed, he fell, he lay down: at her feet he bowed, he fell: where he bowed, there he fell down dead.

(*Lowly was Jael's sphere, but she did for Israel her very best, therefore was she as much blessed as Barak who led the thousands of Israel to battle.*)

28 The mother of Sisera looked out at a window, and cried through the lattice, Why is his chariot *so* long in coming? why tarry the wheels of his chariots? (*This is a beautiful picture of the disappointment of the women at home when their warriors returned not in triumph. They reckoned without God, and therefore their expectation failed them. The next epithet is ironical.*)

29 Her wise ladies answered her, yea, she returned answer to herself,

30 Have they not sped? have they *not* divided the prey; to every man a damsel *or* two; to Sisera a prey of divers colours, a prey of divers colours of needlework, of divers colours of needlework on both sides, *meet* for the necks of *them that take* the spoil?

Thus, in imagination, they divided the spoil of a victory which was never gained. How often have the enemies of the church reckoned upon her overthrow, and rejoiced by anticipation; but hitherto the Lord hath helped us.

31 So let all thine enemies perish, O LORD: but *let* them that love him *be* as the sun when he goeth forth in his might. (*Amen! Amen! Under the gospel we dare say Amen; but our wrestling is with principles, not men; with error, sin, Satan, unbelief. O for brave hands of men and women to smite these foes.*)

The foes of Zion quake for fright,
Where no fear was they quail;
For well they know that sword of might
Which cuts through coats of mail.

The Lord of old defiled their shields,
And all their spears he scorn'd;
Their bones lay scatter'd o'er the fields,
Unburied and unmourn'd.

Let Zion's foes be fill'd with shame;
Her sons are bless'd of God;
Though scoffers now despise his name,
The Lord shall break their rod.

192   "𝔄rise, ☧ 𝔊od! 𝔓lead thine own cause."   APRIL 3.—EVENING.

[*Or July* 5.]

IN *after years, when Israel came into sore trouble, her holy men remembered the Lord's overthrow of Jabin and Sisera, and made it a plea in prayer. We must never doubt that what the Lord did in the olden times for his people he can and will do again. He may alter his mode of action, but he will achieve the same result.*

PSALM LXXXIII.

A Song *or* Psalm of Asaph.

1 Keep not thou silence, O God: hold not thy peace, and be not still, O God.

2 For, lo, thine enemies make a tumult: and they that hate thee have lifted up the head.

O Lord, thine enemies are raging, do not be deaf and dumb to them, but hear thou their furious threats, and rebuke them by thy word. They are very proud, but do thou, O Lord, abase them.

3 They have taken crafty counsel against thy people, and consulted against thy hidden ones.

God's people are hidden as his choice treasure, hidden for protection, hidden in their secret nature, and hidden in the sense of being obscure and un-valued. Against such the wicked plot with cunning and cruelty. Though believers sometimes act without consideration, their enemies seldom do so. In this matter the children of this world are wiser than the children of light.

4 They have said, Come, and let us cut them off from *being* a nation; that the name of Israel may be no more in remembrance.

Only extermination will serve their turn. The powers of evil would not leave a believer on earth if they could help it. Remember the massacre of St. Bartholomew, and be assured that the spirit of Antichrist is unchanged.

5 For they have consulted together with one consent: they are confederate against thee:

6 The tabernacles of Edom, and the Ishmaelites; of Moab, and the Hagarenes;

7 Gebal, and Ammon, and Amalek; the Philistines with the inhabitants of Tyre;

8 Assur also is joined with them: they have holpen the children of Lot. Selah.

Thus relatives and near neighbours, old enemies and new foes, were of one mind against the favoured nation. The wicked often put divided Christians to shame by their unanimity.

9 Do unto them as *unto* the Midianites; as *to* Sisera, as *to* Jabin, at the brook of Kison:

10 *Which* perished at En-dor: they became *as* dung for the earth.

11, 12 Make their nobles like Oreb, and like Zeeb: yea, all their princes as Zebah, and as Zalmunna: Who said, Let us take to ourselves the houses of God in possession. (*They meant to take the tabernacle itself as a prey, and to attack the shrine of God himself. Their total destruction was a fit reward for such ferocious sacrilege.*)

13 O my God, make them like a wheel; as the stubble before the wind. (*Let them have no rest, let them have no power to resist thee.*)

14 As the fire burneth a wood, and as the flame setteth the mountains on fire;

15 So persecute them with thy tempest, and make them afraid with thy storm.

We must love our own enemies, but when we view men as the enemies of God and his glorious cause, we cannot love them nor ought we to do so. May all those who fight against God, truth, love, and holiness, be utterly defeated.

16 Fill their faces with shame; that they may seek thy name, O Lord. (*A sweet prayer, fit for Christian lips, since it asks for the salvation of those who are now the Lord's enemies.*)

17 Let them be confounded and troubled for ever; yea, let them be put to shame and perish:

If wicked men will not bend, then let them break, for it cannot be that all the rights of men and all the laws of God should be set aside to give liberty to unholy minds. If truth and holiness cannot live except bad men be put down, then down let them go.

18 That *men* may know that thou, whose name alone *is* JEHOVAH, *art* the most high over all the earth. (*This is the grand design of providence, and the end to which all events must tend. Let us as a household and as individuals, be ever found upon the Lord's side.*)

O Jesu Christ, thy Church sustain;
Our hearts are wavering, cold and vain;
Then let thy word be strong and clear,
To silence doubt and banish fear.

O guard us all from Satan's wiles,
From worldly threats and worldly smiles,
And let thy saints in unity
Know thee in God and God in thee.

JUDGES VI. 1—16.

AND the children of Israel did evil in the sight of the LORD : *(We commonly say that a burnt child dreads the fire, but Israel, after smarting again and again as the result of her sin, returned to it the moment the chastisement was removed, or the judge was dead. Such is the strange infatuation of men :)* and the LORD delivered them into the hand of Midian seven years. *(This nation was but a puny enemy, and yet it was too much for sinful Israel. The tribes had formerly reduced the Midianites to a very low condition, and now they are themselves unable to stand before them. See how sin weakens men.)*

2, 3 And the hand of Midian prevailed against Israel : *and* because of the Midianites the children of Israel made them the dens which *are* in the mountains, and caves, and strong holds. And *so* it was, when Israel had sown, that the Midianites came up, and the Amalekites, and the children of the east, even they came up against them ;

4 And they encamped against them, and destroyed the increase of the earth, till thou come unto Gaza, and left no sustenance for Israel, neither sheep, nor ox, nor ass.

5, 6 For they came up with their cattle and their tents, and they came as grasshoppers for multitude ; *for* both they and their camels were without number : and they entered into the land to destroy it. And Israel was greatly impoverished because of the Midianites; and the children of Israel cried unto the LORD. *(These wandering plunderers were hard to grapple with, and must have been a dreadful scourge. It is to such marauders that much of the present deserted condition of Palestine is due.)*

7, 8 And it came to pass, when the children of Israel cried unto the LORD because of the Midianites, That the LORD sent a prophet unto the children of Israel, which said unto them, Thus saith the LORD God of Israel, I brought you up from Egypt, and brought you forth out of the house of bondage ; *(The sending of faithful ministers to a people is a token for good from the Lord, even though their testimony should be rather a rebuke than a consolation ;)*

9, 10 And I delivered you out of the hands of the Egyptians, and out of the hand of all that oppressed you, and drave them out from before you, and gave you their land ; And I said unto you, I *am* the LORD your God ; fear not the gods of the Amorites, in whose land ye dwell : but ye have not obeyed my voice. *(Faithful are the wounds of a friend. God had just cause to complain, and in unveiling Israel's great sin, the Lord's servant was going the surest way to build up peace upon a permanent foundation.)*

11 ¶ And there came an angel of the LORD, and sat under an oak which *was* in Ophrah, that *pertained* unto Joash the Abi-ezrite : and his son Gideon threshed wheat by the winepress, to hide *it* from the Midianites.

12 And the angel of the LORD appeared unto him, and said unto him, The LORD *is* with thee, thou mighty man of valour. *(He found Gideon retired, employed, and distressed; three suitable conditions to warrant a celestial interposition. He had very little wheat, for he had no oxen to thresh it ; and he was in great fear of the enemy, and therefore threshed not on the barn floor, but in the winepress ; yet in his poverty he received rich grace. God is no respecter of persons.)*

13 And Gideon said unto him, Oh my Lord, if the LORD be with us, why then is all this befallen us ? and where *be* all his miracles which our fathers told us of, saying, Did not the LORD bring us up from Egypt ? but now the LORD hath forsaken us, and delivered us into the hands of the Midianites. *(These were common-sense questions, and proved that the enquirer had well considered the matter.)*

14 And the LORD looked upon him, and said, Go in this thy might, and thou shalt save Israel from the hand of the Midianites : have not I sent thee ? *(It is clear that the angel was the Lord himself. From such lips what power there is in that question, "Have not I sent thee ?" And what inspiration followed his glance, when " the Lord looked upon Gideon.")*

15 And he said unto him, Oh my Lord, wherewith shall I save Israel ? behold, my family *is* poor in Manasseh, and I *am* the least in my father's house.

16 And the LORD said unto him, Surely I will be with thee, and thou shalt smite the Midianites as one man. *(God called Gideon mighty, and made him so, he sent him and went with him, he taught him faith and then honoured his faith. In what manner will the Lord glorify himself in each of us ?)*

JUDGES VI. 17—32.

A ND Gideon said unto the angel, If now I have found grace in thy sight, then shew me a sign that thou talkest with me.

18 Depart not hence, I pray thee, until I come unto thee, and bring forth my present, and set *it* before thee. And he said, I will tarry until thou come again. *(To one person a sign is denied, and to another it is granted. Herein is manifest not only the sovereignty of God, but also his wisdom in dealing with different men in different manners. Gideon had many signs, yet he was not rebuked for needing them.)*

19 ¶ And Gideon went in, and made ready a kid, and unleavened cakes of an ephah of flour : the flesh he put in a basket, and he put the broth in a pot, and brought *it* out unto him under the oak, and presented *it*.

20 And the angel of God said unto him, Take the flesh and the unleavened cakes, and lay *them* upon this rock, and pour out the broth. And he did so. *(What Gideon meant for a feast was turned into a sacrifice. This was a small matter, so long as the Lord did but accept him.)*

21 ¶ Then the angel of the Lord put forth the end of the staff that *was* in his hand, and touched the flesh and the unleavened cakes ; and there rose up fire out of the rock, and consumed the flesh and the unleavened cakes. Then the angel of the Lord departed out of his sight. *(Here was both a token of divine presence and an intimation of what God could do. He could bring fiery courage out of Gideon's heart, as well as fire out of a rock, and he could consume Midian as readily as he burned up the cakes.)*

22 And when Gideon perceived that he *was* an angel of the Lord, Gideon said, Alas, O Lord God ! for because I have seen an angel of the Lord face to face.

23 And the Lord said unto him, Peace *be* unto thee ; fear not : thou shalt not die.

24 ¶ Then Gideon built an altar there unto the Lord, and called it Jehovah-shalom : *(or "the Lord my peace," in allusion to the Lord's having said, "Peace be unto thee.")*

25, 26 And it came to pass the same night, that the Lord said unto him, Take thy father's young bullock, even the second bullock of seven years old, and throw down the altar of Baal that thy father hath, and cut down the grove that *is* by it : And build an altar unto the Lord thy God upon the top of this rock, in the ordered place, and take the second bullock, and offer a burnt sacrifice with the wood of the grove which thou shalt cut down. *(He was at once to set about cleansing his own house. Those who would serve God abroad should begin at home. He was not commanded to dedicate Baal's grove-temple to God, but to fell it ; nor was he ordered to sacrifice to God upon the idol's altar, but to throw it down. Reformations cannot be too thorough. Unless we down with their nests the foul birds will come back. Gideon had a grand commission which every true believer might rejoice to receive.)*

27 Then Gideon took ten men of his servants, and did as the Lord had said unto him : and *so* it was, because he feared his father's household, and the men of the city, that he could not do *it* by day, that he did *it* by night. *(If we cannot do our duty exactly as we would, we must do it as we can, but anyhow it should be done. Gideon did a glorious night's work.)*

28 ¶ And when the men of the city arose early in the morning, behold, the altar of Baal was cast down, and the grove was cut down that *was* by it, and the second bullock was offered upon the altar *that was* built.

29 And they said one to another, Who hath done this thing ? And when they enquired and asked, they said, Gideon the son of Joash hath done this thing.

30 Then the men of the city said unto Joash, Bring out thy son, that he may die : because he hath cast down the altar of Baal, and because he hath cut down the grove that *was* by it. *Those who themselves deserved to die for idolatry were in a vast hurry to judge and condemn the son of Joash. Frequently those who themselves are most guilty are loudest in accusing others.*

31 And Joash said unto all that stood against him, Will ye plead for Baal ? will ye save him ? he that will plead for him, let him be put to death whilst *it is yet* morning : if he *be* a god, let him plead for himself, because *one* hath cast down his altar. *(His argument was—if Baal be indeed a god he can take care of himself, and if he be not a god, then those who plead for him deserve to die for setting up false deities.)*

32 Therefore on that day he called him Jerubbaal *(or one with whom Baal may plead)*, saying, Let Baal plead against him, because he hath thrown down his altar.

JUDGES VI. 33—40.

THEN all the Midianites and the Amalekites and the children of the east were gathered together, and went over, and pitched in the valley of Jezreel. But the Spirit of the LORD came upon Gideon, and he blew a trumpet; and Abi-ezer was gathered after him. *(When the enemy moved, the Lord moved his chosen servant to meet them, and at his signal many of the downtrodden people plucked up courage and came forth from their hiding places to face the enemy.)*

35 And he sent messengers throughout all Manasseh; who also was gathered after him: and he sent messengers unto Asher, and unto Zebulun, and unto Naphtali; and they came up to meet them. *(The Lord's people are willing in the day of his power.)*

36—40 ¶ And Gideon said unto God, If thou wilt save Israel by mine hand, as thou hast said, Behold, I will put a fleece of wool in the floor; *and* if the dew be on the fleece only, and *it be* dry upon all the earth *beside*, then shall I know that thou wilt save Israel by mine hand, as thou hast said. And it was so: for he rose up early on the morrow, and thrust the fleece together, and wringed the dew out of the fleece, a bowl full of water. And Gideon said unto God, Let not thine anger be hot against me, and I will speak but this once: let me prove, I pray thee, but this once with the fleece; let it now be dry only upon the fleece, and upon all the ground let there be dew. And God did so that night: for it was dry upon the fleece only, and there was dew on all the ground. *(See how tenderly the Lord condescends to the weakness of his servant's faith, and doubly strengthens his confidence. The Lord gives to us similar signs to confirm our faith. Sometimes under the ordinances we are bedewed with grace when others are not, and at other times we feel our natural gracelessness in the very place where others rejoice in abundance of grace. If our religion were mechanical, we could arrange its force; if it were formal, we could maintain its sameness; but since it is of the Lord, it is dependent upon his sovereign grace, and we are made to feel that it is so.)*

CHAPTER VII. 1—8.

1 Then Gideon, and all the people that *were* with him, rose up early, and pitched beside the well of Harod.

2 And the LORD said unto Gideon, The people that *are* with thee *are* too many for me to give the Midianites into their hands, lest Israel vaunt themselves against me, saying, Mine own hand hath saved me. *(Helpers with God are never too few, but we learn from this passage that they may be too many. This is a blow for those who boast their numbers, and an encouragement for the few and feeble.)*

3 Now therefore go to, proclaim in the ears of the people, saying, Whosoever *is* fearful and afraid, let him return and depart early from mount Gilead. And there returned of the people twenty and two thousand; and there remained ten thousand.

4 And the LORD said unto Gideon, The people *are* yet *too* many; bring them down unto the water, and I will try them for thee there: and it shall be, *that* of whom I say unto thee, This shall go with thee, the same shall go with thee; and of whomsoever I say unto thee, This shall not go with thee, the same shall not go. *(This was a great trial for Gideon's faith. If weak in some points, it was mighty in others.)*

5 So he brought down the people unto the water: and the LORD said unto Gideon, Every one that lappeth of the water with his tongue, as a dog lappeth, him shalt thou set by himself; likewise every one that boweth down upon his knees to drink. *(The lappers were men in haste for action, full of passion for the war; men who could not rest till they had smitten their cruel oppressors. Such men the Lord will work with.)*

6 And the number of them that lapped, *putting* their hand to their mouth, were three hundred men: but all the rest of the people bowed down upon their knees to drink water.

7, 8 And the LORD said unto Gideon, By the three hundred men that lapped will I save you, and deliver the Midianites into thine hand: and let all the *other* people go every man unto his place. So the people took victuals in their hand, and their trumpets: and he sent all *the rest of* Israel every man unto his tent, and retained those three hundred men. *(The swordsmen melted away, and only a few trumpeters remained. Now were matters right for conflict, and ripe for victory. When we are weak, then are we strong. Stripped of all such strength as can be seen, we cast ourselves upon the power invisible.)*

JUDGES VII. 9—25.

AND it came to pass the same night, that the LORD said unto him, Arise, get thee down unto the host; for I have delivered it into thine hand. But if thou fear to go down, go thou with Phurah thy servant down to the host. *(See how gently the Lord deals with his servant. He assures him that there is no room for fear, but lest a fear should remain, he removes it.)*

11 And thou shalt hear what they say; and afterward shall thine hands be strengthened to go down unto the host. *(To certain sincere characters, God deigns to give signs and assurances which it might be sinful for others to desire. Because Gideon had so many tokens, we are by no means to expect them, but rather to remember that blessed are they who have not seen and yet have believed.)* Then went he down with Phurah his servant unto the outside of the armed men that were in the host.

12 And the Midianites and the Amalekites and all the children of the east lay along in the valley like grasshoppers for multitude; and their camels were without number, as the sand by the sea side for multitude.

13 And when Gideon was come, behold there was a man that told a dream unto his fellow, and said, Behold, I dreamed a dream, and, lo, a cake of barley bread tumbled into the host of Midian, and came unto a tent, and smote it that it fell, and overturned it, that the tent lay along.

14 And his fellow answered and said, This is nothing else save the sword of Gideon the son of Joash, a man of Israel: for into his hand hath God delivered Midian, and all the host. *(It was a singular providence that one soldier should dream such a dream, that another should give it such an interpretation, and that Gideon should be listening during their conversation. The wonders of providence deserve the careful and adoring eye of the observer. The dream was just what Gideon wanted. He was as despised as a poor barley cake, and yet he should overturn the pavilions of Midian.)*

15 ¶ And it was so, when Gideon heard the telling of the dream, and the interpretation thereof, that he worshipped, and returned into the host of Israel, and said, Arise; for the LORD hath delivered into your hand the host of Midian. *(Note his worshipping under such circumstances. Devotion causes no delay.)*

16, 17 And he divided the three hundred men *into* three companies, and he put a trumpet in every man's hand, with empty pitchers, and lamps within the pitchers. And he said unto them, Look on me, and do likewise: and, behold, when I come to the outside of the camp, it shall be *that*, as I do, so shall ye do.

18 When I blow with a trumpet, I and all that *are* with me, then blow ye the trumpets also on every side of all the camp, and say, The sword of the LORD, and of Gideon.

19, 20, 21 So Gideon, and the hundred men that *were* with him, came unto the outside of the camp in the beginning of the middle watch; and they had but newly set the watch: and they blew the trumpets, and brake the pitchers that *were* in their hands. And the three companies blew the trumpets, and brake the pitchers, and held the lamps in their left hands, and the trumpets in their right hands to blow *withal*: and they cried, The sword of the LORD, and of Gideon. And they stood every man in his place round about the camp: and all the host ran, and cried, and fled. *(Seeing so many torch-bearers, and hearing so many trumpeters, they reckoned that the army itself must be immense, and being smitten with sudden panic they fled.)*

23 And the men of Israel gathered themselves together out of Naphtali, and out of Asher, and out of all Manasseh, and pursued after the Midianites. *(Those who cannot go first, may do good service if they will come in later and aid the good cause.)*

24 ¶ And Gideon sent messengers throughout all mount Ephraim, saying, Come down against the Midianites, and take before them the waters unto Beth-barah and Jordan. Then all the men of Ephraim gathered themselves together, and took the waters unto Beth-barah and Jordan. *(A wise leader is anxious to reap all the fruit he can from a victory. When we have overcome evil of any kind we must labour to make the success a permanent one.)*

25 And they took two princes of the Midianites, Oreb and Zeeb; and they slew Oreb upon the rock Oreb, and Zeeb they slew at the winepress of Zeeb. *(Thus faith wins the day against unnumbered foes. Let us but believe and we shall be established. The Lord is our Captain still, and we shall be more than conquerors.)*

JUDGES VIII. 1—3; 22—27; 32—35.

A ND the men of Ephraim said unto him, Why hast thou served us thus, that thou calledst us not, when thou wentest to fight with the Midianites? And they did chide with him sharply. *(When there is a success, everybody thinks that he ought to have been in it, and blames somebody else that he was away. It is not quite so clear that had these complainers been invited they would have welcomed the invitation. Those who grow angry because they cannot claim a share in the honour, are usually the very persons who would have had least taste for the conflict.)*

2 And he said unto them, What have I done now in comparison of you? *Is* not the gleaning of the grapes of Ephraim better than the vintage of Abi-ezer?

3 God hath delivered into your hands the princes of Midian, Oreb and Zeeb: and what was I able to do in comparison of you? Then their anger was abated toward him, when he had said that. *(A soft answer turneth away wrath. It shewed a noble spirit in Gideon, that though the sole conqueror by right, he covets no monopoly of the praise, but even magnifies the exploits of others beyond his own. Better yield to absurd people, than engender strife among brethren.)*

22 ¶ Then the men of Israel said unto Gideon, Rule thou over us, both thou, and thy son, and thy son's son also: for thou hast delivered us from the hand of Midian.

23 And Gideon said unto them, I will not rule over you, neither shall my son rule over you: the LORD shall rule over you. *Here again Gideon shines. He had no eye to a dynasty, his eye was single for the Lord only. At the same time, it is natural that our deliverer should be our ruler, and if the Lord Jesus has indeed set us free from sin and Satan, it is but meet and right that he should rule over us.*

24 ¶ And Gideon said unto them, I would desire a request of you, that ye would give me every man the earrings of his prey. (For they had golden earrings, because they *were* Ishmaelites.)

25 And they answered, We will willingly give *them.* And they spread a garment, and did cast therein every man the earrings of his prey.

26 And the weight of the golden earrings

that he requested was a thousand and seven hundred *shekels* of gold; beside ornaments, and collars, and purple raiment that *was* on the kings of Midian, and beside the chains that *were* about their camels' necks.

27 And Gideon made an ephod thereof, and put it in his city, *even* in Ophrah: and all Israel went thither a whoring after it; which thing became a snare unto Gideon, and to his house. *What a pity that so good a man, with so good a motive, should do so wrong a thing. What need or right had he to fashion sacerdotal garments, when the only high-priest was elsewhere, and was adorned with all needful priestly robes and ornaments? A world of evil has come into the world through priestly dress. There is One Priest above arrayed in glory; how foolish and how wicked to dream of making priestly vestures for mortal men.*

32 ¶ And Gideon the son of Joash died in a good old age, and was buried in the sepulchre of Joash his father, in Ophrah of the Abi-ezrites.

33 And it came to pass, as soon as Gideon was dead, that the children of Israel turned again, and went a whoring after Baalim, and made Baal-berith their god. *(From worshipping God in a wrong way, to the worship of a wrong god, is an easy step. Alas! Gideon, what evil didst thou do.)*

34 And the children of Israel remembered not the LORD their God, who had delivered them out of the hands of all their enemies on every side:

35 Neither shewed they kindness to the house of Jerubbaal, *namely,* Gideon, according to all the goodness which he had shewed unto Israel. *(It is no wonder if those who forget God, forget also all others to whom they are indebted.)*

This chapter practically admonishes us to keep close to God's rules of worship as laid down in Scripture, for the slightest divergence therefrom may lead to deadly errors and innumerable evils.

Lord, from habits keep me free
Which incline the least to sin,
Lest they prove a snare to me,
And my soul be held therein.

Reverent to thy sacred will,
May I all thy word obey;
Shun the very shade of ill,
From each idol turn away,

JUDGES X. 6, 7; 9—18.

AND the children of Israel did evil again in the sight of the LORD, *(It is clear that afflictions are unavailing to change the heart; their best results are only temporary, and as soon as they are withdrawn, men return to their old ways,)* and served Baalim, and Ashtaroth, and the gods of Syria, and the gods of Zidon, and the gods of Moab, and the gods of the children of Ammon, and the gods of the Philistines, and forsook the LORD, and served not him.

The multiplicity of these idols should have provoked the scorn of those who knew the one only living and true God; but such is the besotting influence of sin that the Israelites became universal image-worshippers. The rites used in the adoration of many of these false deities were to the last degree degrading, and this rendered Israel's sin all the more heinous. Observe, that they forsook Jehovah altogether when they became votaries of idols; men cannot serve God and Mammon; and where falsehood enters, truth leaves in disgust.

7 And the anger of the LORD was hot against Israel, and he sold them into the hands of the Philistines, and into the hands of the children of Ammon. *(As they idolized on all sides, so were they oppressed on all sides—on the west by Philistines, and on the east by Ammonites.)*

9 Moreover the children of Ammon passed over Jordan to fight also against Judah, and against Benjamin, and against the house of Ephraim; so that Israel was sore distressed.

When all alike were crushed beneath the heavy yoke of the oppressor, their cry went up to heaven with great vehemence.

10 And the children of Israel cried unto the LORD, saying, We have sinned against thee, both because we have forsaken our God, and also served Baalim.

11, 12 And the LORD said unto the children of Israel, *Did* not *I deliver you* from the Egyptians, and from the Amorites, from the children of Ammon, and from the Philistines? The Zidonians also, and the Amalekites, and the Maonites, did oppress you; and ye cried to me, and I delivered you out of their hand.

13 Yet ye have forsaken me, and served other gods: wherefore I will deliver you no more. *(Past favours aggravate present rebellion. If God had dealt hardly with them, there might have been some excuse for forsaking him, but it was base to turn from him after so much help received. O how often might the Lord have said to us, "I will deliver you no more.")*

14 Go and cry unto the gods which ye have chosen; let them deliver you in the time of your tribulation. *(This was but justice, but what a dreadful sound it must have made in Israel's ears. Suppose the Lord should deal thus with us and beat us back to the false confidences and sinful pleasures which we have at any time set our hearts upon. Imagine his saying, "Go to your self-righteousness for comfort"—"turn to your merrymakings or to your money bags"—what would desponding souls be able to reply?)*

15 ¶ And the children of Israel said unto the LORD, We have sinned: do thou unto us whatsoever seemeth good unto thee; deliver us only, we pray thee, this day. *(It was their wisest course to confess their sin, and surrender at discretion. Every awakened penitent should do the same.)*

16 And they put away the strange gods from among them, and served the LORD: and his soul was grieved for the misery of Israel.

This practical reformation proved the sincerity of their repentance. True repentance is not only for sin, but from sin. Those who turned to worship the Lord, even though he continued to smite them, were genuine penitents. Not long would the Lord retain his anger when he saw his people in so hopeful a condition of heart. He loves them too well to retain his wrath against them.

17 Then the children of Ammon were gathered together, and encamped in Gilead. And the children of Israel assembled themselves together, and encamped in Mizpeh.

18 And the people *and* princes of Gilead said one to another, What man *is* he that will begin to fight against the children of Ammon? he shall be head over all the inhabitants of Gilead. *(Under renewed invasion the downtrodden Israelites assembled in self-defence, but they were without a leader. They agreed to submit to the rule of any man who would be bold enough to commence the conflict against their cruel enemy. At this juncture the Lord raised up Jephthah, and through his instrumentality answered their prayers.)*

JUDGES XI. 5—10; 12—21; 23—28.

AND when the children of Ammon made war against Israel, the elders of Gilead went to fetch Jephthah out of the land of Tob :

6 And they said unto Jephthah, Come, and be our captain, that we may fight with the children of Ammon.

7 And Jephthah said unto the elders of Gilead, Did not ye hate me, and expel me out of my father's house ? and why are ye come unto me now when ye are in distress ?

We should mind whom we slight, for upon those very persons we may come to be dependent.

9 And Jephthah said unto the elders of Gilead, If ye bring me home again to fight against the children of Ammon, and the LORD deliver them before me, shall I be your head ?

10 And the elders of Gilead said unto Jephthah, The LORD be witness between us, if we do not so according to thy words.

Jephthah asked no more than had been publicly promised, and was naturally his due. So when the Lord Jesus saves us from our sins, it is but just that he should reign over us.

12 ¶ And Jephthah sent messengers unto the king of the children of Ammon, saying, What hast thou to do with me, that thou art come against me to fight in my land ?

Israel might not wantonly make war with Ammon, therefore Jephthah tries first an appeal to reason. Let us follow peace with all men.

13 And the king of the children of Ammon answered unto the messengers of Jephthah, Because Israel took away my land, when they came up out of Egypt, from Arnon even unto Jabbok, and unto Jordan : now therefore restore those *lands* again peaceably. *(This was a mere pretence, but diplomacy abounds with falsehoods. The Ammonites had lost the territory in war with the Amorites, and when Israel captured it from the Amorites, it became theirs.)*

14—21 And Jephthah sent messengers again unto the king of the children of Ammon : *(To try once more what argument would do, he stated the facts of the case:)* And said unto him, Thus saith Jephthah, Israel took not away the land of Moab, nor the land of the children of Ammon : But when Israel came up from Egypt, and walked through the wilderness unto the Red sea, and came to Kadesh ; Then Israel sent messengers unto the king of Edom, saying, Let me, I pray

thee, pass through thy land : but the king of Edom would not hearken *thereto*. And in like manner they sent unto the king of Moab : but he would not *consent:* and Israel abode in Kadesh. Then they went along through the wilderness, and compassed the land of Edom, and the land of Moab, And Israel sent messengers unto Sihon king of the Amorites, the king of Heshbon; and Israel said unto him, Let us pass, we pray thee, through thy land into my place. · But Sihon trusted not Israel to pass through his coast : but Sihon gathered all his people together, and fought against Israel. And the LORD God of Israel delivered Sihon and all his people into the hand of Israel, and they smote them : so Israel possessed all the land of the Amorites, the inhabitants of that country.

23 So now the LORD God of Israel hath dispossessed the Amorites from before his people Israel, and shouldest thou possess it ?

24 Wilt not thou possess that which Chemosh thy god giveth thee to possess ? So whomsoever the LORD our God shall drive out from before us, them will we possess. *(He argued upon their own grounds, and would have convinced them had they been capable of justice.)*

25, 26 And now *art* thou any thing better than Balak the son of Zippor, king of Moab ? did he ever strive against Israel, or did he ever fight against them, While Israel dwelt in Heshbon and her towns, and in Aroer and her towns, and in all the cities that *be* along by the coasts of Arnon, three hundred years ? why therefore did ye not recover *them* within that time ? *(Undisputed possession for three hundred years was certainly a good title enough. It was rather late to revive a dormant claim.)*

27 Wherefore I have not sinned against thee, but thou doest me wrong to war against me : the LORD the Judge be judge this day between the children of Israel and the children of Ammon. *(He did well to make his appeal to heaven. When right is on our side, we may fearlessly leave results with God. If we have done all we can to make peace, and men will not act justly, the sin must rest with them.)*

28 Howbeit the king of the children of Ammon hearkened not unto the words of Jephthah which he sent him.

Lord, for the glory of thy name,
Vouchsafe me now the victory;
Weakness itself, thou knowest I am,
And cannot share the praise with thee:

Because I now can nothing do,
Jesus, do all the work alone,
And bring my soul triumphant through,
To wave its palm before thy throne.

What power against a worm can stand
  Arm'd with Jehovah's sword?
For all who bow to Christ's command
  Are champions of the Lord.

Arm'd with his word and Spirit's might
  We shall the battle gain,
And sin, that tempting Midianite,
  Shall be for ever slain.

Father, though late, I turn to thee,
  With all my idols part;
O let my helpless misery
  Affect thy pitying heart.

Grieved at thine ancient people's woe,
  Be grieved again at mine;
And force my sins to let me go,
  Redeem'd by blood divine.

He who saves us shall be king,
Let him but deliverance bring.
God the Lord our witness be,
He who saves, our king shall be.

Jesus saves us, he shall reign;
Lord, do not the throne disdain;
Since to save us thou hast died,
Thou shalt reign, and none beside.

E'en in my holiest hours,
  My folly I reveal,
I lack a balance for my powers,
  A bridle for my zeal.

Great Spirit teach me how,
  When all my soul is flame,
To guard the purport of my vow,
  Lest I be put to shame.

If unto God I speak
  And pledge the solemn vow,
Thy heavenly guidance I will seek,
  My gentle teacher, thou.

He subdued the powers of hell,
  In the fight he stood alone;
All his foes before him fell,
  By his single arm o'erthrown.

His the battle, his the toil;
  His the honours of the day;
His the glory and the spoil;
  Jesus bears them all way.

Now proclaim His deeds afar,
  Fill the world with his renown:
His alone the victor's car;
  His the everlasting crown!

I can do all things, or can bear
All sufferings, if my Lord be there;
Sweet pleasures mingle with the pains,
While his left hand my head sustains.

But if the Lord be once withdrawn,
And we attempt the work alone;
When new temptations spring and rise,
We find how great our weakness is.

So Samson, when his hair was lost,
Met the Philistines to his cost;
Shook his vain limbs with sad surprise,
Made feeble fight, and lost his eyes.

So Samson Israel's foes o'erthrew,
More than in life by death he slew;
But when our greater Samson fell,
He vanquish'd sin, and death, and hell.

Compass'd with foes, he bow'd his head;
For mercy, not for vengeance pled,
And groaned his last expiring groan,
And pull'd th' infernal kingdom down.

O Lord, our carnal mind control,
  And make us pure within;
Train thou each passion of our soul
  To hate the thought of sin.

Be ours the blessed lot of those
  Who every evil flee;
Whose spirits chaste, as virgins pure,
  In all things follow thee.

JUDGES XI. 29—40.

THEN the Spirit of the LORD came upon Jephthah, and he passed over Gilead, and Manasseh, and passed over Mizpeh of Gilead, and from Mizpeh of Gilead he passed over *unto* the children of Ammon.

Brave man as he was, he needed a divine preparation for his work, and God graciously vouchsafed it to him. When the Spirit of the Lord comes upon a man, it makes him far other than he was before; it elevates, guides, inspires, and strengthens. He who has the Spirit will find his arms upheld, and his strength rendered sufficient for accomplishing the most arduous enterprises. May this same Spirit, in a more gracious manner, rest upon us.

30 And Jephthah vowed a vow unto the LORD, and said, If thou shalt without fail deliver the children of Ammon into mine hands,

31 Then it shall be, that whatsoever cometh forth of the doors of my house to meet me, when I return in peace from the children of Ammon, shall surely be the LORD's, and I will offer it up for a burnt offering. (*This was, doubtless, the warm outburst of an earnest heart, but there was a great want of caution in it. If we vow at all, we should think long and well of what we are about to do, and then express our resolve in the plainest terms. It is most unwise for a Christian man to bring himself into bondage by rash pledges and incautious declarations. Jephthah's case should be a warning to us.*)

32 ¶ So Jephthah passed over unto the children of Ammon to fight against them; and the LORD delivered them into his hands.

33 And he smote them from Aroer, even till thou come to Minnith, *even* twenty cities, and unto the plain of the vineyards, with a very great slaughter. Thus the children of Ammon were subdued before the children of Israel.

Joyfully did the hero return to his home, but alas, how marred was his triumph. His rash vow had become a pit for him.

34 ¶ And Jephthah came to Mizpeh unto his house, and, behold, his daughter came out to meet him with timbrels and with dances : and she *was his* only child ; beside her he had neither son nor daughter.

35 And it came to pass, when he saw her, that he rent his clothes, and said, Alas, my daughter! thou hast brought me very low, and thou art one of them that trouble me : for I have opened my mouth unto the LORD, and I cannot go back. (*Yet it had been far better to break a wrong vow than to keep it. His mistake lay in uttering a vow which might possibly bring about such terrible consequences. He swore that he would offer up for a burnt offering whatsoever came forth of his doors to meet him. Half-instructed as he was, he may have thought that so bold a promise would be acceptable to Jehovah, and now in semi-heathenish fear, he feels he must stand to his word.*)

36 And she said unto him, My father, *if* thou hast opened thy mouth unto the LORD, do to me according to that which hath proceeded out of thy mouth ; forasmuch as the LORD hath taken vengeance for thee of thine enemies, *even* of the children of Ammon. (*It was bravely spoken. Grandly did the hero's daughter yield herself to die, or to remain unmarried, content so long as her country was free.*)

37 And she said unto her father, Let this thing be done for me : Let me alone two months, that I may go up and down upon the mountains, and bewail my virginity, I and my fellows.

38 And he said, Go. And he sent her away *for* two months : and she went with her companions, and bewailed her virginity upon the mountains.

39, 40 And it came to pass at the end of two months, that she returned unto her father, who did with her *according* to his vow which he had vowed : and she knew no man. (*Let us hope that her father did not actually sacrifice her : if he did, it was an act most abhorrent in the sight of God. Her submission to her doom was touchingly beautiful ; let us hope that the vow was capable of a softer construction, and that she lived a celibate life, consecrated to the Lord. Many expressions in the chapter encourage that hope ; at the same time it is sufficiently doubtful, to lead us to repeat our warning against every rash vow. Pause, hot spirit! Consider! Reckon all the consequences, and ere thou open thy mouth unto the Lord, make sure that what thou art covenanting to do is really for his glory, and within the lawful compass of thy power.*) And it was a custom in Israel, *That* the daughters of Israel went yearly to lament the daughter of Jephthah the Gileadite four days in a year.

ISRAEL *by again sinning fell under the tyranny of the Philistines, yet God did not forget his people, but raised them up a champion. An angel appeared to Manoah and his wife, foretelling the birth of a son who should deliver Israel. In due time, his promise was fulfilled by the birth of Samson, some incidents in whose history will now interest us.*

JUDGES XIV.

1 And Samson went down to Timnath, and saw a woman in Timnath of the daughters of the Philistines.

2 And he came up, and told his father and his mother, and said, I have seen a woman in Timnath of the daughters of the Philistines: now therefore get her for me to wife.

Thus the history of this strongest of men begins with an act of weakness; and his whole life is marred by faults in the same direction. An unusually developed animal nature rendered him the easy victim of his passions: if any of us were as vigorous as he, we should probably be even more ready to yield to the temptations which ensnared him. His faith in God was his peculiar virtue; in this, few, if any, of the saints excelled him; but his peculiar physical conformation left an unguarded point in his character, and that proved his downfall.

3 Then his father and his mother said unto him, *Is there* never a woman among the daughters of thy brethren, or among all my people, that thou goest to take a wife of the uncircumcised Philistines? *(It must always be grievous to right-minded parents to see their children marrying ungodly persons No good can possibly come of it. It is most injurious to the soul, and generally leads to heart-rending trials. Surely there are good people enough in the church of God without our looking to the synagogue of Satan for a spouse.)* And Samson said unto his father, Get her for me; for she pleaseth me well. *(This is too often the only reason men will give or can give for the course they pursue. It is the worst reason in the world, for that which pleases our flesh is usually hurtful to our better nature. Let us never be slaves to our animal nature, but govern ourselves by the power of our mental and spiritual manhood.)*

4 But his father and his mother knew not that it *was* of the LORD, that he sought an occasion against the Philistines: for at that time the Philistines had dominion over Israel.

They were not aware that God intended to over-rule this to force him into antagonism with the oppressors of his country.

5 ¶ Then went Samson down, and his father and his mother, to Timnath, and came to the vineyards of Timnath: and, behold, a young lion roared against him.

6 And the Spirit of the LORD came mightily upon him, and he rent him as he would have rent a kid, and *he had* nothing in his hand: but he told not his father or his mother what he had done. *(A supernatural might was given to him, and the strong lion fell before his un-armed strength, yet as he was not proud or desirous of vainglory he left the exploit untold. This was fine exercise for him, a grand preliminary trial of strength before his great battles with the enemy. Like David, he learned to fight Philistines by beginning with beasts.)*

7 And he went down, and talked with the woman; and she pleased Samson well.

8 And after a time he returned to take her, and he turned aside to see the carcase of the lion: and, behold, *there was* a swarm of bees and honey in the carcase of the lion. *(He remembered thankfully how the Lord delivered him, and turned aside to survey the spot, and his memory had its reward, for he found the honey. It is well to recollect past mercies, and learn how easily the Lord can turn our terrors into pleasures.*

" Thus the lion yields us honey;
From the eater food is given.")

9 And he took thereof in his hands, and went on eating, and came to his father and mother, and he gave them, and they did eat: but he told not them that he had taken the honey out of the carcase of the lion. *(He preserved a singular silence, but great doers are frequently little talkers. Dr. Kitto very properly remarks:—" The whole of the affair of the lion is mentioned in the sacred narrative, not merely as an exploit, but on account of the circumstances which grew out of it. Samson, doubtless, performed many mighty feats which are not recorded; those only being mentioned which directly influenced the current of his history, and brought him more or less into collision with the Philistines.*

No one would have thought that out of this slaughter of the lion, and the finding a swarm of bees in the skin-enveloped carcass—occurring, as it did, while the hero was engaged in forming amicable relations with the Philistines, occasion for the exertion of his destroying energies against the oppressors of Israel would have arisen. But so it came to pass. The most unlikely agents— lions, bees, honey-combs, may become the instruments of accomplishing the purposes of God, and of leading or driving a man to his appointed task, when he thinks not of it.")

10 ¶ So his father went down unto the woman : and Samson made there a feast ; for so used the young men to do.

11, 12 And it came to pass, when they saw him, that they brought thirty companions to be with him. *(Probably these thirty men, under the pretence of being boon companions, were set to watch him as spies : the friendship of Philistines should always be mistrusted.)* And Samson said unto them, I will now put forth a riddle unto you : if ye can certainly declare it me within the seven days of the feast, and find *it* out, then I will give you thirty sheets and thirty change of garments :

13 But if ye cannot declare *it* me, then shall ye give me thirty sheets and thirty change of garments. And they said unto him, Put forth thy riddle, that we may hear it.

14 And he said unto them, Out of the eater came forth meat, and out of the strong came forth sweetness. And they could not in three days expound the riddle.

15 And it came to pass on the seventh day, that they said unto Samson's wife, Entice thy husband, that he may declare unto us the riddle, lest we burn thee and thy father's house with fire : have ye called us to take that we have ? *is it* not *so?* *(Thus ill-blood was engendered by the wedding festivities. How can we hope things to go well if we mingle with the unregenerate? Samson was acting very wrongly in all this, but God was overruling it to make him come forth as Philistia's foe, and Israel's champion.)*

16 And Samson's wife wept before him, and said, Thou dost but hate me, and lovest me not : thou hast put forth a riddle unto the children of my people, and hast not told *it* me. And he said unto her, Behold, I have not told *it* my father nor my mother, and shall I tell *it* thee ?

17 And she wept before him the seven days, while their feast lasted : and it came to pass on the seventh day, that he told her, because she lay sore upon him : and she told the riddle to the children of her people.

18 And the men of the city said unto him on the seventh day before the sun went down, What *is* sweeter than honey ? and what *is* stronger than a lion ? And he said unto them, If ye had not plowed with my heifer, ye had not found out my riddle. *(Here he began to learn that a heathen wife was not to be trusted. How could he expect that she, who worshipped a false god, would be true to him ! How sad it was that he did not profit by this experience.)*

19 ¶ And the Spirit of the LORD came upon him, and he went down to Ashkelon, and slew thirty men of them, and took their spoil, and gave change of garments unto them which expounded the riddle. *(As the garments specified would only be worn by persons of wealth, Samson must have dealt the Philistines a heavy blow. Thirty men of rank would be sorely missed.)* And his anger was kindled, and he went up to his father's house.

20 But Samson's wife was *given* to his companion, whom he had used as his friend.

Thus Samson was used as God's executioner among the Philistines, but he himself was made to smart for his folly. His foolish love yielded him small solace ; where he doted he found deceit and desertion. It is perilous to any man to allow his weaker passions to become his guide. Sooner or later sinful joys will curdle into miseries. Never let us run such risks as Samson dared to encounter. Let his wreck be our beacon.

Up believer, face the lion,
Thou shalt rend it like a kid,
Jesus' mighty name rely on,
Face thy foe as thou art bid.

Start not at his loudest roaring,
Slay him in Jehovah's strength :
Then from forth his carcass pouring,
Honey shall be thine at length.

S AMSON'S *marriage led to a complicated quarrel, during which he burned the standing corn of the Philistines by means of firebrands tied to the tails of foxes, and also slaughtered a great number of his enemies. He then went and dwelt at the top of the rock Etam, but God meant him to do far more for the overthrow of Israel's enemies, and therefore gave him but little respite.*

JUDGES XV. 9—20.

9 ¶ Then the Philistines went up, and pitched in Judah, and spread themselves in Lehi. *(This was probably the valley at the foot of Samson's stronghold, afterwards called Lehi, or the place of the jawbone.)*

10 And the men of Judah said, Why are ye come up against us ? And they answered, To bind Samson are we come up, to do to him as he hath done to us. *(The men of Judah had sunk to the condition of vassals, and were forced to be obsequious to their tyrant masters. Sin makes men cowards.)*

11 Then three thousand men of Judah went to the top of the rock Etam, and said to Samson, Knowest thou not that the Philistines are rulers over us ? what is this that thou hast done unto us ? *(O miserable sight, these cowards are friends to their oppressors, and upbraid their best friend. How low were they sunk to talk in this fashion !)* And he said unto them, As they did unto me so have I· done unto them.

12 And they said unto him, We are come down to bind thee, that we may deliver thee into the hand of the Philistines. *(False brethren are our worst enemies, they will ruin us when our enemies cannot. Beware of hypocrites.)* And Samson said unto them, Swear unto me, that ye will not fall upon me yourselves.

13 And they spake unto him, saying, No ; but we will bind thee fast, and deliver thee into their hand : but surely we will not kill thee. And they bound him with two new cords, and brought him up from the rock. *(Does it not remind us of our Lord bound by those whom he came to deliver, and betrayed into the hands of his enemies ?)*

14 ¶ *And* when he came unto Lehi, the Philistines shouted against him. *(This shout came a little too soon. It was soon turned into a shriek of dismay, and then into the silence of death.)* And the Spirit of the LORD came mightily upon him, and the cords that *were* upon his arms became as flax that was burnt with fire, and his bands loosed from off his hands.

15 And he found a new jawbone of an ass, and put forth his hand, and took it, and slew a thousand men therewith. *(The weapon matters little, the force lies in the arm. The Lord can use the weakest to overcome the strongest.)*

16 And Samson said, With the jawbone of an ass, heaps upon heaps, with the jaw of an ass, have I slain a thousand men. *(Like our greater champion, who exclaimed, " I have trodden the winepress alone, and of the people there was none with me.")*

17 And it came to pass, when he had made an end of speaking, that he cast away the jawbone out of his hand, and called that place Ramath-lehi. *(Or the casting away of the jawbone.)*

18 ¶ And he was sore athirst, and called on the LORD, and said, Thou hast given this great deliverance into the hand of thy servant : and now shall I die for thirst, and fall into the hand of the uncircumcised ? *(Samson knew how to pray and to pray in faith too : this was all along the saving point in his character.)*

19 But God clave an hollow place that *was* in the jaw *(or in the place called Lehi or Jawbone),* and there came water thereout ; and when he had drunk, his spirit came again, and he revived ; wherefore he called the name thereof En-hakkore *(the fountain of him who prayed),* which *is* in Lehi *(or the place called Jawbone),* unto this day. *(God, who helps his servants in great matters, sometimes allows them to be greatly tried by comparatively smaller trials, for an exercise of their faith. But he will not leave them in the minor difficulty. Where fell the jawbone from the hero's hand, there rose a refreshing fountain to quench his thirst. God is never at a loss for supplies. We have but to trust him, and we shall do great things, and. receive great things.)*

20 And he judged Israel in the days of the Philistines twenty years. *(By his personal prowess he turned aside Israel's enemies, and established a settled government, God intending in his person to shew Israel how he could make one man chase a thousand, and two put ten thousand to flight.)*

W E *cannot linger over Samson's famous feat at Gaza, where he carried away the city gates upon his shoulders, but must come to the unhappy scene in which that great man fell a victim to his own follies, and was deprived of his power to judge and protect his countrymen. Delilah, the companion of his sin, was the instrument of his downfall.*

JUDGES XVI. 6—20.

6, 7 And Delilah said to Samson, Tell me, I pray thee, wherein thy great strength *lieth*, and wherewith thou mightest be bound to afflict thee. And Samson said unto her, If they bind me with seven green withs that were never dried, then shall I be weak, and be as another man.

8 Then the lords of the Philistines brought up to her seven green withs which had not been dried, and she bound him with them.

9 Now *there were* men lying in wait, abiding with her in the chamber. And she said unto him, The Philistines *be* upon thee, Samson. And he brake the withs, as a thread of tow is broken when it toucheth the fire. So his strength was not known. *(After this deliverance Samson had no excuse for further remaining in traitorous company. "Surely in vain is the net spread in the sight of any bird," but this man was so infatuated that he plunged into the snare after he had once narrowly escaped from it. Sin is madness.)*

10, 11 And Delilah said unto Samson, Behold, thou hast mocked me, and told me lies: now tell me, I pray thee, wherewith thou mightest be bound. And he said unto her, If they bind me fast with new ropes that never were occupied, then shall I be weak, and be as another man.

12 Delilah therefore took new ropes, and bound him therewith, and said unto him, The Philistines *be* upon thee, Samson. And *there were* liers in wait abiding in the chamber. And he brake them from off his arms like a thread. *A second time betrayed! A second time delivered! Will he not fly now from the deceiver's house? Alas! No. You might sooner teach a moth to shun the candle than a man besotted by sin to escape from its wiles.*

13 And Delilah said unto Samson, Hitherto thou hast mocked me and told me lies: tell me wherewith thou mightest be bound. And he said unto her, If thou weavest the seven locks of my head with the web.

14 And she fastened *it* with the pin, and said unto him, The Philistines *be* upon thee, Samson. And he awaked out of his sleep, and went away with the pin of the beam, and with the web. *This time he came dangerously near his secret. The whirlpool in which he was surging was sucking him down. Poor Samson! Who could save thee when thou wast determined to destroy thyself?*

15 16, 17 And she said unto him, How canst thou say, I love thee, when thine heart *is* not with me? thou hast mocked me these three times, and hast not told me wherein thy great strength *lieth*. And it came to pass, when she pressed him daily with her words, and urged him, *so* that his soul was vexed unto death; That he told her all his heart, and said unto her, There hath not come a razor upon mine head; for I *have been* a Nazarite unto God from my mother's womb: if I be shaven, then my strength will go from me, and I shall become weak, and be like any *other* man. *(His consecration was his strength, and when he renounced the unshorn locks, which were the symbol of his dedication, the Lord left him, and he reaped the due reward of his sinful indulgences. He sinned deliberately, and therefore was left to smart for it.)*

18 And when Delilah saw that he had told her all his heart, she sent and called for the lords of the Philistines, saying, Come up this once, for he hath shewed me all his heart. Then the lords of the Philistines came up unto her, and brought money in their hand. *(Bad men and women are always ready to sell for gain those whom they loudly profess to love. They are never to be trusted.)*

19, 20 And she made him sleep upon her knees; and she called for a man, and she caused him to shave off the seven locks of his head; and she began to afflict him, and his strength went from him. And she said, The Philistines *be* upon thee, Samson. And he awoke out of his sleep, and said, I will go out as at other times before, and shake myself. And he wist not that the LORD was departed from him. *(Vainly do we go forth without our God. We may have been valiant and mighty before, but if the Lord shall leave us we shall be captives to our foes. What a warning does this unhappy story present to us. May infinite mercy enable us to profit thereby.)*

206   "𝕹evertheless my lovingkindness will 𝕴 not utterly take from him."

APRIL 9.—EVENING.

[*Or July* 17.]

JUDGES XVI. 21—31.

BUT the Philistines took him, and put out his eyes, *(according to the Arabic Version, they applied fire to them),* and brought him down to Gaza, and bound him with fetters of brass; *(the strongest they could find, and the most painful to the wearer;)* and he did grind in the prison house. *(The great champion was degraded to do a woman's work, work which when performed for others was considered to be the meanest servitude. Milton pictures the fallen hero as describing himself thus—*

" Made of my enemies the scorn and gaze;
To grind in brazen fetters under task
With this Heaven-gifted strength. O glorious strength,
Put to the labour of a beast, debased
Lower than bond slave! Promise was that I
Should Israel from Philistian yoke deliver;
Ask for this great deliverer now, and find him
Eyeless in Gaza at the mill with slaves.")

22 Howbeit the hair of his head began to grow again after he was shaven. *(God's grace casts not off his servants: grace though reduced to the lowest ebb returns again, even as Samson's hair grew, and his strength returned. It is one of the wonders of divine love that it holds on to its object even when he proves unworthy of it.)*

23 Then the lords of the Philistines gathered them together for to offer a great sacrifice unto Dagon their god, and to rejoice : for they said, Our god hath delivered Samson our enemy into our hand.

24 And when the people saw him, they praised their god : for they said, Our god hath delivered into our hands our enemy, and the destroyer of our country, which slew many of us. *(Thus they blasphemed Jehovah by magnifying Baal. They do, however, teach us one lesson, too often forgotten, namely, to ascribe all our victories to God.)*

25 And it came to pass, when their hearts were merry, that they said, Call for Samson, that he may make us sport. And they called for Samson out of the prison house; and he made them sport : and they set him between the pillars.

26 And Samson said unto the lad that held him by the hand, Suffer me that I may feel the pillars whereupon the house standeth, that I may lean upon them. *(The poor blind prisoner made rare mirth for the assembled lords, and they could*

do no other than let him rest a while, while they refilled their cups, and meditated fresh insults.)*

27 Now the house was full of men and women; and all the lords of the Philistines *were* there; and *there were* upon the roof about three thousand men and women, that beheld while Samson made sport.

28 And Samson called unto the LORD, and said, O Lord GOD, remember me, I pray thee, and strengthen me, I pray thee, only this once, O God, that I may be at once avenged of the Philistines for my two eyes. *(How touching is that sweetest of prayers, "Remember me," whether it be Samson or the dying thief who uses it. The Lord indeed did remember him.)*

29 And Samson took hold of the two middle pillars upon which the house stood, and on which it was borne up, of the one with his right hand, and of the other with his left.

30 And Samson said, Let me die with the Philistines. And he bowed himself with *all his* might; and the house fell upon the lords, and upon all the people that *were* therein. So the dead which he slew at his death were more than *they* which he slew in his life.

Milton shall again expound for us—

" Those two massy pillars
With horrible convulsion to and fro
He tugg'd, he shook, till down they came and drew
The whole roof after them, with burst of thunder,
Upon the heads of all who sat beneath,
Lords, ladies, captains, counsellers, or priests,
Their choice nobility and flower, not only
Of this but each Philistian city round.

  •   *   *   *   *   •

O dearly-bought revenge, yet glorious!
Living or dying thou hast fulfill'd
The work for which thou wast foretold
To Israel, and now ly'st victorious
Among thy slain, self-killed,
Not willingly, but tangled in the fold
Of dire necessity, whose law in death conjoin'd
Thee with thy slaughter'd foes."

Thus the Lord God of Israel silenced the boastings of his enemies, as he will do in the last great day.

31 Then his brethren and all the house of his father came down, and took him, and brought *him* up, and buried him between Zorah and Eshtaol in the burying-place of Manoah his father. And he judged Israel twenty years.

THE *sad case of Samson reminds us of the warnings of the book of Proverbs, against that treacherous form of sin. Evil company is always dangerous, but association with persons of impure life is deadly. May the young men of the household lay this day's lesson to heart; it has been hard to write, but a sense of duty forced it upon us.*

PROVERBS VII. 1—18; 21—27. ✓

1 My son, keep my words, and lay up my commandments with thee. *(Treasure up this warning as a precious thing, it may save you from a wretched old age.)*

2, 3 Keep my commandments, and live; and my law as the apple of thine eye. Bind them upon thy fingers, write them upon the table of thine heart. *(Have right principles at your fingers' ends, and in your heart's core.)*

4, 5 Say unto wisdom, Thou *art* my sister; and call understanding *thy* kinswoman: That they may keep thee from the strange woman, from the stranger *which* flattereth with her words. *(As good women are our greatest blessings, so are bad women among the worst curses in the world. Flee from them, listen not to their words. To shew how wicked they are, Solomon tells us a tale of real life, which we will read with earnest prayer, that none of this household may ever imitate the foolish victim.)*

6 7 ¶ For at the window of my house I looked through my casement, And beheld among the simple ones, I discerned among the youths, a young man void of understanding, *(Without grace in his heart, or sense in his head,)*

8 Passing through the street near her corner; and he went the way to her house, *(He had better have gone miles round than pass the spot,)*

9, 10 In the twilight, in the evening, in the black and dark night: *(Late hours lead to no good.)* And, behold, there met him a woman *with* the attire of an harlot, and subtil of heart.

11, 12 (She *is* loud and stubborn; her feet abide not in her house: Now *is she* without, now in the streets, and lieth in wait at every corner.) *(Had she been a fit companion she would have been at home.)*

13 So she caught him, and kissed him, *and* with an impudent face said unto him,

14 *I* have peace offerings with me; this day have I payed my vows. *(O the wickedness of those who mix up religion with their filthiness; but this was a part of the bait with which to entrap the foolish young man.)*

15 Therefore came I forth to meet thee, diligently to seek thy face, and I have found thee. *(This was another falsehood, she cared no more for him than for anybody else. O beware of these deceivers.)*

16, 17, 18 I have decked my bed with coverings of tapestry, with carved *works*, with fine linen of Egypt. I have perfumed my bed with myrrh, aloes, and cinnamon. Come, let us take our fill of love until the morning: let us solace ourselves with loves.

21 With her much fair speech she caused him to yield, with the flattering of her lips she forced him. *(What a servant of Satan was she! There are many like her, who take fools in their nets.)*

22 He goeth after her straightway, as an ox goeth to the slaughter, *(The ox has no idea of what is coming, or he would never enter the slaughter-house: wicked young men little know the terrible results of sin,)* or as a fool to the correction of the stocks; *(The drunkard smiles when set in the stocks, as if it were rare fun; so do foolish men dream that sin is pleasure.)*

23 Till a dart strike through his liver; *(His vital parts shall suffer for his folly, pain shall succeed his pleasures;)* as a bird hasteth to the snare, and knoweth not that it *is* for his life. *The life both of his body and his soul shall be ruined by his vice.*

24 ¶ Hearken unto me now therefore, O ye children, and attend to the words of my mouth.

25 Let not thine heart decline to her ways, go not astray in her paths.

26 For she hath cast down many wounded: yea, many strong *men* have been slain by her. *Samson and Solomon to wit.*

27 Her house *is* the way to hell, going down to the chambers of death. *(Strong language, but none too strong. If young people knew what follows upon unclean actions, they would sooner burn their flesh with fire, or sleep with venomous reptiles, than have any communion with unchaste persons. Young women should loathe those gay fellows whose actions will not bear to be spoken of; and both young and old, male and female, should abhor any indelicacy of thought, word, or deed, in books or mirthful play.)*

JUDGES XVII.

AND there was a man of mount Ephraim, whose name *was* Micah.

2 And he said unto his mother, The eleven hundred *shekels* of silver that were taken from thee, about which thou cursedst, and spakest of also in mine ears, behold, the silver *is* with me; I took it. And his mother said, Blessed *be thou* of the LORD, my son. (*Very little was her blessing worth, since she had been so ready at cursing. Her silver was her god while it was in the form of shekels, quite as much as when it was fashioned into an image, or else she had not cursed because of the loss of it. Her son Micah, who became so ostentatiously religious, was a thief to begin with. A superstitious dread made him restore what his conscience did not forbid him to steal. The man was made of the right material to become a Ritualist.*)

3 And when he had restored the eleven hundred *shekels* of silver to his mother, his mother said, I had wholly dedicated the silver unto the LORD from my hand for my son, to make a graven image and a molten image: now therefore I will restore it unto thee.

An image was to be made contrary to the divine law, and yet it was to be dedicated unto Jehovah. Good intentions are no excuse for disobedience. Image-makers, now-a-days, tell us that they do not worship them, but worship God through them; if this be accepted as an apology, there remains no idolatry in the world. But God thinketh not so.

4 Yet he restored the money unto his mother; and his mother took two hundred *shekels* of silver, and gave them to the founder, who made thereof a graven image and a molten image: and they were in the house of Micah.

5 And the man Micah had an house of gods, and made an ephod, and teraphim, and consecrated one of his sons, who became his priest.

Children imitate their parents. The mother makes one image, the son has a house-full of gods, and the grandson becomes a priest. If we once leave the spiritual worship of God, there is no telling how far we shall wander.

6 In those days *there was* no king in Israel, *but* every man did *that which was* right in his own eyes. (*Which means that every man did what evil he liked.*)

7, 8 And there was a young man out of Beth-lehem-judah of the family of Judah, who *was* a Levite, and he sojourned there. And the man departed out of the city from Beth-lehem-judah to sojourn where he could find *a place:* and he came to mount Ephraim to the house of Micah, as he journeyed.

9 And Micah said unto him, Whence comest thou? And he said unto him, I *am* a Levite of Beth-lehem-judah, and I go to sojourn where I may find *a place.*

10 And Micah said unto him, Dwell with me, and be unto me a father and a priest, and I will give thee ten *shekels* of silver by the year, and a suit of apparel, and thy victuals. So the Levite went in. (*It was but poor pay: two hundred shekels had been spent on an image, and now ten is thought enough for the priest. A rich idol they must have, even though the priest be poor as charity. The pay was worse when we remember that the Levite was selling his soul for the pittance. How degrading for a servant of the living God to be waiting upon dumb idols.*)

11 12 And the Levite was content to dwell with the man; and the young man was unto him as one of his sons. And Micah consecrated the Levite; and the young man became his priest, and was in the house of Micah.

13 Then said Micah, Now know I that the LORD will do me good, seeing I have a Levite to *my* priest. (*So superstition always talks. This was an ordained man and one of the regular clergy, therefore a blessing must attend his performances. Though the images and ephods were all forbidden, and the whole worship was a direct opposition to the Lord's true worship at Jerusalem, yet they looked for a blessing because the priest was in the succession; even as in these days, those who set up crosses, and pictures, and altars—and so insult the Lord Jesus, nevertheless expect peculiar favours because of some imaginary apostolical succession. "God is a spirit, and they that worship him must worship him in spirit and in truth." Outward formalities and performances not commanded in Scripture, we ought not to sanction by our presence, but avoid them lest we partake in the sin of them.*)

JUDGES XVIII. 1—6; 14—26.

IN those days *there was* no king in Israel : and in those days the tribe of the Danites sought them an inheritance to dwell in; for unto that day *all their* inheritance had not fallen unto them among the tribes of Israel.

2 And the children of Dan sent of their family five men from their coasts, men of valour, from Zorah, and from Eshtaol, to spy out the land, and to search it; and they said unto them, Go, search the land : who when they came to mount Ephraim, to the house of Micah, they lodged there.

3 When they *were* by the house of Micah, they knew the voice of the young man the Levite : and they turned in thither, and said unto him, Who brought thee hither ? and what makest thou in this *place ?* and what hast thou here? *(This is generally the worldling's question— " What hast thou here ? " And in this case it was well suited for a hireling priest.)*

4 And he said unto them, Thus and thus dealeth Micah with me, and hath hired me, and I am his priest.

5 And they said unto him, Ask counsel, we pray thee, of God, that we may know whether our way which we go shall be prosperous.

Little did they care whether he was a true servant of God or not. They were like many in our day, who think one religion as good as another. They saw before them a god, an ephod, and a priest, and that was enough for them. One would think that if they cared for religion at all, they would have been anxious to have the right one; but no, the very men who are careful in their eating, their clothing, their medicine, will take their faith second-hand from others, without examination.

6 And the priest said unto them, Go in peace : before the Lord *is* your way wherein ye go.

False priests abound in soft words.

These spies fulfilled their commission, and returned to the Danites with their report; whereupon the men of war marched upon Laish, and on the road stopped at or near Micah's house for the night, as the spies had done previously. They were ungrateful enough to repay his former hospitality by robbing him.

14 ¶ Then answered the five men that went to spy out the country of Laish, and said unto their brethren, Do ye know that there is in these houses an ephod, and teraphim, and a graven image, and a molten image ? now therefore consider what ye have to do. *(This was a hint that perhaps the gods would be worth the stealing.)*

15 And they turned thitherward, and came to the house of the young man the Levite, *even* unto the house of Micah, and saluted him.

16 And the six hundred men appointed with their weapons of war, which *were* of the children of Dan, stood by the entering of the gate.

17 And the five men that went to spy out the land went up, *and* came in thither, *and* took the graven image, and the ephod, and the teraphim, and the molten image : and the priest stood in the entering of the gate with the six hundred men *that were* appointed with weapons of war.

They kept the priest in conversation while they stole the wretched gods which could not protect themselves. Does it not read like a caricature ? How insane a thing, that men should steal what they had worshipped, and afterwards worship what they stole.

18 And these went into Micah's house, and fetched the carved image, the ephod, and the teraphim, and the molten image. Then said the priest unto them, What do ye ?

19 And they said unto him, Hold thy peace, lay thine hand upon thy mouth, and go with us, and be to us a father and a priest : *is it* better for thee to be a priest unto the house of one man, or that thou be a priest unto a tribe and a family in Israel ? *(They knew the most powerful arguments to silence this gentleman, and asked him whether it would not be more profitable to be the priest of a settlement than the private chaplain of a single man. The man who had already sold himself was easily bought.)*

20 And the priest's heart was glad, and he took the ephod, and the teraphim, and the graven image, and went in the midst of the people. *(Bishop Hall says, " He that was won with ten shekels, may be lost with eleven. The Levite had too many gods to make conscience of pleasing one. There is nothing more inconstant than a Levite who seeks nothing but himself.")*

¶ 22 *And* when they were a good way from the house of Micah, the men that *were* in the houses near to Micah's house were gathered together, and overtook the children of Dan.

23 And they cried unto the children of Dan. And they turned their faces, and said unto Micah, What aileth thee, that thou comest with such a company?

24 And he said, Ye have taken away my gods which I made, and the priest, and ye are gone away: and what have I more? and what *is* this *that* ye say unto me, What aileth thee? *(What a mass of superstition and absurdity! Ye have stolen my gods which are my all. They are my own gods, for I made them myself, and very precious are they to my heart, so that nothing can console me for their loss. He was foolish to trust in gods which could not take care of themselves, yet while he did trust in them he showed his sincerity by grieving for their loss. In very deed, if we lose the smile of the living God, we may well say, "What have I more?" To lose the presence of God is to lose all.)*

25 And the children of Dan said unto him, Let not thy voice be heard among us, lest angry fellows run upon thee, and thou lose thy life, with the lives of thy household. *(Those who have power on their side can generally find some-*

thing to say, and they scarcely care to conceal the lion's claw beneath the lion's pad.)

26 And the children of Dan went their way: and when Micah saw that they *were* too strong for him, he turned and went back unto his house.

And if he became a wiser man he was a great gainer by his loss. If Ritualists and others could be cured of their folly by the breaking in pieces of all their altars and the pulling down of every cathedral in the land it would be a cheap remedy. O that the Lord would visit this land, and with his great besom sweep out the priests and their idols. May he also cleanse the temples of our hearts. For this let us pray.

God is King among all nations,
God above all gods is he;
In his hand are earth's foundations,
The strong hills and rolling sea:

He created land and ocean,
He with beauty clothes the sod;
Let us kneel in deep devotion,
Bless our Maker and our God.

From vile idolatry
Preserve my worship clean;
I am the God who set thee free
From slavery and sin.

No symbol shalt thou make,
Or graven image frame;
I am the Lord, Invisible,
Eternal is my name.

Though steeped in midnight dire as death,
The heathen scorn thy name,
And rage with bold blaspheming breath;
Dear Lord, remember them!

Darkly they roam, enslaved by lust,
Devoid of fear and shame;
Before their gods they crouch in dust;
But, oh! remember them!

Why is thy church so much defaced?
Why hast thou laid her fences waste?
Strangers and foes against her join,
And every beast devours thy vine.

Return, Almighty God, return;
Nor let thy bleeding vineyard mourn;
Turn us to thee, thy love restore,
We shall be saved, and sigh no more.

THE *mournfully ludicrous picture of idol-worship afforded by our two last readings, leads us to adore and worship the one only living and true God, who has revealed himself to us as Father, Son, and Holy Spirit, our God in coven-ant, whom alone we reverence. Let us read the devout song of the Jewish church contained in*

PSALM CXV.

1 Not unto us, O LORD, not unto us, but unto thy name give glory, for thy mercy, *and* for thy truth's sake. *(When in trouble, we can find no plea for help in ourselves, but must be humbled, and appeal only to the mercy and faithfulness of God.)*

2 Wherefore should the heathen say, Where *is* now their God ? *(Saints draw arguments from the blasphemies of their enemies, and these are prevalent with God.)*

3 But our God *is* in the heavens : he hath done whatsoever he hath pleased. *(However much the ungodly may rage, God sits upon the throne, they cannot thrust him from the seat of power; and, moreover, amid all their riot the Lord achieves his purposes, and in every jot and tittle his decrees are fulfilled. Sweet comfort this.)*

4 Their idols *are* silver and gold, the work of men's hands. *(At the very best this is all the idols are, mere masses of metal. What scorn is here poured upon the sacred images ! The next sentences are grimly sardonic. Idols are not to be reverenced but despised.)*

5 They have mouths, but they speak not : eyes have they, but they see not :

6 They have ears, but they hear not : noses have they, but they smell not :

7 They have hands, but they handle not : feet have they, but they walk not : neither speak they through their throat. *(Though their features are meant to represent various attributes of power, they are only so many falsehoods, for an eye that cannot see is a poor emblem of know-ledge, a mouth which cannot speak is no symbol of eloquence, and hands which cannot move are a mockery, rather than an ensign of power.)*

8 They that make them are like unto them ; *so is* every one that trusteth in them.
They are as gross and ridiculous as the images they adore.

9 O Israel, trust thou in the LORD : he *is* their help and their shield.

10 O house of Aaron, trust in the LORD : he *is* their help and their shield.

11 Ye that fear the LORD, trust in the LORD : he *is* their help and their shield. *(Thus trust in God is the duty and privilege of all sorts of saints, in all places.)*

12 The LORD hath been mindful of us : he will bless *us* ; *(The past ensures the future, since our God changes not;)* he will bless the house of Israel; he will bless the house of Aaron.

13 He will bless them that fear the LORD, *both* small and great. *(A precious word of comfort for the little in years, in substance, in ability, and in grace; they are not and shall not be forgotten, when God blesses his chosen.)*

14 The LORD shall increase you more and more, you and your children. *(Believers shall be multiplied, the chosen race shall increase.)*

15 Ye *are* blessed of the LORD which made heaven and earth. *(And this is true, whatever men may say, or providence may appoint. Rejoice in it, ye righteous.)*

16 The heaven, *even* the heavens, *are* the LORD'S : but the earth hath he given to the children of men.

17 The dead praise not the LORD, neither any that go down into silence. *(So far as this world is concerned, death ends human praise: let us then resolve to bless the Lord as long as we live, according to the resolution of the next verse.)*

18 But we will bless the LORD from this time forth and for evermore. Praise the LORD.

Formed by human hands, behold
Gods of silver, gods of gold ;
Worship unto these they pay,
Unto these bow down and pray.

Mouths have they, yet not a word
From their speechless lips is heard ;
Eyes they have, yet blind are found ;
Ears,—but cannot hear a sound.

They as void of sense appear,
Who these senseless idols rear ;
All who trust in them for aid,
Miserable dupes are made.

Israel, trust thou in the Lord ;
He alone can help afford :
Make Jehovah's name your shield ;
Sure protection he will yield.

212   " Shall a man make gods unto himself? "

APRIL 12.—MORNING.

[Or July 22.]

ONE *of the most telling satires upon the worship of idols is to be found in the book of the prophet Isaiah.*

ISAIAH XLIV. 9—20.

9, 10, 11, 12 They that make a graven image *are* all of them vanity; and their delectable things *(or favourite idols)* shall not profit; and they *are* their own witnesses; *(If they had any sort of sense they would themselves testify to the uselessness of their idols. They will not allow their minds to be disabused, or else their own experience would undeceive them;)* they see not, nor know; that they may be ashamed. Who hath formed a god, or molten a graven image *that* is profitable for nothing? *(These mighty good-for-nothing gods, when are they made divine? at what period become they worthy of adoration?)* Behold, all his fellows shall be ashamed: *(The stupid idol and its senseless votaries shall be alike laughed to scorn. Let both makers and worshippers, and all who have a hand in the business, come forth and answer a few questions which will shame them:)* and the workmen, they *are* of men: let them all be gathered together, let them stand up; *yet* they shall fear, *and* they shall be ashamed together. The smith with the tongs both worketh in the coals, and fashioneth it with hammers, and worketh it with the strength of his arms: yea, he is hungry, and his strength faileth: he drinketh no water, and is faint. *(The prophet commences with the last workman from whom the idol comes, he takes us to the smith's forge, when the coating of precious metal is fashioned.. But this maker of gods has human weaknesses, he is thirsty, and having no water he faints. A mighty god-maker this! Surely the god is not in the craftsman's shop.)*

13 The carpenter stretcheth out *his* rule; he marketh it out with a line; he fitteth it with planes, and he marketh it out with the compass, and maketh it after the figure of a man, according to the beauty of a man; that it may remain in the house. *(Now he goes a little further back, to the place where the frame-work of the idol is made, and shews us the carpenter with his line, plane and chisel; surely amid this pencilling and marking no trace of god-head is visible.)*

14 He heweth him down cedars, and taketh the cypress and the oak, which he strengtheneth for himself among the trees of the forest: he planteth an ash, and the rain doth nourish *it*.

Lest it should be imagined that there was some antecedent sacredness in the wood before it came into the shop, the prophet takes us a step further and shows it to us growing, planted and watered like other trees.

15 Then shall it be for a man to burn: for he will take thereof, and warm himself; yea, he kindleth *it*, and baketh bread; yea, he maketh a god, and worshippeth *it;* he maketh it a graven image, and falleth down thereto.

Here we see the timber felled, and, lo, it serves the double purpose of baking bread and making a god.

16 He burneth part thereof in the fire; with part thereof he eateth flesh; he roasteth roast, and is satisfied: yea, he warmeth *himself,* and saith, Aha, I am warm, I have seen the fire:

17 And the residue thereof he maketh a god, *even* his graven image: he falleth down unto it, and worshippeth *it,* and prayeth unto it, and saith, Deliver me; for thou *art* my god.

One portion of the tree cooks meat, and blazes on the hearth till men are gladdened with the blaze, the rest is addressed in pleading tones, " Deliver me, for thou art my god." O sottish stupidity!

18 They have not known nor understood: for he hath shut their eyes, that they cannot see; *and* their hearts, that they cannot understand. *(Surely a judicial blindness is over the minds of idolaters. If men were men, and not lovers of sin, they would give up this absurdity.)*

19 And none considereth in his heart, neither *is there* knowledge ·nor understanding to say, I have burned part of it in the fire; yea, also I have baked bread upon the coals thereof; I have roasted flesh, and eaten *it:* and shall I make the residue thereof an abomination? shall I fall down to the stock of a tree?

20 He feedeth on ashes: a deceived heart hath turned him aside, that he cannot deliver his soul, nor say, *Is there* not a lie in my right hand? *(Man has fallen so low through sin that he makes food for himself of that which is unsubstantial as the wind; his reason is perverted, his love of sin has blinded him, he believes lies which are as palpable in their falsehood as if they lay in his open palm. O Lord, have pity on man's madness, and save him from himself. Amen.)*

WE *find the whole history of the book of Judges summed up in brief in*

PSALM CVI. 34—48.

34 They did not destroy the nations, concerning whom the LORD commanded them : *This was their root sin, out of which all the rest of their faults arose. They were led into Canaan on purpose to execute the criminal nations, and they were either too idle, too timid, or too rebellious to carry out their office. Hence all the sin and sorrow which followed. No man can calculate the evils which may spring from the loins of one act of disobedience. If we leave one sin in our nature unsubdued, it will plague us terribly. O for grace to make thorough work, and perfect purging. Only the Holy Spirit can aid us in this.*

35 But were mingled among the heathen, and learned their works. *(Companionship leads to imitation. We cannot live with the wicked without feeling their influence. Those coals which do not burn us may yet blacken us.)*

36 And they served their idols : which were a snare unto them. *(The heathen worship was sometimes tasteful and enticing, and it was frequently licentious and fascinating to the flesh, and so by their tastes and their passions God's own people were entrapped.)*

37, 38 Yea, they sacrificed their sons and their daughters unto devils, And shed innocent blood, *even* the blood of their sons and of their daughters, whom they sacrificed unto the idols of Canaan : and the land was polluted with blood. *(These sacrifices were the culminating point in idolatrous worship, and they were also the most horrible of crimes. What a miserable fact, that a people who had known the Lord should fall so low as to murder their innocent babes at the shrine of demons ! Is not human nature capable of the worst imaginable crimes ? Could even devils perpetrate worse enormities than these ?)*

39 Thus were they defiled with their own works, and went a whoring with their own inventions.

40 Therefore was the wrath of the LORD kindled against his people, insomuch that he abhorred his own inheritance. *(Looking upon their loathsome deeds he loathed them, and determined to let them feel that he would not endure sin even in his own people. Sin was worse in them* than in others, for they knew better, and were under the most solemn bonds to act better.)

41, 42 And he gave them into the hand of the heathen ; and they that hated them ruled over them. Their enemies also oppressed them, and they were brought into subjection under their hand.

43 Many times did he deliver them ; but they provoked *him* with their counsel, and were brought low for their iniquity. *(See the long-suffering of God to deliver them many times, though they returned to their wickedness. Have we not tasted of the same great mercy ?)*

44 Nevertheless he regarded their affliction, when he heard their cry :

45 And he remembered for them his covenant, and repented according to the multitude of his mercies. *(How beautiful is this language! How it sets forth the tender heart of God! O God, who can pardon as thou dost? Who but thyself would keep covenant with such a people? What multitudes of mercies were expended in covering such multitudes of sins ! As in a looking-glass, we may here see our own lives, and it is enough to bring the water into our eyes, as with mingled shame and gratitude we gaze upon our own portraits.)*

46 He made them also to be pitied of all those that carried them captives.

He who brought water out of flints, made even their oppressors sorry for them, and ere long he found means to deliver them.

47 Save us, O LORD our God, and gather us from among the heathen, to give thanks unto thy holy name, *and* to triumph in thy praise.

Thus in after ages other captives profited by the history of ancient times. We should do the same. Let us now join in the doxology which concludes the psalm.

48 Blessed *be* the LORD God of Israel from everlasting to everlasting : and let all the people say, Amen. Praise ye the LORD.

Save, O our God, thine own elect,
From heathen lands thy sons collect ;
We to thy holy name will raise
Our songs, and triumph in thy praise.

Blest be Jehovah, Israel's Lord !
His name be evermore adored !
Amen, let all the people cry !
Praise ye Jehovah, God Most High !

DURING *the bitter tribulations which followed upon the various idolatrous backslidings of Israel, we can imagine the feelings of godly men in the nation as being very similar to those expressed in*

PSALM LXXX.

1 Give ear, O Shepherd of Israel, thou that leadest Joseph like a flock; thou that dwellest *between* the cherubims, shine forth. *(In ancient times thou wast Israel's leader, and even yet thou dwellest above the ark, in the tabernacle of Shiloh; therefore be pleased to display thy power on behalf of thy people.)*

2 Before Ephraim and Benjamin and Manasseh stir up thy strength, and come *and* save us.

The prayer mentions the names of the tribes, even as the Highpriest bore them on his breast for a memorial. O, may God save and bless every section of his one church, and not our own tribe alone.

3 Turn us again, O God, and cause thy face to shine; and we shall be saved. *(All will be right if we are right. A turn of character is better than a turn of circumstances. Turn us, and then turn our captivity.)*

4 O LORD God of hosts, how long wilt thou be angry against the prayer of thy people?

5 Thou feedest them with the bread of tears; and givest them tears to drink in great measure.

Sorrow was both their meat and drink. Would the Lord never end their miseries? This is mighty pleading.

6 Thou makest us a strife unto our neighbours: and our enemies laugh among themselves.

When the wicked find mirth in our miseries, and amusement in our amazement, the Lord will hear and deliver us.

7 Turn us again, O God of hosts, and cause thy face to shine; and we shall be saved.

This is a repetition, but not a vain one, for it was the chief blessing pleaded for.

8 Thou hast brought a vine out of Egypt: thou hast cast out the heathen, and planted it.

9 Thou preparedst *room* before it, and didst cause it to take deep root, and it filled the land.

10 The hills were covered with the shadow of it, and the boughs thereof *were like* the goodly cedars.

11 She sent out her boughs unto the sea, and her branches unto the river. *(Thus the bringing of the nation into Canaan is poetically described, and pathetically dwelt upon. Past favours make present sorrows very bitter, when we know that the change is caused by our sin.)*

12 Why hast thou *then* broken down her hedges, so that all they which pass by the way do pluck her?

13 The boar out of the wood doth waste it, and the wild beast of the field doth devour it.

The state was without order or defence, and the most ferocious enemies devastated the land. What woes were concentrated in this! Only those who know what it is to see invaders in their fields and homesteads can even imagine Israel's low estate.

14 Return, we beseech thee, O God of hosts: look down from heaven, and behold, and visit this vine;

15 And the vineyard which thy right hand hath planted, and the branch *that* thou madest strong for thyself. *(All that was needed was a visit from God, and his anointing upon the judge appointed to deliver. Barak, and Gideon, and Jephthah were nothing without God, but if the Lord appeared they would be fruitful branches.)*

16 *It is* burned with fire, *it is* cut down: they perish at the rebuke of thy countenance.

17 Let thy hand be upon the man of thy right hand, upon the son of man *whom* thou madest strong for thyself. *(This was the great need of Israel—a leader bold and brave, anointed of the Lord to save. Jesus is our great Leader, and he has the might of Jehovah within him. In a minor sense such were the various judges of the tribes. Man sins alone, but he cannot escape from the consequence of sin without help. O, how much do we all need deliveranee from on high.)*

18 So will not we go back from thee: quicken us, and we will call upon thy name. *(Impressed by gratitude, they hoped to be faithful for the future.)*

19 Turn us again, O LORD God of hosts, cause thy face to shine; and we shall be saved.

Bad as their case was, conversion wrought by God's grace would ensure them salvation. It is so with each of us. Let us keep this closing prayer upon our heart and lips for many a day to come.

WE *have now reached the shortest of the historical books, which contains the sweet rustic story of Ruth. Her history is no doubt recorded in the Scriptures because she was one of the ancestors of our Lord Jesus. He who came to save the Gentiles was pleased so to arrange the order of his genealogy, that a foreigner from a heathen land should be one of his progenitors.*

RUTH I. 1—11; 14—18.

1 Now it came to pass in the days when the judges ruled, that there was a famine in the land. And a certain man of Beth-lehem-judah went to sojourn in the country of Moab, he, and his wife, and his two sons.

2 And the name of the man *was* Elimelech, and the name of his wife Naomi, and the name of his two sons Mahlon and Chilion, Ephrathites of Beth-lehem-judah. And they came into the country of Moab, and continued there.

3 And Elimelech Naomi's husband died; and she was left, and her two sons. *(They had escaped the famine, but other troubles overtook them. In every land trial will be our lot.)*

4 And they took them wives of the women of Moab; the name of the one *was* Orpah, and the name of the other Ruth: and they dwelled there about ten years.

5 And Mahlon and Chilion died also both of them; and the woman was left of her two sons and her husband. *(Alas, poor soul! The darts of death wounded her terribly! Yet the Lord did not leave her alone in her widowhood; he prepared a loving heart to yield her sympathy.)*

6 ¶ Then she arose with her daughters in law, that she might return from the country of Moab: for she had heard in the country of Moab how that the Lord had visited his people in giving them bread. *(This was glad news, and it came to her in a good and pious form. No idle gossip would have reported the affair in so holy a shape. Perhaps, however, this was Naomi's way of interpreting the happy event; and it was a most proper one. We ought always to trace good gifts to the giver. Our bread, whether it be temporal or spiritual, comes from the Lord.)*

7 Wherefore she went forth out of the place where she was, and her two daughters in law with her; and they went on the way to return unto the land of Judah.

8, 9, 10 And Naomi said unto her two daughters in law, Go, return each to her mother's house: the Lord deal kindly with you, as ye have dealt with the dead, and with me. The Lord grant you that ye may find rest, each *of you* in the house of her husband. Then she kissed them; and they lifted up their voice, and wept. And they said unto her, Surely we will return with thee unto thy people.

11 And Naomi said, Turn again, my daughters: why will ye go with me? *(And then she reminded them that she had no more sons to become their husbands, and urged them to go back to their own nation, adding,—)* for it grieveth me much for your sakes that the hand of the Lord is gone out against me. *(The aged matron acted wisely in testing the young women. Many say they will join the Lord's people who have not thought of the trials of true religion: they had better count the cost.)*

14 And they lifted up their voice, and wept again; and Orpah kissed her mother in law; but Ruth clave unto her. *(How like these two women are to certain opposite characters we have met with: one, like Orpah, is pleased with religion, and would fain follow the Lord Jesus, but gives it all up because of difficulty or trial; but the other, like Ruth, being really converted, holds on through fair and foul, and perseveres unto the end.)*

15 And she said, Behold, thy sister in law is gone back unto her people, and unto her gods: return thou after thy sister in law.

16 And Ruth said, Intreat me not to leave thee, *or* to return from following after thee: for whither thou goest, I will go; and where thou lodgest, I will lodge: thy people *shall be* my people, and thy God my God:

17 Where thou diest, will I die, and there will I be buried: the Lord do so to me, and more also, *if ought* but death part thee and me. *Thus she joined the Lord's people, and never did she regret it. Those who cast in their lot with Jesus may have to rough it for awhile; but a fair portion surely lies before them.*

18 When she saw that she was steadfastly minded to go with her, then she left speaking unto her. *(She was only too glad to have her for a life-companion. The people of God are glad to welcome sincere souls into their fellowship.)*

RUTH I. 19—22.

SO they two went until they came to Beth-lehem. And it came to pass, when they were come to Beth-lehem, that all the city was moved about them, and they said, *Is* this Naomi ? *(She had been absent ten years, but her character in her better days had stood high with the people; and therefore they were glad to see her return, though they wondered at her poverty. Her many griefs may have so altered her that even her former acquaintances asked, " Is this Naomi ?" Such changes may come to us : may faith and patience prepare us for them.)*

20 And she said unto them, Call me not Naomi *(sweetness or pleasantness)*, call me Mara *(or bitter):* for the Almighty hath dealt very bitterly with me. *(God can soon change our sweets into bitters, therefore let us be humble; but he can with equal ease transform our bitters into sweets, therefore let us be hopeful. It is very usual for Naomi and Mara, sweet and bitter, to meet in the same person. He who was called Benjamin, or " the son of his father's right hand," was first called Benoni, or " the son of sorrow." The comforts of God's grace are all the sweeter when they follow the troubles of life.)*

21 I went out full, and the LORD hath brought me home again empty *(When she had her husband, and sons, and property, she was full, and went her way to a foreign land, perhaps wrongly; but now she was bereft of all, she felt that God was with her in her emptiness, and had himself brought her back):* why *then* call ye me Naomi, seeing the LORD hath testified against me, and the Almighty hath afflicted me ?

It is most wise to observe and own the appointment of God in all that befalls us. Naomi here kissed the rod, and the hand which smote her. This is a most fitting spirit for a chastened believer, and our Lord is the great example of it, for he cried, " The cup which my Father hath given me shall I not drink it?"

22 So Naomi returned, and Ruth the Moabitess, her daughter in law, with her, which returned out of the country of Moab : and they came to Beth-lehem in the beginning of barley harvest.

CHAPTER II. 1—7.

1 And Naomi had a kinsman of her husband's, a mighty man of wealth, of the family of Elimelech ; and his name *was* Boaz.

If it was good for Naomi to have a wealthy relation, how blessed it is for poor sinners to have a rich kinsman in the person of the Lord Jesus.

2 And Ruth the Moabitess said unto Naomi, Let me now go to the field, and glean ears of corn after *him* in whose sight I shall find grace. And she said unto her, Go, my daughter.

These good women were not ashamed of honest and humble labour. They did not take to begging, or idling; but desired to eat the bread of industry. Ruth had been a wealthy lady, but she was not above working to support her mother and herself.

3 And she went, and came, and gleaned in the field after the reapers : and her hap was to light on a part of the field *belonging* unto Boaz, who *was* of the kindred of Elimelech.

It seemed to her a chance, but the hand of the Lord was in it, and directed her to the very best place to promote her future prosperity.

4 ¶ And, behold, Boaz came from Beth-lehem, and said unto the reapers, The LORD *be* with you. And they answered him, The LORD bless thee. *(What a blessing when master and servants commune together on such holy terms. Is not this holy fellowship a very scarce thing?)*

5 Then said Boaz unto his servant that was set over the reapers, Whose damsel *is* this ?

6, 7 And the servant that was set over the reapers answered and said, It *is* the Moabitish damsel that came back with Naomi out of the country of Moab : And she said, I pray you, let me glean and gather after the reapers among the sheaves : so she came, and hath continued even from the morning until now, that she tarried a little in the house.

Boaz was a good master to his servants, and he was also kind to the poor; those who excel in one direction are generally excellent in others. Happy was Ruth to come in the way of such a man. She had given up all for God, and the Lord took care of her. She was busy in the path of duty, and God's love was watching over her.

God is love, his mercy brightens
   All the path in which we rove ;
Bliss he wakes, and woe he lightens ;
   God is wisdom, God is love.

Chance and change are busy ever,
   Man decays and ages move ;
But his mercy waneth never ;
   God is wisdom, God is love.

RUTH II. 8—23.

BOAZ *having asked his servant concerning Ruth, he approached the damsel and addressed her most kindly.*

8 Then said Boaz unto Ruth, Hearest thou not, my daughter ? Go not to glean in another field, neither go from hence, but abide here fast by my maidens :

9 *Let* thine eyes *be* on the field that they do reap, and go thou after them : have I not charged the young men that they shall not touch thee ? and when thou art athirst, go unto the vessels, and drink of *that* which the young men have drawn.

10 Then she fell on her face, and bowed herself to the ground, and said unto him, Why have I found grace in thine eyes, that thou shouldest take knowledge of me, seeing I *am* a stranger ?

11 And Boaz answered and said unto her, It hath fully been shewed me, all that thou hast done unto thy mother in law since the death of thine husband : and *how* thou hast left thy father and thy mother, and the land of thy nativity, and art come unto a people which thou knewest not heretofore.

12 The LORD recompense thy work, and a full reward be given thee of the LORD God of Israel, under whose wings thou art come to trust.

13 Then she said, Let me find favour in thy sight, my lord ; for that thou hast comforted me, and for that thou hast spoken friendly unto thine handmaid, though I be not like unto one of thine handmaidens.

14 And Boaz said unto her, At mealtime come thou hither, and eat of the bread, and dip thy morsel in the vinegar. And she sat beside the reapers : and he reached her parched *corn*, and she did eat, and was sufficed, and left.

15 And when she was risen up to glean, Boaz commanded his young men, saying, Let her glean even among the sheaves, and reproach her not :

16 And let fall also *some* of the handfuls of purpose for her, and leave *them*, that she may glean *them*, and rebuke her not.

17 So she gleaned in the field until even, and beat out that she had gleaned : and it was about an ephah of barley.

Boaz's chief and special reason for doing good to Ruth was that she was a guest in Israel, a dove nestling beneath Jehovah's wings. Religion was uppermost in his soul, and therefore he rejoiced in the woman who had left all to follow the living God. Meanwhile Ruth behaved in the most modest and humble manner, never ceasing to be herself. She toiled on happily all day, supported by the love which she felt towards Naomi at home, for whom she esteemed it to be a great pleasure to work. When children are kind to their parents they are in the way of blessing. Little did Ruth imagine that she would one day be married to the owner of the fields in which she gleaned : there are good things in store for those who walk before God aright.

18 ¶ And she took *it* up, and went into the city : and her mother in law saw what she had gleaned : and she brought forth, and gave to her that she had reserved after she was sufficed.

19 And her mother in law said unto her, Where hast thou gleaned to day ? and where wroughtest thou ? blessed be he that did take knowledge of thee. And she shewed her mother in law with whom she had wrought, and said, The man's name with whom I wrought to day *is* Boaz.

20 And Naomi said unto her daughter in law, Blessed *be* he of the LORD, who hath not left off his kindness to the living and to the dead. And Naomi said unto her, The man *is* near of kin unto us, one of our next kinsmen.

21 And Ruth the Moabitess said, He said unto me also, Thou shalt keep fast by my young men, until they have ended all my harvest.

22 And Naomi said unto Ruth her daughter in law, *It is* good, my daughter, that thou go out with his maidens, that they meet thee not in any other field.

23 So she kept fast by the maidens of Boaz to glean unto the end of barley harvest and of wheat harvest; and dwelt with her mother in law.

Matthew Henry from this passage has drawn the following lessons. " Ruth finished her day's work, (verse 17.) She took care not to lose time, for she gleaned until even. We must not be weary of well-doing, because in due season we shall reap. She did not make an excuse to sit still, or go home till the evening. Let us ' work the works of him that sent us while it is day.'

She scarce used, much less did she abuse the kindness of Boaz, for though he ordered his servants to leave handfuls for her, she continued to glean the scattered ears. She took care not to lose what she had gathered, *but threshed it herself, that she might the easier carry it home, and might have it ready for use.* ' *The slothful man roasteth not that which he took in hunting,' and so loseth the benefit of it; ' but the substance of a diligent man is precious.'* Ruth had *gathered it ear by ear; but when she had put it all together, it was an ephah of barley, or about four pecks. Many a little makes a great deal. It is encouraging to industry, that ' in all labour,' even that of gleaning, ' there is profit;' but ' the talk of the lips tendeth only to penury.' When she had got her corn into as little compass as she could, she took it up herself, and carried it into the city, though had she asked them, it is* likely *some of Boaz's servants would have done that for her. We should study to be as little as possible troublesome to those that are kind to us. She did not think it either too hard or too mean a service, to carry her corn herself into the city; but was pleased with what she had got by her own industry, and careful to secure it. And let us thus take care that ' we lose not those things which we have wrought,' or which we have gained.*"

O Lord how happy should we be
If we could cast our care on thee,
And glean our portion day by day
In fields where thou dost bid us stay.

O teach us this choice way of life,
Serenely free from anxious strife,
To do our heavenly Father's will
And trust his love and bounty still.

Jesus, spotless Lamb of God,
Thou hast bought me with thy blood,
I would value nought beside
Jesus—Jesus crucified.

I am thine, and thine alone,
This I gladly, fully own ;
And, in all my works and ways,
Only now would seek thy praise.

Help me to confess thy name,
Bear with joy thy cross and shame,
Only seek to follow thee,
Though reproach my portion be.

Jesus, our Kinsman and our God,
Array'd in majesty and blood,
Thou art our life ; our souls in thee
Possess a full felicity.

All our immortal hopes are laid
In thee, our surety and our head ;
Thy cross, thy cradle, and thy throne,
Are big with glories yet unknown.

Oh, let my soul for ever lie
Beneath the blessings of thine eye ;
'Tis heaven on earth, 'tis heaven above,
To see thy face, and taste thy love.

Thou, who a tender Parent art,
Regard a parent's plea ;
Our offspring, with an anxious heart,
We now commend to thee.

Our *children* are our greatest care,
A charge which thou hast given :
In all thy graces let them share,
And all the joys of heaven.

BY *the advice of Naomi, Ruth claimed the protection of Boaz, and he at once engaged to take her in marriage, provided the person who was still more nearly akin would waive the right which the Jewish law gave to him. This was brought about and publicly arranged after the custom of the times.*

RUTH IV. 1—17.

1, 2 Then went Boaz up to the gate *(where the court of justice was ordinarily kept)*, and sat him down there: and, behold, the kinsman of whom Boaz spake came by; unto whom he said, Ho, such a one! turn aside, sit down here. And he turned aside, and sat down. And he took ten men of the elders of the city, and said, Sit ye down here. And they sat down. *(To see that everything was done according to law.)*

3, 4 And he said unto the kinsman, Naomi, that is come again out of the country of Moab, selleth a parcel of land, which *was* our brother Elimelech's: And I thought to advertise thee, saying, Buy *it* before the inhabitants, and before the elders of my people. If thou wilt redeem *it*, redeem *it:* but if thou wilt not redeem *it, then* tell me, that I may know; for *there is* none to redeem *it* beside thee; and I *am* after thee. And he said, I will redeem *it. (This he said, not knowing the condition attached to the purchase.)*

5 Then said Boaz, What day thou buyest the field of the hand of Naomi, thou must buy *it* also of Ruth the Moabitess, the wife of the dead, to raise up the name of the dead upon his inheritance. *(Thou canst not have the land without taking the wife of the deceased, and then the children which thou mayest have will be reputed the children of Mahlon, thy deceased kinsman.)*

6 ¶ And the kinsman said, I cannot redeem *it* for myself, lest I mar mine own inheritance: redeem thou my right to thyself; for I cannot redeem *it. (Precisely what Boaz desired to do.)*

7 Now this *was the manner* in former time in Israel concerning redeeming and concerning changing, for to confirm all things; a man plucked off his shoe, and gave *it* to his neighbour: and this *was* a testimony in Israel. *(This law will be found in detail in Deuteronomy xxv.; it was ordained in order that no family might die out in Israel. May God grant that this household may never cease to be represented among the Lord's people.)*

8 Therefore the kinsman said unto Boaz, Buy it for thee. So he drew off his shoe.

9, 10 And Boaz said unto the elders, and *unto* all the people, Ye *are* witnesses this day, that I have bought all that *was* Elimelech's, and all that *was* Chilion's and Mahlon's, of the hand of Naomi. Moreover Ruth the Moabitess, the wife of Mahlon have I purchased to be my wife, to raise up the name of the dead upon his inheritance, that the name of the dead be not cut off from among his brethren, and from the gate of his place: ye *are* witnesses this day.

11, 12 And all the people that *were* in the gate, and the elders, said, *We are* witnesses. The LORD make the woman that is come into thine house like Rachel and like Leah, which two did build the house of Israel: and do thou worthily in Ephratah, and be famous in Bethlehem: And let thy house be like the house of Pharez, whom Tamar bare unto Judah, of the seed which the LORD shall give thee of this young woman.

13 ¶ So Boaz took Ruth, and she was his wife. *(Thus was her self-denying faith rewarded. She left behind her both relatives, country, and prospects, to cast in her lot with the Lord's people, and the Lord not only blessed her, but blessed distant generations through her. Those who follow the Lord at all hazards shall be no losers in the long run. To increase Ruth's joy and crown her happiness, the Lord gave her a son, which son was also a joy to Naomi.)*

14 And the women said unto Naomi, Blessed *be* the LORD, which hath not left thee this day without a kinsman, that his name may be famous in Israel.

15 And he shall be unto thee a restorer of *thy* life, and a nourisher of thine old age: for thy daughter in law, which loveth thee, which is better to thee than seven sons, hath borne him.

16 And Naomi took the child, and laid it in her bosom, and became nurse unto it.

17 And the women her neighbours gave it a name, saying, There is a son born to Naomi; and they called his name Obed: he *is* the father of Jesse, the father of David. *(Thus to point out the line of David, and so of our Lord Jesus this book was written. All the Scriptures are intended to lead us in faith to the great Redeemer. God grant that they may not miss their design in our case.)*

BEFORE *beginning the book of Samuel we will take another portion from David's Holy Alphabet—the hundred and nineteenth Psalm. Luther prized this Psalm so much, that he declared he would not take the whole world in exchange for a single leaf of it. May the Holy Spirit impress it upon our hearts while we read it.*

PSALM CXIX. 49—64.

49 Remember the word unto thy servant, upon which thou hast caused me to hope.

The Christian's hope is wrought in him by the Lord himself, and it is based upon the infallible word of God ; hence it is a sure hope which will never make him ashamed ; for the Lord will certainly remember and fulfil his promises. Yet he does this in answer to prayer : therefore we must plead the handwriting of the Lord.

50 This *is* my comfort in my affliction : for thy word hath quickened me.

Good men have their afflictions, and their best comfort under them is quickening grace. Instead of praying, " Lord, remove the trouble," we should cry, " Lord, quicken me through thy word."

51 The proud have had me greatly in derision : *yet* have I not declined from thy law.

He refused to be laughed out of his religion. Man's jeers are scarcely felt when the Lord Jesus smiles upon us. If we decline from holiness because bad men laugh, we shall make good men weep.

52 I remembered thy judgments of old, O LORD ; and have comforted myself.

53 Horror hath taken hold upon me because of the wicked that forsake thy law.

A holy heart is horrified at sin, at sinners, and at the sinner's doom : those who think lightly of other men's sins will soon sin lightly themselves.

54 Thy statutes have been my songs in the house of my pilgrimage.

The Bible is the believer's song-book, and sweet to his ear are its psalms and hymns. Let us all sing more, and complain less.

55 I have remembered thy name, O LORD, in the night, and have kept thy law.

Singing is for the day, and remembering is for the wakeful hours of night, and in this way the godly make the whole twenty-four hours holiness unto the Lord.

56 This I had, because I kept thy precepts.

Holy songs and devout memories are the fruits of obedience. Many other comforts come to us as rewards while we keep in the right road.

57 Thou art my portion, O LORD : I have said that I would keep thy words. *(The Lord gives himself to us, it is but meet that we should resolve to give ourselves to him.)*

58 I intreated thy favour with *my* whole heart : be merciful unto me according to thy word

59 I thought on my ways, and turned my feet unto thy testimonies.

60 I made haste, and delayed not to keep thy commandments.

Have we done the same? Is there no neglected duty ? In obedience to God, whatever haste we make we shall not be hasty.

61 The bands of the wicked have robbed me : *but* I have not forgotten thy law.

62 At midnight I will rise to give thanks unto thee because of thy righteous judgments.

63 I *am* a companion of all *them* that fear thee, and of them that keep thy precepts.

Those who love good company have some good thing in their own hearts. We ought to choose those for our companions with whom we should be willing to dwell for ever and ever. An aged woman once said, " I cannot believe that the Lord will shut me up with the ungodly, for I have never loved such company. His people have been my friends on earth, and I expect to dwell with them for ever in heaven."

64 The earth, O LORD, is full of thy mercy : teach me thy statutes.

We are full of wants, and sins, and sorrow, therefore it is beyond measure consoling to learn that the Lord has filled the whole earth with his mercy. Let us seek mercy in the most practical form, by asking him graciously to teach us how to live in his fear.

Behold thy waiting servant, Lord,
     Devoted to thy fear ;
Remember and confirm thy word
     For all my hopes are there.

Thou art my portion, O my God,
     Teach me thy righteous way ;
My heart makes haste to obey thy word,
     And suffers no delay.

WE *will take another draught from the overflowing well of David's ever fresh and sparkling Psalm. May the Holy Ghost make it really refreshing to us.*

PSALM CXIX. 65—80.

65 Thou hast dealt well with thy servant, O LORD, according unto thy word. *(Blessed be the name of God, our Father, this is most joyfully true. Some of us here present can say, "Amen, Amen." Every promise has been fulfilled in its season. We have served a good Master and loved a faithful God. Alas! we have not dealt so well with him as we ought to have done.)*

66 Teach me good judgment and knowledge: for I have believed thy commandments. *(One of the Reformers, in a public discussion, was observed to write upon a paper before him. His friend wished to see the notes which had so much helped him, and was surprised to find that they consisted simply of these brief prayers, "More light, Lord; more light, more light." This is just what David asked for, let us seek the same.)*

67 Before I was afflicted I went astray: but now have I kept thy word. *Sweet are the uses of adversity; it pens in the sheep so that they cannot wander as before.*

68 Thou *art* good, and doest good; teach me thy statutes. *(It is the nature of goodness to communicate itself, therefore does the psalmist beseech the good Lord to show him how to be good.)*

69 The proud have forged a lie against me: *but* I will keep thy precepts with *my* whole heart. *(He would answer their calumnies in the most effectual manner, by living them down.)*

70 Their heart is as fat as grease; *but* I delight in thy law. *(They suffered spiritually from fatty degeneration of the heart, and were doltish, gluttonous, lifeless; David made them a warning to himself, and all the more delighted in the law of the Lord.)*

71 *It is* good for me that I have been afflicted; that I might learn thy statutes.

72 The law of thy mouth *is* better unto me than thousands of gold and silver.

73 Thy hands have made me and fashioned me: give me understanding, that I may learn thy commandments. *(Thou hast made me, be*

pleased to new-make me. I am thy work—complete me: I am thy harp, tune me; I am thy child, teach me.)

74 They that fear thee will be glad when they see me: because I have hoped in thy word. *The grace experienced by one believer cheers others; indeed a good man is always a son of consolation to his brethren. He who comes forth perfumed with the spices of God's word, imparts delight to all with whom he associates.*

75 I know, O LORD, that thy judgments *are* right, and *that* thou in faithfulness hast afflicted me. *(This we may be quite sure of, but we are apt to forget it when we are on the bleak side of the hill.)*

76 Let, I pray thee, thy merciful kindness be for my comfort, according to thy word unto thy servant. *(The phrase, "according to thy word," shows us that we should in prayer plead the very words of God, laying our fingers upon them, and by the power of the Holy Spirit, beseeching the Lord to be as good as his own promise. Rest assured he will never deny himself. He is not the son of man that he should repent.)*

77 Let thy tender mercies come unto me, that I may live: for thy law *is* my delight.

78 Let the proud be ashamed; for they dealt perversely with me without a cause: *but* I will meditate in thy precepts. *Under persecution the Psalmist ran at once to the Word. Never begin to argue, or grow angry, but run to your Father in heaven, when men upon earth do you wrong.*

79, 80 Let those that fear thee turn unto me, and those that have known thy testimonies. *(Make thy children willing to help me, and to be helped by me. Let me be a magnet to gather good company, not a besom to sweep them away. May I cultivate love and promote unity; yet not at the expense of truth, therefore do I pray—)* Let my heart be sound in thy statutes; that I be not ashamed.

Father, I bless thy gentle hand;
How kind was thy chastising rod;
That forced my conscience to a stand,
And brought my wandering soul to God!

Foolish and vain I went astray,
Ere I had felt thy scourges, Lord;
I left my guide, and lost my way;
But now I love and keep thy word.

222   " 𝔜e peop𝔩e, pour out your 𝔥eart 𝔟efore 𝔥im."   APRIL 16.—EVENING.

[Or July 31.]

I. SAMUEL I. 1—3; 9—18.

NOW there was a certain man of Rama-thaim-zophim, of mount Ephraim, and his name was Elkanah, the son of Jeroham, the son of Elihu, the son of Tohu, the son of Zuph, an Ephrathite:

2 And he had two wives; the name of the one was Hannah, and the name of the other Peninnah: and Peninnah had children, but Hannah had no children.

It is a sad thing to find a Levite tainted with the error of double marriage, and in this case as in every other it caused much family misery, especially to that wife who was the best and holiest, though denied the blessing of children. Poor Hannah, a woman of great gifts as well as great grace, was so tormented by Peninnah, that her life was made bitter to her. How great a mercy it is that Christianity forbids polygamy, which the old dispensation barely tolerated, and that only because of the hardness of men's hearts.

3 And this man went up out of his city yearly to worship and to sacrifice unto the LORD of hosts in Shiloh. And the two sons of Eli, Hophni and Phinehas, the priests of the LORD, were there.

9 ¶ So Hannah rose up after they had eaten in Shiloh, and after they had drunk. Now Eli the priest sat upon a seat by a post of the temple of the LORD.

10 And she was in bitterness of soul, and prayed unto the LORD, and wept sore.

Her husband loved her, but she needed richer consolation, and she sought it in much earnest prayer. This is the sure fount of comfort.

11 And she vowed a vow, and said, O LORD of hosts, if thou wilt indeed look on the affliction of thine handmaid, and remember me, and not forget thine handmaid, but wilt give unto thine handmaid a man child, then I will give him unto the LORD all the days of his life, and there shall no razor come upon his head.

Bishop Hall well remarks that "the way to obtain any benefit is to devote it, in our hearts, to the glory of that God of whom we ask it; by this means shall God both please his servant, and honour himself; whereas if the scope of our desires be carnal, we may be sure either to fail of our suit, or of a blessing."

12 And it came to pass, as she continued praying before the LORD, that Eli marked her mouth. *(With all his faults, Eli did not neglect his duty, but sat at his post and watched the worshippers. The very presence of the priest helped to keep order in God's house.)*

13 Now Hannah, she spake in her heart; only her lips moved, but her voice was not heard: therefore Eli thought she had been drunken. *(Good men may err. Eli was too indulgent where he ought to have been severe, and too censorious where he should have been charitable. How small a thing it is to be judged of men.)*

14 And Eli said unto her, How long wilt thou be drunken? put away thy wine from thee.

15, 16 And Hannah answered and said, No, my lord, I am a woman of a sorrowful spirit: I have drunk neither wine nor strong drink, but have poured out my soul before the LORD. Count not thine handmaid for a daughter of Belial: for out of the abundance of my complaint and grief have I spoken hitherto.

How gently she replied! Some would have flown into a passion. Meekness is a lovely ornament of piety.

17 Then Eli answered and said, Go in peace: and the God of Israel grant thee thy petition that thou hast asked of him.

Eli was not above confessing his error, and making speedy amends. Let us never be ashamed to acknowledge when we are wrong, nor slow to offer every redress in our power.

18 And she said, Let thine handmaid find grace in thy sight. So the woman went her way, and did eat, and her countenance was no more sad. *(Her faith in the word of God spoken by his servant was so strong, that she began at once to rejoice in the blessing promised to her. Such ought to be our confidence in the divine promise; we should be no more sad, but look out for the blessing, and welcome it with smiling countenance.)*

My heart is resting, O my God;
  I will give thanks and sing;
My soul awaits that joyful hour
  Which shall the blessing bring.

And a "new song" is in my mouth,
  To long-loved music set;
Glory to thee for all the grace
  I have not tasted yet.

I. SAMUEL I. 19—28.

THE *sacrifice was ended, but the devout family did not think of leaving the sacred courts until once more they had bowed before the Lord. They were not tired of worship, but having begun well they would finish well. One heart there was in that family which adored with an unusual joy. Hannah had come up to the tabernacle " a woman of a sorrowful spirit," but not so did she return home. How sweet to leave our burdens behind us after we have joined in worship with the people of God. May our family devotions at this time have the like soothing effect upon any troubled one among us.*

19 ¶ And they rose up in the morning early, and worshipped before the Lord, and returned, and came to their house to Ramah : and Elkanah knew Hannah his wife ; and the Lord remembered her.

20 Wherefore it came to pass, when the time was come about after Hannah had conceived, that she bare a son, and called his name Samuel, *saying*, Because I have asked him of the Lord.

How doubly precious a blessing is when it comes in answer to prayer. Have we nothing to ask for ? Have we not also choice favours which have this increased sweetness in them that we " asked them of the Lord" ?

21 And the man Elkanah, and all his house, went up to offer unto the Lord the yearly sacrifice, and his vow.

Parents must not neglect the service of God because of their children, and when mothers are lawfully detained at home, the rest of the household must not make idle excuses for staying away too.

22 But Hannah went not up ; for she said unto her husband, *I will not go up* until the child be weaned, and *then* I will bring him, that he may appear before the Lord, and there abide for ever.

23 And Elkanah her husband said unto her, Do what seemeth thee good ; tarry until thou have weaned him ; only the Lord establish his word. *(What a choice saying, " Only the Lord establish his word." We ought to think everything less important than this. If God will but deal with us according to promise, other things are of little consequence.)* So the woman abode, and gave her son suck until she weaned him.

24 ¶ And when she had weaned him, she took him up with her, with three bullocks, and one ephah of flour, and a bottle of wine, and brought him unto the house of the Lord in Shiloh : and the child *was* young.

It was natural that the mother should be sorry to part with her dear boy ; yet grace triumphed over nature, and she went up to resign her child to the Lord with a glad heart, which expressed its gratitude in an offering of thanksgiving. What God had lent her she returned to him without reluctance. O that all our dear children may be the Lord's. It were better to part with them to be God's servants, than to keep them with us, and see them graceless.

25 And they slew a bullock, and brought the child to Eli.

26 And she said, Oh, my lord, *as* thy soul liveth, my lord, I *am* the woman that stood by thee here, praying unto the Lord.

27 For this child I prayed ; and the Lord hath given me my petition which I asked of him :

28 Therefore also I have lent him to the Lord ; as long as he liveth he shall be lent to the Lord. *(She gave up this one child, and the Lord sent her five others ere long. The Lord takes care to be in no one's debt, he rewards plenteously those who cheerfully make sacrifices for his cause.)* And he worshipped the Lord there. *(Eli rejoiced in the good woman's piety, and all gracious hearts are glad to see others ardent in love to God. Perhaps, however, the text means that Samuel also worshipped the Lord there, and how delightful it is to see young children truly pray. Is there no little Samuel in this house who will worship the Lord now? Let us all endeavour to do so with our whole hearts.)*

What shall I render to my God
 For all his kindness shown?
My feet shall visit thine abode,
 My songs address thy throne.

Among the saints that fill thine house,
 My offerings shall be paid ;
There shall my zeal perform the vows
 My soul in anguish made.

I. SAMUEL II. 1—11.

A ND Hannah prayed, *(When she had obtained her desire she did not desist from prayer, but the rather she was encouraged to abound in it. Her prayers, however, were no longer salted with sorrow, but were sweetened with the spices of gratitude. She rose from prayer to praise,)* and said, My heart rejoiceth in the LORD, *(Not in my child so much as in my God. God must ever be our exceeding joy),* mine horn is exalted in the LORD : *(Her name and power were lifted up, but she gave the Lord the glory of it:)* my mouth is enlarged over mine enemies ; because I rejoice in thy salvation. *(She knew herself to be in need of salvation, and her faith found all that she wanted in the Lord her God.)*

2 *There is* none holy as the LORD : for *there is* none beside thee : neither *is there* any rock like our God.

Her joy was all in God, in his salvation, in his matchless holiness, and in his eternal strength. Her Samuel did not become her idol, she loved her God better than her boy. Woe unto that mother who permits son or daughter to rival the Lord. God's people must learn to feel and say, " there is none beside thee, O Lord."

3 Talk no more so exceeding proudly ; let *not* arrogancy come out of your mouth : for the LORD *is* a God of knowledge, and by him actions are weighed. *(He does not judge by appearances, his judgments call for sincerity of heart, and will not be content without it.)*

4 The bows of the mighty men *are* broken, and they that stumbled are girded with strength.

5 *They that were* full have hired out themselves for bread ; and *they that were* hungry ceased : so that the barren hath born seven ; and she that hath many children is waxed feeble. *(Thus is it the Lord's way to pull down the lofty, and uplift the lowly. Those who are great and full in themselves he regards with scorn ; but the poor and the empty he looks upon with pity.)*

6 The LORD killeth, and maketh alive : he bringeth down to the grave, and bringeth up.

7 The LORD maketh poor, and maketh rich : he bringeth low, and lifteth up. *(It is the method of his grace to humble those whom he means to exalt. None will ever be rich in Christ*

until they are made to feel that they are bankrupt in themselves.)

8 He raiseth up the poor out of the dust, *and* lifteth up the beggar from the dunghill, to set *them* among princes, and to make them inherit the throne of glory : for the pillars of the earth *are* the LORD's, and he hath set the world upon them. *(He alone is the Creator, and he does as he wills with his own. Who shall question the exercise of his undoubted prerogative ?)*

9 He will keep the feet of his saints, *(He will preserve them from wandering or falling. God's people are too dear to him for him to suffer one of them to perish,)* and the wicked shall be silent in darkness ; for by strength shall no man prevail.

10 The adversaries of the LORD shall be broken to pieces ; out of heaven shall he thunder upon them : the LORD shall judge the ends of the earth ; and he shall give strength unto his king, and exalt the horn of his anointed.

This is a right noble song, breathing not only warm devotion, but the true spirit of poetry. Hannah was a great original poetess, and even the Virgin Mary in her sweet hymn of gratitude will be found to have followed in Hannah's track. Though as yet no Psalms had been written which might serve her as models, her song is exquisitely composed, and has a delightful savour of spiritual religion about it. She is the first who sings of the " anointed" king, and as there was actually no king over Israel in her day, the words would seem to have a prophetic reference to Christ. He is the crown of all the saints' joys, and their songs reach their highest notes when they sing of " the anointed."

11 And Elkanah went to Ramah to his house. And the child did minister unto the LORD before Eli the priest.

My soul doth magnify the Lord,
  My spirit doth rejoice ;
To thee, my Saviour and my God,
  I lift my joyful voice.

My God, I'll praise thee while I live,
  And praise thee when I die,
And praise thee when I rise again,
  And to eternity.

I. SAMUEL II. 12—26.

NOW the sons of Eli *were* sons of Belial; they knew not the LORD.

Yet they were priests and teachers of others. Sad was it for the people to have such ministers. Let our hearts go up to God in gratitude for the great blessing of holy teachers, who practise what they preach. Eli's sons were worse than the worst, when they ought to have been better than the best of common men.

13, 14 And the priest's custom with the people *was, that,* when any man offered sacrifice, the priest's servant came, while the flesh was in seething, with a fleshhook of three teeth in his hand; And he struck *it* into the pan, or kettle, or caldron, or pot; all that the fleshhook brought up the priest took for himself. So they did in Shiloh unto all the Israelites that came thither.

Not satisfied with the breast and shoulder, which were the perquisites of the priests, according to the divine law, they seized a part of the offerer's share of the flesh, and took it before the Lord's portion had been burned upon the altar.

15 Also before they burnt the fat, the priest's servant came, and said to the man that sacrificed, Give flesh to roast for the priest; for he will not have sodden flesh of thee, but raw.

16 And *if* any man said unto him, Let them not fail to burn the fat presently, and *then* take *as much* as thy soul desireth; then he would answer him, *Nay;* but thou shalt give *it me* now: and if not, I will take *it* by force.

17 Wherefore the sin of the young men was very great before the LORD: for men abhorred the offering of the LORD.

Godly people were shocked by such profane greediness, and were grieved by the rudeness of those who ought to have acted with holy courtesy. If ministers become haughty, domineering, and self-seeking, the people will soon loathe the worship. All this involved Eli's sons in great sin.

18 ¶ But Samuel ministered before the LORD, *being* a child, girded with a linen ephod.

It must have been a lovely sight to see the little lad actively engaged in the service of God, wearing the livery of the Great King.

19 Moreover his mother made him a little coat, and brought *it* to him from year to year, when she came up with her husband to offer the yearly sacrifice. (*Remembering that while Samuel was little he could render no very useful service to the tabernacle, she undertook the expense of his clothing, and thus showed both her care for the Lord's house and her love for her dear boy.*)

20 ¶ And Eli blessed Elkanah and his wife, and said, The LORD give thee seed of this woman for the loan which is lent to the LORD. And they went unto their own home.

21 And the LORD visited Hannah, so that she conceived, and bare three sons and two daughters. And the child Samuel grew before the LORD. (*But while this holy child was living near to God, Eli's sons went from bad to worse, till at last Eli spoke to them of their great sins.*)

23, 24 And he said unto them, Why do ye such things? for I hear of your evil dealings by all this people. Nay, my sons; for *it is* no good report that I hear: ye make the LORD's people to transgress.

25 If one man sin against another, the judge shall judge him: but if a man sin against the LORD, who shall intreat for him? Notwithstanding they hearkened not unto the voice of their father, because the LORD would slay them.

They had gone so far that the Lord had resolved to destroy them, and therefore would not grant them grace to repent. Eli ought long before to have put an end to the wickedness of his sons by far stronger measures. Such a tame rebuke as this, which came so late in the day was of no use whatever. Had he chastened his sons betimes, he might have saved their characters and their lives. Children should be grateful for parents who will not let their sins go unpunished. It would be a dreadful thing for a curse to come upon a family, because the sons and daughters were not restrained from sin. A dear little girl who died believing in Jesus affectionately thanked her mother on her death-bed for all her tender love and then added, " But, dear mother, I thank you most of all for having conquered my self-will." Children sometimes think their parents needlessly severe, but when they grow up they will bless them for not indulging them in sin.

26 And the child Samuel grew on, and was in favour both with the LORD, and also with men. (*A sweet way of growing, but to do this a child must be gracious, obedient, and kind.*)

226   " Whom He did predestinate, them He also called."   APRIL 18.—EVENING.

[*Or August* 4.]

I. SAMUEL III. 1—18.

AND the child Samuel ministered unto the LORD before Eli. (*Samuel is said by Josephus to have been about twelve years of age at this time, and so was like our blessed Lord, who at that age said, " Wist ye not that I must be about my Father's business." How charming a sight is a young child serving the Lord.*) And the word of the LORD was precious in those days; *there was* no open vision. (*The sin of the priests and people had made prophetic visions to be very rare.*)

2, 3, 4 And it came to pass at that time, when Eli *was* laid down in his place, and his eyes began to wax dim, *that* he could not see; And ere the lamp of God went out in the temple of the LORD, where the ark of God *was*, and Samuel was laid down *to sleep;* That the LORD called Samuel : and he answered, Here *am* I. (*God calls his servants when he pleases, and it is well for them to be able to reply, " Here am I." Whether it be for duty or suffering, the true child of God says, " Here am I."*)

5 And he ran unto Eli, and said, Here *am* I ; for thou calledst me. And he said, I called not ; lie down again. And he went and lay down.

6 And the LORD called yet again, Samuel. And Samuel arose and went to Eli, and said, Here *am* I ; for thou didst call me. And he answered, I called not, my son ; lie down again.

7 Now Samuel did not yet know the LORD, neither was the word of the LORD yet revealed unto him. (*He did not know the Lord in a prophetical manner, or with the clearness which he afterwards received, but doubtless he was already a godly child.*)

8 And the LORD called Samuel again the third time. And he arose and went to Eli, and said, Here *am* I ; for thou didst call me. (*How lovely was the conduct of Samuel, so simple, so obedient. O that all children were so.*) And Eli perceived that the LORD had called the child.

9 Therefore Eli said unto Samuel, Go, lie down : and it shall be, if he call thee, that thou shalt say, Speak, LORD ; for thy servant heareth. So Samuel went and lay down in his place.

10 And the LORD came, and stood, and called as at other times, Samuel, Samuel. Then Samuel answered, Speak ; for thy servant heareth.

When God speaks to us, a hearing ear is a great mercy ; but a heavy ear is a sad judgment.

11—14 And the LORD said to Samuel, Behold, I will do a thing in Israel, at which both the ears of every one that heareth it shall tingle. In that day I will perform against Eli all *things* which I have spoken concerning his house : when I begin, I will also make an end. For I have told him that I will judge his house for ever for the iniquity which he knoweth ; because his sons made themselves vile, and he restrained them not. And therefore I have sworn unto the house of Eli, that the iniquity of Eli's house shall not be purged with sacrifice nor offering for ever. (*Their day of grace was over, and their doom was sealed. What a warning to those who trifle with holy things, and turn the grace of God into licentiousness as these men did.*)

15 ¶ And Samuel lay until the morning, and opened the doors of the house of the LORD. (*He was not puffed up by having seen a vision, but went about his daily work, even as our Lord returned from Jerusalem with Mary and Joseph, and was subject to them. Holy children are always humble.*) And Samuel feared to shew Eli the vision.

16 Then Eli called Samuel, and said, Samuel, my son. And he answered, Here *am* I.

17 And he said, What *is* the thing that *the* LORD hath said unto thee ? I pray thee hide *it* not from me : God do so to thee, and more also, if thou hide *any* thing from me of all the things that he said unto thee. (*Eli had a wounded conscience, which made him fear something terrible even when the Lord spake.*)

18 And Samuel told him every whit, and hid nothing from him. (*A heavy task for a boy, but grace made him do his duty.*) And he said, It *is* the LORD : let him do what seemeth him good. (*Eli was wrong with his sons, but he was right with God. We must admire the aged man's holy submission, and imitate it.*)

'Twill save us from a thousand snares,
  To mind religion young ;
Grace will preserve our following years,
  And make our virtues strong.

Let the sweet work of prayer and praise,
  Employ our youngest breath ;
Thus we're prepared for longer days,
  Or fit for early death.

I SAMUEL III. 19—21.

AND Samuel grew, and the LORD was with him, and did let none of his words fall to the ground. And all Israel from Dan even to Beersheba knew that Samuel *was* established *to be* a prophet of the LORD. And the LORD appeared again in Shiloh : for the LORD revealed himself to Samuel in Shiloh by the word of the LORD. *(He was faithful when God spake to him once, and therefore he honoured him again. May all young Christians be firm and true from the first, and God will bless them. Meanwhile God was preparing terrible judgment for the wicked sons of Eli.)*

I SAMUEL IV. 1—11.

1, 2 Now Israel went out against the Philistines to battle ; and, when they joined battle, Israel was smitten before the Philistines : and they slew of the army in the field about four thousand men.

3 ¶ And when the people were come into the camp, the elders of Israel said, Wherefore hath the LORD smitten us to day before the Philistines ? Let us fetch the ark of the covenant of the LORD out of Shiloh unto us, that, when it cometh among us, it may save us out of the hand of our enemies. *(They trusted in the outward sign, and forgot that the most holy emblems bring no blessing to ungodly hearts. God will have us know that external religion is nothing worth without inward holiness. It is vain to trust in lying words, saying, " the Temple of the Lord are we." Ceremonies cannot help us if the Lord be not with us. A cross on the bosom is worthless, Christ in the heart is precious.)*

4 So the people sent to Shiloh, that they might bring from thence the ark of the covenant of the LORD of hosts, which dwelleth *between* the cherubims : and the two sons of Eli, Hophni and Phinehas, *were* there with the ark of the covenant of God. *(Thus in the order of providence they were fetched to the field where they were doomed to forfeit their guilty lives. God knows how to reach wicked men, and deal out justice to them.)*

5 And when the ark of the covenant of the LORD came into the camp, all Israel shouted with a great shout, so that the earth rang again. *Presumptuous men are always ready to shout, but ere long they will have to weep and wail as*

did these noisy boasters. *The law was in the ark, but what help could the broken law bring to them, its very presence condemned them ; those who trust in the law are in an evil case.*

6 And when the Philistines heard the noise of the shout, they said, What *meaneth* the noise of this great shout in the camp of the Hebrews ? And they understood that the ark of the LORD was come into the camp.

7, 8, 9 And the Philistines were afraid, for they said, God is come into the camp. And they said, Woe unto us ! for there hath not been such a thing heretofore. Woe unto us ! who shall deliver us out of the hand of these mighty Gods ? these *are* the Gods that smote the Egyptians with all the plagues in the wilderness. Be strong, and quit yourselves like men, O ye Philistines, that ye be not servants unto the Hebrews, as they have been to you : quit yourselves like men, and fight. *The Philistines were heathens, and therefore mistook the ark for God himself, but they knew well enough that if God were indeed with Israel, it would go hard with them. Had they known God to be Almighty, they would not have attempted resistance, but believing him to be only such a god as their own Dagon, they shewed their valour by determining to quit themselves like men. If they were so bold in their apparently desperate condition, how brave ought we to be who are assured of victory, because the Lord of Hosts is with us. To us the Lord says, " Quit you like men, be strong." To be cowardly in the cause of Jesus would be infamous. Never let the fear of man have the slightest power over you, or the reality of your religion will be doubtful.*

10 ¶ And the Philistines fought, and Israel was smitten, and they fled every man into his tent : and there was a very great slaughter.

11 And the ark of God was taken ; *(It was never captured till it was defended by carnal weapons ; true religion always suffers when men would guard it by force ;)* and the two sons of Eli, Hophni and Phinehas, were slain.

Thus did the Lord keep his word. He will be as faithful to his threatenings as to his promises. Woe unto us if we continue in sin ; for the Lord will surely punish us. Are we all saved in Christ Jesus ?

I. SAMUEL IV. 12—18; 20—22.

AND there ran a man of Benjamin out of the army, and came to Shiloh the same day with his clothes rent, and with earth upon his head. (*Bad news is sure to find a messenger and a swift one. Alas, that the good news of the Gospel should so often remain untold.*)

13, 14 And when he came, lo, Eli sat upon a seat by the wayside watching: for his heart trembled for the ark of God. And when the man came into the city, and told *it*, all the city cried out. (*Thus was fulfilled the prophecy that the judgments of the Lord on Eli's sons should make many ears to tingle. Shiloh had been defiled with sin, and it therefore came to be defaced with sorrow.*) And when Eli heard the noise of the crying, he said, What *meaneth* the noise of this tumult? And the man came in hastily, and told Eli.

15 Now Eli was ninety and eight years old; and his eyes were dim, that he could not see.

16 And the man said unto Eli, I *am* he that came out of the army, and I fled to day out of the army. And he said, What is there done, my son?

17 And the messenger answered and said, Israel is fled before the Philistines, and there hath been also a great slaughter among the people, and thy two sons also, Hophni and Phinehas, are dead, and the ark of God is taken. *The venerable old priest, within two years of a century old, heard all the sad news with fortitude and patience till the last item was reached.*

18 And it came to pass, when he made mention of the ark of God, that he fell from off the seat backward by the side of the gate, and his neck brake, and he died: for he was an old man, and heavy. And he had judged Israel forty years. (*His heart was broken and then his neck. He fell in a swoon of grief. No sword of the Philistines could have killed him more certainly than this terrible news that God's ark was captured. Nothing so much affects good men as calamity to the Church, or dishonour brought upon the name of the Lord.*)

The sad tidings that the ark was taken, and that her husband was slain, caused the wife of Phinehas to be seized with deadly pangs.

20, 21, 22 And about the time of her death the women that stood by her said unto her,

Fear not; for thou hast born a son. But she answered not, neither did she regard *it*. And she named the child I-chabod, saying, The glory is departed from Israel: for the ark of God is taken. (*She seems to have been a pious woman, though her husband was a wicked man: her piety led her to forget her own miseries in the greater miseries of the Church of God, and to make her child's name the memorial of the departed glory of Israel. Her death was another stroke at Eli's house, but it was sent in love to her, for she was spared the sight of Israel's sorrows.*)

THE sad story of the destruction of Eli's family is a special warning to all parents not to suffer sin to go unpunished in their households. Want of discipline is want of love. Let us see what Solomon says upon it—

PROVERBS XXIII. 13—18.

13, 14 Withhold not correction from the child: for *if* thou beatest him with the rod, he shall not die. Thou shalt beat him with the rod, and shalt deliver his soul from hell. (*Mr. Bridges in his " Notes on Proverbs," says, " Eli tried gentler means, and the sad issue is written for our instruction. Is it not cruel love that turns away from painful duty? To suffer sin upon a child is tantamount to hating him in our heart. Is it not better that the flesh should smart than that the soul should die? What if thy child should reproach thee throughout eternity, for the neglect of that timely correction which might have saved his soul from hell."*)

15, 16 My son, if thine heart be wise, my heart shall rejoice, even mine. Yea, my reins shall rejoice, when thy lips speak right things. *It is a father's highest happiness to have a son who is not only good himself, but the bold champion of goodness, speaking out bravely for right and truth and God.*

17 Let not thine heart envy sinners: but *be* thou in the fear of the LORD all the day long.

18 For surely there is an end; and thine expectation shall not be cut off. (*This life's trouble will soon be over, and then shall the godly begin their best life. Their hope shall not be ashamed. May the Lord teach us as a family to serve him faithfully, that both here and hereafter we may be blessed.*)

I. SAMUEL V. 1—4; 6—12.

AND the Philistines took the ark of God, and brought it from Eben-ezer unto Ashdod, and they brought it into the house of Dagon, and set it by Dagon.

3 ¶ And when they of Ashdod arose early on the morrow, behold, Dagon *was* fallen upon his face to the earth before the ark of the LORD. *(The true God would not endure that an idol should stand erect in the same temple with his ark, therefore down it must go. The ark was brought into the house as a captive, but immediately became a Conqueror. If the Lord, by his Spirit, comes into the human heart, sin soon falls before him.)* And they took Dagon, and set him in his place again. *(It was a wretched god that needed setting up. If idolatry did not make men foolish, they would see the absurdity of their conduct.)*

4 And when they arose early on the morrow morning, behold, Dagon *was* fallen upon his face to the ground before the ark of the LORD; and the head of Dagon and both the palms of his hands *were* cut off upon the threshold; only *the stump of* Dagon was left to him. *(The second fall was greater than the first, for the fish-god was broken, and only his scaly tail remained. The head and hands which symbolised wisdom and power were dashed to atoms. Thus does grace in the heart destroy the sovereignty and energy of sin.)*

6 But the hand of the LORD was heavy upon them of Ashdod, and he destroyed them, and smote them with emerods, *even* Ashdod and the coasts thereof.

7—9 And when the men of Ashdod saw that *it was* so, they said, The ark of the God of Israel shall not abide with us : for his hand is sore upon us, and upon Dagon our god. They sent therefore and gathered all the lords of the Philistines unto them, and said, What shall we do with the ark of the God of Israel ? And they answered, Let the ark of the God of Israel be carried about unto Gath. And they carried the ark of the God of Israel about *thither*. And it was *so*, that, after they had carried it about, the hand of the LORD was against the city with a very great destruction : and he smote the men of the city, both small and great, and they had emerods in their secret parts.

10 ¶ Therefore they sent the ark of God to Ekron. And it came to pass, as the ark of God came to Ekron, that the Ekronites cried out, saying, They have brought about the ark of the God of Israel to us, to slay us and our people.

11, 12 So they sent and gathered together all the lords of the Philistines, and said, Send away the ark of the God of Israel, and let it go again to his own place, that it slay us not, and our people : for there was a deadly destruction throughout all the city ; the hand of God was very heavy there. And the men that died not were smitten with the emerods : and the cry of the city went up to heaven. *(This disease was not only extremely painful but was meant to put the Philistines to shame, because they insolently dared to seize the ark of God. How glad they would have been to be rid of their captive, which even in captivity triumphed over them.)*

IN *the Psalms we have a summary of this part of Israel's history. Let us read it—*

PSALM LXXVIII. 58—66.

58 For they provoked him to anger with their high places, and moved him to jealousy with their graven images.

59, 60 When God heard *this*, he was wroth, and greatly abhorred Israel : so that he forsook the tabernacle of Shiloh, the tent *which* he placed among men ; *(Shiloh was abandoned, the ark never returned to it, and the place became such a desolation that not one stone was left upon another. The candlestick was removed out of its place.)*

61, 62 And *(the Lord)*, delivered his strength into captivity, and his glory into the enemy's hand. He gave his people over also unto the sword ; and was wroth with his inheritance.

63 The fire consumed their young men ; and their maidens were not given to marriage.

64 Their priests fell by the sword ; and their widows made no lamentation. *(The wife of Phinehas was too much burdened with a heavier sorrow to be able to lament for her husband.)*

65, 66 Then the Lord awaked as one out of sleep, *and* like a mighty man that shouteth by reason of wine. And he smote his enemies in the hinder parts : he put them to a perpetual reproach. *(Not long shall wickedness triumph. God is evermore victorious.)*

I. SAMUEL VI. 1—10; 12—15; 19—21.

AND the ark of the LORD was in the country of the Philistines seven months.

2 And the Philistines called for the priests and the diviners, saying, What shall we do to the ark of the LORD? tell us wherewith we shall send it to his place.

3 And they said, If ye send away the ark of the God of Israel, send it not empty; but in any wise return him a trespass offering: then ye shall be healed, and it shall be known to you why his hand is not removed from you. (*Right wisely did they judge that some acknowledgment of their fault must accompany the return of the ark. If men would be forgiven they must in all possible ways make reparation: even heathens feel this.*)

4, 5 Then said they, What *shall be* the trespass offering which we shall return to him? They answered, Five golden emerods, and five golden mice, *according to* the number of the lords of the Philistines: for one plague *was* on you all, and on your lords. Wherefore ye shall make images of your emerods, and images of your mice that mar the land; and ye shall give glory unto the God of Israel: peradventure he will lighten his hand from off you, and from off your gods, and from off your land.

6 Wherefore then do ye harden your hearts, as the Egyptians and Pharaoh hardened their hearts? when he had wrought wonderfully among them, did they not let the people go, and they departed? (*It is probable that a plague of mice had devoured their crops while hemorrhoids had afflicted their bodies, they therefore acknowledged Jehovah's hand in both judgments.*)

7 Now therefore make a new cart, and take two milch kine, on which there hath come no yoke, and tie the kine to the cart, and bring their calves home from them:

8 And take the ark of the LORD, and lay it upon the cart; and put the jewels of gold, which ye return him *for* a trespass offering, in a coffer by the side thereof; and send it away, that it may go.

9 And see, if it goeth up by the way of his own coast to Beth-shemesh, *then* he hath done us this great evil: but if not, then we shall know that *it is* not his hand *that* smote us; it *was* a chance *that* happened to us.

10 ¶ And the men did so; and took two milch kine, and tied them to the cart, and shut up their calves at home:

12 And the kine took the straight way to the way of Beth-shemesh, *and* went along the highway, lowing as they went, and turned not aside *to* the right hand or *to* the left; and the lords of the Philistines went after them unto the border of Beth-shemesh. (*How wondrously God guided these poor beasts; they went of their own accord away from their calves, lamenting them as they went along, and without a driver they chose the road to the nearest city of the Levites. Who can doubt a special providence in this matter?*)

13 And *they of* Beth-shemesh *were* reaping their wheat harvest in the valley: and they lifted up their eyes, and saw the ark, and rejoiced to see *it*. (*Astonished above measure they must have been to see it brought without human hands to them. God would have them see his hand conspicuously revealed.*)

14, 15 And the cart came into the field of Joshua, a Beth-shemite, and stood there, where *there was* a great stone: and they clave the wood of the cart, and offered the kine a burnt offering unto the LORD. And the Levites took down the ark of the LORD, and the coffer that *was* with it, wherein the jewels of gold *were*, and put *them* on the great stone: and the men of Beth-shemesh offered burnt offerings and sacrificed sacrifices the same day unto the LORD.

19 ¶ And he smote the men of Beth-shemesh, because they had looked into the ark of the LORD, and the people lamented, because the LORD had smitten *many* of the people with a great slaughter. (*God who smote his enemies for their blasphemy, also smites his own people for their presumption. He will be had in reverence of all them that are about him. Let us never trifle with holy things.*)

20 And the men of Beth-shemesh said, Who is able to stand before this holy LORD God? and to whom shall he go up from us? (*Thus instead of confessing their own sin, they laid the blame at the door of God's exceeding great holiness, even as bad men nowadays complain of the preciseness of religion.*)

21 And they sent messengers to the inhabitants of Kirjath-jearim, saying, The Philistines have brought again the ark of the LORD; come ye down, *and* fetch it up to you.

I. SAMUEL VII. 1—13; 15—17. ✓

AND the men of Kirjath-jearim came, and fetched up the ark of the LORD, and brought it into the house of Abinadab in the hill, and sanctified Eleazar his son to keep the ark of the LORD. (*Thus the candlestick was removed from Shiloh, but the candle shone on far more brightly than before.*)

2 And it came to pass, while the ark abode in Kirjath-jearim, that the time was long; for it was twenty years: and all the house of Israel lamented after the LORD. (*This was a happy sorrow. Whenever men lament after God he will soon appear unto them. It should be the business of any of us who have not yet found Jesus, to sigh and cry after him till he appear, and it will not be long before he looks upon us in love. God had already come back to Israel when the people lamented after him, and when a soul sighs for the Lord, the Lord is with it already.*)

3, 4 And Samuel spake unto all the house of Israel, saying, If ye do return unto the LORD with all your hearts, *then* put away the strange gods and Ashtaroth from among you, and prepare your hearts unto the LORD, and serve him only: and he will deliver you out of the hand of the Philistines. Then the children of Israel did put away Baalim, and Ashtaroth, and served the LORD only. (*Their repentance would have been all in vain if it had not been practical. Men cannot keep their sins and have their God; no man can serve two masters.*)

5 And Samuel said, Gather all Israel to Mizpeh, and I will pray for you unto the LORD.

6 And they gathered together to Mizpeh, and drew water, and poured *it* out before the LORD, and fasted on that day, and said there, We have sinned against the LORD. And Samuel judged the children of Israel in Mizpeh.

7 And when the Philistines heard that the children of Israel were gathered together to Mizpeh, the lords of the Philistines went up against Israel. And when the children of Israel heard *it*, they were afraid of the Philistines. (*Yet they had no cause for fear, now that God was reconciled. He who is at peace with God should be fearless.*)

8 And the children of Israel said to Samuel, Cease not to cry unto the LORD our God for us, that he will save us out of the hand of the

Philistines. (*This was a wise speech, and shewed that they had faith as well as fear. Faith in God gave them faith in the power of prayer.*)

9 And Samuel took a sucking lamb, and offered *it for* a burnt offering wholly unto the LORD: and Samuel cried unto the LORD for Israel; and the LORD heard him.

True repentance, prayer, and faith in the great sacrifice, must win the day.

10, 11 And as Samuel was offering up the burnt offering, the Philistines drew near to battle against Israel: but the LORD thundered with a great thunder on that day upon the Philistines, and discomfited them; and they were smitten before Israel. And the men of Israel went out of Mizpeh, and pursued the Philistines, and smote them, until *they came* under Bethcar.

12 Then Samuel took a stone, and set *it* between Mizpeh and Shen, and called the name of it Eben-ezer, saying, Hitherto hath the LORD helped us. (*Samuel won that battle on his knees, and afterwards he recorded with praise what he had won by prayer. Praying men are not ungrateful when their intercession prospers.*)

13 ¶ So the Philistines were subdued, and they came no more into the coast of Israel: and the hand of the LORD was against the Philistines all the days of Samuel.

15, 16 And Samuel judged Israel all the days of his life. (*God does not cast off faithful servants when they grow old, neither do they ask for a retiring pension and for leave to be idle. O to serve God from our childhood to our hoar hairs! May such grace be given to the young members of our family.*) And he went from year to year in circuit to Beth-el, and Gilgal, and Mizpeh, and judged Israel in all those places.

17 And his return *was* to Ramah; for there *was* his house; and there he judged Israel; and there he built an altar unto the LORD.

I my Ebenezer raise
To my kind Redeemer's praise;
With a grateful heart I own
Hitherto thy help I've known.

What may be my future lot
Well I know concerns me not;
This should set my heart at rest,
What thy will ordains is best.

232   "Put not your trust in princes."   APRIL 21.—EVENING.

[*Or August* 10.]

I. SAMUEL VIII. 1; 3—22.

AND it came to pass, when Samuel was old, that he made his sons judges over Israel.

3 And his sons walked not in his ways, but turned aside after lucre, and took bribes, and perverted judgment. *(Grace does not run in the blood, an honoured father may have disgraceful sons. Perhaps Samuel was wrong in making his sons judges, for we do not read that the Lord made them so. Great men ought not to injure the church or the state by putting their sons into offices which they are not fit to fill.)*

4 Then all the elders of Israel gathered themselves together, and came to Samuel,

5 And said unto him, Behold, thou art old, and thy sons walk not in thy ways : now make us a king to judge us like all the nations.

6 ¶ But the thing displeased Samuel, when they said, Give us a king to judge us. And Samuel prayed unto the LORD. *(This little sentence is most instructive. When we are perplexed or displeased, we should resort at once to prayer. Constantly we read of the prayers of the Lord Jesus. We ought to imitate him in this. As the fish loves the stream, and the bird the bough, so the believer loves prayer.)*

7, 8 And the LORD said unto Samuel, Hearken unto the voice of the people in all that they say unto thee : for they have not rejected thee, but they have rejected me, that I should not reign over them. According to all the works which they have done since the day that I brought them up out of Egypt even unto this day, wherewith they have forsaken me, and served other gods, so do they also unto thee.

9 Now therefore hearken unto their voice : howbeit yet protest solemnly unto them, and shew them the manner of the king that shall reign over them. *(If they would have their way they should have it ; but they were to be warned of the consequences that they might not act in ignorance. Many things which men's hearts lust after will be their curse, and although God allows them to have their heart's desire, it is in anger, and it brings them small content.)*

10 And Samuel told all the words of the LORD unto the people that asked of him a king.

11—18 And he said, This will be the manner of the king that shall reign over you : He will take your sons, and appoint *them* for himself, for

his chariots, and *to be* his horsemen ; and *some* shall run before his chariots. And he will appoint him captains over thousands, and captains over fifties ; and *will set them* to ear his ground, and to reap his harvest, and to make his instruments of war, and instruments of his chariots. And he will take your daughters *to be* confectionaries, and *to be* cooks, and *to be* bakers. And he will take your fields, and your vineyards, and your oliveyards, *even* the best *of them,* and give *them* to his servants. And he will take the tenth of your seed, and of your vineyards, and give to his officers, and to his servants. And he will take your menservants, and your maidservants, and your goodliest young men, and your asses, and put *them* to his work. He will take the tenth of your sheep : and ye shall be his servants. And ye shall cry out in that day because of your king which ye shall have chosen you ; and the LORD will not hear you in that day. *(Under the government of God they had been free from exactions and taxations, but if they chose to put their necks under the yoke, they would have to keep them there. When Christians are free from anxiety they had better keep so. Let us not run into spiritual bondage wilfully. King Jesus it is delightful to serve, but it is hard to serve men, or live for ambition, wealth, or custom.)*

19, 20, 21 Nevertheless the people refused to obey the voice of Samuel ; and they said, Nay ; but we will have a king over us ; That we also may be like all the nations ; and that our king may judge us, and go out before us, and fight our battles. And Samuel heard all the words of the people, and he rehearsed them in the ears of the LORD.

22 And the LORD said to Samuel, Hearken unto their voice, and make them a king. And Samuel said unto the men of Israel, Go ye every man unto his city. *(God save us from having our prayers heard as theirs were ! O Lord, if we ask anything amiss of thee, be pleased in mercy to refuse us.)*

All hail the power of Jesus' name !
    Let angels prostrate fall ;
Bring forth the royal diadem,
    And crown him Lord of all

I. SAMUEL IX. 1—6; 14—21; 26, 27.

NOW there was a man of Benjamin, whose name *was* Kish, a Benjamite, a mighty man of power.

2 And he had a son, whose name *was* Saul, a choice young man, and a goodly: *(It would have been better had he been godly as well:)* and *there was* not among the children of Israel a goodlier person than he: from his shoulders and upward *he was* higher than any of the people.

3 And the asses of Kish Saul's father were lost. And Kish said to Saul his son, Take now one of the servants with thee, and arise, go seek the asses. *(A quaint writer says, " Saul's obedience was a fit entrance upon his sovereignty. The service was homely for the son of a great man; yet, he refuseth not to go with his father's servant, upon so mean a search. The disobedient and scornful are good for nothing; they are neither fit to be subjects nor governors. Kish was a great man in his country, yet he disdained not to send his son Saul upon a thrifty errand; neither does Saul plead that it would disgrace him. Pride and wantonness have marred our times. Great parents count it a dishonour to employ their sons in honest labour, and their pampered children think it a shame to do anything, and so behave themselves as if they counted it a glory to be idle or wicked.")*

4, 5 And he passed through mount Ephraim, and passed through the land of Shalisha, but they found *them* not: then they passed through the land of Shalim, and *there they were* not: and he passed through the land of the Benjamites, but they found *them* not. *And* when they were come to the land of Zuph, Saul said to his servant that *was* with him, Come, and let us return; lest my father leave *caring* for the asses, and take thought for us.

6 And he said unto him, Behold now, *there is* in this city a man of God, and *he is* an honourable man; all that he saith cometh surely to pass: now let us go thither; peradventure he can shew us our way that we should go. *(They came to the man of God about asses, and learned something concerning a kingdom, and so many go to hear preachers out of idle curiosity, but God leads them into the kingdom of his dear Son.)*

14, 15 And they went up into the city: *and* when they were come into the city, behold,

Samuel came out against them, for to go up to the high place. Now the LORD had told Samuel in his ear a day before Saul came, saying,

16 To morrow about this time I will send thee a man out of the land of Benjamin, and thou shalt anoint him *to be* captain over my people Israel, that he may save my people out of the hand of the Philistines: for I have looked upon my people, because their cry is come unto me.

17 And when Samuel saw Saul, the LORD said unto him, Behold the man whom I spake to thee of! this same shall reign over my people.

18 Then Saul drew near to Samuel in the gate, and said, Tell me, I pray thee, where the seer's house *is*.

19 And Samuel answered Saul, and said, I *am* the seer: go up before me unto the high place; for ye shall eat with me to day, and to morrow I will let thee go, and will tell thee all that *is* in thine heart. *(That he did, and very much more. God's ministers are enabled by his Spirit to lay bare men's hearts, and then they tell them of the kingdom of heaven.)*

20 And as for thine asses that were lost three days ago, set not thy mind on them; for they are found. And on whom *is* all the desire of Israel? *Is it* not on thee, and on all thy father's house? *(Who cares for asses when a kingdom is in view? Who will regard earthly joys when heaven is to be had? How foolish are those who spend all their thoughts upon this world's straying asses, and lose the unfading crown.)*

21 And Saul answered and said, *Am* not I a Benjamite, of the smallest of the tribes of Israel? and my family the least of all the families of the tribe of Benjamin? wherefore then speakest thou so to me?

26 And they arose early: and it came to pass about the spring of the day, that Samuel called Saul to the top of the house, saying, Up, that I may send thee away. And Saul arose, and they went out both of them, he and Samuel, abroad.

27 *And* as they were going down to the end of the city, Samuel said to Saul, Bid the servant pass on before us, but stand thou still a while, that I may shew thee the word of God. *(This day let each of us endeavour to have a little season for thought and prayer; carrying this text in our hearts, " Stand thou still awhile, that I may shew thee the word of God.")*

Quit ye like men, be strong,
  Fear not the foeman's frown ;
Nor suffer Satan's deadliest blows
  To beat your courage down.

  The battle soon will yield,
  If ye your parts fulfil :
For strong as is the hostile shield,
  Your sword is stronger still.

  Arise, ye saints arise !
  The Lord your leader is ;
The foe before his banner flies,
  The victory is his.

Holy and reverend is the name
  Of our eternal King ;
Thrice holy Lord ! the angels cry ;
  Thrice holy ! let us sing.

The deepest reverence of the mind,
  Pay, O my soul ! to God ;
Lift, with thy hands, a holy heart
  To his sublime abode.

With sacred awe pronounce his name,
  Whom words nor thoughts can reach ;
A broken heart will please him more
  Than noblest forms of speech.

  O Sacred Spirit still
  Abide with all thy saints,
If thou depart the glory's gone,
  And every warrior faints.

  Vain is the outward ark,
  Vain are the means of grace,
The sun is gone, the church is dark,
  If thou dost hide thy face.

  Depart not, gracious Lord,
  Though we have griev'd thee sore
Still all thy sacred help afford,
  Nor let us grieve thee more.

Yes, I will bless thee, O my God !
  Through all my earthly days ;
And to eternity prolong
  Thy vast, thy boundless praise.

Nor shall my tongue alone proclaim
  The honours of my God :
My life with all its active powers,
  Shall spread thy praise abroad.

Soon shall my lips in endless praise,
  Their grateful tribute pay ;
The theme demands an angel's tongue,
  And an eternal day.

These idols tread beneath thy feet,
And to thyself the conquest get ;
Let sin no more oppose my Lord,
Slain by thy Spirit's two-edged sword.

Compel my soul thy sway to own ;
Self-will, self-righteousness dethrone :
Let Dagon fall before thy face,
Destroyed by thine all conquering grace.

  Thy name, almighty Lord,
  Shall sound through distant lands ;
Great is thy grace, and sure thy word ;
  Thy truth for ever stands,

  Far be thine honour spread,
  And long thy praise endure,
Till morning light and evening shade
  Shall be exchanged no more.

I. SAMUEL X. 1; 17—27.

THEN Samuel took a vial of oil, and poured it upon Saul's head, and kissed him, and said, *Is it* not because the LORD hath anointed thee *to be* captain over his inheritance ? *(It has been remarked that only a vial of oil was used, and not a horn as in the case of David; this seemed to foreshadow the shortness of Saul's reign, and his own want of the plenteous grace of God.)*

17, 18 ¶ And Samuel called the people together unto the LORD to Mizpeh; And said unto the children of Israel, Thus saith the LORD God of Israel, I brought up Israel out of Egypt, and delivered you out of the hand of the Egyptians, and out of the hand of all kingdoms, *and* of them that oppressed you :

19 And ye have this day rejected your God, who himself saved you out of all your adversities and your tribulations; and ye have said unto him, *Nay*, but set a king over us. Now therefore present yourselves before the LORD by your tribes, and by your thousands.

This is only one form of a common evil among the Lord's people; they cannot walk by faith pure and simple, but want some intermediate arm to lean upon; they are not spiritual enough to rest content with the invisible God. Providence is not enough for many, they must have visible treasure; neither are they satisfied with the Lord's aid, but cry out for an arm of flesh. To such the Lord often sends that which they seek for, and it becomes a plague to them, just as Saul became rather a curse to Israel than a blessing. When we pray we ought ever to say, "Not as I will, but as thou wilt," lest the Lord should answer us in anger, and give us the desire of our hearts to be a solemn chastisement for our presumption.

20 And when Samuel had caused all the tribes of Israel to come near, the tribe of Benjamin was taken.

21 When he had caused the tribe of Benjamin to come near by their families, the family of Matri was taken, and Saul the son of Kish was taken : and when they sought him, he could not be found. *(He knew from what Samuel had done to him, that the lot must fall upon himself, but he was modest or else fearful to undertake so weighty a business. Crowns are heavy things, and make the wearers' heads ache full often; Saul was by no means to blame for*

hiding from so burdensome an honour. If men knew the trials of the great, they would cease from ambition.)

22 Therefore they enquired of the LORD further, if the man should yet come thither. And the LORD answered, Behold, he hath hid himself among the stuff. *(God knows where we are. Let us never dream of hiding from him. We are like bees in a glass hive, and all we do he observes.)*

23 And they ran and fetched him thence : and when he stood among the people, he was higher than any of the people from his shoulders and upward. *(The kind of man to impress the populace and command respect. They might well look up to one who was taller than themselves by his head and shoulders.)*

24 And Samuel said to all the people, See ye him whom the LORD hath chosen, that *there is* none like him among all the people ? And all the people shouted, and said, God save the king.

25 Then Samuel told the people the manner of the kingdom, and wrote *it* in a book, and laid *it* up before the LORD. *(Saul was to be monarch under God, and to govern constitutionally. The book was the nation's Magna Charta.)* And Samuel sent all the people away, every man to his house.

26 ¶ And Saul also went home to Gibeah; and there went with him a band of men, whose hearts God had touched. *(They saw God's hand in Saul's choice, and stood by him.)*

27 But the children of Belial said, How shall this man save us ? *(No man may hope to please everybody. The man whom God himself points out, is not the man for disaffected people. Saul was of good family, of noble stature, modest and unassuming, but all these things went for nothing with the malcontents. May none of us ever belong to that evil class of persons, who are always in opposition, always faultfinding, never willing to work with anybody. This is not the mind of Christ, nor the fruit of the Spirit, which is ever peaceable.)* And they despised him, and brought him no presents. But he held his peace. *(This was a very sensible course of action. The man who can be quiet will defeat his enemies. Be not hasty to defend yourself, or answer slanderous tongues. Stand still, and see the salvation of God.)*

I. SAMUEL XII. ✓

SAUL *proved his valour by defeating Nahash king of the Ammonites, whereupon the people assembled to establish him more fully in his kingdom. Samuel took advantage of this to end his official life and to warn the people.*

1 And Samuel said unto all Israel, Behold, I have hearkened unto your voice in all that ye said unto me, and have made a king over you.

2, 3 And now I am old and grayheaded; and I have walked before you from my childhood unto this day. Behold, here I *am :* witness against me before the LORD, and before his anointed : whose ox have I taken? or whose ass have I taken? or whom have I defrauded? whom have I oppressed? or of whose hand have I received *any* bribe to blind mine eyes therewith? and I will restore it you.

4, 5, 6, 7 And they said, Thou hast not defrauded us, nor oppressed us, neither hast thou taken ought of any man's hand. And he said unto them, The LORD *is* witness against you, and his anointed *is* witness this day, that ye have not found ought in my hand. And they answered, *He is* witness. And Samuel said unto the people, *It is* the LORD that advanced Moses and Aaron, and that brought your fathers up out of the land of Egypt. Now therefore stand still, that I may reason with you before the LORD of all the righteous acts of the LORD, which he did to you and to your fathers.

8—11 When Jacob was come into Egypt, and your fathers cried unto the LORD, then the LORD sent Moses and Aaron, which brought forth your fathers out of Egypt, and made them dwell in this place. And when they forgat the LORD their God, he sold them into the hand of Sisera, captain of the host of Hazor, and into the hand of the Philistines, and into the hand of the king of Moab, and they fought against them. And they cried unto the LORD, and said, We have sinned, because we have forsaken the LORD, and have served Baalim and Ashtaroth : but now deliver us out of the hand of our enemies, and we will serve thee. And the LORD sent Jerubbaal, and Bedan *(or, as some read it, Barak)*, and Jephthah, and Samuel, and delivered you out of the hand of your enemies on every side, and ye dwelled safe.

12 And when ye saw that Nahash the king of the children of Ammon came against you, ye said unto me, Nay; but a king shall reign over us : when the LORD your God *was* your king.

13 Now therefore behold the king whom ye have chosen, *and* whom ye have desired ! and, behold, the LORD hath set a king over you.

14 If ye will fear the LORD, and serve him, and obey his voice, and not rebel against the commandment of the LORD, then shall both ye and also the king that reigneth over you continue following the LORD your God :

15 But if ye will not obey the voice of the LORD, but rebel against the commandment of the LORD, then shall the hand of the LORD be against you, as it *was* against your fathers.

16 ¶ Now therefore stand and see this great thing, which the LORD will do before your eyes.

17 *Is it* not wheat harvest to day? I will call unto the LORD, and he shall send thunder and rain; that ye may perceive and see that your wickedness *is* great, which ye have done in the sight of the LORD, in asking you a king.

18 So Samuel called unto the LORD; and the LORD sent thunder and rain that day : and all the people greatly feared the LORD and Samuel. *(It seldom or never rains at that period in Palestine. Samuel's prayers were as mighty as those of Elijah.)*

19 And all the people said unto Samuel, Pray for thy servants unto the LORD thy God, that we die not: for we have added unto all our sins *this* evil, to ask us a king.

20, 21, 22 And Samuel said unto the people, Fear not : ye have done all this wickedness : yet turn not aside from following the LORD, but serve the LORD with all your heart; And turn ye not aside : for *then should ye go* after vain *things*, which cannot profit nor deliver; for they *are* vain. For the LORD will not forsake his people for his great name's sake : because it hath pleased the LORD to make you his people.

A precious passage indeed. Election ensures to its objects immutable love, but where the reason for election lies none can tell.

23, 24 Moreover as for me, God forbid that I should sin against the LORD in ceasing to pray for you : Only fear the LORD, and serve him in truth with all your heart : for consider how great *things* he hath done for you.

25 But if ye shall still do wickedly, ye shall be consumed, both ye and your king.

I. SAMUEL XIII. 1—14.

SAUL reigned one year *(during that time no fault was found in him; but he was of that shortwinded race which cannot hold out to the end)*; and when he had reigned two years over Israel, Saul chose him three thousand *men* of Israel; *whereof* two thousand were with Saul in Michmash, and a thousand were with Jonathan in Gibeah of Benjamin : and the rest of the people he sent every man to his tent.

3 And Jonathan smote the garrison of the Philistines that *was* in Geba, and the Philistines heard *of it*. *(Having subdued the country the Philistines put garrisons in the fortresses to keep the people in subjection. Jonathan commenced the war of liberty by destroying one of these garrisons.)* And Saul blew the trumpet throughout all the land, saying, Let the Hebrews hear. *(This was the usual Hebrew war summons, the blast of a trumpet was answered by beacon-fires from hill to hill, and the country rose at once to cast off the Philistine yoke.)*

4 And all Israel heard say *that* Saul had smitten a garrison of the Philistines, and *that* Israel also was had in abomination with the Philistines. And the people were called together after Saul to Gilgal.

5 And the Philistines gathered themselves together to fight with Israel, thirty thousand chariots, and six thousand horsemen, and people as the sand which *is* on the sea shore in multitude : and they came up, and pitched in Michmash, eastward from Beth-aven. *(The Philistines called in their allies, and resolved to put down the Israelitish revolt at once. Such was the terror inspired by so vast a host, that Saul soon found his general levy of the people dispersed; and even his small standing army shrunk from three thousand to seven hundred men.)*

6, 7 When the men of Israel saw that they were in a strait, (for the people were distressed), then the people did hide themselves in caves, and in thickets, and in rocks, and in high places, and in pits. And *some of* the Hebrews went over Jordan to the land of Gad and Gilead. As for Saul, he *was* yet in Gilgal, and all the people followed him trembling. *(Those who remained with Saul in person were faint in heart, and despaired of success.)*

8 ¶ And he tarried seven days, according to the set time that Samuel *had appointed:* but Samuel came not to Gilgal; and the people were scattered from him.

9 And Saul said, Bring hither a burnt offering to me, and peace offerings. And he offered the burnt offering. *(This he had no right to do, for it was an assumption of the priestly office, and a virtual disowning of his position as the viceroy of the Lord. He ought to have waited for directions from the Lord through Samuel; but in his self-will he proceeded to act as if he were quite independent of God's guidance. His impatience cost him his kingdom.)*

10 And it came to pass, that as soon as he had made an end of offering the burnt offering, behold, Samuel came; and Saul went out to meet him, that he might salute him.

11 ¶ And Samuel said, What hast thou done? And Saul said, Because I saw that the people were scattered from me, and *that* thou camest not within the days appointed, and *that* the Philistines gathered themselves together at Michmash;

12 Therefore said I, The Philistines will come down now upon me to Gilgal, and I have not made supplication unto the LORD : I forced myself therefore, and offered a burnt offering.

He was a hypocrite, and tried to cover his rebellious act by pretending great zeal for outward religion.

13 And Samuel said to Saul, Thou hast done foolishly : thou hast not kept the commandment of the LORD thy God, which he commanded thee : for now would the LORD have established thy kingdom upon Israel for ever.

14 But now thy kingdom shall not continue : the LORD hath sought him a man after his own heart, and the LORD hath commanded him *to be* captain over his people, because thou hast not kept *that* which the LORD commanded thee.

At first sight Saul's offence appears little, but no sin is little, because there is no little God to sin against. He had virtually cast off Jehovah's sovereignty, and therefore the Lord would not establish his dynasty.

Keep us, Lord, oh keep us ever,
Vain our hope if left by thee ;
We are thine, oh leave us never,
Till thy face in heaven we see ;
There to praise thee
Through a bright eternity.

I. SAMUEL XV. 1—3 ; 9—11 ; 13—23. ✓

SAMUEL also said unto Saul, The LORD sent me to anoint thee *to be* king over his people, over Israel : now therefore hearken thou unto the voice of the words of the LORD.

2 Thus saith the LORD of hosts, I remember *that* which Amalek did to Israel, how he laid *wait* for him in the way, when he came up from Egypt.

3 Now go and smite Amalek, and utterly destroy all that they have, and spare them not; but slay both man and woman, infant and suckling, ox and sheep, camel and ass.

This wandering people had wantonly attacked the Israelites in the desert, in the most cowardly manner, and this national sin had long been registered in God's book against them. They were moreover a barbarous race of plunderers, most dangerous to their neighbours and to all settled government. The time was come when divine justice required that they should be brought to condign punishment. Saul was therefore sent of God to be the executioner, and was commanded to do his work thoroughly.

9 But Saul and the people spared Agag, and the best of the sheep, and of the oxen, and of the fatlings, and the lambs, and all *that was* good, and would not utterly destroy them : but every thing *that was* vile and refuse, that they destroyed utterly. (*This was half-obedience, which is whole rebellion. Many are ready to slay their disreputable sins, but their fashionable transgressions they cannot give up.*)

10 ¶ Then came the word of the LORD unto Samuel, saying,

11 It repenteth me that I have set up Saul *to be* king : for he is turned back from following me, and hath not performed my commandments. And it grieved Samuel ; and he cried unto the LORD all night. (*The rejection of sinners is a great grief to saints: God has no pleasure in the death of sinners, nor have his people.*)

13 And Samuel came to Saul : and Saul said unto him, Blessed *be* thou of the LORD : I have performed the commandment of the LORD.

He brags most who has most reason for shame.

14 And Samuel said, What *meaneth* then this bleating of the sheep in mine ears, and the lowing of the oxen which I hear ?

15 And Saul said, They have brought them from the Amalekites : for the people spared the best of the sheep and of the oxen, to sacrifice unto the LORD thy God ; and the rest we have utterly destroyed. (*He lays his fault upon others, and pleads the good intention of the act. Neither excuse would avail.*)

16 Then Samuel said unto Saul, Stay, and I will tell thee what the LORD hath said to me this night. And he said unto him, Say on.

17, 18, 19 And Samuel said, When thou *wast* little in thine own sight, *wast* thou not *made* the head of the tribes of Israel, and the LORD anointed thee king over Israel ? And the LORD sent thee on a journey, and said, Go and utterly destroy the sinners the Amalekites, and fight against them until they be consumed. Wherefore then didst thou not obey the voice of the LORD, but didst fly upon the spoil, and didst evil in the sight of the LORD ?

20 And Saul said unto Samuel, Yea, I have obeyed the voice of the LORD, and have gone the way which the LORD sent me, and have brought Agag the king of Amalek, and have utterly destroyed the Amalekites.

21 But the people took of the spoil, sheep and oxen, the chief of the things which should have been utterly destroyed, to sacrifice unto the LORD thy God in Gilgal.

22 And Samuel said, Hath the LORD *as great* delight in burnt offerings and sacrifices, as in obeying the voice of the LORD ? Behold, to obey *is* better than sacrifice, *and* to hearken than the fat of rams.

23 For rebellion *is as* the sin of witchcraft, and stubbornness *is as* iniquity and idolatry. Because thou hast rejected the word of the LORD, he hath also rejected thee from *being* king.

Nothing can compensate for a want of obedience to God's will. We may pretend great zeal for God's glory, but wilful neglect of divine commands will condemn us. External religion cannot be a substitute for holiness. Those who pretended to witchcraft were put to death by Saul, but so long as he himself would not do as the Lord bade him, he was as guilty as the witches whom he slew. Idolatry was known to be overt rebellion against Jehovah, but obstinate disregard of his law was quite as evil a form of rebellion. May the Holy Ghost make us scrupulously obedient, for nothing short of this will prove us to be the true servants of the Lord.

THE *plea of Saul that he had preserved the cattle for sacrifice, when the Lord had bidden him destroy them, reminds us of the folly of those who imagine that religion lies in outward forms, and forget that it is a matter of the heart. To such persons the Lord spake by the mouth of his servant Isaiah, and said—*

ISAIAH I. 10—20.

10 ¶ Hear the word of the LORD, ye rulers of Sodom; give ear unto the law of our God, ye people of Gomorrah. *(The mention of Sodom and Gomorrah was intended to be a warning to them of the certain punishment of their crimes. On account of their forms and ceremonies they reckoned themselves to be the favourites of heaven, but for their hypocrisy they were named after the most accursed of men.)*

11 To what purpose *is* the multitude of your sacrifices unto me? saith the LORD: I am full of the burnt offerings of rams, and the fat of fed beasts; and I delight not in the blood of bullocks, or of lambs, or of he goats. *(They stopped at the outward shell, and never entered upon the kernel of real love to God; hence their religion was useless.)*

12 When ye come to appear before me, who hath required this at your hand, to tread my courts? *(God wants not the superstitious to adore him, he has never invited them to his house. He seeketh those who worship him in spirit and in truth, and not mere formalists.)*

13, 14 Bring no more vain oblations; incense is an abomination unto me; the new moons and sabbaths, the calling of assemblies, I cannot away with; *it is* iniquity, even the solemn meeting. Your new moons and your appointed feasts my soul hateth: they are a trouble unto me; I am weary to bear *them.*

15 And when ye spread forth your hands, I will hide mine eyes from you: yea, when ye make many prayers, I will not hear: your hands are full of blood. *(While they were cruel and oppressive, it was idle to offer elaborate ceremonies, devout postures, holy days and many prayers, for God abhors a heartless worship. Men who do not really believe in the Lord Jesus and obey the Lord's will, might save themselves the trouble of attending upon sacraments, for they only make their case worse, and add to their sins.)*

16, 17 Wash you, make you clean; put away the evil of your doings from before mine eyes; cease to do evil; Learn to do well; seek judgment, relieve the oppressed, judge the fatherless, plead for the widow. *(Repentance, practical and thorough, is a great gospel duty, and a grain of it is better than a ton of ceremonies.)*

18 Come now, and let us reason together, saith the LORD: though your sins be as scarlet, they shall be as white as snow; though they be red like crimson, they shall be as wool.

19 If ye be willing and obedient, ye shall eat the good of the land:

20 But if ye refuse and rebel, ye shall be devoured with the sword: for the mouth of the LORD hath spoken it. *(Have done with the vain boast of your religiousness, and be indeed religious, spiritually and practically. Seek mercy of the Lord with humble heart, since he is ready to bestow it, for the vilest sins can be put away by Jesus' blood; but mere ceremonies avail nothing.)*

To the same purport is that memorable passage in the book of Micah.

MICAH VI. 6—8.

6 ¶ Wherewith shall I come before the LORD, *and* bow myself before the high God? shall I come before him with burnt offerings, with calves of a year old?

7 Will the LORD be pleased with thousands of rams, *or* with ten thousands of rivers of oil? shall I give my firstborn *for* my transgression, the fruit of my body *for* the sin of my soul?

8 He hath shewed thee, O man, what *is* good; and what doth the LORD require of thee, but to do justly, and to love mercy, and to walk humbly with thy God? *(The true proof of godliness is not expensive rites, but hearty obedience; not a loud profession, but holy living; not large subscriptions, but a yielding up of the heart. Have we this vital godliness? Has the Holy Spirit wrought in us a change of heart?)*

Not streaming blood, nor cleansing fire,
Thy righteous anger can appease;
Burnt offerings thou dost not require,
Or gladly I would render these.

The broken heart in sacrifice,
Alone, will thine acceptance meet:
My heart, O God, do not despise,
Abased and contrite at thy feet.

246   " The Lord looketh on the heart."   APRIL 25.—MORNING.

[Or August 17.]

I. SAM. XVI, 1; 4—14; 22, 23.

AND the LORD said unto Samuel, How long wilt thou mourn for Saul, seeing I have rejected him from reigning over Israel? fill thine horn with oil, and go, I will send thee to Jesse the Beth-lehemite: for I have provided me a king among his sons. (*It was both natural and right that the prophet should lament Saul's sin, but he must not repine at the Lord's punishment of him, but rather bestir himself to be God's messenger to the better king who would one day prove a great blessing to Israel. We must lament that any should so sin as to incur God's anger, but at his judgments upon them we must not rebel, for the Judge of all the earth must do right. When the wicked are cast into hell, the saints in heaven do not murmur out of pity to the offenders; but, in obedient sympathy with the most Holy God, they adore with reverential awe.*)

4, 5, 6 And Samuel did that which the LORD spake, and came to Beth-lehem. And he sanctified Jesse and his sons, and called them to the sacrifice. And it came to pass, when they were come, that he looked on Eliab, and said, Surely the LORD's anointed *is* before him. (*Even prophets err when they judge by appearances. Men are not to be valued by their looks but by their hearts.*)

7, 8, 9, 10 But the LORD said unto Samuel, Look not on his countenance, or on the height of his stature; because I have refused him: for *the LORD seeth* not as man seeth; for man looketh on the outward appearance, but the LORD looketh on the heart. Then Jesse called Abinadab, and made him pass before Samuel. And he said, Neither hath the LORD chosen this. Then Jesse made Shammah to pass by. And he said, Neither hath the LORD chosen this. Again, Jesse made seven of his sons to pass before Samuel. And Samuel said unto Jesse, The LORD hath not chosen these.

11 And Samuel said unto Jesse, Are here all *thy* children? And he said, There remaineth yet the youngest, and, behold, he keepeth the sheep. And Samuel said unto Jesse, Send and fetch him: for we will not sit down till he come hither. (*He who was retiring and pious was but little esteemed at home. Parents make great*

mistakes when they undervalue good children because they do not happen to be brilliant and pushing. Despised ones should be comforted when they remember that the Lord knows all about them, and will bring them forward in due time. Verily, there are last who shall be first.*)

12 And he sent, and brought him in. Now he *was* ruddy, *and* withal of a beautiful countenance, and goodly to look to. And the LORD said, Arise, anoint him: for this *is* he.

13 Then Samuel took the horn of oil, and anointed him in the midst of his brethren: and the Spirit of the LORD came upon David from that day forward. (*The horn of oil indicated plenteous grace. We all need the power of the Holy Spirit; may he dwell in us richly, then shall we be kings and priests unto God.*) So Samuel rose up, and went to Ramah.

14 ¶ But the Spirit of the LORD departed from Saul, and an evil spirit from the LORD troubled him. (*We have seen what divine love did for David, and we now learn what divine anger did for Saul. The one thing most needful above all others, is the favour of the Lord. Have that, and we are blessed; be without it, and we are miserable.*)

22 And Saul sent to Jesse, saying, Let David, I pray thee, stand before me; for he hath found favour in my sight.

23 And it came to pass, when the *evil* spirit from God was upon Saul, that David took an harp, and played with his hand: so Saul was refreshed, and was well, and the evil spirit departed from him. (*Saul was probably a monomaniac through remorse of conscience, and needed music to relieve his mind. How much happier was the shepherd youth who had music in his heart and was filled with the good Spirit. God grant that we may live in the fear of God, and so enjoy abiding peace, for even in this life sinful conduct is the root of countless ills.*)

But few among the carnal wise,
    But few of nobler race,
Obtain the favour of thine eyes,
    Almighty King of Grace.

Nature has all her glories lost,
    When brought before thy throne;
No flesh shall in thy presence boast,
    But in the Lord alone.

THE *Holy Spirit has spoken of the election of David in the Psalms more than once, let us read a passage from—*

PSALM LXXVIII. 67—72.

67 He refused the tabernacle of Joseph, and chose not the tribe of Ephraim. (*The ark had been for a long time at Shiloh, in the territory of Ephraim, but the tribe was found unfit for leadership, and the divine residence was therefore removed.*)

68, 69 But chose the tribe of Judah, the mount Zion which he loved. And he built his sanctuary like high *palaces*, like the earth which he hath established for ever.

70, 71 He chose David also his servant, and took him from the sheepfolds : From following the ewes great with young he brought him to feed Jacob his people, and Israel his inheritance.

He exercised the care and art of those who watch for the young lambs, following the ewes in their wanderings; the tenderness· and patience thus acquired, would tend to the development of characteristics most becoming in a king. To the man thus prepared, the office which God had appointed for him came in due season, and he was enabled worthily to fulfil it. It is wonderful how often divine wisdom so arranges the early and obscure portion of a choice life, as to make it a preparatory school for a more active and noble future.

72 So he fed them according to the integrity of his heart; and guided them by the skilfulness of his hands. (*In his reign the people were peaceful and prosperous, and no better king ever sat upon the throne of Israel.*)

WE *will now read a passage in which our Lord Jesus is spoken of as Israel's king, and his reign described.—*

ISAIAH XI. 1—10.

1 And there shall come forth a rod out of the stem of Jesse, and a Branch shall grow out of his roots :

2 And the spirit of the LORD shall rest upon him, the spirit of wisdom and understanding, the spirit of counsel and might, the spirit of knowledge and of the fear of the LORD ;

3, 4 And shall make him of quick understanding in the fear of the LORD : (*Our Lord is very quick to understand the desires and groanings of*

those in whom is the genuine principle of holy fear, even though they be but feebly seeking after God.) and he shall not judge after the sight of his eyes, neither reprove after the hearing of his ears : But with righteousness shall he judge the poor, and reprove with equity for the meek of the earth : and he shall smite the earth with the rod of his mouth, and with the breath of his lips shall he slay the wicked. (*His gospel is the destroyer of evil, and his last sentence will slay the wicked in eternal death.*)

5 And righteousness shall be the girdle of his loins, and faithfulness the girdle of his reins.

6 The wolf also shall dwell with the lamb, and the leopard shall lie down with the kid ; and the calf and the young lion and the fatling together ; and a little child shall lead them.

7 And the cow and the bear shall feed ; their young ones shall lie down together : and the lion shall eat straw like the ox.

8 And the sucking child shall play on the hole of the asp, and the weaned child shall put his hand on the cockatrice' den.

Jesus will in his own good time, deliver this earth from the curse, and restore the purity and peace of Eden. Even the animal creation shall in the latter days feel his elevating power. " The creation itself also shall be delivered from the bondage of corruption, into the glorious liberty of the children of God."

9 They shall not hurt nor destroy in all my holy mountain : for the earth shall be full of the knowledge of the LORD, as the waters cover the sea.

10 ¶ And in that day there shall be a root of Jesse, which shall stand for an ensign of the people ; to it shall the Gentiles seek : and his rest shall be glorious. (*Christ is the rallying point for manhood, he draws all men unto him. To him shall all people offer their allegiance, and the place where he deigns to dwell shall be glorious indeed. What is this but his church, of which he has said, " This is my rest " ?*)

Crown him, the Lord of Peace,
Whose power a sceptre sways
From pole to pole, that wars may cease,
Absorb'd in prayer and praise :
His reign shall know no end,
And round his piercèd feet
Fair flowers of paradise extend
Their fragrance ever sweet.

We love thy church, O God;
Her walls before thee stand
Dear as the apple of thine eye,
And graven on thy hand.

For her our tears shall fall,
For her our prayers ascend,
To her our cares and toils be given,
Till toils and cares shall end.

Jesus, thou Friend divine,
Our Saviour and our King,
Thy hand from every snare and foe,
Shall great deliverance bring.

Rise, ye men of Israel, rise,
Now your routed foe pursue;
Shout his praises to the skies,
Who has conquer'd sin for you.

Jesus doth for you appear,
He his conquering grace affords;
Saves you, not with sword and spear,
For the battle is the Lord's.

Earth and hell shall yet submit,
All his foes before him fall,
Death shall die beneath his feet,
And our God be all in all.

Lord, through the desert drear and wide,
Our erring footsteps need a guide;
Keep us, oh keep us near thy side.
Let us not fall.   Let us not fall.

We have no fear that Thou shouldst lose
One whom eternal love could choose;
But we would ne'er this grace abuse.
Let us not fall.   Let us not fall.

Lord, we are blind, and halt, and lame,
We have no strong-hold but thy name:
Great is our fear to bring it shame.
Let us not fall.   Let us not fall.

To the upright light arises,
    Darkness soon gives place to day;
While the man who truth despises,
    And refuses to obey,
        In a moment,
Cursed of God, shall melt away.

Therefore let us praise Jehovah,
    Sound his glorious name on high,
Sing his praises, and moreover
    By our actions magnify
        Our Redeemer,
Who by blood has brought us nigh.

Who this mighty champion is,
Nature answers from within;
He is my own wickedness,
He my close besetting sin.

In the strength of Jesus' name
With the monster I will fight;
Feeble and unarm'd I am
Save with God's eternal might.

Mindful of his mercies past
Still I trust the same to prove,
Still my helpless soul I cast
On my Lord's redeeming love.

Full oft the clouds of deepest woe,
    So sweet a message bear,
Dark though they seem, 'twere hard to find
    A frown of anger there.

It needs our hearts be wean'd from earth,
    It needs that we be driven,
By loss of every earthly stay,
    To seek our joys in heaven.

For we must follow in the path
    Our Lord and Saviour run;
We must not find a resting-place
    Where he we love had none.

I. SAMUEL XVII. 1—12; 14—18. ✓

N OW the Philistines gathered together their armies to battle, and were gathered together at Shochoh, which *belongeth* to Judah.

Israel had sinned, and her king had cast off his allegiance, and therefore chastisement came. God. has the hearts of wicked Philistines in his hands, and can move them to be a scourge to his offending people.

2, 3 And Saul and the men of Israel were gathered together, and pitched by the valley of Elah, and set the battle in array against the Philistines. And the Philistines stood on a mountain on the one side, and Israel stood on a mountain on the other side: and *there was* a valley between them. *(For forty days they remained gazing upon one another. O, had Israel been faithful to her God, she would soon have been delivered, for then the promise would have been fulfilled, "five of you shall chase an hundred, and an hundred of you shall put ten thousand to flight." When God is gone, the strongest are as weak as water.)*

4, 5 And there went out a champion out of the camp of the Philistines, named Goliath, of Gath, whose height *was* six cubits and a span *(or about ten feet.)* And *he had* an helmet of brass upon his head, and he *was* armed with a coat of mail; and the weight of the coat *was* five thousand shekels of brass.

6 And *he had* greaves of brass upon his legs, and a target of brass between his shoulders.

7 And the staff of his spear *was* like a weaver's beam; and his spear's head *weighed* six hundred shekels of iron: and one bearing a shield went before him.

8 And he stood and cried unto the armies of Israel, and said unto them, Why are ye come out to set *your* battle in array? am not I a Philistine, and ye servants to Saul? choose you a man for you, and let him come down to me.

9 If he be able to fight with me, and to kill me, then will we be your servants: but if I prevail against him, and kill him, then shall ye be our servants, and serve us.

10 And the Philistine said, I defy the armies of Israel this day; give me a man, that we may fight together. *(Goliath is called " the champion," or, in the Hebrew, the middle-man or Mediator, he typifies Satan, our great enemy. Where could*

we have found another Mediator to meet him if the Son of David had not stood in the gap?)

11 When Saul and all Israel heard those words of the Philistine, they were dismayed, and greatly afraid. *(Time was when Saul, who was himself gigantic, would have accepted the challenge, but when God departs from a man he becomes a coward. "Without me ye can do nothing," is a great truth. Many have learned it to their sorrow.)*

12 ¶ Now David *was* the son of that Ephrathite of Beth-lehem-judah, whose name *was* Jesse; and he had eight sons: and the man went among men *for* an old man in the days of Saul.

When made feeble by old age it is a great blessing to have vigorous sons to fill up the ranks of the Lord's army. O ye young men, fill the places of your godly sires.

14 And David *was* the youngest: and the three eldest followed Saul.

15 But David went and returned from Saul to feed his father's sheep at Beth-lehem.

Probably he had long before left the courts of Saul for the solitude he loved so well, just as our Lord after going up to the temple went back to his parents, and was subject unto them.

16 And the Philistine drew near morning and evening, and presented himself forty days.

Even as for forty days Satan tempted our Lord.

17, 18 And Jesse said unto David his son, Take now for thy brethren an ephah of this parched *corn*, and these ten loaves, and run to the camp to thy brethren; And carry these ten cheeses unto the captain of *their* thousand, and look how thy brethren fare, and take their pledge. *(The great Antitype of David visited his brethren below, his Father sending him to us with heavenly food, and messages of love. Alas, like David, he met with a churlish reception, " he came unto his own, and his own received him not." The Lord grant that in our hearts he may ever find a welcome.)*

O Son of Jesse come
Into our camp to day;
Bring with thee much-loved food from home,
And bear our pledge away.

Goliath's threatening words
Oft make thy people fear;
Vain are our numbers, and our swords,
Till thou art with us here.

I. SAMUEL XVII. 20—37.

AND David rose up early in the morning, and left the sheep with a keeper, and took, and went, as Jesse had commanded him ; and he came to the trench, as the host was going forth to the fight, and shouted for the battle. *(He was a good shepherd and did not leave his sheep without a keeper, in this being a fit type of the great Shepherd and Bishop of souls.)*

21 For Israel and the Philistines had put the battle in array, army against army.

22 And David left his carriage *(or baggage)* in the hand of the keeper of the carriage, and ran into the army, and came and saluted his brethren.

23 And as he talked with them, behold, there came up the champion, the Philistine of Gath, Goliath by name, out of the armies of the Philistines, and spake according to the same words : and David heard *them.*

24 And all the men of Israel, when they saw the man, fled from him, and were sore afraid.

25 And the men of Israel said, Have ye seen this man that is come up ? surely to defy Israel is he come up : and it shall be, *that* the man who killeth him, the king will enrich him with great riches, and will give him his daughter, and make his father's house free in Israel. *Such was the prize offered to our champion the Lord Jesus, "the king's daughter all glorious within," was to be the reward of his battle.*

26, 27 And David spake to the men that stood by him, saying, What shall be done to the man that killeth this Philistine, and taketh away the reproach from Israel ? for who *is* this uncircumcised Philistine, that he should defy the armies of the living God ? And the people answered him after this manner, saying, So shall it be done to the man that killeth him.

28 ¶ And Eliab his eldest brother heard when he spake unto the men; and Eliab's anger was kindled against David, and he said, Why camest thou down hither ? and with whom hast thou left those few sheep in the wilderness ? I know thy pride, and the naughtiness of thine heart; for thou art come down that thou mightest see the battle.

29 And David said, What have I now done ? *Is there* not a cause ? *(Brave men may expect to be misunderstood and charged with forward-*

ness ; but it will be to their honour if they bear it patiently and still persevere. Our Lord was rejected by his brethren, but he did not desist from his work of love, neither did he answer them roughly. If we can conquer our own spirits we shall be able to conquer others.)

30,31 And he turned from him toward another, and spake after the same manner : and the people answered him again after the former manner. And when the words were heard which David spake, they rehearsed *them* before Saul : and he sent for him. *(He was at his wit's end, and therefore caught at this which he looked upon as a desperate hope. Despair of all other salvation often drives men to Jesus.)*

32 ¶ And David said to Saul, Let no man's heart fail because of him; thy servant will go and fight with this Philistine.

33 And Saul said to David, Thou art not able to go against this Philistine to fight with him : for thou *art but* a youth, and he a man of war from his youth. *(So the Jewish nation thought our Lord quite unable to save them, and therefore despised him : but nevertheless he won the victory over the dread foe of men.)*

34 And David said unto Saul, Thy servant kept his father's sheep, and there came a lion, and a bear, and took a lamb out of the flock :

35 And I went out after him, and smote him, and delivered *it* out of his mouth : and when he arose against me, I caught *him* by his beard, and smote him, and slew him. *(Christ also delivers his own sheep out of the power of him who goeth about like a roaring lion, and of him it is said, "thou shalt tread upon the lion and adder, the young lion and the dragon shalt thou trample under feet.")*

36 Thy servant slew both the lion and the bear : and this uncircumcised Philistine shall be as one of them, seeing he hath defied the armies of the living God.

37 David said moreover, The LORD that delivered me out of the paw of the lion, and out of the paw of the bear, he will deliver me out of the hand of this Philistine. And Saul said unto David, Go, and the LORD be with thee.

It is wise to conclude that what God has done for us once he can and will do again. We have an unchanging helper to rely upon, and therefore we may reckon on continual help.

I. SAMUEL XVII. 38—51. ✓

AND Saul armed David with his armour, and he put an helmet of brass upon his head; also he armed him with a coat of mail.

39 And David girded his sword upon his armour, and he assayed to go; for he had not proved *it*. And David said unto Saul, I cannot go with these; for I have not proved *them*. And David put them off him. (*Carnal weapons suited not the man whose reliance was upon the Lord, neither did they suit our Lord, to whom they were offered, only to be declined. To this day our Lord's battles are not fought with the weapons of human force, but with those of spiritual energy, his warriors are not clad in martial mail, but in the armour of righteousness.*)

40 And he took his staff in his hand, and chose him five smooth stones out of the brook, and put them in a shepherd's bag which he had, even in a scrip; and his sling *was* in his hand: and he drew near to the Philistine.

These were suitable weapons for a shepherd, and he was accustomed to their use. They were also humble, practical, commonsense weapons, which had no glitter about them, but very much of appropriateness and hopefulness. Brave and believing men act as cautiously in the choice of weapons as if all depended upon themselves, and then trust wholly in the Lord, knowing that their success depends alone upon him.

What a wonderful picture is the scene before us if we read the typical meaning, and see Jesus, the Shepherd, with the pastoral staff in his hand, going forth to sling the smooth stones of the word at the head of the dread enemy of his people. Glorious hero, we bless thee!

41 And the Philistine came on and drew near unto David; and the man that bare the shield *went* before him.

42—44 And when the Philistine looked about, and saw David, he disdained him: for he was *but* a youth, and ruddy, and of a fair countenance. And the Philistine said unto David, *Am* I a dog, that thou comest to me with staves? And the Philistine cursed David by his gods. And the Philistine said to David, Come to me, and I will give thy flesh unto the fowls of the air, and to the beasts of the field.

Bragging words are little worth.

45 Then said David to the Philistine, Thou comest to me with a sword, and with a spear, and with a shield: but I come to thee in the name of the LORD of hosts, the God of the armies of Israel, whom thou hast defied.

46, 47 This day will the LORD deliver thee into mine hand; and I will smite thee, and take thine head from thee; and I will give the carcases of the host of the Philistines this day unto the fowls of the air, and to the wild beasts of the earth; that all the earth may know that there is a God in Israel. And all this assembly shall know that the LORD saveth not with sword and spear: for the battle *is* the LORD's, and he will give you into our hands. (*Here was no boasting, but faith spoke firmly and bravely.*)

48 And it came to pass, when the Philistine arose, and came and drew nigh to meet David, that David hasted, and ran toward the army to meet the Philistine.

His foot and his hand went with his tongue, he was a doer as well as a speaker. Our Lord was a prophet, mighty in deed as well as word.

49 And David put his hand in his bag, and took thence a stone, and slang *it*, and smote the Philistine in his forehead, that the stone sunk into his forehead; and he fell upon his face to the earth. (*How are the mighty fallen! and that too by the hand of a youth, despised and ridiculed! Thus by the foolishness of preaching, the Lord smites his adversary.*)

50 So David prevailed over the Philistine with a sling and with a stone, and smote the Philistine, and slew him; but *there was* no sword in the hand of David. (*He now needed one, and as faith had led him to come forward empty-handed, it was certain that his God would supply his need. If we will only trust God, everything will be supplied as we need it.*)

51 Therefore David ran, and stood upon the Philistine, and took his sword, and drew it out of the sheath thereof, and slew him, and cut off his head therewith. (*Augustine beautifully says, " Our David has cast down our adversary, and cut off his head with his own sword," for " by death he destroyed him that had the power of death, that is the devil." The crucifixion of our Lord was the execution of sin. God's enemies furnish weapons for their own destruction.*) And when the Philistines saw their champion was dead, they fled.

I. SAMUEL XVII. 55—58. ✓

A ND when Saul saw David go forth against
the Philistine, he said unto Abner, the
captain of the host, Abner, whose son *is* this
youth? And Abner said, *As* thy soul liveth,
O king, I cannot tell. And the king said,
Enquire thou whose son the stripling *is*. (*Yet
he ought to have known his former minstrel.
Great men have usually bad memories towards
those who serve them. David's appearance had
much changed, and the king too was almost insane
when he last saw him; and, therefore, was not
likely to remember him. To this day the Jews
cannot answer that question concerning Christ
"Whose son is he?" The blind world, looking
for an outward glory, does not recognise the Son
of the Highest.*)

57, 58 And as David returned from the
slaughter of the Philistine, Abner took him, and
brought him before Saul with the head of the
Philistine in his hand. And Saul said to him,
Whose son *art* thou, *thou* young man? And
David answered *I am* the son of thy servant
Jesse the Beth-lehemite. (*Hard is it to be
honoured with such a victory, and yet remain
humble. David showed his greatness as much
after the fight as he did before and in the conflict.
Had Saul been a man of truth he would have
given the youthful hero his daughter's hand, and
every other possible reward.*)

CHAPTER XVIII. 6—16; 28—30.

6, 7 And it came to pass as they came, when
David was returned from the slaughter of the
Philistine, that the women came out of all cities
of Israel, singing and dancing, to meet king
Saul, with tabrets, with joy, and with instruments
of musick. And the women answered *one another*
as they played, and said, Saul hath slain his
thousands, and David his ten thousands.
*When our Lord returned triumphant over
death and hell, leading captivity captive, the
heavenly ones praised him in their songs. Do
not our hearts also exult in the conquests of
Immanuel our King?*

8, 9 And Saul was very wroth, and the saying
displeased him; and he said, They have ascribed unto David ten thousands, and to me they
have ascribed *but* thousands: and *what* can he
have more but the kingdom? And Saul eyed
David from that day and forward. (*Envy, first-*

*born of hell, whom wilt thou not assail! The
modest behaviour of David ought to have protected
him from Saul's bitterness. We need not wonder
that the old mania came back to Saul. He who
admits an evil temper into his heart, must not
marvel if a melancholy spirit enters with it to
haunt the chambers of his soul.*)

10 ¶ And it came to pass on the morrow,
that the evil spirit from God came upon Saul,
and he prophesied in the midst of the house:
and David played with his hand, as at other
times: and *there was* a javelin in Saul's hand.

11 And Saul cast the javelin; for he said, I
will smite David even to the wall *with it*. And
David avoided out of his presence twice.

12 And Saul was afraid of David, because
the LORD was with him, and was departed from
Saul.

13 Therefore Saul removed him from him,
and made him his captain over a thousand; and
he went out and came in before the people.

14 And David behaved himself wisely in all
his ways; and the LORD *was* with him.

15 Wherefore when Saul saw that he behaved
himself very wisely, he was afraid of him.
*We might have expected to find David afraid
of his powerful enemy, but the case was reversed.
The wicked flee when no man pursueth, but the
righteous are bold as a lion.*

16 But all Israel and Judah loved David,
because he went out and came in before them.
*The more they saw him, the better they loved
him. He was an active leader, and ever at his
post. Diligence and perseverance command the
esteem of the wise.*

28, 29 And Saul saw and knew that the LORD
was with David, and *that* Michal Saul's daughter
loved him. And Saul was yet the more afraid of
David; and Saul became David's enemy continually.

30 Then the princes of the Philistines went
forth: and it came to pass, after they went forth,
that David behaved himself more wisely than
all the servants of Saul; so that his name was
much set by. (*Good conduct is the great thing
in life. The Lord make us followers of him,
who was greater than David, of whom it was
said, "He hath done all things well." Holy
Spirit, fashion us in the image of our Lord, that
he may be glorified in us.*)

SAUL'S *fierce enmity was a sore trial to David, but the Lord found him a solace even in the king's family, for both his eldest son Jonathan and his daughter Michal loved David.*

I. SAMUEL XVIII. 3, 4.

3 Then Jonathan and David made a covenant, because he loved him as his own soul.

Yet Jonathan knew that David was to be king, and that he himself would never wear the crown. His was disinterested affection, most beautiful to witness. Such ought to be our love for Jesus; we should be knit to him in bonds of purest love.

4 And Jonathan stripped himself of the robe that was upon him, and gave it to David, and his garments, even to his sword, and to his bow, and to his girdle. *(Thus should we delight to strip ourselves for Jesus. Let him have all, for he deserves all.)*

CHAPTER XIX. 1; 4—18.

1 And Saul spake to Jonathan his son, and to all his servants, that they should kill David.

He was now worse than ever, or he would not have spoken to others to aid him in a dastardly murder. When God leaves a man, the devil comes to him.

4, 5 And Jonathan spake good of David unto Saul his father, and said unto him, Let not the king sin against his servant, against David; because he hath not sinned against thee, and because his works *have been* to thee-ward very good : For he did put his life in his hand, and slew the Philistine, and the LORD wrought a great salvation for all Israel : thou sawest *it*, and didst rejoice : wherefore then wilt thou sin against innocent blood, to slay David without a cause ? *(Thus Jonathan proved himself a real friend. We ought always to be ready to speak up for those who are falsely condemned.)*

6 And Saul hearkened unto the voice of Jonathan : and Saul sware, *As* the LORD liveth, he shall not be slain. *(Little however did his oath bind him. He was never in a good frame of mind long together. Envy cannot be quiet.)*

7 And Jonathan called David, and Jonathan shewed him all those things. And Jonathan brought David to Saul, and he was in his presence, as in times past.

8 ¶ And there was war again : and David went out, and fought with the Philistines, and slew them with a great slaughter; and they fled from him.

9 And the evil spirit from the LORD was upon Saul, as he sat in his house with his javelin in his hand : and David played with *his* hand.

10 And Saul sought to smite David even to the wall with the javelin; but he slipped away out of Saul's presence, and he smote the javelin into the wall : and David fled, and escaped that night :

*" Not a single shaft can hit,
Till the God of love thinks fit."*

We are safe anywhere while the Lord has work for us to do. Be it ours to live with the harp in our hand, praising God and blessing our fellow-men, and we shall be preserved from the javelins of our foes.

11 Saul also sent messengers unto David's house, to watch him, and to slay him in the morning : and Michal David's wife told him, saying, If thou save not thy life to night, to morrow thou shalt be slain.

12 ¶ So Michal let David down through a window : and he went, and fled, and escaped.

13 And Michal took an image, and laid *it* in the bed, and put a pillow of goats' *hair* for his bolster, and covered *it* with a cloth.

14 And when Saul sent messengers to take David, she said, He *is* sick.

15 And Saul sent the messengers *again* to see David, saying, Bring him up to me in the bed, that I may slay him.

16 And when the messengers were come in, behold, *there was* an image in the bed, with a pillow of goats' *hair* for his bolster. *(We cannot admire Michal's deceit, nor yet her having idols in her house. She was Saul's daughter, and came of a bad stock. The Lord, however, overruled her love for David, so that the persecuted one escaped. God will preserve his own.)*

17 And Saul said unto Michal, Why hast thou deceived me so, and sent away mine enemy, that he is escaped ? And Michal answered Saul, He said unto me, Let me go; why should I kill thee ?

18 ¶ So David fled, and escaped, and came to Samuel to Ramah, and told him all that Saul had done to him. And he and Samuel went and dwelt in Naioth.

PSALM LIX.

THIS *Psalm is entitled* " A golden Psalm of David, when Saul sent, and they watched the house to kill him."

1 Deliver me from mine enemies, O my God : defend me from them that rise up against me. *They were all round the house armed with the royal warrant and with a sufficient force to seize him, yet he had faith enough to pray and not to give up in despair. God has ways of escape for his birds of paradise, even when the fowler's nets are most cunningly spread.*

2 Deliver me from the workers of iniquity, and save me from bloody men. *(When a habitation is beset by thieves, the good man of the house rings the alarm bell, and in these verses we hear it sounding aloud, "deliver me," "defend me," "deliver me," "save me." David could not fall by Saul's hand while he prayed in this fashion.)*

3 For, lo, they lie in wait for my soul : the mighty are gathered against me ; not *for* my transgression, nor *for* my sin, O LORD.

4 They run and prepare themselves without *my* fault : awake to help me, and behold.

5 Thou therefore, O LORD God of hosts, the God of Israel, awake to visit all the heathen : be not merciful to any wicked transgressors. Selah. *(Be merciful to them as men, but not as transgressors, for mercy to such criminals would be cruelty to the inoffensive.)*

6 They return at evening : they make a noise like a dog, and go round about the city.

7 Behold, they belch out with their mouth : swords *are* in their lips : for who, *say they,* doth hear ? *(None are so utterly brutal and abandoned as those who think that God has deserted the world, and no longer takes notice of the words and actions of men.)*

8 But thou, O LORD, shalt laugh at them ; thou shalt have all the heathen in derision.

9 *Because of* his strength will I wait upon thee : for God *is* my defence. *(Is my persecutor strong ? Then, my God, for this very reason I will turn myself to thee, and leave my matters in thy hand. It is our wisdom to see in the greatness of our difficulties a reason for casting ourselves upon the Lord.)*

10 The God of my mercy shall prevent me : God shall let me see *my desire* upon mine enemies.

11 Slay them not, lest my people forget : scatter them by thy power ; and bring them down, O LORD our shield. *(Enemies help to keep God's servants awake, therefore let them live, but let them have no power to do such evil as they desire.)*

12 *For* the sin of their mouth *and* the words of their lips let them even be taken in their pride : and for cursing and lying *which* they speak. *(Swearers are generally liars.)*

13 Consume *them* in wrath, consume *them,* that they *may* not *be :* and let them know that God ruleth in Jacob unto the ends of the earth. Selah.

14 And at evening let them return ; *and* let them make a noise like a dog, and go round about the city.

15 Let them wander up and down for meat, and grudge if they be not satisfied. *(David speaks as a prophet, and not as a man of vindictive spirit seeking revenge ; this was very far from being his character, for when his enemies were in his power he often spared them, taking no vengeance upon them but the sacred one of heaping coals of fire upon their heads by his kindness. These passages may be read as predictions rather than as wishes.)*

16 But I will sing of thy power ; yea, I will sing aloud of thy mercy in the morning : for thou hast been my defence and refuge in the day of my trouble.

17 Unto thee, O my strength, will I sing : for God *is* my defence, *and* the God of my mercy. *(David felt sure of escaping, for he believed that God regarded prayer ; and therefore he began to sing unto his deliverer. This was no easy task. How should we have acted under the circumstances ? Furious murderers were in the street around the house, thirsting for the good man's blood, and yet his faith enabled him to sing praises to God. O for the like confidence !)*

> Thou'rt my rock and my defence ;
> Thou a tower unto Thy saints ;
> Thee I make my confidence,
> Thee I'll trust, though nature faints.
>
> Glad thy mercies will I sing,
> All thy power and love confess ;
> Thou hast been, O heavenly King,
> My safe refuge in distress !

I. SAMUEL XXI. 1—3 ; 6—7.

THEN came David to Nob to Ahimelech the priest : *(David being driven away by Saul from the prophet Samuel, fled at once to the priests. He loved the servants of God, and would not leave their company:)* and Ahimelech was afraid at the meeting of David, and said unto him, Why *art* thou alone, and no man with thee? *(Seeing David alone, and evidently in distress, Ahimelech suspected something wrong.)*

2 And David said unto Ahimelech the priest, The king hath commanded me a business, and hath said unto me, Let no man know anything of the business whereabout I send thee, and what I have commanded thee.

Here David spake falsely, and his error is recorded not to his honour, but for our warning. This sad falsehood led to terrible consequences. O that good men could always trust in the Lord.

3 Now therefore what is under thine hand? give *me* five *loaves of* bread in mine hand, or what there is present.

6 So the priest gave him hallowed *bread :* for there was no bread there but the shewbread, that was taken from before the LORD, to put hot bread in the day when it was taken away.

This act was a violation of the ceremonial law, but in a case of necessity it was justified, for the Lord loves mercy better than sacrifice.

7 Now a certain man of the servants of Saul *was* there that day, and his name *was* Doeg, an Edomite.

This man, being full of enmity, hastened away to accuse the priests of succouring a traitor.

CHAPTER XXII. 9—23.

9, 10 Then answered Doeg the Edomite, and said, I saw the son of Jesse coming to Nob, to Ahimelech. And he enquired of the LORD for him, and gave him victuals, and gave him the sword of Goliath the Philistine.

11,12,13 Then the king sent to call Ahimelech, the priest, and all his father's house, the priests that *were* in Nob : and they came all of them to the king. And Saul said, Hear now, thou son of Ahitub. And he answered, Here I *am*, my lord. And Saul said unto him, Why have ye conspired against me, thou and the son of Jesse, in that thou hast given him bread, and a sword, and hast enquired of God for him, that he should rise against me, to lie in wait, as at this day?

14, 15 Then Ahimelech answered the king, and said, And who *is so* faithful among all thy servants as David, which is the king's son in law, and goeth at thy bidding, and is honourable in thine house? Did I then begin to enquire of God for him? be it far from me : let not the king impute *any* thing unto his servant, *nor* to all the house of my father : for thy servant knew nothing of all this, less or more. *(The simple-minded high priest was blameless, he knew nothing of the feud between Saul and David. David had deceived him, and Doeg knew that he had done so, but did not mention that circumstance. When we report a matter, we are bound to tell it all, or the most innocent may be made to appear guilty.)*

16 And the king said, Thou shalt surely die, Ahimelech, thou, and all thy father's house.

17 ¶ And the king said unto the footmen that stood about him, Turn, and slay the priests of the LORD ; because their hand also *is* with David. But the servants of the king would not put forth their hand to fall upon the priests of the LORD.

18 And the king said to Doeg, Turn thou, and fall upon the priests. And Doeg the Edomite turned, and he fell upon the priests, and slew on that day fourscore and five persons that did wear a linen ephod. *(None but a foreigner would fulfil the cruel edict. Thus the house of Eli was again smitten as the Lord had threatened, but base was the wretched spy whose one-sided report caused so many murders, and hateful the king who commanded the slaughter.)*

19 And Nob, the city of the priests, smote he with the edge of the sword, both men and women, children and sucklings, and oxen, and asses, and sheep, with the edge of the sword.

20 ¶ And one of the sons of Ahimelech, named Abiathar, escaped, and fled after David.

21 And Abiathar shewed David that Saul had slain the LORD's priests.

22 And David said unto Abiathar, I knew *it* that day, when Doeg the Edomite *was* there, that he would surely tell Saul : I have occasioned *the death* of all the persons of thy father's house.

23 Abide thou with me, fear not : for he that seeketh my life seeketh thy life : but with me thou *shalt be* in safeguard. *(David must have been cut to the heart when he saw the result of his falsehood. The Lord keep each of us true in every word that we utter.)*

PSALM LII.

DAVID, *at this time, wrote a psalm, of which the title is—*

To the chief Musician, Maschil, A Psalm of David, when Doeg the Edomite came and told Saul, and said unto him, David is come to the house of Ahimelech.

1 Why boastest thou thyself in mischief, O mighty man? *(Doeg had small room for boasting in having slaughtered a band of defenceless persons who never drew a sword. He ought to have been ashamed of his cowardice. If David here refers to Saul, the words are equally forcible; how could a man who had in former days been valiant in arms, now rejoice in the murder of the helpless?)* the goodness of God endureth continually. *(If priests be slain, their Master lives. God's cause lives on, though good men be hunted down.)*

2 Thy tongue deviseth mischiefs; like a sharp razor, working deceitfully. *(Eastern barbers use the razor so well that a man scarcely knows that his hair is shorn; and so with wily cunning, base men injure the servants of God. Doeg's tongue with its soft but sharp speeches, cut off the priests of the Lord. May the Lord save us from slanderers and backbiters.)*

3 Thou lovest evil more than good; *and* lying rather than to speak righteousness. Selah. *See how low a man can descend so as not only to utter falsehoods, but to love them better than truth. It is a mark of the foulest character when a man actually prefers dishonesty to justice.*

4 Thou lovest all devouring words, O *thou* deceitful tongue. *(Some evil persons have a taste for calumny, they are never better pleased than when they can injure those who are better than themselves. Shun them. Above all never fall into their sin.)*

5 God shall likewise destroy thee for ever, he shall take thee away, and pluck thee out of *thy* dwelling place, and root thee out of the land of the living. Selah. *(God will one day deal out justice to slanderers, he will pull them up like ill-weeds, and cast them into the fire. A terrible portion awaits all liars. They will not let others live, and God will not let them live.)*

6 The righteous also shall see, and fear, and shall laugh at him :

7 Lo, *this is* the man *that* made not God his strength; but trusted in the abundance of his riches, *and* strengthened himself in his wickedness. *(Good men will look down upon plotters and slanderers with supreme contempt, and the Lord will give them good cause to do so, for they shall be taken in their own net, their subtlety shall slay them. Persecutors may be rich, but their wealth shall not save them; justice has ways and methods for bringing the great ones of the earth to its bar. God cannot be bribed; he will avenge his own calumniated servants, and that right early. Therefore let us patiently endure all manner of slander for Christ's sake.)*

8 But I *am* like a green olive tree in the house of God : I trust in the mercy of God for ever and ever. *(Though much abused and hated, David was not plucked up nor destroyed as his enemies would be. He was one of the divine family, and found himself in the household of God everywhere; and yet more, he found himself fresh and vigorous at all seasons like an evergreen olive. If Nob was, as some think, situated upon the Mount of Olives, we can understand why the Psalmist was led to adopt this simile. Though Nob was gone the olives stood, and David also lived on despite Saul's enmity. The psalmist's faith, like an olive, was abiding and perpetual, its leaf did not wither, neither did its fruit fail. It renewed its youth from day to day, and possessed a sacred immortality. He knew God's mercy to be eternal, and in that he trusted. What a rock to build on! What a fortress to fly to!)*

9 I will praise thee for ever, because thou hast done *it:* and I will wait on thy name; for *it is* good before thy saints. *(David's thankfulness was continual, like the mercy in which he rejoiced; he looked upon God's punishment of his foes as already accomplished—"thou hast done it," and therefore he waited patiently till the bright days should dawn for himself and the persecuted church. He felt, as we ought to feel, that quietly to tarry the Lord's leisure, is good for all those who would be accounted the Lord's saints, and is also one of the best means of doing good to our fellow-believers, who from our patient waiting will learn how to possess their souls in peace.)*

AFTER *David had obtained food from the priests, he fled from the country in fear.*

I. SAMUEL XXI. 10—15.

10 ¶ And David arose, and fled that day for fear of Saul, and went to Achish the king of Gath. (*It has an evil look for an Israelite to flee to the Philistines. It was sure to bring the man of God into trouble, to associate with the heathen.*)

11 And the servants of Achish said unto him, *Is* not this David the king of the land? did they not sing one to another of him in dances, saying, Saul hath slain his thousands, and David his ten thousands?

12, 13 And David laid up these words in his heart, and was sore afraid of Achish the king of Gath. And he changed his behaviour before them, and feigned himself mad in their hands, and scrabbled on the doors of the gate, and let his spittle fall down upon his beard.

14 Then said Achish unto his servants, Lo, ye see the man is mad: wherefore *then* have ye brought him to me?

15 Have I need of mad men, that ye have brought this *fellow* to play the mad man in my presence? shall this *fellow* come into my house?

David escaped, but by a very humiliating and unsatisfactory stratagem. When we leave the plain path of faith, there is no telling what shifts we may be put to. How truthful is the Holy Ghost in thus recording the errors of the man after God's own heart: let us take warning.

In the book of Psalms we find a memorial of David's peril and deliverance.

PSALM LVI.

To the chief Musician upon Jonath-elem-rechokim, (*or the silent dove among strangers,*) Michtam of David, when the Philistines took him in Gath.

BE merciful unto me, O God : for man would swallow me up; he fighting daily oppresseth me. (*Saul was always hunting after his life. David told his grief to his Lord, which was a far better method than running to Achish. His narrow escape had taught him wisdom.*)

2 Mine enemies would daily swallow *me* up : for *they be* many that fight against me, O thou most High.

3 What time I am afraid, I will trust in thee. *Those who trust in God when they are afraid, will soon learn to trust and not be afraid. To*

trust *when there is no cause for fear is but the name of faith ; but to be reliant upon God in real danger is the faith of God's elect.*

4 In God I will praise his word, in God I have put my trust; I will not fear what flesh can do unto me. (*Faith, though it may grow dim in a believer, burns up again. See how strong David's trust in God became.*)

5, 6 Every day they wrest my words : all their thoughts *are* against me for evil. They gather themselves together, they hide themselves, they mark my steps, when they wait for my soul.

7 Shall they escape by iniquity? in *thine* anger cast down the people, O God.

8 Thou tellest my wanderings : put thou my tears into thy bottle : *are they* not in thy book?

9 When I cry *unto thee*, then shall mine enemies turn back : this I know; for God *is* for me.

10 In God will I praise *his* word: in the LORD will I praise *his* word.

11 In God have I put my trust : I will not be afraid what man can do unto me.

He had been afraid, and therefore he redoubles his resolution to trust in the Lord for the future. Good men see their faults and avoid them.

12 Thy vows *are* upon me, O God : I will render praises unto thee. (*He had probably made a solemn vow in the time of his peril, and now he owns it. We ought to be true to all the resolves which we have made before the Lord. His Spirit will help us in this.*)

13 For thou hast delivered my soul from death : *wilt* not *thou deliver* my feet from falling, that I may walk before God in the light of the living? (*He saw that he had fallen, and this led him to seek for upholding grace. Let us now confess our own failings, and beseech the Lord to deliver our feet from falling in the future.*)

God counts the sorrows of his saints,
  Their groans affect his ears;
Thou hast a book for my complaints,
  A bottle for my tears.

When to thy throne I raise my cry,
  The wicked fear and flee :
So swift is prayer to reach the sky;
  So near is God to me.

In thee, most holy, just and true,
  I have reposed my trust ;
Nor will I fear what man can do,
  The offspring of the dust.

PSALM XXXIV.

A Psalm of David, when he changed his behaviour before Abimelech ; who drove him away, and he departed.

I WILL bless the LORD at all times : his praise *shall* continually *be* in my mouth.

2 My soul shall make her boast in the LORD : the humble shall hear *thereof,* and be glad.

This is the only kind of boasting which humble people can endure to hear. We may boast in the Lord as much as we can, and neither exceed the bounds of truth, nor cause anyone a moment's pain. Have we not cause to boast in the Lord? Let us not rob him of glory.

3 O magnify the LORD with me, and let us exalt his name together.

4 I sought the LORD, and he heard me, and delivered me from all my fears. *(This shall be our experience if we put the Lord to the same test. Why then do we indulge our fears when prayer is a sure remedy for them. Have we any troubles at this time ? Let us tell them all to our heavenly Father.)*

5 They looked unto him, and were lightened : and their faces were not ashamed. *(Not only David but all others who have looked to the Lord have found help.)*

6 This poor man cried, and the LORD heard *him,* and saved him out of all his troubles.

He describes himself as a poor man, and so he was, for he was driven from home and country. His prayer was only a cry, yet the Lord answered him, and all his troubles vanished. Let the poor in spirit, and the poor in pocket, try the psalmist's plan, and they will soon sing as he did.

7 The angel of the LORD encampeth round about them that fear him, and delivereth them.

8 O taste and see that the LORD *is* good : blessed *is* the man *that* trusteth in him.

No one knows how sweet honey is till he tastes it, and even so the sweetness of true religion cannot be learned by mere hearing, we must try it for ourselves. O Lord, help all in this family to prove the power of faith in Jesus, and the efficacy of prayer to God for themselves.

9 O fear the LORD, ye his saints : for *there is* no want to them that fear him.

10 The young lions do lack, and suffer hunger : but they that seek the LORD shall not want any good *thing. (Lions are strong, fierce,*

and crafty, yet they hunger ; men of the world are also very cunning and full of self-confidence, yet they are not satisfied. But humble believers, though often weak, and in the world's judgment, very foolish, are yet blessed with every needful blessing by their gracious God.)

11 Come, ye children, hearken unto me : I will teach you the fear of the LORD.

The very children in the streets of Gath had laughed at David, therefore when he came back again to his own people, he desired to do good to the little ones, and so make amends for some of the mischief he had done.

12 What man *is he that* desireth life, *and* loveth *many* days, that he may see good ?

13 Keep thy tongue from evil, and thy lips from speaking guile.

14 Depart from evil, and do good ; seek peace, and pursue it. *(Seek after peace, and if it flies from you, follow it up ; be zealous to promote love all around you. It is the way to live happily.)*

15 The eyes of the LORD *are* upon the righteous, and his ears *are* open unto their cry.

16 The face of the LORD *is* against them that do evil, to cut off the remembrance of them from the earth.

17 *The righteous* cry, and the LORD heareth, and delivereth them out of all their troubles.

18 The LORD *is* nigh unto them that are of a broken heart ; and saveth such as be of a contrite spirit. *(What a blessing to have a tender sense of sin. We have heard of persons dying of a broken heart, but if repentance breaks our hearts we shall live eternally.)*

19 Many *are* the afflictions of the righteous : but the LORD delivereth him out of them all.

20 He keepeth all his bones : not one of them is broken.

21 Evil shall slay the wicked : and they that hate the righteous shall be desolate.

22 The LORD redeemeth the soul of his servants : and none of them that trust in him shall be desolate. *(Faith is the great matter. To trust the Lord is the one important point. Beloved ones, are we all trusting in the Lord? The Lord lead us all to do so at this very hour. It would be dreadful indeed to die in unbelief.)*

I. SAMUEL XXII. 1, 2.

FINDING *himself in great danger among the Philistines, David returned to his own land, which he ought never to have left.*

1 David therefore departed thence, and escaped to the cave Adullam: *(where he found huge caverns capable of affording shelter and concealment for large numbers of persons. There David was in his right position, and might look for prosperity. He was in the place of separation, where believers should be found:)* and when his brethren and all his father's house heard *it,* they went down thither to him.

2 And every one *that was* in distress, and every one that *was* in debt, and every one *that was* discontented, gathered themselves unto him ; and he became a captain over them : and there were with him about four hundred men.

In this he became a type of our Lord Jesus, of whom it was said, " This man receiveth sinners and eateth with them." David's followers had been rendered desperate by the oppressions of Saul, but though they were bold and warlike men, they do not appear to have been evil in character; rather from their sympathy with David, and their general conduct, we may believe them to have been the best men in the kingdom, who, from that very cause, had been impoverished by Saul's spiteful treatment. Those who side with Jesus must expect to be treated as he was, and if this drives us into closer fellowship with our despised and rejected Lord, so much the better.

It was at this time that some of his boldest followers joined him.

I. CHRONICLES XI. 15—19.

15, 16, 17, 18, 19 Now three of the thirty captains went down to the rock to David, into the cave of Adullam ; and the host of the Philistines encamped in the valley of Rephaim. And David *was* then in the hold, and the Philistines' garrison *was* then at Beth-lehem. And David longed, and said, Oh that one would give me drink of the water of the well of Beth-lehem, that *is* at the gate ! And the three brake through the host of the Philistines, and drew water out of the well of Beth-lehem, that *was* by the gate, and took *it,* and brought *it* to David : but David would not drink *of* it, but poured it out to the LORD, And said, My God forbid it me, that I should do this thing : shall I drink the blood of these men that have put their lives in jeopardy ? for with *the jeopardy of* their lives they brought it. Therefore he would not drink it. These things did these three mightiest. *(This brave act showed the enthusiastic devotion of David's warriors. They were willing to gratify his smallest wish at the risk of their lives. In such a spirit ought the Lord Jesus to be served by us. David's refusal to drink shewed his tenderness for human life, and revealed one of the sources of his influence over his men. Our great Captain is yet more considerate and compassionate. O to love him more !)*

I. CHRONICLES XI. 10—14.

There came to David during the days of his wanderings several other brave men, some of whose exploits are recorded.

10 ¶ These also *are* the chief of the mighty men whom David had, who strengthened themselves with him in his kingdom, *and* with all Israel, to make him king, according to the word of the LORD concerning Israel.

11 And this *is* the number of the mighty men whom David had ; Jashobeam, an Hachmonite, the chief of the captains : he lifted up his spear against three hundred slain *by him* at one time.

12 And after him *was* Eleazar the son of Dodo, the Ahohite, who *was one* of the three mighties.

13, 14 He was with David at Pas-dammim, and there the Philistines were gathered together to battle, where was a parcel of ground full of barley ; and the people fled from before the Philistines. And they set themselves in the midst of *that* parcel, and delivered it, and slew the Philistines ; and the LORD saved *them* by a great deliverance.

The honours of Christ's kingdom are for those who can fight and suffer, not for idle professors and pretenders. The wonders wrought by these men were due to divine power, and that same might is ready to aid us in all holy conflicts and labours. At the last it will be thought the highest of all honours to have been associated with the Lord Jesus in his humiliations and reproaches. Who among us will take part with Christ in this evil generation, and go without the camp to him, bearing his reproach ? Whose name shall the recording angel place upon the roll this day ? Will not this house yield a man for Jesus?

WE *will now read two of David's cave psalms. He has left behind him the footprints of his wanderings, in his sacred songs. Many record their lives by successive murmurings and rebellions, David by hymns and prayers.*

PSALM CXLII.

Maschil of David (or an instructive Psalm); A Prayer
when he was in the cave.

1 I cried unto the LORD with my voice ; with my voice unto the LORD did I make my supplication.

2 I poured out my complaint before him ; I shewed before him my trouble. *(In his lonely wanderings he made the woods and caverns echo with his prayers.)*

> " *The calm retreat, the silent shade,*
> *With prayer and praise agree,*
> *And seem by thy kind bounty made*
> *For those who worship thee.*"

3 When my spirit was overwhelmed within me, then thou knewest my path. In the way wherein I walked have they privily laid a snare for me. *But since God knew his path, he was not taken in their snares. We owe eternal praises to the Lord for keeping us out of the hands of our enemies.*

4 I looked on *my* right hand, and beheld, but *there was* no man that would know me : refuge failed me ; no man cared for my soul.

5 I cried unto thee, O LORD : I said, Thou *art* my refuge *and* my portion in the land of the living.

6 Attend unto my cry ; for I am brought very low : deliver me from my persecutors ; for they are stronger than I. *(In the worst times all is well if we do not lose our faith in the Lord. No matter how powerful our enemies, we shall overcome if we cling to the divine arm.)*

7 Bring my soul out of prison, that I may praise thy name : the righteous shall compass me about ; for thou shalt deal bountifully with me. *(Very soon, good men and true mustered in great numbers under David's command, and he was no more left in utter loneliness, but became a powerful leader. The Lord can find us friends when we are friendless.)*

LET *us now read :—*

PSALM CXLI.

A Psalm of David.

1 Lord, I cry unto thee : make haste unto me ; give ear unto my voice, when I cry unto thee.

2 Let my prayer be set forth before thee *as* incense ; *and* the lifting up of my hands *as* the evening sacrifice. *(As David could not go to the tabernacle to offer sacrifice and incense, he felt that his prayers would be accepted instead thereof. If we are forced to stay at home on the Lord's day we should none the less worship the Lord in our hearts. The acceptance of prayer and praise does not depend upon place. True spiritual worship even in a cave, is far better than the finest formal service, though offered in a cathedral.)*

3 Set a watch, O LORD, before my mouth ; keep the door of my lips.

4 Incline not my heart to *any* evil thing, to practise wicked works with men that work iniquity : and let me not eat of their dainties. *Even in his lowest case he did not wish to be as the wicked are when at their best.*

5 Let the righteous smite me ; *it shall be* a kindness : and let him reprove me ; *it shall be* an excellent oil, *which* shall not break my head : for yet my prayer also *shall be* in their calamities. *It needs great grace to give reproofs aright, but it needs more to take them aright. Wise men are thankful when their errors are pointed out to them ; but, alas ! wise men are few.*

6 When their judges are overthrown in stony places, they shall hear my words ; for they are sweet. *(When the world is bitter the word is sweet. Those who care not for us now may be glad of our comfort in their distress.)*

7 Our bones are scattered at the grave's mouth, as when one cutteth and cleaveth *wood* upon the earth. *(He was like wood broken and split up for the fire ; he felt that he and his followers were devoted to death, yet he turned to God with hope.)*

8, 9 But mine eyes *are* unto thee, O GOD the Lord : in thee is my trust ; leave not my soul destitute. Keep me from the snares **which** they have laid for me, and the gins of the workers of iniquity.

10 Let the wicked fall into their own nets, whilst that I withal escape. *(His prayer was heard. He was preserved, and even so shall all believers be, if they will but repose their souls upon the faithfulness of God. All is well if faith be firm.)*

Fierce burning coals of juniper,
 And arrows of the strong,
Await those false and cruel tongues
 Which do the righteous wrong.

But as for me my song shall rise
 Before Jehovah's throne,
For he has seen my deep distress,
 And hearken'd to my groan.

In vain the powers of darkness try
 To work the church's ill,
The Friend of sinners reigns on high,
 And checks them at his will.

Though mischief in their hearts may dwell,
 And on their tongues deceit,
A word of his their pride can quell,
 And all their aims defeat.

My trust is in his grace alone;
 His house shall be my home,
How sweet his mercies past to own,
 And hope for more to come.

Oh! taste and see that God is good,
 And that his saints are blest;
Grace never can be understood
 Till in the heart it rest.

Oh! trust the Lord, desponding saint;
 Of all that to him flee,
There's none hath ever been in want,
 And none shall ever be.

Captain of our soul's salvation,
 Perfect made thyself in woe,
Thou didst seek no reputation
 When thou wast with man below:
  'Mid the lowest,
  'Mid the vilest thou didst go.

They whose ills were most distressing,
 They who were of sinners chief,
Gladly sought thy gracious blessing,
 Ran to thee for sure relief:
  Thou didst bless them—
  Thou didst carry all their grief.

All with heavy debts embarrassed,
 Who no hope of pardon see,
All with fears of judgment harass'd,
 Look for help, O Lord, to thee:
  Thou dost freely
  Welcome all who come to thee.

I bow towards thy mercy-seat:
Haste, Lord, thy servant haste to meet,
To thee, addressed, my sorrows rise;
Lord, bend thine ear, accept my cries.

O let my prayer before thee come,
Sweet as the censer's fragrant fume;
And may the hands, which thus I rear,
An evening sacrifice appear!

O glorious hour! O blest abode!
I shall be near and like my God;
And flesh and sin no more control
The sacred pleasures of my soul.

My flesh shall slumber in the ground,
'Till the last trumpet's joyful sound;
Then burst the chains with sweet surprise,
And in my Saviour's image rise.

256   " Thou shalt guide me with thy counsel."   MAY 2.—MORNING.

[Or August 31.]

IN *the passage which we shall now read, we shall see an instance of David's patriotism. Although he was persecuted in his own country, he did not cease from loving his nation, but took a deep interest in all that concerned it. When he found that the Philistines were plundering the granaries of Keilah, he marched with his little army against them.*

I. SAMUEL XXIII. 1—13.

1 Then they told David, saying, Behold, the Philistines fight against Keilah, and they rob the threshingfloors.

2 Therefore David enquired of the LORD, saying, Shall I go and smite these Philistines ? And the LORD said unto David, Go, and smite the Philistines, and save Keilah.

Here we see the deep religiousness of David : he would do nothing till he had waited upon God. O for more of this holy caution.

3 And David's men said unto him, Behold, we be afraid here in Judah : how much more then if we come to Keilah against the armies of the Philistines ? *(Brave as they were, they judged this to be a rash enterprise, for they would have two enemies to fear—the Philistines and the soldiers of Saul. David listened to his men courteously, but he was not ruled by them. He turned to his God again for direction.)*

4 Then David enquired of the LORD yet again. And the LORD answered him and said, Arise, go down to Keilah ; for I will deliver the Philistines into thine hand.

5 So David and his men went to Keilah, and fought with the Philistines, and brought away their cattle, and smote them with a great slaughter. So David saved the inhabitants of Keilah. *(This was a gallant action, and received a reward as far as the spoil of the Philistines was concerned, but the treachery of the people whom David had rescued from their enemies was disgraceful, and shews how base a thing is human nature.)*

6 And it came to pass, when Abiathar the son of Ahimelech fled to David to Keilah, *that* he came down *with* an ephod in his hand.

So that when banished from public worship at the tabernacle, the exiled hero was not without spiritual consolation, for the highpriest himself, and his breast-plate of righteousness were with him. See how God provides for the faithful.

7, 8 And it was told Saul that David was come to Keilah. And Saul said, God hath delivered him into mine hand ; for he is shut in, by entering into a town that hath gates and bars. And Saul called all the people together to war, to go down to Keilah, to besiege David and his men. *(He ought to have honoured him for the eminent service he had rendered to the state, but malice is as a wolf greedy for the blood of its object.)*

9 ¶ And David knew that Saul secretly practised mischief against him ; and he said to Abiathar the priest, Bring hither the ephod.

10 Then said David, O LORD God of Israel, thy servant hath certainly heard that Saul seeketh to come to Keilah, to destroy the city for my sake. *(Observe David's anxiety for the city rather than for himself. Saul had destroyed Nob for sheltering him, and he might do the same to Keilah. Generous spirits cannot bear to bring evil upon others.)*

11 Will the men of Keilah deliver me up into his hand ? will Saul come down, as thy servant hath heard ? O LORD God of Israel, I beseech thee, tell thy servant. And the LORD said, He will come down.

12 Then said David, Will the men of Keilah deliver me and my men into the hand of Saul ? And the LORD said, They will deliver *thee* up.

God so thoroughly knows men, that he can not only tell what they will do, but what they would do under certain circumstances. He knows us better than we know ourselves. Let us always consult his wisdom upon all occasions, and under his direction we shall not err.

13 ¶ Then David and his men, *which were* about six hundred, arose and departed out of Keilah, and went whithersoever they could go. And it was told Saul that David was escaped from Keilah ; and he forbare to go forth.

Thou art near; yes, Lord, I feel it,
    Thou art near where'er I move,
And though sense would fain conceal it,
    Faith oft whispers it to love.

Then, my soul, since God doth love thee,
    Faint not, droop not, do not fear ;
Though his heaven is high above thee,
    He himself is ever near !

DAVID, *for a while, concealed himself in the fastnesses and forests of Ziph. The Ziphites wishing to curry favour with Saul, betrayed the fugitive leader.*

I. SAMUEL XXIII. 19—29.

19 ¶ Then came up the Ziphites to Saul to Gibeah, saying, Doth not David hide himself with us in strong holds in the wood ?

20 Now therefore, O king, come down according to all the desire of thy soul to come down ; and our part *shall be* to deliver him into the king's hand.

21 And Saul said, Blessed *be* ye of the LORD ; for ye have compassion on me.

He had come to regard himself as the injured party, and he dared to introduce God's name into his hypocritical speech ; thus shewing that he had lost all moral sense, and was under a strong delusion to believe a lie. By a course of sin a bad man may at last convince himself that he is right, and even fancy that God himself is in league with him. The Lord save us from so terrible a state of mind. Saul further instructed the Ziphites how to act, so as to secure David.

22 Go, I pray you, prepare yet, and know and see his place where his haunt is, *and* who hath seen him there : for it is told me *that* he dealeth very subtilly.

23 See therefore, and take knowledge of all the lurking places where he hideth himself, and come ye again to me with the certainty, and I will go with you : and it shall come to pass, if he be in the land, that I will search him out throughout all the thousands of Judah.

24 And they arose, and went to Ziph before Saul : but David and his men *were* in the wilderness of Maon.

25 Saul also and his men went to seek *him.* And they told David : wherefore he came down into a rock, and abode in the wilderness of Maon. And when Saul heard *that,* he pursued after David in the wilderness of Maon.

26 And Saul went on this side of the mountain, and David and his men on that side of the mountain : and David made haste to get away for fear of Saul; for Saul and his men compassed David and his men round about to take them.

Now, indeed, David was hunted like a partridge on the mountains. Saul, with his three

thousand men, *chased him, and the treacherous Ziphites beat the bushes before him. It seemed to be all over with the young chieftain, but in his extremity, the Lord interposed.*

27 But there came a messenger unto Saul, saying, Haste thee, and come; for the Philistines have invaded the land.

28 Wherefore Saul returned from pursuing after David, and went against the Philistines : therefore they called that place Selahammahlekoth. *(The pursuer and the pursued were within sight of one another, and yet the victim escaped. The memory of this deliverance was preserved in the name of the Cliff of Divisions, given to the rock down one side of which David climbed while Saul was surrounding the hill on the other side, and was suddenly called away by a panic of the Philistine invasion.)*

29 And David went up from thence, and dwelt in strong holds at En-gedi.

AT *this time David wrote*

PSALM LIV.

1, 2 Save me, O God, by thy name, and judge me by thy strength. Hear my prayer, O God ; give ear to the words of my mouth.

3 For strangers are risen up against me, and oppressors seek after my soul : they have not set God before them. Selah. *(Perhaps the Ziphites were a remnant of the Canaanites, and so were "strangers" ; at any rate they were enemies to David without a cause. If any treat us in this fashion, our best resort is prayer to God.)*

4, 5, 6, 7 Behold, God *is* mine helper : the Lord *is* with them that uphold my soul. He shall reward evil unto mine enemies : cut them off in thy truth. I will freely sacrifice unto thee : I will praise thy name, O LORD ; for *it is* good. For he hath delivered me out of all trouble : and mine eye hath seen *his desire* upon mine enemies.

O lead me to the Rock
That's high above my head !
And make the covert of thy wings
My shelter and my shade.

Within thy presence, Lord,
For ever I'll abide :
Thou art the tower of my defence,
The refuge where I hide.

PSALM XVII.

A Prayer of David.

*S*O *much in this Psalm is illustrated by David's condition in the forests and mountains of Ziph, that it is most appropriate to read it at this time.*

1 Hear the right, O LORD *(Do not suffer might to crush right. Judge my cause and suffer not King Saul to do me wrong),* attend unto my cry, give ear unto my prayer, *that goeth* not out of feigned lips.

2 Let my sentence come forth from thy presence; let thine eyes behold the things that are equal. *(David felt his cause to be so just that he was confident that equity would give a verdict in his favour. We cannot take an unrighteous cause before the Lord, that would be blasphemy; but we may confidently leave a just cause in his hands.)*

3 Thou hast proved mine heart; thou hast visited *me* in the night; *(Like Peter, David uses the argument, " Thou knowest all things, thou knowest that I love thee." It is a most assuring thing to be able to appeal at once to the Lord, and call upon our judge to be a witness for our defence. " Beloved, if our heart condemn us not, then have we confidence towards God." " Thou hast visited me in the night." As if he had said, " Lord, thou hast entered my house at all hours; and thou hast seen me when no one else was nigh; thou hast come upon me unawares and marked my unrestrained actions, and thou knowest whether or no I am guilty of the crimes laid at my door." Happy man, who can thus remember the omniscient eye, and the omnipresent visitor, and find comfort in the remembrance. We too have had our midnight visits from our Lord, and truly they are sweet; so sweet that the recollection of them sets us longing for more of such condescending communings. Lord, if indeed we had been hypocrites, should we have had such fellowship, or have felt such hungerings after a renewal of it?);* thou hast tried me, *and* shalt find nothing; I am purposed *that* my mouth shall not transgress.

4 Concerning the works of men, by the word of thy lips I have kept *me from* the paths of the destroyer. *(Divine guidance had kept him in a safe way, as it will us also, if we seek it.)*

5 Hold up my goings in thy paths, *that* my footsteps slip not.

6 I have called upon thee, for thou wilt hear me, O God : incline thine ear unto me, *and hear* my speech.

7 Shew thy marvellous lovingkindness, O thou that savest by thy right hand them which put their trust *in thee* from those that rise up *against them.*

8, 9 Keep me as the apple of the eye *(No part of the body is more precious, more tender, and more carefully guarded than the eye; and of the eye no portion is more peculiarly protected than the central apple, the pupil, or, as the Hebrew calls it, " the daughter of the eye." The All-wise Creator has placed the eye in a well-protected position; it stands surrounded by projecting bones, like Jerusalem encircled by mountains. Moreover, its great Author has surrounded it with many tunics of inward covering, besides the hedge of the eyebrows, the curtain of the eyelids, and the fence of the eyelashes; and, in addition to this, he has given to every man so high a value for his eyes, and so quick an apprehension of danger that no member of the body is more faithfully cared for than the organ of sight. Thus, Lord, keep thou me, for I trust I am one with Jesus, and so a member of his mystical body),* hide me under the shadow of thy wings, From the wicked that oppress me, *from* my deadly enemies, *who* compass me about.

10 They are enclosed in their own fat : with their mouth they speak proudly.

11 They have now compassed us in our steps : they have set their eyes bowing down to the earth ;

12 Like as a lion *that* is greedy of his prey, and as it were a young lion lurking in secret places. *(A vivid picture of Saul's pursuit of him. He and his men were surrounded, and their enemies followed after them like wild beasts eager in the hunt, tracking their every step.)*

13 Arise, O LORD, disappoint him, cast him down : deliver my soul from the wicked, *which is* thy sword :

14 From men *which are* thy hand, O LORD, from men of the world, *which have* their portion in *this* life, and whose belly thou fillest with thy hid *treasure :* they are full of children, and leave the rest of their *substance* to their babes.

15 As for me, I will behold thy face in righteousness : I shall be satisfied, when I awake, with thy likeness.

PROBABLY *it was in these dark days, when David was still under the fierce displeasure of Saul, that he penned—*

PSALM VII.

This Psalm bears the title of

Shiggaion of David, which he sang unto the LORD, concerning the words of Cush the Benjamite.

It appears probable that Cush had accused David of treasonable conspiracy against Saul's authority, or of some other crime. This the King would be ready enough to credit, both from his jealousy of David, and from the relationship which existed between himself, the son of Kish, and this Cush or Kish the Benjamite.

1 O LORD my God, in thee do I put my trust : save me from all them that persecute me, and deliver me :

2 Lest he tear my soul like a lion, rending *it* in pieces, while *there is* none to deliver.

3 O LORD my God, if I have done this ; if there be iniquity in my hands ;

4 If I have rewarded evil unto him that was at peace with me ; (yea, I have delivered him that without cause is mine enemy :)

5 Let the enemy persecute my soul, and take *it ;* yea, let him tread down my life upon the earth, and lay mine honour in the dust. Selah.

From these verses we may learn that no innocence can shield a man from the calumnies of the wicked. David had been scrupulously careful to avoid any appearance of rebellion against Saul, whom he constantly styled "the Lord's Anointed"; but all this could not protect him from lying tongues. As the shadow follows the substance, so envy pursues goodness. It is only at the tree laden with fruit that men throw stones. If we would live without being slandered, we must wait till we get to heaven. Let us be very heedful not to believe the flying rumours which are always assailing gracious men. If there are no believers in slander, there will be but a dull market in falsehood, and good men's characters will be safe. Ill-will never spoke well. Sinners have an ill-will to saints, and therefore, we may be sure they will not speak well of them.

6 Arise, O LORD, in thine anger, lift up thyself because of the rage of mine enemies : and awake for me *to* the judgment *that* thou hast commanded.

7 So shall the congregation of the people compass thee about : for their sakes therefore return thou on high.

8 The LORD shall judge the people : judge me, O LORD, according to my righteousness, and according to mine integrity *that is* in me.

9 Oh let the wickedness of the wicked come to an end ; but establish the just : for the righteous God trieth the hearts and reins.

10 My defence *is* of God, which saveth the upright in heart.

11 God judgeth the righteous, and God is angry *with the wicked* every day.

12 If he turn not, he will whet his sword ; he hath bent his bow, and made it ready.

13 He hath also prepared for him the instruments of death ; he ordaineth his arrows against the persecutors.

14 Behold, he travaileth with iniquity, and hath conceived mischief, and brought forth falsehood.

15 He made a pit, and digged it, and is fallen into the ditch *which* he made.

16 His mischief shall return upon his own head, and his violent dealing shall come down upon his own pate.

17 I will praise the LORD according to his righteousness : and will sing praise to the name of the LORD most high.

Oh, how good to have a true and upright *heart. Crooked sinners, with all their craftiness, are foiled by honest spirits. God defends the right. Filth will not long abide on the pure white garments of the saints, but shall be brushed off by divine providence, to the vexation of the men by whose base hands it was thrown. The believer should not fear anything which his foes can do or say against him, for the tree which God plants no winds can uproot. God judgeth the righteous, he hath not given them up to their persecutors.*

Delight thyself in God, he'll give
     Thine heart's desire to thee :
Commit thy way to God alone,
     It brought to pass shall be.

And like unto the light he shall
     Thy righteousness display ;
And he thy judgment shall bring forth,
     Like noontide of the day.

I. SAMUEL XXIV. 1—7; 17—19.

AND it came to pass, when Saul was returned from following the Philistines, that it was told him, saying, Behold, David *is* in the wilderness of En-gedi. (*Everybody was ready to act as a spy upon David. The saints of God are always watched by the world, and this should make them all the more careful in their conduct.*)

2 Then Saul took three thousand chosen men out of all Israel, and went to seek David and his men upon the rocks of the wild goats.

Though signally disappointed on former occasions, the envious king must needs be at his cruel work again. No matter where David might conceal himself, or how quiet he might remain, Saul would not let him alone. Envy can never be quiet till it has glutted its revenge.

3 And he came to the sheepcotes by the way, where *was* a cave; and Saul went in to cover his feet: and David and his men remained in the sides of the cave. (*These vast cavernous places could within their dark recesses conceal vast numbers so completely, that an individual might come and go, and never know of their presence.*)

4, 5 And the men of David said unto him, Behold the day of which the LORD said unto thee, Behold, I will deliver thine enemy into thine hand, that thou mayest do to him as it shall seem good unto thee. (*Our best friends will mislead us if we let them. In this case, with the best intentions, David's followers urged him on to murder, but grace restrained his hand.*) Then David arose, and cut off the skirt of Saul's robe privily. And it came to pass afterward, that David's heart smote him, because he had cut off Saul's skirt. (*Good men tremble at doing little wrongs, where others delight in committing great crimes.*)

6 And he said unto his men, The LORD forbid that I should do this thing unto my master, the LORD's anointed, to stretch forth mine hand against him, seeing he *is* the anointed of the LORD.

7 So David stayed his servants with these words, and suffered them not to rise against Saul. But Saul rose up out of the cave, and went on *his* way. (*Dr. Kitto, in his Daily Bible Illustrations, forcibly describes the scene, and that which followed it: " Although under the influence of the master-hand which held back the fierce outlaws, Saul was suffered to ·escape unscathed from that dangerous cave, David was willing to secure some evidence of the fact that Saul's life had been in his power. He therefore approached him softly as he slept, and cut off the skirt of his robe. No sooner, however, did Saul arise and leave the cavern, and his men begin to laugh at the ridiculous figure the sovereign presented in his skirtless robe, than David's heart smote him for the indignity he had been instrumental in inflicting on the royal person. Yielding to the impulse of the moment—which again was right, though it might have been in common calculation, most dangerous, he went boldly forth to the entrance of the cave, and called to the king as he descended into the valley,—' My lord, the king!' Well did the king know that voice. A thunderclap could not have struck him more. He looked up, and David bowed himself very low, in becoming obeisance to his king. He spoke. In a few rapid and strong words, he told what had happened— he described the urgency he had resisted—he held up the skirt in proof how completely had been in his hand the life he spared—saying, ' I have not sinned against thee; yet thou huntest my life to take it. The Lord judge between me and thee; and the Lord avenge me of thee: but mine hand shall not be upon thee.' Behold, now that stern heart is melted. The hard wintry frosts thaw fast before the kindly warmth of his generous nature. Saul weeps; the hot tears—the blessed tears, fall once more from those eyes, dry too long."*)

17 And he said to David, Thou *art* more righteous than I: for thou hast rewarded me good, whereas I have rewarded thee evil.

18, 19 And thou hast shewed this day how that thou hast dealt well with me: forasmuch as when the LORD had delivered me into thine hand, thou killedst me not. For if a man find his enemy, will he let him go well away? wherefore the LORD reward thee good for that thou hast done unto me this day.

Dear Saviour, should our foes defame,
   Or brethren faithless prove
Then, through thy grace, be this our aim,
   To conquer them by love.

Kept peaceful in the midst of strife,
   Forgiving and forgiven;
O may we lead the pilgrim's life,
   And follow thee to heaven!

DAVID *was ever ready to express his grati-tude, and when he had escaped from Saul, he took care to praise the Lord with a new song. He then wrote—*

PSALM LVII.,

which is entitled—

To the chief Musician, Al-taschith, Michtam of David, when he fled from Saul in the cave.

Al-taschith signifies " destroy not," *probably in allusion to his refusing to destroy Saul.*

1 Be merciful unto me, O God, be merciful unto me : for my soul trusteth in thee : yea, in the shadow of thy wings will I make my refuge, until *these* calamities be overpast.

2 I will cry unto God most high ; unto God that performeth *all things* for me.

3 He shall send from heaven, and save me *from* the reproach of him that would swallow me up. Selah. God shall send forth his mercy and his truth.

4 My soul *is* among lions : *and* I lie *even* among them that are set on fire, *even* the sons of men, whose teeth *are* spears and arrows, and their tongue a sharp sword.

5 Be thou exalted, O God, above the heavens ; *let* thy glory *be* above all the earth.

6 They have prepared a net for my steps ; my soul is bowed down : they have digged a pit before me, into the midst whereof they are fallen *themselves*. Selah.

7 My heart is fixed, O God, my heart is fixed : I will sing and give praise.

One would have thought he would have said, " My heart is fluttered;" but no, he is calm, firm, happy, resolute, established. When the central axle is secure, the whole wheel is right. If our great bower anchor holds, the ship cannot drive. " O God, my heart is fixed." I am resolved to trust thee, to serve thee, and to praise thee. Twice does he declare this to the glory of God who thus comforts the souls of his servants. It is surely well with each one of us if our once roving heart is now firmly fixed upon God and the proclamation of his glory. " I will sing and give praise." Vocally and instrumentally will I celebrate thy worship. With lip and with heart will I ascribe honour to thee. Satan shall not stop me, nor **Saul,** *nor the Philistines. I will make Adullam*

ring with music, and all the caverns thereof echo with joyous song.

8 Awake up, my glory ; awake, psaltery and harp : I *myself* will awake early. *(It is as if he had said, " Let the noblest powers of my nature bestir themselves : the intellect which conceives thought, the tongue which expresses it, and the vivid imagination which beautifies it—let all be on the alert now that the hour for praise has come. 'Awake, psaltery and harp.' Let all the music with which I am familiar be well attuned for the hallowed service of praise. ' I myself will awake early.' I will gladden the dawn with my joyous music. No sleepy verses and weary notes shall be heard from me ; I will thoroughly arouse myself for this high employ."*

When we are at our best we fall far short of the Lord's deserts; let us, therefore, make sure that what we bring him is the noblest production of our powers. If it be marred with infirmity, let it not be deteriorated by indolence. Three times the psalmist calls upon himself to awake. Do we need so much arousing, and for such work? Then let us bestir ourselves, for the engagement is too honourable and too important to be left undone, or to be done in a slovenly manner.)

9 I will praise thee, O Lord, among the people : I will sing unto thee among the nations.

10 For thy mercy *is* great unto the heavens, and thy truth unto the clouds. *(Right up from man's low estate to heaven's loftiness mercy reaches. Imagination fails to guess the height of heaven, and even thus the riches of God's mercy exceed our highest thoughts. The psalmist as he sat at the cave's mouth, and looked up to the firmament, rejoiced that God's goodness is vaster, and more sublime than even the vaulted skies.)*

11 Be thou exalted, O God, above the heavens : *let* thy glory *be* above all the earth.

A grand chorus : let us take it up with all our hearts, and lovingly adore the all glorious Lord.

My heart is fix'd, my song shall raise
Immortal honours to thy name ;
Awake my tongue, to sound his praise,
My tongue, the glory of my frame.

Be thou exalted, O my God,
Above the heavens, where angels dwell ;
Thy power on earth be known abroad,
And land to land thy wonders tell.

PERHAPS *it was at this period that David wrote—*

PSALM LXIII.

A Psalm of David, when he was in the wilderness of Judah.

1 O GOD, thou *art* my God; early will I seek thee: my soul thirsteth for thee, my flesh longeth for thee in a dry and thirsty land, where no water is;

2 To see thy power and thy glory, so *as I* have seen thee in the sanctuary.

3 Because thy lovingkindness *is* better than life, my lips shall praise thee.

4 Thus will I bless thee while I live: I will lift up my hands in thy name.

5 My soul shall be satisfied as *with* marrow and fatness; and my mouth shall praise *thee* with joyful lips:

6 When I remember thee upon my bed, *and* meditate on thee in the *night* watches.

7 Because thou hast been my help, therefore in the shadow of thy wings will I rejoice.

8 My soul followeth hard after thee: thy right hand upholdeth me.

9 But those *that* seek my soul, to destroy *it*, shall go into the lower parts of the earth.

10 They shall fall by the sword: they shall be a portion for foxes. (*Or jackals, which in the East are always ready to devour the slain. Saul and his men fell on the battle-field, and David foresaw it would be so, and that then he would be made king.*)

11 But the king shall rejoice in God; every one that sweareth by him shall glory: but the mouth of them that speak lies shall be stopped.

We have refrained from commenting, in order to quote the sweet remarks of our dear friend Andrew Bonar, upon the whole psalm: "*It may have been near the Dead Sea, on his way to the ford of Jordan, that the Psalmist first sung this song. It is a Psalm first heard by David's faithful ones in the wilderness of Judah; but truly a Psalm for every godly man who in the dry world-wilderness can sing: 'All my springs are in thee,'—a Psalm for David—a Psalm for David's Son—a Psalm for the Church in every age—a Psalm for every member of the Church in the weary land! What assurance, what vehement desire, what soul-filling delight in God, in God alone; in God, the only fountain of living water amid a boundless wilderness!*

Hope, too, has its visions here; for it sees the ungodly perish (verses 9, 10), and the King *on the throne surrounded by a company who swear allegiance to Jehovah. Hope sees for itself what Isaiah lxv., 16, describes, every mouth 'swearing by the God of truth;' and what Rev. xxi., 27, has foretold:—the mouth of '*liars*' closed for ever—all who sought other gods, and trusted to other saviours, gone for ever.*

And when we read all this as spoken of Christ, how much does every verse become enhanced. His thirst *for God! His* vision *of Goa! His* estimate *of God's loving-kindness! His* soul satisfied*! His* mouth full of praise*! His* soul following hard after God*! '*O God, thou art my El,' *mighty one.* Thou art my omnipotence. *It is this God he still seeks. The word translated '*so*' in verse 2, and '*thus*' in verse 4, is interesting. In verse 2, the force of it is this: '*No wonder that I so thirst for thee; no wonder that my first thoughts in the morning are toward thee; no wonder that my very flesh longeth for thee! Who would not, that has seen what I have seen? So have I gazed on thee in the sanctuary, seeing thy power and glory!' The '*so*' is like 2 Peter, i. 17. '*Such a voice!' And then, if the past has been thus exquisitely blessed, my prospects for the future are not less so. I see illimitable bliss coming in as a tide; '*so*' will I bless thee while I live!' (ver. 4). Yes; in ages to come, as well as in many a happy moment on earth, my soul shall be satiated as with marrow and fatness! And when verse 7 shews us the soul under the shadow of God's wings, rejoicing, we may say, it is not only like '*the bird, which, sheltered from the heat of the sun amid the rich foliage, sings its merry note,' but it is the soul reposing there as if entering the cloud of glory, like Moses and Elias. O world! come and see* The Righteous One *finding water-springs in God.*"

O God of love, my God thou art;
    To thee I early cry;
Refresh with grace my thirsty heart,
    For earthly springs are dry.

Thy power, thy glory let me see,
    As seen by saints above;
'Tis sweeter, Lord, than life to me,
    To share and sing thy love.

WE *shall again have an instance of David's generous spirit, if we read in—*

I. SAMUEL XXVI. 1—22; 25.

1 And the Ziphites came unto Saul to Gibeah, saying, Doth not David hide himself in the hill of Hachilah, *which is* before Jeshimon?

2 Then Saul arose, and went down to the wilderness of Ziph, having three thousand chosen men of Israel with him, to seek David in the wilderness of Ziph.

3 And Saul pitched in the hill of Hachilah, which *is* before Jeshimon, by the way. But David abode in the wilderness, and he saw that Saul came after him into the wilderness.

4 David therefore sent out spies, and understood that Saul was come in very deed.

5 And David arose, and came to the place where Saul had pitched: and David beheld the place where Saul lay, and Abner the son of Ner, the captain of his host: and Saul lay in the trench, and the people pitched round about him.

6 Then answered David and said to Ahimelech the Hittite, and to Abishai the son of Zeruiah, brother to Joab, saying, Who will go down with me to Saul to the camp? And Abishai said, I will go down with thee.

7 So David and Abishai came to the people by night: and, behold, Saul lay sleeping within the trench, and his spear stuck in the ground at his bolster: but Abner and the people lay round about him.

8 Then said Abishai to David, God hath delivered thine enemy into thine hand this day: now therefore let me smite him, I pray thee, with the spear even to the earth at once, and I will not *smite* him the second time.

9 And David said to Abishai, Destroy him not: for who can stretch forth his hand against the LORD's anointed, and be guiltless?

10, 11, 12 David said furthermore, *As* the LORD liveth, the LORD shall smite him; or his day shall come to die; or he shall descend into battle, and perish. The LORD forbid that I should stretch forth mine hand against the LORD's anointed: but, I pray thee, take thou now the spear that *is* at his bolster, and the cruse of water, and let us go. So David took the spear and the cruse of water from Saul's bolster; and they gat them away, and no man saw *it*, nor knew *it*, neither awaked: for they *were*

all asleep; because a deep sleep from the LORD was fallen upon them.

13 ¶ Then David went over to the other side, and stood on the top of an hill afar off; a great space *being* between them:

14, 15, 16 And David cried to the people, and to Abner the son of Ner, saying, Answerest thou not, Abner? Then Abner answered and said, Who *art* thou *that* criest to the king? And David said to Abner, *Art* not thou a *valiant* man? and who *is* like to thee in Israel? wherefore then hast thou not kept thy lord the king? for there came one of the people in to destroy the king thy lord. This thing *is* not good that thou hast done. As the LORD liveth, ye *are* worthy to die, because ye have not kept your master, the LORD's anointed. And now see where the king's spear *is*, and the cruse of water that *was* at his bolster.

17 And Saul knew David's voice, and said, *Is* this thy voice, my son David? And David said, *It is* my voice, my lord, O king.

18, 19, 20 And he said, Wherefore doth my lord thus pursue after his servant? for what have I done? or what evil *is* in mine hand? Now therefore, I pray thee, let my lord the king hear the words of his servant. If the LORD have stirred thee up against me, let him accept an offering: but if *they be* the children of men, cursed *be* they before the LORD; for they have driven me out this day from abiding in the inheritance of the LORD, saying, Go, serve other gods. Now therefore, let not my blood fall to the earth before the face of the LORD: for the king of Israel is come out to seek a flea, as when one doth hunt a partridge in the mountains.

21 ¶ Then said Saul, I have sinned: return, my son David: for I will no more do thee harm, because my soul was precious in thine eyes this day: behold, I have played the fool, and have erred exceedingly.

22 And David answered and said, Behold the king's spear! and let one of the young men come over and fetch it.

25 Then Saul said to David, Blessed *be* thou, my son David: thou shalt both do great *things*, and also shalt still prevail. So David went on his way, and Saul returned to his place.

Thus David conquered by forbearance, and the lesson for us is, " overcome evil with good."

I. SAMUEL XXX. 1—13; 15—18.

DAVID *again stepped aside from his right position, and went over to Achish the Philistine king, who received him kindly. War soon arose against Israel, and David was expected to march against his own people. When we walk by sight and not by faith, we are sure to be placed in embarrassments ere long, and so was David! Out of this difficulty the Lord delivered him, for the Philistine lords distrusted him, and therefore Achish sent him back to Ziklag, the city which he had allotted to him as his dwelling-place; but the Lord took care to chasten him, for on his return to Ziklag a sad scene awaited him.*

1, 2, 3 And it came to pass, when David and his men were come to Ziklag on the third day, that the Amalekites had invaded the south, and Ziklag, and smitten Ziklag, and burned it with fire; And had taken the women captives, that *were* therein : they slew not any, either great or small, but carried *them* away, and went on their way. So David and his men came to the city, and, behold, *it was* burned with fire; and their wives, and their sons, and their daughters, were taken captives.

4 Then David and the people that *were* with him lifted up their voice and wept, until they had no more power to weep. (*A sad sight to see strong men weep like women, but who would not do so in such a case.*)

5 And David's two wives were taken captives, Ahinoam the Jezreelitess, and Abigail the wife of Nabal the Carmelite.

6 And David was greatly distressed; for the people spake of stoning him, because the soul of all the people was grieved, every man for his sons and for his daughters : but David encouraged himself in the LORD his God.

Some time before, he had said, " There is nothing better for me than that I should speedily escape into the land of the Philistines," but having proved the vanity of all human helps, he turns unto the Lord his God. How different from Saul, who at this time was looking to Satan for aid, and consulting the witch of Endor.

7 And David said to Abiathar the priest, I pray thee, bring me hither the ephod. And Abiathar brought thither the ephod to David. (*It was well that David kept the priest and the ephod always near him, or they would have been carried off with the rest. Whatever we lose, let us hold fast to Christ and his word.*)

8 And David enquired at the LORD, saying, Shall I pursue after this troop ? shall I overtake them ? And he answered him, Pursue : for thou shalt surely overtake *them*, and without fail recover *all*. (*David proved that the God of truth may be trusted, and that the heart which waits upon the Lord will be comforted.*)

9, 10 So David went, he and the six hundred men that *were* with him, and came to the brook Besor, where two hundred abode behind, which were so faint that they could not go over the brook Besor. (*They were not all equally strong, neither are all the followers of the Lord Jesus equally full of grace. Yet our great leader is full of tenderness, and does not disdain to give the feeblest a share of the spoil.*)

11, 12 And they found an Egyptian in the field, and brought him to David, and gave him bread, and he did eat; and they made him drink water ; And they gave him a piece of a cake of figs, and two clusters of raisins : and when he had eaten, his spirit came again to him : for he had eaten no bread, nor drunk *any* water, three days and three nights.

13 And David said unto him, To whom *belongest* thou ? and whence *art* thou ? And he said, I *am* a young man of Egypt, servant to an Amalekite; and my master left me, because three days agone I fell sick. (*Servants are to be cared for in their sickness. Only a heathen master would desert his servant because of illness.*)

15 And David said to him, Canst thou bring me down to this company ? And he said, Swear unto me by God, that thou wilt neither kill me, nor deliver me into the hands of my master, and I will bring thee down to this company.

16, 17, 18 And when he had brought him down, behold, *they were* spread abroad upon all the earth, eating and drinking, and dancing, because of all the great spoil that they had taken out of the land of the Philistines, and out of the land of Judah. And David smote them from the twilight even unto the evening of the next day : and there escaped not a man of them, save four hundred young men, which rode upon camels, and fled. And David recovered all that the Amalekites had carried away : and David rescued his two wives.

Thus faith was honoured, and the clouds of trouble poured forth showers of mercy. To our faith the same blessings shall be granted.

I. SAMUEL XXXI. 1—5 ; 7—13.

NOW the Philistines fought against Israel : and the men of Israel fled from before the Philistines, and fell down slain in mount Gilboa. And the Philistines followed hard upon Saul and upon his sons ; and the Philistines slew Jonathan, and Abinadab, and Melchishua, Saul's sons. And the battle went sore against Saul, and the archers hit him ; and he was sore wounded of the archers.

4 Then said Saul unto his armourbearer, Draw thy sword, and thrust me through therewith ; lest these uncircumcised come and thrust me through, and abuse me. But his armourbearer would not ; for he was sore afraid. Therefore Saul took a sword, and fell upon it. *The unhappy king had forsaken the Lord, and had lost divine protection. He does not appear to have felt the slightest repentance, but to have been left to the hardness of his heart even to the end. His last thoughts had no reference to his sin and his God ; his own poor honour before the world was still his dearest care, as it had been so long. O that he had minded more his reputation in the sight of God, and cared less for human esteem, then had he never been driven to such envy in life or such despair in death. With his sons dead around him, and his bravest warriors slain, the wretched king, in order to escape dishonour, earned the dishonourable name of suicide.*

5 And when his armourbearer saw that Saul was dead, he fell likewise upon his sword, and died with him. *(While we earnestly condemn the self-destruction, we cannot but admire the faithfulness of the armourbearer—faithful unto death. He would not survive his master. Shall this man live and die for Saul, and shall we betray our royal master, Jesus the Lord ?)*

7 ¶ And when the men of Israel that *were* on the other side of the valley, and *they* that *were* on the other side Jordan, saw that the men of Israel fled, and that Saul and his sons were dead, they forsook the cities, and fled ; and the Philistines came and dwelt in them.

8, 9 And it came to pass on the morrow, when the Philistines came to strip the slain, that they found Saul and his three sons fallen in mount Gilboa. And they cut off his head, and stripped off his armour, and sent into the land of the Philistines round about, to publish *it in* the house of their idols, and among the people.

10 And they put his armour in the house of Ashtaroth : and they fastened his body to the wall of Beth-shan. *(To the fallen king there happened the disgrace which he slew himself to escape. The plundering bands of the Philistines came to strip the dead bodies of their clothing, and, lo, upon the mountain side, not far from the corpses of his three sons, they discovered the remains of Saul, swimming in his own blood. Hearts of stone might have softened at the sight, but these barbarians exulted at it. They separated the king's head from the trunk, and stripped off his armour and weapons ; sending the head from city to city as a trophy of their victory, fixing up the armour in the temple of their goddess, as a token of their gratitude to her, and leaving the body as an ignominious relic nailed to a wall.)*

11 ¶ And when the inhabitants of Jabeshgilead heard of that which the Philistines had done to Saul ;

12 All the valiant men arose, and went all night, and took the body of Saul and the bodies of his sons from the wall of Beth-shan, and came to Jabesh, and burnt them there.

13 And they took their bones, and buried *them* under a tree at Jabesh, and fasted seven days. *(It was well and fitly done. Jabesh had been delivered by Saul from the Amorites, and it was honourable on their part to shew this mark of respect to his mangled remains. They burned his bones, that by no future accident they might again be treated with indignity, and then they buried the ashes, and paid the last mournful honours to their former monarch and deliverer.)*

I CHRONICLES X. 13, 14.

13, 14 ¶ So Saul died for his transgression which he committed against the LORD, *even* against the word of the LORD, which he kept not, and also for asking *counsel* of *one that had* a familiar spirit, to enquire *of it* ; And enquired not of the LORD : therefore he slew him, and turned the kingdom unto David the son of Jesse. *(We read that no one enquired at the ark of God all the days of Saul. His evil example did mischief to the whole nation, and therefore his sin was the more grievous. He began well, but his character was based upon love of human approbation, rather than upon the fear of God, and hence it came to nought. Let this be a warning to each one of us.)*

II. SAMUEL I. 1—16.

NOW it came to pass after the death of Saul, when David was returned from the slaughter of the Amalekites, and David had abode two days in Ziklag ;

2 It came even to pass on the third day, that, behold, a man came out of the camp from Saul with his clothes rent, and earth upon his head : and *so* it was, when he came to David, that he fell to the earth, and did obeisance.

3, 4 And David said unto him, From whence comest thou ? And he said unto him, Out of the camp of Israel am I escaped. And David said unto him, How went the matter ? I pray thee, tell me. And he answered, That the people are fled from the battle, and many of the people also are fallen and dead ; and Saul and Jonathan his son are dead also.

5, 6, 7 And David said unto the young man that told him, How knowest thou that Saul and Jonathan his son be dead? And the young man that told him said, As I happened by chance upon mount Gilboa, behold, Saul leaned upon his spear; and, lo, the chariots and horsemen followed hard after him. And when he looked behind him, he saw me, and called unto me. And I answered, Here *am* I.

8 And he said unto me, Who *art* thou ? And I answered him, I *am* an Amalekite.

9 He said unto me again, Stand, I pray thee, upon me, and slay me : for anguish is come upon me, because my life *is* yet whole in me.

10 So I stood upon him, and slew him, because I was sure that he could not live after that he was fallen : and I took the crown that *was* upon his head, and the bracelet that *was* on his arm, and have brought them hither unto my lord. (*The probabilities are that this hypocritical fellow had visited the battle-field for the purpose of plundering the dead, soon after the close of the battle. Either he found Saul dead, or else the monarch's suicidal wound had not yet ended fatally, and the Amalekite finished the deed. His story was told in the hope of winning the thanks of David and a corresponding reward. The crown and bracelet were worth something, but this adventurer hoped to earn a far higher prize by bringing them to the rival leader. He reckoned cunningly ; but little did the Amalekite know that he was not dealing with one like himself but with a man of God. Instead of ingratiating*

himself for life with the new king, he excited David's indignation, and, being condemned by his own story, he met with a speedy doom.)

11, 12 Then David took hold on his clothes, and rent them ; and likewise all the men that *were* with him : And they mourned, and wept, and fasted until even, for Saul, and for Jonathan his son, and for the people of the LORD, and for the house of Israel ; because they were fallen by the sword. (*The man of God felt no joy in his enemy's death, neither will a gracious heart ever rejoice in the misfortune of others, however cruelly they may have acted.)*

13 ¶ And David said unto the young man that told him, Whence *art* thou ? And he answered, I *am* the son of a stranger, an Amalekite.

14 And David said unto him, How wast thou not afraid to stretch forth thine hand to destroy the LORD's anointed ?

15 And David called one of the young men, and said, Go near, *and* fall upon him. And he smote him that he died. (*Whether he spake the truth or not, the sentence was just. As there was now no king in the land, David as captain of the host exercised the office of judge and condemned the man out of his own mouth.)*

16 And David said unto him, Thy blood *be* upon thy head ; for thy mouth hath testified against thee, saying, I have slain the LORD's anointed. (*Thus will all wrong courses sooner or later bring down punishment upon those who enter upon them. The plot looked fair. Who was to discover the falsehood? Were not the plundered ornaments conclusive evidence? David would be sure to ennoble the bearer of such good tidings! The cunning sinner had made one error in his reckoning, and it proved to be a fatal one. Let us take warning and never leave the path of truth. We should abhor every form of deception, for the Lord will not endure liars and will surely overthrow them.)*

The Lord is wise and wonderful,
     As all the ages tell :
O learn of him, learn now of him,
     That all he does is well.

And in his light shall we see light,
     Nor still in darkness roam,
And he shall be to us a rest,
     When evening shadows come.

II SAMUEL I. 17—27.

A ND David lamented with this lamentation over Saul and over Jonathan his son :

18 (Also he bade them teach the children of Judah *the use of* the bow : behold, *it is* written in the book of Jasher.)

The book of Jasher was probably a collection of national songs and records of heroic acts ; it is now lost, for it was not inspired and therefore no special providence preserved its existence. David not only mourned over Saul and Jonathan personally, but he composed an elegy to be sung by the whole nation, and especially by his own tribe. This he entitled "The Bow," in allusion to the skill in archery for which Jonathan was famous, which is alluded to in the dirge itself. David in thus lamenting over the discarded house of Saul, reminds us of Jesus weeping over Jerusalem, whose house is left desolate because it knew not its day.

19 The beauty of Israel is slain upon thy high places :
How are the mighty fallen !

20 Tell *it* not in Gath, publish *it* not in the streets of Askelon ;
Lest the daughters of the Philistines rejoice,
Lest the daughters of the uncircumcised triumph.

21 Ye mountains of Gilboa,
Let there be no dew, neither *let there be* rain, upon you,
Nor fields of offerings :
For there the shield of the mighty is vilely cast away,
The shield of Saul, *as though he had* not *been* anointed with oil.

22 From the blood of the slain, from the fat of the mighty,
The bow of Jonathan turned not back,
And the sword of Saul returned not empty.

23 Saul and Jonathan *were* lovely and pleasant in their lives,
And in their death they were not divided :
They were swifter than eagles,
They were stronger than lions.

24 Ye daughters of Israel, weep over Saul,
Who clothed you in scarlet, with *other* delights,
Who put on ornaments of gold upon your apparel.

25 How are the mighty fallen in the midst of the battle !
O Jonathan, *thou wast* slain in thine high places.

26 I am distressed for thee, my brother Jonathan :
Very pleasant hast thou been unto me :
Thy love to me was wonderful, passing the love of women.

27 How are the mighty fallen, and the weapons of war perished !

Dr. Krummacher, in his " David, the King of Israel," has the following excellent passage, " David did not in his lamentation speak too highly in praise of the King. Was not Saul truly a valiant hero ? Did not also that which was gentle and tender oftentimes find an echo in his soul ? Did not Jonathan and his other sons shew themselves towards him true and faithful children even unto death ? All this at that time hovered before the mind of David. With such recollections as these there was associated a deep, sorrowful compassion for the sad fate of the king. And thus it was David's genuine feeling and sentiment to which he gave full outspoken expression in his lamentation for the dead. These words of the song—' Tell it not in Gath, publish it not in the streets of Askelon,' have, since that time, become a proverb in the circles of the faithful. It is frequently heard when one of their community has failed to take heed to his ways, and, therefore, has given rise to a scandal. Would that the call were more faithfully observed than is usually the case ! Would that the honour of the spiritual Zion lay always as near to the heart of the children of the kingdom as did that of the earthly to the heart of David ! But how often does it happen that they even strive to disclose before the world the weakness of their brethren, and thus, by a repetition of the wickedness of Ham, become traitors to the Church which Christ has purchased with his own blood. They make themselves guilty of bringing dishonour upon the gospel, by opening the gates to such reproach through their tale-bearing, and to their own great prejudice they disown the charity which ' believeth all things and hopeth all things.'"

DAVID *waited seven years and more before he came to the throne of Israel. He reigned meanwhile with great wisdom and justice over that portion of the land which owned his sway, and by his conduct commended himself to general esteem. It was far better to be preparing for the crown than to be plotting to obtain it.*

II. SAMUEL V. 1—3.

1 Then came all the tribes of Israel to David unto Hebron, and spake, saying, Behold, we *are* thy bone and thy flesh.

2 Also in time past, when Saul was king over us, thou wast he that leddest out and broughtest in Israel: and the LORD said to thee, Thou shalt feed my people Israel, and thou shalt be a captain over Israel.

3 So all the elders of Israel came to the king to Hebron; and king David made a league with them in Hebron before the LORD: and they anointed David king over Israel.

Thus without David's having made a single violent grasp at the crown it came to him by general consent. When providence has ripened a blessing for us, it will drop into our lap; but we must not put forth an unholy hand to seize it before the time. David's past conduct, and the fact that he was chosen of the Lord could not always be overlooked. Men have bad memories, but in due time they must and shall remember the deservings of those who have done valiantly. The united tribes were right glad to crown the man who was so worthy to wear the diadem.

I. CHRONICLES XII. 39, 40.

39, 40 And there they were with David three days, eating and drinking: for their brethren had prepared for them. Moreover they that were nigh them, *even* unto Issachar and Zebulun and Naphtali, brought bread on asses, and on camels, and on mules, and on oxen, *and* meat, meal, cakes of figs, and bunches of raisins, and wine, and oil, and oxen, and sheep abundantly: for *there was* joy in Israel. *(Those who were nearest to Hebron had not to bear the expense of a long journey, and therefore they provided the feast. Those who can best afford it should do the most for the honour of our Lord's kingdom.)*

II. SAMUEL V. 4—9.

4 David *was* thirty years old when he began to reign, *and* he reigned forty years.

5 In Hebron he reigned over Judah seven years and six months: and in Jerusalem he reigned thirty and three years over all Israel and Judah.

Being anointed, David was now eager to prove himself a king by clearing his country of lurking enemies; and therefore he determined to expel the Jebusites from their citadel upon mount Zion.

6 And the king and his men went to Jerusalem unto the Jebusites, the inhabitants of the land: which spake unto David, saying, Except thou take away the blind and the lame, thou shalt not come in hither: thinking, David cannot come in hither. *(The probable meaning is that David had called their gods both blind and lame, and now they retorted that their blind and lame gods were quite sufficient to keep him out of their stronghold.)*

7 Nevertheless David took the strong hold of Zion: the same *is* the city of David.

8 And David said on that day, Whosoever getteth up to the gutter, and smiteth the Jebusites, and the lame and the blind, *that are* hated of David's soul, he shall be chief and captain. *(Joab led the van in this fearful fight—fort after fort was captured: the gigantic battlements were scaled, and Israel's warriors climbed over the walls, and smote their enemies in hand to hand encounter.)* Wherefore they said, The blind and the lame shall not come into the house.

That is to say, it became a proverb that Israel would not look to lame and blind deities, and set them up in their houses as a shelter, for they were proved to be worthless defenders.

9 So David dwelt in the fort, and called it the city of David. And David built round about from Millo and inward. *(Thus the sacred mount of Zion was wrested out of the hands of enemies, and became the site of David's palace, and thus the church, saved from all her adversaries is the abode of Jesus her King.)*

Are there no foes for me to face ?
Must I not stem the flood ?
Is this vile world a friend to grace,
To help me on to God ?

Sure I must fight if I would reign ;
Increase my courage, Lord !
I'll bear the toil, endure the pain,
Supported by Thy word.

DAVID *soon found that the honours of royalty brought with them toils and conflicts. It was true of him, as it is also of all believers, that he who would reign must fight.*

II. SAMUEL V. 17—25.

17 ¶ But when the Philistines heard that they had anointed David king over Israel, all the Philistines came up to seek David; and David heard *of it*, and went down to the hold.

18 The Philistines also came and spread themselves in the valley of Rephaim.

Their success against Saul made them bold to attack David, for they knew not the essential difference between the two men. Saul, forsaken of God, was easily overcome; but David, upheld and strengthened by the Lord of Hosts, was a very different antagonist. It is vain to contend against a man who has God for his ally.

19 And David enquired of the LORD, saying, Shall I go up to the Philistines? wilt thou deliver them into mine hand? And the LORD said unto David, Go up: for I will doubtless deliver the Philistines into thine hand.

David's path was plain, but he desired to see God going before him in every step he took. No one ever lost his way by enquiring too often. To seek the Lord's guidance is never superfluous. Every member of our family should follow David's example, and if we do so we shall walk in ways of peace all our days.

20 And David came to Baal-perazim, and David smote them there, and said, The LORD hath broken forth upon mine enemies before me, as the breach of waters. *(David smote them, but he gave all the glory to the Lord. Grace is active and fights, but it is also humble and renders praise to him who gives the victory.)* Therefore he called the name of that place Baal-perazim. *(Or "the master of the breaches," because the Lord had broken the ranks of the enemy, and made a way for David to scatter them.)*

21 And there they left their images; and David and his men burned them.

As the Philistines had once captured the ark, so now the Israelites seized upon the idols of Philistia, and utterly destroyed them, both to shew their detestation, and to prevent their becoming a snare to Israel.

22 ¶ And the Philistines came up yet again, and spread themselves in the valley of Rephaim.

23 And when David enquired of the LORD, he said, Thou shalt not go up; *but* fetch a compass behind them, and come upon them over against the mulberry trees.

24 And let it be, when thou hearest the sound of a going in the tops of the mulberry trees, that then thou shalt bestir thyself: for then shall the LORD go out before thee, to smite the host of the Philistines. *(When the wind rustled among the leaves of the trees, David was to regard it as a sign for battle. God gives to his waiting people hints as to when to bestir themselves more than usual; and surely, whenever we hear that the Spirit of God is moving like the wind through the churches it is time for us to arouse ourselves for sevenfold activity.)*

25 And David did so, as the LORD had commanded him; and smote the Philistines from Geba until thou come to Gazer.

If we do as the Lord commands us, he will command success to attend us.

THUS, *by successfully defeating the invading foe, David was firmly seated on his throne. How he resolved to act in his eminent position he tells us in—*

PSALM CI.

1 I will sing of mercy and judgment: unto thee, O LORD, will I sing.

2 I will behave myself wisely in a perfect way. O when wilt thou come unto me? I will walk within my house with a perfect heart.

3 I will set no wicked thing before mine eyes: I hate the work of them that turn aside; *it* shall not cleave to me.

4 A froward heart shall depart from me: I will not know a wicked *person*.

5 Whoso privily slandereth his neighbour, him will I cut off: him that hath an high look and a proud heart will not I suffer.

6 Mine eyes *shall be* upon the faithful of the land, that they may dwell with me: he that walketh in a perfect way, he shall serve me.

7 He that worketh deceit shall not dwell within my house: he that telleth lies shall not tarry in my sight.

8 I will early destroy all the wicked of the land; that I may cut off all wicked doers from the city of the LORD.

If thou see thy foe in need,
Haste with cheerful hand to feed ;
House him, clothe him, grant him rest,
Bless him as thou wouldst be blest.

If thy foe be in thy hand,
Every vengeful thought withstand ;
Let not anger's sword be bared,
Spare him as thou wouldst be spared,

Oh praise ye the Lord
　With heart and with voice;
His mercies record,
　And round him rejoice.
Ye children of Zion,
　Your Saviour adore !
And learn to rely on
　His grace evermore.

Repose on his arm,
　Ye sheep of his fold !
What terror can harm
　With him to uphold ?
His saints are his treasure,
　Their peace will he seek ;
And pour without measure
　His gifts on the meek.

Go on in his might,
　Ye men of the Lord :
His word be your light,
　His promise your sword.
The king of salvation
　Your foes will subdue ;
And their degradation
　Bring glory to you.

No, I shall envy them no more
　Who grow profanely great,
Though they increase their golden store,
　And rise to wondrous height.

Yes, you must bow your stately head,
　Away your spirit flies,
And no kind angel near your bed,
　To bear it to the skies.

Go now, and boast of all your stores,
　And tell how bright they shine ;
Your heaps of glittering dust are yours,
　And my Redeemer's mine.

If I must die, oh ! let me die
　With hope in Jesus' blood—
The blood that saves from sin and guilt,
　And reconciles to God.

If I must die, then let me die
　In peace with all mankind,
And change these fleeting joys below
　For pleasures all refined.

If I must die—and die I shall—
　Let some kind seraph come,
And bear me on his friendly wing,
　To my celestial home !

Lord, when I lift my voice to Thee,
　To whom all praise belongs,
Thy justice and Thy love shall be
　The subject of my songs.

All sinful ways I will abhor,
　All wicked men forsake ;
And only those who love Thy law
　For my companions take.

Lord ! that I may not go astray,
　Thy constant grace impart;
When wilt Thou come to point my way,
　And fix my roving heart ?

WHEN *David was firmly established, and had routed his enemies, he spake unto the Lord the words of a sacred song which we find in*—

PSALM XVIII. 1—24.

1 I will love thee, O LORD, my strength.

2 The LORD *is* my rock, and my fortress, and my deliverer; my God, my strength, in whom I will trust; my buckler, and the horn of my salvation, *and* my high tower.

3 I will call upon the LORD, *who is worthy* to be praised: so shall I be saved from mine enemies.

4 The sorrows of death compassed me, and the floods of ungodly men made me afraid.

5 The sorrows of hell compassed me about: the snares of death prevented me.

6, 7 In my distress I called upon the LORD, and cried unto my God: he heard my voice out of his temple, and my cry came before him, *even* into his ears. Then the earth shook and trembled; the foundations also of the hills moved and were shaken, because he was wroth.

Oh! the power of prayer, it can move heaven and earth. It can climb to heaven and bring the Lord down to earth to help his people. Thus snares are broken, sorrows removed, death defeated, and Satan foiled. Who would not pray?

8 There went up a smoke out of his nostrils, and fire out of his mouth devoured: coals were kindled by it. *(This is an Oriental method of expressing fierce wrath. God came to help his servant, burning with indignation against his foes. The following verses describe the Lord as interposing in storm and tempest to help his afflicted servant.)*

9 He bowed the heavens also, and came down: and darkness *was* under his feet.

10 And he rode upon a cherub, and did fly: yea, he did fly upon the wings of the wind.

God helps his people speedily. He will be in time, for the winds are the coursers of his car.

11, 12 He made darkness his secret place; his pavilion round about him *were* dark waters *and* thick clouds of the skies. At the brightness *that was* before him his thick clouds passed, hail *stones* and coals of fire.

13, 14 The LORD also thundered in the heavens, and the Highest gave his voice; hail *stones* and coals of fire. Yea, he sent out his arrows, and scattered them; and he shot out lightnings, and discomfited them.

Who can stand against this terrible God? Who can injure those whom he protects?

15 Then the channels of waters were seen, and the foundations of the world were discovered at thy rebuke, O LORD, at the blast of the breath of thy nostrils.

16, 17 He sent from above, he took me, he drew me out of many waters. He delivered me from my strong enemy, and from them which hated me: for they were too strong for me.

18 They prevented me in the day of my calamity: but the LORD was my stay.

His enemies were beforehand with him, but even then God was his all-sufficient aid.

19 He brought me forth also into a large place; he delivered me, because he delighted in me.

20 The LORD rewarded me according to my righteousness; according to the cleanness of my hands hath he recompensed me.

21 For I have kept the ways of the LORD, and have not wickedly departed from my God.

22 For all his judgments *were* before me, and I did not put away his statutes from me.

23 I was also upright before him, and I kept myself from mine iniquity.

24 Therefore hath the LORD recompensed me according to my righteousness, according to the cleanness of my hands in his eyesight.

Happy is the man who can from his heart bless God that he has been kept pure and true; for he shall find, as David did, that the Lord will sooner bow the heavens and dry up the seas, than leave the godly to their enemies.

This Psalm is so long, that we **must** *reserve the remainder for our next worship.*

No change of times shall ever shock
My firm affection, Lord, to Thee;
For Thou hast always been my rock,
A fortress and defence to me.

Thou my deliv'rer art, my God,
My trust is in Thy mighty power;
Thou art my shield from foes abroad,
At home my safeguard and my tower.

W E *will now return to*

PSALM XVIII. 30—50.

and read from verse thirty to the end.

30 *As for* God, his way *is* perfect : *(the experience of all his people bears witness to this. Perfect wisdom, perfect truth, and perfect love, are to be seen in all that he does. Blessed be his name.)* The word of the LORD is tried : *(tried, proved and tested, it has been, but it has never failed. This our soul knoweth right well :)* he *is* a buckler to all those that trust in him. *(And to us among them, feeble though our faith has been.)*

31 For who *is* God save the LORD ? or who *is* a rock save our God ?

32 *It is* God that girdeth me with strength, and maketh my way perfect. *(Believers have a complete armour provided for them, of which the girdle of truth is a principal part.)*

33 He maketh my feet like hinds' *feet*, and setteth me upon my high places.

A believer's feet are shod by a divine hand, the preparation of the gospel of peace makes him tread safely where others fall.

34 He teacheth my hands to war, so that a bow of steel is broken by mine arms.

In conflict, the believer's hands are made mighty to break the enemy's weapons by the force of truth.

35 Thou hast also given me the shield of thy salvation : and thy right hand hath holden me up, and thy gentleness hath made me great.

Above all, we are to take the shield of faith, which is of celestial workmanship, and quenches all the enemy's fiery darts.

36 Thou hast enlarged my steps under me, that my feet did not slip. *(Never let us forget that unless the Lord upheld us, we should fall as others have done, to our shame and ruin.)*

37 I have pursued mine enemies, and overtaken them : neither did I turn again till they were consumed.

38 I have wounded them that they were not able to rise : they are fallen under my feet.

39, 40, 41, 42 For thou hast girded me with strength unto the battle : thou hast subdued under me those that rose up against me. Thou hast also given me the necks of mine enemies ; that I might destroy them that hate me. They cried, but *there was* none to save *them* : even unto the LORD, but he answered them not.

Then did I beat them small as the dust before the wind : I did cast them out as the dirt in the streets. *(David ascribes all his victories to his God. Note how often he repeats the word "Thou." Thou, O Lord, hast done it all.)*

43 Thou hast delivered me from the strivings of the people ; *and* thou hast made me the head of the heathen : a people *whom* I have not known shall serve me. *(The neighbouring nations submitted to David's sway. When God is with us our enemies are at peace, or else they are powerless to harm us.)*

44 As soon as they hear of me, they shall obey me : the strangers shall submit themselves unto me.

45 The strangers shall fade away, and be afraid out of their close places.

46 The LORD liveth ; and blessed *be* my rock ; and let the God of my salvation be exalted.

47, 48 *It is* God that avengeth me, and subdueth the people under me. He delivereth me from mine enemies : yea, thou liftest me up above those that rise up against me : thou hast delivered me from the violent man.

49 Therefore will I give thanks unto thee, O LORD, among the heathen, and sing praises unto thy name.

50 Great deliverance giveth he to his king ; and sheweth mercy to his anointed, to David, and to his seed for evermore. *(As we read all this we should try to appropriate the expressions to ourselves, and personally bless the Lord for all the benefits which our own lives have witnessed. Has not the Lord done great things for us also ? Shall we not also give thanks unto his name ? Yes, verily, we will.)*

His be the "victor's name,"
Who fought our fight alone ;
Triumphant saints no honour claim ;
His conquest was His own.

Sin, Satan, Death appear,
To harass and appal ;
Yet since the gracious Lord is near,
Backward they go, and fall.

We meet them face to face,
Through Jesus' conquest blest ;
March in the triumph of His grace,
Right onward to our rest.

I. CHRONICLES XIII.

AND David consulted with the captains of thousands and hundreds, *and* with every leader.   And David said unto all the congregation of Israel, If *it seem* good unto you, and *that it be* of the LORD our God, let us send abroad unto our brethren every where, *that are* left in all the land of Israel, and with them *also* to the priests and Levites *which are* in their cities *and* suburbs, that they may gather themselves unto us : And let us bring again the ark of our God to us : for we enquired not at it in the days of Saul.   And all the congregation said that they would do so : for the thing was right in the eyes of all the people.   (*The son of Jesse loved the Lord too well to be forgetful of his honour, his earliest thoughts when he was confirmed upon his throne were concerning the glory of his God. How different this from the conduct of those whose wealth and honours render them forgetful of him to whom they owe so much!*)

5 So David gathered all Israel together, from Shihor of Egypt even unto the entering of Hemath, to bring the ark of God from Kirjath-jearim.

6 And David went up, and all Israel, to Baalah, *that is*, to Kirjath-jearim, which *belonged* to Judah, to bring up thence the ark of God the LORD, that dwelleth *between* the cherubims, whose name is called *on it*.

7 And they carried the ark of God in a new cart out of the house of Abinadab : and Uzza and Ahio drave the cart.   (*Here they fell into a grievous error for they neglected the precept of the law which commanded the priests to bear the ark with staves upon their shoulders.   God will be served in his own way and not in ours ; the slightest neglect of this rule may lead to serious consequences.   The two young men that drove the cart had probably grown so familiar with the ark, that they felt little reverence for it, and a solemn lesson was needed to teach all Israel that the Lord is greatly to be feared.*)

8 And David and all Israel played before God with all *their* might, and with singing, and with harps, and with psalteries, and with timbrels, and with cymbals, and with trumpets.

9 ¶ And when they came unto the threshing-floor of Chidon, Uzza put forth his hand to hold the ark ; for the oxen stumbled.

10 And the anger of the LORD was kindled against Uzza, and he smote him, because he put his hand to the ark ; and there he died before God.   (*We have in our day too many among us who commit the sin of Uzza, for they dream that Christianity will suffer greatly unless they bring it into conformity with the ruling taste of society. They alter its doctrines, adorn its worship artistically, overlay its simplicities with philosophy, and its plain speech with oratory, and all with the zealous but presumptuous intent to help Him who needs not such helpers, and to preserve that religion which they only insult by their unbelieving anxiety. We must beware of even imagining that our hand is needed to steady God's ark, the thought is blasphemy.*)

11 And David was displeased, because the LORD had made a breach upon Uzza : wherefore that place is called Perez-uzza to this day.

12 And David was afraid of God that day, saying, How shall I bring the ark of God *home* to me ?

13 So David brought not the ark *home* to himself to the city of David, but carried it aside into the house of Obed-edom the Gittite.

Thus religious joy was interrupted because it had not been sufficiently seasoned with holy awe. This was good for David and all Israel, it suspended their rejoicing, but it purged their hearts from levity and presumption.   It also taught them to be obedient to the Lord's word, as well as zealous in his praise.   Such lessons we all need to be taught.

14 And the ark of God remained with the family of Obed-edom in his house three months. And the LORD blessed the house of Obed-edom, and all that he had.   (*May we as a family always cheerfully open our doors to entertain the Lord's servants and worship, for full many a household has been blessed in so doing.*)

Just and true are all Thy ways,
Great Thy works above our praise ;
Humbled in the dust, we own,
Thou art hóly, Thou alone.

In Thy sight the angel band,
Justly charged with folly stand,
Holiest deeds of creatures lie
Meritless before Thine eye.

II. SAMUEL VI. 12—23.

AND it was told king David, saying, The LORD hath blessed the house of Obed-edom, and all that *pertaineth* unto him, because of the ark of God. So David went and brought up the ark of God from the house of Obed-edom into the city of David with gladness.

Obed-edom's prosperity was a sure token that the Lord was ready to bless all who would treat his ark with reverence. When God blesses men of like passions with ourselves, we are encouraged to expect that he will bless us also.

This time the ark was carried by the priests, for the king said to the priests and Levites, "Sanctify yourselves, that ye may bring up the ark of the Lord God of Israel unto the place that I have prepared for it. For because ye did it not at the first, the Lord our God made a breach upon us, for that we sought him not after the due order."

13 And it was *so*, that when they that bare the ark of the LORD had gone six paces, he sacrificed oxen and fatlings.

14 And David danced before the LORD with all *his* might; and David *was* girded with a linen ephod. *(His royal robes were laid aside, and to shew that he was the Lord's servant he put on the Levite's simple dress, and "danced before the Lord with all his might;" that is, says Krummacher, "he gave expression in outward movements, and by a rhythmic action of his body, to the feelings which swelled in his bosom. The conception which the world of the present day is wont to associate with the word* dance *is here not at all appropriate. The dance was, in Israel, a form of divine worship, in which the highest and holiest inspiration oftentimes expressed itself; as, for example, in the case of Miriam and her companions at the Red Sea. If it had not been so, how would the spirit of prophecy have said by the prophet Jeremiah, 'Again I will build thee, and thou shalt be built, O virgin of Israel: thou shalt again be adorned, and shalt go forth in the* dances *of them that make merry.'" And how would the singer of the hundred-and-fiftieth Psalm have exhorted the pious, saying to them, "Praise ye the Lord: praise him with timbrel and* dance" *!)*

15 So David and all the house of Israel, brought up the ark of the LORD with shouting and with the sound of the trumpet.

16 And as the ark of the LORD came into the city of David, Michal Saul's daughter looked through a window, and saw king David leaping and dancing before the LORD; and she despised him in her heart.

17, 18, 19 ¶ And they brought in the ark of the LORD, and set it in his place, in the midst of the tabernacle that David had pitched for it: and David offered burnt offerings and peace offerings before the LORD. And as soon as David had made an end of offering burnt offerings and peace offerings, he blessed the people in the name of the LORD of hosts. And he dealt among all the people, *even* among the whole multitude of Israel, as well to the women as men, to every one a cake of bread, and a good piece *of flesh*, and a flagon *of wine*. So all the people departed every one to his house.

20 ¶ Then David returned to bless his household. And Michal the daughter of Saul came out to meet David, and said, How glorious was the king of Israel to day, who uncovered himself to day in the eyes of the handmaids of his servants, as one of the vain fellows shamelessly uncovereth himself! *(She could not enter into David's enthusiasm, and doubtless thought him half insane. Even thus at this day, cold, heartless religionists cavil at zeal, and call holy excitement cant and fanaticism.)*

21 And David said unto Michal, *It was* before the LORD, which chose me before thy father, and before all his house, to appoint me ruler over the people of the LORD, over Israel: therefore will I play before the LORD. *(He reminded her of God's electing love; truly, if anything can make a man's heart dance this will.)*

22 And I will yet be more vile than thus, and will be base in mine own sight: and of the maidservants which thou hast spoken of, of them shall I be had in honour. *(One is here reminded of Paul's counting all things but loss for the excellency of the knowledge of Christ Jesus his Lord. To promote God's glory we should rejoice to become less and less esteemed among men.)*

23 Therefore Michal the daughter of Saul had no child unto the day of her death. *(She acted rather as the daughter of Saul than as the wife of David, and therefore like her father she died, leaving no heir to the throne of Israel.)*

II. SAMUEL VII. 1—17.

A ND it came to pass, when the king sat in his house, and the LORD had given him rest round about from all his enemies;

2 That the king said unto Nathan the prophet, See now, I dwell in an house of cedar, but the ark of God dwelleth within curtains.

It was a very gracious thought, and such an one as ought to be upon our own minds, if we know that the worship of God is in need of suitable accommodation. If God gives us a house, let us not be slow to find room for his service.

3 And Nathan said to the king, Go, do all that *is* in thine heart; for the LORD *is* with thee.

Good men naturally like to encourage good designs, and therefore the seer spake out of the fulness of his heart. Yet he was mistaken. It was the prerogative of the Lord Jesus always to speak the mind of God, which he alone perfectly knew; other prophets only spake it when the spirit of prophecy rested upon them; yet, if in anything they were mistaken, the Lord soon rectified their error. Nathan did not refuse to unsay his own words when he was better instructed, neither should any of us be slow to retract if we have unknowingly taught any error.

4, 5, 6 And it came to pass that night, that the word of the LORD came unto Nathan, saying, Go and tell my servant David, Thus saith the LORD, Shalt thou build me an house for me to dwell in? Whereas I have not dwelt in *any* house since the time that I brought up the children of Israel out of Egypt, even to this day, but have walked in a tent and in a tabernacle.

7 In all *the places* wherein I have walked with all the children of Israel spake I a word with any of the tribes of Israel, whom I commanded to feed my people Israel, saying, Why build ye not me an house of cedar?

8, 9 Now therefore so shalt thou say unto my servant David, Thus saith the LORD of hosts, I took thee from the sheepcote, from following the sheep, to be ruler over my people, over Israel: And I was with thee whithersoever thou wentest, and have cut off all thine enemies out of thy sight, and have made thee a great name, like unto the name of the great *men* that *are* in the earth.

10, 11 Moreover I will appoint a place for my people Israel, and will plant them, that they may dwell in a place of their own, and move no more; neither shall the children of wickedness afflict them any more, as beforetime, And as since the time that I commanded judges *to be* over my people Israel, and have caused thee to rest from all thine enemies. Also the LORD telleth thee that he will make thee an house.

The Lord accepts the will for the deed, and pays back his saints in their own coin. Because David willed to build God a house, God built David's house. Truly we serve a good master.

12 ¶ And when thy days be fulfilled, and thou shalt sleep with thy fathers, I will set up thy seed after thee, which shall proceed out of thy bowels, and I will establish his kingdom.

13, 14, 15 He shall build an house for my name, and I will stablish the throne of his kingdom for ever. I will be his father, and he shall be my son. If he commit iniquity, I will chasten him with the rod of men, and with the stripes of the children of men: But my mercy shall not depart away from him, as I took *it* from Saul, whom I put away before thee.

16 And thine house and thy kingdom shall be established for ever before thee: thy throne shall be established for ever. *(This was a glorious covenant even as to its surface meaning, but there was a deeper sense underlying it all, and a special reference to that greater Son of David who shall for ever build up the church. The words, "If he commit iniquity," are by some rendered—"if I make him sin," thus referring the whole passage to him who was made sin for us.)*

17 According to all these words, and according to all this vision, so did Nathan speak unto David. *(In 1 Chron. xxii. 7, 8, David mentions one of the reasons why he was not allowed to build the temple—"As for me, it was in my mind to build an house unto the name of the Lord my God: but the word of the Lord came to me, saying, Thou shalt not build an house unto my name, because thou hast shed much blood upon the earth in my sight." It was not appropriate that he who had been the Lord's executioner on so large a scale should build the temple. God is very jealous of his own honour; and even where there may be no positive sin, yet the blunted feeling incident to some modes of life may disqualify a man for the higher forms of the Lord's service.)*

II. SAMUEL VII. 18—29.

THEN went king David in, and sat before the LORD, (*overwhelmed with gratitude he entered the Lord's tabernacle and reverently sat down and worshipped,*) and he said, Who *am* I, O Lord GOD? and what *is* my house, that thou hast brought me hitherto? (*This is the common feeling of all the Lord's kings and priests. They wonder why they should be chosen, and they adore the sovereign grace which elected them.*)

19 And this was yet a small thing in thy sight, O Lord GOD; but thou hast spoken also of thy servant's house for a great while to come. And *is* this the manner of man, O Lord GOD?

Do men act thus? No, for as far as the heavens are above the earth, so high are the Lord's ways above man's ways. He blesses divinely and not after the stinted measure of man's charity.

20 And what can David say more unto thee? for thou, Lord GOD, knowest thy servant.

This is our comfort, that when our souls are too full for utterance the Lord reads our feelings. If words fail us, God hears the songs or the sighs of our hearts.

21 For thy word's sake, and according to thine own heart, hast thou done all these great things, to make thy servant know *them.*

He disclaims all merit, and ascribes all to the gratuitous bounty of God. He was a free-grace man. He placed the crown upon the right head, and gave glory to God alone.

22 Wherefore thou art great, O LORD God: for *there is* none like thee, neither *is there any* God beside thee, according to all that we have heard with our ears. (*There is none like the Lord, and there are no people like his people. Faith deals with matters which are altogether unique, therefore our gratitude should prompt us to unusual deeds of service. If we receive more than others, we must do more than others.*)

23 And what one nation in the earth *is* like thy people, *even* Israel, whom God went to redeem for a people to himself, and to make him a name, and to do for you great things and terrible, for thy land, before thy people, which thou redeemedst to thee from Egypt, *from* the nations and their gods?

24 For thou hast confirmed to thyself thy people Israel *to be* a people unto thee for ever: and thou, LORD, art become their God.

This is a delightful reflection. God's choice of his people is not temporary, but eternal. He never changes in his relation to his people.

25 And now, O LORD God, the word that thou hast spoken concerning thy servant, and concerning his house, establish *it* for ever, and do as thou hast said. (*These last words contain the essence of prayer—"Do as thou hast said." The only solid foothold for faith is God's word. When a sinner comes before God, he must have nothing else to rely upon except this—"Do as thou hast said." If we cannot plead a promise we cannot ask in confidence; but with God's word before us, we know that his faithfulness will make it good, and therefore we are very bold.*)

26 And let thy name be magnified for ever, saying, The LORD of hosts *is* the God over Israel: and let the house of thy servant David be established before thee.

27 For thou, O LORD of hosts, God of Israel, hast revealed to thy servant, saying, I will build thee an house: therefore hath thy servant found in his heart to pray this prayer unto thee.

What we find promised in God's word we may most fitly find it in our hearts to pray for. Has the Lord said it? then let us seek it.

28 And now, O Lord GOD, thou *art* that God, and thy words be true, and thou hast promised this goodness unto thy servant:

29 Therefore now let it please thee to bless the house of thy servant, that it may continue for ever before thee: for thou, O Lord GOD, hast spoken *it*: and with thy blessing let the house of thy servant be blessed for ever.

Pleading the promises is the sinew and muscle of prayer. As we bring promissory notes to those who have signed them, so should we bring the promises of Holy Scripture before the Lord, and entreat him to make good his word. Let us continually cry to him—"Do as thou hast said."

Lord, for thy name's sake! such the plea,
 With force triumphant fraught,
By which thy saints prevail with thee,
 By thine own Spirit taught.

Oh, for thy name's sake, richly grant
 The unction from above;
Fulfil thy holy covenant,
 And glorify thy love.

WHEN *David was settled upon his throne, his people were accustomed lovingly to pray for him. We find one of their prayer-hymns in the book of Psalms; it is known as—*

PSALM XX.

We shall, as we read it, see Jesus in it, and turn it to spiritual account.

1 The LORD hear thee in the day of trouble; the name of the God of Jacob defend thee;

2 Send thee help from the sanctuary, and strengthen thee out of Zion; *(Out of heaven's sanctuary came the angel to strengthen our Lord, and from the precious remembrance of God's doings in his sanctuary our Lord refreshed himself when on the tree. There is no help like that which is of God's sending, and no deliverance like that which comes out of his sanctuary. The sanctuary to us is the person of our blessed Lord, who was typified by the temple, and is the true sanctuary which God has pitched, and not man: let us fly to the Cross for shelter in all times of need, and help will be sent to us. Men of the world despise sanctuary help, but our hearts have learned to prize it beyond all material aid. They seek help out of the armoury, or the treasury; but we turn to the sanctuary.)* "And strengthen thee out of Zion." *(To the Lord's mystical body the richest good comes in answer to the pleadings of his saints. This verse is a benediction befitting a Sabbath morning, and may be the salutation either of a pastor to his people, or of a Church to its minister. God in the sanctuary of his dear Son's person, and in the city of his chosen Church, is the proper object of his people's prayers, and under such a character they may confidently look to him for promised aid.)*

3 Remember all thy offerings, and accept thy burnt sacrifice; Selah. *(Before war, kings offered sacrifice, upon the acceptance of which they depended for success. Our blessed Lord presented himself as a victim, and was a sweet savour unto the Most High, and then he met and routed the embattled legions of hell. Still does his burnt sacrifice perfume the courts of heaven, and through him the offerings of his people are received as his sacrifices and oblations. We ought in our spiritual conflicts never to march forth to war until first the Lord has given us a token for good at that altar where faith beholds her bleeding Lord.)*

4 Grant thee according to thine own heart, and fulfil all thy counsel.

5 We will rejoice in thy salvation, and in the name of our God we will set up *our* banners: the LORD fulfil all thy petitions.

6 Now know I that the LORD saveth his anointed; he will hear him from his holy heaven with the saving strength of his right hand.

7 Some *trust* in chariots, and some in horses: but we will remember the name of the LORD our God. *(Chariots and horses make such an imposing show, that vain man is much taken with them; yet the discerning eye of faith sees more in an invisible God than in all these. The most dreaded war-engine of David's day was the war-chariot, armed with scythes, which mowed down men like grass: this was the boast and glory of the neighbouring nations; but the saints considered the name of Jehovah to be a far better defence. As the Israelites might not keep horses, it was most natural for them to regard the enemy's cavalry with more than usual dread. It is, therefore, all the greater evidence of faith that the bold songster can here disdain even the horse of Egypt in comparison with the Lord of Hosts. Alas, how many in our day who profess to be the Lord's, are as abjectly dependent upon their fellow-men, or upon an arm of flesh in some shape or other, as if they had never known the name of Jehovah at all!)*

8 They are brought down and fallen: but we are risen, and stand upright.

The enemies of God are uppermost at first, but before long they are brought down by force, or else fall of their own accord. Their foundation is rotten, and therefore when the time comes it gives way under them; their chariots are burned in the fire, and their horses die of pestilence, and where is their boasted strength? As for those who rest on Jehovah, they are often cast down at the first onset, but an Almighty arm uplifts them, and they joyfully stand upright. The victory of Jesus is the inheritance of his people. The world, death, Satan, and sin, shall all be trampled beneath the feet of the champions of faith; while those who rely upon an arm of flesh shall be ashamed and confounded for ever.

9 Save, LORD: let the king hear us when we call.

"His glory is great in thy salvation."

IN another Psalm we find King David exulting in the mercy of the Lord his God.

PSALM XXI.

This has been called the Royal Triumphal Ode. If we can see Jesus the king sweetly prominent in it, we shall be greatly profited.

1 The king shall joy in thy strength, O LORD; and in thy salvation how greatly shall he rejoice!

2 Thou hast given him his heart's desire, and hast not withholden the request of his lips. Selah. *(Souls are saved by Jesus, his people are enriched with all spiritual blessings in him, and this makes him greatly rejoice.)*

3 For thou preventest him with the blessings of goodness : *(The word* prevent *formerly signified to precede or go before, and assuredly Jehovah preceded his Son with blessings. Before he died, saints were saved by the anticipated merit of his death. The Father is so willing to give blessings through his Son, that instead of his being constrained to bestow his grace, he outstrips the Mediatorial march of mercy. " I say not that I will pray the Father for you: for the Father himself loveth you.")*

Thou settest a crown of pure gold on his head. *(Jesus wore the thorn-crown, but now wears the glory-crown. It is a "crown" indicating royal nature, imperial power, deserved honour, glorious conquest, and divine government. The crown is of the richest, rarest, most resplendent, and most lasting order—"gold," and that gold of the most refined and valuable sort, "pure gold," to indicate the excellence of his dominion. This crown is set upon his head most firmly, so that no power can move it, for Jehovah himself has set it upon his brow.)*

4 He asked life of thee, *and* thou gavest *it* him, *even* length of days for ever and ever.

5 His glory *is* great in thy salvation : honour and majesty hast thou laid upon him.

6 For thou hast made him most blessed for ever : thou hast made him exceeding glad with thy countenance.

7 For the king trusteth in the LORD, and through the mercy of the most High he shall not be moved.

8 Thine hand shall find out all thine enemies : thy right hand shall find out those that hate thee. *(None shall escape from the Great King*

when he comes in wrath. Be it ours at once to accept his love.)

9, 10, 11, 12 Thou shalt make them as a fiery oven in the time of thine anger : the LORD shall swallow them up in his wrath, and the fire shall devour them. Their fruit shalt thou destroy from the earth, and their seed from among the children of men. For they intended evil against thee : they imagined a mischievous device, *which* they are not able *to perform.* Therefore shalt thou make them turn their back, *when* thou shalt make ready *thine arrows* upon thy strings against the face of them.

Vain will be all opposition to Jesus, and terrible the overthrow of his enemies. God forbid that we should be among them.

13 Be thou exalted, LORD, in thine own strength : *so* will we sing and praise thy power.

The whole Psalm is meant to show forth the praises of the Lord Jesus. Isaac Ambrose upon this subject writes :—" I remember a dying woman who heard some discourse of Jesus Christ ; ' Oh,' said she, ' speak more of this—let me hear more of this—be not weary of telling his praise; I long to see him, and therefore I love to hear of him'!' Surely I cannot say too much of Jesus Christ. On this blessed subject no man can possibly exaggerate. Had I the tongues of men and angels, I could never fully set forth Christ. It involves an eternal contradiction, that the creature can see to the bottom of the Creator. Suppose all the sands on the sea-shore, all the flowers, herbs, leaves, twigs of trees in woods and forests, all the stars of heaven, were all rational creatures ; and that they had wisdom, and tongues of angels to speak of the loveliness, beauty, glory, and excellency of Christ, as gone to heaven, and sitting at the right-hand of his Father, they would, in all their expressions, stay millions of miles on this side of Jesus Christ. Oh, the loveliness, beauty, and glory of his countenance ! Can I speak, or you hear of such a Christ ? And are we not all in a burning love, in a seraphical love, or at least a conjugal love ? O my heart, how is it thou art not love-sick ? How is it thou dost not charge the daughters of Jerusalem as the spouse did ? I charge you, O daughters of Jerusalem, if ye find my beloved, that ye shall tell him, that I am sick of love."

II. SAMUEL IX.

AND David said, Is there yet any that is left of the house of Saul, that I may shew him kindness for Jonathan's sake?

Good men are grateful men. Jonathan had shown David great kindness, and therefore David sought to return it to his descendants. He who is not faithful in friendship gives no evidence that he is sincere in religion.

2, 3 And *there was* of the house of Saul a servant whose name *was* Ziba. And when they had called him unto David, the king said unto him, *Art* thou Ziba? And he said, Thy servant *is he.* And the king said, *Is* there not yet any of the house of Saul, that I may shew the kindness of God unto him? And Ziba said unto the king, Jonathan hath yet a son, *which is* lame on *his* feet.

4 And the king said unto him, Where *is* he? And Ziba said unto the king, Behold, he *is* in the house of Machir, the son of Ammiel, in Lodebar. *(He was living in the country in great retirement, perhaps in fear that David might seek his life. We are often afraid of the very men who will turn out to be our best friends.)*

5 ¶ Then king David sent, and fetched him out of the house of Machir, the son of Ammiel, from Lo-debar.

6 Now when Mephibosheth, the son of Jonathan, the son of Saul, was come unto David, he fell on his face, and did reverence. *(He was both awed by the splendour of the court, and alarmed lest the king should injure him, but David soon comforted him in the kindest manner.)* And David said, Mephibosheth. And he answered, Behold thy servant!

7 And David said unto him, Fear not: for I will surely shew thee kindness for Jonathan thy father's sake, and will restore thee all the land of Saul thy father; and thou shalt eat bread at my table continually.

8 And he bowed himself, and said, What *is* thy servant, that thou shouldest look upon such a dead dog as I *am*?

9, 10 Then the king called to Ziba, Saul's servant, and said unto him, I have given unto thy master's son all that pertained to Saul and to all his house. Thou therefore, and thy sons, and thy servants, shall till the land for him, and thou shalt bring in *the fruits*, that thy master's son may have food to eat: but Mephibosheth thy

master's son shall eat bread alway at my table. Now Ziba had fifteen sons and twenty servants. *(And therefore he would be able to equip Mephibosheth with a suitable attendance becoming his royal rank.)*

11 Then said Ziba unto the king, According to all that my lord the king hath commanded his servant, so shall thy servant do. As for Mephibosheth, *said the king*, he shall eat at my table, as one of the king's sons.

12, 13 And Mephibosheth had a young son, whose name *was* Micha. And all that dwelt in the house of Ziba *were* servants unto Mephibosheth. So Mephibosheth dwelt in Jerusalem: for he did eat continually at the king's table; and was lame on both his feet.

From this story we learn to remember past kindnesses. If in his prosperity any man has been good to us, let us deal well with him if we ever see either him or his children in want. Never let it be said that a child of God is ungrateful to his fellow-men. If we are to do kindness to those who have treated us ill, much more are we bound to repay the favours of those who have been our friends. A further lesson may be found in the fact that David and Jonathan had made a covenant, and that David was faithful to it, even though Jonathan's son was both obscure in his abode, poor in his estate, and deformed in his person. The Lord also is true to his covenant; he will not forsake those who put their trust in him. Though many of his people are, spiritually, as lame as Mephibosheth, yet he remembers them, and even deigns to invite them to sit at his table in familiar intercourse with him. The Lord is not ashamed of the poor, feeble friends of Jesus, but out of love to their well-beloved Lord and Master he will grant to them to eat continually at the king's table, even though they be lame on both their feet.

Poor, weak, and worthless, though I am,
I have a rich almighty Friend;
Jesus, the Saviour, is His name:
He freely loves, and without end.

He cheers my heart, my wants supplies,
And says that I shall shortly be
Enthroned with him above the skies:
Oh! what a friend is Christ to me!

God is gone up with shouts of joy,
  And angels harping round ;
Our Lord is welcomed to the sky
  With trumpet's joyful sound.

Open, ye heavenly gates, to let
  The King of glory in ;
The Lord of hosts, of saving might,
  Who vanquished death and sin.

And shall not mortals join their songs,
  Though poor their notes may be ?
The lisping of believing tongues,
  Makes heavenly minstrelsy.

Jesus, with thy salvation blest,
We yield the glory to thy name :
Fix'd in thy strength our banners rest,
With joy thy vict'ry we proclaim.

Let men the rattling chariot trust,
Or the swift steed, with courage stored.
In thee our confidence we boast,
Jesus, Messiah, conquering Lord !

Safe shall we stand, nor yield to fear,
When sinners with their hopes shall fall :
Save, Lord, O King Messiah, hear !
Hear, mighty Saviour, when we call.

Jesus, where'er thy people meet,
There they behold thy mercy-seat :
Where'er they seek thee, thou art found
And every place is hallow'd ground.

For thou within no walls confined,
Inhabitest the humble mind ;
Such ever bring thee where they come,
And going, take thee to their home.

Behold, to thee we pour our vow,
Our daily dwelling place art thou!
And whilst the light of life we see,
Our happy souls shall rest in thee.

The head that once was crown'd with thorns
  Is crown'd with glory now ;
A royal diadem adorns
  The mighty victor's brow.

The highest place that heaven affords
  Is his, is his by right,
The King of kings, the Lord of lords,
  And heaven's eternal light.

To him let every tongue be praise,
  And every heart be love :
All grateful honours paid on earth,
  And nobler songs above.

Lead me not, for flesh is frail,
Where fierce trials would assail ;
Leave me not, in darken'd hour,
To withstand the tempter's power.

Save me from the tempter's wiles,
Keep my heart when pleasure smiles ;
On my watch tower may I be,
Lest I should dishonour thee.

While I am a pilgrim here,
Let thy love my spirit cheer :
As my guide, my guard, my friend,
Lead me to my journey's end.

WE *now come to that mournful occurrence in David's life, which changed his whole career from prosperity to sorrow.*

II. SAMUEL XI. 1—3; 6—10; 12—17; 26, 27.

1 And it came to pass, after the year was expired, at the time when kings go forth *to battle,* that David sent Joab, and his servants with him, and all Israel; and they destroyed the children of Ammon, and besieged Rabbah. But David tarried still at Jerusalem. *Perhaps he had begun to indulge himself in ease, and therefore left the battles of his country to be fought by others. If so, we are hereby taught that indolence is the nurse of vice.*

2 And it came to pass in an eveningtide, that David arose from off his bed, and walked upon the roof·of the king's house : (*Did he not rise from his bed till so late in the day? Had he grown self-indulgent? If so, who wonders that he fell?*) and from the roof he saw a woman washing herself; and the woman *was* very beautiful to look upon.

3 And David sent and enquired after the woman. And *one* said, *Is* not this Bath-sheba, the daughter of Eliam, the wife of Uriah the Hittite? (*David at once sent for her and took her to himself, thus committing the grossest sin. Alas! Alas! how were the mighty fallen!*

In a short time David found that his sin would be discovered, and therefore he sent for Uriah to come home, that his shameful conduct might be concealed.)

6, 7 And David sent to Joab, *saying,* Send me Uriah the Hittite. And Joab sent Uriah to David. And when Uriah was come unto him, David demanded *of him* how Joab did, and how the people did, and how the war prospered.

8 And David said to Uriah, Go down to thy house, and wash thy feet. And Uriah departed out of the king's house, and there followed him a mess *of meat* from the king.

9 But Uriah slept at the door of the king's house with all the servants of his lord, and went not down to his house.

10 And when they had told David, saying, Uriah went not down unto his house, David said unto Uriah, Camest thou not from *thy* journey? why *then* didst thou not go down unto thine house? (*To this, Uriah answered that he would not go home to sleep at ease while the ark*

and his fellow-soldiers were in tents, or encamped in the open field. Here we find a common soldier austere and self-denying, while the renowned psalmist had become luxurious and wanton.)

12, 13 And David said to Uriah, Tarry here to day also, and to morrow I will let thee·depart. So Uriah abode in Jerusalem that day, and the morrow. And when David had called him, he did eat and drink before him; and he made him drunk : and at even he went out to lie on his bed with the servants of his lord, but went not down to his house. (*What wickedness was this on David's part to lead honest Uriah into drunkenness! One sin draws on another as links of a chain. With all his cunning, David did not succeed in concealing his crime, and therefore, he went further still, and became guilty of murder to screen himself. " How art thou fallen from heaven, thou beautiful star of the morning!" " Let him that thinketh he standeth take heed lest he fall."*)

14, 15 And it came to pass in the morning, that David wrote a letter to Joab, and sent *it* by the hand of Uriah. And he wrote in the letter, saying, Set ye Uriah in the forefront of the hottest battle, and retire ye from him, that he may be smitten, and die.

16 And it came to pass, when Joab observed the city, that he assigned Uriah unto a place where he knew that valiant men *were.*

17 And the men of the city went out; and fought with Joab : and there fell *some* of the people of the servants of David; and Uriah the Hittite died also. (*The man after God's own heart had fallen so low as to be both an adulterer and a murderer! Other princes in those days did such things commonly, and their people dared not complain, but this was a chosen servant of God, and in him it was foul iniquity.*)

26, 27 And when the wife of Uriah heard that Uriah her husband was dead, she mourned for her husband. And when the mourning was past, David sent and fetched her to his·house, and she became his wife, and bare him a son. But the thing that David had done displeased the LORD. (*Though the sinner may have dreamed that he had cleverly hidden his crime, this last sentence was the death knell of his security. If our conduct displeases the Lord, nothing is well with us.*)

II. SAMUEL XII. 1—10; 13, 14.

AND the LORD sent Nathan unto David. *(Such a sin could not remain unpunished. The Lord sent the same messenger to rebuke who had formerly come to bless. It was great mercy on God's part to send a faithful preacher to David; if he had not loved him, he might have left him to his own hardness of heart. We ought to bless God much for those who will honestly deliver the divine message to us, whether it be sweet or bitter.)* And he came unto him, and said unto him, There were two men in one city; the one rich, and the other poor.

2 The rich *man* had exceeding many flocks and herds:

3 But the poor *man* had nothing, save one little ewe lamb, which he had bought and nourished up: and it grew up together with him, and with his children; it did eat of his own meat, and drank of his own cup, and lay in his bosom, and was unto him as a daughter.

4 And there came a traveller unto the rich man, and he spared to take of his own flock and of his own herd, to dress for the wayfaring man that was come unto him; but took the poor man's lamb, and dressed it for the man that was come to him.

5 And David's anger was greatly kindled against the man; and he said to Nathan, *As* the LORD liveth, the man that hath done this *thing* shall surely die:

6 And he shall restore the lamb fourfold, because he did this thing, and because he had no pity. *(Little did he think that he had pronounced sentence on himself. We are ready enough to condemn others, but, ah! how slow to see sin in ourselves.)*

7, 8 And Nathan said to David, Thou *art* the man. *(The parable was full of wisdom, and the application full of courage. How thunderstruck was the king! How his colour must have changed! How loudly did his conscience say "Amen" to all that the prophet spake. Nathan went on to set forth David's sin, that he might see more of its blackness, and repent the more heartily.)* Thus saith the LORD God of Israel, I anointed thee king over Israel, and I delivered thee out of the hand of Saul; And I gave thee thy master's house, and thy master's wives into thy bosom, and gave thee the house of Israel and of Judah; and if *that had been*

too little, I would moreover have given unto thee such and such things.

9 Wherefore hast thou despised the commandment of the LORD, to do evil in his sight? thou hast killed Uriah the Hittite with the sword, and hast taken his wife *to be* thy wife, and hast slain him with the sword of the children of Ammon.

10 Now therefore the sword shall never depart from thine house; because thou hast despised me, and hast taken the wife of Uriah the Hittite to be thy wife. *(Here was sharp medicine for a foul disease. If we sin, we must smart for it. The Lord's beloved cannot escape the rod if they transgress. In this case, as in most others, the chastisement was of the same nature as the sin. He had slain Uriah with the sword, and the sword was now to waste his family.)*

13 And David said unto Nathan, I have sinned against the LORD. *(A child of God may sin, but he cannot continue in it. If there had been no grace in David, he would have been angry with Nathan, but the spiritual life within him brought him into the dust of repentance at once. Many sin, as David did; but never repent, as he did.)* And Nathan said unto David, The LORD also hath put away thy sin; thou shalt not die.

How quickly the pardon came! "Confess, and live" is God's word to the erring. The Lord our God delighteth in mercy. Let us go to him and acknowledge our transgressions at once, and find immediate pardon.

14 Howbeit, because by this deed thou hast given great occasion to the enemies of the LORD to blaspheme, the child also *that is* born unto thee shall surely die. *(Though David shall live, he shall smart in a tender place. God forgives his children, but he will not suffer them to think lightly of sin; he will smite them heavily, though not mortally. O Lord, keep us from sin.)*

Mercy, mercy, God the Father!
  God the Son, be thou my plea!
God the Holy Spirit, comfort!
  Triune God, deliver me!

Not my sins, O Lord, remember,
  Not thine own avenger be;
But, for thy great tender mercies,
  Saviour God, deliver me!

II. SAMUEL XII. 15—23.

AND Nathan departed unto his house. And the LORD struck the child that Uriah's wife bare unto David, and it was very sick. *(God is true to his word, whether he threatens or promises.)*

16 David therefore besought God for the child; and David fasted, and went in, and lay all night upon the earth. *(We are permitted to pray against coming ills. If David was not forbidden to plead even when the divine will had been declared, how much more may we appeal to God while as yet his purposes are unknown to us.)*

17 And the elders of his house arose, *and went* to him, to raise him up from the earth: but he would not, neither did he eat bread with them. *(They feared for his health, but he was ready to sacrifice himself for his poor suffering babe. He was a tender father, and it pricked him to the heart to see his child suffering through the father's sin. Perhaps it was during this period that repentance was having its perfect work, and he was regaining the smile of his heavenly Father.)*

18 And it came to pass on the seventh day, that the child died. And the servants of David feared to tell him that the child was dead: for they said, Behold, while the child was yet alive, we spake unto him, and he would not hearken unto our voice: how will he then vex himself, if we tell him that the child is dead?

19 But when David saw that his servants whispered, David perceived that the child was dead: therefore David said unto his servants, Is the child dead? And they said, He is dead.

20 Then David arose from the earth, and washed, and anointed *himself*, and changed his apparel, and came into the house of the LORD, and worshipped: then he came to his own house; and when he required, they set bread before him, and he did eat. *(While the child lived he pleaded for its life, but when it was dead he submitted at once to the divine will. He seems also to have realised his pardon by faith in the atoning sacrifice, and therefore with humble gratitude went up again to the house of the Lord to worship, and returned to his palace to pursue the ordinary avocations of life. Some by their long mourning after the loss of children appear to be angry with God, and maintain a spirit of rebellion against him. Such was not David's mind.)*

21 Then said his servants unto him, What thing *is* this that thou hast done? thou didst fast and weep for the child, *while it was* alive; but when the child was dead, thou didst rise and eat bread. *(Those who are not themselves taught of God cannot understand the believer's conduct. He neither rejoices nor mourns according to the world's fashion, but allows his judgment to act, and his better feelings to have full play. This makes independent and consistent Christians appear to be odd and singular.)*

22 And he said, While the child was yet alive, I fasted and wept: for I said, Who can tell *whether* GOD will be gracious to me, that the child may live?

23 But now he is dead, wherefore should I fast? can I bring him back again? I shall go to him, but he shall not return to me.

A great deal is suggested by the words " I shall go to him." David could not have thought his child to be annihilated; it would have given him no comfort to hope to be annihilated too. Far less could David have imagined that the child was in misery, for he did not expect to go there at death. The father believed his babe to be in heaven, and expected to meet him there; and we also believe that all the dear little ones who die in infancy are in glory. We say all little ones, because this child was the offspring of shame, and if it be where David now is, we feel sure that all other departed infants are there also.

" *Millions of infant souls compose
The family above.*"

By the death of his babe the first blow of the rod fell upon David, and throughout the remainder of his life he found his trials multiplied.

It is the Lord whose chast'ning hand
  Has filled the cup of woe;
The shaft of death by his command
  Hath struck the fatal blow.

It is the Lord and he is good,
  Unchangeably the same;
Though sorrow rises like a flood,
  I'll bless his holy name.

284   " Cleanse me from my sin."   MAY 15.—MORNING.

[*Or September 26.*]

HOW *bitterly David lamented his great sin may be seen by the penitential psalms which he composed. Among the most memorable of these is—*

PSALM LI.

It has been often called THE SINNER'S GUIDE.

1 Have mercy upon me, O God, according to thy lovingkindness : according unto the multitude of thy tender mercies blot out my transgressions. (*He appealed to the sweeter attributes. Penitence has a quick eye for the loving and merciful qualities in the divine character. Let us appeal to them.*)

2 Wash me throughly from mine iniquity, and cleanse me from my sin. (*He could not bear to be defiled, he longed for complete pardon.*)

3 For I acknowledge my transgressions : and my sin *is* ever before me.

4 Against thee, thee only, have I sinned, and done *this* evil in thy sight : that thou mightest be justified when thou speakest, *and* be clear when thou judgest. (*The essence of sin lies in its opposition to God, and its impudent defiance of his holy presence. David had wronged Bathsheba and Uriah, but his greatest misery was that he had offended his God. Graceless men care nothing about this.*)

5 Behold, I was shapen in iniquity ; and in sin did my mother conceive me.

6 Behold, thou desirest truth in the inward parts : and in the hidden *part* thou shalt make me to know wisdom. (*His outward act of evil led him to look within, and there he found his inmost nature and his first original to be impure. When our falls lead us to discover and mourn over our inbred sins, we are on the sure way to recovery from them.*)

7 Purge me with hyssop, and I shall be clean : wash me, and I shall be whiter than snow. (*This is a glorious utterance of faith. The humbled soul, while mourning in the dust, yet confides in the blood of sprinkling, and believes that it can remove all stain. Foul as I am yet I am not too filthy for the precious blood of atonement! All manner of sin and of blasphemy the blood of Jesus can remove.*)

8 Make me to hear joy and gladness ; *that* the bones *which* thou hast broken may rejoice.

9 Hide thy face from my sins, and blot out all mine iniquities.

10 Create in me a clean heart, O God ; and renew a right spirit within me. (*Sin destroys, and therefore grace must re-create. Sincere penitents are not content with pardon, they desire to be made holy for the future.*)

11 Cast me not away from thy presence ; and take not thy holy spirit from me.

12 Restore unto me the joy of thy salvation ; and uphold me *with thy* free spirit.

13 *Then* will I teach transgressors thy ways ; and sinners shall be converted unto thee.

None teach so well as those who know the power of forgiving love by personal experience. Pardoned sinners are the best preachers to their rebellious fellow-men.

14 Deliver me from bloodguiltiness, O God, thou God of my salvation : *and* my tongue shall sing aloud of thy righteousness.

15 O Lord, open thou my lips ; and my mouth shall shew forth thy praise.

16 For thou desirest not sacrifice ; else would I give *it :* thou delightest not in burnt offering.

17 The sacrifices of God *are* a broken spirit : a broken and a contrite heart, O God, thou wilt not despise. (*Deep experience led David away from mere forms into the spirit of the gospel. A real sense of sin will never allow men to be content with ordinances, they want the Lord himself to be revealed to them in spiritual worship, as accepting their contrite cries.*)

18 Do good in thy good pleasure unto Zion : build thou the walls of Jerusalem.

19 Then shalt thou be pleased with the sacrifices of righteousness, with burnt offering and whole burnt offering : then shall they offer bullocks upon thine altar. (*Thus he would fain undo the mischief he had wrought and build up the church whose walls he had pulled down by his ill example. The Lord grant that his cause and people may never suffer through our fault. Amen.*)

My soul lies humbled in the dust,
And owns thy dreadful sentence just;
Look down, O Lord, with pitying eye
And save the soul condemn'd to die.

Then will I teach the world thy ways;
Sinners shall learn thy sovereign grace,
I'll lead them to my Saviour's blood,
And they shall praise a pardoning God.

AFTER *David had obtained a sense of pardon, he sang that sweet gospel Psalm, the thirty-second.*

PSALM XXXII.

1 Blessed *is he whose* transgression *is* forgiven, *whose* sin *is* covered.

Yes, even a great sinner may be blessed. When his sin is effectually covered by the great propitiation, he is as blessed as if he had never sinned. Have all the members of this family tasted of this blessedness? Sin has cursed us all, has pardon blessed us all?

2 Blessed *is* the man unto whom the LORD imputeth not iniquity, and in whose spirit *there is* no guile. (*He who is freed from guilt is also cleansed from guile or deceit. David had been very crafty in his endeavours to hide his crime, and he felt it a great relief to escape from the tortuous way of living which arises out of deceit.*)

3 When I kept silence, my bones waxed old through my roaring all the day long.

4 For day and night thy hand was heavy upon me: my moisture is turned into the drought of summer. Selah.

While sin is unconfessed it ferments within the heart, and causes inward anguish; and when God's hand presses from without, the awakened sinner is in a wretched plight indeed. Such are the feelings of all who seek the Lord, in a greater or less degree.

5 I acknowledged my sin unto thee, and mine iniquity have I not hid. I said, I will confess my transgressions unto the LORD; and thou forgavest the iniquity of my sin. Selah.

Forgiveness followed on the heels of confession, for atonement was already made. Who among us will refuse to confess? Let us all acknowledge our sin before the Lord, and the blood of Jesus will put it all away, at once and for ever.

6 For this shall every one that is godly pray unto thee in a time when thou mayest be found: surely in the floods of great waters they shall not come nigh unto him.

7 Thou *art* my hiding place; thou shalt preserve me from trouble; thou shalt compass me about with songs of deliverance. Selah.

He who before he sought the Lord was compassed with sighs is now compassed with songs. If we would be happy we must be pardoned; if

we would be pardoned, we must confess our iniquities, and look to Jesus who covers all our sin.

8 I will instruct thee and teach thee in the way which thou shalt go: I will guide thee with mine eye.

9 Be ye not as the horse, *or* as the mule, *which* have no understanding: whose mouth must be held in with bit and bridle, lest they come near unto thee.

Forgiven men should be tender in heart, and fear to transgress again. We ought not to need rough means to keep us out of mischief, we ought to be sensitive to the faintest touch of the Lord's hand.

10 Many sorrows *shall be* to the wicked: but he that trusteth in the LORD, mercy shall compass him about.

11 Be glad in the LORD, and rejoice, ye righteous: and shout for joy, all *ye that are* upright in heart.

Those who begin with holy weeping shall end with holy rejoicing. If there be one unforgiven one in this family, let him or her go to the heavenly Father and cry for that gracious forgiveness which is given to all who believe in Jesus. It is not given as a reward of good works, or as the fruit of any efforts of our own; but as the free gift of God in Christ Jesus. Paul says that David here describes the blessedness of the man unto whom God imputeth righteousness without works, and he declares most plainly that it is not a matter of merit but of grace. The very worst and vilest sins will be freely and at once forgiven if we will confess them to the Lord, and trust in the infinite merits of his dear Son. Do not linger then, but fly at once to the open fountain.

In Christ I have believed,
And through the spotless Lamb
Grace and salvation have received:
In him complete I am.

My sins, my crimson stains,
Are blotted out each one;
No condemnation now remains!
God views me in his Son.

THE *chastisements of God fell very heavily upon David from the time of his great sin, even to the end of his life. His children became the source of his trials. Amnon fell into the foulest sin, and Absalom his brother slew him on account of it. Absalom having obtained forgiveness for the murder, returned to the court and commenced at once to plot against his own father, who loved him far too well. In his attempts to undermine his father's authority he acted very cunningly, using every art to win popular applause.*

II. SAMUEL XV. 1—12.

1 And it came to pass after this, that Absalom prepared him chariots and horses, and fifty men to run before him. *(Outward pomp often catches the attention of the populace, and therefore Absalom added to the attraction of his own handsome person the unusual magnificence of chariots and running footmen.)*

2, 3 And Absalom rose up early, and stood beside the way of the gate : and it was *so*, that when any man that had a controversy came to the king for judgment, then Absalom called unto him, and said, Of what city *art* thou ? And he said, Thy servant *is* of one of the tribes of Israel. And Absalom said unto him, See, thy matters *are* good and right; but *there is* no man *deputed* of the king to hear thee.

4 Absalom said moreover, Oh that I were made judge in the land, that every man which hath any suit or cause might come unto me, and I would do him justice !

5 And it was *so*, that when any man came nigh *to him* to do him obeisance, he put forth his hand, and took him, and kissed him.

Absalom's ambition led him to take great pains to appear affable and attentive to all. He was early at the palace gate and spoke with all suitors, being "hail-fellow well met" with them all. He flattered each one that his cause was good, and pretended to regret that justice was much neg-lected ; and applicants were kept waiting. If he were king, matters would be seen to at once, and no one should have to complain of delay or injustice. Everybody said "What a courteous prince ! What a just and careful ruler Absalom would be!"

6 And on this manner did Absalom to all Israel that came to the king for judgment : so Absalom stole the hearts of the men of Israel.

The hearts of the people were not won, but stolen, for the vain young prince deceived them. While pretending such zeal for their welfare, he was only advancing his own traitorous schemes.

7, 8 And it came to pass after forty years, that Absalom said unto the king, I pray thee, let me go and pay my vow, which I have vowed unto the LORD, in Hebron. For thy servant vowed a vow while I abode at Geshur in Syria, saying, If the LORD shall bring me again indeed to Jerusalem, then I will serve the LORD.

To crown all his other deceit, Absalom pretended to be exceedingly devout, and declared that he must make a pilgrimage to Hebron, in order to keep a holy vow which he had made in the days of his exile. He is a bad man indeed who uses religion as a stalking horse for his base ambition.

9 And the king said unto him, Go in peace. So he arose, and went to Hebron.

10, 11 But Absalom sent spies throughout all the tribes of Israel, saying, As soon as ye hear the sound of the trumpet, then ye shall say, Absalom reigneth in Hebron. And with Absalom went two hundred men out of Jerusalem, *that were* called ; and they went in their simplicity, and they knew not any thing.

These persons accompanied Absalom to join with him in his devotions, and out of respect for the king's son; but they were not in the secret of the plot. Absalom, however, used their presence for his own ends, by making the common people believe that these honourable men had left David and gone over to his rebel son.

12 And Absalom sent for Ahithophel the Gilonite, David's counsellor, from his city, *even* from Giloh, while he offered sacrifices. And the conspiracy was strong; for the people increased continually with Absalom.

Ahithophel was the intimate friend as well as the counsellor of David ; but he appears to have selfishly gone over to the faction of the young prince, because he judged it to be stronger than the party of the king. Thus David was brought into sore distress, his friends were forsaking him, his enemy was growing stronger and aiming to dethrone him ; and worst of all, that enemy was his favourite son. What mists and black days befell David after he so sadly swerved from the way of holiness.

II. SAMUEL XV. 13—26.

AND there came a messenger to David, saying, The hearts of the men of Israel are after Absalom. (*This must have sounded like a thunder-clap in the ear of David. While rejoicing in the belief that his son was religiously employed in paying his vows, the news of his rebellion was suddenly brought to him. David had rebelled against his God and king, and now he sees his own son in arms against him. How well had God kept his threatening that evil should arise to him out of his own house!*)

14 And David said unto all his servants that *were* with him at Jerusalem, Arise, and let us flee; for we shall not *else* escape from Absalom: make speed to depart, lest he overtake us suddenly, and bring evil upon us, and smite the city with the edge of the sword. (*The city could not be defended, for its walls were not built; therefore, David had prayed, "Build thou the walls of Jerusalem."*)

15 And the king's servants said unto the king, Behold, thy servants *are ready to do* whatsoever my lord the king shall appoint.

16, 17 And the king went forth, and all his household after him, and tarried in a place that was far off. (*He must needs go on foot, though his wicked son had horses: he took his family with him, for he was always a loving father, and would not leave them in danger. Who can tell the sorrow which filled poor David's heart? God's rod smote him heavily.*)

18 And all his servants passed on beside him; and all the Cherethites (*or executioners*), and all the Pelethites (*or messengers*), and all the Gittites, six hundred men which came after him from Gath, passed on before the king. *These were his body-guard, and remained faithful when others deserted to the popular side. May we always adhere to our Lord Jesus, even though all the world should wander after the beast and the false prophet.*

19, 20 Then said the king to Ittai the Gittite, Wherefore goest thou also with us? return to thy place, and abide with the king: for thou *art* a stranger, and also an exile. Whereas thou camest *but* yesterday, should I this day make thee go up and down with us? seeing I go whither I may, return thou, and take back thy brethren: mercy and truth *be* with thee.

David was too generous to wish to bring troubles upon others; much as he needed Ittai's help, he would not impose upon his kindness.

21 And Ittai answered the king, and said, *As* the LORD liveth, and *as* my lord the king liveth, surely in what place my lord the king shall be, whether in death or life, even there also will thy servant be. (*After this true-hearted fashion we ought to follow Jesus.*)

22 And David said to Ittai, Go and pass over. And Ittai the Gittite passed over, and all his men, and all the little ones that *were* with him. (*The Lord did not leave his servant quite alone, but found him friends in his need.*

23 And all the country wept with a loud voice, and all the people passed over: the king also himself passed over the brook Kidron, and all the people passed over, toward the way of the wilderness. (*The common people mourned with their king, and well they might. There was a yet sadder sight when Jesus, "the King, also himself passed over the brook Kidron." O Lord, we see thee typified by David, and our hearts adore thee.*)

24, 25, 26 And lo Zadok also, and all the Levites *were* with him, bearing the ark of the covenant of God: And the king said unto Zadok, Carry back the ark of God into the city: if I shall find favour in the eyes of the LORD, he will bring me again, and shew me *both* it, and his habitation: But if he thus say, I have no delight in thee; behold, *here am* I, let him do to me as seemeth good unto him. (*He was jealous for the safety of the ark and the priests, and therefore would not have them exposed to the same dangers as himself. He was also deeply submissive to the Lord's will, and thereby showed how much his trials had been sanctified to him. It is a blessed thing when the visitations, which God sends upon us for sin, bow us in lowly reverence and humble acquiescence at the Master's feet. So may the Lord always bless our family afflictions to each one of us.*)

Jesus, whom angel hosts adore,
Became a man of griefs for me;
In love, though rich, becoming poor,
That I, through him, enrich'd might be.

II. SAMUEL XV. 29—37.

ZADOK therefore and Abiathar carried the ark of God again to Jerusalem: and they tarried there.

30 ¶ And David went up by the ascent of *mount* Olivet, and wept as he went up, and had his head covered, and he went barefoot : and all the people that *was* with him covered every man his head, and they went up, weeping as they went up. *(This was a mournful procession indeed. To see a good king in his old age fleeing with heavy heart, covered head, weeping eyes, and bare feet, from the rage of his own son—this was a spectacle of woe such as is seldom seen. Well might the people join in the royal lamentation. Little did David think when he acted so wickedly with Bathsheba that his sin would cost him so dear.)*

31 ¶ And *one* told David, saying, Ahithophel *is* among the conspirators with Absalom. And David said, O LORD, I pray thee, turn the counsel of Ahithophel into foolishness.

David was not too sorrowful to pray. He knew where his strength lay, and took care to resort to his strong helper.

32 ¶ And it came to pass, that *when* David was come to the top *of the mount*, where he worshipped God, behold, Hushai the Archite came to meet him with his coat rent, and earth upon his head : *(Perhaps at the brow of the hill the king paused, looked after the ark, and solemnly prostrated himself in worship. Just as he rose from his knees, he found that God had sent him a valuable ally in the person of Hushai, by whose diplomacy Ahithophel's devices were to be defeated. When we most honour God he will be most ready to help us. David was glad to see Hushai, but thought that he would be most useful to his cause by returning to Jerusalem:)*

33, 34 Unto whom David said, If thou passest on with me, then thou shalt be a burden unto me : But if thou return to the city, and say unto Absalom, I will be thy servant, O king ; as I *have been* thy father's servant hitherto, so *will* I now also *be* thy servant : then mayest thou for me defeat the counsel of Ahithophel.

This species of trickery no Christian can approve of, but among Orientals it is highly esteemed. We are sorry that David should fall into it. We must, in this matter, look at him as a warning, rather than as an example.

35, 36 And *hast thou* not there with thee Zadok and Abiathar the priests ? therefore it shall be, *that* what thing soever thou shalt hear out of the king's house, thou shalt tell *it* to Zadok and Abiathar the priests. Behold, *they have* there with them their two sons, Ahimaaz Zadok's *son*, and Jonathan Abiathar's *son ;* and by them ye shall send unto me every thing that ye can hear.

37 So Hushai David's friend came into the city, and Absalom came into Jerusalem.

II. SAMUEL XVII. 22, 24 ; 27—29.

THE *intelligence which Hushai sent by the two young priests induced the king to flee further away, and to retreat beyond the Jordan into the far east of the country.*

22 Then David arose, and all the people that *were* with him, and they passed over Jordan : by the morning light there lacked not one of them that was not gone over Jordan. *(Here was another sad march. It was a gloomy sight to see David and the people fording the Jordan at the dead of night.)*

24 Then David came to Mahanaim. And Absalom passed over Jordan, he and all the men of Israel with him. *(This wicked young prince hotly pursued his father, and could not be content unless he could shed his blood. Yet this was a son of David! What bad sons may come of holy sires!)*

27, 28, 29 And it came to pass, when David was come to Mahanaim, that Shobi the son of Nahash of Rabbah of the children of Ammon, and Machir the son of Ammiel of Lo-debar, and Barzillai the Gileadite of Rogelim, Brought beds, and basons, and earthen vessels, and wheat, and barley, and flour, and parched *corn*, and beans, and lentiles, and parched *pulse,* And honey, and butter, and sheep, and cheese of kine, for David, and for the people that *were* with him, to eat : for they said, The people *is* hungry, and weary, and thirsty, in the wilderness. *(Thus strangers became the good man's friends. There were some sweetening drops in his cup. The Lord never utterly leaves his people. If he smites them, he at the same time supports them. Let us always trust in him.)*

II. SAMUEL XVI. 5—14.

AND when king David came to Bahurim, behold, thence came out a man of the family of the house of Saul, whose name *was* Shimei, the son of Gera : he came forth, and cursed still as he came. (*At the moment when grief had made poor David most sensitive, the foul mouth of Shimei was opened to curse him. It is an evidence of a very cruel disposition when those who need pity are singled out for abuse. It is reckoned a very cowardly thing to strike a man when he is down, and Shimei was just such a coward. All the while that David prospered we hear nothing of Shimei ; but as our trials shew us who are our friends, so do they reveal our enemies.*)

6 And he cast stones at David, and at all the servants of king David : and all the people and all the mighty men *were* on his right hand and on his left. (*His stones and his words were meant not only to hurt the king, but to shew his utter contempt for him,—contempt which he had found it convenient to conceal through so many years.*)

7, 8 And thus said Shimei when he cursed, Come out, come out, thou bloody man, and thou man of Belial : The LORD hath returned upon thee all the blood of the house of Saul, in whose stead thou hast reigned ; and the LORD hath delivered the kingdom into the hand of Absalom thy son : and, behold, thou *art taken* in thy mischief, because thou *art* a bloody man. *This was a base libel, for David had never laid his hand upon Saul or any of his house. Did he not execute the Amalekite who professed to have slain Saul ? Did he not pour out a passionate lament for Saul and Jonathan ? Did he not enquire for any of the house of Jonathan, that he might shew him kindness ? Had he not entertained Mephibosheth at his own table? Evil tongues will not be quiet, and no innocence can ward off their calumnies.*

9 ¶ Then said Abishai the son of Zeruiah unto the king, Why should this dead dog curse my lord the king ? let me go over, I pray thee, and take off his head. (*Nobody can wonder at Abishai's anger. Shimei was barking like a cur, and it seemed only justice to return him iron for his stones ; but David was not of a revengeful mind, and therefore rebuked his angry guardsman.*)

10 And the king said, What have I to do with you, ye sons of Zeruiah ? so let him curse, because the LORD hath said unto him, Curse David. Who shall then say, Wherefore hast thou done so ?

11 And David said to Abishai, and to all his servants, Behold, my son, which came forth of my bowels, seeketh my life : how much more now *may this* Benjamite *do it?* let him alone, and let him curse ; for the LORD hath bidden him.

12 It may be that the LORD will look on mine affliction, and that the LORD will requite me good for his cursing this day. *How humbly did David kiss the Lord's rod, and refuse to avenge himself upon the instrument which smote him so furiously. Nothing helps us to bear a provocation so well as humbly seeing the hand of God in it, chastening us for our former faults. David has well said in the Psalms, " I opened not my mouth because thou didst it." He also consoled himself with the belief that the Lord would not always chide him, but would in due time return and comfort him. Nothing brings God to his children's rescue like the revilings of their enemies. Fathers cannot bear to hear their dear ones abused.*

13 And as David and his men went by the way, Shimei went along on the hill's side over against him, and cursed as he went, and threw stones at him, and cast dust. (*David's patience encouraged Shimei's insolence, so that the base fellow went from bad to worse ; yet he could not provoke the king to revenge. In this forbearance the exiled monarch looks greater than even in his prosperous days. No ermine or gold so well adorn a king as patience and longsuffering. How like was David to our Redeemer who " endured such contradiction of sinners against himself," and answered his revilers with prayers and benedictions.*)

14 And the king, and all the people that *were* with him, came weary, and refreshed themselves there. (*So that at his lowest estate David had some followers ; and when he and his men were weary, providence found them refreshment. Let us hope in the worst times, for better days are in store.*)

When gathering clouds around I view,
And days are dark, and friends are few,
On him I lean, who, not in vain,
Experienced every human pain.

If wounded love my bosom swell,
Deceived by those I prized too well,
He shall his pitying aid bestow
Who felt on earth severer woe.

When trouble, like a gloomy cloud,
Has gather'd thick and thunder'd loud,
He near my soul has always stood,
His loving-kindness, oh, how good!

Calm me, my God, and keep me calm,
Let thine outstretchèd wing,
Be like the shade of Elim's palm
Beside her desert-spring.

Calm in the sufferance of wrong,
Like him who bore my shame;
Calm 'mid the threatening, taunting throng,
Who hate thy holy name.

Calm me, my God, and keep me calm,
Soft resting on thy breast;
Soothe me with holy hymn and psalm,
And bid my spirit rest.

Lord, what a thoughtless wretch was I,
To mourn, and murmur, and repine,
To see the wicked, placed on high,
In pride and robes of honour shine.

But, oh their end! their dreadful end!
Thy sanctuary taught me so;
On slipp'ry rocks I see them stand,
And fiery billows roll below.

Their fancied joys, how fast they flee!
Just like a dream when man awakes:
Their songs of softest harmony
Are but a preface to their plagues.

My God, I feel the mournful scene,
My bowels yearn o'er dying men;
And fain my pity would reclaim,
And snatch the firebrands from the flame.

But feeble my compassion proves,
And can but weep where most it loves;
Thy own all-saving arm employ,
And turn these drops of grief to joy.

Pray that Jerusalem may have
Peace and felicity:
Let them that love thee and thy peace
Have still prosperity.

Therefore I wish that peace may still
Within thy walls remain,
And ever may thy palaces
Prosperity retain.

Now, for my friends' and brethren's sakes,
Peace be in thee, I'll say;
And for the house of God our Lord,
I'll seek thy good alway.

O worship the King,
All glorious above;
O gratefully sing
His power and his love;
Our Shield and Defender,
The Ancient of Days,
Pavilion'd in splendour,
And girded with praise.

Frail children of dust,
And feeble as frail,
In thee do we trust,
Nor find thee to fail;
Thy mercies how tender,
How firm to the end,
Our Maker, Defender,
Redeemer, and Friend!

IN *these sad times the psalmist probably wrote*—
PSALM XXXVIII.
which is entitled—

A Psalm of David, to bring to remembrance.

He feared that he was forgotten by his God, and therefore pleaded to be remembered.

1 O LORD, rebuke me not in thy wrath: neither chasten me in thy hot displeasure.

Rebuked I must be, but Lord deal gently with me; chastening I richly deserve, but do not smite me too heavily lest I utterly perish.

2 For thine arrows stick fast in me, and thy hand presseth me sore.

3 *There is* no soundness in my flesh because of thine anger; neither *is there any* rest in my bones because of my sin. *(Spiritual distress is painful to the last degree. However sweet sin may have been in David's mouth, it was bitter enough when it had once reached his inward parts.)*

4, 5 For mine iniquities are gone over mine head: as an heavy burden they are too heavy for me. My wounds stink *and* are corrupt because of my foolishness. *(Conscience laid on stripe after stripe till his soul was wounded in a thousand places, and the wounds became loathsome as well as painful. No ulcers and putrefying sores can match the unutterable vileness and pollution of iniquity.)*

6 I am troubled; I am bowed down greatly; I go mourning all the day long.

7 For my loins are filled with a loathsome disease: and *there is* no soundness in my flesh.

8 I am feeble and sore broken: I have roared by reason of the disquietness of my heart. *(Thus the penitent are made to feel the smart of sin. The reprobate feel nothing of this, but go singing merrily down to hell; those whom the Lord loves are never allowed to find comfort in sin.)*

9 Lord, all my desire *is* before thee; and my groaning is not hid from thee.

The good Physician understands our case without our needing to explain to him—

"*He takes the meaning of our tears,
The language of our groans.*"

10 My heart panteth, my strength faileth me: as for the light of mine eyes, it also is gone from me. *(Here begins another tale of woe. While he was in pain within, he was forsaken and persecuted without.)*

11 My lovers and my friends stand aloof from my sore; and my kinsmen stand afar off.

12 They also that seek after my life lay snares *for me:* and they that seek my hurt speak mischievous things, and imagine deceits all the day long.

13, 14, 15 But I, as a deaf *man,* heard not; and *I was* as a dumb man *that* openeth not his mouth. *(He would not hear Shimei, so as to punish him. A deaf ear is often a great blessing.)* Thus I was as a man that heareth not, and in whose mouth *are* no reproofs. For in thee, O LORD, do I hope: thou wilt hear, O Lord my God.

16, 17, 18 For I said, *Hear me,* lest *otherwise* they should rejoice over me: when my foot slippeth, they magnify *themselves* against me. For I *am* ready to halt, and my sorrow *is* continually before me. For I will declare mine iniquity: I will be sorry for my sin. *(He would not deny that he had done amiss, although he was innocent of the worst charges which were laid against him.)*

19, 20, 21 But mine enemies *are* lively, *and* they are strong: and they that hate me wrongfully are multiplied. They also that render evil for good are mine adversaries; because I follow *the thing that* good *is.* Forsake me not, O LORD: O my God, be not far from me.

22 Make haste to help me, O Lord my salvation. *(God is not only our Saviour, but our salvation. He who has the Lord upon his side has salvation in present possession. Faith sees in this last sentence the sure result of her prayers, and begins to glorify God for the expected mercy. We shall never be forsaken by our heavenly Father. His grace will come to the rescue, and ere long we shall magnify his name for saving us out of all our troubles. Have we all repented of sin? Are we all resting by faith in him?)*

Jesus, full of every grace,
Now reveal thy smiling face;
Grant the joys of sin forgiven,
Foretaste of the bliss of heaven.

All my guilt to thee is known;
Thou art righteous, thou alone,
All my help is from thy cross;
All beside I count but loss.

Lord, in thee I now believe,
Wilt thou, wilt thou not forgive?
Helpless at thy feet I lie;
Saviour, leave me not to die.

THE *counsel of Hushai, the Archite, was accepted by Absalom instead of that of Ahithophel, whereupon Ahithophel put an end to his own life. Absalom with a great army pursued his father, and a decisive battle was the consequence.*

II. SAMUEL XVIII. 1 ; 5—18.

1 And David numbered the people that *were* with him, and set captains of thousands and captains of hundreds over them. *(But when all were counted, his troops were not one half so numerous as those of his rebellious son.)*

5 And the king commanded Joab and Abishai and Ittai, saying, *Deal* gently for my sake with the young man, *even* with Absalom. And all the people heard when the king gave all the captains charge concerning Absalom. *(This tender charge showed that David expected to gain the victory, but hoped that it would not prove fatal to his son. We have here a type of that gracious King, who, even while his persecutors were scorning and killing him, yet prayed, " Father, forgive them; for they know not what they do.")*

6, 7 So the people went out into the field against Israel : and the battle was in the wood of Ephraim ; Where the people of Israel were slain before the servants of David, and there was there a great slaughter that day of twenty thousand *men.*

8 For the battle was there scattered over the face of all the country : and the wood devoured more people that day than the sword devoured.

9 ¶ And Absalom met the servants of David. And Absalom rode upon a mule, and the mule went under the thick boughs of a great oak, and his head caught hold of the oak, and he was taken up between the heaven and the earth ; and the mule that *was* under him went away.

The very trees of the wood are in arms against the ungodly. Absalom had made his hair his pride, and it became his ruin ; men often perish through that which they idolise. What must have been the thoughts of this unnatural young prince when he found himself caught in the forked branch of the oak, and suspended between heaven and earth to die the death of the accursed ! Let children beware of ingratitude to parents, for it is a sin which peculiarly provokes the wrath of the Most High.

10, 11 And a certain man saw *it*, and told Joab, and said, Behold, I saw Absalom hanged in an oak. And Joab said unto the man that told him, And, behold, thou sawest *him*, and why didst thou not smite him there to the ground ? and I would have given thee ten *shekels* of silver, and a girdle.

12 And the man said unto Joab, Though I should receive a thousand *shekels* of silver in mine hand, *yet* would I not put forth mine hand against the king's son : for in our hearing the king charged thee and Abishai and Ittai, saying, Beware that none *touch* the young man Absalom.

13 Otherwise I should have wrought falsehood against mine own life : for there is no matter hid from the king, and thou thyself wouldest have set thyself against *me*.

14 Then said Joab, I may not tarry thus with thee. And he took three darts in his hand, and thrust them through the heart of Absalom, while he *was* yet alive in the midst of the oak.

15 And ten young men that bare Joab's armour compassed about and smote Absalom, and slew him.

16 And Joab blew the trumpet, and the people returned from pursuing after Israel : for Joab held back the people.

17 And they took Absalom, and cast him into a great pit in the wood, and laid a very great heap of stones upon him : and all Israel fled every one to his tent.

An old writer says, " One death was not enough for Absalom, he was at once hanged, shot, mangled and stoned. Justly was he lifted up by the oak, for he had lifted himself against his father and sovereign ; justly was he pierced with darts, for he had pierced his father's heart with many sorrows ; justly was he mangled, for he had dismembered and divided all Israel ; and justly was he stoned, for he had not only cursed, but pursued his own parent."

18 ¶ Now Absalom in his lifetime had taken and reared up for himself a pillar, which *is* in the king's dale : for he said, I have no son to keep my name in remembrance : and he called the pillar after his own name : and it is called unto this day, Absalom's place.

Absalom's pillar is still pointed out to travellers, but its only purpose is to immortalise the infamy of the unnatural son. Children, love and obey your parents, lest you fall into Absalom's sin and doom.

PSALM LV.

THIS *Psalm most clearly describes David's condition when he had fled far away into the wilderness to escape from his son. He bitterly bewails the treachery of Ahithophel, and prophesies his doom; but his Psalm ends with most faithful and cheerful advice, which we shall all do well to follow.*

1 Give ear to my prayer, O God; and hide not thyself from my supplication.

2 Attend unto me, and hear me : I mourn in my complaint, and make a noise ;

3 Because of the voice of the enemy, because of the oppression of the wicked : for they cast iniquity upon me, and in wrath they hate me.

4 My heart is sore pained within me : and the terrors of death are fallen upon me.

5 Fearfulness and trembling are come upon me, and horror hath overwhelmed me.

6 And I said, Oh that I had wings like a dove! *for then* would I fly away, and be at rest.

7 Lo, *then* would I wander far off, *and* remain in the wilderness. Selah.

8 I would hasten my escape from the windy storm *and* tempest

9 Destroy, O Lord, *and* divide their tongues : for I have seen violence and strife in the city.

10 Day and night they go about it upon the walls thereof : mischief also and sorrow *are* in the midst of it.

11 Wickedness *is* in the midst thereof : deceit and guile depart not from her streets.

12 For *it was* not an enemy *that* reproached me ; then I could have borne *it* : neither *was it* he that hated me *that* did magnify *himself* against me ; then I would have hid myself from him :

13 But *it was* thou, a man mine equal, my guide, and mine acquaintance.

14 We took sweet counsel together, *and* walked unto the house of God in company.

15 Let death seize upon them, *and* let them go down quick into hell : for wickedness *is* in their dwellings, *and* among them.

16 As for me, I will call upon God ; and the LORD shall save me.

17 Evening, and morning, and at noon, will I pray, and cry aloud : and he shall hear my voice.

18 He hath delivered my soul in peace from the battle *that was* against me : for there were many with me.

19 God shall hear, and afflict them, even he that abideth of old. Selah. Because they have no changes, therefore they fear not God.

20 He hath put forth his hands against such as be at peace with him : he hath broken his covenant.

21 *The words* of his mouth were smoother than butter, but war *was* in his heart : his words were softer than oil, yet *were* they drawn swords.

22 Cast thy burden upon the LORD, and he shall sustain thee : he shall never suffer the righteous to be moved.

23 But thou, O God, shalt bring them down into the pit of destruction : bloody and deceitful men shall not live out half their days ; but I will trust in thee.

Let us dwell a moment upon the twenty-second verse, " Thy burden," or what thy God lays upon thee, lay thou it "upon the Lord." His wisdom casts it on thee, it is thy wisdom to cast it on him. He gives thee thy portion of suffering, accept it with cheerful resignation, and then take it back to him with assured confidence. " He shall sustain thee." He who ordains the burden will also ordain strength. Thy bread shall be given thee, thy waters shall be sure. Abundant nourishment shall fit thee to bear all thy labours and trials. "As thy days so shall thy strength be." " He shall never suffer the righteous to be moved." He may move like the boughs of a tree in the tempest, but shall never be moved like the tree torn up by the roots. He stands firm who stands in God. Many would destroy the saints, but God has not suffered them to perish, and he never will. Like pillars, the godly stand " stedfast, unmoveable," to the glory of the Great Architect.

God shall preserve my soul from fear,
 Or shield me when afraid ;
Ten thousand angels must appear,
 If he command their aid.

I cast my burdens on the Lord,
 The Lord sustains them all ;
My courage rests upon his word,
 That saints shall never fall.

WHILE *the great battle was raging in the wood, the aged king was anxiously watching for news.*

II. SAMUEL XVIII. 24—33.

24 And David sat between the two gates: and the watchman went up to the roof over the gate unto the wall, and lifted up his eyes, and looked, and behold a man running alone.

25 And the watchman cried, and told the king. And the king said, If he *be* alone, *there is* tidings in his mouth. *(If there were many men running they would probably be fugitives from the fight, but one would naturally be a herald from the camp.)*

26, 27 And the watchman called unto the porter, and said, Behold *another* man running alone. And the king said, He also bringeth tidings. And the watchman said, Me thinketh the running of the foremost is like the running of Ahimaaz the son of Zadok. And the king said, He *is* a good man, and cometh with good tidings. *(It is a great mercy when this can be said of the son of a priest. So it ought always to be, but so it is not always.)*

28 And Ahimaaz called, and said unto the king, All is well. And he fell down to the earth upon his face before the king, and said, Blessed *be* the LORD thy God, which hath delivered up the men that lifted up their hand against my lord the king.

29 And the king said, Is the young man Absalom safe? *(There was the tender point in the father's heart. If there be such love in an earthly father, how much greater is the affection of our heavenly Father! Surely he takes no delight in the death of any, but had rather that they should turn unto him and live.)* And Ahimaaz answered, When Joab sent the king's servant, and *me* thy servant, I saw a great tumult, but I knew not what *it was. (He had learned to hold his tongue. He was in no haste to grieve the king.)*

30, 31 And the king said *unto him,* Turn aside *and* stand here. And he turned aside, and stood still. And, behold, Cushi came; and Cushi said, Tidings, my lord the king: for the LORD hath avenged thee this day of all them that rose up against thee.

32 And the king said unto Cushi, *Is* the young man Absalom safe? And Cushi ans-

wered, The enemies of my lord the king, and all that rise against thee to do *thee* hurt, be as *that* young man *is. (The honest Ethiopian told his black news as fairly as he could, but a dagger went to the father's heart as he heard it.)*

33 ¶ And the king was much moved, and went up to the chamber over the gate, and wept: and as he went, thus he said, O my son Absalom, my son, my son Absalom! would God I had died for thee, O Absalom, my son, my son! *(Herein was love—great, vehement, passionate; but the love of Jesus to us was greater still; for he did not say, "Would God I had died for you," but he has actually died that we might live. Oh love, amazing and incomprehensible! David weeping is a spectacle of love, but Jesus dying is more wonderful still!)*

II. SAMUEL XIX. 2, 4—8.

2 And the victory that day was *turned* into mourning unto all the people: for the people heard say that day how the king was grieved for his son.

4 But the king covered his face, and the king cried with a loud voice, O my son Absalom, O Absalom, my son, my son!

5, 6 And Joab came into the house to the king, and said, Thou hast shamed this day the faces of all thy servants, in that thou lovest thine enemies, and hatest thy friends. For this day I perceive, that if Absalom had lived, and all we had died this day, then it had pleased thee well.

7 Now therefore arise, go forth, and speak comfortably unto thy servants: for I swear by the LORD, if thou go not forth, there will not tarry one with thee this night: and that will be worse unto thee than all the evil that befel thee from thy youth until now. *(Joab was probably right, but his manner was rough and unfeeling. It is always well to speak gently, even when we are required to be firm.)*

8 Then the king arose, and sat in the gate. And they told unto all the people, saying, Behold, the king doth sit in the gate. And all the people came before the king: for Israel had fled every man to his tent. *(Thus a good end was answered by Joab's harsh interference. Good men follow sound advice, even when it is wrongly presented: we must not act foolishly because our adviser speaks uncourteously.)*

AFTER *many trials, David again enjoyed a period of repose, but his leisure again proved a temptation to him, and he resolved to form an estimate of his own greatness that he might have whereof to glory.*

II. SAMUEL XXIV. 1—4; 9—15.

1 And again the anger of the LORD was kindled against Israel, and he moved David against them to say, Go, number Israel and Judah. *(In the Book of Chronicles, Satan is said to have provoked David to this deed, and so indeed he did, and thus the moral evil of the action belongs to the tempter and his ready victim; but the writer of the present passage saw the hand of the Lord in it, using the sin of David as the means of punishing the sins of the people. Both statements are true, and there is no need to attempt a reconciliation, since one truth must agree with another whether we see it or not.)*

2 For the king said to Joab the captain of the host, which *was* with him, Go now through all the tribes of Israel, from Dan even to Beersheba, and number ye the people, that I may know the number of the people.

3 And Joab said unto the king, Now the LORD thy God add unto the people, how many soever they be, an hundredfold, and that the eyes of my lord the king may see *it*: but why doth my lord the king delight in this thing? *Joab was not only right, but courteous on this occasion. He knew that the people would judge that either a new taxation or a conscription was on foot, and they would become uneasy and rebellious, therefore he thought it unwise. According to the law of Moses, a piece of money as a sin-offering was to be offered by every Israelite when the tribes were counted, but this was neglected. Moses numbered the people at God's bidding, considering them to be the Lord's people, but David counted them at his own will, as if they were his own people, and this the Lord would not endure.*

4 Notwithstanding the king's word prevailed against Joab, and against the captains of the host. And Joab and the captains of the host went out from the presence of the king, to number the people of Israel.

9 And Joab gave up the sum of the number of the people unto the king: and there were in Israel eight hundred thousand valiant men that drew the sword; and the men of Judah *were* five hundred thousand men.

10 ¶ And David's heart smote him after that he had numbered the people. *(That which he looked upon as ground for boasting became reason for humiliation. His army of a million and a quarter of warriors gave him no joy, for he had grieved his God.)* And David said unto the LORD, I have sinned greatly in that I have done: and now, I beseech thee, O LORD, take away the iniquity of thy servant; for I have done very foolishly. *(Grace was in him, and when it came to the front, he was ready enough to mourn his error. O for the like tenderness of conscience!)*

11, 12 For when David was up in the morning, the word of the LORD came unto the prophet Gad, David's seer, saying, Go and say unto David, *(Plain David, not David my servant, as it had formerly been. If we walk contrary to God, he will shew himself contrary to us)* Thus saith the LORD, I offer thee three *things;* choose thee one of them, that I may *do it* unto thee.

13 So Gad came to David, and told him, and said unto him, Shall seven years of famine come unto thee in thy land? or wilt thou flee three months before thine enemies, while they pursue thee? or that there be three days' pestilence in thy land? now advise, and see what answer I shall return to him that sent me.

14 And David said unto Gad, I am in a great strait: let us fall now into the hand of the LORD: for his mercies *are* great: and let me not fall into the hand of man. *(He had a hard alternative, but his choice was wise, and it showed that with all his wanderings he had a sound and loving trust in the Lord his God. A child of God feels always safest in his Father's hands.)*

15 ¶ So the LORD sent a pestilence upon Israel, and there died of the people from Dan even to Beer-sheba seventy thousand men.

O that my chastened heart may smite
  And make me inly groan,
Whene'er I vainly take delight
  In aught I call my own.

Harden'd by sin's deceitfulness
  O may I never be,
But miss my comfort and my peace,
  Whene'er I turn from thee.

296   " It is enough: stay now Thine hand."   MAY 20.—EVENING.

[*Or October* 7.]

OF that great population, in whose number David had sought food for his pride, the plague swept away seventy thousand men.

II. SAMUEL XXIV. 16—25.

16 And when the angel stretched out his hand upon Jerusalem to destroy it, the LORD repented him of the evil, and said to the angel that destroyed the people, It is enough: stay now thine hand. And the angel of the LORD was by the threshingplace of Araunah the Jebusite. (*The angel of pestilence, appearing in visible shape, added a special terror to the judgment. Solemn must have been the state of men's minds as they saw the destroyer unsheathe his sword to smite the capital city of the empire.*)

17 And David spake unto the LORD when he saw the angel that smote the people, and said, Lo, I have sinned, and I have done wickedly: but these sheep, what have they done? let thine hand, I pray thee, be against me, and against my father's house.

Was not this well and bravely spoken? Like a true patriot the king is moved by the woes of his subjects, and, like the father of his country, he would sooner perish himself than see Israel smitten. These people had often acted like wolves to him, but he forgot all their injuries and calls them sheep; they had been guilty of a thousand sins, but, in his zeal for them, he makes himself out to be a far greater sinner, and would have the bolts of vengeance spend themselves upon him and his. Even thus does " that Great Shepherd of the sheep " interpose between the destroying angel and his own redeemed. " If ye seek me," saith he, " let these go their way."

18 ¶ And Gad came that day to David, and said unto him, Go up, rear an altar unto the LORD in the threshingfloor of Araunah the Jebusite. (*On that very spot where the angel held the knife of Abraham from killing his son, there God restrained the sword of the angel from destroying his people.*)

19 And David, according to the saying of Gad, went up as the LORD commanded.

20 And Araunah looked, and saw the king and his servants coming on toward him: and Araunah went out, and bowed himself before the king on his face upon the ground.

21 And Araunah said, Wherefore is my lord the king come to his servant? And David said, To buy the threshingfloor of thee, to build an altar unto the LORD, that the plague may be stayed from the people.

22 And Araunah said unto David, Let my lord the king take and offer up what *seemeth* good unto him: behold, *here be* oxen for burnt sacrifice, and threshing instruments and *other* instruments of the oxen for wood.

23 All these *things* did Araunah, *as* a king, give unto the king. And Araunah said unto the king, The LORD thy God accept thee.

24 And the king said unto Araunah, Nay; but I will surely buy *it* of thee at a price: neither will I offer burnt offerings unto the LORD my God of that which doth cost me nothing. So David bought the threshingfloor and the oxen for fifty shekels of silver.

Here two bountiful spirits entered into holy competition, and one hardly knows which to admire most. True devotion is never niggardly: to godly men that service of God tastes sweetest which costs them most. Nothing is dear enough to give to God; expense is not to be reckoned when the gift is for him. We would not be as those who only bring to God what they can collect from other people. Our gifts shall be from our own store.

25 And David built there an altar unto the LORD, and offered burnt offerings and peace offerings. So the LORD was entreated for the land, and the plague was stayed from Israel.

Thus was the site of the temple marked out in a very special manner. Zion, the church of God, of which the temple was the type, is founded on the hill of sacrifice; it is a monument in praise of sparing mercy; and there the sword of justice is for ever sheathed. Have we come unto mount Zion? Are we resting upon the precious blood of sprinkling? These are grave questions, which it behoves each one to answer on his own account as before the great heart-searching God.

The Lord beheld the sacrifice
There to be offer'd once for all,
He heard his Son's expiring cries
For mercy and forgiveness call.

It is enough—our lives he spares,
For Jesus, our Atonement, died,
He sheathes the sword; he hears our prayers;
His justice now is satisfied.

PSALM CXXXII.

THIS *Psalm fitly closes the active life of David and introduces us to his last thought and care. He longed to see the temple erected upon that spot which had been consecrated by the feet of the celestial messenger when the plague was stayed. He rehearses the story of his former longing to build a house for the Lord, and then dwells upon the covenant which the Lord, in infinite mercy, made with his servant.*

LORD, remember David, *and* all his afflictions:
Many of these afflictions were endured for the Lord's sake and in defence of the Lord's worship, therefore the psalmist dwells upon them; he begs especially that God would remember David's longing to build a temple.

2 How he sware unto the LORD, *and* vowed unto the mighty *God* of Jacob;

3 Surely I will not come into the tabernacle of my house, nor go up into my bed;

4 I will not give sleep to mine eyes, *or* slumber to mine eyelids,

5 Until I find out a place for the LORD, an habitation for the mighty *God* of Jacob.

6 Lo, we heard of it at Ephratah: we found it in the fields of the wood.

In his earliest days, when he dwelt at Bethlehem Ephratah, he had heard of the ark and loved it, and, at last, he found it at Kirjath-jearim, the forest city. Happy are they who love the cause of God in their youth, and are resolved to find out his church and people, even though they should be as much concealed as if hidden in a wood.

7 We will go into his tabernacles: we will worship at his footstool.

Wherever God's worship was, there David resolved to go. Be ours the same holy vow. If the saints be few, poor, and despised, we will sooner worship with them than with the great congregations of the worldly rich.

8 Arise, O LORD, into thy rest; thou, and the ark of thy strength. *(This was the song of Israel when the ark was moved from place to place. We may use it in these days when we are pleading for the presence and power of the Lord in his church.)*

9 Let thy priests be clothed with righteousness; and let thy saints shout for joy.

10 For thy servant David's sake turn not away the face of thine anointed.

Be this our constant prayer, that the church may prosper and the Lord glorify himself in the midst of his people, for the sake of Jesus our greater David, whose face is ever fair in the sight of the Lord.

11 The LORD hath sworn *in* truth unto David; he will not turn from it; Of the fruit of thy body will I set upon thy throne.

12 If thy children will keep my covenant and my testimony that I shall teach them, their children shall also sit upon thy throne for evermore.

13 For the LORD hath chosen Zion; he hath desired *it* for his habitation.

14 This *is* my rest for ever: here will I dwell; for I have desired it.

What God has chosen let us choose, where he dwells let us dwell, and where he rests there let us rest. The church of God should be very dear to our hearts. It should be our anxiety to unite with those who follow the Lord in all things; and when we are joined to their fellowship we should, both by our prayers and efforts, seek to build up the church. What precious promises are those which follow!

15 I will abundantly bless her provision: I will satisfy her poor with bread. *(The gospel is our food, the Lord give us grace to feast on the rich provision, and make us poor in spirit that this heavenly bread may be sweet to us.)*

16 I will also clothe her priests with salvation: and her saints shall shout aloud for joy.

None are so full of joy or so much in a mind to show it as those who dwell where God abides.

17 There will I make the horn of David to bud: I have ordained a lamp for mine anointed.

The glory of Jesus, the Son of David, is great in his church, and in her midst he preserves the light of truth among men.

18 His enemies will I clothe with shame: but upon himself shall his crown flourish.

Jesus shall reign. Oh, to be found among his friends! Who would wish to wear the garments of shame?

Glorious things of thee are spoken,
　　Zion, city of our God!
He whose word cannot be broken,
　　Form'd thee for his own abode:
On the Rock of Ages founded,
　　What can shake thy sure repose?
With salvation's walls surrounded,
　　Thou may'st smile at all thy foes.

DAVID *never turned aside from his desire to see a glorious temple erected to the honour of the Lord his God, and although he was not permitted to build it himself, he diligently provided the materials, earnestly charged Solomon to carry out his design, and at last gathered a solemn council to whom he commended this noble work.*

I. CHRONICLES XXIX. 1—9 ; 20—23.

1 Furthermore David the king said unto all the congregation, Solomon my son, whom alone God hath chosen, *is yet* young and tender, and the work *is* great: for the palace *is* not for man, but for the LORD God. *(God must never be served in a slovenly manner. We should feel under bonds to do our best in all religious work, because the labour is not for man, but for the Lord God.)*

2 Now I have prepared with all my might for the house of my God the gold for *things to be made* of gold, and the silver for *things* of silver, and the brass for *things* of brass, the iron for *things* of iron, and wood for *things* of wood; onyx stones, and *stones* to be set, glistering stones, and of divers colours, and all manner of precious stones, and marble stones in abundance.

He had thought upon the matter, and provided many things, and these were all of the best. Would to God that we all served God in this fashion, with thought and with sacrifice.

3 Moreover, because I have set my affection to the house of my God, I have of mine own proper good, of gold and silver, *which* I have given to the house of my God, over and above all that I have prepared for the holy house,

4, 5 *Even* three thousand talents of gold, of the gold of Ophir, and seven thousand talents of refined silver, to overlay the walls of the houses *withal:* The gold for *things* of gold, and the silver for *things* of silver, and for all manner of work *to be made* by the hands of artificers. And who *then* is willing to consecrate his service this day unto the LORD ? *(He who gives freely himself may justly ask of others. Those who collect but never contribute are inconsistent.)*

6 ¶ Then the chief of the fathers and princes of the tribes of Israel, and the captains of thousands and of hundreds, with the rulers of the king's work, offered willingly,

7 And gave for the service of the house of God of gold five thousand talents and ten thousand drams, and of silver ten thousand talents, and of brass eighteen thousand talents, and one hundred thousand talents of iron.

8 And they with whom *precious* stones were found gave *them* to the treasure of the house of the LORD, by the hand of Jehiel the Gershonite.

He kept the accounts. God's business should be done in order. Church funds should be very carefully accounted for, lest scandal arise.

9 Then the people rejoiced, for that they offered willingly, because with perfect heart they offered willingly to the LORD : and David the king also rejoiced with great joy.

The joy of giving to the Lord is a very great one. Angels might well envy us such bliss.

20 And David said to all the congregation, Now bless the LORD your God. And all the congregation blessed the LORD God of their fathers, and bowed down their heads, and worshipped the LORD, and the king. *(Paying religious homage to God, and respectful honour to the king.)*

21 And they sacrificed sacrifices unto the LORD, and offered burnt offerings unto the LORD, on the morrow after that day, *even* a thousand bullocks, a thousand rams, *and* a thousand lambs, with their drink offerings, and sacrifices in abundance for all Israel : *(Thus the threshing-floor of Araunah was saturated with blood that the foundations of the temple might be laid in sacrifice. Happy are those who are built upon the substitutionary death of Jesus.)*

22 And did eat and drink before the LORD on that day with great gladness. *(So should sacred worship be far removed from sadness, and be regarded as a choice festival.)* And they made Solomon the son of David king the second time, and anointed *him* unto the LORD *to be* the chief governor, and Zadok *to be* priest.

23 Then Solomon sat on the throne of the LORD as king instead of David his father, and prospered ; and all Israel obeyed him.

He was viceroy for his father for awhile, and then succeeded him by the consent of the whole nation.

WE *will now read David's Psalm for Solomon, which still more fully refers to our Lord Jesus Christ.*

PSALM LXXII.

1 Give the king thy judgments, O God, and thy righteousness unto the king's son.

2 He shall judge thy people with righteousness, and thy poor with judgment.

3 The mountains shall bring peace to the people, and the little hills, by righteousness.

4 He shall judge the poor of the people, he shall save the children of the needy, and shall break in pieces the oppressor.

5 They shall fear thee as long as the sun and moon endure, throughout all generations.

6 He shall come down like rain upon the mown grass : as showers *that* water the earth.

7 In his days shall the righteous flourish ; and abundance of peace so long as the moon endureth.

8 He shall have dominion also from sea to sea, and from the river unto the ends of the earth.

9 They that dwell in the wilderness shall bow before him ; and his enemies shall lick the dust.

10 The kings of Tarshish and of the isles shall bring presents : the kings of Sheba and Seba shall offer gifts.

11 Yea, all kings shall fall down before him : all nations shall serve him.

12 For he shall deliver the needy when he crieth ; the poor also, and *him* that hath no helper.

13 He shall spare the poor and needy, and shall save the souls of the needy.

14 He shall redeem their soul from deceit and violence : and precious shall their blood be in his sight.

15 And he shall live, and to him shall be given of the gold of Sheba : prayer also shall be made for him continually ; *and* daily shall he be praised.

16 There shall be an handful of corn in the earth upon the top of the mountains ; the fruit thereof shall shake like Lebanon : and *they* of the city shall flourish like grass of the earth.

17 His name shall endure for ever : his name shall be continued as long as the sun : and *men* shall be blessed in him : all nations shall call him blessed.

18 Blessed *be* the LORD God, the God of Israel, who only doeth wondrous things.

19 And blessed *be* his glorious name for ever : and let the whole earth be filled *with* his glory ; Amen, and Amen.

20 The prayers of David the son of Jesse are ended. *(David's heart was glad at the foresight of the glories of his son Solomon, but far more did he rejoice as his prophetic eye foresaw the greater splendours of the throne of the Messiah. At the second coming of the Lord Jesus, this Psalm will have a grand fulfilment, and meanwhile it is for us by prayer and effort to extend his kingdom. If anything can warm the heart of the Christian, it is the prospect of the Redeemer's universal reign, and reign he will despite all his foes. The Lord Jehovah's power and faithfulness are pledged to give our Lord Jesus the heathen for his inheritance, and, therefore, we may rest fully assured that it will be done. Jesus has fought the fight and won the victory, therefore will the Lord divide him a portion with the great, and he shall divide the spoil with the strong. There is no room for despondency or trembling ; with a covenanted God on our side, sworn to give the victory, all danger of defeat is removed far away. David ended his prayers when he had prayed for the filling of the whole earth with Messiah's glory ; he felt that he had reached the summit of his wishes, and had nothing more to ask. With this prayer upon his lip he is content to die. He strips himself of his royalty, and becomes only " the son of Jesse," thrice happy to subside into nothing before the crowned Messiah. Before his believing eye the reign of Jesus, like the sun, filled all around with light, and exulting therein with all his heart, the holy man felt like Simeon, when he said, " Lord, now lettest thou thy servant depart in peace, for mine eyes have seen thy salvation." May the glory of Jesus in like manner be the one great wish of our souls.)*

Jesus shall reign where'er the sun
Does his successive journeys run ;
His kingdom stretch from shore to shore,
Till moons shall wax and wane no more.

For him shall endless prayer be made,
And praises throng to crown his head ;
His name like sweet perfume shall rise
With every morning sacrifice.

BEFORE *we proceed to the reign of Solomon, we must read two or three of David's choicest Psalms, regretting that we have not time to read them all in our family worship. We must not however omit to study every one of them in private, for they are all more precious than fine gold. One of the sweetest and most notable is*—

PSALM CIII.
A Psalm of David.

BLESS the LORD, O my soul : and all that is within me, *bless* his holy name. *(Soul music is the soul of music ; when we praise the Lord it should be with every faculty we possess.)*

2 Bless the LORD, O my soul, and forget not all his benefits : *(Our memories are frail towards good things : let us stir them up while we bless the Lord.)*

3, 4, 5 Who forgiveth all thine iniquities ; who healeth all thy diseases ; Who redeemeth thy life from destruction ; who crowneth thee with lovingkindness and tender mercies ; Who satisfieth thy mouth with good *things ; so that* thy youth is renewed like the eagle's. *(The sweet singer threads a few of the choicest pearls of mercy upon the string of memory, and casts them around the neck of gratitude, to glitter there while she sings the joyful praises of her God.)*

6 The LORD executeth righteousness and judgment for all that are oppressed. *(No downtrodden one shall ever appeal to him in vain. Woe to those who deal tyrannically with the poor.)*

7 He made known his ways unto Moses, his acts unto the children of Israel.

8 The LORD *is* merciful and gracious, slow to anger, and plenteous in mercy.

9 He will not always chide : neither will he keep *his anger* for ever. *(He must in very love to us chasten us at times, but his hand is soon stayed.)*

10 He hath not dealt with us after our sins ; nor rewarded us according to our iniquities.

11 For as the heaven is high above the earth, *so* great is his mercy toward them that fear him.

12 As far as the east is from the west, *so* far hath he removed our transgressions from us.

What a glorious fact : for the east is infinitely distant from the west, and so to an infinite length is sin removed ; yea, it is blotted out, made an end of, and for ever forgotten.

13 Like as a father pitieth *his* children, *so* the LORD pitieth them that·fear him. *(At their best they want his pity, for they are poor, frail things.)*

14 For he knoweth our frame ; he remembereth that we *are* dust. *(We are not iron, and not even clay, but dust held together by daily miracle.)*

15 *As for* man, his days *are* as grass : as a flower of the field, so he flourisheth.

16 For the wind passeth over it, and it is gone ; and the place thereof shall know it no more.

17 But the mercy of the LORD *is* from everlasting to everlasting upon them that fear him, and his righteousness unto children's children ;

18 To such as keep his covenant, and to those that remember his commandments to do them.

Children who forsake the Lord will derive no benefit from their parentage. It will increase their condemnation, but it cannot remove their guilt ; they must remember his covenant for themselves personally, or they will have no share in it.

19 The LORD hath prepared his throne in the heavens ; and his kingdom ruleth over all.

20 Bless the LORD, ye his angels, that excel in strength, that do his commandments, hearkening unto the voice of his word.

21 Bless ye the LORD, all *ye* his hosts : *ye* ministers of his, that do his pleasure.

22 Bless the LORD, all his works in all places of his dominion : bless the LORD, O my soul.

The psalmist was so full of praise that he desired the aid of all creation to assist him in glorifying the Lord ; but he did not forget that still the main matter is for our own soul to adore the Lord. He concludes on his keynote, as good composers do ; let it be our motto all the day, " Bless the Lord, O my soul."

O bless the Lord, my soul !
Let all within me join,
And aid my tongue to bless his name,
Whose favours are divine.

O bless the Lord, my soul,
Nor let his mercies lie
Forgotten in unthankfulness,
And without praises die.

A NOTHER *of David's grandest Psalms is—*

PSALM CIV.,

which our space compels us to read almost without comment.

1, 2, 3, 4, 5 Bless the LORD, O my soul. O LORD my God, thou art very great; thou art clothed with honour and majesty. Who coverest *thyself* with light as *with* a garment: who stretchest out the heavens like a curtain: who layeth the beams of his chambers in the waters: who maketh the clouds his chariot: who walketh upon the wings of the wind : Who maketh his angels spirits; his ministers a flaming fire: *Who* laid the foundations of the earth, *that* it should not be removed for ever.

6, 7, 8, 9 Thou coveredst it with the deep as *with* a garment : the waters stood above the mountains. *(Probably alluding to the flood.)* At thy rebuke they fled; at the voice of thy thunder they hasted away. They go up by the mountains; *(rising in mists and exhalations)* they go down by the valleys *(rippling in rills, leaping in cataracts)* unto the place which thou hast founded for them. Thou hast set a bound that they may not pass over; that they turn not again to cover the earth.

10, 11, 12 He sendeth the springs into the valleys, *which* run among the hills. They give drink to every beast of the field : the wild asses quench their thirst. By them shall the fowls of the heaven have their habitation, *which* sing among the branches.

13, 14, 15 He watereth the hills from his chambers : the earth is satisfied with the fruit of thy works. He causeth the grass to grow for the cattle, and herb for the service of man : that he may bring forth food out of the earth; And wine *that* maketh glad the heart of man, *and* oil to make *his* face to shine, and bread *which* strengtheneth man's heart.

16 The trees of the LORD are full *of sap;* the cedars of Lebanon, which he hath planted;

17 Where the birds make their nests : *as for* the stork, the fir trees *are* her house.

18 The high hills *are* a refuge for the wild goats ; *and* the rocks for the conies. *(So that each place has its creature, and each creature its place. The loneliest spots are populous.)*

19, 20, 21, 22, 23 He appointed the moon for seasons: the sun knoweth his going down. Thou makest darkness, and it is night : wherein all the beasts of the forest do creep *forth.* The young lions roar after their prey, and seek their meat from God. The sun ariseth, they gather themselves together, and lay them down in their dens. Man goeth forth unto his work and to his labour until the evening. *(Thus each period has its appropriate action, the wheels of providence never stand still.)*

24, 25, 26, 27, 28, 29, 30 O LORD, how manifold are thy works! in wisdom hast thou made them all : the earth is full of thy riches. *So is* this great and wide sea, wherein *are* things creeping innumerable, both small and great beasts. There go the ships : *there is* that leviathan, *whom* thou hast made to play therein. These wait all upon thee; that thou mayest give *them* their meat in due season. *That* thou givest them they gather : thou openest thine hand, they are filled with good. Thou hidest thy face, they are troubled : thou takest away their breath, they die, and return to their dust. Thou sendest forth thy spirit, they are created : and thou renewest the face of the earth. *(God is in all things, great or small. He has not left the world to mere laws and forces, but he is working everywhere. Let us behold him and adore.)*

31 The glory of the LORD shall endure for ever : the LORD shall rejoice in his works.

And if he does so, it is not wise on our part to close our eyes to nature's beauties under the notion of superior spirituality.

32 He looketh on the earth, and it trembleth : he toucheth the hills, and they smoke.

33 I will sing unto the LORD as long as I live : I will sing praise to my God while I have my being.

34 My meditation of him shall be sweet : I will be glad in the LORD.

35 Let the sinners be consumed out of the earth, and let the wicked be no more. *(For they alone spoil creation, and blot the Maker's handiwork.)* Bless thou the LORD, O my soul. Praise ye the LORD.

A NOTHER *Psalm highly characteristic of David is—*

PSALM LXII.

which we are in the habit of calling the ONLY *Psalm, from its containing such frequent repetitions of the word* only. *David rejoiced to place his confidence in God "* only.*"*

1 Truly *(or as it is in the original* only*)* my soul waiteth upon God : from him *cometh* my salvation. *(Our salvation in no measure or degree comes to us from any but the Lord; let us therefore depend alone upon him. If to wait on God be worship, to wait on the creature is idolatry; if to wait on God alone be true faith, to associate an arm of flesh with him is audacious unbelief, yet, how very few of us steer clear of these evils, and look to God alone.)*

2 He only *is* my rock and my salvation ; *he is* my defence ; I shall not be greatly moved.

" Moved," as one says, " but not removed." Moved like a ship at anchor, which swings with the tide, but is not swept away by the current. Nothing stays the soul like a faith which leans alone on God. In faith it is good to have but one string to our bow, one pillar to our house.

3 How long will ye imagine mischief against a man ? ye shall be slain all of you : as a bowing wall *shall ye be, and as* a tottering fence.

4 They only consult to cast *him* down from his excellency : they delight in lies : they bless with their mouth, but they curse inwardly. Selah. *(The world is full of flatterers, and these are plotters against our best prosperity : let us fly from them to the one only confidence of the saints. If we have God for us, who can be against us ?)*

5 My soul, wait thou only upon God ; for my expectation *is* from him. *(Knock at no other door but that of thy God. God is one; let thy hopes look towards him alone. A single eye will fill thee with light.)*

6 He only *is* my rock and my salvation : *he is* my defence ; I shall not be moved.

7 In God *is* my salvation and my glory : the rock of my strength, *and* my refuge, *is* in God.

Notice how David brands his own initials upon every title which he rejoicingly gives to God, my *expectation,* my *rock,* my *salvation,* my *glory, and so on. There are seven* my's *in two verses, and there can never be too many. The*

faith which makes personal appropriation of divine blessings is the faith we all need.

8 Trust in him at all times ; ye people, pour out your heart before him : God *is* a refuge for us. Selah. *(Ye to whom his love is revealed, reveal yourselves to him. Turn the vessel of your soul upside down in his presence, and let your inmost thoughts, desires, sorrows and sins be poured out like water. To keep our griefs to ourselves is to hoard up wretchedness. Give your woe free course before the Lord, and its end is near.)*

9 Surely men of low degree *are* vanity, *and* men of high degree *are* a lie : to be laid in the balance, they *are* altogether *lighter* than vanity.

Men, whether great or small, are still but men, and men are dust. To trust in the many is folly, to rely upon the eminent few is madness ; to depend upon the Lord alone is the only sanity.

10 Trust not in oppression, and become not vain in robbery : if riches increase, set not your heart *upon them. (Here is a difficult precept, for worldly wealth is a slimy thing, and is too apt to cling to the heart. Perhaps this is the reason why so many of the saints are in poverty, because the Lord would spare them from being tempted by increasing riches. God only must be our rest, and not the treasures of time. Wealth is but wind if we make it our confidence.)*

11 God hath spoken once ; twice have I heard this ; that power *belongeth* unto God.

Not to men nor to their possessions may we look for power, that is the prerogative of God alone. Those are wise who look for help alone to him.

12 Also unto thee, O Lord, *belongeth* mercy : for thou renderest to every man according to his work. *(He gives us strength equal to our day. Power is all his own, but he will render as much to us as our work requires. Let us seek it at his hands, and at his hands only.)*

> Ever to the Saviour cling,
> Trust in him and none beside :
> Never let an earthly thing
> Hide from thee the Crucified.
>
> Ever cast on him thy care,
> He invites thee so to do ;
> Never let thy soul despair,
> He will surely help thee through.
>
> Ever live as in the view
> Of the day of glory, near ;
> Never be to Christ untrue,
> Thou shalt soon his glory share.

WE *will now pursue the path of history, and enter upon the reign of Solomon.*

I. KINGS III. 1, 3—15.

1 And Solomon made affinity with Pharaoh king of Egypt, and took Pharaoh's daughter, and brought her into the city of David, until he had made an end of building his own house, and the house of the LORD, and the wall of Jerusalem round about. *(A questionable beginning, a step full of danger.)*

3 And Solomon loved the LORD, walking in the statutes of David his father : only he sacrificed and burnt incense in high places. *(This was contrary to express precept, yet the Lord dealt not severely with Solomon, for he saw that his heart was right before him.)*

4 And the king went to Gibeon to sacrifice there ; for that *was* the great high place : a thousand burnt offerings did Solomon offer upon that altar.

5 ¶ In Gibeon the LORD appeared to Solomon in a dream by night : and God said, Ask what I shall give thee. *(Solomon worships God by day—God appears to Solomon by night. The night cannot but be happy when the day has been holy. The king had offered unto God a thousand burnt-sacrifices, and now the Lord rewards him in godlike fashion by giving him his option. " Ask what I shall give thee !" Nor is God less generous to each one of us under the gospel, for Jesus has said, "Whatsoever ye shall ask the Father in my name, he will give it you.")*

6, 7, 8 And Solomon said, Thou hast shewed unto thy servant David my father great mercy, according as he walked before thee in truth, and in righteousness, and in uprightness of heart with thee ; and thou hast kept for him this great kindness, that thou hast given him a son to sit on his throne, as *it is* this day. And now, O LORD my God, thou hast made thy servant king instead of David my father : and I *am but* a little child : I know not *how* to go out or come in. And thy servant *is* in the midst of thy people which thou hast chosen, a great people, that cannot be numbered nor counted for multitude.

9 Give therefore thy servant an understanding heart to judge thy people, that I may discern between good and bad : for who is able to judge this thy so great a people ? *(It was a wise choice to choose wisdom : young Solomon was already wise when he thus asked of the Lord. He did not ask for grace, which would have been the best gift of all, but he chose the second best, and his reasons for the choice were in the highest degree praiseworthy. He must have often thought upon this matter while awake, or he would not have come to so excellent a decision in his sleep.)*

10 And the speech pleased the Lord, that Solomon had asked this thing.

11, 12 And God said unto him, Because thou hast asked this thing, and hast not asked for thyself long life ; neither hast asked riches for thyself, nor hast asked the life of thine enemies ; but hast asked for thyself understanding to discern judgment ; Behold, I have done according to thy words : lo, I have given thee a wise and an understanding heart ; so that there was none like thee before thee, neither after thee shall any arise like unto thee.

13 And I have also given thee that which thou hast not asked, both riches, and honour : so that there shall not be any among the kings like unto thee all thy days. *(The greater includes the less. Wisdom brings wealth and honour : let us seek the kingdom of God and his righteousness, and then all these things shall be added unto us. Christ Jesus, who is infinite wisdom, is the choice of every believer.)*

14 And if thou wilt walk in my ways, to keep my statutes and my commandments, as thy father David did walk, then I will lengthen thy days.

15 And Solomon awoke ; and, behold, *it was* a dream. And he came to Jerusalem, and stood before the ark of the covenant of the LORD, and offered up burnt offerings, and offered peace offerings, and made a feast to all his servants. *(Gratitude led him to present his sacrifices in the right place. Our love to God should always lead us to a growing attention to his commands. There was now a noble career open before Solomon, and for many years he pursued it most commendably. Those who begin life by seeking wisdom may expect prosperity.)*

> My God, my soul hath one desire,
> I seek for wisdom still,
> Let Jesus be mine all in aii,
> And I'll obey thy will.

SOLOMON *by his wisdom brought great prosperity to his nation, and made the country the centre of trade and commerce. His royal establishment was conducted upon the most sumptuous scale.*

I. KINGS IV., 22—34.

22 ¶ And Solomon's provision for one day was thirty measures of fine flour, and threescore measures of meal,

23 Ten fat oxen, and twenty oxen out of the pastures, and an hundred sheep, beside harts, and roebucks, and fallow-deer, and fatted fowl.

But what is this compared with the provision which loads the table of the King of kings, by whose bounty all the saints are fed?

24 For he had dominion over all *the region* on this side the river, from Tiphsah even to Azzah, over all the kings on this side the river: and he had peace on all sides round about him.

25 And Judah and Israel dwelt safely, every man under his vine and under his fig tree, from Dan even to Beer-sheba, all the days of Solomon. *(So, too, where Jesus rules peace reigns undisturbed.)*

26 ¶ And Solomon had forty thousand stalls of horses for his chariots, and twelve thousand horsemen. *(This was a forbidden luxury, for the Hebrew kings were commanded not to multiply horses. In this Solomon erred.)*

27, 28 And those officers provided victual for king Solomon, and for all that came unto king Solomon's table, every man in his month: they lacked nothing. Barley also and straw for the horses and dromedaries brought they unto the place where *the officers* were, every man according to his charge.

29, 30 ¶ And God gave Solomon wisdom and understanding exceeding much, and largeness of heart, even as the sand that *is* on the sea shore. And Solomon's wisdom excelled the wisdom of all the children of the east country, and all the wisdom of Egypt.

31 For he was wiser than all men; than Ethan the Ezrahite, and Heman, and Chalcol, and Darda, the sons of Mahol: and his fame was in all nations round about.

32, 33 And he spake three thousand proverbs: and his songs were a thousand and five. And he spake of trees, from the cedar tree that *is* in Lebanon even unto the hyssop that springeth out of the wall: he spake also of beasts, and of fowl, and of creeping things, and of fishes.

34 And there came of all people to hear the wisdom of Solomon, from all kings of the earth, which had heard of his wisdom.

See how well the Lord fulfilled his promise. He gave him wisdom in no stinted measure.

I. KINGS X. 14, 15; 18—23.

14, 15 ¶ Now the weight of gold that came to Solomon in one year was six hundred threescore and six talents of gold, Beside *that he had* of the merchantmen, and of the traffick of the spice merchants, and of all the kings of Arabia, and of the governors of the country. *(He built stations for the caravans, and received a toll of the merchants, besides gaining great wealth by purchasing the produce of the East, and selling it to the Western nations.)*

18 ¶ Moreover the king made a great throne of ivory, and overlaid it with the best gold.

19 The throne had six steps, and the top of the throne *was* round behind: and *there were* stays on either side on the place of the seat, and two lions stood beside the stays.

20 And twelve lions stood there on the one side and on the other upon the six steps: there was not the like made in any kingdom.

But how much more glorious will be the throne of our Lord in the day of his appearing!

21 ¶ And all king Solomon's drinking vessels *were of* gold, and all the vessels of the house of the forest of Lebanon *were of* pure gold; none *were of* silver: it was nothing accounted of in the days of Solomon.

22 For the king had at sea a navy of Tharshish with the navy of Hiram: once in three years came the navy of Tharshish, bringing gold, and silver, ivory, and apes, and peacocks.

23 So king Solomon exceeded all the kings of the earth for riches and for wisdom.

Thus again the promise was fulfilled, and wealth followed wisdom. Who would not trust so faithful a God?

Behold your King, your Saviour crown'd
  With glories all divine;
And tell the wondering nations round
  How bright those glories shine.

Infinite power and boundless grace
  In him unite their rays;
You, that have e'er beheld his face,
  Can you forbear his praise?

I. KINGS V. 1—11 ; 13—18.

AND Hiram king of Tyre sent his servants unto Solomon ; for he had heard that they had anointed him king in the room of his father : for Hiram was ever a lover of David. *Fast friends are rare. It was a happy thing for Solomon that his father bequeathed him the love of so useful an ally.*

2 And Solomon sent to Hiram, saying,

3 Thou knowest how that David my father could not build an house unto the name of the LORD his God for the wars which were about him on every side, until the LORD put them under the soles of his feet. *(Like a good son who honoured his father, he does not say that David could not build the temple because he had shed blood, but because he was busy with wars. We ought always to speak the best things of parents.)*

4 But now the LORD my God hath given me rest on every side, *so that there is* neither adversary nor evil occurrent.

5 And, behold, I purpose to build an house unto the name of the LORD my God, as the LORD spake unto David my father, saying, Thy son, whom I will set upon thy throne in thy room, he shall build an house unto my name.

6 Now therefore command thou that they hew me cedar trees out of Lebanon ; and my servants shall be with thy servants : and unto thee will I give hire for thy servants according to all that thou shalt appoint : for thou knowest that *there is* not among us any that can skill to hew timber like unto the Sidonians. *(The tabernacle, which was temporary, could be erected by Jews only; but the temple, which was to be permanent, is not built without the aid of Gentiles. Jews and Gentiles together make up the church which is the temple of God.)*

7, 8 ¶ And it came to pass, when Hiram heard the words of Solomon, that he rejoiced greatly, and said, Blessed *be* the LORD this day, which hath given unto David a wise son over this great people. And Hiram sent to Solomon, saying, I have considered the things which thou sentest to me for : *and* I will do all thy desire concerning timber of cedar, and concerning timber of fir. *(We ought to weigh well what we promise, and then we shall be the more likely to be true to our word. It is well when our second*

thoughts are full of liberality towards the cause of God.)

9 My servants shall bring *them* down from Lebanon unto the sea : and I will convey them by sea in floats unto the place that thou shalt appoint me, and will cause them to be discharged there, and thou shalt receive *them :* and thou shalt accomplish my desire, in giving food for my household. *(Palestine was a fruitful agricultural country, and thus Solomon would do Hiram a service by paying him in provisions.)*

10 So Hiram gave Solomon cedar trees and fir trees *according to* all his desire. *(When God's house is to be built, he will surely find all that is needful for it.)*

11 And Solomon gave Hiram twenty thousand measures of wheat *for* food to his household, and twenty measures of pure oil : thus gave Solomon to Hiram year by year.

13, 14 ¶ And king Solomon raised a levy out of all Israel ; and the levy was thirty thousand men. And he sent them to Lebanon, ten thousand a month by courses : a month they were in Lebanon, *and* two months at home : and Adoniram *was* over the levy.

15, 16 And Solomon had threescore and ten thousand that bare burdens, and fourscore thousand hewers in the mountains ; Beside the chief of Solomon's officers which *were* over the work, three thousand and three hundred, which ruled over the people that wrought in the work.

17 And the king commanded, and they brought great stones, costly stones, *and* hewed stones, to lay the foundation of the house. *Even the foundation stones were not rugged and rough, but hewn and costly. God would have everything which is done for him done well. He careth not so much for that which meets the eye of man, he delights himself with the beauty of those living stones of his spiritual temple which are hidden away from observation.*

18 And Solomon's builders and Hiram's builders did hew *them,* and the stonesquarers : so they prepared timber and stones to build the house. *(So the stones and timbers came to their places prepared, and no sound of axe or hammer was heard. Here below the fitting us for heaven is a work of toil and noise, but in heaven all will be rest and quietness. May the Lord prepare us to be built into his temple above.)*

"Ye also, as lively stones, are built up a spiritual house."

II. CHRONICLES III.

THEN Solomon began to build the house of the LORD at Jerusalem in mount Moriah, where *the LORD* appeared unto David his father, in the place that David had prepared in the threshingfloor of Ornan the Jebusite.

This was the place where Abraham offered up Isaac, and near by the spot where the Lord Jesus suffered as the Lamb which God had provided for sacrifice. The place of sacrifice and atonement is the ordained position of the Church of God.

2 And he began to build in the second *day* of the second month, in the fourth year of his reign.

3 .¶· Now these *are the things wherein* Solomon was instructed for the building of the house of God. The length by cubits after the first measure *was* threescore cubits, and the breadth twenty cubits.

4 And the porch that *was* in the front *of the house*, the length *of it was* according to the breadth of the house, twenty cubits, and the height *was* an hundred and twenty: and he overlaid it within with pure gold.

5 And the greater house he cieled with fir tree, which he overlaid with fine gold, and set thereon palm trees and chains.

6 And he garnished the house with precious stones for beauty : and the gold *was* gold of Parvaim. *(The timber work was costly, but yet it was overlaid with pure gold, of the best kind, and this was adorned with precious stones. The Lord's church is not to be built without vast cost, for it is very precious in his eyes.)*

7, 8, 9 He overlaid also the house, the beams, the posts, and the walls thereof, and the doors thereof, with gold ; and graved cherubims on the walls. And he made the most holy house, the length whereof *was* according to the breadth of the house, twenty cubits, and the breadth thereof twenty cubits: and he overlaid it with fine gold, *amounting* to six hundred talents. And the weight of the nails *was* fifty shekels of gold. And he overlaid the upper chambers with gold.

10 And in the most holy house he made two cherubims of image work, and overlaid them with gold.

11 ¶ And the wings of the cherubims *were* twenty cubits long: one wing *of the one cherub* was five cubits, reaching to the wall· of the house : and the other wing *was likewise* five cubits, reaching to the wing of the other cherub.

12 And *one* wing of the other cherub *was* five cubits, reaching to the wall of the house : and the other wing *was* five cubits *also*, joining to the wing of the other cherub.

13 The wings of these cherubims spread themselves forth twenty cubits·: and they stood on their feet, and their faces *were* inward.

Did these symbolize angels ? We think so : and they are here represented as standing on their feet as servants, and not as sitting upon thrones like gods. We do not worship angels, but we worship with angels, joining in their solemn hymn of praise unto the Lord of all.

14 ¶ And he made the vail *of* blue, and purple, and crimson, and fine linen, and wrought cherubims thereon. *(This veiled the sanctuary, for it was a dark dispensation, and the way into the holiest was not yet manifest.)*

15, 16 Also he made before the house two pillars of thirty and five cubits high, and the chapiter that *was* on the top of each of them *was* five cubits. And he made chains, *as* in the oracle, and put *them* on the heads of the pillars ; and made an hundred pomegranates, and put *them* on the chains.

17 And he reared up the pillars before the temple, one on the right hand, and the other on the left; and called the name of that on the right hand Jachin *(he will establish)*, and the name of that on the left Boaz *(or, in him is strength). These were vast columns intended for glory and for beauty. The Church is the noblest design of the Great Architect. Holy Scripture gives us a full account of the various parts of the temple, and the different articles of furniture. Everything was ordained of God, and full of instruction, and the effect of the whole must have been beyond measure magnificent.)*

Go, worship at Immanuel's feet,
See in himself what glories meet,
No gold or cedar can express
His worth, his glory, and his grace.

Is he a temple ? I adore
Th' indwelling majesty and power ;
And still to this most holy place,
Whene'er I pray I turn my face.

LET us read

PSALM XLV.

A Psalm in which Solomon is just visible in the background as a type, but the Lord Jesus fills the foreground in the fulness of loveliness and majesty.

1 My heart is inditing a good matter : I speak of the things which I have made touching the king : my tongue *is* the pen of a ready writer.

No matter can be so good as that which boils up from a warm heart, and has for its subject the King of saints. The psalmist resolves also to speak only of that which he had made or experienced, for then he felt he could speak fully, deliberately, and wisely, with all the accuracy and force of an accomplished writer. O to have our hearts warm whenever Jesus is the theme! Could we speak of things which we have made our own concerning King Jesus? The question deserves an answer.

2 Thou art fairer than the children of men : grace is poured into thy lips : therefore God hath blessed thee for ever. *(He speaks as though he saw the Well-beloved One. The psalmist falls into raptures at the sight. He hears him speak, and adores him. We shall do the same if he will but reveal himself to us.)*

3 Gird thy sword upon *thy* thigh, O *most* mighty, with thy glory and thy majesty.

4 And in thy majesty ride prosperously because of truth and meekness *and* righteousness ; and thy right hand shall teach thee terrible things. *(This should be our prayer. O Immanuel, the mighty prince, put forth thy power and subdue men to thyself. As Solomon reigned over wide dominions, so also reign thou, O most sweet Prince.)*

5 Thine arrows *are* sharp in the heart of the king's enemies ; *whereby* the people fall under thee. *(His gospel pierces men's hearts, and subdues them to his love.)*

6 Thy throne, O God, *is* for ever and ever : the sceptre of thy kingdom *is* a right sceptre.

7 Thou lovest righteousness, and hatest wickedness : therefore God, thy God, hath anointed thee with the oil of gladness above thy fellows. *(See the divine and human natures here blended in one person. As man the Lord Jesus has his fellows, but as God his throne is for ever and*

ever. Let us make no mistake upon this vital point, but believe in Jesus as God and man.)

8 All thy garments *smell* of myrrh, and aloes, *and* cassia, out of the ivory palaces, whereby they have made thee glad.

9 Kings' daughters *were* among thy honourable women : upon thy right hand did stand the queen in gold of Ophir. *·(The church is arrayed in the best of the best, the righteousness of God. How lovely she is in the loveliness of Jesus!)*

10 Hearken, O daughter, and consider, and incline thine ear ; forget also thine own people, and thy father's house ;

11 So shall the king greatly desire thy beauty : for he *is* thy Lord ; and worship thou him.

The church must be unworldly, and seek first the kingdom of God. Such must each one of us be, and then all other things shall be added unto us, as the next verse teaches.

12 And the daughter of Tyre *shall be there* with a gift ; *even* the rich among the people shall intreat thy favour.

13 The king's daughter *is* all glorious within : her clothing is of wrought gold.

14 She shall be brought unto the king in raiment of needlework : the virgins her companions that follow her shall be brought unto thee.

15 With gladness and rejoicing shall they be brought : they shall enter into the king's palace.

16 Instead of thy fathers shall be thy children, whom thou mayest make princes in all the earth.

The Lord grant that in this house there may be kept up a gracious succession. May pious sons follow godly fathers, and may the King of our hearts have servants in this family as long as the world stands.

17 I will make thy name to be remembered in all generations : therefore shall the people praise thee for ever and ever. *(Jesus can never be forgotten. Solomon is not, but Jesus lives on and reigns on, and shall do for ever and ever ; blessed be his name.)*

The King of saints, how fair his face,
Adorn'd with majesty and grace !
He comes with blessings from above,
And wins the nations to his love.

Let endless honours crown his head ;
Let every age his praises spread ;
While we with cheerful songs approve
The condescensions of his love.

I. KINGS VIII. 1—6 ; 10, 11 ; 22—30.

THEN Solomon assembled the chief of the fathers of the children of Israel, unto King Solomon in Jerusalem, that they might bring up the ark of the covenant of the LORD out of the city of David, which *is* Zion.

Solomon prepared the temple before he brought the ark to it, and an old writer well observes that before we pray we should prepare our heart that it may be a temple for the Lord.

2, 3, 4 And all the men of Israel assembled themselves unto King Solomon ; and the priests took up the ark. And they brought up the ark of the LORD, and the tabernacle of the congregation, and all the holy vessels that *were* in the tabernacle, even those did the priests and the Levites bring up.

5 And king Solomon, and all the congregation of Israel, that were assembled unto him, *were* with him before the ark, sacrificing sheep and oxen, that could not be told nor numbered for multitude. *(They paused on the way at different spots, and offered sacrifices, till, as Josephus tells us, " the ground was moist with drink-offerings and sacrifices." It was the jubilee year, and the season was the feast of tabernacles, so that the crowds were great, and the joy overflowing. When shall we see the whole earth hold jubilee and adore the ascended Saviour ?)*

6 And the priests brought in the ark of the covenant of the LORD unto his place, into the oracle of the house, to the most holy *place, even* under the wings of the cherubims.

10, 11 And it came to pass, when the priests were come out of the holy *place,* that the cloud filled the house of the LORD. So that the priests could not stand to minister because of the cloud : for the glory of the LORD had filled the house of the LORD. *(The cloudy pillar was the token of the presence of God, and its filling the sanctuary was a sign of his graciously accepting the temple. We cannot tell whether it was the dazzling brightness, or the deep, portentous darkness, which overwhelmed the minds of the priests, but assuredly it is a glorious thing to have the Lord so present in the midst of his people that all our works become as nothing, and we feel that no longer do we " stand to minister," but the Lord himself is there.)*

22 ¶ And Solomon stood before the altar of the LORD in the presence of all the congregation of Israel, and spread forth his hands toward heaven. *(He was not a priest, and could not therefore present the sacrifices upon the altar; but as the representative man for the nation he did well to offer up the national prayer.)*

23, 24 And he said, LORD God of Israel, *there is* no God like thee, in heaven above, or on earth beneath, who keepest covenant and mercy with thy servants that walk before thee with all their heart : Who hast kept with thy servant David my father that thou promisedst him : thou spakest also with thy mouth, and hast fulfilled *it* with thine hand, as *it is* this day. *(Observe how he dwells upon the covenant. It is sweet praying when we can plead the promises.)*

25, 26 Therefore now, LORD God of Israel, keep with thy servant David my father that thou promisedst him, saying, There shall not fail thee a man in my sight to sit on the throne of Israel ; so that thy children take heed to their way, that they walk before me as thou hast walked before me. And now, O God of Israel, let thy word, I pray thee, be verified, which thou spakest unto thy servant David my father.

27 But will God indeed dwell on the earth ? behold, the heaven and heaven of heavens cannot contain thee ; how much less this house that I have builded ? *(So even in the dim light of Judaism it was seen that the Lord dwelleth not in temples made with hands ; how astonishing it is that under the Gospel men should still cling to the notion of holy places.)*

28 Yet have thou respect unto the prayer of thy servant, and to his supplication, O LORD my God, to hearken unto the cry and to the prayer, which thy servant prayeth before thee to day :

29 That thine eyes may be open toward this house night and day, *even* toward the place of which thou hast said, My name shall be there : that thou mayest hearken unto the prayer which thy servant shall make toward this place.

30 And hearken thou to the supplication of thy servant, and of thy people Israel, when they shall pray toward this place : and hear thou in heaven thy dwelling place : and when thou hearest, forgive. *(In our highest joys we have still need to say " forgive." Our hearts are out of order when that word does not rise to our lips. Let us plead with God to bless us throughout all our lives, and evermore to forgive.)*

THE *consecration of Solomon's temple brings to our mind his father's delightful Psalm, in which he expressed his love to the worship of the Lord his God.*

PSALM LXXXIV.

1 How amiable *are* thy tabernacles, O LORD of hosts ! *(More delightful than tongue can tell are the assemblies for divine worship. They are lovely in prospect, lovely at the time, and lovely to the memory afterwards. Under heaven, no place is so heavenly as the church of the living God.)*

2 My soul longeth, yea, even fainteth for the courts of the LORD : my heart and my flesh crieth out for the living God.

Do we feel the same burning desire after God? If so, we shall not need urging to attend his worship. Some need to be whipped to worship, but David is here crying for it ; he needed no clatter of bells to ring him in to the service, he carried his bell in his own bosom.

3 Yea, the sparrow hath found an house, and the swallow a nest for herself, where she may lay her young, *even* thine altars, O LORD of hosts, my King, and my God. *(He envied the little birds which lodged about the tabernacle. When far away from the Lord's altars he wished he had wings to fly to them, as the sparrows did, or build near them after the manner of the swallows.)*

4 Blessed *are* they that dwell in thy house : they will be still praising thee. Selah.

He wished he could be always employed about the sacred tent, for he thought that even the menial servants of such a Lord would be always praising him. Dwelling so near him, their joy would never cease, their praises would sound forth both day and night.

5 Blessed *is* the man whose strength *is* in thee ; in whose heart *are* the ways *of them. (Or, " in whose heart are thy ways." None find joy in worship but those who throw their hearts into it. Neither prayer, nor praise, nor the hearing of the word will be profitable to persons who have left their hearts behind them.)*

6 *Who* passing through the valley of Baca make it a well ; the rain also filleth the pools.

The pilgrims who went up to the temple found refreshment in the dreariest part of the road, even the gloomy vale of tears became delightful to them. They made desolate valleys to be as cheerful as the wells where men and women were accustomed to meet for social intercourse. What will not holy fellowship and hearty praises do?

7 They go from strength to strength, *every one of them* in Zion appeareth before God.

God's people hold on their way, grow stronger, and at last reach their journey's end, for they have an almighty Convoy who will not suffer them to fail.

8 O LORD God of hosts, hear my prayer : give ear, O God of Jacob. Selah.

9 Behold, O God our shield, and look upon the face of thine anointed.

10 For a day in thy courts *is* better than a thousand. I had rather be a doorkeeper in the house of my God, than to dwell in the tents of wickedness. *(The doorkeeper is first in and last out, and he has less comfort than anyone, yet David would sooner have the lowest place in God's house, than the highest in the tents of sin. Quaint old Secker says, " Happy are those persons whom God will use as besoms to sweep out the dust from his temple, or who are allowed to tug at an oar of the boat wherein Christ and his people are embarked.")*

11 For the LORD God *is* a sun and shield : the LORD will give grace and glory : no good *thing* will he withhold from them that walk uprightly. *(What a great promise, or set of promises ! Here we have all we need for all time, yea, and for eternity. What an encouragement to pray ! If all things are freely given to us of God, let us open our mouths wide in our petitions. What more can God himself say than he has said in this most precious verse?)*

12 O LORD of hosts, blessed *is* the man that trusteth in thee.

How pleasant, how divinely fair,
O Lord of hosts, thy dwellings are !
With long desire my spirit faints
To meet the assemblies of thy saints.

My flesh would rest in thine abode,
My panting heart cries out for God ;
My God ! my King ! why should I be
So far from all my joys and thee ?

IT *is possible that in those golden days when Solomon walked with God, he was inspired to write the matchless book of Canticles, which is the Holy of holies of the Scriptures, standing like the tree of life in the midst of the garden of inspiration. The song is highly allegorical, and describes Christ and his church as a bride and bridegroom who sing to each other and of each other. The passage we are about to read is a dialogue.*

SOLOMON'S SONG II.

The Bridegroom first speaks, and says—

1 I *AM* the rose of Sharon, *and* the lily of the valleys.

2 As the lily among thorns, so *is* my love among the daughters. *(Who can this be but Jesus, in whose person the rose and lily are combined?*

> "White is his soul, from blemish free,
> Red with the blood he shed for me."

He paints his church as a lone lily growing amidst a wilderness of thorns, among them but not of them, her beauties being all the more conspicuous by contrast.)

Then the Bride or the church exclaims—

3 As the apple tree among the trees of the wood, so *is* my beloved among the sons. I sat down under his shadow with great delight, and his fruit *was* sweet to my taste. *(The golden citron excels all other trees, and Jesus is far more excellent than all others. Shade and fruit, protection and provision, are found in him. He is all in all to us who believe in him.)*

4 He brought me to the banqueting house, and his banner over me *was* love.

5 Stay me with flagons, comfort me with apples: for I *am* sick of love. *(Love to Jesus sometimes becomes so vehement a passion that the soul cannot bear it, and the bodily frame is ready to swoon under the supreme excitement.)*

6 His left hand *is* under my head, and his right hand doth embrace me.

7, 8, 9 I charge you, O ye daughters of Jerusalem, by the roes, and by the hinds of the field, that ye stir not up, nor awake *my* love, till he please. *(The spouse now hears the voice of her husband, and rejoices to see him coming to her with all the sacred haste of omnipotent love.)* The voice of my beloved! behold, he cometh leaping upon the mountains, skipping upon the hills. My beloved is like a roe or a young hart: behold, he standeth behind our wall, he looketh forth at the windows, shewing himself through the lattice.

10 My beloved spake, and said unto me, Rise up, my love, my fair one, and come away.

11 For, lo, the winter is past, the rain is over *and* gone;

12 The flowers appear on the earth; the time of the singing *of birds* is come, and the voice of the turtle is heard in our land;

13 The fig tree putteth forth her green figs, and the vines *with* the tender grape give a *good* smell. Arise, my love, my fair one, and come away. *(When doubts and fears, trials and distresses are over and the heart is full of music, we should go forth in holy fellowship, and delight ourselves with the Lord Jesus. Dark days may come, let us spend our joyful seasons in the most profitable manner, walking with our Lord in the light while the light lasts.)*

The Bridegroom still speaks, and calls to his beloved, saying—

14 ¶ O my dove, *that art* in the clefts of the rock, in the secret *places* of the stairs, let me see thy countenance, let me hear thy voice; for sweet *is* thy voice, and thy countenance *is* comely. *(Come out from the hiding-places of fear or worldliness and own the Lord.)*

15 Take us the foxes, the little foxes, that spoil the vines: for our vines *have* tender grapes.

The church sings again—

16, 17 My beloved *is* mine, and I *am* his: he feedeth among the lilies. Until the day break, and the shadows flee away, turn, my beloved, and be thou like a roe or a young hart upon the mountains of Bether [*or division*]. *(If we have lost the presence of the Lord, it is our duty and our privilege to cry to him to return swiftly and triumphantly, like the fleet roe which overleaps mountains and defies all difficulties.)*

Yes! my Beloved to my sight
Shows a sweet mixture, red and white:
All human beauties, all divine,
In my Beloved meet and shine.

All over glorious is my Lord,
Must be beloved, and yet adored;
His worth if all the nations knew,
Sure the whole earth would love him too.

THAT *the poetical nature of the Song of Solomon may be more clearly seen, we have now before us a passage in which the original form of the Canticle is preserved, and its meaning made more clear by an improved translation.*

SONG III. 6—11.

The first speakers are the DAUGHTERS OF JERUSALEM.

6 What is this coming up from the wilderness,
  As if it were pillars of smoke,
Odorous of myrrh and frankincense,
  With all the fragrant dust of the merchant?

The FRIENDS OF THE BRIDEGROOM *then reply.*

7   Behold his Chariot,
    It is Solomon's;
Sixty valiant men around it
  Of the valiant of Israel;

8 All of them graspers of the sword,
    Trained unto battle;
Every man his sword on his side
  Against alarm by night.

9 The chariot made him King Solomon,
    Of the trees of Lebanon;
10 Its pillars made he silveren,
    The seat thereof golden,
    Its covering of crimson,
  The midst thereof inlaid with LOVE
For the daughters of Jerusalem.

11 Go forth and look, ye daughters of Zion,
    On King Solomon
    In the diadem
Wherewithal his mother crowned him,
Upon the day of his espousal,
  And the day of the gladness of his soul.

Then follows a song of THE KING, *in which he extols the beauty of his bride.*

SONG IV. 1—7.

1   Lo thou fair one,
    My companion,
    Lo thou fair one!
Thine Eyes are doves within thy locks;
Thy Hair like a flock of the goats,
That hang adown Mount Gilead.

2 Thy Teeth like a flock of sheep even shorn,
  That had come up from the washing,
  That are all of them twin-bearing,
  And bereft not one among them.

3 Like a line of scarlet are thy Lips,
    And thy speaking beauteous;
  Like to a pomegranate cloven
    Are thy Temples through thy locks.

4 Like the Tower of David is thy Neck,
    Builded for an armoury,
  With a thousand shields hung upon it,
    All bucklers of the mighty;
5 Twain breasts of thine like a pair of fawns,
    Twinlings of the roe,
  That are feeding among the lilies.

6   Until breathe the day,
    And flee away the shadows,
      I will go my way
      To the Mount of Myrrh,
7 And to the Hill of Frankincense.—
      Thou art all fair,
    My Love, and no spot in Thee.

In the first song the king is seen in his travelling palanquin or chariot-bed, coming up from the wilderness. We may expound the picture as representing our Lord and King going up into his glory from this wilderness world. Mark the sweet odours of his merits, and the smoke of his sacrifice, observe also the attendant angels, as Milton calls them, " the helmed cherubim and the sworded seraphim," who, having kept watch around him in the wilderness, now attend him to swell the pomp of his ascension. Thus will Jesus come a second time, and his church shall go forth and gaze upon him. That glorious chariot of love, whose purple canopy well sets forth the atoning blood, is his salvation in which the church rides and rests with her Lord. Happy those who are in it by faith.

The song in which the king extols his bride will be understood by those who know that the imputed righteousness of the Lord Jesus puts upon the saints a perfect comeliness, so that they are " all fair" in the sight of God. Every single line has its meaning, and spiritual minds will find great delight in reading the works of such writers as Gill, or Durham, or Moody Stuart, upon this priceless book.

312   "Come with me from Lebanon, my spouse."   MAY 28.—EVENING.

[*Or October* 23]

OUR *last reading gave us two parts of a delightful Canticle: we will now read the third portion, in which the King is the chief speaker, and rejoices to extol his bride, even as the Lord Jesus rejoiceth over his church.*

SONG IV. 8—16.

THE KING *thus speaks—*

8 Along with me from Lebanon, my Bride,
  Along with me from Lebanon, come;
Look from off the top of Amana,
  From the top of Shenir and Hermon,
    From the dwellings of the lions,
  From the mountains of the leopards:

Jesus would have us look above the highest earthly delights, and leave all earthly loves for his sake. Shall he say, "Come with me," and shall we refuse to follow? Hear how he sets forth his love to us, his joy over us.

9 Thou hast taken my heart, my Sister, my
                    [Spouse,
  Thou hast taken my heart with one
Of thine eyes, with a single chain of thy
                  [neck;

Though but one grace be seen in us, Jesus spies it out, and is charmed with it; such is his condescending love.

10 How pleasant is thy love, my Sister, my
                    [Spouse,
  How good is thy love above wine,
And the odour of thine ointments above all
                [perfumes!

11 Honey from the comb dropping are thy lips,
                [my Spouse,
  Honey and milk are under thy tongue,
And the scent of thy garments like the scent
              [of Lebanon.

In the esteem of Jesus, the love, the spirit, the words, and the outward conduct of his people are all acceptable.

12   A garden enclosed,
    My Sister, my Bride,
    A spring shut up,
    A fountain sealed:

13   Thy plants a Paradise
    Of granate-apple trees,
    Along with fruits most choice;
    Of henna-plants with nards,
14   The spikenard and the saffron,
    The sweet cane and cinnamon,
    With all trees of frankincense;
    Of myrrh and the lign aloes,
    With all the chief of spices:
15   A fountain for the gardens,
    A well of living waters,
    And streams out of Lebanon.

Jesus thus extols his beloved Church, but having done so, he intercedes for her that the Holy Spirit may visit her, for what would she be without him? Listen to the Redeemer's prayer.

.16   Awake, O North wind;
    And come, thou South;
    Breathe upon my garden,
    Flow its odours forth.

Moved by the love of her Lord, and influenced by the Spirit, the Church begs the Lord to come nearer to her.

  Come, let my Loved One into his garden
  And let him eat his pleasant fruit.

To her he answers lovingly.

SONG V. 1.

1.   I am come into my garden,
    My Sister, my Bride;
    I have gathered my myrrh
    Along with my balm;
    I have eaten my honey
    With my honey-comb;
    I have drunk my wine
    Together with my milk;
    Eat, O friends, drink and quaff ye,
    O well-beloved.

Jesus accepts us and our fruits; let us therefore rejoice in him and feast upon him.

He calls me from the lion's den,
From this wild world of beasts and men,
To Zion, where his glories are—
Not Lebanon is half so fair;

Nor dens of prey, nor flowery plains,
Nor earthly joys, nor earthly pains,
Shall hold my feet, or force my stay,
When Christ invites my soul away.

WE *will again read in the Song, giving the language in its correct form.   The bride hears the Bridegroom knocking at her door, but she excuses herself from rising to admit him, and acts as unkindly to him, as, alas, we too often have done to our Lord Jesus.   The whole story is rehearsed in choicest song in—*

CANTICLES V. 2—16.

THE BRIDE.

2   I am asleep, but my heart is waking ;
The voice of my Well-beloved knocking ;
"Open unto me, my Sister,
My friend, my dove, my innocent,
For my head is filled with the dew,
My locks with the drops of the night."

Observe her indolent excuses.   How cruel she is to her friend !   How selfish !   How self-indulgent !   Have we not cause to blush, as in her conduct we see our own ?

3   I have put off my coat,
How shall I put it on ?
I have washed my feet,
How shall I soil them ?

4   My Well-beloved thrust his hand
Through the wicket of the door,
And my heart was troubled for him.
5   I arose, I to open to my Beloved One,
And my hands were dropping myrrh,
And my fingers myrrh the purest,
On the handles of the bar.

6   I opened,
I unto my Well-beloved ;
But my Well-beloved had withdrawn,
He was gone !
My soul swooned away for his word ;
I sought him, but I found him not ;
Called him but he answered not !

7   Find me did the watchers,
That walk round the city ;
They smote me, wounded me,
Strip my veil from off me
Did the keepers of the walls.

8   I lay a charge upon you,
O daughters of Jerusalem ;
If ye find my Well-beloved,
What are ye to tell him—
That sick of love am I.

Although the spouse had been sadly negligent, and so had grieved her Lord, and made him hide his face from her, yet she still loved him, and therefore was intensely earnest to find him again. She hoped that perhaps her Lord would listen to others, even if he closed his ear for a while to her, and therefore she begged the daughters of Jerusalem to speak to him on her behalf.   When we are in darkness, the prayers of our brethren may be of great service to us.

The song represents the DAUGHTERS OF JERUSALEM *as saying—*

9   What is thy Beloved more than any beloved,
O thou Fair One among women ?
What is thy Beloved more than any beloved,
That in this wise thou chargest us ?

To this enquiry THE BRIDE *replies—*

10   My Beloved is white and red,
The chief amongst a myriad.

11   His head is a mass of gold most fine ;
His locks are branches clustering,
Black as the raven-down.

12   His eyes are like the doves,
By the brooks of waters,
Washing themselves with milk,
Sitting within the floods.

13   His cheeks like beds of balsams,
Flowers of sweetest smell ;
His lips *the scarlet* lilies,
Dropping purest myrrh.

14   His hands have rings of gold
Inset with beryl stones ;
His body is bright ivory,
Overlaid with sapphires ;
15   His legs pillars of marble,
Set on golden sockets.

His look is like to Lebanon,
Noble as the cedars ;
16   His mouth is every sweetness ;
Yea, all of him loveliness.

This is my Beloved One,
And this my Companion,
O daughters of Jerusalem.

IT was in the days of his glory, ere sin had darkened his sun, that Solomon collected and composed the Book of Proverbs, which is a mine of wisdom, and a treasure-house of instruction. Let us read—

PROVERBS I. 20—31.

20 ¶ Wisdom crieth without; she uttereth her voice in the streets : (The right way is not kept a secret, or mentioned only to a few. Everywhere, in these favoured gospel days, we meet with instructions and admonitions. The Bible is in every house, and the preachers of the word are many : if any perish, it will not be because the plan of salvation was not made public. Wisdom is among us, and speaks with earnestness and plainness of speech.)

21 She crieth in the chief place of concourse, in the openings of the gates : in the city she uttereth her words, saying,

22 How long, ye simple ones, will ye love simplicity ? and the scorners delight in their scorning, and fools hate knowledge ?

23 Turn you at my reproof: behold, I will pour out my spirit unto you, I will make known my words unto you. (Thus wisdom, in the person of the Lord Jesus, calls upon the sons of men in pathetic accents. Men are foolish, and love their folly; some of them are so besotted by sin that they scoff at the instruction which alone can save their souls; therefore the Lord expostulates and pleads with them. It is not the will of the Redeemer that the sinner should die, and in infinite love he interposes to prevent their becoming suicides. Note how earnestly he pleads,— "How long" ? and how graciously he promises the aid of his Holy Spirit that they may understand his instructions. Jesus thus pleads with each one of us ; have we obeyed his call ?)

24 ¶ Because I have called, and ye refused ; I have stretched out my hand, and no man regarded ;

25 But ye have set at nought all my counsel, and would none of my reproof :

26 I also will laugh at your calamity ; I will mock when your fear cometh ;

27 When your fear cometh as desolation, and your destruction cometh as a whirlwind ; when distress and anguish cometh upon you.

28 Then shall they call upon me, but I will not answer; they shall seek me early, but they shall not find me :

29 For that they hated knowledge, and did not choose the fear of the LORD :

30 They would none of my counsel : they despised all my reproof.

31 Therefore shall they eat of the fruit of their own way, and be filled with their own devices. (Not until calls of love have failed does the Lord assume the language of stern rebuke ; but when grace has been neglected, and even insulted, justice must speak in tones of thunder. The Lord Jesus wept over sinners in the days of his flesh, and still does he by his Church entreat and warn them, and yearn over them ; but it will not always be so, for the time cometh when he will have no pity, but will utterly reject the cries and petitions of his enemies. They say that the sweetest wine makes the sharpest vinegar, and so the very gentleness and tenderness of Jesus will make him the more terrible when his patience at length turns to wrath. Oh! may none of us ever have addressed to us the terrible words which we have just read, for they are full of weeping, and wailing, and gnashing of teeth. Is it not right that those should perish who refused to be saved ? Should not those be rejected at the last who wilfully rejected the Redeemer throughout their day of grace ? Is it not a most righteous rule that men should reap what they sow, and that those who choose their own delusions should find their choice confirmed ? Shall any one member of our family be so madly wicked as to refuse attention to the invitations of grace ? God forbid that it should be so.)

How they deserve the deepest hell
  That slight the joys above !
What chains of vengeance must they feel
  Who break such cords of love.

Draw us, O God, by sovereign grace,
  And make us wise to-day,
Lest we provoke thy fiercest wrath
  By impudent delay.

PROVERBS VIII. 1—21.

IN *this chapter we hear again the pleadings of heavenly wisdom in the person of the Son of God. Let us not be careless when God himself expostulates with us.*

1 Doth not wisdom cry? and understanding put forth her voice?

2 She standeth in the top of high places, by the way in the places of the paths.

3 She crieth at the gates, at the entry of the city, at the coming in at the doors.

4 Unto you, O men, I call; and my voice *is* to the sons of man. *(Everywhere, in his word, in providence, by his ministers, and by his Spirit, the Incarnate Wisdom still calls to men. Especially in this land of Bibles and of Sabbaths, the Lord Jesus is everywhere heard pleading with old and young, gentle and simple, that they would consider and turn unto him.)*

5 O ye simple, understand wisdom: and, ye fools, be ye of an understanding heart.

Jesus invites the foolish to come to him. How condescending is he in this, for the teachers of old sought wise men for pupils, and few masters now-a-days would invite fools to their schools. Jesus is meek and lowly in heart, he condescends to men of low estate, and is ready to be the teacher of the simple. None need stay away from him because of their ignorance; it should even be a reason for coming to him. But some will enquire, Is his teaching worth hearing? Therefore he says—

6, 7 Hear; for I will speak of excellent things; and the opening of my lips *shall be* right things. *(But does he speak the truth? He does, and he adds)* For my mouth shall speak truth; and wickedness *is* an abomination to my lips.

8, 9 All the words of my mouth *are* in righteousness; *there is* nothing froward or perverse in them. *(But can we understand his teaching? Can poor men comprehend him? Can little children receive his teaching? Yes, his words are simplicity itself.)* They *are* all plain to him that understandeth, and right to them that find knowledge.

10 Receive my instruction, and not silver; and knowledge rather than choice gold.

Soul-saving knowledge is beyond all price.

11 For wisdom *is* better than rubies; and all the things that may be desired are not to be compared to it.

12 I wisdom dwell with prudence, and find out knowledge of witty inventions.

Eternal Wisdom found out the witty invention of the Cross. The plan of salvation by a substitute is the very summit of wisdom: let us give diligence to obtain an interest in it.

13 The fear of the LORD *is* to hate evil: pride, and arrogancy, and the evil way, and the froward mouth, do I hate.

And what God hates, we must also hate with all our heart.

14 Counsel *is* mine, and sound wisdom: I *am* understanding; I have strength.

15 By me kings reign, and princes decree justice.

16 By me princes rule, and nobles, *even* all the judges of the earth.

17 I love them that love me; and those that seek me early shall find me.

This is a portion of meat for the children of our families. Let boys and girls lay hold upon it, and go to Jesus in reliance upon this promise.

18 Riches and honour *are* with me; yea, durable riches and righteousness.

19 My fruit *is* better than gold, yea, than fine gold; and my revenue than choice silver.

Nothing can be so useful, so valuable, so really good for us as to know Christ and to be found in him.

20 I lead in the way of righteousness, in the midst of the paths of judgment: *(In the Via Media, the middle way, which is the path of safety.)*

21 That I may cause those that love me to inherit substance; and I will fill their treasures.

They shall be truly rich in grace, even if their earthly goods be few, and they shall be infinitely rich in the world to come, where there is a kingdom for the very least of them.

If our ways by thee be order'd,
And thy name by us confess'd,
Then thy presence shall go with us,
And thy peace shall give us rest.

If in all the eye be single,
Clean the hands, and pure the breast,
Then thy presence shall go with us,
And thy guidance give us rest.

PROVERBS X. 1—16.

THE *first nine chapters are a kind of introduction to the Book of Proverbs; its short, pithy sentences commence at thè tenth chapter.*

1 The proverbs of Solomon. A wise son maketh a glad father: but a foolish son *is* the heaviness of his mother. *(This is the first of the proverbs, let each child take great notice of it. Who among us would wish to be a life-long grief to father and mother ? Yet such will be the case if we live in sin, and despise the heavenly wisdom.)*

2 Treasures of wickedness profit nothing: but righteousness delivereth from death.

Judas gained his thirty pieces of silver, but what profit had he in them ? Paul obtained the righteousness of Christ, and a crown of life was his portion.

3 The LORD will not suffer the soul of the righteous to famish: but he casteth away the substance of the wicked. *(The godly may hunger, but famish they shall not ; the wicked may increase in wealth, but continue in prosperity they cannot.)*

4 He becometh poor that dealeth *with* a slack hand : but the hand of the diligent maketh rich. *(No pains, no gains ; no sweat, no sweet.)*

5 He that gathereth in summer *is* a wise son: *but* he that sleepeth in harvest *is* a son that causeth shame. *(Neglect of timely industry leads into sin. Our idle days are Satan's busy days. He who will not be thrifty while he may, will find that lost opportunities do not return.)*

6 Blessings *are* upon the head of the just: but violence covereth the mouth of the wicked.

7 The memory of the just *is* blessed : but the name of the wicked shall rót.

8 The wise in heart will receive commandments : but a prating fool shall fall. *(Wise men hear more than they speak, and are willing to listen to practical instruction, but foolish persons talk on till they seal their own condemnation.)*

9 He that walketh uprightly walketh surely : but he that perverteth his ways shall be known.

10 He that winketh with the eye causeth sorrow : but a prating fool shall fall.

Cowardly insinuations, which men dare not utter in words, but covertly express by signs, are the cause of much misery, and no true man will use them. *Those who talk much, and are destitute of real religion, will soon make shipwreck of their profession.*

11 The mouth of a righteous *man is* a well of life : *(sending forth refreshing and saving streams)* but violence covereth the mouth of the wicked. *(Making them like closed wells, full of putrid water, deadly to others, and destructive to themselves.)*

12 Hatred stirreth up strifes : but love covereth all sins. *(Loving spirits will not take offence, but bear and forbear for Christ's sake, but evil-disposed persons make the smallest matter a ground of offence, and are for ever fanning the fires of enmity. Let it not be so among us.)*

13 In the lips of him that hath understanding wisdom is found : but a rod *is* for the back of him that is void of understanding.

14 Wise *men* lay up knowledge : *(for they still feel their own want of it;)* but the mouth of the foolish *is* near destruction. *(He thinks he knows all, and therefore will not learn, but talks himself to ruin.)*

15 The rich man's wealth *is* his strong city : the destruction of the poor *is* their poverty.

Alas ! how often is this the case, even in our own land. Poor men are despised, and few plead their cause. May the Lord send to us such a just spirit that we may always be ready to take the weaker side, and see that the poor man is not trampled upon. It is meanness itself to fawn upon the wealthy ; true religion lifts us above such littleness.

16 The labour of the righteous *tendeth* to life : the fruit of the wicked to sin.

Labour, not idleness, is the stamp of a servant of God. With the wicked, self is always their object and end, and therefore their actions are sinful in the sight of the Lord. O Lord, make thou us to work because of life *within us, so that we may have life yet more abundantly.*

To me, O Lord, be thou "The Way,"
   To me be thou " The Truth ; "
To me, my Saviour, be "The Life,"
   Thou Guardian of my youth !

So shall that Way be my delight,
   That Truth shall make me free ;
That Life shall raise me from the dead,
   And then I'll live to thee.

PROVERBS X. 17—32.

HE *is in* the way of life that keepeth instruction : but he that refuseth reproof erreth. *(No man can do us a greater kindness than to instruct us in the right and warn us of the wrong; but probably it is as difficult to accept advice in a proper spirit as to give it wisely. Be it ours ever to listen to the words of wisdom, and never to be above learning from any one.)*

18 He that hideth hatred *with* lying lips, and he that uttereth a slander, *is* a fool.
The first sentence shows that all hypocritical concealment of hatred is folly as well as sin. The last sentence is a severe blow to very many. May it not apply to some of ourselves? Are we not far too ready to repeat evil reports?

19 In the multitude of words there wanteth not sin : but he that refraineth his lips *is* wise.
How common is the fault of talkativeness. Men talk so much because they think so little. Drums make a great noise because they are hollow. One attribute of a wise man is within the reach of us all—we can be quiet. Let us try it.

20 The tongue of the just *is as* choice silver : the heart of the wicked *is* little worth.
The best part of an ungodly man is little worth; this is God's opinion of him, and it ought to humble him, and cause him serious thought.

21 The lips of the righteous feed many : but fools die for want of wisdom. *(They cannot feed others, for they are famishing themselves for want of the truth.)*

22 The blessing of the LORD, it maketh rich, and he addeth no sorrow with it.
Other riches always bring attendant griefs : none but the Lord's roses are without thorns.

23 *It is* as sport to a fool to do mischief : but a man of understanding hath wisdom.

24 The fear of the wicked, it shall come upon him : but the desire of the righteous shall be granted.

25 As the whirlwind passeth, so *is* the wicked no *more :* but the righteous *is* an everlasting foundation. *(The whirlwind is only remembered by the ruin which it leaves behind it, and the like is true of many a bad man; but the repute of good men is comparable to an ancient castle, whose deep foundations abide the lapse of ages, and remain as enduring monuments from age to age.)*

26 As vinegar to the teeth, and as smoke to the eyes, so *is* the sluggard to them that send him. *(He is obnoxious, objectionable, a nuisance, a provocation. He who would please his employer, must be diligent, quick, and hearty.)*

27 The fear of the LORD prolongeth days : but the years of the wicked shall be shortened.
It cannot be doubted that true religion, by its temperance, peacefulness, and purity, tends to lengthen human life; and it is equally certain that intemperance, vice, irregular habits, and frequent ill-temper, have a powerful tendency to bring men sooner to their graves than would otherwise fall to their lot. Godliness has thus the promise of the life that now is.

28 The hope of the righteous *shall* be gladness : but the expectation of the wicked shall perish.

29 The way of the LORD *is* strength to the upright : but destruction *shall be* to the workers of iniquity.

30 The righteous shall never be removed : but the wicked shall not inhabit the earth.
There will come a day when wicked men shall not be found upon this earth : they will die out, and their places be filled up by a holy seed. We long for the coming of the Lord which will usher in the age of holiness.

31 The mouth of the just bringeth forth wisdom : but the froward tongue shall be cut out.

32 The lips of the righteous know what is acceptable : but the mouth of the wicked *speaketh* frowardness. *(They try to provoke and sadden others : they have no sense of fitness, but talk at random. Far from each of us be that wild, ungovernable tongue which wounds others needlessly : be ours the gentle, holy conversation which blesses both the hearer and the speaker; thus shall this family be a little heaven below.)*

Jesus, the sinner's Friend, to Thee,
Lost and undone, for aid I flee;
Weary of earth, myself, and sin,
Open thine arms and take me in.

Pity and heal my sin-sick soul;
'Tis thou alone canst make me whole;
Fallen, till in me thine image shine,
And lost I am, till thou art mine.

318   " Boast not thyself of to-morrow."   MAY 31.—EVENING.

[*Or October* 29.]

PROVERBS XXVII. 1—18.

BOAST not thyself of to-morrow; for thou knowest not what a day may bring forth. *(To provide for the morrow is duty, to boast of it is sin. Only a worldling will dare to do so, for eternity is near, and we may be ushered into it before the sun goes down or rises again. The rich fool's soul was required of him the very night he gloried in the fulness of his barns. Young people must not make sure of living to ripe years, for there are little graves in the cemetery, and flowers in the bud are taken from the stem. Repentance and faith are our bounden duties to-day; to delay will be a wicked boasting of to-morrow, and may cause our eternal ruin.)*

2 Let another man praise thee, and not thine own mouth; a stranger, and not thine own lips.

3 A stone *is* heavy, and the sand weighty; but a fool's wrath *is* heavier than them both. *Because he will not forgive; he is sullen and revengeful, and his anger oppresses his own heart, and if he has power his wrath becomes a sore burden to others.*

4 Wrath *is* cruel, and anger is outrageous; but who *is* able to stand before envy? *(Adam and Satan both fell by envy of God, and it will surely blot our happiness if we indulge in it. Envy spits its venom on the best of men, and is a horrible and devilish passion, to be fought with and overcome by all who follow the loving Jesus.)*

5 Open rebuke *is* better than secret love.

6 Faithful *are* the wounds of a friend; but the kisses of an enemy *are* deceitful.

7 The full soul loatheth an honeycomb; but to the hungry soul every bitter thing is sweet.

8 As a bird that wandereth from her nest, so *is* a man that wandereth from his place. *Let us not, then, be changeable and unsettled. If we have not succeeded where we are, let us try again, but let us not be for ever shifting. How can a tree grow which is often transplanted?*

9 Ointment and perfume rejoice the heart: so *doth* the sweetness of a man's friend by hearty counsel.

10 Thine own friend, and thy father's friend, forsake not; *(Jesus was our father's best friend, let us not forsake him. We shall never find a better;)* neither go into thy brother's house in the day of thy calamity: *for* better *is* a neighbour *that is* near than a brother far off.

Relationship ought to be a close bond, but alas, selfishness often comes in. Jonathan was kinder to David than Joseph's brethren were to him.

11 My son, be wise, and make my heart glad, that I may answer him that reproacheth me.

12 A prudent *man* forseeth the evil, *and* hideth himself; *but* the simple pass on, *and* are punished.

13 Take his garment that is surety for a stranger, and take a pledge of him for a strange woman. *(Do not trust the licentious man He is bad at heart, and his vices will soon make him a beggar; if you must deal with him, do it on the strictest terms, or he will rob you.)*

14 He that blesseth his friend with a loud voice, rising early in the morning, it shall be counted a curse to him. *(Extravagant praises are distasteful to sensible men, and too often one may suspect that they are uttered with a sinister end. We should wish well to our friends, but vehemently to sound their praises at untimely hours, will do them no service, but rather the reverse.)*

15 A continual dropping in a very rainy day and a contentious woman are alike.

16 Whosoever hideth her hideth the wind, and the ointment of his right hand, *which* bewrayeth *itself.* *Contention with a neighbour is a sharp shower, soon over; but contention with a wife at home is weary work, and makes life a misery; and the worst of it is that the home strife cannot be concealed; the noise and ill-temper of a bad woman reveal themselves; you might as well try to cover up the wind, or hold oil in your hand. Let us never strive, except to make each other happy.*

17 Iron sharpeneth iron; so a man sharpeneth the countenance of his friend. *Good society is a great help to grace. Communion with the saints helps us in the service of God.*

18 Whoso keepeth the fig tree shall eat the fruit thereof: so he that waiteth on his master shall be honoured. *(And if Jesus be that Master, our honour shall be great and long enduring, and our reward shall be sweet indeed.)*

Hear God while he speaks, then hear him to-day;
And pray while he hears, unceasingly pray;
Believe in his promise, rely on his word,
And while he commands you, obey your great Lord.

I. KINGS X. 1—13.

AND when the queen of Sheba heard of the fame of Solomon concerning the name of the LORD, she came to prove him with hard questions. *(Far off as she was, the glory of Solomon reached her, and she was moved to visit him, not only out of curiosity to behold his splendour, but from religious motives, that she might know more concerning the name of the LORD. Alas, there are thousands who show no interest in Jesus, though he is near them, and his gospel is preached in their streets. Sad is it that Solomon should attract a stranger so far away, and Jesus should be neglected by those who are near.)*

2 And she came to Jerusalem with a very great train, with camels that bare spices, and very much gold, and precious stones : and when she was come to Solomon, she communed with him of all that was in her heart.

3 And Solomon told her all her questions : there was not *any* thing hid from the king, which he told her not. *(When sinners come to Jesus he will solve all their difficult questions, and both reveal and remove all their secret disquietudes. He is ever ready to communicate of his wisdom to all who come unto him, and they shall never in any instance find that their difficulties surpass his skill.)*

4 And when the queen of Sheba had seen all Solomon's wisdom, and the house that he had built,

5 And the meat of his table, and the sitting of his servants, and the attendance of his ministers, and their apparel, and his cup-bearers, and his ascent by which he went up unto the house of the LORD ; there was no more spirit in her.

6 And she said to the king, It was a true report that I heard in mine own land of thy acts and of thy wisdom.

7 Howbeit I believed not the words, until I came, and mine eyes had seen *it* : and, behold, the half was not told me : thy wisdom and prosperity exceedeth the fame which I heard.

8, 9 Happy *are* thy men, happy *are* these thy servants, which stand continually before thee, *and* that hear thy wisdom. Blessed be the LORD thy God, which delighted in thee, to set thee on the throne of Israel : because the LORD loved Israel for ever, therefore made he thee king, to do judgment and justice.

In like manner, although the gospel report concerning King Jesus greatly extols him, yet the experience of the believer discovers in him a wealth of grace and goodness which no tongue could have expressed. Jesus must be personally realized by each one of us, or we shall never know him. O that many who now despise the Redeemer would see him for themselves, they would at once change their indifference into adoration.

10 And she gave the king an hundred and twenty talents of gold, and of spices very great store, and precious stones : there came no more such abundance of spices as these which the queen of Sheba gave to king Solomon.

Even so, when a heart truly knows King Jesus it brings tribute to him. Nothing is too good, too costly, too precious for Jesus. If we could lay the whole world at his feet, it would be "a present far too small."

11 And the navy also of Hiram, that brought gold from Ophir, brought in from Ophir great plenty of almug trees, and precious stones.

12 And the king made of the almug trees pillars for the house of the LORD, and for the king's house, harps also and psalteries for singers : there came no such almug trees, nor were seen unto this day.

13 And king Solomon gave unto the queen of Sheba all her desire, whatsoever she asked, beside *that* which Solomon gave her of his royal bounty. So she turned and went to her own country, she and her servants. *(We may also confidently add that our Lord Jesus will be in no one's debt; for all that we can possibly give to him he will make a hundredfold return, yea, he will grant us whatsoever we ask, he will give us the desire of our heart.)*

MATTHEW XII. 42.

The queen of the south shall rise up in the judgment with this generation, and shall condemn it : for she came from the uttermost parts of the earth to hear the wisdom of Solomon ; and, behold, a greater than Solomon *is* here.

The queen of Sheba came from far, with great difficulty, running great risks ; and yet the mass of mankind are utterly careless about a greater than Solomon, and will scarcely cross the streets to see Jesus, who has power to bless them eternally.

Jerusalem the golden,
  With milk and honey blest,
Beneath thy contemplation
  Sink heart and voice oppress'd:
I know not, oh I know not
  What joys await us there:
What radiancy of glory,
  What bliss beyond compare!

They stand, those halls of Sion,
  Conjubilant with song,
And bright with many an angel,
  And all the martyr throng:
The Prince is ever in them,
  The daylight is serene;
The pastures of the blessèd
  Are deck'd in glorious sheen.

Let us pray, the Lord is willing,
  Ever waiting, prayer to hear;
Ready, his kind words fulfilling,
  Loving hearts to help and cheer.

Let us pray! our God with blessing
  Satisfies the praying soul;
Bends to hear the heart's confessing,
  Moulding it to his control.

Let us pray! our life is praying;
  Prayer with time alone may cease:
Then in heaven, God's will obeying,
  Life is praise and perfect peace.

As apple trees among the trees
  Of all the wood appear,
So my Beloved 'mongst the sons
  Is beautiful and dear.

I sat down under his shadow,
  Sat down with great delight,
His fruit was sweet unto my taste
  And pleasant to my sight.

He brought me to his banquet house,
  His banners o'er me move;
Stay me with flagons, comfort me,
  For I am sick of love.

He's chiefest amongst ten thousand
  The fairest of the fair,
His head like gold is glorious,
  Like clouds his raven hair.

His body is like bright iv'ry
  With sapphires overlaid,
His limbs are as marble pillars
  In golden sockets stayed.

His countenance as Lebanon,
  His mouth as cedars moved,
Yea! he's altogether lovely!
  This, this is my Beloved!

T is is my friend, if him ye find,
  Where'er your footsteps rove,
Say, daughters of Jerusalem,
  That I am sick of love.

Judah! lo thy royal Lion,
  Reigns on earth a conquering King:
Come, ye ransom'd tribes of Zion,
  Love's abundant offerings bring;
    There behold him,
  And his ceaseless praises sing.

King of kings! let earth adore him,
  High on his exalted throne;
Fall ye nations, fall before him,
  And his righteous sceptre own:
    All the glory
  Be to him, and him alone!

WE *now come to the mournful part of Solomon's life, in which the wise man played the fool exeedingly, and proved that the greatest of men, apart from the grace of God, may descend to the worst sins. Who would have thought that Solomon would have become licentious, and the son of David an idolator?*

I. KINGS XI. 1—5; 9—13.

1 But king Solomon loved many strange women, together with the daughter of Pharaoh, women of the Moabites, Ammonites, Edomites, Zidonians, *and* Hittites;

2 Of the nations *concerning* which the LORD said unto the children of Israel, Ye shall not go in to them, neither shall they come in unto you: *for* surely they will turn away your heart after their gods: Solomon clave unto these in love.

3 And he had seven hundred wives, princesses, and three hundred concubines: and his wives turned away his heart.

4, 5 For it came to pass, when Solomon was old, *that* his wives turned away his heart after other gods: and his heart was not perfect with the LORD his God, as *was* the heart of David his father. For Solomon went after Ashtoreth the goddess of the Zidonians, and after Milcom the abomination of the Ammonites.

9, 10 And the LORD was angry with Solomon, because his heart was turned from the LORD God of Israel, which had appeared unto him twice, And had commanded him concerning this thing, that he should not go after other gods: but he kept not that which the LORD commanded.

11 Wherefore the LORD said unto Solomon, Forasmuch as this is done of thee, and thou hast not kept my covenant and my statutes, which I have commanded thee, I will surely rend the kingdom from thee, and will give it to thy servant.

12 Notwithstanding in thy days I will not do it for David thy father's sake: *but* I will rend it out of the hand of thy son.

13 Howbeit I will not rend away all the kingdom; *but* will give one tribe to thy son for David my servant's sake, and for Jerusalem's sake which I have chosen. (*Dr. James Hamilton has beautifully described the circumstances of this part of Jewish history.* "*The people murmured. The monarch wheeled along with greater pomp than ever; but the popular prince had soured into the despot, and the crown sat defiant on his moody brow; and stiff were the obeisances, heartless the hosannas, which hailed him as he passed. The ways of Zion mourned; and whilst grass was sprouting in the temple courts, mysterious groves and impious shrines were rising everywhere: and whilst lust defiled the palace, Chemosh and Ashtoreth, and other Gentile abominations, defiled the Holy Land. And in the disastrous eclipse, beasts of the forest crept abroad. From his lurking-place in Egypt Hadad ventured out, and became a life-long torment to the God-forsaken monarch. And Rezon pounced on Damascus, and made Syria his own. And from the Pagan palaces of Thebes and Memphis harsh cries were heard ever and anon, Pharaoh and Jeroboam taking counsel together, screeching forth their threatenings, and hooting insults, at which Solomon could laugh no longer. For amidst all the gloom and misery a message comes from God: the kingdom is rent; and whilst Solomon's successor will only have a fag-end and a fragment, by right Divine ten tribes are handed over to a rebel and a runaway. Luxury and sinful attachments made him an idolater, and idolatry made him yet more licentious; until, in a lazy enervation and languid day-dreaming of the Sybarite, he lost the perspicacity of the sage, and the prowess of the sovereign; and when he woke up from the tipsy swoon, and out of the kennel picked his tarnished diadem, he woke to find his faculties, once so clear and limpid, all perturbed, his strenuous reason paralyzed, and his healthful fancy poisoned. He woke to find the world grown hollow, and himself grown old. He woke to see the sun bedarkened in Israel's sky, and a special gloom encompassing himself. Like one who falls asleep amidst the lights and music of the orchestra, and who awakes amidst empty benches and tattered programmes,—like a man who falls asleep in a flower garden, and who opens his eyes on a bald and locust-blackened wilderness,—the life, the loveliness, was vanished, and all the remaining spirit of the mighty Solomon yawned forth that verdict of the tired voluptuary:—'Vanity of vanities! vanity of vanities! all is vanity!'*")

322   " Vanity of vanities, all is vanity."   JUNE 2.—MORNING.

[Or November 1.]

IN *the book of Ecclesiastes, or The Preacher, Solomon has left us his own biography, the progress of a seeker after pleasure, the history of Solomon the prodigal, written by Solomon the preacher. He gives us in the first chapter not only the preface of the book, but the key-note of its sad contents, for it has well been styled the saddest book in all the Bible.*

ECCLESIASTES I. 1—15.

1 The words of the Preacher, the son of David, king in Jerusalem.

2 Vanity of vanities, saith the Preacher, vanity of vanities; all *is* vanity. (*Thus speaks Solomon the sage, but we love better to hear the voice of Solomon the saint, for he said, " Thy love is better than wine. He brought me into his banqueting-house, and his banner over me was love." How dark are the forbidden ways ! How sweet the roads of holy fellowship !)*

3 What profit hath a man of all his labour which he taketh under the sun ?

4 *One* generation passeth away, and *another* generation cometh : but the earth abideth for ever.

5 The sun also ariseth, and the sun goeth down, and hasteth to his place where he arose.

6 The wind goeth toward the south, and turneth about unto the north ; it whirleth about continually, and the wind returneth again according to his circuits.

7 All the rivers run into the sea ; yet the sea *is* not full ; unto the place from whence the rivers come, thither they return again.

8 All things *are* full of labour ; man cannot utter *it* : the eye is not satisfied with seeing, nor the ear filled with hearing.

9 The thing that hath been, it *is that* which shall be ; and that which is done *is* that which shall be done : and *there is* no new *thing* under the sun.

10 Is there *any* thing whereof it may be said, See, this *is* new ? it hath been already of old time, which was before us.

11 *There is* no remembrance of former *things ;* neither shall there be *any* remembrance of *things* that are to come with *those* that shall come after.

" *As much as if he said, It is all a weary go-round. This system of things is a perpetual*

self-repetition—quite sickening. One generation goes, another comes. The sun rises, and the sun goes down. That was what the sun did yesterday, and what I expect it will do to-morrow. The wind blows north, and the wind blows south ; and this is all it has been doing for these thousand years. The rivers run into the sea, and it would be some relief to find that sea growing fuller ; to perceive the clear waters wetting the dry shingle, and brimming up to the green fields, and floating the boats and fishes up into the forest : but even that inconvenient novelty is denied us ; for though the rill and many a river have been tumbling many a world of water into it, this tide will not overstep its margin ; the flood still bulges, but still refuses to cross its bounds. Words themselves are weariness, and it would tire us to enumerate those everlasting mutations and busy uniformities which make up this endless screw of existence. There are no novelties, no wonders, no discoveries. This universe does not yield an eye-full, or an arm-full to its occupant. The present only repeats the past, the future will repeat them both. The inventions of to-day are the forgotten arts of yesterday, and our children will forget our wisdom, only to have the pleasure of fishing up, as new prodigies, our obsolete truisms. There is no new thing under the sun, yet no repose. Perpetual functions and transient objects—permanent combinations, yet shifting atoms—sameness, yet incessant change, make up the monotonous medley. Woe's me for this weary world ! "*

12 ¶ I the preacher was king over Israel in Jerusalem.

13 And I gave my heart to seek and search out by wisdom concerning all *things* that are done under heaven : (*Solomon began by seeking the Supreme Felicity in knowledge, but the quest was vain. Had he laboured to know Christ he would have found that knowledge a fountain of delight ;)* this sore travail hath God given to the sons of man to be exercised therewith.

14 I have seen all the works that are done under the sun ; and, behold, all *is* vanity and vexation of spirit.

15 *That which is* crooked cannot be made straight : and that which is wanting cannot be numbered.

SOLOMON *gives a description of the ways in which he sought vainly after the chief good. He was placed at a great advantage, for he had a great mind, and vast resources at command: if he found no satisfaction when he had the whole world to ransack, how much less can common men hope to find it in their far narrower estates, and much more limited knowledge? There is no satisfaction apart from God.*

ECCLESIASTES I. 16—18.

16 I communed with mine own heart, saying, Lo, I am come to great estate, and have gotten more wisdom than all *they* that have been before me in Jerusalem : yea, my heart had great experience of wisdom and knowledge.

17 And I gave my heart to know wisdom, and to know madness and folly : I perceived that this also is vexation of spirit. *(He did not confine his researches to graver studies, but gathered all he could from the frivolities and insanities of human nature. We may consider him as devouring the lighter as well as the heavier literature of his times, and studying the comic side of things; yet the result was the same, the hunger of the soul was not satisfied with laughter any more than with hard study. So it ever must be. The library is not heaven, nor is the theatre of broad farce a Paradise.)*

18 For in much wisdom *is* much grief : and he that increaseth knowledge increaseth sorrow.

ECCLESIASTES II. 1—11.

I SAID in mine heart, Go to now, I will prove thee with mirth, therefore enjoy pleasure : and, behold, this also *is* vanity.

2 I said of laughter, *It is* mad : and of mirth, What doeth it ? *(In his mental fever he tossed from side to side, from grave to gay, sobriety to exhilaration, but found no rest, and how could he? for rest is in God alone.)*

3 I sought in mine heart to give myself unto wine, yet acquainting mine heart with wisdom ; and to lay hold on folly, till I might see what *was* that good for the sons of men, which they should do under the heaven all the days of their life. *(But in wine there is madness and not happiness, as drunkards prove.)*

4 I made me great works ; I builded me houses ; I planted me vineyards : *(He had a fit of building, and it amused him till the works*

were completed, and then he was as discontented as before. Had he built high as Babel's tower he would not have reached heaven.)

5 I made me gardens and orchards, and I planted trees in them of all *kind of* fruits :

6 I made me pools of water, to water therewith the wood that bringeth forth trees : *(But in all his gardens he could not grow the tree of life or the plant of content, and therefore he failed here also.)*

7 I got *me* servants and maidens, and had servants born in my house ; also I had great possessions of great and small cattle above all that were in Jerusalem before me :

8 I gathered me also silver and gold, and the peculiar treasure of kings and of the provinces : I gat me men singers and women singers, and the delights of the sons of men, *as* musical instruments, and that of all sorts.

But in all his treasure houses, and halls of music, he could neither lay up the pearl of great price, nor hear the song of sweet peace. The poorest man of faith in his kingdom was happier far than he. Alas, poor rich Solomon !

9 So I was great, and increased more than all that were before me in Jerusalem : also my wisdom remained with me. *(But it remained only to make him more deeply feel the hollowness of earthly joys; it made the void in his heart the more manifest, and by its light he saw the more clearly the "darkness visible" in which he groped.)*

10 And whatsoever mine eyes desired I kept not from them, I withheld not my heart from any joy ; for my heart rejoiced in all my labour : and this was my portion of all my labour.

11 Then I looked on all the works that my hands had wrought, and on the labour that I had laboured to do : and, behold, all *was* vanity and vexation of spirit, and *there was* no profit under the sun. *(The little joy he felt in the pursuit of any one of his various objects vanished when he had realized it. He became a worn out man, jaded, yet altogether unable to take rest. He went round and round like a mill horse, harnessed to his toil, but never advancing beyond the weary circle of unrest. To know Jesus, to love God, to find satisfaction in heavenly things, this is wisdom, and the follies of Solomon should drive us thither. God grant it may be so.)*

324   " In the day of adversity, consider."   JUNE 3.—MORNING.

[*Or November 3.*]

ECCLESIASTES VII. 1—14.

A GOOD name *is* better than precious oint-ment; and the day of death than the day of one's birth. *(After all, there is something even among men worth the having; something which may well justify the choice of the righteous in walking in his integrity. To be enrolled among the martyrs and confessors, or among the humbler saints, is no mean blessing; he whose memory lives after him, in fresh aroma of holi-ness and benevolence has not lived in vain. To such men the day of death is the laying of the top stone of their character, and its shoutings are more joyous than those which celebrated the fix-ing of the foundations.)*

2 ¶ *It is* better to go to the house of mourn-ing, than to go to the house of feasting: for that *is* the end of all men; and the living will lay *it* to his heart.

3 Sorrow *is* better than laughter: for by the sadness of the countenance the heart is made better.

4 The heart of the wise *is* in the house of mourning; but the heart of fools *is* in the house of mirth. *(Experience has proved to all wise men that the solid lessons which they gather in the house of mourning are more valuable, more sustaining, more consoling, and so in the end more fruitful of joy, than the frivolities which merely mask the sadness of the heart, and pass away as in a moment, leaving deeper wretchedness behind them, like the black spots which show where once thorns blazed their little moment.)*

5 *It is* better to hear the rebuke of the wise, than for a man to hear the song of fools.

6 For as the crackling of thorns under a pot, so *is* the laughter of the fool: this also *is* vanity.

7 ¶ Surely oppression maketh a wise man mad; and a gift *(or rather a bribe)* destroyeth the heart. *(By perverting the judgment and killing the conscience.)*

8 Better *is* the end of a thing than the be-ginning thereof: *and* the patient in spirit *is* better than the proud in spirit.

9 Be not hasty in thy spirit to be angry: for anger resteth in the bosom of fools. *(The best man feels the occasional flash of anger, but bad men feed the flame; their wrath smoulders long,* and is ready to burst forth whenever the breath of memory fans it. To be "angry and sin not" is a hard matter. May God grant us grace to rule our temper, or it will be our ruin.)*

10 Say not thou, What is *the cause* that the former days were better than these? for thou dost not enquire wisely concerning this.

Those who cry up the good old times should re-member that time was never older than it is now, and it is a great question if things were ever better than at this present moment. Let us leave off idle complaints, and try to make our times better, and wherein we cannot alter them, let us leave them to God.

11 ¶ Wisdom *is* good with an inheritance: and *by it there is* profit to them that see the sun. *(Men who have an inheritance and no wis dom are in a sad position, for they have great re-sponsibilities, but no grace to meet them; the truest profit is true religion. He is the richest man who has God for his inheritance.)*

12 For wisdom *is* a defence, *and* money *is* a defence: but the excellency of knowledge *is, that* wisdom giveth life to them that have it.

Understand by wisdom, the true wisdom, namely vital godliness, and the meaning of Solomon is clear. There is no real life apart from faith in the Lord Jesus; faith is a defence for our life, as well as the great means of life.

13 Consider the work of God: for who can make *that* straight, which he hath made crooked?

14 In the day of prosperity be joyful, but in the day of adversity consider: God also hath set the one over against the other, to the end that man should find nothing after him.

Trials there must be. This side of heaven there must be thorns with the roses, and clouds with the sunshine. It is our wisdom to act rightly under all circumstances; to bless the Lord when his mercies overflow, and to turn to him penitently when he smites us with the rod. The Lord does not intend that his birds of Paradise should build their nests on any of the trees of this life's forest, therefore he sends his roughest winds to rock the branches to and fro, that his chosen may take wing and fly aloft to the heavenly land, whereupon the tree of life they may sing for ever, and never more be disturbed.

ECCLESIASTES X. 1—14.

DEAD flies cause the ointment of the apothecary to send forth a stinking savour : *so doth* a little folly him that is in reputation for wisdom *and* honour.

No matter though the vase be alabaster, and the perfume the most delicate, dead flies would destroy the precious nard, and even so minor faults will spoil a fine character. Rudeness, irritability, levity, parsimony, egotism, and a thousand other injurious flies have often turned the exquisite perfume of a Christian's life into a pestilent odour to those who were around him. Let us pray for grace to avoid the smaller errors, lest they do us and the gospel serious harm. When a thing is really good it is a pity to spoil it by a small neglect. By little things men are made or ruined as to their influence. Be it ours to watch against the little flies.

2 A wise man's heart *is* at his right hand; but a fool's heart at his left. *(The wise man is practical, and finds a right hand with which to carry out the desires of his soul : the foolish man is left-handed for all that is good, and while he may purpose and plan a right thing, he fails to carry it out, or does it in a left-handed manner.)*

3 Yea also, when he that is a fool walketh by the way, his wisdom faileth *him,* and he saith to every one *that* he *is* a fool.

4 If the spirit of the ruler rise up against thee, leave not thy place ; for yielding pacifieth great offences.

5, 6, 7 There is an evil *which* I have seen under the sun, as an error *which* proceedeth from the ruler : Folly is set in great dignity, and the rich sit in low place. I have seen servants upon horses, and princes walking as servants upon the earth. *(Kings are not always wise in the distribution of honours, and thus it happens that the best men often have the pain of seeing inferior persons thrust over their heads. Moreover, by the events of providence, the least worthy men are often thrown up into position and influence, while persons of character and grace are left to pine in the cold shade of poverty and neglect. So has the Lord ordained it, and the Lord has wise ends to answer by it, therefore let us cheerfully submit. Let us neither envy nor flatter the great, nor be discontented at our own condition. Wrongs will be righted by-and-bye : and*

God's people can afford to wait. Meanwhile it is better to be in the lowest condition, and enjoy the love of God, than to sit among princes, and live without our Father's presence.)

8 He that diggeth a pit shall fall into it ; and whoso breaketh an hedge, a serpent shall bite him. *(Never set traps for others, or violate salutary laws, for evil will come of it.)*

9 Whoso removeth stones shall be hurt therewith ; *and* he that cleaveth wood shall be endangered thereby. *(In all labour there is some risk ; and hence it is well to commend ourselves to the Lord's keeping every day, however free from peril our work may be.)*

10 If the iron be blunt, and he do not whet the edge, then must he put to more strength : but wisdom *is* profitable to direct. *(Knowledge is power : a little common sense will save much toil. It is well to have our wits about us. Christian people should never be stupid : let us sharpen our axes).*

11 Surely the serpent will bite without enchantment ; and a babbler is no better.

12, 13 The words of a wise man's mouth *are* gracious ; but the lips of a fool will swallow up himself. The beginning of the words of his mouth *is* foolishness : and the end of his talk *is* mischievous madness.

14 A fool also is full of words : a man cannot tell what shall be ; and what shall be after him, who can tell him ? *(Still waters run deep, but the babbling brook is shallow. Great talkers are usually little doers. Men of many words are seldom men of great deeds. It is little that we know, and therefore if we talk much we shall most probably enter upon subjects which we do not understand, and so reveal our folly. An ignorant man, if he be quiet, may pass for wise ; but a talkative person advertises his own want of wit. A still tongue shows a wise head. We seldom get into trouble by silence ; but noisy tongues often bring grief to their owners. Our speech should be seasoned with the salt of grace, and be good for the use of edifying ; but this is frequently forgotten, and men talk as if their tongues were their own, forgetting that God will bring them into judgment for every idle word they speak. O Lord, keep thou our lips, that we sin not against thee.)*

326   "At ebening time it shall be light."   JUNE 4.—MORNING.

[*Or November 5.*]

W E *shall read once more in the book of Ecclesiastes, and for that purpose shall select the wise man's famous address to the young in—*

ECCLESIASTES XI. 9, 10.

9 ¶ Rejoice, O young man, in thy youth ; and let thy heart cheer thee in the days of thy youth, and walk in the ways of thine heart, and in the sight of thine eyes : but know thou, that for all these *things* God will bring thee into judgment. *(Solomon does, as it were, dare the young man to seek his own pleasure and throw the reins upon the neck of his passions, but he warns him of the price to be paid, that he may see that the game will not be worth the candle. It can never be worth while to sin, if it be indeed true that every sin will meet with punishment.)*

10 Therefore remove sorrow from thy heart, and put away evil from thy flesh : for childhood and youth *are* vanity. *(There is a way of making youth truly joyous, let the wise young man try it. Our young days will soon be over, let us make them as happy as we can, and live while we live. Everyone agrees with this advice, but few know that the best way of carrying it out is to obtain salvation by believing in Jesus.*)

ECCLESIASTES XII. 1—7; 13, 14.

R EMEMBER now thy Creator in the days of thy youth, while the evil days come not, nor the years draw nigh, when thou shalt say, I have no pleasure in them ; *(Youth is the best time for religious consideration and decision. In old age little heart and little ability are left for the weighty themes of eternity; infirmity and general decay unfit the mind for contemplating subjects to which it has been all its life long unaccustomed. O that young people would beware of delay, and for ever renounce the idea that advanced years are favourable to conversion. No tree is so easily bent as the green sapling.)*

2 While the sun, or the light, or the moon, or the stars, be not darkened, nor the clouds return after the rain : *(meaning that in old age sickness are many, and are more keenly felt than in our prime.)*

3 In the day when the keepers of the house

shall tremble, *(the arms are no longer powerful)* and the strong men shall bow themselves, *(the old man's legs totter beneath his weight)* and the grinders cease because they are few, *(his teeth are almost gone)* and those that look out of the windows be darkened, *(the eyes grow dim.)*

4 And the doors shall be shut in the streets, *(the senses are gradually closed, both ears and eyes become as doors shut up)* when the sound of the grinding is low, and he shall rise up at the voice of the bird, *(his nights are weary, the first crowing of the cock awakes him,)* and all the daughters of musick shall be brought low ; *(his own voice is gone, and he is no longer able to hear the voice of others.)*

5, 6 Also *when* they shall be afraid of *that which is* high, and fears *shall be* in the way, *(aged men are full of anxieties, enterprise and courage fail)* and the almond tree shall flourish, and the grasshopper shall be a burden, and desire shall fail : because man goeth to his long home, and the mourners go about the streets : Or ever the silver cord be loosed, or the golden bowl be broken, or the pitcher be broken at the fountain, or the wheel broken at the cistern. *(The spinal cord, the skull, the heart, and the circulation of the blood are here set forth under beautiful imagery; all these fail us in death.)*

7 Then shall the dust return to the earth as it was : and the spirit shall return unto God who gave it.

13 ¶ Let us hear the conclusion of the whole matter : Fear God, and keep his commandments : for this *is* the whole *duty* of man.

14 For God shall bring every work into judgment, with every secret thing, whether *it be* good, or whether *it be* evil. *(This, then, is the sum of the matter, but the question is, how are we to fulfil the whole duty of man? We may rest assured that it is quite out of our power to do so of ourselves. Only in Christ Jesus can we find the law fulfilled, and he is ours if we believe on him : this is wisdom, Solomon had been wiser had he known nothing but this.)*

II. CHRONICLES IX. 31.

AND Solomon slept with his fathers, and he was buried in the city of David his father : and Rehoboam his son reigned in his stead. *(So ended the wisest man, and so must we all end; there is no discharge in this war. What a change came over the nation when the great ruler passed the sceptre into the hands of his feeble successor. Sad is it when great fathers have foolish sons.)*

II. CHRONICLES X. 1—8 ; 10—16 ; 19.

1 And Rehoboam went to Shechem : for to Shechem were all Israel come to make him king.

2 And it came to pass, when Jeroboam the son of Nebat, who *was* in Egypt, whither he had fled from the presence of Solomon the king, heard *it*, that Jeroboam returned out of Egypt.

3, 4 And they sent and called him. *(The people had felt the government of Solomon to be too despotic, and they determined before they allowed his successor to take the crown, to bind him down to constitutional measures. Their hope of liberty lay in threateni to set up another king if Rehoboam would ot grant them a charter.)* So Jeroboam and all Israel came and spake to Rehoboam, saying, Thy father made our yoke grievous : now therefore ease thou somewhat the grievous servitude of thy father, and his heavy yoke that he put upon us, and we will serve thee.

5 And he said unto them, Come again unto me after three days. And the people departed. *He did well to take time for consideration. Important steps ought not to be taken in a hurry ; we may do in an hour what we cannot undo in a lifetime.*

6 ¶ And king Rehoboam took counsel with the old men that had stood before Solomon his father while he yet lived, saying, What counsel give ye *me* to return answer to this people ?

7 And they spake unto him, saying, If thou be kind to this people, and please them, and speak good words to them, they will be thy servants for ever. *(Full often we must stoop to conquer. To yield a little in order to gain much is wise policy. The people had a right to what they asked, and the young prince should have granted their demands with a hearty good grace, and then he would have been the beloved monarch of an enthusiastic people.)*

8 But he forsook the counsel which the old men gave him, and took counsel with the young men that were brought up with him, that stood before him.

10, 11 And the young men that were brought up with him spake unto him, saying, Thus shalt thou answer the people, My little *finger* shall be thicker than my father's loins. For whereas my father put a heavy yoke upon you, I will put more to your yoke : my father chastised you with whips, but I *will chastise you* with scorpions.

These young aristocrats thought it dangerous to humour the people, for what might they not ask next ? Let them be at once put down with an iron hand ; to consent to their demands would only inflate them with pride, and lead to yet further insubordination. We have heard men talk in this fashion in our own day, but we judged them to be vain fellows. If the people ask for right things, let them have them, and no hurt can come of it.

12 So Jeroboam and all the people came to Rehoboam on the third day, as the king bade, saying, Come again to me on the third day.

13, 14 And the king answered them roughly ; saying, My father made your yoke heavy, but I will add thereto : my father chastised you with whips, but I *will chastise you* with scorpions.

15 So the king hearkened not unto the people : for the cause was of God, that the LORD might perform his word, which he spake by the hand of Ahijah the Shilonite to Jeroboam the son of Nebat.

16, 19 And when all Israel *saw* that the king would not hearken unto them, the people answered the king, saying, What portion have we in David ? and *we have* none inheritance in the son of Jesse : every man to your tents, O Israel : *and* now, David, see to thine own house. So all Israel went to their tents. And Israel rebelled against the house of David unto this day. *(Thus was the sin of Solomon visited on Rehoboam his son, but not unjustly, for the unwise action of Rehoboam naturally led to the breaking away of the ten tribes. God's ways are always just, and we may rest assured that if he seems to act unjustly, it is not really the case. His ways are equal, and in the end men will confess that it is so.)*

When any turn from Zion's way,
(Alas, what numbers do!)
Methinks I hear my Saviour say,
" Wilt thou forsake me too?"

Ah, Lord! with such a heart as mine,
Unless thou hold me fast,
I feel I must, I shall decline,
And prove like them at last.

How vain are all things here below!
How false, and yet how fair!
Each pleasure hath its poison too,
And ev'ry sweet a snare.

Dear Saviour! let thy beauties be
My soul's eternal food ;
And grace command my heart away
From all created good.

I thirst, but not as once I did,
The vain delights of earth to share ;
Thy wounds, Immanuel, all forbid
That I should seek my pleasures there.

It was the sight of thy dear cross
First wean'd my soul from earthly things;
And taught me to esteem as dross
The mirth of fools and pomp of kings.

Jesus, my Saviour, is enough,
When all is gone and spent ;
He fills and over-fills my soul,
Thus I am pure content.

My covenant with flesh and blood,
And every sinful thing,
Is broken, and is stedfast made,
With Jesus Christ my king.

Vanish from me, ye objects vain,
All scenes of lower kind ;
A pleasure equal to my wish
In God alone I find.

Lord, season all my speech
With thine own Spirit's salt,
And never let excess of words
Become my grievous fault.

Let grace dwell in my heart,
So shall it rule my tongue,
And all my faculties for thee
Become a harp well strung.

Each word a note of praise,
Each speech a line of song,
Thus like the angels round thy throne,
I'll praise thee all day long.

Hear ye not a voice from heaven,
To the listening spirit given ?
" Children, come," it seems to say ;
" Give your hearts to me to-day."

While our day is in its dew,
And the clouds of life are few,
Jesu, may we hear thy voice,
And in thy dear love rejoice.

Then, when night and age appear,
Thou wilt chase each doubt and fear :
Thou our glorious Leader be,
When the stars shall fade and flee.

Now to thee, O Lord, we come,
In the morning's early bloom :
Breathe on us thy grace divine ;
Touch our hearts, and keep them thine.

Think gently, and as gently speak,
If thou art strong, respect the weak ;
If thou art weak, from what thou art,
Judge gently of another's heart.

For gentle thoughts and gentle words
Were ever thy dear Saviour Lord's ;
Shall worms a fellow-worm reprove,
When the great holy God is Love?

Therefore be gentle, O my soul !
Thy thoughts and words alike control ;
And if thou must in aught decide,
Err ever on the gentle side.

I KINGS XII. 26—33.

AND Jeroboam said in his heart, Now shall the kingdom return to the house of David:

27 If this people go up to do sacrifice in the house of the LORD at Jerusalem, then shall the heart of this people turn again unto their lord, *even* unto Rehoboam king of Judah, and they shall kill me, and go again to Rehoboam king of Judah. *(He feared that while the tribes went up every year to the temple, the old love to one another would revive, and seeing the palace of the house of David in its magnificence, they might feel regret for having revolted from their ancient line of kings: Jeroboam therefore felt that the temple worship endangered his position. He was a man of a crafty mind, like Ahithophel, and had no fear of God before his eyes, and therefore he resolved to set up a new religion. God's honour was nothing to him. Worldly policy and other base motives have often been the reasons for founding false systems of religion.)*

28 Whereupon the king took counsel, and made two calves *of* gold, and said unto them, It is too much for you to go up to Jerusalem: behold thy gods, O Israel, which brought thee up out of the land of Egypt. *(Men naturally love ease, and prefer a religion which involves little trouble and inconvenience, hence Jeroboam craftily appealed to this degrading propensity of human nature; but how disgraceful it was on the part of Israel that under such a pretext they should forsake the living God and bow before the image of a bullock. May we never leave the good old paths of truth for the sake of honour, position, gain, or ease. Let us cleave unto the Lord with purpose of heart.)*

29 And he set the one in Beth-el, and the other put he in Dan. *(At both ends of the land, so that none might have far to travel.)*

30, 31 And this thing became a sin: for the people went *to worship* before the one, *even* unto Dan. And he made an house of high places, and made priests of the lowest of the people, which were not of the sons of Levi. *(The true priests were faithful and hence he must needs set up others. This speaks well for the Levites. If all other men become idolators, God's ministers must not.)*

32 And Jeroboam ordained a feast in the eighth month, on the fifteenth day of the month, like unto the feast that *is* in Judah, and he offered upon the altar. So did he in Beth-el, sacrificing unto the calves that he had made: and he placed in Beth-el the priests of the high places which he had made.

33 So he offered upon the altar which he had made in Beth-el the fifteenth day of the eighth month, *even* in the month which he had devised of his own heart; and ordained a feast unto the children of Israel: and he offered upon the altar, and burnt incense. *(He dared to take upon himself the priesthood, to change the ordained seasons for worship, to set up a rival altar, and to adore God under a symbolic form. All this was detestable in the sight of God. It is to be feared that in our day many are guilty of Jeroboam's sin, for they invent rites and ceremonies of their own, and forsake the Lord, who is a Spirit, and must be worshipped in spirit and in truth. O for grace to be faithful to the Word of God in all points.)*

I. KINGS XIII. 1—10.

AND, behold, there came a man of God out of Judah by the word of the LORD unto Beth-el: and Jeroboam stood by the altar to burn incense.

2 And he cried against the altar in the word of the LORD, and said, O altar, altar, thus saith the LORD; Behold, a child shall be born unto the house of David, Josiah by name; and upon thee shall he offer the priests of the high places that burn incense upon thee, and men's bones shall be burnt upon thee.

3 And he gave a sign the same day, saying, This is the sign which the LORD hath spoken; Behold, the altar shall be rent, and the ashes that *are* upon it shall be poured out. *(This was bravely spoken. The prophet feared not the wrath of the king or of the crowds around him. Messengers of God must not fear the faces of men.)*

4 And it came to pass, when king Jeroboam heard the saying of the man of God, which had cried against the altar in Beth-el, that he put forth his hand from the altar, saying, Lay hold on him. *(He was greatly irritated to have the first and greatest ceremony of his new religion broken in upon by this zealous messenger of the*

Lord. "*Seize him!*" *cries the king, yea he puts forth his own hand to execute the arrest.*) And his hand, which he put forth against him, dried up, so that he could not pull it in again to him.

5 The altar also was rent, and the ashes poured out from the altar, according to the sign which the man of God had given by the word of the LORD.

6 And the king answered and said unto the man of God, Intreat now the face of the LORD thy God, and pray for me, that my hand may be restored me again. (*The Lord can soon bring down the strongest heart. This proud potentate speedily fell from threatening to entreating. God who withered his hand could have paralyzed his whole body, but in wrath he remembered mercy.*) And the man of God besought the LORD, and the king's hand was restored him again, and became as *it was* before. (*God's servants are easily entreated, and return good for evil.*)

7 And the king said unto the man of God, Come home with me, and refresh thyself, and I will give thee a reward. (*Observe that Jeroboam never uttered a word by way of repentance or humiliation. He was hardened in his proud rebellion against God, and though he was ready to reward the prophet, he would not thank the Lord who sent him.*)

8 And the man of God said unto the king, If thou wilt give me half thine house, I will not go in with thee, neither will I eat bread nor drink water in this place :

9 For so was it charged me by the word of the LORD, saying, Eat no bread, nor drink water, nor turn again by the same way that thou camest.

10 So he went another way, and returned not by the way that he came to Beth-el. (*It was not meet that God's servant should have any fellowship with revolted Israel, no, not even so much as eating a piece of bread or taking a sip of water with them. The true believer's duty is to avoid all unnecessary fellowship with men of sin. "What concord hath Christ with Belial?"*)

Arm of the Lord! awake! awake!
Put on thy strength, the nations shake :
And let the world, adoring, see
Triumphs of mercy wrought by thee.

Say to the heathen, from thy throne,
"I am Jehovah, God alone!"
Thy voice their idols shall confound,
And cast their altars to the ground.

Faith must obey her Father's will
As well as trust his grace ;
A pardoning God is jealous still
For his own holiness.

Though from his wrath he sets us free,
He will be Lord within,
Nor will he let his servants be
Unchastened if they sin.

Lift up a banner in the field
For those that fear thy name ;
Save thy beloved with thy shield,
And put our foes to shame.

Our faith shall gain a wide renown
By thine assisting hand ;
'Tis God that treads the mighty down
And makes the feeble stand.

We bless the Lord of tender love
Who sees the feeblest spark of grace,
And sends his Spirit from above
To bless the babes that seek his face.

His quick approving eye discerns
Where "some good thing" for God is found ;
On that good thing his eye he turns,
And there he makes his gifts abound.

Well may the Lord that good espy,
'Tis he who works all good within ;
Faith's healing look, prayer's childlike cry,
And love which weeps o'er pardon'd sin.

Ye fearful saints fresh courage take,
The clouds ye so much dread
Are big with mercies, and shall break
With blessings on your head.

Judge not the Lord by feeble sense,
But trust him for his grace ;
Behind a frowning providence,
He hides a smiling face.

I. KINGS XIII. 11—30.

NOW there dwelt an old prophet in Beth-el; and his sons came and told him all the works that the man of God had done that day in Beth-el : the words which he had spoken unto the king, them they told also to their father.

12, 13, 14 And their father said unto them, What way went he ? For his sons had seen what way the man of God went, which came from Judah. And he said unto his sons, Saddle me the ass. So they saddled him the ass : and he rode thereon, and went after the man of God, and found him sitting under an oak : and he said unto him, *Art* thou the man of God that camest from Judah ? And he said, I *am*.

15 Then he said unto him, Come home with me, and eat bread.

16, 17 And he said, I may not return with thee, nor go in with thee : neither will I eat bread nor drink water with thee in this place : For it was said to me by the word of the LORD, Thou shalt eat no bread nor drink water there, nor turn again to go by the way that thou camest.

18 He said unto him, I *am* a prophet also as thou *art ;* and an angel spake unto me by the word of the LORD, saying, Bring him back with thee into thine house, that he may eat bread and drink water. *But* he lied unto him.

19 So he went back with him, and did eat bread in his house, and drank water.

20 ¶ And it came to pass, as they sat at the table, that the word of the LORD came unto the prophet that brought him back :

21 And he cried unto the man of God that came from Judah, saying, Thus saith the LORD, Forasmuch as thou hast disobeyed the mouth of the LORD, and hast not kept the commandment which the LORD thy God commanded thee,

22 But camest back, and hast eaten bread and drunk water in the place, of which *the LORD* did say to thee, Eat no bread, and drink no water ; thy carcase shall not come unto the sepulchre of thy fathers.

23, 24 And it came to pass, after he had eaten bread, and after he had drunk, that he saddled for him the ass, *to wit,* for the prophet whom he had brought back. And when he was gone, a lion met him by the way, and slew him : and his carcase was cast in the way, and the ass stood by it, the lion also stood by the carcase.

25 And, behold, men passed by, and saw the carcase cast in the way, and the lion standing by the carcase : and they came and told *it* in the city where the old prophet dwelt.

26 And when the prophet that brought him back from the way heard *thereof,* he said, It *is* the man of God, who was disobedient unto the word of the LORD : therefore the LORD hath delivered him unto the lion, which hath torn him, and slain him, according to the word of the LORD, which he spake unto him.

27 And he spake to his sons, saying, Saddle me the ass. And they saddled *him*.

28 And he went and found his carcase cast in the way, and the ass and the lion standing by the carcase : the lion had not eaten the carcase, nor torn the ass.

29 And the prophet took up the carcase of the man of God, and laid it upon the ass, and brought it back : and the old prophet came to the city, to mourn and to bury him.

30 And he laid his carcase in his own grave ; and they mourned over him, *saying,* Alas, my brother ! *(This is a very solemn illustration of the great truth that the Lord our God is a jealous God. He will be obeyed by those whom he honours to become his servants. He has expressly said, " I will be sanctified in them that come nigh me." To trifle with his commands in the smallest degree may involve even the best of men in solemn chastisement. The old prophet at Bethel must have backslidden very far from God, or he would not have tempted the man of God so wickedly ; the man of God ought not, however, to have believed him so readily, seeing that his declaration contradicted the express command of the Lord, which he had personally received. The Lord saw fit to slay him, but let us hope that as a righteous man he had hope in his death. Let us hope also that the death of the prophet from Judah became a warning to the old prophet at Bethel, and was the means of restoring him to his right state before God. It may have been one of those terrible things in righteousness whereby the Lord calls back his wanderers. Its lesson to us is to walk before God with holy jealousy and fear to offend.)*

332   " The root of the matter is found in him."   JUNE 6.—MORNING.

[Or November 9.]

I. KINGS XIV. 1—9 ; 12, 13 ; 17, 18.

A T that time Abijah the son of Jeroboam fell sick. And Jeroboam said to his wife, Arise, I pray thee, and disguise thyself, that thou be not known to be the wife of Jeroboam ; and get thee to Shiloh : behold, there *is* Ahijah the prophet, which told me that *I should be* king over this people. And take with thee ten loaves, and cracknels, and a cruse of honey, and go to him : he shall tell thee what shall become of the child. *Bad men cannot help respecting God's true messengers. Why did not Jeroboam go to the prophets of the calves? The ungodly and those who follow false religions lose all confidence in their notions in times of necessity, and begin to look about them for better comfort. Ahijah's word had been powerful with the king before, and therefore he sent to him again. Many a sinner has a something in his conscience which bears witness to the Lord's minister, for his word has in former times been full of power.*

4 And Jeroboam's wife did so, and arose, and went to Shiloh, and came to the house of Ahijah. But Ahijah could not see ; for his eyes were set by reason of his age.

5, 6 And the LORD said unto Ahijah, Behold, the wife of Jeroboam cometh to ask a thing of thee for her son ; for he *is* sick : thus and thus shalt thou say unto her : for it shall be when she cometh in, that she shall feign herself *to be* another *woman.* And it was *so,* when Ahijah heard the sound of her feet, as she came in at the door, that he said, Come in, thou wife of Jeroboam ; why feignest thou thyself *to be* another ? for I *am* sent to thee *with* heavy tidings. *(Those who think to hide themselves from God will be utterly confounded, for he will unmask them to their everlasting shame. Sinners now appear in the garb of saints, but the Lord knoweth them that are his.)*

7, 8, 9 Go, tell Jeroboam, Thus saith the LORD God of Israel, Forasmuch as I exalted thee from among the people, and made thee prince over my people Israel, And rent the kingdom away from the house of David, and gave it thee : and *yet* thou hast not been as my servant David, who kept my commandments, and who followed me with all his heart, to do *that* only *which was* right in mine eyes ; But hast done evil above all that were before thee : for thou hast gone and

made thee other gods, and molten images, to provoke me to anger, and hast cast me behind thy back : *(Therefore the Lord declared that there should be no sons left of the family of Jeroboam, and none to perpetuate his name and race. The whole family was devoted to utter destruction and erasure from among the households of Israel. God knows how to punish as well as how to bless.)*

12, 13 Arise thou therefore, get thee to thine own house : *and* when thy feet enter into the city, the child shall die. And all Israel shall mourn for him, and bury him : for he only of Jeroboam shall come to the grave, because in him there is found *some* good thing toward the LORD God of Israel in the house of Jeroboam.

17 ¶ And Jeroboam's wife arose, and departed, and came to Tirzah : *and* when she came to the threshold of the door, the child died ;

18 And they buried him ; and all Israel mourned for him, according to the word of the LORD, which he spake by the hand of his servant Ahijah the prophet. *(Upon this incident Matthew Henry remarks :—" Those are good in whom are good things towards the Lord God of Israel ; good inclinations, good intentions, good desires towards him. Where there is but some good thing of that kind, it will be found ; God who seeks it sees it, be it never so little, and is pleased with it. A little grace goes a great way with great folks. It is so rare to find princes well affected to religion, that when they are so, they are worthy of double honour. Pious dispositions are in a peculiar manner amiable and acceptable when they are found in those that are young. The divine image in miniature has a peculiar lustre and beauty in it. A good child in the house of Jeroboam is a miracle of divine grace : to be there untainted is like being in the fiery furnace unhurt, unsinged. Observe the care taken of him : he only of all Jeroboam's family shall be buried, and shall be lamented, as one that lived desired. Those that are distinguished by the divine grace shall be distinguished by the divine providence." In this family we trust there are some who have in them hopeful signs of grace : let such be encouraged by observing that the Lord notices the smallest measure of grace which may be found in any one of us.)*

WHILE *the new kingdom of the ten tribes was under the sway of Jeroboam, Rehoboam died and was succeeded by his son.*

II. CHRONICLES XIII. 1—16; 18; 20.

1 Now in the eighteenth year of king Jeroboam began Abijah to reign over Judah.

2 He reigned three years in Jerusalem. And there was war between Abijah and Jeroboam.

3 And Abijah set the battle in array with an army of valiant men of war, *even* four hundred thousand chosen men: Jeroboam also set the battle in array against him with eight hundred thousand chosen men, *being* mighty men of valour. *(Who can imagine the horrors of a civil war conducted upon such a scale as this. Surely every male in the two nations must have been draughted into one or other of the armies. Blessed are we in this matter since no alarms of war are heard in our streets. May the Lord cause wars to cease unto the ends of the earth.)*

4, 5, 6, 7, 8 And Abijah stood up upon mount Zemaraim, which *is* in mount Ephraim, and said, Hear me, thou Jeroboam, and all Israel; Ought ye not to know that the LORD God of Israel gave the kingdom over Israel to David for ever, *even* to him and to his sons by a covenant of salt? Yet Jeroboam the son of Nebat, the servant of Solomon the son of David, is risen up, and hath rebelled against his lord. And there are gathered unto him vain men, the children of Belial, and have strengthened themselves against Rehoboam the son of Solomon, when Rehoboam was young and tender-hearted, and could not withstand them. And now ye think to withstand the kingdom of the LORD, in the hand of the sons of David; and ye *be* a great multitude, and *there are* with you golden calves, which Jeroboam made you for gods. *(It was wise on Abijah's part so to state the cause of battle. When it is a question between God and golden calves the result of the dispute is certain.)*

9 Have ye not cast out the priests of the LORD, the sons of Aaron, and the Levites, and have made you priests after the manner of the nations of *other* lands? so that whosoever cometh to consecrate himself with a young bullock and seven rams, *the same* may be a priest of *them that are* no gods.

10, 11 But as for us, the LORD *is* our God, and we have not forsaken him; and the priests, which minister unto the LORD, *are* the sons of Aaron, and the Levites *wait* upon *their* business: And they burn unto the LORD every morning and every evening burnt sacrifices and sweet incense: the shewbread also *set they in order* upon the pure table; and the candlestick of gold with the lamps thereof, to burn every evening: for we keep the charge of the LORD our God; but ye have forsaken him.

12 And, behold, God himself *is* with us for *our* captain, and his priests with sounding trumpets to cry alarm against you. O children of Israel, fight ye not against the LORD God of your fathers; for ye shall not prosper. *(This was a worthy speech, and very commendable as intended to prevent bloodshed. We cannot be sure that Abijah was a spiritual man, but he and the nation of Judah as yet held to the worship of Jehovah, and therefore had the Lord on their side.)*

13 ¶ But Jeroboam caused an ambushment to come about behind them: so they were before Judah, and the ambushment *was* behind them. *(Jeroboam was not a man of words, but of deeds, and was surrounding his foe while Abijah was delivering his oration.)*

14, 15, 16 And when Judah looked back, behold, the battle *was* before and behind: and they cried unto the LORD, and the priests sounded with the trumpets. Then the men of Judah gave a shout: and as the men of Judah shouted, it came to pass, that God smote Jeroboam and all Israel before Abijah and Judah. And the children of Israel fled before Judah: and God delivered them into their hand. *(Praying and praising are noble weapons; no wonder that the Lord interposed when his people drew him into the fight by their two hands of pleading and blessing.)*

18 Thus the children of Israel were brought under at that time, and the children of Judah prevailed, because they relied upon the LORD God of their fathers.

20 Neither did Jeroboam recover strength again in the days of Abijah: and the LORD struck him, and he died. *(He was made to feel at last how unequal was his conflict with God, yet he persevered in it, and died impenitent, leaving the divine curse as a legacy to his descendants. May the good Lord save us from such an end.)*

II. CHRONICLES XIV. 1—4 ; 6—15.

SO Abijah slept with his fathers, and they buried him in the city of David : and Asa his son reigned in his stead. In his days the land was quiet ten years. (*This was a change for the better, for Abijah had tolerated idols, though he had not neglected the worship of Jehovah, and during his reign the godless party had multiplied, and polluted the nation with their heathenish and licentious practices. Abijah and his favourite queens had aided and abetted the evil faction, and the people had very greatly degenerated. It is singular that, though both father and mother were bad, Asa did that which was good ; it is clear from this that the children need not be wicked because their parents are so.*)

2, 3, 4 And Asa did *that which was* good and right in the eyes of the LORD his God : For he took away the altars of the strange *gods*, and the high places, and brake down the images, and cut down the groves : And commanded Judah to seek the LORD God of their fathers, and to do the law and the commandment. (*He made a thorough reformation, sweeping away not only the images of the false gods, but the sacred groves in which they were worshipped. O that we might live to see such a thorough purging of our own land ! Let us pray for it.*)

6 ¶ And he built fenced cities in Judah : for the land had rest, and he had no war in those years ; because the LORD had given him rest.

7 Therefore he said unto Judah, Let us build these cities, and make about *them* walls, and towers, gates, and bars, *while* the land *is* yet before us ; because we have sought the LORD our God, we have sought *him*, and he hath given us rest on every side. So they built and prospered. (*Obedience to God brought blessing with it ; yet even with this fact before them they did not long remain faithful.*)

8 And Asa had an army *of men* that bare targets and spears, out of Judah three hundred thousand ; and out of Benjamin, that bare shields and drew bows, two hundred and fourscore thousand : all these *were* mighty men of valour.

9 ¶ And there came out against them Zerah the Ethiopian with an host of a thousand thousand, and three hundred chariots ; and came unto Mareshah.

10 Then Asa went out against him, and they set the battle in array in the valley of Zephathah at Mareshah. (*The good king had his trials ; even when obedience insured prosperity it did not screen him from a measure of affliction.*)

11 And Asa cried unto the LORD his God, and said, LORD, *it is* nothing with thee to help, whether with many, or with them that have no power : help us, O LORD our God ; for we rest on thee, and in thy name we go against this multitude. O LORD, thou *art* our God ; let not man prevail against thee.

This is a grand specimen of the prayer of faith. The million soldiers of Zerah are not enough to daunt faith, for it sees the Lord's all-sufficiency, and therefore makes no account of his adversaries. The small force at hand is not permitted to act as a discouragement, for faith knows that the Lord works by his own strength, and does not depend upon the strength of instruments. It is a glorious thing to be able to call the Lord our God, and then to rest in him without care or fear, being certain that our cause is safe because it is bound up with his honour, and is in his own hands. After Asa's example, let us trust and not be afraid when brought into great trials and difficulties.

12 So the LORD smote the Ethiopians before Asa, and before Judah ; and the Ethiopians fled.

13 And Asa and the people that *were* with him pursued them unto Gerar : and the Ethiopians were overthrown, that they could not recover themselves ; for they were destroyed before the LORD, and before his host ; and they carried away very much spoil.

14 And they smote all the cities round about Gerar ; for the fear of the LORD came upon them : and they spoiled all the cities ; for there was exceeding much spoil in them.

15 They smote also the tents of cattle, and carried away sheep and camels in abundance, and returned to Jerusalem. (*They were more than conquerors, as believers always are. They gained greatly by that which threatened to be their destruction. If we will but trust in the like manner, the like experience shall certainly be ours. Greater is he that is for us than all they that be against us.*)

II. CHRONICLES XV. 1—17.

AND the Spirit of God came upon Azariah the son of Oded :

2 And he went out to meet Asa, and said unto him, Hear ye me, Asa, and all Judah and Benjamin ; The LORD *is* with you, while ye be with him ; and if ye seek him, he will be found of you ; but if ye forsake him, he will forsake you. *(While they were flushed with victory it was a fit time to remind them where their great strength lay, and urge them to continue in obedience while the rewards of it were before their eyes. The prophet did not congratulate and flatter the monarch, but impressed upon him his obligations to the Lord, who had so greatly favoured him. Ministers are not sent· to please us, but tŏ profit us.)*

3, 4, 5, 6, 7 Now for a long season Israel *hath been* without the true God, and without a teaching priest, and without law. But when they in their trouble did turn unto the LORD God of Israel, and sought him, he was found of them. And in those times *there was* no peace to him that went out, nor to him that came in, but great vexations *were* upon all the inhabitants of the countries. And nation was destroyed of nation, and city of city : for God did vex them with all adversity. Be ye strong therefore, and let not your hands be weak : for your work shall be rewarded. *(It was matter of plain history that the condition of the people depended entirely upon their fidelity to God. They made or unmade their own fortunes. Have we not also learned by this time that we are happy when we live near to God, and are in an evil case when we backslide from him ? Let us lay this fact to heart.)*

8 And when Asa heard these words, he took courage, and put away the abominable idols out of all the land of Judah and Benjamin, and renewed the altar of the LORD, that *was* before the porch of the LORD. *(The best swept room will bear cleansing again, and thèrefore Asa made another and further investigation and reformation, for idolators here and there had kept up their idols by stealth, but down they must go at this second search.)*

9 And he gathered all Judah and Benjamin, and the strangers with them out of Ephraim and Manasseh, and out of Simeon : for they fell to him out of Israel in abundance, when they saw that the LORD his God *was* with him.

10 So they gathered themselves together at Jerusalem in the third month, in the fifteenth year of the reign of Asa.

11 And they offered unto the LORD the same time, of the spoil *which* they had brought, seven hundred oxen and seven thousand sheep.

12 And they entered into a covenant to seek the LORD God of their fathers with all their heart and with all their soul ;

13 That whosoever would not seek the LORD God of Israel should be put to death, whether small or great, whether man or woman.

14, 15 And they sware unto the LORD with a loud voice, and with shouting, and with trumpets, and with cornets. And all Judah rejoiced at the oath : for they had sworn with all their heart, and sought him with their whole desire ; and he was found of them : and the LORD gave them rest round about. *(The people were great at promising, but slow in performing; their hearts were fickle, and what they resolved upon one day with great enthusiasm they forgot the next, and were again mad upon their idols. How much were they like ourselves !)*

16 And also *concerning* Maachah the mother of Asa the king, he removed her from *being* queen, because she had made an idol in a grove : and Asa cut down her idol, and stamped *it,* and burnt *it* at the brook Kidron. *(This was a masterstroke; he deposed the queen-mother and demolished her idol in the most ignominious manner. The king would not connive at sin in those nearest and dearest to him. It must have caused him much pain, but he loved his God too well to shrink from the deed.)*

17 But the high places were not taken away out of Israel : nevertheless the heart of Asa was perfect all his days. *(Even in the best work there is a flaw, which has to be spoken of with a " but." The false gods were put down, but the unauthorized altars to the true God were still untouched. This may be thought to be a lesser evil, but it had been better to have gone through with the work. It was well, however, that in heart and intention Asa was sound before God.)*

336   *" Cursed be the man that trusteth in man."*   JUNE 8.—MORNING.

[*Or November* 13.]

II. CHRONICLES XVI. 1—14.

IN the six and thirtieth year of the reign of Asa Baasha king of Israel came up against Judah, and built Ramah, to the intent that he might let none go out or come in to Asa king of Judah. (*For he was vexed that on account of the peace and prosperity of Judah, and its attachment to the true God, so many of his subjects removed into the territory of Asa.*)

2, 3 Then Asa brought out silver and gold out of the treasures of the house of the LORD and of the king's house, and sent to Ben-hadad king of Syria, that dwelt at Damascus, saying, There is a league between me and thee, as there was between my father and thy father: behold, I have sent thee silver and gold; go, break thy league with Baasha king of Israel, that he may depart from me.

4, 5 And Ben-hadad hearkened unto king Asa, and sent the captains of his armies against the cities of Israel; and they smote Ijon, and Dan, and Abel-maim, and all the store cities of Naphtali. And it came to pass, when Baasha heard it, that he left off building of Ramah, and let his work cease.

6 Then Asa the king took all Judah; and they carried away the stones of Ramah, and the timber thereof, wherewith Baasha was building; and he built therewith Geba and Mizpah. (*What a proof is this that the best believers may fall into unbelief, and trust for awhile in an arm of flesh. Asa was for awhile relieved from fear by turning to Syria for help, and therefore no doubt he thought himself right, but we greatly err if we estimate the correctness of our actions by their result. The Lord was angry with Asa, and as a chastisement his life was a troubled one from that day forward. He took the temple gold to bribe a heathen king to break his treaties, but his great fault was that he trusted in man rather than in God.*)

7, 8 ¶ And at that time Hanani the seer came to Asa king of Judah, and said unto him, Because thou hast relied on the king of Syria, and not relied on the LORD thy God, therefore is the host of the king of Syria escaped out of thine hand. Were not the Ethiopians and the Lubims a huge host, with very many chariots and horsemen? yet, because thou didst rely on the LORD, he delivered them into thine hand.

9 For the eyes of the LORD run to and fro throughout the whole earth, to shew himself strong in the behalf of *them* whose heart *is* perfect toward him. Herein thou hast done foolishly: therefore from henceforth thou shalt have wars. (*This was faithful dealing, and ought to have touched the conscience of the pious king, but he was in a bad condition of soul, and did not receive the rebuke as a gracious man should have done.*)

10 Then Asa was wroth with the seer, and put him in a prison house; for *he was* in a rage with him because of this thing. And Asa oppressed *some* of the people the same time.

His reliance upon an arm of flesh had apparently led to good results, and hence the king resented the prophet's warning. He became irritated, and the old nature in him came sadly into prominence. Though hitherto a just monarch, he at this time acted like a tyrant. We must not judge any man by his solitary actions, but by the general tenor of his life; Asa was, after all, one of the best of the kings of Judah.

11 ¶ And, behold, the acts of Asa, first and last, lo, they *are* written in the book of the kings of Judah and Israel.

12 And Asa in the thirty and ninth year of his reign was diseased in his feet, until his disease *was* exceeding great: yet in his disease he sought not to the LORD, but to the physicians. (*As a child of God he could not be left unchastened for such sins, and the gout in his feet became a heavy rod with which the Lord smote him. It was sad to see him at this time, repeating his folly of reliance upon the creature instead of the Creator. We may call in the physician, but we must not forget our God, or the most skilful doctor will do us no good.*)

13 ¶ And Asa slept with his fathers, and died in the one and fortieth year of his reign.

14 And they buried him in his own sepulchres, which he had made for himself in the city of David, and laid him in the bed which was filled with sweet odours and divers kinds of spices prepared by the apothecaries' art: and they made a very great burning for him.

The people knew how to value a good king. His memory was very fragrant among them. May our names also " smell sweet and blossom from the dust."

A SA *died under a cloud, but the Lord had mercy upon his people and found them a worthy ruler in Jehoshaphat, the good son of a good father, of whose early days we read in—*

II. CHRONICLES XVII. 1—11.

1 And Jehoshaphat his son reigned in his stead, and strengthened himself against Israel.

For Ahab, who had been some years upon the throne of Israel, was an active and warlike prince, and could only be held in check by vigorous measures. Jehoshaphat did not, like his father, trust in Syria, but used lawful means for defence.

2 And he placed forces in all the fenced cities of Judah, and set garrisons in the land of Judah, and in the cities of Ephraim, which Asa his father had taken.

3 And the LORD was with Jehoshaphat, because he walked in the first ways of his father David, and sought not unto Baalim ;

Observe the distinction between David's first and last ways. What a pity that such a distinction had to be made. Alas, many good people have their first warm, zealous, consistent ways, but gradually decline from their first love and grow cold and worldly. In every man's character we should imitate only that which is good, and we should not allow the faults of good men to influence us for evil. Jehoshaphat was clear of idolatry, and was not seduced to worship Baal by the example of his neighbours.

4 But sought to the LORD God of his father, and walked in his commandments, and not after the doings of Israel.

5 Therefore the LORD stablished the kingdom in his hand ; and all Judah brought to Jehoshaphat presents ; and he had riches and honour in abundance.

6 And his heart was lifted up in the ways of the LORD : moreover he took away the high places and groves out of Judah.

The lifting up of Jehoshaphat's heart is meant to set forth his zeal and delight in obedience to Jehovah. It is well when it is our joy to serve God, for then our service is real and from the heart. The Lord made the king popular with his people, so that they gave him many voluntary presents, but this did not make him proud; rather, by God's grace, the more he was exalted the more he exulted in the Lord.

7 ¶ Also in the third year of his reign he sent to his princes, *even* to Ben-hail, and to Obadiah, and to Zechariah, and to Nethaneel, and to Michaiah, to teach in the cities of Judah.

Princes and judges have great influence, and when they give their minds to the promotion of virtue they can accomplish great things. May God teach our princes and great men, and then they will become beneficial to the nation.

8 And with them *he* sent Levites, *even* Shemaiah, and Nethaniah, and Zebadiah, and Asahel, and Shemiramoth, and Jehonathan, and Adonijah, and Tobijah, and Tob-adonijah, Levites ; and with them Elishama and Jehoram, priests.

9 And they taught in Judah, and *had* the book of the law of the LORD with them, and went about throughout all the cities of Judah, and taught the people.

The instruction given by the judge was backed up and sanctified by the sacred teaching of the priests and Levites. Education is of small value if separated from religion ; there is more need that the people should know their Bibles than anything else. Ministers, when they teach, should carry their Bibles with them, to give weight to their words, and force conviction upon all who hear them.

10 ¶ And the fear of the LORD fell upon all the kingdoms of the lands that *were* round about Judah, so that they made no war against Jehoshaphat. *(When we are right with God he will make things right all around. He stills the raging of the sea, and the tumult of the people; and when he gives peace none can disquiet us.)*

11 Also *some* of the Philistines brought Jehoshaphat presents, and tribute silver ; and the Arabians brought him flocks, seven thousand and seven hundred rams, and seven thousand and seven hundred he-goats.

O greatly bless'd the people are
  The joyful sound that know ;
In brightness of thy face, O Lord,
  They ever on shall go.
They in thy name shall all the day
  Rejoice exceedingly ;
And in thy righteousness shall they
  Exalted be on high.
For God is our defence ; and He
  To us doth safety bring :
The Holy One of Israel
  Is our Almighty King.

WE *must now turn from the comparative quiet of the history of Judah to the troublous annals of the more sinful nation of Israel. The house of Jeroboam was rooted out by Baasha, who reigned wickedly twenty-four years, but was not able to found a dynasty, because his sins brought upon his house the same doom as that which had befallen Jeroboam's family. His son Elah, and all his descendants, were murdered by his captain, Zimri, while drinking at Tirzah. After a week's reign, Zimri was vanquished by Omri, a rival commander, and perished among the blazing ruins of the palace at Tirzah. Omri had a troubled and wicked reign of twelve years, and was then succeeded by the notorious Ahab, of whom we shall now read.*

I. KINGS XVI. 29—34.

29, 30 In the thirty and eighth year of Asa king of Judah began Ahab the son of Omri to reign over Israel : and Ahab the son of Omri reigned over Israel in Samaria twenty and two years. And he did evil in the sight of the LORD above all that *were* before him.

31 And it came to pass, as if it had been a light thing for him to walk in the sins of Jeroboam the son of Nebat, that he took to wife Jezebel the daughter of Ethbaal king of the Zidonians, and went and served Baal, and worshipped him. *(The strong-minded Jezebel completely mastered the vacillating Ahab, and became the real ruler of the land, slaying the prophets of Jehovah, and compelling the people to reverence her demon deities.)*

32, 33 And he reared up an altar for Baal in the house of Baal, which he had built in Samaria. And Ahab made a grove ; and Ahab did more to provoke the LORD God of Israel to anger than all the kings of Israel that were before him.

34 ¶ In his days did Hiel the Beth-elite build Jericho : he laid the foundation thereof in Abiram his firstborn, and set up the gates thereof in his youngest *son* Segub, according to the word of the LORD, which he spake by Joshua the son of Nun. *(It was a time of monstrous deeds of evil, when the fear of God was disregarded, and men gloried in defying the Most High. Infidelity usually flourishes side by side with superstition, and where some are worshipping a thousand deities, others are always to be found who deride the one only Lord : yet even in such days the purposes of the Lord are being accomplished. Hiel, the Beth-elite, in his arrogance, did exactly as the Lord had declared.)*

I. KINGS XVII. 1—6.

AND Elijah the Tishbite, *who was of the* inhabitants of Gilead, said unto Ahab, *As* the LORD God of Israel liveth, before whom I stand, there shall not be dew nor rain these years, but according to my word. *(He leaps into the arena, like a lion from the hills. Who he was, or what he had been, we are not told. He comes in thunder, and speaks lightning. The times were fit for an Elijah, and Elijah was fit for them.)*

2, 3, 4 And the word of the LORD came unto him, saying, Get thee hence, and turn thee eastward, and hide thyself by the brook Cherith, that *is* before Jordan. And it shall be, *that* thou shalt drink of the brook ; and I have commanded the ravens to feed thee there. *(God is a good master, and never suffers his servants to starve. He will provide for his own, even if all the land be wasted by drought.)*

5 So he went and did according unto the word of the LORD : for he went and dwelt by the brook Cherith, that *is* before Jordan.

6 And the ravens brought him bread and flesh in the morning, and bread and flesh in the evening ; and he drank of the brook.

He had plain but sufficient fare, but what unlikely providers ! Ravens are rather robbers than caterers, yet they forgot their own hunger and the cries of their young to feed the prophet. Perhaps they fetched the bread and meat out of Ahab's larder; there was very little to be found anywhere else. Well does an old writer observe, " O God ! thou that providest meat for the fowls of the air, wilt make the fowls of the air provide meat for man, rather than his dependence on thee shall be disappointed : O let not our faith be wanting to thee, since thy care can never be wanting to us."

More likely to rob than to feed,
Were ravens, who live upon prey,
But when the Lord's people have need,
His goodness will find out a way.

He lions and ravens can tame,
All creatures obey his command :
Then let me rejoice in his name,
And leave all my cares in his hand.

I. KINGS XVII. 7—24.

AND it came to pass after a while, that the brook dried up, because there had been no rain in the land. And the word of the LORD came unto Elijah, saying, Arise, get thee to Zarephath, which *belongeth* to Zidon,-and dwell there : behold, I have commanded a widow woman there to sustain thee. *(When one door shuts, another opens. God is not confined to one method of supplying his servants. It was wonderful that Elijah was fed by ravens ; it was a new wonder to find him fed by a poor widow, and she a foreigner.)*

10 So he arose and went to Zarephath. *(He did not question the command, but obeyed it ; this is the walk of faith.)* And when he came to the gate of the city, behold, the widow woman *was* there gathering of sticks. *(How unlikely it seemed that she would be able to sustain the prophet, yet Elijah confidently addressed himself to her.)* And he called to her, and said, Fetch me, I pray thee, a little water in a vessel, that I may drink.

11, 12 And as she was going to fetch *it*, he called to her, and said, Bring me, I pray thee, a morsel of bread in thine hand. And she said, *As* the LORD thy God liveth, I have not a cake, but an handful of meal in a barrel, and a little oil in a cruse : and, behold, I *am* gathering two sticks, that I may go in and dress it for me and my son, that we may eat it, and die. *(The good woman had recognised Jehovah's servant, and was ready enough to serve him, but his request for bread touched her in a tender place, for she had barely enough meal for one scanty repast, and then she expected to die with her child.)*

13, 14 And Elijah said unto her, Fear not; go *and* do as thou hast said : but make me thereof a little cake first, and bring *it* unto me, and after make for thee and for thy son. For thus saith the LORD God of Israel, The barrel of meal shall not waste, neither shall the cruse of oil fail, until the day *that* the LORD sendeth rain upon the earth. *(She was to exercise obedient faith first, and then her needs would be supplied. Many try to reverse this order.)*

15, 16 And she went and did according to the saying of Elijah : and she, and he, and her house, did eat *many* days. *And* the barrel of meal wasted not, neither did the cruse of oil fail, according to the word of the LORD, which he spake by Elijah. *(Thus shall our little always be enough. We shall often scrape the bottom of the barrel, but there will always be a handful left. It may be that we shall never have much in hand, but this is no evil, for then our provision will never grow stale, but come to us fresh from our heavenly Father's hand.)*

17, 18 And it came to pass after these things, *that* the son of the woman, the mistress of the house, fell sick ; and his sickness was so sore, that there was no breath left in him. And she said unto Elijah, What have I to do with thee, O thou man of God ? art thou come unto me to call my sin to remembrance, and to slay my son? *(We are all too apt to mistake the grounds of our afflictions, and to blame second causes. The child had been preserved from starving by the prophet, how then could the woman blame him for his death ? Sorrow makes us hasty. Elijah knew this, and was very tender towards her.)*

19, 20 And he said unto her, Give me thy son. And he took him out of her bosom, and carried him up into a loft, where he abode, and laid him upon his own bed. And he cried unto the LORD, and said, O LORD my God, hast thou also brought evil upon the widow with whom I sojourn, by slaying her son ?

21 And he stretched himself upon the child three times, and cried unto the LORD, and said, O LORD my God, I pray thee, let this child's soul come into him again.

22 And the LORD heard the voice of Elijah; and the soul of the child came into him again, and he revived. *(If the prophet obtained miracles in answer to prayer, how much more may we expect good things which are according to the common course of nature ! If we pray like Elias, we shall have like Elias.)*

23 And Elijah took the child, and brought him down out of the chamber into the house, and delivered him unto his mother : and Elijah said, See, thy son liveth.

24 And the woman said to Elijah, Now by this I know that thou *art* a man of God, *and* that the word of the LORD in thy mouth *is* truth.

Love divine, all joys excelling,
  Joy of heaven, to earth come down ;
Fix in us thy humble dwelling,
  All thy faithful mercies crown ;
Jesus, thou art all compassion ;
  Pure, unbounded love thou art ;
Visit us with thy salvation,
  Enter every trembling heart.

Finish, then, thy new creation,
  Pure and spotless let us be ;
Let us see thy great salvation,
  Perfectly restored in thee :
Changed from glory into glory,
  Till in heaven we take our place,
Till we cast our crowns before thee,
  Lost in wonder, love, and praise !

God only my salvation is,
  And my strong rock is he ;
He only is my sure defence,
  I shall not movèd be.

Ye people, place your confidence
  In God, your God, alone,
And you shall see your enemies
  Each one of them o'erthrown.

In holy contemplation,
  We sweetly now pursue
The theme of God's salvation,
  And find it ever new.
Set free from present sorrow
  We cheerfully can say,
E'en let the unknown morrow
  Bring with it what it may ;

It can bring with it nothing
  But he will bear us through :
Who gives the lilies clothing,
  Will clothe his people too :
Beneath the spreading heavens,
  No creature but is fed ;
And he who feeds the ravens,
  Will give his children bread.

Though vine nor fig-tree neither
  Their wonted fruit should bear,
Though all the field should wither,
  Nor flocks nor herds be there ;
Yet God the same abiding,
  His praise shall tune my voice ;
For while in him confiding,
  I cannot but rejoice.

Fear not the face of man,
  But bravely serve the Lord ;
Stand forth and bear thy witness well,
  According to his word.

Thou art thyself a king,
  Girt with majestic power,
Thy foe is but a puny thing,
  A creature of an hour.

Saw ye not the cloud arise,
Little as a human hand ?
Now it spreads along the skies,
Hangs o'er all the thirsty land :

Lo, the promise of a shower
Drops already from above ;
But the Lord will shortly pour
All the Spirit of his love.

Stand up ! Stand up for Jesus !
  The trumpet-call obey ;
Forth to the mighty conflict,
  In this his glorious day ;
Ye that are men, now serve him,
  Against unnumber'd foes ;
Your courage rise with danger,
  And strength to strength oppose.

Stand up ! Stand up for Jesus !
  Stand in his strength alone :
The arm of flesh will fail you ;
  Ye dare not trust your own :
Put on the gospel armour,
  And watching unto prayer,
Where duty calls, or danger,
  Be never wanting there.

Stand up ! Stand up for Jesus !
  The strife will not be long ;
This day the noise of battle,
  The next the victor's song.
To him that overcometh
  A crown of life shall be ;
He with the king of Glory
  Shall reign eternally.

I. KINGS XVIII. 1—15; 17—20.

AND it came to pass *after* many days, that the word of the LORD came to Elijah in the third year, saying, Go, shew thyself unto Ahab ; and I will send rain upon the earth.

To unbelief this would have appeared like a command to plunge into the raging waves of the sea, or to walk into a lion's den, but soldiers of the Heavenly King do not reason, but obey.

2, 3, 4 And Elijah went to shew himself unto Ahab. And *there was* a sore famine in Samaria. And Ahab called Obadiah, which *was* the governor of *his* house. (Now Obadiah feared the LORD greatly: For it was *so*, when Jezebel cut off the prophets of the LORD, that Obadiah took an hundred prophets, and hid them by fifty in a cave, and fed them with bread and water.) *(Here was a dove living in the eagle's nest. Obadiah was not a half-and-half man, but feared the Lord fully, hence his character won him confidence even from ungodly Ahab, and in his great trouble the king did not trust any of his idolatrous nobles as he trusted holy Obadiah. He lived in a wicked court, and yet was zealous for his God, and shewed his zeal by feeding the prophets when food was dear, and kindness to them might have cost him his life. If in so difficult a position Obadiah was so earnest, what manner of persons ought we to be who are so much more happily situated?)*

5 And Ahab said unto Obadiah, Go into the land, unto all fountains of water, and unto all brooks : peradventure we may find grass to save the horses and mules alive, that we lose not all the beasts. *(Judgment alone cannot soften the heart, for all that Ahab cared for when under the chastising hand of God was to preserve his stud. He thought more of his horses than of his soul, or his starving subjects.)*

6, 7 So they divided the land between them to pass throughout it : Ahab went one way by himself, and Obadiah went another way by himself. And as Obadiah was in the way, behold, Elijah met him : and he knew him, and fell on his face, and said, *Art* thou that my lord Elijah ?

8 And he answered him, I *am* : go, tell thy lord, Behold, Elijah *is here*.

9, 10, 11, 12 And he said, What have I sinned, that thou wouldest deliver thy servant into the hand of Ahab, to slay me ? *As the*

LORD thy God liveth, there is no nation or kingdom, whither my lord hath not sent to seek thee : and when they said, *He is* not *there;* he took an oath of the kingdom and nation, that they found thee not. And now thou sayest, Go, tell thy lord, Behold, Elijah *is here*. And it shall come to pass, *as soon as* I am gone from thee, that the Spirit of the LORD shall carry thee whither I know not ; and *so* when I come and tell Ahab, and he cannot find thee, he shall slay me : but I thy servant fear the LORD from my youth.

13, 14 Was it not told my lord what I did when Jezebel slew the prophets of the LORD, how I hid an hundred men of the LORD's prophets by fifty in a cave, and fed them with bread and water ? And now thou sayest, Go, tell thy lord, Behold, Elijah *is here :* and he shall slay me. *(The good man was timid, for he had not been living the separated life, and therefore was far inferior in faith to the lonely Elijah, but the prophet bore with his weakness, for he knew him to be right at heart. We that are strong must bear the infirmities of the weak, and not expect all men to be equally bold.)*

15 And Elijah said, *As* the LORD of hosts liveth, before whom I stand, I will surely shew myself unto him to-day.

17 ¶ And it came to pass, when Ahab saw Elijah, that Ahab said unto him, *Art* thou he that troubleth Israel ?

18, 19 And he answered, I have not troubled Israel ; but thou, and thy father's house, in that ye have forsaken the commandments of the LORD, and thou hast followed Baalim. Now therefore send, *and* gather to me all Israel unto mount Carmel, and the prophets of Baal four hundred and fifty, and the prophets of the groves four hundred, which eat at Jezebel's table.

20 So Ahab sent unto all the children of Israel, and gathered the prophets together unto mount Carmel. *(Mark the holy boldness of Elijah, and how it awed the king. Elijah was far more royal than Ahab, for faith made him a king before the Lord. Be it ours to act in the same heroic spirit, never fearing the face of man, but facing the Lord's foes with unflinching valour. So shall we win the "well done, good and faithful servant," which should be the highest object of our ambition.)*

I. KINGS XVIII. 20—29.

SO Ahab sent unto all the children of Israel, and gathered the prophets together unto mount Carmel. *(The whole band of eight hundred and fifty priests, in all their gaudy attire, gathered upon the mountain's brow to confront the one lone prophet of the living God.)*
21 And Elijah came unto all the people, and said, How long halt ye between two opinions? if the LORD *be* God, follow him: but if Baal, *then* follow him. And the people answered him not a word. *(In silent awe the crowd listened to the one undaunted man of God, as he offered them the great choice of God or Baal, and proposed by one grand test to prove which was truly God.)*
22 Then said Elijah unto the people, I, *even* I only, remain a prophet of the Lord; but Baal's prophets *are* four hundred and fifty men.
Numbers are no test of right; but brave is he who dares to hold the truth, where thousands love the lie.
23 Let them therefore give us two bullocks; and let them choose one bullock for themselves, and cut it in pieces, and lay *it* on wood, and put no fire *under*: and I will dress the other bullock, and lay *it* on wood, and put no fire *under*:
24 And call ye on the name of your gods, and I will call on the name of the LORD: and the God that answereth by fire, let him be God. And all the people answered and said, It is well spoken.
" As when a wave,
That rears itself, a wall of polished glass,
For leagues along the shore, and hangs in air,
Falls with one deafening crash, so rose the shout
Of answering acclamation from the crowd.
White-faced, with restless lips and anxious eyes,
Baal's prophets heard, their hundreds cowed and mute
Before one man. They dared not, in mere shame,
Decline the challenge."

25 And Elijah said unto the prophets of Baal, Choose you one bullock for yourselves, and dress *it* first; for ye *are* many; and call on the name of your gods, but put no fire *under*.
He knew their cunning, and that by sleight of hand they would cheat if they could; hence he said, suggestively, " but put no fire under."
26 And they took the bullock which was given them, and they dressed *it*, and called on the name of Baal from morning even until noon, saying, O Baal, hear us. But *there was* no voice, nor any that answered. And they leaped upon the altar which was made. *(They multiplied their litanies and genuflections; they exhausted their whole round of performances, but the sun-god lent them not a spark of his fires.)*
27 And it came to pass at noon, that Elijah mocked them, and said, Cry aloud: for he *is* a god; either he is talking, or he is pursuing, or he is in a journey, *or* peradventure he sleepeth, and must be awaked. *(Idolatry deserves contempt. The irony of Elijah was holy, though bitter as gall. How would Elijah laugh now at the Papists with their god of bread; and the Ritualists with their magical sacraments. His scorn would be unbounded as ours may well be; only as followers of Jesus we mix pity with our indignation.)*
28 And they cried aloud, and cut themselves after their manner with knives and lancets, till the blood gushed out upon them. *(How much torture is there in false religion: our God takes no pleasure in the miseries of his children. Hair-shirts, lacerated backs, and skeletons macerated with fasting, are fit worship for a demon god; but the blessed God loves them not.)*
29 And it came to pass, when midday was past, and they prophesied until the *time* of the offering of the *evening* sacrifice, that *there was* neither voice, nor any to answer, nor any that regarded.
" They writhed and tore
In ecstasies of grief and rage. At last
They hung their heads in mute despair, and looked
Upon the ground."

Baal could do nothing: our next reading will show us what Jehovah did.

The God we serve maintains his throne
Above the clouds, beyond the skies;
Through all the earth his will is done;
He knows our groans, he hears our cries.

But the vain idols men adore
Are senseless shapes of stone or wood;
At best a mass of glittering ore,
A silver saint, or golden god.

Shine forth in all thy dreadful name!
Why should a Papist's haughty tongue
Insult us, and to bring us shame,
Set up the gods dethroned so long?

I. KINGS XVIII. 30—40.

AND Elijah said unto all the people, Come near unto me. And all the people came near unto him. And he repaired the altar of the LORD *that was* broken down. *(Now was Elijah's turn, and the time for Jehovah to work.)*

31 And Elijah took twelve stones, according to the number of the tribes of the sons of Jacob, unto whom the word of the LORD came, saying, Israel shall be thy name :

32 And with the stones he built an altar in the name of the LORD : *(The challenge was made in the name of all Israel; therefore were twelve stones set up ; the whole nation was now to put the grand question to the test, and see whether Jehovah would answer by fire. The prophet would have nothing to do with Baal's altar ; Christ has no concord with Belial)* and he made a trench about the altar, as great as would contain two measures of seed.

33 And he put the wood in order, and cut the bullock in pieces, and laid *him* on the wood, and said, Fill four barrels with water, and pour *it* on the burnt sacrifice, and on the wood.

34 And he said, Do *it* the second time. And they did *it* the second time. And he said, Do *it* the third time. And they did *it* the third time. *(Till twelve barrels of water filled the trench, and damped all the materials for sacrifice; thus every notion of any concealed fire was effectually removed, and the trial was proved to be a fair and honest one.)*

35 And the water ran round about the altar ; and he filled the trench also with water.

36 And it came to pass at *the time of* the offering of the *evening* sacrifice, that Elijah the prophet came near, and said, LORD God of Abraham, Isaac, and of Israel, let it be known this day that thou *art* God in Israel, and *that* I *am* thy servant, and *that* I have done all these things at thy word.

37 Hear me, O LORD, hear me, that this people may know that thou *art* the LORD God, and *that* thou hast turned their heart back again. *(Bishop Hall well observes, " The Baalites' prayers were not more tedious than Elijah's was short, and yet it was more pithy than short, charging God with the care of his covenant, of his truth, and of his own glory."* The priests of

Baal were full of outward vehemence and fantastic action; Elijah's vehemence was inward, and his manner simple, but devout. His faith was the power of his prayer. His God helped him to pray believingly, and the issue was certain. Faith uses no machinery but that of prayer, but superstition overflows with ceremonials.)*

38 Then the fire of the LORD fell, and consumed the burnt sacrifice, and the wood, and the stones, and the dust, and licked up the water that *was* in the trench.

The author of " The Days of Jezebel" has described this in noble language :—

" *Scarce had he spoken when a broad white glare,*
Scattering earth's light, like darkness in its path,
Keener than lightning, calmer than the dawn,
The sword of God, that proveth him by fire,
That proveth him by fire in every age,
Stooped from above, and touched the sacrifice.
In the white blaze the sun grew wan, and hung
Like a pale moon upon the glimmering sky.
The fierce flame licked the water up, the wood
Crackled aloft, the very altar stones
Glowed fiery red ! * * * * * * *
Clear broke the shout from that great multitude,
' *Jah is the God ! Jehovah, he is God.'* "

39 And when all the people saw *it*, they fell on their faces : and they said, The LORD, he *is* the God ; the LORD, he *is* the God.

40 And Elijah said unto them, Take the prophets of Baal ; let not one of them escape. And they took them : and Elijah brought them down to the brook Kishon, and slew them there.

Elijah had the law of God at his back in performing this execution ; the men were false prophets, and were justly doomed to die. How Elijah bared his arm for that dread task, and made the dry bed of Kishon run with blood ! Not thus smite we at men, but oh that sin's errors and superstitions were thus slain, every one of them. Not one of them should be allowed to escape. Lord, do this killing work among evil systems at this hour !

O that the fire from heaven might fall,
Our sins its ready victims find,
Seize on our lusts and burn up all,
Nor leave the least remains behind!

Then would our prostrate hearts adore,
And own the Lord our righteousness;
He is the God of saving power,
The Lord Jehovah we confess.

I. KINGS XVIII. 41—46.

AND Elijah said unto Ahab, Get thee up, eat and drink; for *there is* a sound of abundance of rain. *(Only the prophet's ears heard that sound, but faith is quick of hearing. Though not a cloud relieved the burning sky, and no wind had yet arisen from the quarter whence the rain usually came, the prophet was strong in confidence, and did not hesitate to declare it. Faith never goes beyond her warrant when she declares that the Lord will fulfil his word.)*

42 So Ahab went up to eat and to drink. And Elijah went up to the top of Carmel; *(Different men go to different engagements. Ahab to eat and drink, and Elijah to wrestle and prevail with his God.)* And he cast himself down upon the earth, and put his face between his knees.

43 And said to his servant, Go up now, look toward the sea. *(Faith keeps a watch; she bows to the earth in humility, but she sets expectation at work to look toward the sea.)* And he went up, and looked, and said, *There is* nothing. And he said, Go again seven times. *(True faith can wait; her importunity gathers strength from her Lord's delays, and her expectation remains still on its watch-tower. It is a brave thing to be able to say, " Go again seven times.")*

44 And it came to pass at the seventh time, that he said, Behold, there ariseth a little cloud out of the sea, like a man's hand. And he said, Go up, say unto Ahab, Prepare *thy chariot,* and get thee down, that the rain stop thee not. *Prayer was heard, the little cloud was a sufficient token, faith was now fully assured and made her boast yet more courageously.*

45 And it came to pass in the mean while, that the heaven was black with clouds and wind, and there was a great rain. And Ahab rode, and went to Jezreel.

46 And the hand of the LORD was on Elijah; and he girded up his loins, and ran before Ahab to the entrance of Jezreel. *(To shew his loyalty, he acted as a running footman. Stern as he was in his obedience to Jehovah, he was willing to serve the king if the king would serve the Lord.)*

I. KINGS XIX. 1—8.

AND Ahab told Jezebel all that Elijah had done, and withal how he had slain all the prophets with the sword. *(Ahab's pliable nature was always impelled towards evil by his haughty spouse. Woe to the man who mates a Jezebel.)*

2 Then Jezebel sent a messenger unto Elijah, saying, So let the gods do *to me,* and more also, if I make not thy life as the life of one of them by to morrow about this time.

3 And when he saw *that,* he arose, and went for his life, and came to Beer-sheba, which *belongeth* to Judah, and left his servant there.

4 ¶ But he himself went a day's journey into the wilderness, and came and sat down under a juniper tree: and he requested for himself that he might die; and said, It is enough; now, O LORD, take away my life; for I *am* not better than my fathers. *(His intense excitement had been followed by languor, his exhilaration by depression: man is but dust. He prayed to die, and yet the Lord did not intend that he should ever die. Truly, we often know not what we ask.)*

5 And as he lay and slept under a juniper tree, behold, then an angel touched him, and said unto him, Arise *and* eat.

6 And he looked, and, behold, *there was* a cake baken on the coals, and a cruse of water at his head. And he did eat and drink, and laid him down again. *(The Lord pitied his weary and disappointed servant, and as he had before fed him by ravens, he now honours him by supplying his need by angels. We often receive our best consolations in our worst times, and then how sweet they are!)*

7 And the angel of the LORD came again the second time, and touched him, and said, Arise *and* eat; because the journey *is* too great for thee. *(Twice came the sacred refreshment; the Lord doubles our comforts when our sorrows are multiplied.)*

8 And he arose, and did eat and drink, and went in the strength of that meat forty days and forty nights unto Horeb the mount of God.

A glorious march, a heavenly fast, a divine sustaining. Carmel's struggles and Samaria's disappointments were all to be rewarded by the communion of Horeb. Blessed are all they who wait upon the Lord; he will make them " a people near unto him."

ELIJAH, *when he fled from Jezebel, sought communion with the Lord at Horeb. He felt greatly aggrieved and sorely wounded in soul that, after the great decision of Carmel, Israel remained idolatrous, bound by a woman's will to Baal and the calves: he therefore sought the loneliness of Horeb, wherein to give his indignation vent.*

I. KINGS XIX. 9—18.

9 ¶ And he came thither unto a cave, and lodged there; and, behold, the word of the LORD *came* to him, and he said unto him, What doest thou here, Elijah? *(Thou, the brave Elijah, wherefore hast thou fled to this place? Leader in Israel, wherefore hast thou deserted thy post? There are none to instruct or rebuke in these rocky solitudes, what art thou doing in this place?)*

10 And he said, I have been very jealous for the LORD God of hosts: for the children of Israel have forsaken thy covenant, thrown down thine altars, and slain thy prophets with the sword; and I, *even* I only, am left; and they seek my life, to take it away. *(His sorrows were too much for him. He could have borne hunger, and thirst, and pain; but to see the Lord blasphemed was more than his great spirit could brook. He seems vexed with the Lord for not interposing to save his servants, the prophets. His secret heart longs to see terrible things in righteousness by which the ungodly nation may be awed into adoration.)*

11 And he said, Go forth, and stand upon the mount before the LORD. *(Come out of the cave, breathe the fresh air, and see what the Lord would teach thee.)* And, behold, the LORD passed by, and a great and strong wind rent the mountains, and brake in pieces the rocks before the LORD; *but* the LORD *was* not in the wind: and after the wind an earthquake; *but* the LORD *was* not in the earthquake:

12 And after the earthquake a fire; *but* the LORD *was* not in the fire: and after the fire a still small voice. *(Thus he learned that not by terrors and judgments are men's hearts won to God, but by the gentler force of loving persuasion. Elijah was like earthquake and fire, and his ministry was powerful, but it was not successful; there needed a gentler soul, with more plaintive pleadings to win the revolting people to their God.)*

13 And it was *so*, when Elijah heard *it*, that he wrapped his face in his mantle, and went out, and stood in the entering in of the cave. And, behold, *there came* a voice unto him, and said, What doest thou here, Elijah?

14 And he said, I have been very jealous for the LORD God of hosts: because the children of Israel have forsaken thy covenant, thrown down thine altars, and slain thy prophets with the sword; and I, *even* I only, am left; and they seek my life, to take it away.

15 And the LORD said unto him, Go, return on thy way to the wilderness of Damascus: and when thou comest, anoint Hazael *to be* king over Syria:

16 And Jehu the son of Nimshi shalt thou anoint *to be* king over Israel: and Elisha the son of Shaphat of Abel-meholah shalt thou anoint *to be* prophet in thy room.

17 And it shall come to pass, *that* him that escapeth the sword of Hazael shall Jehu slay: and him that escapeth from the sword of Jehu shall Elisha slay. *(The best cure for depressed spirits is more work to do for God. Elijah soon recovered his cheerfulness when he had commissions to fulfil for the Lord he loved so well. After the lesson he had received, he did not again leave his field of labour through fear of Jezebel, but sternly fought the battles of the Lord till his time of service was ended. Moreover, great was his joy to find that in the apostate nation there was yet a faithful remnant, for the Lord said to him)—*

18 Yet I have left *me* seven thousand in Israel, all the knees which have not bowed unto Baal, and every mouth which hath not kissed him. *(The Lord knows his own. They may be driven to hide themselves through cruel persecution, but they are not hidden from him. In these evil days, when Ritualism has set up her false gods, and turned the heart of our nation away from the gospel, be it ours to remain faithful unto the Lord; and in no sense or manner to aid or abet the wretched idolatries now so much in vogue. May we be among the thousands "which have not bowed unto Baal.")*

346   " Shall not God avenge his own elect ? "   JUNE 12.—EVENING.

[*Or November 22.*]

I. KINGS XXI. 1—16.

AND it came to pass after these things, that Naboth the Jezreelite had a vineyard, which *was* in Jezreel, hard by the palace of Ahab king of Samaria.

2 And Ahab spake unto Naboth, saying, Give me thy vineyard, that I may have it for a garden of herbs, because it *is* near unto my house : and I will give thee for it a better vineyard than it ; *or*, if it seem good to thee, I will give thee the worth of it in money.

3 And Naboth said to Ahab, The LORD forbid it me, that I should give the inheritance of my fathers unto thee. (*Naboth did not refuse to sell his vineyard merely because of a natural attachment to the inheritance of his fathers, but because the law of God forbade such a sale. The land might not be transferred from one tribe to another. Naboth knew this law, and bravely resolved to obey it.*)

4 And Ahab came into his house heavy and displeased because of the word which Naboth the Jezreelite had spoken to him : for he had said, I will not give thee the inheritance of my fathers. And he laid him down upon his bed, and turned away his face, and would eat no bread. (*Acting like a spoiled, self-willed child, he fumed and fretted because he could not have his way. How miserable are men who have not learned to bridle their desires.*)

5 ¶ But Jezebel his wife came to him, and said unto him, Why is thy spirit so sad, that thou eatest no bread ?

6 And he said unto her, Because I spake unto Naboth the Jezreelite, and said unto him, Give me thy vineyard for money ; or else, if it please thee, I will give thee *another* vineyard for it : and he answered, I will not give thee my vineyard.

7 And Jezebel his wife said unto him, Dost thou now govern the kingdom of Israel ? arise, *and* eat bread, and let thine heart be merry : I will give thee the vineyard of Naboth the Jezreelite. (*An imperious woman is a fit tool for the Evil One. Ahab was bad enough, but he was a mere novice in evil compared with his fierce Sidonian queen. Bad women are often very bad; even as good women are the best of the human race.*)

8, 9, 10 So she wrote letters in Ahab's name, and sealed *them* with his seal, and sent the letters unto the elders and to the nobles that *were* in his city, dwelling with Naboth. And she wrote in the letters, saying, Proclaim a fast, and set Naboth on high among the people : And set two men, sons of Belial, before him, to bear witness against him, saying, Thou didst blaspheme God and the king. And *then* carry him out, and stone him, that he may die.

11, 12 And the men of his city, *even* the elders and the nobles who were the inhabitants in his city, did as Jezebel had sent unto them, *and* as it *was* written in the letters which she had sent unto them. They proclaimed a fast, and set Naboth on high among the people.

13 And there came in two men, children of Belial, and sat before him : and witnessed against Naboth, in the presence of the people, saying, Naboth did blaspheme God and the king. Then they carried him forth out of the city, and stoned him with stones, that he died. (*Both the nobles and the witnesses were utterly devoid of honesty ; they were willing and apt disciples of the vicious court of Jezebel.*)

14 Then they sent to Jezebel, saying, Naboth is stoned, and is dead.

A cold-blooded message indeed. Murder was in their eyes a trifle, yet these very men had just celebrated a fast. Superstition has no conscience.

15 ¶ And it came to pass, when Jezebel heard that Naboth was stoned, and was dead, that Jezebel said to Ahab, Arise, take possession of the vineyard of Naboth the Jezreelite, which he refused to give thee for money : for Naboth is not alive, but dead.

16 And it came to pass, when Ahab heard that Naboth was dead, that Ahab rose up to go down to the vineyard of Naboth the Jezreelite, to take possession of it. (*He claimed it as a forfeit to the crown for Naboth's alleged treason, but how could he have looked for a blessing upon it ? Never let us dare to take to ourselves anything unjustly, for it will be a curse to us.*)

Rest in the Lord and keep his way,
Nor let thine anger rise,
Though providence should long delay
To punish haughty vice.

Thine innocence shall God display
And make his judgments known
Fair as the light of dawning day,
And glorious as the noon.

I. KINGS XXI. 17—29.

AND the word of the LORD came to Elijah the Tishbite, saying,

18 Arise, go down to meet Ahab king of Israel, which *is* in Samaria : behold, *he is* in the vineyard of Naboth, whither he is gone down to possess it. *(Short is the triumph of the wicked. Before Ahab can enjoy his plunder, he is to be served with a writ of ejectment of a terrible kind.)*

19 And thou shalt speak unto him, saying, Thus saith the LORD, Hast thou killed, and also taken possession ? And thou shalt speak unto him, saying, Thus saith the LORD, In the place where dogs licked the blood of Naboth shall dogs lick thy blood, even thine. *(Admire the dauntless courage of Elijah, who does not hesitate to confront the haughty king in the very moment of his joy. Who would like to take the prey from between the lion's jaws ? Yet this heroic man advances to the task.)*

20 And Ahab said to Elijah, Hast thou found me, O mine enemy? *(Ungodly men often count faithful ministers to be their enemies, when indeed they are their truest friends. We should count him our benefactor who has the courage to tell us unpleasant truth.)* And he answered, I have found *thee :* because thou hast sold thyself to work evil in the sight of the LORD. *(Had it not been for his iniquity, Elijah would not have troubled the king; but because Ahab offended the Lord, therefore Elijah offended him. In our ministry, if men's consciences are touched, they ought not to blame the preacher, but their sins. Elijah went on to declare the utter destruction of the race of Ahab.)*

21, 22 Behold, I will bring evil upon thee, and will take away thy posterity. And will make thine house like the house of Jeroboam the son of Nebat, and like the house of Baasha the son of Ahijah, for the provocation wherewith thou hast provoked *me* to anger, and made Israel to sin. *(The same sins were to be followed by the same judgments. Let us take heed, for it is written, "Except ye repent ye shall all likewise perish."*

23 And of Jezebel also spake the LORD, saying, The dogs shall eat Jezebel by the wall of Jezreel. *(Here was a special word for the proud queen, and the prophet feared not now to*

utter it, though once he had fled from her. God makes his servants brave when they are on his errands. Nature may fail them, but grace will not.)*

24 Him that dieth of Ahab in the city the dogs shall eat ; and him that dieth in the field shall the fowls of the air eat.

25 ¶ But there was none like unto Ahab, which did sell himself to work wickedness in the sight of the LORD, whom Jezebel his wife stirred up. *(Unconverted men have each one his price : give them what they ask, and they will sin as Satan may prescribe.)*

26 And he did very abominably in following idols, according to all *things* as did the Amorites, whom the LORD cast out before the children of Israel.

27 And it came to pass, when Ahab heard those words, that he rent his clothes, and put sackcloth upon his flesh, and fasted, and lay in sackcloth, and went softly.

28 And the word of the LORD came to Elijah the Tishbite, saying,

29 Seest thou how Ahab humbleth himself before me ? because he humbleth himself before me, I will not bring the evil in his days : *but* in his son's days will I bring the evil upon his house. *(The doom pronounced on Ahab was most terrible, and the threat of it evidently had a great effect upon the vacillating king. He had no grace, and did not therefore savingly repent ; but even his natural fear had something in it which the Lord approved, and therefore the doom was postponed a little. What power there is in humility and repentance ! God grant us grace to approach him by Jesus Christ in a still more acceptable manner, adding faith to our trembling, and we may be quite sure that he who respited Ahab will altogether save us.)*

And lo ! he vanish'd from the ground,
  Destroyed by hands unseen ;
Nor root, nor branch, nor leaf was found
  Where all that pride had been.

But mark the man of righteousness,
  His sev'ral steps attend ;
True pleasure runs through all his ways,
  And peaceful is his end.

I. KINGS XXII. 1—9; 13, 14; 28; 30—35; 37, 38.

AND they continued three years without war between Syria and Israel.

This seems to be noted as a remarkably long season of rest. To wha a wretched state must the poor but sinful people have been reduced by perpetual war. Scarcely a family could have escaped either plunder or the loss of its father and sons.

2, 3 And it came to pass in the third year, that Jehoshaphat the king of Judah came down to the king of Israel. And the king of Israel said unto his servants, Know ye that Ramoth in Gilead *is* ours, and we *be* still, *and* take it not out of the hand of the king of Syria?

4 And he said unto Jehoshaphat, Wilt thou go with me to battle to Ramoth-gilead? And Jehoshaphat said to the king of Israel, I *am* as thou *art*, my people as thy people, my horses as thy horses. (*Alas, that a good man should so readily make a league with an idolator.*)

5 And Jehoshaphat said unto the king of Israel, Enquire, I pray thee, at the word of the LORD to day.

6 Then the king of Israel gathered the prophets together, about four hundred men, and said unto them, Shall I go against Ramoth-gilead to battle, or shall I forbear? And they said, Go up; for the Lord shall deliver *it* into the hand of the king. (*False prophets are always plentiful, for the business pays.*)

7 And Jehoshaphat said, *Is there* not here a prophet of the LORD besides, that we might enquire of him?

8 And the king of Israel said unto Jehoshaphat, *There is* yet one man, Micaiah the son of Imlah, by whom we may enquire of the LORD: but I hate him; for he doth not prophesy good concerning me, but evil. And Jehoshaphat said, Let not the king say so. (*This was far too mild a rebuke, but evil communications lower the tone of the best men.*)

9, 13 Then the king of Israel called an officer and said, Hasten *hither* Micaiah the son of Imlah. And the messenger that was gone to call Micaiah spake unto him, saying, Behold now, the words of the prophets *declare* good unto the king with one mouth: let thy word, I pray thee, be like the word of one of them, and speak *that which is* good. (*This was a base attempt to pervert the prophet, but he was a true disciple of Elijah, and could not be turned aside.*)

14 And Micaiah said, *As* the LORD liveth, what the LORD saith unto me, that will I speak.

28 And Micaiah said, If thou return at all in peace, the LORD hath not spoken by me. And he said, Hearken, O people, every one of you. *He spake like a man of God, and called on all around to bear him witness.*

30 And the king of Israel said unto Jehoshaphat, I will disguise myself, and enter into the battle; but put thou on thy robes. And the king of Israel disguised himself, and went into the battle. (*Thus in a dastardly manner he exposed his friend to screen himself. Bad companions will not hesitate to compass our ruin if it will answer their purpose.*)

31 But the king of Syria commanded his captains, saying, Fight neither with small nor great, save only with the king of Israel.

32, 33 And it came to pass, when the captains of the chariots saw Jehoshaphat, that they said, Surely it *is* the king of Israel. And they turned aside to fight against him: and Jehoshaphat cried out. And it came to pass, when the captains of the chariots perceived that it *was* not the king of Israel, that they turned back from pursuing him. (*This was a special deliverance, for we are told in the Chronicles that God moved them to depart from him. His great peril must have made him feel the evil of his association with Ahab.*)

34 And a *certain* man drew a bow at a venture, and smote the king of Israel between the joints of the harness: wherefore he said unto the driver of his chariot, Turn thine hand, and carry me out of the host; for I am wounded.

35, 37, 38 And the battle increased that day: and the king was stayed up in his chariot against the Syrians, and died at even: and the blood ran out of the wound into the midst of the chariot. So the king died, and was brought to Samaria; and they buried the king in Samaria. And *one* washed the chariot in the pool of Samaria; and the dogs licked up his blood; and they washed his armour; according unto the word of the LORD which he spake.

That chance arrow was guided by divine vengeance, and every syllable of Elijah's threatening proved true. Who would not fear thee, thou just and holy God!

II. CHRONICLES XIX. 1—11.

AND Jehoshaphat the king of Judah returned to his house in peace to Jerusalem. *(Very special had been his deliverance from death; let us hope that he felt deeply grateful for it. He had by his own folly put himself into harm's way, and it was great mercy which rescued him from peril. We find, however, that he did not go unrebuked.)*

2 And Jehu the son of Hanani the seer went out to meet him, and said to king Jehoshaphat, Shouldest thou help the ungodly, and love them that hate the LORD? therefore *is* wrath upon thee from before the LORD.

3 Nevertheless there are good things found in thee, in that thou hast taken away the groves out of the land, and hast prepared thine heart to seek God. *(The father had rebuked Asa, and had been roughly used for so doing, but this did not prevent the son from doing his duty. He spake very plainly and personally to Jehoshaphat, and did not hesitate to deliver to him the solemn threatening of the Lord: nor was his message a fruitless one, for the king saw his sin, and set about doing all the good he could, as a token of his hearty repentance.)*

4 And Jehoshaphat dwelt at Jerusalem: and he went out again through the people from Beer-sheba to mount Ephraim, and brought them back unto the LORD God of their fathers.

When we turn to God ourselves, we cannot do better than use all our influence to convert others.

5 And he set judges in the land throughout all the fenced cities of Judah, city by city,

6 And said to the judges, Take heed what ye do: for ye judge not for man, but for the LORD, who *is* with you in the judgment.

7 Wherefore now let the fear of the LORD be upon you; take heed and do *it:* for *there is* no iniquity with the LORD our God, nor respect of persons, nor taking of gifts.

In all our dealings we are bound to be strictly just, and never should we allow ourselves to be perverted by the threats or smiles of any man. Our heavenly Father is righteous, and so should all his children be. It is not only judges who may be bribed, but servants may be bribed to allow tradesmen to rob their masters; masters may be tempted to be unjust to servants; and children may be led to be untruthful in their statements by gifts and threats. Such things must not be, or we shall grieve the Holy Spirit of God.

8 ¶ Moreover in Jerusalem did Jehoshaphat set of the Levites, and *of* the priests, and of the chief of the fathers of Israel, for the judgment of the LORD, and for controversies, when they returned to Jerusalem.

This was to be a central court of judicature where hard cases would be decided. What a blessing is it that in the New Jerusalem we have one who is called Wonderful Counsellor, and no case is too hard for him.

9 And he charged them, saying, Thus shall ye do in the fear of the LORD, faithfully, and with a perfect heart.

10 And what cause soever shall come to you of your brethren that dwell in their cities, between blood and blood, between law and commandment, statutes and judgments, ye shall even warn them that they trespass not against the LORD, and *so* wrath come upon you, and upon your brethren: this do, and ye shall not trespass. *(Very needful is it even now to exhort one another to do the right whether we offend or please. Disciples of Jesus should be strictly upright: if honour be banished from all the rest of the world, it should still dwell in the bosom of believers.)*

11 And, behold, Amariah the chief priest *is* over you in all matters of the LORD; and Zebadiah the son of Ishmael, the ruler of the house of Judah, for all the king's matters: also the Levites *shall be* officers before you. Deal courageously, and the LORD shall be with the good. *(Let this be our motto in all our dealings. He who acts uprightly has never any cause to fear, for God is with him. Children, learn this line by heart, "Deal courageously, and the Lord shall be with the good.")*

I send the joys of earth away,
Away, ye tempters of the mind;
False as the smooth deceitful sea,
And empty as the whistling wind.

Lord, I adore thy matchless grace,
That warn'd me of that dark abyss,
That drew me from those treacherous seas,
And bade me seek superior bliss.

II. CHRONICLES XX. 1—19.

IT came to pass after this also, *that* the children of Moab, and the children of Ammon, and with them *other* beside the Ammonites, came against Jehoshaphat to battle.

This was a chastisement upon him for joining with Ahab, for now the wicked join against him ; but it was sent in love, and therefore ended well.

2, 3 Then there came some that told Jehoshaphat, saying, There cometh a great multitude against thee. And Jehoshaphat feared, and set himself to seek the LORD, and proclaimed a fast throughout all Judah. *(He did not only fear because of the vast number of the invaders, but because the Lord had told him by the mouth of the prophet that wrath would be upon him. His fears, however, drove him to prayer, and whenever this is the case matters will be sure to mend.)*

4 And Judah gathered themselves together, to ask *help* of the LORD : even out of all the cities of Judah they came to seek the LORD. *(Great troubles can only be met by great prayer. Let us use this certain remedy when trial comes upon us.)*

5—12 And Jehoshaphat stood in the congregation of Judah and Jerusalem, in the house of the LORD, before the new court. And said, O LORD God of our fathers, *art* not thou God in heaven ? and rulest *not* thou over all the kingdoms of the heathen ? and in thine hand *is there not* power and might, so that none is able to withstand thee ? *Art* not thou our God, *who* didst drive out the inhabitants of this land before thy people Israel, and gavest it to the seed of Abraham thy friend for ever ? And they dwelt therein, and have built thee a sanctuary therein for thy name, saying, If, *when* evil cometh upon us, *as* the sword, judgment, or pestilence, or famine, we stand before this house, and in thy presence, (for thy name *is* in this house,) and cry unto thee in our affliction, then thou wilt hear and help. And now, behold, the children of Ammon and Moab and mount Seir, whom thou wouldest not let Israel invade, when they came out of the land of Egypt, but they turned from them, and destroyed them not ; Behold, *I say, how* they reward us, to come to cast us out of thy possession, which thou hast given us to inherit. O our God, wilt thou not judge them ? for we have no might against this great company that cometh against us ; neither know we what to do : but our eyes *are* upon thee. *(This was a noble prayer ; the king pleaded the divine power and sovereignty, he reminded the Lord of his former favours to his people, and then he pleaded the promise and covenant. After this manner also should we pray. The last sentence is peculiarly sweet : " our eyes are upon thee." For direction, help, protection, and encouragement they looked alone to the Lord. We shall be sure to see good when our eyes are fixed upon God alone.)*

13 And all Judah stood before the LORD, with their little ones, their wives, and their children. *(The prayers even of little ones are powerful with God. All our family should learn to pray, and in times of distress each one should assist in calling upon the Lord for help.)*

14 ¶ Then upon Jahaziel, a Levite of the sons of Asaph, came the spirit of the LORD in the midst of the congregation.

God will soon send a loving word when all his people humbly cry unto him.

15, 17 And he said, Hearken ye, all Judah, and ye inhabitants of Jerusalem, and thou king Jehoshaphat, Thus saith the LORD unto you, Be not afraid nor dismayed by reason of this great multitude ; for the battle *is* not yours, but God's. Ye shall not *need* to fight in this *battle :* set yourselves, stand ye *still,* and see the salvation of the LORD with you, O Judah and Jerusalem : fear not, nor be dismayed ; to morrow go out against them : for the LORD *will be* with you. *(When the Lord undertakes for his people he makes short work of their enemies.)*

18 And Jehoshaphat bowed his head with *his* face to the ground : and all Judah and the inhabitants of Jerusalem fell before the LORD, worshipping the LORD.

God's great mercy humbled them into lowliest adoration. They did not question the truth of the promise, but worshipped gratefully at once.

19 And the Levites, of the children of the Kohathites, and of the children of the Korhites, stood up to praise the LORD God of Israel with a loud voice on high.

This was real faith. Cannot we also praise the Lord for favours yet to come ? He will bless us, let us even now bless him.

II. CHRONICLES XX. 20—30.

AND they rose early in the morning, and went forth into the wilderness of Tekoa : and as they went forth, Jehoshaphat stood and said, Hear me, O Judah, and ye inhabitants of Jerusalem ; Believe in the LORD your God, so shall ye be established ; believe his prophets, so shall ye prosper.

21 And when he had consulted with the people, he appointed singers unto the LORD, and that should praise the beauty of holiness, as they went out before the army, and to say, Praise the LORD ; for his mercy *endureth* for ever. (*Here was a march in faith, a song of faith, and preparations of faith for yet further praise. O that we could all advance to our daily trials in such a spirit, we should then experience great deliverances from the Lord's hand.*)

22 ¶ And when they began to sing and to praise, the LORD set ambushments against the children of Ammon, Moab, and mount Seir, which were come against Judah ; and they were smitten. (*The people sang more or less all the way they went, from the time they set out, but when they came near the enemy they sang louder and louder, and then the Lord began to work, for the various nations mistook one another for enemies, and the Lord turned their own ambushments against themselves.*)

23 For the children of Ammon and Moab stood up against the inhabitants of mount Seir, utterly to slay and destroy *them :* and when they had made an end of the inhabitants of Seir, every one helped to destroy another.

24 And when Judah came toward the watch tower in the wilderness, they looked unto the multitude, and, behold, they *were* dead bodies fallen to the earth, and none escaped. (*They marched with hallelujahs, and were more than conquerors, for they needed not to strike a blow. Let us as a family make up a hallelujah band, and continually magnify the Lord.*)

25 And when Jehoshaphat and his people came to take away the spoil of them, they found among them in abundance both riches with the dead bodies, and precious jewels, which they stripped off for themselves, more than they could carry away : and they were three days in gathering of the spoil, it was so much. (*Faith wins even more than she expects, a blessing which she has not room enough to receive.*)

26 ¶ And on the fourth day they assembled themselves in the valley of Berachah ; (*or Blessing*) for there they blessed the LORD.

27, 28 Then they returned, every man of Judah and Jerusalem, and Jehoshaphat in the forefront of them, to go again to Jerusalem with joy ; for the LORD had made them to rejoice over their enemies. And they came to Jerusalem with psalteries and harps and trumpets unto the house of the LORD. (*Those who praise before the blessing are sure to praise afterwards. What a glorious Te Deum did they chant before the Lord.*)

29, 30 And the fear of God was on all the kingdoms of *those* countries, when they had heard that the LORD fought against the enemies of Israel. So the realm of Jehoshaphat was quiet : for his God gave him rest round about.

WE *will now read the Psalm which in all probability was sung by the people upon their triumphant return to the temple.*

PSALM XLVII.

1 O clap your hands, all ye people ; shout unto God with the voice of triumph.

2 For the LORD most high *is* terrible ; *he is* a great King over all the earth.

3 He shall subdue the people under us, and the nations under our feet.

4 He shall choose our inheritance for us, the excellency of Jacob whom he loved. Selah.

5 God is gone up with a shout, the LORD with the sound of a trumpet.

6 Sing praises to God, sing praises : sing praises unto our King, sing praises.

7 For God *is* the King of all the earth : sing ye praises with understanding.

8 God reigneth over the heathen : God sitteth upon the throne of his holiness.

9 The princes of the people are gathered together, *even* the people of the God of Abraham : for the shields of the earth *belong* unto God : he is greatly exalted.

When the Lord Jesus shall return a second time from overcoming all his foes, and ours, we shall rejoice in some such words as these. Even now we may sing unto the Lord, for he hath triumphed gloriously. His own right hand and his holy arm have gotten him the victory.

WE *now return to the history of the kingdom of Israel.*

II. KINGS I. 2—13 ; 15—17.

2 And Ahaziah *(the son of Ahab)* fell down through a lattice in his upper chamber that *was* in Samaria, and was sick : and he sent messengers, and said unto them, Go, enquire of Baal-zebub the god of Ekron whether I shall recover of this disease. *(Shame that an Israelite should go to the Philistines for a deity, and leave the God of heaven for the god of flies.)*

3, 4 But the angel of the LORD said to Elijah the Tishbite, Arise, go up to meet the messengers of the king of Samaria, and say unto them, *Is it* not because *there is* not a God in Israel, *that* ye go to enquire of Baal-zebub the god of Ekron? Now therefore thus saith the LORD, Thou shalt not come down from that bed on which thou art gone up, but shalt surely die. And Elijah departed. *(His appearance was abrupt and his departure sudden. How astonished must the messengers of Ahaziah have been to meet with a man who knew their business, and gave them an answer to a question which they had never mentioned to him.)*

5 ¶ And when the messengers turned back unto him, he said unto them, Why are ye now turned back ?

6 And they said unto him, There came a man up to meet us, and said unto us, Go, turn again unto the king that sent you, and say unto him, Thus saith the LORD, *Is it* not because *there is* not a God in Israel, *that* thou sendest to enquire of Baal-zebub the god of Ekron ? therefore thou shalt not come down from that bed on which thou art gone up, but shalt surely die.

7 And he said unto them, What manner of man *was* he which came up to meet you, and told you these words ?

8 And they answered him, *He was* an hairy man, and girt with a girdle of leather about his loins. And he said, It *is* Elijah the Tishbite.

Then, like a true son of Jezebel, he resolved to slay Elijah, reckoning that he would never rest so long as the troublesome prophet survived.

9 Then the king sent unto him a captain of fifty with his fifty. And he went up to him : and, behold, he sat on the top of an hill. And he spake unto him, Thou man of God, the king hath said, Come down.

10 And Elijah answered and said to the captain of fifty, If I *be* a man of God, then let fire come down from heaven, and consume thee and thy fifty. And there came down fire from heaven, and consumed him and his fifty.

We have to deal with another and gentler prophet who rebuked his disciples when they spoke of calling down fire from heaven upon his enemies. Elijah, under a different dispensation, met the wrath of a king by a calm act of faith, and the band who came to take him lay dead at his feet.

11 Again also he sent unto him another captain of fifty with his fifty. And he answered and said unto him, O man of God, thus hath the king said, Come down quickly. *(He was more peremptory than the first, and would have the prophet hasten to surrender. He thus courted destruction.)*

12 And Elijah answered and said unto them, If I *be* a man of God, let fire come down from heaven, and consume thee and thy fifty. And the fire of God came down from heaven, and consumed him and his fifty.

13 And he sent again a captain of the third fifty with his fifty. And the third captain of fifty went up, and came and fell on his knees before Elijah, and besought him, and said unto him, O man of God, I pray thee, let my life, and the life of these fifty thy servants, be precious in thy sight. *(This captain was wise, and being forced to perform a dangerous task, cast himself on the prophet's mercy. Humility turns aside the sword of vengeance. It is well to be lowly before the Lord.)*

15 And the angel of the LORD said unto Elijah, Go down with him : be not afraid of him. And he arose, and went down with him unto the king. *(Boldly he entered the gates of Samaria, and passed into the royal palace, fearless of Jezebel: the Lord put such dignity upon his servant that no man laid hands upon him.)*

16 And he said unto him, Thus saith the LORD, Forasmuch as thou hast sent messengers to enquire of Baal-zebub the god of Ekron, *is it* not because *there is* no God in Israel to enquire of his word ? therefore thou shalt not come down off that bed on which thou art gone up, but shalt surely die.

17 So he died according to the word of the LORD which Elijah had spoken.

II. KINGS II. 1—14.

AND it came to pass, when the Lord would take up Elijah into heaven by a whirlwind, that Elijah went with Elisha from Gilgal.

2 And Elijah said unto Elisha, Tarry here, I pray thee; for the Lord hath sent me to Beth-el. (*Elijah made the visitation of the schools of the prophets his last earthly work. No one can over-estimate the importance of our theological colleges being filled with holy men. Do we pray for students as we ought?*) And Elisha said *unto him, As* the Lord liveth, and *as* thy soul liveth, I will not leave thee. So they went down to Beth-el. (*Elijah, in prospect of departure, wished for solitude that he might pour out his soul before the Lord; and moreover he was a man of humble spirit, and did not desire others to see his glorious departure, lest they should think too much of him: Elisha, however, was appointed to be a witness of his translation. Those believers who most desire to escape observation are nevertheless known and read, for the Lord does not design that his choicest works should be hidden.*)

3 And the sons of the prophets that *were* at Beth-el came forth to Elisha, and said unto him, Knowest thou that the Lord will take away thy master from thy head to day? And he said, Yea, I know *it;* hold ye your peace.

4 And Elijah said unto him, Elisha, tarry here, I pray thee; for the Lord hath sent me to Jericho. And he said, *As* the Lord liveth, and *as* thy soul liveth, I will not leave thee. So they came to Jericho.

5 And the sons of the prophets that *were* at Jericho came to Elisha, and said unto him, Knowest thou that the Lord will take away thy master from thy head to day? And he answered, Yea, I know *it;* hold ye your peace.

6 And Elijah said unto him, Tarry, I pray thee, here; for the Lord hath sent me to Jordan. And he said, *As* the Lord liveth, and *as* thy soul liveth, I will not leave thee. And they two went on. (*Elisha could not be shaken off: he felt that he must see the last of his master, and must obtain from him a parting blessing.*)

7, 8 And fifty men of the sons of the prophets went, and stood to view afar off: and they two stood by Jordan. And Elijah took his mantle, and wrapped *it* together, and smote the waters, and they were divided hither and thither, so that they two went over on dry ground. (*That river had aforetime been swollen or dried up, according as the prophet had opened or shut up heaven, and now it opened to give him a dry passage. In this, as in many other respects, Elijah resembled Moses, who divided the waters of the Red Sea.*)

9 ¶ And it came to pass, when they were gone over, that Elijah said unto Elisha, Ask what I shall do for thee, before I be taken away from thee. And Elisha said, I pray thee, let a double portion of thy spirit be upon me.

He felt the difficulty of succeeding such a man as Elijah, and reckoned that he would need a double measure of grace to follow in his footsteps. His request shows that his heart was in his life-work, and that he had abandoned every selfish desire: his sole ambition was to serve his God.

10 And he said, Thou hast asked a hard thing: *nevertheless*, if thou see me *when I am* taken from thee, it shall be so unto thee; but if not, it shall not be *so.* (*It was not in Elijah's power to give the Spirit; he could but ask it for his friend, and give him a parting sign that the petition was granted.*)

11 And it came to pass, as they still went on, and talked, that, behold, *there appeared* a chariot of fire, and horses of fire, and parted them both asunder; and Elijah went up by a whirlwind into heaven. (*A fit departure for one whose fiery spirit and whirlwind force had made all Israel tremble. None beside of mortal men were thus carried in visible state to heaven. Singular fidelity was honoured by a singular translation.*)

12, 13, 14 And Elisha saw *it*, and he cried, My father, my father, the chariot of Israel, and the horsemen thereof. (*Elijah had been the protector of Israel, the chariot and horseman of the nation, and when he is gone, what will Israel do? This was Elisha's uppermost thought.*) And he saw him no more: and he took hold of his own clothes, and rent them in two pieces. He took up also the mantle of Elijah that fell from him, and went back, and stood by the bank of Jordan; And he took the mantle of Elijah that fell from him, and smote the waters, and said, Where *is* the Lord God of Elijah? and when he also had smitten the waters, they parted hither and thither: and Elisha went over.

II. KINGS IV. 1—14.

NOW there cried a certain woman of the wives of the sons of the prophets unto Elisha, saying, Thy servant my husband is dead ; and thou knowest that thy servant did fear the Lord : and the creditor is come to take unto him my two sons to be bondmen.

This was the hard custom of the age, that a man's sons should serve his creditor till his debts were discharged, even though their father was dead. How thickly did sorrows crowd upon this poor woman; her husband was dead, her estate hampered with debts, and her children were to be taken from her to serve another.

2 And Elisha said unto her, What shall I do for thee ? tell me, what hast thou in the house ? *(Whatever she had she was bound to give it up to pay the debts.)* And she said, Thine handmaid hath not any thing in the house, save a pot of oil. *(Her poverty was great indeed, and yet she was a prophet's wife : the people were too fond of their idols to give much to the Lord's servants.)*

3 Then he said, Go, borrow thee vessels abroad of all thy neighbours, *even* empty vessels ; borrow not a few.

4 And when thou art come in, thou shalt shut the door upon thee and upon thy sons, and shalt pour out into all those vessels, and thou shalt set aside that which is full.

5 So she went from him, and shut the door upon her and upon her sons, who brought *the vessels* to her ; and she poured out.

6 And it came to pass, when the vessels were full, that she said unto her son, Bring me yet a vessel. And he said unto her, *There is* not a vessel more. And the oil stayed.

In the same way the grace of God will fill up all our emptiness if we have but faith in him. When we can receive no more, the blessing will stay ; not because the Lord has come to an end of his power, but because we are not able to contain more. " According to your faith be it unto you," great faith shall have great supplies. If we are stinted, the fault lies wholly with ourselves.

7 Then she came and told the man of God. And he said, Go, sell the oil, and pay thy debt, and live thou and thy children of the rest.

She must pay her debts first, and then the remainder would be hers : she had no right to any of the oil till the creditors were satisfied. It was

no sin for her to bear her husband's debts when she had no means of paying, but the moment it was in her power to meet the claim, she was bound to do so. It would be well if all Christian people remembered this. We are bidden to owe no man anything, and yet debts are shamefully common.*

8 ¶ And it fell on a day, that Elisha passed to Shunem, where *was* a great woman ; and she constrained him to eat bread. And *so* it was, *that* as oft as he passed by, he turned in thither to eat bread.

9, 10 And she said unto her husband, Behold now, I perceive that this *is* an holy man of God, which passeth by us continually. Let us make a little chamber, I pray thee, on the wall ; and let us set for him there a bed, and a table, and a stool, and a candlestick : and it shall be, when he cometh to us, that he shall turn in thither.

11 And it fell on a day, that he came thither, and he turned into the chamber, and lay there.

Elisha had relieved a poor woman, and now he is entertained by a rich woman ; providence compensates the merciful. It was a great honour to the Shunammite to be allowed to entertain the Lord's servant, and she shewed her true piety by doing this spontaneously, and providing for the good man all necessaries, and above all a quiet room to himself, where he would be undisturbed by the business of the house.

12 And he said to Gehazi his servant, Call this Shunammite. And when he had called her, she stood before him.

13 And he said unto him, Say now unto her, Behold, thou hast been careful for us with all this care ; what *is* to be done for thee ? wouldest thou be spoken for to the king, or to the captain of the host ? And she answered, I dwell among mine own people. *(She was contented with her lot, and wished for no royal favour.)*

14 And he said, What then *is* to be done for her ? And Gehazi answered, Verily she hath no child, and her husband is old.

Thus it was suggested to the prophet that the birth of a child would fill the house with joy, and the Lord granted the generous woman her desire. Those who serve the Lord and are kind to his people shall meet with a large return. May our house ever be open to the ministers of Christ, for their Lord's sake.

II. KINGS IV. 18—23 ; 25—37.

THE *greatest earthly blessings are uncertain; the son who had made the Shunammite so glad was now to cause her grief.*

18, 19, 20 And when the child was grown, it fell on a day, that he went out to his father to the reapers. And he said unto his father, My head, my head. *(Perhaps the harvest sun was too hot for him, and he suffered from sunstroke, as many do in the east.)* And he said to a lad, Carry him to his mother. And when he had taken him, and brought him to his mother, he sat on her knees till noon, and *then* died.

21 And she went up, and laid him on the bed of the man of God, and shut *the door* upon him, and went out. *(Full of grief she was, for she had lost her son ; but she had a hope left, for she had not lost her faith.)*

22 And she called unto her husband, and said, Send me, I pray thee, one of the young men, and one of the asses, that I may run to the man of God, and come again.

23 And he said, Wherefore wilt thou go to him to day ? *it is* neither new moon, nor sabbath. And she said, *It shall be* well.

Her answer was the one word "well." Her heart was full and her faith sorely tried, therefore she said but little, and would not pain her husband by mentioning their crushing loss until she had proved the power of the prophet's God.

25, 26 So she went and came unto the man of God to mount Carmel. And it came to pass, when the man of God saw her afar off, that he said to Gehazi his servant, Behold, *yonder is* that Shunammite : Run now, I pray thee, to meet her, and say unto her, *Is it* well with thee ? *is it* well with thy husband ? *is it* well with the child ? And she answered, *It is* well.

27 And when she came to the man of God to the hill, she caught him by the feet : but Gehazi came near to thrust her away. *(She was in an agony, tossed to and fro between faith and fear, therefore she acted not in the manner usual to her, but fell passionately at the prophet's feet.)* And the man of God said, Let her alone ; for her soul *is* vexed within her : and the Lord hath hid *it* from me, and hath not told me.

28 Then she said, Did I desire a son of my lord ? did I not say, Do not deceive me ?

She argued that surely the son was not sent to mock her and break her heart, yet she felt that if he were to be soon removed it looked very like it, and this she could not believe to be the Lord's intention. Thus her faith and her anguish pleaded with Elisha.

29 Then he said to Gehazi, Gird up thy loins, and take my staff in thine hand, and go thy way : if thou meet any man, salute him not ; and if any salute thee, answer him not again : and lay my staff upon the face of the child.

30 And the mother of the child said, *As* the LORD liveth, and *as* thy soul liveth, I will not leave thee. And he arose, and followed her.

31 And Gehazi passed on before them, and laid the staff upon the face of the child ; but *there was* neither voice, nor hearing. Wherefore he went again to meet him, and told him, saying, The child is not awaked.

God would not grant this blessing to a mere form ; there must be mighty prayer.

32, 33, 34 And when Elisha was come into the house, behold, the child was dead, *and* laid upon his bed. He went in therefore, and shut the door upon them twain, and prayed unto the LORD. And he went up, and lay upon the child, and put his mouth upon his mouth, and his eyes upon his eyes, and his hands upon his hands : and he stretched himself upon the child ; and the flesh of the child waxed warm.

35 Then he returned, and walked in the house to and fro ; and went up, and stretched himself upon him : and the child sneezed seven times, and the child opened his eyes. *(By faith this woman received her child raised to life again as the woman of Sarepta had done before. Although a miracle will not be wrought for us, we ought to have a like faith, and we shall then see things equally worthy of our gratitude.)*

36 And he called Gehazi, and said, Call this Shunammite. So he called her. And when she was come in unto him, he said, Take up thy son.

37 Then she went in, and fell at his feet, and bowed herself to the ground, and took up her son, and went out. *(We must imitate this good woman, and in all times of trouble go with it to the Lord, and he will surely help us through. " Trust ye in the Lord for ever.")*

Shall I, for fear of feeble man,
Thy Spirit's course in me restrain ?
Or, undismay'd in deed and word,
Be a true witness for my Lord ?

Awed by a mortal's frown, shall I
Conceal the Word of God Most High ?
How then before thee shall I dare
To stand, or how thy anger bear ?

Give me thy strength, O God of power !
Then let winds blow, or thunders roar,
Thy faithful witness will I be :
'Tis fixed ! I can do all through thee.

Zion stands by hills surrounded,
Zion kept by power divine ;
All her foes shall be confounded,
Though the world in arms combine :
Happy Zion,
What a favour'd lot is thine !

Zion's Friend in nothing alters,
Though all others may, and do ;
His is love that never falters,
Always to its object true.
Happy Zion !
Crown'd with mercies ever new.

God is our refuge, tried and proved,
Amid a stormy world :
We will not fear though earth be moved,
And hills in ocean hurl'd.

When earth and hell against us came,
He spake, and quell'd their powers ;
The Lord of hosts is still the same,
The God of grace is ours.

Jesus our Lord is love,
All gentle are his ways,
And since he suffered in our stead,
No fear our heart dismays.

No fiery vengeance now,
No burning wrath comes down ;
If justice call for sinner's blood,
The Saviour shows his own.

Before his Father's eye
Our humble suit he moves ;
The Father lays his thunder by,
And looks, and smiles, and loves.

Our soaring spirits upward rise
To the celestial throne,
Fain would we see the blessed Three,
And the Almighty One.

Lord, how our souls are all on fire
To see thy bless'd abode ;
Our tongues rejoice in tunes of praise
To our incarnate God !

And while our faith enjoys this sight,
We long to leave our clay,
And wish thy fiery chariots, Lord,
To fetch our souls away.

Straiten'd in God we cannot be,
No bounds his power and bounty know,
His grace is an exhaustless sea,
Which flows, and shall for ever flow ;
And if its course suspended seem,
The hindrance is in us, not Him.

Long as our faith's capacity
Is stretch'd to admit the blessing given,
We drink the streaming Deity,
And gasp for larger draughts of heaven !
But when we lose our emptiness,
The oil, the joy, the Spirit stays !

Empty us, then, most gracious Lord,
And keep us always empty here,
Till thee, according to thy word,
We see upon the clouds appear,
Thy glorious fulness to reveal,
And all thy saints for ever fill.

Since like the weeping Shunammite,
For many dead in sin we grieve ;
Now, Lord, display thine arm of might,
Cause them to hear thy voice and live.

Thy preachers bear the staff in vain,
Though at thine own command they go ;
Lord, they have tried and tried again,
They find them dead, and leave them so.

Come, then, thyself to ev'ry heart,
The glory of thy name make known ;
The means are our appointed part,
The pow'r and grace are thine alone.

II. KINGS IV. 38—44.

A ND Elisha came again to Gilgal: and *there was* a dearth in the land; and the sons of the prophets *were* sitting before him: and he said unto his servant, Set on the great pot, and seethe pottage for the sons of the prophets.

Though there was nothing to put in the pot except a very little meal, the man of God was persuaded that the Lord would send provision, and therefore ordered the pot to be placed on the fire in readiness. We have heard of one who had no bread and much faith; and therefore after prayer he caused the cloth to be laid, to show his practical belief that the Lord would send supplies: such faith Elisha had.

39 And one went out into the field to gather herbs, and found a wild vine, and gathered thereof wild gourds his lap full, and came and shred *them* into the pot of pottage: for they knew *them* not. (*Unbelief is vainly active: this person could not wait for the Lord to fill the pot, but must needs come to the Lord's assistance, and so did mischief. Faith does better with her patient waiting than mistrust with her vain activity.*)

40 So they poured out for the men to eat. And it came to pass, as they were eating of the pottage, that they cried out, and said, O *thou* man of God, *there is* death in the pot. And they could not eat *thereof.*

41 But he said, Then bring meal. And he cast *it* into the pot; and he said, Pour out for the people, that they may eat. And there was no harm in the pot. (*Thus for every evil the Lord finds an antidote. In the great cauldron of society at this moment there are deadly evils, such as ritualism and infidelity: the way to counteract their pernicious influence is to cast in the meal of gospel truth until the error is neutralised by the wonder-working grace of God.*)

42 ¶ And there came a man from Baal-shalisha, and brought the man of God bread of the firstfruits, twenty loaves of barley, and full ears of corn in the husk thereof *(or rather—in his scrip).* And he said, Give unto the people, that they may eat. (*Elisha's faith had enabled him to believe that God could provide when there was nothing in the house; and therefore he was convinced that divine power could multiply their slender store now that they had a little in hand.*)

43 And his servitor said, What, should I set this before an hundred men? He said again, Give the people, that they may eat: for thus saith the Lord, They shall eat, and shall leave *thereof.*

44 So he set *it* before them, and they did eat, and left *thereof,* according to the word of the LORD. (*We are to use what we have, and God will give us more. As our needs so shall our supply be, for we are promised strength equal to our days.*)

II. KINGS VI. 1—7.

A ND the sons of the prophets said unto Elisha, Behold now, the place where we dwell with thee is too strait for us. Let us go, we pray thee, unto Jordan, and take thence every man a beam, and let us make us a place there, where we may dwell. And he answered, Go ye.

3 And one said, Be content, I pray thee, and go with thy servants. And he answered, I will go. (*His company would cheer them, and his holy conversation would improve them: they loved him, and therefore desired to have him with them; he loved them, and therefore consented to join them in their labours.*)

4 So he went with them. And when they came to Jordan, they cut down wood.

5 But as one was felling a beam, the ax head fell into the water: and he cried, and said, Alas, master! for it was borrowed. (*He was poor, and had been compelled to borrow; he was honest, and was doubly grieved to lose what had been lent to him.*)

6 And the man of God said, Where fell it? And he showed him the place. And he cut down a stick, and cast *it* in thither; and the iron did swim. (*Yes, and God can still make iron swim; things impossible to us are possible to him. Out of every difficulty Omnipotence can bring us, only let us in childlike confidence cast our burden upon the Lord. Whatever our family trial may be, the Lord will help us through it.*)

7 Therefore said he, Take *it* up to thee. And he put out his hand, and took it. (*Joyful enough was this son of the prophets. May we have like work, like society, like faith, and like joy.*)

II. KINGS V. 1—14.

NOW Naaman, captain of the host of the king of Syria, was a great man with his master, and honourable, because by him the LORD had given deliverance unto Syria: he was also a mighty man in valour, *but he was* a leper.

In every lot there is a crook ; no man can be described without a "but." Naaman's "but" was one which embittered his life, for his disease was loathsome, deadly, and incurable.

2 And the Syrians had gone out by companies, and had brought away captive out of the land of Israel a little maid ; and she waited on Naaman's wife.

3 And she said unto her mistress, Would God my lord *were* with the prophet that *is* in Samaria ! for he would recover him of his leprosy. *(Who knows how this girl came to know of the prophet of the true God ? Perhaps a holy mother had made her familiar with the true faith and its ministers. Mothers cannot tell where their children may be cast in after years ; they ought therefore to prepare them for every contingency by storing their minds with the truth of God.)*

4 And *one* went in, and told his lord, saying, Thus and thus said the maid that *is* of the land of Israel. *(Naaman was a kind master, for all his servants took an interest in him: it is very pleasant when each one of the family seeks the good of the rest. Masters should care for the good of their servants, and servants should make their masters' interests their own.)*

5 And the king of Syria said, Go to, go, and I will send a letter unto the king of Israel. And he departed, and took with him ten talents of silver, and six thousand *pieces* of gold, and ten changes of raiment.

6 And he brought the letter to the king of Israel, saying, Now when this letter is come unto thee, behold, I have *therewith* sent Naaman my servant to thee, that thou mayest recover him of his leprosy. *(This was an error. The poor idolatrous king could do nothing.)*

7 And it came to pass, when the king of Israel had read the letter, that he rent his clothes, and said, *Am* I God, to kill and to make alive, that this man doth send unto me to recover a man of his leprosy ? wherefore, consider, I pray you, and see how he seeketh

a quarrel against me. *(He was alarmed, and feared that his powerful neighbour sought a pretext for another war.)*

8 ¶ And it was *so*, when Elisha the man of God had heard that the king of Israel had rent his clothes, that he sent to the king, saying, Wherefore hast thou rent thy clothes ? let him come now to me, and he shall know that there is a prophet in Israel.

9 So Naaman came with his horses and with his chariot, and stood at the door of the house of Elisha. *(Full of pomp and pride.)*

10 And Elisha sent a messenger unto him, saying, Go and wash in Jordan seven times, and thy flesh shall come again to thee, and thou shalt be clean. *(To cure Naaman of pride Elisha did not come out to him personally, but sent him a simple message.)*

11 But Naaman was wroth, and went away, and said, Behold, I thought, He will surely come out to me, and stand, and call on the name of the LORD his God, and strike his hand over the place, and recover the leper. *(He wanted rites and ceremonies, as many do now.)*

12 *Are* not Abana and Pharpar, rivers of Damascus, better than all the waters of Israel ? may I not wash in them, and be clean ? So he turned and went away in a rage. *(Just as those do who neglect the great gospel command, "Believe on the Lord Jesus Christ," and go about to find out a way of being saved by their own doings, or by priestly ritual.)*

13 And his servants came near, and spake unto him, and said, My father, *if* the prophet had bid thee *do some* great thing, wouldest thou not have done *it?* how much rather then, when he saith to thee, Wash, and be clean ? *Good reasoning this ! If Jesus had said to us, "Go on pilgrimage and be saved," we would have traversed the world ; shall we not obey him when he says, "Believe and live?"*

14 Then went he down, and dipped himself seven times in Jordan, according to the saying of the man of God : and his flesh came again like unto the flesh of a little child, and he was clean. *God is always as good as his word, but he will have us obey him. Faith will save us ; but if we will not believe neither shall we inherit eternal life. How is it with each one of us ? Have we washed in Jesus' blood or no?*

II. KINGS V. 15—27.

AND *Naaman* returned to the man of God, he and all his company, and came, and stood before him : and he said, Behold, now I know that *there is* no God in all the earth, but in Israel : now therefore, I pray thee, take a blessing of thy servant. *(Gratitude was in the stranger's bosom, he was not like those who receive great benefits and then go away to forget the giver. His gratitude prompted him to reward the prophet as well as to praise his Master.)*

16 But he said, *As* the LORD liveth, before whom I stand, I will receive none. And he urged him to take *it ;* but he refused.

He wished Naaman to see that he was not like the mercenary priests who swarmed around him. Freely he had received, and freely he gave. From others Elisha received presents, he only declined in this case because he saw it to be best.

17 And Naaman said, Shall there not then, I pray thee, be given to thy servant two mules' burden of earth ? for thy servant will henceforth offer neither burnt offering nor sacrifice unto other gods, but unto the LORD. *(Did he want this earth to make an altar with, according to the law ? We may suppose so, but we cannot be sure.)*

18 In this thing the LORD pardon thy servant, *that* when my master goeth into the house of Rimmon to worship there, and he leaneth on my hand, and I bow myself in the house of Rimmon : when I bow down myself in the house of Rimmon, the LORD pardon thy servant in this thing. *(His faith was very weak, and he wanted some indulgence in a matter which would involve his position at court. It was a wrong request, and was passed over in silence. It may be that in due time Naaman outgrew all fear, and became as decided for Jehovah as we could wish to have seen him at the first.)*

19 And he said unto him, Go in peace. So he departed from him a little way.

20 ¶ But Gehazi, the servant of Elisha the man of God, said, Behold, my master hath spared Naaman this Syrian, in not receiving at his hands that which he brought : but, *as* the LORD liveth, I will run after him, and take somewhat of him. *(How profane to mix up the name of the Lord with his covetousness and falsehood. A man may live with a prophet, and yet be no better than he should be.)*

21 So Gehazi followed after Naaman. And when Naaman saw *him* running after him, he lighted down from the chariot to meet him, and said, *Is* all well ?

22 And he said, All *is* well. My master hath sent me, saying, Behold, even now there be come to me from mount Ephraim two young men of the sons of the prophets : give them, I pray thee, a talent of silver, and two changes of garments. *(Wilful falsehood, every word of it !)*

23 And Naaman said, Be content, take two talents. And he urged him, and bound two talents of silver in bags, with two changes of garments, and laid *them* upon two of his servants ; and they bare *them* before him.

24 And when he came to the tower, he took *them* from their hand, and bestowed *them* in the house : and he let the men go, and they departed.

What benefit could these things be when he had to hide them away and leave them. Men lose their souls to get for themselves goods which are a trouble to them.

25 But he went in, and stood before his master. And Elisha said unto him, Whence comest thou, Gehazi ? And he said, Thy servant went no whither.

One lie requires another to support it. The beginning of falsehood is as the breaking out of fire ; no one knows where it will end.

26 And he said unto him, Went not mine heart *with thee,* when the man turned again from his chariot to meet thee ? *Is it* a time to receive money, and to receive garments, and oliveyards, and vineyards, and sheep, and oxen, and menservants, and maidservants ?

27 The leprosy therefore of Naaman shall cleave unto thee, and unto thy seed for ever. And he went out from his presence a leper *as* white as snow. *(God in infinite mercy forbid that any one of us should provoke him by untruth. Liars are not in these days punished with leprosy, but they will at the last have their portion in the lake which burneth with fire and brimstone : who can contemplate such a doom without trembling ?)*

Since lying lips and all deceit
　Are hateful in thy sight,
From crooked ways, Lord, keep my feet,
　For truth is my delight.

360   "The Strength of Israel will not lie."   JUNE 19.—MORNING.

[Or December 5.]

SOME *time after the cure of Naaman, the king of Syria besieged Samaria and reduced the people to such famine that mothers ate their own children. At last Elisha was permitted to assure the miserable people of deliverance.*

II. KINGS VII. 1—17.

1 Then Elisha said, Hear ye the word of the LORD; Thus saith the LORD, To morrow about this time *shall* a measure of fine flour *be sold* for a shekel, and two measures of barley for a shekel, in the gate of Samaria.

2 Then a lord on whose hand the king leaned answered the man of God, and said, Behold, *if* the LORD would make windows in heaven, might this thing be? And he said, Behold, thou shalt see *it* with thine eyes, but shalt not eat thereof. *(He was profane as well as unbelieving. This sarcasm was a specimen of his usual sneers at the Lord and his prophet.)*

3 ¶ And there were four leprous men at the entering in of the gate: and they said one to another, Why sit we here until we die?

4 If we say, We will enter into the city, then the famine *is* in the city, and we shall die there: and if we sit still here, we die also. Now therefore come, and let us fall unto the host of the Syrians: if they save us alive, we shall live; and if they kill us, we shall but die.

5 And they rose up in the twilight, to go unto the camp of the Syrians: and when they were come to the uttermost part of the camp of Syria, behold, *there was* no man there.

6, 7 For the Lord had made the host of the Syrians to hear a noise of chariots, and a noise of horses, *even* the noise of a great host: and they said one to another, Lo, the king of Israel hath hired against us the kings of the Hittites, and the kings of the Egyptians, to come upon us. Wherefore they arose and fled in the twilight, and left their tents, and their horses, and their asses, even the camp as it *was*, and fled for their life. *(If the Lord wills it, the most valiant foes of his church will run away like frightened hares. Why should we fear those who so soon become afraid of themselves?)*

8 And when these lepers came to the uttermost part of the camp, they went into one tent, and did eat and drink, and carried thence silver, and gold, and raiment, and went and hid *it;* and

came again, and entered into another tent, and carried thence *also,* and went and hid *it.*

9 Then they said one to another, We do not well: this day *is* a day of good tidings, and we hold our peace: if we tarry till the morning light, some mischief will come upon us: now therefore come, that we may go and tell the king's household.

10, 11 So they came and called unto the porter of the city: And he called the porters; and they told it to the king's house within.

12 ¶ And the king arose in the night, and said unto his servants, I will now shew you what the Syrians have done to us. They know that we *be* hungry; therefore are they gone out of the camp to hide themselves in the field, saying, When they come out of the city, we shall catch them alive, and get into the city.

13 And one of his servants answered and said, Let *some* take, I pray thee, five of the horses that remain, and let us send and see. *(God's promise was forgotten or smothered in its effect by their fears; however they did well to send and see. Some will not take the trouble even to look when a blessing is given, they feel so certain that it cannot be possible.)*

14, 15, 16 They took therefore two chariot horses; and the king sent after the host of the Syrians, saying, Go and see. And they went after them unto Jordan: and, lo, all the way *was* full of garments and vessels, which the Syrians had cast away in their haste. And the messengers returned, and told the king. And the people went out, and spoiled the tents of the Syrians. So a measure of fine flour was *sold* for a shekel, and two measures of barley for a shekel, according to the word of the LORD. *(God's word was fulfilled to the penny and to the hour.)*

17 ¶ And the king appointed the lord on whose hand he leaned to have the charge of the gate: and the people trode upon him in the gate, and he died, as the man of God had said, who spake when the king came down to him.

Providence fulfils the threats as well as the promises of heaven: the fine flour is sold, and the infidel nobleman is crushed. Dreadful will it be if any one of us should perish after the same example of unbelief, yet we shall do so if we see the blessings of the gospel all around us *and lose them ourselves from want of faith.*

II. KINGS VIII. 1—15.

THEN spake Elisha unto the woman, whose son he had restored to life, saying, Arise, and go thou and thine household, and sojourn wheresoever thou canst sojourn : for the LORD hath called for a famine ; and it shall also come upon the land seven years. *(She had gloried that she dwelt among her own people, and now she must be tried by a temporary banishment; but doubtless she knew that faith's path is not an easy one, and yet is always the way of safety.)*

2 And the woman arose, and did after the saying of the man of God : and she went with her household, and sojourned in the land of the Philistines seven years. *(She bore the trial well, entering upon it without question, and waiting under it without complaint.)*

3 And it came to pass at the seven years' end, that the woman returned out of the land of the Philistines : and she went forth to cry unto the king for her house and for her land. *(In her absence others had seized her heritage, and she appealed to royal authority for its restoration.)*

4 And the king talked with Gehazi the servant of the man of God, saying, Tell me, I pray thee, all the great things Elisha hath done.

5 And it came to pass, as he was telling the king how he had restored a dead body to life, that, behold, the woman, whose son he had restored to life, cried to the king for her house and for her land. And Gehazi said, My lord, O king, this *is* the woman, and this *is* her son, whom Elisha restored to life.

This was a noticeable providence. There were, as men would say, many chances to one against such a singular meeting of events. The king must talk to Gehazi, and the subject must be the woman's son, and lo ! just in the nick of time, the heroine of the story puts in an appearance. Wonderful, was it not ? And yet, if we will but open our eyes, such wonders happen in our own case more times than we can tell.

6 And when the king asked the woman, she told him. So the king appointed unto her a certain officer, saying, Restore all that *was* hers, and all the fruits of the field since the day that she left the land, even until now. *(Thus God repaid her a hundredfold the cup of cold water which she gave to Elisha when she hospitably entertained him. God will be in no one's debt.)*

7 ¶ And Elisha came to Damascus; *(marching right into the teeth of Israel's enemies: bravely did he perform the Lord's errands, even as Elijah had done before him)* ; and Ben-hadad the king of Syria was sick ; and it was told him, saying, The man of God is come hither.

8 And the king said unto Hazael, Take a present in thine hand, and go, meet the man of God, and enquire of the LORD by him, saying, Shall I recover of this disease ?

9 So Hazael went to meet him, and took a present with him, even of every good thing of Damascus, forty camels' burden, and came and stood before him, and said, Thy son Ben-hadad king of Syria hath sent me to thee, saying, Shall I recover of this disease ?

10 And Elisha said unto him, Go, say unto him, Thou mayest certainly recover : howbeit the LORD hath shewed me that he shall surely die. *(He might recover as far as his disease went, but he would die because Hazael would murder him. The statements were quite consistent.)*

11 And he settled his countenance steadfastly, until he was ashamed : and the man of God wept.

12 And Hazael said, Why weepeth my lord ? And he answered, Because I know the evil that thou wilt do unto the children of Israel :

13 And Hazael said, But what, *is* thy servant a dog, that he should do this great thing ? *(Hypocritically he denied that he would do it, yet in his heart he was already plotting.)* And Elisha answered, The LORD hath shewed me that thou *shalt be* king over Syria.

14 So he departed from Elisha, and came to his master ; who said to him, What said Elisha to thee ? And he answered, He told me *that* thou shouldest surely recover.

15 And it came to pass on the morrow, that he took a thick cloth, and dipped *it* in water, and spread *it* on his face, so that he died : and Hazael reigned in his stead.

Thus he proved himself to be worse than a dog, though he had spoken so fairly. Fine professions go for nothing when the heart is wrong. We must have new hearts and right spirits, or we cannot tell what crimes we may yet commit. Who knows the amount of evil which any one of us may do if grace does not prevent ? O Lord, save us from ourselves.

II. KINGS IX. 1—7; 14; 21—26; 30—37.

AND Elisha the prophet called one of the children of the prophets, and said unto him, Gird up thy loins, and take this box of oil in thine hand, and go to Ramoth-gilead : And when thou comest thither, look out there Jehu the son of Jehoshaphat the son of Nimshi, and go in, and make him arise up from among his brethren, and carry him to an inner chamber; Then take the box of oil, and pour *it* on his head, and say, Thus saith the Lord, I have anointed thee king over Israel. Then open the door, and flee, and tarry not. *(He was not to wait for fee or reward. Those who do the Lord's business must not be loiterers or saunterers. God's angels fly swiftly, and God's prophets must go on his errands with speed.)*

4 So the young man, *even* the young man the prophet, went to Ramoth-gilead.

5 And when he came, behold, the captains of the host *were* sitting; and he said, I have an errand to thee, O captain. And Jehu said, Unto which of all us ? And he said, To thee, O captain.

6 And he arose, and went into the house; and he poured the oil on his head, and said unto him, Thus saith the Lord God of Israel, I have anointed thee king over the people of the Lord, *even* over Israel.

7 And thou shalt smite the house of Ahab thy master, that I may avenge the blood of my servants the prophets, and the blood of all the servants of the Lord, at the hand of Jezebel.

14 So Jehu the son of Jehoshaphat the son of Nimshi conspired against Joram. *(He was probably the commander-in-chief, and it was no new thing in the history of Israel for such persons to dethrone the monarch.)* Now Joram had kept Ramoth-gilead, he and all Israel, because of Hazael king of Syria. *(Therefore he had left Jehu in command in Ramoth-gilead, and Jehu, having revolted, hastened with all his cavalry to Jezreel, to attack Joram, who lay there sick of wounds received in battle. When Jehu was perceived by the watchmen on the walls of the palace, the king sent messengers who at once deserted to Jehu's side. The king therefore resolved to confront his rebellious captain, but it was a foolhardy action, and ended in his death. The deadly encounter is thus described:*

21 And Joram said, Make ready. And his chariot was made ready. And Joram king of Israel and Ahaziah king of Judah went out, each in his chariot, and they went out against Jehu, and met him in the portion of Naboth the Jezreelite.

22 And it came to pass, when Joram saw Jehu, that he said, *Is it* peace, Jehu ? *(Meaning, dost thou return defeated ? Or hast thou conquered the Syrians and established peace ? He little dreamed of the doom upon which he was rushing: the greatest sinners are generally the most secure, secure even on the brink of ruin.)* And he answered, What peace, so long as the whoredoms of thy mother Jezebel and her witchcrafts *are so* many ? *(What peace can any sinner expect to have with God while he lives in sin ?)*

23 And Joram turned his hands, and fled, and said to Ahaziah, *There is* treachery, O Ahaziah.

24 And Jehu drew a bow with his full strength, and smote Jehoram between his arms, and the arrow went out at his heart, and he sunk down in his chariot.

25 Then said *Jehu* to Bidkar his captain, Take up, *and* cast him in the portion of the field of Naboth the Jezreelite : for remember how that, when I and thou rode together after Ahab his father, the Lord laid this burden upon him ;

26 Surely I have seen yesterday the blood of Naboth, and the blood of his sons, saith the Lord ; and I will requite thee in this plat, saith the Lord. Now therefore take *and* cast him into the plat *of ground,* according to the word of the Lord. *(Thus the Lord is known by the judgments which he executeth. It was singular that he who had years before heard the prophecy, as it were by accident, should himself become the fulfiller of it.)*

30 ¶ And when Jehu was come to Jezreel, Jezebel heard *of it;* and she painted her face, and tired her head, and looked out at a window.

31 And as Jehu entered in at the gate, she said, *Had* Zimri peace, who slew his master ?

Her haughty spirit quailed not. She taunted the Lord's avenger, and perhaps hoped to intimidate him by her insolence; but he had a commission from God, and this made him bold to proceed to execute the wicked queen.

32, 33 And he lifted up his face to the window, and said, Who *is* on my side? who? And there looked out to him two *or* three eunuchs. And he said, Throw her down. So they threw her down: and *some* of her blood was sprinkled on the wall, and on the horses: and he trode her under foot. *(Her murder of the Lord's prophets thus came home to her; the body which she pampered was trampled upon as straw is trodden for the dunghill.)*

34—36 And when he was come in, he did eat and drink, and said, Go, see now this cursed *woman*, and bury her: for she *is* a king's daughter. And they went to bury her: but they found no more of her than the skull, and the feet, and the palms of *her* hands. Wherefore they came again, and told him. And he said, This *is* the word of the LORD, which he spake by his servant Elijah the Tishbite, saying, In the portion of Jezreel shall dogs eat the flesh of Jezebel:

37 And the carcase of Jezebel shall be as dung upon the face of the field in the portion of Jezreel; *so* that they shall not say, This *is* Jezebel. *(This had been the cry in her pompous days; her heralds cried, " This is Jezebel," but they would say this no more. They could not even say, This is Jezebel's body, this is Jezebel's tomb, or, this is Jezebel's heir. Thus the name of the wicked shall rot. Lord, we bow before thee in reverence, trembling at thy justice.)*

The Lord Jehovah reigns!
Let all the nations fear;
Let sinners tremble at his throne
Nor tempt his wrath severe.

Jesus the Saviour reigns!
Let earth adore its Lord;
As with an iron rod he breaks
The haters of his word.

How holy is his name!
How terrible his praise!
Justice, and truth, and judgment join
In all his works of grace.

O'er earth and wave our God is Lord,
Let all his saints confide in him;
The sunken axe His power restored,
And faith can make the iron swim.

O sit not down when efforts fail,
And weep beside the river's brim,
Faith still is mighty to prevail;
Believe, and make the iron swim.

Have I that faith which looks to Christ,
O'ercomes the world and sin,
Receives him, Prophet, Priest, and King,
And makes the conscience clean?

If I this precious grace possess,
All praise is due to thee;
If not, I seek it from thy hands;
Now grant it, Lord, to me.

The fountain of Christ, assist me to sing,
The blood of our Priest, our crucified King:
Which perfectly cleanses from sin and from filth;
And richly dispenses salvation and health.

This fountain, though rich, from charge is quite clear;
The poorer the wretch, the welcomer here:
Come needy and guilty, come loathsome and bare;
You can't come too filthy, come just as you are.

This fountain in vain has never been tried;
It takes out all stain whenever applied:
The water flows sweetly with virtue divine,
To cleanse souls completely, though leprous as mine.

Ourselves so skilful to conceal,
So exquisite our art,
God only knows the utmost hell
Of the deceitful heart.

But now with shame I clearly see
That but for sovereign grace,
In lowest deeps of infamy
My soul had found her place.

Ah, do not Lord, forsake thy child,
And I shall never fall;
By no transgressions be defil'd,
Though capable of all.

364   " The wicked are overthrown, and are not."   JUNE 20.—EVENING.

[*Or December 8.*]

HAVING *seen the end of the house of Ahab, we will now glance at the kingdom of Judah, where we shall find evil kings upon the throne, the sad result of good Jehoshaphat's too friendly alliance with the idolatrous monarchs of Israel.*

II. CHRONICLES XXI. 1, 4, 6; 18—20.

1 Now Jehoshaphat slept with his fathers, and Jehoram his son reigned in his stead.

4 Now when Jehoram was risen up to the kingdom of his father, he strengthened himself, and slew all his brethren with the sword, and *divers* also of the princes of Israel. *(He followed the cruel policy of many oriental despots who are afraid of rivals, and therefore put to death all who are either by rank or influence, likely to obtain power. Jehoram's brothers were better than he; and this perhaps made him the more inveterate against them.)*

6 And he walked in the way of the kings of Israel, like as did the house of Ahab: for he had the daughter of Ahab to wife: and he wrought *that which was* evil in the eyes of the LORD. *(How much depends upon a man's marriage; for good or for evil it will influence his entire life. Jehoram acted wickedly, for he had the daughter of Ahab to wife. May all the marriages of our family be "in the Lord.")*

On account of Jehoram's sin his country was plundered, his palace sacked, and his wives and children carried into captivity, yet he repented not.

18 ¶ And after all this the LORD smote him in his bowels with an incurable disease.

19 So he died of sore diseases. And his people made no burning for him, like the burning of his fathers.

20 Thirty and two years old was he when he began to reign, and· he reigned in Jerusalem eight years, and departed without being desired. *(Nobody valued him in life, or mourned him in death.)* Howbeit they buried him in the city of David, but not in the sepulchres of the kings.

Counting him unworthy to sleep with godly princes. They that despise God shall be lightly esteemed.

II. CHRONICLES XXII. 1—9.

AND the inhabitants of Jerusalem made Ahaziah his youngest son king in his stead. Forty and two years old *was* Ahaziah when he began to reign, and he reigned one year in Jerusalem. His mother's name also *was* Athaliah the daughter of Omri. He also walked in the ways of the house of Ahab: for his mother was his counsellor to do wickedly.

She who had ruined her husband had also perverted her son. Mothers have much in their power: they are the queens of the household, and shape the future of their children.

4 Wherefore he did evil in the sight of the LORD like the house of Ahab: for they were his counsellors after the death of his father to his destruction. *(Counsellors to wickedness are counsellors to destruction.)*

5 He walked also after their counsel, and went with Jehoram the son of Ahab king of Israel to war against Hazael king of Syria at Ramoth-gilead: and the Syrians smote Joram.

6 And he returned to be healed in Jezreel because of the wounds which were given him at Ramah, when he fought with Hazael king of Syria. And Azariah the son of Jehoram king of Judah went down to see Jehoram the son of Ahab at Jezreel, because he was sick.

7, 8 And the destruction of Ahaziah was of God by coming to Joram: for when he was come, he went out with Jehoram against Jehu the son of Nimshi, whom the LORD had anointed to cut off the house of Ahab. And it came to pass, that, when Jehu was executing judgment upon the house of Ahab, and found the princes of Judah, and the sons of the brethren of Ahaziah, that ministered to Ahaziah, he slew them.

9 And he sought Ahaziah: and they caught him, (for he was hid in Samaria,) and brought him to Jehu: *(He had been like the house of Ahab in sin, and he was therefore overthrown in their destruction. His mother and his wife were both of the evil race of Ahab, and being thus doubly allied to it, he must fall with it. We should never form unions on earth with those from whom we should wish to be separated at the day of judgment:)* and when they had slain him, they buried him: Because, said they, he *is* the son of Jehoshaphat, who sought the LORD with all his heart. *(They buried him out of respect for his pious grandsire, or else his body would have been left to the dogs: the memory of the just is blessed, but the name of the wicked shall rot.)*

II. KINGS XI. 1—4; 10—18; 20.

AND when Athaliah the mother of Ahaziah saw that her son was dead, she arose and destroyed all the seed royal. *(Like a true descendant of Ahab, she stopped at nothing which could promote her own ambition. Well might she be called "Athaliah that wicked woman." The seed of David was almost destroyed by her, but the Lord interposed, for the sceptre could not depart from Judah until Messiah came. The covenant promise to David was bound up in a single life, but it did not fail.)*

2, 3 But Jehosheba, the daughter of king Joram, sister of Ahaziah, took Joash the son of Ahaziah and stole him from among the king's sons *which were* slain; and they hid him, *even* him and his nurse, in the bedchamber from Athaliah, so that he was not slain. And he was with her hid in the house of the LORD six years. And Athaliah did reign over the land. *(Athaliah was not likely to go to the Lord's house to find the child, for she seldom troubled that sacred place. David had lovingly cared for God's house, and now the Lord shelters the hope of his servant's race in the chambers of the temple.)*

4 ¶ And the seventh year Jehoiada *(the high priest)* sent and fetched the rulers over hundreds, with the captains and the guard, and brought them to him into the house of the LORD, and made a covenant with them, and took an oath of them in the house of the LORD, and shewed them the king's son. *These he appointed to act as a body-guard to the king, when he should be brought forth publicly to be crowned.*

Matthew Henry remarks that Jehoiada was a man of great wisdom, for he kept the prince in the background till the fit time when the people were weary of Athaliah's tyranny; a man of great influence, for the Levites and all Judah did as he commanded; a man of great faith, for in the darkest times he said, "Behold, the king's son shall reign as the Lord hath said;" a man of great religion, for he re-established the worship of the Lord all over the land; a man of great resolution, for he went boldly through with his loyal resolve, and carried it out to final success.

10 And to the captains over hundreds did the priest give king David's spears and shields, that *were* in the temple of the LORD.

11 And the guard stood, every man with his weapons in his hand, round·about the king.

12 And he brought forth the king's son, and put the crown upon him, and *gave him* the testimony; and they made him king, and anointed him; and they clapped their hands, and said, God save the king.

13 ¶ And when Athaliah heard the noise of the guard *and* of the people, she came to the people into the temple of the LORD.

14 And when she looked, behold, the king stood by a pillar, as the manner *was*, and the princes and the trumpeters by the king, and all the people of the land rejoiced, and blew with trumpets: and Athaliah rent her clothes, and cried, Treason, Treason. *(Yet she was herself the greatest traitor. Vain were her cries; her despotism and cruelty had alienated all her friends; neither hands nor voices were lifted in her defence.)*

15 But Jehoiada the priest commanded the captains of the hundreds, the officers of the host, and said unto them, Have her forth without the ranges: and him that followeth her kill with the sword. For the priest had said, Let her not be slain in the house of the LORD.

16 And they laid hands on her; and she went by the way by the which the horses came into the king's house: and there was she slain.

Thus the last of Ahab's seed died an unhallowed death: imperious to the last, the fierce woman, like Jezebel before her, rushed upon destruction.

17, 18 And Jehoiada made a covenant between the LORD and the king and the people, that they should be the LORD's people; between the king also and the people. And all the people of the land went into the house of Baal, and brake it down; his altars and his images brake they in pieces thoroughly, and slew Mattan the priest of Baal before the altars.

20 And all the people of the land rejoiced, and the city was in quiet. *(Thus by the holy influence of one eminently good man, the nation was brought back again to its former condition, and purged of idols. When God's Spirit is in a man he can sway the hearts of thousands. Lord, send us such men both in church and state.)*

366   " Freely ye have received, freely give."   JUNE 21.—EVENING.

[*Or December* 10.]

II. KINGS XII. 1—15.

IN the seventh year of Jehu Jehoash began to reign ; and forty years reigned he in Jerusalem. And Jehoash did *that which was* right in the sight of the LORD all his days wherein Jehoiada the priest instructed him.

But alas! he had no root in himself ; he was the creature of influences, and was only good so long as the reins of his conduct were in godly hands. Men should have minds of their own, and possess principles which will guide them, whether their instructors are with them or removed from them. Jehoiada deserves great honour for the way in which he managed the affairs of the kingdom.

3 But the high places were not taken away : the people still sacrificed and burnt incense in the high places.

4 And Jehoash said to the priests, All the money of the dedicated things that is brought into the house of the LORD, *even* the money of every one that passeth *the account*, the money that every man is set at, *and* all the money that cometh into any man's heart to bring into the house of the LORD,

5 Let the priests take *it* to them, every man of his acquaintance : and let them repair the breaches of the house, wheresoever any breach shall be found. *(The king had been brought up in the temple, and therefore felt a great love for it ; he had but a form of godliness, but he was very zealous for that form, and even shamed the priests themselves. Those who have nothing but external religion are often more eager for it than those who possess the reality of godliness.)*

6 But it was *so, that* in the three and twentieth year of king Jehoash the priests had not repaired the breaches of the house.

7 Then king Jehoash called for Jehoiada the priest, and the *other* priests, and said unto them, Why repair ye not the breaches of the house ? now therefore receive no *more* money of your acquaintance, but deliver it for the breaches of the house. *(Ministers ought not to be burdened with the raising of money, they have higher duties. Through leaving it to the priests, things were badly managed, and contributions were thrown into one fund which ought to have been separately appropriated ; the king therefore resolved upon another plan. If we cannot provide means for a good work in one way, we must try another.)*

8 And the priests consented to receive no *more* money of the people, neither to repair the breaches of the house.

9 But Jehoiada the priest took a chest, and bored a hole in the lid of it, and set it beside the altar, on the right side as one cometh into the house of the LORD : and the priests that kept the door put therein all the money *that was* brought into the house of the LORD.

10 And it was *so*, when they saw that *there was* much money in the chest, that the king's scribe and the high priest came up, and they put up in bags, and told the money that was found in the house of the LORD.

This method was novel, and commended itself to the judgment of the people. It is most important that persons should be sure that whatever is given to the cause of God is honestly used.

11, 12 And they gave the money, being told, into the hands of them that did the work, that had the oversight of the house of the LORD : and they laid it out to the carpenters and builders, that wrought upon the house of the LORD, And to masons, and hewers of stone, and to buy timber and hewed stone to repair the breaches of the house of the LORD, and for all that was laid out for the house to repair *it*.

13 Howbeit there were not made for the house of the LORD bowls of silver, snuffers, basons, trumpets, any vessels of gold, or vessels of silver, of the money *that was* brought into the house of the LORD :

14 But they gave that to the workmen, and repaired therewith the house of the LORD.

Here it will be well to ask whether we as a family are doing our part for the support of divine worship. Let us not dwell in our ceiled houses while the house of God lies waste.

15 Moreover they reckoned not with the men, into whose hand they delivered the money to be bestowed on workmen : for they dealt faithfully. *(Faithfulness is a great virtue. Whatever may happen to us, we must be exact to a farthing in the keeping of accounts. A Christian should be one whom all can trust with untold gold. Whether we are household servants, or lords of the land, our first duty to our fellow men is scrupulous honesty.)*

II. CHRONICLES XXIV. 2; 15—25.

AND Joash did *that which was* right in the sight of the Lord all the days of Jehoiada the priest.

But he had never acted from love to God; what he had done was out of complaisance to Jehoiada, who had helped him to the crown. The religious party had set him up, and therefore so long as they were in power he held with them, but when the idolatrous faction became strong he went over to their side. He who is blown one way by the wind will turn to another quarter if the wind changes. How important to possess deep-seated principles.

15 ¶ But Jehoiada waxed old, and was full of days when he died; an hundred and thirty years old *was he* when he died.

16 And they buried him in the city of David among the kings, because he had done good in Israel, both toward God, and toward his house.

17 Now after the death of Jehoiada came the princes of Judah, and made obeisance to the king. Then the king hearkened unto them.

No doubt the princes congratulated Joash upon his deliverance from the oversight of the aged priest, and "now," said they, "let us leave the dull and severe religion of Jehovah for the gay and pleasurable worship of the idols. We have had enough of this Puritanism, let us fall in with the ways of other nations, and enjoy the festive rites and more liberal morals of Baal and Ashtaroth." To this the king gave willing ear.

18 And they left the house of the Lord God of their fathers, and served groves and idols: and wrath came upon Judah and Jerusalem for this their trespass.

19 Yet he sent prophets to them, to bring them again unto the Lord; and they testified against them: but they would not give ear.

20 And the Spirit of God came upon Zechariah the son of Jehoiada the priest, which stood above the people, and said unto them, Thus saith God, Why transgress ye the commandments of the Lord, that ye cannot prosper? because ye have forsaken the Lord, he hath also forsaken you.

21 And they conspired against him, and stoned him with stones at the commandment of the king in the court of the house of the Lord.

Thus polluting with murder the sanctuary itself. They could not bear to be reproved for their faults. Some children show the same spirit, and are very angry if they are spoken to. Such bad temper would lead to murder if it were not restrained. He who is angry with another for telling him of his faults is a murderer.

22 Thus Joash the king remembered not the kindness which Jehoiada his father had done to him, but slew his son. And when he died, he said, The Lord look upon *it*, and require *it*.

An ungrateful man is capable of any crime. After the father had done so much for the king it was disgraceful to kill the son for doing his duty. Such a crime could not go unpunished.

23 ¶ And it came to pass at the end of the year, *that* the host of Syria came up against him: and they came to Judah and Jerusalem, and destroyed all the princes of the people, from among the people, and sent all the spoil of them unto the king of Damascus.

The dying martyr's blood brought speedy vengeance on the land. The princes had been first in the sin and therefore they were conspicuous in the punishment, and the city wherein the murder had been perpetrated was made to feel the brunt of the war.

24 For the army of the Syrians came with a small company of men, and the Lord delivered a very great host into their hand, because they had forsaken the Lord God of their fathers. So they executed judgment against Joash.

25 And when they were departed from him, (for they left him in great diseases,) his own servants conspired against him for the blood of the sons of Jehoiada the priest, and slew him on his bed, and he died: and they buried him in the city of David, but they buried him not in the sepulchres of the kings.

Thus Joash was first despoiled by his enemies, then his land was invaded by them, and as a climax he became personally diseased. Since all this did not lead him to repentance, the Lord put an end to his wicked reign by well deserved punishment. He had slain the sons of his benefactor, and soon his own servants assassinated him in his bed. "Evil shall slay the wicked, and they that hate the righteous shall be desolate."

ABOUT *this time occurred the visit of the prophet Jonah to Nineveh, of which we will now read, and, as we do so, we may note the honest way in which the prophet describes himself, and reveals his own infirmities and faults.*

JONAH I. 1—7.

1 Now the word of the LORD came unto Jonah the son of Amittai, saying,

2 Arise, go to Nineveh, that great city, and cry against it; for their wickedness is come up before me. (*The city is said to have measured sixty miles round the walls, and to have contained a million of inhabitants. It was full of idols, and its wealth was obtained by plundering other nations. It was very gracious on the Lord's part to send a prophet to warn such a city; but it was no slight task for one man to venture on so unwelcome an errand.*)

3 But Jonah rose up to flee unto Tarshish from the presence of the LORD, (*Who would have thought that a prophet would act so wickedly? Let him that thinketh he standeth take heed lest he fall. We are much weaker than a prophet, and more likely to fall; let us therefore cry to the Lord to keep us.*) And (*Jonah*) went down to Joppa; and he found a ship going to Tarshish: (*The finding of the ship was one of those providences which some think it right to follow in the teeth of God's express commands. Old Thomas Adams says, "If thou wilt fly from God, the devil will lend thee both spurs and a horse; yea, a post-horse that will carry thee swiftly." It is our duty to follow God's orders, and not the apparent leading of circumstances.*) So he paid the fare thereof, and went down into it, to go with them unto Tarshish from the presence of the LORD. (*Sin is expensive; the fare thereof must be paid, and men care not how much they pay to gratify their wrong desires, though they will grumble at any little which the cause of God asks from them. What a mad errand was Jonah upon when he hoped to fly from the Lord, who is alike present in all places, as much present in Tarshish as in Nineveh!*)

4 ¶ But the LORD sent out a great wind into the sea, and there was a mighty tempest in the sea, so that the ship was like to be broken.

If we run from God he will send rough messengers after us: we may flee away in a calm, but a storm will soon be sent as an officer from heaven to arrest us.

5 Then the mariners were afraid, and cried every man unto his god, and cast forth the wares that *were* in the ship into the sea, to lighten *it* of them. (*On this, Adams remarks: "Mariners living in the sea almost as fishes in their element, are commonly men devoid of fear, venturous, and contemners of danger. Yet now seeing the tempest so vehement on a sudden that their goodly and tall ship was tossed like a cockboat, and cracked so that it was like to be torn all to pieces, they were persuaded that it was no ordinary storm, but a revenging tempest, sent out by some great power which had been provoked: now they tremble for fear, like little children when they are frightened, lest their ship break, or leak, and so sink, and they lose their ship, lives and all. These fearless fellows were brought down by danger, and quaked like a young soldier who starteth at the sound of a gun. They did well to pray, but they prayed not well, for they turned to idol gods which could not even help themselves."*) But Jonah was gone down into the sides of the ship; and he lay, and was fast asleep. (*He for whom the storm was sent was the last to hear its message. When good men fall into sin they are generally in such a slumbering state of heart that it is hard to bring them to repentance.*)

6 So the shipmaster came to him, and said unto him, What meanest thou, O sleeper? arise, call upon thy God, if so be that God will think upon us, that we perish not. (*How well these words may be applied to those who are careless hearers of the gospel; they are asleep, and asleep in awful danger. Even a heathen might rebuke them as this shipmaster chided Jonah. O that they would awake and call upon God for their own sakes, and the sake of their families who are perishing with them.*)

7 And they said every one to his fellow, Come, and let us cast lots, that we may know for whose cause this evil *is* upon us. So they cast lots, and the lot fell upon Jonah. (*What men call chances are all in the hands of God. How sad that the best man on board the vessel should be convicted as being, for the time, the worst of all! When good men sin their offence is very great. Let us pray God to preserve us, lest we also be put to shame before the ungodly.*)

JONAH I. 8—16.

THEN said *(the mariners)* unto *(Jonah),*
Tell us, we pray thee, for whose cause
this evil *is* upon us; *(They put him to the question,
and did not condemn him without a hearing.
There was more justice among these heathen sailors
than we often find among professed Christians,
who will judge by appearances and condemn
in haste.)* What *is* thine occupation? and
whence comest thou? what *is* thy country? and
of what people *art* thou?

9 And he said unto them, I *am* an Hebrew;
and I fear the LORD, the God of heaven, which
hath made the sea and the dry *land.*

*He spoke out like an honest man, as he was.
He owned that his occupation was the fear of the
Lord, and he hesitated not to claim for his God
supremacy over all the Babel of gods to whom they
had been praying. He was ashamed of himself,
but not of his religion.*

10 Then were the men exceedingly afraid,
and said unto him, Why hast thou done this?
For the men knew that he fled from the presence
of the LORD, because he had told them.

*They knew what he had done, but they asked
his motive for so doing. What could have induced
him to flee from one who had made the sea and
the dry land, and could therefore overtake him in
his flight, wherever he might go?*

11 ¶ Then said they unto him, What shall
we do unto thee, that the sea may be calm unto
us? for the sea wrought, and was tempestuous.

*They were loth to lift up their hands against
him; they dreaded to injure him, though his guilt
was clear; they did not even insult him, as some
would have done. From this let us learn never
to be severe with our brethren, even though their
faults should cause us great trouble and danger;
let us rather appeal to their better judgment, and
lead them to suggest a remedy themselves.*

12 And he said unto them, Take me up, and
cast me forth into the sea; so shall the sea be
calm unto you; for I know that for my sake
this great tempest *is* upon you.

*Herein Jonah, who was an eminent type of
our Lord Jesus, sets before us the doctrine of
substitution, in a figure. Jesus is cast into the
sea of wrath, and it becomes calm to us. This is
the most glorious of all revealed truths, and most
needful to be believed and personally rested in.*

*Jonah, in the verse before us, appears in an
amiable light, as clothed with humility, a true
penitent, ready to receive chastisement without
complaint.*

13 Nevertheless the men rowed hard to bring
it to the land; but they could not: for the sea
wrought, and was tempestuous against them.

*The mildness of Jonah and his deep concern
for their safety touched their hearts, and they
resolved to save him if they could, but all in vain.
In a figure, we are here taught the spiritual
truth, that no toiling of our own can save us; it
is by the death of the Substitute alone that we can
be delivered.*

14 Wherefore they cried unto the LORD, and
said, We beseech thee, O LORD, we beseech
thee, let us not perish for this man's life, and lay
not upon us innocent blood: for thou, O LORD,
hast done as it pleased thee.

*They forsook their false gods and prayed only
to Jehovah. Their efforts to save Jonah were
unavailing, therefore they were driven to cast him
overboard, but they would not do it till they had
made one last solemn appeal to heaven. What a
sight it must have been, to see these men on their
knees, amidst the fury of the storm, and what a
pleasure to hear them cry, "We beseech thee, O
Lord, we beseech thee." Nor did they forget all
this when the tempest subsided; their fulfilment
of their vows is the most pleasing point in the
case.*

15 So they took up Jonah, and cast him forth
into the sea: and the sea ceased from her raging.

*This was one of the most solemn funerals that
ever took place. Into the raging billows the living
man was cast as into his grave, and lo, all was
still. The sacrifice was offered, and peace returned.
Marvellous type of our redemption! Do we all
understand that it is by Jesus' death that we
must live?*

16 Then the men feared the LORD exceedingly, and offered a sacrifice unto the LORD, and
made vows. *(When men are saved from destruction they are bound to give glory unto God,
both with words and gifts. Let us at this time
honour the Lord by our songs and our thank-
offerings, for he alone is the Rock of our salvation.)*

How shall I praise th' eternal God,
　That infinite Unknown ?
Who can ascend his high abode,
　Or venture near his throne ?

Sinners before his presence die ;
　How holy is his name !
His anger and his jealousy
　Burn like devouring fiame.

Justice upon a dreadful throne
　Maintains the rights of God ;
While mercy sends her pardons down,
　Bought with a Saviour's blood.

Come, ye that love the Saviour's name,
　And joy to make it known ;
The Sovereign of your heart proclaim,
　And bow before his throne.

Lo he on David's ancient throne,
　His power and grace displays,
While Salem with its echoing hills,
　Sends forth the voice of praise.

Sing, ye redeem'd ! Before the throne,
　Ye white-robed myriads fall ;
Sing, for the Lord of glory reigns,
　The Christ, the heir of all.

To the Lord we all things owe,
To the Lord we love to give :
Day by day his mercies flow,
Day by day to him we'll live.

Thus we sanctify our store
Cleanse the canker from our gold ;
And the Lord returns us more,
Fifty and a hundred-fold.

Our best offering is small,
But in condescending love,
He who is the Lord of all
Smiles upon it from above.

Never leave us, nor forsake us,
　Thou on whom our souls rely,
Till thou shalt for ever take us
　To behold that glory nigh ;
　　Which, though distant,
　Fills thy people's hearts with joy.

All our strength at once would fail us,
　If deserted, Lord, by thee ;
Nothing then could aught avail us,
　Certain our defeat would be :
　　Those who hate us
　Thenceforth their desire would see.

But we look to thee as able,
　Grace to give in time of need :
Heaven we know is not more stable,
　Than the promise which we plead :
　　'Tis thy promise
　Gives thy people hope indeed.

Could I so false, so faithless prove,
　To quit thy service and thy love ;
Where, Lord, could I thy presence shun,
　Or from thy dreadful glory run ?

If mounted on a morning ray
I fly beyond the Western sea,
Thy swifter hand would first arrive,
And there arrest thy fugitive.

O may these thoughts possess my breast
Where'er I rove, where'er I rest !
Nor let my weaker passions dare
Consent to sin, for God is there.

From a heart by sin deceivèd,
　Bent with froward will, to take
Its own downward course of madness,
　Save us for thy mercies' sake.

From a soul whose deathlike slumber
　Will not at thy voice awake,
But sleep on, nor heed its danger,
　Save us for thy mercies' sake.

JONAH I. 17.

NOW the Lord had prepared a great fish to swallow up Jonah. *(He who prepared the storm prepared the fish. It was expressly prepared for his divine purpose. What species it belonged to it is idle to enquire.)*

And Jonah was in the belly of the fish three days and three nights. *(Thomas Jones, in his "Jonah's Portrait," well observes, "He must be a preacher whether he will or no. When he was sent to preach to one city only, he refused; and now the Lord compels him to preach, not to one city, but to the whole world, by making him a type of Christ in his death, burial, and resurrection. 'As Jonah was three days and three nights in the whale's belly; so shall the Son of man be three days and three nights in the heart of the earth.' When the servants of God run away from an easy service, their Master frequently appoints them a harder task. If Jonah will not preach up and down the streets of Nineveh, he shall preach from the bottom of the sea. Man's highest wisdom is to obey his God, whatever work he appoints for him to do. If they who are sent to preach will not preach willingly, storms and tempests shall prepare them for their work. Many have fallen into dismal darkness and the deep, for want of more zeal and fidelity in their Master's service; when they are tried they come forth as gold. Let those who desert God and his service learn how necessary it is to return; and let those who repent see that 'with the Lord there is mercy, and with him is plenteous redemption.'")*

JONAH. II.

THEN Jonah prayed unto the Lord his God out of the fish's belly, *(He had lost all heart for prayer on board ship, but he began anew when plunged in sore distress.)*

2 And said, I cried by reason of mine affliction unto the Lord, and he heard me; out of the belly of hell cried I, *and* thou heardest my voice. *(Out of the centre of the unseen world which the belly of the fish resembled, Jonah sent up his plaintive cry and was heard. Prayer can reach the ear of God from the depths of the sea.)*

3, 4 For thou hadst cast me into the deep, in the midst of the seas; and the floods compassed me about: all thy billows and thy waves passed over me. Then I said, I am cast out of thy sight; yet I will look again toward thy holy temple. *(If thou wilt not look on me, yet will I keep mine eyes upon thee, if peradventure grace should yet be shewed me.)*

5 The waters compassed me about, *even* to the soul: the depth closed me round about, the weeds were wrapped about my head. *(He felt as if the seaweeds had become his winding-sheet.)*

6 I went down to the bottoms of the mountains; the earth with her bars *was* about me for ever: yet hast thou brought up my life from corruption, O Lord my God. *(Low as he went, he might have gone far lower had not divine power and mercy intervened. He lived on still, and this made him glad. Even in the belly of the fish he uttered his thankfulness.)*

7, 8 When my soul fainted within me I remembered the Lord: and my prayer came in unto thee, into thine holy temple. They that observe lying vanities forsake their own mercy.

9 But I will sacrifice unto thee with the voice of thanksgiving; I will pay *that* that I have vowed. *(He anticipates his deliverance, and commences to rejoice in it.)* Salvation *is* of the Lord. *(This is a summary of sound theology, and perhaps if more Christians had felt the depth of soul trouble, there would be more of such solid divinity preached and believed.)*

10 ¶ And the Lord spake unto the fish, and it vomited out Jonah upon the dry *land.*

A word was enough, the fish was glad to be rid of his burden; and at the word of the Lord the enemies of his people shall be glad to let them go, that they may escape the judgments which else would come upon them.

Salvation! oh, the joyful sound!
'Tis pleasure to our ears;
A sovereign balm for every wound,
A cordial for our fears.

Buried in sorrow and in sin,
At hell's dark door we lay;
But we arise, by grace divine,
To see a heavenly day.

Salvation! let the echo fly
The spacious earth around,
While all the armies of the sky
Conspire to raise the sound.

372   " A greater than Jonas is here."   JUNE 24.—MORNING.

[*Or December 15.*]

JONAH III.

AND the word of the LORD came unto Jonah the second time, saying,

2 Arise, go unto Nineveh, that great city, and preach unto it the preaching that I bid thee. (*This was a gracious sign that the Lord had forgiven his servant's disobedience, but it shewed also that the Lord would not alter his purpose to please the whim of man, nor change his servant's work because he quarrelled with it. Jonah was forced to go to Nineveh after all ; his rebellion had been of no avail.*)

3 So Jonah arose, and went unto Nineveh, according to the word of the LORD. (*This time there was no delay and no demur. Five hundred miles was not too long a march, nor were rivers and deserts any impediment ; the prophet had learned obedience by the things which he had suffered.*) Now Nineveh was an exceeding great city of three days' journey.

4 And Jonah began to enter into the city a day's journey, and he cried, and said, Yet forty days, and Nineveh shall be overthrown.

How startled must the people have been as they saw the strange, stern man, and heard his monotonous warning cry. The news ran through the city ; and the people crowded to hear the terrible voice which declared to them their speedy doom.

5 ¶ So the people of Nineveh believed God, and proclaimed a fast, and put on sackcloth, from the greatest of them even to the least of them.

6 For word came unto the king of Nineveh, and he arose from his throne, and he laid his robe from him, and covered *him* with sackcloth, and sat in ashes.

7 And he caused *it* to be proclaimed and published through Nineveh by the decree of the king and his nobles, saying, Let neither man nor beast, herd nor flock, taste any thing : let them not feed, nor drink water :

8 But let man and beast be covered with sackcloth, and cry mightily unto God : yea, let them turn every one from his evil way, and from the violence that *is* in their hands.

9 Who can tell *if* God will turn and repent, and turn away from his fierce anger, that we perish not ? (*The kings of Assyria assumed the air of gods, and were adored by their people, yet the great potentate then reigning reverenced the*

divine message. *It might have been concluded that he would strike off the prophet's head, but a sacred awe withheld him, and a sense of terror led him to become a suppliant. Faint was the hope of respite for the doomed capital, yet on that hope they ventured to try the effect of repentance. " Who can tell ?" was all they could say, and the fierce messenger who warned them gave them no encouragement. Shall these men rise up in judgment against us ? They had only the law, and yet sought mercy ; shall we remain impenitent when the gospel is daily preached to us ? They had neither promise nor invitation, we have both in abundance ; shall we refuse to come to that banquet of grace to which they so eagerly pressed ? They made even their children and their cattle feel the bitterness of sin and repentance, and shall we make mirth for ourselves upon the brink of eternal perdition ? Woe unto us if it should be more tolerable for the men of Nineveh than for us at the last great day.*)

10 ¶ And God saw their works, that they turned from their evil way ; and God repented of the evil, that he had said that he would do unto them ; and he did *it* not. (*If threatenings will suffice, judgment shall be averted. God tries words before he comes to blows.*)

THE *Lord Jesus made mention of the repentance of the Ninevites when he addressed the unbelievers of his own day. Let us read the passage in—*

MATTHEW XII. 38—41.

38 Then certain of the scribes and of the Pharisees answered, saying, Master, we would see a sign from thee.

39 But he answered and said unto them, An evil and adulterous generation seeketh after a sign ; and there shall no sign be given to it, but the sign of the prophet Jonas :

40 For as Jonas was three days and three nights in the whale's belly ; so shall the Son of man be three days and three nights in the heart of the earth.

41 The men of Nineveh shall rise in judgment with this generation, and shall condemn it : because they repented at the preaching of Jonas ; and, behold, a greater than Jonas *is* here.

JONAH IV.

BUT it displeased Jonah exceedingly, and he was very angry. *(His reputation as a prophet was everything in his eyes, and how would it be maintained now that the city would be spared? Besides, he abhorred the idolatrous people, and thought it absurd to spare them : they were in his eyes only fit to be destroyed.)*

2 And he prayed unto the LORD, and said, I pray thee, O LORD, *was* not this my saying, when I was yet in my country ? Therefore I fled before unto Tarshish : for I knew that thou *art* a gracious God, and merciful, slow to anger, and of great kindness, and repentest thee of the evil.

3 Therefore now, O LORD, take, I beseech thee, my life from me ; for *it is* better for me to die than to live. *(We cannot love Jonah when we see him so peevish ; but we must remember that he is the writer of this description of himself, and therefore we must admire the fidelity with which he paints his own portrait in the blackest colours, and offers no excuse or extenuation for his moroseness. He was a man of stern integrity, and extremely sensitive as to his personal character for truthfulness, and therefore fearing that his repute would be marred, he fell into a grievously bad temper, and sulked as a good man should not have done.)*

4 ¶ Then said the LORD, Doest thou well to be angry ? *(A question which we may reprovingly ask of ourselves if we are soon angry, often angry, long angry, or bitterly angry. How could it be right of Jonah to be angry because a million lives were spared ?)*

5 So Jonah went out of the city, and sat on the east side of the city, and there made him a booth, and sat under it in the shadow, till he might see what would become of the city.

Possibly he still expected to see his prophecy fulfilled ; at least he lingered with a forlorn and horrible hope that, to save his reputation, a great city would be destroyed.

6 And the LORD God prepared a gourd, and made *it* to come up over Jonah, that it might be a shadow over his head, to deliver him from his grief. So Jonah was exceeding glad of the gourd. *(Being sensitive and nervous, the great heat distressed him, and the cool shade which the leafy shelter yielded him was a great comfort to him.)*

7 But God prepared a worm when the morning rose the next day, and it smote the gourd that it withered. *(The God who prepared a whale prepared a gourd, and then prepared a worm to destroy it, and all with the view of preparing Jonah to submit to the divine will.)*

8 And it came to pass, when the sun did arise, that God prepared a vehement east wind ; and the sun beat upon the head of Jonah, that he fainted, and wished in himself to die, and said, *It is* better for me to die than to live.

How like to Elijah is Jonah in his weak points. One inclines to believe the tradition which makes him to have been the son of the widow of Sarepta and the scholar of Elijah.

9 And God said to Jonah, Doest thou well to be angry for the gourd ? And he said, I do well to be angry, *even* unto death. *(Poor Jonah, how bitterly he spoke even to his God ! Surely he had forgotten the whale's belly.)*

10, 11 Then said the LORD, Thou hast had pity on the gourd, for the which thou hast not laboured, neither madest it grow ; which came up in a night, and perished in a night. And should not I spare Nineveh, that great city, wherein are more than sixscore thousand persons that cannot discern between their right hand and their left hand ; and *also* much cattle ? *(This was a convincing argument, and doubtless led the prophet to shake himself clear of petulance. If he would spare a gourd, how much more should the Lord spare a vast city, with so great a host of children in it ? Perhaps some one of us may be inclined to selfishness, or may be unduly sensitive and peevish, let us resort to the Lord Jesus for instruction, and take his yoke upon us, for he is meek and lowly of heart. Never can we find rest till the demon of self-will is utterly cast out.)*

Alas ! how often I complain,
Imagine ills, and fret at pain,
E'en ask for death with peevish heart,
Because self-will is made to smart.

Now, Lord, rebuked my spirit stands,
My times are ever in thy hands,
Here all my will I now submit,
And cast my pride beneath thy feet.

374   *"They limited the Holy One of Israel."*   JUNE 25.—MORNING.

[*Or December* 17.]

WE shall now take another glimpse at the guilty kingdom of Israel. When *Jehu* had swept away the worship of Baal, he restored the worship of God under the figure of an ox, which the sacred writers always describe contemptuously as a calf. His sons after him maintained that forbidden worship which bore the same relation to the true religion as Romanism does to the faith of the gospel.

II. KINGS XIII. 1—6; 9—11; 14—19.

1, 2 In the three and twentieth year of Joash king of Judah Jehoahaz the son of Jehu began to reign over Israel in Samaria, *and reigned* seventeen years. And he did evil in the sight of the LORD, and followed the sins of Jeroboam the son of Nebat, which made Israel to sin.

3 And the anger of the LORD was kindled against Israel, and he delivered them into the hand of Hazael king of Syria, and into the hand of Ben-hadad the son of Hazael, all *their* days.

The Syrians reduced Israel so low that no army was left to defend the country, and the poor people are described as being made "like the dust by threshing." Wretched are the wages of iniquity.

4, 5 And Jehoahaz besought the LORD, and the LORD hearkened unto him : for he saw the oppression of Israel, because the king of Syria oppressed them. And the LORD gave Israel a saviour, so that they went out from under the hand of the Syrians : and the children of Israel dwelt in their tents, as beforetime.

God sometimes hears the prayers of the wicked for temporal things. Who can set bounds to his mercy? Let us seek him for spiritual blessings.

6 Nevertheless they departed not from the sins of the house of Jeroboam, who made Israel sin, *but* walked therein : and there remained the grove also in Samaria. *(Perhaps spared for its beauty, even as at this time, foolish persons reverence the images of Popery because they are works of art.)*

9 And Jehoahaz slept with his fathers; and Joash his son reigned in his stead.

10 11 In the thirty and seventh year of Joash king of Judah began Jehoash the son of Jehoahaz to reign over Israel in Samaria, *and reigned* sixteen years. And he did evil in the sight of the LORD; he departed not from all the sins of Jeroboam the son of Nebat, who made Israel sin : *but* he walked therein.

14 Now Elisha was fallen sick of his sickness whereof he died. And Joash the king of Israel came down unto him, and wept over his face, and said, O my father, my father, the chariot of Israel, and the horsemen thereof.

After sixty or seventy years of service, rest came to the faithful prophet. Good men, when they come to die, are often honoured by those who have rejected their living testimony. Bad as Joash was, he knew that Elisha was the only defence of the country, and therefore wept at the prospect of his loss.

15, 16 And Elisha said unto him, Take bow and arrows. And he took unto him bow and arrows. And he said to the king of Israel, Put thine hand upon the bow. And he put his hand *upon it:* and Elisha put his hands upon the king's hands.

17 And he said, Open the window eastward. And he opened *it.* Then Elisha said, Shoot. And he shot. And he said, The arrow of the LORD's deliverance, and the arrow of deliverance from Syria : for thou shalt smite the Syrians in Aphek, till thou have consumed *them.*

18 And he said, Take the arrows. And he took *them.* And he said unto the king of Israel, Smite upon the ground. And he smote thrice, and stayed.

19 And the man of God was wroth with him, and said, Thou shouldest have smitten five or six times; then hadst thou smitten Syria till thou hadst consumed *it* : whereas now thou shalt smite Syria *but* thrice. *(Though a dying man, Elisha was angry at unbelief, and well he might be, for God himself is angry with it, and in this case it robbed Israel of great victories, and of all hope of permanent peace. If our faith can shoot many arrows by asking great things of God, expecting great things from God, and attempting great things for God, we shall see mighty marvels; but want of faith stints the blessing; we win but thrice when we might go forth conquering and to conquer. Wretched are the men who rob themselves, and stop the flow of blessing; yet such a course of action is common with us. Lord, send us great family blessings. Convert every one of us. Bless our work for thee, and do great things for us and by us.)*

WE come back *to the history of the king-dom of Judah, and find Joash succeeded by Amaziah.*

II. CHRONICLES XXV. 1—11.

1 Amaziah *was* twenty and five years old *when* he began to reign, and he reigned twenty and nine years in Jerusalem. And his mother's name *was* Jehoaddan of Jerusalem.

2 And he did *that which was* right in the sight of the LORD, but not with a perfect heart. *Like his father Joash, he lacked steady principle, and therefore, though he began well, he turned aside in his later days and suffered for his apostacy.*

3 ¶ Now it came to pass, when the kingdom was established to him, that he slew his servants that had killed the king his father.

4 But he slew not their children, but *did* as *it is* written in the law in the book of Moses, where the LORD commanded, saying, The fathers shall not die for the children, neither shall the children die for the fathers, but every man shall die for his own sin. *(This just law was obeyed by the king, though in other eastern courts the entire families of regicides are usually put to death. It spoke well for Amaziah that he broke through prevailing customs to obey the law of the Lord.)*

5 ¶ Moreover Amaziah gathered Judah together, and made them captains over thousands, and captains over hundreds, according to the houses of *their* fathers, throughout all Judah and Benjamin : and he numbered them from twenty years old and above, and found them three hundred thousand choice *men, able* to go forth to war, that could handle spear and shield. *This was only one-fourth of the number of Jehoshaphat's army in former times, and shews how greatly the kingdom of Judah had suffered by the wars which had fallen upon it for its sins.*

6 He hired also an hundred thousand mighty men of valour out of Israel for an hundred talents of silver. *(This amount was paid to the king of Israel for leave to use his troops. It amounted to about fifty thousand pounds or ten shillings a man, a very paltry pay. The soldiers were not paid, but expected to remunerate themselves from the spoil. What must war have been when carried on upon such principles? Human*

life was a trifle, and the tenure of property was not worth a day's purchase.)

7 But there came a man of God to him, saying, O king, let not the army of Israel go with thee ; for the LORD *is* not with Israel, *to wit, with* all the children of Ephraim.

8 But if thou wilt go, do *it,* be strong for the battle : God shall make thee fall before the enemy : for God hath power to help, and to cast down. *(God would not have his people joining with idolaters ; all the help we can get from the ungodly will prove to be hindrance.)*

9 And Amaziah said to the man of God, But what shall we do for the hundred talents which I have given to the army of Israel ? And the man of God answered, The LORD is able to give thee much more than this. *(This text should be remembered when religion appears to involve us in present loss ; God can make it up to us in many ways, both in temporals and spirituals. We may count the cost as rigidly as we please, and we shall find that it is always best to obey the Lord.)*

10 Then Amaziah separated them, *to wit,* the army that was come to him out of Ephraim, to go home again : wherefore their anger was greatly kindled against Judah, and they returned home in great anger.

11 And Amaziah strengthened himself, and led forth his people, and went to the valley of salt, and smote of the children of Seir ten thousand. *(Alone he was victorious. If we will trust in God, and no longer lean on the arm of flesh, we shall be conquerors too ; and as for any loss which we may have to put up with for Christ's sake, we may rejoice in it.)*

Alone relying on the Lord,
  The battle we shall win ;
But if we trust an arm of flesh,
  We fall a prey to sin.

Away, then, carnal confidence,
  Let pride be overthrown ;
Jesus shall be our sole defence ;
  We rest in him alone.

II. CHRONICLES XXV. 14—24 ; 27, 28.

NOW it came to pass, after that Amaziah was come from the slaughter of the Edomites, that he brought the gods of the children of Seir, and set them up *to be* his gods, and bowed down himself before them, and burned incense unto them.

This was madness itself, for if the gods of Edom had been worth anything they would have helped their former worshippers. It is wonderful that a man can bow down before that which he carries away captive, but is it not even more strange that others should adore a piece of bread, which they afterwards eat ?

15 Wherefore the anger of the LORD was kindled against Amaziah, and he sent unto him a prophet, which said unto him, Why hast thou sought after the gods of the people, which could not deliver their own people out of thine hand ?

16 And it came to pass, as he talked with him, that *the king* said unto him, Art thou made of the king's counsel ? forbear ; why shouldest thou be smitten ? Then the prophet forbare, and said, I know that God hath determined to destroy thee, because thou hast done this, and hast not hearkened unto my counsel. *(Those who will not hear must feel ; no sign of evil is more sure than a refusal to listen to the Lord's warnings. Victory had made Amaziah proud, and pride became the mother of many sins : the lower we are in our own esteem the better.)*

17 ¶ Then Amaziah king of Judah took advice, and sent to Joash, the son of Jehoahaz, the son of Jehu, king of Israel, saying, Come, let us see one another in the face.

Probably because the hired Israelitish soldiers, whom he had dismissed, had plundered the towns and villages on their way home, Amaziah desired vengeance ; therefore in his pride he sent a haughty challenge to the king of Israel.

18 And Joash king of Israel sent to Amaziah king of Judah, saying, The thistle that *was* in Lebanon sent to the cedar that *was* in Lebanon, saying, Give thy daughter to my son to wife : and there passed by a wild beast that *was* in Lebanon, and trode down the thistle.

A proud challenge provoked a contemptuous answer. Joash as good as said, " You petty king, you are but a thistle, how dare you challenge such

a powerful monarch as I am ? You are not worthy of my arms."

19 Thou sayest, Lo, thou hast smitten the Edomites ; and thine heart lifteth thee up to boast : abide now at home ; why shouldest thou meddle to *thine* hurt, that thou shouldest fall, *even* thou, and Judah with thee ?

20 But Amaziah would not hear ; for it *came* of God, that he might deliver them into the hand *of their enemies*, because they sought after the gods of Edom.

21 So Joash the king of Israel went up ; and they saw one another in the face, *both* he and Amaziah king of Judah, at Beth-shemesh, which *belongeth* to Judah.

22 And Judah was put to the worse before Israel, and they fled every man to his tent.

23, 24 And Joash the king of Israel took Amaziah king of Judah, at Beth-shemesh, and brought him to Jerusalem, and brake down the wall of Jerusalem from the gate of Ephraim to the corner gate, four hundred cubits. And *he took* all the gold and the silver, and all the vessels that were found in the house of God with Obed-edom, and the treasures of the king's house, the hostages also, and returned to Samaria. *(One pitched battle ended the war, and left Amaziah a prisoner, the walls of Jerusalem broken down, the temple pillaged, and the nation bound down under penalties to keep the peace. Thus the vainglorious monarch was laid low. Having lost the respect of all around him, it was not long before there were plots against his crown and his life.)*

27 Now after the time that Amaziah did turn away from following the LORD they made a conspiracy against him in Jerusalem ; and he fled to Lachish : but they sent to Lachish after him, and slew him there.

28 And they brought him upon horses, and buried him with his fathers in the city of Judah.

Thus in dishonour ended the life of the unstable son of an unstable father. Many start well and bid fair for heaven, yet fall short of it because there is no vitality in their religion, it has never changed their nature. Nothing short of a new heart and a right spirit will enable a man to weather the storm and reach the haven of eternal rest.

AGAIN *we glance at the Israel kingdom, and find Jeroboam the Second reigning with his father, and afterwards succeeding him on the throne.*

II. KINGS XIV. 23—27 ; 29.

23, 24 In the fifteenth year of Amaziah the son of Joash king of Judah Jeroboam the son of Joash king of Israel began to reign in Samaria, *and reigned* forty and one years. And he did *that which was* evil in the sight of the LORD : he departed not from all the sins of Jeroboam the son of Nebat, who made Israel to sin.

25 He restored the coast of Israel from the entering of Hamath unto the sea of the plain, according to the word of the LORD God of Israel, which he spake by the hand of his servant Jonah, the son of Amittai, the prophet, which *was* of Gath-hepher.

So that Jonah had other and more pleasant work to do after he had returned from Nineveh. Those who execute difficult tasks shall have easier work ere long.

26 For the LORD saw the affliction of Israel, *that it was* very bitter : for *there was* not any shut up, nor any left, nor any helper for Israel.

27 And the LORD said not that he would blot out the name of Israel from under heaven : but he saved them by the hand of Jeroboam the son of Joash. *(God has respect to the sufferings of his people; he is a tender father, and cannot endure to look upon the miseries of his children. He stays his justice as long as ever it is consistent for him to forbear.)*

29 And Jeroboam slept with his fathers, *even* with the kings of Israel ; and Zachariah his son reigned in his stead.

DURING *this reign the herdsman prophet, Amos, delivered messages from the Lord. His utterances are short, sharp, and decisive, and are generally conveyed in rural figures, such as were suggested by his rustic occupations. His prophecy is not adorned with the graces of style, being composed of short questions, sudden exclamations, and claps of thundering threatening ; we select a specimen from—*

AMOS III. 1—8.

1 Hear this word that the LORD hath spoken against you, O children of Israel, against the whole family which I brought up from the land of Egypt, saying,

2 You only have I known of all the families of the earth : therefore I will punish you for all your iniquities. *(Others sin against less light, and therefore their fault may be winked at ; but justice grows severe where transgression is wilful and malicious.)*

3, 4 Can two walk together, except they be agreed ? Will a lion roar in the forest, when he hath no prey ? will a young lion cry out of his den, if he have taken nothing ?

God's voice is not mere noise, it means something, and woe to those who despise it. He does not threaten without cause.

5 Can a bird fall in a snare upon the earth, where no gin *is* for him ? shall *one* take up a snare from the earth, and have taken nothing at all ? *(Evil does not come to men by chance, neither will God withdraw his hand till he has wrought his design.)*

6 Shall a trumpet be blown in the city, and the people not be afraid ? shall there be evil in a city, and the LORD hath not done *it* ?

Do not think that God sends false alarms ; be sure that he is the author of the troubles which afflict the ungodly.

7 Surely the Lord GOD will do nothing, but he revealeth his secret unto his servants the prophets.

8 The lion hath roared, who will not fear ? the Lord GOD hath spoken, who can but prophesy ? *(The drift of this series of questions is to remind the people of their God, and of the certainty that he was speaking to them by his prophets and by the judgments which so sorely tried them. We need the same arousing now, and if the Lord should send it by a herdsman, we ought to be ready to receive it. God, who chooseth the things that are despised, was pleased to send a peasant to warn a king. Who was more fit to deal with a brutish people than a keeper of cattle ?)*

The Lord Jehovah speaks,
How dreadful is his voice !
But if the Saviour's face be seen,
We tremble, yet rejoice.

Almighty God, pronounce
The word of conquering grace ;
So shall the flint dissolve to tears,
And mourners seek thy face.

O UR *present lesson consists of another portion of the prophecies of Amos.*

AMOS V. 14—27.

14 Seek good, and not evil, that ye may live :
and so the LORD, the God of hosts, shall be
with you, as ye have spoken.

*You boast of his being with you, but if you
wish him to be really so, you must seek him and
follow his ways. To boast of our religious
privileges, as though God was certainly with us
because we go to a place of worship is mere vain
glory ; God dwells only with the contrite in
heart.*

15 Hate the evil, and love the good, and
establish judgment in the gate : *(where courts of
justice were held :)* it may be that the LORD God
of hosts will be gracious unto the remnant of
Joseph. *(If men have only a* may be, *they
ought to be earnest in seeking salvation ; how
much more should we be eager for eternal life
when we have sure promises and divine* shalls
and wills.*)*

16 Therefore the LORD, the God of hosts,
the Lord, saith thus ; Wailing *shall be* in all
streets ; and they shall say in all the highways,
Alas! alas! and they shall call the husbandman
to mourning, and such as are skilful of lamentation to wailing. *(The husbandman shall be so
disappointed in his harvest that he shall lament
as those do who bury the dead. Harvest home
shall be mournful as a funeral.)*

17 And in all vineyards *shall be* wailing : for
I will pass through thee, saith the LORD.

*In the place where joy was most manifest shall
be most sorrow.*

18 Woe unto you that desire the day of the
LORD ! to what end *is* it for you ? the day of
the LORD *is* darkness, and not light. *(Bitterly
will they lament that they said, " Where is the
promise of his coming ?" They will find the day
of which they spoke so jestingly to be overwhelm-
ingly terrible to them.)*

19 As if a man did flee from a lion, and a
bear met him ;· or went into the house, and
leaned his hand on the wall, and a serpent bit
him. *(It shall be to the wicked a going from
bad to worse, from danger to destruction.)*

20 *Shall* not the day of the LORD *be* darkness, and not light ? even very dark, and no
brightness in it ? *(No gleams of mercy shall
light up the day of visitation ; justice shall reign*

alone, and spread unmingled terror through the
ranks of the rebellious.)*

21 ¶ I hate, I despise your feast days, and I
will not smell in your solemn assemblies.

*Formal worship where sin is loved is detestable
to God ; he is insulted by the outward homage of
those who love the wages of iniquity.*

22 Though ye offer me burnt offerings and
your meat offerings, I will not accept *them :*
neither will I regard the peace offerings of your
fat beasts.

23 Take thou away from me the noise of thy
songs ; for I will not hear the melody of thy
viols. *(Costly offerings and the charms of melody
are not the things which God desires : holiness is
his music, and a broken heart his chosen sacrifice.)*

24 But let judgment run down as waters, and
righteousness as a mighty stream.

*This he demands, and this he will have ; and
all short of this is a mockery of him.*

25 Have ye offered unto me sacrifices and
offerings in the wilderness forty years, O house
of Israel ? *(Even at the first they were idolaters :
at the outset they could not hold on in the right
way for a single generation : idolatry was rooted
in them, nothing could wean them from it.)*

26 But ye have borne the tabernacle of your
Moloch and Chiun your images, the star of
your god, which ye made to yourselves. *(Even
Moloch, the most bloody of the idols, they adored ;
no worship was too vile for them.)*

27 Therefore will I cause you to go into
captivity beyond Damascus, saith the LORD,
whose name *is* The God of hosts.

*Idolatry, injustice, and uncleanness provoke the
Lord, and he will not suffer such evils to go unpunished. O Lord God of hosts, wash us in the
blood of Jesus ; renew us by thy Spirit, and
keep us true to thee all our days.*

Alone upon the means of grace
  Our souls must not depend ;
Theirs simply is the handmaid's place
  Of means unto an end.

Nor must we only for a while
  Put off the sins we mourn,
To flatter conscience, and beguile
  The hours till they return ;

But low in penitence must lie,
  In deed as well as word ;
And then must turn to Calvary,
  And trust our bleeding Lord.

AMOS *had many visions, and he told them to the people boldly.*

AMOS VII.

1, 2 Thus hath the Lord God shewed unto me; and, behold, he formed grasshoppers *(or locusts)* in the beginning of the shooting up of the latter growth; and, lo, *it was* the latter growth after the king's mowings. And it came to pass, *that* when they had made an end of eating the grass of the land, then I said, O Lord God, forgive, I beseech thee : by whom shall Jacob arise ? for he *is* small.

3 The Lord repented for this : It shall not be, saith the Lord. *(A famine was threatened by means of locusts, but the prophet's intercession turned aside the evil. We cannot set too much store by the earnest prayers of holy men.)*

4, 5 Thus hath the Lord God shewed unto me : and, behold, the Lord God called to contend by fire, and it devoured the great deep, and did eat up a part. Then said I, O Lord God, cease, I beseech thee : by whom shall Jacob arise ? for he *is* small.

6 The Lord repented for this : This also shall not be, saith the Lord God. *(The fire indicated devouring judgments, but the prophet again pleaded, urging the low estate of Israel, and a second time he prevailed. The prayers of the righteous are the shields of the nation.)*

7 Thus he shewed me : and, behold, the Lord stood upon a wall *made* by a plumbline, with a plumbline in his hand.

8 And the Lord said unto me, Amos, what seest thou ? And I said, A plumbline. Then said the Lord, Behold, I will set a plumbline in the midst of my people Israel : I will not again pass by them any more:

9 And the high places of Isaac shall be desolate, and the sanctuaries of Israel shall be laid waste; and I will rise against the house of Jeroboam with the sword. *(He would judge the nation as a builder tests a wall to see if it is upright, and after that he would break down all that was out of line and unfit to stand. The sinful house of Jehu had now ruled for four generations, there would be but one more king, and then like the dynasty of Ahab, it would be swept away. This prophecy was delivered at Bethel, in the very centre of idolatrous worship.)*

10, 11 Then Amaziah the priest of Beth-el sent to Jeroboam king of Israel, saying, Amos hath conspired against thee in the midst of the house of Israel : the land is not able to bear all his words. For thus Amos saith, Jeroboam shall die by the sword, and Israel shall surely be led away captive out of their own land.

This was only in part true: Amos had not said that Jeroboam would be slain. We can never hope to have our case fairly stated; our enemies will exaggerate.

12 Also Amaziah said unto Amos, O thou seer, go, flee thee away into the land of Judah, and there eat bread, and prophesy there :

13 But prophesy not again any more at Beth-el : for it *is* the king's chapel, and it *is* the king's court. *(As much as to say, " You are not wanted here. Judah is the place for those of your way of thinking; and besides, your rough manners are not fit for this courtly shrine." Little did the false priest dream of the rejoinder he would receive.)*

14, 15 Then answered Amos, and said to Amaziah, I *was* no prophet, neither *was* I a prophet's son; but I *was* an herdman, and a gatherer of sycomore fruit : And the Lord took me as I followed the flock, and the Lord said unto me, Go, prophesy unto my people Israel. *(He spoke not out of any wilful ambition, but by divine commission, and was not therefore at all likely to be silenced by the threats of men.)*

16 Now therefore hear thou the word of the Lord : Thou sayest, Prophesy not against Israel, and drop not *thy word* against the house of Isaac.

17 Therefore thus saith the Lord ; Thy wife shall be an harlot in the city, and thy sons and thy daughters shall fall by the sword, and thy land shall be divided by line ; and thou shalt die in a polluted land : and Israel shall surely go into captivity forth of his land. *(In a few years these words came true. Woe unto those who stand up against the Lord and oppose his servants.)*

O Lord, thy chosen servants bless,
   That they may faithful be ;
Thy truth upon the conscience press,
   And sinners win to thee !

In holy watchfulness and prayer,
   O keep them near thy side ;
May they with loving zeal declare,
   A Saviour crucified.

Great God! to thee I'll make
My griefs and sorrows known;
And with a humble hope
Approach thine awful throne;
Though by my sins deserving hell,
I'll not despair;—for, "Who can tell?"

Vile unbelief, begone;
Ye doubts, fly swift away;
God hath an ear to hear,
While I've a heart to pray;
If he be mine, all will be well—
For ever so; and, "Who can tell?"

Then let us not despond,
Inquiring "Who can tell?"
For in the sacred word
The question's answer'd well:
That all who come to Christ *shall* be
Saved now, and through eternity.

Since from our faith thou dost withhold
No blessing of thy grace,
Make us in confidence most bold
Thy promise to embrace.

Full many an arrow may we aim
With faith's most mighty bow,
Strengthened by thine all-conquering name,
Our sins to overthrow.

At twice or thrice let us not stay,
But the full number dare;
Since thou dost not a limit lay,
Why should our hands forbear?

Is there ambition in my heart?
Search, gracious God, and see:
Or do I act a haughty part?
Lord, I appeal to thee.

I charge my thoughts, be humble still,
And all my carriage mild,
Content, my Father, with thy will,
And quiet as a child.

The patient soul, the lowly mind,
Shall have a large reward:
Let saints be humble and resigned;
And ne'er provoke the Lord.

Jehovah hath spoken!
The nations shall hear;
From the east to the west
Shall his glory appear;
With thunders and tempest
To judgment he'll come;
And all men before him
Shall wait for their doom.

Woe, woe to the sinners!
To what shall they trust?
In the day of God's vengeance,
The holy and just!
How meet all the terrors
That flame in his path,
When the mountains shall melt
At the glance of his wrath!

O God, ere the day
Of thy mercy be past,
With trembling our souls
On that mercy we cast:
O guide us in wisdom;
For aid we implore;
Till, saved with thy people,
Thy grace we adore.

Long hath the night of sorrow reign'd;
The dawn shall bring us light:
God shall appear, and we shall rise
With gladness in his sight.

Our hearts, if God we seek to know,
Shall know him, and rejoice;
His coming like the morn shall be,
Like morning songs his voice.

So shall his presence bless our souls,
And shed a joyful light;
That hallow'd morn shall chase away
The sorrows of the night.

With broken heart and contrite sigh,
A trembling sinner, Lord, I cry;
Thy pardoning grace is rich and free;
O God! be merciful to me.

I smite upon my troubled breast,
With deep and conscious guilt oppress'd:
Christ and his cross my only plea;
O God! be merciful to me.

AGAIN *we will read in the book of Amos.*

AMOS IX.

He first foretells the sure destruction of Israel.

1 I saw the Lord standing upon the altar : *(Trampling upon the idolatrous altar at Bethel :)* and he said, Smite the lintel of the door, that the posts may shake : and cut them in the head, all of them ; *(The pillars of the temple were to be cleft asunder, and in their fall to destroy their worshippers; while those who escaped would be pursued by justice ;)* and I will slay the last of them with the sword : he that fleeth of them shall not flee away, and he that escapeth of them shall not be delivered.

2 Though they dig into hell, thence shall mine hand take them ; though they climb up to heaven, thence will I bring them down :

3 And though they hide themselves in the top of Carmel, I will search and take them out thence ; and though they be hid from my sight in the bottom of the sea, thence will I command the serpent, and he shall bite them :

4 And though they go into captivity before their enemies, thence will I command the sword, and it shall slay them : and I will set mine eyes upon them for evil, and not for good.

The passage we have just read is one of the most wonderful descriptions of omnipresence ever written, even by an inspired pen.

5 And the Lord God of hosts *is* he that toucheth the land, and it shall melt, and all that dwell therein shall mourn : and it shall rise up wholly like a flood ; and shall be drowned, as *by* the flood of Egypt.

6 *It is* he that buildeth his stories in the heaven, and hath founded his troop in the earth ; he that calleth for the waters of the sea, and poureth them out upon the face of the earth : The Lord *is* his name.

7 *Are* ye not as children of the Ethiopians unto me, O children of Israel ? saith the Lord. Have not I brought up Israel out of the land of Egypt ? and the Philistines from Caphtor, and the Syrians from Kir ?

They were thus warned not to rely upon past privileges. When they ceased to regard him as peculiarly their God, he made light of all that he had done for them, and reminded them of great things which he had done for other nations.

8 Behold, the eyes of the Lord God *are* upon the sinful kingdom, and I will destroy it from off the face of the earth ; saving that I will not utterly destroy the house of Jacob, saith the Lord.

9 For, lo, I will command, and I will sift the house of Israel among all nations, like as *corn* is sifted in a sieve, yet shall not the least grain fall upon the earth.

10 All the sinners of my people shall die by the sword, which say, The evil shall not overtake nor prevent us.

The prophecy we are now reading is not unmingled evil, it has also joyful tidings concerning glorious times to come.

11 In that day will I raise up the tabernacle of David that is fallen, and close up the breaches thereof ; and I will raise up his ruins, and I will build it as in the days of old :

12 That they may possess the remnant of Edom, and of all the heathen, which are called by my name, saith the Lord that doeth this.

David's royal house in the person of the Lord Jesus shall obtain more than its ancient glory ; not only revolted Israel, but the heathen also shall submit to his sway.

13 Behold, the days come, saith the Lord, that the plowman shall overtake the reaper, and the treader of grapes him that soweth seed ; and the mountains shall drop sweet wine, and all the hills shall melt. *(Palestine will be fruitful once again, yea, it will become the garden of the world when Jesus reigns over it.)*

14, 15 And I will bring again the captivity of my people of Israel, and they shall build the waste cities, and inhabit *them ;* and they shall plant vineyards, and drink the wine thereof : they shall also make gardens, and eat the fruit of them. And I will plant them upon their land, and they shall no more be pulled up out of their land which I have given them, saith the Lord thy God. *(Is it not clear from this that Israel will be gathered together under the reign of Jesus the Son of David, and restored to their own land ? There is a glorious future for the Lord's ancient people, and for us also who have come to trust in the great Son of David.)*

IN the days of the second Jeroboam, Hosea lived in Samaria, and prophesied concerning the sins and woes of Israel and Judah. His utterances are passionately earnest, and therefore are often abrupt and broken. In the following chapter, having described the sin of Israel, he very touchingly represents the Lord as winning her heart by his lovingkindness.

HOSEA II. 14—23.

14 ¶ Therefore, behold, I will allure her, and bring her into the wilderness, and speak comfortably unto her.

15 And I will give her her vineyards from thence, and the valley of Achor (or trouble) for a door of hope: and she shall sing there, as in the days of her youth, and as in the day when she came up out of the land of Egypt.

The time of the nation's trial would be a season of hearty reformation, and so all her former joy would come back to her.

16 And it shall be at that day, saith the LORD, that thou shalt call me Ishi (my husband); and shalt call me no more Baali (my Lord). (The name of love shall take the place of the name of law. This is the spirit of the gospel.)

17 For I will take away the names of Baalim out of her mouth, and they shall no more be remembered by their name. (It is well when the very name of sin becomes detestable, when vices once delighted in are not even named among us, as becometh saints.)

18 And in that day will I make a covenant for them with the beasts of the field, and with the fowls of heaven, and with the creeping things of the ground: and I will break the bow and the sword and the battle out of the earth, and will make them to lie down safely.

19, 20 And I will betroth thee unto me for ever; yea, I will betroth thee unto me in righteousness, and in judgment, and in loving kindness, and in mercies. I will even betroth thee unto me in faithfulness: and thou shalt know the LORD. (A superlative verse. A bottomless mine of love. It is more suitable to be enjoyed in silence than to be expounded in words. Blessed are those who are married unto the Lord, for his love admits of no change, his espousals never end in divorce.)

21 And it shall come to pass in that day, I will hear, saith the LORD, I will hear the heavens, and they shall hear the earth;

22 And the earth shall hear the corn, and the wine, and the oil; and they shall hear Jezreel.

23 And I will sow her unto me in the earth; and I will have mercy upon her that had not obtained mercy; and I will say to them which were not my people, Thou art my people; and they shall say, Thou art my God.

These are new covenant blessings,—shalls and wills of sovereign grace, full of abounding mercy. Such promises should lead the sinful to seek the Lord repentingly: let us see how Hosea exhorted the people to this.

HOSEA VI. 1—7.

COME, and let us return unto the LORD: for he hath torn, and he will heal us; he hath smitten, and he will bind us up.

2 After two days will he revive us: in the third day he will raise us up, and we shall live in his sight. (When the Holy Spirit convinces of sin he has designs of love, and intends to reveal the Saviour's healing power. God will not torment men before their time, and if now he terrifies their consciences, it is with the design of leading them to his dear Son for refuge.)

3 Then shall we know, if we follow on to know the LORD: his going forth is prepared as the morning; and he shall come unto us as the rain, as the latter and former rain unto the earth. (If we come to God, he will reveal himself to us in forgiving love.)

4 O Ephraim, what shall I do unto thee? O Judah, what shall I do unto thee? for your goodness is as a morning cloud, and as the early dew it goeth away. (Fickleness is the crying fault of many hearers; they are impressed, but the impression soon departs.)

5 Therefore have I hewed them by the prophets; I have slain them by the words of my mouth: and thy judgments are as the light that goeth forth.

6 For I desired mercy, and not sacrifice; and the knowledge of God more than burnt offerings.

7 But they like men have transgressed the covenant: there have they dealt treacherously against me. (Let not this charge lie against us, but with truly broken hearts let us seek unto the Lord of Hosts by Jesus Christ.)

HOSEA VII.

WHEN I would have healed Israel, then the iniquity of Ephraim was discovered, and the wickedness of Samaria : for they commit falsehood ; and the thief cometh in, *and* the troop of robbers spoileth without.

Notwithstanding the goodness of God, and his sending prophets to warn and instruct the people, they went on with all the vices so common to idolatrous nations ; they plundered one another, and justice was utterly perverted.

2 And they consider not in their hearts *that* I remember all their wickedness : now their own doings have beset them about ; they are before my face.

3 They make the king glad with their wickedness, and the princes with their lies.

Sad is it when the great ones of a nation are patrons of iniquity and take pleasure in falsehood. What can be expected of the common people when the princes delight in crime ?

4 They *are* all adulterers, as an oven heated by the baker, *who* ceaseth from raising after he hath kneaded the dough, until it be leavened.

They were as hot with depraved desires as a baker's oven when prepared for baking.

5 In the day of our king the princes have made *him* sick with bottles of wine ; he stretched out his hand with scorners.

Drunkenness and blasphemy were common in the court. Have we not these sins even among us in all ranks of society ?

6 For they have made ready their heart like an oven, whiles they lie in wait : their baker sleepeth all the night ; in the morning it burneth as a flaming fire. *(As the baker, though he sleeps, rises early to light his fire, so were they, even when they were quiet, meditating fresh sin.)*

7 They are all hot as an oven, and have devoured their judges ; all their kings are fallen : *there is* none among them that calleth unto me.

8 Ephraim, he hath mixed himself among the people ; Ephraim is a cake not turned.

He is neither one thing nor the other ; he professes to fear God and yet worships idols. This double-mindedness is common now-a-days, and is very distasteful to God, who says, " I would thou wert cold or hot."

9 Strangers have devoured his strength, and he knoweth *it* not : yea, gray hairs are here and there upon him, yet he knoweth not.

The nation did not know its own decays, even as sinners do not know how sad is their condition.

10 And the pride of Israel testifieth to his face : and they do not return to the LORD their God, nor seek him for all this.

Bad as they were, they yet had a high opinion of themselves, and therefore did not repent nor cry for mercy ; this is the secret cause of all impenitence and rejection of Christ.

11 Ephraim also is like a silly dove without heart : they call to Egypt, they go to Assyria.

They ran after many false trusts, and instead of relying upon God they veered from one of the great rival nations to another.

12 When they shall go, I will spread my net upon them ; I will bring them down as the fowls of the heaven ; I will chastise them, as their congregation hath heard.

13 Woe unto them ! for they have fled from me : destruction unto them ! because they have transgressed against me : though I have redeemed them, yet they have spoken lies against me. *(When God cries, " Woe," it is woe indeed. Against every impenitent sinner, such words as these are levelled. It is a dreadful thing to remain at enmity with the Lord.)*

14 And they have not cried unto me with their heart, when they howled upon their beds : they assemble themselves for corn and wine, *and* they rebel against me. *(Men can be loud enough in their cups, but they are dumb as to prayer or praise.)*

15 Though I have bound *and* strengthened their arms, yet do they imagine mischief against me. *(The strength which God gave them they used to rebel against him. Are any of us acting in this manner ?)*

16 They return, *but* not to the most High : they are like a deceitful bow : their princes shall fall by the sword for the rage of their tongue : this *shall be* their derision in the land of Egypt.

Their punishment would have an element of shame in it, for the heathen nation to which they looked for help would treat them with supreme contempt. If we will make earthly things our gods, we shall be for ever clothed with shame. Lord save us from this. Amen.

HOSEA X.

ISRAEL *is* an empty vine, he bringeth forth fruit unto himself: according to the multitude of his fruit he hath increased the altars; according to the goodness of his land they have made goodly images.

If all that we do is for ourselves and to serve our sins, we are worse than fruitless, yet many very active and busy persons deserve no better description. They work for self, and toil for sin.

2 Their heart is divided; now shall they be found faulty: he shall break down their altars, he shall spoil their images.

3 For now they shall say, We have no king, because we feared not the LORD; what then should a king do to us?

For a time Israel had no king. Jeroboam the Second was dead, and his son was kept from the throne by civil strife. A king was necessary to keep the land in order, but without God the best human arrangements are useless.

4 They have spoken words, swearing falsely in making a covenant: thus judgment springeth up as hemlock in the furrows of the field.

They made a covenant with Shalmaneser in the days of king Hoshea, and broke it basely; their justice was no better than a poisonous weed, it was rank villainy.

5 The inhabitants of Samaria shall fear because of the calves of Beth-aven: *(or the cow-calf of the house of vanity, a contemptuous description of the calf of Bethel:)* for the people thereof shall mourn over it, and the priests thereof *that* rejoiced on it, for the glory thereof, because it is departed from it.

6 It shall be also carried unto Assyria *for* a present to king Jareb *(or the strifeful king)*: Ephraim shall receive shame, and Israel shall be ashamed of his own counsel.

7 *As for* Samaria, her king is cut off as the foam upon the water. *(He floated aloft like a bubble, and was destroyed as readily.)*

8 The high places also of Aven, the sin of Israel, shall be destroyed: the thorn and the thistle shall come up on their altars; and they shall say to the mountains, Cover us; and to the hills, Fall on us.

The mountains which they selected for their confidence shall be called upon by themselves to overwhelm them, and hide them from the armies of the terrible king of Assyria.

9 O Israel, thou hast sinned from the days of Gibeah: there they stood: the battle in Gibeah against the children of iniquity did not overtake them. *(Once they fought for God against Benjamin, but from that day and onward they had been found upon the side of evil. On which side are we?)*

10 *It is* in my desire that I should chastise them; and the people shall be gathered against them, when they shall bind themselves in their two furrows. *(Though they unite like two oxen which tread the furrows, when yoked together, they shall be unable to escape.)*

11 And Ephraim *is as* an heifer *that is* taught, *and* loveth to tread out *the corn;* but I passed over upon her fair neck: I will make Ephraim to ride: *(or to carry. They had been luxuriously employed like oxen in treading out the corn, but a yoke shall be put upon them, and they shall be burdened:)* Judah shall plow, *and* Jacob shall break his clods.

12 Sow to yourselves in righteousness, reap in mercy; break up your fallow ground: for it *is* time to seek the LORD, till he come and rain righteousness upon you.

13, 14 Ye have plowed wickedness, ye have reaped iniquity; ye have eaten the fruit of lies: because thou didst trust in thy way, in the multitude of thy mighty men. Therefore shall a tumult arise among thy people, and all thy fortresses shall be spoiled, as Shalman *(or Shalmaneser)* spoiled Beth-arbel in the day of battle: the mother was dashed in pieces upon *her* children. *(The fierce Assyrian king appears to have made a terrible example of a certain city, and in such a manner would he deal with all the land of Israel if they continued in their sin.)*

15 So shall Beth-el do unto you because of your great wickedness: in a morning shall the king of Israel utterly be cut off.

Speedily would their idolatrous calf be the ruin both of themselves and their king. All this was fulfilled when the Assyrian devastated the land, carried away their king, Hoshea, imprisoned him till he died, and put a final end to the very existence of the kingdom of the ten tribes. Thus will the Lord deal out justice to those who sin against him; let us cry to him for mercy, and turn from every evil way.

HOSEA XI. 1—11.

WHEN Israel *was* a child, then I loved him, and called my son out of Egypt. *The ancient love and grace of God ought to have been a powerful motive for obedience, but it was not.*

2 *As* they called them, so they went from them : they sacrificed unto Baalim, and burned incense to graven images. *(The more they were warned, the more they sinned. Alas, how many do the same!)*

3, 4 I taught Ephraim also to go, taking them by their arms ; but they knew not that I healed them. I drew them with cords of a man, with bands of love : and I was to them as they that take off the yoke on their jaws, and I laid meat unto them. *(As the husbandman gives rest to the oxen, removes their yoke, and feeds them, so the Lord set his people free and supplied their needs, and yet they revolted from him.)*

5 ¶ He shall not return into the land of Egypt, but the Assyrian shall be his king, because they refused to return.

6 And the sword shall abide on his cities, and shall consume his branches, and devour *them,* because of their own counsels.

7 And my people are bent to backsliding from me : though they called them to the most High, none at all would exalt *him.*

8 How shall I give thee up, Ephraim ? *how* shall I deliver thee, Israel ? how shall I make thee as Admah ? *how* shall I set thee as Zeboim ? mine heart is turned within me, my repentings are kindled together.

9 I will not execute the fierceness of mine anger, I will not return to destroy Ephraim : for I *am* God, and not man ; the Holy One in the midst of thee : and I will not enter into the city. *(Mark the tender love of God, and his unwillingness to smite his people. The same conflict is in his soul still towards sinners. Such compassion should lead us to repentance.)*

10 They shall walk after the LORD : he shall roar like a lion : when he shall roar, then the children shall tremble from the west.

11 They shall tremble as a bird out of Egypt, and as a dove out of the land of Assyria : and I will place them in their houses, saith the LORD. *At last in alarm they would fly to God, and he would save them. Even if sinners come to God entirely out of fear, he will not reject them.*

HOSEA XIV.

O ISRAEL, return unto the LORD thy God ; for thou hast fallen by thine iniquity. *What gracious pleading! Can we reject it as Israel did? If we do, we shall fall as they did.*

2, 3 Take with you words, and turn to the LORD : say unto him, Take away all iniquity, and receive *us* graciously : so will we render the calves of our lips. Asshur shall not save us ; we will not ride upon horses : neither will we say any more to the work of our hands, Ye are our gods : for in thee the fatherless findeth mercy. *Words are put into the sinner's lips—will he not use them? He has only to give up his sins, and his false trusts, and God will pity him as he does children in distress. The next words are mercy itself written out in capitals.*

4 ¶ I will heal their backsliding, I will love them freely : for mine anger is turned away from him.

5 I will be as the dew unto Israel : he shall grow as the lily, and cast forth his roots as Lebanon. *(He shall be beautiful and enduring.)*

6 His branches shall spread, and his beauty shall be as the olive tree, and his smell as Lebanon. *(He shall flourish and yield shade to others, he shall be fruitful, and therefore fair to look upon, and the fame of his happiness and excellence shall fly abroad like sweet perfume.)*

7 They that dwell under his shadow shall return ; they shall revive *as* the corn, and grow as the vine : the scent thereof *shall be* as the wine of Lebanon. *(His children and dependents shall be blest also ; and shall enjoy divine favour in a manner most choice and sweet.)*

8 Ephraim *shall say,* What have I to do any more with idols? I have heard *him,* and observed him : I *am* like a green fir tree. From me is thy fruit found. *(All our goodness comes from God's grace ; we must for ever be barren without him. Let us study well these passages of sacred writ, for the next verse very solemnly calls us to devout attention.)*

9 Who *is* wise, and he shall understand these *things?* prudent, and he shall know them ? for the ways of the LORD *are* right, and the just shall walk in them : but the transgressors shall fall therein.

JUNE 30.—EVENING.

"Thou hast destroyed thyself, but in Me is thine help." [*Or December* 28.]

HOSEA XIII. 1—14.

WHEN Ephraim spake trembling, he exalted himself in Israel; but when he offended in Baal, he died. *(Humble walking before God brings honour, but proud and wilful sin is deadly. O for grace to maintain a lowly spirit before the Lord.)*

2, 3 And now they sin more and more, and have made them molten images of their silver, *and* idols according to their own understanding, all of it the work of the craftsmen: they say of them, Let the men that sacrifice kiss the calves. Therefore they shall be as the morning cloud, and as the early dew that passeth away, as the chaff *that* is driven with the whirlwind out of the floor, and as the smoke out of the chimney. *(If men will have transitory trusts they must have transitory joys. If we love gold our joy will melt; if we live for fame, which is only the breath of man, it will dissolve and be gone as a vapour. God alone provides us an enduring portion, yet how few confide in him!)*

4 Yet I *am* the LORD thy God from the land of Egypt, and thou shalt know no god but me: for *there is* no saviour beside me. *(Vainly do we look to our own works, or to false priests, Jesus alone can save.)*

5 ¶ I did know thee in the wilderness, in the land of great drought. *(The Lord has not failed us in distress. We have tried and proved his faithfulness in times of great need; let us, then, be faithful to him in return.)*

6 According to their pasture, so were they filled; they were filled, and their heart was exalted; therefore have they forgotten me. *Oh, shameful ingratitude, the more mercies they enjoyed the more wickedly they behaved! Because God remembered them in his goodness they forgot him and grew proud.*

7 Therefore I will be unto them as a lion: as a leopard by the way will I observe *them:*

8 I will meet them as a bear *that is* bereaved *of her whelps,* and will rend the caul of their heart, and there will I devour them like a lion: the wild beast shall tear them. *(Our God is just, and terrible in vengeance. Sin provokes him, and though he is slow to anger, he is mighty to punish when the time of retribution is fully come.)*

9 ¶ O Israel, thou hast destroyed thyself; but in me *is* thine help. *(This is the sum of the whole matter. Man ruins himself; God alone saves him. Damnation is all of sin; salvation is all of grace.)*

10, 11 I will be thy king: where *is any other* that may save thee in all thy cities? and thy judges of whom thou saidst, Give me a king and princes? I gave thee a king in mine anger, and took *him* away in my wrath. *(Saul was such a king: men often covet useless things.)*

12 The iniquity of Ephraim *is* bound up; his sin *is* hid. *(It is not forgotten, but laid away for future judgment, as men bind up their title deeds and place them in a secure place. All our sins will be remembered at the last great day, unless they are blotted out by the blood of Jesus.)*

13 The sorrows of a travailing woman shall come upon him: he *is* an unwise son; for he should not stay long in *the place of* the breaking forth of children. *(He is slow to be born again, he puts off conversion. This charge can be brought against many awakened sinners. Why halt ye between two opinions? Death and judgment do not tarry. Hasten, O sinner, to be wise.)*

14 I will ransom them from the power of the grave; I will redeem them from death: O death, I will be thy plagues; O grave, I will be thy destruction: repentance shall be hid from mine eyes. *(Though first to be applied to the national resurrection of Israel, this passage has a grand outlook towards the resurrection of the dead. Believing in this promise, we hate our sins, and knowing that they are pardoned, we meet death with joy, expecting to rise from the grave in the glorious image of the Redeemer.)*

I knew thee when the world was waste,
　And thou alone wast fair,
On thee my heart its fondness placed,
　My soul reposed its care.

Can I forget the cloudy days
　Of grief in which we met,
When in life's lone and friendless ways
　Thou didst not me forget.

Can I forget those words of love,
　So tender and so true,
With which, when thou must needs reprove,
　Thou didst so comfort too?

O never, never let me choose
　Freedom from thy control;
O never, never let me lose
　Thy sunshine from my soul.

IT is most probable that while Amos and Hosea were messengers from the Lord to Israel, Joel was prophesying in Judah. One of his most memorable prophecies relates to a plague of locusts which fell upon the land.

JOEL II. 1—14.

1 Blow ye the trumpet in Zion, and sound an alarm in my holy mountain : let all the inhabitants of the land tremble : for the day of the LORD cometh, for it is nigh at hand ;

It was such a visitation as might well create alarm, and call to humiliation and prayer.

2 A day of darkness and of gloominess, a day of clouds and of thick darkness, as the morning spread upon the mountains : a great people and a strong ; there hath not been ever the like, neither shall be any more after it, *even* to the years of many generations.

The locusts were so many that they clouded the sun and caused darkness at midday. Vast flights of these destructive creatures are not unusual in our day, but the prophet's description relates to some special and unusual plague.

3 A fire devoureth before them ; and behind them a flame burneth : the land is as the garden of Eden before them, and behind them a desolate wilderness ; yea, and nothing shall escape them. *(It is so ; locusts devour every green thing as completely as a raging fire.)*

4, 5 The appearance of them is as the appearance of horses ; and as horsemen, so shall they run. Like the noise of chariots on the tops of mountains shall they leap, like the noise of a flame of fire that devoureth the stubble, as a strong people set in battle array. *(The Italians call a locust* cavalette, *or little horse : they are for number, speed, order, and noise, very similar to troops of cavalry.)*

6 Before their face the people shall be much pained : all faces shall gather blackness.

7 They shall run like mighty men ; they shall climb the wall like men of war ; and they shall march every one on his ways, and they shall not break their ranks :

8 Neither shall one thrust another ; they shall walk every one in his path : and *when* they fall upon the sword, they shall not be wounded.

The order with which they march is wonderful to the last degree ; no disciplined troops could possibly preserve their ranks more accurately.

9 They shall run to and fro in the city ; they shall run upon the wall, they shall climb up upon the houses ; they shall enter in at the windows like a thief.

Nothing can turn them aside ; their march is onward, over walls and fences, hills and valleys.

10 The earth shall quake before them ; the heavens shall tremble : the sun and the moon shall be dark, and the stars shall withdraw their shining : *(Such is the misery of the poor people who see the fruit of their fields devoured before their eyes by a remorseless and irresistible foe, that for them all things are full of terror, and they feel as if the end of the world were come.)*

11 And the LORD shall utter his voice before his army : for his camp is very great : for *he is* strong that executeth his word : for the day of the LORD *is* great and very terrible ; and who can abide it ? *(Though unheard of human ear, their Commander-in-chief, even the Lord of Hosts, makes his voice to be heard by the dense battalions of devouring locusts, so that at his bidding they push forward in their awful course. Well might the prophet say, " Who can abide it ?")*

12, 13 ¶ Therefore, also now, saith the LORD, turn ye *even* to me with all your heart, and with fasting, and with weeping, and with mourning : And rend your heart, and not your garments, and turn unto the LORD your God : for he *is* gracious and merciful, slow to anger, and of great kindness, and repenteth him of the evil.

14 Who knoweth *if* he will return and repent, and leave a blessing behind him ; *even* a meat offering and a drink offering unto the LORD your God ? *(If anything could avert so terrible a calamity, prayer would do it. True repentance is the only way to remove the rod from any people. O Lord, help us to cast out our sins, lest they compel thee to chasten us with sore affliction. Accept us, for our hope is in thy Son.)*

When distractions, fear and doubt,
Come from all the world without,
And like locusts plague the soul,
Lord, do thou their power control.

When the clouds of grief and care,
Darken down into despair,
When by grief we are laid low,
Then thy gracious kindness show.

IN *returning to the history of Judah, we are glad to find that a good king was placed upon the throne, and ruled for many years.*

II. CHRONICLES XXVI. 1 ; 4—8 ; 16—21.

1, 4 Then all the people of Judah took Uzziah, who *was* sixteen years old, and made him king in the room of his father Amaziah. And he did right in the sight of the LORD, according to all that his father Amaziah did. *(But he did not fall into idol-worship, as his father had so foolishly done. Children should follow their parents so far as they follow the commands of God, and no further.)*

5 And he sought God in the days of Zechariah, who had understanding in the visions of God : and as long as he sought the LORD, God made him to prosper. *(God alone can give true prosperity ; seeking the Lord with all our heart is the surest way to be blest.)*

6, 7 And he went forth and warred against the Philistines, and brake down the wall of Gath, and the wall of Jabneh, and the wall of Ashdod, and built cities about Ashdod, and among the Philistines. And God helped him against the Philistines, and against the Arabians that dwelt in Gur-baal, and the Mehunims.

8 And the Ammonites gave gifts to Uzziah : and his name spread abroad *even* to the entering in of Egypt ; for he strengthened *himself* exceedingly. *(He was a skilful man, and a great inventor of engines of war, besides being an excellent cultivator of the soil. The country rose to a high pitch of prosperity under his rule.)*

16 But when he was strong, his heart was lifted up to *his* destruction : *(What a warning is this to prosperous Christians. When we are weak we lean upon the Lord and are safe, but when we are strong the temptation is to become self-important, and then a fall is near. More fall among the strong than among the timid and trembling. His offence was intrusion into the priestly office :)* for he transgressed against the LORD his God, and went into the temple of the LORD to burn incense upon the altar of incense.

Most of the heathen kings united royalty and priesthood in their own persons, and Uzziah, no doubt, judged that it would strengthen his influence if he did the same, but in this he acted wickedly, and angered the Lord.

17, 18 And Azariah the priest went in after him, and with him fourscore priests of the LORD, *that were* valiant men : And they withstood Uzziah the king, and said unto him, *It appertaineth* not unto thee, Uzziah, to burn incense unto the LORD, but to the priests the sons of Aaron, that are consecrated to burn incense : go out of the sanctuary ; for thou hast trespassed ; neither *shall it be* for thine honour from the LORD God. *(They boldly told the intruding king that his act was not right, and was not safe. Korah and his accomplices paid dear for offering incense, which was the work of the priests only, and the king would not find it to his honour to usurp their office. The incense of our prayers and praises must come up before the Lord from the hand of Jesus, our great High-priest, or it can never be accepted by the Lord.)*

19 Then Uzziah was wroth, and *had* a censer in his hand to burn incense : and while he was wroth with the priests, the leprosy even rose up in his forehead before the priests in the house of the LORD, from beside the incense altar.

The Lord ended the controversy once for all ; the king would not listen to the Lord's word, and therefore was made to feel his hand. Woe unto those who pretend to offer a sacrifice for sin, now that the one offering of Jesus has put away transgression ; the leprosy of heresy is on their brows even now ; let us shun their company.

20 And Azariah the chief priest, and all the priests, looked upon him, and, behold, he *was* leprous in his forehead, and they thrust him out from thence ; yea, himself hasted also to go out, because the LORD had smitten him.

21 And Uzziah the king was a leper unto the day of his death, and dwelt in a several house, *being* a leper ; for he was cut off from the house of the LORD : and Jotham his son *was* over the king's house, judging the people of the land. *(His punishment was merciful, for it gave him long space for repentance, but it was a suitable rebuke for his sin. He was proud, and the disease humbled him ; he invaded the office of the priests, and became subject to their inspection, for they had the care of lepers ; he coveted a dignity to which he had no right, and so lost the monarchy which was lawfully his. Let us reverence the priesthood of our Lord Jesus, and never dream of intruding into it.)*

UZZIAH *lived for some time shut up as a leper. The year in which he died was the occasion of one of Isaiah's visions: that eminent prophet exercised his ministry in this and the next three reigns.*

ISAIAH VI.

1 In the year that king Uzziah died I saw also the Lord sitting upon a throne, high and lifted up, and his train filled the temple. *(Isaiah saw the Messiah, as we learn from John xii. 41. His glorious apparel and magnificent state filled the Holy of Holies with splendour.)*

2 Above it stood the seraphims : *(Those holy ministers stood around the throne of glory, adoring, and waiting as servants to obey their King's behests:)* each one had six wings ; with twain he covered his face, and with twain he covered his feet, and with twain he did fly.

Milton thus poetically describes a seraph :—

> " *Six wings he wore to shade*
> *His lineaments divine ; the pair that clad*
> *Each shoulder broad, came mantling o'er his breast*
> *With regal ornament ; the middle pair*
> *Girt like a starry zone his waist, and round*
> *Skirted his loins and thighs with downy gold,*
> *And colours dipt in heaven ; the third his feet*
> *Shadowed from either heel with feathered mail,*
> *Sky tinctured grain.*"

3 4, And one cried unto another, and said, Holy, holy, holy, *is* the LORD of hosts : the whole earth *is* full of his glory. And the posts of the door moved at the voice of him that cried, and the house was filled with smoke.

5 ¶ Then said I, Woe *is* me! for I am undone; because I *am* a man of unclean lips, and I dwell in the midst of a people of unclean lips : for mine eyes have seen the King, the LORD of hosts. *(A sense of the Lord's presence humbles even the best of men : we cannot see the glory of God and continue to glory in ourselves. Humility is an indispensable preparation for the Lord's work. Isaiah must first feel his sinfulness before the live coal can touch his lips.)*

6 Then flew one of the seraphims unto me, having a live coal in his hand, *which* he had taken with the tongs from off the altar :

7 And he laid *it* upon my mouth, and said, Lo, this hath touched thy lips ; and thine iniquity is taken away, and thy sin purged.

8 Also I heard the voice of the Lord, saying, Whom shall I send, and who will go for us ? Then said I, Here *am* I ; send me.

When a man's lips have felt the sacrificial flame, he is bold to go upon the Lord's errands, though it were to the world's end.

9, 10 ¶ And he said, Go, and tell this people, Hear ye indeed, but understand not ; and see ye indeed, but perceive not. Make the heart of this people fat, and make their ears heavy, and shut their eyes ; lest they see with their eyes, and hear with their ears, and understand with their heart, and convert, and be healed.

11, 12 Then said I, Lord, how long ? And he answered, Until the cities be wasted without inhabitant, and the houses without man, and the land be utterly desolate. And the LORD have removed men far away, and *there be* a great forsaking in the midst of the land. *(On account of their sin the people could find no blessing in the ministry, but even the voice of God was a savour of death unto death unto them.)*

13 ¶ But yet in it *shall be* a tenth, and *it* shall return, and shall be eaten : as a teil tree, and as an oak, whose substance *is* in them, when they cast *their leaves : so* the holy seed *shall be* the substance thereof. *(As a tree has life in it when the leaves are gone, so would the nation still live on, to be in due season restored to its former glory.)*

THE *evangelist John applied these words of Isaiah to the times of our Lord, and in that connection they were solemnly fulfilled.*

JOHN XII. 37—41.

37, 38 But though he had done so many miracles before them, yet they believed not on him : That the saying of Esaias the prophet might be fulfilled, which he spake, Lord, who hath believed our report ? and to whom hath the arm of the Lord been revealed ?

39, 40, 41 Therefore they could not believe, because that Esaias said again, He hath blinded their eyes, and hardened their heart ; that they should not see with *their* eyes, nor understand with *their* heart, and be converted, and I should heal them. These things said Esaias, when he saw his glory, and spake of him.

Sovereign Ruler, Lord of all,
Prostrate at thy feet I fall ;
Hear, oh, hear my earnest cry ;
Frown not, lest I faint and die.

Vilest of the sons of men,
Chief of sinners I have been :
Oft have sinn'd before thy face,
Trampled on thy richest grace.

Justly might thy fatal dart
Pierce this bleeding, broken heart;
Justly might thy angry breath
Blast me in eternal death.

Jesus, save my dying soul ;
Make my broken spirit whole ;
Humbled in the dust I lie ;
Saviour, leave me not to die.

Sinful, sighing to be blest,
Bound, and longing to be free,
Weary, waiting for my rest ;
" God be merciful to me ! "

Holiness ! I've none to plead,
Sinfulness in all I see ;
I can only bring my need ;
" God be merciful to me ! "

Broken heart, and downcast eyes,
Dare not lift themselves to thee,
Yet thou canst interpret sighs ;
" God be merciful to me ! "

There is One beside the throne,
And my only hope and plea
Are in him, and him alone ;
" God be merciful to me ! "

Thou art my refuge, Lord, I flee
From other safeguard unto thee ;
Now by thy hand of power divine,
Sustain this feeble soul of mine.

Uphold my feet, so quick to fail,
And in thy strength I shall prevail ;
Go thou before me, lead me on,
Until the heavenly home be won.

Thy wisdom every day I prove,
And learn thy endless, quenchless love !
By grace upheld, by grace restored,
Thou knowest that I love thee, Lord.

A good High Priest is come,
Supplying Aaron's place,
And, taking up his room,
Dispensing life and grace.
Woe to the man who dares pretend
His sacrifice with Christ's to blend.

He died ; but lives again,
And by the altar stands ;
There shows how he was slain,
Opening his piercèd hands.
Our Priest abides ; 'tis he alone
Who can for guilty man atone.

I other priests disclaim,
And laws, and offerings too,
None but the bleeding Lamb,
The mighty work can do.
Away, ye base pretenders all,
Ere yet the vengeance on you fall !

O thou who didst the temple fill
With thy resplendent, awful train,
The glory of thine Israel still,
Appear in those bright robes again.

Thrice holy, holy, holy Lord,
Thou art by seraphim adored ;
And, while they stand around thy seat,
They veil their faces and their feet.

Lord, how can sinful lips proclaim
The honours of so great a name !
O for thine altar's glowing coal
To touch my lips, to fire my soul !

Then, if a messenger thou ask,
A labourer for the hardest task,
Through all my weakness and my fear,
Love shall reply, " Thy servant's here."

I will praise thee every day !
Now thine anger's turn'd away,
Comfortable thoughts arise
From the bleeding sacrifice.

Jesus is become at length,
My salvation and my strength ;
And his praises shall prolong,
While I live, my pleasant song.

Raise again the joyful sound,
Let the nations roll it round !
Zion shout, for this is he,
God the Saviour dwells in thee.

UZZIAH, *king of Judah, who became a leper, was succeeded by his son Jotham.*

II. CHRONICLES XXVII.

1 Jotham *was* twenty and five years old when he began to reign, and he reigned sixteen years in Jerusalem. His mother's name also *was* Jerushah, the daughter of Zadok.

2 And he did *that which was* right in the sight of the LORD, according to all that his father Uzziah did : howbeit he entered not into the temple of the LORD. *(We should imitate our parents' excellencies, but not their failings. It is well that Jotham took warning from his father's sin.)* And the people did yet corruptly. *(They would have followed the king had he been a worshipper of idols, but they would not go with him in adoring the Lord. There was even a conspiracy hatched against him to set up the son of Tabeal, but it came to nothing.)*

3 He built the high gate of the house of the LORD, and on the wall of Ophel he built much.

4 Moreover he built cities in the mountains of Judah, and in the forests he built castles and towers. *(He did what he could for the material benefit of the people, greatly mourning that they were so indifferent to their own spiritual good.)*

5 He fought also with the king of the Ammonites, and prevailed against them. And the children of Ammon gave him the same year an hundred talents of silver, and ten thousand measures of wheat, and ten thousand of barley. So much did the children of Ammon pay unto him, both the second year, and the third.

For one good man's sake God blessed the whole nation. It is sad to think that this did not lead them to follow the example of their pious king; yet how many children there are with godly parents who nevertheless continue to sin against the Lord, and grieve their father's heart. May there never be any such in this house; and if there be, may the Lord Jesus look upon them and grant them repentance unto life.

6 So Jotham became mighty, because he prepared his ways before the LORD his God.

He was careful and thoughtful in his conduct, and fearful lest he should sin by inadvertence, and therefore he became strong. There is a great deal of meaning in the expression " he prepared his ways before the Lord his God;" it implies that he did not follow men, or seek their approbation, but lived as in the immediate presence of the Lord, and desired above all things to please him.

7 Now the rest of the acts of Jotham, and all his wars, and his ways, lo, they *are* written in the book of the kings of Israel and Judah.

8, 9 He was five and twenty years old when he began to reign, and reigned sixteen years in Jerusalem. And Jotham slept with his fathers, and they buried him in the city of David : and Ahaz his son reigned in his stead.

Thus passed away one of the six best kings of Judah; happy nation to have known such a ruler.

It may be for our instruction to notice that, during the long reign of Uzziah over Judah, the unhappy kingdom of Israel had been a scene of strife. For many years no king sat upon the throne, and when at last Zechariah, the fourth descendant from Jehu, assumed the crown, his reign was ended in six months by Shallum, who killed him in the presence of the people. Shallum also destroyed all the members of the family of Jehu, and thus the prophetic threatening was fulfilled. Shallum, the murderer, enjoyed the throne for only one month, and was in his turn murdered by Menahem, who for the next ten years oppressed the people, who were wholly given to their idols. At this period we hear, for the first time, of an Assyrian invasion, and Menahem purchased peace by paying a heavy subsidy and yielding a number of his subjects as captives. At Menahem's death his son Pekahiah mounted the guilty throne, to pursue the same course of sin as his predecessors, but in the brief space of two years his reign was over, for Pekah, one of his captains, assassinated him, and began to reign at about the same period, or a little before Jotham; so that Pekah, as king of Israel, was contemporary with Jotham and Ahaz kings of Judah. Do not feel troubled by these details, for nothing in God's word is trivial. Those who love the Lord love every letter of his Book. The prophecy of Hosea will lose much of its interest to us if we are not acquainted with the times in which he lived. The histories of Scripture are as much inspired as the Psalms or the Gospels, and it is a shame for Christians not to be well acquainted with them.

IN the days of Jotham, as in the reign of Uzziah, the great prophet Isaiah was pouring forth his eloquent utterances. He is the great gospel seer, who spake more of Jesus Christ than all the rest. We will now read three of his prophecies, which he gave forth in the form of songs. The first song describes Israel under the figure of a vineyard, and was, from its form and beauty, well fitted to win the attention of the people.

ISAIAH V. 1—7.

1 Now will I sing to my wellbeloved a song of my beloved touching his vineyard. My wellbeloved hath a vineyard in a very fruitful hill:

2 And he fenced it, and gathered out the stones thereof, and planted it with the choicest vine, and built a tower in the midst of it, and also made a winepress therein: and he looked that it should bring forth grapes, and it brought forth wild grapes.

3 And now, O inhabitants of Jerusalem, and men of Judah, judge, I pray you, betwixt me and my vineyard.

4 What could have been done more to my vineyard, that I have not done in it? wherefore, when I looked that it should bring forth grapes, brought it forth wild grapes?

5 And now go to; I will tell you what I will do to my vineyard: I will take away the hedge thereof, and it shall be eaten up; and break down the wall thereof, and it shall be trodden down:

6 And I will lay it waste: it shall not be pruned, nor digged; but there shall come up briers and thorns: I will also command the clouds that they rain no rain upon it.

7 For the vineyard of the Lord of hosts is the house of Israel, and the men of Judah his pleasant plant: and he looked for judgment, but behold oppression; for righteousness, but behold a cry.

How much is our condition like that of Israel and Judah! What more could God have done for us? We have the Bible and the ministry of the gospel: as a family we are a garden walled around, and our country is the fruitful field of true religion. What fruit are we yielding? If we are barren, what must we expect? Judgment is always in proportion to privilege misused. May grace be upon us all, that we may bear much fruit unto the Lord our God.

SPEAKING of the coming of the Lord Jesus, the prophet says:—

ISAIAH XII.

1, 2 And in that day thou shalt say, O Lord, I will praise thee: though thou wast angry with me, thine anger is turned away, and thou comfortedst me. Behold, God is my salvation; I will trust, and not be afraid: for the Lord JEHOVAH is my strength and my song; he also is become my salvation.

3 Therefore with joy shall ye draw water out of the wells of salvation. (What a sweet gospel song. None can sing it but those whose sins have been washed away in the blood of Jesus, and to them it is a rapturous hymn. They are no longer afraid to believe the promises, and to go to the Lord for blessings: the wells are free to the citizens of Zion, and they draw water exultingly.)

4 And in that day shall ye say, Praise the Lord, call upon his name, declare his doings among the people, make mention that his name is exalted.

5 Sing unto the Lord; for he hath done excellent things: this is known in all the earth.

6 Cry out and shout, thou inhabitant of Zion: for great is the Holy One of Israel in the midst of thee. (It is the delight of saved souls to magnify the Lord; they cannot contain their joy, they shout as those who divide the spoil.)

WHEN God has rebuked his people's enemies, another song shall be on their lips.

ISAIAH XXVI. 1—4.

1 In that day shall this song be sung in the land of Judah; We have a strong city; salvation will God appoint for walls and bulwarks.

2 Open ye the gates, that the righteous nation which keepeth the truth may enter in.

3 Thou wilt keep him in perfect peace, whose mind is stayed on thee: because he trusteth in thee.

4 Trust ye in the Lord for ever: for in the Lord JEHOVAH is everlasting strength.

Happy are those who are protected and kept in peace by their Omnipotent God. Is there one in our house who does not trust in the Lord? Let us pray that all our minds may be stayed on God.

II. KINGS XVI. 1—4.

IN the seventeenth year of Pekah the son of Remaliah, *(king of Israel,)* Ahaz the son of Jotham king of Judah began to reign.

He was the bad son of a good father, and under him the kingdom of Judah relapsed into the sad state out of which Jotham had raised it.

2, 3 Twenty years old *was* Ahaz when he began to reign, and reigned sixteen years in Jerusalem, and did not right in the sight of the LORD his God, like David his father. But he walked in the way of the kings of Israel, yea, and made his son to pass through the fire, according to the abominations of the heathen, whom the LORD cast out from before the children of Israel.

4 And he sacrificed and burnt incense in the high places, and on the hills, and under every green tree. *(He was not satisfied with the ordinary idolatries, but sought out the vilest forms of superstition, and practised the unnatural and cruel rites peculiar to the demon Moloch. Old historians assert that the image of Moloch was of brass, and when heated red-hot, children were placed in its arms to be consumed. What shame that the ruler of the chosen people should be guilty of so terrible a crime as to expose his own son to such a death! We may well blush for human nature: an old divine once quaintly said that it was half beast and half devil, and he was very near the mark.)*

IN such times as those of Ahaz the word of the Lord, as contained in the first chapter of Isaiah, was greatly needed.

ISAIAH I. 2—9.

2 Hear, O heavens, and give ear, O earth: for the LORD hath spoken, I have nourished and brought up children, and they have rebelled against me. *(It is not the heathen nor strangers that the Lord here upbraids, but his own highly-favoured people, his lovingly-nurtured children, in whom sin was doubly sinful.)*

3 The ox knoweth his owner, and the ass his master's crib: *but* Israel doth not know, my people doth not consider. *(Men are more brutish than the beasts. They receive all at the Lord's hands, and then utterly forget him. Alas, Lord God, that thou shouldst thus be treated!)*

4 Ah sinful nation, a people laden with iniquity, a seed of evildoers, children that are corrupters : they have forsaken the LORD, they have provoked the Holy One of Israel unto anger, they are gone away backward.

5, 6 ¶ Why should ye be stricken any more ? ye will revolt more and more : the whole head is sick, and the whole heart faint. From the sole of the foot even unto the head *there is* no soundness in it ; *but* wounds, and bruises, and putrifying sores : they have not been closed, neither bound up, neither mollified with ointment. *(During the reign of Ahaz the troubles of the people were extreme, as we shall see in succeeding readings, but they were none the better for being afflicted. The nation was like a man who had been beaten till there remained no place for another stripe; yet still they loved their idols and their sins.)*

7, 8 Your country *is* desolate, your cities *are* burned with fire : your land, strangers devour it in your presence, and *it is* desolate, as overthrown by strangers. And the daughter of Zion is left as a cottage in a vineyard, as a lodge in a garden of cucumbers, as a besieged city.

Jerusalem stood alone, and in great dilapidation, like the temporary hut which the keepers of a vineyard put up hurriedly to shield them from the sun. Their palace city was like a hovel, and where once cities clustered in every vale and hung on every hillside, all was desolation.

9 Except the LORD of hosts had left unto us a very small remnant, we should have been as Sodom, *and* we should have been like unto Gomorrah. *(So wicked were they, that, but for the faithful few, God would have cursed the land as he did the cities of the plain. Oh, wretched plight of a favoured people. The Lord save our country from the same backsliding!)*

Oh, shall I never feel
The meltings of thy love ?
Am I of such hell-harden'd steel
That mercy cannot move ?

Chasten'd full sore I am,
And bruised in every part,
But judgments fail to break me down
And subjugate my heart.

Look on me, Lord of love !
O turn thy gracious eyes !
Then all my soul to penitence
Shall melt with sweet surprise.

ISAIAH VII. 1—17.

AND it came to pass in the days of Ahaz the son of Jotham, king of Judah, *that* Rezin the king of Syria, and Pekah the son of Remaliah, king of Israel, went up toward Jerusalem to war against it, but could not prevail against it. *(These petty kings had troubles enough of their own from the greater powers, yet they could not be at peace, plunder was sweet to them.)*

2 And it was told the house of David, *(or the representative of David's royal house,)* saying, Syria is confederate with Ephraim. And his heart was moved, and the heart of his people, as the trees of the wood are moved with the wind. *(The object of the invasion by Syria and Israel was to put down the kings of the line of David once for all, and set up the son of Tabeal, a creature of their own. There was so much discontented feeling abroad among his own subjects that Ahaz was at his wit's end with fear.)*

3 Then said the LORD unto Isaiah, Go forth now to meet Ahaz, thou, and Shear-jashub thy son, at the end of the conduit of the upper pool in the highway of the fuller's field ; *(Ahaz was probably going there to see that water was secured for Jerusalem in case of siege, or that it was cut off from the besiegers : at the conduit the prophet was bidden to meet the king.)*

4, 5, 6 And say unto him, Take heed, and be quiet ; fear not, neither be fainthearted for the two tails of these smoking firebrands, for the fierce anger of Rezin with Syria, and of the son of Remaliah. Because Syria, Ephraim, and the son of Remaliah, have taken evil counsel against thee, saying, Let us go up against Judah, and vex it, and let us make a breach therein for us, and set a king in the midst of it, *even* the son of Tabeal :

7 Thus saith the Lord GOD, It shall not stand, neither shall it come to pass.

8 For the head of Syria *is* Damascus, and the head of Damascus *is* Rezin ; and within threescore and five years shall Ephraim be broken, that it be not a people.

9 And the head of Ephraim *is* Samaria, and the head of Samaria *is* Remaliah's son. If ye will not believe, surely ye shall not be established. *(Here was a most encouraging message, and a noble opportunity for Ahaz ; he had but to trust in the Lord, and have his kingdom established about him, but he was at that moment*

meditating an appeal to the great Assyrian monarch, and preferred to lean upon an arm of flesh rather than upon the Lord of Hosts.)

10, 11 Moreover the LORD spake again unto Ahaz, saying, Ask thee a sign of the LORD thy God ; ask it either in the depth, or in the height above.

12 But Ahaz said, I will not ask, neither will I tempt the LORD. *(This was a mere evasion. He knew that if he accepted a sign it would be fulfilled, and then he would have no excuse for distrusting the Lord, but he did not wish to commit himself to the course of action which faith would involve ; he preferred to continue his negotiations with Tiglath-pileser. How universally do men prefer the crooked road of policy to the straight path of faith ; such conduct never prospers.)*

13 And he said, Hear ye now, O house of David ; *Is it* a small thing for you to weary men, but will ye weary my God also ?

14 Therefore the Lord himself shall give you a sign ; Behold, a virgin shall conceive, and bear a son, and shall call his name Immanuel.

15 Butter and honey shall he eat, that *(or until)* he may know to refuse the evil, and choose the good.

16 For before the child shall know to refuse the evil, and choose the good, the land that thou abhorrest shall be forsaken of both her kings. *(As Ahaz had refused a sign, God appointed one far above anything he could have imagined. A son would be born of a virgin, a divine child, whose name should be " God with us." Such a child would naturally reach years of discretion very early, but in even less space than it would take for this heaven-born son to arrive at a responsible age, the two enemies of Judah would both be dethroned. Blessed be the Lord for granting to his people so glorious a sign of grace ; nothing can afford such comfort to the troubled as the fact that the Word was made flesh and dwelt among us.)*

Ahaz rejected the way of faith, and therefore the prophet added the following threatening sentence—

17 The LORD shall bring upon thee, and upon thy people, and upon thy father's house, days that have not come, from the day that Ephraim departed from Judah.

A HAZ *rejected the message of the Lord by Isaiah—*

II. CHRONICLES XXVIII. 5—15.

5 Wherefore the LORD his God delivered him into the hand of the king of Syria; and they smote him, and carried away a great multitude of them captives, and brought *them* to Damascus. And he was also delivered into the hand of the king of Israel, who smote him with a great slaughter. *(His enemies, though they could not take Jerusalem, were suffered by God to devastate the country, and so Ahaz gathered bitter fruit from trusting in man. The king of Assyria was slow in coming to his help, and meanwhile the confederate princes despoiled him.)*

6 For Pekah the son of Remaliah slew in Judah an hundred and twenty thousand in one day, *which were* all valiant men ; because they had forsaken the LORD God of their fathers.

7 And Zichri, a mighty man of Ephraim, slew Maaseiah the king's son, and Azrikam the governor of the house, and Elkanah *that was* next to the king. *(So that judgment came home to the king, and death was busy in his own household ; a due reward for passing others of his children through the fire to Moloch.)*

8 And the children of Israel carried away captive of their brethren two hundred thousand, women, sons, and daughters, and took also away much spoil from them, and brought the spoil to Samaria. *(All suffered for the common sin, for " the children gathered wood, and the fathers kindled the fire, and the women kneaded dough to make cakes for the queen of heaven, and to pour out drink-offerings unto other gods, to provoke the Lord to anger." God has ways of punishing sinners of all ages.)*

9, 10 But a prophet of the LORD was there, whose name *was* Oded : and he went out before the host that came to Samaria, *(With holy courage he confronted the host in the name of God who sent him,)* and said unto them, Behold, because the LORD God of your fathers was wroth with Judah, he hath delivered them into your hand, and ye have slain them in a rage *that* reacheth up unto heaven. And now ye purpose to keep under the children of Judah and Jerusalem for bondmen and bondwomen unto you : *but are there* not with you, even with you, sins against the LORD your God ?

A humbling question for any of us when we are severe upon others. Is there no beam in our own eye ? Why, then, are we so censorious concerning the mote in our brother's eye ?

11 Now hear me therefore, and deliver he captives again, which ye have taken captive of your brethren : for the fierce wrath of the LORD *is* upon you.

12, 13 Then certain of the heads of the children of Ephraim stood up against them that came from the war, And said unto them, Ye shall not bring in the captives hither : for whereas we have offended against the LORD *already,* ye intend to add *more* to our sins and to our trespass : for our trespass is great, and *there is* fierce wrath against Israel.

The prophet's expostulation was thus backed up by some of the leading men, and speedily had a most delightful effect. If all who hold positions of influence would support the Lord's servants by co-working with their ministry, a world of good would be effected.

14 So the armed men left the captives and the spoil before the princes and all the congregation.

15 And the men which were expressed by name rose up, and took the captives, and with the spoil clothed all that were naked among them, and arrayed them, and shod them, and gave them to eat and to drink, and anointed them, and carried all the feeble of them upon asses, and brought them to Jericho, the city of palm trees, to their brethren. *(This is one of the happiest incidents in the gloomy history of the ten tribes. It shewed a tenderness little to be expected, and makes us the more deeply regret that they had not grace enough to throw down the calves, and turn unto the Lord. Fine actions are sometimes performed by ungodly men, just as one now and then sees a lovely rose blooming upon a dunghill.)*

Lord, we all look up to thee,
As one favoured family ;
May all strife between us cease,
As we love thee, Prince of Peace.

Free from all that hearts divide,
Let us all in love abide ;
All the power of grace express,
All the heights of holiness.

II. CHRONICLES XXVIII. 16—19.

AT that time did king Ahaz send unto the kings of Assyria to help him.

17 For again the Edomites had come and smitten Judah, and carried away captives.

18 The Philistines also had invaded the cities of the low country, and of the south of Judah, and had taken *(many towns and villages)* and they dwelt there.

19 For the LORD brought Judah low because of Ahaz king of Israel ; for he made Judah naked, and transgressed sore against the LORD.

The kingdom had flourished greatly under Jotham, but the Lord who raised it up could just as easily bring it down. Those who will not be humble must be humbled. Remark the expression, —" he made Judah naked." Sin strips man of all his beauty, exposes him to contempt, and robs him of protection. The smallest powers were able to oppress Judah ; insignificant nations, which had been tributaries to it before, did with it as they pleased.

II. KINGS XVI. 7—11.

SO Ahaz sent messengers to Tiglath-pileser king of Assyria, saying, I *am* thy servant and thy son : come up, and save me out of the hand of the king of Syria, and out of the hand of the king of Israel, which rise up against me.

8, 9 And Ahaz took the silver and gold that was found in the house of the LORD, and in the treasures of the king's house, and sent *it for* a present to the king of Assyria. And the king of Assyria hearkened unto him : for the king of Assyria went up against Damascus, and took it, and carried *the people of* it captive to Kir, and slew Rezin.. *(Trust in man is an expensive business, for those we look to will be pretty sure to look to their own interests, and will not serve us unless they can serve themselves at the same time. Carnal confidences lead men to rob God: Ahaz thought nothing of stripping the temple in order to purchase the aid of his great patron, who cared nothing for him, but only for the plunder he could obtain by the war.)*

10 And king Ahaz went to Damascus to meet Tiglath-pileser king of Assyria, and saw an altar that *was* at Damascus : and king Ahaz sent to Urijah the priest the fashion of the altar, and the pattern of it, according to all the workmanship thereof.

11 And Urijah the priest built an altar according to all that king Ahaz had sent from Damascus : so Urijah the priest made *it* against king Ahaz came from Damascus. *(Foolish indeed was this to borrow the altar of a vanquished monarch. If his gods had been of any service to Benhadad, he would not have been crushed by the Assyrian. Idolaters are mad.)*

II. CHRONICLES. XXVIII. 20; 22—25; 27.

AND Tilgath-pilneser king of Assyria came unto him, and distressed him, but strengthened him not. *(He quartered his troops upon him, and impoverished his people. Ahaz now felt the curse of trusting in man.)*

22, 23 ¶ And in the time of his distress did he trespass yet more against the LORD : this *is* that king Ahaz. *(This brand is set upon him, for it is a special sin when a man grows worse under affliction.)* For he sacrificed unto the gods of Damascus, which smote him : and he said, Because the gods of the kings of Syria help them, *therefore* will I sacrifice to them, that they may help me. But they were the ruin of him, and of all Israel.

24 And Ahaz gathered together the vessels of the house of God, and cut in pieces the vessels of the house of God, and shut up the doors of the house of the LORD, and he made him altars in every corner of Jerusalem.

Those who will not worship at God's altar will set up a hundred shrines of their own ; men who will not believe the gospel will yield credence to a thousand lying superstitions.

25 And in every several city of Judah he made high places to burn incense unto other gods, and provoked to anger the LORD God of his fathers.

27 And Ahaz slept with his fathers, and they buried him in the city, *even* in Jerusalem : but they brought him not into the sepulchres of the kings of Israel : and Hezekiah his son reigned in his stead. *(He died impenitent and inglorious, and by a sort of holy censorship which appears to have been exercised over Judah's dead kings, he was denied burial in the royal tombs.)*

WHILE *Ahaz was setting up his idols the eloquent rebukes of Isaiah were remembered by the godly remnant. With what energy does he extol the Lord and denounce all attempts to set him forth by symbols.*

ISAIAH XL. 12—31.

12 Who hath measured the waters in the hollow of his hand, and meted out heaven with the span, and comprehended the dust of the earth in a measure, and weighed the mountains in scales, and the hills in a balance ?

13, 14 Who hath directed the Spirit of the LORD, or *being* his counsellor hath taught him ? With whom took he counsel, and *who* instructed him, and taught him in the path of judgment, and taught him knowledge, and shewed to him the way of understanding ?

15, 16 Behold, the nations *are* as a drop of a bucket, and are counted as the small dust of the balance : behold, he taketh up the isles as a very little thing. And Lebanon *is* not sufficient to burn, nor the beasts thereof sufficient for a burnt offering.

17 All nations before him *are* as nothing ; and they are counted to him less than nothing, and vanity.

18 To whom then will ye liken God ? or what likeness will ye compare unto him ?

To confound idolaters, the prophet describes the process of god-making, that he may shame them out of such foolish worship.

19 The workman melteth *(or carveth)* a graven image, and the goldsmith spreadeth it over with gold, and casteth silver chains. *(Think of worshipping a piece of wood plated by the goldsmith, which needs to be fastened in its place lest it fall or be stolen ! Is not this insanity ?)*

20 He that *is* so impoverished that he hath no oblation chooseth a tree *that* will not rot ; he seeketh unto him a cunning workman to prepare a graven image, *that* shall not be moved.

21 Have ye not known ? have ye not heard ? hath it not been told you from the beginning ? have ye not understood from the foundations of the earth ?

22 *It is* he that sitteth upon the circle of the earth, and the inhabitants thereof *are* as grasshoppers ; that stretcheth out the heavens as a curtain, and spreadeth them out as a tent to dwell in :

23 That bringeth the princes to nothing ; he maketh the judges of the earth as vanity.

24 Yea, they shall not be planted ; yea, they shall not be sown : yea, their stock shall not take root in the earth : and he shall also blow upon them, and they shall wither, and the whirlwind shall take them away as stubble. *(The greatest empires wither when God forbids their prospering; is he, then, like to an image of wood ?)*

25 To whom then will ye liken me, or shall I be equal ? saith the Holy One.

26 Lift up your eyes on high, and behold who hath created these *things*, that bringeth out their host by number : he calleth them all by names by the greatness of his might, for that *he is* strong in power ; not one faileth. *(Let every star rebuke the worshipper of wood and stone.)*

27 Why sayest thou, O Jacob, and speakest, O Israel, My way is hid from the LORD, and my judgment is passed over from my God ?

28 Hast thou not known ? hast thou not heard, *that* the everlasting God, the LORD, the Creator of the ends of the earth, fainteth not, neither is weary ? *there is* no searching of his understanding.

29 He giveth power to the faint ; and to *them that have* no might he increaseth strength.

30 Even the youths shall faint and be weary, and the young men shall utterly fall :

31 But they that wait upon the LORD shall renew *their* strength ; they shall mount up with wings as eagles ; they shall run, and not be weary ; *and* they shall walk, and not faint. *(Be it ours, then, to trust the unseen Lord, and never shall we fail. Glorious Lord, we believe; help thou our unbelief.)*

Fear not, nor longer be dismayed,
Lo, I, the mighty God, am nigh ;
Thou shalt, each moment, feel my aid,
If thou wilt on mine arm rely.

Why shouldst thou fear, when I am thine—
When all I am, I am for thee ?
If thou art weak, my strength divine
Is perfect in infirmity.

Without my help thou canst not stand,
But thee I will not leave alone ;
I'll hold thee up by my right hand,
Till thou shalt reach my heavenly throne.

II. KINGS XVII. 1—7; 12—18; 24—29; 33.

IN the twelfth year of Ahaz king of Judah
began Hoshea the son of Elah to reign in
Samaria over Israel nine years. And he did
evil in the sight of the LORD, but not as the
kings of Israel that were before him. *(Though
best of all the kings of Israel, he was bad; and
though bad, he was the best. God takes care to
give men their due, and say all in their favour
that can be said.)*

3, 4 ¶ Against him came up Shalmaneser king
of Assyria; and Hoshea became his servant,
and gave him presents. And the king of Assyria found conspiracy in Hoshea: for he had
sent messengers to So king of Egypt, and
brought no present to the king of Assyria, as *he
had done* year by year: therefore the king of
Assyria shut him up, and bound him in prison.
*Egypt was the rival power to Assyria, and
the petty kings were first on one side and then on
the other, as they hoped to gain advantage.*

5 ¶ Then the king of Assyria came up
throughout all the land, and went up to Samaria,
and besieged it three years.

6 In the ninth year of Hoshea the king
of Assyria took Samaria, and carried Israel
away into Assyria. *(This was the close of the
guilty career of the kingdom of Israel.)*

7 For *so* it was, that the children of Israel
had sinned against the LORD their God, which
had brought them up out of the land of Egypt,
and had feared other gods.

12 For they served idols, whereof the LORD
had said unto them, Ye shall not do this thing.

13—18 Yet the LORD testified against Israel,
and against Judah, by all the prophets, *and by*
all the seers, saying, Turn ye from your evil
ways, and keep my commandments *and* my
statutes, according to all the law which I commanded your fathers, and which I sent to you
by my servants the prophets. Notwithstanding
they would not hear, but hardened their necks,
like to the neck of their fathers, that did not
believe in the LORD their God. And they rejected his statutes, and his covenant that he
made with their fathers, and his testimonies
which he testified against them; and they
followed vanity, and became vain, and went
after the heathen that *were* round about them,
concerning whom the LORD had charged them,

that they should not do like them. And they
left all the commandments of the LORD their
God, and made them molten images, *even* two
calves, and made a grove, and worshipped all
the host of heaven, and served Baal. And they
caused their sons and their daughters to pass
through the fire, and used divination and enchantments, and sold themselves to do evil in
the sight of the LORD, to provoke him to anger.
Therefore the LORD was very angry with Israel,
and removed them out of his sight: there was
none left but the tribe of Judah only.

24 ¶ And the king of Assyria brought *men*
from Babylon, and placed *them* in the cities of
Samaria instead of the children of Israel. *(Thus
the land was peopled by a motley company collected from several conquered nations. This was
a part of the policy of the Assyrian monarch,
in order to keep the nations his slaves.)*

25 And *so* it was at the beginning of their
dwelling there, *that* they feared not the LORD:
therefore the LORD sent lions among them, which
slew *some* of them. *(Still has God some champions
left: lions prove loyal if men are traitors.)*

26 Wherefore they spake to the king of Assyria, saying, The nations which thou hast removed, and placed in the cities of Samaria,
know not the manner of the God of the land:
therefore he hath sent lions among them, and,
behold, they slay them.

27 Then the king of Assyria commanded,
saying, Carry thither one of the priests whom
ye brought from thence; and let him teach
them the manner of the God of the land.
*They imagined that there was a deity for each
country, and that Israel's god must be appeased.*

28, 29 Then one of the priests whom they had
carried away from Samaria came and dwelt in
Beth-el, and taught them how they should fear
the LORD. Howbeit every nation made gods of
their own, and put *them* in the houses of the high
places which the Samaritans had made, every
nation in their cities wherein they dwelt.

33 So they feared the LORD, and served their
own gods, after the manner of the nations whom
they carried away from thence. *(And this mon-
grel religion is fashionable still: men try to serve
God and Mammon, but in vain. God will have
no rival, he will be all or nothing. May God deliver us from this Samaritan mixture. Amen.)*

WHEN *Ahaz was dead, and Hezekiah had newly ascended the throne of Judah, we* can well conceive of Isaiah as pleading with the people to reform. *Observe the gentleness of his persuasions.*

ISAIAH XLII. 24, 25.

24, 25 Who gave Jacob for a spoil, and Israel to the robbers ? did not the LORD, he against whom we have sinned ? for they would not walk in his ways, neither were they obedient unto his law. Therefore he hath poured upon him the fury of his anger, and the strength of battle : and it hath set him on fire round about, yet he knew not; and it burned him, yet he laid *it* not to heart. *(Both Israel and Judah had suffered severely through their sins. Israel was uprooted by the Assyrian, and Judah had been deprived of its men by hundreds of thousands, till only a mere handful remained. Surely it was time to learn wisdom and give up the idols which so greatly provoked the Lord.)*

LEST *they should fear that the Lord would not be favourable to them if they returned,* the prophet poured forth a stream of gracious promises in his Master's name.

ISAIAH XLIII. 1—7; 22—28.

1 But now thus saith the LORD that created thee, O Jacob, and he that formed thee, O Israel, Fear not : for I have redeemed thee, I have called *thee* by thy name ; thou *art* mine.

2 When thou passest through the waters, I *will be* with thee ; and through the rivers, they shall not overflow thee : when thou walkest through the fire, thou shalt not be burned ; neither shall the flame kindle upon thee.

3 For I *am* the LORD thy God, the Holy One of Israel, thy Saviour : I gave Egypt *for* thy ransom, Ethiopia and Seba for thee.

4—7 Since thou wast precious in my sight, thou hast been honourable, and I have loved thee : therefore will I give men for ·thee, and people for thy life. Fear not : for I *am* with thee : I will bring thy seed from the east, and gather thee from the west. I will say to the north, Give up ; and to the south, Keep not back : bring my sons from far, and my daughters from the ends of the earth ; *Even* every one that is called by my name : for I have created him for my glory, I have formed him ; yea, I have made him.

Sin had made them captives, but eternal love had redeemed them, and in the time appointed the banished ones would return. Ought not such loving words to have touched the hearts of the men to whom they were spoken ? Do they touch ours ? They belong to all believers : do we love God for speaking so graciously to us ?

22—24 But thou hast not called upon me, O Jacob ; but thou hast been weary of me, O Israel. Thou hast not brought me the small cattle of thy burnt offerings ; neither hast thou honoured me with thy sacrifices. I have not caused thee to serve with an offering, nor wearied thee with incense. Thou hast bought me no sweet cane with money, neither hast thou filled me with the fat of thy sacrifices : but thou hast made me to serve with thy sins, thou hast wearied me with thine iniquities.

The temple had been shut up. None cared to honour the good Lord, but all were bent on provoking him. What a charge these words contain ! We naturally expect to hear sentence pronounced, and the criminals led forth to execution ; but mark and marvel at the unexpected love, the boundless grace !

25 I, *even* I, *am* he that blotteth out thy transgressions for mine own sake, and will not remember thy sins. *(This the Lord proved to be true by the blessing which he gave to his repenting people under Hezekiah. But O the depths of the mercy set forth in this verse. Jehovah himself has pardoned his people, for his own name's sake ! He has voluntarily passed an act of indemnity and oblivion which buries all their sins. Who can now despair ? Whosoever believeth on the Lord Jesus is already reconciled, and his sins are gone for ever. Glory be to God for this ! yea, glory for ever.)*

26—28 Put me in remembrance : let us plead together : declare thou, that thou mayest be justified. Thy first father hath sinned, and thy teachers have transgressed against me. Therefore I have profaned the princes of the sanctuary, and have given Jacob to the curse, and Israel to reproaches. *(Their former miseries were the fruit of their sins, and therefore they were bound to confess their transgressions, and plead the promise of pardon. Lord, we will do the same.)*

Till God in human flesh I see,
    My thoughts no comfort find ;
The holy, just, and sacred Three
    Are terrors to my mind.

But if Immanuel's face appear,
    My hope, my joy begins ;
His name forbids my slavish fear,
    His grace removes my sins.

Lord, I, too, wandered from thy ways,
    And knelt at stranger shrine :
I've called another name, " belov'd,"
    And nigh forgotten thine.

The feeble reed on which I leaned
    A sword of judgment proved,
And pierced the soul that wandered far
    From him whom still I loved.

Behold mine idols, perish'd all !
    Here mourning now I stand :
I lift my contrite heart to thee,
    And bless thy chastening hand.

We praise, we worship thee, O God ;
Thy sovereign power we sound abroad :
All nations bow before thy throne,
And thee, the great Jehovah, own.

O holy, holy, holy Lord,
Thou God of Hosts, by all adored ;
Earth and the heavens are full of thee,
Thy light, thy power, thy Majesty.

Glory to thee, O God, most high !
Father, we praise thy Majesty ;
The Son, the Spirit, we adore ;
One Godhead, blest for evermore.

" Fear not, I am with thee, oh be not dismay'd !
I, I am thy God, and will still give thee aid ;
I'll strengthen thee, help thee, and cause thee to stand,
Upheld by my righteous omnipotent hand.

" When through the deep waters I call thee to go,
The rivers of grief shall not thee overflow ;
For I will be with thee, thy troubles to bless,
And sanctify to thee thy deepest distress.

" The soul that on Jesus hath lean'd for repose,
I will not, I will not desert to his foes ;
That soul, though all hell should endeavour to shake,
I'll never, no never, no never forsake ! "

Captain of thine enlisted host,
Display thy glorious banner high ;
The summons send from coast to coast,
And call a numerous army nigh.

A solemn jubilee proclaim,
Proclaim the great sabbatic day ;
Assert the glories of thy name ;
Spoil Satan of his wish'd-for prey.

Bid, bid thy heralds publish loud
The peaceful blessings of thy reign ;
And when they speak of sprinkled blood,
The mystery to the heart explain.

Chase the usurper from his throne,
Oh ! chase him to his destined hell ;
Stout-hearted sinners overcome ;
And glorious in thy temple dwell.

Music, bring thy sweetest treasures,
    Dulcet melody and chord,
Link the notes with loveliest measures
    To the glory of the Lord.

Wing the praise from every nation,
    Sweetest instruments employ,
Raise the chorus of creation,
    Swell the universal joy.

Far away be gloom and sadness ;
    Spirits with seraphic fire,
Tongues with hymns, and hearts with gladness,
    Higher sound the chords and higher.

To the Father, to the Saviour,
    To the Spirit, source of light,
As it was, is now, and ever,
    Praise in heaven's supremest height.

II. CHRONICLES XXIX. 1—5; 15—19.

HEZEKIAH began to reign *when he was five and twenty years old*, and he reigned nine and twenty years in Jerusalem. And he did right in the sight of the LORD, according to all that David his father had done. *(It is quite a relief to get rid of Ahaz and meet with one of the best of kings. Now Judah will prosper again.)*

3 ¶ He in the first year of his reign, in the first month, opened the doors of the house of the LORD, and repaired them. *(Those who mean to do well cannot begin too early; the first year of this king's reign was full of good.)*

4, 5 And he brought in the priests and the Levites, and gathered them together into the east street, And said unto them, Hear me, ye Levites, sanctify now yourselves, and sanctify the house of the LORD God of your fathers, and carry forth the filthiness out of the holy *place*.

15 And they gathered their brethren, and sanctified themselves, and came, according to the commandment of the king, by the words of the LORD, to cleanse the house of the LORD. *(Those who are to sanctify God's house must themselves first be sanctified; we cannot cleanse others if our own hands are foul.)*

16 And the priests went into the inner part of the house of the LORD, to cleanse *it*, and brought out all the uncleanness that they found in the temple of the LORD into the court of the house of the LORD. And the Levites took *it*, to carry *it* out abroad into the brook Kidron. *(That memorable brook which our Lord crossed when he once for all sanctified his people. All the uncleanness of our holy things he has beheld; and by passing over that brook in sorrow he has put it all away.)*

17, 18 So they sanctified the house of the LORD in eight days. Then they went in to Hezekiah the king, and said, We have cleansed all the house of the LORD, and the altar of burnt offering, with all the vessels thereof, and the shewbread table, with all the vessels thereof.

19 Moreover all the vessels, which king Ahaz in his reign did cast away in his transgression, have we prepared and sanctified, and, behold, they *are* before the altar of the LORD. *(The house being purged, worship could begin; our hearts also must be purified before we can offer acceptable homage to the Lord.)*

II. CHRONICLES XXX. 1; 6—12.

AND Hezekiah sent to all Israel and Judah, and wrote letters also to Ephraim and Manasseh, that they should come to the house of the LORD God of Israel. *(Those who love God desire others to join with them in his service: true revivals create a missionary spirit. The kingdom of Israel was dissolving, and the poor people who remained could be reached by Hezekiah.)*

6—9 So the posts went with the letters from the king and his princes throughout all Israel and Judah, and according to the commandment of the king, saying, Ye children of Israel, turn again unto the LORD God of Abraham, Isaac, and Israel, and he will return to the remnant of you, that are escaped out of the hand of the kings of Assyria. And be not ye like your fathers, and like your brethren, which trespassed against the LORD God of their fathers, *who* therefore gave them up to desolation, as ye see. Now be ye not stiffnecked, as your fathers *were, but* yield yourselves unto the LORD, and enter into his sanctuary, which he hath sanctified for ever: and serve the LORD your God, that the fierceness of his wrath may turn away from you. For if ye turn again unto the LORD, your brethren and your children *shall find* compassion before them that lead them captive, so that they shall come again into this land: for the LORD your God *is* gracious and merciful, and will not turn away *his* face from you, if ye return unto him.

10 So the posts passed from city to city through the country of Ephraim and Manasseh even unto Zebulun: but they laughed them to scorn, and mocked them. *(And no wonder. Ridicule is the favourite weapon of wicked men. Let us not marvel if the world scorns us and our entreaties; it only acts after its own nature.)*

11 Nevertheless divers of Asher and Manasseh and of Zebulun humbled themselves, and came to Jerusalem. *(Thank God, there is always some good soil for the divine seed to fall upon. Let us not be weary in well-doing.)*

12 Also in Judah the hand of God was to give them one heart to do the commandment of the king and of the princes, by the word of the LORD. *(The hand of the Lord works wonders: our churches and our nation need it. Lord, stretch out thy saving arm and glorify thy Son.)*

II. CHRONICLES XXX. 13—15; 17—23; 26, 27.

AND there assembled at Jerusalem much people to keep the feast of unleavened bread in the second month, a very great congregation.

14 And they arose and took away the altars that *were* in Jerusalem, and all the altars for incense took they away, and cast *them* into the brook Kidron. *(It was meet to cast out the old leaven before they kept the feast. A purified temple led to a purified city; good things grow. Here is mention of the Kidron again, and so we are once more reminded of the atonement of our Lord Jesus, which removes all impurities.)*

15 Then they killed the passover on the fourteenth *day* of the second month: and the priests and the Levites were ashamed, and sanctified themselves, and brought in the burnt offerings into the house of the LORD.

17 For *there were* many in the congregation that were not sanctified: therefore the Levites had the charge of the killing of the passovers for every one *that was* not clean, to sanctify *them* unto the LORD. *(The irregularities were unavoidable and not wilful, and therefore the Lord looked at the heart and forgave them. It would be a sad wrong done to the divine mercy if we were to argue from this that we may alter the ordinances of God at our pleasure. If we do so without the reasons which were present in this case, we shall meet with rebuke, and not remission.)*

18, 19 For a multitude of the people, *even* many of Ephraim, and Manasseh, Issachar, and Zebulun, had not cleansed themselves, yet did they eat the passover otherwise than it was written. But Hezekiah prayed for them, saying, The good LORD pardon every one *that* prepareth his heart to seek God, the LORD God of his fathers, though *he be* not *cleansed* according to the purification of the sanctuary. *(A short but sweet prayer: sin is confessed, mercy sought, and the goodness of the Lord pleaded.)*

20—22 And the LORD hearkened to Hezekiah, and healed the people. And the children of Israel that were present at Jerusalem kept the feast of unleavened bread seven days with great gladness: and the Levites and the priests praised the LORD day by day, *singing* with loud instruments unto the LORD. *(So there was much singing: the more praise the better.)* And

Hezekiah spake comfortably unto all the Levites that taught the good knowledge of the LORD. *(There was much preaching; the people needed it, and were right glad to attend upon it.)* And they did eat throughout the feast seven days, offering peace offerings, and making confession to the LORD God of their fathers.

Best of all, there was much praying and confessing of sin, and so we may be sure there was plenteous forgiveness, and this led the people to desire yet more fellowship with their God.

23, 26 And the whole assembly took counsel to keep other seven days: and they *kept* other seven days with gladness. So there was great joy in Jerusalem: for since the time of Solomon the son of David king of Israel *there was* not the like in Jerusalem. *(Holy duties should be sweetened with holy gladness.)*

27 Then the priests the Levites arose and blessed the people: and their voice was heard, and their prayer came *up* to his holy dwelling place, *even* unto heaven. *(They ended well; every man went home with a blessing in his ears, and prayer also reached the ear of the God of heaven, which was the greatest mercy of all.)*

II. CHRONICLES XXXI. 1, 2.

NOW when all this was finished, all Israel that were present went out to the cities of Judah, and brake the images in pieces, and cut down the groves, and threw down the high places and the altars out of all Judah and Benjamin, in Ephraim also and Manasseh, until they had utterly destroyed them all. Then all the children of Israel returned, every man to his possession, into their own cities. *Those have profited indeed who go home to break their idols. Is this the result of our hearing? Do we make an end of our sins?*

2 And Hezekiah appointed the courses of the priests and the Levites after their courses, every man according to his service, the priests and Levites for burnt offerings and for peace offerings, to minister, and to give thanks, and to praise in the gates of the tents of the LORD. *The best way to keep out error and sin is to promote truth and holiness by gospel ordinances and earnest ministers. Sound gospel preaching alone can defeat the inroads of Popery. The Lord send it in our day.*

II. CHRONICLES. XXXII. 1—3; 5—12; 14,
16, 17, 19, 20.

AFTER these things, and the establishment thereof, Sennacherib king of Assyria came, and entered into Judah, and encamped against the fenced cities, and thought to win them for himself. *(Notwithstanding the glorious reformation made by Hezekiah, he and his people must be tried; the trial became a test of their faith, and an opportunity for the Lord to shew himself strong on their behalf. They were none the less approved of God because they were tried: good trees are pruned because they are good, and in order to make them better.)*

2, 3 And when Hezekiah saw that Sennacherib was come, and that he was purposed to fight against Jerusalem, He took counsel with his princes and his mighty men to stop the waters of the fountains which *were* without the city : and they did help him. *(To a vast host the want of water would be a great peril, hence the wisdom of cutting off the supplies in the region which Sennacherib would traverse. Faith is near akin to common sense.)*

5 Also he strengthened himself, and built up all the wall that was broken, and raised *it* up to the towers, and another wall without, and repaired Millo *in* the city of David, and made darts and shields in abundance.

Here again were common-sense preparations : faith trusts in God, but repairs her bulwarks.

6, 7, 8 And he set captains of war over the people, and gathered them together to him in the street of the gate of the city, and spake comfortably to them saying, Be strong and courageous, be not afraid nor dismayed for the king of Assyria, nor for all the multitude that *is* with him : for *there be* more with us than with him : With him *is* an arm of flesh; but with us *is* the LORD our God to help us, and to fight our battles. And the people rested themselves upon the words of Hezekiah king of Judah.

They were inspired with confidence by their leader's heroic language ; and shall not we, the soldiers of Christ, be cheered by that which he has spoken—" Let not your hearts be troubled"?

9 ¶ After this did Sennacherib king of Assyria send his servants to Jerusalem, unto Hezekiah king of Judah, and unto all Judah that *were* at Jerusalem, saying,

10, 11 Thus saith Sennacherib king of Assyria, Whereon do ye trust, that ye abide in the siege in Jerusalem ? Doth not Hezekiah persuade you to give over yourselves to die by famine and by thirst, saying, The LORD our God shall deliver us out of the hand of the king of Assyria ?

12 Hath not the same Hezekiah taken away his high places and his altars, and commanded Judah and Jerusalem, saying, Ye shall worship before one altar, and burn incense upon it ?

The tyrant king treated Hezekiah meanly by appealing to his people to revolt from him and look to their own interests ; charging him with deceiving them, and with profanity in putting an end to the unlawful worship upon the high places. Hezekiah's greatest virtue is here mentioned as a crime, so common is it for saints to be misrepresented by sinners.

14 Who *was there* among all the gods of those nations that my fathers utterly destroyed, that could deliver his people out of mine hand, that your God should be able to deliver you out of mine hand ? *(He spake exceeding proudly, as if he regarded Jehovah as inferior to the idols whose worshippers he had vanquished. The Lord would surely be moved to jealousy by such taunts.)*

16, 17 And his servants spake yet *more* against the LORD God, and against his servant Hezekiah. He wrote also letters to rail on the LORD God of Israel, and to speak against him, saying, As the gods of the nations of *other* lands have not delivered their people out of mine hand, so shall not the God of Hezekiah deliver his people out of mine hand.

Writing is deliberate, and therefore doubly profane. It was well for Hezekiah to have so foul-mouthed an enemy, for his insolent blasphemies stirred up the indignation of the Lord.

19 And they spake against the God of Jerusalem, as against the gods of the people of the earth, *which were* the work of the hands of man.

20 And for this *cause* Hezekiah the king, and the prophet Isaiah the son of Amoz, prayed and cried to heaven. *(Deliverance was not far off when king and prophet both cried to heaven. Is any troubled, or in fear of trouble? Let him pray.)*

A TERRIBLY *blasphemous letter written by Rabshakeh, Sennacherib's captain, caused Hezekiah great distress, but he knew where to take his trouble.*

II. KINGS XIX. 14—34.

14 And Hezekiah received the letter of the hand of the messengers, and read it: and Hezekiah went up into the house of the LORD, and spread it before the LORD. *(This was a much better plan than attempting to answer his enemy in the same insulting language: an angry answer to an angry letter shews that the weakness and sin are not confined to one side of the quarrel. Praying over a letter is an infinitely wiser thing than going to law about it.)*

15, 16, 17, 18, 19 And Hezekiah prayed before the LORD, and said, O LORD God of Israel, which dwellest *between* the cherubims, thou art the God, *even* thou alone, of all the kingdoms of the earth; thou hast made heaven and earth. LORD, bow down thine ear, and hear: open, LORD, thine eyes, and see: and hear the words of Sennacherib, which hath sent him to reproach the living God. Of a truth, LORD, the kings of Assyria have destroyed the nations and their lands, And have cast their gods into the fire: for they *were* no gods, but the work of men's hands, wood and stone: therefore they have destroyed them. Now therefore, O LORD our God, I beseech thee, save thou us out of his hand, that all the kingdoms of the earth may know that thou *art* the LORD God, *even* thou only. *(After acknowledging the power of the invader, and ascribing the overthrow of the gods of other nations to the fact that they were dead idols, the king appeals to Jehovah, the God of Israel, to prove his own reality and power by saving his people, lest the heathen should reckon him to be a God only in name. Appeals to God's honour have much power in them; it ought to be our greatest concern and our surest confidence. We are taught to begin prayer with "Hallowed be thy name," and close it with "Thy kingdom come.")*

20, 21 Then Isaiah the son of Amoz sent to Hezekiah, saying, Thus saith the LORD God of Israel, *That* which thou hast prayed to me against Sennacherib king of Assyria I have heard. This *is* the word that the LORD hath spoken concerning him; The virgin the daughter

of Zion hath despised thee, *and* laughed thee to scorn; the daughter of Jerusalem hath shaken her head at thee. *(Weak as she is, she is under the Lord's protection and defies thee.)*

22, 23, 24 Whom hast thou reproached and blasphemed? and against whom hast thou exalted *thy* voice, and lifted up thine eyes on high? *even* against the Holy *One* of Israel. By thy messengers thou hast reproached the Lord, and hast said, With the multitude of my chariots I am come up to the height of the mountains, to the sides of Lebanon, and will cut down the tall cedar trees thereof, *and* the choice fir trees thereof: and I will enter into the lodgings of his borders, *and into* the forest of his Carmel. I have digged and drunk strange waters, and with the sole of my feet have I dried up all the rivers of besieged places. *(These were Sennacherib's feats of war, which he emblazoned on his palace walls; he gloried in the devastations he had caused. Vain glory this! More becoming a demon than one born of a woman. The lust of conquest obliterates compassion. Great, however, as Sennacherib thought himself to be, he was now to find his superior, and to learn whence his power had been derived.)*

25, 26 Hast thou not heard long ago *how* I have done it, *and* of ancient times that I have formed it? now have I brought it to pass, that thou shouldest be to lay waste fenced cities *into* ruinous heaps. Therefore their inhabitants were of small power, they were dismayed and confounded; they were *as* the grass of the field, and *as* the green herb, *as* the grass on the housetops, and *as corn* blasted before it be grown up. *(It had been by Jehovah's power that he had conquered, he had been used as a scourge in the Lord's hand, to chastise the wickedness of the nations.)*

27, 28 But I know thy abode, and thy going out, and thy coming in, and thy rage against me. Because thy rage against me and thy tumult is come up into mine ears, therefore I will put my hook in thy nose, and my bridle in thy lips, and I will turn thee back by the way by which thou camest. *(Like a huge monster, he might rage and roar, but he would be made to know his master, and go back to his den at the word of command.)*

29 And this *shall be* a sign unto thee, Ye shall eat this year such things as grow of themselves, and in the second year that which

springeth of the same ; and in the third year sow ye, and reap, and plant vineyards, and eat the fruits thereof. *(Provisions were at famine prices, and it was too late to sow the fields, therefore the Lord sustained the people for two years, by giving the earth an unusual fertility, thus fulfilling his promise, "so shalt thou dwell in the land, and verily thou shalt be fed.")*

30, 31 And the remnant that is escaped of the house of Judah shall yet again take root downward, and bear fruit upward. For out of Jerusalem shall go forth a remnant, and they that escape out of mount Zion : the zeal of the LORD *of hosts* shall do this. *(Yet again would the kingdom revive, the people would again take root in the soil, and grow upward in prosperity. It is well in spiritual things to unite the two growths, so as to take root downward in humility and experience, while we grow upward in zeal and enthusiasm.)*

32, 33, 34 Therefore thus saith the LORD concerning the king of Assyria, He shall not come into this city, nor shoot an arrow there, nor come before it with shield, nor cast a bank against it. By the way that he came, by the same shall he return, and shall not come into this city, saith the LORD. For I will defend this city, to save it, for mine own sake, and for my servant David's sake.

Ye that love the cause of Zion,
  Though despis'd of men, and few,
Arm'd with boldness like the lion,
  Fear not all that men can do.
What though all the world oppose ;
God is stronger than her foes.

Now, ye people, walk around her,
  View her walls, and count her towers ;
See how God, her King and founder,
  Keeps her safe from hostile powers :
Zion's children live secure ;
God has made their dwelling sure.

Foes of Zion, fight no longer ;
  Here submission will be gain :
Zion's King will prove the stronger,
  And with power her cause maintain.
He secures her gates and walls :
'Tis on you the ruin falls.

Lord, I forego all anxious thought,
  And cast on thee my care ;
Content that thou art over all,
  And rulest everywhere.

Teach me to listen for thy voice
  When the storm howleth loud ;
Help me to look for light from thee,
  Beneath the darkest cloud.

Thy face I seek with earnest prayer,
  For thou art all my stay,
Now let thy mighty arm appear
  And drive my griefs away.

At thy rebuke, O Jacob's God,
  Both horse and chariot fell :
Who knows the terrors of thy rod ?
  Thy vengeance who can tell ?

What power can stand before thy sight,
  When once thy wrath appears ?
When heaven shines round with dreadful light,
  The earth lies still and fears.

Happy the church, thou sacred place,
The seat of thy Creator's grace ;
Thine holy courts are his abode,
Thou earthly palace of our God !

Thy walls are strength, and at thy gates
A guard of heavenly warriors waits ;
Nor shall thy deep foundations move
Fix'd on his counsels and his love.

Thy foes in vain designs engage,
Against his throne in vain they rage ;
Like rising waves, with angry roar,
That dash and die upon the shore.

Then let our souls in Zion dwell,
Nor fear the wrath of Rome nor hell ;
His arms embrace this happy ground,
Like brazen bulwarks built around.

HEZEKIAH *had prayed, and Isaiah had been sent with a message in which Sennacherib's overthrow was promised: the king had not long to wait to see what he desired. God's actions are prompt, for his preparations for war are always made; his arsenal is well stored. It was a word and a blow, and Assyria was smitten never to trouble Hezekiah again.*

II. KINGS XIX. 35—37.

35 ¶ And it came to pass that night, that the angel of the LORD went out, and smote in the camp of the Assyrians an hundred four score and five thousand : and when they arose early in the morning, behold, they *were* all dead corpses. *(The few who survived looked upon the myriads of dead, lying " like the leaves of the forest when autumn has blown.")*

36 So Sennacherib king of Assyria departed, and went and returned, and dwelt at Nineveh.

Now that this terrible robber was no longer able to roam abroad with his marauding host, there was some rest to the surrounding nations, who thus profited by Hezekiah's prayer.

37 And it came to pass, as he was worshipping in the house of Nisroch his god, that Adrammelech and Sharezer his sons smote him with the sword : and they escaped into the land of Armenia. And Esarhaddon his son reigned in his stead. *(Thus at the feet of his own idol he poured out his heart's blood, and his blasphemies were heard no more.)*

THAT *jubilant Psalm, the seventy-sixth, was probably written at the time of the destruction of Sennacherib's army; at any rate it is singularly descriptive of it. Let us sympathise in the holy joy of the writer as he triumphs in the triumph of his God.*

PSALM LXXVI.

1 In Judah *is* God known : his name *is* great in Israel. *(If unknown in all the world beside he is famous among his people. Because the world knows him not, it blasphemes as Rab-shakeh did, but the Lord's people delight to sound forth his praises to the world's end.)*

2 In Salem also is his tabernacle, and his dwelling place in Zion.

3 There brake he the arrows of the bow, the shield, and the sword, and the battle. Selah. *(Without leaving his peaceful abode in the temple,*

he sent forth his word and snapped the arrows of his enemies before they could fit them upon the string, he ended the fight ere they could begin it. They did not cast up a bank nor shoot an arrow there. And shall not the Lord defend his church? Assuredly ! She is safe, come what may.)

4 Thou *art* more glorious *and* excellent than the mountains of prey. *(Heaps upon heaps, Assyria had stowed away her plunder, and the fame thereof went abroad, but Israel's God eclipsed the mighty deeds of the destroying invader. Glory be to his name !)*

5 The stouthearted are spoiled, *(They came to spoil, and were spoiled themselves,)* they have slept their sleep : *(their last sleep, the sleep of death :)* and none of the men of might have found their hands. *(Their arms were palsied, the rigour of death stiffened their fingers.)*

6 At thy rebuke, O God of Jacob, both the chariot and horse are cast into a dead sleep. *(Never to neigh or rattle again ; still were the trampings of the horses and the crash of the cars.)*

7, 8 Thou, *even* thou, *art* to be feared : and who may stand in thy sight when once thou art angry ? Thou didst cause judgment to be heard from heaven ; the earth feared, and was still. *(So complete a destruction was evidently a judgment from heaven, and those who heard of it cried out, " This is the finger of God !" Such a blow will yet be struck at the Papacy, for fall it must, to the astonishment of all mankind.)*

9 When God arose to judgment, to save all the meek of the earth. Selah.

10 Surely the wrath of man shall praise thee: the remainder of wrath shalt thou restrain.

Enemies are held in by God's will, and when allowed to rage, God's glory will be enhanced by their overthrow. Let us never yield to fear. The Lord of hosts is mightier than the mightiest foes of his church.

11 Vow, and pay unto the LORD your God : let all that be round about him bring presents unto him that ought to be feared.

12 He shall cut off the spirit of princes : *he is* terrible to the kings of the earth. *(As men slip off a tender shoot from a plant, so can the Lord remove the proudest monarchs ; be it ours to worship, love, and serve the King of kings. To his name be endless praises.)*

HOW *gloriously did Isaiah speak at this time; let us read his eloquent words—*

ISAIAH XXXIII. 1, 2 ; 7—24.

1 Woe to thee that spoilest, and thou *wast* not spoiled; and dealest treacherously, and they dealt not treacherously with thee! when thou shalt cease to spoil, thou shalt be spoiled; *and* when thou shalt make an end to deal treacherously, they shall deal treacherously with thee. *(Assyria had gained power by treachery, and by treachery she should fall.)*

2 O LORD, be gracious unto us; we have waited for thee: be thou their arm every morning, our salvation also in the time of trouble.

7 Behold, their valiant ones shall cry without: the ambassadors of peace shall weep bitterly. *(The Assyrian king refused all terms of peace, and made valiant men weep for fear, at the remembrance of his power and cruelty.)*

8 The highways lie waste, the wayfaring man ceaseth: he hath broken the covenant, he hath despised the cities, he regardeth no man.

9 The earth mourneth *and* languisheth: Lebanon is ashamed *and* hewn down: Sharon is like a wilderness; and Bashan and Carmel shake off *their fruits. (Devastation and desolation followed the invader's track.)*

10 Now will I rise, saith the LORD; now will I be exalted; now will I lift up myself.

11 Ye shall conceive chaff, ye shall bring forth stubble: your breath, *as* fire, shall devour you.

12 And the people shall be *as* the burnings of lime: *as* thorns cut up shall they be burned in the fire. *(At God's rebuke the mighty adversary would be consumed, consumed by his own fury, gone like thorns in the fire.)*

13 ¶ Hear, ye *that are* far off, what I have done; and, ye *that are* near, acknowledge my might.

14 The sinners in Zion are afraid; fearfulness hath surprised the hypocrites. Who among us shall dwell with the devouring fire? who among us shall dwell with everlasting burnings? *(Their terror at Sennacherib led them to enquire how they could endure the yet greater wrath of God, whose wrath is like a fire which devours, and yet burns on. Everlasting burnings are more to be feared than death itself;*

be it our great business to escape from them. The righteous were at ease while the hypocrites were alarmed, and so we read)—

15 He that walketh righteously, and speaketh uprightly; he that despiseth the gain of oppressions, that shaketh his hands from holding of bribes, that stoppeth his ears from hearing of blood, and shutteth his eyes from seeing evil ;.

16 He shall dwell on high: his place of defence *shall be* the munitions of rocks: bread shall be given him; his waters *shall be* sure.

17 Thine eyes shall see the king in his beauty: they shall behold the land that is very far off. *(Hezekiah came forth in his robes again, and the people, being free from the invader, could travel as far abroad as they chose.)*

18 Thine heart shall meditate terror. Where *is* the scribe? where *is* the receiver? where *is* he that counted the towers?

19 Thou shalt not see a fierce people, a people of a deeper speech than thou canst perceive; of a stammering tongue, *that thou canst* not understand. *(The proud Assyrian engineers and accountants were disappointed, and his harsh-speaking soldiery came not near the city.)*

20, 21 Look upon Zion, the city of our solemnities: thine eyes shall see Jerusalem a quiet habitation, a tabernacle *that* shall not be taken down; not one of the stakes thereof shall ever be removed, neither shall any of the cords thereof be broken.   But there the glorious LORD *will be* unto us a place of broad rivers *and* streams; wherein shall go no galley with oars, neither shall gallant ship pass thereby.

22 For the LORD *is* our judge, the LORD *is* our lawgiver, the LORD *is* our king; he will save us. *(They had all the advantages of broad rivers without being exposed to attacks by vessels of war, for the Lord was with them.   Not so Assyria, for its state was like a vessel in a storm.)*

23 Thy tacklings are loosed; they could not well strengthen their mast, they could not spread the sail: then is the prey of a great spoil divided; the lame take the prey.

24 And the inhabitant shall not say, I am sick: the people that dwell therein *shall be* forgiven *their* iniquity. *(Jerusalem healed, restored, forgiven, was blessed indeed. Such blessings have all the saints.)*

408   "The Lord is good, a stronghold in the day of trouble."   JULY 10.—MORNING.

[*Or January* 16.]

SOMEWHERE *about this time the prophet Nahum was called to speak for the Lord : we will read his declaration against Assyria.*

NAHUM I.

1 The burden of Nineveh. The book of the vision of Nahum the Elkoshite.

2 God *is* jealous, and the LORD revengeth ; *(He loves his people too well to see them trampled upon and not avenge their wrongs. Assyria had carried away the ten tribes, and now threatened Judah, and therefore God in love to his people interposed;)* the LORD revengeth, and *is* furious ; the LORD will take vengeance on his adversaries, and he reserveth *wrath* for his enemies.

He had borne patiently with the insolence of Sennacherib, but he was not insensible, and would ere long pour out his indignation.

3, 4 The LORD *is* slow to anger, and great in power, and will not at all acquit *the wicked : (His longsuffering is often misunderstood, and the wicked dream that their crimes are overlooked, but they will speedily be undeceived.)* the LORD *hath* his way in the whirlwind and in the storm, and the clouds *are* the dust of his feet. He rebuketh the sea, and maketh it dry, and drieth up all the rivers: Bashan languisheth, and Carmel, and the flower of Lebanon languisheth.

He can withhold the clouds, and then the most fruitful lands will be barren with drought.

5, 6 The mountains quake at him, and the hills melt, and the earth is burned at his presence, yea, the world, and all that dwell therein. Who can stand before his indignation ? and who can abide in the fierceness of his anger ? his fury is poured out like fire, and the rocks are thrown down by him.

Lightning and earthquake are his servants, and none can stand against them.

7 The LORD *is* good, a strong hold in the day of trouble ; and he knoweth them that trust in him. *(This is a note of soft, sweet music, amid the thunder of divine power, falling most refreshingly upon the ear of faith.)*

8 But with an overrunning flood he will make an utter end of the place thereof, and darkness shall pursue his enemies.

9 What do ye imagine against the LORD ? he will make an utter end : affliction shall not rise up the second time. *(His one stroke would be enough to break Assyria once for all.)*

10 For while *they be* folden together *as* thorns, and while they are drunken *as* drunkards, they shall be devoured as stubble fully dry. *(While gathered together as thorns in a heap, a single flame from heaven would be enough to consume them.)*

11 There is *one* come out of thee, that imagineth evil against the LORD, a wicked counsellor. *(Sennacherib is here described and denounced.)*

12, 13 Thus saith the LORD ; Though *they be* quiet, and likewise many, yet thus shall they be cut down, when he shall pass through. *(In one night the deed was done, and Judah was delivered. Therefore the Lord says to his people :)* Though I have afflicted thee, I will afflict thee no more. For now will I break his yoke from off thee, and will burst thy bonds in sunder.

As for the foe, he declares—

14 And the LORD hath given a commandment concerning thee, *that* no more of thy name be sown : out of the house of thy gods will I cut off the graven image and the molten image : I will make thy grave ; for thou art vile.

Once had Nineveh been warned, and it for a while repented ; but since it had returned to its old ways its doom was sealed, and as a city it would soon be dead and buried. Let travellers tell how fully this threatening has been fulfilled.

15 Behold upon the mountains the feet of him that bringeth good tidings, that publisheth peace ! O Judah, keep thy solemn feasts, perform thy vows : for the wicked shall no more pass through thee : he is utterly cut off.

Joyful obedience was required of Judah on account of such a deliverance. We have been set free from a worse tyrant than Sennacherib, therefore let us rejoice in the Lord our God, and magnify his Son Jesus, the angel which redeemed us out of all evil.

Sinners, with joy look up !
The herald's feet appear ;
He comes from Zion's sacred top,
A gospel-messenger.

The end of war and sin,
In Christ, your peace, obtain :
And when his kingdom reigns within,
It shall for ever reign.

MICAH *also came forward to support Isaiah's testimony. Quite a company of holy seers shone forth like stars in the evening of Judah's history. In the chapter which we are about to read, Micah's far-seeing eye beheld the Lord Jesus in the glory of the latter days.*

MICAH IV.

1, 2 But in the last days it shall come to pass, *that* the mountain of the house of the LORD shall be established in the top of the mountains, and it shall be exalted above the hills; and people shall flow unto it. And many nations shall come, and say, Come, and let us go up to the mountain of the LORD, and to the house of the God of Jacob; and he will teach us of his ways, and we will walk in his paths: for the law shall go forth of Zion, and the word of the LORD from Jerusalem.

God reserves his best things to the last. In Messiah's days the true faith and the true church will have wide dominion; that which the material temple typified shall be fully revealed and reverenced far and wide.

3 And he shall judge among many people, and rebuke strong nations afar off; and they shall beat their swords into plowshares, and their spears into pruninghooks: nation shall not lift up a sword against nation, neither shall they learn war any more.

4 But they shall sit every man under his vine and under his fig tree; and none shall make *them* afraid: for the mouth of the LORD of hosts hath spoken it. *(For this unbroken peace we sigh; it will not come by means of civilisation, commerce and moral advancement: Jesus alone is the world's Peacemaker.)*

5 For all people will walk every one in the name of his god, and we will walk in the name of the LORD our God for ever and ever.

6 In that day, saith the LORD, will I assemble her that halteth, and I will gather her that is driven out, and her that I have afflicted;

7 And I will make her that halted a remnant, and her that was cast far off a strong nation: and the LORD shall reign over them in mount Zion from henceforth, even for ever. *(From the poor relics of the Jewish nation we have received the gospel, and so in a spiritual sense mount Zion triumphs in her reigning Lord.)*

8 And thou, O tower of the flock, the strong hold of the daughter of Zion, unto thee shall it come, even the first dominion; the kingdom shall come to the daughter of Jerusalem.

9, 10 Now why dost thou cry out aloud? *is there* no king in thee? is thy counsellor perished? for pangs have taken thee as a woman in travail. Be in pain, and labour to bring forth, O daughter of Zion, like a woman in travail: for now shalt thou go forth out of the city, and thou shalt dwell in the field, and thou shalt go *even* to Babylon; there shalt thou be delivered; there the LORD shall redeem thee from the hand of thine enemies. *(Jerusalem was troubled sorely, but good would come of it; the people would be carried into Babylon, but God would deliver them. While Jesus lives, his church is safe.)*

11, 12 Now also many nations are gathered against thee, that say, Let her be defiled, and let our eye look upon Zion. But they know not the thoughts of the LORD, neither understand they his counsel: for he shall gather them as the sheaves into the floor. *(Faith beholds her enemies as sheaves for her to thresh, and by divine help she treads them down. We are more than conquerors, through our loving God.)*

13 Arise and thresh, O daughter of Zion: for I will make thine horn iron, and I will make thy hoofs brass: and thou shalt beat in pieces many people: and I will consecrate their gain unto the LORD, and their substance unto the Lord of the whole earth.

No strife shall vex Messiah's reign
 Or mar those peaceful years;
To ploughshares men shall beat their swords,
 To pruning-hooks their spears.

No longer hosts encountering hosts,
 Their millions slain deplore;
They hang the trumpet in the hall,
 And study war no more.

Come, then! oh come from every land,
 To worship at his shrine,
And, walking in the light of God,
 With holy beauties shine.

THE *whole of the prophecies of Isaiah are precious, and should be read by us constantly in private. To whet our desires to read the whole book, we shal take a few of the choicer portions. He gives a very wonderful description of the pilgrims to heaven, and their joyful march. We find it in—*

ISAIAH XXXV.

1 The wilderness and the solitary place shall be glad for them; and the desert shall rejoice, and blossom as the rose.

Though oftentimes despised and oppressed, there will come a time when the people of God shall be known to be the greatest blessings to men, for the most waste and desolate parts of society shall be cheered and benefitted by their presence and influence. It has been so already in a measure, but better days are in store.

2 It shall blossom abundantly, and rejoice even with joy and singing: the glory of Lebanon shall be given unto it, the excellency of Carmel and Sharon, they shall see the glory of the Lord, *and* the excellency of our God.

Spiritual blessings in heavenly things shall be enjoyed by them in Christ Jesus, and so shall all men see how glorious a God they serve.

3 ¶ Strengthen ye the weak hands, and confirm the feeble knees.

4 Say to them *that are* of a fearful heart, Be strong, fear not: behold, your God will come *with* vengeance, *even* God *with* a recompence; he will come and save you.

He will execute vengeance on his foes; but as for you who trust in him, though you are weak and timid, he will come and save you. What comfort these words are calculated to afford!

5 Then the eyes of the blind shall be opened, and the ears of the deaf shall be unstopped.

6 Then shall the lame *man* leap as an hart, and the tongue of the dumb sing: for in the wilderness shall waters break out, and streams in the desert. *(These are the miracles which attest the gospel now, and these shall be more abundantly multiplied in the golden age, which is on its way. Believers know what these miracles mean, for they have experienced the gracious cures which Jesus works, and in their wants and needs the Lord daily gives them "streams in the desert.")*

7 And the parched ground shall become a pool, and the thirsty land springs of water: in the habitation of dragons, where each lay, *shall be* grass with reeds and rushes.

Salvation can gladden desolation; places and hearts abandoned to every unclean thing, and empty of all good, shall yet, through divine grace, become fruitful in every good word and work.

8 And an highway shall be there, and a way, and it shall be called The way of holiness; the unclean shall not pass over it; but it *shall be* for those: the wayfaring men, though fools, shall not err *therein.*

9 No lion shall be there, nor *any* ravenous beast shall go up thereon, it shall not be found there; but the redeemed shall walk *there:*

The Lord has cast up a way of grace for simple souls, and in it they are safe from sin and Satan, and every foe. Are we travelling this sacred road? If so we are redeemed by blood, and are striving after holiness; for those who love sin cannot be journeying to heaven. How thankful we ought to be that the road to heaven is for plain people, and how gladly ought we to forsake sin and walk therein!

10 And the ransomed of the Lord shall return, and come to Zion with songs and everlasting joy upon their heads: they shall obtain joy and gladness, and sorrow and sighing shall flee away. *(This is the end of holy pilgrimage; it ends in bliss which knows no end. Crowns of joy will be placed upon the heads of all who follow the Lamb of God, their mourning shall be ended, and they shall rest with him for ever. Happy pilgrims, fain would we all go with you: father, mother, children, and servants, we would all march to the celestial city by the pathway of faith.)*

Jesus, my all, to heaven is gone,
He whom I fix'd my hopes upon,
His track I see, and I'll pursue
The narrow way, till him I view.

The way the holy prophets went,
The road that leads from banishment,
The King's highway of holiness,
I'll go, for all his paths are peace.

Lo! glad I come; and thou, blest Lamb,
Shalt take me to thee, as I am:
Nothing but sin have I to give;
Nothing but love shall I receive.

WE *shall now listen to Isaiah while he speaks partly of Cyrus, and principally of Christ in—*

ISAIAH XLII. 1—16.

1 Behold my servant, whom I uphold ; mine elect *(or my choice one), in whom* my soul delighteth ; I have put my spirit upon him : he shall bring forth judgment to the Gentiles. *This Jesus has done in our case, for we who were sinners of the Gentiles rejoice in his righteousness. Glory be to his name !*

2 He shall not cry, nor lift up, nor cause his voice to be heard in the street. *(Jesus was meek and lowly, and no clamorous hunter for popularity.)*

3 A bruised reed shall he not break, and the smoking flax shall he not quench : he shall bring forth judgment unto truth. *(The poor, useless, feeble heart, which, like a crushed reed, can yield no music, Jesus binds up; and the soul in which only a spark of grace lingers, and out of which only a smoke of desire arises, he will preserve and fan into a flame. How encouraging is this ! Oh, for faith to lay hold upon it !)*

4 He shall not fail nor be discouraged, till he have set judgment in the earth : and the isles shall wait for his law.

5 ¶ Thus saith God the Lord, he that created the heavens, and stretched them out ; he that spread forth the earth, and that which cometh out of it ; he that giveth breath unto the people upon it, and spirit to them that walk therein :

6 I the Lord have called thee in righteousness, and will hold thine hand, and will keep thee, and give thee for a covenant of the people, for a light of the Gentiles ;

7 To open the blind eyes, to bring out the prisoners from the prison, *and* them that sit in darkness out of the prison house. *(See what a Saviour we have, and how the Lord is with him. He works wonders of grace, and why may we not share in them ? Will he not bring out our captive spirits to gospel liberty?)*

8 I *am* the Lord : that *is* my name : and my glory will I not give to another, neither my praise to graven images.

9 Behold, the former things are come to pass, and new things do I declare : before they spring forth I tell you of them.

10 Sing unto the Lord a new song, *and* his praise from the end of the earth, ye that go down to the sea, and all that is therein ; the isles, and the inhabitants thereof.

11 Let the wilderness and the cities thereof lift up *their voice*, the villages *that* Kedar doth inhabit : let the inhabitants of the rock sing, let them shout from the top of the mountains.

12 Let them give glory unto the Lord, and declare his praise in the islands. *The finished work of Jesus is enough to fill the universe with the praises of the Eternal God. We will daily pray that it may be made known, till the whole earth shall rejoice in it and bring glory to God.*

13 The Lord shall go forth as a mighty man, he shall stir up jealousy like a man of war : he shall cry, yea, roar ; he shall prevail against his enemies. *(The gospel is the cry of the mighty God, and those who do not receive it will be overthrown by it. To the unbelieving its voice is terrible as the roaring of a lion.)*

14, 15 I have long time holden my peace ; I have been still, *and* refrained myself : *now* will I cry like a travailing woman ; I will destroy and devour at once. I will make waste mountains and hills, and dry up all their herbs ; and I will make the rivers islands, and I will dry up the pools. *(Longsuffering has its limits ; and when God begins to deal with sinful nations and ungodly men, his works of justice will be beyond measure dreadful. No comforts will be left to those who refused comfort in Christ.)*

16 And I will bring the blind by a way *that* they knew not ; I will lead them in paths *that* they have not known : I will make darkness light before them, and crooked things straight. These things will I do unto them, and not forsake them. *(In the midst of judgment, mercy and truth shall not be forgotten; God's chosen shall be led safely, and their afflictions shall be removed. Specially precious are the last words, " and not forsake them." Why are we sorrowful? for God is our friend still. Never has he deserted a sincerely believing heart, and he never will, come what may. Let us, then, rest in his love, and go forward to our life's end with exulting courage.)*

412   "The Lord will help me."   JULY 12.—MORNING.

[Or January 20.]

ISAIAH L.

THUS saith the LORD, Where *is* the bill of your mother's divorcement, whom I have put away ? or which of my creditors *is it* to whom I have sold you ? Behold, for your iniquities have ye sold yourselves, and for your transgressions is your mother put away.

When Israel was carried into captivity it was not because God had forgotten his covenant, or wantonly cast off his people. He was not like a cruel husband who divorces his wife in anger, or like a poor needy father compelled to give up his children to his creditors for debt. No, it was sin which brought every evil upon Israel; sin, and nothing else. This also is true in our case. Sin is the root of misery; if we rebel against God, he will surely make us smart under his displeasure.

2, 3 Wherefore, when I came, *was there* no man ? when I called, *was there* none to answer ? *(When Jesus came to the Jews they received him not; this was their condemnation. They were lost, not because he could not save, but because they would not receive him.)* Is my hand shortened at all, that it cannot redeem ? or have I no power to deliver ? behold, at my rebuke I dry up the sea, I make the rivers a wilderness : their fish stinketh, because *there is* no water, and dieth for thirst. I clothe the heavens with blackness, and I make sackcloth their covering.

God has wrought these marvels and can work them again. By these deeds of power he delivered his people, and he is quite as able to save them now. Their sinful unbelief shuts men out from seeing the great power and love of God.

4 The Lord GOD hath given me the tongue of the learned, that I should know how to speak a word in season to *him that is* weary : he wakeneth morning by morning, he wakeneth mine ear to hear as the learned.

Jesus, as man, was endowed with wisdom without measure, for the Spirit in his fulness rested upon him. He knows how to comfort mourners, he is learned in the art of consolation.

5, 6 The Lord GOD hath opened mine ear, and I was not rebellious, neither turned away back. I gave my back to the smiters, and my cheeks to them that plucked off the hair : I hid not my face from shame and spitting. *(No sufferings daunted our blessed Redeemer; his*

testimony brought him into shame, but he would not cease from it till he had fulfilled his Father's will, and accomplished our redemption. Who would not trust such a Saviour ?)

7 For the Lord GOD will help me; therefore shall I not be confounded : therefore have I set my face like a flint, and I know that I shall not be ashamed. *(This is true, not only of our Lord, but of all his witnesses; the Lord makes them bold, and they tremble not at persecution. They expect to suffer, for Jesus suffered; they are confident of victory, for he overcame.)*

8 *He is* near that justifieth me ; who will contend with me ? let us stand together : who *is* mine adversary ? let him come near to me.

9 Behold, the Lord GOD will help me; who *is* he *that* shall condemn me ? lo, they all shall wax old as a garment ; the moth shall eat them up. *(The gospel, like its founder, laughs at opposition. Men are but puny things, so feeble that the worm will devour them. The righteous have no cause to fear, they may bear witness for God in spite of the most furious adversaries, for the Lord will triumph in them and by them.)*

10, 11 Who *is* among you that feareth the LORD, that obeyeth the voice of his servant, that walketh *in* darkness, and hath no light ? let him trust in the name of the LORD, and stay upon his God. Behold, all ye that kindle a fire, that compass *yourselves* about with sparks : walk in the light of your fire, and in the sparks *that* ye have kindled. This shall ye have of mine hand ; ye shall lie down in sorrow. *(Children of light often walk in darkness; let them trust in the Lord, and their joy will return. Children of darkness walk in a light of their own kindling, but they have good cause to be afraid; for when the night comes in which they most need a candle, they must go to the bed of the grave in the dark. How solemn a threatening ! To lie down in sorrow, sorrow from God's own hand. Let us escape from such a doom.)*

When we cannot see our way,
Let us trust, and still obey;
He who bids us forward go,
Cannot fail the way to show.

ISAIAH LI. 1—13.

HEARKEN to me, ye that follow after righteousness, ye that seek the LORD : look unto the rock *whence* ye are hewn, and to the hole of the pit *whence* ye are digged.

2 Look unto Abraham your father, and unto Sarah *that* bare you : for I called him alone, and blessed him, and increased him.

Lest they should grow dejected at the low estate of the nation, they are bidden to remember whence it came. One man was chosen, and one woman, they were both old before a child was born to them, they were a lone family in the earth ; yet out of them sprang a great nation ; nothing could be more apparently hopeless, yet the covenant was fulfilled, and therefore the like could and would be done again, and poor, downtrodden Israel would yet arise.

3 For the LORD shall comfort Zion : he will comfort all her waste places ; and he will make her wilderness like Eden, and her desert like the garden of the LORD ; joy and gladness shall be found therein, thanksgiving, and the voice of melody.

4 ¶ Hearken unto me, my people ; and give ear unto me, O my nation : for a law shall proceed from me, and I will make my judgment to rest for a light of the people.

5 My righteousness *is* near ; my salvation is gone forth, and mine arms shall judge the people ; the isles shall wait upon me, and on mine arm shall they trust.

6 Lift up your eyes to the heavens, and look upon the earth beneath : for the heavens shall vanish away like smoke, and the earth shall wax old like a garment, and they that dwell therein shall die in like manner : but my salvation shall be for ever, and my righteousness shall not be abolished. *(God is faithful, and will be true to his covenant ; it is no agreement for days and years, its tenure is everlasting. The salvation which this covenant promises shall not be hidden in a corner, afar off it shall be published, even as it is at this day in our own fair island of the sea. Nothing can be more delightful than to have this salvation in possession, and to see its stable foundation in the covenant of grace.)*

7 ¶ Hearken unto me, ye that know righteousness, the people in whose heart *is* my law ; fear ye not the reproach of men, neither be ye afraid of their revilings.

8 For the moth shall eat them up like a garment, and the worm shall eat them like wool : but my righteousness shall be for ever, and my salvation from generation to generation. *(Fear not dying man, trust in the ever-living God.)*

9 ¶ Awake, awake, put on strength, O arm of the LORD ; awake, as in the ancient days, in the generations of old. *Art* thou not it that hath cut Rahab *(or Egypt), and* wounded the dragon ? *(or the crocodile, the emblem of Egypt.)*

10 *Art* thou not it which hath dried the sea, the waters of the great deep ; that hath* made the depths of the sea a way for the ransomed to pass over ? *(This is a bold prayer. It lays hold upon that glorious arm which wrought such marvels in Egypt on behalf of the Lord's elect, and its plea is that he can do like deeds again, and that the time has come for him to do them.)*

11 Therefore the redeemed of the LORD shall return, and come with singing unto Zion ; and everlasting joy *shall be* upon their head : they shall obtain gladness and joy ; *and* sorrow and mourning shall flee away. *(Assured faith here quotes the promise which had been given in a previous prophecy, and confidently asserts that it will be ever so. It is always well to have a promise at our fingers' ends.)*

12, 13 I, *even* I, *am* he that comforteth you : who *art* thou, that thou shouldest be afraid of a man *that* shall die, and of the son of man *which* shall be made *as* grass ; And forgettest the LORD thy maker, that hath stretched forth the heavens, and laid the foundations of the earth ; and hast feared continually every day because of the fury of the oppressor, as if he were ready to destroy ? and where *is* the fury of the oppressor ? *(It is in God's hands. No oppressor can rage against us unless the Lord permits ; why then do we fear ? He who gives our foe permission to annoy us in measure, holds the other end of his chain and will keep him within bounds. In holy confidence let us stand still and see the salvation of God.)*

Awake, all-conquering Arm, awake,
And Satan's mighty empire shake ;
Assert the honours of thy throne,
And make this ruin'd world thine own.

WE *will now read Isaiah's prophecy of the glory of the church in the latter days through the ingathering of the Gentiles. There is neither space for comment, nor need of it.*

ISAIAH LX.

1 Arise, shine; for thy light is come, and the glory of the LORD is risen upon thee.

2 For, behold, the darkness shall cover the earth, and gross darkness the people : but the LORD shall arise upon thee, and his glory shall be seen upon thee.

3 And the Gentiles shall come to thy light, and kings to the brightness of thy rising.

4 Lift up thine eyes round about, and see : all they gather themselves together, they come to thee : thy sons shall come from far, and thy daughters shall be nursed at *thy* side.

5 Then thou shalt see, and flow together, and thine heart shall fear, and be enlarged ; because the abundance of the sea shall be converted unto thee, the forces of the Gentiles shall come unto thee.

6, 7 The multitude of camels shall cover thee, the dromedaries of Midian and Ephah; all they from Sheba shall come : they shall bring gold and incense ; and they shall shew forth the praises of the LORD. All the flocks of Kedar shall be gathered together unto thee, the rams of Nebaioth shall minister unto thee : they shall come up with acceptance on mine altar, and I will glorify the house of my glory.

8 Who *are* these *that* fly as a cloud, and as the doves to their windows ?

9 Surely the isles shall wait for me, and the ships of Tarshish first, to bring thy sons from far, their silver and their gold with them, unto the name of the LORD thy God, and to the Holy One of Israel, because he hath glorified thee.

10 And the sons of strangers shall build up thy walls, and their kings shall minister unto thee : for in my wrath I smote thee, but in my favour have I had mercy on thee.

11, 12 Therefore thy gates shall be open continually ; they shall not be shut day nor night; that *men* may bring unto thee the forces of the Gentiles, and *that* their kings *may be* brought. For the nation and kingdom that will not serve thee shall perish ; yea, *those* nations shall be utterly wasted.

13 The glory of Lebanon shall come unto thee, the fir tree, the pine tree, and the box together, to beautify the place of my sanctuary ; and I will make the place of my feet glorious.

14 The sons also of them that afflicted thee shall come bending unto thee ; and all they that despised thee shall bow themselves down at the soles of thy feet; and they shall call thee The city of the LORD, The Zion of the Holy One of Israel.

15 Whereas thou hast been forsaken and hated, so that no man went through *thee*, I will make thee an eternal excellency, a joy of many generations.

16 Thou shalt also suck the milk of the Gentiles, and shalt suck the breast of kings : and thou shalt know that I the LORD *am* thy Saviour and thy Redeemer, the mighty One of Jacob.

17 For brass I will bring gold, and for iron I will bring silver, and for wood brass, and for stones iron : I will also make thy officers peace, and thine exactors *(or gatherers of tribute)* righteousness.

18 Violence shall no more be heard in thy land, wasting nor destruction within thy borders; but thou shalt call thy walls Salvation, and thy gates Praise.

19, 20 The sun shall be no more thy light by day ; neither for brightness shall the moon give light unto thee : but the LORD shall be unto thee an everlasting light, and thy God thy glory. Thy sun shall no more go down ; neither shall thy moon withdraw itself: for the LORD shall be thine everlasting light, and the days of thy mourning shall be ended.

21, 22 Thy people also *shall be* all righteous : they shall inherit the land for ever, the branch of my planting, the work of my hands, that I may be glorified. A little one shall become a thousand, and a small one a strong nation : I the LORD will hasten it in his time.

Hasten, Lord! the promised hour ;
Come in glory and in power ;
Still thy foes are unsubdued ;
Nature sighs to be renew'd.

Time has nearly reach'd its sum,
All things with thy bride say "Come;"
Jesus, whom all worlds adore,
Come, and reign for evermore!

ISAIAH LXI.

THE Spirit of the Lord God *is* upon me; because the Lord hath anointed me to preach good tidings unto the meek; he hath sent me to bind up the broken-hearted, to proclaim liberty to the captives, and the opening of the prison to *them that are* bound;

2 To proclaim the acceptable year of the Lord, and the day of vengeance of our God; to comfort all that mourn;

3 To appoint unto them that mourn in Zion, to give unto them beauty for ashes, the oil of joy for mourning, the garment of praise for the spirit of heaviness; that they might be called trees of righteousness, the planting of the Lord, that he might be glorified. *(The opening words of this chapter were quoted by our Lord Jesus as his credentials, when he stood up to read in the synagogue of Nazareth. The description which is here given is applicable to none but Jesus, and in him every word is verified. Note also how the whole Trinity unite in the work of grace. Jehovah the Father—the Lord God, anoints his Son to his glad office; the Spirit rests upon him; and the Son himself performs divine acts. This glorious gospel of the sacred Trinity is not for the proud and boastful, but for mourners and those who are in heaviness for sin. If we belong to that class, Jesus has come to bless us.)*

4 And they shall build the old wastes, they shall raise up the former desolations, and they shall repair the waste cities, the desolations of many generations.

5 And strangers shall stand and feed your flocks, and the sons of the alien *shall be* your plowmen and your vinedressers. *(Set free from care, we let the dead bury their dead, and those who are of the earth, mind earthly things; as for us, our business is in another world.)*

6 But ye shall be named the Priests of the Lord: *men* shall call you the Ministers of our God: ye shall eat the riches of the Gentiles, and in their glory shall ye boast yourselves.

It is our highest honour to be servants of God, and priests devoted to his honour, sacrificing prayer and praise.

7 For your shame *ye shall have* double: and *for* confusion they shall rejoice in their portion: therefore in their land they shall possess the double: everlasting joy shall be unto them.

Every sorrow of the Lord's own people shall blossom into a double joy. The winter of grief will soon be over, and the eternal summer of bliss will be all the brighter.

8 For I the Lord love judgment, I hate robbery for burnt offering; and I will direct their work in truth, and I will make an everlasting covenant with them. *(Once let a people become sincere in heart, spiritual in worship, and upright before the Lord, and he will cause infinite blessings to be their portion, world without end.)*

9 And their seed shall be known among the Gentiles, and their offspring among the people: all that see them shall acknowledge them, that they *are* the seed *which* the Lord hath blessed.

Believers who walk with God shall be noted and noticed as being truly what they profess to be. It is a sad thing when men of the world do not know what to call us: it is to be feared that hundreds of professors are so inconsistent, that they will never be recognised by the world as being the blessed of the Lord, if indeed they be such.

10 I will greatly rejoice in the Lord, my soul shall be joyful in my God; for he hath clothed me with the garments of salvation, he hath covered me with the robe of righteousness, as a bridegroom decketh *himself* with ornaments, and as a bride adorneth *herself* with her jewels.

How happy the church is as she surveys the righteousness in which she is clothed. She is overjoyed, and well she may be, for when the Lord covers our nakedness with his perfections, it is enough to make the stones sing.

11 For as the earth bringeth forth her bud, and as the garden causeth the things that are sown in it to spring forth; so the Lord God will cause righteousness and praise to spring forth before all the nations. *(We are God's husbandry, and he will take care that the fair fruit of righteousness and peace shall be produced in us. So let it be, good Lord.)*

Where'er the sun begins its race,
  Or ends its swift career,
Both east and west shall own his grace
  And Christ be honoured there.

Ten thousand crowns upon his brow,
  Declare his victories won:
O may his conquests ever grow,
  While time its course shall run.

IN *vision Isaiah beheld the Lord Jesus in the latter days destroying all the foes of his people, and as he saw him returning in triumph from the field of battle, he exclaimed—*

ISAIAH LXIII.

1 Who *is* this that cometh from Edom, with dyed garments from Bozrah? this *that is* glorious in his apparel, travelling in the greatness of his strength? I that speak in righteousness, mighty to save.

2 Wherefore *art thou* red in thine apparel, and thy garments like him that treadeth in the winefat?

3 I have trodden the winepress alone; and of the people *there was* none with me: for I will tread them in mine anger, and trample them in my fury; and their blood shall be sprinkled upon my garments, and I will stain all my raiment.

4 For the day of vengeance *is* in mine heart, and the year of my redeemed is come.

5 And I looked, and *there was* none to help; and I wondered that *there was* none to uphold: therefore mine own arm brought salvation unto me; and my fury, it upheld me.

6 And I will tread down the people in mine anger, and make them drunk in my fury, and I will bring down their strength to the earth.

7, 8, 9 I will mention the lovingkindnesses of the LORD, *and* the praises of the LORD, according to all that the LORD hath bestowed on us, and the great goodness toward the house of Israel, which he hath bestowed on them according to his mercies, and according to the multitude of his lovingkindnesses. For he said, Surely they *are* my people, children *that* will not lie: so he was their Saviour. In all their affliction he was afflicted, and the angel of his presence saved them: in his love and in his pity he redeemed them; and he bare them, and carried them all the days of old.

10 ¶ But they rebelled, and vexed his holy Spirit: therefore he was turned to be their enemy, *and* he fought against them.

11—14 Then he remembered the days of old, Moses, *and* his people, *saying,* Where *is* he that brought them up out of the sea with the shepherd of his flock? where *is* he that put his holy Spirit within him? That led *them* by the right hand of Moses with his glorious arm, dividing the water before them, to make himself an everlasting name? That led them through the deep, as an horse in the wilderness, *that* they should not stumble? As a beast goeth down into the valley, the Spirit of the LORD caused him to rest: so didst thou lead thy people, to make thyself a glorious name.

15 Look down from heaven, and behold from the habitation of thy holiness and of thy glory: where *is* thy zeal and thy strength, the sounding of thy bowels and of thy mercies toward me? are they restrained?

16 Doubtless thou *art* our father, though Abraham be ignorant of us, and Israel acknowledge us not: thou, O LORD, *art* our father, our redeemer; thy name *is* from everlasting.

17, 18 O LORD, why hast thou made us to err from thy ways, *and* hardened our heart from thy fear? Return for thy servants' sake, the tribes of thine inheritance. The people of thy holiness have possessed *it* but a little while: our adversaries have trodden down thy sanctuary.

19 We are *thine:* thou never barest rule over them; they were not called by thy name.

Upon this very wonderful chapter Dr. Hawker has the following spiritual reflections:—" *Who is this that cometh up with salvation, but the* LORD *mighty to save? He is one with Jehovah in the divine nature, and no less one with us in the human, bone of our bone, and flesh of our flesh. Surely,* LORD, *thine own arm brought salvation, and of the people there was none with thee; though in all things it behoved thee to be made like unto thy brethren, yet in redemption-work thou troddest the winepress of the wrath of God alone. And amidst all our rebellions and forgetfulness of thee, never didst thou forget us, or forego our interests. In all our afflictions thou wast afflicted. Thy love and thy pity allowed of no abatement, for thou wast always* Jesus; '*the same yesterday, and to day, and for ever.' Oh! then,* Lord! *let not the waywardness of thy children thwart the gracious designs of thy love; but remember that we are but dust, and let thy strength and thy zeal, and the sounding of thy bowels, never be restrained. We throw ourselves upon covenant relationship, and beseech of thee, our God, to remember that most blessed promise, in which thou hast said,* '*I will not turn away from them to do them good;' and,* '*I will put my fear in their hearts, that they shall not depart from me.'* "

II. KINGS XX. 1—19 ; 21.

IN those days was Hezekiah sick unto death. And the prophet Isaiah the son of Amoz came to him, and said unto him, Thus saith the LORD, Set thine house in order ; for thou shalt die, and not live. *(Well was it for Hezekiah to have so faithful a chaplain in his dying moments. Too often when men are near to death, their friends feel so much cruel delicacy, that they dare not tell them the truth as to their state.)*

2, 3 Then he turned his face to the wall, and prayed unto the LORD, saying, I beseech thee, O LORD, remember now how I have walked before thee in truth and with a perfect heart, and have done *that which is* good in thy sight. And Hezekiah wept sore. *(He longed for a little more time below, he had begun to love the world too well, and moreover, he was too anxious about an heir to the throne.)*

4, 5, 6 And it came to pass, afore Isaiah was gone out into the middle court, that the word of the LORD came to him, saying, Turn again, and tell Hezekiah the captain of my people, Thus saith the LORD, the God of David thy father, I have heard thy prayer, I have seen thy tears: behold, I will heal thee : on the third day thou shalt go up unto the house of the LORD. And I will add unto thy days fifteen years ; and I will deliver thee and this city out of the hand of the king of Assyria; and I will defend this city for mine own sake, and for my servant David's sake.

7 And Isaiah said, take a lump of figs. And they took and laid *it* on the boil, and he recovered. *(A poultice must be used. Although the Lord could heal us without medicine and surgery, he does not choose to do so.)*

8 ¶ And Hezekiah said unto Isaiah, What *shall be* the sign that the LORD will heal me, and that I shall go up into the house of the LORD the third day ?

9 And Isaiah said, This sign shalt thou have of the LORD, that the LORD will do the thing that he hath spoken: shall the shadow go forward ten degrees, or go back ten degrees ?

10, 11 And Hezekiah answered, It is a light thing for the shadow to go down ten degrees : nay, but let the shadow return backward ten degrees. And Isaiah the prophet cried unto the LORD : and he brought the shadow ten degrees backward, by which it had gone down in the dial of Ahaz. *(There is no use in enquiring how this was done ; it is another instance of the omnipotence of God.)*

12, 13 At that time Berodach-baladan, king of Babylon, sent letters and a present unto Hezekiah : for he had heard that Hezekiah had been sick. And Hezekiah hearkened unto them, and shewed them all the house of his precious things, the silver, and the gold, and the spices, and the precious ointment, and *all* the house of his armour, and all that was found in his treasures: there was nothing in his house, nor in all his dominion, that Hezekiah shewed them not. *(At first sight this looks harmless enough, but the Lord saw that the king was proud, delighted in the flatteries of heathen strangers, and perhaps hoped to strengthen himself by alliance with their rising kingdom. God is jealous of those he loves, and is severe with them in proportion to his love to them. This sad fault of good Hezekiah led a devout writer to cry, "O God ! if thou do not keep us as well in our sunshine as in our storm, we are sure to perish: as in all time of our tribulation, so in all time of our wealth, good Lord, deliver us !")*

14, 15 Then came Isaiah the prophet unto king Hezekiah, and said unto him, What said these men ? and from whence came they unto thee ? And Hezekiah said, They are come from a far country, *even* from Babylon. And he said, What have they seen in thine house ? And Hezekiah answered, All *the things* that *are* in mine house have they seen : there is nothing among my treasures that I have not shewed them.

16, 17, 18 And Isaiah said unto Hezekiah, Hear the word of the LORD. Behold, the days come, that all that *is* in thine house, and that which thy fathers have laid up in store unto this day, shall be carried into Babylon : nothing shall be left, saith the LORD. And of thy sons that shall issue from thee, which thou shalt beget, shall they take away ; and they shall be eunuchs in the palace of the king of Babylon.

19 Then said Hezekiah unto Isaiah, Good *is* the word of the LORD which thou hast spoken. And he said, *Is it* not *good,* if peace and truth be in my days ? *(The rod was heavy, but Hezekiah kissed it like a true-born child of God. Lord, teach us the like patience.)*

21 And Hezekiah slept with his fathers : and Manasseh his son reigned in his stead.

418

JULY 15.—MORNING.

"All manner of sin and blasphemy shall be forgiven unto men."

[Or January 26.]

II. CHRONICLES XXXIII. 1—6; 9—13; 15, 16; 20—25.

MANASSEH *was* twelve years old when he began to reign. (*So that he was born three years after his father's recovery, and perhaps it was the absence of an heir which rendered Hezekiah so loth to die.*) He reigned fifty and five years in Jerusalem : But did *that which was* evil in the sight of the LORD, like unto the abominations of the heathen, whom the LORD had cast out before the children of Israel. (*So that could his father have foreseen what his son would be like, he might have been content to die childless.*)

3—6 For he built again the high places which Hezekiah his father had broken down, and he reared up altars for Baalim, and made groves, and worshipped all the host of heaven, and served them. Also he built altars in the house of the LORD, whereof the LORD had said, In Jerusalem shall my name be for ever. And he built altars for all the host of heaven in the two courts of the house of the LORD. And he caused his children to pass through the fire in the valley of the son of Hinnom : also he observed times, and used enchantments, and used witchcraft, and dealt with a familiar spirit, and with wizards : he wrought much evil in the sight of the LORD, to provoke him to anger. (*He went from bad to worse, he rioted in evil, nothing was too bad for him, he heaped up the most daring impieties, and yet he was the son of a saint. Children may have the best examples, and yet fall into the worst sins.*)

9 So Manasseh made Judah and the inhabitants of Jerusalem to err, *and* to do worse than the heathen, whom the LORD had destroyed before the children of Israel.

10 And the LORD spake to Manasseh, and to his people : but they would not hearken. *They persecuted the prophets and " shed innocent blood very much." It is a sign of great hardness of heart when warnings are despised.*

11 ¶ Wherefore the LORD brought upon them the captains of the host of the king of Assyria, which took Manasseh among the thorns, and bound him with fetters, and carried him to Babylon. (*His kingdom thus became so reduced that it was " as when a man wipeth a dish and turneth it upside down." His great sin was* visited *with a punishment which made men's ears to tingle as they heard of it.*)

12, 13 And when he was in affliction, he besought the LORD his God, and humbled himself greatly before the God of his fathers, And prayed unto him : and he was intreated of him, and heard his supplication, and brought him again to Jerusalem into his kingdom. Then Manasseh knew that the LORD he *was* God. (*Who can say that God is not ready to pardon, when he sees such a sinner saved? No man could be worse than Manasseh, and yet he obtained mercy. Oh, the depths of divine love! Let every sinner in the universe come and welcome to Jesus, for the chief of sinners has been saved.*)

15, 16 And he took away the strange gods, and the idol out of the house of the LORD, and all the altars that he had built in the mount of the house of the LORD, and in Jerusalem, and cast *them* out of the city. And he repaired the altar of the LORD, and sacrificed thereon peace offerings and thank offerings, and commanded Judah to serve the LORD God of Israel.

He ceased to do evil and learned to do well, and this was the best evidence of his sincerity. The Lord grant us also to bring forth fruits meet for repentance.

20 ¶ So Manasseh slept with his fathers, and they buried him in his own house : and Amon his son reigned in his stead.

21—23 Amon *was* two and twenty years old when he began to reign, and reigned two years in Jerusalem. But he did *that which was* evil in the sight of the LORD, as did Manasseh his father : for Amon sacrificed unto all the carved images which Manasseh his father had made, and served them ; And humbled not himself before the LORD, as Manasseh his father had humbled himself ; but Amon trespassed more and more. (*How little does one man learn from the experience of another, even though it be his own father! Electing love is here to be seen. Manasseh sins, and grace gives him repentance ; Amon sins, and continues in it till he perishes.*)

24 And his servants conspired against him, and slew him in his own house.

25 But the people of the land slew all them that had conspired against king Amon ; and the people of the land made Josiah his son king in his stead.

II. CHRONICLES XXXIV. 1—4.

JOSIAH *was* eight years old when he began to reign, and he reigned in Jerusalem one and thirty years. And he did *that which was* right in the sight of the LORD, and walked in the ways of David his father, and declined *neither* to the right hand, nor to the left.

What a vast difference can grace make in persons of the same age. Manasseh began to reign at twelve and Josiah at eight; Manasseh was piously trained by Hezekiah, Josiah was brought up under wicked Amon; yet Manasseh plunged into foul idolatries, and Josiah was tender and holy. The Spirit of God bloweth where he chooses.

3 ¶ For in the eighth year of his reign, while he was yet young, Josiah began to seek after the God of David his father: and in the twelfth year he began to purge Judah and Jerusalem from the high places, and the groves, and the carved images, and the molten images.

He did not wait a moment longer than his juvenile age compelled him, but as soon as ever he was a man he acted the part of a man of God.

4 And they brake down the altars of Baalim in his presence; and the images, that *were* on high above them, he cut down; and the groves, and the carved images, and the molten images, he brake in pieces, and made dust *of them*, and strowed *it* upon the graves of them that had sacrificed unto them. *(Thus shewing contempt for idolatry in every possible manner.)*

II. KINGS XXIII. 15—20.

MOREOVER the altar that *was* at Beth-el, *and* the high place which Jeroboam the son of Nebat, who made Israel to sin, had made, both that altar and the high place he brake down, and burned the high place, *and* stamped *it* small to powder, and burned the grove. And as Josiah turned himself, he spied the sepulchres that *were* there in the mount, and sent, and took the bones out of the sepulchres, and burned *them* upon the altar, and polluted it, according to the word of the LORD which the man of God proclaimed, who proclaimed these words.

17 Then he said, What title *is* that that I see? And the men of the city told him, *It is* the sepulchre of the man of God, which came from Judah, and proclaimed these things that thou hast done against the altar of Beth-el.

18 And he said, Let him alone; let no man move his bones. So they let his bones alone, with the bones of the prophet that came out of Samaria.

19 And all the houses also of the high places that *were* in the cities of Samaria, which the kings of Israel had made to provoke *the LORD* to anger, Josiah took away, and did to them according to all the acts that he had done in Beth-el.

20 And he slew all the priests of the high places that *were* there upon the altars, and burned men's bones upon them, and returned to Jerusalem. *(This was gloriously thorough work. We need such a man now to cleanse our land from the images of Rome which are everywhere being set up by misguided men. If God does not soon interpose, our beloved country will be a Popish land once more. O Lord, frustrate the knavish tricks of Jesuits and others who are now perverting our fellow-countrymen!)*

II. KINGS XXII. 3—7.

AND it came to pass in the eighteenth year of king Josiah, *that* the king sent Shaphan the son of Azaliah, the son of Meshullam, the scribe, to the house of the LORD saying, Go up to Hilkiah the high priest, that he may sum the silver which is brought into the house of the LORD, which the keepers of the door have gathered of the people: And let them deliver it into the hand of the doers of the work, that have the oversight of the house of the LORD: and let them give it to the doers of the work which *is* in the house of the LORD, to repair the breaches of the house, Unto carpenters, and builders, and masons, and to buy timber and hewn stone to repair the house.

7 Howbeit there was no reckoning made with them of the money that was delivered into their hand, because they dealt faithfully. *(Pulling down is not enough; there should be building up. Many are hasty to amend abuses, but are not half as ready to help the good cause. Former kings had used the temple as a sort of bank, from which to take gold and silver in their times of distress; but Josiah was anxious to restore it to its former splendour. It is pleasing to find one so young doing so great a work for the Lord. May the sons of our family be Josiahs.)*

420   "*My heart standeth in awe of Thy Word.*"   JULY 16.—MORNING.

[*Or January* 28.]

II. KINGS XXII. 8—20.

AND Hilkiah the high priest said unto Shaphan the scribe, I have found the book of the law in the house of the LORD. And Hilkiah gave the book to Shaphan, and he read it. *(Perhaps this was the authentic original of the word of God, which some godly priest had hidden away in persecuting times. Copies had always been scarce, and in the bad times they had been hunted out and destroyed. Highly privileged are we who have Bibles in all our houses, and none to take them from us. With what eagerness did these holy men search this precious volume, though among its contents they found a terrible prophecy of coming judgment.)*

9 And Shaphan the scribe came to the king, and said, Thy servants have gathered the money that was found in the house, and have delivered it into the hand of them that do the work, that have the oversight of the house of the LORD.

10 And Shaphan the scribe shewed the king, saying, Hilkiah the priest hath delivered me a book. And Shaphan read it before the king. *They were not like those Popish shavelings who would keep the Bible from the people; they anxiously desired that God's message should be known, and its power felt.*

11 And it came to pass, when the king had heard the words of the book of the law, that he rent his clothes. *(He was of a tender spirit, and trembled at the word of the Lord, when he saw the evils sin had brought upon the nation.)*

12, 13 And the king commanded Hilkiah the priest, and Ahikam the son of Shaphan, and Achbor the son of Michaiah, and Shaphan the scribe, and Asahiah a servant of the king's, saying, Go ye, enquire of the LORD for me, and for the people, and for all Judah, concerning the words of this book that is found: for great *is* the wrath of the LORD that is kindled against us, because our fathers have not hearkened unto the words of this book, to do according unto all that which is written concerning us. *This was practical wisdom. He would know whether the Lord would, in answer to prayer, withdraw the curses which were threatened in the law. After this manner ought we to seek unto the Lord whenever in reading the Scriptures we perceive that we have transgressed.*

14 So Hilkiah the priest, and Ahikam, and Achbor, and Shaphan, and Asahiah, went unto Huldah the prophetess, the wife of Shallum the son of Tikvah, the son of Harhas, keeper of the wardrobe; (now she dwelt in Jerusalem in the college;) and they communed with her. *Huldah was both housewife and prophetess, but the great ones were not too proud to consult her. Perhaps Jeremiah was absent upon the Lord's errands, and in his great alarm the king applied to that servant of God who was near at hand.*

15, 16, 17 And she said unto them, Thus saith the LORD God of Israel, Tell the man that sent you to me, Thus saith the LORD, Behold, I will bring evil upon this place, and upon the inhabitants thereof, *even* all the words of the book which the king of Judah hath read: Because they have forsaken me, and have burned incense unto other gods, that they might provoke me to anger with all the works of their hands; therefore my wrath shall be kindled against this place, and shall not be quenched. *Josiah was king among the people, but he was only a man before God, and so the prophetess called him; she knew not how to flatter, but spoke out as it was her duty to do. Grace makes the feeblest bold.*

18, 19, 20 But to the king of Judah which sent you to enquire of the LORD, thus shall ye say to him, Thus saith the LORD God of Israel, *As touching* the words which thou hast heard; Because thine heart was tender, and thou hast humbled thyself before the LORD, when thou heardest what I spake against this place, and against the inhabitants thereof, that they should become a desolation and a curse, and hast rent thy clothes, and wept before me; I also have heard *thee*, saith the LORD. Behold, therefore, I will gather thee unto thy fathers, and thou shalt be gathered into thy grave in peace; and thine eyes shall not see all the evil which I will bring upon this place. And they brought the king word again. *(Severity to Judah was tempered by mercy to Josiah. He was humble while others were proud. He bowed like a reed before the storm, and the tempest of wrath left him unharmed. See the benefit of submission to God. May the like tenderness of heart be found in each of us, and may the Lord deal graciously with his servants.)*

Joy to the world; the Lord is come!
Let earth receive her King:
Let every heart prepare him room,
And heaven and nature sing.

Joy to the earth; the Saviour reigns!
Let men their songs employ:
While fields, and floods, rocks, hills, and plains,
Repeat the sounding joy.

No more let sins and sorrows grow,
Nor thorns infest the ground;
He comes to make his blessings flow
Far as the curse is found.

He rules the world with truth and grace,
And makes the nations prove
The glories of his righteousness,
And wonders of his love.

When shall thy lovely face be seen?
When shall our eyes behold our God?
What lengths of distance lie between,
And hills of guilt!—a heavy load!

Ye heavenly gates, loose all your chains:
Let the eternal pillars bow!
Blest Saviour, cleave the starry plains,
And make the crystal mountains flow!

Put thy bright robes of triumph on,
And bless our eyes, and bless our ears,
Thou absent Love, thou dear unknown,
Thou fairest of ten thousands fairs.

Jehovah speaks the healing word,
And no disease withstands;
Fevers and plagues obey the Lord,
And fly at his commands.

If half the strings of life should break,
He can our frame restore;
He casts our sins behind his back,
And they are found no more.

Great God of wonders! all thy ways
Are matchless, God-like, and divine;
But the fair glories of thy grace
More God-like and unrivall'd shine:
Who is a pardoning God like thee?
Or who has grace so rich and free?

Crimes of such horror to forgive,
Such guilty, daring worms to spare;
This is thy grand prerogative,
And none shall in the honour share:
Who is a pardoning God like thee?
Or who has grace so rich and free?

Fall, ye idols, fall before him,
Lo, the living God appears;
All ye gods around adore him,
Tremble and confess your fears;
Prostrate from your places hurl'd,
Own the God that made the world.

Hark! a cry among the nations,
"Come, and let us seek the Lord:
Vain our former expectations;
Vain the idols we ador'd:
Zion's King is God alone:
Let us bow before his throne."

Great God, I love thy sacred word;
What light and joy its leaves afford!
Thy precepts guide my doubtful way,
Thy fear forbids my feet to stray.

Thy threatenings wake my slumbering eyes,
And warn me where my danger lies;
They show me all my guilt and shame,
And make me prize the Saviour's name.

May this blest volume ever lie,
Close to my heart and near my eye;
Till life's last hour my thoughts engage,
And be my chosen heritage.

422   "𝕷et your heart be perfect with the 𝕷ord our 𝔊od."   JULY 16 —EVENING.

[*Or January* 29.]

II. CHRONICLES XXXV. 1, 2 ; 7, 8 ; 10—18.

MOREOVER Josiah kept a passover unto the LORD in Jerusalem : and they killed the passover on the fourteenth *day* of the first month. (*This was the day appointed in the law, and Josiah determined to be exact to the letter.*)

2 And he set the priests in their charges, and encouraged them to the service of the house of the LORD. (*Arranging them in proper order with the Levites, so that all things might be performed without disorder. The Lord's service should be rendered to him with all care and reverence ; his work ought never to be performed in a slovenly manner. "Let all things be done decently and in order," is a precept not to be forgotten.*)

7 And Josiah gave to the people, of the flock, lambs and kids, all for the passover offerings, for all that were present, to the number of thirty' thousand, and three thousand bullocks : these were of the king's substance.

8 And his princes gave willingly unto the people, to the priests, and to the Levites. *Many of the people were too poor to bring their own sacrifices, and therefore the generous king provided them ; he thought no expense too great in honour of his God. Liberality towards the good cause is a noble fruit of grace in the heart.*

10, 11 So the service was prepared, and the priests stood in their place, and the Levites in their courses, according to the king's commandment. And they killed the passover, and the priests sprinkled *the blood* from their hands, and the Levites flayed them. (*Thus Judah renewed its covenant, and rejoiced in the grand type of the promised Saviour. No feast is so precious to believers as feeding upon the Lamb of God's passover.*)

12 And they removed the burnt offerings, that they might give according to the divisions of the families of the people, to offer unto the LORD, as *it is* written in the book of Moses. And so *did they* with the oxen.

13 And they roasted the passover with fire, according to the ordinance : but the *other* holy *offerings* sod they in pots, and in caldrons, and in pans, and divided *them* speedily among all the people. (*There were so many to be served, and so few of the priests and Levites, that they used all*

expedition. *When the king's business requireth haste, we must not be tardy.*)

14 And afterward they made ready for themselves, and for the priests : because the priests the sons of Aaron *were busied* in offering of burnt offerings and the fat until night ; therefore the Levites prepared for themselves, and for the priests the sons of Aaron.

15 And the singers the sons of Asaph *were* in their place, according to the commandment of David, and Asaph, and Heman and Jeduthun the king's seer ; and the porters *waited* at every gate ; they might not depart from their service ; for their brethren the Levites prepared for them. (*Singing was not forgotten, nor any other part of the holy office, even the doors were kept. One duty did not jostle another. It is always bad when, while serving God in one way, we become negligent of other duties. Doors must be kept as well as psalms sung.*)

16 So all the service of the LORD was prepared the same day, to keep the passover, and to offer burnt offerings upon the altar of the LORD, according to the commandment of king Josiah.

17 And the children of Israel that were present kept the passover at that time, and the feast of unleavened bread seven days.

18 And there was no passover like to that kept in Israel from the days of Samuel the prophet ; neither did all the kings of Israel keep such a passover as Josiah kept, and the priests, and the Levites, and all Judah and Israel that were present, and the inhabitants of Jerusalem.

There may have been greater numbers present on former occasions, but at no other time were the rules laid down in the word of God so exactly observed, and this is a point in the Lord's eyes of far greater importance than numbers or pomp. It is our duty to worship the Lord in his own way. The closer we keep to Scripture the better ; any departure therefrom mars our worship. Carefully let us remember this, and zealously put away all will-worship, and adore the Lord in spirit and in truth, for the Father seeketh such to worship him. Let others do as they will, but as for this household, let us serve the Lord with our whole hearts.

THE *prophet Zephaniah appeared at the close of Josiah's reign. We will read a portion from his prophecy.*

ZEPHANIAH III. 8—20.

8 Wait ye upon me, saith the LORD, until the day that I rise up to the prey: for my determination *is* to gather the nations, that I may assemble the kingdoms, to pour upon them mine indignation, *even* all my fierce anger: for all the earth shall be devoured with the fire of my jealousy.

9 For then will I turn to the people a pure language, that they may all call upon the name of the LORD, to serve him with one consent. *After wrath will come mercy. The language of men has become impure with sin, and their tongues are confounded with diverse forms of speech; but when the Spirit of God descended at Pentecost he sanctified human lips to the Lord's service, and gave an earnest of that future day in which with one voice all nations shall praise God.*

10 From beyond the rivers of Ethiopia my suppliants, *even* the daughter of my dispersed, shall bring mine offering. *From afar shall Israel return to their land, and the most distant nations shall be converted to the Lord. O long-expected day, begin!*

11 In that day shalt thou not be ashamed for all thy doings, wherein thou hast transgressed against me: for then I will take away out of the midst of thee them that rejoice in thy pride, and thou shalt no more be haughty because of my holy mountain. *(The cause of shame would be removed by sanctifying grace, and then they would enjoy peace with God.)*

12 I will also leave in the midst of thee an afflicted and poor people, and they shall trust in the name of the LORD. *When boasting is excluded, trust begins, and the poorest are then made rich in grace.*

13 The remnant of Israel shall not do iniquity, nor speak lies; neither shall a deceitful tongue be found in their mouth: for they shall feed and lie down, and none shall make *them afraid. (What a choice promise! Sin both starves and disturbs the soul, but grace brings both food and rest.)*

14, 15 Sing, O daughter of Zion; shout, O Israel; be glad and rejoice with all the heart, O daughter of ·Jerusalem. The LORD hath taken away thy judgments, he hath cast out thine enemy: the king of Israel, *even* the LORD, *is* in the midst of thee: thou shalt not see evil any more. *(Joyful is the presence of God: what evil can harm us when Jesus is near? The fulfilment of this promise to Israel is yet to come, but believers in their measure enjoy it even now.)*

16, 17 In that day it shall be said to Jerusalem, Fear thou not: and to Zion, Let not thine hands be slack. The LORD thy God in the midst of thee *is* mighty; he will save, he will rejoice over thee with joy; he will rest in his love, he will joy over thee with singing. *(A marvellous expression. Think of God himself as singing! " As the bridegroom rejoiceth over the bride so shall thy God rejoice over thee !" Creation could not make Him sing, but the work of grace is above measure dear to his heart, and makes him " rejoice with joy"—a very vivid and forcible expression.)*

18 I will gather *them that are* sorrowful for the solemn assembly, *who* are of thee, *to whom* the reproach of it *was* a burden. *(When in exile they could not hold their solemn feasts, and this was a burdensome reproach to them; but God will gather them, and their reproach shall be rolled away.)*

19 Behold, at that time I will undo all that afflict thee: and I will save her that halteth, and gather her that was driven out; and I will get them praise and fame in every land where they have been put to shame.

20 At that time will I bring you *again*, even in the time that I gather you: for I will make you a name and a praise among all people of the earth, when I turn back your captivity before your eyes, saith the LORD. *Persecution and contempt will come to an end, and the saints shall in the latter days be accounted the excellent of the earth. Shame and reproach are the cross which Christians must carry for their Lord's sake, but the loving providence of God will change all this ere long, to the confusion of our adversaries and his own eternal glory. Let us hope and quietly wait, resting in the love of God.*

The covenant of grace all blessings secures,
Believer, rejoice, for all things are yours;
And God from his purpose will never remove,
But love thee, and bless thee, and rest in his love.

424   " Thou, ☩ Lord, remainest for ever."   JULY 17.—EVENING.

[Or January 31.]

II. CHRONICLES XXXV. 20—27.

AFTER all this, when Josiah had prepared the temple, Necho king of Egypt came up to fight against Charchemish by Euphrates : and Josiah went out against him.

Probably he thought he had good reasons for so doing: it may be that he was bound by treaty to side with the Assyrian king; but it would have been far better to have let the matter alone. God's people were separated for himself, and they did well when they remained so. What had they to do with the quarrels of these two great kings? They had better have said, " Let the potsherds strive with the potsherds of the earth;" as for us, we will abide under the shadow of the Almighty.

21 But he sent ambassadors to him, saying, What have I to do with thee, thou king of Judah? *I come* not against thee this day, but against the house wherewith I have war : for God commanded me to make haste : forbear thee from *meddling with* God, who *is* with me, that he destroy thee not. *(Pharaoh knew that Josiah was a devout man, and therefore hoped to keep him quiet by a pretended message from God. It was not likely that the true God would send a message to his own favoured servant by a heathen like Necho; and Josiah is by no means to be blamed for disregarding the cunning advice of the Egyptian.)*

22, 23, 24 Nevertheless Josiah would not turn his face from him, but disguised himself, that he might fight with him, and hearkened not unto the words of Necho from the mouth of God, and came to fight in the valley of Megiddo. And the archers shot at king Josiah; and the king said to his servants, Have me away; for I am sore wounded. His servants therefore took him out of that chariot, and put him in the second chariot, that he had; and they brought him to Jerusalem and he died, and was buried in *one of the sepulchres of his fathers. (Though Pharaoh had only intended deceit, the event proved that God had resolved to take his servant home by an honourable death, removing him speedily from the evil to come. Josiah intended no wrong in fighting with Necho; but felt in honour bound to oppose his march against the Assyrian king, to whom his grandfather owed his restoration to the throne: the fact that he was killed by no means shows that he was in error, for in the best of causes a man may die.)* And all Judah and Jerusalem mourned for Josiah.

25 ¶ And Jeremiah lamented for Josiah : and all the singing men and the singing women spake of Josiah in their lamentations to this day, and made them an ordinance in Israel : and, behold, they *are* written in the lamentations. *(This is not that Book of Lamentations which forms part of Holy Scripture, but some other volume which is now lost. There were many books extant in those days which were not inspired, and the fact that these are lost should make us the more grateful for the special providence which has preserved the sacred volume entire.)*

26 Now the rest of the acts of Josiah, and his goodness, according to *that which was* written in the law of the LORD,

27 And his deeds, first and last, behold, they *are* written in the book of the kings of Israel and Judah.

THOUGH *not written in sole reference to Josiah, the following portion of Jeremiah's Lamentations is appropriate.*

LAMENTATIONS V. 15—22.

15 The joy of our heart is ceased ; our dance is turned into mourning.

16 The crown is fallen *from* our head : woe unto us, that we have sinned !

17 For this our heart is faint; for these *things* our eyes are dim.

18 Because of the mountain of Zion, which is desolate, the foxes walk upon it.

19 Thou, O LORD, remainest for ever; thy throne from generation to generation.

Though the king is dead, the Lord lives on; and this is our comfort: to him will we appeal.

20 Wherefore dost thou forget us for ever, *and* forsake us so long time ?

21 Turn thou us unto thee, O LORD, and we shall be turned ; renew our days as of old.

22 But thou hast utterly rejected us ; thou art very wroth against us.

Child of sorrow, do they leave thee,
 Those on whom thy hopes were stayed ?
Jesus calls, and will receive thee
 With a love which cannot fade ;
  Hark, he bids thee
 Seek the home for sinners made.

UPON *the death of Josiah the people crowned the king's second son, Jehoahaz, who was the very opposite of his pious father.*

II. KINGS. XXIII. 31—33.

31—33 Jehoahaz *was* twenty and three years old when he began to reign ; and he reigned three months in Jerusalem. And he did evil in the sight of the LORD, according to all that his fathers had done. And Pharaoh-nechoh put him in bands at Riblah in the land of Hamath, that he might not reign in Jerusalem ; and put the land to a tribute of an hundred talents of silver, and a talent of gold.

THIS *young king appears to have been of a very warlike and energetic character, so that he provoked his neighbours round about him, and therefore Pharaoh Necho soon deprived him of his crown. The prophet Ezekiel thus described him :—*

EZEKIEL XIX. 1—4.

1 Moreover take thou up a lamentation for the princes of Israel,

2 And say, What *is* thy mother ? A lioness : she lay down among lions, she nourished her whelps among young lions.

3 And she brought up one of her whelps : it became a young lion, and it learned to catch the prey ; it devoured men.

4 The nations also heard of him ; he was taken in their pit, and they brought him with chains unto the land of Egypt.

JEREMIAH *had given Jehoahaz fair warning, but it had been lost upon him. After Jehoahaz had been carried away prisoner, Jeremiah went to the new king with a message concerning himself and his predecessor.*

JEREMIAH XXII. 1—5; 7—12.

1—4 Thus saith the LORD ; Go down to the house of the king of Judah, and speak there this word, And say, Hear the word of the LORD, O king of Judah, that sittest upon the throne of David, thou, and thy servants, and thy people that enter in by these gates : Thus saith the LORD ; Execute ye judgment and righteousness, and deliver the spoiled out of the hand of the oppressor : and do no wrong, do no violence to the stranger, the fatherless, nor the widow, neither shed innocent blood in this place.

For if ye do this thing indeed, then shall there enter in by the gates of this house kings sitting upon the throne of David, riding in chariots and on horses, he, and his servants, and his people. (*Which promise is the more remarkable because the Jewish kingdom was reduced to the lowest possible ebb, and it seemed scarcely possible that it should recover. It gave them also one more opportunity of repentance, with the prospect of escape from the doom which had long been threatened.*)

5 But if ye will not hear these words, I swear by myself, saith the LORD, that this house shall become a desolation. (*The alternative was set before them of life or death, even as heaven and hell are set before us this day.*)

7, 8 And I will prepare destroyers against thee, every one with his weapons : and they shall cut down thy choice cedars, and cast *them* into the fire. And many nations shall pass by this city, and they shall say every man to his neighbour, Wherefore hath the LORD done thus unto this great city ?

9 Then they shall answer, Because they have forsaken the covenant of the LORD their God, and worshipped other gods and served them.

God will make the impenitent to be monuments of wrath, and trophies of justice. · O may it never be so with us !

10—12 Weep ye not for the dead, neither bemoan him : *but* weep sore for him that goeth away : for he shall return no more, nor see his native country. For thus saith the LORD touching Shallum (*Jehoahaz*) the son of Josiah king of Judah, which reigned instead of Josiah his father, which went forth out of this place ; He shall not return thither any more : But he shall die in the place whither they have led him captive, and shall see this land no more. (*Three months of his sin had been more than enough, he would never return, though the people doted upon him. The career of some sinners is soon over.*)

The Lord hath eyes to give the blind ;
The Lord supports the sinking mind ;
He helps the stranger in distress,
The widow and the fatherless.

His truth for ever stands secure :
He saves the oppress'd, he feeds the poor;
He sends the labouring conscience peace,
And grants the prisoners sweet release.

426   "The Lord God is my strength."   JULY 18.—EVENING.

[*Or February 2.*]

IN *all probability the prophet Habakkuk flourished about the time of the short reign of Jehoahaz. We will read his prayer.*

HABAKKUK III. 2—19.

2 O LORD, I have heard thy speech, *and* was afraid: O LORD, revive thy work in the midst of the years, in the midst of the years make known ; in wrath remember mercy. *(This prayer well suits the case of the Church of God at this time; may the Lord graciously hear it. The prophet describes the Lord's appearance to his people at Sinai, and the way in which he conducted them to the promised land through the Jordan, subduing all their foes before them. Thus he strengthened his confidence that the Lord would again appear to deliver his people.)*

3, 4 God came from Teman, and the Holy One from mount Paran. Selah. His glory covered the heavens, and the earth was full of his praise. And *his* brightness was as the light; he had horns *coming* out of his hand : *(Or beams like those of the sun :)* and there *was* the hiding of his power. *(Even this glory was not a full display of his power : the horns or emblems of his power, and the beamings of his glory were seen, but not the power and glory themselves, for these are insufferably bright. It has been well said that even the clearest revelation of God is also an obvelation or concealment. If the face of Moses needed a veil before men could look on it, much more does the glory of the Lord.)*

5 Before him went the pestilence, and burning coals went forth at his feet. *(To destroy the Canaanites and make room for Israel.)*

6 He stood, and measured the earth : he beheld, and drove asunder the nations; and the everlasting mountains were scattered, the perpetual hills did bow : his ways *are* everlasting.

7 I saw the tents of Cushan in affliction : *and* the curtains of the land of Midian did tremble. *Nations hitherto unconquerable trembled at his might ; none could stand before him.*

8, 9 Was the LORD displeased against the rivers ? *was* thine anger against the rivers ? *was* thy wrath against the sea, that thou didst ride upon thine horses *and* thy chariots of salvation ? Thy bow was made quite naked, *according* to the oaths of the tribes, *even thy* word. Selah. *(God's bow was taken from its case, and used for*

war, *even as he had sworn to his chosen.)* Thou didst cleave the earth with rivers.

10 The mountains saw thee, *and* they trembled : the overflowing of the water passed by : the deep uttered his voice, *and* lifted up his hands on high.

11 The sun *and* moon stood still in their habitation : at the light of thine arrows they went, *and* at the shining of thy glittering spear.

12, 13 Thou didst march through the land in indignation, thou didst thresh the heathen in anger. Thou wentest forth for the salvation of thy people, *even* for salvation with thine anointed; thou woundedst the head out of the house of the wicked, by discovering the foundation unto the neck. Selah. *(Deadly were his blows of vengeance; he smote nations as when the axe severs the neck and smites off the head.)*

14 Thou didst strike through with his staves the head of his villages : they came out as a whirlwind to scatter me : their rejoicing *was* as to devour the poor secretly.

15 Thou didst walk through the sea with thine horses, *through* the heap of great waters.

16 When I heard, my belly trembled ; my lips quivered at the voice : rottenness entered into my bones, and I trembled in myself, that I might rest in the day of trouble : when he cometh up unto the people, he will invade them with his troops. *(All holy men have thus trembled at the sight of God, yet faith has given them rest. How sweet are the closing verses !)*

17 ¶ Although the fig tree shall not blossom, neither *shall* fruit *be* in the vines ; the labour of the olive shall fail, and the fields shall yield no meat ; the flock shall be cut off from the fold, and *there shall be* no herd in the stalls :

18, 19 Yet I will rejoice in the LORD, I will joy in the God of my salvation. The LORD God *is* my strength, and he will make my feet like hinds' *feet*, and he will make me to walk upon mine high places. To the chief singer on my stringed instruments. *(Though war and famine should cause a failure of all comforts, yet would the prophet find joy enough in his God; yea, he would leap with exultation like a hind upon the rocks. Should the worst come to the worst, he would still attune his heart to magnify the Lord. May this devoutly trustful spirit rule in all our hearts !)*

WE now find another of Josiah's sons upon the throne, but he was no better than his brother. Alas, poor Judah!

II. KINGS XXIII. 34—37.

34—37 And Pharaoh-nechoh made Eliakim the son of Josiah king, and turned his name to Jehoiakim, and took Jehoahaz away: and he came to Egypt, and died there. And Jehoiakim gave the silver and gold to Pharaoh; but he taxed the land to give the money according to the commandment of Pharaoh. Jehoiakim was twenty and five years old when he began to reign; and he reigned eleven years in Jerusalem. And he did evil in the sight of the LORD, according to all that his fathers had done.

EZEKIEL has described his character and reign in a parable. Jehoahaz was the first lion cub which had been destroyed, and then the nation found another in Jehoiakim.

EZEKIEL XIX. 5—9.

5 Now when she saw that she had waited, and her hope was lost, then she took another of her whelps, and made him a young lion.

6, 7 And he went up and down among the lions, he became a young lion, and learned to catch the prey, and devoured men. And he knew their desolate palaces, and he laid waste their cities; and the land was desolate, and the fulness thereof, by the noise of his roaring. (Jehoiakim was evidently a plunderer of the poor nations around him, a common freebooter, living by the sword.)

8 Then the nations set against him on every side from the provinces, and spread their net over him: he was taken in their pit.

9 And they put him in ward in chains, and brought him to the king of Babylon: they brought him into holds, that his voice should no more be heard upon the mountains of Israel.

II. KINGS XXIV. 1—4.

IN his days Nebuchadnezzar king of Babylon came up, and Jehoiakim became his servant three years: then he turned and rebelled against him. (No doubt tempted by the promises of the Egyptian king. Judah lay between the territories of the two great rivals, and both were anxious to secure it as a border country.)

2—4 And the LORD sent against him bands of the Chaldees, the Syrians, the Moabites, and the children of Ammon. Surely at the commandment of the LORD came this upon Judah, to remove them out of his sight, for the sins of Manasseh, according to all that he did; And also for the innocent blood that he shed: for he filled Jerusalem with innocent blood; which the LORD would not pardon. (Jehoiakim and his people endorsed the sin of Manasseh, and the accumulated wrath of God fell upon them.)

THIS king was a great oppressor, and built a palace for himself by the unpaid toil of his subjects, making it sumptuous with the spoils which he took as a border robber. Jeremiah thus bravely rebuked him—

JEREMIAH XXII. 13—19.

13, 14 Woe unto him that buildeth his house by unrighteousness, and his chambers by wrong; that useth his neighbour's service without wages, and giveth him not for his work; That saith, I will build me a wide house and large chambers, and cutteth him out windows; and it is cieled with cedar, and painted with vermilion.

15 Shalt thou reign, because thou closest thyself in cedar? did not thy father (Josiah) eat and drink, and do judgment and justice, and then it was well with him?

16, 17 He judged the cause of the poor and needy; then it was well with him: was not this to know me? saith the LORD. But thine eyes and thine heart are not but for thy covetousness, and for to shed innocent blood, and for oppression, and for violence, to do it.

18 Therefore thus saith the LORD concerning Jehoiakim the son of Josiah king of Judah; They shall not lament for him, saying, Ah my brother! or, Ah sister! they shall not lament for him, saying, Ah lord! or, Ah his glory!

19 He shall be buried with the burial of an ass, drawn and cast forth beyond the gates of Jerusalem. (None lamented this tyrannical monarch. Consigned to infamy, his carcase was left to rot like that of an ass, none caring to cast a handful of earth over his detested person. The poor should be paid fair wages for their labour, and never should the rich and mighty dare to wrong them, for God is the avenger of all such. Woe unto those who grind the faces of the needy!)

428   "Be ye followers of God as dear children."   JULY 19.—EVENING.

[*Or February* 4.]

JEREMIAH XXXV. 1—3 ; 5—19.

THE word which came unto Jeremiah from the LORD in the days of Jehoiakim the son of Josiah king of Judah, saying, Go unto the house of the Rechabites, and speak unto them, and bring them into the house of the LORD, into one of the chambers, and give them wine to drink. (*The Rechabites were descendants of Jethro, and maintained a separate existence as a nation by continuing their wandering habits and dwelling only in tents.*)

3—5 Then I took Jaazaniah the son of Jeremiah, the son of Habaziniah, and his brethren, and all his sons, and the whole house of the Rechabites ; And I set before the sons of the house of the Rechabites pots full of wine, and cups, and I said unto them, Drink ye wine.

6, 7 But they said, We will drink no wine : for Jonadab the son of Rechab our father commanded us, saying, Ye shall drink no wine, *neither* ye, nor your sons for ever : Neither shall ye build house, nor sow seed, nor plant vineyard, nor have *any :* but all your days ye shall dwell in tents ; that ye may live many days in the land where ye *be* strangers.

8—11 Thus have we obeyed the voice of Jonadab the son of Rechab our father in all that he hath charged us, to drink no wine all our days, we, our wives, our sons, nor our daughters ; Nor to build houses for us to dwell in : neither have we vineyard, nor field, nor seed : But we have dwelt in tents, and have obeyed, and done according to all that Jonadab our father commanded us. But it came to pass, when Nebuchadrezzar king of Babylon came up into the land, that we said, Come, and let us go to Jerusalem for fear of the army of the Chaldeans, and for fear of the army of the Syrians : so we dwell at Jerusalem.

12 ¶ Then came the word of the LORD unto Jeremiah, saying,

13 Thus saith the LORD of hosts, the God of Israel ; Go and tell the men of Judah and the inhabitants of Jerusalem, Will ye not receive instruction to hearken to my words ? saith the LORD.

14 The words of Jonadab the son of Rechab, that he commanded his sons not to drink wine, are performed ; for unto this day they drink none, but obey their father's commandment :

notwithstanding I have spoken unto you, rising early and speaking ; but ye hearkened not unto me.

15 I have sent also unto you all my servants the prophets, rising up early and sending *them,* saying, Return ye now every man from his evil way, and amend your doings, and go not after other gods to serve them, and ye shall dwell in the land which I have given to you and to your fathers : but ye have not inclined your ear, nor hearkened unto me.

16, 17 Because the sons of Jonadab the son of Rechab have performed the commandment of their father, which he commanded them ; but this people hath not hearkened unto me : Therefore thus saith the LORD God of hosts, the God of Israel ; Behold, I will bring upon Judah, and upon all the inhabitants of Jerusalem all the evil that I have pronounced against them : because I have spoken unto them, but they have not heard ; and I have called unto them, but they have not answered.

The reasoning is very forcible. If the sons of Jonadab so exactly and continuously obeyed their father, how great was the sin of Judah in refusing to obey her God!

18 ¶ And Jeremiah said unto the house of the Rechabites, Thus saith the LORD of hosts, the God of Israel ; Because ye have obeyed the commandment of Jonadab your father, and kept all his precepts, and done according unto all that he hath commanded you :

19 Therefore thus saith the LORD of hosts, the God of Israel ; Jonadab the son of Rechab shall not want a man to stand before me for ever.

The Rev. Joseph Wolf, missionary in the east, thus writes :—" On my arrival in Mesopotamia, some Jews that I saw there pointed me to one of the ancient Rechabites. He stood before me, wild like an Arab, holding the bridle of his horse in his hand. I showed him the Bible in Hebrew and Arabic, which he was much rejoiced to see, as he could read both languages, but had no knowledge of the New Testament. After having proclaimed to him the tidings of salvation, and made him a present of the Hebrew and Arabic Bibles and Testaments, I asked him, 'Whose descendant are you?' 'Mousa,' said he, boisterously, 'is my name, and I will show you who were my ancestors ;' on which he immediately began to read from the fifth to the eleventh verse of Jeremiah-xxxv. 'Where do you reside' ? said I. 'At Mesha, now called Mecca, in the deserts around those places. We drink no wine, and plant no vineyard, and sow no seed; and live in tents, as Jonadab our father commanded us. Hobab was our father too. Come to us, and you will find us sixty thousand in number; and you see thus the prophecy has been fulfilled.' ' Therefore thus saith the Lord of hosts, the God of Israel; Jonadab the son of Rechab shall not want a man to stand before me for ever ;' and saying this, Mousa the Rechabite mounted his horse and fled away, and left behind a host of evidence in favour of sacred writ."

O that God's children here below,
  Might thus his laws fulfil,
And each, where God has placed him, know
  And do his holy will.

Guide us, O Lord, by grace divine,
  That we may never stray ;
May Christ our Sun, for ever shine,
  Upon our heavenward way.

With one consent let all the earth
  To God their cheerful voices raise ;
Glad homage pay with awful mirth,
  And sing before him songs of praise.

Convinced that he is God alone,
  From whom both we and all proceed ;
We, whom he chooses for his own,
  The flock that he vouchsafes to feed.

For he's the Lord, supremely good,
  His mercy is for ever sure ;
His truth, which always firmly stood,
  To endless ages shall endure.

The Lord, the Judge, before his throne
  Bids the whole world draw nigh ;
The nations near the rising sun,
  And near the western sky.

No more shall bold blasphemers say,
  " Judgment will ne'er begin ;"
No more abuse his long delay
  To impudence and sin.

Thron'd on a cloud our God shall come,
  Bright flames prepare his way ;
Thunder and darkness, fire and storm,
  Lead on the dreadful day.

What though no flowers the fig-tree clothe,
  Though vines their fruit deny,
The labour of the olive fail,
  And fields no meat supply :

Though from the fold, with sad surprise,
  My flock cut off I see ;
Though famine pine in empty stalls,
  Where herds were wont to be ;

Yet in the Lord will I be glad,
  And glory in his love ;
In him I'll joy, who will the God
  Of my salvation prove.

God is the treasure of my soul ;
  The source of lasting joy ;
A joy which want shall not impair,
  Nor death itself destroy.

O Zion, when I think on thee,
I wish for pinions like the dove,
And mourn to think that I should be
So distant from the place I love.

But yet we shall behold the day,
When Zion's children shall return ;
Our sorrows then shall flee away,
And we shall never, never mourn.

The hope that such a day will come,
Makes e'en the captives' portion sweet ;
Tho' now we wander far from home,
In Zion soon we all shall meet.

LET *us now read that famous prophecy of Jeremiah in which a period of seventy years was indicated as the time of the captivity in Babylon.*

JEREMIAH XXV. 1—14.

1--3 The word that came to Jeremiah concerning all the people of Judah in the fourth year of Jehoiakim the son of Josiah king of Judah, that *was* the first year of Nebuchadrezzar king of Babylon; The which Jeremiah the prophet spake unto all the people of Judah, and to all the inhabitants of Jerusalem, saying, I have spoken unto you, rising early and speaking; but ye have not hearkened. (*It is a great grief to a minister when his earnestness is disregarded, and men still turn a deaf ear to his appeals. This is, moreover, a great aggravation of sin; for every rejected reproof adds a new degree of sinfulness to transgression. Are any of our household resisting the voice of God, and sinning against light and knowledge? If so, may the Lord turn them by his grace.*)

4 And the LORD hath sent unto you all his servants the prophets, rising early and sending *them;* but ye have not hearkened, nor inclined your ear to hear. (*When parents, teachers, brothers, and sisters have spoken to us, and we remain hardened, we have much to answer for.*)

5—7 They said, Turn ye again now every one from his evil way, and from the evil of your doings, and dwell in the land that the LORD hath given unto you and to your fathers for ever and ever : And go not after other gods to serve them, and to worship them, and provoke me not to anger with the works of your hands; and I will do you no hurt. Yet ye have not hearkened unto me, saith the LORD; that ye might provoke me to anger with the works of your hands to your own hurt. (*Wrong-doing always hurts those who are guilty of it. Every man who sins is an enemy to himself.*)

8, 9 ¶ Therefore thus saith the LORD of hosts; Because ye have not heard my words, Behold, I will send and take all the families of the north, saith the LORD, and Nebuchadrezzar the king of Babylon, my servant, and will bring them against this land, and against the inhabitants thereof, and against all these nations round about, and will utterly destroy them, and make them an astonishment, and an hissing, and perpetual desolations.

The Medes and other northern people were confederate with Babylon, and by their ferocious destructiveness turned Judea into a desert, and made its cities heaps of ruins.

10 Moreover I will take from them the voice of mirth, and the voice of gladness, the voice of the bridegroom, and the voice of the bride, the sound of the millstones, and the light of the candle. (*The houses which remained standing were uninhabited; in the morning no grinding of the handmill proclaimed the preparation of the early meal, and in the evening no night lamp was lit at the time when labour ends. Destruction reigned supreme.*)

11 And this whole land shall be a desolation, *and* an astonishment; and these nations shall serve the king of Babylon seventy years.

12—14 And it shall come to pass, when seventy years are accomplished, *that* I will punish the king of Babylon, and that nation, saith the LORD, for their iniquity, and the land of the Chaldeans, and will make it perpetual desolations. And I will bring upon that land all my words which I have pronounced against it, *even* all that is written in this book, which Jeremiah hath prophesied against all the nations. For many nations and great kings shall serve themselves of them also : and I will recompense them according to their deeds, and according to the works of their own hands.

Seventy years Judah must be captive, the exact amount of the Sabbaths of the 490 years from the reign of Saul to the captivity, and therefore a most righteous retribution for violated Sabbaths. God's judgments are by rule and measure, but his mercy knows no bounds. To Babylon judgment came more terribly than to Judah, according to the spirit of that text: "If judgment begin at the house of God, what shall the end be of them that obey not the gospel of God?" Judah rose again, but Babylon never; the Lord utterly consumed the rod with which he had so sorely smitten his chosen nation. Lord, when thou dost chasten us, deal with us as with sons, and not as thou dost with aliens and enemies.

IN those evil days Jeremiah continued to plead with the people and mourn for their hardness of heart. Let us hear him speak—

JEREMIAH XVII. 1—17.

1, 2 The sin of Judah *is* written with a pen of iron, *and* with the point of a diamond : *it is* graven upon the table of their heart, and upon the horns of your altars ; Whilst their children remember their altars and their groves by the green trees upon the high hills. *(They were as keen after idols as if the propensity to idolatry had been graven into them with an iron pen never to be erased, and they were as confident in it as if it had been sanctioned by a law inscribed with a diamond-point upon their altars. Upon the tablets of men's hearts, where God's holy law should be, all manner of evil is written.)*

3, 4 O my mountain in the field, I will give thy substance *and* all thy treasures to the spoil, *and* thy high places for sin, throughout all thy borders. And thou, even thyself, shalt discontinue from thine heritage that I gave thee ; and I will cause thee to serve thine enemies in the land which thou knowest not : for ye have kindled a fire in mine anger, *which* shall burn for ever.

5, 6 ¶ Thus saith the LORD ; Cursed *be* the man that trusteth in man, and maketh flesh his arm, and whose heart departeth from the LORD. For he shall be like the heath in the desert, and shall not see when good cometh ; but shall inhabit the parched places in the wilderness, *in* a salt land and not inhabited. *(The Jews were prone to trust in Egypt as the rival of Babylon. Creature confidence is essentially idolatry, and if it be found in us we are guilty of that sin, even though no image be set up in our house. The dreary junipers of the desert are more to be envied than men who trust in men.)*

7, 8 Blessed *is* the man that trusteth in the LORD, and whose hope the LORD is. For he shall be as a tree planted by the waters, and *that* spreadeth out her roots by the river, and shall not see when heat cometh, but her leaf shall be green ; and shall not be careful in the year of drought, neither shall cease from yielding fruit. *(Trials will come, even as heat and drought try every tree, but faith sets the believer above circumstances, and makes him always flourish.)*

9 ¶ The heart *is* deceitful above all *things*, and desperately wicked : who can know it ?

10 I the LORD search the heart, *I* try the reins, even to give every man according to his ways, *and* according to the fruit of his doings.

11 *As* the partridge sitteth *on* eggs, and hatcheth *them* not ; *so* he that getteth riches, and not by right, shall leave them in the midst of his days, and at his end shall be a fool.

The bird, with all her care, often fails to hatch her eggs ; and so Jehoiakim and other oppressors gathered together what they were not permitted to enjoy.

12 ¶ A glorious high throne from the beginning *is* the place of our sanctuary. *(High places for sin he had condemned, but his soul rejoices in the glorious high place of everlasting love. To that sacred mount let us daily resort.)*

13 O LORD, the hope of Israel, all that forsake thee shall be ashamed, *and* they that depart from me shall be written in the earth, because they have forsaken the LORD, the fountain of living waters.

14 Heal me, O LORD, and I shall be healed ; save me, and I shall be saved : for thou *art* my praise. *(I praise thee for past mercies. O be gracious to me now in this time of need!).*

15 ¶ Behold, they say unto me, Where *is* the word of the LORD ? let it come now. *(In taunting mockery they challenged the prophet's message, and defied the Lord to fulfil his threats ; this made him a man of sorrows.)*

16 As for me, I have not hastened from *being* a pastor to follow thee : neither have I desired the woeful day ; thou knowest : that which came out of my lips was *right* before thee. *(He foretold their destruction, but he did not desire it. When ministers preach of hell, unthinking persons call them harsh, but it would be far greater harshness if they suffered men to live in false peace, and to die unwarned.)*

17 Be not a terror unto me : thou *art* my hope in the day of evil. *(He felt the unkindness of his hearers, for he had a very sensitive heart, but he feared most of all being left of God. It is not likely that so good a Master would cast off his faithful servants, and yet when we are hard pushed grievous doubts will intrude. Lord, increase our faith.)*

DANIEL I. 1—16.

IN the third year of the reign of Jehoiakim king of Judah came Nebuchadnezzar king of Babylon unto Jerusalem, and besieged it.

2 And the Lord gave Jehoiakim king of Judah into his hand, with part of the vessels of the house of God : which he carried into the land of Shinar to the house of his god ; and he brought the vessels into the treasure house of his god.

3, 4 And the king spake unto Ashpenaz the master of his eunuchs, that he should bring *certain* of the children of Israel, and of the king's seed, and of the princes ; Children in whom *was* no blemish, but well favoured, and skilful in all wisdom, and cunning in knowledge, and understanding science, and such as *had* ability in them to stand in the king's palace, and whom they might teach the learning and the tongue of the Chaldeans. *(This prudent monarch sought to increase the splendour and influence of the Chaldean court by having men of intelligence near at hand. He had probably made a selection from the noble families of other subjugated nations, and now he did the same with the captives brought from Judah.)*

5 And the king appointed them a daily provision of the king's meat *(or food)*, and of the wine which he drank : so nourishing them three years, that at the end thereof they might stand before the king. *(They were to be thus honourably sustained and duly educated, till their personal beauty and mental gifts would be developed, and they would become fit attendants upon his majesty.)*

6 Now among these were of the children of Judah, Daniel, Hananiah, Mishael, and Azariah :

7 Unto whom the prince of the eunuchs gave names : for he gave unto Daniel *(whose name signifies* "judge of God" *) the name* of Belteshazzar *(or Bel's favourite)*, and to Hananiah, of Shadrach *(or young friend of the king)*; and to Mishael, of Meshach *(which probably means the lamb)*; and to Azariah, of Abed-nego *(or servant of Nebo. There may be little in a name to some persons, but upon others titles have very great influence ; nevertheless, these three holy youths were not perverted from their faith : their names were changed, but not their natures.)*

8 ¶ But Daniel purposed in his heart that he would not defile himself with the portion of the king's meat, nor with the wine which he drank : therefore he requested of the prince of the eunuchs that he might not defile himself.

The king's food was such as Hebrews were forbidden to eat, and his wine had most probably been consecrated to idols by libations, therefore Daniel endeavoured to avoid defilement.

9 Now God had brought Daniel into favour and tender love with the prince of the eunuchs.

10 And the prince of the eunuchs said unto Daniel, I fear my lord the king, who hath appointed your meat and your drink : for why should he see your faces worse liking than the children which *are* of your sort ? then shall ye make *me* endanger my head to the king.

11 Then said Daniel to Melzar, whom the prince of the eunuchs had set over Daniel, Hananiah, Mishael, and Azariah,

12, 13 Prove thy servants, I beseech thee, ten days ; and let them give us pulse *(or vegetable diet only)* to eat, and water to drink. Then let our countenances be looked upon before thee, and the countenance of the children that eat of the portion of the king's meat : and as thou seest, deal with thy servants.

14 So he consented to them in this matter, and proved them ten days.

15 And at the end of ten days their countenances appeared fairer and fatter in flesh than all the children which did eat the portion of the king's meat. *(Their temperate living had promoted rather than injured their health, an experience which has been confirmed in hundreds of instances ; moreover, the Lord whom they so scrupulously obeyed, saw to it that they should not suffer. Be it ours to follow the right course with care, and no harm can come of it.)*

16 Thus Melzar took away the portion of their meat, and the wine that they should drink ; and gave them pulse. *(Thus by courteously requesting the favour, and submitting cheerfully to the officer's test, Daniel and his friends gained their point, which they might not have done had they been rude and rash. Gentleness wins where roughness would utterly fail. The decision and wisdom shown by these four young men are an example to us all.)*

DANIEL II. 1—9; 12—24.

AND in the second year of the reign of Nebuchadnezzar Nebuchadnezzar dreamed dreams, wherewith his spirit was troubled, and his sleep brake from him.

2 Then the king commanded to call the magicians, and the astrologers, and the sorcerers, and the Chaldeans, for to shew the king his dreams. So they came and stood before the king.

3 And the king said unto them, I have dreamed a dream, and my spirit was troubled to know the dream.

4 Then spake the Chaldeans to the king in Syriack, O king, live for ever : tell thy servants the dream, and we will shew the interpretation.

5, 6 The king answered and said to the Chaldeans, The thing is gone from me : if ye will not make known unto me the dream, with the interpretation thereof, ye shall be cut in pieces, and your houses shall be made a dunghill. But if ye shew the dream, and the interpretation thereof, ye shall receive of me gifts and rewards and great honour : therefore shew me the dream, and the interpretation thereof.

7 They answered again and said, Let the king tell his servants the dream, and we will shew the interpretation of it.

8, 9 The king answered and said, I know of certainty that ye would gain the time, (*or get a respite during which the king might calm down,*) because ye see the thing is gone from me. But if ye will not make known unto me the dream, *there is but* one decree for you : for ye have prepared lying and corrupt words to speak before me, till the time be changed : therefore tell me the dream, and I shall know that ye can shew me the interpretation thereof. (*He argued rightly, that persons who could really foretell things to come by interpreting a dream could also tell the dream itself ; and if they failed to do so, they were self-condemned as base impostors, for whom no sentence could be too severe. The Chaldeans pleaded their inability and the unreasonableness of the king's request, but all in vain.*)

12 For this cause the king was angry and very furious, and commanded to destroy all the wise *men* of Babylon.

13 And the decree went forth that the wise *men* should be slain ; and they sought Daniel and his fellows to be slain.

14, 15 ¶ Then Daniel answered with counsel and wisdom to Arioch the captain of the king's guard, which was gone forth to slay the wise *men* of Babylon : He answered and said to Arioch the king's captain, Why *is* the decree *so* hasty from the king ? Then Arioch made the thing known to Daniel.

16 Then Daniel went in, and desired of the king that he would give him time, and that he would shew the king the interpretation.

17, 18 Then Daniel went to his house, and made the thing known to Hananiah, Mishael, and Azariah, his companions : That they would desire mercies of the God of heaven concerning this secret ; that Daniel and his fellows should not perish with the rest of the wise *men* of Babylon. (*Prayer appealed to the omniscient One, and discovered the key of the mystery. In our worst plights let us pray.*)

19 ¶ Then was the secret revealed unto Daniel in a night vision. Then Daniel blessed the God of heaven.

20, 21, 22 Daniel answered and said, Blessed be the name of God for ever and ever : for wisdom and might are his : And he changeth the times and the seasons : he removeth kings, and setteth up kings : he giveth wisdom unto the wise, and knowledge to them that know understanding : He revealeth the deep and secret things : he knoweth what *is* in the darkness, and the light dwelleth with him.

23 I thank thee, and praise thee, O thou God of my fathers, who hast given me wisdom and might, and hast made known unto me now what we desired of thee : for thou hast *now* made known unto us the king's matter. (*Prayer went before, and praise follows after. Prayer obtains the blessing, and praise acknowledges it : never let us fail to praise the Lord for mercies received.*)

24 ¶ Therefore Daniel went in unto Arioch, whom the king had ordained to destroy the wise *men* of Babylon : he went and said thus unto him ; Destroy not the wise *men* of Babylon : bring me in before the king, and I will shew unto the king the interpretation.

Faith, assured that her prayer was heard, acted with courage. Daniel did not fear a failure, he knew in whom his faith reposed. May the like faith be in us.

"There is a God in heaven that revealeth secrets."

DANIEL, *having been instructed by God as to Nebuchadnezzar's dream, now went in unto the king.*

DANIEL II. 26—45; 48.

26 The king answered and said to Daniel, Art thou able to make known unto me the dream which I have seen, and the interpretation thereof?

27—29 Daniel answered in the presence of the king, and said, The secret which the king hath demanded cannot the wise *men*, the astrologers, the magicians, the soothsayers, shew unto the king; But there is a God in heaven that revealeth secrets, and maketh known to the king Nebuchadnezzar what shall be in the latter days. Thy dream, and the visions of thy head upon thy bed, are these; As for thee, O king, thy thoughts came *into thy mind* upon thy bed, what should come to pass hereafter: and he that revealeth secrets maketh known to thee what shall come to pass.

30 But as for me, this secret is not revealed to me for *any* wisdom that I have more than any living, but for *their* sakes that shall make known the interpretation to the king, and that thou mightest know the thoughts of thy heart.

31 ¶ Thou, O king, sawest, and behold a great image. This great image, whose brightness *was* excellent, stood before thee; and the form thereof *was* terrible.

32, 33 This image's head *was* of fine gold, his breast and his arms of silver, his belly and his thighs of brass, his legs of iron, his feet part of iron and part of clay (*or earthenware*).

34, 35 Thou sawest till that a stone was cut out without hands, which smote the image upon his feet *that were* of iron and clay, and brake them to pieces. Then was the iron, the clay, the brass, the silver, and the gold, broken to pieces together, and became like the chaff of the summer threshingfloors; and the wind carried them away, that no place was found for them: and the stone that smote the image became a great mountain, and filled the whole earth.

36 ¶ This *is* the dream; and we will tell the interpretation thereof before the king.

37, 38 Thou, O king, *art* a king of kings: for the God of heaven hath given thee a kingdom, power, and strength, and glory. And wheresoever the children of men dwell, the beasts of the field and the fowls of the heaven hath he given into thine hand, and hath made thee ruler over them all. Thou *art* this head of gold. (*The first great empire was the Babylonian or Assyrio-Chaldean—a majestic despotism.*)

39 And after thee shall arise another kingdom inferior to thee, (*this was the Medo-Persian monarchy,*) and another third kingdom of brass, which shall bear rule over all the earth. (*Indicating the Macedonian empire of Alexander.*)

40 And the fourth kingdom shall be strong as iron: forasmuch as iron breaketh in pieces and subdueth all *things*: and as iron that breaketh all these, shall it break in pieces and bruise. (*Thus was the Roman power predicted.*)

41 And whereas thou sawest the feet and toes, part of potters' clay, and part of iron, the kingdom shall be divided; but there shall be in it of the strength of the iron, forasmuch as thou sawest the iron mixed with miry clay.

42, 43 And *as* the toes of the feet *were* part of iron, and part of clay, *so* the kingdom shall be partly strong, and partly broken. And whereas thou sawest iron mixed with miry clay, they shall mingle themselves with the seed of men: but they shall not cleave one to another, even as iron is not mixed with clay. (*The Roman empire was a mixture of many nations, and not a uniform whole, and in due time it fell to pieces.*)

44 And in the days of these kings shall the God of heaven set up a kingdom, which shall never be destroyed: and the kingdom shall not be left to other people, *but* it shall break in pieces and consume all these kingdoms, and it shall stand for ever. (*This fifth monarchy is no other than the divine empire of King Jesus, which shall subdue all things to itself.*)

45 Forasmuch as thou sawest that the stone was cut out of the mountain without hands, and that it brake in pieces the iron, the brass, the clay, the silver, and the gold; the great God hath made known to the king what shall come to pass hereafter: and the dream *is* certain, and the interpretation thereof sure.

48 Then the king made Daniel a great man, and gave him many great gifts, and made him ruler over the whole province of Babylon, and chief of the governors over all the wise *men* of Babylon. (*So was the Lord honoured among the heathen, and a friend provided at court for the poor despised Jews.*)

WE must now leave Daniel at Babylon, and return to the wicked king *Jehoiakim* and the prophet *Jeremiah* at *Jerusalem*. *Jeremiah*, at the command of God, wrote all his prophecies in a book, that the king and people might yet be moved to repentance. Great is the patience of the Lord. He waiteth to be gracious.

JEREMIAH XXXVI. 5, 6 ; 8 ; 21—31.

5, 6 And Jeremiah commanded Baruch, saying, I *am* shut up ; I cannot go into the house of the LORD : Therefore go thou, and read in the roll, which thou hast written from my mouth, the words of the LORD in the ears of the people in the LORD's house upon the fasting day : and also thou shalt read them in the ears of all Judah that come out of their cities.

When good men cannot do the work of God personally, they are glad to call in others. How glad we ought to be to do anything for the Lord: if we cannot preach like Jeremiah, we can read like Baruch, and if so, we must be sure to do it.

8 And Baruch the son of Neriah did according to all that Jeremiah the prophet commanded him, reading in the book the words of the LORD in the LORD's house. *(Baruch's reading in the temple attracted the attention of the scribes and nobles, and after they had heard him read the roll in private, they carried it to the king.)*

21 And Jehudi read it in the ears of the king and in the ears of all the princes which stood beside the king.

22 Now the king sat in the winterhouse in the ninth month : and *there* was a *fire* on the hearth burning before him.

23 And it came to pass, *that* when Jehudi had read three or four leaves, he cut it with the penknife, and cast *it* into the fire that *was* on the hearth, until all the roll was consumed in the fire that *was* on the hearth.

As Jehudi read the roll, the king cut off the portion, and scornfully burned it piece by piece.

24 Yet they were not afraid, nor rent their garments, *neither* the king, nor any of his servants that heard all these words. *(Contrast this wicked defiance with the tenderness of Josiah when he received the book of the Lord.)*

25 Nevertheless Elnathan and Delaiah and Gemariah had made intercession to the king that he would not burn the roll : but he would not hear them. *(God here takes kindly note of those who were of a better spirit, but their protests only aggravated the king's sin.)*

26 But the king commanded Jerahmeel the son of Hammelech, and Seraiah the son of Azriel, and Shelemiah the son of Abdeel, to take Baruch the scribe and Jeremiah the prophet ; but the LORD hid them.

If we help good men as Baruch did Jeremiah we must expect to suffer with them, but we shall also share with them the guardian care of heaven. See the obstinacy of Jehoiakim ; he will not repent, but becomes a persecutor of his best friends.

27 ¶ Then the word of the LORD came to Jeremiah, after that the king had burned the roll, and the words which Baruch wrote at the mouth of Jeremiah, saying,

28—30 Take thee again another roll, and write in it all the former words that were in the first roll, which Jehoiakim the king of Judah hath burned. And thou shalt say to Jehoiakim king of Judah, Thus saith the LORD ; Thou hast burned this roll, saying, Why hast thou written therein, saying, The king of Babylon shall certainly come and destroy this land, and shall cause to cease from thence man and beast ? Therefore thus saith the LORD of Jehoiakim king of Judah ; He shall have none to sit upon the throne of David : and his dead body shall be cast out in the day to the heat, and in the night to the frost.

He was not succeeded by any of his posterity except his son Jehoiachin, whose three months' reign was counted as nothing. This wicked king had treated the prophetic roll contemptuously, and therefore his dead body was subjected to ignominy. The second roll contained more threatenings than the first: sinners multiply their miseries when they add to their sins.

31 And I will punish him and his seed and his servants for their iniquity ; and I will bring upon them, and upon the inhabitants of Jerusalem, and upon the men of Judah, all the evil that I have pronounced against them ; but they hearkened not. *(The king gained nothing by burning the roll, for all its threatenings remained. A man who hates the Bible for threatening the wicked with eternal punishment cannot quench the flames of hell by raging against the book. He would act far more wisely if he would escape from the wrath to come by repentance and faith.)*

As parchèd in the barren sands,
  Beneath a burning sky,
The worthless bramble with'ring stands,
  And only grows to die;

Such is the sinner's awful case,
  Who makes the world his trust,
And dares his confidence to place
  In vanity and dust.

A secret curse destroys his root,
  And dries his moisture up;
He lives a while, but bears no fruit,
  Then dies without a hope.

Reason's glimmering light is vain
  Till thy Spirit I receive:
He thy language must explain
  He must give me to believe.

Then thy wisdom's gift is mine
  When thou dost the truth reveal;
Then I see the Lamb divine,
  All the mysteries unseal.

All the seven seals he breaks,
  Every truth of grace makes known;
All his children wise he makes,
  But their wisdom is his own.

Preserve me from the snares of sin
  Through my remaining days;
And in me let each virtue shine
  To my Redeemer's praise.

Let deep repentance, faith and love,
  Be join'd with godly fear;
And all my conversation prove
  My heart to be sincere.

Teach thou my soul all sin to hate,
  And loathe the thing unclean;
Thine image in me new-create,
  And keep me pure from sin.

Jesus, thy mighty kingdom rear,
  A stone unhewn of mortal hands,
Let the fifth monarchy appear,
  And spread its sway o'er all the lands.

Now let that stone the image smite,
  And break the iron, and the clay;
Conquer by thy blest Spirit's might,
  And force the nations to obey.

Lord, let thy kingdom now prevail,
  And all opposing power disperse;
Soon to a boundless mountain swell,
  And fill the happy universe.

Father of mercies! in thy word
  What endless glory shines!
For ever be thy name adored,
  For these celestial lines.

The best relief that mourners have,
  It makes our sorrows blest;
Our fairest hope beyond the grave,
  And our eternal rest.

O may these heavenly pages be
  My ever dear delight;
And still new beauties may I see,
  And still increasing light!

Divine Instructor, gracious Lord!
  Be thou for ever near:
Teach me to love thy sacred word,
  And view my Saviour there!

II. KINGS XXIV. 6—9; 11, 12.

SO Jehoiakim slept with his fathers : and Jehoiachin his son reigned in his stead.

7 And the king of Egypt came not again any more out of his land : for the king of Babylon had taken from the river of Egypt unto the river Euphrates all that pertained to him.

8, 9 Jehoiachin *was* eighteen years old when he began to reign, and he reigned in Jerusalem three months. And he did evil in the sight of the LORD, according to all that his father had done.

11, 12 And Nebuchadnezzar king of Babylon came against the city, and his servants did besiege it. And Jehoiachin the king of Judah went out to the king of Babylon, he and his mother, and his servants, and his princes, and his officers : and the king of Babylon took him in the eighth year of his reign. (*That is to say, the eighth year of the reign of Nebuchadnezzar. Jehoiachin saw the utter uselessness of holding out against the potent Babylonian, and probably hoped that he would be reinstated as a vassal prince, but Nebuchadnezzar's temper had been too much tried by Judah's affinity with Egypt, and he took both the king and all the better part of the population of Jerusalem as prisoners to Babylon. This was a second and more sweeping captivity. All this had been foretold by the prophet Jeremiah, though they would not hearken to him. Those who will not regard warnings must perish hopelessly. Thus plainly and plaintively had the messenger of the Lord spoken.*)

JEREMIAH XXII. 21—30.

I SPAKE unto thee in thy prosperity ; *but* thou saidst, I will not hear. This *hath been* thy manner from thy youth, that thou obeyedst not my voice. The wind shall eat up all thy pastors, and thy lovers shall go into captivity : surely then shalt thou be ashamed and confounded for all thy wickedness. (*Like a parching wind, the Chaldeans would wither all ; not pasture only, but pastors also, would be destroyed ; Judah's helpers should all fail her. The hope of the wicked is gone like dew from the grass when the summer's sun burns overhead.*)

23 O inhabitant of Lebanon, that makest thy nest in the cedars, how gracious shalt thou be when pangs come upon thee, the pain as of a woman in travail ! (*The cedar palace could not shelter the king. He was very graceful in his pomp, but little grace would he or his people get from the invader.*)

24—27 *As* I live, saith the LORD, though Coniah the son of Jehoiakim king of Judah were the signet upon my right hand, yet would I pluck thee thence ; and I will give thee into the hand of them that seek thy life, and into the hand *of them* whose face thou fearest, even into the hand of Nebuchadrezzar king of Babylon, and into the hand of the Chaldeans. And I will cast thee out, and thy mother that bare thee, into another country, where ye were not born ; and there shall ye die. But to the land whereunto they desire to return, thither shall they not return.

28 *Is* this man Coniah a despised broken idol ? (*His people idolized him, and God broke down his power and pride :*) is he a vessel wherein *is* no pleasure ? (*a broken, worthless pot :*) wherefore are they cast out, he and his seed, and are cast into a land which they know not ?

29, 30 O earth, earth, earth, hear the word of the LORD. Thus saith the LORD, Write ye this man childless, a man *that* shall not prosper in his days : for no man of his seed shall prosper, sitting upon the throne of David, and ruling any more in Judah. (*Sad doom for a grandson of holy Josiah. His own sin and his father's sin, blotted out their names from the roll of genealogy, for had not the prophetic roll been destroyed by them ? May none of our household provoke the Lord. May a godly father be followed by pious sons, for Jesus' sake, Amen.*)

Kingdoms and thrones to God belong,
Crown him, ye nations, in your song :
His wondrous names and powers rehearse ;
His honours shall enrich your verse.

Proclaim him king, pronounce him bless'd ;
He's your defence, your joy, your rest ;
When terrors rise and nations faint,
God is the strength of every saint.

AFTER *Jehoiakim's son had been removed, another son of Josiah came to the throne.*

JEREMIAH XXXVII. 1—8; 11—21.

1, 2 And king Zedekiah the son of Josiah reigned instead of Coniah the son of Jehoiakim, whom Nebuchadrezzar king of Babylon made king in the land of Judah. But neither he, nor his servants, nor the people of the land, did hearken unto the words of the LORD, which he spake by the prophet Jeremiah. *(Amazing folly! They would not see, though the judgments of God stared them in the face.)*

3 And Zedekiah the king sent to the prophet Jeremiah, saying, Pray now unto the LORD our God for us. *(He wanted his prayers, but not his sermons. How like the ungodly of our days! Zedekiah had broken his solemn oath to the Babylonian king, and well might he fear his just anger; and moreover the people had followed the abominations of the heathen, so that the eleven years' reign of Zedekiah had been a great provocation to the Lord.)*

4 Now Jeremiah came in and went out among the people: for they had not put him into prison.

5—8 Then Pharaoh's army was come forth out of Egypt: and when the Chaldeans that besieged Jerusalem heard tidings of them, they departed from Jerusalem. Then came the word of the LORD unto the prophet Jeremiah, saying, Thus saith the LORD, the God of Israel; Thus shall ye say to the king of Judah, that sent you unto me to enquire of me; Behold, Pharaoh's army, which is come forth to help you, shall return to Egypt into their own land. And the Chaldeans shall come again, and fight against this city, and take it, and burn it with fire.

11, 12 And it came to pass, that when the army of the Chaldeans was broken up from Jerusalem for fear of Pharaoh's army, Then Jeremiah went forth out of Jerusalem to go into the land of Benjamin, to separate himself thence in the midst of the people. *(Intending to wander hither and thither as a witness that Jerusalem was unsafe to dwell in.)*

13 And when he was in the gate of Benjamin, a captain of the ward *was* there, whose name *was* Irijah, and he took Jeremiah the prophet, saying, Thou fallest away to the Chaldeans.

14, 15 Then said Jeremiah, *It is* false; I fall not away to the Chaldeans. But he hearkened not to him: so Irijah took Jeremiah, and brought him to the princes. Wherefore the princes were wroth with Jeremiah, and smote him, and put him in prison in the house of Jonathan the scribe: for they had made that the prison.

They were willing to make prisons of their private houses, but they had no room for the worship of the Lord.

16, 17 When Jeremiah was entered into the dungeon, and into the cabins, *(or vaulted cells in the pit,)* and Jeremiah had remained there many days; Then Zedekiah the king sent, and took him out: and the king asked him secretly in his house, and said, Is there *any* word from the LORD? And Jeremiah said, There is: for, said he, thou shalt be delivered into the hand of the king of Babylon. *(Thus boldly did the good man speak: we should always be brave in the Lord's cause.)*

18—20 Moreover Jeremiah said unto king Zedekiah, What have I offended against thee, or against thy servants, or against this people, that ye have put me in prison? Where *are* now your prophets which prophesied unto you, saying, The king of Babylon shall not come against you, nor against this land? Therefore hear now, I pray thee, O my lord the king, let my supplication, I pray thee, be accepted before thee; that thou cause me not to return to the house of Jonathan the scribe, lest I die there.

21 Then Zedekiah the king commanded that they should commit Jeremiah into the court of the prison, and that they should give him daily a piece of bread out of the bakers' street, until all the bread in the city were spent. Thus Jeremiah remained in the court of the prison.

Thus was the promise fulfilled, "in the days of famine they shall be satisfied." God takes care that those who serve him well shall not starve.

TO BE SUNG OR READ.   104th.

Though troubles assail, and dangers affright,
Though friends should all fail, and foes all unite;
Yet one thing secures us, whatever betide,
The Scripture assures us, "The Lord will provide."

When Satan appears, to stop up our path,
And fill us with fears, we triumph by faith:
He cannot take from us, though oft he has tried,
This heart cheering promise, "The Lord will provide."

WHILE *the prophet was in the court of the prison, he continued to warn and advise the people for their good, bidding them yield themselves to Nebuchadnezzar. On this account the princes complained of him to the king, as disheartening the people.*

JEREMIAH XXXVIII. 5—18 ; 24, 28.

5 Then Zedekiah the king said, Behold, he *is* in your hand : for the king *is* not *he that* can do *any* thing against you.

Poor vacillating monarch ! He had no mind of his own, and was a mere tool in the hands of the princes. Many fall into great sin from want of manly firmness. They do wrong because they have not the courage to say " No."

6 Then took they Jeremiah, and cast him into the dungeon that ˙*was* in the court of the prison : and they let down Jeremiah with cords. And in the dungeon *there was* no water, but mire : so Jeremiah sunk in the mire. *(What a loathsome place ! Truly, through much tribulation many holy men have inherited the kingdom.)*

7—10 Now when Ebed-melech the Ethiopian, one of the eunuchs which was in the king's house, heard that they had put Jeremiah in the dungeon, he went forth out of the king's house, and spake to the king, saying, My lord the king, these men have done evil in all that they have done to. Jeremiah the prophet, whom they have cast into the dungeon ; and he is like to die for hunger in the place where he is : for *there is* no more bread in the city. *(A Gentile was more gentle than a Jew. He had a black skin, but a tender heart.)* Then the king commanded Ebed-melech the Ethiopian, saying, Take from hence thirty men with thee, and take up Jeremiah the prophet out of the dungeon, before he die. *(Easily led, the king turned round in a moment.)*

11 So Ebed-melech took the men with him, and went into the house of the king under the treasury, and took thence old cast clouts and old rotten rags, and let them down by cords into the dungeon to Jeremiah.

Good deeds should be done tenderly ; the bare cords would have hurt the emaciated prophet. Ebed-melech was thoughtful for his comfort.

12 And Ebed-melech the Ethiopian said unto Jeremiah, Put now *these* old cast clouts and rotten rags under thine armholes under the cords. And Jeremiah did so.

13 So they drew up Jeremiah with cords, and took him up out of the dungeon : and Jeremiah remained in the court of the prison.

14 ¶ Then Zedekiah the king sent, and took Jeremiah the prophet unto him : and the king said unto Jeremiah, I will ask thee a thing ; hide nothing from me.

15 Then Jeremiah said unto Zedekiah, If I declare *it* unto thee, wilt thou not surely put me to death ? and if I give thee counsel, wilt thou not hearken unto me ?

16 So Zedekiah the king sware secretly unto Jeremiah, saying, *As* the LORD liveth, that made us this soul, I will not put thee to death, neither will I give thee into the hand of these men that seek thy life.

This was said in private, for the timid prince was afraid of his nobles. What a wretched, cringing spirit he had ; the courage of the prophet stands out in grand contrast.

17, 18 Then said Jeremiah unto Zedekiah, Thus saith the LORD, the God of hosts, the God of Israel ; If thou wilt assuredly go forth unto the king of Babylon's princes, then thy soul shall live, and this city shall not be burned with fire ; and thou shalt live, and thine house : But if thou wilt not go forth to the king of Babylon's princes, then shall this city be given into the hands of the Chaldeans, and they shall burn it with fire, and thou shalt not escape out of their hand.

24 Then said Zedekiah unto Jeremiah, Let no man know of these words, and thou shalt not die. *(Never let us thus tremble, and fear wicked men. Moral courage can be gained by prayer to God, and timid spirits should seek it daily, for the want of it may prove their ruin. A soldier of Jesus ought never to be a coward.)*

28 So Jeremiah abode in the court of the prison until the day that Jerusalem was taken : and he was *there* when Jerusalem was taken.

Am I a soldier of the cross,
    A follower of the Lamb ?
And shall I fear to own his cause,
    Or blush to speak his name ?

Sure I must fight if I would reign ;
    Increase my courage, Lord !
I'll bear the toil, endure the pain,
    Supported by thy word.

E VEN *in those gloomy days, the Lord did not leave the faithful few to pine, without a promise of brighter days.*

JEREMIAH XXXI. 1—9; 31—37.

1 At the same time, *(namely, in the latter days,)* saith the LORD, will I be the God of all the families of Israel, and they shall be my people.

2 Thus saith the LORD, The people *which were* left of the sword found grace in the wilderness ; *even* Israel, when I went to cause him to rest. *(Continually does the Lord refer to his former loving kindnesses to assure his people that he is still ready to deliver them.)*

3 The LORD hath appeared of old unto me, *saying,* Yea, I have loved thee with an everlasting love : therefore with loving kindness have I drawn thee. *(Meditate much on this sentence.)*

4 Again I will build thee, and thou shalt be built, O virgin of Israel : thou shalt again be adorned with thy tabrets, and shalt go forth in the dances of them that make merry. *(Victory should again awaken the songs of virgins, and the sound of timbrels, as of old at the Red Sea.)*

5 Thou shalt yet plant vines upon the mountains of Samaria : the planters shall plant, and shall eat *them* as common things.

6, 7 For there shall be a day, *that* the watchmen upon the mount Ephraim shall cry, Arise ye, and let us go up to Zion unto the LORD our God. For thus saith the LORD : Sing with gladness for Jacob, and shout among the chief of the nations : publish ye, praise ye, and say, O LORD, save thy people, the remnant of Israel.

8, 9 Behold, I will bring them from the north country, and gather them from the coasts of the earth, *and* with them the blind and the lame, the woman with child and her that travaileth with child together : a great company shall return thither. They shall come with weeping, and with supplications will I lead them : I will cause them to walk by the rivers of waters in a straight way, wherein they shall not stumble : for I am a father to Israel, and Ephraim *is* my firstborn. *Though awakened sinners are sad when they come to God, yet their way is a safe and a straight one, and leads them into the full enjoyment of divine adoption.*

31 ¶ Behold, the days come, saith the LORD, that I will make a new covenant with the house of Israel, and with the house of Judah :

32 Not according to the covenant that I made with their fathers in the day *that* I took them by the hand to bring them out of the land of Egypt ; which my covenant they brake, although I was an husband unto them, saith the LORD : *In the old covenant something remained to be done upon man's side, and therefore it failed; a covenant founded alone upon grace is the only one which will save a sinful people.*

33 But this *shall be* the covenant that I will make with the house of Israel ; After those days saith the LORD, I will put my law in their inward parts, and write it in their hearts ; and will be their God and they shall be my people.

34 And they shall teach no more every man his neighbour, and every man his brother, saying, Know the LORD : for they shall all know me, from the least of them unto the greatest of them, saith the LORD : for I will forgive their iniquity, and I will remember their sin no more. *The tenor of the covenant of grace is, " I will," and " they shall ;" there are no ifs or buts in it. It is made up of absolute promises upon God's part, and cannot be put in jeopardy by the acts of man, hence it is sure ; mark well the seal and token of it in the following verses.*

35 ¶ Thus saith the LORD, which giveth the sun for a light by day, *and* the ordinances of the moon and of the stars for a light by night, which divideth the sea when the waves thereof roar ; The LORD of hosts *is* his name.

36 If those ordinances depart from before me, saith the LORD, *then* the seed of Israel also shall cease from being a nation before me for ever.

37 Thus saith the LORD ; If heaven above can be measured, and the foundations of the earth searched out beneath, I will also cast off all the seed of Israel for all that they have done, saith the LORD.

He by himself hath sworn ;
I on his oath depend ;
I shall on eagles' wings upborne
At last to heav'n ascend.

Though sun and moon decay,
And earth and hell withstand,
To Canaan's bounds I force my way
By his divine command.

July 25.—Morning.
[*Or February* 15.]
" 𝔅𝔢𝔥𝔬𝔩𝔡 𝔱𝔥𝔢 𝔴𝔦𝔠𝔨𝔢𝔡 𝔞𝔟𝔬𝔪𝔦𝔫𝔞𝔱𝔦𝔬𝔫𝔰 𝔱𝔥𝔞𝔱 𝔱𝔥𝔢𝔶 𝔡𝔬."

441

D URING *the reign of Zedekiah, the prophet Ezekiel was upon the banks of the Chebar with the exiles who had been carried away in the days of Jehoiachin. Let us read one of his prophetic visions.*

EZEKIEL VIII.

2 I beheld, and lo a likeness as the appearance of fire : from the appearance of his loins even downward, fire ; and from his loins even upward, as the appearance of brightness, as the colour of amber.

3 And he put forth the form of an hand, and took me by a lock of mine head ; and the spirit lifted me up between the earth and the heaven, and brought me in the visions of God to Jerusalem, to the door of the inner gate that looketh toward the north ; where *was* the seat of the image of jealousy, which provoketh to jealousy. *Probably the image of Astarte, the queen of heaven, or the Syrian Venus; idolaters have usually had some favourite female idol, and the Romanists have followed closely in their track.*

4. And, behold, the glory of the God of Israel *was* there, according to the vision that I saw in the plain.

5 ¶ Then said he unto me, Son of man, lift up thine eyes now the way toward the north. So I lifted up mine eyes the way toward the north, and behold northward at the gate of the altar this image of jealousy in the entry.

6—8 He said furthermore unto me, Son of man, seest thou what they do ? *even* the great abominations that the house of Israel committeth here, that I should go far off from my sanctuary ? *(To set up the image of a licentious divinity in the temple itself was enough to move the Lord to withdraw his glorious presence from the temple for ever. Are there not also sins in us which might lead the Holy Spirit to depart from us ?)* but turn thee yet again, *and* thou shalt see greater abominations. And he brought me to the door of the court ; and when I looked, behold a hole in the wall. Then said he unto me, Son of man, dig now in the wall : and when I had digged in the wall, behold a door.

9 And he said unto me, Go in, and behold the wicked abominations that they do here.

10 So I went in and saw ; and behold every form of creeping things, and abominable beasts, and all the idols of the house of Israel, pourtrayed upon the wall round about. *(They practised the degrading worship of the Egyptians, by whom loathsome animals and insects were reverenced.)*

11 And there stood before them seventy men of the ancients of the house of Israel, and in the midst of them stood Jaazaniah the son of Shaphan, with every man his censer in his hand ; and a thick cloud of incense went up.

12 Then said he unto me, Son of man, hast thou seen what the ancients of the house of Israel do in the dark, every man in the chambers of his imagery ? for they say, The Lord seeth us not ; the Lord hath forsaken the earth. *These seventy represented the whole nation which had fallen into the basest superstition.*

13 ¶ He said also unto me, Turn thee yet again, *and* thou shalt see greater abominations that they do.

14 Then he brought me to the door of the gate of the Lord's house, which *was* toward the north ; and, behold, there sat women weeping for Tammuz. *(Celebrating a most lascivious festival, too wicked to be described. It is terrible when vice is made a part of religion. The popish confessional leads to much the same results.)*

15 ¶ Then said he unto me, Hast thou seen *this*, O son of man ? turn thee yet again, *and* thou shalt see greater abominations than these.

16 And he brought me into the inner court of the Lord's house, and, behold, at the door of the temple of the Lord, between the porch and the altar, *were* about five and twenty men, with their backs toward the temple of the Lord, and their faces toward the east ; and they worshipped the sun toward the east. *(The leaders of the twenty-five courses of the priests had gone over to sun worship ! This was worst of all.)*

17, 18 Then he said unto me, Hast thou seen *this*, O son of man ? Is it a light thing to the house of Judah that they commit the abominations which they commit here ? for they have filled the land with violence, and have returned to provoke me to anger : and lo, they put the branch to their nose. Therefore will I also deal in fury : mine eye shall not spare, neither will I have pity : and though they cry in mine ears with a loud voice, *yet* will I not hear them. *Such provoking sins demanded punishment. We cannot make idols for ourselves without storing up trouble for a future time. Flee idolatry.*

THE *divine messenger, who had shown to Ezekiel the sin of Jerusalem, afterwards showed him the punishment of that erring city.*

EZEKIEL IX.

1 He cried also in mine ears with a loud voice, saying, Cause them that have charge over the city to draw near, even every man *with* his destroying weapon in his hand. *(God has messengers of vengeance, and these are fully armed to effect his terrible purpose. What would become of us if he were to send them forth at this moment?)*

2 And, behold, six men came from the way of the higher gate, which lieth toward the north, and every man a slaughter weapon in his hand; *(Two destroyers were enough for Sodom, but Jerusalem must have six, one at each gate.)* and one man among them *was* clothed with linen, with a writer's inkhorn by his side *(He was among the six, but not of them: he was distinguished by his priestly robe, and from him some hope of mercy might come. Who is this but our Prophet and Priest, the Lord Jesus?)* And they went in, and stood beside the brasen altar. *(To protect it, and avenge the defilements it had suffered.)*

3, 4 And the glory of the God of Israel was gone up from the cherub, whereupon he was, to the threshold of the house. And he called to the man clothed with linen, which *had* the writer's inkhorn by his side; And the LORD said unto him, Go through the midst of the city, through the midst of Jerusalem, and set a mark upon the foreheads of the men that sigh and that cry for all the abominations that be done in the midst thereof. *(Our great High Priest keeps the book of life, and seals his own, so that no evil shall touch them. He is best fitted for this work, for he knows them that are his. Mercy's pen does its work, and takes precedence of the sword of vengeance. Penitence is the peculiar mark of grace: those who sigh and cry on account of sin shall live.)*

5, 6 And to the others he said in mine hearing, Go ye after him through the city, and smite: let not your eye spare, neither have ye pity: Slay utterly old *and* young, both maids, and little children, and women: but come not near any man upon whom *is* the mark; and begin at my sanctuary. *(Dreadful words, "begin at my sanctuary." If the house of God is the starting-point of judgment, where will the ungodly and the wicked appear? Yet see how safe are those whom grace has set apart! Their deliverer goes before the destroyer, and saves his own.)* Then they began at the ancient men which *were* before the house.

7 And he said unto them, Defile the house, and fill the courts with the slain: go ye forth. And they went forth, and slew in the city.

8 And it came to pass, while they were slaying them, and I was left, that I fell upon my face, and cried, and said, Ah Lord GOD! wilt thou destroy all the residue of Israel in thy pouring out of thy fury upon Jerusalem?

What gratitude filled the prophet's heart when he saw that he was left; but he was not selfish, he began at once to intercede for the people. Do we attend to this?

9 Then said he unto me, The iniquity of the house of Israel and Judah *is* exceeding great, and the land is full of blood, and the city full of perverseness: for they say, The LORD hath forsaken the earth, and the LORD seeth not.

10 And as for me also, mine eye shall not spare, neither will I have pity, *but* I will recompense their way upon their head.

Sin may have become so aggravated that intercession is powerless, for wrath is determined.

11 And, behold, the man clothed with linen, which *had* the inkhorn by his side, reported the matter, saying, I have done as thou hast commanded me. *(See how faithful Christ is. Is he bidden to secure deliverance to the righteous remnant? He has so done, and exclaims, "Of all that thou hast given me, I have lost none.")*

Though destruction stalk around us,
And th' avenger marches by,
God's own power and love surround us,
We are safe, for Christ is nigh.

Holy Ghost, with light divine,
Shine upon this heart of mine;
Chase the shades of sin away,
Turn my darkness into day.

Light up every dark recess
Of my heart's ungodliness;
Cast down every idol throne,
Reign supreme, and reign alone.

THE *judgment of God hung over Jerusalem for a long time, as though the Lord were loath to strike the final blow. During that period Jeremiah prophesied that after the city had been destroyed the people would yet return, and in token of his faith he purchased a piece of ground.*

JEREMIAH XXXII. 1—15.

1, 2 The word that came to Jeremiah from the Lord in the tenth year of Zedekiah king of Judah, For then the king of Babylon's army besieged Jerusalem: and Jeremiah the prophet was shut up in the court of the prison, which *was* in the king of Judah's house.

3—5 For Zedekiah king of Judah had shut him up, saying, Wherefore dost thou prophesy, and say, Thus saith the Lord, Behold, I will give this city into the hand of the king of Babylon, and he shall take it; and Zedekiah king of Judah shall not escape out of the hand of the Chaldeans, but shall surely be delivered into the hand of the king of Babylon, and shall speak with him mouth to mouth, and his eyes shall behold his eyes; and he shall lead Zedekiah to Babylon, and there shall he be until I visit him, saith the Lord: though ye fight with the Chaldeans, ye shall not prosper.

6, 7 And Jeremiah said, The word of the Lord came unto me, saying, Behold, Hanameel the son of Shallum thine uncle shall come unto thee, saying, Buy thee my field that *is* in Anathoth: for the right of redemption *is* thine to buy *it*. *(This was a forlorn request indeed, for a piece of land in a country devastated by war and occupied by the enemy, is hardly worth accepting as a gift.)*

8 So Hanameel mine uncle's son came to me in the court of the prison according to the word of the Lord, and said unto me, Buy my field I pray thee, that *is* in Anathoth, which *is* in the country of Benjamin: for the right of inheritance *is* thine, and the redemption *is*·thine; buy *it* for thyself. Then I knew that this *was* the word of the Lord. *(Therefore, he proceeded at once to the purchase, and thus made the people see that he believed that which he preached. We are bound, not only to have faith in God's promises, but also to act accordingly. It is not every man who would give up good money for land which he could not reach, in the midst of a destructive war; no one indeed would do so, unless he believed that*

better days would come when the reversion would be valuable.)

9, 10 And I bought the field of Hanameel my uncle's son, that *was* in Anathoth, and weighed him the money, *even* seventeen shekels of silver. And I subscribed the evidence, and sealed *it*, and took witnesses, and weighed *him* the money in the balances.

11 So I took the evidence of the purchase, *both* that which was sealed *according* to the law and custom, and that which was open:

12 And I gave the evidence of the purchase unto Baruch, in the sight of Hanameel mine uncle's *son*, and in the presence of the witnesses that subscribed the book of the purchase, before all the Jews that sat in the court of the prison.

The business was honestly and thoroughly done. It was no sham purchase, and Jeremiah's faith was no mere pretence. It is related in Roman history, that when Hannibal's army was near to Rome, a field upon which the enemy lay was purchased in the full belief that Roman valour would raise the siege. Surely we have far more reason to venture our all upon the word of God, and prove our faith by our actions.

13—15 And I charged Baruch before them, saying, Thus saith the Lord of hosts, the God of Israel; Take these evidences, this evidence of the purchase, both which is sealed, and this evidence which is open; and put them in an earthen vessel, that they may continue many days. For thus saith the Lord of hosts, the God of Israel; Houses and fields and vineyards shall be possessed again in this land.

Jeremiah's purchase would be talked of in all directions, and would be more convincing than any sermon. If we act in firm reliance upon our faithful God, our conduct will go far to arouse and to convert those among whom we dwell.

O for the living faith,
The real, active trust,
Which looks to what Jehovah saith,
Though trampled in the dust.

It plays not with the word,
Nor hesitates to act;
Pleading, it reckons to be heard,
And finds the promise fact.

ALTHOUGH *Jeremiah had without hesi-
tation obeyed the word of the Lord, and
declared his faith, yet he was in great mental
perplexity, and therefore he resorted to the consoling exercise of prayer.*

JEREMIAH XXXII. 16, 17; 24—30; 36—44.

16 Now when I had delivered the evidence
of the purchase unto Baruch the son of Neriah,
I prayed unto the LORD, saying,

17 Ah Lord GOD! behold, thou hast made
the heaven and the earth by thy great power
and stretched out arm, *and* there is nothing too
hard for thee. *(Then he went on to recount the
Lord's mighty acts in Egypt and in Canaan, and
at last came to that which so much tried his
faith, namely, the presence of the Chaldeans, and
their earthworks, whereby the city was threatened. He pleaded with the Lord and said,)*

24 Behold the mounts, they are come unto
the city to take it ; and the city is given into the
hand of the Chaldeans, that fight against it, because of the sword, and of the famine, and of
the pestilence : and what thou hast spoken is
come to pass ; and, behold, thou seest *it.*

25 And thou hast said unto me, O Lord GOD,
Buy thee the field for money, and take witnesses ; for the city is given into the hand of the
Chaldeans. *(This is the way to pray. State the
trouble—" behold the mounts," and plead the
promise. The Lord will make the mystery
clear, and turn darkness into light.)*

26 ¶ Then came the word of the LORD unto
Jeremiah, saying,

27—29 Behold, I *am* the LORD, the God of all
flesh : is there any thing too hard for me ?
Therefore thus saith the LORD ; Behold, I will
give this city into the hand of Nebuchadrezzar
king of Babylon, and he shall take it : And the
Chaldeans, that fight against this city, shall
come and set fire on this city, and burn it with
the houses, upon whose roofs they have offered
incense unto Baal, and poured out drink offerings unto other gods, to provoke me to anger.

30 For the children of Israel and the children of Judah have only done evil before me
from their youth, saith the LORD.

*Thus judgment was threatened, but after
a while mercy would come to the front again, and
that in a manner most marvellous.*

36 And now therefore thus saith the LORD,
the God of Israel, concerning this city, whereof
ye say, it shall be delivered into the hand of the
king of Babylon by the sword, and by the
famine, and by the pestilence ;

37—40 Behold, I will gather them out
of all countries, whither I have driven them in
mine anger, and in my fury, and in great wrath ;
and I will bring them again unto this place, and
I will cause them to dwell safely : And they
shall be my people, and I will be their God :
And I will give them one heart, and one way,
that they may fear me for ever, for the good of
them, and of their children after them : And I
will make an everlasting covenant with them,
that I will not turn away from them, to do them
good ; but I will put my fear in their hearts,
that they shall not depart from me.

*These are charming words, and belong as much
to every child of God as to restored Israel, for
there can be but one everlasting covenant, and in
that all believers have an interest. The people
of God are favoured with new natures, which incline towards God and holiness, and must do so
for ever : this is an unspeakable blessing. If we
might fall away and perish even after conversion,
we should have no security ; but if the Lord declares " they shall not depart from me," our final
perseverance is secured.*

41—44 Yea, I will rejoice over them to do
them good, and I will plant them in this land
assuredly with. my whole heart and with my
whole soul. For thus saith the LORD ; Like as I
have brought all this great evil upon this
people, so will I bring upon them all the good
that I have promised them. And fields shall be
bought in this land, whereof ye say, *It is* desolate without man or beast ; it is given into the
hand of the Chaldeans. Men shall buy fields
for money, and subscribe evidences, and seal
them, and take witnesses in the land of Benjamin, and in the places about Jerusalem, and in
the cities of Judah, and in the cities of the
mountains, and in the cities of the valley, and
in the cities of the south : for I will cause their
captivity to return, saith the LORD.

*So Jeremiah's prayer brought him a cheering
answer, and, man of sorrows as he was, he had
abounding reasons for thankfulness.*

JEREMIAH XXXIX. 1; 4—18.

IN the ninth year of Zedekiah king of Judah, in the tenth month, came Nebuchadrezzar king of Babylon and all his army against Jerusalem, and they besieged it. *(In a very short time they forced their way through the outer wall, and began to assail the inner fortifications.)*

4 ¶ And it came to pass, *that* when Zedekiah the king of Judah saw them, and all the men of war, then they fled, and went forth out of the city by night, by the way of the king's garden, by the gate betwixt the two walls : and he went out the way of the plain.

5 But the Chaldeans' army pursued after them, and overtook Zedekiah in the plains of Jericho : and when they had taken him, they brought him up to Nebuchadnezzar king of Babylon to Riblah in the land of Hamath, where he gave judgment upon him. *(The feeble-minded and vicious monarch had now before him conclusive evidence of the truthfulness of Jeremiah, and no doubt his anguish was great as he remembered how many warnings he had despised.)*

6 Then the king of Babylon slew the sons of Zedekiah in Riblah before his eyes : also the king of Babylon slew all the nobles of Judah.

To see his babes slain, and his friends put to death by hundreds, must have been worse than death, especially to so timid a man as Zedekiah.

7 Moreover he put out Zedekiah's eyes, and bound him with chains, to carry him to Babylon.

He had shut his eyes to the light, and now God for ever shuts him up in darkness; he had chosen the bondage of sin, and now he must wear the chains of misery. God has effectual ways of punishing rebels.

8 ¶ And the Chaldeans burned the king's house, and the houses of the people, with fire, and brake down the walls of Jerusalem.

9, 10 Then Nebuzar-adan the captain of the guard carried away captive into Babylon the remnant of the people that remained in the city, and those that fell away, that fell to him, with the rest of the people that remained. But Nebuzar-adan the captain of the guard left of the poor of the people, which had nothing, in the land of Judah, and gave them vineyards and fields at the same time.

11, 12 Now Nebuchadrezzar king of Babylon gave charge concerning Jeremiah to Nebuzar-adan the captain of the guard, saying, Take him, and look well to him, and do him no harm ; but do unto him even as he shall say unto thee.

The mighty monarch cared kindly for the poor prophet. No doubt he had heard who he was, and how he had counselled the people to submit. The mark of the man with the inkhorn was on the prophet, and that was the secret of his safety.

13, 14 So Nebuzar-adan the captain of the guard sent, and Nebushasban, Rab-saris, and Nergal-sharezer, Rab-mag, and all the king of Babylon's princes ; Even they sent, and took Jeremiah out of the court of the prison, and committed him unto Gedaliah the son of Ahikam the son of Shaphan, that he should carry him home : so he dwelt among the people.

15, 16 ¶ Now the word of the LORD came unto Jeremiah, while he was shut up in the court of the prison, saying, Go and speak to Ebed-melech, the Ethiopian, saying, Thus saith the LORD of hosts, the God of Israel ; Behold, I will bring my words upon this city for evil, and not for good ; and they shall be *accomplished* in that day before thee.

17 But I will deliver thee in that day, saith the LORD : and thou shalt not be given into the hand of the men of whom thou *art* afraid.

18 For I will surely deliver thee, and thou shalt not fall by the sword, but thy life shall be for a prey unto thee : because thou hast put thy trust in me, saith the LORD. *(He had been kind to a prophet, and therefore he received a prophet's reward, and moreover he had put his trust in the Lord, and therefore the saving mark was set upon him. If we cannot be prophets or ministers, let us be their friends, and the friends of Jesus, and we shall share in their salvation.)*

There is a safe and secret place
  Beneath the wings divine,
Reserved for all the heirs of grace,
  Oh ! be that refuge mine !

The least, the feeblest there may hide
  Uninjured and unawed ;
While thousands fall on every side,
  He rests secure in God.

Believer, here thy comfort stands,
From first to last salvation's free ;
And everlasting love demands
An everlasting song from thee.

A SHORT *time after Jerusalem had been taken by Nebuchadnezzar, the Edomites were also overthrown. This was foretold by the prophet Obadiah. We shall have time to read almost the whole of his little book.*

OBADIAH 1—12; 15—19; 21.

1, 2 Thus saith the Lord GOD concerning Edom ; We have heard a rumour from the LORD, and an ambassador is sent among the heathen, Arise ye, and let us rise up against her in battle. Behold, I have made thee small among the heathen : thou art greatly despised.

Boasting generally ends in the boaster's being despised.

3 ¶ The pride of thine heart hath deceived thee, thou that dwellest in the clefts of the rock, whose habitation *is* high ; that saith in his heart, Who shall bring me down to the ground ?

4 Though thou exalt *thyself* as the eagle, and though thou set thy nest among the stars, thence will I bring thee down, saith the LORD.

Pride must come down : neither God nor man can bear it.

5 If thieves came to thee, if robbers by night, (how art thou cut off!) would they not have stolen till they had enough ? if the grapegatherers came to thee, would they not leave *some* grapes ? *(But nothing would be left, the destruction would be complete.)*

6 How are *the things* of Esau searched out ! *how* are his hidden things sought up !

7 All the men of thy confederacy have brought thee *even* to the border : the men that were at peace with thee have deceived thee, *and* prevailed against thee ; *they that eat* thy bread have laid a wound under thee : *there is* none understanding in him.

8 Shall I not in that day, saith the LORD, even destroy the wise *men* out of Edom, and understanding out of the mount of Esau ?

9 And thy mighty *men*, O Teman, shall be dismayed, to the end that every one of the mount of Esau may be cut off by slaughter.

10, 11 For *thy* violence against thy brother Jacob shame shall cover thee, and thou shalt be cut off for ever. In the day that thou stoodest on the other side, in the day that the strangers carried away captive his forces, and foreigners entered into his gates, and cast lots upon Jerusalem, even thou *wast* as one of them.

12 But thou shouldest not have looked on the day of thy brother in the day that he became a stranger ; neither shouldest thou have rejoiced over the children of Judah in the day of their destruction ; neither shouldest thou have spoken proudly in the day of distress.

If we are hard to others in their distress, it will be sure to come home to us. With what measure we mete, it shall be measured to us again ; and especially so if we have rejoiced in the sorrows of God's people.

15 For the day of the LORD *is* near upon all the heathen : as thou hast done, it shall be done unto thee : thy reward shall return upon thine own head.

16 For as ye have drunk upon my holy mountain, *so* shall all the heathen drink continually, yea, they shall drink, and they shall swallow down, and they shall be as though they had not been. *(As they drank in derision, so shall they drink to confusion. Woe unto them !)*

17 ¶ But upon mount Zion shall be deliverance, and there shall be holiness ; and the house of Jacob shall possess their possessions.

18 And the house of Jacob shall be a fire, and the house of Joseph a flame, and the house of Esau for stubble, and they shall kindle in them, and devour them ; and there shall not be *any* remaining of the house of Esau ; for the LORD hath spoken *it*. *(Israel must live, but Edom must die. The election survives, the enemy perishes utterly. Happy those who are of the true believing seed.)*

19, 21 And *they of* the south shall possess the mount of Esau ; and *they of* the plain the Philistines : and they shall possess the fields of Ephraim, and the fields of Samaria : and Benjamin *shall possess* Gilead. And saviours shall come up on mount Zion to judge the mount of Esau ; and the kingdom shall be the LORD's.

A most sweet ending. It is the inspired answer to our prayer, "Thy kingdom come."

> O Lord, thine is the kingdom,
>   Thine shall it ever be,
> And all thy foes like Edom,
>   Shall perish utterly.
>
> Long have they mock'd thy nation,
>   But thou hast mark'd their pride ;
> With crushing devastation
>   Thou wilt their boasts deride

DANIEL III. 1, 3, 7—9, 12—28; 30.

NEBUCHADNEZZAR the king made an image of gold, and he set it up in the plain of Dura, in the province of Babylon.

3, 7 Then the princes, the governors, and captains, the judges, the treasurers, the counsellors, the sheriffs, and all the rulers of the provinces, were gathered together unto the dedication of the image that Nebuchadnezzar the king had set up. And at that time, when all the people heard the sound of the cornet, flute, harp, sackbut, psaltery, and all kinds of musick, all the people, the nations, and the languages, fell down *and* worshipped the golden image that Nebuchadnezzar the king had set up.

8 Wherefore at that time certain Chaldeans came near, and accused the Jews.

9 They spake and said to the king Nebuchadnezzar, O king, live for ever.

12 There are certain Jews whom thou hast set over the affairs of the province of Babylon, Shadrach, Meshach, and Abed-nego ; these men, O king, have not regarded thee : they serve not thy gods, nor worship the golden image which thou hast set up.

13 Then Nebuchadnezzar in *his* rage and fury commanded to bring Shadrach, Meshach, and Abed-nego. Then they brought these men before the king.

14, 15 Nebuchadnezzar spake and said unto them, *Is it* true, O Shadrach, Meshach, and Abed-nego, do not ye serve my gods, nor worship the golden image which I have set up ? Now if ye be ready that at what time ye hear the sound of the cornet, flute, harp, sackbut, psaltery, and dulcimer, and all kinds of musick, ye fall down and worship the image which I have made ; *well :* but if ye worship not, ye shall be cast the same hour into the midst of a burning fiery furnace ; and who *is* that God that shall deliver you out of my hands ?

16—18 Shadrach, Meshach, and Abed-nego answered and said to the king, O Nebuchadnezzar, we *are* not careful to answer thee in this matter. If it be *so*, our God whom we serve is able to deliver us from the burning fiery furnace, and he will deliver *us* out of thine hand, O king. But if not, be it known unto thee, O king, that we will not serve thy gods, nor worship the golden image which thou hast set up.

19 ¶ Then was Nebuchadnezzar full of fury, and the form of his visage was changed against Shadrach, Meshach, and Abed-nego : *therefore*, he spake, and commanded that they should heat the furnace one seven times more than it was wont to be heated.

20 And he commanded the most mighty men that *were* in his army to bind Shadrach, Meshach, and Abed-nego, *and* to cast *them* into the burning fiery furnace.

21 Then these men were bound in their coats, their hosen, and their hats, and their *other* garments, and were cast into the midst of the burning fiery furnace.

22 Therefore because the king's commandment was urgent, and the furnace exceeding hot, the flame of the fire slew those men that took up Shadrach, Meshach, and Abed-nego.

23 And these three men, Shadrach, Meshach, and Abed-nego, fell down bound into the midst of the burning fiery furnace.

24 Then Nebuchadnezzar the king was astonied, and rose up in haste, *and* spake, and said unto his counsellors, Did not we cast three men bound into the midst of the fire ? They answered and said unto the king, True, O king.

25 He answered and said, Lo, I see four men loose, walking in the midst of the fire, and they have no hurt ; and the form of the fourth is like the Son of God.

26 ¶ Then Nebuchadnezzar came near to the mouth of the burning fiery furnace, *and* spake, and said, Shadrach, Meshach, and Abed-nego, ye servants of the most high God, come forth, and come *hither*. Then Shadrach, Meshach, and Abed-nego came forth of the midst of the fire.

27 And the princes, governors, and captains, and the king's counsellors, being gathered together, saw these men, upon whose bodies the fire had no power, nor was an hair of their head singed, neither were their coats changed, nor the smell of fire had passed on them.

28 *Then* Nebuchadnezzar spake, and said, Blessed *be* the God of Shadrach, Meshach, and Abed-nego, who hath sent his angel and delivered his servants that trusted in him, and have changed the king's word, and yielded their bodies, that they might not serve nor worship any god, except their own God.

30 Then the king promoted Shadrach, Meshach, and Abed-nego, in the province of Babylon. *(The unfaltering fidelity of the three holy children is worthy of our imitation. They never hesitated or parleyed with the tyrant. Fixed were their hearts in God, and confidently stayed on him; and so they conquered the proud monarch; yea, and vanquished death itself, quenching the violence of the flames. Rich was their reward. Jesus walked the glowing coals with them, and turned the furnace into a fair pavilion. In his name let us also abide by the truth without flinching, and no evil shall come nigh unto us. Never let us debate or question,* *but for God and his holy gospel let us be bold to sacrifice even life itself. May the sons of this family be such young men as Shadrach, Meshach, and Abed-nego. Amen.)*

Tempted and persecuted here,
Afflicted and distress'd,
With steadfast faith we persevere,
And stand the fiery test:

The fire shall all our bands consume,
And in the furnace tried,
Out of the flames we soon shall come,
Unhurt and purified.

Throughout my sinful soul I feel
The strength of pride invincible;
But thou th' Almighty God of grace
Can all my haughty thoughts abase.

All things are possible to thee,
Display thy humbling grace in me;
And in thy tender love impart
My Saviour's lowliness of heart.

I freely feed them now
With tokens of my love;
But richer pastures I prepare,
And sweeter streams above.

Unnumber'd years of bliss
I to my sheep will give
And, while my throne unshaken stands,
Shall all my chosen live.

This tried almighty hand
Is raised for their defence;
Where is the power shall reach them there?
Or what shall force them thence?

Your harps, ye trembling saints,
Down from the willows take:
Loud to the praise of love divine,
Bid every string awake.

Though in a foreign land,
We are not far from home;
And nearer to our house above
We every moment come.

Blest is the man, O God,
That stays himself on thee!
Who waits for thy salvation, Lord,
Shall thy salvation see.

THE *book of Daniel contains a memorable incident in the life of Nebuchadnezzar. He dreamed a dream, which the prophet thus interpreted to him.*

DANIEL IV. 20—30; 33—37.

20 The tree that thou sawest, which grew, and was strong, whose height reached unto the heaven, and the sight thereof to all the earth;

21 Whose leaves *were* fair, and the fruit thereof much, and in it *was* meat for all; under which the beasts of the field dwelt, and upon whose branches the fowls of the heaven had their habitation:

22, 23 It *is* thou, O king, that art grown and become strong: for thy greatness is grown, and reacheth unto heaven, and thy dominion to the end of the earth. And whereas the king saw a watcher and an holy one coming down from heaven, and saying, Hew the tree down, and destroy it; yet leave the stump of the roots thereof in the earth, even with a band of iron and brass, in the tender grass of the field; and let it be wet with the dew of heaven, and *let* his portion *be* with the beasts of the field, till seven times pass over him;

24 This *is* the interpretation, O king, and this *is* the decree of the most High, which is come upon my lord the king:

25 That they shall drive thee from men, and thy dwelling shall be with the beasts of the field, and they shall make thee to eat grass as oxen, and they shall wet thee with the dew of heaven, and seven times shall pass over thee, till thou know that the most High ruleth in the kingdom of men, and giveth it to whomsoever he will.

26 And whereas they commanded to leave the stump of the tree roots; thy kingdom shall be sure unto thee, after that thou shalt have known that the heavens do rule.

27 Wherefore, O king, let my counsel be acceptable unto thee, and break off thy sins by righteousness, and thine iniquities by shewing mercy to the poor; if it may be a lengthening of thy tranquillity. (*The proud monarch was thus fairly warned, but such is the infatuation of sin that he did not repent or reform, and therefore full soon the threatened judgment came upon him.*)

28 ¶ All this came upon the king Nebuchadnezzar.

29 At the end of twelve months he walked in the palace of the kingdom of Babylon.

30 The king spake, and said, Is not this great Babylon, that I have built for the house of the kingdom by the might of my power, and for the honour of my majesty?

33 The same hour was the thing fulfilled upon Nebuchadnezzar: and he was driven from men, and did eat grass as oxen, and his body was wet with the dew of heaven, till his hairs were grown like eagles' *feathers*, and his nails like birds' *claws*. (*The king was insane, and the form of his disease was that known as Lycan-thropy, a melancholy madness in which the patient imagines himself to be transformed into an animal, and acts accordingly. Many similar cases are on record, and some exist at the present moment. We ought to bless God every day for our reason, for if it were gone from us we might in an hour's time be no better than the beasts of the field.*)

34 And at the end of the days I Nebuchadnezzar lifted up mine eyes unto heaven, and mine understanding returned unto me, and I blessed the most High, and I praised and honoured him that liveth for ever, whose dominion *is* an everlasting dominion, and his kingdom *is* from generation to generation:

35 And all the inhabitants of the earth *are* reputed as nothing: and he doeth according to his will in the army of heaven, and *among* the inhabitants of the earth: and none can stay his hand, or say unto him, What doest thou?

36 At the same time my reason returned unto me; and for the glory of my kingdom, mine honour and brightness returned unto me; and my counsellors and my lords sought unto me; and I was established in my kingdom, and excellent majesty was added unto me.

37 Now I Nebuchadnezzar praise and extol and honour the King of heaven, all whose works *are* truth, and his ways judgment: and those that walk in pride he is able to abase.

Thus humbly did the proud Nebuchadnezzar bow before the Lord, and confess before all men that the Lord alone is God. If he was not a converted man he certainly wrote like one. Let us shun his pride, and if we have been guilty of it, let us henceforth imitate his humility.

450   " **I will raise up for them a plant of renown.**"   JULY 2G.—MORNING.

[*Or February* 23.]

EZEKIEL *continued to cheer the captivity of his brethren with comfortable words. After complaining of the unfaithful shepherds, who had scattered his people, the Lord promised to gather his chosen by his own hand.*

EZEKIEL XXXIV. 11—31.

11, 12 Thus saith the Lord GOD; Behold, I, *even* I, will both search my sheep, and seek them out. As a shepherd seeketh out his flock in the day that he is among his sheep *that* are scattered; so will I seek out my sheep and will deliver them out of all places where they have been scattered in the cloudy and dark day.

Because they are his own people he will not suffer them to be lost. The Lord's elect shall be gathered by efficacious grace and brought to Jesus.

13 And I will bring them out from the people, and gather them from the countries, and will bring them to their own land, and feed them upon the mountains of Israel by the rivers, and in all the inhabited places of the country.

14, 15 I will feed them in a good pasture, and upon the high mountains of Israel shall their fold be : there shall they lie in a good fold, and *in* a fat pasture shall they feed upon the mountains of Israel. I will feed my flock, and I will cause them to lie down, saith the Lord GOD.

Provision and rest are two great necessities. We have in Christ Jesus both of these blessings.

16 I will seek that which was lost, and bring again that which was driven away, and will bind *that which was* broken, and will strengthen that which was sick : but I will destroy the fat and the strong ; I will feed them with judgment.

Proud, self-sufficient, and self-righteous persons have neither part nor lot in the covenant; for them judgment is reserved.

17 And *as for* you, O my flock, thus saith the Lord GOD; Behold, I judge between cattle and cattle, between the rams and the he goats.

18, 19 *Seemeth it* a small thing unto you to have eaten up the good pasture, but ye must tread down with your feet the residue of your pastures ? and to have drunk of the deep waters, but ye must foul the residue with your feet ? And *as for* my flock, they eat that which ye have trodden with your feet ; and they drink that which ye have fouled with your feet.

A hard, overbearing spirit towards weaker brethren always brings chastisement with it.

20—23 Therefore thus saith the Lord GOD unto them ; Behold, I, *even* I, will judge between the fat cattle and between the lean cattle. Because ye have thrust with side and with shoulder, and pushed all the diseased with your horns, till ye have scattered them abroad Therefore will I save my flock, and they shall no more be a prey ; and I will judge between cattle and cattle. And I will set up one shepherd over them, and he shall feed them, *even* my servant David; he shall feed them, and he shall be their shepherd. *(Who is this but Jesus, the true David, the gentle Shepherd who tenderly cares for the weak ?)*

24—26 And I the LORD will be their God, and my servant David a prince among them ; I the LORD have spoken *it*. And I will make with them a covenant of peace, and will cause the evil beasts to cease out of the land, and they shall dwell safely in the wilderness, and sleep in the woods. And I will make them and the places round about my hill a blessing ; and I will cause the shower to come down in his season ; there shall be showers of blessing.

27, 28 And the tree of the field shall yield her fruit, and the earth shall yield her increase, and they shall be safe in their land, and shall know that I *am* the LORD, when I have broken the bands of their yoke, and delivered them out of the hand of those that served themselves of them. And they shall no more be a prey to the heathen, neither shall the beast of the land devour them ; but they shall dwell safely, and none shall make *them* afraid.

29 And I will raise up for them a plant of renown, and they shall be no more consumed with hunger in the land, neither bear the shame of the heathen any more. *(What a plant of renown is Jesus, the tree of life! Blessed are those who rejoice in his shadow and his fruit.)*

30, 31 Thus shall they know that I the LORD their God *am* with them, and *that* they, *even* the house of Israel, *are* my people, saith the Lord GOD. And ye my flock, the flock of my pasture, *are* men, *and I am* your God, saith the Lord GOD. *(This last sentence is the grandest ever uttered. Nothing more can be desired when the Lord has once said unto us, " I am your God.")*

EZEKIEL XXXVII. 1—14.

THE hand of the Lord was upon me, and carried me out in the spirit of the Lord, and set me down in the midst of the valley which *was* full of bones, And caused me to pass by them round about : and, behold, *there were very many in the open valley; and, lo, they were* very dry. *(Such were the captives among whom Ezekiel dwelt: they were spiritually and nationally dead; their recovery seemed hopeless.)*

3—6 And he said unto me, Son of man, can these bones live? And I answered, O Lord God, thou knowest. Again he said unto me, Prophesy upon these bones, and say unto them, O ye dry bones, hear the word of the Lord. Thus saith the Lord God unto these bones; Behold, I will cause breath to enter into you, and ye shall live : And I will lay sinews upon you, and will bring up flesh upon you, and cover you with skin, and put breath in you, and ye shall live ; and ye shall know that I *am* the Lord. *It seemed an idle thing to prophesy to dry bones ; and it appears equally useless to preach to unregenerate sinners : but it is ours to do as God bids us, and leave the result to him.*

7, 8 So I prophesied as I was commanded : and as I prophesied, there was a noise, and behold a shaking, and the bones came together, bone to his bone. And when I beheld, lo, the sinews and the flesh came up upon them, and the skin covered them above : but *there was* no breath in them. *(Preaching arouses man's moral nature, but it cannot give him spiritual life until the Holy Spirit breathes upon him.)*

9 Then said he unto me, Prophesy unto the wind, prophesy, son of man, and say to the wind, Thus saith the Lord God; Come from the four winds, O breath, and breathe upon these slain, that they may live.

10 So I prophesied as he commanded me, and the breath came into them, and they lived, and stood up upon their feet, an exceeding great army. *(Easily enough is the miracle wrought when the Spirit descends. May the Lord bless the word of our minister to the salvation of thousands.)*

11—14 Then he said unto me, Son of man, these bones are the whole house of Israel : behold, they say, Our bones are dried, and our

hope is lost : we are cut off for our parts. Therefore prophesy and say unto them, Thus saith the Lord God; Behold, O my people, I will open your graves, and cause you to come up out of your graves, and bring you into the land of Israel. And ye shall know that I *am* the Lord, when I have opened your graves, O my people, and brought you up out of your graves, And shall put my spirit in you, and ye shall live, and I shall place you in your own land : then shall ye know that I the Lord have spoken *it*, and performed *it*, saith the Lord.

Israel would live again, though as a nation it was politically and even morally dead. God had not given up his people, nor forgotten his covenant, and ere long he would restore the national life, and give the remnant to dwell in their own land.

May the Lord also quicken our souls into vigorous spiritual life.

WHAT *good news must this have been to the banished ones, whose sadness is so well depicted in—*

PSALM CXXXVII. 1—6.

1 By the rivers of Babylon, there we sat down, yea, we wept, when we remembered Zion.

2 We hanged our harps upon the willows in the midst thereof.

3 For there they that carried us away captive required of us a song ; and they that wasted us *required of us* mirth, *saying*, Sing us *one* of the songs of Zion.

4 How shall we sing the Lord's song in a strange land ?

5 If I forget thee, O Jerusalem, let my right hand forget *her cunning*.

6 If I do not remember thee, let my tongue cleave to the roof of my mouth ; if I prefer not Jerusalem above my chief joy.

Love to Zion had not died out with the faithful. Some Jews settled in ignoble comfort in their captor's land, but not the spiritual among them ; to them the land of promise was dear as to the patriarchs of old. Let us never call this Babylonian world our rest, but keep our eye upon the heavenly Jerusalem, where our portion is reserved.

WE *will now read one of Ezekiel's most interesting and instructive visions.*

EZEKIEL XLVII. 1—12.

1, 2 Afterward he brought me again unto the door of the house; and, behold, waters issued out from under the threshold of the house eastward: for the forefront of the house *stood toward* the east, and the waters came down from under from the right side of the house, at the south *side* of the altar. Then brought he me out of the way of the gate northward, and led me about the way without unto the utter gate by the way that looketh eastward; and, behold, there ran out waters on the right side. *(Here we see the river of the water of life, the divine outpouring of the Holy Spirit in gospel days. It rises at the sacrificial altar.)*

3 And when the man that had the line in his hand went forth eastward, he measured a thousand cubits, and he brought me through the waters; the waters *were* to the ancles.

4, 5 Again he measured a thousand, and brought me through the waters; the waters *were* to the knees. Again he measured a thousand, and brought me through; the waters *were* to the loins. Afterward he measured a thousand; *and it was* a river that I could not pass over: for the waters were risen, waters to swim in, a river that could not be passed over.

The power and influence of the life-giving gospel grows each day. The streams of Palestine frequently lessen as they run, but the river of grace becomes deeper and wider. The grain of mustard grows into a tree. The drops which oozed from beneath the altar deepened and widened into an impassable torrent.

6 ¶ And he said unto me, Son of man, hast thou seen *this?* Then he brought me, and caused me to return to the brink of the river.

7 Now, when I had returned, behold, at the bank of the river *were* very many trees on the one side and on the other.

Fertility is produced by grace, blessings spring up like fruitful trees wherever the gospel comes.

8 Then said he unto me, These waters issue out toward the east country, and go down into the desert, and go into the sea: *which being* brought forth into the sea, the waters shall be healed. *(Almost within sight of Jerusalem lay the loathsome Dead Sea, which covered the ruins*

of the doomed cities of the plain, a sad memorial and type of sin. Into this horrid pool the living water flowed and made it so sweet and clear that it swarmed with fish—a beautiful emblem of the way in which the worst parts of the earth are reclaimed by the gospel when it comes in the power of the Spirit of God.)

9, 10 And it shall come to pass, *that* every thing that liveth, which moveth, whithersoever the rivers shall come, shall live: and there shall be a very great multitude of fish, because these waters shall come thither: for they shall be healed; and every thing shall live whither the river cometh. And the fishers shall stand upon it from En-gedi even unto En-eglaim; they shall be a *place* to spread forth nets; their fish shall be according to their kinds, as the fish of the great sea, exceeding many.

11 But the miry places thereof and the marishes thereof shall not be healed; they shall be given to salt. *(To some the gospel is not a savour of life. They reject the truth, and so miss its healing power, their wills are set upon evil, and they are given over to a reprobate mind. These are not always apparently the worst characters, they are not foul deeps like the Dead Sea, but marshy places only; perhaps their sense of fancied excellence prevents their humbly accepting the grace which bringeth salvation.)*

12 And by the river upon the bank thereof, on this side and on that side, shall grow all trees for meat, whose leaf shall not fade, neither shall the fruit thereof be consumed: it shall bring forth new fruit according to his months, because their waters they issued out of the sanctuary: and the fruit thereof shall be for meat, and the leaf thereof for medicine.

So Ezekiel's vision melts into that of John in the Revelation, and we are made to rejoice in the ever fresh, varied, satisfying, and soul-delighting blessings of the covenant of grace. Be it ours to drink of this water and never thirst again.

Behold of grace the quickening streams,
Their course with countless blessings teems;
Their founts hard by that altar rise
Where bled th' atoning sacrifice.

Down to the foul and loathsome sea
Of human guilt and misery,
The deepening floods in mercy roll,
And make the death-struck waters whole.

DANIEL V. 1—8 ; 13 ; 16—28 ; 30.

BELSHAZZAR the king made a great feast to a thousand of his lords, and drank wine before the thousand. Belshazzar, whiles he tasted the wine, commanded to bring the golden and silver vessels which his father Nebuchadnezzar had taken out of the temple which *was* in Jerusalem ; that the king, and his princes, his wives, and his concubines, might drink therein.

3 Then they brought the golden vessels that were taken out of the temple of the house of God which *was* at Jerusalem; and the king, and his princes, his wives, and his concubines, drank in them.

4 They drank wine, and praised the gods of gold, and of silver, of brass, of iron, of wood, and of stone.

5 ¶ In the same hour came forth fingers of a man's hand, and wrote over against the candlestick upon the plaister of the wall of the king's palace : and the king saw the part of the hand that wrote.

6, 7 Then the king's countenance was changed, and his thoughts troubled him, so that the joints of his loins were loosed, and his knees smote one against another. The king cried aloud to bring in the astrologers, the Chaldeans, and the soothsayers. *And* the king spake, and said to the wise *men* of Babylon, Whosoever shall read this writing, and shew me the interpretation thereof, shall be clothed with scarlet, and *have* a chain of gold about his neck, and shall be the third ruler in the kingdom.

8 Then came in all the king's wise *men :* but they could not read the writing, nor make known to the king the interpretation thereof.

13 Then was Daniel brought in before the king. *And* the king spake and said unto Daniel, *Art* thou that Daniel which *art* of the children of the captivity of Judah, whom the king my father brought out of Jewry ?

16 And I have heard of thee, that thou canst make interpretations, and dissolve doubts : now if thou canst read the writing, and make known to me the interpretation thereof, thou shalt be clothed with scarlet, and *have* a chain of gold about thy neck, and shalt be the third ruler in the kingdom.

17 ¶ Then Daniel answered and said before the king, Let thy gifts be to thyself, and give thy rewards to another ; yet I will read the writing unto the king, and make known to him the interpretation.

18—20 O thou king, the most high God gave Nebuchadnezzar thy father a kingdom, and majesty, and glory, and honour : And for the majesty that he gave him, all people, nations, and languages, trembled and feared before him : whom he would he slew ; and whom he would he kept alive ; and whom he would he set up ; and whom he would he put down. But when his heart was lifted up, and his mind hardened in pride, he was deposed from his kingly throne, and they took his glory from him :

21 And he was driven from the sons of men : and his heart was made like the beasts, and his dwelling *was* with the wild asses : they fed him with grass like oxen, and his body was wet with the dew of heaven ; till he knew that the most high God ruled in the kingdom of men, and *that* he appointeth over it whomsoever he will.

22 And thou his son, O Belshazzar, hast not humbled thine heart, though thou knewest all this ;

23 But hast lifted up thyself against the Lord of heaven ; and they have brought the vessels of his house before thee, and thou, and thy lords, thy wives, and thy concubines, have drunk wine in them ; and thou hast praised the gods of silver, and gold, of brass, iron, wood, and stone, which see not, nor hear, nor know : and the God in whose hand thy breath *is*, and whose *are* all thy ways, hast thou not glorified :

24 Then was the part of the hand sent from him ; and this writing was written.

25 ¶ And this *is* the writing that was written, MENE, MENE, TEKEL, UPHARSIN.

26 This *is* the interpretation of the thing : MENE ; God hath numbered thy kingdom, and finished it.

27 TEKEL ; Thou art weighed in the balances, and art found wanting.

28 PERES ; Thy kingdom is divided, and given to the Medes and Persians.

30 In that night was Belshazzar the king of the Chaldeans slain.

To be Sung or Read.

Condemn'd when in the balance weigh'd,
My soul might well be sore afraid ;
But to my Substitute I flee,
And Jesus fills the scale for me.

DARIUS *made Daniel the prime minister of his empire, and this excited the envy of those beneath him.*

DANIEL VI. 4—24.

4 Then the presidents and princes sought to find occasion against Daniel concerning the kingdom; but they could find none occasion nor fault; forasmuch as he *was* faithful, neither was there any error or fault found in him.

5 Then said these men, We shall not find any occasion against this Daniel, except we find *it* against him concerning the law of his God.

6, 7 Then these presidents and princes assembled together to the king, and said thus unto him, King Darius, live for ever. All the presidents of the kingdom, the governors, and the princes, the counsellors, and the captains, have consulted together to establish a royal statute, and to make a firm decree, that whosoever shall ask a petition of any God or man for thirty days, save of thee, O king, he shall be cast into the den of lions. *(This would be highly flattering to the king, and it was cunningly framed to entrap him. It would sound so grandly that no prayer was made on earth by the space of one month, save that which was addressed to the great Darius. How often are men snared by their own pride!)*

8, 9 Now, O king, establish the decree, and sign the writing, that it be not changed, according to the law of the Medes and Persians, which altereth not. Wherefore king Darius signed the writing and the decree. *(Little dreaming what he had thereby done. It is wise to consider a long time before we set our hands to any writing, otherwise we may soon sign away the inheritance of our children.)*

10 ¶ Now when Daniel knew that the writing was signed, he went into his house; and his windows being open in his chamber toward Jerusalem, he kneeled upon his knees three times a day, and prayed, and gave thanks before his God, as he did aforetime. *(He made no alteration, not even in the mode of his worship, lest there should be thought to be any wavering in him. To him life or death was not the question, but loyalty to his Lord was all in all. He would not bate one jot in his adherence to his God, and he took care that his enemies should know this at the very outset.)*

11 Then these men assembled, and found Daniel praying and making supplication before his God.

12 Then they came near and spake before the king concerning the king's decree; Hast thou not signed a decree, that every man that shall ask *a petition* of any God or man within thirty days, save of thee, O king, shall be cast into the den of lions? The king answered and said, The thing *is* true, according to the law of the Medes and Persians, which altereth not.

13 Then answered they and said before the king, That Daniel, which *is* of the children of the captivity of Judah, regardeth not thee, O king, nor the decree that thou hast signed, but maketh his petition three times a day.

14 Then the king, when he heard *these* words, was sore displeased with himself, and set *his* heart on Daniel to deliver him : and he laboured till the going down of the sun to deliver him.

15 Then these men assembled unto the king, and said unto the king, Know, O king, that the law of the Medes and Persians *is*, That no decree nor statute which the king establisheth may be changed. *(This rule was an affectation of grandeur, and a very foolish one. Immutability is for God, and not for men.)*

16, 17 Then the king commanded, and they brought Daniel, and cast *him* into the den of lions. *Now* the king spake and said unto Daniel, Thy God whom thou servest continually, he will deliver thee. And a stone was brought, and laid upon the mouth of the den ; and the king sealed it with his own signet, and with the signet of his lords ; that the purpose might not be changed concerning Daniel.

18 ¶ Then the king went to his palace, and passed the night fasting : neither were instruments of musick brought before him : and his sleep went from him. *(He was far more wretched in his palace than Daniel in the den. What a grand night the prophet must have spent : no wonder that he afterwards saw visions of terrible beasts, and yet felt no fear.)*

19, 20 Then the king arose very early in the morning, and went in haste unto the den of lions. And when he came to the den, he cried with a lamentable voice unto Daniel : *and* the king spake and said to Daniel, O Daniel,

(455)

servant of the living God, is thy God, whom thou servest continually, able to deliver thee from the lions?

21, 22 Then said Daniel unto the king, O king, live for ever. *(Well, kindly and courteously spoken. He did not blame the king, but saluted him right loyally.)* My God hath sent his angel, and hath shut the lions' mouths, that they have not hurt me : forasmuch as before him innocency was found in me; and also before thee, O king, have I done no hurt.

23 Then was the king exceeding glad for him, and commanded that they should take Daniel up out of the den, and no manner of hurt was found upon him, because he believed in his God.

God can still shut lions' mouths. Let us do the right at all hazards, and the Lord will deliver us. Daniel's God still lives: are we prepared to be Daniels?

24 ¶ And the king commanded, and they brought those men which had accused Daniel, and they cast *them* into the den of lions, them, their children, and their wives; and the lions had the mastery of them, and brake all their bones in pieces or ever they came at the bottom of the den.

The Christian, like his Lord of old,
Must look for foes and trials here;
Yet may the weakest saint be bold,
With such a friend as Jesus near.

The lion's roar need not alarm,
O Lord, the feeblest of thy sheep;
Nor can the fiercest monster harm,
While thou art nigh to watch and keep.

Therefore I will thy foes defy,
And own thee as my God, my friend;
No fear shall make me e'er deny
The God on whom my hopes depend.

Thus saith God of his Anointed;
He shall let my people go;
'Tis the work for him appointed,
'Tis the work that he shall do;
And my city
He shall found, and build it too.

He shall humble all the scorners,
He shall fill his foes with shame;
He shall raise and comfort mourners
By the sweetness of his name;
To the captives
He shall liberty proclaim.

He shall gather those that wander'd;
When they hear the trumpet's sound,
They shall join his sacred standard,
They shall come and flock around:
He shall save them;
They shall be with glory crown'd.

Praise ye the Lord; 'tis good to raise
Our hearts and voices in his praise:
His nature and his works invite
To make this duty our delight.

The Lord builds up Jerusalem,
And gathers nations to his name:
His mercy melts the stubborn soul,
And makes the broken spirit whole.

His church is precious in his sight;
He makes her glory his delight,
His treasures on her head are pour'd;
O Zion's children, praise the Lord.

There is a fountain fill'd with blood,
Drawn from Immanuel's veins:
And sinners, plunged beneath that flood,
Lose all their guilty stains.

Dear dying Lamb, thy precious blood
Shall never lose its power,
Till all the ransom'd church of God
Be saved to sin no more.

E'er since by faith I saw the stream
Thy flowing wounds supply,
Redeeming love has been my theme,
And shall be till I die.

Many times since days of youth,
May Israel truly say,
Foes devoid of love and truth
Afflict me day by day;
Yet they never can prevail,
God defends his people still;
Jesus' power can never fail
To save from all that's ill.

God hath Zion set apart
For his abiding place;
Sons of wrath and guileful art
He'll banish from his face:
God for Israel doth fight;
Israel, on thy God depend;
Christ shall keep thee day and night,
Till all thy troubles end.

BABYLON *had overthrown Judah, and now in its turn it was vanquished by Cyrus: this was greatly for the good of the Jews, for the Persian king became their friend and patron, according to ancient prophecies. Thus the Lord's purposes were fulfilled. When his time is come, all things work together to accomplish his designs.*

EZRA I.

1 Now in the first year of Cyrus king of Persia, that the word of the LORD by the mouth of Jeremiah might be fulfilled, the LORD stirred up the spirit of Cyrus king of Persia, that he made a proclamation throughout all his kingdom, and *put it* also in writing, saying,

2 Thus saith Cyrus king of Persia, The LORD God of heaven hath given me all the kingdoms of the earth ; and he hath charged me to build him an house at Jerusalem, which *is* in Judah.

It is delightful to hear such an acknowledgment from so great a king, and to see him so cheerfully take up his allotted work. We also have received all that we have from God, and should be prompt to do his bidding.

3 Who *is there* among you of all his people ? his God be with him, and let him go up to Jerusalem, which *is* in Judah, and build the house of the LORD God of Israel, (he *is* the God,) which *is* in Jerusalem.

4 And whosoever remaineth in any place where he sojourneth, let the men of his place help him with silver, and with gold, and with goods, and with beasts, beside the freewill offering for the house of God that is in Jerusalem.

5 ¶ Then rose up the chief of the fathers of Judah and Benjamin, and the priests, and the Levites, with all *them* whose spirit God had raised, to go up to build the house of the LORD which *is* in Jerusalem.

6 And all they that *were* about them strengthened their hands with vessels of silver, with gold, with goods, and with beasts, and with precious things, beside all *that* was willingly offered. *(The king's word and example excited a good feeling towards the Jews, so that they went out of Babylon as aforetime they had gone out of Egypt, laden with silver and gold.)*

7, 8 Also Cyrus the king brought forth the vessels of the house of the LORD, which Nebuchadnezzar had brought forth out of Jerusalem,

and had put them in the house of his gods ; Even those did Cyrus king of Persia bring forth by the hand of Mithredath the treasurer, and numbered them unto Sheshbazzar, the prince of Judah. *(These vessels were the lawful spoil of Cyrus when he captured the city of Babylon and its temples : a generous spirit prompted him to restore them to their ancient use. God knows how to provide for his own temple ; Cyrus restored the vessels, but the Lord's hand was in the matter.)*

9 And this *is* the number of them : thirty chargers of gold, a thousand chargers of silver, nine and twenty knives,

10 Thirty basons of gold, silver basons of a second *sort* four hundred and ten, *and* other vessels a thousand.

11 All the vessels of gold and of silver *were* five thousand and four hundred. All *these* did Sheshbazzar bring up with *them of* the captivity that were brought up from Babylon unto Jerusalem.

ENCOURAGED *by the Persian king, a considerable number returned to Jerusalem with Zerubbabel, though not such a company as might have been expected when affairs were so favourable.*

EZRA II. 64, 65; 68, 69.

64 The whole congregation together *was* forty and two thousand three hundred *and* threescore.

65 Beside their servants and their maids, of whom *there were* seven thousand three hundred thirty and seven : and *there were* among them two hundred singing men and singing women.

68 And *some* of the chief of the fathers, when they came to the house of the LORD which *is* at Jerusalem, offered freely for the house of God to set it up in his place :

69 They gave after their ability unto the treasure of the work threescore and one thousand drams of gold, and five thousand pound of silver, and one hundred priests' garments.

They had brought generous hearts with them, and at the sight of the sacred site they laid down their voluntary offerings that the Lord's house might be restored. God's house should be considered before our own house.

ABOUT *this time the seventy weeks of the prophet were complete, and the time had come for the return from captivity; the Lord therefore raised up Cyrus, and moved his heart to set his people free, and help them to go back to Jerusalem. Of this we have already learned in our last lesson, and therefore let us read those psalms in which the feelings of the returning exiles are set forth.*

PSALM LXXXV.

1, 2 LORD, thou hast been favourable unto thy land: thou hast brought back the captivity of Jacob. Thou hast forgiven the iniquity of thy people, thou hast covered all their sin. Selah. *(All goes well when sin is pardoned. This is the one fatal hindrance to prosperity; and, this removed, all is well.)*

3 Thou hast taken away all thy wrath: thou hast turned *thyself* from the fierceness of thine anger.

4 Turn us, O God of our salvation, and cause thine anger toward us to cease.

When God turns to us in love, it is high time that we turned to him in faith and repentance; and, indeed, we very soon do so. Love is the great converting force: when the love of Jesus turns us, we are turned indeed.

5 Wilt thou be angry with us for ever? wilt thou draw out thine anger to all generations?

6 Wilt thou not revive us again: that thy people may rejoice in thee?

7 Shew us thy mercy, O LORD, and grant us thy salvation.

8 I will hear what God the LORD will speak: for he will speak peace unto his people, and to his saints: but let them not turn again to folly.

9 Surely his salvation *is* nigh them that fear him; that glory may dwell in our land.

10 Mercy and truth are met together; righteousness and peace have kissed *each other.*

This it is our privilege to see fulfilled in the atonement of the Lord Jesus, by which our captivity is turned, and peace is made between God and our souls.

11 Truth shall spring out of the earth; and righteousness shall look down from heaven.

Earth looks up in sincerity, and heaven looks down in mercy.

12 Yea, the LORD shall give *that which is* good; and our land shall yield her increase.

13 Righteousness shall go before him; and shall set *us* in the way of his steps.

Re-established in their land, which was made fruitful once again, they desired to obey the Lord in all things and to follow closely the path of obedience.

WE *can imagine the restored exiles at this time singing—*

PSALM CXXVI.

1 When the LORD turned again the captivity of Zion, we were like them that dream.

It seemed too good to be true, they could not realise that so good a thing had befallen them.

2 Then was our mouth filled with laughter, and our tongue with singing: then said they among the heathen, The LORD hath done great things for them.

3 The LORD hath done great things for us; *whereof* we are glad.

What others declared concerning them was true, and they boldly avowed it; they did not bury the Lord's mercies in forgetfulness, or cast doubts upon them by mock modesty. We too often say " We hope and we trust," when we ought rather to say, " The Lord hath done great things for us."

4 Turn again our captivity, O LORD, as the streams in the south.

5 They that sow in tears shall reap in joy.

6 He that goeth forth and weepeth, bearing precious seed, shall doubtless come again with rejoicing, bringing his sheaves *with him.*

When God revealed his gracious name
And changed our mournful state,
The rapture seem'd a pleasing dream,
The grace appeared so great.

"Great is the work," my neighbours cried,
And own'd the power divine;
"Great is the work," my heart replied,
"And be the glory thine."

The Lord can clear the darkest skies,
Can give us day for night;
Make drops of sacred sorrow rise
To rivers of delight.

458   "𝔥e gathereth together the outcasts of Israel."   AUGUST 1.—EVENING.

[*Or March* 1.]

EZRA III.

AND when the seventh month was come, and the children of Israel *were* in the cities, the people gathered themselves together as one man to Jerusalem. *(There was a spirit of unity among the returned exiles, and a warm love to the worship of God, and therefore as soon as they had made such arrangements as were absolutely needed for their own living, they met to consult concerning the rebuilding of the temple. Things will be sure to go well with the cause of God when all the people are as one man.)*

2 Then stood up Jeshua the son of Jozadak, and his brethren the priests, and Zerubbabel the son of Shealtiel, and his brethren, and builded the altar of the God of Israel, to offer burnt offerings thereon, as *it is* written in the law of Moses the man of God. *(Atonement for sin must be presented, and thanks must be rendered. The Lord's people love the altar of sacrifice.)*

3 And they set the altar upon his bases *(or upon its former foundation)*; for fear *was* upon them because of the people of those countries : and they offered burnt offerings thereon unto the LORD, *even* burnt offerings morning and evening.

4, 5 They kept also the feast of tabernacles, as *it is* written, and *offered* the daily burnt offerings by number, according to the custom, as the duty of every day required; And afterward *offered* the continual burnt offering, both of the new moons, and of all the set feasts of the LORD that were consecrated, and of every one that willingly offered a freewill offering unto the LORD. *(Though but few and poor, they were very earnest, and very careful to do as the law commanded them. In this they are our teachers.)*

6, 7 From the first day of the seventh month began they to offer burnt offerings unto the LORD. But the foundation of the temple of the LORD was not *yet* laid. They gave money also unto the masons, and to the carpenters ; and meat, and drink, and oil, unto them of Zidon, and to them of Tyre, to bring cedar trees from Lebanon to the sea of Joppa, according to the grant that they had of Cyrus king of Persia.

8 ¶ Now in the second year of their coming unto the house of God at Jerusalem, in the second month, began Zerubbabel the son of Shealtiel, and Jeshua the son of Jozadak, and the remnant of their brethren the priests and the Levites, and all they that were come out of the captivity unto Jerusalem ; and appointed the Levites, from twenty years old and upward, to set forward the work of the house of the LORD. *(They were probably the best educated men and the fittest for overseeing the work.)*

9 Then stood Jeshua *with* his sons and his brethren, Kadmiel and his sons, the sons of Judah, together, to set forward the workmen in the house of God : the sons of Henadad, *with* their sons and their brethren the Levites.

It was an honour to these men to have their names recorded, and it will be equally honourable to us if we do anything for the church of God.

10, 11 And when the builders laid the foundation of the temple of the LORD, they set the priests in their apparel with trumpets, and the Levites the sons of Asaph, with cymbals to praise the LORD, after the ordinance of David king of Israel. And they sang together by course in praising and giving thanks unto the LORD ; because *he is* good, for his mercy *endureth* for ever toward Israel. And all the people shouted with a great shout, when they praised the LORD, because the foundation of the house of the LORD was laid. *(The laying of the foundation was celebrated with much sacred pomp and praising of the Lord. Who will not be glad when the Lord's temple is being builded?)*

12, 13 But many of the priests and Levites and chief of the fathers, *who were* ancient men, that had seen the first house, when the foundation of this house was laid before their eyes, wept with a loud voice ; and many shouted aloud for joy : So that the people could not discern the noise of the shout of joy from the noise of the weeping of the people : for the people shouted with a loud shout, and the noise was heard afar off. *(It was a noble structure; but for the size and costliness of the stones, and the preciousness of the metals, it was far inferior to Solomon's. Moreover, it had not the ark, nor the Shechinah light, nor the Urim and Thummim. In all that we do for God we shall see cause to mingle regret with rejoicing; we serve the Lord with gladness, but we sorrow that we serve him so ill. May the blood of Jesus cleanse our holy things.)*

IT *would appear from the chapter which we last read that the singers at the founding of the temple sang—*

PSALM CXVIII.

1 O give thanks unto the LORD; for *he is* good : because his mercy *endureth* for ever.

2 Let Israel now say, that his mercy *endureth* for ever.

3 Let the house of Aaron now say, that his mercy *endureth* for ever.

4 Let them now that fear the LORD say, that his mercy *endureth* for ever.

5 I called upon the LORD in distress ; the LORD answered me, *and set me* in a large place. *Out of the Babylonish captivity had they come to the freedom of their own land, beneath the patronage of Cyrus.*

6 The LORD *is* on my side ; I will not fear : what can man do unto me ?

7 The LORD taketh my part with them that help me : therefore shall I see *my desire* upon them that hate me. *(For there were such : the Samaritans and other envious neighbours looked on with jealous eyes.)*

8 *It is* better to trust in the LORD than to put confidence in man.

9 *It is* better to trust in the LORD than to put confidence in princes.

10 All nations compassed me about : but in the name of the LORD will I destroy them.

11 They compassed me about ; yea, they compassed me about : but in the name of the LORD I will destroy them.

12 They compassed me about like bees ; they are quenched as the fire of thorns : for in the name of the LORD I will destroy them.

Faith is more than a conqueror, and sings a song of victory before the battle is over.

13 Thou hast thrust sore at me that I might fall : but the LORD helped me.

14 The LORD *is* my strength and song, and is become my salvation.

15 The voice of rejoicing and salvation *is* in the tabernacles of the righteous : the right hand of the LORD doeth valiantly.

16 The right hand of the LORD is exalted : the right hand of the LORD doeth valiantly.

17 I shall not die, but live, and declare the works of the LORD. *(Israel was not quite dead :*

the nation would yet revive : even in her ashes lived her wonted fires.)

18 The LORD hath chastened me sore : but he hath not given me over unto death.

19 Open to me the gates of righteousness : I will go into them, *and* I will praise the LORD:

20 This gate of the LORD, into which the righteous shall enter.

21 I will praise thee : for thou hast heard me, and art become my salvation.

22 The stone *which* the builders refused is become the head *stone* of the corner.

23 This is the LORD's doing : it *is* marvellous in our eyes. *(Thus, as they looked on their once despised leader, they were led to sing in mystic prophecy of Jesus, the Messiah, who is now to us our chief corner-stone.)*

24 This *is* the day *which* the LORD hath made ; we will rejoice and be glad in it.

25 Save now, I beseech thee, O LORD : O LORD, I beseech thee, send now prosperity.

26 Blessed *be* he that cometh in the name of of the LORD : we have blessed you out of the house of the LORD. *(They blessed the priest, and the priest returned the benediction, and then they proceeded to sacrifice.)*

27 God *is* the LORD, which hath shewed us light : bind the sacrifice with cords, *even* unto the horns of the altar.

28 Thou *art* my God, and I will praise thee : *thou art* my God, I will exalt thee.

29 O give thanks unto the LORD ; for *he is* good : for his mercy *endureth* for ever.

Let us treasure up this golden sentence, and when we are in any difficulty or trouble let us at once repair to Him, whose mercy endureth for ever.

Praise ye the Lord, how kind, how nigh !
His mercy fills eternity.
Let Israel now adoring cry,
" His mercy fills eternity."

Let Aaron's line new anthems try,
" His mercy fills eternity,"
Who fear the Lord, sing deep and high,
" His mercy fills eternity."

Thou art my God, 'tis thee I praise ;
My Lord, on high thy name I raise ;
Praise to the Lord, for good is he,
" His mercy fills eternity."

AFTER *the foundations of the temple had been laid, the work was opposed, and the people grew dispirited; the prophet Haggai was sent to exhort them to begin again.*

HAGGAI I.

1, 2 In the second year of Darius the king, in the first day of the month, came the word of the LORD by Haggai the prophet unto Zerubbabel the son of Shealtiel, governor of Judah, and to Joshua the son of Josedech, the high priest, saying, Thus speaketh the LORD of hosts, saying, This people say, The time is not come, the time that the LORD's house should be built. *(The difficulties placed in their way by their enemies had discouraged the people, and led them to believe that the set time, mentioned in the book of Jeremiah, had not yet come. When we do not like a work it is easy to find an excuse for postponing it.)*

3 Then came the word of the LORD by Haggai the prophet, saying,

4 *Is it* time for you, O ye, to dwell in your cieled houses, and this house *lie* waste ?

They had made their own houses luxurious, but the temple was as yet little better than a ruin. Its unfinished and unroofed walls accused them of want of zeal for the Lord.

5 Now therefore thus saith the LORD of hosts ; Consider your ways.

6 Ye have sown much, and bring in little ; ye eat, but ye have not enough ; ye drink, but ye are not filled with drink ; ye clothe you, but there is none warm ; and he that earneth wages earneth wages *to put it* into a bag with holes.

Meanness towards God's work had kept them poor. If men are selfish and keep their wealth to themselves, and rob God of his portion, they shall not prosper, or if they do, no blessing shall come with it.

7 ¶ Thus saith the LORD of hosts ; Consider your ways. *(Judge whether you are acting honestly and fairly with the Lord, and consider whether your poverty may not be sent as a punishment for your robbing God of his due.)*

8 Go up to the mountain, and bring wood, and build the house ; and I will take pleasure in it, and I will be glorified, saith the LORD.

9, 10 Ye looked for much, and, lo, *it came* to little : and when ye brought *it* home, I did blow upon it. Why ? saith the LORD of hosts.

Because of mine house that *is* waste, and ye run every man unto his own house. Therefore the heaven over you is stayed from dew, and the earth is stayed *from* her fruit.

11 And I called for a drought upon the land, and upon the mountains, and upon the corn, and upon the new wine, and upon the oil, and upon *that* which the ground bringeth forth, and upon men, and upon cattle, and upon all the labour of the hands. *(They gave little, and therefore received little. When men are bad stewards, their great Lord refuses to trust them with his estate ; if they deprive the great Owner of all things of his quit-rent of grateful offering, he will take away their vineyard, and let it out to others. This is but just and right.)*

12 ¶ Then Zerubbabel the son of Shealtiel, and Joshua the son of Josedech, the high priest, with all the remnant of the people, obeyed the voice of the LORD their God, and the words of Haggai the prophet, as the LORD their God had sent him, and the people did fear before the LORD.

13 Then spake Haggai the LORD's messenger in the LORD's message unto the people, saying, I *am* with you, saith the LORD.

14 And the LORD stirred up the spirit of Zerubbabel the son of Shealtiel, governor of Judah, and the spirit of Joshua the high priest, and the spirit of all the remnant of the people ; and they came and did work in the house of the LORD of hosts, their God,

15 In the four and twentieth day of the sixth month, in the second year of Darius the king.

See the value of a man of God! His voice calls others to their duty, who else would have quite neglected it. If we have been niggardly to the cause of God, let Haggai's voice sound across the centuries, and quicken us also to diligence in service and liberality in gift to the work of the Lord.

Wake thy slumbering children, wake them,
  Bid them to thy harvest go ;
Blessings, O our Father, make them ;
  Round their steps let blessings flow.

Give reviving—give refreshing—
  Give the look'd-for Jubilee ;
To thyself may crowds be pressing,
  Bringing glory unto thee.

EZRA IV. 1—6.

NOW when the adversaries of Judah and Benjamin heard that the children of the captivity builded the temple unto the Lord God of Israel; Then they came to Zerubbabel, and to the chief of the fathers, and said unto them, Let us build with you : for we seek your God, as ye *do;* and we do sacrifice unto him since the days of Esar-haddon king of Assur, which brought us up hither.

3 But Zerubbabel, and Jeshua, and the rest of the chief of the fathers of Israel, said unto them, Ye have nothing to do with us to build an house unto our God ; but we ourselves together will build unto the Lord God of Israel, as king Cyrus the king of Persia hath commanded us.

They resolved to maintain their separate position according to the Lord's will. Christians also should be separate from the world.

4—6 Then the people of the land weakened the hands of the people of Judah, and troubled them in building, And hired counsellors against them, to frustrate their purpose, all the days of Cyrus king of Persia, even until the reign of Darius king of Persia. And in the reign of Ahasuerus, *(or Cambyses,)* in the beginning of his reign, wrote they *unto him* an accusation against the inhabitants of Judah and Jerusalem.

The result of this letter was, not only an order to refrain from building the wall of the city, but the temple also was left till the reign of Darius. Then the prophets Haggai and Zechariah stirred up the people, and the work re-commenced. Opposition was again excited, and appeal was made to Darius. He ordered a search to be made, and the original edict of Cyrus was found, whereupon the king issued a decree that none should oppose the work. The wording of it was as follows :—

EZRA VI. 6—14.

NOW *therefore,* Tatnai, governor beyond the river, Shethar-boznai, and your companions the Apharsachites, which *are* beyond the river, be ye far from thence :

7 Let the work of this house of God alone ; let the governor of the Jews and the elders of the Jews build this house of God in his place.

8 Moreover I make a decree what ye shall do to the elders of these Jews for the building of this house of God : that of the king's goods,

even of the tribute beyond the river, forthwith expences be given unto these men, that they be not hindered. *(Signally had all opposition failed, for their very enemies were compelled under pains and penalties to supply them with money for building the temple. Little did they expect this, but God can always do for his people exceeding abundantly above what they ask or even think. The king also ordered that animals for sacrifice should be supplied to them.)*

9 And that which they have need of, both young bullocks, and rams, and lambs, for the burnt offerings of the God of heaven, wheat, salt, wine, and oil, according to the appointment of the priests which *are* at Jerusalem, let it be given them day by day without fail :

10 That they may offer sacrifices of sweet savours unto the God of heaven, and pray for the life of the king, and of his sons.

11, 12 Also I have made a decree, that whosoever shall alter this word, let timber be pulled down from his house, and being set up, let him be hanged thereon ; and let his house be made a dunghill for this. And the God that hath caused his name to dwell there destroy all kings and people, that shall put to their hand to alter *and* to destroy this house of God which *is* at Jerusalem. I Darius have made a decree; let it be done with speed. *(This was a very peremptory decree in the Jews' favour, and the work went on gloriously when the people had been fully aroused by the prophets to do the work.)*

13, 14 Then Tatnai, governor on this side the river, Shethar-boznai, and their companions, according to that which Darius the king had sent, so they did speedily. And the elders of the Jews builded, and they prospered through the prophesying of Haggai the prophet and Zechariah the son of Iddo. And they builded, and finished *it,* according to the commandment of the God of Israel, and according to the commandment of Cyrus, and Darius, and Artaxerxes king of Persia. *(May the Lord also build up his church in these days and glorify his son Jesus Christ our Lord.)*

To be Sung or Read.

Thus saith the Lord to Jacob's seed,
In me, the mighty God, rejoice ;
No hostile weapon shall succeed
Against the people of my choice.

HAGGAI II. 1—19.

IN the seventh *month*, in the one and twentieth *day* of the month, came the word of the LORD by the prophet Haggai, saying, Speak now to Zerubbabel, governor of Judah, and to Joshua, the high priest, and to the residue of the people, saying, Who *is* left among you that saw this house in her first glory? and how do ye see it now? *is it* not in your eyes in comparison of it as nothing? *(This was another cause of the discouragement of the people. They pleaded that the building would be a very poor affair in comparison with the first temple. Many now-a-days excuse themselves from doing their best by pleading that they can do so little.)*

4 Yet now be strong, O Zerubbabel, saith the LORD; and be strong, O Joshua, son of Josedech, the high priest; and be strong, all ye people of the land, saith the LORD, and work: for I *am* with you, saith the LORD of hosts:

The very best encouragement in all the world.

5 *According to* the word that I covenanted with you when ye came out of Egypt, so my spirit remaineth among you: fear ye not.

6, 7 For thus saith the LORD of hosts; Yet once, it *is* a little while, and I will shake the heavens, and the earth, and the sea, and the dry *land;* And I will shake all nations, and the desire of all nations shall come: and I will fill this house with glory, saith the LORD of hosts.

8 The silver *is* mine, and the gold *is* mine, saith the LORD of hosts. *(Their poverty need not hinder them; for God could find them means, as indeed he did, for he laid the treasures of Darius at their feet. It is ours to do our best for God's cause, and believe that the Lord will provide.)*

9 The glory of this latter house shall be greater than of the former, saith the LORD of hosts: and in this place will I give peace, saith the LORD of hosts. *(And so it was, for there the Lord Jesus appeared, " a light to lighten the Gentiles, and the glory of his people Israel.")*

10, 11 In the four and twentieth *day* of the ninth *month*, in the second year of Darius, came the word of the LORD by Haggai the prophet, saying, Thus saith the LORD of hosts; Ask now the priests *concerning* the law, saying,

12 If one bear holy flesh in the skirt of his garment, and with his skirt do touch bread, or pottage, or wine, or oil, or any meat, shall it be holy? And the priests answered and said, No. *(Legal sanctity is not easily transmitted. Holy flesh sanctified the garment in which it was wrapped, but did not cleanse anything beyond. Men are not rendered holy by outward ritual.)*

13 Then said Haggai, If *one that is* unclean by a dead body touch any of these, shall it be unclean? And the priests answered and said, It shall be unclean.

14 Then answered Haggai, and said, So *is* this people, and so *is* this nation before me, saith the LORD; and so *is* every work of their hands; and that which they offer there *is* unclean. *(The uncleanness of the offerer spoils the sacrifice. There is a spreading power in the defilement of sin, though not in legal sanctity. Oh, to be clean before the Lord! for if we are not so, all that we do will be unaccepted.)*

15—19 And now, I pray you, consider from this day and upward, from before a stone was laid upon a stone in the temple of the LORD: Since those *days* were, when *one* came to an heap of twenty *measures*, there were *but* ten: when *one* came to the pressfat for to draw out fifty *vessels* out of the press, there were *but* twenty. I smote you with blasting and with mildew and with hail in all the labours of your hands; yet ye *turned* not to me, saith the LORD. Consider now from this day and upward, from the four and twentieth day of the ninth *month*, even from the day that the foundation of the LORD's temple was laid, consider *it* Is the seed yet in the barn? yea, as yet the vine, and the fig tree, and the pomegranate, and the olive tree, hath not brought forth: from this day will I bless *you.*

When they began to serve the Lord with holy zeal, then would he enrich them; but until then they would have a curse on their granaries and their crops. God save us as a family from this!

Lord, bless me from this day,
As thou alone canst bless;
Take mine iniquity away,
And give thy righteousness.

Lord, bless me from this day,
Thy sovereign grace impart;
Teach me thy sacred law t' obey
With all my willing heart.

ZECHARIAH *the prophet was a fellow-worker with Haggai, and aided him in bringing about the completion of the temple. His prophecy is full of visions, and worthy of our careful study.*

ZECHARIAH I. 1—13; 18—21.

1—3 In the eighth month, in the second year of Darius, came the word of the LORD unto Zechariah, the son of Berechiah, the son of Iddo the prophet, saying, The LORD hath been sore displeased with your fathers. Therefore say thou unto them, Thus saith the LORD of hosts; Turn ye unto me, saith the LORD of hosts, and I will turn unto you, saith the LORD of hosts.

4 Be ye not as your fathers, unto whom the former prophets have cried, saying, Thus saith the LORD of hosts; Turn ye now from your evil ways, and *from* your evil doings: but they did not hear, nor hearken unto me, saith the LORD.

5 Your fathers, where *are* they? and the prophets, do they live for ever?

6 But my words and my statutes, which I commanded my servants the prophets, did they not take hold of your fathers? and they returned and said, Like as the LORD of hosts thought to do unto us, according to our ways, and according to our doings, so hath he dealt with us.

7, 8 Upon the four and twentieth day of the eleventh month, which *is* the month Sebat, in the second year of Darius, came the word of the LORD unto Zechariah, the son of Berechiah, the son of Iddo the prophet, saying, I saw by night, and behold a man riding upon a red horse, and he stood among the myrtle trees that *were* in the bottom; and behind him *were there* red horses, speckled, and white. (*He saw the Lord of providence, attended by his ministering spirits, surveying the kingdoms. The red horses probably represented distress and war; the speckled, mingled events; and the white, times of prosperity.*)

9 Then said I, O my lord, what *are* these? And the angel that talked with me said unto me, I will shew thee what these *be*.

10, 11 And the man that stood among the myrtle trees answered and said, These *are they* whom the LORD hath sent to walk to and fro through the earth. And they answered the angel of the LORD that stood among the myrtle trees, and said, We have walked to and fro through the earth, and, behold, all the earth sitteth still, and is at rest. (*He who guards his church, which he calls his myrtle, summons his servants to give in their account of what is going on upon the face of the earth, and they report a general peace.*)

12 Then the angel of the LORD answered and said, O LORD of hosts, how long wilt thou not have mercy on Jerusalem and on the cities of Judah, against which thou hast had indignation these threescore and ten years? (*Would not poor Israel share in the wide-spread peace? Her intercessor does not forget to plead for her.*)

13 And the LORD answered the angel that talked with me *with* good words *and* comfortable words. (*Yes, better times were in store, and the Lord declared their coming.*)

18 Then lifted I up mine eyes, and saw, and behold four horns.

19 And I said unto the angel that talked with me, What *be* these? And he answered me, These *are* the horns which have scattered Judah, Israel, and Jerusalem.

20 And the LORD shewed me four carpenters.

21 Then said I, What come these to do? And he spake, saying, These *are* the horns which have scattered Judah, so that no man did lift up his head: but these are come to fray (*or fright*) them, to cast out the horns of the Gentiles, which lifted up *their* horn over the land of Judah to scatter it.

God will always find men to do his work; there were horns to be cut off, and here are the carpenters or artificers. God will always find the right sort of men: they were smiths, not fishermen: and he will always find enough men, for as there were four horns, so are there four smiths to beat them to pieces. Empires which have opposed the Lord have been crushed to powder, and so will it always be: no power can stand against the Lord of Hosts. Are we upon his side? Have we believed in his Son Jesus? If so, none can harm us; but if not, his wrath will overthrow us.

TO BE SUNG OR READ.

Through all thy works thy wisdom shines,
And baffles Satan's deep designs;
Thy power is sovereign to fulfil
The noblest counsels of thy will.

L ET *us read for our personal instruction:*

ZECHARIAH III.

1 And he shewed me Joshua the high priest standing before the angel of the LORD, and Satan standing at his right hand to resist him.

Every believer is a priest, and his standing is before the angel of the Lord, for in the presence of God and unto him alone is our ministry rendered. The enemy of souls is ever ready to act as the accuser of the brethren, and as the hinderer of all holy service. Often when we know it not he comes forward to oppose our soul's best interests.

2 And the LORD said unto Satan, The LORD rebuke thee, O Satan; even the LORD that hath chosen Jerusalem rebuke thee : *is* not this a brand plucked out of the fire?

We have a divine Advocate to plead our cause; he pleads our election and our effectual calling. If the Lord has chosen us and snatched us from sure destruction, will he not accept the service which we render to him? To what end then should the adversary oppose us?

3 Now Joshua was clothed with filthy garments, and stood before the angel.

Alas! this is our condition also, for we have not kept ourselves unspotted from the world; but mark the care and love of the great Advocate.

4 And he answered and spake unto those that stood before him, saying, Take away the filthy garments from him. And unto him he said, Behold, I have caused thine iniquity to pass from thee, and I will clothe thee with change of raiment. (*Gone, for ever gone, is the iniquity of the believer; he is no longer condemned, but accepted in the sight of God. The goodly raiment of Christ's righteousness is ours.*)

5 And I said, Let them set a fair mitre upon his head. So they set a fair mitre upon his head, and clothed him with garments. And the angel of the LORD stood by. (*Sin is removed, righteousness is bestowed, honour is conferred, and all through the omnipotent word of that Angel of the covenant in whom our soul delights. He stands by, and therefore all is well. We owe everything to Jesus. To him be glory for ever.*)

6 And the angel of the LORD protested unto Joshua, saying,

7 Thus saith the LORD of hosts ; If thou wilt walk in my ways, and if thou wilt keep my charge, then thou shalt also judge my house, and shalt also keep my courts, and I will give thee places to walk among these that stand by.

Believers who act obediently are honoured with service, and are enabled to glorify God by bringing forth the fruits of grace among their brethren. Would to God that more of us were eminent for holiness and usefulness!

8 Hear now, O Joshua the high priest, thou, and thy fellows that sit before thee : for they *are* men wondered at : for, behold, I will bring forth my servant the BRANCH. (*This is the grand announcement of all, Jesus is* THE BRANCH *from David's root, the fruitful bough on which we hang all our hopes. He shall build the true temple of God, and upon him, as the one goodly foundation-stone, shall all eyes be fixed.*)

9 For behold the stone that I have laid before Joshua; upon one stone *shall be* seven eyes: behold, I will engrave the graving thereof, saith the LORD of hosts, and I will remove the iniquity of that land in one day.

God and men, angels and devils, saints and sinners, are all gazing upon Jesus. What a graving was that which he endured when justice cut deep into his hands, and feet, and side; then, indeed, iniquity was removed in one day.

10 In that day, saith the LORD of hosts, shall ye call every man his neighbour under the vine and under the fig tree.

Jesus will bring peace. His reign shall end the woes and discords of the chosen people. Sin being wholly removed, peace will be restored and established for ever. Are we each of us looking to the Lord Jesus for all things? Do we trust in him as our Advocate, and is his righteousness our glorious dress?

Guilty we plead before thy throne,
    And low in dust we lie,
Till Jesus stretch his gracious arm
    To bring the guilty nigh.

The sins of one most righteous day
    Might plunge us in despair ;
Yet all the crimes of numerous years
    Shall our great Surety clear.

That spotless robe, which he hath wrought,
    Shall deck us all around ;
Nor by the piercing eye of God
    One blemish shall be found.

ZECHARIAH IV. 1—10.

AND the angel that talked with me came again, and waked me, as a man that is wakened out of his sleep, And said unto me, What seest thou ? And I said, I have looked, and behold a candlestick all *of* gold, with a bowl upon the top of it, and his seven lamps thereon, and seven pipes to the seven lamps, which *are* upon the top thereof : And two olive trees by it, one upon the right *side* of the bowl, and the other upon the left *side* thereof.

4 So I answered and spake to the angel that talked with me, saying, What *are* these, my lord ?

The Jewish church was aptly set forth by the golden candlestick ; and the two olive trees, mysteriously supplying the lamps with oil, were admirable emblems of the secret manner in which grace is infused into the saints by the energy of the Holy Ghost. Other lamps must be fed with oil by human labour, but the Lord himself supplies the golden candlestick of his church.

5 Then the angel that talked with me answered and said unto me, Knowest thou not what these be ? And I said, No, my lord.

6 Then he answered and spake unto me, saying, This *is* the word of the LORD unto Zerubbabel, saying, Not by might, nor by power, but by my spirit, saith the LORD of hosts.

God will work in his own way despite the feebleness of his people, or the power of their foes. The vision was intended to teach Zerubbabel that, by secret means, God would keep his cause safe from decay by poverty, or destruction by opponents.

7—9 Who *art* thou, O great mountain ? before Zerubbabel *thou shalt become* a plain : and he shall bring forth the headstone *thereof with* shoutings, *crying*, Grace, grace unto it. *(The Samaritan opposition came to nothing, and by the aid of Darius the house was joyfully completed.)* Moreover the word of the LORD came unto me, saying, The hands of Zerubbabel have laid the foundation of this house; his hands shall also finish it; and thou shalt know that the LORD of hosts hath sent me unto you.

10 For who hath despised the day of small things ? for they shall rejoice, and shall see the plummet in the hand of Zerubbabel *with* those seven; they *are* the eyes of the LORD, which run to and fro through the whole earth.

God blessed the work, and it went on under his supreme protection, angels watching over it. The spirit of the people was stimulated so that they did not flag, their enemies were restrained, and all materials for the temple were given them ; and all this not by their own might, but by the Spirit of God. Let us learn to trust in God when we are most weak, and friends are most few, for he will appear and glorify himself in us.

THE *prophet also uttered a remarkable prophecy as to the future conversion of the Jewish people.*

ZECHARIAH XII. 9—14.

9 And it shall come to pass in that day, *that* I will seek to destroy all the nations that come against Jerusalem.

10 And I will pour upon the house of David, and upon the inhabitants of Jerusalem, the spirit of grace and of supplications : and they shall look upon me whom they have pierced, and they shall mourn for him, as one mourneth for *his* only *son*, and shall be in bitterness for him, as one that is in bitterness for *his* firstborn.

O that this long-expected day would come, that so poor Israel might take her proper place in the household of grace !

11 In that day shall there be a great mourning in Jerusalem, as the mourning of Hadadrimmon in the valley of Megiddon.

12—14 And the land shall mourn, every family apart ; the family of the house of David apart, and their wives apart ; the family of the house of Nathan apart, and their wives apart ; The family of the house of Levi apart, and their wives apart ; the family of Shimei apart, and their wives apart ; All the families that remain, every family apart, and their wives apart.

Repentance must be personal and private, or it cannot be real. Do we understand such repentance ? Have we felt it for ourselves ?

ZECHARIAH XIII. 1.

1 In that day there shall be a fountain opened to the house of David and to the inhabitants of Jerusalem for sin and for uncleanness. *(When a soul mourns for sin, its pardon is near. True repentance weeps at the foot of the cross. We sorrow not as despairing sinners do, for we have washed in the atoning blood, and are clean.)*

MANY *Jews preferred to live in Persia and forget their fathers' land. These fell into a low state of grace, but were nevertheless the subjects of very remarkable providential deliverances, which are recorded in the Book of Esther. King Ahasuerus, or Xerxes, commanded Vashti, his queen, to show herself at a drinking bout. This immodest act she refused to do, and therefore the king divorced her. Beautiful women were gathered from every land that he might choose a new queen, and among others Esther was presented by her uncle Mordecai. Very far had Mordecai turned aside from the purity which becomes a child of God when he did this, but the Lord overruled it for his people's good, for Esther became the queen of Ahasuerus, and was thus able to interpose to save the Jews.*

ESTHER III. 1—13.

1 After these things did king Ahasuerus promote Haman the son of Hammedatha the Agagite, and advanced him, and set his seat above all the princes that *were* with him.

2 And all the king's servants, that *were* in the king's gate, bowed, and reverenced Haman : for the king had so commanded concerning him. But Mordecai bowed not, nor did *him* reverence. (*The Persians ascribed religious honours to their rulers, and these the godly Jew would not render.*)

3 Then the king's servants, which *were* in the king's gate, said unto Mordecai, Why transgressest thou the king's commandment ?

4, 5 Now it came to pass, when they spake daily unto him, and he hearkened not unto them, that they told Haman, to see whether Mordecai's matters would stand : for he had told them that he *was* a Jew. And when Haman saw that Mordecai bowed not, nor did him reverence, then was Haman full of wrath.

6 And he thought scorn to lay hands on Mordecai alone ; for they had shewed him the people of Mordecai : wherefore Haman sought to destroy all the Jews that *were* throughout the whole kingdom of Ahasuerus, *even* the people of Mordecai. (*What a mean and cruel spirit dwelt in this great lord ! He might very well have allowed the Jew to act as he pleased, for how could so great a man be injured by missing the nod of a poor Jew ? But no, he plots a horrible* revenge—*a whole nation must die to atone for the brusque manners of one man.*)

7 ¶ In the first month, that *is* the month Nisan, in the twelfth year of king Ahasuerus, they cast Pur, that *is*, the lot, before Haman from day to day, and from month to month, *to* the twelfth *month*, that *is*, the month Adar.

He superstitiously waited for a lucky day in which to wreak vengeance on Mordecai's nation, and happily the lot fell twelve months forward, which gave time to reverse the king's decree.

8, 9 And Haman said unto king Ahasuerus, There is a certain people scattered abroad and dispersed among the people in all the provinces of thy kingdom ; and their laws *are* diverse from all people ; neither keep they the king's laws : therefore it *is* not for the king's profit to suffer them. If it please the king, let it be written that they may be destroyed : and I will pay ten thousand talents of silver to the hands of those that have the charge of the business, to bring *it* into the king's treasuries.

10 And the king took his ring from his hand and gave it unto Haman the son of Hammedatha the Agagite, the Jews' enemy.

11 And the king said unto Haman, The silver *is* given to thee, the people also, to do with them as it seemeth good to thee. (*Unhappy were the people who were subject to such a hasty, thoughtless king. Well was it for the world that Xerxes did not conquer the Greeks at Salamis !*)

12, 13 Then were the king's scribes called on the thirteenth day of the first month, and there was written according to all that Haman had commanded unto the rulers of every people of every province according to the writing thereof, and *to* every people after their language ; in the name of king Ahasuerus was it written, and sealed with the king's ring. And the letters were sent by posts into all the king's provinces, to destroy, to kill, and to cause to perish, all Jews, both young and old, little children and women, in one day, *even* upon the thirteenth *day* of the twelfth month, which *is* the month Adar, and *to take* the spoil of them for a prey. (*To gratify a favourite's malice an ancient race must be massacred. God be thanked that under a constitutional government our lives are not at the mercy of one man as the poor Israelites were.*)

TO *please his favourite, the king had doomed all the Jews to destruction : we can imagine the universal distress which it created.*

ESTHER IV.

1, 2 When Mordecai perceived all that was done, Mordecai rent his clothes, and put on sackcloth with ashes, and went out into the midst of the city, and cried with a loud and a bitter cry ; And came even before the king's gate : for none *might* enter into the king's gate clothed with sackcloth. *(He felt as if he had been the cause of the overthrow of his people, since it was for his sake that Haman had determined to massacre every one of them.)*

3 And in every province, whithersoever the king's commandment and his decree came, *there was* great mourning among the Jews, and fasting, and weeping, and wailing ; and many lay in sackcloth and ashes. *(As well they might, since they were all doomed to die by the sword. The Lord's people were in great jeopardy.)*

4—6 So Esther's maids and her chamberlains came and told *it* her. Then was the queen exceedingly grieved ; and she sent raiment to clothe Mordecai, and to take away his sackcloth from him : but he received *it* not. Then called Esther for Hatach, *one* of the king's chamberlains, whom he had appointed to attend upon her, and gave him a commandment to Mordecai, to know what it *was*, and why it *was*. So Hatach went forth to Mordecai unto the street of the city, which *was* before the king's gate.

7 And Mordecai told him of all that had happened unto him, and of the sum of the money that Haman had promised to pay to the king's treasuries for the Jews, to destroy them.

8 Also he gave him the copy of the writing of the decree that was given at Shushan to destroy them, to shew *it* unto Esther, and to declare *it* unto her, and to charge her that she should go in unto the king, to make supplication unto him, and to make request before him for her people.

9 And Hatach came and told Esther the words of Mordecai. *(Evidence of the great danger of her race was supplied to her both by word of mouth and by the copy of the decree which she could read for herself. No one could now help the poor doomed nation but Esther ; for*

her it would be a dangerous task, and she had no great measure of that high all-daring faith which had dwelt in some of her ancestors. Her position as queen, in an alien court, was not one which fostered the highest form of spiritual life.)

10 Again Esther spake unto Hatach, and gave him commandment unto Mordecai ;

11 All the king's servants, and the people of the king's provinces, do know, that whosoever, whether man or woman, shall come unto the king into the inner court, who is not called, *there is* one law of his to put *him* to death, except such to whom the king shall hold out the golden sceptre, that he may live : but I have not been called to come in unto the king these thirty days.

12 And they told to Mordecai Esther's words.

13, 14 Then Mordecai commanded to answer Esther, Think not with thyself that thou shalt escape in the king's house, more than all the Jews. For if thou altogether holdest thy peace at this time, *then* shall there enlargement and deliverance arise to the Jews from another place ; but thou and thy father's house shall be destroyed : and who knoweth whether thou art come to the kingdom for *such* a time as this ?

Mordecai was sure that God would deliver his people in some way or other, and he warned Esther that if she missed the honour of being her nation's deliverer, she would not herself escape, for the king's edict would operate even in the palace.

15 Then Esther bade *them* return Mordecai this answer,

16 Go, gather together all the Jews that are present in Shushan, and fast ye for me, and neither eat nor drink three days, night or day : I also and my maidens will fast likewise ; and so will I go in unto the king, which *is* not according to the law : and if I perish, I perish.

17 So Mordecai went his way, and did according to all that Esther had commanded him.

If they would pray for her, she would venture. Surely, if she thus plucked up courage to approach a hasty, imperious tyrant, no penitent sinner need fear to come to God by Jesus Christ.

Thy church through every past alarm
In thee has found a Friend
And, Lord, on thine Almighty arm
We now for all depend.

468   " If ye have bitter envying ni your hearts, glory not."   AUGUST 6.—EVENING.

[*Or March* 11.]

THE *three days of prayer and fasting were over, and the time came for Esther to risk all, and go in unto the king unbidden, and plead for her nation.*

ESTHER V.

1 Now it came to pass oh the third day, that Esther put on *her* royal *apparel,* and stood in the inner court of the king's house, over against the king's house : and the king sat upon his royal throne in the royal house, over against the gate of the house. *(These kings affected great state, and, partly to impress their people with awe, and partly for their own safety, none dared approach them on peril of their lives, if they had not been expressly called. For Israel's sake Esther encountered this mortal danger.)*

2 And it was so, when the king saw Esther the queen standing in the court, *that* she obtained favour in his sight : and the king held out to Esther the golden sceptre that *was* in his hand. So Esther drew near, and touched the top of the sceptre.

3 Then said the king unto her, What wilt thou, queen Esther ? and what *is* thy request ? it shall be even given thee to the half of the kingdom. *(She had good speed at the outset. If we will but act boldly, the Lord will help us.)*

4 And Esther answered, If *it seem* good unto the king, let the king and Haman come this day unto the banquet that I have prepared for him.

5 Then the king said, Cause Haman to make haste, that he may do as Esther hath said. So the king and Haman came to the banquet that Esther had prepared.

6 And the king said unto Esther at the banquet of wine, What *is* thy petition ? and it shall be granted thee : and what *is* thy request ? even to the half of the kingdom it shall be performed.

7, 8 Then answered Esther, and said, My petition and my request *is ;* If I have found favour in the sight of the king, and if it please the king to grant my petition, and to perform my request, let the king and Haman come to the banquet that I shall prepare for them, and. I will do to morrow as the king hath said.

Either she had not yet the courage to speak out, or else she wisely judged that. her influence over

the king needed to be strengthened before it would outweigh that of the cunning favourite.

9 ¶ Then went Haman forth that day joyful and with a glad heart : but when Haman saw Mordecai in the ·king's gate, that he stood not up, nor moved for him, he was full of indignation against Mordecai. *(Sternly would Mordecai gaze upon him, viewing him now with utter abhorrence, as intending to murder all the Jews.)*

10 Nevertheless Haman refrained himself : and when he came home, he sent and called for his friends, and Zeresh his wife.

11 And Haman told them of the glory of his riches, and the multitude of his children, and all *the things* wherein the king had promoted him, and how he had advanced him above the princes and servants of the king.

12, 13 Haman said moreover, Yea, Esther the queen did let no man come in with the king unto the banquet that she had prepared but myself ; and to morrow am I invited unto her also with the king. Yet all this availeth me nothing, so long as I see Mordecai the Jew sitting at the king's gate. *(Pride is a pitiful thing, and so hungry that all the world cannot satisfy it if some one little matter go amiss.)*

14 ¶ Then said Zeresh his wife and all his friends unto him, Let a gallows be made of fifty cubits high, and to morrow speak thou unto the king that Mordecai may be hanged thereon : then go thou in merrily with the king unto the banquet. And the thing pleased Haman ; and he caused the gallows to be made.

He was such a favourite that he had only to ask and have, so that he would make short work with sulky Mordecai. Next morning he would go to court and get the king's warrant for the man's execution. We shall see what happened.

But no such rigid law we fear,
Who to the King of kings draw near,
Boldly approach his gracious throne,
And freely our requests make known.

Beyond the inner court we press,
Enter within the holiest place ;
Sure to obtain the peace of God,
And all we ask through Jesu's blood.

ESTHER VI.

ON that night could not the king sleep ; *(he who commanded a hundred and twenty-seven provinces, could not command a little sleep ;)* and he commanded to bring the book of records of the chronicles ; and they were read before the king. *(To while away the weary hours, and help him to slumber.)*

2 And it was found written, that Mordecai had told of Bigthana and Teresh, two of the king's chamberlains, the keepers of the door, who sought to lay hand on the king Ahasuerus. *Singular was the providence which led to the reading of this record ; the hand of the Lord was in it.*

3 And the king said, What honour and dignity hath been done to Mordecai for this ? Then said the king's servants that ministered unto him, There is nothing done for him. *The monarch was impressed with the great service which Mordecai had rendered, and perhaps struck with the stern uprightness for which he was famous ; and he felt that so loyal an adherent ought not to have been passed over and left unrewarded.*

4 ¶ And the king said, Who *is* in the court ? Now Haman was come into the outward court of the king's house, to speak unto the king to hang Mordecai on the gallows that he had prepared for him.

5 And the king's servants said unto him, Behold, Haman standeth in the court. And the king said, Let him come in. *(He was up betimes to make a halter for the man he hated, but the Lord thought not so. Providence had brought him where he would mix for himself a bitter cup.)*

6 So Haman came in. And the king said unto him, What shall be done unto the man whom the king delighteth to honour ? Now Haman thought in his heart, To whom would the king delight to do honour more than to myself ?

7 And Haman answered the king, For the man whom the king delighteth to honour,

8 Let the royal apparel be brought which the king *useth* to wear, and the horse that the king rideth upon, and the crown royal which is set upon his head :

9 And let this apparel and horse be delivered to the hand of one of the king's most noble princes, that they may array the man *withal* whom the king delighteth to honour, and bring him on horseback through the street of the city, and proclaim before him, Thus shall it be done to the man whom the king delighteth to honour. *He went as far as he well could, imagining that all these honours were intended for himself.*

10 Then the king said to Haman, Make haste, *and* take the apparel and the horse, as thou hast said, and do even so to Mordecai the Jew, that sitteth at the king's gate : let nothing fail of all that thou hast spoken.

11 Then took Haman the apparel and the horse, and arrayed Mordecai, and brought him on horseback through the street of the city, and proclaimed before him, Thus shall it be done unto the man whom the king delighteth to honour.

12 And Mordecai came again to the king's gate. *(Not at all elated, he took his old place.)* But Haman hasted to his house mourning, and having his head covered. *(As full of spleen and malice as he could hold.)*

13 And Haman told Zeresh his wife and all his friends every *thing* that had befallen him. Then said his wise men and Zeresh his wife unto him, If Mordecai *be* of the seed of the Jews, before whom thou hast begun to fall, thou shalt not prevail against him, but shalt surely fall before him. *(This was cold comfort. He had been the dupe of the soothsayers, and now they render him no consolation.)*

14 And while they *were* yet talking with him, came the king's chamberlains, and hasted to bring Haman unto the banquet that Esther had prepared. *(Little did he know how that banquet would end, and little do the enemies of the Lord know how surely and terribly they will be overthrown. May grace prevent our ever fighting against God !)*

He can raise the poor to stand
With the princes of the land ;
Wealth upon the needy shower ;
Set the meanest high in power.

He the broken spirit cheers ;
Turns to joy the mourner's tears ;
Such the wonders of his ways :
Praise his name--for ever praise.

470   *" So let all thine enemies perish, O Lord."*   AUGUST 7.—EVENING.

[*Or March* 13.]

ESTHER VII.

SO the king and Haman came to banquet with Esther the queen. And the king said again unto Esther, What *is* thy petition, queen Esther? and it shall be granted thee: and what *is* thy request? and it shall be performed, *even* to the half of the kingdom.

3, 4 Then Esther the queen answered and said, If I have found favour in thy sight, O king, and if it please the king, let my life be given me at my petition, and my people at my request: For we are sold, I and my people, to be destroyed, to be slain, and to perish. But if we had been sold for bondmen and bondwomen, I had held my tongue, although the enemy could not countervail the king's damage.

This was well and boldly spoken, and Haman must have writhed in agony as he heard it.

5 Then the king answered and said unto Esther the queen, Who is he, and where is he, that durst presume in his heart to do so?

6 And Esther said, The adversary and enemy *is* this wicked Haman. Then Haman was afraid before the king and the queen.

7 And the king arising from the banquet of wine in his wrath *went* into the palace garden: and Haman stood up to make request for his life to Esther the queen; for he saw that there was evil determined against him by the king.

8 Then the king returned out of the palace garden into the place of the banquet of wine; and Haman was fallen upon the bed whereon Esther *was*. Then said the king, Will he force the queen also before me in the house? As the word went out of the king's mouth, they covered Haman's face. *(As a condemned man, who would no more see the sun. He was so proud that the courtiers were glad to see his downfall; and as his malice towards Mordecai was common talk, they hastened to mention it to the king.)*

9 And Harbonah, one of the chamberlains, said before the king, Behold also, the gallows fifty cubits high, which Haman had made for Mordecai, who·had spoken good for the king, standeth in the house of Haman. Then the king said, Hang him thereon.

10 So they hanged Haman on the gallows· that he had prepared for Mordecai. Then was the king's wrath pacified.

But though Haman was dead, the edict for the slaughter of the Jews remained in force.

ESTHER VIII. 3—11; 15; 16.

AND Esther spake yet again before the king, and fell down at his feet, and besought him with tears to put away the mischief of Haman the Agagite, and his device that he had devised against the Jews.

4—6 Then the king held out the golden sceptre toward Esther. So Esther arose, and stood before the king, And said, If it please the king, and if I have found favour in his sight, and the thing *seem* right before the king, and I *be* pleasing in his eyes, let it be written to reverse the letters· devised by Haman the Agagite, which he wrote to destroy the Jews which *are* in all the king's provinces: For how can I endure to see the evil that shall come unto my people? or how can I endure to see the destruction of my kindred?

7 Then the king Ahasuerus said unto Esther the queen and to Mordecai the Jew,

8—11 Write ye also for the Jews, as it liketh you, in the king's name, and seal *it* with the king's ring: And Mordecai wrote in the king Ahasuerus' name, and sent letters by posts on horseback, *and* riders on mules, camels, *and* young dromedaries: Wherein the king granted the Jews which *were* in every city to gather themselves together, and to stand for their life, to destroy, to slay, and to cause to perish, all the power of the people and province that would assault them, *both* little ones and women, and *to take* the spoil of them for a prey. *(The decree to slay the Jews could not be reversed, but its sting was extracted by the new decree that the Jews might defend themselves, and slay their foes.)*

15, 16 And Mordecai went out from the presence of the king in royal apparel of blue and white, and with a great crown of gold: and the city of Shushan rejoiced and was glad. The Jews had light, and gladness, and joy, and honour.

Thus the seed of Abraham lived on, despite the plots of Satan and of Haman; and so shall the Church of the living God triumph over all the assaults of Rome and hell. Praise ye the Lord!

Crowns and thrones shall perish, kingdoms rise and
    wane,
But the church of Jesus constant will remain;
Gates of hell can never 'gainst that church prevail,
We have God's own promise, and it cannot fail.

M ORE *than seventy years after Sheshbazzar had led the first exiles back to Jerusalem, according to the decree of Cyrus, the Lord stirred up Ezra, a priest, to conduct another company to the beloved city. Leaving all the ease and comfort of the land in which they dwelt, believing men and women joined together to return to the sacred place where their fathers had aforetime worshipped the true God. The company started with the full sanction of Artaxerxes, the Persian king. Ezra, acting as his own historian, says—*

EZRA VIII. 15—35.

15—17 And I gathered them together to the river that runneth to Ahava ; and there abode we in tents three days : and I viewed the people, and the priests, and found there none of the sons of Levi. Then sent I for men of understanding. And I sent them with commandment unto Iddo the chief at the place Casiphia, that they should bring unto us ministers for the house of our God. *(Ezra felt that they must have the priests of the Lord with them. What can righteous men do without the ordinances of religion ?)*
18—20 And by the good hand of our God upon us they brought us a man of understanding of the sons of Mahli, the son of Levi, and Sherebiah, with his sons and his brethren, eighteen ; And Hashabiah, and with him Jeshaiah of the sons of Merari, his brethren and their sons, twenty ; Also of the Nethinims, whom David and the princes had appointed for the service of the Levites, two hundred and twenty Nethinims : all of them were expressed by name.
21 Then I proclaimed a fast there, at the river of Ahava, that we might afflict ourselves before our God, to seek of him a right way for us, and for our little ones, and for all our substance.
He begins well who begins with prayer.
22, 23 For I was ashamed to require of the king a band of soldiers and horsemen to help us against the enemy in the way : because we had spoken unto the king, saying, The hand of our God *is* upon all them that seek him ; but his power and his wrath *is* against all them that forsake him. So we fasted and besought our God for this : and he was intreated of us.
Prayer is both shield and sword. Faith in this case bore herself bravely in refusing to com-

promise the honour of God by begging protection of the Persian king.
24—27 Then I separated twelve of the chief of the priests, and weighed unto them the silver, and the gold, and the vessels, *even* the offering of the house of our God, which the king, and his counsellors, and his lords, and all Israel *there* present had offered :
28—30 And I said unto them, Ye *are* holy unto the LORD ; the vessels *are* holy also ; and the silver and the gold *are* a freewill offering unto the LORD God of your fathers. Watch ye, and keep *them*, until ye weigh *them* before the chief of the priests and the Levites, and chief of the fathers of Israel, at Jerusalem, in the chambers of the house of the LORD. So took the priests and the Levites the weight of the silver, and the gold, and the vessels, to bring *them* to Jerusalem unto the house of our God.
31 ¶ Then we departed from the river of Ahava on the twelfth *day* of the first month, to go unto Jerusalem : and the hand of our God was upon us, and he delivered us from the hand of the enemy, and of such as lay in wait by the way. *(He travels safely who has the Lord of Hosts for his convoy.)*
32—34 And we came to Jerusalem, and abode there three days. Now on the fourth day was the silver and the gold and the vessels weighed in the house of our God by the hand of Meremoth the son of Uriah the priest ; By number *and* by weight of every one : and all the weight was written at that time. *(Care should always be taken that all that belongs to the Lord's house should be exactly accounted for.)*
35 *Also* the children of those that had been carried away, which were come out of the captivity, offered burnt offerings unto the God of Israel, twelve bullocks for all Israel, ninety and six rams, seventy and seven lambs, twelve he goats *for* a sin offering : all *this was* a burnt offering unto the LORD. *(Thus with devout hearts they commenced a new and happy era for Jerusalem. Those who act with an eye to the glory of God shall receive honour at his hands.)*

My soul shall pray for Zion still,
   While life or breath remains,
There my best friends, my kindred dwell,
   There God, my Saviour reigns.

WHILE *matters were being conducted so well by Ezra and his friends, and their great care was for the house of God, the Lord was mindful of them, and found them a friend at court, who speedily came to Jerusalem with reinforcements, and, what was best of all, with permission from the Persian king to build the walls of Jerusalem, for the city had remained unfortified all these long years. We shall now read the story of Nehemiah.*

NEHEMIAH I. 1—4.

1—3 The words of Nehemiah the son of Hachaliah. *(A grand court dignitary, cupbearer to the king.)* And it came to pass in the month Chisleu, in the twentieth year, as I was in Shushan the palace, That Hanani, one of my brethren, came, he and *certain* men of Judah ; and I asked them concerning the Jews that had escaped, which were left of the captivity, and concerning Jerusalem. And they said unto me, The remnant that are left of the captivity there in the province *are* in great affliction and reproach : the wall of Jerusalem also *is* broken down, and the gates thereof are burned with fire. *Great good came of this pious conversation. It is well when good men talk of good things.*

4 And it came to pass, when I heard these words, that I sat down and wept, and mourned *certain* days, and fasted, and prayed before the God of heaven.

NEHEMIAH II. 1—13.

AND it came to pass in the month Nisan. in the twentieth year of Artaxerxes the king, *that* wine *was* before him : and I took up the wine, and gave *it* unto the king. Now I had not been *beforetime* sad in his presence. *See the providence which called him to do his office just at this time.*

2, 3 Wherefore the king said unto me, Why *is* thy countenance sad, seeing thou *art* not sick ? this *is* nothing *else* but sorrow of heart. Then I was very sore afraid, And said unto the king, Let the king live for ever : why should not my countenance be sad, when the city, the place of my fathers' sepulchres, *lieth* waste, and the gates thereof are consumed with fire ?

4 Then the king said unto me, For what dost thou make request ? So I prayed to the God of heaven. *(This was well done. Silent prayer works wonders, and wastes no time.)*

5 And I said unto the king, If it please the king, and if thy servant have found favour in thy sight, that thou wouldest send me unto Judah, unto the city of my fathers' sepulchres, that I may build it.

6 And the king said unto me, (the queen also sitting by him,) For how long shall thy journey be ? and when wilt thou return ? So it pleased the king to send me ; and I set him a time. *(He was highly esteemed, and the king was loth to part with him.)*

7, 8 Moreover, I said unto the king, If it please the king, let letters be given me to the governors beyond the river, that they may convey me over till I come into Judah ; And a letter unto Asaph the keeper of the king's forest, that he may give me timber to make beams for the gates of the palace which *appertained* to the house, and for the wall of the city, and for the house that I shall enter into. And the king granted me, according to the good hand of my God upon me.

9 ¶ Then I came to the governors beyond the river, and gave them the king's letters. Now the king had sent captains of the army and horsemen with me. *So that he came as governor in due state.*

10 When Sanballat the Horonite, and Tobiah the servant, the Ammonite, heard *of it*, it grieved them exceedingly that there was come a man to seek the welfare of the children of Israel. *(Enemies always come forward when good is to be done. We must reckon on this, and we shall not then be troubled about it.)*

11 So I came to Jerusalem, and was there three days.

12, 13 And I arose in the night, I and some few men with me ; neither told I *any* man what my God had put in my heart to do at Jerusalem : neither *was there any* beast with me, save the beast that I rode upon. And I went out by night by the gate of the valley, and viewed the walls of Jerusalem, which were broken down, and the gates thereof were consumed with fire. *(This night survey was wise. Plans are best kept secret till they are matured We must serve the Lord prudently as well as zealously. Lord, teach us how to do this.)*

I N *the rebuilding of Jerusalem several circumstances deserve our notice. We are unable to read the full record of all the workers, and therefore we will select verses of an interesting nature from—*

NEHEMIAH III. 1—3; 5; 8; 10; 12; 20; 27—29; 31, 32.

1 Then Eliashib the high priest rose up with his brethren the priests, and they builded the sheep gate ; they sanctified it, and set up the doors of it ; even unto the tower of Meah they sanctified it, unto the tower of Hananeel.

Those who were chief in office led the way ; they did the work most appropriate to them, for they repaired the gate by which the sheep entered the city for sacrifice, and they did it in a most commendable manner, sanctifying all that they did. Both in our service, and in the manner of it, all believers, being priests unto God, should be examples to others.

2 And next unto him builded the men of Jericho. *(They had less interest in the work, being men of another town, but they lent their aid cheerfully. If we help ourselves, others will be the more inclined to help us.)* And next to them builded Zaccur the son of Imri.

3 But the fish gate did the sons of Hassenaah build, who *also* laid the beams thereof, and set up the doors thereof, the locks thereof, and the bars thereof. *(They did their work thoroughly in its details, and this is the right way to act in the service of the Lord. Nothing should be done in a slovenly manner.)*

5 And next unto them the Tekoites repaired ; but their nobles put not their necks to the work of their Lord. *(They were too haughty to work, but the people would not be discouraged by them. Nobles are never so ignoble as when they despise the work of the Lord.)*

8 Next unto him repaired Uzziel the son of Harhaiah, of the goldsmiths. Next unto him also repaired Hananiah the son of *one of* the apothecaries, and they fortified Jerusalem unto the broad wall. *(Goldsmiths and apothecaries carry on most honourable trades, and happily these had both wealth and hearts to give it.)*

10 And next unto them repaired Jedaiah the son of Harumaph, even over against his house. *And where could he work more suitably?*

Whatever we do, let us try to serve God at home, and do good in our own neighbourhood.

12 And next unto him repaired Shallum the son of Halohesh, the ruler of the half part of Jerusalem, he and his daughters. *(Good women can take their share in the Lord's work, and it is highly honourable to them when they do so. In our houses let the daughters serve the cause of Jesus.)*

20 After him Baruch the son of Zabbai earnestly repaired the other piece, from the turning *of the wall* unto the door of the house of Eliashib the high priest. *(Baruch was so eager and zealous that he finished two measures of the wall. We can never do too much for the good cause.)*

27 After them the Tekoites repaired another piece, over against the great tower that lieth out, even unto the wall of Ophel. *(Though forsaken by their nobles, the Tekoites did double work. If great men will not serve God, the poorer sort must shame them by doing double.)*

28 From above the horse gate repaired the priests, every one over against his house.

29 After them repaired Zadok the son of Immer over against his house.

31 After him repaired Malchiah the goldsmith's son unto the place of the Nethinims, and of the merchants, over against the gate Miphkad, and to the going up of the corner.

32 And between the going up of the corner unto the sheep gate repaired the goldsmiths and the merchants. *(And so, by the labours of all, the circle of the wall was complete, and Jerusalem was protected. The church of God in our day needs building up, and it is the duty of each believer to take his share in the work. What can we do? Let the question go round among us, What can I do? Do I really love the Lord, and trust in his Son Jesus? If so, what shall I do, my Saviour to praise?)*

As labourers on thy church's walls,
Lord, give us grace to be
Content to lift the heaviest load
Through life's long day for Thee.

Of wages we will ask no more,
When thou shalt call us home,
Than to have shared that travail sore,
Which makes thy kingdom come.

474   " The builders, every one had his sword girded by his side."   AUGUST 9.—EVENING.

[Or March 17.]

NEHEMIAH IV. 1—9; 11—15; 17—21.

BUT it came to pass, that when Sanballat heard that we builded the wall, he was wroth, and took great indignation, and mocked the Jews. And he spake before his brethren and the army of Samaria, and said, What do these feeble Jews ? will they fortify themselves ? will they sacrifice ? will they make an end in a day ? will they revive the stones out of the heaps of the rubbish which are burned ?

Mockery has always been the favourite weapon of ungodly men. In this case Sanballat scoffed at the zealous eagerness of the people. " See," said he, " they work as if a city could be built in a day." That which was eminently to their honour he made the theme of his jeering—a very common habit to this day.

3 Now Tobiah the Ammonite *was* by him, and he said, Even that which they build, if a fox go up, he shall even break down their stone wall. *(This bird of the same feather sang the same note. He scoffed because he was afraid.)*

4, 5 Hear, O our God ; for we are despised : and turn their reproach upon their own head, and give them for a prey in the land of captivity : And cover not their iniquity, and let not their sin be blotted out from before thee : for they have provoked *thee* to anger before the builders. *(A prayer more after the spirit of the law than the gospel. It is full of Nehemiah's zeal for right, but lacks the gentleness of Jesus.)*

6—8 So built we the wall ; and all the wall was joined together unto the half thereof : for the people had a mind to work. But it came to pass, *that* when Sanballat, and Tobiah, and the Arabians, and the Ammonites, and the Ashdodites, heard that the walls of Jerusalem were made up, *and* that the breaches began to be stopped, then they were very wroth, And conspired all of them together to come *and* to fight against Jerusalem, and to hinder it.

9 Nevertheless we made our prayer unto our God, and set a watch against them day and night, because of them. *(Cromwell bade his soldiers trust in God, and keep their powder dry. Nehemiah was equally practical.)*

11 And our adversaries said, They shall not know, neither see, till we come in the midst among them, and slay them, and cause the work to cease. *(They intended to take them by surprise, but in this they were foiled.)*

12 And it came to pass, that when the Jews which dwelt by them came, they said unto us ten times, From all places whence ye shall return unto us *they will be upon you. (It was well done of these outlying Jews to warn their brethren so often ; they acted as sentinels.)*

13, 14 Therefore set I in the lower places behind the wall, *and* on the higher places, I even set the people after their families with their swords, their spears, and their bows. And I looked, and rose up, and said unto the nobles, and to the rulers, and to the rest of the people, Be not ye afraid of them : remember the Lord, *which is* great and terrible, and fight for your brethren, your sons, and your daughters, your wives, and your houses. *(He set before them the terribleness of God as a reason for having no terror of men. " Fear him, ye saints, and ye will then have nothing else to fear.")*

15 And it came to pass, when our enemies heard that it was known unto us, and God had brought their counsel to nought, that we returned all of us to the wall, every one unto his work. *(They lost no time in holidays and congratulations ; they were in earnest, and kept to their business.)*

17, 18 They which builded on the wall, and they that bare burdens, with those that laded, *every one* with one of his hands wrought in the work, and with the other *hand* held a weapon. For the builders, every one had his sword girded by his side, and *so* builded. And he that sounded the trumpet *was* by me. *(So must Christians both labour and fight, watch and pray, build up the good, and guard against the evil.)*

19, 20 And I said unto the nobles, and to the rulers, and to the rest of the people, The work *is* great and large, and we are separated upon the wall, one far from another. In what place *therefore* ye hear the sound of the trumpet, resort ye thither unto us : our God shall fight for us. *(Here was the best reason for courage. If God be for us, who can be against us ? O God, our God, fight for us this day !)*

21 So we laboured in the work : and half of them held the spears from the rising of the morning till the stars appeared. *(In God's work we may well make long days. Time is short, and the Lord's work deserves all our strength.)*

AFTER *Jerusalem had been walled in, Nehemiah took great care to reform the manners of the people, and to celebrate the ordinances of religion as the law of God directed. We will read of one of their great assemblies.*

NEHEMIAH VIII. 1—17.

1 And all the people gathered themselves together as one man into the street that *was* before the water gate; and they spake unto Ezra the scribe to bring the book of the law of Moses, which the LORD had commanded to Israel.

2 And Ezra the priest brought the law before the congregation both of men and women, and all that could hear with understanding, upon the first day of the seventh month.

3 And he read therein before the street that *was* before the water gate from the morning until midday, before the men and the women, and those that could understand; and the ears of all the people *were attentive* unto the book of the law. *(They were not wearied with five or six hours' devotion, whereas in these times there is much complaint if the service lasts longer than an hour and a half.)*

4 And Ezra the scribe stood upon a pulpit of wood, which they had made for the purpose; and beside him stood Mattithiah, and Shema and Anaiah, and Urijah, and Hilkiah, and Maaseiah, on his right hand; and on his left hand, Pedaiah, and Mishael, and Malchiah, and Hashum, and Hashbadana, Zechariah, *and* Meshullam. *(So that the pulpit was a roomy one. The presence of these eminent persons added authority and honour to the preacher's office before the eyes of the people.)*

5, 6 And Ezra opened the book in the sight of all the people; (for he was above all the people;) and when he opened it, all the people stood up : And Ezra blessed the LORD, the great God. And all the people answered, Amen, Amen, with lifting up their hands : and they bowed their heads, and worshipped the LORD with *their* faces to the ground.

7 Also Jeshua, and Bani, and Sherebiah, Jamin, Akkub, Shabbethai, Hodijah, Maaseiah, Kelita, Azariah, Jozabad, Hanan, Pelaiah, and the Levites, caused the people to understand the law : and the people *stood* in their place.

As they could not all hear the same person's voice, they were divided into companies, and were instructed by the good men just named.

8 So they read in the book in the law of God distinctly, and gave the sense, and caused *them* to understand the reading.

The reading of difficult passages of Scripture in public is of small use to the many : the preacher should explain what he reads.

9 ¶ And Nehemiah, which *is* the Tirshatha, and Ezra the priest the scribe, and the Levites that taught the people, said unto all the people, This day *is* holy unto the LORD your God; mourn not, nor weep. For all the people wept, when they heard the words of the law.

10 Then he said unto them, Go your way, eat the fat, and drink the sweet, and send portions unto them for whom nothing is prepared : for *this* day *is* holy unto our Lord : neither be ye sorry ; for the joy of the LORD is your strength. *(Even our sorrow for sin must not prevent our grateful joy. While God is so good, we ought to rejoice in him, however much we may see to weep over in ourselves.)*

11 So the Levites stilled all the people, saying, Hold your peace, for the day *is* holy ; neither be ye grieved.

12 And all the people went their way to eat, and to drink, and to send portions, and to make great mirth, because they had understood the words that were declared unto them.

Good cause for gladness have those who understand the Scriptures. A service which is above our comprehension must be dreary to us; but if we can enter into it, we may well be glad.

13—15 And on the second day were gathered together the chief of the fathers of all the people, the priests, and the Levites, unto Ezra the scribe, even to understand the words of the law. And they found written in the law which the LORD had commanded by Moses, that the children of Israel should dwell in booths in the feast of the seventh month : And that they should publish and proclaim in all their cities, and in Jerusalem, saying, Go forth unto the mount, and fetch olive branches, and pine branches, and myrtle branches, and palm branches, and branches of thick trees, to make booths, as *it is* written.

16, 17 So the people went forth, and brought *them*, and made themselves booths, every one upon the roof of his house, and in their courts, and in the courts of the house of God, and in the street of the water gate, and in the street of the gate of Ephraim. And all the congregation of them that were come again out of the captivity made booths, and sat under the booths: for since the days of Jeshua the son of Nun unto that day had not the children of Israel done so. And there was very great gladness.

The joyous feast of Tabernacles followed the day of atonement, and on this occasion the people, having entered, by deep sorrow, into the humiliation of the atonement, were all the more ready to enjoy the delights of the after feast. They kept it after a better fashion than in any former period. Let us also keep the feast, for our sins have been put away by our great Substitute. Let us joyfully sojourn here below in these frail tabernacles till we enter into our house eternal in the heavens.

O my soul, what means this sadness?
  Wherefore art thou thus cast down?
Let thy griefs be turned to gladness,
  Bid thy restless fears be gone:
    Look to Jesus,
  And rejoice in his dear name.

Oh that I could now adore him,
  Like the heavenly host above,
Who for ever bow before him,
  And unceasing sing his love!
    Happy songsters!
  When shall I your chorus join?

Thou shalt arise, and mercy have
  Upon thy Sion yet;
The time to favour her is come,
  The time that thou hast set.

For in her rubbish and her stones
  Thy servants pleasure take;
Yea, they the very dust thereof
  Do favour for her sake.

When Sion by the mighty Lord
  Built up again shall be,
Then shall her gracious God appear
  In glorious majesty.

Oft in sorrow, oft in woe,
Onward, Christians, onward go;
Fight the fight, maintain the strife,
Strengthen'd with the bread of life.

Let your drooping hearts be glad;
March in heavenly armour clad;
Fight, nor think the battle long,
Soon shall victory tune your song.

Let not sorrow dim your eye,
Soon shall every tear be dry;
Let not fears your course impede,
Great your strength if great your need.

Onward, then, to glory move,
More than conquerors ye shall prove;
Though opposed by many a foe,
Christian soldiers, onward go.

Now doth my soul resolve indeed
  To wound her Lord no more;
Hence from my heart, ye sins, begone,
  For Jesus I adore.

Furnish me, Lord, with heav'nly arms
  From grace's magazine,
And I'll proclaim eternal war
  With every darling sin.

No more, ye lusts, shall ye command,
  No more will I obey;
Stretch out, O God, thy conqu'ring hand,
  And drive thy foes away!

Look upon me, Lord, I pray thee,
  Let thy Spirit dwell in mine;
Thou hast sought me, thou hast bought me,
  Only thee to know I pine.
    Let me find thee!
  Take my heart, and own me thine!

Nought I ask for, nought I strive for,
  But thy grace so rich and free;
That thou givest whom thou lovest,
  And who truly cleave to thee.
    Let me find thee!
  He hath all things who hath thee.

NEHEMIAH *was a very strict disciplinarian, and very earnest to prevent breaches of the divine law. He narrates instances of his determined action.*

NEHEMIAH XIII. 15—31.

15 In those days saw I in Judah *some* treading wine presses on the sabbath, and bringing in sheaves, and lading asses ; as also wine, grapes, and figs, and all *manner of* burdens, which they brought into Jerusalem on the sabbath day : and I testified *against them* in the day wherein they sold victuals. *(They made a market of the Sabbath, but the godly governor would not permit it ; he warned them to desist.)*

16 — 18 There dwelt men of Tyre also therein, which brought fish, and all manner of ware, and sold on the sabbath unto the children of Judah, and in Jerusalem. Then I contended with the nobles of Judah, and said unto them, .What evil thing *is* this that ye do, and profane the sabbath day ? Did not your fathers thus, and did not our God bring all this evil upon us, and upon this city ? yet ye bring more wrath upon Israel by profaning the sabbath. *(He blamed the buyers more than the sellers. The men of Tyre were heathen, and knew no better, but the nobles of Judah were instructed, and should not have encouraged Sabbath-breaking.)*

19 And it came to pass, that when the gates of Jerusalem began to be dark before the sabbath, I commanded that the gates should be shut, and charged that they should not be opened till after the sabbath : and *some* of my servants set I at the gates, *that* there should no burden be brought in on the sabbath day

20 So the merchants and sellers of all kind of ware lodged without Jerusalem once or twice. *(Hoping to do a sly trade in the suburbs.)*

21 Then I testified against them, and said unto them, Why lodge ye about the wall ? if ye do *so* again, I will lay hands on you. From that time forth came they no *more* on the sabbath.

He used his authority vigorously, and would not be trifled with ; fathers and masters should be equally resolved to have the Lord's day observed in their households.

22 And I commanded the Levites that they should cleanse themselves, and *that* they should come *and* keep the gates, to sanctify the sabbath day. Remember me, O my God, *concern-*

ing this also, and spare me according to the greatness of thy mercy.

23, 24 In those days also saw I Jews *that* had married wives of Ashdod, of Ammon. *and* of Moab : And their children spake half in the speech of Ashdod, and could not speak in the Jews' language, but according to the language of each people.

Marriages of Christians with the ungodly are highly injurious to their children, who are sure to follow the worse side of the house.

25—27 And I contended with them, and cursed them *(or denounced God's curse upon them),* and smote certain of them, and plucked off their hair, and made them swear by God, *saying,* Ye shall not give your daughters unto their sons, nor take their daughters unto your sons, or for yourselves. Did not Solomon king of Israel sin by these things ? yet among many nations was there no king like him, who was beloved of his God, and God made him king over all Israel : nevertheless even him did outlandish women cause to sin. Shall we then hearken unto you to do all this great evil, to transgress against our God in marrying strange wives ? *(This stern ruler saw that the mixed marriages placed the whole nation in jeopardy, and therefore he was indignant. Love to his country made him intolerant of that which would prove its ruin.)*

28, 29 And *one* of the sons of Joiada, the son of Eliashib the high priest, *was* son in law to Sanballat the Horonite : therefore I chased him from me. Remember them, O my God, because they have defiled the priesthood, and the covenant of the priesthood, and of the Levites. ·

30, 31 Thus cleansed I them from all strangers, and appointed the wards of the priests and the Levites, every one in his business ; And for the wood offering, at times appointed, and for the firstfruits. Remember me, O my God, for good. *(Here we leave this true patriot, and eminently conscientious ruler. We are not called to govern, as he did, with an iron hand, but we ought to be equally inflexible, decided, and resolute for God, and for his holy will. The sin of other men will lie upon us if we do not bear our protest in every possible manner, for the Lord has said, " Thou shalt in any wise rebuke thy neighbour, and not suffer sin upon him.")*

478   *" If I be a Father, where is mine honour?"*   AUGUST 11.—MORNING.

[*Or March* 20.]

WE *have now arrived at the period when the last of the prophets came with a divine message, Malachi is called by the Hebrews. "The seal of the prophets," because he closes the prophetical canon of the old dispensation. Malachi followed close on the heels of Zechariah, and found the people no longer idolatrous, but formal, cold, self-righteous, and unspiritual. His censures are very bold, and his prophecies of the coming era of the gospel very clear.*

MALACHI I. 1—14.

1—5 The burden of the word of the LORD to Israel by Malachi. I have loved you, saith the LORD. Yet ye say, Wherein hast thou loved us? *(They were discouraged because the temple had been built but the Messiah had not come, nor had the nation risen from its poverty into the glory which had been foretold; they therefore questioned the special love of God to them. The Lord replies by asking them:)* Was not Esau Jacob's brother? saith the LORD: yet I loved Jacob, And I hated Esau, and laid his mountains and his heritage waste for the dragons of the wilderness. Whereas Edom saith, We are impoverished, but we will return and build the desolate places; thus saith the LORD of hosts, They shall build, but I will throw down; and they shall call them, The border of wickedness, and, The people against whom the LORD hath indignation for ever. And your eyes shall see, and ye shall say, The LORD will be magnified from the border of Israel. *(The overthrow of Edom was final, but Israel would revive. Was not this a sign of special love?)*

6 ¶ A son honoureth *his* father, and a servant his master: if then I *be* a father, where *is* mine honour? and if I *be* a master, where *is* my fear? saith the LORD of hosts unto you, O priests, that despise my name. *(Notice how thickly close questions follow each other all through the chapter. Shall we be able to answer the Lord when at the last he searches us?)* And ye say, Wherein have we despised thy name?

7 Ye offer polluted bread upon mine altar; and ye say, Wherein have we polluted thee? In that ye say, The table of the LORD *is* contemptible. *(You do not serve me with your hearts; ye slur my service, and bring the worst offerings ye can find.)*

8 And if ye offer the blind for sacrifice, *is it* not evil? and if ye offer the lame and sick, *is it* not evil? offer it now unto thy governor; will he be pleased with thee, or accept thy person? saith the LORD of hosts. *(To give to God what we should be ashamed to present to man is a grievous insult to his majesty.)*

9, 10 And now, I pray you, beseech God that he will be gracious unto us: this hath been by your means: will he regard your persons? saith the LORD of hosts. Who *is there* even among you that would shut the doors *for nought?* neither do ye kindle *fire* on mine altar for nought. I have no pleasure in you, saith the LORD of hosts, neither will I accept an offering at your hand.

Nothing was done out of love; no one had enough respect unto the Lord to worship him voluntarily. They were unspiritual formalists.

11 For from the rising of the sun even unto the going down of the same my name *shall be* great among the Gentiles; and in every place incense *shall* be offered unto my name, and a pure offering: for my name *shall be* great among the heathen, saith the LORD of hosts.

Good news is this for us. When Jewish worship became unacceptable, a door of hope was opened for the Gentiles. Glory be to divine grace.

12—14 But ye have profaned it, in that ye say, The table of the LORD *is* polluted; and the fruit thereof, *even* his meat, *is* contemptible. Ye said also, Behold, what a weariness *is it!* and ye have snuffed at it, saith the LORD of hosts; and ye brought *that which was* torn, and the lame, and the sick; thus ye brought an offering: should I accept this of your hand? saith the LORD. But cursed *be* the deceiver, which hath in his flock a male, and voweth, and sacrificeth unto the LORD a corrupt thing: *(he has the best, and yet gives God the worst:)* for I *am* a great King, saith the LORD of hosts, and my name *is* dreadful among the heathen.

This chapter warns us not to worship God coldly and heartlessly. If we do indeed love him, let us give heartily to his cause, work for him zealously, pray to him fervently, and count his service our supreme delight, for without this our religion will be offensive in the sight of the Lord.

M ALACHI *signifies* messenger, *or angel. His office it was to hand over the prophetic charge into the hand of another messenger, who heralded the Lord, the Messiah himself, the Messenger of the Covenant. Malachi is the evening star of the Old Testament.*

MALACHI III. 1—12.

1 Behold, I will send my messenger, and he shall prepare the way before me : *(" There was a man sent from God, whose name was John:")* and the Lord, whom ye seek, shall suddenly come to his temple, even the messenger of the covenant, whom ye delight in : behold, he shall come, saith the LORD of hosts.

Since the temple is destroyed in which Messiah was to come, it is quite certain that he has come. He came when few were looking for him, when only an aged man and a venerable woman were in the temple expecting his arrival.

2, 3 But who may abide the day of his coming? and who shall stand when he appeareth? for he *is* like a refiner's fire, and like fullers' sope : And he shall sit *as* a refiner and purifier of silver : and he shall purify the sons of Levi, and purge them as gold and silver, that they may offer unto the LORD an offering in righteousness. *(Malachi saw the future Judge in the present Saviour. He saw that the people were not ready for the Messiah, and that his coming would be the severest trial to which Israel had been put, and would more terribly than ever reveal the false-heartedness of the people. He saw, with prophetic eye, the end as well as the beginning, and looked onward to those better days in which Israel will yet be holiness unto the Lord.)*

4, 5 Then shall the offering of Judah and Jerusalem be pleasant unto the LORD, as in the days of old, and as in former years. And I will come near to you to judgment; and I will be a swift witness against the sorcerers, and against the adulterers, and against false swearers, and against those that oppress the hireling in *his* wages, the widow, and the fatherless, and that turn aside the stranger *from his right,* and fear not me, saith the LORD of hosts.

Jesus in the Gospel overthrows all forms of wickedness and oppression; he is the great reformer, the hope of all people.

6 For I *am* the LORD, I change not ; therefore ye sons of Jacob are not consumed.

The Jewish nation has passed through the fire, but exists still, because the Lord does not change, and will not cast off his people.

7—9 Even from the days of your fathers ye are gone away from mine ordinances, and have not kept *them.* Return unto me, and I will return unto you, saith the LORD of hosts. But ye said, Wherein shall we return ? Will a man rob God ? Yet ye have robbed me. But ye say, Wherein have we robbed thee ? In tithes and offerings. Ye *are* cursed with a curse : for ye have robbed me, *even* this whole nation.

They were no longer idolaters, but they were mean in their gifts, and heartless in their worship; hence their woes.

10—12 Bring ye all the tithes into the storehouse, that there may be meat in mine house, and prove me now herewith, saith the LORD of hosts, if I will not open you the windows of heaven, and pour you out a blessing, that *there* shall not *be room* enough *to receive it.* And I will rebuke the devourer *(or the locust)* for your sakes, and he shall not destroy the fruits of your ground ; neither shall your vine cast her fruit before the time in the field, saith the LORD of hosts. And all nations shall call you blessed : for ye shall be a delightsome land, saith the LORD of hosts. *(How happy would it have been for the Jews had they listened to this encouraging admonition ! They disregarded it, and perished. Let us take warning from their example. We cannot expect to prosper if we are dishonest to the Lord : he can easily enough measure back to us as we measure out to him ; and if he sees us slack-handed in his service, he can soon send forth a devouring providence which will empty our purse, impoverish our trade, enfeeble our body, and sadden our spirits. Happy are they who, being saved by grace, bring him all their tithes, for peace and prosperity shall be their portion.)*

O thou whom we delight in,
  The messenger of love !
Come to thy temple quickly
  Back from thy throne above :
But who may bide thy coming,
  Who hear thy footstep's tread,
Who stand when thou appearest,
  Thou Judge of quick and dead ?

HERE *we conclude our Old Testament readings; the Lord grant that we may not have read in vain.*

MALACHI III. 13—18.

13 ¶ Your words have been stout against me, saith the LORD. Yet ye say, What have we spoken *so much* against thee?

The people were far too ready to justify themselves and deny the charges which were so justly brought against them. We are never right while we try to clear ourselves before God.

14 Ye have said, It *is* vain to serve God: and what profit *is it* that we have kept his ordinance, and that we have walked mournfully before the LORD of hosts? (*They looked for temporal benefit from their outward religiousness. Like hirelings they would be paid for everything they did, and had no real love to God.*)

15 And now we call the proud happy; yea, they that work wickedness are set up; yea, *they that* tempt God are even delivered.

Thus they envied the condition of the wicked, and thought God's dealings were unjust.

16 ¶ Then they that feared the LORD spake often one to another: and the LORD hearkened, and heard *it*, and a book of remembrance was written before him for them that feared the LORD, and that thought upon his name.

While sinners were murmuring, a few saints of a better temper were communing about the best things. They spake often together, and spake so sweetly that the Lord listened, and recorded what he heard. Holy conversation is both edifying to us and pleasing to God.

17 And they shall be mine, saith the LORD of hosts, in that day when I make up my jewels; and I will spare them, as a man spareth his own son that serveth him. (*The Lord made these holy talkers to be his crown jewels, his peculiar treasure, and he promised that at the last great judgment day he would own them as his choice ones. May we all be among them.*)

18 Then shall ye return, and discern between the righteous and the wicked, between him that serveth God and him that serveth him not.

Men will be seen in their true colours at the last, and hypocrisy will come to an end.

MALACHI IV.

FOR, behold, the day cometh, that shall burn as an oven; and all the proud, yea, and all that do wickedly, shall be stubble: and the day that cometh shall burn them up, saith the LORD of hosts, that it shall leave them neither root nor branch. But unto you that fear my name shall the Sun of righteousness arise with healing in his wings; and ye shall go forth, and grow up as calves of the stall. (*Carefully attended and bountifully supplied.*)

3 And ye shall tread down the wicked; for they shall be ashes under the soles of your feet in the day that I shall do *this*, saith the LORD of hosts. (*This shall be the result of Christ's coming, that the wicked shall be overcome, while the righteous shall rise to glory and happiness.*)

4 ¶ Remember ye the law of Moses my servant, which I commanded unto him in Horeb for all Israel, *with* the statutes and judgments.

5, 6 Behold, I will send you Elijah the prophet before the coming of the great and dreadful day of the LORD: And he shall turn the heart of the fathers to the children, and the heart of the children to their fathers, lest I come and smite the earth with a curse. (*John did come in the power of Elias; he began to preach the glad news which bids all discord cease. That gospel word has continued its peace-giving power, and will do so for ever.*

The Old Testament concludes with the word "curse." The Jews have wished to alter this, but there it stands. Let us look away from the law which can only curse us to that better covenant which blesses us in Christ Jesus.)

How will my heart endure
The terrors of that day,
When earth and heaven, before his face,
Astonish'd shrink away?

Ye sinners, seek his grace,
Whose wrath ye cannot bear;
Fly to the shelter of his cross,
And find salvation there.

So shall that curse remove,
By which the Saviour bled;
And the last awful day shall pour
His blessings on your head.

SELECTIONS FOR READING AT FAMILY PRAYER,

MAINLY FROM THE

NEW TESTAMENT

OF

OUR LORD AND SAVIOUR

JESUS CHRIST.

WITH BRIEF NOTES AND COMMENTS

BY

C. H. SPURGEON.

LET *us not commence our reading of the New Testament without earnest prayer that it may prove a blessing to us by the teaching of the Holy Spirit. These things are written that we may believe in the Lord Jesus, and we shall read to no purpose unless we do in very deed believe in him to the salvation of our souls. It will be well to remember that four hundred years had passed since the days of Malachi, and that Judea formed a part of the great Roman Empire, with Herod the Great as its tributary king. Now was the time appointed for the coming of John, the fore-runner of the promised Messiah.*

LUKE I. 5—25.

5—9 There was in the days of Herod, the king of Judæa, a certain priest named Zacharias, of the course of Abia: and his wife *was* of the daughters of Aaron, and her name *was* Elisabeth. And they were both righteous before God, walking in all the commandments and ordinances of the Lord blameless. And they had no child, because that Elisabeth was barren, and they both were *now* well stricken in years. And it came to pass, that while he executed the priest's office before God in the order of his course, According to the custom of the priest's office, his lot was to burn incense when he went into the temple of the Lord. *(This was done twice every day, at the time of the morning and evening sacrifices, and was an emblem of the merits of Jesus, and of the prayers of saints, which ascend like sweet perfume to the throne of God.)*

10 And the whole multitude of the people were praying without at the time of incense.

11, 12 And there appeared unto him an angel of the Lord standing on the right side of the altar of incense. And when Zacharias saw *him,* he was troubled, and fear fell upon him.

13—16 But the angel said unto him, Fear not, Zacharias: for thy prayer is heard; and thy wife Elisabeth shall bear thee a son, and thou shalt call his name John. And thou shalt have joy and gladness; and many shall rejoice at his birth. For he shall be great in the sight of the Lord, and shall drink neither wine nor strong drink; and he shall be filled with the Holy Ghost, even from his mother's womb. And many of the children of Israel shall he turn to the Lord their God.

17 And he shall go before him in the spirit and power of Elias, to turn the hearts of the fathers to the children, and the disobedient to the wisdom of the just; to make ready a people prepared for the Lord.

18 And Zacharias said unto the angel, Whereby shall I know this? for I am an old man, and my wife well stricken in years. *(His faith was staggered by the apparent impossibility of the case, as ours too often is when outward providences appear to contradict the promise.)*

19 And the angel answering said unto him, I am Gabriel, that stand in the presence of God; and am sent to speak unto thee, and to shew thee these glad tidings.

20 And, behold, thou shalt be dumb, and not able to speak, until the day that these things shall be performed, because thou believest not my words, which shall be fulfilled in their season.

Unbelief is very displeasing to God, and cannot be indulged in, even by the best of men, without involving them in chastisement. If we will not believe a promise, we shall not be permitted the comfort of it, and its fulfilment will be attended with some humiliating circumstance which will mark the Lord's displeasure at our unbelief.

21 And the people waited for Zacharias, and marvelled that he tarried so long in the temple.

22 And when he came out, he could not speak unto them: and they perceived that he had seen a vision in the temple: for he beckoned unto them, and remained speechless.

23 And it came to pass, that, as soon as the days of his ministration were accomplished, he departed to his own house. *(He did not make his infirmity an excuse for leaving his office, as many would have done. We must work on for the Lord as long as we have any ability left.)*

24 And after those days his wife Elisabeth conceived, and hid herself five months, saying,

25 Thus hath the Lord dealt with me in the days wherein he looked on *me,* to take away my reproach among men.

The mother of John had more faith than her husband, but both were excellent persons. We may reasonably expect the best preachers to be born of pious parents. Would to God that in our household might be raised up those who will cry, "Behold the Lamb of God, which taketh away the sin of the world."

THE *birth of the forerunner being near, it was now time for the Lord himself to be spoken of.*

LUKE I. 26—33; 35; 38—40; 46—55.

26, 27 And in the sixth month the angel Gabriel was sent from God unto a city of Galilee, named Nazareth, to a virgin espoused to a man whose name was Joseph, of the house of David; and the virgin's name *was* Mary.

28 And the angel came in unto her, and said, Hail *thou that art* highly favoured, the Lord *is* with thee: blessed *art* thou among women.

29 And when she saw *him,* she was troubled at his saying, and cast in her mind what manner of salutation this should be.

30 And the angel said unto her, Fear not, Mary: for thou hast found favour with God.

31 And, behold, thou shalt conceive in thy womb, and bring forth a son, and shalt call his name JESUS.

32 He shall be great, and shall be called the Son of the Highest: and the Lord God shall give unto him the throne of his father David:

33 And he shall reign over the house of Jacob for ever; and of his kingdom there shall be no end.

35 And the angel said unto her, The Holy Ghost shall come upon thee, and the power of the Highest shall overshadow thee: therefore also that holy thing which shall be born of thee shall be called the Son of God.

38 And Mary said, Behold the handmaid of the Lord; be it unto me according to thy word. And the angel departed from her.

39, 40 And Mary arose in those days, and went into the hill country with haste, into a city of Juda; And entered into the house of Zacharias, and saluted Elisabeth.

46—48 And Mary said, My soul doth magnify the Lord, And my spirit hath rejoiced in God my Saviour. For he hath regarded the low estate of his handmaiden: for, behold, from henceforth all generations shall call me blessed.

49 For he that is mighty hath done to me great things; and holy *is* his name.

50 And his mercy *is* on them that fear him from generation to generation.

51 He hath shewed strength with his arm; he hath scattered the proud in the imagination of their hearts.

52 He hath put down the mighty from *their* seats, and exalted them of low degree.

53 He hath filled the hungry with good things; and the rich he hath sent empty away.

54, 55 He hath holpen his servant Israel, in remembrance of *his* mercy; As he spake to our fathers, to Abraham, and to his seed for ever.

The person chosen to be the mother of the Lord Jesus was a lowly maid, but she was also a godly woman of no mean ability of mind, for her song is written in the highest style of poetry. To the humble and devout the visitations of the Holy Spirit are granted. The manner in which the angel saluted Mary was highly honourable to her, but affords no ground for the superstitious reverence of the Papists, for " he saluted her as a saint, and did not pray to her as a goddess." Mary confessed herself a sinner needing salvation, for she rejoiced in God her Saviour; it never entered into her mind to claim the homage of mankind.

It is a great blessing that in answer to earnest prayer the Holy Spirit will come into our hearts, and make us sing as joyfully as Mary did. Christ will dwell in our hearts by faith, and we shall be numbered with those favoured ones of whom Jesus said, " The same is my brother, and sister, and mother."

My soul doth magnify the Lord,
  My spirit doth rejoice;
To thee my Saviour and my God
  I lift my joyful voice.

Down from above the blessèd dove
  Is come into my breast,
To witness thine eternal love,
  And give my spirit rest.

Hark, the glad sound, the Saviour comes,
  The Saviour promised long!
Let every heart prepare a throne,
  And every voice a song.

Our glad hosannas, Prince of Peace,
  Thy welcome shall proclaim;
And heaven's eternal arches ring
  With thy beloved name.

T HE *time soon arrived for John to be born, and Elisabeth became a joyful mother.*

LUKE I. 58—80.

58 And her neighbours and her cousins heard how the Lord had shewed great mercy upon her; and they rejoiced with her. (*This is a very beautiful way of stating the case, "The Lord had shewed great mercy upon her." Family events should be looked at in this light, and made the occasion of pious thanksgiving.*)

59, 60 And it came to pass, that on the eighth day they came to circumcise the child; and they called him Zacharias, after the name of his father. And his mother answered and said, Not *so;* but he shall be called John (*or the Lord's gracious gift*).

61 And they said unto her, There is none of thy kindred that is called by this name.

62 And they made signs to his father, how he would have him called. (*For he was deaf as well as dumb, a double chastisement for his unbelief, which was now to be graciously removed.*)

63 And he asked for a writing table, and wrote, saying, His name is John. (*He had not heard what the mother had said, but he confirmed her wish, and obeyed the divine command which had been brought by the angel.*) And they marvelled all.

64 And his mouth was opened immediately, and his tongue *loosed,* and he spake, and praised God. (*The dumb man in a moment not only spake, but sang for very joy. The Lord is a God of wonders.*)

65, 66 And fear came on all that dwelt round about them : and all these sayings were noised abroad throughout all the hill country of Judæa. And all they that heard *them* laid *them* up in their hearts, saying, What manner of child shall this be ! And the hand of the Lord was with him.

67 And his father Zacharias was filled with the Holy Ghost, and prophesied, saying,

68 Blessed *be* the Lord God of Israel ; for he hath visited and redeemed his people,

69 And hath raised up an horn of salvation for us in the house of his servant David ;

70 As he spake by the mouth of his holy prophets, which have been since the world began:

71 That we should be saved from our enemies, and from the hand of all that hate us ;

72 To perform the mercy *promised* to our fathers, and to remember his holy covenant ;

73, 74 The oath which he sware to our father Abraham, that he would grant unto us, that we being delivered out of the hand of our enemies might serve him without fear,

75 In holiness and righteousness before him, all the days of our life. (*So that there is not a word in this noble song of Zacharias concerning John, or his own relationship to him ; he reserves that until he has poured forth his whole soul concerning the Lord's Christ. Jesus must be first and foremost in his people's hearts; even our highest spiritual joys must stand second to him. Him will we praise with our best music.*)

76 And thou, child, shalt be called the prophet of the Highest: for thou shalt go before the face of the Lord to prepare his ways ;

77 To give knowledge of salvation unto his people by the remission of their sins,

78 Through the tender mercy of our God ; whereby the dayspring from on high hath visited us,

79 To give light to them that sit in darkness and *in* the shadow of death, to guide our feet into the way of peace. (*Delightful is the object of the Saviour's coming ; no longer need any believer be in bondage through fear of death. Light has sprung up in the vale of deathshade, and peace smooths our pathway even there.*)

80 And the child grew, and waxed strong in spirit, and was in the deserts till the day of his shewing unto Israel. (*Great minds are reared in solitude. Lone places are fit nurses for God's heroes. We should be all the better if we were oftener alone; in the solemn silence of nature sanctified spirits find a congenial atmosphere.*)

Light of those whose dreary dwelling
  Borders on the shades of death,
Come, and by thyself revealing,
  Dissipate the clouds beneath :

The new heaven and earth's Creator,
  In our deepest darkness rise,
Scattering all the night of nature,
  Pouring day upon our eyes.

Still we wait for thy appearing;
  Life and joy thy beams impart,
Chasing all our fears, and cheering
  Every poor benighted heart.

Save us in thy great compassion,
  O thou mild pacific Prince ;
Give the knowledge of salvation,
  Give the pardon of our sins.

L ET us read with great joy of the birth of Jesus, the incarnate God.

LUKE II. 1—20.

1 And it came to pass in those days, that there went out a decree from Cæsar Augustus, that all the world should be taxed.

2 (*And* this taxing was first made when Cyrenius was governor of Syria.) *(The census was taken by Augustus, but the actual collecting of the tax was not carried out till the time of Cyrenius.)*

3—6 And all went to be taxed, every one into his own city. And Joseph also went up from Galilee, out of the city of Nazareth, into Judæa, unto the city of David, which is called Bethlehem ; (because he was of the house and lineage of David :) To be taxed with Mary his espoused wife, being great with child. And so it was, that, while they were there, the days were accomplished that she should be delivered.

The decree of Cæsar was made to fulfil the decree of Jehovah, that Jesus should be born in Bethlehem.

7 And she brought forth her firstborn son, and wrapped him in swaddling clothes, and laid him in a manger ; because there was no room for them in the inn.

Little love had the world for the Redeemer. It could find no room for him, no, not even in the place where the meanest traveller had free accommodation.

" No peaceful home upon his cradle smiled,
  Guests rudely went and came where slept the royal child."

8 And there were in the same country shepherds abiding in the field, keeping watch over their flock by night.

To simple minds, humbly doing their duty, the good news first came.

9—12 And, lo, the angel of the Lord came upon them, and the glory of the Lord shone round about them : and they were sore afraid. And the angel said unto them, Fear not : for, behold, I bring you good tidings of great joy, which shall be to all people. For unto you is born this day in the city of David a Saviour, which is Christ the Lord. And this *shall be* a sign unto you ; Ye shall find the babe wrapped in swaddling clothes, lying in a manger.

The heavenly messenger had scarcely concluded his announcement before he was joined by others who had hastened after him to swell the glory of the proclamation of the new-born king.

13, 14 And suddenly there was with the angel a multitude of the heavenly host praising God, and saying, Glory to God in the highest, and on earth peace, good will toward men.

15 And it came to pass, as the angels were gone away from them into heaven, the shepherds said one to another, Let us now go even unto Bethlehem, and see this thing which is come to pass, which the Lord hath made known unto us. *(They believed the news, were interested in it, and went to see. If we believe the gospel, let us show our faith practically.)*

16—18 And they came with haste, and found Mary, and Joseph, and the babe lying in a manger. And when they had seen *it*, they made known abroad the saying which was told them concerning this child. And all they that heard *it* wondered at those things which were told them by the shepherds.

19 But Mary kept all these things, and pondered *them* in her heart.

20 And the shepherds returned, glorifying and praising God for all the things that they had heard and seen, as it was told unto them.

Here were three ways of treating the news concerning Jesus. Some wondered, and there the matter ended, as, it is to be feared, it ends with many who hear it in these days. Mary weighed all these things in her heart ; to her they would be a perpetual source of blessing. The shepherds showed their piety in another manner, for they glorified God by telling the glad tidings to others. Have we not good cause to follow their example?

Hark, the herald angels sing,
Glory to the new-born King,
" Peace on earth and mercy mild ;
God and sinners reconciled."

Veil'd in flesh the Godhead see ;
Hail the incarnate Deity !
Pleased as man with men to appear,
Jesus our Immanuel here.

Mild he lays his glory by ;
Born, that men no more might die ;
Born, to raise the sons of earth ;
Born, to give them second birth.

LUKE II. 21, 22 ; 24—38.

AND when eight days were accomplished for the circumcising of the child, his name was called JESUS, which was so named of the angel before he was conceived in the womb. *(Jesus signifies "Jehovah the Saviour," and is the most melodious of all names in the ears of penitent sinners.)*

22 And when the days of her purification according to the law of Moses were accomplished, they brought him to Jerusalem, to present *him* to the Lord ;

24 And to offer a sacrifice according to that which is said in the law of the Lord, A pair of turtledoves, or two young pigeons.

Our Lord having placed himself, for our sakes, under the law, was obedient to it in all points, thus fulfilling all righteousness on our behalf. The poverty of his parents is showed by their presenting the second poorest offering accepted by the law ; there was one offering poorer still, but they were not in abject poverty, that worst distress was reserved for Jesus in his after years, when he would not have where to lay his head. Though he was rich, for our sakes he became poor.

25 And, behold, there was a man in Jerusalem, whose name *was* Simeon ; and the same man *was* just and devout, waiting for the consolation of Israel : and the Holy Ghost was upon him. *(He was just before men and devout towards God, and his faith looked steadily forward for the coming of the Messiah, whom those who believingly searched the Scriptures were daily expecting.)*

26 And it was revealed unto him by the Holy Ghost, that he should not see death, before he had seen the Lord's Christ.

27—29 And he came by the Spirit into the temple : and when the parents brought in the child Jesus, to do for him after the custom of the law, Then took he him up in his arms, and blessed God, and said, Lord, now lettest thou thy servant depart in peace, according to thy word :

30 For mine eyes have seen thy salvation,

31, 32 Which thou hast prepared before the face of all people ; A light to lighten the Gentiles, and the glory of thy people Israel.

33 And Joseph and his mother marvelled at those things which were spoken of him.

34 And Simeon blessed them, and said unto Mary his mother, Behold, this *child* is set for the fall and rising again of many in Israel ; and for a sign which shall be spoken against ;

35 (Yea, a sword shall pierce through thy own soul also,) that the thoughts of many hearts may be revealed. *(The highly-favoured mother had to endure unusually sharp and killing griefs as she saw the sorrows and the death of her blameless son.)*

36 And there was one Anna, a prophetess, the daughter of Phanuel, of the tribe of Aser : she was of a great age, and had lived with an husband seven years from her virginity ;

37 And she *was* a widow of about fourscore and four years, which departed not from the temple, but served *God* with fastings and prayers night and day. *(Having lost her husband for eighty-four years, she had devoted herself to the continual worship of God, and had, no doubt, as a prophetess, been spiritually useful to many. Women are much more honoured under the gospel than under the law. It was meet that two of the first witnesses to our Lord should be an aged man and a venerable woman.)*

38 And she coming in that instant gave thanks likewise unto the Lord, and spake of him to all them that looked for redemption in Jerusalem. *(O for grace to embrace Jesus, to love Jesus, to testify to Jesus, and to be so joyful in Jesus that we may be willing, like Simeon, to die, or, like Anna, to speak of him to all around !)*

Saints, before the altar bending,
  Waiting long with hope and fear,
Suddenly the Lord descending
  In his temple shall appear ;
    Come and worship,
  Worship Christ, the new-born King.

Sinners, wrung with true repentance,
  Doom'd for guilt to endless pains,
Justice now repeals the sentence,
  Mercy calls you—break your chains ;
    Come and worship,
  Worship Christ, the new-born King.

488   " Unto us a child is born, unto us a son is given."   AUGUST 15.—MORNING.

[Or March 28.]

MATTHEW II. 1—18.

NOW when Jesus was born in Bethlehem of Judæa in the days of Herod the king, behold, there came wise men from the east to Jerusalem, Saying, Where is he that is born king of the Jews ? for we have seen his star in the east, and are come to worship him. *(They had seen a bright particular star, which tradition connected with the birth of a great king. The wise men missed their way, and went to Jerusalem ; the shepherds did not. The wise are often less able to find Jesus than the poor and simple.)*

3—6 When Herod the king had heard *these things,* he was troubled, and all Jerusalem with him. And when he had gathered all the chief priests and scribes of the people together, he demanded of them where Christ should be born. And they said unto him, In Bethlehem of Judæa : for thus it is written by the prophet, And thou Bethlehem, *in* the land of Juda, art not the least among the princes of Juda : for out of thee shall come a Governor, that shall rule my people Israel. *(Thus by means of a cruel enemy the Lord obtained a grand public testimony from all the great teachers of the Jews that Messiah was to be born at Bethlehem, and by this means it was noised abroad that a star had appeared, and strangers had come from far to see the newly-born king of the Jews. Truly, God glorifies his Son even by his foes.)*

7 Then Herod, when he had privily called the wise men, enquired of them diligently what time the star appeared.

8 And he sent them to Bethlehem, and said, Go and search diligently for the young child ; and when ye have found *him,* bring me word again, that I may come and worship him also.

9—11 When they had heard the king, they departed ; and, lo, the star, which they saw in the east, went before them, till it came and stood over where the young child was. When they saw the star, they rejoiced with exceeding great joy. And when they were come into the house, they saw the young child with Mary his mother, and fell down, and worshipped him : and when they had opened their treasures, they presented unto him gifts ; gold, and frankincense, and myrrh. *(True faith is not disappointed at the lowliness of the Saviour. Though the wise men found Jesus in a mean abode, they discerned his majesty, and adored him with offerings suitable to a prophet, priest, and king.)*

12 And being warned of God in a dream that they should not return to Herod, they departed into their own country another way.

13 And when they were departed, behold, the angel of the Lord appeareth to Joseph in a dream, saying, Arise, and take the young child and his mother, and flee into Egypt, and be thou there until I bring thee word : for Herod will seek the young child to destroy him.

14, 15 When he arose, he took the young child and his mother by night, and departed into Egypt : And was there until the death of Herod : that it might be fulfilled which was spoken of the Lord by the prophet, saying, Out of Egypt have I called my son. *(Providence both watched over the safety of the Lord, and enabled Joseph to support the mother and child by the offerings of the eastern sages. In the same manner is the church the peculiar care of heaven in all its persecutions and needs.)*

16, 17 Then Herod, when he saw that he was mocked of the wise men, was exceeding wroth, and sent forth, and slew all the children that were in Bethlehem, and in all the coasts thereof, from two years old and under, according to the time which he had diligently enquired of the wise men. Then was fulfilled that which was spoken by Jeremy the prophet, saying,

18 In Rama was there a voice heard, lamentation, and weeping, and great mourning, Rachel weeping *for* her children, and would not be comforted, because they are not.

Thus did our Lord narrowly escape a cruel death. He had poor welcome among men, whom he came to redeem. Angels celebrated his birth with songs, but among men the malice of the wicked greeted him with the blood of infants and the wailings of bereaved mothers. O dear Redeemer, how sorrowfully did thy life for us begin ! Alas ! how sorrowfully did it end !

As with gladness men of old
Did the guiding star behold,
As with joy they hailed its light,
Leading onward, beaming bright,
So, most gracious God, may we
Evermore be led by thee !
As with joyful steps they sped
To that lowly manger-bed,
There to bend the knee before
Him whom heaven and earth adore,
So may we, with willing feet,
Ever seek thy mercy-seat,

MATTHEW II. 19—23.

BUT when Herod was dead, behold, an angel of the Lord appeareth in a dream to Joseph in Egypt, Saying, Arise, and take the young child and his mother, and go into the land of Israel : for they are dead which sought the young child's life.

21—23 And he arose, and took the young child and his mother, and came into the land of Israel. But when he heard that Archelaus did reign in Judæa in the room of his father Herod, he was afraid to go thither : notwithstanding, being warned of God in a dream, he turned aside into the parts of Galilee : And he came and dwelt in a city called Nazareth : that it might be fulfilled which was spoken by the prophets, He shall be called a Nazarene.

Every step the Saviour took was a fulfilment of prophecy. How blind were those who would not acknowledge him as indeed the Messiah! Our Lord spent nearly thirty years of his life in a city which bestowed upon him a title of scorn. "The Nazarene" is still his name of contempt among the Jews. How ready ought we to be to endure any measure of reproach for his sake!

LUKE II. 40—52.

40 And the child grew, and waxed strong in spirit, filled with wisdom : and the grace of God was upon him. *(What a child was this, with the fulness of divine grace upon him! Lord Jesus, make our sons and daughters to be like thee while they are yet children.)*

41, 42 Now his parents went to Jerusalem every year at the feast of the passover. And when he was twelve years old, they went up to Jerusalem after the custom of the feast.

43, 44 And when they had fulfilled the days, as they returned, the child Jesus tarried behind in Jerusalem ; and Joseph and his mother knew not *of it*. But they, supposing him to have been in the company, went a day's journey ; and they sought him among *their* kinsfolk and acquaintance.

45 And when they found him not, they turned back again to Jerusalem, seeking him.

46, 47 And it came to pass, that after three days they found him in the temple, sitting in the midst of the doctors, both hearing them and asking them questions. And all that heard him were astonished at his understanding and answers.

He did not set up for a teacher, but listened and eagerly enquired. No doubt there was more in his questions than in their replies, and when they catechized him in return, he gave such answers that they marvelled at the wondrous boy, whose surprising intelligence and holiness beamed forth in his countenance, and spoke in every word.

48 And when they saw him, they were amazed : and his mother said unto him, Son, why hast thou thus dealt with us ? behold, thy father and I have sought thee sorrowing.

49 And he said unto them, How is it that ye sought me ? wist ye not that I must be about my Father's business ? *(He knew the secret of his birth, which perhaps his mother had never told him, and he marvelled that his parents should think him unkind in following his manifest destiny. How sweetly does our Lord here teach us in our earliest youth to serve our heavenly Father!)*

50 And they understood not the saying which he spake unto them.

51 And he went down with them, and came to Nazareth, and was subject unto them : but his mother kept all these sayings in her heart.

52 And Jesus increased in wisdom and stature, and in favour with God and man.

For eighteen years longer he continued in the obscurity of Nazareth, a matchless man, in holiness unrivalled, spending his days at his father's handicraft, and in preparation for his great work. He was for thirty years emptying himself of all glory, that afterwards he might be filled with reproach for our sake. We ought exceedingly to admire our Lord in the lowliness of these preparatory years.

> How beautiful his childhood was!
>   Harmless and undefiled ;
> Oh! dear to his young mother's heart
>   Was this pure, sinless child.
>
> Kindly in all his deeds and words,
>   And gentle as the dove;
> Obedient, affectionate :
>   His very soul was love.
>
> Oh! is it not a blessed thought,
>   Ye men of human birth,
> That once the Saviour was a child,
>   And lived upon the earth ?

490   "𝔥e recei𝔟e𝔡 from 𝔊o𝔡 t𝔥e 𝔉at𝔥er 𝔥onour an𝔡 glor𝔶."   AUGUST 16.—MORNING.

[*Or March* 30.]

MATTHEW III.

IN those days came John the Baptist, preaching in the wilderness of Judæa, And saying, Repent ye: for the kingdom of heaven is at hand. For this is he that was spoken of by the prophet Esaias, saying, The voice of one crying in the wilderness, Prepare ye the way of the Lord, make his paths straight. (*As the priests commenced their service at thirty, it was probably at that age that John began publicly to teach. He commenced with a message most appropriate to the coming of the Saviour.*)

4 And the same John had his raiment of camel's hair, and a leathern girdle about his loins; and his meat was locusts and wild honey. *He was dressed as Elijah had been, and lived a self-denying, ascetic life, in keeping with the ministry of repentance.*

5, 6 Then went out to him Jerusalem, and all Judæa, and all the region round about Jordan, And were baptized of him in Jordan, confessing their sins. (*All ranks and classes came to him; he stirred the whole south of Palestine with his energetic ministry. To all men he addressed suitable words of rebuke and warning.*)

7—9 But when he saw many of the Pharisees and Sadducees come to his baptism, he said unto them, O generation of vipers, who hath warned you to flee from the wrath to come? Bring forth therefore fruits meet for repentance: And think not to say within yourselves, We have Abraham to *our* father: for I say unto you, that God is able of these stones to raise up children unto Abraham. (*He bade them lay aside their boastings, and seriously give themselves up to repentance. This bold address would be sure to make them very angry, but John, like Elias, feared them not.*)

10 And now also the axe is laid unto the root of the trees: therefore every tree which bringeth not forth good fruit is hewn down, and cast into the fire. (*There was to be an end of all pretence and hypocrisy. For many years formalists and boastful professors had been great in Israel; the new dispensation would destroy all this, and require truth in the inward parts.*)

11, 12 I indeed baptize you with water unto repentance: but he that cometh after me is mightier than I, whose shoes I am not worthy to bear: he shall baptize you with the Holy Ghost, and *with* fire: Whose fan *is* in his hand, and he will throughly purge his floor, and gather his wheat into the garner; but he will burn up the chaff with unquenchable fire.

Thus the forerunner pointed to the Coming One, and bade the people look for one who in the power of the Spirit would scatter to the winds all the vainglory of learned Sadducees and boastful Pharisees, by proclaiming a spiritual religion in which repentance and faith would far outweigh external religiousness.

13 ¶ Then cometh Jesus from Galilee to Jordan unto John, to be baptized of him.

Perhaps six months after John had commenced, when Jesus would be himself thirty years of age. Our Lord came after the people had been baptized, and offered himself for baptism.

14 But John forbad him, saying, I have need to be baptized of thee, and comest thou to me?

Shall the Lord be baptized by the servant? How canst thou receive anything from me?

15 And Jesus answering said unto him, Suffer *it to be so* now: for thus it becometh us to fulfil all righteousness. Then he suffered him.

Jesus would set an example to all his disciples, and would in a figure set forth his own sufferings, death, burial, and resurrection, in which all righteousness is comprehended.

16 And Jesus, when he was baptized, went up straightway out of the water: and, lo, the heavens were opened unto him, and he saw the Spirit of God descending like a dove, and lighting upon him:

17 And lo a voice from heaven, saying, This is my beloved Son, in whom I am well pleased.

Thus while in the act of prayer, and while yielding obedience to his Father's will, the Lord received his first great public attestation from above, and the anointing with which he should discharge his work. Let no believer neglect the ordinance which his Lord so highly honoured, lest he lose some special sealing and anointing.

Didst thou the great example lead,
    In Jordan's swelling flood?
And shall my pride disdain the deed
    That's worthy of my God?

Hast thou for me the cross endured,
    And all the shame despised?
And shall I be ashamed, O Lord,
    With thee to be baptized?

MATTHEW IV. 1—11.

THEN was Jesus led up of the spirit into the wilderness to be tempted of the devil. *(After the blessing of the Spirit comes trial. When the soul is enriched with grace, Satan bestirs himself to rob it of its treasure; While our Lord was hidden, the evil one might be still; now that he comes forth to his life's battle, he finds his foe awaiting him. Now was the seed of the woman to commence his combat with the old serpent.)*

2 And when he had fasted forty days and forty nights, he was afterward an hungred.

And while thus suffering, the tempter thought he had him at an advantage, and might assail him through his bodily needs. The arch-enemy avails himself of every weakness of our body, hoping thereby to overcome us.

3 And when the tempter came to him, he said, If thou be the Son of God, command that these stones be made bread.

He urged him to unbelief, to mistrust of his Father, and so to the use of unfit means to obtain food. Jesus had come to obey, not to command. How often, when we have been in need, has Satan tempted us to help ourselves, because God did not seem to help us! Mark that word, "If," that cruel doubt of his sonship. It could not wound the Perfect One, but it may sorely injure us if it be allowed a lodgment. Beware of this shaft of hell.

4 But he answered and said, It is written, Man shall not live by bread alone, but by every word that proceedeth out of the mouth of God.

He would not doubt. What if bread was lacking? God can sustain life without it, he is not dependent upon secondary causes. It was a grand blow which our champion here struck at his crafty antagonist.

5 Then the devil taketh him up into the holy city, and setteth him on a pinnacle of the temple,

6 And saith unto him, If thou be the Son of God, cast thyself down: for it is written, He shall give his angels charge concerning thee: and in *their* hands they shall bear thee up, lest at any time thou dash thy foot against a stone.

The enemy here went to the opposite pole, and tempted the Lord to presume. Because the promise guaranteed security, therefore he was to leap from the pinnacle. This presuming upon the promise is a common temptation, and Scripture, perverted and misquoted, is brought to back it May we have grace to see through the snare, and never become vain confident.

7 Jesus said unto him, It is written again, Thou shalt not tempt the Lord thy God.

The sword of the Spirit, which is the word of God, here made another glorious and conquering cut at the enemy. How grandly our Lord defeated the foe! Let us learn never to tempt the Lord by wickedly presuming upon his mercy, or his faithfulness.

8 Again, the devil taketh him up into an exceeding high mountain, and sheweth him all the kingdoms of the world, and the glory of them;

9 And saith unto him, All these things will I give thee, if thou wilt fall down and worship me. *(In this case the deceiver laboured to inflame the Saviour with ambition, and made him a tempting but blasphemous offer. Alas! how many have idolized evil for the sake of power, and so have ruined their own souls! There was no vulnerable place in the Redeemer: this third arrow, like the former two, glanced harmlessly from him, and he smote a third most telling blow at his adversary.)*

10 Then saith Jesus unto him, Get thee hence, Satan: for it is written, Thou shalt worship the Lord thy God, and him only shalt thou serve.

A well-chosen passage, and worthy to be always before our eyes. Are we living wholly unto God? This is the only safeguard against self-worship, mammon-worship, and other forms of idolatry.

11 Then the devil leaveth him, and, behold, angels came and ministered unto him.

After the devil the angels. Only let us be steadfast, and, like our Lord, we shall receive celestial consolations. O thou who wast tempted for us, help us in temptation. Amen.

Jesus, more than conqueror
O'er the thrice-embattled foe,
Fill'd with thine own Spirit's power,
Thou wilt power on us bestow.

By thy conquering Spirit led,
We shall put the fiend to flight;
Bruise again the serpent's head,
Triumph in Messiah's might.

WHILE *Jesus was absent, John continued his ministry as before.*

JOHN I. 19—42.

19 ¶ And this is the record of John, when the Jews sent priests and Levites from Jerusalem to ask him, Who art thou ?

20 And he confessed, and denied not; but confessed, I am not the Christ.

21 And they asked him, What then ? Art thou Elias ? And he saith, I am not. Art thou that prophet ? And he answered, No.

He was not literally Elias, nor any other departed prophet. The Jews did not see the true import of the promises which foretold the coming of the Messiah's forerunner, but vainly expected Elijah to return in person.

22 Then said they unto him, Who art thou ? that we may give an answer to them that sent us. What sayest thou of thyself ?

23 He said, I *am* the voice of one crying in the wilderness, Make straight the way of the Lord, as said the prophet Esaias. *(Jesus is the Word, John only the voice declaring the word.)*

24 And they which were sent were of the Pharisees. *(For Sadducees in their unbelief would have taken no interest in such things.)*

25 And they asked him, and said unto him, Why baptizest thou then, if thou be not that Christ, nor Elias, neither that prophet ?

26, 27 John answered them, saying, I baptize with water : but there standeth one among you, whom ye know not; He it is, who coming after me is preferred before me, whose shoe's latchet I am not worthy to unloose. *(So did he honour his Lord that he felt unworthy to perform the menial service of unloosing and carrying his shoes. To do anything for Jesus is a great honour.)*

28 These things were done in Bethabara beyond Jordan, where John was baptizing.

29 ¶ The next day John seeth Jesus coming unto him, and saith, Behold the Lamb of God, which taketh away the sin of the world.

This was a true gospel note. Jesus is the great victim sacrificed for human guilt, not a lamb but the Lamb, and the Lamb of God— " God-ordained, God-given, God-accepted." The sin of the world is viewed as one huge burden which he takes away as a sacrifice. This verse is the substance of the gospel message, and is the burden of all true preaching.

30, 31 This is he of whom I said, After me cometh a man which is preferred before me : for he was before me. And I knew him not : but that he should be made manifest to Israel, therefore am I come baptizing with water.

32—34 And John bare record, saying, I saw the Spirit descending from heaven like a dove, and it abode upon him. And I knew him not : but he that sent me to baptize with water, the same said unto me, Upon whom thou shalt see the Spirit descending, and remaining on him, the same is he which baptizeth with the Holy Ghost. And I saw, and bare record that this is the Son of God. *(Jesus and John had lived apart, and John did not know Jesus till the Spirit had spoken to him; there was therefore no collusion between them, and the witness of John is rendered all the more valuable.)*

35—37 Again the next day after John stood, and two of his disciples; And looking upon Jesus as he walked, he saith, Behold the Lamb of God ! And the two disciples heard him speak, and they followed Jesus. *(That is good preaching, which leads men away from the preacher himself to his Lord.)*

38 Then Jesus turned, and saw them following, and saith unto them, What seek ye ? They said unto him, Rabbi, (which is to say, being interpreted, Master,) where dwellest thou ?

Meaning, " We desire to converse with thee in some quiet place, and learn what John means."

39 He saith unto them, Come and see. They came and saw where he dwelt, and abode with him that day : for it was about the tenth hour.

40, 41 One of the two which heard John *speak*, and followed him, was Andrew, Simon Peter's brother. He first findeth his own brother Simon, and saith unto him, We have found the Messias, which is, being interpreted, the Christ.

42 And he brought him to Jesus. *(Blessed is the man who having found the Lord for himself brings his brother also. These first disciples were John and Andrew; John says nothing about himself, but is careful to record the zealous act of Andrew; true humility is as glad to display the virtues of others as it is anxious to conceal its own. Andrew brought to Jesus a convert of greater mark than himself, and so may the least be the means of the conversion of the greatest.)*

JOHN I. 43—51.

THE day following Jesus would go forth into Galilee, and findeth Philip, and saith unto him, Follow me. *(That simple word won the heart of the fourth disciple. Has Jesus never said the same to us ?)*

44, 45 Now Philip was of Bethsaida, the city of Andrew and Peter. Philip findeth Nathanael, and saith unto him, We have found him, of whom Moses in the law, and the prophets, did write, Jesus of Nazareth, the son of Joseph. *(So the good work goes on by one telling another. If each Christian would try to bring another to Jesus, how much would be done!)*

46 And Nathanael *(who is elsewhere called Bartholomew)* said unto him, Can there any good thing come out of Nazareth ? Philip saith unto him, Come and see.

47 Jesus saw Nathanael coming to him, and saith of him, Behold an Israelite indeed, in whom is no guile ! *(A man of a simple-hearted, frank, open spirit.)*

48 Nathanael saith unto him, Whence knowest thou me ? Jesus answered and said unto him, Before that Philip called thee, when thou wast under the fig tree, I saw thee. *(There he had probably been seeking divine light by much earnest secret prayer, and the Lord Jesus knew this. How startled must Nathanael have been when his secret habit was thus openly spoken of.)*

49 Nathanael answered and saith unto him, Rabbi, thou art the Son of God ; thou art the King of Israel.

50 Jesus answered and said unto him, Because I said unto thee, I saw thee under the fig tree, believest thou ? Thou shalt see greater things than these.

51 And he saith unto him, Verily, verily, I say unto you, Hereafter ye shall see heaven open, and the angels of God ascending and descending upon the Son of man. *(Like a guileless Jacob, he had believed, and like him he shall see the mediatorial ladder which connects earth with heaven. Those who are willing to learn shall be graciously taught.*

Very quiet was the work of Jesus, and yet he had in two days gathered five choice men, who became his faithful disciples, and the pioneers of his kingdom. Jesus now removed from the Judean valley to Galilee. The journey would occupy him two days.)

JOHN II. 1—12.

AND the third day there was a marriage in Cana of Galilee, and the mother of Jesus was there : And both Jesus was called, and his disciples to the marriage. *(Marriage was thus honoured. Jesus would not have his people despise social joys and duties.)*

3 And when they wanted wine, the mother of Jesus saith unto him, They have no wine.

4 Jesus saith unto her, Woman, what have I to do with thee ? mine hour is not yet come.

The word for " Woman" in the Greek is far more respectful than would appear from the English ; but still the sentence was a rebuke, and was meant to prevent Mary's overstepping her position. No human relationship could give any man or woman the right to dictate, or even suggest what Jesus should do.

5 His mother saith unto the servants, whatsoever he saith unto you, do *it.*

6 And there were set there six waterpots of stone, after the manner of the purifying of the Jews, containing two or three firkins apiece.

7, 8 Jesus saith unto them, Fill the waterpots with water. And they filled them up to the brim. And he saith unto them, Draw out now, and bear unto the governor of the feast. And they bare *it.*

9, 10 When the ruler of the feast had tasted the water that was made wine, and knew not whence it was : (but the servants which drew the water knew ;) the governor of the feast called the bridegroom, And saith unto him, Every man at the beginning doth set forth good wine ; and when men have well drunk, then that which is worse : *but* thou hast kept the good wine until now.

By turning water into wine our Lord showed the difference between his teaching and that of John, and also drew a line between his spiritual kingdom and the sects whose righteousness lay in meats and drinks.

11 This beginning of miracles did Jesus in Cana of Galilee, and manifested forth his glory ; and his disciples believed on him. *(So the presence of Jesus elevates our household joys and turns them from water into wine.)*

12 ¶ After this he went down to Capernaum, he, and his mother, and his brethren, and his disciples : and they continued there not many days.

JOHN II. 13—25.

AND the Jews' passover was at hand, and Jesus went up to Jerusalem, *(We have seen him there once before as a son in his own house, and here we see him in riper years as a son over his own house, the heir, exercising authority in the Father's palace.)*

14 And found in the temple those that sold oxen and sheep and doves, and the changers of money sitting: *(They were necessary for public convenience that the worshippers might purchase offerings, and might exchange Roman for Jewish money, since that alone could be presented to the priests; but they had no right to transact this business within the house of God.)*

15 And when he had made a scourge of small cords, he drove them all out of the temple, and the sheep, and the oxen; and poured out the changers' money, and overthrew the tables;

16 And said unto them that sold doves, Take these things hence; make not my Father's house an house of merchandise. *(Now was fulfilled in measure the prophecy of Malachi: "Behold, I will send my messenger, and he shall prepare the way before me: and the Lord, whom ye seek, shall suddenly come to his temple, even the messenger of the covenant, whom ye delight in: behold, he shall come, saith the Lord of hosts. But who may abide the day of his coming? and who shall stand when he appeareth? for he is like a refiner's fire, and like fullers' sope: and he shall sit as a refiner and purifier of silver: and he shall purify the sons of Levi, and purge them as gold and silver, that they may offer unto the Lord an offering in righteousness." With like zeal will he drive out of his church all who seek their own advancement, and turn the worship of God into a means of gain for themselves. This was the first occasion upon which our Lord purged the temple, and he had to repeat the work a second time. Nothing is so hard to cleanse as a place which has once been holy and has become defiled. It does not seem that any one opposed the Lord Jesus; the majesty of his appearance probably held all in check.)*

17 And his disciples remembered that it was written, The zeal of thine house hath eaten me up.

18 Then answered the Jews and said unto him, What sign shewest thou unto us, seeing that thou doest these things?

19 Jesus answered and said unto them, Destroy this temple, and in three days I will raise it up.

20, 21 Then said the Jews, Forty and six years was this temple in building, and wilt thou rear it up in three days? But he spake of the temple of his body. *(The resurrection is the surest seal of our Lord's mission, and the fact that he rose by his own power is a clear evidence of his deity. Who but he could say of his own dead body, "I will raise it up"? Since Jesus has risen we ought most heartily to believe on him.)*

22 When therefore he was risen from the dead, his disciples remembered that he had said this unto them; and they believed the scripture, and the word which Jesus had said. *(They no doubt before this believed both their Master's word and the Scriptures, but when they understood them better, in the light of their accomplishment, they were as if they believed anew.)*

23 ¶ Now when he was in Jerusalem at the passover, in the feast *day*, many believed in his name, when they saw the miracles which he did. *(The gospel wins many converts, and some of them in after days do not turn out to be stable; this however we must look for, as Jesus did, for the next verse tells us that he did not trust those who were so eager to profess allegiance; for he understood the fickleness of human hearts, the superficial nature of much which passes for true religion, and the ease with which hasty conversions are turned into sudden and final apostacies. May the Lord cleanse our hearts and keep us to the end.)*

24 But Jesus did not commit himself unto them, because he knew all *men*,

25 And needed not that any should testify of man: for he knew what was in man.

Saviour, who dost with anger see
The lusts which steal my heart from thee,
The thieves out of thy temple chase,
And cleanse my soul by sovereign grace.

Thy blood hath made me wholly thine,
My body is thy Spirit's shrine;
And now my God is dwelling there
My soul shall be a house of prayer.

JOHN III. 1—21.

THERE was a man of the Pharisees, named Nicodemus, a ruler of the Jews:

2 The same came to Jesus by night, and said unto him, Rabbi, we know that thou art a teacher come from God: for no man can do these miracles that thou doest, except God be with him. *(Perhaps he came by night because he was busy all the day, or because he would make private inquiries before he committed himself to the new teacher. Jesus did not refuse him a midnight audience, and Nicodemus came to him in courteous and candid spirit.)*

3 Jesus answered and said unto him, Verily, verily, I say unto thee, Except a man be born again, he cannot see the kingdom of God. *Thus he tried the faith which the inquiring ruler already had. The doctrine of regeneration has been a test question and a stone of stumbling to many, and always will be so. Jesus tried Nicodemus at the outset with this vital question, for he never suppresses truth to win followers.*

4 Nicodemus saith unto him, How can a man be born when he is old? can he enter the second time into his mother's womb, and be born?

5, 6 Jesus answered, Verily, verily, I say unto thee, Except a man be born of water and *of* the Spirit, he cannot enter into the kingdom of God. That which is born of the flesh is flesh; and that which is born of the Spirit is spirit. *Flesh at its best can only produce flesh; and since we must become spiritual in order to enter the spiritual kingdom of Jesus, it is inevitable that we must be born again, or else remain strangers to the things of God. Every man must be born twice or die twice: let this never be forgotten.*

7, 8 Marvel not that I said unto thee, Ye must be born again. The wind bloweth where it listeth, and thou hearest the sound thereof, but canst not tell whence it cometh, and whither it goeth: so is every one that is born of the Spirit. *(The regenerate man is a mystery, and whence his new nature came, and whither it tends, are both spiritual questions which the carnal mind is unable to answer.)*

9 Nicodemus answered and said unto him, How can these things be?

10---12 Jesus answered and said unto him, Art thou a master of Israel, and knowest not these things? Verily, verily, I say unto thee, We speak that we do know, and testify that we have seen; and ye receive not our witness. If I have told you earthly things *(or things belonging to this world)*, and ye believe not, how shall ye believe, if I tell you *of* heavenly things? *The higher truths are not opened up to those who are staggered by the simpler doctrines. It would be idle to attempt it.*

13 And no man hath ascended up to heaven, but he that came down from heaven, *even* the Son of man which is in heaven.

14, 15 And as Moses lifted up the serpent in the wilderness, even so must the Son of man be lifted up: That whosoever believeth in him should not perish, but have eternal life. *It is remarkable that the same chapter which so strongly teaches us the need of the new birth is that which most clearly sets forth the gospel of faith in Christ Jesus. Both truths are to be cordially believed. We must be born again, and yet whosoever believeth in Jesus is not condemned.*

16, 17 For God so loved the world, that he gave his only begotten Son, that whosoever believeth in him should not perish, but have everlasting life. For God sent not his Son into the world to condemn the world; but that the world through him might be saved.

18 ¶ He that believeth on him is not condemned: but he that believeth not is condemned already, because he hath not believed in the name of the only begotten Son of God. *(Let this be well marked. All this family who have not believed are already condemned.)*

19 And this is the condemnation, that light is come into the world, and men loved darkness rather than light, because their deeds were evil.

20, 21 For every one that doeth evil hateth the light, neither cometh to the light, lest his deeds should be reproved. But he that doeth truth cometh to the light, that his deeds may be made manifest, that they are wrought in God. *With such simple teaching before us, it will be terrible if any one of us should live and die in unbelief. It becomes us at once to believe in Jesus, for ere long we shall be gone where gospel promises are no longer presented as a ground of hope. Lord, we believe, and by grace we are saved.*

496   " He that believeth on the Son hath everlasting life."   AUGUST 19.—MORNING.

[Or April 5.]

JOHN III. 22—36.

AFTER these things came Jesus and his disciples into the land of Judæa; and there he tarried with them, and baptized.

23, 24 And John also was baptizing in Ænon near to Salim, because there was much water there: and they came and were baptized. For John was not yet cast into prison. *(John had chosen a spot suitable for the sacred rite. As Milton puts it:*

" Them who shall believe,
Baptizing in the profluent stream."

He would not have needed much water if he had merely sprinkled the people.)

25 ¶ Then there arose a question between *some* of John's disciples and the Jews about purifying.

26 And they came unto John, and said unto him, Rabbi, he that was with thee beyond Jordan, to whom thou barest witness, behold, the same baptizeth, and all *men* come to him.

27 John answered and said, A man can receive nothing, except it be given him from heaven. *(Each one has his appointed place, and John had no desire to usurp that of another, least of all that of his Lord. The truth stated in this verse should act as an effectual cure for envy and emulation.)*

28 Ye yourselves bear me witness, that I said, I am not the Christ, but that I am sent before him. *(He felt clear upon this point, and it will be well for all ministers if they are equally sure that they have never exalted themselves, but their Master only.)*

29 He that hath the bride is the bridegroom: but the friend of the bridegroom, *(his best man, or paranymph)* which standeth and heareth him, rejoiceth greatly because of the bridegroom's voice: this my joy therefore is fulfilled.

30 He must increase, but I *must* decrease.

31 He that cometh from above is above all: he that is of the earth is earthly, and speaketh of the earth: he that cometh from heaven is above all.

32 And what he hath seen and heard, that he testifieth: and no man receiveth his testimony. *(John's disciples said that all men went after Jesus, and that seemed a great thing to them; John, on the other hand, thought little of*
the crowds which heard Jesus, he desired something far higher, and sighed because men did not in their hearts receive the Son of God.)

33 He that hath received his testimony hath set to his seal that God is true. *(John eagerly turns men's minds to the Redeemer. He is willing to be nothing so that they will but believe in the Saviour. Indeed, all who love their fellow-men must desire the same, for only as Jesus is received in the heart can men be saved.)*

34 For he whom God hath sent speaketh the words of God: for God giveth not the Spirit by measure *unto him.*

35 The Father loveth the Son, and hath given all things into his hand.

36 He that believeth on the Son hath everlasting life: and he that believeth not the Son shall not see life; but the wrath of God abideth on him. *(This is the one grand distinction,—believer or unbeliever, how does it affect this family? Have we believed, or are we now under divine wrath because of unbelief?)*

LUKE III. 18—20.

AND many other things in his exhortation preached he unto the people.

19 But Herod the tetrarch, being reproved by him for Herodias his brother Philip's wife, and for all the evils which Herod had done,

20 Added yet this above all, that he shut up John in prison. *(Herod had been a willing hearer of John till he touched his conscience, and then he would have no more of his preaching. A man is in a sad state when he hates the ministry which is meant to lead him to repentance. May God preserve us from so wicked a spirit. It is a sure mark of condemnation.)*

That Jesus saves from sin and hell,
  Is truth divinely sure;
And on this rock our faith may rest
  Immoveably secure.

Oh let these tidings be received
  With universal joy,
And let the high angelic praise
  Our tuneful powers employ!

" Glory to God who gave his Son
  To bear our shame and pain;
Hence peace on earth, and grace to men,
  In endless blessings reign."

JOHN IV. 1—26.

WHEN therefore the Lord knew how the Pharisees had heard that Jesus made and baptized more disciples than John, (though Jesus himself baptized not, but his disciples,) he left Judæa, and departed again into Galilee. *Not wishing to provoke opposition unnecessarily, or evoke controversy at this early stage.*

4 And he must needs go through Samaria. *Not only as the nearest road, but because he had a work of mercy to perform. He felt a necessity laid upon him to seek a poor guilty woman of that country.*

5, 6 Then cometh he to a city of Samaria, which is called Sychar, near to the parcel of ground that Jacob gave to his son Joseph. Now Jacob's well was there. Jesus therefore, being wearied with *his* journey, sat thus on the well: *and* it was about the sixth hour.

7—9 There cometh a woman of Samaria to draw water: Jesus saith unto her, Give me to drink. (For his disciples were gone away unto the city to buy meat.) Then saith the woman of Samaria unto him, How is it that thou, being a Jew, askest drink of me, which am a woman of Samaria? for the Jews have no dealings with the Samaritans.

10 Jesus answered and said unto her, If thou knewest the gift of God, and who it is that saith to thee, Give me to drink; thou wouldest have asked of him, and he would have given thee living water. *(Mark the connection, " Thou wouldest have asked, and he would have given." It is always so, asking and giving are rivetted together. Who would not ask, when the answer is so sure and the boon so precious?)*

11, 12 The woman saith unto him, Sir, thou hast nothing to draw with, and the well is deep: from whence then hast thou that living water? Art thou greater than our father Jacob, which gave us the well, and drank thereof himself, and his children, and his cattle? *(She could not read the Lord's riddle, she thought only of water which she could carry in her bucket.)*

13, 14 Jesus answered and said unto her, Whosoever drinketh of this water shall thirst again: But whosoever drinketh of the water that I shall give him shall never thirst; but the water that I shall give him shall be in him a well of water springing up into everlasting life.

15, 16 The woman saith unto him, Sir, give me this water, that I thirst not, neither come hither to draw. Jesus saith unto her, Go, call thy husband, and come hither. *(Hitherto nothing had reached her heart, but this sentence startled her: yet it was a very natural one, and such as eastern custom suggested, for a religious teacher was not allowed to instruct a married woman for any length of time unless her husband was present.)*

17, 18 The woman answered and said, I have no husband. Jesus said unto her, Thou hast well said, I have no husband: for thou hast had five husbands; and he whom thou now hast is not thy husband: in that saidst thou truly. *(This revealed her history; a woman often divorced, and probably not for the best of reasons. Her vicious career was thus unveiled for her own inspection.)*

19 The woman saith unto him, Sir, I perceive that thou art a prophet. *(She starts aside to talk of external rites. Like ourselves before conversion, she did not wish to have her conscience probed too much. She was curious to know whether the Jews or the Samaritans had the true temple: even ungodly people dispute on such questions.)*

20 Our fathers worshipped in this mountain; and ye say, that in Jerusalem is the place where men ought to worship.

21—24 Jesus saith unto her, Woman, believe me, the hour cometh, when ye shall neither in this mountain, nor yet at Jerusalem, worship the Father. Ye worship ye know not what: we know what we worship: for salvation is of the Jews. But the hour cometh, and now is, when the true worshippers shall worship the Father in spirit and in truth: for the Father seeketh such to worship him. God *is* a Spirit: and they that worship him must worship *him* in spirit and in truth. *(This was new light to her. Spiritual worship she had not thought of. It is well when we begin to see that all true religion must be heart work.)*

25 The woman saith unto him, I know that Messias cometh, which is called Christ: when he is come he will tell us all things.

26 Jesus saith unto her, I that speak unto thee am he. *(Thus did the Sun of Righteousness shine full upon her in condescending grace, and in his own light she saw and believed.)*

498   "𝔍 will call them my people which were not my people."   AUGUST 20.—MORNING.

[Or April 7.]

JOHN IV. 27—42.

AND upon this came his disciples, and marvelled that he talked with the woman: yet no man said, What seekest thou? or, Why talkest thou with her? *(Their Jewish prejudices were aroused by his large-hearted care for a Samaritan woman, for they would have scorned to speak to her; yet they were awed by his appearance, and felt too much esteem for their Master to enquire too boldly.)*

28, 29 The woman then left her waterpot, and went her way into the city, and saith to the men, Come, see a man, which told me all things that ever I did: is not this the Christ?

The convert becomes a missionary. Her worldly cares are all forgotten; she cares only for the souls of others.

30 Then they went out of the city, and came unto him. *(God blessed the woman's testimony so that their curiosity was excited, and she thus became one link in the chain of causes which led to the conversion of many. We might all be useful if we would but try.)*

31 ¶ In the mean while his disciples prayed him, saying, Master, eat.

32 But he said unto them, I have meat to eat that ye know not of. *(He was so happy in his work that he forgot the calls of appetite; the soul conquered the body.)*

33 Therefore said the disciples one to another, Hath any man brought him *ought* to eat?

34 Jesus saith unto them, My meat is to do the will of him that sent me, and to finish his work. *(This occupied all his thoughts, and success in it was refreshing to his heart.)*

35 Say not ye, There are yet four months, and *then* cometh harvest? behold, I say unto you, Lift up your eyes, and look on the fields; for they are white already to harvest.

The people were streaming out of Sychar, eager to hear; the Samaritans were as ready for the word as the corn for the sickle. This was a goodly sight, but it called for further effort. When the people are willing to receive the word, they bring great responsibility upon their ministers.

36, 37 And he that reapeth receiveth wages, and gathereth fruit unto life eternal: that both he that soweth and he that reapeth may rejoice together. And herein is that saying true, One soweth, and another reapeth.

38 I sent you to reap that whereon ye bestowed no labour: other men laboured, and ye are entered into their labours. *(So is it with us all. We are reapers of what was sown in ages gone by, and especially of that which Jesus has sown by his agonies and death.)*

39 ¶ And many of the Samaritans of that city believed on him for the saying of the woman, which testified, He told me all that ever I did.

Very imperfect instruments may be used by the Holy Spirit to lay the foundations of faith. Foxe tells us that some were brought to a knowledge of the truth in his day by reading Chaucer's works: "And in that rarity of books and want of teachers, this one thing I greatly marvel at," says he, "that the word of God did multiply so exceedingly, for I find that one neighbour conversing with others did soon win and turn their minds to the truth."

40—42 So when the Samaritans were come unto him, they besought him that he would tarry with them: and he abode there two days. And many more believed because of his own word; and said unto the woman, Now we believe, not because of thy saying: for we have heard *him* ourselves, and know that this is indeed the Christ, the Saviour of the world.

They outgrew their first instructor, and rose to a firmer basis of faith and a clearer understanding of the Gospel. If they learned so much in two days, how much ought we to have learned who have had Jesus teaching in our streets these many years.

Let us learn from this deeply interesting Scripture to live to do good, and let us also learn that no service which we can render to our fellow-creatures is so really beneficial as to bear witness to them concerning Jesus.

Help me, O Lord, thy love to show,
   Thy saving truth proclaim;
'Tis all my business here below
   To cry, "Behold the Lamb!"

Happy, if with my latest breath
   I may but gasp thy name;
Preach thee in life, and cry in death,
   "Behold, behold the Lamb!"

LUKE IV. 14—30.

AND Jesus returned in the power of the Spirit into Galilee: and there went out a fame of him through all the region round about. And he taught in their synagogues, being glorified of all. (*Highly favoured was that rural region to have Christ himself going on circuit through its towns. It is a great privilege to have the gospel preached in the place wherein we dwell: let us prize it if we have it.*)

16 And he came to Nazareth, where he had been brought up: and, as his custom was, he went into the synagogue on the sabbath day, and stood up for to read. (*Synagogue worship was not all that could be wished, but it was better than none; and our Lord therefore set the example of attendance upon it, as the recognised way of reverencing the Sabbath and of praising God. Never should we forsake the assembling of ourselves together, even if we be but two or three.*)

17—19 And there was delivered unto him the book of the prophet Esaias. And when he had opened the book, he found the place where it was written, The Spirit of the Lord *is* upon me, because he hath anointed me to preach the gospel to the poor; he hath sent me to heal the brokenhearted, to preach deliverance to the captives, and recovering of sight to the blind, to set at liberty them that are bruised, To preach the acceptable year of the Lord. (*He paused there, and did not read on, or he would have read of " the day of vengeance of our God." That would have been inappropriate just then, for his errand was purely one of mercy.*)

20 And he closed the book, and he gave *it* again to the minister, and sat down. And the eyes of all them that were in the synagogue were fastened on him.

21 And he began to say unto them, This day is this scripture fulfilled in your ears.

22 And all bare him witness, and wondered at the gracious words which proceeded out of his mouth. (*Their first thoughts were best. While they thought of* what *he said, they were charmed; but when they considered* who *he was that had said it, they changed their minds for the worse, as many other foolish persons have done.*) And they said, Is not this Joseph's son?

23 And he said unto them, Ye will surely say unto me this proverb, Physician, heal thyself:

whatsoever we have heard done in Capernaum, do also here in thy country.

24 And he said, Verily I say unto you, No prophet is accepted in his own country.

25, 26 But I tell you of a truth, many widows were in Israel in the days of Elias, when the heaven was shut up three years and six months, when great famine was throughout all the land; But unto none of them was Elias sent, save unto Sarepta, *a city* of Sidon, unto a woman *that was* a widow.

27 And many lepers were in Israel in the time of Eliseus the prophet; and none of them was cleansed, saving Naaman the Syrian.

He declared to them the doctrines of divine sovereignty and electing grace, and these truths the carnal mind always kicks at. Men will hear anything rather than a proclamation that the Lord dispenses his mercy as seemeth good in his sight. His mentioning the blessing of the Gentiles was another point in our Lord's address which was sure to enrage his hearers, for men are as wroth with the freeness of grace as with the sovereignty of it. Jesus did not come there to flatter them; he told them the truth, whether they approved of it or no.

28—30 And all they in the synagogue, when they heard these things, were filled with wrath, And rose up, and thrust him out of the city, and led him unto the brow of the hill whereon their city was built, that they might cast him down headlong. But he passing through the midst of them went his way.

They were admirers one hour, and murderers at heart the next. Honest servants of Christ must not wonder if warm friends become bitter foes because of the truth. Man is fickle, and those are wisest who do not lean upon him.

> The world his abject poverty
> And low estate disdain,
> And nothing great in Jesus see,
> The humble Son of Man.
>
> But we who Christ aright have known,
> And seen with inward eyes,
> Adore him as th' Almighty One
> Who made both earth and skies.

Behold the sin-atoning Lamb,
With wonder, gratitude, and love:
To take away our guilt and shame,
See him descending from above.

Our sins and griefs on him were laid;
He meekly bore the mighty load;
Our ransom-price he fully paid
In groans and tears, in sweat and blood.

To save a guilty world he dies;
Sinners, behold the bleeding Lamb!
To him lift up your longing eyes,
And hope for mercy in his name.

Of old at Cana's marriage feast
As guest behold the Lord!
Joy from his gentle presence flowed,
And plenty from his word.

He check'd no gladness, such as might
The Christian's heart become;
From him no shadow ever fell
Upon a Christian home.

And so let all our festal joy
Be in his presence found,
And so let every spot on earth
Be counted " holy ground."

Not all the outward forms on earth,
Nor rites that God has given,
Nor will of man, nor blood, nor birth,
Can raise a soul to heaven.

The sovereign will of God alone
Creates us heirs of grace;
Born in the image of his Son,
A new peculiar race.

The Spirit, like some heavenly wind,
Blows on the sons of flesh;
Creates a new—a heavenly mind,
And forms the man afresh.

Our quicken'd souls awake and rise
From the long sleep of death;
On heavenly things we fix our eyes,
And praise employs our breath.

I heard the voice of Jesus say,
" Behold I freely give
The living water—thirsty one,
Stoop down, and drink, and live."

I came to Jesus, and I drank
Of that life-giving stream;
My thirst was quench'd, my soul revived,
And now I live in him.

Fain would I be often reading
In the ancient holy Book,
Of my Saviour's gentle pleading,
Truth in every word and look.

How to all the sick and tearful
Help was ever gladly shown;
How he sought the poor and fearful,
Called them brothers and his own.

Still I read the ancient story,
And my joy is ever new,
How for us he left his glory,
How he still is kind and true.

How the flock he gently leadeth,
Whom his Father gave him here;
How his arms he widely spreadeth
To his heart to draw us near.

Our flesh and sense must be denied,
Passion and envy, lust, and pride,
Whilst justice, temp'rance, truth, and love,
Our inward piety approve.

Tender and kind be all our thoughts,
Through all our lives let mercy run:
Since God forgives our numerous faults,
For the dear sake of Christ his Son.

WHEN *driven from one city Jesus displayed his healing power in another. Ingratitude could not make him cease to bless mankind.*

JOHN IV. 46—54.

46, 47 So Jesus came again into Cana of Galilee, where he made the water wine. And there was a certain nobleman, whose son was sick at Capernaum. When he heard that Jesus was come out of Judæa into Galilee, he went unto him, and besought him that he would come down, and heal his son : for he was at the point of death. *(It is a rare sight to see the great ones of the earth coming to Jesus ; but they must come as well as the poorest, if they would be blest.)*

48 Then said Jesus unto him, Except ye see signs and wonders, ye will not believe.

49 The nobleman saith unto him, Sir, come down ere my child die.

In his vehement desire he took the rebuke in silence, and then cried out again for mercy.

50, 51 Jesus saith unto him, Go thy way ; thy son liveth. And the man believed the word that Jesus had spoken unto him, and he went his way. And as he was now going down, his servants met him, and told *him*, saying, Thy son liveth. *(Faith and the cure were wrought at the same moment. From Cana to Capernaum, like a flash of lightning, the power to heal travelled the moment that the father believed.)*

52 Then enquired he of them the hour when he began to amend. And they said unto him, Yesterday at the seventh hour the fever left him.

53 So the father knew that *it was* at the same hour, in the which Jesus said unto him, Thy son liveth : and himself believed, and his whole house.

54 This *is* again the second miracle *that* Jesus did, when he was come out of Judæa into Galilee. *(The first dealt with marriage, and the second with children. Jesus is the true "Family Friend." Parents, believingly go to him for your children! He waits to answer you.)*

WE *now turn to another event which happened about this time.*

LUKE V. 1—11.

1—3 And it came to pass, that, as the people pressed upon him to hear the word of God, he stood by the lake of Gennesaret, And saw two ships standing by the lake : but the fishermen were gone out of them, and were washing *their* nets. And he entered into one of the ships, which was Simon's, and prayed him that he would thrust out a little from the land. And he sat down, and taught the people out of the ship.

4 Now when he had left speaking, he said unto Simon, Launch out into the deep, and let down your nets for a draught.

5 And Simon answering said unto him, Master, we have toiled all the night, and have taken nothing : nevertheless at thy word I will let down the net. *(Whatever may have happened, it is ours to obey, and in obeying we shall meet with a reward.)*

6, 7 And when they had this done, they inclosed a great multitude of fishes : and their net brake. And they beckoned unto *their* partners, which were in the other ship, that they should come and help them. And they came, and filled both the ships, so that they began to sink.

8 When Peter saw *it*, he fell down at Jesus' knees, saying, Depart from me ; for I am a sinful man, O Lord. *(He felt that he was not fit for such holy company, and expressed the feeling in all simplicity. He was always outspoken.)*

9, 10 For he was astonished, and all that were with him, at the draught of the fishes which they had taken : And so *was* also James, and John, the sons of Zebedee, which were partners with Simon. And Jesus said unto Simon, Fear not ; from henceforth thou shalt catch men.

11 And when they had brought their ships to land, they forsook all, and followed him.

And wonderful man-catchers they became, taking whole nations in their gospel nets. The Lord help all his spiritual fishermen to cast the net on the right side of the ship.

O Lord our God, thy servants bless,
And crown their labours with success ;
For they will cast the net in vain
If thou the Spirit dost restrain.

But if thou guide their willing hand,
Obedient to thy wise command,
Then will they bring the sons of men
Back to their Lord and God again.

MARK I. 21—39.

AND they went into Capernaum; and straightway on the sabbath day he entered into the synagogue, and taught.

22 And they were astonished at his doctrine : for he taught them as one that had authority, and not as the scribes.

23—25 And there was in their synagogue a man with an unclean spirit; and he cried out, Saying, Let *us* alone; what have we to do with thee, thou Jesus of Nazareth ? art thou come to destroy us ? I know thee who thou art, the Holy One of God. And Jesus rebuked him, saying, Hold thy peace, and come out of him. (*Christ would not have praise from the devil, it has an ill savour about it.*)

26, 27 And when the unclean spirit had torn him, and cried with a loud voice, he came out of him. And they were all amazed, insomuch that they questioned among themselves, saying, What thing is this ? what new doctrine *is* this ? for with authority commandeth he even the unclean spirits, and they do obey him.

28 And immediately his fame spread abroad throughout all the region round about Galilee.

29 And forthwith, when they were come out of the synagogue, they entered into the house of Simon and Andrew, with James and John.

30 But Simon's wife's mother lay sick of a fever, and anon they tell him of her.

Luke says it was "a great fever," so that she was too ill to speak for herself. We must tell Jesus of those who do not plead for themselves.

31 And he came and took her by the hand, and lifted her up; and immediately the fever left her, and she ministered unto them.

Usually a person healed of fever is long in recovering strength, but our Lord's cures are perfect as well as immediate. Those whom the Lord heals spiritually are sure to be grateful, they minister both to him and to his people. If he serves us, it is but meet that we should serve him.

32, 33 And at even, when the sun did set, they brought unto him all that were diseased, and them that were possessed with devils. And all the city was gathered together at the door.

34 And he healed many that were sick of divers diseases, and cast out many devils; and suffered not the devils to speak, because they knew him.

35 And in the morning, rising up a great while before day, he went out, and departed into a solitary place, and there prayed. (*He had much work before him, and therefore desired much communion with God. Press of business should not excuse us from prayer, but rather urge us to have more of it.*)

36, 37 And Simon and they that were with him followed after him. And when they had found him, they said unto him, All *men* seek for thee. (*Simon was always too forward. We shall often meet with interruptions in prayer, even from well-meaning men; therefore let us, like Jesus, get alone and choose early hours.*)

38 And he said unto them, Let us go into the next towns, that I may preach there also: for therefore came I forth.

39 And he preached in their synagogues throughout all Galilee, and cast out devils.

He did not stay to receive honour for his wonderful miracles, but posted on to other fields of labour. Let us also press forward, for we have much to do, and but one short life to do it in.

MATTHEW IV. 23—25.

AND Jesus went about all Galilee, teaching in their synagogues, and preaching the gospel of the kingdom, and healing all manner of sickness and all manner of disease among the people. (*What a blessed mixture, "preaching and healing"! Now-a-days we have them both spiritually in the gospel. He who preaches Jesus is a healer, for that sacred name is medicine.*)

24 And his fame went throughout all Syria : and they brought unto him all sick people that were taken with divers diseases and torments, and those which were possessed with devils, and those which were lunatick, and those that had the palsy; and he healed them. (*What a list of maladies, and how sweet the footnote, "and he healed them"!*)

25 And there followed him great multitudes of people from Galilee, and *from* Decapolis, and *from* Jerusalem, and *from* Judæa, and *from* beyond Jordan. (*Well might they do so, since he scattered such priceless boons. Let us follow him in a higher sense, for none are sick in soul who abide in fellowship with him. Walk with "the beloved physician," and thou shalt no more say "I am sick."*)

MATTHEW V. 1—12.

AND seeing the multitudes, he went up into a mountain : *(Where he could find a suitable position for an audience. How different was this hill of the gospel from the Sinai of the law ! Israel trembled before a mountain of curses, we rejoice in the mount of beatitudes.)* and when he was set, his disciples came unto him : *(Sitting was the usual posture of an oriental teacher ; he spake as from the chair of authority, and his learners gathered at his feet.)*

2 And he opened his mouth, and taught them, saying, *(Now was opened the richest fountain of instruction which had ever flowed for the good of mankind. He who had aforetime opened the mouths of prophets now opened his own mouth. Speaking distinctly and earnestly, as all should do who have an important message to deliver, he went on to pronounce seven benedictions upon seven sorts of persons. These seven descriptions make up a perfect character, and the seven blessings appended thereto when combined constitute perfect bliss. The whole seven rise one above another like the steps of a ladder of light, and the blessings appropriate to each grow out of the virtues described. At the close of the seven beatitudes of character comes an eighth and double benediction bestowed upon that persecuted condition which is the present result of holiness. The whole make up a celestial octave of benediction.)*

3 Blessed *are* the poor in spirit: for their's is the kingdom of heaven. *(The first step of the ladder is low, and therefore the more readily reached. It begins where the law ends. The law reveals our poverty, and Jesus removes it. Men who know their spiritual poverty are the only ones who by faith can lay hold upon the true riches of grace.)*

4 Blessed *are* they that mourn : for they shall be comforted. *(To their sense of need is now added holy sorrow for sin ; this leads them to Jesus, and he consoles them.)*

5 Blessed *are* the meek : for they shall inherit the earth. *(Men who are repentant cannot be proud, hence the next blessing is to the gentle in spirit. These enjoy what they have, and, being content with the divine will, they possess by birthright both this world and worlds to come.)*

6 Blessed *are* they which do hunger and thirst after righteousness : for they shall be filled.

Pining for more holiness, they press forward towards it, and reach it, while the self-satisfied miss it by self-conceit. The Lord will be sure to fill us if we long after the best things.

7 Blessed *are* the merciful : for they shall obtain mercy. *(They do good, and get good. Being filled with righteousness, they are empty of all malice, and are loving to others, and so win their love. God will show no mercy to those who are unmerciful to their fellow men.)*

8 Blessed *are* the pure in heart : for they shall see God. *(Sin puts out our eyes. When the heart is pure, the spiritual eye grows bright, and the pure and holy Lord reveals himself.)*

9 Blessed *are* the peacemakers : for they shall be called the children of God. *This is a high attainment, and follows upon purity : "first pure, then peaceable." He who reaches it shall have clear evidence of his adoption into God's household. May each one of us try to be a peacemaker in the family, in the church, and in the world.*

10, 11 Blessed *are* they which are persecuted for righteousness' sake : for their's is the kingdom of heaven. Blessed are ye, when *men* shall revile you, and persecute *you*, and shall say all manner of evil against you falsely, for my sake.

12 Rejoice, and be exceeding glad : for great *is* your reward in heaven : for so persecuted they the prophets which were before you. *The world cannot appreciate those traits of character which the Lord delights in, hence its opposition and spite. Be it ours to endure hardness as good soldiers of Jesus, never for a moment flinching from cross-bearing for Jesus' sake.*

Bless'd are the humble souls that see
Their emptiness and poverty ;
Treasures of grace to them are giv'n,
And crowns of joy laid up in heaven.

Bless'd are the men of broken heart,
Who mourn for sin with inward smart ;
The blood of Christ divinely flows,
A healing balm for all their woes.

Bless'd are the men of peaceful life,
Who quench the coals of growing strife ;
They shall be called the heirs of bliss,
The sons of God, the God of peace.

MATTHEW V. 13—30.

YE are the salt of the earth : but if the salt have lost his savour, wherewith shall it be salted ? it is thenceforth good for nothing, but to be cast out, and to be trodden under foot of men. *(If those who have grace could lose it altogether, they could never be restored. When a church becomes a den of evil, it is in a hopeless plight, even as is the Church of Rome at this present time.)*

14 Ye are the light of the world. A city that is set on an hill cannot be hid.

15 Neither do men light a candle, and put it under a bushel, but on a candlestick ; and it giveth light unto all that are in the house.

16 Let your light so shine before men, that they may see your good works, and glorify your Father which is in heaven. *(Do not shine by proud pretensions, but by real holiness, not for your own glory, but the glory of God.)*

17, 18 Think not that I am come to destroy the law, or the prophets : I am not come to destroy, but to fulfil. For verily I say unto you, Till heaven and earth pass, one jot or one tittle shall in no wise pass from the law till all be fulfilled. *(The gospel honours and establishes the law. The life and death of Jesus show both the beauty of righteousness and the evil of sin, and thus cause the principles of right and truth to triumph eternally.)*

19 Whosoever therefore shall break one of these least commandments, and shall teach men so, he shall be called the least in the kingdom of heaven : but whosoever shall do and teach *them,* the same shall be called great in the kingdom of heaven.

20 For I say unto you, That except your righteousness shall exceed *the righteousness* of the scribes and Pharisees, ye shall in no case enter into the kingdom of heaven.

Grace makes better men than self-righteousness ever does. The day of judgment will show that the saints are holier men than Pharisees ever were with all their boastings of superior sanctity.

21, 22 Ye have heard that it was said by them of old time, Thou shalt not kill ; and whosoever shall kill shall be in danger of the judgment : But I say unto you, That whosoever is angry with his brother without a cause shall be in danger of the judgment *(or the sentence of the criminal courts in the various towns :)* and whosoever shall say to his brother, Raca, *(or brainless one,)* shall be in danger of the council *(or to be summoned before the Sanhedrim :)* but whosoever shall say, Thou fool, shall be in danger of hell fire.

23, 24 Therefore if thou bring thy gift to the altar, and there rememberest that thy brother hath ought against thee ; Leave there thy gift before the altar, and go thy way ; first be reconciled to thy brother, and then come and offer thy gift. *(An unforgiving spirit is fatal to worship. Till every offence against us is pardoned, our approach to the altar is an insult to the God of love.)*

25, 26 Agree with thine adversary quickly, whiles thou art in the way with him ; lest at any time the adversary deliver thee to the judge, and the judge deliver thee to the officer, and thou be cast into prison. Verily I say unto thee, Thou shalt by no means come out thence, till thou hast paid the uttermost farthing. *(Those who refuse to do justice shall have judgment to the full, both in time and in eternity.)*

27, 28 Ye have heard that it was said by them of old time, Thou shalt not commit adultery : But I say unto you, That whosoever looketh on a woman to lust after her hath committed adultery with her already in his heart.

Heart and eye can sin as well as the hand ; the law is spiritual, and condemns for wishes and lustings. How greatly may we be under condemnation even when no deed of ill has polluted our character !

29, 30 And if thy right eye offend thee, pluck it out, and cast *it* from thee : for it is profitable for thee that one of thy members should perish, and not *that* thy whole body should be cast into hell. And if thy right hand offend thee, cut it off, and cast *it* from thee : for it is profitable for thee that one of thy members should perish, and not *that* thy whole body should be cast into hell. *(Any loss, any self-denial, any pain is better than to lose our souls for ever. We must mortify ourselves and forsake that which is most pleasing to our corrupt nature, sooner than be castaways for ever. May the Lord help us to enter in at the strait gate.)*

MATTHEW V. 33—48.

AGAIN, ye have heard that it hath been said by them of old time, Thou shalt not forswear thyself, but shalt perform unto the Lord thine oaths :

34 But I say unto you, Swear not at all ; neither by heaven ; for it is God's throne :

35, 36 Nor by the earth ; for it is his footstool : neither by Jerusalem ; for it is the city of the great King. Neither shalt thou swear by thy head, because thou canst not make one hair white or black.

37 But let your communication be, Yea, yea ; Nay, nay : for whatsoever is more than these cometh of evil. *(Does not this forbid every kind of oath, not only profane swearing, but even that which is generally enjoined by civil governments? It would be hard to prove the contrary. Certainly, Christians ought to avoid all such expressions as "upon my honour," "upon my word," and the like, for such language goes beyond the "yea and nay" which is allowed them. Men who swear profanely greatly err when they imagine that thus they secure credence, for every sensible person knows that a man who is accustomed to common swearing is quite able both to lie and to steal. Clean language becomes those who have been washed in the blood of Jesus. The tongue is an index of the health both of soul and body. He who is not pure in word is assuredly not pure in heart, and shall not see the Lord.)*

38 Ye have heard that it hath been said, An eye for an eye, and a tooth for a tooth :

39 But I say unto you, That ye resist not evil : but whosoever shall smite thee on thy right cheek, turn to him the other also.

Retaliation is not a Christian word, and revenge is only fit to be spoken of by the devil and his children. To bear and yet to bear still more is the mark of a soul renewed by grace.

40—42 And if any man will sue thee at the law, and take away thy coat, let him have *thy* cloke also. And whosoever shall compel thee to go a mile, go with him twain. Give to him that asketh thee, and from him that would borrow of thee turn not thou away.

Generosity and willing sympathy are beauties of the sanctified character. It is far better to suffer a great wrong than to provoke litigation,

and manifest a contentious spirit. Those who are always standing up for their rights, and will never put up with an injury, have not yet caught the spirit of the Lord Jesus.

43—45 Ye have heard that it hath been said, Thou shalt love thy neighbour, and hate thine enemy. But I say unto you, Love your enemies, bless them that curse you, do good to them that hate you, and pray for them which despitefully use you, and persecute you ; That ye may be the children of your Father which is in heaven : for he maketh his sun to rise on the evil and on the good, and sendeth rain on the just and on the unjust.

Good for evil is to be our only weapon, and with this we are to fight perpetually, cost us what it may. The love of God falls on men who deserve it not, and so also must our kindness. It would be far better that a hundred evil persons deceived us, and so obtained our aid, than that one suffering fellow-creature should be neglected because of the wickedness of others. Hardness of heart gradually grows upon men through contact with a deceitful and oppressive world; but we must not allow evil influences to mastery us, and steel our hearts against our fellows.

46—48 For if ye love them which love you, what reward have ye ? do not even the publicans the same ? And if ye salute your brethren only, what do ye more *than others?* do not even the publicans so ? Be ye therefore perfect, even as your Father which is in heaven is perfect.

Lofty is this ideal, but we must aim to reach it. Universal benevolence and unconquerable love are the crown and glory of a holy character; without it we are still deficient, whatever virtues we may possess. The sternly just man must rise higher, and become the meek forgiver of injuries, and the generous friend of the needy. O God of love, educate us to this, for Jesus' sake.

Father ! I see thy sun arise
To cheer thy friends and enemies ;
And when thy voice from heaven descends,
Thy bounty both alike befriends.

I hope for pardon through thy Son,
For all the crimes which I have done ;
Oh, may the grace that pardons me,
Constrain me to forgive like thee.

WE *will continue reading from the Sermon on the Mount.*

MATTHEW VI. 1—15.

1 Take heed that ye do not your alms *(or, as many versions have it),* " your righteousness" before men, to be seen of them : otherwise ye have no reward of your Father which is in heaven. *(If the action is not done in the Lord's service, but with a view to our own honour, we cannot expect a reward from above.)*

2 Therefore when thou doest *thine* alms, do not sound a trumpet before thee, as the hypocrites do in the synagogues and in the streets, that they may have glory of men. Verily I say unto you, They have their reward.

Those who blaze abroad their charity enjoy a sort of recompense in the public approbation which they gain, and having thus obtained the reward they seek after, they cannot reasonably expect any other.

3 But when thou doest alms, let not thy left hand know what thy right hand doeth :

Do not let what you have done be so known, even to yourself, as to become the subject of self-approbation. Do not count over what has been given, rather go on to give more.

4 That thine alms may be in secret : and thy Father which seeth in secret himself shall reward thee openly.

Those who are anxious to have their donations publicly acknowledged, and will give nothing unless it be put down upon a printed list, should take warning from these words. We also should learn to give to the cause of God and to the poor in the quietest manner possible.

5 And when thou prayest, thou shalt not be as the hypocrites *are :* for they love to pray standing in the synagogues and in the corners of the streets, that they may be seen of men. Verily I say unto you, They have their reward.

6 But thou, when thou prayest, enter into thy closet, and when thou hast shut thy door, pray to thy Father which is in secret ; and thy Father which seeth in secret shall reward thee openly.

7, 8 But when ye pray, use not vain repetitions, as the heathen *do :* for they think that they shall be heard for their much speaking. Be not ye therefore like unto them : for your Father knoweth what things ye have need of, before ye ask him. *(The heathen repeat over*

and over again the same words, as also do the Papists and Semipapists of our own land. This is sheer mockery. God is not deaf or forgetful, neither does he delight in mere sounds. Prayer is the intelligent approach of the mind of man to the mind of God, and in that coming we must not think of adding to the divine knowledge, which is infinite, or dictating to the divine will, which is sovereign.)

9 After this manner therefore pray ye : *(This is the perfect model by which to shape your prayers.)* Our Father which art in heaven, Hallowed be thy name.

10 Thy kingdom come. Thy will be done in earth, as *it is* in heaven. *(Out of seven petitions the first three concern the name, kingdom, and will of God. The Lord must occupy the highest place in our prayers, and indeed in our whole lives.*

The four petitions for ourselves rise by degrees from " bread" up to "deliverance from evil," teaching us that we ought not to grovel in prayer, but to increase in spirituality while we plead.)

11 Give us this day our daily bread.

Give us necessary food, bread for the day, our own bread, yet thy gracious gift. Give it not only to me, but to all of us, thy children.

12, 13 And forgive us our debts, as we forgive our debtors. *(We are willing to make this the measure of thy forgiveness.)* And lead us not into temptation, *(Do not in thy providence allow us to be placed where we shall be severely tried,)* but deliver us from evil : *(especially the Evil One,)* For thine is the kingdom, and the power, and the glory, for ever. Amen.

14 For if ye forgive men their trespasses, your heavenly Father will also forgive you :

15 But if ye forgive not men their trespasses, neither will your Father forgive your trespasses.

> Our Father, God, who art in heaven,
>   All hallowed be thy name !
> Thy kingdom come ; thy will be done,
>   In earth and heaven the same.
> Give us, this day, our daily bread ;
>   And, as we those forgive
> Who sin against us, so may we
>   Forgiving grace receive.
> Into temptation lead us not :
>   From evil set us free ;
> The kingdom, power, and glory, Lord,
>   Ever belong to thee.

OUR *Lord in his Sermon on the Mount further said:—*

MATTHEW VI. 19—24.

19—21 Lay not up for yourselves treasures upon earth, where moth and rust doth corrupt, and where thieves break through and steal : But lay up for yourselves treasures in heaven, where neither moth nor rust doth corrupt, and where thieves do not break through nor steal : For where your treasure is, there will your heart be also. *(Whatever we make to be our treasure will be sure to become the attraction of our heart. If we accumulate earthly riches, our hearts will by degrees be tied up in our money-bags; and, on the other hand, if our chief possessions are in heavenly things, our hearts will rise into the higher and more spiritual region. The position of the heart is sure to be affected by the place where the treasure is laid up. Shall sons of God give their hearts away to passing joys, which decay if they remain ours, and are liable at any moment to be taken from us?)*

22, 23 The light of the body is the eye : if therefore thine eye be single, thy whole body shall be full of light. But if thine eye be evil, thy whole body shall be full of darkness. If therefore the light that is in thee be darkness, how great *is* that darkness! *(A heart professedly set upon heaven but held in bondage to earth is like an eye blinded by the intrusion of a foreign substance, involving the unfortunate owner of it in darkness. There is no such thing as seeing spiritual things while the soul's windows are fastened up with shutters of worldliness.)*

24 ¶ No man can serve two masters : for either he will hate the one, and love the other ; or else he will hold to the one, and despise the other. Ye cannot serve God and mammon.

Two leading principles cannot rule in one heart; they cannot both be master. Either sin or grace will engross the whole heart; neither will submit to compromise.

MATTHEW VII. 1—12.

1 Judge not, that ye be not judged.

2 For with what judgment ye judge, ye shall be judged : and with what measure ye mete, it shall be measured to you again.

3—5 And why beholdest thou the mote that is in thy brother's eye, but considerest not the beam that is in thine own eye? Or how wilt thou say to thy brother, Let me pull out the mote out of thine eye ; and, behold, a beam *is* in thine own eye? Thou hypocrite, first cast out the beam out of thine own eye ; and then shalt thou see clearly to cast out the mote out of thy brother's eye. *(Yet are we all too ready to condemn others and to be lenient to ourselves. It will be wise to act upon the precisely opposite principle, making every excuse for others, and accepting none for ourselves.)*

6 ¶ Give not that which is holy unto the dogs, neither cast ye your pearls before swine. lest they trample them under their feet, and turn again and rend you.

7 ¶ Ask, and it shall be given you ; seek, and ye shall find ; knock, and it shall be opened unto you :

8 For every one that asketh receiveth ; and he that seeketh findeth ; and to him that knocketh it shall be opened.

9 Or what man is there of you, whom if his son ask bread, will he give him a stone?

10 Or if he ask a fish, will he give him a serpent?

11 If ye then, being evil, know how to give good gifts unto your children, how much more shall your Father which is in heaven give good things to them that ask him?

Prayer is thus urgently recommended to us ; we are asking of a Father, not of a tyrant, and that Father will employ all his wisdom and judgment not in repelling our pleas, but in doing for us exceeding abundantly above all that we ask or even think.

12 Therefore all things whatsoever ye would that men should do to you, do ye even so to them : for this is the law and the prophets.

This last verse is the golden rule, and those who follow it will live truly noble lives.

What enchants you, gain or pleasure?
　Pluck right eyes, with right hands part ;
Ask your conscience, where's your treasure?
　For, be certain, there's your heart.

God and Mammon? O be wiser.
　Serve them both? It cannot be ;
Ease in warfare, saint and miser,
　These will never well agree.

MATTHEW VII. 13—29.

ENTER ye in at the strait gate: for wide *is* the gate, and broad *is* the way, that leadeth to destruction, and many there be which go in thereat: *(Choose not your religion because it is easy, and is patronised by the multitude, for the evil way is that which has charms for the crowd, since it is prepared by the Evil One so as to be pleasant to flesh and blood.)*

14 Because strait *is* the gate and narrow *is* the way, which leadeth unto liïe, and few there be that find it. *(Perhaps few absolutely, certainly few comparatively take the right road. If we would be saved we must swim against the stream, we must bear the cross and deny ourselves: this is not the popular course and never will be, but gracious souls choose it.)*

15—20 Beware of false prophets, which come to you in sheep's clothing, but inwardly they are ravening wolves. Ye shall know them by their fruits. Do men gather grapes of thorns, or figs of thistles? Even so every good tree bringeth forth good fruit; but a corrupt tree bringeth forth evil fruit. A good tree cannot bring forth evil fruit, neither *can* a corrupt tree bring forth good fruit. Every tree that bringeth not forth good fruit is hewn down, and cast into the fire. Wherefore by their fruits ye shall know them.

Judge religious teachers not by their claims to apostolical descent, or episcopal ordination, but by their doctrines and actions. He who glorifies God by gracious preaching and holy living has the best certificate of ordination in the world; while he who promulgates error, or lives unrighteously, is no servant of the Lord, however loud his pretensions may be.

21 ¶ Not every one that saith unto me, Lord, Lord, shall enter into the kingdom of heaven; but he that doeth the will of my Father which is in heaven. *(Religion must be practical, or it will prove worthless at the last.)*

22, 23 Many will say to me in that day, Lord, Lord, have we not prophesied in thy name? and in thy name have cast out devils? and in thy name done many wonderful works? And then will I profess unto them, I never knew you: depart from me, ye that work iniquity.

24, 25 Therefore whosoever heareth these sayings of mine, and doeth them, I will liken him unto a wise man, which built his house upon a rock: And the rain descended, and the floods came, and the winds blew, and beat upon that house; and it fell not: for it was founded upon a rock. *(Even to the doer of the word trial will come, rains of affliction will fall from above, floods of persecution or trouble will arise from the earth, and mysterious winds of spiritual temptation will beat upon him from all quarters; but he has a good foundation of real, vital, practical faith, and therefore he survives every test. Not so the mere hearer of the word, his case comes to a very different end.)*

26 And every one that heareth these sayings of mine, and doeth them not, shall be likened unto a foolish man, which built his house upon the sand:

27 And the rain descended, and the floods came, and the winds blew, and beat upon that house; and it fell: and great was the fall of it.

He endured no severer trials than the righteous; but for lack of foundation he could not sustain the shock; his great profession only made his ruin the more remarkable. Oh, to be on the rock, that is the main matter! Vital godliness outlives all mere imitations of grace.

28, 29 And it came to pass, when Jesus had ended these sayings, the people were astonished at his doctrine: For he taught them as *one* having authority, and not as the scribes.

He was no doctor of doubts, no questioner and quibbler; he spake boldly, for he spake the truth. We need greatly in these days a ministry of the same kind. Send it, good Lord, we beseech thee.

Strait the gate, the way is narrow,
To the realms of endless bliss;
Sinful men and vain professors,
Self-deceived, the passage miss;
Rushing headlong,
Down they sink the dread abyss.

Thou who art thy people's guardian,
Condescend my guide to be;
By thy Spirit's light unerring,
Let me thy salvation see:
May I never
Miss the way that leads to thee.

MARK I. 35—45.

AND in the morning, rising up a great while before day, he went out, and departed into a solitary place, and there prayed.

The Sun of Righteousness was up before the sun. How much must our Lord have loved prayer to renounce his needed rest in sleep, in order to hold converse with his heavenly Father. He was sinless, and yet needed prayer : far be it from us to dream that we can do without it. In private we must, like our Lord, equip ourselves for the public battle of life.

36, 37 And Simon and they that were with him followed after him. And when they had found him, they said unto him, All *men* seek for thee.

38 And he said unto them, Let us go into the next towns, that I may preach there also : for therefore came I forth. *(Seclusion was not used as a luxury by him, nor did he plead his devotions as an excuse for escaping public duties. He was ready to preach or to pray, according to the demand of the hour. In such readiness for service should all his followers excel.)*

39 And he preached in their synagogues throughout all Galilee, and cast out devils.

40 And there came a leper to him, beseeching him, and kneeling down to him, and saying unto him, If thou wilt, thou canst make me clean.

Probably this poor man in his eagerness to be healed had broken the rules which kept him in seclusion, and dared to enter the house where Jesus was, contrary to the law of leprosy. His was a venturesome faith. It was no small confidence which could believe the Lord Jesus to be able to heal a disease so loathsome and incurable. It will be well if we can have the same assurance with regard to our sin.

41 And Jesus, moved with compassion, put forth *his* hand, and touched him, and saith unto him, I will ; be thou clean. *(That touch bespoke the sympathy of Jesus. Any one else would have been made unclean by contact with diseased flesh ; with him it was otherwise, for his touch and word removed the cause of uncleanness.)*

42 And as soon as he had spoken, immediately the leprosy departed from him, and he was cleansed. *(Time is not wanted for divine cures. One word is enough to blot out all sin, and make the loathsomeness of lust depart. If we can but trust him, Jesus is able to heal.)*

43, 44 And he straitly charged him, and forthwith sent him away ; And saith unto him, See thou say nothing to any man : but go thy way, shew thyself to the priest, and offer for thy cleansing those things which Moses commanded, for a testimony unto them.

45 But he went out, and began to publish *it* much, and to blaze abroad the matter, insomuch that Jesus could no more openly enter into the city, but was without in desert places : and they came to him from every quarter.

The healed leper had better have obeyed his Lord and held his peace, for his grateful declarations hindered the Lord's work of mercy, and took him away from hundreds who needed him. However generous and natural the promptings of our grateful hearts may be, it is always wisest to do exactly as we are bidden. Lord, heal us, and make us thy servants for ever.

Now, Lord, to whom for help I call,
  Thy miracles repeat ;
With pitying eye behold me fall
  A leper at thy feet.

Loathsome, and foul, and self-abhorr'd,
  I sink beneath my sin ;
But if thou wilt, a gracious word,
  Of thine, can make me clean.

Whene'er the angry passions rise,
And tempt our thoughts or tongues to strife,
To Jesus let us lift our eyes,
Bright pattern of the Christian life.

Oh how benevolent and kind !
How mild, how ready to forgive !
Be this the temper of our mind,
And these the rules by which we live.

To do his heavenly Father's will,
Was his employment and delight ;
Humility and holy zeal
Shone through his life, divinely bright.

Dispensing good where'er he came,
The labours of his life were love :
Oh, if we love the Saviour's name,
Let his divine example move.

MARK II. 1—22.

AND again he entered into Capernaum after some days; and it was noised that he was in the house. And straightway many were gathered together, insomuch that there was no room to receive *them*, no, not so much as about the door: and he preached the word unto them.

3 And they come unto him, bringing one sick of the palsy, which was borne of four. *That man is highly favoured who has godly neighbours labouring for his salvation.*

4 And when they could not come nigh unto him for the press, they uncovered the roof where he was: and when they had broken *it* up, they let down the bed wherein the sick of the palsy lay. *(Feeling that all they had to do was to bring their sick friend under the eye of Jesus, they did not stick at difficulties. If we loved men's souls better, we should oftener seek out unusual methods of bringing them to the Saviour.)*

5 When Jesus saw their faith, he said unto the sick of the palsy, Son, thy sins be forgiven thee. *(He struck his disease at the root. When sin is forgiven, every other evil is a small matter.)*

6 But there were certain of the scribes sitting there, and reasoning in their hearts,

7 Why doth this *man* thus speak blasphemies? who can forgive sins but God only?

8—11 And immediately when Jesus perceived in his spirit that they so reasoned within themselves, he said unto them, Why reason ye these things in your hearts? Whether is it easier to say to the sick of the palsy, *Thy* sins be forgiven thee; or to say, Arise, and take up thy bed, and walk? But that ye may know that the Son of man hath power on earth to forgive sins, (he saith to the sick of the palsy,) I say unto thee, Arise, and take up thy bed, and go thy way into thine house.

12 And immediately he arose, took up the bed, and went forth before them all; insomuch that they were all amazed, and glorified God, saying, We never saw it on this fashion.

13, 14 And he went forth again by the sea side; and all the multitude resorted unto him, and he taught them. And as he passed by, he saw Levi the *son* of Alphæus sitting at the receipt of custom, and said unto him, Follow me. And he arose and followed him. *(This was Matthew, the tax gatherer. The Master's voice said little, but effected much. Two words are enough to win a man to Jesus if they are attended by the power of the Spirit. As soon as he was converted, Matthew gave a feast, that his former friends might see Jesus.)*

15 And it came to pass, that as Jesus sat at meat in his house, many publicans and sinners sat also together with Jesus and his disciples: for there were many, and they followed him.

16 And when the scribes and Pharisees saw him eat with publicans and sinners, they said unto his disciples, How is it that he eateth and drinketh with publicans and sinners?

17 When Jesus heard *it*, he saith unto them, They that are whole have no need of the physician, but they that are sick: I came not to call the righteous, but sinners to repentance.

18 And the disciples of John and of the Pharisees used to fast: and they come and say unto him, Why do the disciples of John and of the Pharisees fast, but thy disciples fast not.

19 And Jesus said unto them, Can the children of the bridechamber fast, while the bridegroom is with them? as long as they have the bridegroom with them, they cannot fast.

20 But the days will come, when the bridegroom shall be taken away from them, and then shall they fast in those days.

21, 22 No man also seweth a piece of new cloth on an old garment: else the new piece that filled it up taketh away from the old, and the rent is made worse. And no man putteth new wine into old bottles: else the new wine doth burst the bottles, and the wine is spilled, and the bottles will be marred: but new wine must be put into new bottles.

Everything should be in harmony. To make babes in grace live in the same manner as aged veterans would be unnatural. Rigid forms no more suit the free spirit of Christianity, than an old skin bottle would suit new, fermenting wine.

From fisher's net, from fig-tree's shade,
  God gathers whom he will:
Touched by his grace, th' elect are made
  His purpose to fulfil.

O grant us grace, that to thy call
  We may obedient be;
And, cheerfully forsaking all,
  May follow only thee.

JOHN V. 1—14.

AFTER this there was a feast of the Jews ; and Jesus went up to Jerusalem.

Honouring his Father's law, and at the same time availing himself of the concourse of people to spread the gospel.

2 Now there is at Jerusalem by ,the sheep *market* a pool, which is called in the Hebrew tongue Bethesda, having five porches.

3 In these lay a great multitude of impotent folk, of blind, halt, withered, waiting for the moving of the water.

Jesus was sure to go where he was most needed, seeking those who could not come to him.

4 For an angel went down at a certain season into the pool, and troubled the water : whosoever then first after the troubling of the water stepped in was made whole of whatsoever disease he had.

5 And a certain man was there, which had an infirmity thirty and eight years.

6 When Jesus saw him lie, and knew that he had been now a long time *in that case,* he saith unto him, Wilt thou be made whole ?

A question probably needed to excite his hope, which had grown languid through long waiting and frequent disappointments. The question may well be put to those who have for years been seeking salvation in the use of the outward means of grace without success.

7 The impotent man answered him, Sir, I have no man, when the water is troubled, to put me into the pool : but while I am coming, another steppeth down before me.

As if to prove his anxiety to be healed, the man mentioned his friendless condition in a very pitiful and humble manner. Sinners should imitate this man, and lay their helpless cases before the Good Physician.

8 Jesus saith unto him, Rise, take up thy bed, and walk. *(Leave off watching and waiting, believe my word, and rise. This is the way in which the gospel ends all our natural endeavours and tarryings by an immediate and saving command. " Believe in the Lord Jesus, and wait no longer at the pool," is the one precept of the gospel.)*

9 And immediately the man was made whole, and took up his bed, and walked : and on the same day was the sabbath.

Faith in the almighty word of Jesus brings immediate healing to our souls. Why, then, do so many linger year after year, waiting for they know not what ? Angels will not now come from heaven, nor could they save us if they did; but there is life eternal in the message of mercy, and if we will obey it, salvation is ours at once.

10 ¶ The Jews therefore said unto him that was cured, It is the sabbath day : it is not lawful for thee to carry *thy* bed.

11 He answered them, He that made me whole, the same said unto me, Take up thy bed, and walk. *(He could not quote better authority for what he had done than the word of one who was proved to be divine by the cure which he had wrought. Observe that where Jesus works a gracious cure he also bestows an obedient mind, so that his commands become law to us henceforth.)*

12 Then asked they him, What man is that which said unto thee, Take up thy bed, and walk ?

13 And he that was healed wist not who it was : for Jesus had conveyed himself away, a multitude being in *that* place.

Salvation may come to those who have but scanty knowledge. If we believe in the person and word of Jesus we shall be taught more of both by-and-by.

14 Afterward Jesus findeth him in the temple, and said unto him, Behold, thou art made whole : sin no more, lest a worse thing come unto thee.

Those who are healed need to be instructed, lest they err again. It becomes all who have received any measure of grace to watch against the returns of sin, which may bring them into yet deeper trouble. Happy for us is it that our Lord does not leave us after he has restored us, but visits us with his divine teachings by the Holy Spirit.

Lame at the pool I long have been,
 Waiting to find relief ;
Lord, I have none to put me in
 And wash away my grief.

Speak thou, and give my soul to hear;
 Thy word can make me whole.
Lord, I believe, and leap for joy,
 For thou hast saved my soul.

512   " Jesus Christ is Lord."   AUGUST 26.—EVENING.

[*Or April* 20.]

WHEN *the Jews upbraided our Lord for working a miracle upon the Sabbath, he replied with overwhelming arguments.*

JOHN V. 17—42.

17 But Jesus answered them, My Father worketh hitherto, and I work. *(The processes of nature, which are the work of God, are not stopped upon the Sabbath. God and his Christ are above all law. Men themselves could not keep the Sabbath if the power of God were not in action to keep them alive.)*

18 Therefore the Jews sought the more to kill him, because he not only had broken the sabbath, but said also that God was his Father, making himself equal with God.

19, 20 Then answered Jesus and said unto them, Verily, verily, I say unto you, The Son can do nothing of himself, but what he seeth the Father do: for what things soever he doeth, these also doeth the Son likewise. For the Father loveth the Son, and sheweth him all things that himself doeth: and he will shew him greater works than these, that ye may marvel. *(He declared his own unity and equality with God, even though it excited yet greater wrath against him.)*

21—23 For as the Father raiseth up the dead, and quickeneth *them;* even so the Son quickeneth whom he will. For the Father judgeth no man, but hath committed all judgment unto the Son: that all *men* should honour the Son, even as they honour the Father. He that honoureth not the Son honoureth not the Father which hath sent him.

24 Verily, verily, I say unto you, He that heareth my word, and believeth on him that sent me, hath everlasting life, and shall not come into condemnation; but is passed from death unto life.

25—29 Verily, verily, I say unto you, The hour is coming, and now is, when the dead shall hear the voice of the Son of God: and they that hear shall live. For as the Father hath life in himself; so hath he given to the Son to have life in himself; And hath given him authority to execute judgment also, because he is the Son of man. Marvel not at this: for the hour is coming, in the which all that are in the graves shall hear his voice, And shall come forth; they that have done good, unto the resurrection of life; and they that have done evil, unto the resurrection of damnation.

30 I can of mine own self do nothing. *(He never acted apart from the Father; he was always the Word of God.)* As I hear, I judge: and my judgment is just; because I seek not mine own will, but the will of the Father which hath sent me.

31—35 If I bear witness of myself, my witness is not true. *(He waives the usual objection that a man cannot bear witness to himself, and cites other evidence.)* There is another that beareth witness of me; and I know that the witness which he witnesseth of me is true. Ye sent unto John, and he bare witness unto the truth. But I receive not testimony from man: but these things I say, that ye might be saved. He was a burning and a shining light: and ye were willing for a season to rejoice in his light.

36—38 But I have greater witness than *that* of John: for the works which the Father hath given me to finish, the same works that I do, bear witness of me, that the Father hath sent me. And the Father himself, which hath sent me, hath borne witness of me. Ye have neither heard his voice at any time, nor seen his shape. And ye have not his word abiding in you: for whom he hath sent, him ye believe not.

39 Search the scriptures; for in them ye think ye have eternal life: and they are they which testify of me. *(His appeal is to the Scripture which they themselves reverenced. Truly it teems with testimony concerning him.)*

40 And ye will not come to me, that ye might have life. *(Alas, this is still true of mankind!)*

41 I receive not honour from men.

42 But I know you, that ye have not the love of God in you.

Of the Father's love begotten,
  Ere the world began to be,
He is Alpha and Omega,
  He the source, the ending he.

This is that divine Messiah
  Promised in the faithful word,
Whom the voices of the prophets
  Heralded with one accord.

Christ, to thee, with God the Father,
  And, O Holy Ghost, to thee,
Hymn, and psalm, and high thanksgiving,
  And unwearied praises be!

MATTHEW XII. 1—21.

A T that time Jesus went on the sabbath day through the corn; and his disciples were an hungred, and began to pluck the ears of corn, and to eat. (*Not from any idle feeling of passing away time, but because of necessity, the disciples took ears of corn to eat as they passed through the fields. This they were allowed to do by the Jewish law, and no one found fault with them for it, only it happened to be the Sabbath, and therefore the Pharisees renewed the old quarrel.*)

2 But when the Pharisees saw *it*, they said unto him, Behold, thy disciples do that which is not lawful to do upon the sabbath day.

One would have thought that it was surely permissible to relieve hunger on the Sabbath; but the Pharisees made it out to be an act of harvesting, and even of threshing when they saw them rub the ears in their hands. Some men are great at making much ado about nothing.

3, 4 But he said unto them, Have ye not read what David did, when he was an hungred, and they that were with him; How he entered into the house of God, and did eat the shewbread, which was not lawful for him to eat, neither for them which were with him, but only for the priests? (*Necessity has no law. It was never intended that men should die of hunger in order to preserve the sanctity of a day.*)

5, 6 Or have ye not read in the law, how that on the sabbath days the priests in the temple profane the sabbath, and are blameless? But I say unto you, That in this place is *one* greater than the temple. (*Works done for God are commendable on the Sabbath, and if the Lord himself was present, and had not blamed his disciples, it was not for others to complain.*)

7, 8 But if ye had known what *this* meaneth, I will have mercy, and not sacrifice, ye would not have condemned the guiltless. For the Son of man is Lord even of the sabbath day.

God has not intended the fourth commandment to be used cruelly, so as to forbid the doing of that which is absolutely needful. The institution of the Sabbath is under the power of Jesus, the Lord of love, and is not a burden, but a delight.

9, 10 And when he was departed thence, he went into their synagogue: And, behold, there was a man which had *his* hand withered. And they asked him, saying, Is it lawful to heal on the sabbath days? that they might accuse him.

11 And he said unto them, What man shall there be among you, that shall have one sheep, and if it fall into a pit on the sabbath day, will he not lay hold on it, and lift *it* out?

12 How much then is a man better than a sheep? Wherefore it is lawful to do well on the sabbath days.

13 Then saith he to the man, Stretch forth thine hand. And he stretched *it* forth; and it was restored whole, like as the other. (*Thus he emphatically showed the true position of the Sabbath, and his own resolve not to be bound in the fetters of Jewish tradition with regard to it.*)

14—19 Then the Pharisees went out, and held a council against him, how they might destroy him. But when Jesus knew *it*, he withdrew himself from thence: (*going to the borders of the sea of Gennesaret*) and great multitudes followed him, and he healed them all; And charged them that they should not make him known. That it might be fulfilled which was spoken by Esaias the prophet, saying, Behold my servant, whom I have chosen; my beloved, in whom my soul is well pleased: I will put my spirit upon him, and he shall shew judgment to the Gentiles. He shall not strive, nor cry; neither shall any man hear his voice in the streets. (*He neither sought popularity nor controversy.*)

20 A bruised reed shall he not break, and smoking flax shall he not quench, till he send forth judgment unto victory. (*He left those fuming Pharisees, and the weak reeds of scribes and doctors, till a future time, not caring utterly to quench or crush their broken power.*)

21 And in his name shall the Gentiles trust. *Quiet as he was, he is our hope and joy, and our soul rests upon him.*

Help us, through good report and ill,
  Our daily cross to bear;
Like thee, to do our Father's will,
  Our brethren's griefs to share.

Let grace our selfishness expel,
  Our earthliness refine;
And kindness in our bosoms dwell,
  As free and true as thine.

LUKE VI. 12—36.

AND it came to pass in those days, *(while he was by the sea, near Capernaum)* that he went out into a mountain to pray, and continued all night in prayer to God.

It was his wont to spend a season in special prayer before any great act of his life. He was about to send out the first missionaries, but he would do nothing till he had prayed.

13—16 And when it was day, he called *unto him* his disciples : and of them he chose twelve, whom also he named apostles ; Simon, (whom he also named Peter), and Andrew his brother, James and John, Philip and Bartholomew, Matthew and Thomas, James the *son* of Alphæus, and Simon called Zelotes, And Judas *the brother* of James, and Judas Iscariot, which also was the traitor.

17—19 And he came down with them, and stood in the plain, and the company of his disciples, and a great multitude of people out of all Judæa and Jerusalem, and from the sea coast of Tyre and Sidon, which came to hear him, and to be healed of their diseases ; And they that were vexed with unclean spirits : and they were healed. And the whole multitude sought to touch him : for there went virtue out of him, and healed *them* all. *(Now was another great opportunity for preaching, and our Lord availed himself of it. We now find him delivering the Sermon on the Plain which, in many points, resembles the Sermon on the Mount. It has four beatitudes and four woes, and repeats in almost the same words the former discourse.)*

20 ¶ And he lifted up his eyes on his disciples, and said, Blessed *be ye* poor : for your's is the kingdom of God. *(Poor though they were, they were his disciples, and were poor in spirit as well as in pocket, and therefore blessed. We must understand all these beatitudes spiritually, or we shall make grave mistakes.)*

21 Blessed *are ye* that hunger now : for ye shall be filled. Blessed *are ye* that weep now : for ye shall laugh.

22 Blessed are ye, when men shall hate you, and when they shall separate you *from their company*, and shall reproach *you*, and cast out your name as evil, for the Son of man's sake.

23 Rejoice ye in that day, and leap for joy : for, behold, your reward *is* great in heaven : for

in the like manner did their fathers unto the prophets.

24 But woe unto you that are rich ! for ye have received your consolation. *(For the most part those who are rich despise religion. "Gold and the gospel seldom do agree," says Bunyan.)*

25 Woe unto you that are full ! for ye shall hunger. *(If satisfied with earth's good things, they will soon be gone, and eternal want will follow.)* Woe unto you that laugh now ! for ye shall mourn and weep. *(To spend life in frivolous mirth and gaiety is to store up sorrow.)*

26 Woe unto you, when all men shall speak well of you ! for so did their fathers to the false prophets. *(Dangerous then is the position of the favourite of mankind. If the ungodly mass love a man, God loves him not.)*

27 ¶ But I say unto you which hear, Love your enemies, do good to them which hate you.

28—30 Bless them that curse you, and pray for them which despitefully use you. And unto him that smiteth thee on the *one* cheek offer also the other ; and him that taketh away thy cloke forbid not *to take thy* coat also. Give to every man that asketh of thee ; and of him that taketh away thy goods ask *them* not again.

Better suffer any loss than wrangle and go to courts of law, where indeed one is apt to increase his loss rather than repair it.

31 And as ye would that men should do to you, do ye also to them likewise.

32—36 For if ye love them which love you, what thank have ye ? for sinners also love those that love them. And if ye do good to them which do good to you, what thank have ye ? for sinners also do even the same. And if ye lend *to them* of whom ye hope to receive, what thank have ye ? for sinners also lend to sinners, to receive as much again. But love ye your enemies, and do good, and lend, hoping for nothing again ; and your reward shall be great, and ye shall be the children of the Highest : for he is kind unto the unthankful and *to* the evil. Be ye therefore merciful, as your Father also is merciful. *(This noble godlike principle of doing good without prospect of return should be better exhibited by professed Christians than it is. Let it be our prayer that we may act by its rule.)*

MATTHEW XI. 2—19.

NOW when John had heard in the prison the works of Christ, he sent two of his disciples, And said unto him, Art thou he that should come, or do we look for another?

Had his sufferings depressed his spirit? We think not. He probably sent his disciples, that their faith might be confirmed.

4—6 Jesus answered and said unto them, Go and shew John again those things which ye do hear and see: The blind receive their sight, and the lame walk, the lepers are cleansed, and the deaf hear, the dead are raised up, and the poor have the gospel preached to them. And blessed is *he,* whosoever shall not be offended in me. *(These are the attesting proofs of the true Messiah's mission, and among them all there is no greater wonder of grace than the preaching of the gospel to the poor. Other teachers had shut them out, but Jesus specially sought them out.)*

7 And as they departed, Jesus began to say unto the multitudes concerning John, What went ye out into the wilderness to see? A reed shaken by the wind? *(Was he a man easily moved, pliant and yielding? By no means. John was very far from being fickle or cowardly.)*

8—11 But what went ye out for to see? A man clothed in soft raiment? behold, they that wear soft *clothing* are in kings' houses. But what went ye out for to see? A prophet? yea, I say unto you, and more than a prophet. For this is *he,* of whom it is written, Behold, I send my messenger before thy face, which shall prepare thy way before thee. Verily I say unto you, Among them that are born of women there hath not risen a greater than John the Baptist: notwithstanding he that is least in the kingdom of heaven is greater than he.

His was but a twilight dispensation, and we who live in the full blaze of day have greater privileges than he had. John had never heard the words, " It is finished," as we have done, to our hearts' joy.

12 And from the days of John the Baptist until now the kingdom of heaven suffereth violence, and the violent take it by force. *(There is no such thing as winning this kingdom by half-hearted endeavours. Energy is needed for success in this life, and much more for the life to come. Grace in the heart leads men to strive to enter in*

at the strait gate. Oh that we could see more holy violence in the church of God. Sloth and lethargy are robbing Jesus of his honour, and the church of its success.)

13—15 For all the prophets and the law prophesied until John. And if ye will receive *it,* this is Elias, which was for to come. He that hath ears to hear, let him hear.

16 ¶ But whereunto shall I liken this generation? It is like unto children sitting in the markets, and calling unto their fellows,

17 And saying, We have piped unto you, and ye have not danced; we have mourned unto you, and ye have not lamented.

They could not agree as to what they should play. Some of them proposed to imitate a wedding, and began to pipe, but the others would not dance. " Well, then," said they, " let us perform a funeral," and they commenced to mourn, but their wayward companions would not respond with lamentations. Even so it is hard to find ministers to please men: one is too rambling, and another too logical; and if one preacher be condemned for being vulgar, another is censured for his flowery style. There is no satisfying fastidious tastes. If we are in a right state of heart, we shall remember George Herbert's words: " Judge not the preacher, he is thy judge."

18 For John came neither eating nor drinking, and they say, He hath a devil.

19 The Son of man came eating and drinking, and they say, Behold a man gluttonous, and a winebibber, a friend of publicans and sinners. But wisdom is justified of her children.

God knows best whom to send, and we ought to be on the watch to profit by them all.

'Tis not a cause of small import
  The pastor's care demands;
But what might fill an angel's heart,
  And fill'd a Saviour's hands.

They watch for souls for which the Lord
  Did heavenly bliss forego;
For souls which must for ever live
  In raptures, or in woe.

May they *that* Jesus, whom they preach,
  Their own Redeemer see:
And watch thou daily o'er their souls,
  That they may watch for thee.

LUKE VII. 1—17.

NOW when he had ended all his sayings in the audience of the people, he entered into Capernaum.

2 And a certain centurion's servant, who was dear unto him, was sick, and ready to die.

He was a good master, and had a good servant, therefore there was much affection between them, which is a rare thing in these days.

3 And when he heard of Jesus, he sent unto him the elders of the Jews, beseeching him that he would come and heal his servant.

4—6 And when they came to Jesus, they besought him instantly, saying, That he was worthy for whom he should do this : For he loveth our nation, and he hath built us a synagogue. Then Jesus went with them. And when he was now not far from the house, the centurion sent friends to him, saying unto him, Lord, trouble not thyself : for I am not worthy that thou shouldest enter under my roof : *(The Jews called him worthy, but he did not think himself so. He who enjoys the good opinion of others, and is not thereby lifted up, possesses a sound mind.)*

7 Wherefore neither thought I myself worthy to come unto thee : but say in a word, and my servant shall be healed. *(Give the word, and the disease will fly without thy needing to come personally. This was grand faith.)*

8 For I also am a man set under authority, having under me soldiers, and I say unto one, Go, and he goeth ; and to another, Come, and he cometh ; and to my servant, Do this, and he doeth it. *(Although only a petty officer, yet his word was law, and therefore he rightly concluded that the word of the Lord Jesus would be equally powerful over all the realms of nature. He had only to say to the disease " Go," and it would be gone. This was such good reasoning as only grace could have taught him.)*

9 When Jesus heard these things, he marvelled at him, and turned him about, and said unto the people that followed him, I say unto you, I have not found so great faith, no, not in Israel.

10 And they that were sent, returning to the house, found the servant whole that had been sick. *(The Jews had praised the centurion's works, but the Lord fixed his eye upon his faith.*

This is the jewel which Jesus prizes most. Do we each and all possess it ?)

11, 12 And it came to pass the day after, that he went into a city called Nain ; and many of his disciples went with him, and much people. Now when he came nigh to the gate of the city, behold, there was a dead man carried out, the only son of his mother, and she was a widow : and much people of the city was with her.

Death takes away the young full often. Had it been the Lord's will, one of us might have been this day a corpse, and to-day would have been mournfully spent by the rest of the family at the tomb. The poor widowed mother who mourned her only son was at once observed by the tender Jesus, and addressed in tones of deepest sympathy.

13, 14 And when the Lord saw her, he had compassion on her, and said unto her, Weep not. And he came and touched the bier : and they that bare *him* stood still. And he said, Young man, I say unto thee, Arise.

15 And he that was dead sat up, and began to speak. And he delivered him to his mother.

Oh, that he would give spiritual life to those of this family who are dead in sin ! Young and fair, excellent and amiable as young men and women may be, they must be quickened by the Holy Spirit, or else they will remain dead in trespasses and sins. Jesus can give the spiritual life, and a mother's tears will go far to touch his heart and win the blessing.

16, 17 And there came a fear on all : and they glorified God, saying, That a great prophet is risen up among us ; and, That God hath visited his people. And this rumour of him went forth throughout all Judæa, and throughout all the region round about.

So was his name renowned, even as it is among his own saints at this hour. Blessed, for ever blessed, be the Friend of Man !

Thou art the *Life :* the empty bier
Proclaims thy conquering arm ;
And those who put their trust in thee,
Nor death nor hell shall harm.

Thou art *the Way, the Truth, the Life :*
Grant us that Way to know,
That Truth to keep, that Life to win,
Whose joys eternal flow.

THE *remarkable portion of Scripture which we are about to read contains in a small space the three great truths of human responsibility, the sovereignty of electing love, and the free proclamation of the gospel. If we cannot reconcile them, we must, nevertheless, believe them, and wait for clearer light.*

MATTHEW XI. 20—30.

20 Then began he to upbraid the cities wherein most of his mighty works were done, because they repented not: *Therefore it is clear that they ought to have repented. Jesus would not have upbraided them for impenitence, if penitence were not their duty.*

21 Woe unto thee, Chorazin! woe unto thee, Bethsaida! for if the mighty works, which were done in you, had been done in Tyre and Sidon, they would have repented long ago in sackcloth and ashes. *(A very mysterious statement, since it involves the singular fact that the mighty works were not done among those who would have repented, and were done among those who refused to repent. The way of the Lord is far above the comprehension of men.)*

22 But I say unto you, It shall be more tolerable for Tyre and Sidon at the day of judgment, than for you. *(Though as to open sin the Sidonians were beyond measure vile, yet they were not so guilty as those who had wilfully refused the gospel, and therefore their punishment would be less. This the Lord repeated, varying the words.)*

23, 24 And thou, Capernaum, which art exalted unto heaven, shalt be brought down to hell: for if the mighty works, which have been done in thee, had been done in Sodom, it would have remained until this day. But I say unto you, That it shall be more tolerable for the land of Sodom in the day of judgment, than for thee. *Yet Sodom's doom is fearful beyond imagination—where then will despisers of the gospel appear? Our Lord now changed the theme and discoursed upon sovereign grace.*

25, 26 At that time Jesus answered and said, I thank thee, O Father, Lord of heaven and earth, because thou hast hid these things from the wise and prudent, and hast revealed them unto babes. Even so, Father: for so it seemed good in thy sight.

27 All things are delivered unto me of my Father; and no man knoweth the Son, but the Father; neither knoweth any man the Father, save the Son, and *he* to whomsoever the Son will reveal *him.*

Here is the author of election—the Father, his right to choose—Lord of heaven and earth, the objects of his choice—babes, and the only reason of his choice which he deigns to give us—"so it seemed good in thy sight." Our Lord next bore testimony to himself as the great channel by which the blessings of electing love flow down to those whom he has chosen. The doctrines of grace are as true as the fact of our responsibility, and the two agree in one, though few can see where they meet. Salvation is all of grace, damnation is man's fault, and his fault alone.

The third part of our reading contains a full, free, personal, present invitation to sinners to come to Jesus. No ministry is complete where this is kept in the background. As we read it may we feel the drawing influence of the Holy Spirit, and find rest in Jesus at once.

28 Come unto me, all *ye* that labour and are heavy laden, and I will give you rest.

29, 30 Take my yoke upon you, and learn of me; for I am meek and lowly in heart: and ye shall find rest unto your souls. For my yoke *is* easy, and my burden is light. *(Is there one here, who has hitherto refused the invitation? Let him come now! Come, and welcome. Remember it is not to sacraments, or to priests that you are to come, but to Jesus himself. He, and he alone, can give perfect rest to all who are obedient to him.)*

"Come hither, all ye weary souls,
Ye heavy laden sinners come;
I'll give you rest from all your toils,
And raise you to my heavenly home.

"They shall find rest that learn of me,
I'm of a meek and lowly mind;
But passion rages like the sea,
And pride is restless as the wind.

"Bless'd is the man whose shoulders take
My yoke, and bear it with delight;
My yoke is easy to his neck,
My grace shall make the burden light."

Jesus, we come at thy command;
With faith, and hope, and humble zeal,
Resign our spirits to thy hand,
To mould and guide us at thy will.

LUKE VII. 36—50.

AND one of the Pharisees desired him that he would eat with him. And he went into the Pharisee's house, and sat down to meat.

37 And, behold, a woman in the city, which was a sinner, when she knew that *Jesus* sat at meat in the Pharisee's house, brought an alabaster box of ointment,

38 And stood at his feet behind *him* weeping, and began to wash his feet with tears, and did wipe *them* with the hairs of her head, and kissed his feet, and anointed *them* with the ointment.

We are not informed as to how she came to know and love the Saviour. It may be that some gracious word of his had recalled her from a life of infamy and shame, which was fast ending in misery and despair. Filled with deep repentance, and moved with holy reverence for her Lord, she brought the greatest treasure she possessed, and used it all for him, standing behind him in her bashfulness, washing his feet in her humility, weeping for penitence, kissing his feet for love, and unbraiding her tresses and using them as a towel, out of supreme devotion to him, to whom she owed her all. Happy woman, to be able thus to show her devout attachment to her Lord.

39 Now when the Pharisee which had bidden him saw *it*, he spake within himself, saying, This man, if he were a prophet, would have known who and what manner of woman *this is* that toucheth him : for she is a sinner.

He had never thought of our Lord as he should have done, and now his respect quite fails. He could not think that any good man would allow such a woman to come so near him. Simon did not understand Jesus, but Jesus well enough understood Simon, and therefore spoke to him.

40 And Jesus answering said unto him, Simon, I have somewhat to say unto thee. And he saith, Master, say on.

41, 42 There was a certain creditor which had two debtors : the one owed five hundred pence, and the other fifty. And when they had nothing to pay, he frankly forgave them both. Tell me therefore, which of them will love him most ?

43 Simon answered and said, I suppose that *he*, to whom he forgave most. And he said unto him, Thou hast rightly judged.

44—47 And he turned to the woman, and said unto Simon, Seest thou this woman ? I entered into thine house, thou gavest me no water for my feet : but she hath washed my feet with tears, and wiped *them* with the hairs of her head. Thou gavest me no kiss : but this woman since the time I came in hath not ceased to kiss my feet. My head with oil thou didst not anoint : but this woman hath anointed my feet with ointment. Wherefore I say unto thee, Her sins, which are many, are forgiven ; for she loved much : but to whom little is forgiven, *the same* loveth little. *(Self-righteousness can never serve after the same fashion as love. It does its duty in the formal style of force work, and not with the zest and delight of true affection. The attempt to save ourselves by our own merits never brings forth those emotions of entire devotion which arise from a sense of grace bestowed and sin pardoned. Are there not in our own case reasons for fervent love ? He who writes this exposition feels that, above all men, he is bound to love his forgiving Master. Do not the same feelings occur to others ?)*

48 And he said unto her, Thy sins are forgiven. *(Her love brought her a fresh token for good, another assurance of forgiveness. Gratitude for former favours is the sure method to obtain more.)*

49 And they that sat at meat with him began to say within themselves, Who is this that forgiveth sins also ?

50 And he said to the woman, Thy faith hath saved thee ; go in peace. *(He did not take the trouble to rebuke the impudent murmurers, but he persisted in consoling the loving penitent. He honoured her faith, and bade her go, with his peace resting upon her, for he did not wish her to be disturbed by cruel tongues.*

Learn hence how delighted Jesus is to forgive great sinners, since they bring him great love in return, and see also how free his mercy is, since he frankly forgives those who have nothing to pay.)

Love and grief my heart dividing,
    With my tears-his feet I'll bathe,
Constant still in faith abiding,
    Life deriving from his death.

Here it is I find my heaven,
    While upon the cross I gaze.
Love I much ? I've more forgiven ;
    I'm a miracle of grace.

MATTHEW XII. 22—37.

THEN was brought unto him one possessed with a devil, blind, and dumb: and he healed him, insomuch that the blind and dumb both spake and saw.

It would seem that the devil had special licence to do his worst among men during the days of our Lord's sojourn upon earth. Thus was he the more gloriously defeated by the Son of God in many pitched battles between the two champions.

23 And all the people were amazed, and said, Is not this the son of David?

They spoke honestly, but their leaders were prejudiced, and refused to see what was clear enough to the most ordinary understandings. It is a dreadful thing to be so warped by education as to refuse to admit what is plain to all.

24 But when the Pharisees heard *it*, they said, This *fellow* doth not cast out devils but by Beelzebub the prince of the devils.

25, 26 And Jesus knew their thoughts, and said unto them, Every kingdom divided against itself is brought to desolation; and every city or house divided against itself shall not stand: And if Satan cast out Satan, he is divided against himself; how shall then his kingdom stand?

27—29 And if I by Beelzebub cast out devils, by whom do your children cast *them* out? therefore they shall be your judges. *(For some of the sons of the Pharisees pretended to be able to heal possessed persons.)* But if I cast out devils by the Spirit of God, then the kingdom of God is come unto you. Or else how can one enter into a strong man's house, and spoil his goods, except he first bind the strong man? and then he will spoil his house.

30 He that is not with me is against me; and he that gathereth not with me scattereth abroad.

Let this always be remembered, and let each one ask himself, "Am I with Christ?" If not, remember you are against him. Can you bear this?

31 Wherefore I say unto you, All manner of sin and blasphemy shall be forgiven unto men: but the blasphemy *against* the *Holy* Ghost shall not be forgiven unto men.

32 And whosoever speaketh a word against the Son of man, it shall be forgiven him: but whosoever speaketh against the Holy Ghost, it shall not be forgiven him, neither in this world, neither in the *world* to come.

A terrible doom which fell upon these Pharisees and destroyed them. How careful we ought to be to render all reverence and obedience to the Holy Spirit, lest by grieving him away we should be left to final perdition! While the Spirit of God still continues to strive with us we have not committed this deadly sin.

33 Either make the tree good, and his fruit good; or else make the tree corrupt, and his fruit corrupt: for the tree is known by *his* fruit.

Nothing will suffice but a change of nature. The very root and sap of the soul must be renewed by grace.

34 O generation of vipers, how can ye, being evil, speak good things? for out of the abundance of the heart the mouth speaketh.

35 A good man out of the good treasure of the heart bringeth forth good things: and an evil man out of the evil treasure bringeth forth evil things. *(That which is in comes out. The stream declares the character of the fountain.)*

36 But I say unto you, That every idle word that men shall speak, they shall give account thereof in the day of judgment.

37 For by thy words thou shalt be justified, and by thy words thou shalt be condemned.

This makes common talk a solemn matter. Who among us can bear such a test? Let us fly to the blood of Jesus for cleansing from sins of the tongue, and to the Spirit of God to bridle that unruly member.

Sovereign of heaven! thine empire spreads
   O'er all the world on high,
And at thy frown the infernal powers
   In wild confusion fly.

Like lightning, from his glittering throne
   The great arch-traitor fell,
Driven with enormous ruin down
   To infamy and hell.

Permitted now to range at large,
   And traverse earth and air,
O'er captive human souls he reigns,
   And boasts his kingdom there.

Yet thence thy grace can drive him out,
   With one almighty word;
O send thy potent sceptre forth,
   And reign victorious, Lord!

LUKE VIII. 1—3.

A ND it came to pass afterward, that he went throughout every city and village, preaching and shewing the glad tidings of the kingdom of God : and the twelve *were* with him,

2 And certain women, which had been healed of evil spirits and infirmities, Mary called Magdalene, out of whom went seven devils,

3 And Joanna the wife of Chuza, Herod's steward, and Susanna, and many others, which ministered unto him of their substance.

So that our Lord was supported by the voluntary offerings of his followers. He did no more work at the carpenter's bench, when he began to preach the gospel: his ministry required all his time and strength. It is noble in men, like Paul, to labour at their trade while preaching, but if believers were as generous as they should be, such drudgery would not long be necessary.

MATTHEW XII. 38—40; 43—50.

T HEN certain of the scribes and of the Pharisees answered, saying, Master, we would see a sign from thee.

39 But he answered and said unto them, An evil and adulterous generation seeketh after a sign; and there shall no sign be given to it, but the sign of the prophet Jonas :

40 For as Jonas was three days and three nights in the whale's belly ; so shall the Son of man be three days and three nights in the heart of the earth.

43 When the unclean spirit is gone out of a man, he walketh through dry places, seeking rest, and findeth none. *(The evil spirit cannot rest. He is so malicious that unless he is doing mischief he cannot bear himself.)*

44 Then he saith, I will return into my house from whence I came out; *(The devil is represented as going out of the man of his own will, and, therefore, when he wills he returns. He calls it "my house" because he had not been expelled from it by divine grace, neither had Jesus taken possession. So men who become moralised and improved entirely of their own accord, and in their own strength, return to their old sins. When grace comes and turns out the devil by force of divine love, he never returns, but unrenewed nature soon welcomes back the tempter.)* and when

he is come, he findeth *it* empty, swept, and garnished. *(Many men's lives are swept from the fouler vices, and garnished with pretty human virtues; but they are not inhabited by the Spirit of God, and hence evil soon gets the upper hand, and the soul becomes worse than before.)*

45 Then goeth he, and taketh with himself seven other spirits more wicked than himself, and they enter in and dwell there : and the last *state* of that man is worse than the first. Even so shall it be also unto this wicked generation.

Idolatry left the Jewish nation after the captivity in Babylon, but formalism, superstition, and self-righteousness ruled over them, and made them harder to deal with than their idolatrous fathers.

46 ¶ While he yet talked to the people, behold, *his* mother and his brethren stood without, desiring to speak with him.

47 Then one said unto him, Behold, thy mother and thy brethren stand without, desiring to speak with thee. *(His nightly watches and daily labours were wearing him out, and his relations, conceiving the idea that he must be out of his mind, planned to seize him, and withdraw him from public work. The kindest of men cannot comprehend the zeal of a real fervent heart ; they call it enthusiasm, and speak of the possibility of "going too far," and being too earnest : so are the best men least understood. Our Lord's mother seems to have had some hand in this mistaken project : blessed as she was she was, not infallible.)*

48, 49 But he answered and said unto him that told him, Who is my mother ? and who are my brethren ? And he stretched forth his hand toward his disciples, and said, Behold my mother and my brethren !

50 For whosoever shall do the will of my Father which is in heaven, the same is my brother, and sister, and mother.

The spiritual relationship outweighs the natural one. Believers are the true "Holy Family."

Lord, what are we and what our race,
That thou dost us for brethren own,
Crown'd thus with dignity and grace
To brightest cherubim unknown ?

What can we do to make return,
Or half our gratitude express?
To thee our souls' affections turn,
With all our hearts thy name we bless.

MATTHEW XIII. 1—23.

THE same day went Jesus out of the house, and sat by the sea side.

2 And great multitudes were gathered together unto him, so that he went into a ship, and sat; and the whole multitude stood on the shore. *A most delightful instance of out-of-door preaching, of which the more the better, for without it great numbers of our fellow-men will never hear the gospel. The natural objects around him no doubt supplied the Lord with his illustrations, and these were so homely and full of meaning, that they arrested the attention of all.*

3, 4 And he spake many things unto them in parables, saying, Behold, a sower went forth to sow; And when he sowed, some *seeds* fell by the way side, *(on the trodden pathway)* and the fowls came and devoured them up:

5, 6 Some fell upon stony places *(or spots where the rock was near the surface)* where they had not much earth: and forthwith they sprung up, because they had no deepness of earth: And when the sun was up, they were scorched; and because they had no root, they withered away.

7 And some fell among thorns; and the thorns sprung up and choked them:

8 But other fell into good ground, and brought forth fruit, some an hundredfold, some sixtyfold, some thirtyfold.

9 Who hath ears to hear, let him hear.

10 And the disciples came, and said unto him, Why speakest thou unto them in parables?

11 He answered and said unto them, Because it is given unto you to know the mysteries of the kingdom of heaven, but to them it is not given. *(Carnal minds foolishly put a literal meaning upon expressions which are evidently figurative, and so discern not the meaning. To understand the gospel is a gift of divine grace.)*

12 For whosoever hath, to him shall be given, and he shall have more abundance: but whosoever hath not, from him shall be taken away even that he hath.

13 Therefore speak I to them in parables: because they seeing see not; and hearing they hear not, neither do they understand.

14 And in them is fulfilled the prophecy of Esaias, which saith, By hearing ye shall hear, and shall not understand; and seeing ye shall see, and shall not perceive:

15 For this people's heart is waxed gross, and *their* ears are dull of hearing, and their eyes they have closed; lest at any time they should see with *their* eyes, and hear with *their* ears, and should understand with *their* heart, and should be converted, and I should heal them. *Those who will not see may expect to fall into such a state that they cannot see.*

16—21 But blessed *are* your eyes, for they see: and your ears, for they hear. For verily I say unto you, That many prophets and righteous *men* have desired to see *those things* which ye see, and have not seen *them;* and to hear *those things* which ye hear, and have not heard *them.* Hear ye therefore the parable of the sower. When any one heareth the word of the kingdom, and understandeth *it* not, then cometh the wicked *one,* and catcheth away that which was sown in his heart. This is he which received seed by the way side. But he that received the seed into stony places, the same is he that heareth the word, and anon with joy receiveth it; Yet hath he not root in himself, but dureth for a while: for when tribulation or persecution ariseth because of the word, by and by he is offended.

22 He also that received seed among the thorns is he that heareth the word; and the care of this world, and the deceitfulness of riches, choke the word, and he becometh unfruitful.

23 But he that received seed into the good ground is he that heareth the word, and understandeth *it;* which also beareth fruit, and bringeth forth, some an hundredfold, some sixty, some thirty. *(Four bad soils are mentioned, and only one which is good. A lesson to us to examine ourselves carefully, lest we be found barren.)*

> Sow in the morn thy seed,
> At eve hold not thy hand;
> To doubt and fear give thou no heed;
> Broadcast it o'er the land!
>
> Thou canst not toil in vain:
> Cold, heat, and moist, and dry
> Shall foster and mature the grain,
> For garners in the sky.
>
> Then, when the glorious end,
> The day of God, shall come,
> The angel reapers shall descend,
> And heaven sing, " Harvest home! "

522   " He shall separate them one from another."   AUGUST 31.—EVENING.

[Or April 30.]

MATTHEW XIII. 24—30 ; 36—43.

ANOTHER parable put he forth unto them, saying, The kingdom of heaven is likened unto a man which sowed good seed in his field :

25 But while men slept, his enemy came and sowed tares among the wheat, and went his way.

26 But when the blade was sprung up, and brought forth fruit, then appeared the tares also.

27 So the servants of the householder came and said unto him, Sir, didst not thou sow good seed in thy field ? from whence then hath it tares ?

28 He said unto them, An enemy hath done this. The servants said unto him, Wilt thou then that we go and gather them up ?

29 ·But he said, Nay ; lest while ye gather up the tares, ye root up also the wheat with them.

30 Let both grow together until the harvest : and in the time of harvest I will say to the reapers, Gather ye together first the tares, and bind them in bundles to burn them : but gather the wheat into my barn.

36 Then Jesus sent the multitude away, and went into the house : and his disciples came unto him, saying, Declare unto us the parable of the tares of the field.

37 He answered and said unto them, He that soweth the good seed is the Son of man ; *All the spiritual good in the world comes from him. Whoever the servants may be, the Master who sent them to sow good seed is Jesus, our Lord.*

38 The field is the world; *(for everywhere is the gospel to be preached, and the church to be formed is in the world, though not of it. The whole world belongs to Jesus : let Satan rage as he may, he is only an usurper. Despite all opposition, it is in this great field of the world that the Lord has sown a church, and maintained it in being.)* the good seed are the children of the kingdom; but the tares are the children of the wicked *one; (Satan is a busy agent, and is always doing his best to hinder the good work of Jesus. The seed of the serpent, and the seed of the woman are at deadly enmity.)*

39 The enemy that sowed them is the devil ; *(Our Saviour did not mean such tares as grow in our country, but a sort of mock wheat common in the east. The evil one could not prevent the springing up of the good seed, and therefore he tried to impede its growth, and spoil its harvest by throwing in among it noxious seed. The devil cannot destroy the church, and therefore he endeavours to mar its beauty by the introduction of hypocrites. These are in many respects so like to true Christians that it is not possible to remove them without expelling genuine believers with them by mistake. Open sinners we can easily remove from the church ; but not those who have the outward manners of Christians ; however wrong at heart they may be, we are unable to judge them, and must let them remain.)* the harvest is the end of the world ; and the reapers are the angels.

40 As therefore the tares are gathered and burned in the fire ; so shall it be in the end of this world.

41 The Son of man shall send forth his angels, and they shall gather out of his kingdom all things that offend, and them which do iniquity ;

42 And shall cast them into a furnace of fire : there shall be wailing and gnashing of teeth.

The true character of men will develop itself in due season, and will be clearly seen at the last day. Angels will have no difficulty in discerning between sincere believers and mere formalists. Men may deceive the church to-day, and do it much mischief by creeping into it while they are unconverted ; they ought, however, to tremble, for the hour comes in which the unquenchable fires of divine wrath will consume all pretenders.

43 Then shall the righteous shine forth as the sun in the kingdom of their Father. Who hath ears to hear, let him hear.

The church, while yet she ripens here,
Mix'd and imperfect must appear ;
Sinners and saints together meet,
The tares are mingled with the wheat.

But a dividing day will come,
And hypocrites must hear their doom,
" Depart, accurs'd, to endless woe,
Prepared for devils and for you."

Lord, may I then accepted stand
Among the wheat at thy right hand ;
Before the angels stand confest,
And hear thy lips proclaim me blest.

OUR *loving Lord has left us many priceless parables, in which great truths are made plain to our understandings. He deserves our love for thus condescending to our dulness.*

MATTHEW XIII. 31—33; 44—58.

31 Another parable put he forth unto them, saying, The kingdom of heaven is like to a grain of mustard seed, which a man took, and sowed in his field :

32 Which indeed is the least of all seeds : but when it is grown, it is the greatest among herbs, and becometh a tree, so that the birds of the air come and lodge in the branches thereof. *Mustard of this kind is common in Palestine. Nothing at its commencement could be smaller, or less conspicuous, than the church of Christ; nothing in the end shall be so great and honourable. Already many happy souls, like birds, are resting in its branches.*

33 ¶ Another parable spake he unto them; The kingdom of heaven is like unto leaven, which a woman took, and hid in three measures of meal, till the whole was leavened. *Silently, mysteriously, and potently it works, and so do good or evil influences in society.*

44 ¶ Again, the kingdom of heaven is like unto treasure hid in a field; the which when a man hath found, he hideth, and for joy thereof goeth and selleth all that he hath, and buyeth that field.

45, 46 Again, the kingdom of heaven is like unto a merchant man, seeking goodly pearls : who, when he had found one pearl of great price, went and sold all that he had, and bought it. *(The first man is the suddenly converted sinner, who finds Jesus, though he looked not for him; the second is the diligent seeker, who at last discovers Jesus for whom he had sought. They both agree in setting the highest value upon the treasure. Do we value Jesus thus? Say, Is he very precious to our hearts?)*

47 ¶ Again, the kingdom of heaven is like unto a net, that was cast into the sea, and gathered of every kind :

48 Which, when it was full, they drew to shore, and sat down, and gathered the good into vessels, but cast the bad away.

49—52 So shall it be at the end of the world : the angels shall come forth, and sever the wicked from among the just, And shall cast them into the furnace of fire : there shall be wailing and gnashing of teeth. *(No church will be perfect here; the unmixed church is above.)* Jesus saith unto them, Have ye understood all these things? They say unto him, Yea, Lord. Then said he unto them, Therefore every scribe *which is* instructed unto the kingdom of heaven is like unto a man *that is* an householder, which bringeth forth out of his treasure *things* new and old.

53 ¶ And it came to pass, *that* when Jesus had finished these parables, he departed thence.

54—56 And when he was come into his own country, he taught them in their synagogue, insomuch that they were astonished, and said, Whence hath this *man* this wisdom, and *these* mighty works? Is not this the carpenter's son? is not his mother called Mary? and his brethren, James, and Joses, and Simon, and Judas? and his sisters, are they not all with us? Whence then hath this *man* all these things?

57 And they were offended in him. But Jesus said unto them, A prophet is not without honour, save in his own country, and in his own house. *(Foolish people live in all ages. They like things with hard names, which come from great distances; they would despise gold itself if they could dig it up in their own garden. Such folly led the people of Nazareth to do the Lord a great injustice, and to rob themselves of many priceless blessings; and if we allow prejudice or fancy to rule our judgments we may fall into like errors.)*

58 And he did not many mighty works there because of their unbelief. *(Unbelief ties the hands of the incarnate God. It is to be feared that the reason of the slow progress of true religion, at this time, is to be found in the unbelief of the people of God.)*

The volume of my Father's grace
Does all my griefs assuage;
Here I behold my Saviour's face
Almost in every page.

This is the field where hidden lies
The pearl of price unknown;
That merchant is divinely wise
Who makes that pearl his own.

MATTHEW VIII. 18—22.

NOW when Jesus saw great multitudes about him, he gave commandment to depart unto the other side. *(He avoided popularity. To be followed by an admiring crowd was no joy to him; he gave orders to sail at once, but did not start for some time afterwards.)*

19 And a certain scribe came, and said unto him, Master, *(or teacher,)* I will follow thee whithersoever thou goest.

It was a rare thing to meet with a scribe who had any respect for the Lord, and it is to be feared that even this well-disposed member of that profession was not a spiritually enlightened person. He thought himself capable of making any sacrifice. It is the mark of those who have not the Spirit of God that they think themselves able to do everything, whereas when taught of God they discover that of themselves they can do nothing.

20 And Jesus saith unto him, The foxes have holes, and the birds of the air *have* nests; but the Son of man hath not where to lay *his* head.

Was the scribe willing to share such deep poverty? We fear not. Could we ourselves follow Jesus whithersoever he goeth?

> "Have ye counted the cost?
> Have ye counted the cost,
> Ye warriors of the cross?
> Are ye fixed in heart, for your Master's sake,
> To suffer all earthly loss?
> Can ye bear the scoff of the worldy-wise,
> As ye pass by pleasure's bower,
> To watch with your Lord on the mountain-top
> Through the dreary midnight hour?"

21, 22 And another of his disciples said unto him, Lord, suffer me first to go and bury my father. But Jesus said unto him, Follow me; and let the dead bury their dead.

Jesus saw that he was merely offering an excuse for delay. There are always people enough to attend to earthly business, and when the Lord calls us to do his work, we must leave all lower concerns to those whose proper calling it is to attend to them.

MARK IV. 35—41.

AND the same day, when the even was come, he saith unto them, Let us pass over unto the other side. And when they had sent away the multitude, they took him even as he was in the ship. *(They hurried him off, weary as he was, for the crowd increased. He was quite worn out with toil.)* And there were also with him other little ships.

37, 38 And there arose a great storm of wind, and the waves beat into the ship, so that it was now full. And he was in the hinder part of the ship, asleep on a pillow: and they awake him, and say unto him, Master, carest thou not that we perish? *(Jesus always cares for us. Even though he seems to sleep, and allows our troubles to multiply, all is well.)*

39 And he arose, and rebuked the wind, and said unto the sea, Peace, be still. And the wind ceased, and there was a great calm.

Who but God could speak thus? Where are the senses of those who cannot see his Godhead?

40 And he said unto them, Why are ye so fearful? how is it that ye have no faith?

41 And they feared exceedingly, and said one to another, What manner of man is this, that even the wind and the sea obey him?

Awe came over them, and well it might; they saw that no mere man could act as he had done. Jesus, Master, in all our troubles we will call upon thee, and thou wilt answer us! Our heart rejoices in thee, and sings:—

> "Away, despair; my gracious Lord doth hear!
> Though winds and waves assault my keel,
> He doth preserve it; he doth steer,
> Even when the boat seems most to reel.
> Storms are the triumph of his art;
> Well may he close his eyes, but not his heart."

Fear was within the tossing bark,
When stormy winds grew loud,
And waves came rolling high and dark,
And the tall mast was bowed.

And men stood breathless in their dread,
And baffled in their skill,
But one was there, who rose and said
To the wild sea, "Be still!"

And the wind ceased—it ceased: that word
Passed through the gloomy sky;
The troubled billows knew their Lord,
And fell beneath his eye.

And slumber settled on the deep,
And silence on the blast;
They sank, as flowers that fold to sleep,
When sultry day is past.

MARK V. 1—21.

AND they came over unto the other side of the sea, into the country of the Gadarenes. And when he was come out of the ship, immediately there met him out of the tombs a man with an unclean spirit, Who had *his* dwelling among the tombs; and no man could bind him, no, not with chains : Because that he had been often bound with fetters and chains, and the chains had been plucked asunder by him, and the fetters broken in pieces : neither could any *man* tame him, *(The evil spirit had made him wildly insane, and given him supernatural strength, so that he was a terror to the district over which he roamed, making night and day hideous with his terrible outcries.)*

5 And always, night and day, he was in the mountains, and in the tombs, crying, and cutting himself with stones.

6 But when he saw Jesus afar off, he ran and worshipped him. *(The evil spirit was compelled to crouch at the Redeemer's feet; this was a token of the casting of Satan beneath our feet which shall be accomplished shortly.)*

7, 8 And cried with a loud voice, and said, What have I to do with thee, Jesus, *thou* Son of the most high God ? I adjure thee by God, that thou torment me not. For he said unto him, Come out of the man, *thou* unclean spirit.

9 And he asked him, What *is* thy name ? And he answered, saying, My name *is* Legion : for we are many. *(It would seem as if all the fallen angels were let loose upon men at that time, so that many crowded into one poor creature: but our Lord was more than a match for them. A legion of soldiers numbered six thousand men ; how many devils there were within this poor man we cannot tell, but if there had been six millions Jesus could have conquered them.)*

10 And he besought him much that he would not send them away out of the country.
They cling to this world and dread to return to their prison house.

11 Now there was there nigh unto the mountains a great herd of swine feeding.

12 And all the devils besought him, saying, Send us into the swine, that we may enter into them. *(They had sooner plague poor swine than have no ill work on hand.)*

13 And forthwith Jesus gave them leave. And the unclean spirits went out, and entered into the swine : and the herd ran violently down a steep place into the sea, (they were about two thousand ;) and were choked in the sea.
A most just judgment upon their owners, who, as Jews, had no right to keep unclean animals.

14 And they that fed the swine fled, and told *it* in the city, and in the country. And they went out to see what it was that was done.

15 And they come to Jesus, and see him that was possessed with the devil, and had the legion, sitting, and clothed, and in his right mind : and they were afraid.

16, 17 And they that saw *it* told them how it befel to him that was possessed with the devil, and *also* concerning the swine. And they began to pray him to depart out of their coasts. *(What folly ! Yet many do this. They had rather not be impressed by the gospel, and therefore politely request it to go elsewhere. It will be an evil day for them if Jesus grants their request, and leaves them for ever to themselves.)*

18 And when he was come into the ship, he that had been possessed with the devil prayed him that he might be with him.

19 Howbeit Jesus suffered him not, but saith unto him, Go home to thy friends, and tell them how great things the Lord hath done for thee, and hath had compassion on thee.
Here was happy, holy, useful work for him. Such a task as Jesus has allotted to each of us.

20 And he departed, and began to publish in Decapolis how great things Jesus had done for him : and all *men* did marvel.

21 And when Jesus was passed over again by ship unto the other side, much people gathered unto him : and he was nigh unto the sea.

The powers of hell agree
To hold our souls in vain ;
He sets the sons of bondage free,
And breaks the cursed chain.

Th' Almighty king of saints
Our tyrant lusts subdues,
Expels the demons from our minds,
And all our soul renews.

For our own cheerful voice
Shall loud hosannas raise ;
Our hearts shall glow with gratitude,
Our lips proclaim his praise.

526   " If I may touch but His clothes, I shall be whole."   SEPTEMBER 2.—EVENING.

[*Or May* 4.]

MARK V. 22—43.

AND, behold, there cometh one of the rulers of the synagogue, Jairus by name ; and when he saw him, he fell at his feet, And besought him greatly, saying, My little daughter lieth at the point of death : *I pray thee,* come and lay thy hands on her, that she may be healed ; and she shall live. *(She was his only daughter, and therefore very dear. Her father's faith was of the boldest kind, for he hoped to see her raised up even though at her last gasp ; but it was not equal to that of the centurion who thought that Jesus could cure by a word without coming near.)*

24 And *Jesus* went with him ; and much people followed him, and thronged him.

25—28 And a certain woman, which had an issue of blood twelve years, And had suffered many things of many physicians, and had spent all that she had, and was nothing bettered, but rather grew worse, When she had heard of Jesus, came in the press behind, and touched his garment. For she said, If I may touch but his clothes, I shall be whole. *(Contact with Jesus is life, the touch of faith conveys healing virtue to the soul. Her disease rendered her timid, so that she came behind, and stole the cure ; and yet her faith was unusually strong,—many believed that Jesus could heal with a word, she alone believed that the very hem of his garment had healing power in it.)*

29 And straightway the fountain of her blood was dried up ; and she felt in *her* body that she was healed of that plague.

30—32 And Jesus, immediately knowing in himself that virtue had gone out of him, turned him about in the press, and said, Who touched my clothes ? And his disciples said unto him, Thou seest the multitude thronging thee, and sayest thou, Who touched me ? And he looked round about to see her that had done this thing.

33 But the woman fearing and trembling, knowing what was done in her, came and fell down before him, and told him all the truth. *This was for her benefit. She might else have gone away believing that there was a power resident in Christ's dress irrespective of his will ; the Lord by showing that he knew what was done gave her clearer views of himself.*

34 And he said unto her, Daughter, thy faith hath made thee whole ; go in peace, and be whole of thy plague.

35 While he yet spake, there came from the ruler of the synagogue's *house certain* which said, Thy daughter is dead : why troublest thou the Master any further ?

36 As soon as Jesus heard the word that was spoken, he saith unto the ruler of the synagogue, Be not afraid, only believe.

37, 38 And he suffered no man to follow him, save Peter, and James, and John the brother of James. And he cometh to the house of the ruler of the synagogue, and seeth the tumult, and them that wept and wailed greatly. *These were hired mourners who mimicked sorrow, and made loud lamentations.*

39 And when he was come in, he saith unto them, Why make ye this ado, and weep ? the damsel is not dead, but sleepeth.

40 And they laughed him to scorn. *(Being quite sure that she was dead. Thus they became the best witnesses that there was no deception in her restoration to life.)* But when he had put them all out, he taketh the father and the mother of the damsel, and them that were with him, and entereth in where the damsel was lying.

41 And he took the damsel by the hand, and said unto her, Talitha cumi ; which is, being interpreted, Damsel, I say unto thee, arise.

42 And straightway the damsel arose, and walked ; for she was *of the age* of twelve years. And they were astonished with a great astonishment. *(Oh that Jesus in the power of his Spirit would go to the houses of his people, and raise all the spiritually dead. There are dear little maids whom we much love who have not the new life within them ; we will pray for them, and hope that the word of the gospel will save them.)*

43 And he charged them straitly that no man should know it ; and commanded that something should be given her to eat. *When we see young people converted, we should try to feed them with those truths which are intended to support and comfort their hearts.*

In secret fear she came behind
     And healing virtue stole,
But Jesus spake a loving word,
     " Thy faith hath made thee whole."

Like her, with hopes and fears I come
     To touch thee if I may,
Oh ! do not on thy servant frown,
     But send me healed away.

MATTHEW IX. 27—33; 35—38.

AND when Jesus departed thence, two blind men followed him, crying, and saying, *Thou* son of David, have mercy on us.

Dr. Adam Clarke has well said, "That man has already a measure of heavenly light who knows that he has no merit; that his cry *should be a cry for* mercy; *that he must be* fervent, *and that, in praying, he must* follow *Jesus Christ as the true Messiah—the* son of David *expected from heaven."*

28 And when he was come into the house, the blind men came to him : and Jesus saith unto them, Believe ye that I am able to do this? They said unto him, Yea, Lord.

29, 30 Then touched he their eyes, saying, According to your faith be it unto you. And their eyes were opened; and Jesus straitly charged them, saying, See *that* no man know *it.*

31 But they, when they were departed, spread abroad his fame in all that country.

They had been earnestly bidden not to do so, and therefore they were blameworthy. Our case is exactly the reverse, for if we do not *bear testimony to the power of divine grace in our souls we shall be greatly guilty.*

32 ¶ As they went out, behold, they brought to him a dumb man possessed with a devil.

33 And when the devil was cast out, the dumb spake : and the multitudes marvelled, saying, It was never so seen in Israel.

35 And Jesus went about all the cities and villages, teaching in their synagogues, and preaching the gospel of the kingdom, and healing every sickness and every disease among the people. *(Diligent effort to do good was our Lord's best reply to carping enemies. Imitate him.)*

36 ¶ But when he saw the multitudes, he was moved with compassion on them, because they fainted, and were scattered abroad, as sheep having no shepherd.

37, 38 Then saith he unto his disciples, The harvest truly *is* plenteous, but the labourers *are* few; pray ye therefore the Lord of the harvest, that he will send forth labourers into his harvest. *(A prayer very seldom offered, and therefore real labourers for God are so few. It ought to be our daily petition. Our Lord used the fit means to answer his own prayer.)*

MATTHEW X. 1—15.

AND when he had called unto *him* his twelve disciples, he gave them power *against* unclean spirits, to cast them out, and to heal all manner of sickness and all manner of disease. Now the names of the twelve apostles are these; The first, Simon, who is called Peter, and Andrew his brother; James *the son* of Zebedee, and John his brother; Philip, and Bartholomew; Thomas, and Matthew the publican; James *the son* of Alphæus, and Lebbæus, whose surname was Thaddæus; Simon the Canaanite, and Judas Iscariot, who also betrayed him.

5—7 These twelve Jesus sent forth, and commanded them, saying, Go not into the way of the Gentiles, and into *any* city of the Samaritans enter ye not : But go rather to the lost sheep of the house of Israel. And as ye go, preach, saying, The kingdom of heaven is at hand.

8—10 Heal the sick, cleanse the lepers, raise the dead, cast out devils : freely ye have received, freely give. Provide neither gold, nor silver, nor brass in your purses, Nor scrip for *your* journey, neither two coats, neither shoes nor yet staves : for the workman is worthy of his meat.

They were not to provide for themselves, others supply their needs. God's servants are to be supported by those among whom they labour.

11—13 And into whatsoever city or town ye shall enter, enquire who in it is worthy; and there abide till ye go thence. And when ye come into an house, salute it. And if the house be worthy, let your peace come upon it : but if it be not worthy, let your peace return to you.

14 And whosoever shall not receive you, nor hear your words, when ye depart out of that house or city, shake off the dust of your feet.

15 Verily I say unto you, It shall be more tolerable for the land of Sodom and Gomorrha in the day of judgment, than for that city.

So doth the Lord set most solemn sanctions upon the preaching of the gospel, that none may dare to despise it. Have we received the glad tidings, or shall we die in our sins? These questions need to be pressed home, and answered prayerfully.

528   "Fear not them which kill the body."   SEPTEMBER 3.—EVENING.

[Or May 6.]

WE *will continue reading our Lord's address to those whom he sent forth to preach the gospel.*

MATTHEW X. 16—39.

16 Behold, I send you forth as sheep in the midst of wolves : be ye therefore wise as serpents, and harmless as doves. *(Peculiar qualities are needed for a life involving undeserved suffering. We need the prudence which prevents others from wronging us, as well as the gentleness which does no wrong to others.)*

17, 18 But beware of men : for they will deliver you up to the councils, and they will scourge you in their synagogues ; And ye shall be brought before governors and kings for my sake, for a testimony against them and the Gentiles.

19, 20 But when they deliver you up, take no thought how or what ye shall speak : for it shall be given you in that same hour what ye shall speak. For it is not ye that speak, but the Spirit of your Father which speaketh in you. *Though ignorant of this world's wisdom they were not to be anxious as to how they should reply to their learned accusers : the gospel is its own defence, and the Spirit the best pleader.*

21, 22 And the brother shall deliver up the brother to death, and the father the child : and the children shall rise up against *their* parents, and cause them to be put to death. And ye shall be hated of all *men* for my name's sake : but he that endureth to the end shall be saved.

23 But when they persecute you in this city, flee ye into another : for verily I say unto you, Ye shall not have gone over the cities of Israel, till the Son of man be come.

24, 25 The disciple is not above *his* master, nor the servant above his lord. It is enough for the disciple that he be as his master, and the servant as his lord. If they have called the master of the house Beelzebub, how much more *shall they call* them of his household ?

26 Fear them not therefore : for there is nothing covered, that shall not be revealed ; and hid, that shall not be known.

27 What I tell you in darkness, *that* speak ye in light : and what ye hear in the ear, *that* preach ye upon the housetops. *(Our business is to publish the gospel, whether we suffer for it or not. To suppress our testimony would be deadly sin.)*

28 And fear not them which kill the body, but are not able to kill the soul : but rather fear him which is able to destroy both soul and body in hell.

29—31 Are not two sparrows sold for a farthing ? and one of them shall not fall on the ground without your Father. But the very hairs of your head are all numbered. Fear ye not therefore, ye are of more value than many sparrows. *(The care of our heavenly Father is so minute that we ought to dismiss for ever all our fears. If he takes care of us even down to the hairs of our head, we are secure indeed.)*

32, 33 Whosoever therefore shall confess me before men, him will I confess also before my Father which is in heaven. But whosoever shall deny me before men, him will I also deny before my Father which is in heaven.

34—36 Think not that I am come to send peace on earth : I came not to send peace, but a sword. For I am come to set a man at variance against his father, and the daughter against her mother, and the daughter in law against her mother in law. And a man's foes *shall be* they of his own household. *(The ultimate end of the gospel will be peace, but before it reaches that there must be a struggle. Carnal men will oppose the truth, and hence a warfare will arise.)*

37, 38 He that loveth father or mother more than me is not worthy of me : and he that loveth son or daughter more than me is not worthy of me. And he that taketh not his cross, and followeth after me, is not worthy of me.

39 He that findeth his life shall lose it : and he that loseth his life for my sake shall find it. *Some have refused to burn at the stake, and have been burned in their own beds ; and many more have dreaded the pains of persecution, and so have plunged into the flames of hell by apostacy.*

Should persecution rage and flame,
Still trust in thy Redeemer's name ;
In fiery trials thou shalt see
That, "as thy days, thy strength shall be."

When call'd to bear the weighty cross,
Of sore affliction, pain, or loss,
Or deep distress, or poverty,
Still, "as thy days, thy strength shall be."

THE *stir made by the mission of the twelve reached all classes of society.*

MARK VI. 14—29.

14 And king Herod heard *of him ;* (for his name was spread abroad :) and he said, That John the Baptist was risen from the dead, and therefore mighty works do shew forth themselves in him. *(Where there is an idle faith there is generally a busy imagination: Herod would not obey John's religion, and yet became the slave of superstition. His conscience was not powerful enough to prevent his murdering the good man, yet it was not so dead as to allow him to rest in peace after the cruel deed.)*

15 Others said That it is Elias. And others said, That it is a prophet, or as one of the prophets.

16, 17 But when Herod heard *thereof,* he said, It is John, whom I beheaded : he is risen from the dead. For Herod himself had sent forth and laid hold upon John, and bound him in prison for Herodias' sake, his brother Philip's wife : for he had married her.

18 For John had said unto Herod, It is not lawful for thee to have thy brother's wife. *This was faithful preaching. What is the good of a minister if he does not tell us our faults?*

19, 20 Therefore Herodias had a quarrel against him, and would have killed him ; but she could not; For Herod feared John, knowing that he was a just man and an holy, and observed him; and when he heard him, he did many things, and heard him gladly. *(Herod is a warning to us. He was not a mere hearer of John. He was an attentive and delighted hearer, and up to a certain point a doer of the word. Surely he bade fair for good things ; and yet he became the murderer of the very man to whom he had listened with so much respect. If hearing the gospel does not change our nature, it has done little or nothing for us.)*

21, 22 And when a convenient day was come, that Herod on his birthday made a supper to his lords, high captains, and chief *estates* of Galilee ; And when the daughter of the said Herodias came in, and danced, and pleased Herod and them that sat with him, the king said unto the damsel, Ask of me whatsoever thou wilt, and I will give *it* thee.

23 And he sware unto her, Whatsoever thou shalt ask of me, I will give *it* thee, unto the half of my kingdom. *(Probably he had become drunken while feasting, and so uttered the rash promise and confirmed it with an oath. When vice dances in the presence of drunkenness no good can come of it. This young girl danced off the prophet's head: we have never read that any good at all proportionate to this evil ever came of dancing. For a child of God to join with the frivolous in their idle dances, would be as unbecoming as for an angel to wallow in the mire.)*

24 And she went forth, and said unto her mother, What shall I ask ? And she said, The head of John the Baptist.

25 And she came in straightway with haste unto the king, and asked, saying, I will that thou give me by and by in a charger *(or a large dish)* the head of John the Baptist.

26 And the king was exceeding sorry ; yet for his oath's sake, and for their sakes which sat with him, he would not reject her.

27, 28 And immediately the king sent an executioner, and commanded his head to be brought : and he went and beheaded him in the prison, And brought his head in a charger, and gave it to the damsel : and the damsel gave it to her mother.

29 And when his disciples heard *of it,* they came and took up his corpse, and laid it in a tomb. *(Or as another evangelist tells us, " they went and told Jesus," which was the very best thing they could do. Happy are they who have learned to take all their trials to Jesus. Let us speak with him now in our prayer.)*

Come, my soul, thy suit prepare,
Jesus loves to answer prayer ;
He himself has bid thee pray,
Therefore will not say thee nay.

With my burden I begin,
Lord, remove this load of sin ;
Let thy blood, for sinners spilt,
Set my conscience free from guilt.

Lord, I cast on thee my care,
Thou hast bid me leave it there ;
For my heavenly Father knows
All my griefs, and wants, and woes.

MARK VI. 30—44.

AND the apostles gathered themselves together unto Jesus, and told him all things, both what they had done, and what they had taught. *(Ministers are accountable to their Lord both for their doings and sayings, and they should neither do nor teach anything which they will be ashamed to relate to their Master.)*

31, 32 And he said unto them, Come ye yourselves apart into a desert place, and rest a while : for there were many coming and going, and they had no leisure so much as to eat. And they departed into a desert place by ship privately.

The most active servants of God cannot always have their minds upon the stretch ; they must have relaxation. Their tender Master was careful to provide it for the apostles, and those who are of a kindred spirit should enable poor ministers at set times to enjoy a little needful retirement. Jesus took his apostles to a place where they could be alone, for rest in a crowd is not the rest ministers need.

33 And the people saw them departing, and many knew him, and ran afoot thither out of all cities, and outwent them, and came together unto him. *(No bell was wanted to call them together. The spirit of hearing was abroad, and the people flocked like doves to their windows, and this all the more eagerly because the preacher was going away. If we knew how soon good ministers will be called home to heaven, we should be far more eager to profit by them while they are spared to us.)*

34 And Jesus, when he came out, saw much people, and was moved with compassion toward them, because they were as sheep not having a shepherd : and he began to teach them many things. *(He was not angry at losing his rest, but ready to bless the people, for he saw their need.)*

35, 36 And when the day was now far spent, his disciples came unto him, and said, This is a desert place, and now the time is far passed : Send them away, that they may go into the country round about, and into the villages, and buy themselves bread : for they have nothing to eat. *(This is the disciples' way out of the difficulty. No doubt they can take care of themselves :—"send them away." We hope something may be done for the masses, and there we leave it.)*

37 He answered and said unto them, Give ye them to eat. *(Meet their wants yourselves. Alas! the command sounds very hard when the exchequer is low!)* And they say unto him, Shall we go and buy two hundred pennyworth of bread, and give them to eat ? *(They calculate the need, but forget the omnipotence which is at hand to meet it.)*

38 He saith unto them, How many loaves have ye? go and see. And when they knew, they say, Five, and two fishes.

39 And he commanded them to make all sit down by companies upon the green grass.

The Lord had thus provided a noble banqueting hall, splendidly carpeted, and of vast dimensions, and there his guests sat in order, as became a royal entertainment.

40 And they sat down in ranks, by hundreds, and by fifties. *(For it was not a scramble, but a royal feast.)*

41 And when he had taken the five loaves and the two fishes, he looked up to heaven, and blessed, and brake the loaves, and gave *them* to his disciples to set before them ; and the two fishes divided he among them all.

42 And they did all eat, and were filled.

43 And they took up twelve baskets full of the fragments, and of the fishes.

44 And they that did eat of the loaves were about five thousand men.

When Jesus blesses our slender gifts, he makes them sufficient for the feeding of thousands. It is ours to do our best, and trust in the Lord to make it useful. Lord, help us so to do.

Thy providence is kind and large,
Both man and beast thy bounty share ;
The whole creation is thy charge,
But saints are thy peculiar care.

My God! how excellent thy grace,
Whence all our hope and comfort springs ;
The sons of Adam, in distress,
Fly to the shadow of thy wings.

Ye servants of God, your Master proclaim,
And publish abroad his wonderful name ;
The name all-victorious of Jesus extol ;
His kingdom is glorious, and rules over all.

Salvation to God, who sits on the throne,
Let all cry aloud, and honour the Son ;
The praises of Jesus the angels proclaim,
Fall down on their faces and worship the Lamb.

JOHN VI. 14—17.

THEN those men, when they had seen the miracle that Jesus did, said, This is of a truth that prophet that should come into the world. When Jesus therefore perceived that they would come and take him by force, to make him a king, he departed again into a mountain himself alone. *(He again put away the crown of temporal sovereignty, just as he had done when the devil tempted him in the wilderness.)*

16 And when even was *now* come, his disciples went down unto the sea,

17 And entered into a ship, and went over the sea toward Capernaum.

MATTHEW XIV. 24—33.

BUT the ship was now in the midst of the sea, tossed with waves : for the wind was contrary. *(Their sails could not help them, and they made so little headway that by midnight they were only in the middle of the lake.)*

25 And in the fourth watch of the night *(when the morning was drawing near)* Jesus went unto them, walking on the sea. *(Trench has beautifully said: " In the first storm (Matthew viii. 24) he was present in the ship with them ; and thus they must have felt all along that, if it came to the worst, they might rouse him ; while the mere sense of his presence must have given them the sense of a comparative security. But he will not have them to be clinging only to the sense of his bodily presence ; they must not be as ivy, needing always an outward support, but as hardy forest trees, which can brave a blast ; and this time he puts them forth into the danger alone, even as some loving mother-bird thrusts her fledglings from the nest, that they may find their own wings and learn to use them. And by the issue he will awaken in them a confidence in his ever-ready help ; for as his walking on the sea must have been altogether unimagined by them, they may have easily despaired of that help reaching them, and yet it does not fail them. When he has tried them to the uttermost, " in the fourth watch of the night," he appears beside them, thus teaching them for all their after life, in all coming storms of temptation, that he is near them ; that, however he may not be seen always by their bodily eyes, and however they may seem cut off from his*

assistance, yet is he indeed a very present help in time of trouble.")

26 And when the disciples saw him walking on the sea, they were troubled, saying, It is a spirit ; and they cried out for fear.

27, 28 But straightway Jesus spake unto them, saying, Be of good cheer ; it is I ; be not afraid. And Peter answered him and said, Lord, if it be thou, bid me come unto thee on the water.

29 And he said, Come. *(He gave him permission.)* And when Peter was come down out of the ship, he walked on the water, to go to Jesus. *(How remarkable his sensations! How joyful and yet how trembling, must Peter have been ! What wonders his faith performed!)*

30 But when he saw the wind boisterous, he was afraid ; and beginning to sink, he cried, saying, Lord, save me. *(Where he had half hoped to be distinguished for superior courage he reveals his timidity, and is humbled thereby. Unbelief alone made him sink, he removed his eye from his Lord to the billows. Have we not acted in a similar manner more than once?)*

31 And immediately Jesus stretched forth *his* hand, and caught him, and said unto him, O thou of little faith, wherefore didst thou doubt ? *(Saving him first, and then gently chiding him. If he spoke thus to Peter, what would he say to some of us who are far more unbelieving?)*

32, 33 And when they were come into the ship, the wind ceased. Then they that were in the ship came and worshipped him, saying, Of a truth thou art the Son of God. *(His Godhead was clear to them, and they adored him.)*

" If it be thou "—oh ! bid me come,
  Dark though the waters be ;
I will not fear, if thou art near,
  And bid'st me come to thee.

" If it be thou," the storm may swell
  Obedient to thy will ;
For thou canst all its fury quell,
  And bid its waves " Be still."

" If it be thou !" Oh yes, it is !
  My Saviour's voice I hear,
He tells my soul that I am his,
  And he is ever near.

532   " **Lord, ebermore gibe us this bread.** "   SEPTEMBER 5.—EVENING.

[*Or May* 10.]

T HOSE *who followed Jesus with a wrong motive soon found that he did not care for their company, and was gone from them, they knew not how. If we attend places of worship with worldly motives, we shall one day find out as these people did, that "Jesus was not there."*

JOHN VI. 22—34.

22 The day following, when the people which stood on the other side of the sea saw that there was none other boat there, save that one whereinto his disciples were entered, and that Jesus went not with his disciples into the boat, but *that* his disciples were gone away alone ;

23 (Howbeit there came other boats from Tiberias nigh unto the place where they did eat bread, after that the Lord had given thanks :)

John is particular in noticing our Lord's thanksgiving ; spiritual minds remark and remember most the spiritual parts of any action. The Jews noticed the bread and the fish, but the beloved disciple was most pleased with the giving of thanks. Oh for a spiritual eye !

24 When the people therefore saw that Jesus was not there, neither his disciples, they also took shipping, and came to Capernaum, seeking for Jesus.

25 And when they had found him on the other side of the sea, they said unto him, Rabbi, when camest thou hither ? *(Here was much zeal and outward respect, but it was blind and selfish, and therefore the Lord set no store by it.)*

26 Jesus answered them and said, Verily, verily, I say unto you, Ye seek me, not because ye saw the miracles, but because ye did eat of the loaves, and were filled.

With an unerring glance he read their hearts. They fancied that they were fond of him and his kingdom ; he knew that far grosser affections ruled them ; this he told them plainly to their faces, and bade them seek more noble objects.

27 Labour not for the meat which perisheth, but for that meat which endureth unto everlasting life, which the Son of man shall give unto you : for him hath God the Father sealed.

28 Then said they unto him, What shall we do, that we might work the works of God ?

29 Jesus answered and said unto them, This is the work of God, that ye believe on him whom he hath sent. *(The most godlike work,*

the greatest, and most acceptable, is that we believe in Jesus. Faith is, after all, the noblest of works, and none have it but those in whom God himself has placed it.)

30 They said therefore unto him, What sign shewest thou then, that we may see, and believe thee ? what dost thou work ?

31 Our fathers did eat manna in the desert ; as it is written, He gave them bread from heaven to eat. *(They wanted feeding again, and thought that by such talk they would induce the Lord to make them another banquet. They spoke of bread from heaven, little caring where it came from, so long as they might but be filled with it. It is wonderful that Jesus had patience to listen to their greedy and crafty insinuations.)*

32 Then Jesus said unto them, Verily, verily, I say unto you, Moses gave you not that bread from heaven ; but my Father giveth you the true bread from heaven.

33 For the bread of God is he which cometh down from heaven, and giveth life unto the world.

34 Then said they unto him, Lord, evermore give us this bread. *(Some thus prayed in honest ignorance, expecting to have food for nothing from his hand every day ; but others merely said this in taunt, deridingly setting it before the Lord as the test of his Messiahship that he should give them bread all their lives. Yet they have, unwittingly, furnished us with a petition which we may hourly use ; it is full of meaning, and exactly expresses our need and our desire. Let us carry it with us all this day as our heart's wish and prayer—"Lord, evermore give us this bread.")*

Oh ! labour ye not for perishing meat ;
For Jesus hath brought his body to eat ;
Himself the true leaven, the life-giving bread,
He came down from heaven to quicken the dead.

To hearts unrenew'd 'tis hard to believe
His body for food how Jesus can give ;
But he who partaketh doth inwardly feed,
And knows that it maketh a banquet indeed !

JOHN VI. 35—50.

AND Jesus said unto them, I am the bread of life : he that cometh to me shall never hunger ; and he that believeth on me shall never thirst. (*Here he spake plainly, and made his meaning clear to all who wished to understand it. Faith feeds on Jesus and satisfies the soul.*)

36 But I said unto you, That ye also have seen me, and believe not.

37 All that the Father giveth me shall come to me ; and him that cometh to me I will in no wise cast out. (*Their unbelief was proof that they were not his ; but though they rejected him, others would come to him, so that he would not be left without followers. Moreover, all who came to him believingly he would receive, whoever they might be. This text is as full of consolation as a honeycomb is full of sweetness.*)

38 For I came down from heaven, not to do mine own will, but the will of him that sent me.

39 And this is the Father's will which hath sent me, that of all which he hath given me I should lose nothing, but should raise it up again at the last day.

40 And this is the will of him that sent me, that every one which seeth the Son, and believeth on him, may have everlasting life : and I will raise him up at the last day. (*Some are very much taken up with the decrees of God ; here is one which they will do well always to bear in mind—every believer has everlasting life. No secret decree can contradict this published ordinance of heaven.*)

41, 42 The Jews then murmured at him, because he said, I am the bread which came down from heaven. And they said, Is not this Jesus, the son of Joseph, whose father and mother we know ? how is it then that he saith, I came down from heaven ?

43 Jesus therefore answered and said unto them, Murmur not among yourselves.

44 No man can come to me, except the Father which hath sent me draw him : and I will raise him up at the last day.

45 It is written in the prophets, And they shall be all taught of God. Every man therefore that hath heard, and hath learned of the Father, cometh unto me. (*They needed not to excite themselves and grow angry, for his preaching did not concern them ; they had neither part nor lot in the matter. If they had been his own elect, they would have believed, but their wicked unbelief was sufficient evidence that the bread he came to give was not of the kind which they cared for, and that they were not the people for whom it was provided.*)

46 Not that any man hath seen the Father, save he which is of God, he hath seen the Father.

47 Verily, verily, I say unto you, He that believeth on me hath everlasting life.

This plain and unlimited statement from the mouth of Jesus himself ought greatly to encourage and comfort all who believe. Do you trust alone in him ? Then you have life, life which can never die, life which will be fully developed in eternal happiness. Do you not feel that you have everlasting life ? Nevertheless, if you are trusting in Jesus, the fact is sure, and you are certainly in possession of it. Whatever your feelings may be, Jesus knows what he says, and his witness is true. Believe it because he says so. What better witness can you require ?

48 I am that bread of life. (*The real bread, the soul bread, the bread of immortality. Jesus is that to all who trust him.*)

49 Your fathers did eat manna in the wilderness, and are dead.

50 This is the bread which cometh down from heaven, that a man may eat thereof, and not die. (*They only ate bread for the body, and the body died. Jesus gives soul bread, and he who eats of it lives in joy for ever. Have all in this household trusted Jesus ? Are we all feeding upon him ? If not, may the Lord work faith in us at this very moment.*)

Not to myself I owe
That I, O Lord, am thine;
Free grace hath all the shades broke through,
And caused the light to shine.

Me thou hast willing made
Thy offers to receive ;
Call'd by the voice that wakes the dead,
I come to thee and live.

Because thy sovereign love
Was bent the worst to save ;
Jesus who reigns enthroned above,
To me salvation gave.

OUR *Lord continued his address upon the bread of life and openly declared—*

JOHN VI. 51—64; 66—71.

51, 52 I am the living bread which came down from heaven : if any man eat of this bread he shall live for ever: and the bread that I will give is my flesh, which I will give for the life of the world. The Jews therefore strove among themselves, saying, How can this man give us *his* flesh to eat? *(They understood him literally, just as Papists do now. They were too carnally minded to comprehend that the soul feeds upon the great truth that God took upon himself our flesh.)*

53 Then Jesus said unto them, Verily, verily, I say unto you, Except ye eat the flesh of the Son of man, and drink his blood, ye have no life in you. *(He did not refer to the Lord's Supper, for it was not instituted, neither is it absolutely essential to salvation : the dying thief received no sacrament, yet was he with his Lord in Paradise so soon as he expired. The eating and drinking are spiritual, and only regenerated persons can have part in them. How searching, then, is this word of Jesus, for multitudes of professors have no personal experience of such feeding as our Lord intended.)*

54, 55 Whoso eateth my flesh, and drinketh my blood, hath eternal life ; and I will raise him up at the last day. For my flesh is meat indeed, and my blood is drink indeed.

56 He that eateth my flesh, and drinketh my blood, dwelleth in me, and I in him.

Participation in the person and work of Jesus leads to an abiding union with him, and to near and dear communion with him.

57 As the living Father hath sent me, and I live by the Father : so he that eateth me, even he shall live by me.

This truth cannot too often be repeated— eternal life can only be ours as we embrace by faith the incarnate God, and make him the life of our soul.

58 This is that bread which came down from heaven : not as your fathers did eat manna, and are dead : he that eateth of this bread shall live for ever.

59 These things said he in the synagogue, as he taught in Capernaum.

60 Many therefore of his disciples, when they had heard *this*, said, This is an hard saying ; who can hear it ? *(Carnal minds first misread the Lord's words, and then kick against them. None but those enlightened by the Spirit of God will see the beauty of the mystery of faith; others will, by-and-by, cavil and be gone.)*

61 When Jesus knew in himself that his disciples murmured at it, he said unto them, Doth this offend you ?

62 *What* and if ye shall see the Son of man ascend up where he was before ?

63 It is the spirit that quickeneth ; the flesh profiteth nothing : the words that I speak unto you, *they* are spirit, and *they* are life.

64 But there are some of you that believe not. For Jesus knew from the beginning who they were that believed not, and who should betray him. *(He knew that to many the Spirit did not go with the word, and therefore it would only be to them 'a savour of death unto death : but in this he was by no means disappointed, he foresaw that it would be so.)*

66 ¶ From that *time* many of his disciples went back, and walked no more with him.

67, 68 Then said Jesus unto the twelve, Will ye also go away ? Then Simon Peter answered him, Lord, to whom shall we go ? thou hast the words of eternal life.

69 And we believe and are sure that thou art that Christ, the Son of the living God.

70 Jesus answered them, Have not I chosen you twelve, and one of you is a devil ?

71 He spake of Judas Iscariot *the son* of Simon : for he it was that should betray him, being one of the twelve. *(The eternal purpose of God to save his chosen, works its way by sending forth the enlightening Spirit upon those ordained to life. These being quickened believe the gospel, and are thereby known to be the chosen of God. The rest do not receive the truth, and never will; by this, then, may each of us judge whether he has a part in electing love or no.)*

> Lord, the hunger of my soul
> Is for food which thou dost give ;
> Other appetite control,
> Teach me on thyself to live.
>
> Jesus, great incarnate God,
> Be thou ever dear to me,
> May thy precious flesh and blood
> Daily drink and manna be.

September 7.—Morning.

[*Or May* 13.]   "Set your heart and your soul to seek the Lord your God."

535

MARK VII. 1—23.

THEN came together unto him the Pharisees, and certain of the scribes, which came from Jerusalem. (*It was a sign of stormy weather when these ill birds came together.*)

2—4 And when they saw some of his disciples eat bread with defiled, that is to say, with unwashen, hands, they found fault. For the Pharisees, and all the Jews, except they wash *their* hands oft, eat not, holding the tradition of the elders. And *when they come* from the market, except they wash, they eat not. And many other things there be, which they have received to hold, *as* the washing of cups, and pots, brasen vessels, and of tables.

5 Then the Pharisees and scribes asked him, Why walk not thy disciples according to the tradition of the elders, but eat bread with unwashen hands?

6—8 He answered and said unto them, Well hath Esaias prophesied of you hypocrites, as it is written, This people honoureth me with *their* lips, but their heart is far from me. Howbeit in vain do they worship me, teaching *for* doctrines the commandments of men. For laying aside the commandment of God, ye hold the tradition of men, *as* the washing of pots and cups: and many other such like things ye do. (*These were the ancestors of our modern Ritualists, who are fast bound with idle forms and vain ceremonials, and make a great matter of the cut of a garment, or the colour of a robe.*)

9 And he said unto them, Full well ye reject the commandment of God, that ye may keep your own tradition. (*The keeping of human commands always leads to the neglect of the divine. Superstition strangles true religion.*)

10—13 For Moses said, Honour thy father and thy mother; and, Whoso curseth father or mother, let him die the death: but ye say, If a man shall say to his father or mother, *It is* Corban, that is to say, a gift, by whatsoever thou mightest be profited by me; *he shall be free.* And ye suffer him no more to do ought for his father or his mother; making the word of God of none effect through your tradition, which ye have delivered: and many such like things do ye. (*If an ungrateful son did not care to give his parents what they asked, he had only to say that he had made an offering of it,*

and he was free from all obligation to succour his parents. This was a forcible example of the way in which tradition made void the law of God; but many such might have been quoted, for the Rabbis openly exalted their precepts above the law of Moses. In their Talmud we read, "The words of the scribes are more noble than the words of the law; for the words of the law are both hard and easy, but the words of the scribes are all easy to be understood.")*

14, 15 ¶ And when he had called all the people *unto him*, he said unto them, Hearken unto me every one *of you*, and understand: There is nothing from without a man, that entering into him can defile him: but the things which come out of him, those are they that defile the man. (*Godliness does not consist in meats or drinks, in feasting or fasting. No food, unless it be the means of gluttony or drunkenness, has a defiling effect. Tradition makes much of externals, the gospel makes very little.*)

16 If any man have ears to hear, let him hear.

17 And when he was entered into the house from the people, his disciples asked him concerning the parable.

18, 19 And he saith unto them, Are ye so without understanding also? Do ye not perceive, that whatsoever thing from without entereth into the man, *it* cannot defile him; because it entereth not into his heart, but into the belly, and goeth out into the draught, purging all meats?

20—23 And he said, That which cometh out of the man, that defileth the man. For from within, out of the heart of men, proceed evil thoughts, adulteries, fornications, murders, thefts, covetousness, wickedness, deceit, lasciviousness, an evil eye, blasphemy, pride, foolishness: all these evil things come from within, and defile the man. (*Thus did he set forth the true spiritual religion, wherein holy hearts are everything, and peculiar meats are nothing; obedient lives are acceptable, and rigid abstinences little worth. We do not need salt fish, but salt in ourselves; not unleavened cakes, but hearts free from malice and hypocrisy.*)

Not different food, nor different dress,
Compose the kingdom of our Lord;
But peace, and joy, and righteousness,
Faith, and obedience to his word.

MATTHEW XV. 21—28.

THEN Jesus went thence, and departed into the coasts of Tyre and Sidon.

Though he did not go out of Palestine, which was the sphere of his ministry, he took care to go to the very edge of it.

22 And, behold, a woman of Canaan came out of the same coasts, and cried unto him, saying, Have mercy on me, O Lord, *thou* son of David; my daughter is grievously vexed with a devil.

23 But he answered her not a word. And his disciples came and besought him, saying, Send her away; for she crieth after us.

His silence tried her faith, but did not conquer it; she pleaded still.

24 But he answered and said, I am not sent but unto the lost sheep of the house of Israel.

He seemed to deny her, and to give a reason for the denial; yet she would not be put off.

25 Then came she and worshipped him, saying, Lord, help me.

Short, urgent, and to the point was this petition. As we grow more earnest our words usually become fewer.

26 But he answered and said, It is not meet to take the children's bread, and to cast *it* to dogs. *(The miracles were for the Jews, the favoured children, and not for Gentile dogs.)*

27 And she said, Truth, Lord: yet the dogs eat of the crumbs which fall from their masters' table. *(As much as to say, the boon which I ask, though very great to me, is but as a crumb to thee. Favour me with a dog's portion, since thou hast called me a dog. She broke the hard bone of our Lord's apparently harsh speech, and speedily found marrow of comfort in it. Oh, blessed faith which will not be repulsed!)*

28 Then Jesus answered and said unto her, O woman, great *is* thy faith: be it unto thee even as thou wilt. And her daughter was made whole from that very hour.

MARK VII. 31—37.

AND again, departing from the coasts of Tyre and Sidon, he came unto the sea of Galilee, through the midst of the coasts of Decapolis.

32 And they bring unto him one that was deaf, and had an impediment in his speech; and they beseech him to put his hand upon him.

33 And he took him aside from the multitude, and put his fingers into his ears, and he spit, and touched his tongue;

34 And looking up to heaven, he sighed, and saith unto him, Ephphatha, that is, Be opened.

35 And straightway his ears were opened, and the string of his tongue was loosed, and he spake plain. *(This was an acted sermon suitable for a deaf and dumb man. He took him aside—for grace makes men feel their personality, and sets them as units before God; he put his fingers into his ears and touched his tongue to let him know where the evil lay, for we must know something of the disease, or we shall not value the remedy; he spit—for the means of grace are simple, and to some even disgusting; he looked up to heaven, for thence our help must come; he sighed, for he heals us by bearing our sorrows in his own person. The whole gospel is set forth in this deaf and dumb man's alphabet.)*

36 And he charged them that they should tell no man: but the more he charged them, so much the more a great deal they published *it;*

37 And were beyond measure astonished, saying, He hath done all things well: he maketh both the deaf to hear, and the dumb to speak. *(When a beggar is relieved at any door he tells others, and so many more come; thus the crowds around our Lord increased daily, but he was able to meet all their needs. Blessed be his name, he is still quite as able and willing to supply all our necessities. Let us tell him at this time all our wants and woes, and we too shall soon be astonished by his wonders of grace.)*

The men of a place where Jesus hath been,
Acknowledge his grace which saves them from sin,
To others discover the power of his word,
And all the land over they publish their Lord.

The cure we have found through faith in his name,
The country around we gladly proclaim,
The worst, if he pleases, to Christ may draw near,
Who heals our diseases, and hushes our fear.

To those that believe salvation is sure,
Come all and receive immediate cure.
Ye now may approach him, and calling him Lord,
The moment ye touch him your souls are restored.

MARK VIII. 1—9.

I N those days the multitude being very great, and having nothing to eat, Jesus called his disciples *unto him*, and saith unto them, I have compassion on the multitude, because they have now been with me three days, and have nothing to eat : And if I send them away fasting to their own houses, they will faint by the way : for divers of them came from far.

Some spiritual teachers think it beneath them to devise anything for the temporal good of their hearers, but our Lord was intensely human and humane. He could not look on hunger and faintness without pity.

4 And his disciples answered him, From whence can a man satisfy these *men* with bread here in the wilderness ?

5 And he asked them, How many loaves have ye ? And they said, Seven.

That is the question—How much ability have you ? To calculate how much agency would be necessary to evangelize the thousands, may be mere speculation : to resolve each one of us to do our own share of the work is sound sense.

6, 7 And he commanded the people to sit down on the ground : and he took the seven loaves, and gave thanks, and brake, and gave to his disciples to set before *them ;* and they did set *them* before the people. And they had a few small fishes : and he blessed, and commanded to set them also before *them.*

8 So they did eat, and were filled : and they took up of the broken *meat* that was left seven baskets. *(Those hands which multiplied the food were surely those of the world's Creator. Who can doubt the Godhead of Jesus ? Lord, prove thy Deity by making the labours of thy poor church to be a rich blessing to millions.)*

9 And they that had eaten were about four thousand.

MATTHEW XV. 39 : XVI. 1—12.

A ND he sent away the multitude, and took ship, and came into the coasts of Magdala.

1 The Pharisees also with the Sadducees came, and tempting desired him that he would shew them a sign from heaven.

How trying it must have been to his holy and ardent soul to be haunted by these spies ! Yet he

never *fell into their snares. His holy wisdom is an example for us. We too are watched.*

2 He answered and said unto them, When it is evening, ye say, It *will be* fair weather : for the sky is red.

3 And in the morning, It *will be* foul weather to day : for the sky is red and lowring. O *ye* hypocrites, ye can discern the face of the sky ; but can ye not *discern* the signs of the times ?

The signs of coming judgment were clear enough. None are so blind as those who will not see.

4 A wicked and adulterous generation seeketh after a sign ; and there shall no sign be given unto it, but the sign of the prophet Jonas. And he left them, and departed.

5 And when his disciples were come to the other side, they had forgotten to take bread.

6 Then Jesus said unto them, Take heed and beware of the leaven of the Pharisees and of the Sadducees. *(Meaning their sour, hypocritical, carping spirit, and erroneous teaching.)*

7 And they reasoned among themselves, saying, *It is* because we have taken no bread.

8 *Which* when Jesus perceived, he said unto them, O ye of little faith, why reason ye among yourselves, because ye have brought no bread ?

9 Do ye not yet understand, neither remember the five loaves of the five thousand, and how many baskets ye took up ?

10 Neither the seven loaves of the four thousand, and how many baskets ye took up ?

11 How is it that ye do not understand that I spake *it* not to you concerning bread, that ye should beware of the leaven of the Pharisees and of the Sadducees ?

12 Then understood they how that he bade *them* not beware of the leaven of bread, but of the doctrine of the Pharisees and of the Sadducees. *(What mere children the disciples were, yet Jesus bore with them very kindly, and so will he do with us.)*

Canst thou, then, without compassion,
Me thy faint disciple see,
Hungering after thy salvation,
Perishing for want of thee ?

Dying, till the grace is given,
Only for thy life I pine ;
Feed me, Lord, with bread from heaven.
Fill my soul with love divine.

MARK VIII. 22—38.

AND he cometh to Bethsaida; and they bring a blind man unto him, and besought him to touch him.

Our Lord was never long without a case of sickness or infirmity to deal with, and if we are wise we shall each one keep him well employed by taking our own infirmities and sins to him. One touch of that dear hand will make us whole.

23 And he took the blind man by the hand and led him out of the town; and when he had spit on his eyes, and put his hands upon him, he asked him if he saw ought.

24 And he looked up, and said, I see men as trees, walking. *(He saw indistinctly, as some of us do now in spiritual things; but when our Lord begins a cure he makes a perfect work of it. Meanwhile it is a great mercy to see at all.)*

25 After that he put *his* hands again upon his eyes, and made him look up: and he was restored, and saw every man clearly.

26 And he sent him away to his house, saying, Neither go into the town, nor tell *it* to any in the town.

27 ¶ And Jesus went out, and his disciples, into the towns of Cæsarea Philippi: and by the way he asked his disciples, saying unto them, Whom do men say that I am?

28 And they answered, John the Baptist: but some *say*, Elias: and others, One of the prophets.

29 And he saith unto them, But whom say ye that I am? And Peter answereth and saith unto him, Thou art the Christ.

30 And he charged them that they should tell no man of him. *(Then he desired to avoid notoriety, and had wise reasons for commanding silence, but now we may publish his fame as much as we please; yea, the more we sound abroad his praises the better will he be pleased.)*

31, 32 And he began to teach them, that the Son of man must suffer many things, and be rejected of the elders, and *of* the chief priests, and scribes, and be killed, and after three days rise again. And he spake that saying openly. And Peter took him, and began to rebuke him.

In his great love he could not bear to hear his Lord talk of suffering even unto death; but still his affection did not excuse his gross presumption.

33 But when he had turned about and looked on his disciples, he rebuked Peter, saying, Get thee behind me, Satan *(or thou adversary)*: for thou savourest not the things that be of God, but the things that be of men.

It was great impudence on Peter's part to chide his Lord, nor could the Master endure that his servant should put a stumbling-block in his way by urging him to forego suffering and death. He counted even his best friend to be an adversary when he stood in the way of his work of love. Lord, thou wast angry with Peter because thou wast too fond of us to spare thyself.

34, 35 And when he had called the people unto *him* with his disciples also, he said unto them, Whosoever will come after me, let him deny himself, and take up his cross, and follow me. For whosoever will save his life shall lose it; but whosoever shall lose his life for my sake and the gospel's, the same shall save it.

Not only must Jesus make a sacrifice of himself, but the spirit of selfishness must be driven out of all who will be saved by him, and they also must be willing to die for the gospel's sake. Nor need they be ashamed to do so, for in the end he will prove to have acted wisely who gave up all earthly things to gain the heavenly treasure.

36 For what shall it profit a man, if he shall gain the whole world, and lose his own soul?

37 Or what shall a man give in exchange for his soul?

38 Whosoever therefore shall be ashamed of me and of my words in this adulterous and sinful generation; of him also shall the Son of man be ashamed, when he cometh in the glory of his Father with the holy angels.

Solemn words. Let us not go forth from this room till we have asked for grace, never to be ashamed of the name, people, doctrine, ordinances, or commands of Jesus.

Jesus! and shall it ever be?
A mortal man ashamed of thee!
Ashamed of thee, whom angels praise,
Whose glories shine through endless days.

Ashamed of Jesus! that dear Friend
On whom my hopes of heaven depend!
No; when I blush, be this my shame,
That I no more revere his name.

OUR *blessed Lord for the most part led a life of humiliation; but occasionally, lest men should altogether forget his divine nature, he drew aside the curtain, and revealed a measure of his majesty. This he did in a special manner upon the holy mount.*

MATTHEW XVII. 1—9.

1 And after six days Jesus taketh Peter, James, and John his brother, and bringeth them up into an high mountain apart, *(A quaint writer says our Lord took Peter because he loved Christ most, John because Christ loved him most, and James because, next to these, he loved and was loved most. The Lord knew the men whom he had chosen, and judged these three to be the fittest eye-witnesses of his glory.)*

2 And was transfigured before them: and his face did shine as the sun, and his raiment was white as the light. *(As a foretaste of the glory in which he will shine hereafter, he put on the robes of his excellency for a moment, and dazzled his disciples' eyes. How great was the condescension which kept him closely veiled while here below. Brighter than the sun is he, and yet he deigned to be despised and rejected of men.)*

3 And, behold, there appeared unto them Moses and Elias talking with him.

The law and the prophets are in harmony with Christ, and when we see the glory of Jesus we behold their light sweetly blending with his own.

4 Then answered Peter, and said unto Jesus, Lord, it is good for us to be here: if thou wilt, let us make here three tabernacles; one for thee, and one for Moses, and one for Elias.

Not knowing what he said, but feeling as we have often done, that we would gladly remain in sweet meditation and hallowed fellowship, and go no more down into the rude world.

5 While he yet spake, behold, a bright cloud overshadowed them: and behold a voice out of the cloud, which said, This is my beloved Son, in whom I am well pleased; hear ye him.

6 And when the disciples heard *it*, they fell on their face, and were sore afraid.

Astonished and overcome, they fell down as in the stupor of deep sleep.

> " *When, in ecstasy sublime,*
> *Tabor's glorious steep I climb,*
> *At the too transporting light*
> *Darkness rushes o'er my sight.*"

We are not able as yet to bear too clear a view of the glory of our Lord. Before we enter heaven we shall be strengthened to bear the strain of the beatific vision.

7 And Jesus came and touched them, and said, Arise, and be not afraid.

8 And when they had lifted up their eyes, they saw no man, save Jesus only.

And that sight was enough. To see Jesus only is all that saint or sinner need desire.

9 And as they came down from the mountain, Jesus charged them, saying, Tell the vision to no man, until the Son of man be risen again from the dead.

The mind of Jesus rushed forward to his death and resurrection. Tabor could not make him forget Calvary. Christ crucified should ever be most dear to us, since for our sakes he despised the shame of death, and counted dishonour as glory, that he might redeem us to himself.

OF *this transfiguration of our Lord and the attesting voice of the Father, Peter speaks in his epistle.*

II. PETER I. 16—18.

16 For we have not followed cunningly devised fables, when we made known unto you the power and coming of our Lord Jesus Christ, but were eyewitnesses of his majesty.

17 For he received from God the Father honour and glory, when there came such a voice to him from the excellent glory, This is my beloved Son, in whom I am well pleased.

18 And this voice which came from heaven we heard, when we were with him in the holy mount.

The apostles, by seeing the transfiguration, were confirmed in faith and enabled to bear witness concerning their Lord to all generations.

O thou, who once on Tabor's hill
Didst shine before the favoured three,
The souls which love thee favour still
Thy nearer glory, Lord, to see.

E'en now let faith's far-gazing eye
The brightness of thy Godhead scan,
And view thee, throned in heaven on high,
The Almighty Lord, the Son of Man.

540   " **Lord, I believe; help Thou mine unbelief.**"   September 9.—Evening.

[*Or May 18.*]

MARK IX. 14—29.

AND when he came to *his* disciples, he saw a great multitude about them, and the scribes questioning with them. (*From glory upon the mountain to conflict in the valley is a very usual transition.*)

15 And straightway all the people, when they beheld him, were greatly amazed, and running to *him* saluted him. (*No doubt his face was resplendent with some relics of the glory which had beamed from him upon the holy mount: yet it is remarkable that the people were not terrified, but ran to him and not from him: the glories of Jesus are always attractive.*)

16 And he asked the scribes, What question ye with them?

17, 18 And one of the multitude answered and said, Master, I have brought unto thee my son, which hath a dumb spirit; and wheresoever he taketh him, he teareth him: and he foameth, and gnasheth with his teeth, and pineth away: and I spake to thy disciples that they should cast him out; and they could not.

Without their Master they could do nothing; they were like soldiers assailed by the enemy in the absence of their commander. His coming soon turned the tide of battle.

19 He answereth him, and saith, O faithless generation, how long shall I be with you? how long shall I suffer you? bring him unto me.

20 And they brought him unto him: and when he saw him, straightway the spirit tare him; and he fell on the ground, and wallowed foaming. (*Matters often come to their worst before they mend. The devil had great wrath, and put forth all his power, because he perceived that his time was short.*)

21, 22 And he asked his father, How long is it ago since this came unto him? And he said, Of a child. And ofttimes it hath cast him into the fire, and into the waters, to destroy him: but if thou canst do any thing, have compassion on us, and help us.

23 Jesus said unto him, If thou canst believe, all things *are* possible to him that believeth.

The Saviour returned the unbelieving " if thou canst" to its right place; the want of power never lies in Jesus, but in our faith.

24 And straightway the father of the child cried out, and said with tears, Lord, I believe;

help thou mine unbelief. (*A prayer most fitting for many struggling believers, in whom faith and unbelief are striving for the mastery.*)

25 When Jesus saw that the people came running together, he rebuked the foul spirit, saying unto him, *Thou* dumb and deaf spirit, I charge thee, come out of him, and enter no more into him. (*Our Lord spake divinely, charging demons as one having authority over them. Let us confide in him, for all power is given unto him in heaven and in earth.*)

26 And *the spirit* cried, and rent him sore, and came out of him: and he was as one dead; insomuch that many said, He is dead.

27 But Jesus took him by the hand, and lifted him up; and he arose.

28 And when he was come into the house, his disciples asked him privately, Why could not we cast him out?

29 And he said unto them, This kind can come forth by nothing, but by prayer and fasting. (*God reserves certain blessings, and determines to bestow them only upon those who offer importunate prayer and practise self-denial. Yet where disciples fail, their Master succeeds. We may take the most desperate case to him; we may take our own.*)

How sad our state by nature is!
Our sin, how deep its stains!
And Satan binds our captive minds
Fast in his slavish chains.

But lo, we hear the Saviour call,
He comes to our relief:
" We would believe thy promise, Lord,
Oh, help our unbelief."

Stretch out thine arm, victorious King!
Our reigning sins subdue;
Drive the old dragon from his seat,
With all his hellish crew.

Shall we anger's deep defilement
Cherish in despite of heaven?
Shall we spurn at reconcilement,
Who so oft have been forgiven?

If offence that folly gave us
Should our faith and patience try,
Like our Lord, who died to save us,
Let us meekly pass it by.

MARK IX. 33—44; 49, 50.

AND he came to Capernaum: and being in the house he asked them, What was it that ye disputed among yourselves by the way? But they held their peace : for by the way they had disputed among themselves, who *should be the greatest.* (*This was the old evil, and it broke forth in many ways and at singular times. The Master spoke of his death, and the disciples spoke of pre-eminence. He was infinitely superior to the best of his followers, and in nothing more evidently so than in the unselfishness of his nature. Oh that we may have grace to keep clear of the apostles' fault!*)

35—37 And he sat down, and called the twelve, and saith unto them, If any man desire to be first, *the same* shall be last of all, and servant of all. And he took a child, and set him in the midst of them : and when he had .taken him in his arms, he said unto them, Whosoever shall receive one of such children in my name, receiveth me : and whosoever shall receive me, receiveth not me, but him that sent me.

38 ¶ And John answered him, saying, Master, we saw one casting out devils in thy name, and he followeth not us : and we forbad him, because he followeth not us. (*Surely this was a case of schism ! John had in his bosom all the zeal of the high-churchman, and his fellow apostles shared the feeling. This unknown worker honoured the name of Jesus and was clothed in his power, and one would have thought that the apostles would have recognised him as a brother : but no, "he followeth not us" was enough to sour all their brotherly kindness, and they forbad the good man to cast out any more devils, or to do anything more in the name of Jesus. This was after the approved model of church*ianity*; we shall see in the next verse that it was* not* Christ*ianity.)*

39 But Jesus said, Forbid him not ; for there is no man which shall do a miracle in my name, that can lightly speak evil of me.

40 For he that is not against us is on our part.

Even if the man himself were not sincere, yet, for his own credit's sake, he could not become an open opposer of the Lord. His aid was secured, so far, at least, that he could not become a reviler of that name by which he had wrought

wonders. *If the proud professors who reject all who dissent from them would at least remember that those whom they despise are not enemies of Christ, they might treat them with a little more consideration than they now do.*

41, 42 For whosoever shall give you a cup of water to drink in my name, because ye belong to Christ, verily I say unto you, he shall not lose his reward. And whosoever shall offend *(or cause to stumble)* one of *these* little ones that believe in me, it is better for him that a millstone were hanged about his neck, and he were cast into the sea. *(Beware, then, lest by word or act we cause any child of God to sin.)*

43 And if thy hand offend thee, cut it off : it is better for thee to enter into life maimed, than having two hands to go into hell, into the fire that never shall be quenched :

44 Where their worm dieth not, and the fire is not quenched. *(There is a worm undying, and a fire unquenchable. Let men say what they will, the wrath of God abides for ever upon those who die unsaved. It is worth while to make any sacrifice rather than fall for ever into hell.)*

49 For every one shall be salted with fire, and every sacrifice shall be salted with salt.

Either we must be tried with fire here or hereafter. Self-denial and endurance of our Lord's will must be the salt and the fire of our sacrifice in this life, or else the endless woes of the wrath of God shall be both preserving salt and consuming fire to us in another world. Far better to accept the light afflictions of to-day, than to endure the fierce flames of perdition.

50 Salt *is* good : but if the salt have lost his saltness, wherewith will ye season it ? Have salt in yourselves, and have peace one with another.

To be Sung or Read.

Behold, how good a thing it is,
    And how becoming well,
Together, such as brethren are,
    In unity to dwell !

Like precious ointment on the head,
    That down the beard did flow,
E'en Aaron's beard, and to the skirts
    Did of his garments go.

As Hermon's dew, the dew that doth
    On Sion's hills descend ;
For there the blessing God commands,
    Life that shall never end.

MATTHEW XVII. 22—27.

AND while they abode in Galilee, Jesus said unto them, The Son of man shall be betrayed into the hands of men. And they shall kill him, and the third day he shall be raised again. And they were exceeding sorry.

He often spoke to them upon this point, and as they gradually comprehended his meaning their sorrow increased. He kept his death always before his mind's eye, and frequently reminded his followers of it before it was accomplished; and now that his suffering work is finished, he would have it always present to the hearts of his people.

24, 25 And when they were come to Capernaum, they that received tribute *money* came to Peter, and said, Doth not your master pay tribute ? He saith, Yes. *(But, as usual, he spake too quickly. He ought not to have committed his Master to the payment of a doubtful exaction.)* And when he was come into the house, Jesus prevented *(or anticipated)* him, saying, What thinkest thou, Simon ? of whom do the kings of the earth take custom or tribute ? of their own children, or of strangers ?

26 Peter saith unto him, Of strangers. Jesus saith unto him, Then are the children free.

This tribute had not the divine sanction. The services of the temple, and the maintenance of the priests were otherwise provided for by the Mosaic law, and no annual poll tax had ever been instituted by God. Eastern kings in our Lord's day levied tribute only upon the natives of conquered lands, and did not exact from their own people. It could not be supposed that the King of Grace would tax his own family.

27 Notwithstanding, lest we should offend them, go thou to the sea, and cast an hook, and take up the fish that first cometh up ; and when thou hast opened his mouth, thou shalt find a piece of money : that take, and give unto them for me and thee. *(He paid the demand, but in such a way as to prove his own sovereign status. He paid as only God could do.)*

MATTHEW XVIII. 21—35.

THEN came Peter to him, and said, Lord, how oft shall my brother sin against me, and I forgive him ? till seven times ? Jesus saith unto him, I say not unto thee, Until seven times : but, Until seventy times seven.

23, 24 Therefore is the kingdom of heaven likened unto a certain king, which would take account of his servants. And when he had begun to reckon, one was brought unto him, which owed him ten thousand talents. *(If of silver, these talents were worth between three and four millions sterling ; if of gold, sixty millions.)*

25—28 But forasmuch as he had not to pay, his lord commanded him to be sold, and his wife, and children, and all that he had, and payment to be made. The servant therefore fell down, and worshipped him, saying, Lord, have patience with me, and I will pay thee all. Then the Lord of that servant was moved with compassion, and loosed him, and forgave him the debt. But the same servant went out, and found one of his fellowservants, which owed him an hundred pence : *(or about three pounds :)* and he laid hands on him, and took *him* by the throat, saying, Pay me that thou owest. *(This debt at the most was the millionth part of the former one.)*

29 And his fellowservant fell down at his feet, and besought him, saying, Have patience with me, and I will pay thee all. *(The attitude and words which had drawn compassion from his master were addressed to him in vain.)*

30 And he would not : but went and cast him into prison, till he should pay the debt.

31 So when his fellowservants saw what was done, they were very sorry, and came and told unto their lord all that was done.

32, 33 Then his lord, after that he had called him, said unto him, O thou wicked servant, I forgave thee all that debt, because thou desiredst me : shouldest not thou also have had compassion on thy fellowservant, even as I had pity on thee ?

34 And his lord was wroth, and delivered him to the tormentors, till he should pay all that was due unto him.

35 So likewise shall my heavenly Father do also unto you, if ye from your hearts forgive not every one his brother their trespasses.

God will deal with each of us upon the principle which sways our own life, and if we adopt a stern and severe mode of action, we must expect the same rule to be carried out in our case.

JOHN VII. 2—24.

NOW the Jews' feast of tabernacles was at hand.

3—5 His brethren therefore said unto him, Depart hence, and go into Judæa, that thy disciples also may see the works that thou doest. For *there is* no man *that* doeth any thing in secret, and he himself seeketh to be known openly. If thou do these things, shew thyself to the world. For neither did his brethren believe in him.

6—8 Then Jesus said unto them, My time is not yet come: but your time is alway ready. The world cannot hate you; but me it hateth, because I testify of it, that the works thereof are evil. Go ye up unto this feast: I go not up yet unto this feast; for my time is not yet full come. *(Our Lord's relatives did not yet understand him. Any trembling faith in his commission which they possessed, was exercised selfishly in wishing to see him become a man of influence, in whose honours they might share. Meanwhile he was bringing upon his own head enmity and abuse for honestly rebuking the sins of the times. So wide a difference was there between the Lord Jesus and his nearest kindred. He lived for others, and they, until they became renewed in heart, sought only themselves.)*

9 When he had said these words unto them, he abode *still* in Galilee.

10 But when his brethren were gone up, then went he also up unto the feast, not openly, but as it were in secret.

11, 12 Then the Jews sought him at the feast, and said, Where is he? And there was much murmuring among the people concerning him: for some said, He is a good man: others said, Nay; but he deceiveth the people.

13 Howbeit no man spake openly of him for fear of the Jews. *(By whom is chiefly meant the rulers. The people were so much in fear of these great ones, that they spoke with bated breath in reference to the object of their enmity.)*

14 ¶ Now about the midst of the feast Jesus went up into the temple, and taught.

15 And the Jews marvelled, saying, How knoweth this man letters, having never learned?

16 Jesus answered them, and said, My doctrine is not mine, but his that sent me.

His doctrine was not from himself, it was authorised by the Father, who had sent him.

17—19 If any man will do his will, he shall know of the doctrine, whether it be of God, or *whether* I speak of myself. He that speaketh of himself seeketh his own glory: but he that seeketh his glory that sent him, the same is true, and no unrighteousness is in him. Did not Moses give you the law, and *yet* none of you keepeth the law? Why go ye about to kill me?

How plaintive are these words! The loving heart of Jesus was wounded at their ingratitude and wanton malice.

20 The people answered and said, Thou hast a devil: who goeth about to kill thee?

21, 22 Jesus answered and said unto them, I have done one work, and ye all marvel. Moses therefore gave unto you circumcision; (not because it is of Moses, but of the fathers;) and ye on the sabbath day circumcise a man.

23, 24 If a man on the sabbath day receive circumcision, that the law of Moses should not be broken; are ye angry at me, because I have made a man every whit whole on the sabbath day? Judge not according to the appearance, but judge righteous judgment.

Excellent advice, which we should all do well to follow. We ought not to allow ourselves to be swayed by prejudice and influenced by superficial appearances. Good men and good things are often despised. Truth and holiness have had to run the gauntlet of mankind. All is not gold that glitters, and there is much true gold which never glitters at all. May we be taught by the Holy Spirit to abhor that which is evil, and cleave only to that which is good and true. On the Saviour's side may we always be found.

Faithful amid unfaithfulness,
'Mid darkness only light,
Thou didst thy Father's name confess,
And in his will delight.

Unmov'd by threats or flatt'ring wiles,
Or suffering, shame, and loss:
Thy path uncheer'd by earthly smiles,
Led only to the cross.

Give us thy meek and lowly mind;
We would obedient be;
And all our rest and pleasure find
In learning, Lord, of thee.

SEPTEMBER 11.—EVENING.

544   *" If any man thirst, let him come unto Me, and drink."*   [*Or May* 22.]

JOHN VII. 25—39.

THEN said some of them of Jerusalem, Is not this he, whom they seek to kill? But, lo, he speaketh boldly, and they say nothing unto him. Do the rulers know indeed that this is the very Christ?

There were various opinions and conjectures. All those who had come up to the feast were interested in him. Jesus always creates a stir; men cannot remain indifferent, but must take one side or the other in reference to him. The dauntless manner in which our Lord faced the crowd led many to ask whether, after all, the rulers were not afraid of him.

27 Howbeit we know this man whence he is: but when Christ cometh, no man knoweth whence he is. *(There was a vague notion current among the Jews that the origin of the Messiah would be veiled in mystery—a notion in which there was a large amount of truth, hence their knowledge of the family at Nazareth was a stumbling-block in the way of their receiving the claims of Jesus.)*

28, 29 Then cried Jesus in the temple as he taught, saying, Ye both know me, and ye know whence I am: and I am not come of myself, but he that sent me is true, whom ye know not. But I know him: for I am from him, and he hath sent me.

30 Then they sought to take him: but no man laid hands on him, because his hour was not yet come.

31 And many of the people believed on him, and said, When Christ cometh, will he do more miracles than these which this *man* hath done?

Well might they make the inquiry. If men will not have Christ for a Saviour, what sort of a Saviour would they have?

32 The Pharisees heard that the people murmured such things concerning him; and the Pharisees and the chief priests sent officers to take him.

33, 34 Then said Jesus unto them, Yet a little while am I with you, and *then* I go unto him that sent me. Ye shall seek me, and shall not find *me:* and where I am, *thither* ye cannot come. *(They need not be in a hurry to put him away, for he would soon be gone.)*

35 Then said the Jews among themselves, Whither will he go, that we shall not find him? will he go unto the dispersed among the Gentiles, and teach the Gentiles?

There was such a large-heartedness about his teaching that it was adapted for all mankind, and a sense of this may have caused much of the irritated feeling of the Jews towards him.

36 What *manner of* saying is this that he said, Ye shall seek me, and shall not find *me:* and where I am, *thither* ye cannot come?

37 In the last day, that great *day* of the feast, Jesus stood and cried, saying, If any man thirst, let him come unto me and drink.

38, 39 He that believeth on me, as the scripture hath said, out of his belly shall flow rivers of living water. (But this spake he of the Spirit, which they that believe on him should receive: for the Holy Ghost was not yet *given;* because that Jesus was not yet glorified.)

Jesus kept in the background till the fitting moment, and then he came boldly forward to deliver one of the freest and fullest gospel discourses upon record. On a day when no servile work might be done, and consequently no water could be drawn, he freely proclaimed his salvation. His grace is free, it is effectual in its operation, and its results are abiding, elevating, purifying, and saving. Faith receives the grace of God, and the soul lives. Without money and without price the boon of eternal life is bestowed. Let us bless that dear Redeemer who at this moment still cries aloud, "If any man thirst, let him come unto me, and drink."

The Saviour calls, let every ear
   Attend the heavenly sound;
Ye doubting souls, dismiss your fear,
   Hope smiles reviving round.

For every thirsty, longing heart,
   Here streams of bounty flow,
And life and health and bliss impart,
   To banish mortal woe.

Ye sinners, come; 'tis mercy's voice,
   The gracious call obey;
Mercy invites to heavenly joys;
   And can you yet delay?

Dear Saviour, draw reluctant hearts,
   To thee let sinners fly,
And take the bliss thy love imparts,
   And drink, and never die.

JOHN VII. 40—53.

MANY of the people therefore, when they heard this saying, said, Of a truth this is the Prophet.

41 Others said, This is the Christ. But some said, Shall Christ come out of Galilee?

42 Hath not the scripture said, That Christ cometh of the seed of David, and out of the town of Bethlehem, where David was?

43 So there was a division among the people because of him. *(Sermons do not produce the same effect upon all minds. Even when the Lord himself was the preacher some believed and some believed not, and among those who did believe there were several degrees of faith. May God grant that when we hear the word we may be led to embrace it, and feel its power in our inmost souls. One ground of unbelief in our Lord's day appears to have been ignorance; his hearers knew that the Messiah would be born at Bethlehem, and supposing that Jesus was a native of Galilee, they could not believe in him. Had they taken the trouble to inquire, this stumbling-block would soon have been taken out of their way, for they would have learned that he was of the house and lineage of David, and was born in Bethlehem, according to the word of prophecy. If we remain in unbelief through wilful ignorance, we shall have no one but ourselves to blame.)*

44 And some of them would have taken him; but no man laid hands on him.

Yes, even in the Redeemer's congregation there were malicious hearts which remained unsoftened by his message of love, and would have repaid his affectionate zeal by making him their prisoner, if fear had not held them in check.

The Lord's enemies among the rulers now resolved to seize him and put an end to his teaching, and therefore they sent officers to arrest him; but these returned empty-handed to those who sent them.

45 Then came the officers to the chief priests and Pharisees; and they said unto them, Why have ye not brought him?

46 The officers answered, Never man spake like this man. *(They had been spell-bound both by his matter and his manner, and the Pharisees were compelled to hear their own servants sing his praises. If we have ever heard the Lord Jesus speak in our hearts, we shall fully agree with the verdict of the officers. Speak to us now, O Lord, and we shall rejoice with joy unspeakable.)*

47, 48 Then answered them the Pharisees, Are ye also deceived? Have any of the rulers or of the Pharisees believed on him?

This is an old and foolish objection. Rulers and eminent men are quite as often wrong as right, and human authority is a very doubtful rule.

49 But this people who knoweth not the law are cursed. *(This again is another stale form of opposition to the truth. The adversaries represent those who believed in Jesus as an ignorant rabble, a contemptible and cursed crew. We may well be content to share the world's scorn with the despised saints, for it has always been the lot of the godly to be sneered at.)*

50 Nicodemus saith unto them, (he that came to Jesus by night, being one of them,)

51 Doth our law judge any man before it hear him, and know what he doeth?

This was well spoken. Nicodemus may have been timid, but when he saw that his help was needed, he spoke out right well and wisely. What a blow was here aimed at the heart of prejudice! Prejudiced persons would do well to answer the question of Nicodemus.

52 They answered and said unto him, Art thou also of Galilee? Search, and look: for out of Galilee ariseth no prophet.

53 And every man went unto his own house.

JOHN VIII. 1.

JESUS went unto the mount of Olives.

He had no other resort. Sleep was for all except the Saviour: he went to meditation and to prayer. Blessed Lord, what an example dost thou set us by thus resorting to sacred solitude!

Never mortal spake like him!
More than man he needs must be,
Sure he is the God supreme,
For I feel his power in me.

He hath changed me by his word,
By his charms my soul subdued;
Ever since his voice I heard,
All my nature is renew'd!

JOHN VIII. 2—11.

A ND early in the morning he came again into the temple, and all the people came unto him ; and he sat down, and taught them.

By a night of prayer he had prepared himself for a day of labour and opposition. It is wise, whenever we expect double work or conflict, to gird up our loins by special devotion. He who has overcome heaven by prayer has no cause to dread the face of his enemies. Calmly did our Lord begin his teaching, though he knew that his enemies were planning his destruction.

3 And the scribes and Pharisees brought unto him a woman taken in adultery ; and when they had set her in the midst,

4 They say unto him, Master, this woman was taken in adultery, in the very act.

5 Now Moses in the law commanded us that such should be stoned : but what sayest thou ?

See the cunning of these foxes. If the Lord condemned the woman to die, they would then tax him with going beyond his province, and setting up for a ruler; and if he let her go, they would charge him with being the friend of vice.

6 This they said, tempting him, that they might have to accuse him. But Jesus stooped down, and with *his* finger wrote on the ground, *as though he heard them not. (These last words are added by the translators, and are not needed. He wrote on the ground to show his unwillingness to meddle with the matter, and to give time for their consciences to work. He did not at once unmask them, but gave them time to retreat if they were wise, or to invite a crushing defeat by their persevering folly.)*

7 So when they continued asking him, he lifted up himself, and said unto them, He that is without sin among you, let him first cast a stone at her.

8 And again he stooped down, and wrote on the ground. *(He stooped this second time to allow the accusers time to slink away unobserved by him, and they quietly availed themselves of the opportunity.)*

9 And they which heard *it*, being convicted by *their own* conscience, went out one by one, beginning at the eldest, *(Or at the elders, or chief elders,) even* unto the last : and Jesus was left alone, and the woman standing in the midst.

The trap had failed to secure the victim, but it caught those who had prepared it. Stunned by the blow which Jesus laid home upon them, the vile hypocrites took to their heels, feeling themselves to have been grossly foolish to have provoked such a disclosure.

10 When Jesus had lifted up himself, and saw none but the woman, he said unto her, Woman, where are those thine accusers ? hath no man condemned thee ?

11 She said, No man, Lord. *(Dr. Brown well observes : "What inimitable tenderness and grace ! Conscious of her own guilt, and till now in the hands of men who had talked of stoning her, wondering at the* skill *with which her accusers had been dispersed, and the* grace *of the few words addressed to herself, she would be disposed to listen, with a reverence and teachableness before unknown, to our Lord's admonition.* 'And Jesus said unto her, Neither do I condemn thee : go, and sin no more.' *He pronounces no pardon upon the woman, like* 'Thy sins are forgiven thee; Go in peace.' *Much less does he say that she had done nothing condemnable: he simply leaves the matter where it was. He meddles not with the magistrate's office, nor acts the* judge *in any sense: but in saying,* ' Go, and sin no more,' *which had been before said to one who undoubtedly believed (ch. v. 14), more is probably implied than expressed. If brought suddenly to conviction of sin, to admiration of her Deliverer, and to a willingness to be admonished and guided by him, this call to begin a new life may have carried with it what would ensure and naturally bring about a permanent change.")*

Thine advocate in Jesus see!
'Tis he that speaks the word ; 'tis he
   That takes the prisoner's part :
Not to condemn the world he came ;
Believing now in Jesus' name,
   E'en now absolved thou art.

Who shall accuse th' elect of God,
Protected by th' atoning blood ?
   'Tis God that justifies,
That bids thee go and sin no more—
Go in thy Saviour's peace and power,
   And trace him to the skies.

O UR *Lord pleaded with the Jewish people and set the truth clearly before them, but they cavilled at him and rejected him. Of this we have an instance in—*

JOHN VIII. 31—59.

31 Then said Jesus to those Jews which believed on him, If ye continue in my word, *then* are ye my disciples indeed ;

32 And ye shall know the truth, and the truth shall make you free.

The contentious party among the Jews here interrupted him, boastfully extolling themselves as freemen. They were under the dominion of the Romans, and yet gloried in never having been in bondage.

33 They answered him, We be Abraham's seed, and were never in bondage to any man : how sayest thou, Ye shall be made free ?

34—36 Jesus answered them, Verily, verily, I say unto you, Whosoever committeth sin is the servant of sin. And the servant abideth not in the house for ever : *but* the Son abideth ever. If the Son therefore shall make you free, ye shall be free indeed.

37, 38 I know that ye are Abraham's seed ; but ye seek to kill me, because my word hath no place in you. I speak that which I have seen with my Father : and ye do that which ye have seen with your father.

39, 40 They answered and said unto him, Abraham is our father. Jesus saith unto them, If ye were Abraham's children, ye would do the works of Abraham. But now ye seek to kill me, a man that hath told you the truth, which I have heard of God : this did not Abraham.

41 Ye do the deeds of your father. Then said they to him, We be not born of fornication ; we have one Father, *even* God.

42 Jesus said unto them, If God were your Father, ye would love me : for I proceeded forth and came from God ; neither came I of myself, but he sent me.

43 Why do ye not understand my speech ? *even* because ye cannot hear my word.

44, 45 Ye are of *your* father the devil, and the lusts of your father ye will do. He was a murderer from the beginning, and abode not in the

truth, because there is no truth in him. When he speaketh a lie, he speaketh of his own : for he is a liar, and the father of it. And because I tell *you* the truth, ye believe me not.

46, 47 Which of you convinceth me of sin ? And if I say the truth, why do ye not believe me ? He that is of God heareth God's words : ye therefore hear *them* not, because ye are not of God.

48 Then answered the Jews, and said unto him, Say we not well that thou art a Samaritan, and hast a devil ? *(When they cannot argue, men usually take to railing. A bad case when hard pushed is very apt to employ abuse as its defence.)*

49, 50 Jesus answered, I have not a devil ; but I honour my Father, and ye do dishonour me. And I seek not mine own glory : there is one that seeketh and judgeth.

51 Verily, verily, I say unto you, If a man keep my saying, he shall never see death.

52, 53 Then said the Jews unto him, Now we know that thou hast a devil. Abraham is dead, and the prophets ; and thou sayest, If a man keep my saying, he shall never taste of death. Art thou greater than our father Abraham, which is dead ? and the prophets are dead ; whom makest thou thyself ?

54—56 Jesus answered, If I honour myself, my honour is nothing: it is my Father that honoureth me ; of whom ye say, that he is your God : Yet ye have not known him ; but I know him : and if I should say, I know him not, I shall be a liar like unto you : but I know him, and keep his saying. Your father Abraham rejoiced to see my day : and he saw *it*, and was glad.

57 Then said the Jews unto him, Thou art not yet fifty years old, and hast thou seen Abraham ? *(The sorrows of our Lord made him appear to be nearly fifty, though he was only a little over thirty.)*

58 Jesus said unto them, Verily, verily, I say unto you, Before Abraham was, I am.

Thus did he declare his Godhead and eternal existence, but they would not believe in him.

59 Then took they up stones to cast at him : but Jesus hid himself, and went out of the temple, going through the midst of them, and so passed by.

548   "The eyes of the blind shall see."   SEPTEMBER 13.—EVENING.

[Or May 26.]

JOHN IX. 1—23.

AND as *Jesus* passed by, he saw a man which was blind from *his* birth.

2 And his disciples asked him, saying, Master, who did sin, this man, or his parents, that he was born blind ?

3 Jesus answered, Neither hath this man sinned, nor his parents : *(that is to say, neither his own sin nor that of his parents is the cause of his blindness,)* but that the works of God should be made manifest in him.

4, 5 I must work the works of him that sent me, while it is day : the night cometh, when no man can work. As long as I am in the world, I am the light of the world.

6 When he had thus spoken, he spat on the ground, and made clay of the spittle, and he anointed the eyes of the blind man with the clay,

7 And said unto him, Go, wash in the pool of Siloam, (which is by interpretation, Sent.) He went his way therefore, and washed, and came seeing. *(Means were used, but they were such as had no efficacy of their own, and would tend rather to impede than assist. Often does the Lord use the most unlikely instrumentalities.)*

8 The neighbours therefore, and they which before had seen him that he was blind, said, Is not this he that sat and begged ?

9 Some said, This is he: others *said*, He is like him: *but* he said, I am *he.* *(He was a plain blunt man of unusually sound sense. He ended the controversy by two words of the most positive kind—"I am.")*

10 Therefore said they unto him, How were thine eyes opened ?

11 He answered and said, A man that is called Jesus made clay, and anointed mine eyes, and said unto me, Go to the pool of Siloam, and wash : and I went and washed, and I received sight. *(His statement was as clear as it could be, and as brief as possible.)*

12 Then said they unto him, Where is he ? He said, I know not.

13, 14 They brought to the Pharisees him that aforetime was blind. And it was the sabbath day when Jesus made the clay, and opened his eyes. *(And so the old quarrel was revived, and fresh ground found for opposing the Lord Jesus.)*

15 Then again the Pharisees also asked him how he had received his sight. He said unto them, He put clay upon mine eyes, and I washed, and do see. *(Here is not a word to spare, yet the statement is full and accurate.)*

16 Therefore said some of the Pharisees, This man is not of God, because he keepeth not the sabbath day. Others said, How can a man that is a sinner do such miracles ? And there was a division among them.

17 They say unto the blind man again, What sayest thou of him, that he hath opened thine eyes ? He said, He is a prophet. *(So much he felt sure of, and was not ashamed to declare. When he knew more, he was equally definite and decided. If the Lord hath given us our spiritual sight, it will be a happy circumstance if we are just as positive and outspoken as this remarkable man. The cause of God needs many champions just now who will speak out whether they offend or please. The Lord make us such.)*

18 But the Jews did not believe concerning him, that he had been blind, and received his sight, until they called the parents of him that had received his sight.

19 And they asked them, saying, Is this your son, who ye say was born blind ? how then doth he now see ?

20—23 His parents answered them and said, We know that this is our son, and that he was born blind : but by what means he now seeth, we know not ; or who hath opened his eyes, we know not: he is of age, ask him: he shall speak for himself. These *words* spake his parents, because they feared the Jews: for the Jews had agreed already, that if any man did confess that he was Christ, he should be put out of the synagogue. Therefore said his parents, He is of age ; ask him.

Yes, the Lord has healed my blindness,
    Pitying my infirmity.
Trophy of his loving-kindness,
    I was blind, but now I see !

Oh that all the blind but knew him,
    And would be advised by me ;
Surely they would hasten to him,
    He would cause them all to see.

JOHN IX. 24—41.

THEN again called they the man that was blind, and said unto him, Give God the praise : we know that this man is a sinner.

Smooth words, but full of malice ; they did not, however, deceive the resolute man to whom they were spoken.

25 He answered and said, Whether he be a sinner *or no,* I know not : one thing I know, that, whereas I was blind, now I see.

That was enough for him, and he could not be beaten out of it. Surely the man who had opened eyes which had never seen the light before could not be a guilty person.

26 Then said they to him again, What did he to thee ? how opened he thine eyes ?

27 He answered them, I have told you already, and ye did not hear : wherefore would ye hear *it* again ? will ye also be his disciples ?

He turned from his defensive position and warmly assailed his questioners. They were so determined to cavil that he refused to go over his story again.

28, 29 Then they reviled him, and said, Thou art his disciple ; but we are Moses' disciples. We know that God spake unto Moses : *as for* this *fellow,* we know not from whence he is.

30—33 The man answered and said unto them, Why herein is a marvellous thing, that ye know not from whence he is, and *yet* he hath opened mine eyes. Now we know that God heareth not sinners : but if any man be a worshipper of God, and doeth his will, him he heareth. Since the world began was it not heard that any man opened the eyes of one that was born blind. If this man were not of God he could do nothing. *(This was splendid reasoning. The man's eyes were opened in more senses than one.)*

34 They answered and said unto him, Thou wast altogether born in sins, and dost thou teach us ? And they cast him out. *(Railing and persecution are the old arguments of those who are silenced, but refuse to be convinced. We must expect such things just in proportion as our enemies feel the power of our words.)*

35 Jesus heard that they had cast him out ; and when he had found him, he said unto him, Dost thou believe on the Son of God ?

Happy is it for us that Jesus is sure to come to us when we are cast out by men for his sake.

36 He answered and said, Who is he, Lord, that I might believe on him ?

37 And Jesus said unto him, Thou hast both seen him, and it is he that talketh with thee.

38 And he said, Lord, I believe. And he worshipped him. *(Being no Socinian, the divinity of Jesus was clear to him, and he acted accordingly. If the eyes of Unitarians were opened, they also would worship Jesus.)*

39 ¶ And Jesus said, For judgment I am come into this world, that they which see not might see ; and that they which see might be made blind. *(The process is going on—the wise are made fools, and the fools are made wise. Men who boast of what they know have their folly rendered more conspicuous, while self-distrusting honest-minded confessors of their ignorance are taught of God. Lord, make us to be among those whose eyes rejoice in thy light.)*

40, 41 And *some* of the Pharisees which were with him heard these words, and said unto him, Are we blind also ? Jesus said unto them, If ye were blind, ye should have no sin : but now ye say, We see ; therefore your sin remaineth.

If they really could not see, they might be excused, but, sinning against the light of which they boasted, they were guilty indeed.

To be Sung or Read.

Light of the world, our eyes unseal,
Thy miracles in us recount ;
Now on our eyelids place the clay,
And send us to Siloah's fount.

Light of the world, our praises hear ;
Thou hast our darkness turn'd to day.
Though foes may mock, we will not fear,
But all thy glorious work display.

'Tis no surprising thing
That we should be unknown,
The Jewish world knew not their king,
God's everlasting Son.

Though we endure the sneer
And jest of wicked men,
We'll patient wait till Christ appear,
For he will come again.

550   "𝕵 know 𝕸y sheep, and am known of 𝕸ine."   SEPTEMBER 14.—EVENING.

[*Or May* 28.]

JOHN X. 1—18.

VERILY, verily, I say unto you, He that entereth not by the door into the sheepfold, but climbeth up some other way, the same is a thief and a robber. *(Those pretended shepherds who came not as the Scriptures had appointed were robbers seeking only their own advantage.)*

2 But he that entereth in by the door is the shepherd of the sheep. *(Jesus came according to prophecy, in the right and ordained manner.)*

3 To him the porter openeth: *(John the Baptist knew him and opened the door for him.)* and the sheep hear his voice: and he calleth his own sheep by name, and leadeth them out.

Outside an eastern village there was a stone enclosure, within which the flocks of the inhabitants were penned at night. When the owner of any one of the flocks desired to lead forth his sheep the porter admitted him, and he soon separated his own sheep from the rest.

4, 5 And when he putteth forth his own sheep, he goeth before them, and the sheep follow him: for they know his voice. And a stranger will they not follow, but will flee from him: for they know not the voice of strangers.

The shepherd has only to call his own sheep, and they rise and follow. No one can deceive them; if a stranger were dressed in their shepherd's clothes, they would detect him by his voice.

6 This parable spake Jesus unto them: but they understood not what things they were which he spake unto them.

7, 8 Then said Jesus unto them again, Verily, verily, I say unto you, I am the door of the sheep. All that ever came before me are thieves and robbers: but the sheep did not hear them.

The elect of God were not duped, but waited till the true Christ came.

9, 10 I am the door: by me if any man enter in, he shall be saved, and shall go in and out, and find pasture. The thief cometh not, but for to steal, and to kill, and to destroy: I am come that they might have life, and that they might have *it* more abundantly.

11 I am the good shepherd: the good shepherd giveth his life for the sheep.

Best token of goodness! Noblest deed of love!

The false shepherds were all for gain, but Jesus loved us, and gave himself for us.

12, 13 But he that is an hireling, and not the shepherd, whose own the sheep are not, seeth the wolf coming, and leaveth the sheep, and fleeth: and the wolf catcheth them, and scattereth the sheep. The hireling fleeth, because he is an hireling, and careth not for the sheep.

14 I am the good shepherd, and know my *sheep,* and am known of mine. *(Mutual knowledge exists between Jesus and his people. He never mistakes one of them, neither do they follow a pretender under the supposition that he is their Lord. Grace bestows discernment upon the saints, and they know their leader from all others.)*

15 As the Father knoweth me, even so know I the Father: and I lay down my life for the sheep.

16 And other sheep I have, which are not of this fold: them also I must bring, and they shall hear my voice; and there shall be one fold, *(or rather flock)* and one shepherd. *(The Gentiles were not folded, and were like stray sheep. They are now by grace united with the chosen Jews in one flock.)*

17 Therefore doth my Father love me, because I lay down my life, that I might take it again.

18 No man taketh it from me, but I lay it down of myself. I have power to lay it down, and I have power to take it again. This commandment have I received of my Father.

As God, our Lord Jesus held his life absolutely at his own disposal, and no power could compel him to die, but he became our sin-bearer, and for our sake the servant of the Father, and therefore, to carry out his office, he even laid down his life for us. Blessed be his glorious name for evermore.

Loving Shepherd of thy sheep,
Keep me, Lord, in safety keep;
Nothing can thy power withstand,
None can pluck me from thy hand.
Loving Shepherd, thou didst give
Thine own life that I might live;
May I love thee day by day,
Gladly thy sweet will obey.
Where thou leadest me I go,
Walking in thy steps below;
Then before thy Father's throne,
Jesu, claim me for thy own.

JOHN X. 19—40.

THERE was a division therefore again among the Jews for these sayings. *Christ thus called out his own sheep from the flocks of others. The gospel is a great separator, and every Sabbath day it reveals its power in dividing the sheep from the goats. Those who hear and obey are saved; those who are disobedient are condemned in their own consciences.*

20, 21 And many of them said, He hath a devil, and is mad; why hear ye him? Others said, These are not the words of him that hath a devil. Can a devil open the eyes of the blind?

22, 23 And it was at Jerusalem the feast of the dedication, and it was winter *(or stormy, wintry weather).* And Jesus walked in the temple in Solomon's porch. *(Sheltering himself from the cold, and reaching the people who would there assemble.)*

24 Then came the Jews round about him, and said unto him, How long dost thou make us to doubt? If thou be the Christ, tell us plainly.

25, 26 Jesus answered them, I told you, and ye believed not : the works that I do in my Father's name, they bear witness of me. But ye believe not, because ye are not of my sheep, as I said unto you. *(This was plain, bold speech. They were none of his, and therefore they had not discerned him. Had they been his chosen, they would have received him joyfully. This doctrine is very irksome to the pride of man.)*

27 My sheep hear my voice, and I know them, and they follow me :

28—31 And I give unto them eternal life; and they shall never perish, neither shall any *man* pluck them out of my hand. My Father, which gave *them* me, is greater than all ; and no *man* is able to pluck *them* out of my Father's hand. *(The chosen are doubly secure; two hands have grasped them, and in that double security they are beyond all danger.)* I and *my* Father are one. Then the Jews took up stones again to stone him. *(They would not hear of his being one with the Father; and, alas, there are persons still living who will honour Jesus as man, but when we speak of his Godhead they are filled with anger.)*

32 Jesus answered them, Many good works have I shewed you from my Father; for which of those works do ye stone me?

33 The Jews answered him, saying, For a good work we stone thee not; but for blasphemy; and because that thou, being a man, makest thyself God. *(He was assuredly God, or else, being so good a man, he would never have claimed to be what he was not. If Christ Jesus be not God, he is an impostor, and we are idolaters.)*

34—36 Jesus answered them, Is it not written in your law, I said, Ye are gods? If he called them gods, unto whom the word of God came, and the scripture cannot be broken; Say ye of him, whom the Father hath sanctified, and sent into the world, Thou blasphemest; because I said, I am the Son of God? *(This was an argument intended to cool their rage, for, if in some sense the chosen people had been called gods, they ought not to have been so sure that it was blasphemy for Jesus to claim to be the Son of God.)*

37 If I do not the works of my Father, believe me not.

38 But if I do, though ye believe not me, believe the works : that ye may know, and believe, that the Father *is* in me, and I in him.

39, 40 Therefore they sought again to take him : but he escaped out of their hand; And went away again beyond Jordan into the place where John at first baptized; and there he abode.

Having borne his testimony, our Lord again retired. How does his declaration affect us? Are we his sheep? Do we follow in his steps? Let each answer as before the all-knowing Lord.

Thou Shepherd of Israel divine,
The joy of the upright in heart,
For closer communion we pine,
Still, still to reside where thou art.

Ah! show us that happiest place—
That place of thy people's abode,
Where saints in an ecstasy gaze,
Adoring their crucified God.

'Tis there, with the lambs of thy flock,
Our spirits would covet to rest;
To lie at the foot of the rock,
Or rise to be hid in thy breast.

'Tis there we would always abide,
And never a moment depart;
Preserv'd evermore by thy side,
Eternally hid in thine heart.

JOHN XI. 1—19.

NOW a certain *man* was sick, *named* Lazarus, of Bethany, the town of Mary and her sister Martha.

2 (It was *that* Mary which anointed the Lord with ointment, and wiped his feet with her hair, whose brother Lazarus was sick.)

3 Therefore his sisters sent unto him, saying, Lord, behold, he whom thou lovest is sick.

Sickness is no stranger in the homes of the saints. However much we may be the Lord's favourites we can claim no exemption from bodily affliction: but in our case it bears an aspect full of consolation, it is sent not as a punishment, but as a means of blessing.

4 When Jesus heard *that,* he said, This sickness is not unto death, *(death will not be the ultimate end of it,)* but for the glory of God, that the Son of God might be glorified thereby.

Blessed is that illness of which this can be said: such sickness is better than health.

5, 6 Now Jesus loved Martha, and her sister, and Lazarus. When he had heard therefore that he was sick, he abode two days still in the same place where he was.

His love made him slow! This seems strange. We should have hastened on to our friend's chamber, but Jesus, who loved better than we do, was in no hurry. Omnipotence is the source of divine patience.

7 Then after that saith he to *his* disciples, Let us go into Judæa again.

8 *His* disciples say unto him, Master, the Jews of late sought to stone thee; and goest thou thither again? *(Very rightly they wished to keep him from danger, more rightly still he shrank not from exposing himself when duty called.)*

9, 10 Jesus answered, Are there not twelve hours in the day? If any man walk in the day, he stumbleth not, because he seeth the light of this world. But if a man walk in the night, he stumbleth, because there is no light in him.

He was safe till his hour came, and therefore worked on in defiance of Jewish malice. He had his allotted day, and he meant to work to the end of it despite all opposition.

11 These things said he: and after that he saith unto them, Our friend Lazarus sleepeth; but I go, that I may awake him out of sleep.

12—15 Then said his disciples, Lord, if he sleep, he shall do well. Howbeit Jesus spake of his death: but they thought that he had spoken of taking of rest in sleep. Then said Jesus unto them plainly, Lazarus is dead. And I am glad for your sakes that I was not there, to the intent ye may believe; nevertheless let us go unto him. *(Anything which helps our faith is a blessing for which to thank God.)*

16 Then said Thomas, which is called Didymus, unto his fellowdisciples, Let us also go, that we may die with him. *(Bravely did he say, "Since our Master will expose himself to such peril, let us go with him, if it be only to share his fate." Better far to die with Christ than to desert him in the hour of trial.)*

17 Then when Jesus came, he found that he had *lain* in the grave four days already.

18 Now Bethany was nigh unto Jerusalem, about fifteen furlongs off:

19 And many of the Jews came to Martha, and Mary, to comfort them concerning their brother. *(These were formal visits, customary in those times, but they were of very little use to the two bereaved sisters, who above all things longed to see the Lord. Without Jesus our friends are miserable comforters. A little while ago we read of Jesus at a wedding, and in this passage we find him on the road to a funeral: he shares in all that concerns us, and most of all in our griefs. Have we a family trouble? Let us send for the Master. His presence will make all things work for good.)*

Saviour! I can welcome sickness
  If these words be said of me:
Can rejoice midst pain and weakness,
  If I am but loved by thee.
    Love so precious,
  Balm for every wound will be.

Though that love sends days of sadness
  In a life so brief as this,
It prepares me days of gladness
  And a life of perfect bliss.
    Love so precious
  Bids me every fear dismiss.

JOHN XI. 20—37.

THEN Martha, as soon as she heard that Jesus was coming, went and met him : but Mary sat *still* in the house. *(Martha had earnestly expected the Lord's coming, and her active spirit led her to meet him. In this she is an example to us: our faith and hope and prayer, should go forth to meet the Lord in his ways of providence and grace. We may not judge Mary, but we may do well to remember that it is a temptation to contemplative Christians to sit too still in hours of sorrow. Martha was cumbered with much serving, and there have been Marys who have been cumbered with much fretting.)*

21, 22 Then said Martha unto Jesus, Lord, if thou hadst been here, my brother had not died. But I know, that even now, whatsoever thou wilt ask of God, God will give *it* thee.

Her complaint of his absence was very gentle, and her faith in his power to restore her brother was far too pleasing to Jesus for him to be displeased by what she said. How apt are we all to think that if the Lord were with us we should not be in trouble, whereas it is in affliction that he is most graciously manifest.

23, 24 Jesus saith unto her, Thy brother shall rise again. Martha saith unto him, I know that he shall rise again in the resurrection at the last day.

25, 26 Jesus said unto her, I am the resurrection, and the life : he that believeth in me, though he were dead, yet shall he live : And whosoever liveth and believeth in me shall never die. Believest thou this? *(It would be well after hearing any scriptural truth, to put this question to ourselves : " Believest thou this ? " Especially should we be well established in the truth that Jesus is the source, substance, and first-fruits of the resurrection.)*

27 She saith unto him, Yea, Lord : I believe that thou art the Christ, the Son of God, which should come into the world.

28 And when she had so said, she went her way, and called Mary her sister secretly, saying, The Master is come, and calleth for thee.

Jesus had probably said more than is here recorded, and had asked for Mary particularly. In the gospel he asks after each one of us.

29—31 As soon as she heard *that*, she arose quickly, and came unto him. Now Jesus was not yet come into the town, but was in that place where Martha met him. The Jews then which were with her in the house, and comforted her, when they saw Mary, that she rose up hastily and went out, followed her, saying, She goeth unto the grave to weep there.

32 Then when Mary was come where Jesus was, and saw him, she fell down at his feet, saying unto him, Lord, if thou hadst been here, my brother had not died. *(Her posture indicated the deepest reverence, yet her complaint was couched in the same words as that of her sister. We all find it hard to understand why the Lord permits heavy trials to overtake us.)*

33 When Jesus therefore saw her weeping, and the Jews also weeping which came with her, he groaned in the spirit, and was troubled.

34 And said, Where have ye laid him? They said unto him, Lord, come and see.

35 Jesus wept. *(This little verse is full of great teaching. It shows both the humanity and the sympathy of Jesus, and is for ever the mourner's choicest gem of consolation.)*

36 Then said the Jews, Behold how he loved him ! *(A word of astonishment which may as truly be used in reference to his love to each of his servants. His love to us is wonderful.)*

37 And some of them said, Could not this man, which opened the eyes of the blind, have caused that even this man should not have died? *(Of course he could, but they had not the wit to argue that he who could preserve life could also restore it. Often men stand on the verge of faith, and yet at last die in unbelief.)*

" See how he loved !" exclaimed the Jews,
As tender tears from Jesus fell ;
My grateful heart the thought pursues,
And on the theme delights to dwell.

" See how he loved," who travelled on,
And taught the doctrine from the skies !
Who bade disease and pain begone,
And called the sleeping dead to rise.

" See how he loved," who never shrank
From toil or danger, pain or death !
Who all the cup of sorrow drank,
And meekly yielded up his breath.

Such love, can we, unmoved, survey ?
Oh, may our breasts with ardour glow,
To tread his steps, his laws obey,
And thus our warm affections show !

554   "I have the keys of hell and of death."   SEPTEMBER 16.—EVENING.

[Or June 1.]

JOHN XI. 38—57.

JESUS therefore again groaning in himself cometh to the grave. *(We hear more about his groaning in this case, than in all his own personal sufferings. He never groaned so much for his own trials as for the troubles of his friends.)* It was a cave, and a stone lay upon it.

39 Jesus said, Take ye away the stone. *(All that man* can *do, man must do : the miracle begins only where natural forces end.)* Martha, the sister of him that was dead, saith unto him, Lord, by this time he stinketh : for he hath been dead four days. *(In that hot climate, putrefaction would soon set in. Could not Martha, who believed Jesus to be almighty in power, believe that even out of corruption her brother could be raised? Faith has strange weaknesses, and while leaping one way will limp another.)*

40 Jesus saith unto her, Said I not unto thee, that, if thou wouldest believe, thou shouldest see the glory of God ?

41, 42 Then they took away the stone *from the place* where the dead was laid. And Jesus lifted up *his* eyes, and said, Father, I thank thee that thou hast heard me. And I knew that thou hearest me always : but because of the people which stand by I said *it*, that they may believe that thou hast sent me.

43 And when he thus had spoken, he cried with a loud voice, Lazarus, come forth.

44 And he that was dead came forth, bound hand and foot with graveclothes : and his face was bound about with a napkin. Jesus saith unto them, Loose him, and let him go. *(When Jesus calls dead sinners out of their graves of sin into newness of life they are often bound by habits arising out of their former lives, it is our duty by example and instruction to lead them into the full liberty of the gospel.)*

45, 46 Then many of the Jews which came to Mary, and had seen the things which Jesus did, believed on him. But some of them went their ways to the Pharisees, and told them what things Jesus had done. *(Some people are mean enough for anything. How base these must have been!)*

47, 48 Then gathered the chief priests and the Pharisees a council, and said, What do we ? for this man doeth many miracles. If we let him thus alone, all *men* will believe on him : and the Romans shall come and take away both our place and nation.

49, 50 And one of them, *named* Caiaphas, being the high priest that same year, said unto them, Ye know nothing at all, nor consider that it is expedient for us, that one man should die for the people, and that the whole nation perish not. *(For mere political expediency, he would kill Jesus that the nation might not be destroyed by the Romans : but in this, like Balaam, he said far more than he himself understood, and was the mouthpiece of the Holy Spirit to declare the doctrine of the substitutionary sacrifice, by which atonement is made.)*

51, 52 And this spake he not of himself : but being high priest that year, he prophesied that Jesus should die for that nation ; and not for that nation only, but that also he should gather together in one the children of God that were scattered abroad.

53 Then from that day forth they took counsel together for to put him to death.

54—57 Jesus therefore walked no more openly among the Jews ; but went thence unto a country near to the wilderness, into a city called Ephraim, and there continued with his disciples. And the Jews' passover was nigh at hand : and many went out of the country up to Jerusalem before the passover, to purify themselves. Then sought they for Jesus, and spake among themselves, as they stood in the temple, What think ye, that he will not come to the feast? Now both the chief priests and the Pharisees had given a commandment, that, if any man knew where he were, he should shew *it*, that they might take him. *(What a proof have we here of the madness of depraved nature, when we see men eager to put to death one whose divine power had been so clearly proved by his raising the dead ! Such madness is in us all till grace removes it.)*

Jesus, thou Prince of life!
Thy chosen cannot die ;
Like thee, they conquer in the strife,
To reign with thee on high.

It is not death to fling
Aside this sinful dust,
And rise on strong exulting wing,
To live among the just.

LUKE IX. 51—62.

AND it came to pass, when the time was come that he should be received up, he stedfastly set his face to go to Jerusalem. *He looked beyond his death to his ascension, and for the joy that was set before him he was resolute to go through with the appointed suffering. Oh that we were equally stedfast to perform all the will of the Lord!*

52, 53 And sent messengers before his face: and they went, and entered into a village of the Samaritans, to make ready for him. And they did not receive him, because his face was as though he would go to Jerusalem. *(They were prejudiced against the Jewish worship. The Samaritans often attacked Galileans who passed through their country to go up to the feasts at Jerusalem.)*

54 And when his disciples James and John saw *this*, they said, Lord, wilt thou that we command fire to come down from heaven, and consume them, even as Elias did? *(They thought it holy indignation, and so perhaps it was, but that is not to be paramount under the gospel. Love reigns in Christ's kingdom.)*

55, 56 But he turned, and rebuked them, and said, Ye know not what manner of spirit ye are of. For the Son of man is not come to destroy men's lives, but to save *them*. And they went to another village.

57 And it came to pass, that, as they went in the way, a certain *man* said unto him, Lord, I will follow thee whithersoever thou goest.

58 And Jesus said unto him, Foxes have holes, and birds of the air *have* nests; but the Son of man hath not where to lay *his* head. *He hoped to share the glories of the great prophet and the honours of the Messiah. Jesus honestly told him that he would have not only to fare hard but to lie hard, and this did not suit the new professor. He had chosen Christ in ignorance, but Christ had not chosen him, and therefore away he went.*

59, 60 And he said unto another, Follow me. But he said, Lord, suffer me first to go and bury my father. Jesus said unto him, Let the dead bury their dead: but go thou and preach the kingdom of God. *(Christ himself called this man, and therefore, though he raised difficulties, grace overcame them. Nature's love was strong in him,* *but grace gained the victory. We must make everything else secondary to serving the Lord. Ministers should leave worldly business to others, and give themselves to the preaching of the gospel.)*

61, 62 And another also said, Lord, I will follow thee; but let me first go bid them farewell which are at home at my house. And Jesus said unto him, No man, having put his hand to the plough, and looking back, is fit for the kingdom of God. *(He who is called to the ministry should go through with it. As long as lungs and life hold out, no preacher may cease his testimony. If God has called him he must not, yea, he cannot, leave his sacred work.)*

WE are surprised to learn that it was James and John who thought of destroying the unfriendly Samaritans. Had it been Peter we should not have wondered, but how could the loving John act thus? Is not this another instance of the fact that most good men, at some time or other, fail in the very grace for which they are most remarkable? How differently did the beloved disciple act and write in after days! To show the contrast let us read—

I. JOHN IV. 10—14.

10 Herein is love, not that we loved God, but that he loved us, and sent his Son *to be* the propitiation for our sins.

11 Beloved, if God so loved us, we ought also to love one another.

12, 13 No man hath seen God at any time. If we love one another, God dwelleth in us, and his love is perfected in us. Hereby know we that we dwell in him, and he in us, because he hath given us of his Spirit.

14 And we have seen and do testify that the Father sent the Son *to be* the Saviour of the world. *(He was an eyewitness that Jesus did not come to destroy men's lives; this he had seen, and could testify to it with authority.)*

> Not to condemn the sons of men,
> Did Christ, the Son of God, appear;
> No weapons in his hands were seen,
> No fire from heaven nor thunder there.
>
> He came to save and not destroy,
> He from opposers turned away;
> Forbearing love became his joy.
> And, "Be it ours henceforth," we pray.

556   "𝔓eace be to this house."   September 17.—Evening.

[*Or June* 3.]

LUKE X. 1—20.

AFTER these things the Lord appointed other seventy also, and sent them two and two before his face into every city and place, whither he himself would come. (*The twelve had succeeded so well that our Lord enlarged the number of his evangelists, and sent them forth as itinerant preachers all over the land.*)

2 Therefore said he unto them, The harvest truly *is* great, but the labourers *are* few : pray ye therefore the Lord of the harvest, that he would send forth labourers into his harvest.

This prayer was to be offered by preachers themselves. In any other calling men are afraid of being crowded out if too many engage in it ; but there is no fear of this in the Christian ministry ; there cannot be too many soul-winners.

3 Go your ways : behold, I send you forth as lambs among wolves. (*They must therefore expect trouble, and look to a higher power than their own for protection.*)

4 Carry neither purse, nor scrip, nor shoes : and salute no man by the way. (*The king's business required haste, and therefore the needless courtesies of life were to be omitted.*)

5, 6 And into whatsoever house ye enter, first say, Peace *be* to this house. And if the son of peace be there, your peace shall rest upon it : if not, it shall turn to you again.

No blessing can be lost, if not well bestowed it will come home to the giver.

7 And in the same house remain, eating and drinking such things as they give : for the labourer is worthy of his hire. Go not from house to house. (*They were neither to be beggars nor feasters ; but, being refreshed at one hospitable table, they were to go on with their work.*)

8—12 And into whatsoever city ye enter, and they receive you, eat such things as are set before you : and heal the sick that are therein, and say unto them, The kingdom of God is come nigh unto you. But into whatsoever city ye enter, and they receive you not, go your ways out into the streets of the same, and say, Even the very dust of your city, which cleaveth on us, we do wipe off against you : notwithstanding be ye sure of this, that the kingdom of God is come nigh unto you. But I say unto you, that it shall be more tolerable in that day for Sodom, than for that city.

13, 14 Woe unto thee, Chorazin ! woe unto thee, Bethsaida ! for if the mighty works had been done in Tyre and Sidon, which have been done in you, they had a great while ago repented, sitting in sackcloth and ashes. But it shall be more tolerable for Tyre and Sidon at the judgment, than for you.

15 And thou, Capernaum, which art exalted to heaven, shalt be thrust down to hell.

Matthew Henry says, " To understand the wisdom of God in giving the means of grace to those who would not improve them, and denying them to those who would, we must wait for the great day of discovery."

16 He that heareth you heareth me ; and he that despiseth you despiseth me ; and he that despiseth me despiseth him that sent me.

Christ judges himself to be treated as his ministers are, and therefore it will go hard with those who reject their message and cause them pain.

17 And the seventy returned again with joy, saying, Lord, even the devils are subject unto us through thy name.

18 And he said unto them, I beheld Satan as lightning fall from heaven. (*He saw him fall from his power like a meteor, suddenly and hopelessly.*)

19 Behold, I give unto you power to tread on serpents and scorpions, and over all the power of the enemy : and nothing shall by any means hurt you.

20 Notwithstanding in this rejoice not, that the spirits are subject unto you ; but rather rejoice, because your names are written in heaven.

To be elect is better than to be endowed with the greatest gifts. When we are likely to become too elated by what the Lord does by us, it will be well to remember that what he has done for us is a far greater and safer reason for joy.

Bid, Lord, thy heralds publish loud
The peaceful blessings of thy reign ;
And when they speak of sprinkled blood,
The mystery to the heart explain.

Chase the usurper from his throne,
Oh ! chase him to his destined hell ;
Stout-hearted sinners overcome,
And glorious in thy temple dwell.

LUKE X. 23—37.

AND he turned him unto *his* disciples, and said privately, Blessed *are* the eyes which see the things that ye see : For I tell you, that many prophets and kings have desired to see those things which ye see, and have not seen *them ;* and to hear those things which ye hear, and have not heard *them.* (*Gospel times are happy times. Do we think enough of our privilege in being permitted to live in an age when salvation is fully revealed and plainly preached in all our streets? It is to be feared that the commonness of the blessing has made it cheap in our esteem.*)

25 ¶ And, behold, a certain lawyer stood up, and tempted him, saying, Master, what shall I do to inherit eternal life ? (*Or, what is the way to heaven by my own doings and merits ?*)

26 He said unto him, What is written in the law ? how readest thou ?

27 And he answering said, Thou shalt love the Lord thy God with all thy heart, and with all thy soul, and with all thy strength, and with all thy mind ; and thy neighbour as thyself.

28 And he said unto him, Thou hast answered right : this do, and thou shalt live. *For " the man that* doeth *these things shall live in them ;" but who has ever thus loved the Lord his God? Who among the fallen sons of men can thus honour his Maker? Our Lord thus laid open the impossibility of salvation by works. The labours of Hercules are nothing to the work which is required to merit heaven. To love God and our neighbour, according to the measure of the law, has never yet been accomplished by any mere man.*

29 But he, willing to justify himself, said unto Jesus, And who is my neighbour ? *Expecting the Lord to tell him that his fellow Jew was such ; instead of which, the Lord tells him that he ought to be a neighbour to any man and every man in need.*

30 And Jesus answering said, A certain *man* went down from Jerusalem to Jericho, and fell among thieves, which stripped him of his raiment, and wounded *him,* and departed, leaving *him* half dead.

31 And by chance there came down a certain priest that way : and when he saw him, he passed by on the other side. (*He had too much to do at the temple to act the part of a man.*

Official religiousness often kills common humanity.)

32 And likewise a Levite, when he was at the place, came and looked *on him,* and passed by on the other side.

33, 34 But a certain Samaritan, as he journeyed, came where he was : and when he saw him, he had compassion *on him,* And went to *him,* and bound up his wounds, pouring in oil and wine, and set him on his own beast, and brought him to an inn, and took care of him.

35, 36 And on the morrow when he departed, he took out two pence, and gave *them* to the host, and said unto him, Take care of him ; and whatsoever thou spendest more, when I come again, I will repay thee. Which now of these three, thinkest thou, was neighbour unto him that fell among the thieves ?

37 And he said, He that shewed mercy on him. Then said Jesus unto him, Go, and do thou likewise. (*Compassion is a great gospel duty, and it must be hearty and practical. When we see a man in distress, we must not pass him by as the priest and Levite did, for thus we shall show that our religion is only skin-deep, and has never affected our hearts. We must pity, go near, help, and befriend. All that is needed we must do, so far as it lies in our power, and never leave the needy one till we have seen the matter through. The good Samaritan has earned for himself immortal honour. Let us imitate him by manifesting a brother's love to those who are in trouble, even though they should happen to be opposed to us in religion, or have been regarded as our enemies. Such conduct will bring glory to God, and go far to recommend the holy religion which we profess. The Lord help us to do so, for Jesus' sake. Amen.*)

How beauteous are their feet
Who stand on Zion's hill !
Who bring salvation on their tongues,
And words of peace reveal !

How happy are our ears,
That hear this joyful sound,
Which kings and prophets waited for,
And sought but never found.

How blessed are our eyes,
That see this heavenly light !
Prophets and kings desired it long,
But died without the sight.

LUKE X. 38—42.

NOW it came to pass, as they went, that he entered into a certain village: and a certain woman named Martha received him into her house.

39 And she had a sister called Mary, which also sat at Jesus' feet, and heard his word.

40 But Martha was cumbered about much serving, and came to him, and said, Lord, dost thou not care that my sister hath left me to serve alone? bid her therefore that she help me. (*Martha was not blamable for serving, nor for serving much, but for being distracted with care, when she should have been listening to her Lord. Mary wisely judged that it would better please the Lord for her to hearken to his teaching than to offer him a grand entertainment. What were joints and dishes to him! He had far rather receive an attentive ear than any or all the other attentions which the kindest hostesses could offer him.*)

41, 42 And Jesus answered and said unto her, Martha, Martha, thou art careful and troubled about many things: But one thing is needful: and Mary hath chosen that good part, which shall not be taken away from her. (*She was more spiritual than her sister, and was wise for so being. The active Christian must one day cease from his activity, but the contemplative spiritual believer may continue to sit at Jesus' feet throughout the whole of life, and even in death itself. To learn of Jesus and live in communion with him is the highest privilege of saints.*)

LUKE XI. 1—13.

AND it came to pass, that, as he was praying in a certain place, when he ceased, one of his disciples said unto him, Lord, teach us to pray, as John also taught his disciples.

2 And he said unto them, When ye pray, say, Our Father which art in heaven, Hallowed be thy name. Thy kingdom come. Thy will be done, as in heaven, so in earth.

3 Give us day by day our daily bread.

4 And forgive us our sins; for we also forgive every one that is indebted to us. And lead us not into temptation; but deliver us from evil. (*This is the model for our prayers, and the more closely we copy its fulness, order, brevity, and spirituality, the better we shall pray.*)

5—7 And he said unto them, Which of you shall have a friend, and shall go unto him at midnight, and say unto him, Friend, lend me three loaves; For a friend of mine in his journey is come to me, and I have nothing to set before him? And he from within shall answer and say, Trouble me not: the door is now shut, and my children are with me in bed; I cannot rise and give thee.

8 I say unto you, Though he will not rise and give him, because he is his friend, yet because of his importunity he will rise and give him as many as he needeth.

Importunity will prevail where friendship fails; how much more will it succeed with our ever-faithful heavenly friend!

9, 10 And I say unto you, Ask, and it shall be given you; seek, and ye shall find; knock, and it shall be opened unto you. For every one that asketh receiveth; and he that seeketh findeth; and to him that knocketh it shall be opened. (*Prayer is not a vain exercise; it is heard and answered. Where it fails there is a reason for that failure. "Ye have not because ye ask not, or because ye ask amiss."*)

11 If a son shall ask bread of any of you that is a father, will he give him a stone? (*There were stones near the Saviour which looked like thin cakes of bread. Will a father deceive his child with these?*) or if he ask a fish, will he for a fish give him a serpent? (*Some fishes may be mistaken for serpents. Will a father give his child a poisonous serpent instead of a fish?*)

12 Or if he shall ask an egg, will he offer him a scorpion?

13 If ye then, being evil, know how to give good gifts unto your children: how much more shall *your* heavenly Father give the Holy Spirit to them that ask him? (*We do not make mistakes and give our children deadly things when they ask for good things, neither will the Lord refuse us, or send us the counterfeits of blessings. We shall obtain real boons, and that which is the essence of all benedictions, the life of grace, and the soul of holiness, namely, the Holy Spirit. We may ask for him, and we may expect to receive him in answer to our petition.*)

LUKE XI. 37—54.

AND as he spake, a certain Pharisee besought him to dine with him : and he went in, and sat down to meat. *(If he meant the invitation kindly, our Lord accepted of it in kindness to him ; and if he intended it as a means of watching him, the Lord showed that he was not afraid of his keenest glances. Truth baffles spies, and therefore fears them not.)*

38 And when the Pharisee saw *it*, he marvelled that he had not first washed before dinner. *(The merely outward ceremony of bathing their hands before eating was made so much of by the Pharisees that our Lord purposely abstained from it. He came to teach the religion which cleanses the heart, not that which begins and ends with the body. It is the duty of the followers of Jesus to discourage in all possible ways the superstitious observances of modern Ritualists, who are the Pharisees of the period.)*

39 And the Lord said unto him, Now do ye Pharisees make clean the outside of the cup and the platter ; but your inward part is full of ravening and wickedness.

40 *Ye* fools, did not he that made that which is without make that which is within also ?

41 But rather give alms of such things as ye have ; and, behold, all things are clean unto you. *(When benevolence offers a portion of her substance to the poor, she sanctifies the rest. To wash ones hands of greediness is better than a hundred washings in water.)*

42 But woe unto you, Pharisees ! for ye tithe mint and rue and all manner of herbs, and pass over judgment and the love of God : these ought ye to have done, and not to leave the other undone. *(Only a hypocrite will exalt trifles above important duties, and he only does so to be thought exceedingly strict. The tithe of small herbs could not amount to much, and was only paid in order to make men say, "How scrupulous the Pharisees are !")*

43 Woe unto you, Pharisees ! for ye love the uppermost seats in the synagogues, and greetings in the markets.

44 Woe unto you, scribes and Pharisees, hypocrites ! for ye are as graves which appear not, and the men that walk over *them* are not aware *of them. (Their hearts were full of wickedness, and yet they bore a high repute; and*

so were like graves which are green above ground, but are full of rottenness within, where the eye of man cannot see.)

45 ¶ Then answered one of the lawyers *(or teachers of the law)* and said unto him, Master, thus saying thou reproachest us also. *(It touched his conscience as the Lord intended it should.)*

46 And he said, Woe unto you also, *ye* lawyers ! for ye lade men with burdens grievous to be borne, and ye yourselves touch not the burdens with one of your fingers.

47, 48 Woe unto you ! for ye build the sepulchres of the prophets, and your fathers killed them. Truly ye bear witness that ye allow the deeds of your fathers : for they indeed killed them, and ye build their sepulchres.

They pretended to honour the prophets by erecting memorials to them; but inasmuch as they continued in the sins of their persecuting sires, he accuses them of perpetrating and perfecting their parents' acts; the fathers killed and buried the saints, and the sons built their sepulchres.

49 Therefore also said the wisdom of God, I will send them prophets and apostles, and *some* of them they shall slay and persecute :

50 That the blood of all the prophets, which was shed from the foundation of the world, may be required of this generation ;

51 From the blood of Abel unto the blood of Zacharias, which perished between the altar and the temple : verily I say unto you, It shall be required of this generation. *(Read the story of the siege of Jerusalem, and the just vengeance of God upon the Jews will be before you.)*

52 Woe unto you, lawyers ! for ye have taken away the key of knowledge : ye entered not in yourselves, and them that were entering in ye hindered.

53, 54 And as he said these things unto them, the scribes and the Pharisees began to urge *him* vehemently, and to provoke him to speak of many things : Laying wait for him, and seeking to catch something out of his mouth, that they might accuse him. *(Burkitt, in his Commentary, here writes, " When any lie in wait to catch something out of our mouth that they may ensnare us, give us thy prudence and thy patience, O Lord, that we may not give occasion to those who seek occasion against us.")*

LUKE XII. 1—21.

IN the mean time, when there were gathered together an innumerable multitude of people, insomuch that they trode one upon another, he began to say unto his disciples first of all, Beware ye of the leaven of the Pharisees, which is hypocrisy. For there is nothing covered, that shall not be revealed; neither hid, that shall not be known. *(How vain, then, is it to play the hypocrite! If God did not see, and nothing more were known of us than what our fellow men can detect, hypocrisy might answer its purpose; but what folly it is to try to deceive when everything is observed by the Lord, and will in due time be published before all men.)*

3 Therefore whatsoever ye have spoken in darkness shall be heard in the light; and that which ye have spoken in the ear in closets shall be proclaimed upon the housetops. *(Therefore it becomes us to behave in our private life just as we would do if all men were gazing upon us. Since we cannot conceal our true character, let us not be so foolish as to seem to be what we are not.)*

4, 5 And I say unto you my friends, Be not afraid of them that kill the body, and after that have no more that they can do. But I will forewarn you whom ye shall fear: Fear him, which after he hath killed hath power to cast into hell; yea, I say unto you, Fear him.

6 Are not five sparrows sold for two farthings, and not one of them is forgotten before God?

7 But even the very hairs of your head are all numbered. Fear not therefore: ye are of more value than many sparrows. *(The doctrine of a special providence is here plainly taught. It is full of richest comfort.)*

8 Also I say unto you, Whosoever shall confess me before men, him shall the Son of man also confess before the angels of God:

9 But he that denieth me before men shall be denied before the angels of God.

10 And whosoever shall speak a word against the Son of man, it shall be forgiven him: but unto him that blasphemeth against the Holy Ghost it shall not be forgiven. *He will be left to impenitence and therefore be lost. Those who can and do repent have not committed this sin.*

11, 12 And when they bring you unto the synagogues, and *unto* magistrates, and powers, take ye no thought how or what thing ye shall answer, or what ye shall say: For the Holy Ghost shall teach you in the same hour what ye ought to say.

13 And one of the company said unto him, Master, speak to my brother, that he divide the inheritance with me.

14 And he said unto him, Man, who made me a judge or a divider over you? *(He kept to his own work, and did not interfere with the duty of the magistrate. Christian ministers should in this imitate their Lord and mind their own proper business.)*

15—17 And he said unto them, Take heed, and beware of covetousness: for a man's life consisteth not in the abundance of the things which he possesseth. And he spake a parable unto them, saying, The ground of a certain rich man brought forth plentifully: And he thought within himself, saying, What shall I do, because I have no room where to bestow my fruits? *(Why not give the overplus to the poor? There were twenty good ways of disposing of his superfluous wealth.)*

18, 19 And he said, This will I do: I will pull down my barns, and build greater; and there will I bestow all my fruits and my goods. And I will say to my soul, Soul, thou hast much goods laid up for many years; take thine ease, eat, drink, *and* be merry. *(It was all self. He talked only of "I," and "My goods." Alas, such language is common enough when covetous men talk to themselves.)*

20, 21 But God said unto him, *Thou fool,* this night thy soul shall be required of thee: then whose shall those things be, which thou hast provided? So *is* he that layeth up treasure for himself, and is not rich toward God. *(He is a fool too. He puts the body before the soul, he hopes to find ease on the thorny bed of wealth, and makes sure of a long life in a dying world. O Lord, keep all of us from being so foolish.)*

Almighty Father of mankind!
  On thee my hopes remain;
And when the day of trouble comes,
  I shall not trust in vain.

In all thy mercies, may my soul
  A Father's bounty see;
Nor let the gifts thy hand bestows
  Estrange my heart from thee.

LUKE XII. 35—48

L ET your loins be girded about, and *your* lights burning; (*Eastern garments require to be girded up when a man begins to work. The Saviour tells us to be prepared for service towards God, and for testimony before men. We are to get ready, and to keep ready.*)

36 And ye yourselves like unto men that wait for their lord, when he will return from the wedding; that when he cometh and knocketh, they may open unto him immediately. *We are to live in expectation, waiting to hear the knock of our Master at the door. Are we so living? Do we look for the coming of the Lord?*

37 Blessed *are* those servants, whom the lord when he cometh shall find watching: verily I say unto you, that he shall gird himself, and make them to sit down to meat, and will come forth and serve them. (*This is not according to the manner of men, for what master will wait upon his servants? Yet the condescending love of Jesus promises to us this high honour. Who would not cheerfully obey such a Lord?*)

38 And if he shall come in the second watch, or come in the third watch, and find *them* so, blessed are those servants.

39 And this know, that if the good man of the house had known what hour the thief would come, he would have watched, and not have suffered his house to be broken through.

40 Be ye therefore ready also: for the Son of man cometh at an hour when ye think not. *Watch and wait: at any moment Jesus may be here. What manner of persons ought we to be, who live in such an expectation?*

41 ¶ Then Peter said unto him, Lord, speakest thou this parable unto us, or even to all? (*It had a bearing upon all, but the Lord, in answer to Peter's question, proceeded to show its special bearing upon ministers of the gospel.*)

42 And the Lord said, Who then is that faithful and wise steward, whom *his* lord shall make ruler over his household, to give *them their* portion of meat in due season? *It was anciently the steward's duty to allot to every member of the family his regular portion, and so are the stewards of Christ to instruct all classes of persons, giving to each the teaching most appropriate.*

43 Blessed *is* that servant, whom his lord when he cometh shall find so doing.

44 Of a truth I say unto you, that he will make him ruler over all that he hath.

45, 46 But and if that servant say in his heart, My lord delayeth his coming; and shall begin to beat the menservants and maidens, and to eat and drink, and to be drunken; The lord of that servant will come in a day when he looketh not for *him*, and at an hour when he is not aware, and will cut him in sunder, and will appoint him his portion with the unbelievers. *The most terrible punishments will be richly deserved by those who, being placed in the responsible position of caring for the souls of others, shall dare to neglect them, and shall even use their power and influence to tyrannise over them and oppress them. May the Lord send us faithful ministers, and keep them faithful.*

47, 48 And that servant, which knew his lord's will, and prepared not *himself*, neither did according to his will, shall be beaten with many *stripes*. But he that knew not, and did commit things worthy of stripes, shall be beaten with few *stripes*. For unto whomsoever much is given, of him shall be much required: and to whom men have committed much, of him they will ask the more. (*God's judgments will be exactly according to right, and none shall have cause to complain. The highest degree of punishment will fall to the lot of some of us if we neglect the gospel, for we have much light and knowledge; and therefore, our sin will be the greater.*)

Ye servants of the Lord,
  Each in his office wait,
Observant of his heavenly word,
  And watchful at his gate.

Let all your lamps be bright,
  And trim the golden flame:
Gird up your loins as in his sight,
  For awful is his name.

Watch! 'tis your Lord's command;
  And while we speak he's near;
Mark the first signal of his hand,
  And ready all appear.

562   *" Thou art loosed from thine infirmity."*   SEPTEMBER 20.—EVENING.

[*Or June* 9.]

WE *are now about to consider one of our Lord's miracles, wrought upon a woman who had long been in sorrow. May it comfort any who are spiritually in a like condition.*

LUKE XIII. 11—17.

11 And, behold, there was a woman which had a spirit of infirmity eighteen years, and was bowed together, and could in no wise lift up *herself. (Poor creature, to be so long deformed, so long made to suffer at every step she took! Her condition was very grievous, but she did not stay away from public worship. If she had done so, she would not have been found by Jesus in the synagogue.)*

12, 13 And when Jesus saw her, he called *her to him,* and said unto her, Woman, thou art loosed from thine infirmity. And he laid *his* hands on her : and immediately she was made straight, and glorified God. *(When souls which have long been bowed down are graciously made upright, they never fail to give praise to God.)*

14 And the ruler of the synagogue answered with indignation, because that Jesus had healed on the sabbath day, and said unto the people, There are six days in which men ought to work : in them therefore come and be healed, and not on the sabbath day.

15—17 The Lord then answered him, and said, *Thou* hypocrite, doth not each one of you on the sabbath loose his ox or *his* ass from the stall, and lead *him* away to watering? And ought not this woman, being a daughter of Abraham, whom Satan hath bound, lo, these eighteen years, be loosed from this bond on the sabbath day? And when he had said these things, all his adversaries were ashamed : and all the people rejoiced for all the glorious things that were done by him.

THERE *are many persons to be found who are bowed down with despondency of spirit, and cannot lift up themselves to enjoy a comfortable hope. Let such take heart from the case before us ; and let them also remember that the Lord does not now forget the sorrowful and broken-hearted. We see this expressly stated in—*

ISAIAH XLIX. 13—16.

13 Sing, O heavens ; and be joyful, O earth ; and break forth into singing, O mountains : for the LORD hath comforted his people, and will have mercy upon his afflicted.

14 But Zion said, the LORD hath forsaken me, and my Lord hath forgotten me.

15, 16 Can a woman forget her sucking child, that she should not have compassion on the son of her womb? yea, they may forget, yet will I not forget thee. Behold, I have graven thee upon the palms of *my* hands ; thy walls *are* continually before me.

THAT *he might be able to sympathise with downcast souls, and bear with their infirmities, Jesus himself became a man like ourselves. Troubled hearts should think of this, and be of good cheer. The Holy Spirit speaks of him most sweetly in—*

HEBREWS II. 14—18.

14 Forasmuch then as the children are partakers of flesh and blood, he also himself likewise took part of the same ; that through death he might destroy him that had the power of death, that is, the devil ;

15 And deliver them who through fear of death were all their lifetime subject to bondage.

16 For verily he took not on *him the nature of* angels ; but he took on *him* the seed of Abraham.

17 Wherefore in all things it behoved him to be made like unto *his* brethren, that he might be a merciful and faithful high priest in things *pertaining* to God, to make reconciliation for the sins of the people.

18 For in that he himself hath suffered being tempted, he is able to succour them that are tempted.

Darkness and doubts had veil'd my mind,
    And drown'd my eyes in tears,
Till, like the sun, my Saviour's face,
    Dispell'd my gloomy fears.

Oh, what immortal joys I felt,
    And raptures all divine,
When Jesus told me I was his,
    And my beloved mine!

In vain the tempter frights my soul,
    And breaks my peace in vain ;
One glimpse, dear Saviour, of thy face
    Revives my joys again.

LUKE XIII. 23—35.

THEN said one unto him, Lord, are there few that be saved? *(A question which has been asked many times since. If a book could be published by authority detailing the number of the saved, many would hasten to read it. It would be far more wise to ask, "Shall I be saved?" We may get a clear answer to that personal inquiry, but upon the larger question we are not yet in possession of more than clouded light. "If but three persons are to be saved, why should not I be one of them?" was a sensible remark we once heard from an earnest seeker.)* And he said unto them, Strive to enter in at the strait gate: for many, I say unto you, will seek to enter in, and shall not be able. *(Now is the accepted time, but ere long the day of grace and of this mortal life will end, and then it will be too late to seek for mercy.)*

25, 26 When once the master of the house is risen up, and hath shut to the door, and ye begin to stand without, and to knock at the door, saying, Lord, Lord, open unto us; and he shall answer and say unto you, I know you not whence ye are: Then shall ye begin to say, We have eaten and drunk in thy presence, and thou hast taught in our streets. *(No doubt many rely upon the means of grace and participation in the sacraments; their confidence will utterly fail them at the last.)*

27 But he shall say, I tell you, I know you not whence ye are; depart from me, all *ye* workers of iniquity.

28 There shall be weeping and gnashing of teeth, when ye shall see Abraham, and Isaac, and Jacob, and all the prophets, in the kingdom of God, and you *yourselves* thrust out. *Pushed out with indignation, because the gospel was rejected by them. It will be a great loss to lose the company of prophets and saints for ever.*

29 And they shall come from the east, and *from* the west, and from the north, and *from* the south, and shall sit down in the kingdom of God. *(It will very much aggravate the sorrows of the lost to see so many saved whose prospects did not appear to be one half so hopeful as their own.)*

30 And, behold, there are last which shall be first, and there are first which shall be last.

31 The same day there came certain of the Pharisees, saying unto him, Get thee out, and depart hence: for Herod will kill thee.

32, 33 And he said unto them, Go ye, and tell that fox, Behold, I cast out devils, and I do cures to day and to morrow, and the third *day* I shall be perfected. Nevertheless I must walk to day, and to morrow, and the *day* following: for it cannot be that a prophet perish out of Jerusalem. *(He called Herod a fox because that crafty person was trying to frighten him out of his dominions by employing the Pharisees to alarm him with fear of death. Jesus, as Lord over all kings, had a right thus to describe the cunning monarch whose character was exactly that of the scheming, artful fox. Jesus defied his threats, and went on with his holy mission.)*

34 O Jerusalem, Jerusalem, which killest the prophets, and stonest them that are sent unto thee; how often would I have gathered thy children together, as a hen *doth gather* her brood under *her* wings, and ye would not!

35 Behold, your house is left unto you desolate: and verily I say unto you, Ye shall not see me, until *the time* come when ye shall say, Blessed *is* he that cometh in the name of the Lord. *(Wonderful sight! The Son of God in tears! He could not think of the ruin of men without deep sympathy, nor should we. We must not allow our hearts to become unfeeling in this matter, or we shall be very unlike our Lord and Master.)*

Did Christ o'er sinners weep,
And shall our cheeks be dry?
Let floods of penitential grief
Burst forth from every eye.

The Son of God in tears,
Angels with wonder see!
Be thou astonish'd, O my soul,
He shed those tears for thee.

He wept that we might weep;
Each sin demands a tear;
In heaven alone no sin is found,
And there's no weeping there.

LUKE XIV. 1; 7—24.

AND it came to pass, as he went into the house of one of the chief Pharisees to eat bread on the sabbath day, that they watched him. *(It must have been a great vexation to the open-hearted Saviour to be thus perpetually surrounded by spies. None but he would have endured it with so much meekness. Instead of being distracted by their mean enmity, he calmly sought the good of the guests around him.)*

7 And he put forth a parable to those which were bidden, when he marked how they chose out the chief rooms ; saying unto them,

8, 9 When thou art bidden of any *man* to a wedding, sit not down in the highest room ; lest a more honourable man than thou be bidden of him ; And he that bade thee and him come and say to thee, Give this man place ; and thou begin with shame to take the lowest room.

10 But when thou art bidden, go and sit down in the lowest room ; that when he that bade thee cometh, he may say unto thee, Friend, go up higher : then shalt thou have worship in the presence of them that sit at meat with thee.

11 For whosoever exalteth himself shall·be abased ; and he that humbleth himself shall be exalted. *(The parable is self-evident common sense, and the lesson from it is most important spiritual truth. Let us not lose its practical teaching.)*

12 ¶ Then said he also to him that bade him, When thou makest a dinner or a supper, call not thy friends, nor thy brethren, neither thy kinsmen, nor *thy* rich neighbours ; lest they also bid thee again, and a recompence be made thee.

13 But when thou makest a feast, call the poor, the maimed, the lame, the blind :

14 And thou shalt be blessed ; for they cannot recompense thee : for thou shalt be recompensed at the resurrection of the just. *(We give to the rich, and think it a pleasure to do them service ; and yet, they do not need it. Who would refuse anything to the queen? Yet the poor are not so welcome. Is this right?)*

15 ¶ And when one of them that sat at meat with him heard these things, he said unto him, Blessed *is* he that shall eat bread in the kingdom of God.

16 Then said he unto him, A certain man made a great supper, and bade· many :

17 And sent his servant at supper time to say to them that were bidden, Come ; for all things are now ready.

18 And they all with one *consent* began to make excuse. The first said unto him, I have bought a piece of ground, and I must needs go and see it : I pray thee have me excused. *Why not go to see the ground at another time? Had he bought it without seeing it?*

19 And another said, I have bought five yoke of oxen, and I go to prove them : I pray thee have me excused. *(Did he mean to plough at night? These bad excuses were worse than none.)*

20 And another said, I have married a wife, and therefore I cannot come. *(Why not bring his wife with him? This was a pretence too flimsy to conceal his unfriendly feeling to the giver of the feast.)*

21 So that servant came, and shewed his lord these things. Then the master of the house being angry said to his servant, Go out quickly into the streets and lanes of the city, and bring in hither the poor, and the maimed, and the halt, and the blind. *(The anger of our Lord against some brought good to others. If those first bidden will not come to the feast, we Gentile sinners are enabled to fill the vacant room.)*

22 And the servant said, Lord, it is done as thou hast commanded, and yet there is room.

23 And the Lord said unto the servant, Go out into the highways and hedges, and compel *them* to come in, that my house may be filled.

24 For I say unto you, That none of those men which were bidden shall taste of my supper. *(If mercy be refused by us now, we shall be refused mercy ere long. The Lord is very patient ; but he will not always bear to have his love despised. May none of us delay accepting the gospel call, lest the Lord should declare that we shall not taste of his supper.)*

" All things are ready," Come,
    Come to the supper spread ;
Come rich and poor, come old and young,
    Come, and be richly fed.
" All things are ready," Come,
    The invitation's given,
Through him who now in glory sits
    At God's right hand in heaven.
" All things are ready," Come,
    The door is open wide ;
Oh feast upon the love of God,
    For Christ, his Son, has died.

Oh that I could for ever sit
With Mary at the Master's feet ;
 Be this my happy choice :
My only care, delight, and bliss,
My joy, my heaven on earth, be this,
 To hear the Bridegroom's voice.

God only knows the love of God :
Oh that it now were shed abroad
 In this poor stony heart :
For love I sigh, for love I pine :
This only portion, Lord be mine,
 Be mine this better part.

To wash the hands or bow the knee
 While all is foul within,
Is but a base hypocrisy,
 And addeth sin to sin.
Lord, search my heart and try my ways
 And make my soul sincere ;
Then shall I stand before thy face,
 And find acceptance there.

Is there a thing beneath the sun
That strives with thee my heart to share ?
Ah, tear it thence, and reign alone,
The Lord of every motion there !
Then shall my heart from earth be free,
When it hath found repose in thee.

Each moment draw from earth away
My heart, that lowly waits thy call ;
Speak to my inmost soul, and say,
"I am thy Love, thy God, thy All !"
To feel thy power, to hear thy voice,
To taste thy love, be all my choice.

Lord, teach our sympathising breasts
 That sacred joy to know,
Which lies in sharing others' joys,
 And cheering others' woe.
To homes of want, and beds of pain,
 We cheerfully repair ;
And with the gift thy hand bestows,
 Relieve the mourner's care.
The widow's heart shall sing for joy,
 The orphan's tongue shall sing ;
And thus to thee our loving Lord,
 We will new glory bring.

He comes with sudden stroke to smite
 The busy sons of men ;
He cometh as a thief at night,
 But no man knoweth when.

Watch, therefore, since you cannot tell
 Th' appointed hour nor day ;
Watch, that he find you girded well,
 Watch, ye, I say, and pray.

Ask not for self a crown,
 Let all ambition die ;
Remember how thy Lord came down
 And laid his glories by.

Drink thou with him the cup,
 With him the baptism share ;
Be this thy truest lifting up
 Like to thy Lord to fare.

Jesus ! Master ! hear my cry ;
Save me, heal me with a word ;
Fainting at thy feet I lie ;
Thou my whispered plaint hast heard.

Jesus ! Master ! mercy show ;
Thou art passing near my soul ;
Thou my inward grief dost know,
Thou alone canst make me whole.

Jesus ! Master ! as of yore
Thou didst bid the blind man see,
Light upon my spirit pour ;
Jesus ! Master ! heal thou me.

LUKE XIV. 25—35.

AND there went great multitudes with him : and he turned, and said unto them,

26 If any *man* come to me, and hate not his father, and mother, and wife, and children, and brethren, and sisters, yea, and his own life also, he cannot be my disciple. *(Jesus did not wish to win disciples by mistake. He would not have men follow him without knowing the terms upon which he would receive them as disciples. He therefore told them plainly that he must be everything or nothing; he claims the first place in the heart; even parents and children must be second to him. He must be so paramount that for his sake all other dear ones would be abandoned, if need be, and life itself would be relinquished for love of him. Less love to Jesus than this is no love at all. Do we love him with an all-absorbing, masterly affection? If not, we have not yet learned to be his disciples.)*

27 And whosoever doth not bear his cross, and come after me, cannot be my disciple.

Still further, our Lord proceeds to lay down the terms of discipleship. His followers must suffer loss and shame, and be willing to do so, or they have not learned the first elements of the faith. Jesus denied himself for the good of others, and for the truth's sake, and so must we, or we cannot be his followers. What say we to this?

28 For which of you, intending to build a tower, sitteth not down first, and counteth the cost, whether he have *sufficient* to finish *it?*

29, 30 Lest haply, after he hath laid the foundation, and is not able to finish *it*, all that behold *it* begin to mock him, Saying, This man began to build, and was not able to finish.

To make a profession of religion and not to consider what it will cost us is to subject ourselves to ridiculous failure. We must give Jesus all our heart, and be willing to suffer for his sake. Can we carry this out by the Spirit's help? If not, it is better not to profess to be Christians.

31, 32 Or what king, going to make war against another king, sitteth not down first, and consulteth whether he be able with ten thousand to meet him that cometh against him with twenty thousand? Or else, while the other is yet a great way off, he sendeth an ambassage, and desireth conditions of peace.

33 So likewise, whosoever he be of you that forsaketh not all that he hath, he cannot be my disciple. *(We may not be called actually to do so, but we must be quite ready to lose all for Jesus' sake, or else we are not his true followers. What martyrs have actually done we must be willing to do, or we have not the grace of God in us.)*

34 ¶ Salt *is* good : but if the salt have lost his savour, wherewith shall it be seasoned?

35 It is neither fit for the land, nor yet for the dunghill; *but* men cast it out. He that hath ears to hear, let him hear. *(If Christianity itself could become powerless, of what good would it be? If a man renewed by grace could become like other men, how could he be saved? If the Spirit of God and his regeneration could fail, what would remain? Blessed be God, such a failure shall never occur; but if it could, the result must be final and total destruction.)*

THE *apostles and the first believers were ready to sacrifice all things for Jesus; they did not ask to walk with the truth in its silver slippers, but were willing to go through the mire with her. Paul is a notable instance of this, for he says,—*

PHILIPPIANS III. 7—11.

7 But what things were gain to me, those I counted loss for Christ.

8 Yea doubtless, and I count all things *but* loss for the excellency of the knowledge of Christ Jesus my Lord : for whom I have suffered the loss of all things, and do count them *but* dung, that I may win Christ,

9 And be found in him, not having mine own righteousness, which is of the law, but that which is through the faith of Christ, the righteousness which is of God by faith :

10 That I may know him, and the power of his resurrection, and the fellowship of his sufferings, being made conformable unto his death.

11 If by any means I might attain unto the resurrection of the dead. *(Better far to die for Christ than live by apostacy. Gain by selling Christ would be deadly loss; loss for him is gain. May the Lord enable us calmly to choose Christ and his cross and to forsake sin and its transitory pleasures. Amen.)*

LUKE XV. 1—10.

THEN drew near unto him all the publicans *(or tax-gatherers)* and sinners for to hear him. *(They filled the inner circle, being anxious to catch every word. The Lord Jesus was so kind and affable, that they felt at home with him. He had none of the repelling pride of the Pharisaic doctors, but his loving interest in the fallen classes, like a loadstone, drew them around him.)*

2 And the Pharisees and scribes murmured, saying, This man receiveth sinners, and eateth with them. *(They formed an outer ring of grumbling spies, carping at all that he said and did. In their zeal to find fault with him, they uttered that which has ever remained as his highest praise. It is for us poor sinners a signal mercy that Jesus does receive the guilty, and commune with them. Let us ask him to receive us again at this moment, and eat with us, for it is still true, that " this man receiveth sinners."*

The cavilling of the Pharisees drew from our Lord that richest of all his gospel parables, which we are now about to read. It is but one picture, though painted in three panels.)

3, 4 And he spake this parable unto them, saying, What man of you, having an hundred sheep, if he lose one of them, doth not leave the ninety and nine in the wilderness, and go after that which is lost, until he find it ?

5 And when he hath found *it*, he layeth *it* on his shoulders, rejoicing.

6 And when he cometh home, he calleth together *his* friends and neighbours, saying unto them, Rejoice with me ; for 1 have found my sheep which was lost.

7 I say unto you, that likewise joy shall be in heaven over one sinner that repenteth, more than over ninety and nine just persons, which need no repentance. *(This first picture describes the joy of the Son of God in man's salvation. He is the Good Shepherd, and cares for each one of his sheep. To rescue the lost, he left the saints and angels in heaven, and traversed this wilderness world. He finds those who are not seeking him, and, with hands of love and shoulders of power, brings them home, making himself and all holy beings glad at the finding of the lost. If for*

us to be saved gives to the Saviour so much joy, there must be hope for the very worst. Is it not so?)

8, 9 Either what woman having ten pieces of silver, if she lose one piece, doth not light a candle, and sweep the house, and seek diligently till she find *it ?* And when she hath found *it*, she calleth *her* friends and *her* neighbours together, saying, Rejoice with me ; for I have found the piece which I had lost.

10 Likewise, I say unto you, there is joy in the presence of the angels of God over one sinner that repenteth. *(The second picture of the one great parable sets forth the work of the Holy Spirit through the church. Man is a precious thing; he bears the image of God; but he is lost. The Spirit, by the church, seeks the lost treasure. The candle of truth is brought, and much trouble is taken by the preaching of the searching word to seek for the lost. Lost souls are found, and then the church is glad, and God himself, before whom angels stand, is full of rejoicing. Whatever we may do, he values the pieces minted in his own mint, and has no pleasure in their being lost. What comfort it ought to be to anxious souls when they learn that their salvation will give joy to the heart of him whom angels adore. One repenting sinner is more joy to God than a new-made world. Let us return to our loving Lord, and grieve him no more.*

Those who are once found by divine grace are saved, for the angels would not rejoice prematurely over one who might yet be lost. Heavenly joy is never rash ; angels cannot be supposed to have rejoiced too soon. True penitents are saved, and therefore, before they enter heaven holy beings rejoice over them with unalloyed delight, expecting to see them ere long in glory.)

> To see a sinner saved,
>   Makes glad th' angelic choir ;
> O'erwhelmed with mightier ecstasies
>   They lift their praises higher.
>   From every golden string
>   Sublimer praises sound,
> The dead restored to life they sing,
>   The wandering sinner found—
>   Found, to be lost no more,
>   Alive, in life to stay,
> And love, and wonder, and adore
>   Through one eternal day.

WE *will now look at the third of the three pictures which make up our Lord's parable: it represents the divine Father's part in salvation.*

LUKE XV. 11—32.

11, 12 And he said, A certain man had two sons: And the younger of them said to *his* father, Father, give me the portion of goods that falleth *to me.* And he divided unto them *his* living.

13 And not many days after the younger son gathered all together, and took his journey into a far country, and there wasted his substance with riotous living.

14—16 And when he had spent all, there arose a mighty famine in that land; and he began to be in want. And he went and joined himself to a citizen of that country; and he sent him into his fields to feed swine. And he would fain have filled his belly with the husks that the swine did eat: and no man gave unto him. *This is the best the world can do for an awakened sinner. Its richest joys and its best religious teachings are only swines' meat, and cannot satisfy the soul's cravings.*

17—19 And when he came to himself, he said, How many hired servants of my father's have bread enough and to spare, and I perish with hunger! I will arise and go to my father, and will say unto him, Father, I have sinned against heaven, and before thee, And am no more worthy to be called thy son: make me as one of thy hired servants.

20 And he arose, and came to his father. But when he was yet a great way off, his father saw him, and had compassion, and ran, and fell on his neck, and kissed him.

21 And the son said unto him, Father, I have sinned against heaven, and in thy sight, and am no more worthy to be called thy son. (*He did not say, "Make me as one of thy hired servants:" his father smothered that legal prayer with a kiss.*)

22—24 But the father said to his servants, Bring forth the best robe, and put *it* on him; and put a ring on his hand, and shoes on *his* feet: And bring hither the fatted calf, and kill *it;* and let us eat and be merry: For this my son was dead, and is alive again; he was lost, and is found. And they began to be merry.

25, 26 Now his elder son was in the field: and as he came and drew nigh to the house, he heard musick and dancing. And he called one of the servants, and asked what these things meant. (*He was in a bad state, and had grown self-conceited, as even good people are apt to do.*)

27 And he said unto him, Thy brother is come; and thy father hath killed the fatted calf, because he hath received him safe and sound.

28 And he was angry, and would not go in: therefore came his father out, and intreated him.

29, 30 And he answering said to *his* father, Lo, these many years do I serve thee, neither transgressed I at any time thy commandment: and yet thou never gavest me a kid, that I might make merry with my friends: But as soon as this thy son was come, which hath devoured thy living with harlots, thou hast killed for him the fatted calf. (*He complained that his religion brought him but little joy, and yet the newly converted sinner was made the receiver of great delights. We have often heard this from grumbling professors who have sunk into an ill condition of heart.*)

31 And he said unto him, Son, thou art ever with me, and all that I have is thine. (*If we do not rejoice, it is our own fault for living below our privileges, for all things are ours.*)

32 It was meet that we should make merry, and be glad: for this thy brother was dead, and is alive again; and was lost, and is found.

Joy over new converts is most proper and seemly, and it is unlovely for any to grudge them the delights of new found grace. Let us imitate the heavenly Father, and not the elder brother.

Who can describe the joys that rise
Through all the courts of Paradise,
To see a prodigal return,
To see an heir of glory born?

With joy the Father doth approve
The fruit of his eternal love;
The Son with joy looks down, and sees
The purchase of his agonies.

The Spirit takes delight to view
The holy soul he formed anew;
And saints and angels join to sing
The growing empire of their King.

LUKE XVI. 1—17.

AND he said also unto his disciples, There was a certain rich man, which had a steward; and the same was accused unto him that he had wasted his goods.

2 And he called him, and said unto him, How is that I hear this of thee? give an account of thy stewardship; for thou mayest be no longer steward.

3, 4 Then the steward said within himself, What shall I do? for my lord taketh away from me the stewardship: I cannot dig; to beg I am ashamed. I am resolved what to do, that, when I am put out of the stewardship, they may receive me into their houses.

5 So he called every one of his lord's debtors *unto him,* and said unto the first, How much owest thou unto my lord?

6 And he said, An hundred measures of oil. And he said unto him, Take thy bill, and sit down quickly, and write fifty.

7 Then said he to another, and how much owest thou? And he said, An hundred measures of wheat. And he said unto him, Take thy bill, and write fourscore.

8 And the lord *(not Jesus, but the steward's master),* commended the unjust steward, because he had done wisely: for the children of this world are in their generation wiser than the children of light. *(It was not his dishonesty which was commended, but his shrewdness. The steward's business was to get as much as he could for his lord out of the tenants; and finding that he was to be dismissed he used his remaining tenure of office to earn their friendship, by remitting their rents. In this he was sharp and far seeing; and we, though we must never act dishonestly, should also look before us, and act with our worldly treasure in such a way as to win the friendship of others. Money is never better used than when we do good to others with it, so that in persecuting times, even the ungodly may think of us in a friendly spirit, while the gracious will love us, and welcome us into the mansions above. Hoarding gets poor interest; giving is true thrift.)*

9 And I say unto you, Make to yourselves friends of the mammon of unrighteousness; that, when ye fail, they may receive you into everlasting habitations.

10, 11 He that is faithful in that which is least is faithful also in much: and he that is unjust in the least is unjust also in much. If therefore ye have not been faithful in the unrighteous mammon, who will commit to your trust the true *riches?* *(A man who does not use money well will not employ higher gifts discreetly. To use wealth to promote the good of others is wisdom, and he who fails in this, does not know how to use the true riches, and will not be trusted therewith. It needs much grace to use money well, and those who make it their care to do so, are among the best of Christians.)*

12 And if ye have not been faithful in that which is another man's, who shall give you that which is your own? *(If you are not faithful when you are under obligation to be so, you will be far more unwise in matters in which you think that you may do as you please. The bad steward of another will make a bad manager for himself.)*

13 ¶ No servant can serve two masters: for either he will hate the one, and love the other; or else he will hold to the one, and despise the other. Ye cannot serve God and mammon.

Two principles cannot both be master in the heart. God and mammon will neither of them accept a divided empire. We must serve the one or the other; the two will never agree.

14 And the Pharisees also, who were covetous, heard all these things: and they derided him. *(Men are very apt to pretend to ridicule that which troubles their consciences. No person is more hopeless than the man who jests at the Word of the Lord.)*

15 And he said unto them, Ye are they which justify yourselves before men; but God knoweth your hearts: for that which is highly esteemed among men is abomination in the sight of God. *(This we should always remember, for it will save us from loving the fashions of the day, or trembling at the frowns of men. If God abhors what man esteems, man's judgment should be of small account with us.)*

16 The law and the prophets *were* until John: since that time the kingdom of God is preached, and every man presseth into it.

17 And it is easier for heaven and earth to pass, than one tittle of the law to fail.

OUR *present reading opens up to a terrible view of the state of the ungodly in the world to come, when all their earthly riches will be taken from them, and their guilty souls will be driven from the presence of the Lord.*

LUKE XVI. 19—31.

19 There was a certain rich man, which was clothed in purple and fine linen, and fared sumptuously every day : *(He was a worldling in a choice position. The world does not always yield its servants such present comforts and enjoyments, for even the ungodly are often poor and sick. This man thought himself fortune's favourite, and he cared nothing for the favour of God. He was rich, and showed it in his clothing and his feeding. Self-indulgence and earthly honour were the gods which he worshipped every day. Many envied him, but could they have known his latter end, they would have pitied him.)*

20 And there was a certain beggar named Lazarus, which was laid at his gate, full of sores.

21 And desiring to be fed with the crumbs which fell from the rich man's table : moreover the dogs came and licked his sores.

They were more pitiful than their master, and lent the moisture of their tongues where he refused his aid. Here was a saint at his worst, and yet it went well with him.

22 And it came to pass, that the beggar died, and was carried by the angels into Abraham's bosom : the rich man also died, and was buried ; *(With gilded hearse, and plumes, and pall, and marble tomb, perhaps ; but what of that ?)*

23 And in hell he lift up his eyes, being in torments, and seeth Abraham afar off, and Lazarus in his bosom. *(This makes hell the more unbearable, that the lost can behold the bliss of the blessed.)*

24 And he cried and said, Father Abraham, have mercy on me, and send Lazarus, that he may dip the tip of his finger in water, and cool my tongue ; for I am tormented in this flame.

Into what a case had he now come ! His rare wines were far away, and even a drop of water was prayed for as a luxury. How sad to be rich here, and to be lost hereafter !

25 But Abraham said, Son, remember that thou in thy lifetime receivedst thy good things,

and likewise Lazarus evil things : but now he is comforted, and thou art tormented.

26 And beside all this, between us and you there is a great gulf fixed : so that they which would pass from hence to you cannot; neither can they pass to us, that *would come* from thence.

The division is eternal. Once saved for ever saved : once lost for ever lost. The partings of the judgment are final : saint and sinner will never meet again when once their dooms are fixed.

27, 28 Then he said, I pray thee therefore, father, that thou wouldest send him to my father's house : For I have five brethren ; that he may testify unto them, lest they also come into this place of torment. *(Their coming into hell would increase his wretchedness ; their upbraidings would flog his conscience and increase his woe. It was not that he had any spiritual love for their souls, but he had love for himself, and did not wish to hear their reproaches.)*

29 Abraham saith unto him, They have Moses and the prophets ; let them hear them.

30 And he said, Nay, father Abraham : but if one went unto them from the dead, they will repent.

31 And he said unto him, If they hear not Moses and the prophets, neither will they be persuaded, though one rose from the dead.

If the Word of God and the ministry of the gospel be not enough to convert men, there is no hope for them ; even a preacher sent from the eternal world would have no power over them, they would scorn his message. Are any of us unsaved ? Let us see our condition, and yield to the gospel's call. However happy our life may be in this world, it were better for us that we had never been born than that we should live and die unsaved. O Eternity, Eternity ! what must it be to lose thy heavenly joys ! What must it be to sink into thine infinite woes !

Ah ! who can speak the vast dismay
   Which fills the sinner's mind,
When torn by death's strong hand away,
   He leaves his all behind.

Wretches who cleave to earthly things,
   But are not rich to God,
Their dying hour is full of stings,
   And hell their dark abode.

LUKE XVII. 3—19.

TAKE heed to yourselves : If thy brother trespass against thee, rebuke him ; and if he repent, forgive him.

4 And if he trespass against thee seven times in a day, and seven times in a day turn again to thee, saying, I repent ; thou shalt forgive him. *(We are not to pretend to do so, but to do it really and from our hearts. Though the provocation may be cruel and frequently repeated, still we are to meet it with love, and thus overcome evil with good. Is not this a hard task? The apostles evidently thought it so difficult that they placed it out of the region of common actions, and regarded it as a marvel which only great faith could perform.)*

5 And the apostles said unto the Lord, Increase our faith. *(They felt that to forgive as their Lord bade them needed mighty faith ; and Jesus, pleased with their prayer, explained to them that faith would enable them to work both this and other spiritual wonders.)*

6 And the Lord said, If ye had faith as a grain of mustard seed, ye might say unto this sycamine tree, Be thou plucked up by the root, and be thou planted in the sea ; and it should obey you. *(To remove a tree from the earth and plant it in the unstable ocean would not be so great a marvel as to transplant the forgiving nature of the Lord Jesus and make it flourish in our hearts : yet faith can achieve the miracle. Lord, work this in each of us.)*

7, 8 But which of you having a servant plowing or feeding cattle, will say unto him by and by, when he is come from the field, Go, and sit down to meat ? And will not rather say unto him, Make ready wherewith I may sup, and gird thyself, and serve me, till I have eaten and drunken ; and afterward thou shalt eat and drink ? *(This is the season for service, and if grace enables us to be zealous and diligent, we are only acting as our position requires. To wish the Lord to give us honour and ease in this life, is as unreasonable as if a servant should expect his master to wait upon him.)*

9, 10 Doth he thank that servant because he did the things that were commanded him ? I trow not. So likewise ye, when ye shall have done all those things which are commanded you, say, We are unprofitable servants : we have done that which was our duty to do. *(Boasting is excluded. If we have reached the highest degree of holiness, we are no better than we should be.)*

11—13 And it came to pass, as he went to Jerusalem, that he passed through the midst of Samaria and Galilee. And as he entered into a certain village, there met him ten men that were lepers, which stood afar off : and they lifted up *their* voices, and said, Jesus, Master, have mercy on us.

14—16 And when he saw *them*, he said unto them, Go shew yourselves unto the priests. And it came to pass, that, as they went, they were cleansed. And one of them, when he saw that he was healed, turned back, and with a loud voice glorified God, And fell down on *his* face at his feet, giving him thanks : and he was a Samaritan.

17 And Jesus answering said, Were there not ten cleansed ? but where *are* the nine ?

18 There are not found that returned to give glory to God, save this stranger. *(It is a good rule never to expect gratitude from any one, for it is a rare thing in the earth ; and when we do receive it, it generally comes from those of whom we least expected it. Let us not ourselves forget to show our thankfulness to God for mercies received, for although gratitude to the Lord may not be in itself a sufficient sign of grace, yet its absence is a sure token of an unrenewed heart. In the case before us the thankful Samaritan was the only one of the ten who had true faith, and therefore he received the Saviour's blessing.)*

19 And he said unto him, Arise, go thy way, thy faith hath made thee whole.

Ten lepers felt the Saviour's power
    And straightway were restored,
But only one of ten returned
    To bless the healing Lord.

So all among the sons of men,
    His bounteous gifts obtain,
But few return with thankful love
    To bless the Lord again.

Lord, let me not ungrateful prove,
    For this were deepest shame,
But teach me how with all my heart
    To magnify thy name.

MATTHEW XIX. 1—2.

AND it came to pass, *that* when Jesus had finished these sayings, he departed from Galilee, and came into the coasts of Judæa beyond Jordan;

2 And great multitudes followed him; and he healed them there. (*This is a most encouraging fact. If Jesus cures multitudes why should he not save each one of us? Why should we not cry to him for help, and expect to receive it? The healing virtue in Jesus is not diminished: seek it, and it will be freely given.*)

LUKE XVII. 20—37.

20 And when he was demanded of the Pharisees, when the kingdom of God should come, he answered them and said, The kingdom of God cometh not with observation:

21 Neither shall they say, Lo here! or, lo there! for, behold, the kingdom of God is within you. (*They looked for an outward reign, as many do still, and so they missed the glory of the inward spiritual kingdom. Outward pomp and show in religion are still the main things with many, but they forget the words before us; "Behold, the kingdom of God is within you."*)

22 And he said unto the disciples, The days will come, when ye shall desire to see one of the days of the Son of man, and ye shall not see *it*. (*No doubt many a time the apostles said, "Would God our Lord were here," especially in those dark days when the Romans compassed the city.*)

23 And they shall say to you, See here; or, see there: go not after *them*, nor follow *them*.

24 For as the lightning, that lighteneth out of the one *part* under heaven, shineth unto the other *part* under heaven; so shall also the Son of man be in his day. (*There will be no need of inquiries then. His coming will be plain to all. Yet there was need of this caution, for in all ages deceivers have risen up, and have misled many by prophecies concerning the second advent. Vain dreamers often go insane upon this matter.*)

25 But first must he suffer many things, and be rejected of this generation.

26 And as it was in the days of Noe, so shall it be also in the days of the Son of man.

27 They did eat, they drank, they married wives, they were given in marriage, until the day that Noe entered into the ark, and the flood came, and destroyed them all.

28—30 Likewise also as it was in the days of Lot; they did eat, they drank, they bought, they sold, they planted, they builded; But the same day that Lot went out of Sodom it rained fire and brimstone from heaven, and destroyed *them* all. Even thus shall it be in the day when the Son of man is revealed.

31 In that day, he which shall be upon the housetop, and his stuff in the house, let him not come down to take it away: and he that is in the field, let him likewise not return back. *The most valued property must be sacrificed to save life. Loitering has cost many a man his soul.*

32 Remember Lot's wife. (*She looked, she longed, she lingered, and she died, yet she was Lot's wife, and was on the way to escape. Alas, how many are near to salvation and yet perish. This little verse should be often before our eyes.*)

33 Whosoever shall seek to save his life shall lose it; and whosoever shall lose his life shall preserve it. (*Those who die for Christ's sake have saved their lives, and those who are cowards and deny their Lord to escape from death have in the highest sense lost life.*)

34—36 I tell you, in that night there shall be two *men* in one bed; the one shall be taken, and the other shall be left. Two *women* shall be grinding together; the one shall be taken, and the other left. Two *men* shall be in the field; the one shall be taken, and the other left. *When the Romans came only a few escaped, and so even now death finds many unprepared. Families will not be saved in the bulk. True religion is a personal matter; one by faith will live, and another will perish in unbelief. Who among us will escape from hell when the Lord shall summon us to judgment?*

37 And they answered and said unto him, Where, Lord? And he said unto them, Wheresoever the body *is*, thither will the eagles be gathered together. (*The first fulfilment of this prophecy was at the siege of Jerusalem, when the Roman eagles gathered around the dead body of the Jewish state. Then did the Lord come forth to punish impenitent Israel, and then his disciples, being warned, fled in haste from the condemned city. Never, however, let us forget that his great coming is yet future, and that we ought to be hourly prepared for it.*)

ONE *of the most beautiful events in the life of the Redeemer is recorded in—*

MARK X. 13—16.

13 And they brought young children to him, that he should touch them : and *his* disciples rebuked those that brought *them.*

No doubt their mothers rightly judged that the Saviour's blessing would in the best sense enrich their children, and conduce to their future happiness, and so they led their boys and girls to him. The disciples thought that he would be annoyed with the little ones, but they did not know what a kind heart he had. No fathers or mothers should think their children too little to be converted. While they are boys and girls, Jesus can bless them.

14 But when Jesus saw *it*, he was much displeased, and said unto them, Suffer the little children to come unto me, and forbid them not : for of such is the kingdom of God. *(We do not often find him much displeased, and therefore we may learn that to discourage a child from coming to Jesus is beyond all other things displeasing to him.)*

15 Verily I say unto you, Whosoever shall not receive the kingdom of God as a little child, he shall not enter therein. *(We must possess the simplicity, teachableness, and trustfulness of children, or else grace is not in us. Like them also we must be free from avarice and ambition.)*

16 And he took them up in his arms, put *his* hands upon them, and blessed them.

DAVID *in his day was well aware that the grace of God makes men childlike. This will be clearly seen, if we read—*

PSALM CXXXI.

1 Lord, my heart is not haughty, nor mine eyes lofty : neither do I exercise myself in great matters, or in things too high for me.

2 Surely I have behaved and quieted myself, as a child that is weaned of his mother : my soul *is* even as a weaned child.

3 Let Israel hope in the LORD from henceforth and for ever.

THE *tenderness of Jesus to the little ones proved him to be the Messiah, for we read—*

ISAIAH XL. 10, 11.

10 Behold, the Lord GOD will come with strong *hand*, and his arm shall rule for him: behold, his reward *is* with him, and his work before him.

11 He shall feed his flock like a shepherd : he shall gather the lambs with his arm, and carry *them* in his bosom, *and* shall gently lead those that are with young.

NOW *that we have before us this choice act of Jesus' love in receiving children, let us pray that all in this house may be blessed of him, and that the children may be saved while yet young. Have we not the promise of it? Is not the promise to us and to our children? For our encouragement let us read and pray over—*

PSALM CXXVIII.

1 Blessed *is* every one that feareth the LORD ; that walketh in his ways.

2, 3 For thou shalt eat the labour of thine hands: happy *shalt* thou *be*, and *it shall be* well with thee. Thy wife *shall be* as a fruitful vine by the sides of thine house : thy children like olive plants round about thy table.

4 Behold, that thus shall the man be blessed that feareth the LORD.

5 The LORD shall bless thee out of Zion : and thou shalt see the good of Jerusalem all the days of thy life.

6 Yea, thou shalt see thy children's children, *and* peace upon Israel.

Full of love was Jesus found
To the little ones around ;
And his tender, loving eye
Would not pass an infant by.

When the young to him were led,
Gracious gentle words he said ;
While he took them up and smiled
Kindly on each little child.

" Let the young ones come to me,
And forbid them not," said he ;
" Many such, in heaven above,
Dwell with God and share his love."

MARK X. 17—31.

AND when he was gone forth into the way, there came one running, and kneeled to him, and asked him, Good Master, what shall I do that I may inherit eternal life ? *(An inquiry which had been put to him before, but this time it came from one who thought that he had already done all that would entitle him to eternal bliss. The question was not "What is the way of salvation?" but, "How can I merit heaven?")*

18 And Jesus said unto him, Why callest thou me good ? *there is* none good but one, *that is,* God. *(The questioner did not know that Jesus was God, and therefore he ought not to have called him good.)*

19 Thou knowest the commandments, Do not commit adultery, Do not kill, Do not steal, Do not bear false witness, Defraud not, Honour thy father and mother. *(If a man would win heaven by works he must keep these commands and more.)*

20 And he answered and said unto him, Master, all these have I observed from my youth.

21 Then Jesus beholding him loved him, and said unto him, One thing thou lackest : go thy way, sell whatsoever thou hast, and give to the poor, and thou shalt have treasure in heaven : and come, take up the cross, and follow me.

If he loved God supremely, as the law required, here was a test for him. We are not all called to relinquish our property; but if Jesus bade us do so, and we refused, it would prove that we loved the world better than God, and therefore were very far from keeping the commandments.

22 And he was sad at that saying, and went away grieved : for he had great possessions.

He could not stand the test. He thought that he loved God best, but soon discovered that he did not.

23 And Jesus looked round about, and saith unto his disciples, How hardly shall they that have riches enter into the kingdom of God !

24 And the disciples were astonished at his words. *(For the Rabbis gave the rich all the advantage, and thought the salvation of the poor almost hopeless.)* But Jesus answereth again, and saith unto them, Children, how hard is it for them that trust in riches to enter into the kingdom of God ! *(Trusting in riches is the great evil rather than the having of them, though the two things often go together.)*

25, 26 It is easier for a camel to go through the eye of a needle, than for a rich man to enter into the kingdom of God. And they were astonished out of measure, saying among themselves, Who then can be saved ?

27 And Jesus looking upon them saith, With men *it is* impossible, but not with God : for with God all things are possible.

28 ¶ Then Peter began to say unto him, Lo, we have left all, and have followed thee.

But it was a poor little all—an old ship and a few worn out nets. Peter's usual rashness led him to mention the sacrifice he and his friends had made; in after years he was more modest.

29, 30 And Jesus answered and said, Verily I say unto you, There is no man that hath left house, or brethren, or sisters, or father, or mother, or wife, or children, or lands, for my sake, and the gospel's, But he shall receive an hundredfold now in this time, houses, and brethren, and sisters, and mothers, and children, and lands, with persecutions ; and in the world to come eternal life. *(Even here the Lord Jesus is to us a hundredfold more than houses or relatives could be, and when he is near we rejoice to suffer for his sake.)*

31 But many *that are* first shall be last; and the last first.

Ye glittering toys of earth, adieu,
   A nobler choice be mine ;
A real prize attracts my view,
   A treasure all divine.

Jesus to multitudes unknown,
   Oh, name divinely sweet !
Jesus, in thee, in thee alone,
   Wealth, honour, pleasure, meet.

Should both the Indies at my call,
   Their boasted stores resign,
With joy I would renounce them all,
   For leave to call thee mine.

Should earth's vain treasures all depart,
   Of this dear gift possess'd,
I'd clasp it to my joyful heart,
   And be for ever bless'd.

MATTHEW XX. 1—16.

FOR the kingdom of heaven is like unto a man *that is* an householder, which went out early in the morning to hire labourers into his vineyard. And when he had agreed with the labourers for a penny a day, he sent them into his vineyard. (*Each man is called upon to work for the Lord, and in doing so he will find an abundant reward. The penny promised was sufficient maintenance for the day, and was regarded as a fair wage. No man shall ever have cause to complain that he served God for nought. Those are happiest who enter his service early in the morning.*)

3, 4 And he went out about the third hour, and saw others standing idle in the market place, And said unto them ; Go ye also into the vineyard, and whatsoever is right I will give you. And they went their way. (*Till we serve God we are idlers. However busy we may be we do nothing till we live for God.*)

5 Again he went out about the sixth and ninth hour, and did likewise. (*The half of the day was gone, yea, three-fourths of it, and yet this patient householder engaged the labourers. If half our life, or even three-fourths, be gone, the Lord will still receive us, for his hirings are not after the manner of men.*)

6 And about the eleventh hour he went out, and found others standing idle, and saith unto them, Why stand ye here all the day idle ?

7 They say unto him, Because no man hath hired us. He saith unto them, Go ye also into the vineyard ; and whatsoever is right, *that* shall ye receive. (*This showed that the hiring of labourers in this case was not an act of necessity but of bounty, or surely the householder would not have hired men just as the sun was setting. In the Lord's vineyard grace alone chooses, calls, hires, and pays the workers.*)

8 So when even was come, the lord of the vineyard saith unto his steward, Call the labourers, and give them *their* hire, beginning from the last unto the first.

9 And when they came that *were hired* about the eleventh hour, they received every man a penny. (*However late in life a man may be converted he shall enjoy the same privileges and promises as others. Free grace gives freely and does not upbraid.*)

10 But when the first came, they supposed that they should have received more ; and they likewise received every man a penny.

11 And when they had received *it*, they murmured against the goodman of the house.

12 Saying, These last have wrought *but* one hour, and thou hast made them equal unto us, which have borne the burden and heat of the day. (*This ungenerous spirit will creep in even among the servants of God, but it deserves to be cast out with detestation. We ought to rejoice in the richness of divine love to aged converts. Envy of another's spiritual privileges is most unseemly in a child of God.*)

13—15 But he answered one of them, and said, Friend, I do thee no wrong : didst not thou agree with me for a penny ? Take *that* thine *is*, and go thy way : I will give unto this last, even as unto thee. Is it not lawful for me to do what I will with mine own ? Is thine eye evil, because I am good ? (*The sovereignty of God is vindicated as much in the enjoyments and privileges of saints as in their election to eternal life. In making all his people equally dear to his heart, equally safe in Christ, and equal in justification and adoption, the Lord as much displays his undoubted right to do as he wills with his own, as when he chooses a certain number of sinners, and allows others to continue in their sins.*)

16 So the last shall be first, and the first last : for many be called, but few chosen.

Those who start in religion and promise great things frequently disappoint us, while others of whom we despaired bring forth good fruit. Many are called by the Gospel, but few are really elect of God, and so obey the call from the heart ; and out of these only a remnant become eminent for grace. Choice men are rare even among the chosen.

While our days on earth are lengthen'd,
  May we give them, Lord, to thee ;
Cheer'd by hope, and daily strengthen'd,
  May we run, nor weary be ;
    Till thy glory,
  Without clouds in heaven we see.

576   " Ye shall indeed drink of the cup that I drink of."   SEPTEMBER 27.—MORNING.

[*Or June* 22.]

MARK X. 32—45.

AND they were in the way going up to Jerusalem ; and Jesus went before them: and they were amazed ; and as they followed, they were afraid. *(Like a brave captain the Lord led the way, and like brave followers his disciples, despite their fears, kept close to their leader. It is well if, when we experience any alarm, we have faith enough still to press 'forward where Jesus points out the road.)* And he took again the twelve, and began to tell them what things should happen unto him, *Saying,* Behold we go up to Jerusalem ; and the Son of man shall be delivered unto the chief priests, and unto the scribes; and they shall condemn him to death, and shall deliver him to the Gentiles : And they shall mock him, and shall scourge him, and shall spit upon him, and shall kill him : and the third day he shall rise again. *(The Lord was very explicit, and gave more of the details of his sufferings and death than he had ever mentioned before. He was very familiar with his friends, and told them all things ; he was very honest with them, and plainly warned them of the evils which would happen to him, lest they should follow him with mistaken expectations. Jesus familiarised his disciples with his death before it happened, and much more would he now have it before our minds, since its bitterness is past, and the fruits of it are surpassingly precious.)*

35 ¶ And James and John, the sons of Zebedee, come unto him, saying, Master, we would that thou shouldest do for us whatsoever we shall desire.

36 And he said unto them, What would ye that I should do for you ? *(He would not grant them a request thus put to him in the dark. He wisely allowed them to go on with their suit, that, upon further consideration, they might be made ashamed of it.)*

37 They said unto him, Grant unto us that we may sit, one on thy right hand, and the other on thy left hand, in thy glory. *(When he should take his kingdom, they desired to be the first peers in his realm. Not, perhaps, because they wished to be above their brethren, but because they loved him so well that they desired to be very near and dear to him, and to enjoy the same distinguished position which he had in some*

measure given to them already, when with Peter they had formed a favoured trio upon the mount of transfiguration.)

38 But Jesus said unto them, Ye know not what ye ask : can ye drink of the cup that I drink of ? and be baptized with the baptism that I am baptized with ?

39 And they said unto him, We can. And Jesus said unto them, Ye shall indeed drink of the cup that I drink of; and with the baptism that I am baptized withal shall ye be baptized :

40 But to sit on my right hand and on my left hand is not mine to give ; but *it shall be given to them* for whom it is prepared.

Our ignorance often shows itself in our prayers. We ask for a crown when we ought to pray for grace to bear our cross.

41 And when the ten heard *it,* they began to be much displeased with James and John.

This was very natural, but it did not last long. Partly through the influence of our Lord's words, and partly through the humble and loving conduct of these two gracious brethren, all jealousy subsided, and we do not detect even a trace of it in the after history of the apostles.

42—44 But Jesus called them *to him,* and saith unto them, Ye know that they which are accounted to rule over the Gentiles exercise lordship over them ; and their great ones exercise authority upon them. But so shall it not be among you : but whosoever will be great among you, shall be your minister *(or servant):* And whosoever of you will be the chiefest, shall be servant of all. *(In the church of God, he is greatest who renders most service, and is willing to take the lowest place for the good of the rest. Those who are really eminent have to work harder and endure far more reproach than their less honoured brethren, and so it should be, since thus it was with our Lord.)*

45 For even the Son of man came not to be ministered unto, but to minister, and to give his life a ransom for many. *(He gave up all and took the lowest service for our sakes; thus teaching his followers not to look for honour or service from their fellow Christians, but to stand ready to be the servants of all. Lord, teach us to serve, and save us from the pride which would expect others to pay us homage.)*

LUKE XIX. 1—10.

A ND *Jesus* entered and passed through Jericho. And, behold, *there was* a 'man named Zacchæus, which was the chief among the publicans, and he was rich.

3, 4 And he sought to see Jesus who he was; and could not for the press, because he was little of stature. And he ran before, and climbed up into a sycomore tree to see him : for he was to pass that *way*.

5 And when Jesus came to the place, he looked up, and saw him, and said unto him, Zacchæus, make haste, and come down ; for to day I must abide at thy house. (*Here was sovereign, free, effectual grace. Jesus sought the heart which else would never have sought him. The eternal purpose had rendered it necessary that Zacchæus should be saved; there was a divine* must *in the way, and therefore called and saved he was, though apparently one of the most unlikely of converts.*)

6 And he made haste, and came down, and received him joyfully.

Oh that each one of us might with equal willingness receive Jesus, who is now calling us to himself. May the mighty word of everlasting love make us willing in the day of its power.

7 And when they saw *it*, they all murmured, saying, That he was gone to be guest with a man that is a sinner. (*Not only the Pharisees, but others also were astonished at the Saviour's visit to this member of the tax-collecting band, for the publicans were despised and hated by all their countrymen. Free grace thus delights to astonish men by choosing and calling the base things of this world.*)

8 And Zacchæus stood, and said unto the Lord ; Behold, Lord, the half of my goods I give to the poor ; and if I have taken any thing from any man by false accusation, I restore *him* fourfold. (*Thus he gave evidence of a change of heart by a change of way. Restitution is first due to all whom we may have wronged, and then, over and above that, charity to the poor becomes our duty. Zacchæus attended to both obligations, he was just as well as generous. Thus by his righteous and liberal conduct he cleared the Saviour from all charges of conniving at sin. The Lord had not winked at his conduct, but had made him repent of it, and for ever turn from it, to become an honourable man.*)

9 And Jesus said unto him, This day is salvation come to this house, forsomuch as he also is a son of Abraham.

10 For the Son of man is come to seek and to save that which was lost. (*A publican was looked upon as a lost man, who had forfeited his privileges as a son of Abraham; but Jesus restored the lost one, and raised him to a higher position than that which he had occupied by birth. Sin has not lost us so much as Jesus gives us.*)

MARK X. 46—52.

A ND as he went out of Jericho with his disciples and a great number of people, blind Bartimæus, the son of Timæus, sat by the highway side begging.

47 And when he heard that it was Jesus of Nazareth, he began to cry out, and say, Jesus, *thou* son of David, have mercy on me.

Though he could not see, he could hear and speak, and he earnestly used what power he had. Some who are unsaved neglect the use of the means which are within their power, and do not ask for salvation.

48 And many charged him that he should hold his peace : but he cried the more a great deal, *Thou* son of David, have mercy on me.

When a soul is really anxious it cannot refrain from prayer. It must and will cry for mercy.

49 And Jesus stood still, and commanded him to be called. And they call the blind man, saying unto him, Be of good comfort, rise ; he calleth thee.

50 And he, casting away his garment, rose, and came to Jesus. (*He cared no more for his old cloak, he expected to receive his sight. The hope of mercy makes all other things seem trivial.*)

51 And Jesus answered and said unto him, What wilt thou that I should do unto thee ? The blind man said unto him, Lord, that I might receive my sight.

52 And Jesus said unto him, Go thy way ; thy faith hath made thee whole. And immediately he received his sight, and followed Jesus in the way.

How quick the cure. The man believed and prayed, and Jesus spake the healing word. Exercise such faith each one of you, and the like healing shall be yours.

578   "𝕺ccupy till 𝕴 come."   SEPTEMBER 28.—MORNING.

[*Or June* 24.]

LUKE XIX. 11—27.

AND as they heard these things, he added and spake a parable, because he was nigh to Jerusalem, and because they thought that the kingdom of God should immediately appear. *(He would turn their thoughts away from the thrones and glories, which they fondly expected, to the service and duty which really lay before them.)*

12, 13 He said therefore, A certain nobleman went into a far country to receive for himself a kingdom, and to return. And he called his ten servants, and delivered them ten pounds, and said unto them, Occupy till I come.

Use my money in trade till I return.

14 But his citizens hated him, and sent a message after him, saying, We will not have this *man* to reign over us.

15 And it came to pass, that when he was returned, having received the kingdom, then he commanded these servants to be called unto him, to whom he had given the money, that he might know how much every man had gained by trading.

16 Then came the first, saying, Lord, thy pound hath gained ten pounds. *(Great grace is modest. He did not say I have gained ten pounds, but thy pound hath gained it. Good men say as Paul did, "I laboured, yet not I, but the grace of God which was in me.")*

17 And he said unto him, Well, thou good servant: because thou hast been faithful in a very little, have thou authority over ten cities.

18 And the second came, saying, Lord, thy pound hath gained five pounds.

19 And he said likewise to him : Be thou also over five cities. *(Those who are alike faithful may not be all equally successful; there is a sovereignty in the results of service as well as in the gifts of grace. Yet all faithful servants are acceptable to their Master.)*

20, 21 And another came, saying, Lord, behold, *here is* thy pound, which I have kept laid up in a napkin: For I feared thee, because thou art an austere man: thou takest up that thou layedst not down, and reapest that thou didst not sow.

22, 23 And he saith unto him, Out of thine own mouth will I judge thee, *thou* wicked servant. Thou knewest that I was an austere man, taking up that I laid not down, and reaping that I did not sow : Wherefore then gavest not thou my money into the bank, that at my coming I might have required mine own with usury ? *(or interest.)*

He met him on his own ground, and condemned him out of his own mouth. The character of the master is no rule for the servant, he was bound to do his lord's will, and if he knew that lord to be severe, this should have quickened him into greater diligence.

24—26 And he said unto them that stood by, Take from him the pound, and give *it* to him that hath ten pounds. (And they said unto him, Lord, he hath ten pounds.) For I say unto you, that unto every one which hath shall be given ; and from him that hath not, even that he hath shall be taken away from him.

It is always so ; the gracious and faithful man obtains more grace and more means of usefulness, while the unfaithful man sinks lower and lower, and grows worse and worse. We must either make progress or else lose what we have attained. There is no such thing as standing still in religion.

27 But those mine enemies, which would not that I should reign over them, bring hither, and slay *them* before me. *(Will there be one of this dear family among those unhappy rebels who will miserably perish ? O Lord, forbid it !)*

There is an hour when I must stand,
  Before the judgment seat ;
And all my sins, and all my crimes,
  In awful vision meet.

There is an hour, when I must look
  On one eternity ;
And nameless woe, or blissful life,
  My endless portion be.

O Saviour, then, in all my need
  Be near, be near to me ;
And let my soul, by steadfast faith,
  Find life and heaven in thee.

JOHN XII. 1—11.

THEN Jesus six days before the passover came to Bethany, where Lazarus was which had been dead, whom he raised from the dead. (*Our Lord never seems more lovely than when reposing in the delightful family circle of Bethany. We there see his gentle heart unveiled amid domestic joys and sorrows, and we perceive how near akin he is to us, how much at home with us, and how able to bless us. Jesus in the heart and Jesus in the house make up heaven below.*)

2 There they made him a supper; and Martha served : but Lazarus was one of them that sat at the table with him. (*Christ had once reproved Martha for being cumbered about much serving, but we find her serving still; she had not taken it amiss, and peevishly forsaken her post of duty, as some would have done; she loved her Lord too well for that. This time she served within hearing of the Lord's gracious words, and served without complaining, or exhibiting over-anxiety. It is well when good people grow better. As for Lazarus, he was highly favoured, and yet his lot was only such as the Lord gives to all whom he quickens, for those who are made alive by him are made to sit together with him.*)

3 Then took Mary a pound of ointment of spikenard, very costly, and anointed the feet of Jesus, and wiped his feet with her hair : and the house was filled with the odour of the ointment. *This was her grand testimonial of love. She thought nothing too good for her Lord. The expense was nothing in her esteem; she brought him the best she had, for her love was generous. She poured out the precious ointment with her own hands, for she desired to render him personal service, and she poured it not on his head but on his feet, to show both her own deep humility and her Lord's superlative worth. There was also in her loving act an intelligent faith, which recognised his office as Priest and King, and treated him as the anointed of the Lord. Her loving lowliness in wiping his feet with her hair, set forth her entire devotion to his service. Enlightened affection suggested the whole deed, and we shall do well to imitate her therein, by giving our best treasure, and our most intense personal service without stint to him who has redeemed us with his blood.*

4 Then saith one of his disciples, Judas Iscariot, Simon's *son*, which should betray him,

5 Why was not this ointment sold for three hundred pence, and given to the poor ?

6 This he said, not that he cared for the poor ; but because he was a thief, and had the bag, and bare what was put therein. (*Here was a devil condemning a saint, and charity to the poor made into an argument against an act of piety. Many in these days argue in the same manner if a liberal heart gives largely to the cause of Christ. To their question, " Why was not this money given to the poor?" we reply, Because it was better still to give it to Jesus.*)

7 Then said Jesus, Let her alone : against the day of my burying hath she kept this. (*Her act had gone beyond her own intention. Christ places his people's actions in the best possible light.*)

8 For the poor always ye have with you ; but me ye have not always. (*We can always give to the poor, for as long as the church lasts there will be such; but Jesus in his flesh was only once on earth, and it was meet that he should have honour done him by those who loved him.*)

9 Much people of the Jews therefore knew that he was there : and they came not for Jesus' sake only, but that they might see Lazarus also, whom he had raised from the dead.

10, 11 But the chief priests consulted that they might put Lazarus also to death ; Because that by reason of him many of the Jews went away, and believed on Jesus. (*This was concentrated wickedness. Did they hope to baffle Omnipotence itself? Were they so enraged at the Lord's success as even to defy the life-giving God? To what extremities of sin will men go!*)

Though all the world my choice deride,
Yet Jesus shall my portion be ;
For I am pleased with none beside;
The fairest of the fair is he.

Sweet is the vision of thy face,
And kindness o'er thy lips is shed;
Lovely art thou, and full of grace,
And glory beams around thy head.

Thy sufferings I embrace with thee,
Thy poverty and shameful cross;
The pleasures of the world I flee,
And deem its treasures only dross.

Be daily dearer to my heart,
And ever let me feel thee near;
Then willingly with all I'd part,
Nor count it worthy of a tear.

MATTHEW XXI. 1—16.

AND when they drew nigh unto Jerusalem, and were come to Bethphage, unto the mount of Olives, then sent Jesus two disciples,

2 Saying unto them, Go into the village over against you, and straightway ye shall find an ass tied, and a colt with her : loose *them*, and bring *them* unto me.

3 And if any *man* say ought unto you, ye shall say, The Lord hath need of them ; and straightway he will send them.

He had the hearts of all men under his control, and at once moved the owner to lend his ass. The colt came and its mother at its side, for Jesus would not cause even the meanest creature a needless pain by separating it from its young.

4 All this was done, that it might be fulfilled which was spoken by the prophet, saying,

5 Tell ye the daughter of Sion, Behold, thy King cometh unto thee, meek, and sitting upon an ass, and a colt the foal of an ass.

He came in state as a judge, but it was in fitting state, and such as was becoming in a true ruler in Israel; for he did not ride upon the horse which was the boast of Egypt, but on the humbler ass, which ancient lawgivers had been content with.

6 And the disciples went, and did as Jesus commanded them,

7 And brought the ass, and the colt, and put on them their clothes, and they set *him* thereon.

8 And a very great multitude spread their garments in the way ; others cut down branches from the trees, and strawed *them* in the way.

9 And the multitudes that went before, and that followed, cried, saying, Hosanna to the son of David *(or, "Save now, we beseech thee")*: Blessed *is* he that cometh in the name of the Lord ; Hosanna in the highest.

10 And when he was come into Jerusalem, all the city was moved, saying, Who is this ?

Bishop Hall has well said : " The attending disciples need be at no loss for an answer. Which of the prophets has not put it into their mouths? Who is this? Ask Moses, and he shall tell you, the seed of the woman who shall bruise the serpent's head. Ask your father Jacob, and he shall tell you, the Shiloh of the tribe of Judah. Ask David, and he shall tell you, the King of Glory. Ask Isaiah, and he shall tell you, Emmanuel, Wonderful, the mighty God, the Prince of Peace. Ask Jeremiah, and he shall tell you, the righteous Branch. Ask Daniel, and he shall tell you, the Messiah. Ask John the Baptist, he shall tell you, the Lamb of God. The God of the prophets hath told you, This is my beloved Son, in whom I am well pleased. Yea, the very devils themselves have been forced to confess, I know thee who thou art, the Holy One of God. On no side hath Christ left himself without a full and plain testimony."

11 And the multitude said, This is Jesus the prophet of Nazareth of Galilee.

12, 13 And Jesus went into the temple of God, and cast out all them that sold and bought in the temple, and overthrew the tables of the moneychangers, and the seats of them that sold doves, And said unto them, It is written, My house shall be called the house of prayer ; but ye have made it a den of thieves.

This was his second purgation of the temple. He had cleansed it once before in his earlier ministry. Alas! when good things begin to be perverted they need many cleansings before they are set right again.

14 And the blind and the lame came to him in the temple ; and he healed them.

15 And when the chief priests and scribes saw the wonderful things that he did, and the children crying in the temple, and saying, Hosanna to the son of David ; they were sore displeased,

16 And said unto him, Hearest thou what these say ? and Jesus saith unto them, Yea ; have ye never read, Out of the mouth of babes and sucklings thou hast perfected praise ?

Let children learn from this that Jesus values their praises, and let them give him their hearts while they are yet young.

Ride on, ride on in majesty !
In lowly pomp ride on to die :
O Christ ! thy triumphs now begin
O'er captive death and conquered sin.

Ride on, ride on in majesty !
Thy last and fiercest strife is nigh :
The Father, on his sapphire throne,
Expects his own anointed Son.

Ride on, ride on in majesty !
In lowly pomp ride on to die :
Bow thy meek head to mortal pain ;
Then, take, O God, thy power, and reign !

JOHN XII. 20—36.

AND there were certain Greeks among them that came up to worship at the feast: The same came therefore to Philip, which was of Bethsaida of Galilee, and desired him, saying, Sir, we would see Jesus.

22 Philip cometh and telleth Andrew: and again Andrew and Philip tell Jesus.

These Greeks did well to desire to see the great teacher, and we shall do still better if in all our attendances upon religious worship our chief desire shall be to see Jesus. We should desire this that we may know him better, trust him more readily, and become more like him. We miss the end of public worship if we fail to see Jesus.

23, 24 And Jesus answered them, saying, The hour is come, that the Son of man should be glorified. Verily, verily, I say unto you, Except a corn of wheat fall into the ground and die, it abideth alone: but if it die, it bringeth forth much fruit. *(Our Lord showed that he could only reach his mediatorial glory through death, and he then went on to teach the Greeks, and us, that, in like manner, by self-denial only can any of us attain to glory.)*

25, 26 He that loveth his life shall lose it; and he that hateth his life in this world shall keep it unto life eternal. If any man serve me, let him follow me; and where I am, there shall also my servant be: if any man serve me, him will *my* Father honour.

27 Now is my soul troubled; and what shall I say? Father, save me from this hour: but for this cause came I unto this hour.

28 Father, glorify thy name. Then came there a voice from heaven, *saying*, I have both glorified *it*, and will glorify *it* again.

29 The people therefore, that stood by, and heard *it*, said that it thundered: others said, An angel spake to him.

30 Jesus answered and said, This voice came not because of me, but for your sakes.

This was the third time the heavenly voice had borne witness to him. First, when as our Priest he commenced his life-work at his baptism; a second time upon the mount of transfiguration, when his Father said "Hear ye him," thus marking him out as the prophet long foretold; and now a third time when he had just entered Jerusalem as

King. Thus in each of his three offices the Father bare witness concerning him.

31 Now is the judgment of this world: now shall the prince of this world be cast out.

32, 33 And I, if I be lifted up from the earth, will draw all *men* unto me. This he said, signifying what death he should die. *(Thus by his death Satan is conquered and cast down from the seat of power, and souls are saved by myriads).*

34 The people answered him, We have heard out of the law that Christ abideth for ever: and how sayest thou, The Son of man must be lifted up? who is this Son of man?

35 Then Jesus said unto them, Yet a little while is the light with you. Walk while ye have the light, lest darkness come upon you: for he that walketh in darkness knoweth not whither he goeth.

36 While ye have light, believe in the light, that ye may be the children of light. These things spake Jesus, and departed, and did hide himself from them.

MATTHEW XXI. 17.

AND he left them, and went out of the city into Bethany; and he lodged there. *He loved the quiet of the village and the domestic love of the household of Lazarus. Those of us who are wise will find in retirement our strength for public service.*

We would see Jesus, for we know
His sovereign grace alone
Can on us hearts of flesh bestow,
And for our sins atone.

We would see Jesus, does not he
Bid contrite sinners come?
And to such guilty souls as we
Proclaim "There yet is room!"

We would see Jesus, for his saints
May lean upon his breast;
Pour out with confidence their plaints,
And find celestial rest.

We would see Jesus, and would pray
For those unhappy friends,
Who still pursue that crooked way
Which in perdition ends.

MARK XI. 12—26.

AND on the morrow, when they were come from Bethany, he was hungry : And seeing a fig tree afar off having leaves, he came, if haply he might find any thing thereon : and when he came to it, he found nothing but leaves ; for the time of figs was not *yet.*

14 And Jesus answered and said unto it, No man eat fruit of thee hereafter for ever. And his disciples heard *it. (Fig trees put forth their fruit before their leaves : it was not yet time for figs, and yet this pretentious tree was covered with leaves. It promised far more than other trees, and then deceived those who came to it for fruit. It was meet that a blight should fall upon this type of hypocrisy, this symbol of boastful falsehood. Proud professors of religion, whose actions are not right in the sight of God, should tremble lest the like curse should light on them.)*

15 ¶ And they come to Jerusalem : and Jesus went into the temple, and began to cast out them that sold and bought in the temple, and overthrew the tables of the moneychangers, and the seats of them that sold doves ;

16 And would not suffer that any man should carry *any* vessel through the temple.

17 And he taught, saying unto them, Is it not written, My house shall be called of all nations the house of prayer ? but ye have made it a den of thieves.

18 And the scribes and chief priests heard *it*, and sought how they might destroy him : for they feared him, because all the people was astonished at his doctrine.

Though purged so short a time before, the temple was foul again. Nothing is so hard to make clean and keep clean as a degenerate church. It should be the daily prayer of all who love the pure gospel that in these degenerate times the Lord Jesus would by his Holy Spirit, and the power of divine truth, cleanse out of our churches all false doctrines, Popish practices, and worldly fashions. May the Lord also purge the temple of our hearts and make our inmost nature the house of prayer, the palace of the living God.

19 And when even was come, he went out of the city. *(Seeking again the quiet of Bethany, so refreshing to his devout and gentle spirit.)*

20 ¶ And in the morning, as they passed by, they saw the fig tree dried up from the roots.

21 And Peter calling to remembrance saith unto him, Master, behold, the fig tree which thou cursedst is withered away.

22, 23 And Jesus answering saith unto them, Have faith in God. For verily I say unto you, That whosoever shall say unto this mountain, Be thou removed, and be thou cast into the sea ; and shall not doubt in his heart, but shall believe that those things which he saith shall come to pass ; he shall have whatsoever he saith.

When faith concerning anything is given to us, by the Lord, it is the shadow of the coming event and its prayer is always heard; but faith is not in all cases bestowed, nor can we always pray in full assurance, and in such cases it would be base presumption to pretend to have unlimited power in supplication. The limit of prayer is the will of God, our guides as to that limit are the promise of God and the faith which we are enabled to exercise.

24 Therefore I say unto you, What things soever ye desire, when ye pray, believe that ye receive *them,* and ye shall have *them.*

This of course is to be understood as taking for granted that we pray for right things, otherwise we shall ask and have not, because we ask amiss. What latitude is here given us in prayer! How slow we are to use the power thus entrusted to us!

25, 26 And when ye stand praying, forgive, if ye have aught against any : that your Father also which is in heaven may forgive you your trespasses. But if ye do not forgive, neither will your Father which is in heaven forgive your trespasses. *(Remember this when anger tries to hold you in its evil power. Flee from it as from your mortal foe.)*

Thy mansion is my cleansèd heart,
O Lord, thy dwelling-place secure !
Bid the unruly throng depart,
And leave the consecrated floor.

Devoted though I am to thee,
A thievish swarm my soul annoys,
They grieve my Lord away from me,
And rob my heart of all its joys.

O Lord, what bliss thy presence gives !
What peace shall reign when thou art here !
Thy presence makes this den of thieves
A calm, delightful house of prayer.

MATTHEW XXI. 23—46.

AND when he was come into the temple, the chief priests and the elders of the people came unto him as he was teaching, and said, By what authority doest thou these things? and who gave thee this authority?

24—26 And Jesus answered and said unto them, I also will ask you one thing, which if ye tell me, I in likewise will tell you by what authority I do these things. The baptism of John, whence was it? from heaven, or of men? And they reasoned with themselves, saying, If we shall say, From heaven; he will say unto us, Why did ye not then believe him? But if we shall say, Of men; we fear the people; for all hold John as a prophet.

27 And they answered Jesus, and said, We cannot tell. And he said unto them, Neither tell I you by what authority I do these things. *Thus were they taken in their own craftiness and utterly silenced.*

28 ¶ But what think ye? A *certain* man had two sons; and he came to the first, and said, Son, go work to day in my vineyard.

29—32 He answered and said, I will not: but afterward he repented, and went. And he came to the second, and said likewise. And he answered and said, I *go*, sir: and went not. Whether of them twain did the will of *his* father? They say unto him, The first. Jesus saith unto them, Verily I say unto you, That the publicans and the harlots go into the kingdom of God before you. For John came unto you in the way of righteousness, and ye believed him not: but the publicans and the harlots believed him: and ye, when ye had seen *it*, repented not afterward, that ye might believe him. *(This was a home thrust, and right well deserved by them. It may also be a lesson to us if we see great sinners converted while we ourselves remain undecided. Is there one of us in this condition?)*

33 ¶ Hear another parable: There was a certain householder, which planted a vineyard, and hedged it round about, and digged a winepress in it, and built a tower, and let it out to husbandmen, and went into a far country:

34, 35 And when the time of the fruit drew near, he sent his servants to the husbandmen, that they might receive the fruits of it. And the husbandmen took his servants, and beat one, and killed another, and stoned another.

36 Again, he sent other servants more than the first: and they did unto them likewise.

37 But last of all he sent unto them his son, saying, They will reverence my son.

38, 39 But when the husbandmen saw the son, they said among themselves, This is the heir; come, let us kill him, and let us seize on his inheritance. And they caught him, and cast *him* out of the vineyard, and slew *him*.

40 When the lord therefore of the vineyard cometh, what will he do unto those husbandmen?

41 They say unto him, He will miserably destroy those wicked men, and will let out *his* vineyard unto other husbandmen, which shall render him the fruits in their seasons.

42—43 Jesus saith unto them, Did ye never read in the scriptures, The stone which the builders rejected, the same is become the head of the corner: this is the Lord's doing, and it is marvellous in our eyes? Therefore say I unto you, The kingdom of God shall be taken from you, and given to a nation bringing forth the fruits thereof.

44 And whosoever shall fall on this stone shall be broken: but on whomsoever it shall fall, it will grind him to powder. *(If we oppose the Saviour we shall hurt only ourselves, but if we provoke him to punish us we shall be crushed as completely as if a huge rock had rolled upon us. Who will dare to be at enmity with Jesus?)*

45, 46 And when the chief priests and Pharisees had heard his parables, they perceived that he spake of them. But when they sought to lay hands on him, they feared the multitude, because they took him for a prophet.

Lo, the stone which once aside
By the builder's hand was thrown,
See it now the building's pride,
See it now the corner stone!

Lo, we hail Jehovah's deed,
Strange and wondrous in our eyes!
Jesus Christ is Lord decreed,
Bid the voice of gladness rise.

MATTHEW XXII. 1—14.

AND Jesus answered and spake unto them again by parables, and said,

2, 3 The kingdom of heaven is like unto a certain king, which made a marriage for his son, And sent forth his servants to call them that were bidden to the wedding : and they would not come. *(It was their sovereign who invited them, and to refuse his invitation was an act of rebellion. Their presence was intended to render honour to the marriage of their prince, and their resolution to be absent was a studied insult both to the king and his son. God in infinite condescension has decreed to glorify his Son by bestowing his rich grace upon undeserving man, and when man wilfully rejects the favour, he is guilty of insulting the Lord of love. Will any of us live and die in this sin?)*

4 Again, he sent forth other servants, saying, Tell them which are bidden, Behold, I have prepared my dinner : my oxen and *my* fatlings *are* killed, and all things *are* ready : come unto the marriage. *(He was very patient, and condescended to reason with his erring subjects, hoping that perhaps their second thoughts might correct their hasty words. He even pleaded with them, though he might have sent forth his armies at once to destroy them. How true a representation is this of the great Father of mercy!)*

5 But they made light of *it*, and went their ways, one to his farm, another to his merchandise :

6 And the remnant took his servants, and entreated *them* spitefully, and slew *them*. *Only a few were persecutors, the many were despisers only, but they perished in the general doom, for they had despised their prince.*

7 But when the king heard *thereof*, he was wroth : and he sent forth his armies, and destroyed those murderers, and burned up their city.

8 Then saith he to his servants, The wedding is ready, but they which were bidden were not worthy.

9 Go ye therefore into the highways, and as many as ye shall find, bid to the marriage.

10 So those servants went out into the highways, and gathered together all as many as they found, both bad and good : and the wedding was furnished with guests.

Those who hear the gospel regularly are often found rejecting it, yet the Lord's purposes of grace will not fail, Jesus shall see of the travail of his soul, and heaven shall be tenanted by rejoicing millions. Out of the poorest and meanest of mankind sovereign grace will select its favoured ones, and make them partakers of its bounty.

11 ¶ And when the king came in to see the guests, he saw there a man which had not on a wedding garment :

12 And he saith unto him, Friend, how camest thou in hither not having a wedding garment? And he was speechless.

His conduct was as gross an insult as that of those who refused to come. A dress was provided for each guest, but he would not put it on, he despised the royal livery, and defied the regal law in the palace itself. Thus do those act who unite themselves with the church, and yet are not holy, nor obedient to Jesus. They insult the Redeemer to his face and defy him in his own house. Are any of us guilty of this? Do we profess to be Christians, and go to the communion table, though we do not wear the garments of sanctification! If so, let us tremble at the doom which awaits us.

13 Then said the king to the servants, Bind him hand and foot, and take him away, and cast *him* into outer darkness ; there shall be weeping and gnashing of teeth.

14 For many are called, but few *are* chosen. *Even in the visible church all are not the Lord's elect. What need of careful self-examination! Lord, make us to be truly thine own.*

Oh! why do mortals yet despise
This Bridegroom from above?
And for their farms and merchandise
Neglect the feast of love?

Send forth thy messengers, O Lord,
Through all the haunts of sin ;
And, hailing sinners by thy word,
Compel them to come in.

For they, who once this supper taste,
Shall thirst for sin no more ;
And they, who see The Bridegroom's face,
Eternally adore.

MATTHEW XXII. 15—46.

THEN went the Pharisees, and took counsel how they might entangle him in *his* talk.

16 And they sent out unto him their disciples with the Herodians, saying, Master, we know that thou art true, and teachest the way of God in truth, neither carest thou for any *man :* for thou regardest not the person of men.

Men who wish to ensnare us begin with flattery. Let us beware of smooth speeches.

17 Tell us therefore, What thinkest thou ? Is it lawful to give tribute unto Cæsar, or not ?

18 But Jesus perceived their wickedness, and said, Why tempt ye me, *ye* hypocrites ?

19 Shew me the tribute money. And they brought unto him a penny.

20 And he saith unto them, Whose *is* this image and superscription ?

21 They say unto him, Cæsar's. Then saith he unto them, Render therefore unto Cæsar the things which are Cæsar's ; and unto God the things that are God's. *(By using Cæsar's coinage they confessed their subjection to his authority, and they were bound to act accordingly. Civil rulers are to be obeyed in civil things, but they must not touch religion, that is the sphere of God alone. Attention to this rule would be a great blessing both to Church and State.)*

22 When they had heard *these words*, they marvelled, and left him, and went their way.

23 ¶ The same day came to him the Sadducees, which say that there is no resurrection, and asked him,

24 Saying, Master, Moses said, If a man die, having no children, his brother shall marry his wife, and raise up seed unto his brother.

25—27 Now there were with us seven brethren : and the first, when he had married a wife, deceased, and, having no issue, left his wife unto his brother : Likewise the second also, and the third, unto the seventh. And last of all the woman died also.

28 Therefore in the resurrection whose wife shall she be of the seven ? for they all had her.

29—32 Jesus answered and said unto them, Ye do err, not knowing the scriptures, nor the power of God. For in the resurrection they neither marry, nor are given in marriage, but are as the angels of God in heaven. But as touching the resurrection of the dead, have ye not read that which was spoken unto you by God, saying, I am the God of Abraham, and the God of Isaac, and the God of Jacob ? God is not the God of the dead, but of the living.

A most conclusive reply, which shut the mouths of the Sadducees, and showed the Saviour's infinite superiority to their fancied wisdom.

33 And when the multitude heard *this*, they were astonished at his doctrine.

34 ¶ But when the Pharisees had heard that he had put the Sadducees to silence, they were gathered together.

35 Then one of them, *which was* a lawyer, asked *him a question*, tempting him, and saying,

36 Master, which *is* the great commandment in the law ?

37—40 Jesus said unto him, Thou shalt love the Lord thy God with all thy heart, and with all thy soul, and with all thy mind. This is the first and great commandment. And the second *is* like unto it, Thou shalt love thy neighbour as thyself. On these two commandments hang all the law and the prophets.

41, 42 While the Pharisees were gathered together, Jesus asked them, Saying, What think ye of Christ ? whose son is he ? They say unto him, *The son* of David.

43—45 He saith unto them, How then doth David in spirit call him Lord, saying, The Lord said unto my Lord, Sit thou on my right hand, till I make thine enemies thy footstool ? If David then call him Lord, how is he his son ? *(This was a puzzle for them, out of which they could not see their way, and thus Jesus left the field victorious over all his foes.)*

46 And no man was able to answer him a word, neither durst any *man* from that day forth ask him any more *questions*.

If ask'd what of Jesus I think,
Though still my best thoughts are but poor,
I say, he's my meat and my drink,
My life, and my strength, and my store,
My Shepherd, my Husband, my Friend,
My Saviour from sin and from thrall,
My Hope from beginning to end,
My Portion, my Lord, and my All.

MARK XII. 38—44.

AND he said unto them in his doctrine, Beware of the scribes, which love to go in long clothing, and *love* salutations in the market-places, And the chief seats in the synagogues, and the uppermost rooms at feasts : Which devour widows' houses, and for a pretence make long prayers : these shall receive greater damnation. (*Mark the honesty of Jesus; he never flinched from declaring the truth concerning the highest in the land. No fear of man ever fettered his speech. The object of his rebuke was pride, pride of dress and rank, and the outward display of religion. Let us avoid these things, for the Lord abhors them. Shall pardoned sinners be proud? God forbid.*)

41 ¶ And Jesus sat over against the treasury, and beheld how the people cast money into the treasury : and many that were rich cast in much.

42 And there came a certain poor widow, and she threw in two mites, which make a farthing.

43 And he called *unto him* his disciples, and saith unto them, Verily I say unto you, That this poor widow hath cast more in, than all they which have cast into the treasury :

44 For all *they* did cast in of their abundance; but she of her want did cast in all that she had, *even* all her living. (*How often do we hear persons speak of "giving their mite," when they know that they are doing no such thing. This poor woman gave her all; where do we find such givers now-a-days? We must measure our generosity not by what we give, but by what remains. Jesus sat over against the treasury, and he is sitting there still. He knows what we bring to him, and he sees whether it is a fair proportion of our means. He measures our offerings not by their amount, but by the will of the giver.*)

JOHN XII. 37—50.

BUT though he had done so many miracles before them, yet they believed not on him:

38 That the saying of Esaias the prophet might be fulfilled, which he spake, Lord, who hath believed our report? and to whom hath the arm of the Lord been revealed?

39, 40 Therefore they could not believe, because that Esaias said again, He hath blinded their eyes, and hardened their heart; that they should not see with *their* eyes, nor understand with *their* heart, and be converted, and I should heal them. (*Continued sin and pride brought on a judicial blindness, so that the plainest truth was not seen by them. Have we believed in Jesus? If not, is there not great danger that we shall be blinded too?*)

41 These things said Esaias, when he saw his glory, and spake of him. (*We shall find a description of the prophet's vision in the sixth chapter of Isaiah. It is worthy of note that the prophet says, "I saw also the Lord, sitting upon his throne," and that he heard the seraphim adore him. Yet the passage is here used in reference to Jesus, who is therefore Lord and God.*)

42, 43 ¶ Nevertheless among the chief rulers also many believed on him; but because of the Pharisees they did not confess *him*, lest they should be put out of the synagogue : For they loved the praise of men more than the praise of God. (*Alas, that men should be such shameful cowards as to be ashamed of the Lord of glory.*)

44—46 Jesus cried and said, He that believeth on me, believeth not on me, but on him that sent me. And he that seeth me seeth him that sent me. I am come a light into the world, that whosoever believeth on me should not abide in darkness.

47 And if any man hear my words, and believe not, I judge him not : for I came not to judge the world, but to save the world.

48, 49 He that rejecteth me, and receiveth not my words, hath one that judgeth him : the word that I have spoken, the same shall judge him in the last day. For I have not spoken of myself; but the Father which sent me, he gave me a commandment, what I should say and what I should speak.

50 And I know that his commandment is life everlasting : whatsoever I speak therefore, even as the Father said unto me, so I speak.

Most gracious Lord, what can we pay
    For favours so divine?
We consecrate our every power,
    To be for ever thine.

Had we ten thousand hearts and lives,
    We'd give them all to thee;
Had we ten thousand tongues, they all
    Should join the harmony.

MATTHEW XXIII. 1—12; 23—31.

THEN spake Jesus to the multitude, and to his disciples, Saying, The scribes and the Pharisees sit in Moses' seat: All therefore whatsoever they bid you observe, *that* observe and do; but do not ye after their works: for they say, and do not. (*In what a sad plight is the teacher concerning whom such advice must be given—"do as he says and not as he does." From such teachers may the Lord save our country.*)

4 For they bind heavy burdens and grievous to be borne, and lay *them* on men's shoulders; but they *themselves* will not move them with one of their fingers.

5—7 But all their works they do for to be seen of men: they make broad their phylacteries, and enlarge the borders of their garments, And love the uppermost rooms at feasts, and the chief seats in the synagogues, And greetings in the markets, and to be called of men, Rabbi, Rabbi. (*The love of applause is a very common sin, and we may easily fall into it. Let us pray to be kept from seeking honour from men in our religious or charitable acts, for the influence of such a motive will be most pernicious. Self-seeking makes virtue itself a vice.*)

8 But be not ye called Rabbi: for one is your Master, *even* Christ; and all ye are brethren.

9, 10 And call no *man* your father upon the earth: for one is your Father, which is in heaven. Neither be ye called masters: for one is your Master, *even* Christ. (*All titles and honours in the church which exalt men and give occasion for pride are here forbidden. In the Christian church we should seek to realise a truer "Liberty, Equality, and Fraternity," than that for which the world clamours in vain.*)

11, 12 But he that is greatest among you shall be your servant. And whosoever shall exalt himself shall be abased; and he that shall humble himself shall be exalted.

23 Woe unto you, scribes and Pharisees, hypocrites! for ye pay tithe of mint and anise and cummin, and have omitted the weightier *matters* of the law, judgment, mercy, and faith: these ought ye to have done, and not to leave the other undone.

24 *Ye* blind guides, which strain at a gnat, and swallow a camel. (*A strong expression* setting forth the fact that they regarded trifles and neglected weighty duties; they strained out gnats from their wine, but cared nothing for huge sins.)

25 Woe unto you, scribes and Pharisees, hypocrites! for ye make clean the outside of the cup and of the platter, but within they are full of extortion and excess.

26 *Thou* blind Pharisee, cleanse first that *which is* within the cup and platter, that the outside of them may be clean also.

27, 28 Woe unto you, scribes and Pharisees, hypocrites! for ye are like unto whited sepulchres, which indeed appear beautiful outward, but are within full of dead *men's* bones, and of all uncleanness. Even so ye also outwardly appear righteous unto men, but within ye are full of hypocrisy and iniquity.

29—31 Woe unto you, scribes and Pharisees, hypocrites! because ye build the tombs of the prophets, and garnish the sepulchres of the righteous, And say, If we had been in the days of our fathers we would not have been partakers with them in the blood of the prophets. Wherefore ye be witnesses unto yourselves, that ye are the children of them which killed the prophets. (*Here we have much the same teaching as we have read before. The faults denounced are hard to remove, hence the Saviour exposes them again and again. He was not ashamed to preach many times upon the same topic when there was need to do so. Let us learn from this passage to avoid all self-seeking and hypocrisy in religion. May the Lord make us true and humble.*)

O Lord, if I have not begun
To tread the sacred road,
Now teach my wandering feet the way
To reach thy blest abode.

Or if I'm truly in the path,
Assist me with thy strength,
That I may swift advances make,
And reach thy house at length.

My care, my hope, my sole request,
Are all comprised in this,
Truly to follow Christ my Lord,
And then to share his bliss.

588

"He that shall endure unto the end, the same shall be saved."

OCTOBER 3.—MORNING.

[Or July 4.]

MARK XIII. 1—12.

AND as he went out of the temple, one of his disciples saith unto him, Master, see what manner of stones and what buildings *are here! (They thought that he would be as much pleased with noble architecture as they were; but he looked on the temple with very different eyes. To him nothing was beautiful which was polluted with sin.)*

2 And Jesus answering said unto him, Seest thou these great buildings? there shall not be left one stone upon another, that shall not be thrown down. *(Our Lord sorrowfully foresaw the total overthrow of the rebellious city, and warned his disciples, so that when the evil day came, they were prepared for it, and were confirmed in their faith in him by the remembrance of his prophecy.)*

3 And as he sat upon the mount of Olives over against the temple, Peter and James and John and Andrew asked him privately,

4 Tell us, when shall these things be? and what *shall be* the sign when all these things shall be fulfilled?

5 And Jesus answering them began to say, Take heed lest any *man* deceive you:

6 For many shall come in my name, saying, I am *Christ;* and shall deceive many.

7, 8 And when ye shall hear of wars and rumours of wars, be ye not troubled; for *such things* must needs be; but the end *shall* not *be* yet. For nation shall rise against nation, and kingdom against kingdom: and there shall be earthquakes in divers places, and there shall be famines and troubles: these *are* the beginnings of sorrows. *(And only the beginnings compared with the overwhelming destruction which would sweep over the city of Jerusalem and the nation of the Jews.)*

9 ¶ But take heed to yourselves: for they shall deliver you up to councils; and in the synagogues ye shall be beaten: and ye shall be brought before rulers and kings for my sake, for a testimony against them. *(The various parties among the Jews, however much they warred against each other, would combine against the followers of Jesus, and seek to crush them with all their might.)*

10 And the gospel must first be published among all nations. *(Persecuted they would be, but they would conquer; the Gospel would be* proclaimed all over the world, and *neither men nor devils could hinder its course.)*

11 But when they shall lead *you,* and deliver you up, take no thought beforehand what ye shall speak, neither do ye premeditate: but whatsoever shall be given you in that hour, that speak ye: for it is not ye that speak, but the Holy Ghost. *(Those whom Jesus calls to be his advocates shall have full instructions from him, and divine help in pleading his cause. This promise has been most faithfully fulfilled, as all the books of martyrs most plainly show. Poor and illiterate men have baffled the learned in controversy, being helped to proclaim the truth without fear.)*

12 Now the brother shall betray the brother to death, and the father the son; and children shall rise up against *their* parents, and shall cause them to be put to death. *(Saddest of all is the betrayal of good men by their own relatives, but this they have had to bear for Jesus' sake. Ought we not to be able to bear those petty persecutions which in these times are all that the enemy can do against us? Sneers, jests, and slanders are light crosses compared with those which the martyrs carried.)*

MATTHEW XXIV. 11—13.

AND many false prophets shall rise, and shall deceive many. *(Evils never come alone: while the church would be persecuted by those outside of her bounds, it would be disturbed within by heretics, and weakened by want of love and zeal.)*

12 And because iniquity shall abound, the love of many shall wax cold.

13 But he that shall endure unto the end, the same shall be saved. *(This sums it all up. Come what may, if we hold on we shall conquer. Lord, grant us persevering grace.)*

Let not thy heart despond and say,
How shall I stand the trying day?
He has engaged by firm decree,
That, "as thy day, thy strength shall be."

Should persecution rage and flame,
Still trust in thy Redeemer's name;
In fiery trials thou shalt see
That, "as thy day, thy strength shall be."

OUR *Lord gave his disciples warning as to the destruction of Jerusalem, so that they might escape from the slaughter.*

MATTHEW XXIV. 15—35.

15, 16 When ye therefore shall see the abomination of desolation, spoken of by Daniel the prophet, stand in the holy place, (whoso readeth, let him understand :) Then let them which be in Judæa flee into the mountains : *(This advice the disciples followed, and as soon as the armies surrounded Jerusalem, they escaped to the little mountain of Pella while the inhabitants of Jerusalem were slain by the Romans.)*

17, 18 Let him which is on the housetop not come down to take any thing out of his house : Neither let him which is in the field return back to take his clothes. *(They were not to linger to save their property, but flee for their lives at once.)*

19 And woe unto them that are with child, and to them that give suck in those days!

20—22 But pray ye that your flight be not in the winter, neither on the sabbath day : For then shall be great tribulation, such as was not since the beginning of the world to this time, no, nor ever shall be. And except those days should be shortened, there should no flesh be saved : but for the elect's sake those days shall be shortened.

23—25 Then if any man shall say unto you, Lo, here *is* Christ, or there ; believe *it* not. For there shall arise false Christs, and false prophets, and shall show great signs and wonders : insomuch that, if *it were* possible, they shall deceive the very elect. Behold, I have told you before.

26 Wherefore if they shall say unto you, Behold, he is in the desert ; go not forth : behold *he is* in the secret chambers ; believe *it* not.

27 For as the lightning cometh out of the east, and shineth even unto the west ; so shall also the coming of the Son of man be.

28 For wheresoever the carcase is, there will the eagles be gathered together. *(So far our Lord spoke of the siege of Jerusalem. After this he referred to the last great day.)*

29, 30 Immediately after the tribulation of those days shall the sun be darkened, and the moon shall not give her light, and the stars shall fall from heaven, and the powers of the heavens shall be shaken : And then shall appear the sign of the Son of man in heaven : and then shall all the tribes of the earth mourn, and they shall see the Son of man coming in the clouds of heaven with power and great glory.

This is the glorious appearing of our Lord at the last. No sun or moon will be needed when he shines forth ; his glory will be brighter than the sun in the heavens. He will find the nations still unsaved, and horror will be their portion. If he were to come now, should we have to mourn, or could we meet him in peace ?

31 And he shall send his angels with a great sound of a trumpet, and they shall gather together his elect from the four winds, from one end of heaven to the other. *(They shall be saved from the terrible destruction, and as soon as they are removed, wrath shall break forth on the ungodly.*

Our Lord then returned to speak of the overthrow of Jerusalem, and gave his disciples warning to watch the signs of the times.)

32 Now learn a parable of the fig tree ; When his branch is yet tender, and putteth forth leaves, ye know that summer *is* nigh :

33 So likewise ye, when ye shall see all these things, know that it is near, *even* at the doors.

34 Verily I say unto you, this generation shall not pass, till all these things be fulfilled.

35 Heaven and earth shall pass away, but my words shall not pass away.

When the gospel race is run,
When the Gentile day is done,
Signs and wonders there shall be
In the heaven, and earth, and sea.

Lo ! mid terror and mid tears,
Jesus in the clouds appears,
While the trump's tremendous blast
Peals, the loudest and the last.

East and west, and south and north,
Speeds each glorious angel forth,
Gathering in with glittering wing
Zion's saints to Zion's King.

Man nor angel knows that day ;
Heaven and earth shall pass away ;
Still shall stand the Saviour's word,
Deathless as its deathless Lord.

THE apostles had asked the Lord concerning the day of his coming, " When shall these things be?" He made answer as follows :—

MATTHEW XXIV. 36—51.

36 Of that day and hour knoweth no *man*, no, not the angels of heaven, but my Father only. *(Let us not therefore be troubled by idle prophecies as to the end of the world, even if they claim to be interpretations of Scripture, for what angels do not know has certainly not been revealed to hair-brained fanatics. " The veil which covers the face of futurity is woven by the hand of mercy ;" let us not countenance those who attempt to tear it away. Augustine has well said, " God will not suffer man to have the knowledge of things to come; for if he had foresight of his prosperity he would be careless, and if he foreknew his adversity he would be hopeless." The day of the Lord will find many unprepared, and will make a final division in our race.)*

37 But as the days of Noe *were*, so shall also the coming of the Son of man be.

38 For as in the days that were before the flood they were eating and drinking, marrying and giving in marriage, until the day that Noe entered into the ark,

39 And knew not until the flood came, and took them all away ; so shall also the coming of the Son of man be.

40 Then shall two be in the field ; the one shall be taken, and the other left. *(Comrades in labour will not therefore be companions in eternity : the workman who loved the Lord will dwell in glory while his fellow-servant who lived and died an unbeliever will perish for ever.)*

41 Two *women shall be* grinding at the mill; the one shall be taken, and the other left. *Servants in the same family must be parted as wide asunder as heaven is from hell, unless their hearts have been renewed by grace.*

42 ¶ Watch therefore : for ye know not what hour your Lord doth come.

43 But know this, that if the goodman of the house had known in what watch the thief would come, he would have watched, and would not have suffered his house to be broken up.

44 Therefore be ye also ready : for in such an hour as ye think not the Son of man cometh. *Mr. Wesley was once asked by a lady, " Suppose that you knew that you were to die at twelve o'clock to-morrow night, how would you spend the intervening time?" " How, madam ?" he replied, " why just as I intend to spend it now. I should preach this night at Gloucester, and again at five to-morrow morning. After that I should ride to Tewkesbury, preach in the afternoon, and meet the societies in the evening. I should then repair to friend Martin's house, who expects to entertain me, converse and pray with the family as usual, retire to my room at ten o'clock, commend myself to my heavenly Father, lie down to rest, and wake up in glory." To be prepared for the coming of Jesus we need not leave our daily callings, and stand gazing upward into heaven ; but with grace in our hearts we shall do well to continue in the path of service with steadfast souls.*

45 Who then is a faithful and wise servant, whom his lord hath made ruler over his household, to give them meat in due season ?

46 Blessed *is* that servant, whom his lord when he cometh shall find so doing.

47 Verily I say unto you, That he shall make him ruler over all his goods.

48—51 But and if that evil servant shall say in his heart, My lord delayeth his coming ; And shall begin to smite *his* fellowservants, and to eat and drink with the drunken ; The lord of that servant shall come in a day when he looketh not for *him*, and in an hour that he is not aware of, And shall cut him asunder, and appoint *him* his portion with the hypocrites : there shall be weeping and gnashing of teeth. *(When professors neglect their own work they often pass hard judgments and cruel criticisms upon Christians. They would not do this if they remembered that the Lord is close at hand, and will visit such evils with the severest punishment.)*

Man may disbelieve the tidings,
  Or in anger turn away ;
'Tis foretold there shall be scoffers
  Rising in the latter day :

Yet he'll come, the Lord from heaven,
  Not to suffer, or to die ;
But to take his waiting people
  To their glorious rest on high.

Yet in mercy still he lingers,
  Lengthening out the day of grace ;
Till he comes, inviting sinners
  To his welcome, fond embrace.

OUR *Saviour continued to instruct his disciples as to the solemn judgment of the last great day, and in so doing he delivered the instructive parable which follows:*—

MATTHEW XXV. 1—13.

1 Then shall the kingdom of heaven be likened unto ten virgins, which took their lamps, and went forth to meet the bridegroom. *As attendants on the bride they represented her, and went forward to meet the Bridegroom, even as many profess to belong to the church and to be waiting for the coming of the Lord.*

2 And five of them were wise, and five *were* foolish.

3 They that *were* foolish took their lamps, and took no oil with them:

4 But the wise took oil in their vessels with their lamps. *(" The oil which the wise virgins carried in their vessels, as distinguished from that which burned in their lamps, points to the Holy Spirit, as a spirit of grace and supplication dwelling in a believer's heart. All the ten virgins experienced convictions, and made profession, as is indicated by the lamps lighted and borne aloft; but some had nothing more than convictions and professions, while others had passed from death unto life, and had received that life which is hid with Christ in God.")*

5 While the bridegroom tarried, they all slumbered and slept. *(Either having grown weary through the weakness of nature, or else having given way to sloth they fell asleep.)*

6 And at midnight there was a cry made, Behold, the bridegroom cometh; go ye out to meet him.

7 Then all those virgins arose, and trimmed their lamps. *(When the Lord is proclaimed as near at hand all classes of professors begin to examine themselves to see if they are really ready for his presence.)*

8 And the foolish said unto the wise, Give us of your oil; for our lamps are gone out.

9 But the wise answered, saying, *Not so;* lest there be not enough for us and you: but go ye rather to them that sell, and buy for yourselves. *(As an old writer says, " They turn themselves to the wise, whom, perhaps, they had lately laughed at, with the prayer 'Give*

us of your oil, for our lamps are gone out.' They betake themselves, if they are Catholics, to the dead saints, if they are Protestants, to the living, whom they have been accustomed to revere as their guides on account of their wisdom and grace, and they plead, Help us, comfort us, pray for us, that we may be brought into a state of grace. In vain. They answer, Not so, lest there be not enough for us and you. What you desire is impossible. None of us has any surplus merit out of which he could give a portion to another.")*

10 And while they went to buy, the bridegroom came; and they that were ready went in with him to the marriage: and the door was shut.

11 Afterward came also the other virgins, saying, Lord, Lord, open to us.

12 But he answered and said, Verily I say unto you, I know you not. *(Their fate was wretched indeed, they were so near heaven and yet lost, so much associated with saints and yet shut out of their bliss. It is vain to be a hearer of the word, a Bible reader, a church member, or a teacher of others, unless the oil of grace be in our hearts.)*

13 Watch therefore, for ye know neither the day nor the hour wherein the Son of man cometh. *(" Short is life; fleeting is time; quick is death; sure is judgment; long is eternity. Therefore, what thou desirest to do, do it quickly.")*

Ye virgin souls, arise,
With all the dead awake!
Unto salvation wise,
Oil in your vessels take:
Upstarting at the midnight cry,
"Behold your heavenly Bridegroom nigh!"

He comes, he comes, to call
The nations to his bar,
And raise to glory all
Who fit for glory are:
Make ready for your full reward;
Go forth with joy to meet your Lord.

592   "The Lord of those servants cometh and reckoneth with them."

OCTOBER 5.—MORNING.

[Or July 8.]

STILL *further to warn us of his coming, our Lord delivered the parable of the talents.*

MATTHEW XXV. 14—30.

14 For *the kingdom of heaven is* as a man travelling into a far country, *who* called his own servants, and delivered unto them his goods.

15 And unto one he gave five talents, to another two, and to another one; to every man according to his several ability; and straightway took his journey. *(We have all some talent. It may be only one, but we are responsible for it. Are we acting up to the measure of our ability? Many wish they had more talents, but this is wrong, for the Lord has entrusted us with quite as many gifts as we shall be able to give a good account of. Our great concern should be to be found faithful stewards of such things as we have.)*

16 Then he that had received the five talents went and traded with the same, and made *them* other five talents.

17 And likewise he that *had received* two, he also gained other two.

18 But he that had received one went and digged in the earth, and hid his lord's money. *He probably thought that as he could not do much he would not do anything, and there are thousands of his opinion; they fancy that their little is not needed and will never be missed, and therefore they make no attempt to serve their Lord. Are we of that kind?*

19 After a long time the lord of those servants cometh, and reckoneth with them.

20 And so he that had received five talents came and brought other five talents, saying, Lord, thou deliveredst unto me five talents: behold, I have gained beside them five talents more.

21 His lord said unto him, Well done, *thou* good and faithful servant: thou hast been faithful over a few things, I will make thee ruler over many things: enter thou into the joy of thy lord.

22 He also that had received two talents came and said, Lord, thou deliveredst unto me two talents: behold, I have gained two other talents beside them.

23 His lord said unto him, Well done, good and faithful servant; thou hast been faithful over a few things, I will make thee ruler over many things: enter thou into the joy of thy lord.

24, 25 Then he which had received the one talent came and said, Lord, I knew thee that thou art an hard man, reaping where thou hast not sown, and gathering where thou hast not strawed: And I was afraid, and went and hid thy talent in the earth: lo, *there* thou hast *that is* thine. *(Deep down in all unregenerate hearts there lurks the idea that God is too severe upon poor erring mortals, expecting more of them than is reasonable. Yet, if they think so they ought to be roused to greater carefulness to render to the Lord full obedience; their knowledge of what the Lord demands will make their disobedience the more criminal.)*

26 His lord answered and said unto him, *Thou* wicked and slothful servant, thou knewest that I reap where I sowed not, and gather where I have not strawed:

27 Thou oughtest therefore to have put my money to the exchangers, and *then* at my coming I should have received mine own with usury *(or interest).*

28 Take therefore the talent from him, and give *it* unto him which hath ten talents.

29 For unto every one that hath shall be given, and he shall have abundance: but from him that hath not shall be taken away even that which he hath.

30 And cast ye the unprofitable servant into outer darkness: there shall be weeping and gnashing of teeth. *(He was not rebellious, but only unprofitable, and that condemned him. How does this solemn truth bear upon us? Let us search and see.)*

> Make haste, O man, to live,
> For thou so soon must die;
> Time hurries past thee like the breeze;
> How swift its moments fly!
>
> Make haste, O man, to live,
> Thy time is almost o'er;
> Oh, sleep not, dream not, but arise;
> The Judge is at the door!

M AY *our hearts be earnestly attentive while we read our-Lord's own account of the Day of Judgment.*

MATTHEW XXV. 31—46.

31 When the Son of man shall come in his glory, and all the holy angels with him, then shall he sit upon the throne of his glory:

32 And before him shall be gathered all nations: and he shall separate them one from another, as a shepherd divideth *his* sheep from the goats:

33 And he shall set the sheep on his right hand, but the goats on the left. *(Here we are mixed together, but the keen eye of the Great Shepherd will detect our real characters and place us in one or other of the two flocks into which all mankind will be divided. There will be no middle company, we shall be placed either with saints or sinners in that day. To which do we now belong?)*

34 Then shall the King say unto them on his right hand, Come, ye blessed of my Father, inherit the kingdom prepared for you from the foundation of the world:

35 For I was an hungred, and ye gave me meat: I was thirsty, and ye gave me drink: I was a stranger, and ye took me in:

36 Naked, and ye clothed me: I was sick, and ye visited me: I was in prison, and ye came unto me. *(All these are deeds of love; not one of them consists of words, or ceremonial acts. The truest worship of God is charity to the needy: does not the apostle James say, "Pure religion and undefiled before God and the Father is this, to visit the fatherless and widows in their affliction and to keep himself unspotted from the world.")*

37 Then shall the righteous answer him, saying, Lord, when saw we thee an hungred, and fed *thee?* or thirsty, and gave *thee* drink?

38 When saw we thee a stranger, and took *thee* in? or naked, and clothed *thee?*

39 Or when saw we thee sick, or in prison, and came unto thee? *(They were modest, and had never set so high a value upon their own virtues as to have seen that excellence in them which the Judge had long ago discovered, and which he now declares publicly before men and angels. They had only been kind to poor and afflicted men and women, and were surprised to hear that* the Lord regarded their actions as rendered to himself.)

40 And the King shall answer and say unto them, Verily I say unto you, Inasmuch as ye have done *it* unto one of the least of these my brethren, ye have done it unto me. *(How this ennobles charity! "He that giveth to the poor lendeth unto the Lord." Who would not show kindness to his Redeemer?)*

41 Then shall he say also unto them on the left hand, Depart from me, ye cursed, into everlasting fire, prepared for the devil and his angels:

42 For I was an hungred, and ye gave me no meat: I was thirsty, and ye gave me no drink:

43 I was a stranger, and ye took me not in: naked, and ye clothed me not: sick, and in prison, and ye visited me not.

They were not condemned for what they had done amiss, but for what they had not done. Sins of omission are glaring evidences of want of grace, especially the omission of those duties which common humanity requires of us.

44 Then shall they also answer him, saying, Lord, when saw we thee an hungred, or athirst, or a stranger, or naked, or sick, or in prison, and did not minister unto thee? *(They were self-righteous and had no eye to see their faults. Fain would they have justified themselves. Those who deny their sins may be sure that they are of the goats.)*

45 Then shall he answer them, saying, Verily I say unto you, Inasmuch as ye did *it* not to one of the least of these, ye did *it* not to me.

46 And these shall go away into everlasting punishment: but the righteous into life eternal.

There is no temporary punishment any more than temporary reward. As sure as heaven is everlasting, so also is hell. Flee, O flee from the wrath to come.

Thou Judge of quick and dead,
Before whose bar severe,
With holy joy or guilty dread,
We all shall soon appear!

Our caution'd souls prepare
For that tremendous day;
And fill us now with watchful care,
And stir us up to pray.

594.   "𝔍𝔣 𝔞𝔫𝔶 𝔪𝔞𝔫 𝔬𝔭𝔢𝔫 𝔱𝔥𝔢 𝔡𝔬𝔬𝔯, 𝔍 𝔴𝔦𝔩𝔩 𝔠𝔬𝔪𝔢 𝔦𝔫 𝔱𝔬 𝔥𝔦𝔪."   OCTOBER 6.—MORNING.

[Or July 10.]

MATTHEW XXVI. 1—5; 14—16.

AND it came to pass, when Jesus had finished all these sayings, he said unto his disciples, Ye know that after two days is *the feast of* the passover, and the Son of man is betrayed to be crucified.

3, 4 Then assembled together the chief priests, and the scribes, and the elders of the people, unto the palace of the high priest, who was called Caiaphas, And consulted that they might take Jesus by subtilty, and kill *him*. (*"The kings of the earth set themselves, and the rulers take counsel together against the Lord, and against his anointed." Oh, that the friends of Jesus were half as earnest to concert measures for glorifying him, as these men were when they resolved upon his death.)*

5 But they said, Not on the feast *day*, lest there be an uproar among the people.

The enemies of Christ's cause have never ceased to oppose him by meanness and treachery; the truth fears not the day, but evil is underhanded and works by secret plots. Still do the opponents of the gospel conspire to take Jesus by subtlety. Let us, like our Lord, oppose to their cunning nothing but holy courage and truthful simplicity.

14, 15 Then one of the twelve, called Judas Iscariot, went unto the chief priests, And said *unto them*, What will ye give me, and I will deliver him unto you? And they covenanted with him for thirty pieces of silver. (*The price of a slave. This showed the contempt of the rulers for Jesus and the avarice of Judas, which permitted him to sell his Master for so small a sum. How strikingly does all this correspond with the voice of prophecy in Zech. xi. "So they weighed for my price thirty pieces of silver; a goodly price that I was prised at of them." It is to be feared that thousands are selling Jesus for a less price than Judas received. A smile from the world has been a bribe sufficient to seduce many.)*

16 And from that time he sought opportunity to betray him.

MARK XIV. 12—16.

AND the first day of unleavened bread, when they killed the passover, his disciples said unto him, Where wilt thou that we go and prepare that thou mayest eat the passover? (*They knew that their Lord observed all the commands of the law, but as he had no house of his own, and it was usual for the inhabitants of Jerusalem to lend their rooms to strangers, they wished for his orders as to where he would keep the feast.)*

13 And he sendeth forth two of his disciples, and saith unto them, Go ye into the city, and there shall meet you a man bearing a pitcher of water: follow him.

14 And wheresoever he shall go in, say ye to the goodman of the house, The Master saith, Where is the guestchamber, where I shall eat the passover with my disciples?

15 And he will shew you a large upper room furnished *and* prepared: there make ready for us. (*Among his friends he had a secret foe, but in the city of his foes he had also a secret friend: the time was come for both to be discovered, for the death of Jesus is that by which the thoughts of many hearts are revealed. The directions given to Peter and John, whom he sent, must have established in them the full conviction that he knew all things, and this would deepen their belief that his prophecy of his death would be fulfilled: thus they would be led to see how voluntarily he submitted himself to the death which awaited him.)*

16 And his disciples went forth, and came into the city, and found as he had said unto them: and they made ready the passover.

The room in which Jesus was entertained is the emblem of a heart into which the Lord comes to sup; such a heart is enlarged by grace with love and joy and gratitude; it is an upper room lifted up from the world and sin, it is prepared and furnished by the Holy Spirit, and is freely opened to the great Master, who comes to feast with his beloved. Lord make our hearts such a room and we will receive both thee and thy disciples into our truest love.

If still thou dost with sinners eat,
Let my poor heart thy chamber be,
With gladness such a guest I'll greet,
And keep the paschal feast with thee.

If thou wilt come to me below,
My heart shall purge out sinful leaven
And every day more meet I'll grow
To keep the paschal feast in heaven.

LUKE XXII. 14—18; 24—30.

AND when the hour was come, he sat down, *(or reclined upon a couch after the Eastern manner,)* and the twelve apostles with him.

15 And he said unto them, With desire I have desired to eat this passover with you before I suffer : *(Strong was his longing to commune with his beloved ones, as also to finish his great work, and to become the lamb of God's passover.)*

16 For I say unto you, I will not any more eat thereof, until it be fulfilled in the kingdom of God. *(The passover was now to cease. Our Lord observed the outward sign one night before the proper time, because it was to be fulfilled on the morrow. This change was a sign that it had waxed old, and was ready to vanish away.)*

17, 18 And he took the cup, and gave thanks, and said, Take this, and divide *it* among yourselves : For I say unto you, I will not drink of the fruit of the vine, until the kingdom of God shall come. *(While the thoughts of the Master were thus taken up with his sufferings, it is painful to find that the apostles were disputing about pre-eminence. Alas, poor human nature!)*

24 ¶ And there was also a strife among them, which of them should be accounted the greatest.

25—27 And he said unto them, The kings of the Gentiles exercise lordship over them ; and they that exercise authority upon them are called benefactors. But ye *shall* not *be* so : but he that is greatest among you, let him be as the younger ; and he that is chief, as he that doth serve. For whether *is* greater, he that sitteth at meat, or he that serveth ? *is* not he that sitteth at meat ? but I am among you as he that serveth.

28—30 Ye are they which have continued with me in my temptations. And I appoint unto you a kingdom, as my Father hath appointed unto me ; That ye may eat and drink at my table in my kingdom, and sit on thrones judging the twelve tribes of Israel.

HOW *sweetly did he end their envious disputing by his words, but he went further and dealt it a final death blow by the condescending acts recorded in—*

JOHN XIII. 1—19.

1 Now before the feast of the passover, when Jesus knew that his hour was come that he should depart out of this world unto the Father, having loved his own which were in the world, he loved them unto the end.

2—5 And supper being ended, the devil having now put into the heart of Judas Iscariot, Simon's *son*, to betray him ; Jesus knowing that the Father had given all things into his hands, and that he was come from God, and went to God ; He riseth from supper, and laid aside his garments ; and took a towel, and girded himself. After that he poureth water into a bason, and began to wash the disciples' feet, and to wipe *them* with the towel wherewith he was girded.

6 Then cometh he to Simon Peter : and Peter saith unto him, Lord, dost thou wash my feet ?

7 Jesus answered and said unto him, What I do thou knowest not now ; but thou shalt know hereafter.

8 Peter saith unto him, Thou shalt never wash my feet. Jesus answered him, If I wash thee not, thou hast no part with me.

9 Simon Peter saith unto him, Lord, not my feet only, but also *my* hands and *my* head.

10, 11 Jesus saith to him, He that is washed needeth not save to wash *his* feet, but is clean every whit : and ye are clean, but not all. For he knew who should betray him ; therefore said he, Ye are not all clean.

12—15 So after he had washed their feet, and had taken his garments, and was set down again, he said unto them, Know ye what I have done to you ? Ye call me Master and Lord : and ye say well; for *so* I am. If I then, *your* Lord and Master, have washed your feet ; ye also ought to wash one another's feet. For I have given you an example, that ye should do as I have done to you.

16, 17 Verily, verily, I say unto you, The servant is not greater than his lord ; neither he that is sent greater than he that sent him. If ye know these things, happy are ye if ye do them.

18 I speak not of you all : I know whom I have chosen : but that the scripture may be fulfilled, He that eateth bread with me hath lifted up his heel against me.

19 Now I tell you before it come, that, when it is come to pass, ye may believe that I am *he*.

No comment is needed, and we have given none. Let us practise what is here so clearly taught.

JOHN XIII. 21—30.

WHEN Jesus had thus said, he was troubled in spirit, and testified, and said, Verily, verily, I say unto you, that one of you shall betray me. *(He could not but be troubled as he quoted the words of David, " He that eateth bread with me hath lifted up his heel against me." He who has been deserted by his friend and betrayed by a beloved companion will best be able to sympathise with the Lord. How different from us was he when he found himself betrayed. He did not turn in anger on the traitor, and upbraid him to his face; but he spoke indefinitely of one then present; as if he would give the offender an opportunity to repent, by gently hinting to him that his evil covenant was known to his innocent victim. Hard was the heart which could be hardened under that tender and delicate appeal.)*

22 Then the disciples looked one on another, doubting of whom he spake. *(We read that they each one said, " Lord, is it I?" No one suspected his fellow, none thought of Judas. It is well when we take warnings home to ourselves :—*

" If a traitor was found 'midst the privileged few,
If in Jesus' own presence a Judas was nigh;
Let my poor startled conscience this moment renew,
The anxious enquiry of ' Lord, is it I?'")

23 Now there was leaning on Jesus' bosom one of his disciples, whom Jesus loved.

With true modesty John conceals his name, but with fond remembrance of his Master's favour, he uses a title dearer to him than the name his father gave him. To be " that disciple whom Jesus loved" was greater honour than to be an emperor.

24 Simon Peter therefore beckoned to him, that he should ask who it should be of whom he spake. *(If any man may expect to know the secret of the Lord it is the disciple who lives in fellowship with his Lord. He may ask questions when others dare not.)*

25 He then lying on Jesus' breast saith unto him, Lord, who is it?

26 Jesus answered, He it is, to whom I shall give a sop, when I have dipped *it.* And when he had dipped the sop, he gave *it* to Judas Iscariot, *the son* of Simon. *(And yet the hardened sinner was not moved to repentance. Son of perdition, indeed, he was. Yet Jesus gave*

him a sop from his own dish. *Outward gifts from the Lord's hand are not always proofs of love. There was but one traitor at the table, and he alone had a sop given him from Christ's own hand; let us not envy those ungodly ones to whom the dainty morsels fall, they are only eating to their own condemnation.)*

27 And after the sop Satan entered into him. *(His irritation was great at being discovered, and as he was already a devil in covetousness, so Satan came to him and filled him with malice.)* Then said Jesus unto him, That thou doest, do quickly. *(He did not bid him do it, but since he would do it, he charged him to waste no time. Oh, the admirable meekness of the Lamb of God! Not one angry word fell from his lips. Why are we so full of wrath when we are ill-used?)*

28 Now no man at the table knew for what intent he spake this unto him.

29 For some *of them* thought, because Judas had the bag, that Jesus had said unto him, Buy *those things* that we have need of against the feast; or, that he should give something to the poor. *(This shows that the Redeemer showed no resentment, he spoke so calmly that the disciples thought that he referred to some ordinary business.)*

30 He then having received the sop went immediately out : and it was night.

Leave thee! no, my dearest Saviour,
   Thee whose blood my pardon bought ;
Slight thy mercy, scorn thy favour!
   Perish such an impious thought :
      Leave thee—never !
   Where for peace could I resort ?

But, O Lord, thou know'st my weakness,
   Know'st how prone I am to stray ;
God of love, of truth, of meekness,
   Guide and keep me in thy way;
      Blest Redeemer !
   Let me never from thee stray.

My God, my God, was ever love,
Was ever lowliness like thine?
Amazed I beg thee to explain
Thine own mysterious love's design.

Wondering I ask how can it be
That God should wait on man below?
That God's own Son should stoop to me,
And wash a sinner white as snow?

JOHN XIII. 31—37.

THEREFORE when *Judas* was gone out, Jesus said, Now is the Son of man glorified, and God is glorified in him. *(In spirit he had already triumphed. At the sight of Judas he had suffered pangs unutterable, but his soul had overcome the trial, and had gained an earnest of complete victory in the battle which lay before him. The traitor also was driven out of his church, and he saw in this a prophecy of the overthrow of Antichrist.)*

32 If God be glorified in him, God shall also glorify him in himself, and shall straightway glorify him. *(His eye is on the glory as he enters upon his passion; "for the joy that was set before him he endured the cross, despising the shame.")*

33 Little children, yet a little while I am with you. Ye shall seek me : and as I said unto the Jews, Whither I go, ye cannot come; so now I say to you. *(Now that Judas is gone, he unbosoms his heart, and speaks to the eleven under the tender term of "little children." He tells them that just now they are not to die with him and for a while they cannot follow him into heaven, but must tarry below; and he teaches them how to behave to one another in his absence, and leaves them the law of love as one of his last words.)*

34 A new commandment I give unto you, That ye love one another; as I have loved you, that ye also love one another.

35 By this shall all *men* know that ye are my disciples, if ye have love one to another.

36 Simon Peter said unto him, Lord, whither goest thou ? Jesus answered him, Whither I go, thou canst not follow me now; but thou shalt follow me afterwards. *(Peter would one day die a martyr's death, but not just then. This ought to have satisfied and silenced him, but his loving heart outran his judgment.)*

37 Peter said unto him, Lord, why cannot I follow thee now ? I will lay down my life for thy sake.

LUKE XXII. 31—38.

AND the Lord said, Simon, Simon, behold, Satan hath desired *to have* you, that he may sift *you* as wheat : But I have prayed for thee, that thy faith fail not : and when thou art converted, strengthen thy brethren. *(This solemn warning and gracious declaration were* meant to set the bold disciple on his guard, but he was self-confident, and again declared his strength of purpose.)*

33 And he said unto him, Lord, I am ready to go with thee, both into prison, and to death.

34 And he said, I tell thee, Peter, the cock shall not crow this day, before that thou shalt thrice deny that thou knowest me. *(Never was man more hearty and sincere, but the Lord knew he would waver. Let none of us talk of what we will do, but pray for grace to do it.)*

35 And he said unto them, When I sent you without purse, and scrip, and shoes, lacked ye any thing ? And they said, Nothing.

36 Then said he unto then, But now, he that hath a purse, let him take *it*, and likewise *his* scrip : and he that hath no sword, let him sell his garment, and buy one. *(Now all was changed, no one would entertain them, every one would harm them, and they would be as men needing defence against deadly foes. He did not, however, mean that they should fight with carnal weapons, as we shall see immediately. It was only an intimation that they were now to be assailed by force.)*

37 For I say unto you, that this that is written must yet be accomplished in me, And he was reckoned amongst the transgressors : for the things concerning me have an end.

38 And they said, Lord, behold, here *are* two swords. And he said unto them, It is enough. *(If they were literally to fight, two swords were not enough, but they were enough to express the Saviour's idea. They were now to go out as warriors to conquer the world, and the swords represented their militant condition. One sword was rashly used by Peter, and his Lord bade him put it away, to show that armed force is not to be employed; there was another sword not then wielded, which typified the Word of God, with which nations are subdued.)*

Boast not thy strength of faith and zeal
  For trials yet unknown ;
Or thou wilt soon by falling feel
  Thou canst not stand alone.

To Jesus now confide thy heart,
  He only can defend,
He will his mighty grace impart,
  And keep thee to the end.

THE *same night in which he was betrayed our divine Lord instituted the sacred Supper, which is to his people the perpetual memorial of his death, and is to be celebrated till he shall come again.*

MATTHEW XXVI. 26—30.

26 And as they were eating *(that is to say, while yet the Paschal feast was proceeding; so that the one feast might melt into the other)*, Jesus took bread, and blessed *it*, and brake *it*, and gave *it* to the disciples, and said, Take, eat; this is my body. *(He could not have meant that the bread was actually his body, for in his body he was sitting at the table, and he could not have two bodies. Nobody could misunderstand these words of Jesus unless they wished to do so, or were too devoid of reason to comprehend anything. Jesus meant evidently the bread represented his body, and should be to them in future the sign that he was really incarnate.)*

27 And he took the cup, and gave thanks, and gave *it* to them, saying, Drink ye all of it;

As if he foresaw that the Papists would take away the cup from the people, he expressly bade them all drink of it. The plainest language of command is no bond to those who are given over to the delusions of Rome.

28 For this is my blood of the new testament, which is shed for many for the remission of sins. *(The cup was the instructive token of his blood, for it was filled with the blood of the grape. Jesus is meat and drink to his people; their necessary food, their dainty luxury; their staff of life, their exhilaration and joy. How sweet to reflect that the memorial of our dying Lord is not a funeral wailing, but a festival of rest; not a superstitious rite, but a simple, joyful commemoration. It is a pity that by kneeling some of our brethren have missed the instruction which an easy reclining or sitting posture would have given them,—in Jesus, believers have entered into rest.)*

29 But I say unto you, I will not drink henceforth of this fruit of the vine, until that day when I drink it new with you in my Father's kingdom. *(Symbols were not for him, though useful to us: we shall ere long with him enjoy the reality which the emblem could but feebly typify.)*

30 And when they had sung an hymn, they went out into the mount of Olives.

Brave was the heart which could sing with death before him: surely that hymn was a battle psalm defying death and hell. In like manner let us sing in all times of trial and temptation, and so glorify our God.

THE *apostle Paul gives us a full account of this Supper, which he received by express revelation. He thus writes:—*

I. CORINTHIANS XI. 23—29.

23, 24 For I have received of the Lord that which also I delivered unto you, That the Lord Jesus the *same* night in which he was betrayed took bread: And when he had given thanks, he brake *it*, and said, Take, eat: this is my body, which is broken for you: this do in remembrance of me.

25 After the same manner also *he took* the cup, when he had supped, saying, This cup is the new testament in my blood: this do ye, as oft as ye drink *it*, in remembrance of me.

26 For as often as ye eat this bread, and drink this cup, ye do shew the Lord's death till he come.

27 Wherefore whosoever shall eat this bread, and drink *this* cup of the Lord, unworthily, shall be guilty of the body and blood of the Lord.

28 But let a man examine himself and so let him eat of *that* bread, and drink of *that* cup.

29 For he that eateth and drinketh unworthily *(without faith, reverence, and sincerity of soul)*, eateth and drinketh damnation *(or condemnation)* to himself, not discerning the Lord's body. *(He insults the ordinance by staying in the emblem and seeing no further; his heart is not occupied with the death of Jesus, he does not use the Supper as the Lord intended. Let us pay great attention to this, and mind how we behave at the Lord's table.)*

According to thy gracious word,
  In meek humility,
This will I do, my dying Lord,
  I will remember thee.

Thy body, broken for my sake,
  My bread from heaven shall be;
Thy testamental cup I take,
  And thus remember thee.

AFTER *the supper was over our Lord addressed his disciples in language full of loving concern for them. He knew that his absence would greatly distress them, and therefore he poured forth a stream of consolations. How many thousands of tried believers have been comforted by these gracious words? All Scripture is as a garden of sweet flowers, but this passage may be compared to the rose, for its marvellous beauty and sweetness.*

JOHN XIV. 1—14.

1 Let not your heart be troubled : ye believe in God, believe also in me. *(Though I die do not doubt me, rest in your Saviour as you do in your God.)*

2 In my Father's house are many mansions : if *it were* not *so*, I would have told you. I go to prepare a place for you. *(His absence would not grieve them if they remembered the errand on which he was gone. We may well spare the bodily presence of Jesus from this world now that we know he has gone to prepare our eternal resting place.)*

3, 4 And if I go and prepare a place for you, I will come again, and receive you unto myself; that where I am, *there* may ye be also. And whither I go ye know, and the way ye know.

5 Thomas saith unto him, Lord, we know not whither thou goest ; and how can we know the way? *(Probably his notion was that our Lord would go to Nazareth or Galilee or some remote place to be anointed king, and prepare places for his followers, and therefore in his cool, thoughtful, practical way he sought for information. He did not know that the Lord referred to his return to glory.)*

6, 7 Jesus saith unto him, I am the way, the truth, and the life : no man cometh unto the Father, but by me. If ye had known me, ye should have known my Father also : and from henceforth ye know him, and have seen him.

8 Philip saith unto him, Lord, shew us the Father, and it sufficeth us.

Here another good disciple betrayed his ignorance, he had not yet grasped the idea of the essential union of the Father and the Son.

9 Jesus saith unto him, Have I been so long time with you, and yet hast thou not known me,

Philip? he that hath seen me hath seen the Father ; and how sayest thou *then*, Shew us the Father ? *(Till the Spirit of God illuminates the mind we learn little even from the best of teachers. God was in Christ most evidently, and yet Philip did not perceive it.)*

10, 11 Believest thou not that I am in the Father, and the Father in me? the words that I speak unto you I speak not of myself : but the Father that dwelleth in me, he doeth the works. Believe me that I *am* in the Father, and the Father in me : or else believe me for the very works' sake. *(What meaning can there be in these words if Jesus be not Divine, and one with the Father? No clearer statement of his Godhead could be given.)*

12 Verily, verily, I say unto you, He that believeth on me, the works that I do shall he do also ; and greater *works* than these shall he do ; because I go unto my Father.

As God, the Lord Jesus not only had infinite power in himself, but he was able to delegate it to others. His apostles wrought great miracles, and his believing disciples worked mighty spiritual works, so that more converts were brought to the faith by their testimony, than were called by the personal ministry of the Lord himself ; and this, because through the Lord's ascension into glory the Spirit of God was more fully given.

13, 14 And whatsoever ye shall ask in my name, that will I do, that the Father may be glorified in the Son. If ye shall ask anything in my name, I will do *it*. *("Good prayers," says Bishop Hall, "never come weeping home. I am sure that I shall receive either what I ask or what I should ask." If the best of blessings are to be had for the asking, he who will not ask deserves to go without.)*

Can we mourn as broken-hearted,
  We who hang upon thy love,
Jesus for our sake departed
  To thy Father's house above?

Source of all our consolations,
  There we our Forerunner see :
In those lasting habitations
  Thou hast found a place for me.

All our hopes and souls we venture
  On thy never-failing word,
Sure into thy joy to enter,
  Sure to triumph with our Lord.

600   "𝔍𝔣 𝔶𝔢 𝔩𝔬𝔳𝔢 𝔐𝔢, 𝔨𝔢𝔢𝔭 𝔐𝔶 𝔠𝔬𝔪𝔪𝔞𝔫𝔡𝔪𝔢𝔫𝔱𝔰."   OCTOBER 9.—MORNING.

[*Or July* 16.]

WE were obliged to pause in the middle of that delightful chapter, the fourteenth of *John*; let us now read the concluding portion of it :—

JOHN XIV. 15—31.

15 If ye love me, keep my commandments.

It becomes us to take note of this short text. True love to Jesus always shows itself by obedience, all other love is only a thing of the lips, and betrays a hypocritical heart. Are we daily giving proof of our love to Jesus by doing as he has bidden us?

16, 17 And I will pray the Father, and he shall give you another Comforter, that he may abide with you for ever; *Even* the Spirit of truth; whom the world cannot receive, because it seeth him not, neither knoweth him : but ye know him ; for he dwelleth with you, and shall be in you.

18 I will not leave you comfortless *(or orphans)*: I will come to you.

19 Yet a little while, and the world seeth me no more; but ye see me : because I live, ye shall live also.

20 At that day ye shall know that I *am* in my Father, and ye in me, and I in you.

21 He that hath my commandments, and keepeth them, he it is that loveth me : and he that loveth me shall be loved of my Father, and I will love him, and will manifest myself to him.

22 Judas saith unto him, not Iscariot, Lord, how is it that thou wilt manifest thyself unto us, and not unto the world ? *(The Holy Spirit is careful to preserve the name of the gracious Jude from being confused with that of the traitor. Our characters are safe in his keeping. Jude asked a very proper question. How is it that the Lord reveals himself to us and not to others? Often when overwhelmed with a sense of the Lord's love to us, we have been ready to ask the same question, and say "Why me, Lord? why me?")*

23 Jesus answered and said unto him, If a man love me, he will keep my words : and my Father will love him, and we will come unto him, and make our abode with him.

Here is the reason for special manifestation, namely, special and mutual love. The Father and the Son love to abide where they are welcomed by humble and affectionate hearts, for these are habitations which they have themselves prepared for their own indwelling.

24 He that loveth me not keepeth not my sayings : and the word which ye hear is not mine, but the Father's which sent me.

25, 26 These things have I spoken unto you, being *yet* present with you. But the Comforter, *which is* the Holy Ghost, whom the Father will send in my name, he shall teach you all things, and bring all things to your remembrance, whatsoever I have said unto you. *(Value the Holy Spirit therefore, and give ear to his teaching at all times.)*

27 Peace I leave with you, my peace I give unto you : not as the world giveth, give I unto you. Let not your heart be troubled, neither let it be afraid. *(He was close upon his own sufferings, yet his main anxiety was to cheer the hearts of the dear ones he was about to leave; he had not one selfish thought.)*

28 Ye have heard how I said unto you, I go away, and come *again* unto you. If ye loved me, ye would rejoice, because I said, I go unto the Father : for my Father is greater than I.

29 And now I have told you before it come to pass, that, when it is come to pass, ye might believe.

30 Hereafter I will not talk much with you : for the prince of this world cometh, and hath nothing in me.

31 But that the world may know that I love the Father ; and as the Father gave me commandment, even so I do. Arise, let us go hence. *(With unfaltering footsteps he advanced to his agony : he did not wait to be seized, he was a willing victim and went forward to take up his cross.)*

Jesus is gone up on high ;
But his promise still is here,
"I will all your wants supply ;
I will send the Comforter."

Let us now his promise plead,
Let us to his throne draw nigh ;
Jesus knows his people's need,
Jesus hears his people's cry.

Send us, Lord, the Comforter,
Pledge and witness of thy love;
Dwelling with thy people here,
Leading them to joys above.

OUR *reading is taken from our Lord's parting discourse, which is full of every precious thing, a mine of wealth, a treasure-house of gems.*

JOHN XVI. 1—15.

1 These things have I spoken unto you, that ye should not be offended.

2 They shall put you out of the synagogues: yea, the time cometh, that whosoever killeth you will think that he doeth God service.

3 And these things will they do unto you, because they have not known the Father, nor me. *(Fully has this warning been verified: the blood of martyrs has flowed in rivers, yet the Church has not been offended with her Lord. He is so glorious that, she follows him even to prison and to death.)*

4 But these things have I told you, that when the time shall come, ye may remember that I told you of them. And these things I said not unto you at the beginning, because I was with you.

And therefore they were safe at his side; now he was about to leave them and they would need to be doubly on their guard.

5 But now I go my way to him that sent me; and none of you asketh me, Whither goest thou?

6 But because I have said these things unto you, sorrow hath filled your heart. *(They were too bowed down with grief at what he had told them to be able to make any more enquiries. It is an evil connected with excessive sorrow that it often closes the eyes to facts which are full of consolation.)*

7 Nevertheless I tell you the truth; It is expedient for you that I go away: for if I go not away, the Comforter will not come unto you; but if I depart, I will send him unto you.

If Jesus were here in one place we could not all reach him, and for this reason the presence of the Holy Spirit is more valuable than the bodily presence of the Redeemer would be. The Comforter can be in all the assemblies of the saints at the same time, and can teach at one moment all the disciples of the Lord; he can prompt prayers and inspire praises in myriads of souls at once, and apply the word with power to millions of hearts at the same instant. The glory of the church is the abiding power of the Holy Ghost, comforting the church and convincing the world.

8 And when he is come, he will reprove the world of sin, and of righteousness, and of judgment:

9 Of sin, because they believe not on me;
The most heinous of all sins, for it reveals the deep enmity of the heart to God. Men are enemies to God indeed, since they will sooner perish than be saved in God's way.

10 Of righteousness, because I go to my Father, and ye see me no more;
By God's raising him from the dead and receiving him into glory the perfection and acceptance of the righteousness of Jesus were proved.

11 Of judgment, because the prince of this world is judged. *(The life, death, and teachings of Jesus pronounce the clearest judgment upon the powers of evil and their unfruitful works.)*

12 I have yet many things to say unto you, but ye cannot bear them now.
Ye are not yet baptized with the Spirit, and are not able to grasp the higher mysteries.

13 Howbeit when he, the Spirit of truth, is come, he will guide you into all truth: for he shall not speak of himself; but whatsoever he shall hear, *that* shall he speak: and he will shew you things to come.

14 He shall glorify me: for he shall receive of mine, and shall shew *it* unto you.

15 All things that the Father hath are mine: therefore said I, that he shall take of mine, and shall shew *it* unto you. *(May the Holy Spirit reveal to us the person, work, and love of Jesus. He can teach the dullest scholar. His teachings all tend to glorify Jesus; they are no novelties, but the doctrines of Jesus laid home to the heart. Most blessed Spirit, teach thou each one of us!)*

The Holy Ghost is here,
Where saints in prayer agree,
As Jesu's parting gift he's near
Each pleading company.

He dwells within our soul,
An ever welcome Guest;
He reigns with absolute control,
As Monarch in the breast.

Our bodies are his shrine,
And he th' indwelling Lord;
All hail, thou Comforter divine!
Be evermore adored!

OUR *Lord continued to cheer and warn the little band around him, telling them of the sorrows they might expect, and of the consolations which would be given them.*

JOHN XVI. 16—33.

16 A little while, and ye shall not see me: and again, a little while, and ye shall see me, because I go to the Father. *(Because the Holy Spirit would enlighten them, they would see him in the truest sense, and would be prepared in a little while to see him for ever in glory.)*

17, 18 Then said *some* of his disciples among themselves, What is this that he saith unto us, A little while, and ye shall not see me : and again, a little while, and ye shall see me : and, Because I go to the Father ? They said therefore, What is this that he saith, A little while ? we cannot tell what he saith.

19 Now Jesus knew that they were desirous to ask him, and said unto them, Do ye enquire among yourselves of that I said, A little while and ye shall not see me : and again, a little while, and ye shall see me ?

20 Verily, verily, I say unto you, That ye shall weep and lament, but the world shall rejoice : and ye shall be sorrowful, but your sorrow shall be turned into joy. *(When the Lord was gone they were full of grief, but as soon as his great representative, the Comforter, had come to them, they were filled with holy joy, triumphing greatly because the Lord had ascended and had bestowed gifts upon men.)*

21, 22 A woman when she is in travail hath sorrow, because her hour is come : but as soon as she is delivered of the child, she remembereth no more the anguish, for joy that a man is born into the world. And ye now therefore have sorrow : but I will see you again, and your heart shall rejoice, and your joy no man taketh from you. *(No longer do the saints sorrow over the departure of their Lord, for they see the joyful result of his death, resurrection, and ascension, and are filled with a sacred delight which cannot be damped by persecution.)*

23 And in that day ye shall ask me nothing. *(They would be so well instructed that they would put no more childish questions to him, being led by the Spirit into the mysteries of the kingdom.)* Verily, verily, I say unto you, What-

soever ye shall ask the Father in my name, he will give *it* you. *(Blessed assurance, sealed with a double Verily ! Who will dare to doubt the efficacy of prayer ?)*

24 Hitherto have ye asked nothing in my name : ask, and ye shall receive, that your joy may be full. *(They had not yet learned the power of the name of Jesus, but when taught of the Spirit they would plead the name of Jesus with great prevalence.)*

25 These things have I spoken unto you in proverbs : but the time cometh, when I shall no more speak unto you in proverbs, but I shall shew you plainly of the Father.

26, 27 At that day ye shall ask in my name : and I say not unto you, that I will pray the Father for you : For the Father himself loveth you, because ye have loved me, and have believed that I came out from God.

28 I came forth from the Father, and am come into the world : again, I leave the world, and go to the Father.

29 His disciples said unto him, Lo, now speakest thou plainly, and speakest no proverb.

30 Now are we sure that thou knowest all things, and needest not that any man should ask thee : by this we believe that thou camest forth from God.

31 Jesus answered them, Do ye now believe ? *He reminded them by this question that their faith was not so strong as they imagined. When we are not under immediate trial we fancy our faith to be far greater than it really is.*

32 Behold, the hour cometh, yea, is now come, that ye shall be scattered, every man to his own, and shall leave me alone : and yet I am not alone, because the Father is with me.

33 These things I have spoken unto you, that in me ye might have peace. In the world ye shall have tribulation : but be of good cheer ; I have overcome the world. *(We have found our Lord's words to be true, for tribulation has been our portion ; let us be confident that the rest of his words are true also.)*

O love of God, our shield and stay,
Through all the perils of our way ;
Eternal love, in thee we rest,
For ever safe, for ever blest!

WE *have listened to our Lord's farewell sermon, let us now attend to his farewell prayer. Melancthon says of it, " There is no voice which has ever been heard either in heaven or on earth, more exalted, more holy, more fruitful, more sublime than this prayer offered by the Son of God himself." Beyond all other forms of supplication it deserves to be known as " the Lord's Prayer." Our time will only permit us to read one half of it on this occasion, but we will meditate upon the remainder when next we gather at the family altar.*

JOHN XVII. 1—12.

1 These words spake Jesus, and lifted up his eyes to heaven *(Our Lord, with holy calmness, looked into the face of the Father, and John, who seldom records the gestures of his beloved Lord, saw the upward glancing of his eye, and never forgot that impressive look. As Jesus looked up he prayed),* and said, Father, the hour is come *(This the Father knew, but Jesus loved to have fellowship with his Father in that knowledge. Prayer is not only the asking for favours, it is the intercourse of the soul with God, the drawing near of the heart to the Lord. Our Lord went on to cry)* glorify thy Son, that thy Son also may glorify thee :

2 As thou hast given him power over all flesh, that he should give eternal life to as many as thou hast given him. *(All men are in the hands of the Mediator—here is the universality of his redemption ; he will, however, save only his own people—here is the speciality of it.)*

3 And this is life eternal, that they might know thee the only true God, and Jesus Christ, whom thou hast sent. *(Do we know by experience what this eternal life is ? Do we know the only true God and Jesus Christ the sent one ? Let conscience answer. It is worthy of note that this is the only place in which our Lord applies to himself the compound name of Jesus Christ the Anointed Saviour.)*

4 I have glorified thee on the earth : I have finished the work which thou gavest me to do.

5 And now, O Father, glorify thou me with thine own self with the glory which I had with thee before the world was.

6 I have manifested thy name unto the men which thou gavest me out of the world: thine they were, and thou gavest them me ; and they have kept thy word.

7 Now they have known that all things whatsoever thou hast given me are of thee.

8 For I have given unto them the words which thou gavest me ; and they have received *them,* and have known surely that I came out from thee, and they have believed that thou didst send me.

9 I pray for them : I pray not for the world, but for them which thou hast given me ; for they are thine. *(The special blessings sought for by our Lord would not be prized by the ungodly world even could they obtain them, hence our Lord does not ask his Father to give such boons to any but his own disciples. He specially pleads that his beloved ones may be kept from the evil of the world, a prayer which evidently could not be offered for those who are themselves the cause of the evil and are living in it.)*

10 And all mine are thine, and thine are mine ; and I am glorified in them.

11 And now I am no more in the world, but these are in the world, and I come to thee. *(This is, as it were, a prayer from within the veil. The Saviour pleads as if he were already entered into the heavens.)* Holy Father, keep through thine own name those whom thou hast given me, that they may be one, as we *are.*

12 While I was with them in the world, I kept them in thy name : those that thou gavest me I have kept, and none of them is lost, but the son of perdition ; that the scripture might be fulfilled. *(The Redeemer's petition is, that his people may be kept from sin. How carefully ought we to behave ourselves lest we go astray into that which would grieve his heart. If he pleaded with God that we might be kept from sin, God forbid that we should take pleasure in it.)*

There is a Shepherd kind and strong,
  Still watchful for his sheep ;
Nor shall the infernal lion rend
  Whom he vouchsafes to keep.

Blest Jesus, intercede for us,
  That we may fall no more ;
Oh, raise us, when we prostrate lie,
  And comfort lost restore.

Thy sacred energy impart,
  That faith may never fail :
But under showers of fiery darts,
  That temper'd shield prevail.

604   "𝔗hou hast loved them as 𝔗hou hast loved 𝔐e."   OCTOBER 11.—MORNING.

[*Or July* 20.]

A T *this time we shall read the remainder of our Lord's departing prayer. May the Holy Spirit lead each one of us into its meaning.*

JOHN XVII. 13—26.

Our Lord had already said to his Father, " I come to thee," but such was the yearning of his soul after the Father, that once again he said,

13 And now come I to thee *(and then he added words full of anticipated triumph, from which it is clear that the joy which was set before him was not hidden from his eyes, for he desired his beloved ones to be sharers in it) ;* and these things I speak in the world, that they might have my joy fulfilled in themselves.

14 I have given them thy word ; and the world hath hated them, because they are not of the world, even as I am not of the world.

15 I pray not that thou shouldest take them out of the world, but that thou shouldest keep them from the evil.

16 They are not of the world, even as I am not of the world.

17 Sanctify them through thy truth : thy word is truth. *(The teaching of Jesus is the word of the Father, and that teaching is the great means of making believers to be " Holiness unto the Lord.")*

18 As thou hast sent me into the world, even so have I also sent them into the world.

He has commissioned us to glorify the Father by the salvation of men. The pierced hands of Jesus have ordained each one of us to minister for the good of those around us.

19 And for their sakes I sanctify myself, that they also might be sanctified through the truth. *(Our Lord consecrated himself, and set himself apart for the sake of his own elect, that they also might be consecrated to the glory of God.)*

20, 21 Neither pray I for these alone, but for them also which shall believe on me through their word ; that they all may be one ; as thou, Father, *art* in me, and I in thee, that they also may be one in us : that the world may believe that thou hast sent me. *(Where there is real grace in the heart, true unity is manifested. All the truly spiritual are one, and no party names can divide them ; one touch of grace has made all*

the saints more than kin, for they are one body in Christ.)

22, 23 And the glory which thou gavest me I have given them ; that they may be one, even as we are one : I in them, and thou in me, that they may be made perfect in one ; and that the world may know that thou hast sent me, and hast loved them, as thou hast loved me.

What a wonderful sentence is this last one. The Father loves his chosen even as he loves Jesus. Wonder of wonders ! Unspeakable grace !

24 Father, I will that they also, whom thou hast given me, be with me where I am ; that they may behold my glory, which thou hast given me : for thou lovedst me before the foundation of the world. *(Jesus here pleads with authority, " Father, I will," and we may be sure that his petition will succeed. All who are resting in him shall ere long be with him in glory.)*

25 O righteous Father, the world hath not known thee : but I have known thee, and these have known that thou hast sent me.

26 And I have declared unto them thy name, and will declare *it :* that the love wherewith thou hast loved me may be in them, and I in them. *(Dwelling thus upon his union with his church, our dear Redeemer entered upon that awful agony which preceded his passion. Was ever such a prayer heard before or since, either in heaven or in earth ?)*

> So near, so very near to God,
>   I cannot nearer be ;
> For in the person of his Son
>   I am as near as he.
>
> So dear, so very dear to God,
>   More dear I cannot be ;
> The love wherewith he loves his Son,
>   Such is his love to me.

> Softly to the garden lead us,
>   To behold thy bloody sweat
> Though thou from the curse hast freed us,
>   Let us not the curse forget.
>
> Be thy groans and cries rehearsèd
>   By thy Spirit in our ears,
> Till we, viewing whom we piercèd,
>   Melt in sympathetic tears.

MARK XIV. 32—42.

AND they came to a place which was named Gethsemane (*or the olive-press*): and he saith to his disciples, Sit ye here, while I shall pray. (*Company yields solace to a heavy heart; the disciples could not bear any part of our Lord's griefs, but they might have watched with him.*)

33, 34 And he taketh with him Peter and James and John, and began to be sore amazed, and to be very heavy: and saith unto them, My soul is exceeding sorrowful unto death: tarry ye here, and watch. (*He wished to have them near, but not too near: his woes were not to be seen of mortal man. The Man of Sorrows now began to enter the great deeps of woe.*)

35 And he went forward a little and fell on the ground, and prayed that, if it were possible, the hour might pass from him.

36 And he said, Abba, Father, all things *are* possible unto thee; take away this cup from me: nevertheless not what I will, but what thou wilt. (*Blessed prayer! Its sweet resignation to the Father's will should be an example to every tried child of God.*)

37 And he cometh, and findeth them sleeping, and saith unto Peter, Simon, sleepest thou? couldest not thou watch one hour?

38 Watch ye and pray, lest ye enter into temptation. The spirit truly *is* ready, but the flesh *is* weak. (*It is said by Luke that they were sleeping* FOR SORROW. *Their kind Master, knowing this, was ready with an excuse for them, and did not chide them for what looked unkind.*)

39 And again he went away, and prayed, and spake the same words.

40 And when he returned, he found them asleep again, (for their eyes were heavy,) neither wist they what to answer him. (*Luke tells us, "Being in an agony, he prayed more earnestly, and his sweat was as it were great drops (or clots) of blood falling down to the ground." Oh, the amazing griefs which were laid upon Jesus when our sins became his burden. We bless him with all our hearts for agonizing thus for us.*)

41 And he cometh the third time, and saith unto them, Sleep on now, and take *your* rest: it is enough, the hour is come; behold, the Son of man is betrayed into the hands of sinners.

42 Rise up, let us go; lo, he that betrayeth me is at hand. (*His agony in the garden was over, and he went calmly on to meet death and finish the great work of our redemption.*)

MATTHEW XXVI. 47—56.

AND while he yet spake, lo, Judas, one of the twelve, came, and with him a great multitude with swords and staves, from the chief priests and elders of the people.

48 Now he that betrayed him gave them a sign, saying, Whomsoever I shall kiss, that same is he: hold him fast.

49 And forthwith he came to Jesus, and said, Hail, Master; and kissed him.

50 And Jesus said unto him, Friend, wherefore art thou come? (*Still did the traitor mix a hypocritical respect with his baseness, as betrayers of Jesus are ever apt to do. How would such a kiss have provoked us! and yet our gentle Lord spake not one harsh word, his meekness endured to the end.*) Then came they, and laid hands on Jesus, and took him.

51 And, behold, one of them which were with Jesus stretched out *his* hand, and drew his sword, and struck a servant of the high priest's, and smote off his ear.

52, 53 Then said Jesus unto him, Put up again thy sword into his place: for all they that take the sword shall perish with the sword. Thinkest thou that I cannot now pray to my Father, and he shall presently give me more than twelve legions of angels?

54 But how then shall the scriptures be fulfilled, that thus it must be?

55 In that same hour said Jesus to the multitudes, Are ye come out as against a thief with swords and staves for to take me? I sat daily with you teaching in the temple, and ye laid no hold on me.

56 But all this was done, that the scriptures of the prophets might be fulfilled. Then all the disciples forsook him, and fled.

Where now were brave Peter and loving John? Alas for poor human nature! Far be it from us to imagine that we should have done better. These flying disciples warn us to pray that we may be kept faithful in the hour of trial.

MATTHEW XXVI. 57—75.

AND they that had laid hold on Jesus led him away to Caiaphas the high priest, where the scribes and the elders were assembled. *(Waiting for his blood, his enemies were spending the night in watching, until news should come that he was taken.)*

58 But Peter followed him afar off unto the high priest's palace, and went in, and sat with the servants, to see the end.

59—61 Now the chief priests, and elders, and all the council, sought false witness against Jesus, to put him to death; but found none: yea, though many false witnesses came, *yet* found they none. At the last came two false witnesses, And said, This *fellow* said, I am able to destroy the temple of God, and to build it in three days. *(This was a perversion of his meaning, and a wresting of his words. He had spoken of his own body and said, " Destroy this temple." It is no strange thing if the wicked misrepresent what we say, for they did the same by our Master and Lord.)*

62, 63 And the high priest arose, and said unto him, Answerest thou nothing? what *is it which* these witness against thee? but Jesus held his peace. *(Like a sheep before her shearers, he opened not his mouth.)* And the high priest answered and said unto him, I adjure thee by the living God, that thou tell us whether thou be the Christ, the Son of God.

64 Jesus saith unto him, Thou hast said: nevertheless I say unto you, Hereafter shall ye see the Son of man sitting on the right hand of power, and coming in the clouds of heaven.

65, 66 Then the high priest rent his clothes, saying, He hath spoken blasphemy; what further need have we of witnesses? behold, now ye have heard his blasphemy. What think ye? They answered and said, He is guilty of death. *(How could God's own Son blaspheme? His works had proved him to be God, and yet they called him a blasphemer.)*

67, 68 Then did they spit in his face, and buffeted him; and others smote *him* with the palms of their hands, saying, Prophesy unto us, thou Christ, Who is he that smote thee? *(Having rejected his Deity, they now mock at his prophetic claims. Those who deny Jesus to be God, do not long accept his teaching. See the*

shame our Lord endured! Our sins brought it upon him.)

69, 70 Now Peter sat without in the palace : and a damsel came unto him, saying, Thou also wast with Jesus of Galilee. But he denied before *them* all, saying, I know not what thou sayest. *(Brave Peter trembles before a maid-servant.)*

71, 72 And when he was gone out into the porch, another *maid* saw him, and said unto them that were there, This *fellow* was also with Jesus of Nazareth. And again he denied with an oath, I do not know the man. *(He uttered an oath, that they might no longer suspect him, for followers of Jesus abhor swearing. Poor Peter, what a fall was thine!)*

73 And after a while came unto *him* they that stood by, and said to Peter, Surely thou also art *one* of them; for thy speech bewrayeth thee. *(His Galilean brogue revealed him. If a believer sins he will not be able to do it as others do, and is sure to be detected.)*

74 Then began he to curse and to swear, saying, I know not the man. And immediately the cock crew. *(Providence controls what men call accidents. Surely the cock could crow when it willed, and yet the will of the Lord was done.)*

75 And Peter remembered the word of Jesus, which said unto him, Before the cock crow, thou shalt deny me thrice. And he went out, and wept bitterly. *(There was grace in his heart, and therefore the crow of a cock affected him, and the look of his Lord broke his heart. May the Lord by some means bring us also to repentance if at any time we are so base as to deny him.)*

If near the pit I rashly stray,
Before I fall, as fall I may,
   The keen conviction dart !
Recall me by that pitying look,
That kind, upbraiding glance which broke
   Unfaithful Peter's heart.

In me thine utmost mercy show,
And make me like thyself below,
   Unblamable in grace ;
Preserv'd, prepar'd, and fitted here,
In full perfection to appear
   Before thy glorious face.

SORROWFULLY *let us now see our Lord accused before the Jewish council, standing alone before his cruel enemies. After the council had condemned Jesus in a preliminary examination, they seem to have separated, to meet again in a more formal manner in the morning.*

LUKE XXII. 66—71.

66—69 And as soon as it was day *(which was then about five in the morning)*, the elders of the people and the chief priests and the scribes came together, and led him into their council, saying, Art thou the Christ? tell us. And he said unto them, If I tell you, ye will not believe: and if I also ask *you*, ye will not answer me, nor let *me* go. *(They would neither hear his arguments nor reply fairly to any questions which he might put to them, by which his claims might be proved. He had, in former days, proved to them that he was the Christ, and that the Christ was the Son of God, and yet they had refused to believe. He, therefore, bore his testimony, and left the issue to the last great day, saying,)* Hereafter shall the Son of man sit on the right hand of the power of God.

70 Then said they all, Art thou then the Son of God? *(He had called himself " the Son of man," but they saw at once that his claim to sit at God's right hand involved his Deity, and, therefore, they pushed the question yet further, that they might accuse him.)* And he said unto them, Ye say that I am. *(Which means, " Ye say rightly that I am.")*

71 And they said, What need we any further witness? for we ourselves have heard of his own mouth. *(From the boldness of our Lord let us take example, and never conceal the truth from fear of men.)*

MATTHEW XXVII. 1—10.

WHEN the morning was come, all the chief priests and elders of the people took counsel against Jesus to put him to death :

The day was more advanced, but it was yet early, and a third time the Sanhedrim held a sitting, not to try the Lord Jesus, but to consider how to secure his destruction. The Romans had taken away from them the power of life and death, and, therefore, they were forced to carry their prisoner to the Roman governor.

2 And when they had bound him, they led *him* away, and delivered him to Pontius Pilate the governor.

3, 4 Then Judas, which had betrayed him, when he saw that he was condemned, repented himself, and brought again the thirty pieces of silver to the chief priests and elders, Saying, I have sinned in that I have betrayed the innocent blood. And they said, What *is that* to us? see thou *to that*.

5 And he cast down the pieces of silver in the temple, and departed, and went and hanged himself. *(From the place whereon he hung himself he fell headlong and was dashed in pieces; thus every circumstance of horror attended his self-murder. Unhappy man! How short-lived was his profit! How eternal his loss! Will we give up Christ for gain or pleasure! O Lord, forbid it.)*

6 And the chief priests took the silver pieces, and said, It is not lawful for to put them into the treasury, because it is the price of blood.

Base hypocrites. They had a qualmish conscience about the harmless pieces of money, but none concerning the murder they had perpetrated! They remind us of those who are zealous for their church, and yet continue in sin.

7 And they took counsel, and bought with them the potter's field, to bury strangers in.

8—10 Wherefore that field was called, The field of blood, unto this day. Then was fulfilled that which was spoken by Jeremy the prophet, saying, And they took the thirty pieces of silver, the price of him that was valued, whom they of the children of Israel did value ; and gave them for the potter's field, as the Lord appointed me.

Lord! when I read the traitor's doom,
    To his own place consign'd,
What holy fear, and humble hope,
    Alternate fill my mind!

Traitor to thee I too have been,
    But saved by matchless grace,
Or else the lowest, hottest hell
    Had surely been my place.

Blest Lamb of God! thy sovereign grace
    To all around I'll tell,
Which made a place in glory mine,
    Whose just desert was hell.

608   *" My kingdom is not of this world."*   OCTOBER 13.—MORNING.

[*Or July 24.*]

W E *shall now attend our dear Redeemer to the judgment seat of the Roman ruler.*

JOHN XVIII. 28—40.

28 Then led they Jesus from Caiaphas unto the hall of judgment : and it was early ; and they themselves went not into the judgment hall, lest they should be defiled ; but that they might eat the passover. *(For the passover had not yet been celebrated. Our Lord observed a kind of paschal feast one day before the usual time, but the real passover he kept in a higher manner, being then made to be the Lamb of God, whose blood procures the salvation of the chosen. The Jewish counsellors little knew that they were already far too defiled to have any real fellowship with God's passover, and were unconsciously slaughtering the true Lamb, whose flesh they were not privileged to eat.)*

29 Pilate then went out unto them, and said, What accusation bring ye against this man ?

30 They answered and said unto him, If he were not a malefactor, we would not have delivered him up unto thee. *(They would hurry Pilate to pronounce sentence without a trial, as if the mere fact of their bringing a charge was quite enough. In what a hurry man is to do despite to his God !)*

31, 32 Then said Pilate unto them, Take ye him, and judge him according to your law. The Jews therefore said unto him, It is not lawful for us to put any man to death : That the saying of Jesus might be fulfilled, which he spake, signifying what death he should die.

33 Then Pilate entered into the judgment hall again, and called Jesus, and said unto him, Art thou the king of the Jews ?

34 Jesus' answered him, Sayest thou this thing of thyself, or did others tell it thee of me ?

35 Pilate answered, Am I a Jew ? Thine own nation and the chief priests have delivered thee unto me : what hast thou done ?

Well might he ask this. What, indeed, hadst thou done, O blessed Master, that men should clamour for thy blood?

36 Jesus answered, My kingdom is not of this world : if my kingdom were of this world, then would my servants fight, that I should not be delivered to the Jews : but now is my kingdom not from hence. *(Thus our Lord wit-*

nessed a good confession, and showed Pilate that his claims were spiritual, and that he was no rival of Cæsar.)

37 Pilate therefore said unto him, Art thou a king then ? Jesus answered, Thou sayest that I am a king. To this end was I born, and for this cause came I into the world, that I should bear witness unto the truth. Every one that is of the truth heareth my voice.

38 Pilate saith unto him, What is truth ? And when he had said this, he went out again unto the Jews, and saith unto them, I find in him no fault *at all. (Poor Pilate ! he was interested and favourably impressed, and went out to try and clear his prisoner, towards whom he had a mingled feeling of wonder, pity, and awe.)*

39 But ye have a custom, that I should release unto you one at the passover : will ye therefore that I release unto you the King of the Jews ? *(By this he hoped to succeed in delivering Jesus, but vain was the attempt. His enemies meant to put him to death, and would not be turned from their purpose.)*

40 Then cried they all again, saying, Not this man, but Barabbas. Now Barabbas was a robber. *(Thus having valued the Lord Jesus at the price of a slave, they now prefer a robber to him, and are anxious to see him die a felon's death. Well does Herbert put it :—*

> *" Pilate, a stranger, holdeth off ; but they,*
> *Mine own dear people, cry* 'away, away,'
> *With noise confusèd frightening the day.*
> *Was ever grief like mine ?")*

Rejected and despised of men,
    Behold a man of woe !
And grief his close companion still
    Through all his life below !

Yet all the griefs he felt were ours,
    Ours were the woes he bore ;
Pangs, not his own, his spotless soul
    With bitter anguish tore.

We held him as condemn'd of heaven,
    An outcast from his God ;
While for our sins he groaned, he bled,
    Beneath his Father's rod.

His sacred blood hath wash'd our souls
    From sin's polluting stain ;
His stripes have heal'd us, and his death
    Revived our souls again.

IT was vain for Pilate to attempt to appease the Jews; they were bent on the death of Jesus, and nothing else would satisfy them.

LUKE XXIII. 5—16.

5 And they were the more fierce, saying, He stirreth up the people, teaching throughout all Jewry, beginning from Galilee to this place.

6 When Pilate heard of Galilee, he asked whether the man were a Galilæan.

7 And as soon as he knew that he belonged unto Herod's jurisdiction, he sent him to Herod, who himself also was at Jerusalem at that time. *(He hoped by this means to rid himself of this troublesome affair. He knew the Lord to be innocent, and he ought to have set him free, but had not the moral courage to do so; he, therefore, welcomed the chance of transferring the case to other hands. How wretched is that man who is afraid to do right.)*

8 ¶ And when Herod saw Jesus, he was exceeding glad : for he was desirous to see him of a long *season*, because he had heard many .things of him ; and he hoped to have seen some miracle done by him.

9 Then he questioned with him in many words ; but he answered him nothing.

It was no part of our Lord's business to gratify idle curiosity, neither could it be of any avail to explain his doctrine to a man of Herod's character, and, therefore, his wisdom was seen in his silence.

10 And the chief priests and scribes stood and vehemently accused him. *(As they saw that Herod was not bitter against him, they grew more violent in their charges, hoping that our Lord's silence would enrage him, and so they might procure his death.)*

11 And Herod with his men of war set him at nought, and mocked *him*, and arrayed him in a gorgeous robe, and sent him again to Pilate.

Herod saw that Jesus could not be guilty in the manner laid to his charge, but the silence of the Lord excited his angry contempt, and he therefore ridiculed his claims to be the Messiah.

12 ¶ And the same day Pilate and Herod were made friends together : for before they were at enmity between themselves.

13, 14 ¶ And Pilate, when he had called together the chief priests and the rulers and the people, Said unto them, Ye have brought this man unto me, as one that perverteth the people : and, behold, I, having examined *him* before you, have found no fault in this man touching those things whereof ye accuse him :

15 No, nor yet Herod : for I sent you to him ; and, lo, nothing worthy of death is done unto him.

16 I will therefore chastise him, and release *him*. *(A compromise, but a very wicked one. If guilty the prisoner ought not to be released, if innocent he ought not to be chastised. Attempts to compromise between right and wrong are always failures and should be shunned by all honest men.)*

MATTHEW XXVII. 19, 20, 24, 25.

WHEN he was set down on the judgment seat, his wife sent unto him, saying, Have thou nothing to do with that just man : for I have suffered many things this day in a dream because of him. *(This was a warning to him. Heathens paid much respect to dreams, and, therefore, this must have greatly moved him, yet he dared not oppose the priests.)*

20 But the chief priests and elders persuaded the multitude that they should ask Barabbas, and destroy Jesus.

24 ¶ When Pilate saw that he could prevail nothing, but *that* rather a tumult was made, he took water, and washed *his* hands before the multitude, saying, I am innocent of the blood of this just person : see ye to *it*. *(The washing availed him nothing, the blood of Jesus lay at his door, for had he been just he would have released the innocent.)*

25 Then answered all the people, and said, His blood *be* on us, and on our children.

A terrible imprecation, which has doomed Israel to her long sorrows. The blood of Jesus will either be upon us to cleanse, or on us to condemn. Which will it be?

Power and dominion are his due
Who stood condemn'd at Pilate's bar ;
Wisdom belongs to Jesus too,
Though he was charged with madness here.

Honour immortal must be paid,
Instead of scandal and of scorn ;
While glory shines around his head,
And a bright crown without a thorn.

JOHN XIX. 1—15.

THEN Pilate therefore took Jesus, and scourged *him.*

2 And the soldiers platted a crown of thorns, and put *it* on his head, and they put on him a purple robe,

3 And said, Hail, King of the Jews! and they smote him with their hands.

Even as Isaiah had prophesied: " I gave my back to the smiters, and my cheeks to them that plucked off the hair ; I hid not my face from shame and spitting." An old writer says, concerning this shameful spitting, " What couldest thou have found on earth more vile and loathsome in order to thy abasement than that man should spit on thee? and this, moreover, with such railing and insult, as though thou wert the pest of mankind, a blasphemer and an outcast unworthy of the merest decencies of life ! What, Lord, was there in thee to be loathed ? Why, then, do they thus contemn and spit upon thee? Oh, my God, it is my due, not thine ! Truly do I, Lord, deserve to be spitted on by every creature, as a vile and harmful thing, a wretched sinner, unworthy to live ; but thou, Infinite Mercy, dost promote me to honour, dost spare me, and, for my sake, dost yield up the majesty of thy person and thy divine countenance to be humbled by such loathsome affronts and insults!"

4 Pilate therefore went forth again, and saith unto them, Behold, I bring him forth to you, that ye may know that I find no fault in him.

5 Then came Jesus forth, wearing the crown of thorns, and the purple robe. And *Pilate* saith unto them, Behold the man !

A spectacle which ought to have broken their hearts, and melted them to pity. Can we look on our suffering Lord and not love him ? If so, we are as base as they.

6 When the chief priests therefore and officers saw him, they cried out, saying, Crucify *him,* crucify *him.* Pilate saith unto them, Take ye him, and crucify *him :* for I find no fault in him.

7 The Jews answered him, We have a law, and by our law he ought to die, because he made himself the Son of God.

They first charged him with a civil, and then with an ecclesiastical offence. They cared not

how they compassed his death so that they could be rid of him.

8 ¶ When Pilate therefore heard that saying, he was the more afraid ; *(The mention of so august a claim as that of being* SON OF GOD *co-operated with his wife's dream to arouse his fears.)*

9 And went again into the judgment hall, and saith unto Jesus, Whence art thou ? But Jesus gave him no answer.

10 Then saith Pilate unto him, Speakest thou not unto me ? knowest thou not that I have power to crucify thee, and have power to release thee ?

11 Jesus answered, Thou couldest have no power *at all* against me, except it were given thee from above : therefore he that delivered me unto thee hath the greater sin.

12 And from thenceforth Pilate sought to release him : but the Jews cried out, saying, If thou let this man go, thou art not Cæsar's friend : whosoever maketh himself a king speaketh against Cæsar. *(Now they come back to the old charge. When men hate Jesus and his religion they will say anything ; a wicked tongue is never short of arguments.)*

13 ¶ When Pilate therefore heard that saying, he brought Jesus forth, and sat down in the judgment seat in a place that is called the Pavement, but in the Hebrew, Gabbatha.

14 And it was the preparation of the passover, and about the sixth hour : and he saith unto the Jews, Behold your King !

15 But they cried out, Away with *him,* away with *him,* crucify him. Pilate saith unto them, Shall I crucify your king ? The chief priests answered, We have no king but Cæsar.

What a sarcasm was that ! " Shall I crucify your King ?" It was clear as noonday that he was no dangerous rival of Cæsar, for how could he be really a temporal king of the Jews when the Jews themselves were clamouring for his execution ?

Are any of us, like these Jews, rejecting the kingship of Jesus ? We may be doing so practically, and that will be as fatal to our souls as if we did so in words. Lord Jesus, thou art our King, reign over us and in us, that we may one day reign with thee.

LUKE XXIII. 24—34.

AND Pilate gave sentence that it should be as they required. And he released unto them him that for sedition and murder was cast into prison, whom they had desired; but he delivered Jesus to their will. *(He had not courage to stem the stream, he feared that they might accuse him to Cæsar if he suffered Jesus to go free, and, therefore, he sold himself to do evil. We need to be firm in our principles or we shall soon be driven into great sin.)*

26 And as they led him away, they laid hold upon one Simon, a Cyrenian, coming out of the country, and on him they laid the cross, that he might bear *it* after Jesus.

Wherein he was highly privileged. Such honour have all true saints.

> *Shall Simon bear the cross alone,*
> *And all the rest go free?*
> *No, there's a cross for every one,*
> *And there's a cross for me.*

27 ¶ And there followed him a great company of people, and of women, which also bewailed and lamented him. *(No woman is mentioned as having spoken against Jesus in his life, or as having had a share in his death. Of woman born, by a woman was he anointed for his burial; a woman—Pilate's wife—pleaded for him, and here women wept over him. Women ministered to him in life, laid him in the grave, and were the first to meet him at his rising.)*

28 But Jesus turning unto them said, Daughters of Jerusalem, weep not for me, but weep for yourselves, and for your children.

29 For, behold, the days are coming, in the which they shall say, Blessed *are* the barren, and the wombs that never bare, and the paps which never gave suck.

30, 31 Then shall they begin to say to the mountains, Fall on us; and to the hills, Cover us. For if they do these things in a green tree, what shall be done in the dry?

Our Lord foresaw the terrors of the siege of Jerusalem, and bade the women prepare for overwhelming sorrows. If the innocent thus suffered, what would become of the guilty?

32 And there were also two other malefactors, led with him to be put to death.

33 And when they were come to the place, which is called Calvary, there they crucified him, and the malefactors, one on the right hand, and the other on the left.

34 Then said Jesus, Father, forgive them; for they know not what they do.

JOHN XIX. 19—27.

AND Pilate wrote a title, and put *it* on the cross. And the writing was, JESUS OF NAZARETH THE KING OF THE JEWS.

20 This title then read many of the Jews: for the place where Jesus was crucified was nigh to the city: and it was written in Hebrew, *and* Greek, *and* Latin.

21 Then said the chief priests of the Jews to Pilate, Write not, The King of the Jews; but that he said, I am King of the Jews.

22 Pilate answered, What I have written I have written. *(He could be firm when he liked, and his sin was, therefore, all the greater.)*

23 ¶ Then the soldiers, when they had crucified Jesus, took his garments, and made four parts, to every soldier a part; and also *his* coat: now the coat was without seam, woven from the top throughout.

24 They said therefore among themselves, Let us not rend it, but cast lots for it, whose it shall be: that the scripture might be fulfilled, which saith, They parted my raiment among them, and for my vesture they did cast lots. These things therefore the soldiers did.

Gambling hardens the heart, none but gamblers could have been brutish enough to rattle dice where the blood of Jesus was falling. The very sound of dice and the sight of cards should be loathed by a follower of the Crucified.

25 ¶ Now there stood by the cross of Jesus his mother, and his mother's sister, Mary the *wife* of Cleophas, and Mary Magdalene.

26, 27 When Jesus therefore saw his mother, and the disciple standing by, whom he loved, he saith unto his mother, Woman, behold thy son! Then saith he to the disciple, Behold thy mother! And from that hour that disciple took her unto his own *home.* *(To whose care should he commit his mother, but to that of the beloved John? He has handed over the widow and the orphan to the care of his people; let us not forget them.)*

LUKE XXIII. 39—43.

AND one of the malefactors which were hanged railed on him, saying, If thou be Christ, save thyself and us.

40, 41 But the other answering rebuked him, saying, Dost not thou fear God, seeing thou art in the same condemnation? And we indeed justly; for we receive the due reward of our deeds: but this man hath done nothing amiss.

42 And he said unto Jesus, Lord, remember me when thou comest into thy kingdom.

Dr. Hanna has beautifully said : " Here, amid the triumph of enemies, and the failure of the faith of friends, is one who discerns, even through the dark envelope which covers it, the hidden glory of the Redeemer, and openly hails him as his Lord and King. Marvellous, indeed, the faith in our Lord's divinity which sprung up so suddenly in such an unlikely region. Are we wrong in saying that, at the particular moment when that testimony to Christ's divinity was borne, there was not another full believer in that divinity but the dying thief ? . . . And what a tenderness of conscience is here ; what deep reverence for God ; what devout submission to the divine will ; what entire relinquishment of all personal grounds of confidence before God ; what a vivid realising of the world of spirits ; what a humble trust in Jesus ; what a zeal for the Saviour's honour ; what an indignation at the unworthy treatment he was receiving ! May we not take that catalogue of the fruits of genuine repentance which an apostle has drawn up for us, and applying it here, say of this man's repentance : Behold what carefulness it wrought in him ; yea, what clearing of himself ; yea, what indignation ; yea, what fear ; yea, what vehement desire ; yea, what zeal ; yea, what revenge ! In all things he approved himself to be a changed man, in all the desires and dispositions and purposes of his heart."

43 And Jesus said unto him, Verily I say unto thee, To day shalt thou be with me in paradise. *(The dying Saviour reigns on the cross, and allots a place in paradise to his companion in death. Here is no hint of purgatory, the pardoned thief is with Jesus that very day. So also shall all believers be with Jesus immediately they leave the body.)*

MATTHEW XXVII. 45—49.

NOW from the sixth hour there was darkness over all the land unto the ninth hour.

46 And about the ninth hour Jesus cried with a loud voice, saying, Eli, Eli, lama sabachthani? that is to say, My God, my God, why hast thou forsaken me ? *(A cry in which every word is emphatic. Read it over as many times as there are words, and see a new force of meaning each time. Jesus cried in this manner, that none of his saints might ever need to do so.)*

47 Some of them that stood there, when they heard *that,* said, This *man* calleth for Elias. *(Thus jesting at his prayer. Oh, horric cruelty !)*

48 And straightway one of them ran, and took a spunge, and filled *it* with vinegar, and put *it* on a reed, and gave him to drink.

49 The rest said, Let be, let us see whether Elias will come to save him.

JOHN XIX. 28—30.

AFTER this, Jesus knowing that all things were now accomplished, that the scripture might be fulfilled, saith, I thirst.

29 Now there was set a vessel full of vinegar : and they filled a spunge with vinegar, and put *it* upon hyssop, and put *it* to his mouth.

30 When Jesus therefore had received the vinegar, he said, It is finished : and he bowed his head, and gave up the ghost.

What a grand utterance ! Now are we safe, for salvation is complete.

MATTHEW XXVII. 51—54.

AND, behold, the veil of the temple was rent in twain from the top to the bottom; and the earth did quake, and the rocks rent ;

52 And the graves were opened ; and many bodies of the saints which slept arose,

53 And came out of the graves after his resurrection, and went into the holy city, and appeared unto many. *(These were early proofs of his resurrection power. These first-fruits prove that the harvest is sure.)*

54 Now when the centurion, and they that were with him, watching Jesus, saw the earthquake, and those things that were done, they feared greatly, saying, Truly this was the Son of God.

JOHN XIX. 31—42.

THE Jews therefore, because it was the preparation, that the bodies should not remain upon the cross on the sabbath day, (for that sabbath day was an high day,) besought Pilate that their legs might be broken, and *that* they might be taken away. *(The men who could commit this murder without shame were, nevertheless, great sticklers for every point of ceremony, whatever cruelty it might involve. This proves that rites and ceremonies leave men as bad as they find them. Romanists, with a thousand pompous performances, yet rejoiced in the burning of pious men and women, and invented racks and tortures for them. Let this teach us to mind most the spiritual requirements of the gospel, and remember that the religion which does not change the heart and teach us to be merciful is good for nothing.)*

32 Then came the soldiers, and brake the legs of the first, and of the other which was crucified with him. *(This was done to hasten death. Verily, the tender mercies of the wicked are cruel.)*

33 But when they came to Jesus, and saw that he was dead already, they brake not his legs :

34 But one of the soldiers with a spear pierced his side, and forthwith came there out blood and water.

35 And he that saw *it* bare record *(that is to say, John himself)*, and his record is true : and he knoweth that he saith true, that ye might believe. *(He was sure of what he saw, he was under no delusion, he asserts it with the utmost confidence.)*

36 For these things were done, that the scripture should be fulfilled, A bone of him shall not be broken.

37 And again another scripture saith, They shall look on him whom they pierced.

38 ¶ And after this Joseph of Arimathæa, being a disciple of Jesus, but secretly for fear of the Jews, besought Pilate that he might take away the body of Jesus : and Pilate gave *him* leave. He came therefore, and took the body of Jesus.

39 And there came also Nicodemus, which at the first came to Jesus by night, and brought a mixture of myrrh and aloes, about an hundred pound *weight*. *(The two secret but true followers of our Lord now came out in their true colours. The cross is the great revealer of the thoughts of men's hearts. Blessed are they who are not ashamed of Christ Crucified.)*

40 Then took they the body of Jesus, and wound it in linen clothes with the spices, as the manner of the Jews is to bury.

41 Now in the place where he was crucified there was a garden ; and in the garden a new sepulchre, wherein was never man yet laid.

42 There laid they Jesus therefore because of the Jews' preparation *day ;* for the sepulchre was nigh at hand.

MATTHEW XXVII. 62—66.

NOW the next day, that followed the day of the preparation, the chief priests and Pharisees came together unto Pilate,

63 Saying, Sir, we remember that that deceiver said, while he was yet alive, After three days I will rise again.

64 Command therefore that the sepulchre be made sure until the third day, lest his disciples come by night, and steal him away, and say unto the people, He is risen from the dead : so the last error shall be worse than the first.

Their jealous hatred led them to mar their own Sabbath and Passover by appeals to a heathen ruler. Little did they know of that spiritual Sabbath-keeping, which makes us lay aside our cares and even our own thoughts upon the hallowed day of rest.

65 Pilate said unto them, Ye have a watch : go your way, make *it* as sure as ye can.

66 So they went, and made the sepulchre sure, sealing the stone, and setting a watch.

Thus, unwittingly, helping to secure testimony for the resurrection such as none could gainsay. It was now impossible for his body to be stolen, and if he came forth it must be by supernatural power. Oh, blind Jews, thus to ensure their own confusion ! Blinder yet are they who believe that Jesus rose, and yet do not put their trust in him.

LET us read a selection of verses from the sixty-ninth Psalm, in which David was led to set forth the Redeemer's sufferings before and upon the cross.

PSALM LXIX. 1—4; 6—21.

1 Save me, O God; for the waters are come in unto *my* soul. *(Sorrows, deep, abounding, deadly, had penetrated his inner nature. Bodily anguish is not his first complaint; he begins not with the gall which embittered his lips, but with the mighty griefs which broke into his heart.)*

2 I sink in deep mire, where *there is* no standing: I am come into deep waters, where the floods overflow me. *(His sufferings were unlike all others in degree, the waters were such as soaked into the soul; the mire was the mire of the abyss itself, and the floods were deep and overflowing.)*

3 I am weary of my crying: my throat is dried: *(Long pleading, with awful fervour, had scorched his throat as with flames of fire:)* mine eyes fail while I wait for my God.

4 They that hate me without a cause are more than the hairs of mine head: they that would destroy me, *being* mine enemies wrongfully, are mighty: then I restored *that* which I took not away. *(It may be truly said that he restores what he took not away; for he gives back to the injured honour of God a recompense, and to man his lost happiness, though the insult of the one and the fall of the other, were neither of them, in any sense, his doings.)*

6 Let not them that wait on thee, O Lord GOD of hosts, be ashamed for my sake: let not those that seek thee be confounded for my sake, O God of Israel. *(Our blessed Lord ever had a tender concern for his people, and would not have his own oppression of spirit become a source of discouragement to them.)*

7 Because for thy sake I have borne reproach; shame hath covered my face.

They first covered our Lord with a veil of opprobrious accusation, and then hurried him away to be crucified. They passed him through the trial of cruel mockings, besmeared his face with spittle, and covered it with bruises, so that Pilate's "Ecce Homo" called the world's attention to an unexampled spectacle of woe and shame. Ah, blessed Lord, it was our shame which thou wast made to bear! Nothing more deserves to be reproached and despised than sin, and lo, when thou wast made sin for us, thou wast called

to endure abuse and scorn. *Blessed be thy name, it is over now, but we owe thee more than heart can conceive for thine amazing stoop of love.*

8 I am become a stranger unto my brethren, and an alien unto my mother's children.

9 For the zeal of thine house hath eaten me up; and the reproaches of them that reproached thee are fallen upon me.

10 When I wept, *and chastened* my soul with fasting, that was to my reproach.

11 I made sackcloth also my garment; and I became a proverb to them.

12 They that sit in the gate speak against me; and I *was* the song of the drunkards.

What amazing sin that he whom seraphs worship with veiled faces, should be a scornful proverb among the most abandoned of men.

13, 14 But as for me, my prayer *is* unto thee O LORD, *in* an acceptable time: O God, in the multitude of thy mercy hear me, in the truth of thy salvation. Deliver me out of the mire, and let me not sink: let me be delivered from them that hate me, and out of the deep waters.

15 Let not the waterflood overflow me, neither let the deep swallow me up, and let not the pit shut her mouth upon me.

16 Hear me, O LORD; for thy lovingkindness *is* good: turn unto me according to the multitude of thy tender mercies.

17 And hide not thy face from thy servant; for I am in trouble: hear me speedily.

18 Draw nigh unto my soul, *and* redeem it: deliver me because of mine enemies.

19 Thou hast known my reproach, and my shame, and my dishonour: mine adversaries *are* all before thee.

20 Reproach hath broken my heart *(our Lord died of a broken heart, and reproach had done the deed)*; and I am full of heaviness *(the heaviness of our Lord in the garden is expressed by many and forcible words in the four gospels, and each term goes to show that the agony was beyond measure great):* and I looked *for some* to take pity, but *there was* none; and for comforters, but I found none.

21 They gave me also gall for my meat; and in my thirst they gave me vinegar to drink.

A criminal's draught was offered to our innocent Lord, a bitter portion to our dying Master. Sorry entertainment had earth for her King.

Behold the Man ! by all condemn'd,
Assaulted by a host of foes ;
His person and his claims contemn'd,
A man of sufferings and woes.

Behold the Man ! he stands alone,
His foes are ready to devour ;
Not one of all his friends will own
Their Master in this trying hour.

Behold the Man ! though scorn'd below,
He bears the greatest name above ;
The angels at his footstool bow,
And all his royal claims approve.

Here lies of life th' immortal Prince,
Under arrest for all our sins ;
Prisoner of death, and silent here
He lies till the third morn appear.

My faith with joy and wonder sees,
Jesus, thy sacred obsequies ;
A burial which has power to save
From death, a burial of the grave !

Oh, that I now my wish might have,
And sink into my Saviour's grave ;
Then with my Head triumphant rise,
And wear his glories in the skies.

My heart dissolves to see thee bleed.
This heart so hard before.
I hear thee for the guilty plead,
And grief o'erflows the more.

'Twas for the sinful thou didst die,
And I a sinner stand :
What love speaks from thy dying eye,
And from each piercèd hand !

I know this cleansing blood of thine
Was shed, dear Lord, for me,—
For me, for all—oh, grace divine !—
Who look by faith on thee.

'Twas not the insulting voice of scorn
So deeply wrung his heart ;
The piercing nail, the pointed thorn,
Caused not the saddest smart :

But every struggling sigh betray'd
A heavier grief within,
How on his burden'd soul was laid
The weight of human sin.

O thou who hast vouchsafed to bear
Our sins' oppressive load,
Grant us thy righteousness to wear,
And lead us to our God.

'Tis finish'd ! all the debt is paid ;
Justice divine is satisfied ;
The grand and full atonement made ;
God for his people's guilt hath died.

Saved from the legal curse I am,
My Saviour hangs on yonder tree :
See there the meek expiring Lamb !
'Tis finish'd ! He expired for me !

Accepted in the Well-Beloved,
And clothed in righteousness divine,
I see the bar to heaven removed,
For all thy merits, Lord, are mine.

The enormous load of human guilt
Was on my Saviour laid ;
With woes as with a garment, he
For sinners was array'd.

And in the horrid pangs of death
He wept, he pray'd for me ;
Loved and embraced my guilty soul
When nailèd to the tree.

Oh, love amazing ! love beyond
The reach of human tongue ;
Love which shall be the subject of
An everlasting song.

616   "*My God, my God, why hast Thou forsaken me?*"   OCTOBER 16.—EVENING.

[*Or July* 31.]

PSALM XXII. 1—3; 11—24; 27, 28, 30, 31.

THE *most wonderful description of our Lord's sufferings on the cross itself is contained in the 22nd Psalm, from which we will now select portions for reading.*

The Psalm opens with our Lord's cry upon the cross, and it may be regarded throughout as his soliloquy while bleeding on the tree.

1 My God, my God, why hast thou forsaken me? *why art thou so* far from helping me, *and from* the words of my roaring? *(He prayed until he almost lost the power of articulate utterance.)*

2 O my God, I cry in the daytime, but thou hearest not; and in the night season, and am not silent.

3 But thou *art* holy, *O thou* that inhabitest the praises of Israel. *(Whatever the Father may do, the Mediator will not murmur; he holds fast his faith in the holiness of God.)*

11 Be not far from me; for trouble *is* near; for *there is* none to help. *(None either could or would help him, he trod the wine-press alone; yet was it a sore trial to find that all his disciples had forsaken him, and lover and friend were put far from him.)*

12 Many bulls have compassed me: strong *bulls* of Bashan have beset me round.

The mighty ones in the crowd are here marked by the tearful eye of their victim.

13 They gaped upon me *with* their mouths, *as* a ravening and a roaring lion. *(Like hungry cannibals they opened their blasphemous mouths as if to swallow the man they abhorred.)*

14 I am poured out like water, and all my bones are out of joint: *(As if distended upon a rack. Is it not most probable that the fastening of the hands and feet, and the jar occasioned by fixing the cross in the earth, may have dislocated the bones of the Crucified One? If this is not intended, we must refer the expression to that extreme weakness which would occasion relaxation of the muscles, and a general sense of parting asunder throughout the whole system)* my heart is like wax; it is melted in the midst of my bowels. *(Dr. Gill wisely observes: "If the heart of Christ, the Lion of the tribe of Judah, melted at it, what heart can endure, or hands be strong, when God deals with men in his wrath?")*

15 My strength is dried up like a potsherd; and my tongue cleaveth to my jaws; and thou hast brought me into the dust of death.

16 For dogs have compassed me: *(Here he marks the more ignoble crowd, who, while less strong than their brutal leaders, were not less ferocious, for they were howling and barking like unclean and hungry dogs)* the assembly of the wicked have inclosed me: they pierced my hands and my feet.

17, 18 I may tell all my bones: they look *and* stare upon me. They part my garments among them, and cast lots upon my vesture.

19 But be not thou far from me, O LORD: O my strength, haste thee to help me.

20 Deliver my soul from the sword; my darling from the power of the dog.

Meaning his soul, his life, which is most dear to every man. The original is "My only one," and therefore is our soul dear, because it is our only soul. Would that all men made their souls their darlings, but many treat them as if they were not worth so much as the mire of the streets.

21 Save me from the lion's mouth: for thou hast heard me from the horns of the unicorns.

22 I will declare thy name unto my brethren: in the midst of the congregation will I praise thee. *(The transition is very marked; darkness passed away from the Redeemer's soul and light broke in. The ruling passion, strong in death, led him to joyous thoughts of his beloved people.)*

23 Ye that fear the LORD, praise him; all ye the seed of Jacob, glorify him; and fear him, all ye the seed of Israel.

24 For he hath not despised nor abhorred the affliction of the afflicted; neither hath he hid his face from him; but when he cried unto him, he heard.

27 All the ends of the world shall remember and turn unto the LORD: and all the kindreds of the nations shall worship before thee.

28 For the kingdom *is* the LORD's: and he *is* the governor among the nations.

Jesus rejoiced in the glorious reign of the Lord over all nations of men.

30 A seed shall serve him; it shall be accounted to the Lord for a generation.

31 They shall come, and shall declare his righteousness unto a people that shall be born, that he hath done *this*. *(Or "It is finished." Salvation's glorious work is done.)*

JOHN XX. 1—17.

THE first *day* of the week cometh Mary Magdalene early, when it was yet dark, unto the sepulchre, and seeth the stone taken away from the sepulchre. *(She and her companions had inquired, " Who shall roll us away the stone?" and lo, they found it gone. God often removes our difficulties out of the way long before we come to them.)*

2 Then she runneth, and cometh to Simon Peter, and to the other disciple, whom Jesus loved, and saith unto them, They have taken away the Lord out of the sepulchre, and we know not where they have laid him.

3 Peter therefore went forth, and that other disciple, and came to the sepulchre.

4 So they ran both together : and the other disciple did outrun Peter, and came first to the sepulchre.

5 And he stooping down, *and looking in,* saw the linen clothes lying ; yet went he not in.

6 Then cometh Simon Peter following him, and went into the sepulchre, and seeth the linen clothes lie,

7 And the napkin, that was about his head, not lying with the linen clothes, but wrapped together in a place by itself. *(If any had stolen the body by night, they certainly would not have left the grave-clothes, much less have folded them up. Our Lord came forth at his leisure, not as one who breaks his prison, but as a captive lawfully delivered. Jesus has made the grave a furnished chamber for our repose, and the napkin by itself may serve to dry the mourner's tears.)*

8 Then went in also that other disciple, which came first to the sepulchre, and he saw, and believed.

9 For as yet they knew not the scripture, that he must rise again from the dead.

Though repeated to them so often, they had not seen the real meaning. What need there is of the Holy Spirit's teaching !

10 Then the disciples went away again unto their own home.

11, 12 ¶ But Mary stood without at the sepulchre weeping : and as she wept, she stooped down, *and looked* into the sepulchre, and seeth two angels in white sitting, the one at the head, and the other at the feet, where the body of Jesus had lain.

13 And they say unto her, Woman, why weepest thou ? *(Heaven was rejoicing over the risen Lord, the glad fact was an assurance of joy to earth, why then did this holy woman weep ? It was ignorance which kept her in sorrow. If we would learn more of the truth concerning Jesus, we should soon find consolation.)* She saith unto them, Because they have taken away my Lord, and I know not where they have laid him.

14 And when she had thus said, she turned herself back, and saw Jesus standing, and knew not that it was Jesus.

15 Jesus saith unto her, Woman, why weepest thou ? whom seekest thou ? She, supposing him to be the gardener, saith unto him, Sir, if thou have borne him hence, tell me where thou hast laid him, and I will take him away.

Her love made her feel equal to anything ; however ghastly and heavy the burden she would bear it, love would make it light.

16 Jesus saith unto her, Mary. She turned herself, and saith unto him, Rabboni ; which is to say, Master.

17 Jesus saith unto her, Touch me not ; for I am not yet ascended to my Father : but go to my brethren, and say unto them, I ascend unto my Father, and your Father ; and *to* my God, and your God. *(There will be time enough for another interview. Do not attempt to detain me, for I am not yet ascended. Go, tell those whom I still love, that I have called them brethren, and desire to see them before I rise into my Father's glory. Observe the tender love of Jesus, and remember that he has carried the same loving heart to heaven.)*

" Christ, the Lord, is risen to-day !"
Sons of men and angels say !
Raise your joys and triumphs high ;
Sing, ye heavens ; and earth reply.

Love's redeeming work is done ;
Fought the fight, the battle won :
Lo ! the sun's eclipse is o'er ;
Lo ! he sets in blood no more !

Vain the stone, the watch, the seal,
Christ has burst the gates of hell ;
Death in vain forbids his rise,
Christ hath open'd paradise.

WHILE *our Lord remained upon earth he showed himself often to his disciples.*

LUKE XXIV. 13—35.

13, 14 And, behold, two of them went that same day, *(the day on which the Lord arose,)* to a village called Emmaus, which was from Jerusalem *about* threescore furlongs. *(Or about seven miles and a half.)* And they talked together of all these things which had happened.

15 And it came to pass, that, while they communed *together* and reasoned, Jesus himself drew near, and went with them. *(When Christians make their Lord the subject of discourse they may hope to be favoured with his company.)*

16 But their eyes were holden that they should not know him. *(And the Lord himself also appeared to them " in another form," so that they did not recognise him. Jesus sometimes hides himself from those whom he loves best. He may be very near us and yet we may not know him.)*

17, 18 And he said unto them, What manner of communications *are* these that ye have one to another, as ye walk, and are sad ? And the one of them, whose name was Cleopas, answering said unto him, Art thou only a stranger in Jerusalem, and hast not known the things which are come to pass there in these days ?

19—24 And he said unto them, What things ? And they said unto him, Concerning Jesus of Nazareth, which was a prophet mighty in deed and word before God and all the people : And how the chief priests and our rulers delivered him to be condemned to death, and have crucified him. But we trusted that it had been he which should have redeemed Israel : and beside all this, to day is the third day since these things were done. Yea, and certain women also of our company made us astonished, which were early at the sepulchre ; And when they found not his body, they came, saying, that they had also seen a vision of angels, which said that he was alive. And certain of them which were with us went to the sepulchre, and found *it* even so as the women had said : but him they saw not.

25, 26 Then he said unto them, O fools, and slow of heart to believe all that the prophets have spoken : *(He called them fools, or wanting in thought and understanding. The original words do not imply contempt ; our Lord gently rebuked them for not seeing what was so plainly revealed in Scripture.)* Ought not Christ to have suffered these things, and to enter into his glory ? *(Is it not so predicted in the prophets ? How could it be otherwise ?)*

27 And beginning at Moses and all the prophets, he expounded unto them in all the scriptures the things concerning himself.

28 And they drew nigh unto the village, whither they went : and he made as though he would have gone further. *(No doubt he would have done so if they had been indifferent to his company : Jesus never forces his society upon us.)*

29 But they constrained him, saying, Abide with us : for it is toward evening, and the day is far spent. And he went in to tarry with them. *(Love can always find a plea to which her Lord will yield, for he is always most willing to commune with his people.)*

30, 31 And it came to pass, as he sat at meat with them, he took bread, and blessed *it*, and brake, and gave to them. And their eyes were opened, and they knew him ; and he vanished out of their sight. *(The precious ordinance of " breaking of bread," is that in which Jesus manifests himself full often to his chosen, and therefore they greatly delight in it. Let none of us forget to do this in remembrance of him.)*

32—34 And they said one to another, Did not our heart burn within us, while he talked with us by the way, and while he opened to us the scriptures ? And they rose up the same hour, and returned to Jerusalem, and found the eleven gathered together, and them that were with them, Saying, The Lord is risen indeed, and hath appeared to Simon. *(This testimony of the apostles the returning travellers were able to confirm, and they did so at once.)*

35 And they told what things *were done* in the way, and how he was known of them in breaking of bread.

Abide with me ! Fast falls the eventide ;
The darkness deepens : Lord, with me abide !
When other helpers fail, and comforts flee,
Help of the helpless, O abide with me !

Swift to its close ebbs out life's little day ;
Earth's joys grow dim ; its glories pass away :
Change and decay in all around I see ;
O thou, who changest not, abide with me !

I need thy presence every passing hour.
What but thy grace can foil the tempter's power ?
Who like thyself my guide and stay can be ?
Through cloud and sunshine, O abide with me !

OUR *Lord showed himself to an assembly of his disciples after his resurrection.*

JOHN XX. 19—31.

19 Then the same day at evening, being the first *day* of the week, when the doors were shut where the disciples were assembled for fear of the Jews, came Jesus and stood in the midst, and saith unto them, Peace *be* unto you. *(His presence among them when the doors were closed must have astonished and delighted them. While they were trembling he came to re-assure them both by his words and his smiles.)*

20 And when he had so said, he shewed unto them *his* hands and his side. Then were the disciples glad, when they saw the Lord.

And well might they be, for his presence is ever a well-spring of joy. Mark the loving familiarity which thus unveiled his scars, and note the full proofs of his identity which those wounds afforded them. Even now the Lord reveals himself unto his chosen as he doth not unto the world. Oh, for a view of him by faith.

21, 22 Then said Jesus to them again, Peace *be* unto you : as *my* Father hath sent me, even so send I you. And when he had said this, he breathed on *them*, and saith unto them, Receive ye the Holy Ghost :

23 Whose soever sins ye remit, they are remitted unto them ; *and* whose soever *sins* ye retain, they are retained. *(He gave them a commission and added the power to carry it out by the gift of the Holy Ghost. Moreover he promised to put force into the sentences which they pronounced in his name, so that when they preached remission to penitents, the Lord granted that remission, and when in the name of Jesus they declared that the sins of unbelievers remained upon them, it was so. The gospel is not our word, but the word of Jesus who has sent us.)*

24 ¶ But Thomas, one of the twelve, called Didymus, was not with them when Jesus came.

He neglected the week-night service and lost a blessing, as many have done since.

25 The other disciples therefore said unto him, We have seen the Lord. But he said unto them, Except I shall see in his hands the print of the nails, and put my finger into the print of the nails, and thrust my hand into his side, I will not believe. *(He had no right to claim such a proof ; unbelief is unreasonable in its demands.)*

26 ¶ And after eight days again his disciples were within, and Thomas with them : *then* came Jesus, the doors being shut, and stood in the midst, and said, Peace *be* unto you.

27 Then saith he to Thomas, Reach hither thy finger, and behold my hands ; and reach hither thy hand, and thrust *it* into my side : and be not faithless, but believing. *(Infinite was the Redeemer's condescension. Knowing the doubts of Thomas he stooped to meet them, for he knew him to be sincere and willing to be convinced.)*

28 And Thomas answered and said unto him, My Lord and my God. *(Thus in a moment reading the Deity of Jesus in wounds. A sweet lesson. Oh, to learn it every day afresh.)*

29 Jesus saith unto him, Thomas, because thou hast seen me, thou hast believed : blessed *are* they that have not seen, and *yet* have believed. *(The richest blessing falls to the share of those simple minds who believe the word of God, even when surrounded with difficulty and unsupported by signs and evidences. The more childlike the faith the happier the heart.)*

30, 31 And many other signs truly did Jesus in the presence of his disciples, which are not written in this book : But these are written, that ye might believe that Jesus is the Christ, the Son of God ; and that believing ye might have life through his name. *(Have we so believed? If not, the Bible has been read by us in vain.)*

Crown him, the Lord of Love ;
Behold his hands and side,
Rich wounds, yet visible above
In beauty glorified.

Crown him, the Lord of Peace,
Whose power a sceptre sways
From pole to pole, that wars may cease,
Absorb'd in prayer and praise :

His reign shall know no end,
And round his piercèd feet
Fair flowers of Paradise extend
Their fragrance ever sweet.

All hail ! Redeemer, hail !
For thou hast died for me :
Thy praise shall never, never fail
Throughout eternity.

JOHN XXI. 1—6 ; 9—13 ; 15—19.

AFTER these things Jesus shewed himself again to the disciples at the sea of Tiberias ; and on this wise shewed he *himself.*

2 There were together Simon Peter, and Thomas called Didymus, and Nathanael of Cana in Galilee, and the *sons* of Zebedee, and two other of his disciples. *(It was well to keep together and enjoy the communion of saints. Good society makes good men better.)*

3 Simon Peter saith unto them, I go a fishing. They say unto him, We also go with thee. They went forth, and entered into a ship immediately ; and that night they caught nothing. *(As they had as yet no directions to go upon their spiritual business, they acted commendably in following their daily callings, for nothing is more dangerous than indolence.)*

4 But when the morning was now come, Jesus stood on the shore : but the disciples knew not that it was Jesus.

5 Then Jesus saith unto them, Children, have ye any meat ? They answered him, No.

6 And he said unto them, Cast the net on the right side of the ship, and ye shall find. They cast therefore, and now they were not able to draw it for the multitude of fishes.

9 As soon then as they were come to land, they saw a fire of coals there, and fish laid thereon, and bread. *(Everything tended to remind them of their old times with their Lord. Fishing in the old place, the old failures, the old miracles, and the old repast, would all help them to identify their Master. But what a new light was over all !)*

10 Jesus saith unto them, Bring of the fish which ye have now caught.

11 Simon Peter went up, and drew the net to land full of great fishes, an hundred and fifty and three : and for all there were so many, yet was not the net broken. *("Be of use ! Forward ! To Christ !" These were the watchwords of Peter, and should be ours.)*

12 Jesus saith unto them, Come *and* dine. And none of the disciples durst ask him, Who art thou ? knowing that it was the Lord.

13 Jesus then cometh, and taketh bread, and giveth them, and fish likewise. *(Jesus here showed himself to be what he still is. the Provider, the Host, the Husband of his Church.)*

15 ¶ So when they had dined, Jesus saith to Simon Peter, Simon, *son·* of Jonas, lovest thou me more than these ? He saith unto him, Yea, Lord ; thou knowest that I love thee. He saith unto him, Feed my lambs.

16 He saith to him again the second time, Simon, *son* of Jonas, lovest thou me ? He saith unto him, Yea, Lord ; thou knowest that I love thee. He saith unto him, Feed my sheep.

17 He saith unto him the third time, Simon, *son* of Jonas, lovest thou me ? *(The Greek word means in this third question more than before, and might be rendered, "Lovest thou me dearly?")* Peter was grieved because he said unto him the third time, Lovest thou me ? And he said unto him, Lord, thou knowest all things ; thou knowest that I love thee. Jesus saith unto him, Feed my sheep. *(He had three times denied, and he must three times avow his Lord.)*

18, 19 Verily, verily, I say unto thee, When thou wast young, thou girdedst thyself, and walkedst whither thou wouldest : but when thou shalt be old, thou shalt stretch forth thy hands, and another shall gird thee, and carry *thee* whither thou wouldest not. This spake he, signifying by what death he should glorify God *(namely, by crucifixion).* And when he had spoken this, he saith unto him, Follow me.

Thus was erring Peter fully restored. How mightily would that word "follow me" ring in his ears and influence his whole future. Follow me in doctrine, follow me in practice, follow me in sufferings, follow me in death, follow me to glory. May the Lord say to each one of us with power, FOLLOW ME.

Do not I love thee, O my Lord ?
   Then let me nothing love :
Dead be my heart to every joy,
   When Jesus cannot move.

Hast thou a lamb in all thy flock
   I would disdain to feed ?
Hast thou a foe, before whose face
   I fear thy cause to plead ?

Thou know'st I love thee, dearest Lord ;
   But oh, I long to soar
Far from the sphere of mortal joys,
   And learn to love thee more.

THE *apostle Paul has collected the evidence of our Lord's resurrection, and has drawn from it the grand doctrine of the resurrection of all believers. His wonderful words have cheered mourners in all ages, and confirmed the faith of the saints. Let us read with deep attention—*

I. CORINTHIANS XV. 1—18.

1 Moreover, brethren, I declare unto you the gospel which I preached unto you, which also ye have received, and wherein ye stand;

2 By which also ye are saved, if ye keep in memory what I preached unto you, unless ye have believed in vain.

3 For I delivered unto you first of all that which I also received, how that Christ died for our sins according to the scriptures;

4—7 And that he was buried, and that he rose again the third day according to the scriptures:

This, then, is the gospel. It consists in great facts. Christ died for our sins, he has made atonement for our transgressions; Christ was buried and has risen from the dead;—this is the gospel in a nutshell;—those who heartily believe these facts, and rely upon the risen substitute for sinners, are saved.

(Paul goes on to say that Jesus really rose,) And that he was seen of Cephas, *(or Peter)* then of the twelve: After that, he was seen of above five hundred brethren at once; of whom the greater part remain unto this present, but some are fallen asleep. After that, he was seen of James; then of all the apostles. *(Nothing in history was ever better attested. The witnesses had nothing to gain, and many of them even lost their lives for maintaining their belief.)*

8 And last of all he was seen of me also, as of one born out of due time. *(He refers here to the time of his conversion, when Jesus spoke to him out of heaven and plainly revealed himself to him.)*

9 For I am the least of the apostles, that am not meet to be called an apostle, because I persecuted the church of God. *(God had forgiven Paul, but he never forgave himself; tears were ever in his eyes at the remembrance of his sin.)*

10 But by the grace of God I am what I am: and his grace which *was bestowed* upon me was not in vain; but I laboured more abundantly than they all: yet not I, but the grace of God which was with me. *(His modesty did not lead him to deny the grace of God. We ought to think little of ourselves, but it would be dishonouring to God to depreciate what he has done for us.)*

11 Therefore whether *it were* I or they, so we preach, and so ye believed.

12 Now if Christ be preached that he rose from the dead, how say some among you that there is no resurrection of the dead?

13 But if there be no resurrection of the dead, then is Christ not risen:

14 And if Christ be not risen, then *is* our preaching vain, and your faith *is* also vain.

Christianity stands or falls with the resurrection of its founder. No man can be a Christian and doubt the resurrection of the Lord; if that had not happened, the whole matter would have been proved an imposture.

15 Yea, and we are found false witnesses of God; because we have testified of God that he raised up Christ: whom he raised not up, if so be that the dead rise not. *(Who can believe the apostles to have been guilty of deliberate falsehood on this point? Their characters, their holy teaching, and their martyr deaths all forbid us to rank them with common cheats and liars. Their testimony is in all respects worthy of credit. Jesus did rise from the dead.)*

16, 17 For if the dead rise not, then is not Christ raised: And if Christ be not raised, your faith *is* vain; ye are yet in your sins.

18 Then they also which are fallen asleep in Christ are perished. *(If Jesus did not rise, those who died resting upon him were deceived, and have found no advocate at the bar of God; they are therefore lost for ever. The Corinthian Christians were not prepared to believe this, and yet so it must be if Jesus did not rise.)*

Bless'd be the everlasting God,
   The Father of our Lord;
Be his abounding mercy praised,
   His majesty adored.

When from the dead he raised his Son,
   And call'd him to the sky,
He gave our souls a lively hope
   That they should never die.

What though our inbred sins require
   Our flesh to see the dust;
Yet as the Lord our Saviour rose,
   So all his followers must.

622   "But now is Christ risen from the dead."   OCTOBER 19.—EVENING,

[*Or August 6.*]

THE *apostle Paul proceeds with his argument upon the resurrection, and declares for himself and brethren*—

I. CORINTHIANS XV. 19—34.

19 If in this life only we have hope in Christ, we are of all men most miserable.

If after all there is no resurrection, then the apostles suffered for nothing, they were wretched dupes, and having higher expectations than others their disappointment was proportionately bitter.

20 But now is Christ risen from the dead, *and* become the firstfruits of them that slept.

The risen Saviour is the pledge and guarantee of our resurrection ; we shall surely live again.

21 For since by man *came* death, by man *came* also the resurrection of the dead.

22 For as in Adam all die, even so in Christ shall all be made alive. (*By Adam's sin all who are in him die, and by Christ's righteousness all who are in him shall be made alive. There are two great covenant headships : the first was Adam's headship under the covenant of works, by which we have fallen, and the second is the headship of the Lord Jesus under the covenant of grace, by which we rise to eternal life.*)

23, 24 But every man in his own order : Christ the firstfruits ; afterward they that are Christ's at his coming. Then *cometh* the end, when he shall have delivered up the kingdom to God, even the Father ; when he shall have put down all rule and all authority and power.

25, 26 For he must reign, till he hath put all enemies under his feet. The last enemy *that* shall be destroyed *is* death.

27 For he hath put all things under his feet. But when he saith all things are put under *him,* it is manifest that he is excepted, which did put all things under him.

28 And when all things shall be subdued unto him, then shall the Son also himself be subject unto him that put all things under him, that God may be all in all. (*As Mediator, all power is given to our Lord Jesus in heaven and in earth, and this he will exercise until he has vanquished every foe. Then shall his mediatorial reign cease, the universe shall come under the direct sovereignty of God as God ; and the Blessed Trinity shall shine forth before all the redeemed, and enter into immediate fellowship with them.*)

29 Else what shall they do which are baptized for the dead, if the dead rise not at all ? why are they then baptized for the dead ?

As one believer died another came forward to occupy his place, and so the ranks were filled up by fresh converts. Where was the reason for such enthusiasm if in death men cease to be? Baptism is itself a picture of burial and resurrection, and it loses all its meaning if there be no rising from the tomb.

30, 31 And why stand we in jeopardy every hour ? I protest by your rejoicing which I have in Christ Jesus our Lord, I die daily.

His life was always in jeopardy : what was the use of enduring such perils if, after all, death turned out to be an endless sleep? The suffering Christian is the greatest of fools if the dead rise not.

32 If after the manner of men I have fought with beasts at Ephesus, what advantageth it me, if the dead rise not ? let us eat and drink; for to morrow we die. (*The most sensible thing to do if this life is all and there is nought beyond it, is to enjoy all the pleasures we can while the days fly by us. The apostle had been exposed in the amphitheatre and had escaped : but why run such risks for a mere dream ?*)

33 Be not deceived : evil communications corrupt good manners.

34 Awake to righteousness, and sin not; for some have not the knowledge of God : I speak *this* to your shame. (*Living among philosophical sceptics, the Corinthian Christians had learned to doubt. Paul here warns them of the danger of such company, and rebukes them for having so shamefully called in question the fundamental doctrine of their religion. God save us from the evil communications of this infidel generation.*)

My life's a shade, my days
Apace to death decline ;
My Lord is Life, he'll raise
My dust again, even mine.
Sweet truth to me ! I shall arise,
And with these eyes my Saviour see.

My peaceful grave shall keep
My bones till that sweet day ;
I wake from my long sleep
And leave my bed of clay.
Sweet truth to me ! I shall arise,
And with these eyes my Saviour see.

WE will now finish Paul's wonderful resurrection chapter.

I. CORINTHIANS XV. 35—58.

35—38 But some *man* will say, How are the dead raised up? and with what body do they come? *(The insinuation is, that a dead-body decays and cannot be raised again. Paul has little patience with the sceptical question, and cries,)* Thou fool, that which thou sowest is not quickened, except it die: And that which thou sowest, thou sowest not that body that shall be, but bare grain, it may chance of wheat, or of some other *grain:* But God giveth it a body as it hath pleased him, and to every seed his *(or rather its)* own body. *(You cannot tell from looking at a seed what the plant is to be, neither can we determine from our present bodies what their future form will be. How lovely is the flower compared with the shrivelled grain! How fair will our bodies be in comparison with these trembling frames!)*

39 All flesh *is* not the same flesh: but *there is* one *kind of* flesh of men, another flesh of beasts, another of fishes, *and* another of birds.

40 *There are* also celestial bodies, and bodies terrestrial: but the glory of the celestial *is* one, and the *glory* of the terrestrial *is* another.

41 *There is* one glory of the sun, and another glory of the moon, and another glory of the stars: for *one* star differeth from *another* star in glory. *(As all these things differ from each other, so will the resurrection body differ from that in which we now live. It will be the same body as to identity, yet will it differ in many important points.)*

42, 43 So also *is* the resurrection of the dead. It is sown in corruption; it is raised in incorruption: It is sown in dishonour; it is raised in glory: it is sown in weakness; it is raised in power:

44 It is sown a natural body *(or a soulish body, animated by the animal life);* it is raised a spiritual body *(fit for the immortal spirit which will quicken it).* There is a natural *(or soulish)* body, and there is a spiritual body.

45 And so it is written, The first man Adam was made a living soul; the last Adam *was made* a quickening spirit.

46 Howbeit that *was* not first which is spiritual, but that which is natural *(or for the soul);* and afterward that which is spiritual.

47 The first man *is* of the earth, earthy: the second man *is* the Lord from heaven.

48, 49 As *is* the earthy, such *are* they also that are earthy: and as *is* the heavenly, such *are* they also that are heavenly. And as we have borne the image of the earthy, we shall also bear the image of the heavenly. *(Blessed assurance!)*

50 Now this I say, brethren, that flesh and blood cannot inherit the kingdom of God; neither doth corruption inherit incorruption.

51, 52 Behold, I shew you a mystery; We shall not all sleep, but we shall all be changed, In a moment, in the twinkling of an eye, at the last trump: for the trumpet shall sound, and the dead shall be raised incorruptible, and we shall be changed. *(Those who are alive when Jesus comes must undergo a transformation ere they can enter heaven.)*

53—55 For this corruptible must put on incorruption, and this mortal *must* put on immortality. So when this corruptible shall have put on incorruption, and this mortal shall have put on immortality, then shall be brought to pass the saying that is written, Death is swallowed up in victory. O death, where *is* thy sting? O grave, where *is* thy victory?

56 The sting of death *is* sin; and the strength of sin *is* the law.

57 But thanks *be* to God, which giveth us the victory through our Lord Jesus Christ.

58 Therefore, my beloved brethren, be ye stedfast, unmoveable, always abounding in the work of the Lord, forasmuch as ye know that your labour is not in vain in the Lord.

The saints who now in Jesus sleep,
His own almighty power shall keep,
Till dawns the bright illustrious day,
When death itself shall die away.

How loud shall our glad voices sing,
When Christ his risen saints shall bring
From beds of dust and silent clay,
To realms of everlasting day!

624   It is good to sing praises unto our God.   OCTOBER 20.—EVENING.

[*Or August* 8.]

HAVING *now completed our reading of the life of our Lord up to his resurrection, we will meditate upon a few choice psalms. The first is full of praise and adoration.*

PSALM CXLVII.

1 Praise ye the LORD : for *it is* good to sing praises unto our God ; for *it is* pleasant ; *and* praise is comely. *(Few things are both good and pleasant. Medicine is good, but not pleasant ; sin, to the ungodly, is pleasant, but it can never be good. In the praise of God both the good and the pleasant are combined.)*

2 The LORD doth build up Jerusalem : he gathereth together the outcasts of Israel. *With poor self-condemned outcast souls he builds up his church. His grace delights to select such, and to do great things for them.*

3 He healeth the broken in heart, and bindeth up their wounds.

4 He telleth the number of the stars ; he calleth them all by *their* names. *(It will be well to read these two verses over again. The Lord who tells the stars, bends over wounded sinners, and binds up broken hearts—condescension like this is amazing. In the contemplation of it we are lost in love and wonder.)*

5 Great *is* our Lord, and of great power : his understanding *is* infinite.

6 The LORD lifteth up the meek : he casteth the wicked down to the ground.

7 Sing unto the LORD with thanksgiving ; sing praise upon the harp unto our God :

8 Who covereth the heaven with clouds, who prepareth rain for the earth, who maketh grass to grow upon the mountains.

9 He giveth to the beast his food, *and* to the young ravens which cry. *(The Creator cares for the work of his own hands. Does he hear the ravens cry and will he not hear us when we confess our sins and ask for pardon ? Ay, that he will.)*

10, 11 He delighteth not in the strength of the horse : he taketh not pleasure in the legs of a man. The LORD taketh pleasure in them that fear him, in those that hope in his mercy. *We value men by their strength, God cares more for their weakness ; we admire those who can run with speed : he favours those who have learned to rest in his mercy. Let the weak in*

body and mind be consoled by the fact that the *Lord of Mercy cares for them.*

12 Praise the LORD, O Jerusalem ; praise thy God, O Zion.

13 For he hath strengthened the bars of thy gates ; he hath blessed thy children within thee.

14 He maketh peace *in* thy borders, *and* filleth thee with the finest of the wheat.

15 He sendeth forth his commandment *upon* earth : his word runneth very swiftly. *Whether it be in the realm of nature or grace the word of the Lord brooks no hindrance, yields to no obstacle.*

16 He giveth snow like wool *(so that the tender plants are protected from the frost)* : he scattereth the hoarfrost like ashes.

17 He casteth forth his ice like morsels : who can stand before his cold ? *(Dwellers in severe climates feel the force of this. It is a striking expression. If the comforts of grace and nature were removed from us we should soon perish. Who can stand before his cold ?)*

18 He sendeth out his word, and melteth them *(ice, snow, hoarfrost, all vanish at his bidding)* ; he causeth his wind to blow, *and* the waters flow.

19 He sheweth his word unto Jacob, his statutes and his judgments unto Israel.

20 He hath not dealt so with any nation : and *as for his* judgments, they have not known them. Praise ye the LORD. *(We who dwell in this land of privileges ought to be as grateful as ancient Israel. As a family we have been highly favoured, and let us, one and all, unite in praising the Lord.)*

From all that dwell below the skies
Let the Creator's praise arise ;
Let the Redeemer's name be sung
Through every land, by every tongue.

Eternal are thy mercies, Lord ;
Eternal truth attends thy word :
Thy praise shall sound from shore to shore
Till suns shall rise and set no more.

WE *shall read for our instruction a part of that devout hymn of praise—*

PSALM CVII. 1—22.

1 O give thanks unto the LORD, for *he is* good : for his mercy *endureth* for ever.

2 Let the redeemed of the LORD say *so,* whom he hath redeemed from the hand of the enemy ;

3 And gathered them out of the lands, from the east, and from the west, from the north, and from the south. *(If all the rest of mankind should be dumb, the redeemed must not be. It is theirs to lead the song, and tell how the Lord conducts them through the wilderness to the promised rest. The psalmist speaks of the Lord's goodness to travellers across the desert, and such are we.)*

4 They wandered in the wilderness in a solitary way ; they found no city to dwell in.

5 Hungry and thirsty, their soul fainted in them.

6 Then they cried unto' the LORD in their trouble, *and* he delivered them out of their distresses. *(Necessity is often the mother of prayer, and prayer is the forerunner of deliverance. Our soul may faint, but so long as we can pray we shall not perish.)*

7 And he led them forth by the right way, that they might go to a city of habitation.

8 Oh that *men* would praise the LORD *for* his goodness, and *for* his wonderful works to the children of men !

9 For he satisfieth the longing soul, and filleth the hungry soul with goodness. *Here ends the paragraph which refers to pilgrims, the song now tells of the Lord's goodness to prisoners. All the saints have been spiritual captives, and are all bound to praise the Lord as they remember how he set them free.*

10 Such as sit in darkness and in the shadow of death, *being* bound in affliction and iron ;

11 Because they rebelled against the words of God, and contemned the counsel of the most High :

12 Therefore he brought down their heart with labour ; they fell down, and *there was* none to help.

13 Then they cried unto the LORD in their trouble, *and* he saved them out of their distresses. *(Bondage under conviction, weariness through legal labour, and a sense of utter help-*

lessness, compel men to pray, and then their deliverance comes. God has made his grace illustrious in the liberation of the prisoners of hope.)

14 He brought them out of darkness and the shadow of death, and brake their bands in sunder.

15 Oh that *men* would praise the LORD *for* his goodness, and *for* his wonderful works to the children of men !

16 For he hath broken the gates of brass, and cut the bars of iron in sunder. *Now the psalm deals with the sick, especially those whose sickness is brought on by their own folly, and here again we are all portrayed.*

17 Fools because of their transgression, and because of their iniquities, are afflicted.

18 Their soul abhorreth all manner of meat ; and they draw near unto the gates of death. *Sick people are whimsical as to their food, for their appetite is gone ; and even so under soul sickness, men refuse the best of comforts, and cannot believe those promises which would cheer them.*

19 Then they cry unto the LORD in their trouble, *and* he saveth them out of their distresses.

20 He sent his word, and healed them, and delivered *them* from their destructions.

21 Oh that *men* would praise the LORD *for* his goodness, and *for* his wonderful works to the children of men !

22 And let them sacrifice the sacrifices of thanksgiving, and declare his works with rejoicing. *(See the order here : the soul is sore sick, it begins to pray ; the Lord sends his word, the soul is healed ; praise is presented, and God is glorified. May this become a matter of experience with each one of us.)*

He feeds and clothes us all the way,
He guides our footsteps lest we stray ;
He guards us with a powerful hand,
And brings us to the heavenly land.

O let the saints with joy record
The truth and goodness of the Lord !
How great his works ! how kind his ways !
Let every tongue pronounce his praise.

626   *" He setteth the poor on high from affliction."*   OCTOBER 21.—EVENING.

[*Or August* 10.]

I T *will be profitable to read the rest of the psalm which furnished us with our last lesson. May the Holy Spirit sweetly bless it to all of us.*

PSALM CVII. 23—43.

The divine poet now sings of the Lord's mercy to sailors in time of tempest.

23 They that go down to the sea in ships, that do business in great waters ;

24 These see the works of the LORD, and his wonders in the deep.

25 For he commandeth, and raiseth the stormy wind, which lifteth up the waves thereof.

26 They mount up to the heaven, they go down again to the depths : their soul is melted because of trouble.

27 They reel to and fro, and stagger like a drunken man, and are at their wits' end.

28 Then they cry unto the LORD in their trouble, and he bringeth them out of their distresses. *(What a pity that they had not prayed before ! What condescension on the Lord's part to hear them now ! However long we may have neglected prayer, it is never too late. If the ship is sinking we may even then cry to God.)*

29 He maketh the storm a calm, so that the waves thereof are still. *(He does it all. He commanded the stormy wind to blow and he bids it cease. Some wise men attribute all this to abstract laws. The wisdom which puts God further off is wretched folly ; our bliss lies in feeling him to be near.)*

30 Then are they glad because they be quiet ; so he bringeth them unto their desired haven.

31 Oh that *men* would praise the LORD *for* his goodness, and *for* his wonderful works to the children of men !

32 Let them exalt him also in the congregation of the people, and praise him in the assembly of the elders. *(Sailors should go to the house of God as soon as they land, and unite with the general praise. It is to be feared that many who prayed on the sea curse on shore.)*

The song now treats of the various changes of human life and the mercy seen in them all.

33 He turneth rivers into a wilderness, and the watersprings into dry ground ;

34 A fruitful land into barrenness, for the wickedness of them that dwell therein.

35 He turneth the wilderness into a standing water, and dry ground into watersprings.

God who turned the fruitful land into a wilderness, also transforms the wilderness into a garden. He can bless or curse most effectually. Who would not be agreed with him ? If we are in the worst condition, let us have hope, for the Lord turns dry ground into watersprings.

36 And there he maketh the hungry to dwell, that they may prepare a city for habitation ;

37 And sow the fields, and plant vineyards, which may yield fruits of increase.

38 He blesseth them also, so that they are multiplied greatly ; and suffereth not their cattle to decrease.

39 Again, they are minished and brought low through oppression, affliction, and sorrow.

40 He poureth contempt upon princes, and causeth them to wander in the wilderness, *where there is* no way.

41 Yet setteth he the poor on high from affliction, and maketh *him* families like a flock.

This contrast is continually dwelt upon in Scripture, and is especially noticeable in the songs of Hannah and Mary. The Lord casts down the high and lifts up the low : let his name be praised, for thus he rectifies the wrongs of this evil world.

42 The righteous shall see *it*, and rejoice : and all iniquity shall stop her mouth.

43 Whoso *is* wise, and will observe these *things*, even they shall understand the lovingkindness of the LORD. *(The psalm is a spiritual riddle, and those who are taught of God will spy out the meaning. Providence also is often an enigma, but faith interprets it, and sees the love of God in everything.)*

Amidst the roaring of the sea,
My soul still hangs her hope on thee ;
Thy constant love, thy faithful care,
Is all that saves me from despair.

O Lord ! the pilot's part perform,
And guide and guard me through the storm ;
Defend me from each threatening ill,
Control the waves, say, " Peace—be still ! "

Though tempest-tossed, and half a wreck,
My Saviour through the floods I seek ;
Let neither winds nor stormy main
Force back my shattered bark again.

WE *have upon former occasions read por-tions of the one hundred and nineteenth Psalm. It is so precious that we will continue to study it, and now read from verse eighty-one to verse one hundred and four.*

PSALM CXIX. 81—104.

81 My soul fainteth for thy salvation : *but* I hope in thy word.

82 Mine eyes fail for thy word, saying, When wilt thou comfort me? *(We have the word in the Bible, but we want it to be applied by the Holy Spirit to our hearts, and we eagerly long to have it so. O Lord, grant our desire.)*

83 For I am become like a bottle in the smoke ; *yet* do I not forget thy statutes.

Like an old wine-skin blackened and shrivelled by smoke, he was worn with pain and anxiety, yet he did not leave the way of holiness, nor should we think of doing so, come what may.

84, 85 How many *are* the days of thy servant? when wilt thou execute judgment on them that persecute me? The proud have digged pits for me, which *are* not after thy law.

86 All thy commandments *are* faithful : they persecute me wrongfully ; help thou me.

A prayer as sweet as it is short ; let us use it : " Help thou me."

87 They had almost consumed me upon earth ; but I forsook not thy precepts.

88 Quicken me after thy lovingkindness ; so shall I keep the testimony of thy mouth.

We are always in need of the Spirit's quickening influences. Our hearts cannot keep fast hold upon the truth if they become paralysed by worldliness.

89 For ever, O LORD, thy word is settled in heaven. *(Other things are fleeting and changeable, thy promise is fixed and sure ; and this is our soul's stay in time of trouble. What should we do if the promise could fail?)*

90, 91 Thy faithfulness *is* unto all generations : thou hast established the earth, and it abideth. They continue this day according to thine ordinances : for all *are* thy servants.

Nature fulfils thy purposes, thou givest fixity to its laws, and even so shall the plans and promises of grace abide for ever.

92 Unless thy law *had been* my delights, I should then have perished in mine affliction.

93, 94 I will never forget thy precepts : for

with them thou hast quickened me. I *am* thine, save me ; for I have sought thy precepts.

95 The wicked have waited for me to destroy me : *but* I will consider thy testimonies.

This was far better than considering his danger and devising plans for escape. Faith continues her meditations undisturbed by the rage of her adversaries.

96 I have seen an end of all perfection : *but* thy commandment *is* exceeding broad.

Perfect happiness in this world, or perfection in the flesh, are dreams, but the law is perfect, and so also is the glorious plan of salvation, therefore do we turn away from all else to rest in the Lord.

97 O how love I thy law ! it *is* my meditation all the day.

98—100 Thou through thy commandments hast made me wiser than mine enemies : for they *are* ever with me. I have more understanding than all my teachers : for thy testimonies *are* my meditation. I understand more than the ancients, because I keep thy precepts. *(He became wiser than " his enemies " in subtlety, than "his teachers" in doctrine, than " the ancients" in experience. What a fruitful harvest did David reap in the field of Scripture. The same wisdom may be found by each of us if we learn from the same testimonies.)*

101 I have refrained my feet from every evil way, that I might keep thy word.

102 I have not departed from thy judgments: for thou hast taught me. *(No other teaching is so practically effectual. He teacheth us to profit.)*

103 How sweet are thy words unto my taste ! *yea, sweeter* than honey to my mouth !

104 Through thy precepts I get understanding : therefore I hate every false way.

May such a holy abhorrence of sin be found in each of us evermore.

The men that keep thy law with care,
    And meditate thy word,
Grow wiser than their teachers are,
    And better know the Lord.

Thy precepts make me truly wise ;
    I hate the sinners' road ;
I hate my own vain thoughts that rise ;
    But love thy law, O God.

PSALM CXIX. 105—128.

THY word *is* a lamp unto my feet, and a light unto my path. *(It is a practical guide, not a book for my study only, but for my daily walk.)*

106 I have sworn, and I will perform *it*, that I will keep thy righteous judgments.

107 I am afflicted very much : quicken me, O LORD, according unto thy word. *(Our greatest need in times of trouble is more spiritual life. Afflictions will be a gain to us if they are sanctified to our more thorough arousing and enlivening. We have a promise that it shall be so, for the psalmist says, "according unto thy word.")*

108 Accept, I beseech thee, the freewill offerings of my mouth, O LORD, and teach me thy judgments.

109 My soul *is* continually in my hand : yet do I not forget thy law. *(Fear often drives away holy thought, and urges men to sin ; faith enables the believer to remain in quiet communion with God, even when life itself is in danger.)*

110 The wicked have laid a snare for me : yet I erred not from thy precepts.

111, 112 Thy testimonies have I taken as an heritage for ever : for they *are* the rejoicing of my heart. I have inclined mine heart to perform thy statutes alway, *even unto* the end.

113 I hate *vain* thoughts : but thy law do I love.

114 Thou *art* my hiding place and my shield : I hope in thy word.

115 Depart from me, ye evil doers: for I will keep the commandments of my God.

Bad companions must be chased away, for they are great enemies to holy living. We must be plain with the ungodly, and tell them that their company will never please us till they learn to please God.

116—119 Uphold me according unto thy word, that I may live: and let me not be ashamed of my hope. Hold thou me up, and I shall be safe : and I will have respect unto thy statutes continually. Thou hast trodden down all them that err from thy statutes: for their deceit *is* falsehood. Thou puttest away all the wicked of the earth *like* dross : therefore I love thy testimonies. *(God's justice in treading down and destroying the wicked is not distasteful to a holy mind ; on the contrary, we love him for being*

angry with evil, and relieving the world of those who are given over to it. A God without justice would be no God to just men.)

120 My flesh trembleth for fear of thee ; and I am afraid of thy judgments. *(Seeing others punished, we feel a holy awe in our own souls, and fear lest we also should be deceived by sin.)*

121 I have done judgment and justice : leave me not to mine oppressors.

122 Be surety for thy servant for good : let not the proud oppress me.

123 Mine eyes fail for thy salvation, and for the word of thy righteousness.

124 Deal with thy servant according unto thy mercy, and teach me thy statutes. *(We dare not court justice, yet we do not ask for a mercy which would allow us to sin ; we crave the grace which teaches us to follow after holiness.)*

125 I *am* thy servant ; give me understanding, that I may know thy testimonies.

A good master will teach his young servant his business and bear with his ignorance ; he cannot, however, give him understanding ; but this our heavenly Master can perform.

126 *It is* time for *thee*, LORD, to work : *for* they have made void thy law. *(When bad living and bad doctrine cast a slur upon religion, we may importunately beg the Lord to interfere to protect the interests of his own word. Are we not living in precisely such times ?)*

127, 128 Therefore I love thy commandments above gold ; yea, above fine gold. Therefore I esteem all *thy* precepts *concerning* all *things to be* right ; *and* I hate every false way. *(David was a decided man, he took strong ground and did not compromise, he loved right and hated wrong. That is the only safe position : there let us be found.)*

Great is their peace who love thy law,
  How firm their souls abide !
Nor can a bold temptation draw
  Their steady feet aside.

Thou hast inclined this heart of mine,
  Thy statutes to fulfil ;
And thus, till mortal life shall end,
  Would I perform thy will.

PSALM XLII.

THIS *is a very favourite psalm, and has many thousands of times cheered the hearts of the people of God.*

1 As the hart panteth after the water brooks, so panteth my soul after thee, O God. *(As the hunted hart instinctively seeks after the river to lave its smoking flanks and to escape the dogs, even so my weary, persecuted soul pants after the Lord my God.)*

2 My soul thirsteth for God, for the living God: when shall I come and appear before God? *(How he repeats and reiterates his desire! After his God, he pined even as the drooping flowers for the dew, or the moaning turtle for her mate. It were well if all our resortings to public worship were viewed as appearances before God; delight in them would then be a sure mark of grace.)*

3 My tears have been my meat day and night, while they continually say unto me, Where *is* thy God? *(His appetite was gone; his tears not only seasoned his meat, but became his only food. It was well for him that the heart could open the safety-valves; there is a dry grief far more terrible than showery sorrows. His tears, since they were shed because God was blasphemed were " honourable dew," drops of holy water, such as Jehovah putteth into his bottle.)*

4 When I remember these *things*, I pour out my soul in me: for I had gone with the multitude, I went with them to the house of God, with the voice of joy and praise, with a multitude that kept holyday.

" I sigh to think of happier days
 When thou, O God, wast nigh;
 When every heart was tuned to praise;
 And none more blest than I."

5 Why art thou cast down, O my soul? and *why* art thou disquieted in me? hope thou in God: for I shall yet praise him *for* the help of his countenance. *(As though he were two men, the psalmist talks to himself. His faith reasons with his fears, his hope argues with his sorrows. These present troubles, are they to last for ever? My absence from the solemn feasts, is that a perpetual exile? Why this deep depression, this faithless fainting? As Trapp says, " David chideth David out of the dumps;" and herein he is an example for all desponding ones. To search out the*

cause of our sorrow is often the best surgery for grief. Self-ignorance is not bliss; in this case it is misery.)

6 O my God, my soul is cast down within me: therefore will I remember thee from the land of Jordan, and of the Hermonites, from the hill Mizar. *(He recalls his seasons of choice communion by the river and among the hills, and especially that dearest hour upon the little hill, where love spake her sweetest language and revealed her nearest fellowship. It is great wisdom to store up in memory our choice occasions of converse with heaven; we may want them another day, when the Lord is slow in bringing back his banished ones.)*

7 Deep calleth unto deep at the noise of thy waterspouts: all thy waves and thy billows are gone over me. *(As in a waterspout the deeps above and below clasp hands, so it seemed to David that heaven and earth united to create a tempest around him. His woes were incessant and overwhelming.)*

8 *Yet* the Lord will command his lovingkindness in the daytime, and in the night his song *shall be* with me, *and* my prayer unto the God of my life.

9 I will say unto God my rock, Why hast thou forgotten me? why go I mourning because of the oppression of the enemy?

To know the reason for sorrow is in part to know how to escape it, or, at least, how to endure it.

10 *As* with a sword in my bones, mine enemies reproach me: while they say daily unto me, Where *is* thy God?

11 Why art thou cast down, O my soul? and why art thou disquieted within me? hope thou in God: for L shall yet praise him, *who is* the health of my countenance, and my God.

This sentence is peculiarly sweet. The enemies had said "Where is thy God," and the persecuted one replies, " He is here, as my joy and my all." Faith is not ashamed to own that God is her God even when he is greatly testing her. If we can keep our hold upon the Lord when in the midst of trial we shall come out of it safely.

For yet I know I shall him praise,
  Who graciously to me
The health is of my countenance,
  Yea, mine own God is he.

WE *shall now read that very choice experimental song*—

PSALM XXVII.

1 The LORD *is* my light and my salvation; whom shall I fear? the LORD *is* the strength of my life; of whom shall I be afraid?

2 When the wicked, *even* mine enemies and my foes, came upon me to eat up my flesh, they stumbled and fell. *(Past experience is a great help to faith. If fierce and powerful enemies have been defeated before, we need not fear now.)*

3 Though an host should encamp against me, my heart shall not fear; though war should rise against me, in this *will* I *be* confident.

4 One *thing* have I desired of the LORD, that will I seek after; that I may dwell in the house of the LORD all the days of my life, to behold the beauty of the LORD, and to enquire in his temple. *(Divided aims tend to distraction, weakness, disappointment. The man of one book is eminent, the man of one pursuit is successful. Let all our affections be bound up in one affection, and that affection set upon heavenly things. David desired above all things to be one of the household of God, a home-born child, living at home with his Father. This is our dearest wish, only we extend it to those days of our immortal life which have not yet dawned. We pine for our Father's house above, the home of our souls; if we may but dwell there for ever, we care but little for the goods or ills of this poor life. What a day will that be when every faithful follower of Jesus shall behold " the King in his beauty." Oh, for that infinitely blessed vision!)*

5 For in the time of trouble he shall hide me in his pavilion: in the secret of his tabernacle shall he hide me; he shall set me up upon a rock. *(In the pavilion of sovereignty, the holy place of sacrifice, and the rock of divine immutability we dwell securely.)*

6 And now shall mine head be lifted up above mine enemies round about me: therefore will I offer in his tabernacle sacrifices of joy; I will sing, yea, I will sing praises unto the LORD.

To sing in time of trouble is faith's glory. We need not wait till full deliverance comes, but even while our foes surround us we may shout the victory, for it is sure.

7 Hear, O LORD *when* I cry with my voice: have mercy also upon me, and answer me.

8 *When thou saidst,* Seek ye my face; my heart said unto thee, Thy face, LORD, will I seek. *(If we would have the Lord hear our voice, we must be careful to respond to his voice. The true heart should echo the will of God, as the rocks among the Alps repeat, in sweetest music, the notes of the peasant's horn.)*

9 Hide not thy face *far* from me; put not thy servant away in anger: thou hast been my help; leave me not, neither forsake me, O God of my salvation. *(A prayer for the future, and an inference from the past. If the Lord had meant to leave us, why did he begin with us?)*

10 When my father and my mother forsake me, then the LORD will take me up.

These dear relations will be the last to desert me; but if the milk of human kindness should dry up even from their breasts, there is a Father who never forgets. Some of the greatest of the saints have been cast out by their families, and persecuted for righteousness' sake.

11 Teach me thy way, O LORD, and lead me in a plain path, because of mine enemies.

These will entrap us if they can, but the way of simple honesty is safe from their rage. It is wonderful to observe how honest simplicity baffles and outwits the craftiness of wickedness.

12 Deliver me not over unto the will of mine enemies: for false witnesses are risen up against me, and such as breathe out cruelty.

13 *I had fainted,* unless I had believed to see the goodness of the LORD in the land of the living. *(We must believe to see, not see to believe; we must stay our soul's hunger with foretastes of the Lord's eternal goodness, which shall soon be our feast and our song.)*

14 Wait on the LORD: be of good courage, and he shall strengthen thine heart: wait, I say, on the LORD. *(David, in the words " I say," sets his own private seal to the word which, as an inspired man, he had been moved to write. At this moment he says to us as a family, " Wait, I say, on the Lord.")*

The Lord of glory is my light,
    And my salvation too;
God is my strength, nor will I fear
    What all my foes can do.

When troubles rise, and storms appear,
    In him his children hide:
God has a strong pavilion, where
    He makes my soul abide.

L UKE *commences the Acts of the Apostles with a kind of preface which runs thus* :

ACTS I.

1—5 The former treatise have I made, O Theophilus, of all that Jesus began both to do and teach, Until the day in which he was taken up, after that he through the Holy Ghost had given commandments unto the apostles whom he had chosen: To whom also he shewed himself alive after his passion by many infallible proofs, being seen of them forty days, and speaking of the things pertaining to the kingdom of God: And, being assembled together with *them*, commanded them that they should not depart from Jerusalem, but wait for the promise of the Father, which, *saith he*, ye have heard of me. For John truly baptized with water ; but ye shall be baptized with the Holy Ghost not many days hence.

6 When they therefore were come together, they asked of him, saying, Lord, wilt thou at this time restore again the kingdom to Israel ?

7, 8 And he said unto them, It is not for you to know the times or the seasons, which the Father hath put in his own power. But ye shall receive power, after that the Holy Ghost is come upon you : and ye shall be witnesses unto me both in Jerusalem and in all Judæa, and in Samaria, and unto the uttermost part of the earth. *(Humble waiting upon God, and joyful work for him, are the best cures for excessive curiosity.)*

9 And when he had spoken these things, while they beheld, he was taken up ; and a cloud received him out of their sight.

10, 11 And while they looked stedfastly toward heaven as he went up, behold, two men stood by them in white apparel ; Which also said, Ye men of Galilee, why stand ye gazing up into heaven ? this same Jesus, which is taken up from you into heaven, shall so come in like manner as ye have seen him go into heaven. *(When we stand gazing and trifling, the consideration of our Master's second coming should quicken and awaken us ; when we stand gazing and trembling, the same truth should comfort and encourage us.)*

12, 14 Then returned they unto Jerusalem from the mount called Olivet, which is from Jerusalem a sabbath day's journey. And they continued with one accord in prayer and supplication, with the women, and Mary the mother of Jesus, and with his brethren.

Prayer welded them together ; we hear no more of those strifes, which were once so frequent, as to which of them should be the greatest.

15, 16 And in those days Peter stood up in the midst of the disciples, and said, Men *and* brethren, this scripture must needs have been fulfilled, which the Holy Ghost by the mouth of David spake before concerning Judas, which was guide to them that took Jesus. *(What a gentle way of putting it. Harsh words are not to be used even of the worst of men. One is glad to hear Peter speaking thus calmly, surely he was made tender by the memory of his own fall.)*

17 For he was numbered with us, and had obtained part of this ministry.

18—22 Now this man purchased a field with the reward of iniquity ; and falling headlong, he burst asunder in the midst, and all his bowels gushed out. And it was known unto all the dwellers at Jerusalem ; insomuch as that field is called in their proper tongue, Aceldama, that is to say, The field of blood. For it is written in the book of Psalms, Let his habitation be desolate, and let no man dwell therein : and his bishoprick let another take. Wherefore of these men which have companied with us all the time that the Lord Jesus went in and out among us, Beginning from the baptism of John, unto that same day that he was taken up from us, must one be ordained to be a witness with us of his resurrection.

23—25 And they appointed two, Joseph called Barsabas, who was surnamed Justus, and Matthias. And they prayed, and said, Thou, Lord, which knowest the hearts of all *men*, shew whether of these two thou hast chosen, That he may take part of this ministry and apostleship, from which Judas by transgression fell, that he might go to his own place.

26 And they gave forth their lots ; and the lot fell upon Matthias ; and he was numbered with the eleven apostles.

No instance of the use of the lot occurs after the Spirit was given. It was an Old Testament custom, and to use it now would be idle superstition.

632   " **Lift up your heads, O ye gates.** "   OCTOBER 24.—EVENING.

[*Or August 16.*]

THE *psalmist David saw by the eye of prophecy the ascension of our Lord, and* sang *of it in—*

PSALM XXIV.

1 The earth *is* the LORD's, and the fulness thereof ; the world, and they that dwell therein.

2 For he hath founded it upon the seas, and established it upon the floods.

3 Who shall ascend into the hill of the LORD ? or who shall stand in his holy place ?

All creation belongs unto the Lord, and the whole universe is his domain ; but there is an abode of special glory where he more fully reveals himself to those whom he regards as peculiarly his own. The psalmist asks who these can be, and how it is that they are qualified to climb the hill whereon the divine palace is built. He describes their character and their leader.

4, 5 He that hath clean hands, and a pure heart ; who hath not lifted up his soul unto vanity, nor sworn deceitfully. He shall receive the blessing from the LORD, and righteousness from the God of his salvation. *(None can enter but the altogether pure in life and motive, the faithful and the upright. Jesus alone of our race perfectly answers to this description, and therefore he it is who leads the way and opens heaven's gate for those whom he has made meet to enter.)*

6 This *is* the generation of them that seek him, that seek thy face, O Jacob. Selah.

7 Lift up your heads, O ye gates ; and be ye lift up, ye everlasting doors ; and the King of glory shall come in. *(These verses reveal to us the great representative man, who answered to the full character laid down, and therefore by his own right ascended the holy hill of Zion. We see him rising from amidst the little group upon Olivet, and as the cloud receives him, angels reverently escort him to the gates of heaven. The ancient gates of the eternal temple are personified and called upon " to lift up their heads," as though, with all their glory, they were not great enough for the all-glorious King. Let the highest heavens put on unusual loftiness in honour of " the King of glory.")*

8 Who *is* this King of glory ? The LORD strong and mighty, the LORD mighty in battle.

The watchers at the gate, hearing the song, look over the battlements and ask " Who is this King of glory ? " *A question full of meaning and worthy of the meditation of eternity. Who is he in person, nature, character, office, and work ? What is his pedigree ? what his rank and what his race ? The answer given in a mighty wave of music is, " The Lord strong and mighty, the Lord mighty in battle." We know the might of Jesus by his victories over sin, death, and hell, and we clap our hands as we see him leading captivity captive in the majesty of his strength.*

9 Lift up your heads, O ye gates ; even lift *them* up, ye everlasting doors ; and the King of glory shall come in. *(The words are repeated with a pleasing variation. There are times of deep, earnest feeling when repetitions are not vain, but full of force. Doors were often taken from their hinges when easterns would show welcome to a guest, and some doors were drawn up like a portcullis, and may possibly have protruded from the top ; thus literally lifting up their heads. The picture is highly poetical, and shows how wide heaven's gate is set by the ascension of our Lord. Blessed be God, it has never since been closed. The open gates of heaven invite the weakest believer to enter.)*

10 Who is this King of glory ? The LORD of hosts, he *is* the King of glory. Selah.

The closing note is inexpressibly grand. Jehovah of hosts, Lord of men and angels, is the King of glory, and he it is who, having once descended to earth, now returns to his throne. The ascended Saviour is here declared to be the Head and Crown of the universe, the King of Glory. Our Immanuel is hymned in sublimest strains : Jesus of Nazareth is Jehovah Sabaoth.

Our Lord is risen from the dead ;
Our Jesus is gone up on high ;
The powers of hell are captive led—
Dragg'd to the portals of the sky.

There his triumphal chariot waits,
And angels chant the solemn lay ;—
" Lift up your heads, ye heavenly gates !
Ye everlasting doors, give way."

" Who is the King of glory, who ? "
The Lord of glorious power possess'd,
The King of saints and angels too :
God over all, for ever bless'd !

ACTS II. 1—21.

AND when the day of Pentecost was fully come, they were all with one accord in one place. *(Ancient Israel celebrated at Pentecost the feast of harvest: behold, here by the outpouring of the Spirit three thousand souls are to be in one day gathered into the granary of the Lord. Observe how unity and prayerfulness prevailed when the blessing of God descended upon the church.)*

2 And suddenly there came a sound from heaven as of a rushing mighty wind, and it filled all the house where they were sitting. *This appealed to their hearing, and was a fit accompaniment of the sacred breath of the Spirit.*

3 And there appeared unto them cloven tongues like as of fire, and it sat upon each of them. *(The fire appealed to their sight. It is an instructive emblem of the spiritual energy of the Holy Ghost. A tongue set on fire of hell is Satan's choice weapon; but tongues inflamed from above are the special instruments of grace.)*

4 And they were all filled with the Holy Ghost, and began to speak with other tongues, as the Spirit gave them utterance.

5—8 And there were dwelling at Jerusalem Jews, devout men, out of every nation under heaven. Now when this was noised abroad, the multitude came together, and were confounded, because that every man heard them speak in his own language. And they were all amazed and marvelled, saying one to another, Behold, are not all these which speak Galilæans? And how hear we every man in our own tongue, wherein we were born?

9—11 Parthians, and Medes, and Elamites, and the dwellers in Mesopotamia, and in Judæa, and Cappadocia, in Pontus, and Asia, Phrygia, and Pamphylia, in Egypt, and in the parts of Libya about Cyrene, and strangers of Rome, Jews and proselytes, Cretes and Arabians, we do hear them speak in our tongues the wonderful works of God.

12, 13 And they were all amazed, and were in doubt, saying one to another, What meaneth this? Others mocking said, These men are full of new wine. *(Men are sure to be divided in opinion upon the best and divinest things. Some wonder ignorantly, others ridicule maliciously, and a few adore reverently.)*

14, 15 ¶ But Peter, standing up with the eleven, lifted up his voice, and said unto them, Ye men of Judæa, and all *ye* that dwell at Jerusalem, be this known unto you, and hearken to my words: For these are not drunken, as ye suppose, seeing it is *but* the third hour of the day. *(Again we notice the mildness of Peter, he does not grow indignant at the charge of drunkenness, but answers it with the gentlest argument. His discourse which follows is most of it quoted from the Old Testament. Christ's scholars never become wiser than the Bible; the Spirit is given, not to supersede the Scriptures, but to enable us to understand and use them.)*

16—20 But this is that which was spoken by the prophet Joel; And it shall come to pass in the last days, saith God, I will pour out of my Spirit upon all flesh: and your sons and your daughters shall prophesy, and your young men shall see visions, and your old men shall dream dreams: And on my servants and on my handmaidens I will pour out in those days of my Spirit; and they shall prophesy: And I will shew wonders in heaven above, and signs in the earth beneath; blood, and fire, and vapour of smoke: The sun shall be turned into darkness, and the moon into blood, before that great and notable day of the Lord come: *These signs of wrath began to show themselves when Israel slew its King upon the cross; then the sun was turned into darkness. Yet more powerfully did they occur at the destruction of Jerusalem: blood, fire, and vapour of smoke filled the whole city. The year of the redeemed is also the day of vengeance of our God.*

21 And it shall come to pass, *that* whosoever shall call on the name of the Lord shall be saved.

This portion from Joel is read in the service of the Karaite Jews on the day of Pentecost, and it is extremely probable that it was the lesson for the day in Peter's time; he was therefore doubly wise in making it his text.

The last verse is so encouraging that we will read it again: And it shall come to pass, *that* whosoever shall call on the name of the Lord shall be saved. *Is any one of us now seeking the Lord? Let him find comfort in this gracious assurance, for no soul ever perished calling upon the name of the Lord.*

OCTOBER 25.—EVENING.

634   ' 𝔚𝔥𝔬 𝔞𝔯𝔢 𝔱𝔥𝔢𝔰𝔢 𝔱𝔥𝔞𝔱 𝔣𝔩𝔶 𝔞𝔰 𝔞 𝔠𝔩𝔬𝔲𝔡, 𝔞𝔫𝔡 𝔞𝔰 𝔱𝔥𝔢 𝔡𝔬𝔟𝔢𝔰 𝔱𝔬 𝔱𝔥𝔢𝔦𝔯 𝔴𝔦𝔫𝔡𝔬𝔴𝔰 ? "   [Or August 18.]

PETER *having begun to preach, soon came to the marrow of his subject, and testified concerning Jesus.*

ACTS II. 22—42 ; 47.

22—24 Ye men of Israel, hear these words ; Jesus of Nazareth, a man approved of God among you by miracles and wonders and signs, which God did by him in the midst of you, as ye yourselves also know : Him, being delivered by the determinate counsel and foreknowledge of God, ye have taken, and by wicked hands have crucified and slain. *(This was plain speech. Peter had no fear of man, he pressed the truth home upon the conscience. Pray for all ministers that they may be equally courageous.)* Whom God hath raised up, having loosed the pains of death : because it was not possible that he should be holden of it.

25—28 For David speaketh concerning him, I foresaw the Lord always before my face, for he is on my right hand, that I should not be moved : Therefore did my heart rejoice, and my tongue was glad ; moreover also my flesh shall rest in hope : Because thou wilt not leave my soul in hell, neither wilt thou suffer thine Holy One to see corruption. Thou hast made known to me the ways of life ; thou shalt make me full of joy with thy countenance.

29—32 Men *and* brethren, let me freely speak unto you of the patriarch David, that he ·is both dead and buried, and his sepulchre is with us unto this day. Therefore being a prophet, and knowing that God had sworn with an oath to him, that of the fruit of his loins, according to the flesh, he would raise up Christ to sit on his throne ; He seeing this before spake of the resurrection of Christ, that his soul was not left in hell, neither his flesh did see corruption. This Jesus hath God raised up, whereof we all are witnesses. *(David's prophecy and the witness of the apostles agreed together ; here was convincing evidence for all devout inquirers. Nor was this all, for the miraculous gifts now manifestly bestowed were further proofs of the Messiahship of Jesus. Peter proceeded to dwell upon that argument.)*

33 Therefore being by the right hand of God exalted, and having received of the Father the promise of the Holy Ghost, he hath shed forth this, which ye now see and hear.

34, 35 For David is not ascended into the heavens : but he saith himself, The LORD said unto my Lord, Sit thou on my right hand, Until I make thy foes thy footstool. *David could not have referred to himself, but to one who was his Lord, even to Jesus, now risen and ascended.*

36 Therefore let all the house of Israel know assuredly, that God hath made that same Jesus, whom ye have crucified, both Lord and Christ.

37 ¶ Now when they heard *this*, they were pricked in their heart, and said unto Peter and to the rest of the apostles, Men *and* brethren, what shall we do ? *(The concluding words, " Him have ye crucified," were the sharp hook by which, as a good fisher of men, Peter caught their hearts. The first word of the awakened showed a right feeling ; Peter's love in calling them " men and brethren," had created love in them, and they, in return, address the despised disciples by the same name. If there are any unconverted ones in this family, may they even now inquire, " What shall we do to be saved ?")*

38 Then Peter said unto them, Repent, and be, baptized every one of you in the name of Jesus Christ for the remission of sins, and ye shall receive the gift of the Holy Ghost.

39 For the promise is unto you, and to your children, and to all that are afar off, *even* as many as the Lord our God shall call.

40 And with many other words did he testify and exhort, saying, Save yourselves from this untoward generation. *(His gospel was very simple ; believing repentance, and baptismal profession were required, and nothing more. This same gospel belonged to their children as well as to themselves.)*

41, 42 Then they that gladly received his word were baptized : and the same day there were added *unto them* about three thousand souls. And they continued stedfastly in the apostles' doctrine and fellowship, and in breaking of bread, and in prayers.

47 Praising God, and having favour with all the people. And the Lord added to the church daily such as should be saved. *(Let us pray that such a state of things may again be seen among the people of God, and let us try to produce it.)*

Thou art gone up on high,
To mansions in the skies;
And round thy throne unceasingly
The songs of praise arise.

Thou art gone up on high;
But thou wilt come again,
With all the bright ones of the sky
Attendant in thy train.

Forthwith a tongue of fire
Is seen on every brow;
Each heart receives the Father's light,
The Word's enkindling glow.

The Holy Ghost on all
Is mightily outpoured,
Who straight in divers tongues declare
The wonders of the Lord.

The Father and the Son,
And Spirit we adore;
Oh, may the Spirit's gifts be poured
On us for evermore.

What a beautiful sight, when the children of light
In their primitive purity shone!
The disciples of old never strayed from the fold,
But they all were united in one.

The affections of grace were with prayer and with
Carried on with their every employ;   [praise
Their meals were all blest, and their hearts they
In songs of angelical joy.   [expressed

Their impotent foes could no longer oppose,
Or withhold their extorted esteem;
But were forced to give place to a torrent of grace,
And were all carried down with the stream.

Our hearts adore the matchless name,
Omnipotent to bless,
The name of Jesus, still the same
Despite our feebleness.

Once in the temple gate we lay
Crippled, till he restored;
But lo, we stand and walk to-day,
Yea, leap to praise the Lord.

All hail, thou dear restoring name,
We will our tongues employ,
To bid the souls which still are lame,
Believe and leap for joy.

Though sinners boldly join against the Lord to rise,
Against his Christ combine, th' Anointed to despise;
Though earth disdain, and hell engage,
Vain is their rage, their counsel vain.

Jesus the Saviour reigns! on Sion is his throne;
The Lord's decree sustains his own begotten Son:
Up from the grave he bids him rise,
And mount the skies, with power to save.

Oh, serve the Lord with fear, and rev'rence his command;
With sacred joy draw near, with solemn trembling stand;
Kneel at his throne, your homage bear,
His power declare, and kiss the Son.

Be the matter what it may,
Speak the honest truth alway;
He who lies a pain to waive,
Is at heart a coward slave.

He who speaks with lying tongue
Adds to wrong a greater wrong,
Much provoked is God Most High,
When we dare to tell a lie.

Unaw'd by man's authority,
Unable to forbear,
What we have seen and heard of thee,
O Lord, we must declare.

The balmy virtue of thy death
We must through life proclaim,
And publish with our latest breath,
Salvation through thy name.

Jesus stands with arms extended,
(Risen from his dazzling throne),
Sees his servants' warfare ended,
Sends his flaming chariot down,
Smiles triumphant,
Reaches out the palm and crown.

Should he call e'en us t'inherit
Joys for martyr'd saints prepared,
He will fill us with his Spirit,
Pledge of our supreme reward;
Sinking, dying,
We shall view our heavenly Lord.

636   *" Declare His glory among the heathen."*   OCTOBER 26.—MORNING.

[*Or August* 19.]

THE *spread of the gospel among men of all nations had been the theme of sacred song in the days of the psalmist. We shall read two of the psalms which refer thereto.*

PSALM XCVI.

1 O sing unto the LORD a new song : sing unto the LORD, all the earth. *(Not Israel only, as in the olden times, but all mankind.)*

2, 3 Sing unto the LORD, bless his name ; shew forth his salvation from day to day. Declare his glory among the heathen, his wonders among all people. *(This was the business of Pentecost, and is the duty of all the saints at all times.)*

4 For the LORD *is* great, and greatly to be praised : he *is* to be feared above all gods.

5 For all the gods of the nations *are* idols *(or nothings)*: but the LORD made the heavens.

6 Honour and majesty *are* before him : strength and beauty *are* in his sanctuary.

7 Give unto the LORD, O ye kindreds of the people, give unto the LORD glory and strength.

8 Give unto the LORD the glory *due unto* his name : bring an offering, and come into his courts. *(Prayers and praises are to be presented by all mankind ; the sacrifice of Jesus has ended all other offerings.)*

9 O worship the LORD in the beauty of holiness : fear before him, all the earth.

10 Say among the heathen *that* the LORD reigneth : the world also shall be established that it shall not be moved : he shall judge the people righteously.

11—13 Let the heavens rejoice, and let the earth be glad ; let the sea roar, and the fulness thereof. Let the field be joyful, and all that *is* therein : then shall all the trees of the wood rejoice Before the LORD : for he cometh, for he cometh to judge the earth : he shall judge the world with righteousness, and the people with his truth. *(The reign of Jesus ends oppression, war, and crime, hence it is the cause of joy to all mankind.)*

PSALM XCVII.

THE LORD reigneth ; let the earth rejoice ; let the multitude of isles be glad *thereof.*

2 Clouds and darkness *are* round about him :

righteousness and judgment *are* the habitation of his throne. *(Our Lord's birth was obscure, and his doctrine was to the world's judgment mysterious as though wrapt in cloud ; yet is it perfect holiness.)*

3 A fire goeth before him, and burneth up his enemies round about. *(The fire of his Spirit destroyed idols and false philosophies.)*

4 His lightnings enlightened the world : the earth saw, and trembled. *(The truth lit up the nations, and amazed all people.)*

5 The hills melted like wax at the presence of the LORD, at the presence of the Lord of the whole earth. *(All difficulties vanished, all enemies were subdued, the gospel triumphed over all.)*

6 The heavens declare his righteousness, and all the people see his glory. *(Under the whole heaven the gospel was published : it was as well known as if written across the skies.)*

7 Confounded be all they that serve graven images, that boast themselves of idols : worship him, all ye gods.

8, 9 Zion heard, and was glad ; and the daughters of Judah rejoiced because of thy judgments, O LORD. For thou, LORD, *art* high above all the earth : thou art exalted far above all gods.

10 Ye that love the LORD, hate evil : he preserveth the souls of his saints ; he delivereth them out of the hand of the wicked.

11 Light is sown for the righteous, and gladness for the upright in heart. *(Glad times are in store for us, the seed which shall produce them is already sown and will soon yield its harvest.)*

12 Rejoice in the LORD, ye righteous ; and give thanks at the remembrance of his holiness.

Joy is the privilege and the duty of a Christian, and he cannot have too much of it if it be of the right kind. Never let us give way to repining, rather let our holy cheerfulness cause others to inquire, " Whence comes their happiness ? "

All that remains for me
Is but to love and sing,
And wait until the angels come
To bear me to the King.

ACTS III. 1—21.

NOW Peter and John went up together into the temple at the hour of prayer, *being* the ninth *hour.* And a certain man lame from his mother's womb was carried, whom they laid daily at the gate of the temple which is called Beautiful, to ask alms of them that entered into the temple ; Who seeing Peter and John about to go into the temple asked an alms. *(They were interrupted on their way to their devotions, but it was a blessed interruption, for in the end they themselves were able to worship all the more fervently, and another was added to the number of those who praised the Lord. May we have grace to turn every incident we meet with to good account for promoting the glory of God. A beggar's cry would not annoy us if we were looking out for opportunities of doing good.)*

4 And Peter, fastening his eyes upon him with John, said, Look on us.

5 And he gave heed unto them, expecting to receive something of them.

6 Then Peter said, Silver and gold have I none ; but such as I have give I thee : In the name of Jesus Christ of Nazareth rise up and walk. *(Oh, the power of that name ! If we did but believe in it as Peter did, we also should bless poor sinners, and be enriched ourselves with something better than silver and gold.)*

7 And he took him by the right hand, and lifted *him* up : and immediately his feet and ancle bones received strength.

8 And he leaping up stood, and walked, and entered with them into the temple, walking, and leaping, and praising God. *(His joy was too great for him to go at an ordinary pace. When souls are healed by grace they overflow with enthusiasm. If we remembered our obligations to the Lord Jesus for making us whole, we also should often tread his courts with rapture, and feel as if we must dance for joy.)*

9, 10 And all the people saw him walking and praising God : And they knew that it was he which sat for alms at the Beautiful gate of the temple : and they were filled with wonder and amazement at that which had happened unto him.

11 And as the lame man which was healed held Peter and John, all the people ran together unto them in the porch that is called Solomon's, greatly wondering.

12 ¶ And when Peter saw *it,* he answered unto the people, Ye men of Israel, why marvel ye at this ? or why look ye so earnestly on us, as though by our own power or holiness we had made this man to walk ?

13 The God of Abraham, and of Isaac, and of Jacob, the God of our fathers, hath glorified his Son Jesus ; whom ye delivered up, and denied him in the presence of Pilate, when he was determined to let *him* go. *(He points them away from himself and John to the Lord Jesus. This is very different from those Popish priests who bid us look to saints, and even urge us to seek blessings from their poor sinful selves.)*

14, 15 But ye denied the Holy One and the Just, and desired a murderer to be granted unto you ; And killed the Prince of life, whom God hath raised from the dead ; whereof we are witnesses. *(He charges them with their sin. As the sharp needle makes way for the silken thread, so does conviction of sin prepare men for the glorious gospel.)*

16 And his name through faith in his name hath made this man strong, whom ye see and know : yea, the faith which is by him hath given him this perfect soundness in the presence of you all.

17, 18 And now, brethren, I wot that through ignorance ye did *it,* as *did* also your rulers. But those things, which God before had shewed by the mouth of all his prophets, that Christ should suffer, he hath so fulfilled.

See how he woos them, as a mother does her child, and interprets their wicked conduct as kindly as he can.

19 ¶ Repent ye therefore, and be converted, that your sins may be blotted out, when the times of refreshing shall come from the presence of the Lord ;

20 And he shall send Jesus Christ, which before was preached unto you :

21 Whom the heaven must receive until the times of restitution of all things, which God hath spoken by the mouth of all his holy prophets since the world began. *(Jesus will come again to restore this fallen earth ; till then he reigns above.)*

638

"We cannot but speak the things which we have seen and heard." [*Or August* 21.]

OCTOBER 27.—MORNING.

AFTER *Peter and John had healed the lame man, they preached the gospel in the courts of the temple.*

ACTS IV. 1—21 ; 23—30.

1, 2 And as they spake unto the people, the priests, and the captain of the temple, and the Sadducees, came upon them, Being grieved that they taught the people, and preached through Jesus the resurrection from the dead.

3, 4 And they laid hands on them, and put *them* in hold unto the next day : for it was now eventide. Howbeit many of them which heard the word believed ; and the number of the men was about five thousand. *(Quesnel says, "Truth may be oppressed, but it cannot be suppressed; the preacher may be bound, but not the word.")*

5—7 ¶ And it came to pass on the morrow, that their rulers, and elders, and scribes, and as many as were of the kindred of the high priest, were gathered together at Jerusalem. And when they had set them in the midst, they asked, By what power, or by what name, have ye done this ?

8—12 Then Peter, filled with the Holy Ghost, said unto them, Ye rulers of the people, and elders of Israel, If we this day be examined of the good deed done to the impotent man, by what means he is made whole; Be it known unto you all, and to all the people of Israel, that by the name of Jesus Christ of Nazareth, whom ye crucified, whom God raised from the dead, *even* by him doth this man stand here before you whole. This is the stone which was set at nought of you builders, which is become the head of the corner. Neither is there salvation in any other : for there is none other name under heaven given among men, whereby we must be saved. *(How Peter glories in the name of Jesus ; how he brandishes it in the face of the foe ! Almighty power lies in it, and blessed is he who has made it his trust.)*

13, 14 Now when they saw the boldness of Peter and John, and perceived that they were unlearned and ignorant men, they marvelled ; and they took knowledge of them, that they had been with Jesus. And beholding the man which was healed standing with them, they could say nothing against it.

15—17 But when they had commanded them to go aside out of the council, they conferred among themselves, Saying, What shall we do to these men ? for that indeed a notable miracle hath been done by them *is* manifest to all them that dwell in Jerusalem ; and we cannot deny *it*. But that it spread no further among the people, let us straitly threaten them, that they speak henceforth to no man in this name.

18—20 And they called them, and commanded them not to speak at all nor teach in the name of Jesus. But Peter and John answered and said unto them, Whether it be right in the sight of God to hearken unto you more than unto God, judge ye. For we cannot but speak the things which we have seen and heard. *(The sun might as easily leave off shining as good men desist from speaking of Jesus.)*

21—23 So when they had further threatened them, they let them go, finding nothing how they might punish them, because of the people : for all *men* glorified God for that which was done. And being let go, they went to their own company, and reported all that the chief priests and elders had said unto them.

24—26 And when they heard that, they lifted up their voice to God with one accord, and said, Lord, thou *art* God, which hast made heaven, and earth, and the sea, and all that in them is : Who by the mouth of thy servant David hast said, Why did the heathen rage, and the people imagine vain things ? The kings of the earth stood up, and the rulers were gathered together against the Lord, and against his Christ.

27, 28 For of a truth against thy holy child Jesus, whom thou hast anointed, both Herod, and Pontius Pilate, with the Gentiles, and the people of Israel, were gathered together, For to do whatsoever thy hand and thy counsel determined before to be done.

29, 30 And now, Lord, behold their threatenings : and grant unto thy servants, that with all boldness they may speak thy word, By stretching forth thine hand to heal ; and that signs and wonders may be done by the name of thy holy child Jesus. *(Thus psalms and prayers were presented to the Lord by the united church, and the work went on triumphantly. We, too, have equal cause for adoration, for the Lord of Hosts is with us, working for the glory of his Son.)*

ACTS IV. 32—37.

AND the multitude of them that believed were of one heart and of one soul : neither said any *of them* that ought of the things which he possessed was his own ; but they had all things common. *(There was need of such liberality, for the Christians were mostly poor, and liable to be deprived of everything by persecution. Covetous men would have been very uncomfortable in the early church, indeed they are not fit to be in any church at any time.)*

33 And with great power gave the apostles witness of the resurrection of the Lord Jesus : and great grace was upon them all.

34, 35 Neither was there any among them that lacked : for as many as were possessors of lands or houses sold them, and brought the prices of the things that were sold, And laid *them* down at the apostles' feet ; and distribution was made unto every man according as he had need. *(Thus when Jerusalem was destroyed and Judea devastated, the Christians had the less to lose, and the less sorrow in being scattered abroad.)*

36, 37 And Joses, who by the apostles was surnamed Barnabas, (which is, being interpreted, The son of consolation,) a Levite, *and* of the country of Cyprus, Having land, sold *it*, and brought the money and laid *it* at the apostles' feet. *(Yet while some were acting so nobly there were tares among the wheat, professed disciples who could act the liar's part.)*

ACTS V. 1—14.

BUT a certain man named Ananias, with Sapphira his wife, sold a possession,

2 And kept back *part* of the price, his wife also being privy *to it*, and brought a certain part, and laid *it* at the apostles' feet. *(Intending to make others believe that he had given all, as Barnabas had done. He was not required to give all unless he chose to do so, his sin lay in pretending to be more generous than he really was.)*

3, 4 But Peter said, Ananias, why hath Satan filled thine heart to lie to the Holy Ghost, and to keep back *part* of the price of the land ? Whiles it remained, was it not thine own ? and after it was sold, was it not in thine own power ? why hast thou conceived this thing in thine heart ? thou hast not lied unto men, but unto God.

5 And Ananias hearing these words fell down, and gave up the ghost : and great fear came on all them that heard these things.

This was the first act of divine church discipline, a discipline which is still carried out by him who walks among the golden candlesticks. On account of church sins even now some are sickly among us, and many sleep. The nearer we come to God the more truly shall we find that he is a jealous God who will not wink at sin. It was not Peter's word, but the judgment of God, which slew Ananias.

6 And the young men arose, wound him up, and carried *him* out, and buried *him*.

7, 8 And it was about the space of three hours after, when his wife, not knowing what was done, came in. And Peter answered unto her, Tell me whether ye sold the land for so much ? And she said, Yea, for so much.

9 Then Peter said unto her, How is it that ye have agreed together to tempt the Spirit of the Lord ? behold, the feet of them which have buried thy husband *are* at the door, and shall carry thee out.

10 Then fell she down straightway at his feet, and yielded up the ghost : and the young men came in, and found her dead, and, carrying *her* forth, buried *her* by her husband.

She had time for reflection, yet she stuck to the falsehood. It is a sad thing when husband and wife go hand in hand to hell, and most of all so when they make a profession of religion.

11 And great fear came upon all the church, and upon as many as heard these things. *(Well may such fear fall on us also, lest we should be found false to God, and perish in our sin.)*

12 ¶ And by the hands of the apostles were many signs and wonders wrought among the people ; (and they were all with one accord in Solomon's porch.

13 And of the rest durst no man join himself to them : but the people magnified them.

14 And believers were the more added to the Lord, multitudes both of men and women.)

The chaff was driven out, and kept out, but the true saints were all the more ready to join the church. Holy discipline does not diminish the church, it is the sure means of increasing it with the right people.

640   " 𝕎e ought to obey 𝔊od rather than men."   OCTOBER 28.—MORNING.

[Or August 23.]

ACTS V. 17—36; 38—42.

THEN the high priest rose up, and all they that were with him, (which is the sect of the Sadducees,) and were filled with indignation, And laid their hands on the apostles, and put them in the common prison. *(The Sadducees were the Broad Churchmen of their day, yet their liberal views did not prevent their persecuting the lovers of the truth. Men of no religion are frequently the greatest bigots in the world.)*

19, 20 But the angel of the Lord by night opened the prison doors, and brought them forth, and said, Go, stand and speak in the temple to the people all the words of this life.

21 And when they heard *that,* they entered into the temple early in the morning, and taught. But the high priest came, and they that were with him, and called the council together, and all the senate of the children of Israel, and sent to the prison to have them brought.

22, 23 But when the officers came, and found them not in the prison, they returned, and told, Saying, The prison truly found we shut with all safety, and the keepers standing without before the doors : but when we had opened, we found no man within.

24 Now when the high priest and the captain of the temple and the chief priests heard these things, they doubted of them whereunto this would grow. *(Staggered but not converted, they went madly on with their persecution. Truly, when a sinner is set on mischief nothing will stop him but the grace of God.)*

25 Then came one and told them, saying, Behold, the men whom ye put in prison are standing in the temple, and teaching the people.

26—28 Then went the captain with the officers, and brought them without violence : for they feared the people, lest they should have been stoned. And when they had brought them, they set *them* before the council : and the high priest asked them, Saying, Did not we straitly command you that ye should not teach in this name ? and, behold, ye have filled Jerusalem with your doctrine, and intend to bring this man's blood upon us. *(As in Æsop's fable, the sheep of Jesus are charged by the wolf with troubling the water.)*

29, 30 ¶ Then Peter and the *other* apostles answered and said, We ought to obey God rather than men. The God of our fathers raised up Jesus, whom ye slew and hanged on a tree. *(Peter does not flinch; he lays the great crime of Jesus' death at their door.)*

31, 32 Him hath God exalted with his right hand *to be* a Prince and a Saviour, for to give repentance to Israel, and forgiveness of sins. And we are his witnesses of these things ; and *so is* also the Holy Ghost, whom God hath given to them that obey him.

33 ¶ When they heard *that,* they were cut *to the heart,* and took counsel to slay them.

34—36 Then stood there up one in the council, a Pharisee, named Gamaliel, a doctor of the law, had in reputation among all the people, and commanded to put the apostles forth a little space ; And said unto them, Ye men of Israel, take heed to yourselves what ye intend to do as touching these men. For before these days rose up Theudas, boasting himself to be somebody ; to whom a number of men, about four hundred, joined themselves : who was slain ; and all, as many as obeyed him, were scattered, and brought to nought.

38, 39 And now I say unto you, Refrain from these men, and let them alone : for if this counsel or this work be of men, it will come to nought : But if it be of God, ye cannot overthrow it ; lest haply ye be found even to fight against God.

Bad but prudent men have frequently, for policy's sake, advocated toleration, and so have been in the hands of God the means of delivering his people from persecution. We should admire the great Head of the church who can find a protector for her, even in the enemy's camp.

40 And to him they agreed : and when they had called the apostles, and beaten *them,* they commanded that they should not speak in the name of Jesus, and let them go.

41, 42 And they departed from the presence of the council, rejoicing that they were counted worthy to suffer shame for his name. And daily in the temple, and in every house, they ceased not to teach and preach Jesus Christ. *(Those who had been scourged rejoiced, but their enemies went home envious and wretched. We ought to rejoice if we bear reproach for Christ ; and we should persevere in serving the Lord, however furiously we may be opposed.)*

ACTS VI. 1—15.

AND in those days, when the number of the disciples was multiplied, there arose a murmuring of the Grecians *(or Christian Jews who had lived in foreign parts)* against the Hebrews *(or Palestine Jews)*, because their widows were neglected in the daily ministration. *(Perhaps, being strangers, they were not well known, and so were overlooked; we have no reason to believe that the neglect was intentional. Mistakes will occur, and if not rectified they may create ill-will and division.)*

2 Then the twelve called the multitude of the disciples *unto them*, and said, It is not reason that we should leave the word of God, and serve tables. *(Others can do such work; ministers have enough to do to mind their own business.)*

3, 4 Wherefore, brethren, look ye out among you seven men of honest report, full of the Holy Ghost and wisdom, whom we may appoint over this business. But we will give ourselves continually to prayer, and to the ministry of the word. *(Prayer and preaching make up the entire life of a minister; by prayer he receives the word from God, and by preaching he communicates it to his people. Other church officers should take care that the minister's mind is not burdened with temporal anxieties.)*

5, 6 And the saying pleased the whole multitude: and they chose Stephen, a man full of faith and of the Holy Ghost, and Philip, and Prochorus, and Nicanor, and Timon, and Parmenas, and Nicolas a proselyte of Antioch: Whom they set before the apostles: and when they had prayed, they laid *their* hands on them.

7, 8 And the word of God increased; and the number of the disciples multiplied in Jerusalem greatly; and a great company of the priests were obedient to the faith. And Stephen, full of faith and power, did great wonders and miracles among the people.

9, 10 ¶ Then there arose certain of the synagogue, which is called *the synagogue* of the Libertines, disputing with Stephen. And they were not able to resist the wisdom and the spirit by which he spake.

11 Then they suborned men, which said, We have heard him speak blasphemous words against Moses, and *against* God.

12, 13 And they stirred up the people, and the elders, and the scribes, and came upon *him*, and caught him, and brought *him* to the council, And set up false witnesses, which said, This man ceaseth not to speak blasphemous words against this holy place, and the law:

14 For we have heard him say, that this Jesus of Nazareth shall destroy this place, and shall change the customs which Moses delivered us.

15 And all that sat in the council, looking stedfastly on him, saw his face as it had been the face of an angel. *(His holy and glad heart beamed forth in his countenance, a flash of coming glory lit up his face, and even his foes were forced to see it; yet neither this sight nor his eloquent address could touch their cruel hearts, for they thirsted for his blood, and would have it.)*

ACTS VII. 54—60.

WHEN they heard these things, they were cut to the heart, and they gnashed on him with *their* teeth.

55, 56 But he, being full of the Holy Ghost, looked up stedfastly into heaven, and saw the glory of God, and Jesus standing on the right hand of God, And said, Behold, I see the heavens opened, and the Son of man standing on the right hand of God. *(Jesus was seen standing to receive the martyr's soul. What a vision! It removed the bitterness of death.)*

57, 58 Then they cried out with a loud voice, and stopped their ears, and ran upon him with one accord, And cast *him* out of the city, and stoned *him*: and the witnesses laid down their clothes at a young man's feet, whose name was Saul.

59 And they stoned Stephen, calling upon *God*, and saying, Lord Jesus, receive my spirit.

60 And he kneeled down, and cried with a loud voice, Lord, lay not this sin to their charge. And when he had said this, he fell asleep.

Asleep amid the falling stones! He slept not till he had left the church the legacy of his prayers. Augustine says, "If Stephen had not thus prayed, the church had not received that young man named Saul." We have no other description of martyrdom in the New Testament, the Holy Spirit foreseeing that the church would have an abundance of such records in after times.

OCTOBER 29.—MORNING.

642   " They that were scattered abroad went everywhere preaching the Word."   [Or August 25.]

ACTS VIII. 1—24.

AND Saul was consenting unto his death. *(He took pleasure in the execution of Stephen, being zealously resolute to put down the church.)* And at that time there was a great persecution against the church which was at Jerusalem; and they were all scattered abroad throughout the regions of Judæa and Samaria, except the apostles.

2 And devout men carried Stephen *to his burial,* and made great lamentation over him.

It is not wrong to lament the death of holy men, for they are a great loss to the community.

3 As for Saul, he made havock of the church, entering into every house, and haling men and women committed *them* to prison.

4 Therefore they that were scattered abroad went everywhere preaching the word. *(Driven yet further afield, they carried the gospel into other lands. The winds of persecution fan the fire of faith in the church, and carry the sparks of truth to a distance. The Devil destroys his own kingdom, while he thinks he is crushing the rising empire of Christ.)*

5 Then Philip went down to the city of Samaria, and preached Christ unto them.

Stephen is gone, but Philip comes forward; the church will not fail for want of men to bear her standard.

6—8 And the people with one accord gave heed unto those things which Philip spake, hearing and seeing the miracles which he did. For unclean spirits, crying with loud voice, came out of many that were possessed *with them:* and many taken with palsies, and that were lame, were healed. And there was great joy in that city. *(Joy in forgiven sin, joy in healing mercy, joy in God's gracious presence. See how Christians, though persecuted themselves, make others glad.)*

9—11 But there was a certain man, called Simon, which beforetime in the same city used sorcery, and bewitched the people of Samaria, giving out that himself was some great one: To whom they all gave heed, from the least to the greatest, saying, This man is the great power of God. And to him they had regard, because that of long time he had bewitched them with sorceries.

12 But when they believed Philip preaching the things concerning the kingdom of God, and the name of Jesus Christ, they were baptized, both men and women.

13 Then Simon himself believed also: and when he was baptized, he continued with Philip, and wondered, beholding the miracles and signs which were done. *(But he did not savingly believe, as is clear from his conduct. He was baffled by Philip, and therefore believed his doctrine to be true, made a profession of faith and entered the church, and might have done immense mischief, had he not been detected by his own greed. The church of God has many foes: Saul vexes her without, and Simon within.)*

14—17 Now when the apostles which were at Jerusalem heard that Samaria had received the word of God, they sent unto them Peter and John: Who, when they were come down, prayed for them, that they might receive the Holy Ghost: (For as yet he was fallen upon none of them: only they were baptized in the name of the Lord Jesus.) Then laid they *their* hands on them, and they received the Holy Ghost.

18, 19 And when Simon saw that through laying on of the apostles' hands the Holy Ghost was given, he offered them money, Saying, Give me also this power, that on whomsoever I lay hands, he may receive the Holy Ghost. *(Hence the purchase of office in the church is called Simony. Wretched distinction, to furnish a name for a new sin.)*

20—22 But Peter said unto him, Thy money perish with thee, because thou hast thought that the gift of God may be purchased with money. Thou hast neither part nor lot in this matter: for thy heart is not right in the sight of God. Repent therefore of this thy wickedness, and pray God, if perhaps the thought of thine heart may be forgiven thee.

23 For I perceive that thou art in the gall of bitterness, and *in* the bond of iniquity.

24 Then answered Simon, and said, Pray ye to the Lord for me, that none of these things which ye have spoken come upon me. *(He did not say, "Pray that I may be forgiven," his heart only throbbed with carnal desires for power, or slavish fears of judgment. All around him the divine light was spreading, but he remained blinded by sordid feelings. The Lord grant us to rise far above everything mercenary in religion.)*

ACTS VIII. 26—40.*

AND the angel of the Lord spake unto Philip, saying, Arise, and go toward the south unto the way that goeth down from Jerusalem unto Gaza, which is desert. *(How precious is one single soul in the sight of the Lord! In order to bring one person to the faith, he sends an angel to Philip, and sends Philip from populous Samaria to the desert.)*

27, 28 And he arose and went : *(A teacher of the gospel must go in the obedience of faith, although the call leads him into the wilderness.)* and, behold, a man of Ethiopia, an eunuch of great authority under Candace queen of the Ethiopians, who had the charge of all her treasure, and had come to Jerusalem for to worship, was returning, and sitting in his chariot read Esaias the prophet. *(The word of God is the best reading on a journey; not only on the desert way from Jerusalem, but on the way through time to eternity. We forget thereby the hardships of the way, we look not aside to forbidden paths, we make thereby blessed travelling acquaintances, and we go forward on the right path to the blessed goal.)*

29 Then the Spirit said unto Philip, Go near and join thyself to this chariot.

30 And Philip ran thither to *him*, and heard him read the prophet Esaias, and said, Understandest thou what thou readest?

If a teacher, on his visit, finds people occupied with the word of God, he must not long waste time with digressions about the weather and the state of their health, but take the word of God for his text and introduction, as it lies open.

31 And he said, How can I, except some man should guide me? And he desired Philip that he would come up and sit with him.

32, 33 The place of the scripture which he read was this, He was led as a sheep to the slaughter; and like a lamb dumb before his shearer, so opened he not his mouth : In his humiliation his judgment was taken away : and who shall declare his generation? for his life is taken from the earth.

It was the finger of God which pointed to this passage; for the sum of all Christian truth is

Christ, both humbled and exalted. *In this is contained an admonition for all teachers to lead souls, as the chief matter, to the knowledge of Christ, the Crucified and the Risen One. This, as a rule, is much more effective than moral preaching. The missionaries in Greenland who, with discourses on the living God and his holy commandments, preached for a whole year to deaf ears, struck home when they commenced with the evangelical message, "Behold the Lamb of God, that taketh away the sins of the world!"*

34 And the eunuch answered Philip, and said, I pray thee, of whom speaketh the prophet this? of himself, or of some other man?

35, 36 Then Philip opened his mouth, and began at the same scripture, and preached unto him Jesus. And as they went on *their* way, they came unto a certain water : and the eunuch said, See, *here is* water; what doth hinder me to be baptized?

37 And Philip said, If thou believest with all thine heart, thou mayest. And he answered and said, I believe that Jesus Christ is the Son of God. *(See the order: the word is understood, then comes faith, and then baptism. Is the Lord's order right? Then let no man alter it. None can have any right to church ordinances but those who believe with all their hearts that Jesus is the Son of God.)*

38, 39 And he commanded the chariot to stand still : and they went down both into the water, both Philip and the eunuch; and he baptized him. And when they were come up out of the water, the Spirit of the Lord caught away Philip, that the eunuch saw him no more : and he went on his way rejoicing. *(When the good man's work was done, the new convert needed him no more, for he had the key of the scriptures in his own hands.)*

40 But Philip was found at Azotus : and passing through he preached in all the cities, till he came to Cæsarea. *(This chapter should be read candidly, and its teachings accepted: what they are is so clear that there is little need of explanation. Take heed how ye read.)*

* In this reading the first five notes are from Lange's Commentary. All through the work we have gathered from every available source.

Obedience fills the soul with joy,
　Then let us now obey;
Our heart believes, our duty's clear,
　And Jesus leads the way.

ACTS IX. 1—22.

AND Saul, yet breathing out threatenings and slaughter against the disciples of the Lord, went unto the high priest, And desired of him letters to Damascus to the synagogues, that if he found any of this way, whether they were men or women, he might bring them bound unto Jerusalem.

His very breath was threatening; all Judea was not a large enough hunting ground for him. What a rebel he was! What a saint he became! How mighty is divine grace!

3, 4 And as he journeyed, he came near Damascus: and suddenly there shined round about him a light from heaven: And he fell to the earth, and heard a voice saying unto him, Saul, Saul, why persecutest thou me?

5 And he said, Who art thou, Lord? And the Lord said, I am Jesus whom thou persecutest: *it is* hard for thee to kick against the pricks. *(What surprise filled the soul of Saul when he perceived that the Nazarene whom he had hated was really divine. Little had he dreamed of persecuting the Son of God, he thought he was crushing out a troublesome imposture. O Lord, open the eyes of any other sincere bigot who may be persecuting thy cause without knowing it to be thine!)*

6 And he trembling and astonished said, Lord, what wilt thou have me to do? And the Lord *said* unto him, Arise, and go into the city, and it shall be told thee what thou must do.

He rises a changed man, he has seen the Lord and is conquered; he has become the willing servant of Jesus whom he persecuted. His hectoring has ended, his submission is complete.

7—9 And the men which journeyed with him stood speechless, hearing a voice, but seeing no man. And Saul arose from the earth: and when his eyes were opened, he saw no man: but they led him by the hand, and brought *him* into Damascus. And he was three days without sight, and neither did eat nor drink. *(And no wonder. The light had blinded him, and the revelation from heaven so possessed him that he forgot everything else.)*

10—12 And there was a certain disciple at Damascus, named Ananias; and to him said the Lord in a vision, Ananias. And he said, Behold, I *am here*, Lord. And the Lord *said* unto him, Arise, and go into the street which is called Straight, and enquire in the house of Judas for *one* called Saul, of Tarsus: for, behold, he prayeth, And hath seen in a vision a man named Ananias coming in, and putting *his* hand on him, that he might receive his sight.

13, 14 Then Ananias answered, Lord, I have heard by many of this man, how much evil he hath done to thy saints at Jerusalem: And here he hath authority from the chief priests to bind all that call on thy name.

Do we wonder that the good man doubted? Should not we be slow to believe if we were told that the Pope of Rome had given up his superstition, and was humbly seeking a Saviour? Yet the case would not be more wonderful.

15, 16 But the Lord said unto him, Go thy way: for he is a chosen vessel unto me, to bear my name before the Gentiles, and kings, and the children of Israel: For I will shew him how great things he must suffer for my name's sake. *(Paul was not merely to be a saint, but an eminent one. Great sinners usually love much when they are forgiven.)*

17 And Ananias went his way, and entered into the house; and putting his hands on him said, Brother Saul, the Lord, *even* Jesus, that appeared unto thee in the way as thou camest, hath sent me, that thou mightest receive thy sight, and be filled with the Holy Ghost.

18 And immediately there fell from his eyes as it had been scales: and he received sight forthwith, and arose, and was baptized.

He did not neglect baptism, as some do. What the Lord ordains we must not despise.

19 And when he had received meat, he was strengthened. Then was Saul certain days with the disciples which were at Damascus.

20—22 And straightway he preached Christ in the synagogues, that he is the Son of God. But all that heard *him* were amazed, and said; Is not this he that destroyed them which called on this name in Jerusalem, and came hither for that intent, that he might bring them bound unto the chief priests? But Saul increased the more in strength, and confounded the Jews which dwelt at Damascus, proving that this is very Christ. *(Thus electing love chose a persecutor; almighty grace made him a penitent; the Holy Spirit made him a believer, and by divine authority he became a minister and an apostle. Grace works miracles.)*

Lo Satan trembles and gives place
  Before the Spirit's might!
The power of efficacious grace
  Puts all his hosts to flight.

His kingdom falls, his spells and charms
  By Jesus are o'erthrown,
The Spirit wields victorious arms,
  And holds the field alone.

Ah, Grace! into unlikeliest hearts
  It is thy boast to come;
The glory of thy light to find
  In darkest spots a home.

Thy choice, O God of goodness! then
  We lovingly adore;
Oh, give us grace to keep thy grace,
  And grace to long for more!

They who feed thy sick and faint
  For thyself a banquet find;
They who clothe the naked saint
  Round *thy* loins the raiment bind.

Thou wilt deeds of love repay;
Grace shall gen'rous hearts reward
Here on earth, and in the day
When they meet their reigning Lord.

O Spirit of the Lord, prepare
All the round earth her God to meet;
Breathe thou abroad like morning air,
Till hearts of stone begin to beat.

Baptize the nations far and nigh;
The triumphs of the cross record:
The name of Jesus glorify,
Till every kindred call him Lord.

Come, guilty souls, and flee away
  Like doves to Jesu's wounds;
This is the welcome gospel-day,
  Wherein free grace abounds.

God loved the church, and gave his Son
  To drink the cup of wrath:
And Jesus says he'll cast out none
  That come to him by faith.

Fly abroad, thou mighty Gospel,
  Win and conquer, never cease;
May thy lasting, wide dominion
  Multiply, and still increase.
    Sway thy sceptre,
  Saviour, all the world around.

When he first the work begun,
Small and feeble was his day:
Now the word doth swiftly run,
Now it wins its widening way:

More and more it spreads and grows,
Ever mighty to prevail;
Sin's strongholds it now o'erthrows,
Shakes the trembling gates of hell.

From Greenland's icy mountains,
  From India's coral strand,
Where Afric's sunny fountains
  Roll down their golden sand;
From many an ancient river,
  From many a palmy plain,
They call us to deliver
  Their land from error's chain.

To Father, Son, and Holy Ghost,
  One God, whom we adore,
Be glory as it was, is now,
  And shall be evermore.

ACTS IX. 23—43.

PAUL'S *bold preaching soon aroused the enmity of those who had formerly admired him.*

23 And after that many days were fulfilled, the Jews took counsel to kill him :

24 But their laying await was known of Saul. And they watched the gates day and night to kill him.

25 Then the disciples took him by night, and let *him* down by the wall in a basket.

26 And when Saul was come to Jerusalem, he assayed to join himself to the disciples : but they were all afraid of him, and believed not that he was a disciple. *(This was three years after his conversion, after he had been in retirement in Arabia. It must have been a hard lesson for Paul to find himself suspected by brethren whom he loved.)*

27 But Barnabas took him, and brought *him* to the apostles, and declared unto them how he had seen the Lord in the way, and that he had spoken to him, and how he had preached boldly at Damascus in the name of Jesus. *(This was a right brotherly deed. New converts need a friend.)*

28—30 And he was with them coming in and going out at Jerusalem. And he spake boldly in the name of the Lord Jesus, and disputed against the Grecians : but they went about to slay him. *Which* when the brethren knew, they brought him down to Cæsarea, and sent him forth to Tarsus.

31 Then had the churches rest throughout all Judæa and Galilee and Samaria, and were edified ; and walking in the fear of the Lord, and in the comfort of the Holy Ghost, were multiplied.

32—35 And it came to pass, as Peter passed throughout all *quarters,* he came down also to the saints which dwelt at Lydda. And there he found a certain man named Æneas, which had kept his bed eight years, and was sick of the palsy. And Peter said unto him, Æneas, Jesus Christ maketh thee whole : arise, and make thy bed. And he arose immediately. And all that dwelt at Lydda and Saron saw him, and turned to the Lord. *(Christians are always ready to do good to the sick. We cannot now restore them by miracle, and, therefore, by kind nursing and* care to *provide hospitals, we must do the best we can to show that we care for them. Spiritual healing is, however, still among us, and it is our joy to whisper in the despairing sinner's ear, " Jesus Christ maketh thee whole.")*

36 ¶ Now there was at Joppa a certain disciple named Tabitha, which by interpretation is called Dorcas *(or gazelle):* this woman was full of good works and almsdeeds which she did.

Peter healed and Dorcas clothed ; grace prompts the saints to help the helpless.

37 And it came to pass in those days, that she was sick, and died : whom when they had washed, they laid *her* in an upper chamber.

38 And forasmuch as Lydda was nigh to Joppa, and the disciples had heard that Peter was there, they sent unto him two men, desiring *him* that he would not delay to come to them.

39 Then Peter arose and went with them. When he was come, they brought him into the upper chamber : and all the widows stood by him weeping, and shewing the coats and garments *(or upper and under garments)* which Dorcas made, while she was with them.

These are the best relics of the saints. Many leave behind them wealth wrung out of the poor : hers was a noble legacy.

40, 41 But Peter put them all forth, and kneeled down, and prayed *(nothing can be done without prayer, not even by an apostle);* and turning *him* to the body said, Tabitha, arise. And she opened her eyes : and when she saw Peter, she sat up. And he gave her *his* hand, and lifted her up, and when he had called the saints and widows, presented her alive. *(Luke describes the weeping of the widows at her death ; he relates nothing concerning their joy at her being raised, for that was indescribable. Have we so lived that the poor would rejoice to see us back again when we die ? Christian women should make Dorcas their example, and labour according to their ability for the needy ones around them.)*

42 And it was known throughout all Joppa ; and many believed in the Lord.

43 And it came to pass, that he tarried many days in Joppa with one Simon a tanner.

Whose hospitality has immortalized his name. It matters little what trade a man is, if he serves the Lord in it. Are we doing so in ours ?

WE *have now to read a chapter peculiarly interesting to us Gentiles, because it shows how the middle wall of partition between Jews and Gentiles, which our Lord broke down by his death, was in due time practically removed by the calling of a Gentile household to the faith of Jesus. Before this time only Jews, proselytes, and Samaritans, all branches of the older family, had been converted, but now a Roman captain and his house were to be saved.*

ACTS X. 1—23.

1, 2 There was a certain man in Cæsarea called Cornelius, a centurion of the band called the Italian *band, A* devout *man,* and one that feared God with all his house, which gave much alms to the people, and prayed to God alway.

3 He saw in a vision evidently about the ninth hour of the day an angel of God coming in to him, and saying unto him, Cornelius.

4 And when he looked on him, he was afraid, and said, What is it, Lord ? And he said unto him, Thy prayers and thine alms are come up for a memorial before God. *(Yet something more was wanted, and he must send for one who would tell him of Jesus, the Saviour.)*

5, 6 And now send men to Joppa, and call for *one* Simon, whose surname is Peter: he lodgeth with one Simon a tanner, whose house is by the sea side : he shall tell thee what thou oughtest to do.

7, 8 And when the angel which spake unto Cornelius was departed, he called two of his household servants, and a devout soldier of them that waited on him continually ; And when he had declared all *these* things unto them, he sent them to Joppa. *(The tanner's trade was greatly despised, but this did not prejudice the centurion. Better to learn the way of God from one who lodged with a poor tanner than remain in ignorance. Meanwhile God was preparing Peter to comply with the centurion's request.)*

9—13 On the morrow, as they went on their journey, and drew nigh unto the city, Peter went up upon the housetop to pray about the sixth hour : And he became very hungry, and would have eaten : but while they made ready, he fell into a trance, And saw heaven opened, and a certain vessel descending unto him, as it had been a great sheet knit at the four corners, and let down to the earth : Wherein were all

manner of four-footed beasts of the earth, and wild beasts, and creeping things, and fowls of the air. And there came a voice to him, Rise, Peter; kill, and eat.

14 But Peter said, Not so, Lord ; for I have never eaten anything that is common or unclean.

The same Peter who formerly would not permit his Lord to wash the feet of his sinful servant now doubts whether that can be cleansed which, by the Jewish law, was unclean. How the old self comes up, even in the regenerated.

15, 16 And the voice *spake* unto him again the second time, What God hath cleansed, *that* call not thou common. This was done thrice : and the vessel was received up again into heaven.

Do not wonder if you have to teach children many times the same thing, for even an apostle needed to have his lesson repeated three times.

17, 18 Now while Peter doubted in himself what this vision which he had seen should mean, behold, the men which were sent from Cornelius had made enquiry for Simon's house, and stood before the gate, And called, and asked whether Simon, which was surnamed Peter, were lodged there. *(See the hand of Providence. How well-timed were the vision and the arrival of the messengers!)*

19, 20 While Peter thought on the vision, the Spirit said unto him, Behold, three men seek thee. Arise therefore, and get thee down, and go with them, doubting nothing : for I have sent them.

21 Then Peter went down to the men which were sent unto him from Cornelius ; and said, Behold, I am he whom ye seek : what *is* the cause wherefore ye are come ?

22 And they said, Cornelius the centurion, a just man, and one that feareth God, and of good report among all the nation of the Jews, was warned from God by an holy angel to send for thee into his house, and to hear words of thee.

These servants spoke well of their master, and that fact speaks well for them. God will surely bless those families in which the heads of the house and the servants love one another because they all love the Lord.

23 Then called he them in, and lodged *them.*

Humble as the lodging was, he offered it to them, and they accepted it. Christians should be hospitable even if they are poor.

648

OCTOBER 31.—EVENING.

"𝔗𝔥𝔞𝔱 𝔱𝔥𝔢 𝔊𝔢𝔫𝔱𝔦𝔩𝔢𝔰 𝔰𝔥𝔬𝔲𝔩𝔡 𝔟𝔢 𝔣𝔢𝔩𝔩𝔬𝔴 𝔥𝔢𝔦𝔯𝔰, 𝔞𝔫𝔡 𝔬𝔣 𝔱𝔥𝔢 𝔰𝔞𝔪𝔢 𝔟𝔬𝔡𝔶."

[*Or August* 30.]

ACTS X. 23—29; 33—48.

THE *messengers of Cornelius were not long detained by the apostle, for* On the morrow Peter went away with them, and certain brethren from Joppa accompanied him.

24 And the morrow after they entered into Cæsarea. *(It was a journey of thirty miles, but no doubt the apostle and his six brethren had sweet fellowship on the road, and found kind companions in the three attendants.)* And Cornelius waited for them, and had called together his kinsmen and near friends.

25, 26 And as Peter was coming in, Cornelius met him, and fell down at his feet, and worshipped *him.* But Peter took him up, saying, Stand up; I myself also am a man.

Had he been like his pretended successor, he would have bidden him kiss his toe.

27 And as he talked with him, he went in, and found many that were come together.

28, 29 And he said unto them, Ye know how that it is an unlawful thing for a man that is a Jew to keep company, or come unto one of another nation; but God hath shewed me that I should not call any man common or unclean. Therefore came I *unto you* without gainsaying, as soon as I was sent for: I ask therefore for what intent ye have sent for me? *(Note how he longs to be at work, he wastes no time in idle compliments. Soul matters are weighty and should be at once attended to. Cornelius was ready at once to tell Peter how the Lord had appeared to him, and directed him to send to Joppa, and he added:)*—

33 Immediately therefore I sent to thee; and thou hast well done that thou art come. Now therefore are we all here present before God, to hear all things that are commanded thee of God. *The best kind of congregation a preacher can have. Bogatzky says, "These words should be inscribed on all our church-doors and pulpits, that men may consider well wherefore they ought to be in the house of God." Peter's congregation was unbroken—"we are all here;" it was devout—"present before God;" it was attentive—"to hear all things;" it was teachable, for they desired to know "all things that are commanded thee of God." We should always go to divine service in this spirit.*

34, 35 Then Peter opened *his* mouth, and said, Of a truth I perceive that God is no respecter of persons: But in every nation he that feareth him, and worketh righteousness, is accepted with him. *(Not in such a way as to supersede the gospel, but to secure them the privilege of hearing it. If there are among the heathen any like Cornelius, the Lord will be sure to send a Peter to them, for he has accepted them.)*

36—41 The word which *God* sent unto the children of Israel, preaching peace by Jesus Christ: (he is Lord of all:) That word, *I say,* ye know, which was published throughout all Judæa, and began from Galilee, after the baptism which John preached; How God anointed Jesus of Nazareth with the Holy Ghost and with power: who went about doing good, and healing all that were oppressed of the devil; for God was with him. And we are witnesses of all things which he did both in the land of the Jews, and in Jerusalem; whom they slew and hanged on a tree: Him God raised up the third day, and shewed him openly; Not to all the people, but unto witnesses chosen before of God, *even* to us, who did eat and drink with him after he rose from the dead.

42, 43 And he commanded us to preach unto the people, and to testify that it is he which was ordained of God *to be* the Judge of quick and dead. To him give all the prophets witness, that through his name whosoever believeth in him shall receive remission of sins.

44, 45 While Peter yet spake these words, the Holy Ghost fell on all them which heard the word. And they of the circumcision which believed were astonished, as many as came with Peter, because that on the Gentiles also was poured out of the gift of the Holy Ghost.

46, 47 For they heard them speak with tongues, and magnify God. Then answered Peter, Can any man forbid water, that these should not be baptized, which have received the Holy Ghost as well as we?

48 And he commanded them to be baptized in the name of the Lord. *(The fact that they had already received the Holy Spirit so abundantly did not set aside the divine ordinance, it was rather the ground of their right to it. This passage is instructive to those who wish to learn.)* Then prayed they him to tarry certain days.

PETER *had baptized the Gentile household of Cornelius, and so novel an action could not pass unnoticed: the report soon reached the apostles at Jerusalem, and Peter was called upon to explain; he did so, and all were satisfied, and rejoiced in what the Lord had done.*

ACTS XI. 1—4; 18—30.

1—3 And the apostles and brethren that were in Judæa heard that the Gentiles had also received the word of God. And when Peter was come up to Jerusalem, they that were of the circumcision contended with him, Saying, Thou wentest in to men uncircumcised, and didst eat with them. (*It would seem that a number of Jewish Christians attached an undue importance to circumcision, and made a kind of party in the church. The Holy Spirit does not conceal the faults and mistakes of good men; no histories and biographies are so impartial as those written by inspiration. Peter was no pope, for the common disciples called him to account; but he did not become angry, or claim to be infallible.*)

4 But Peter rehearsed *the matter* from the beginning, and expounded *it* by order unto them. *See here a beautiful example of humility and patience. Peter had been directed by the Lord in what he did, and the act itself was most commendable, yet he rose and defended his conduct without anger, in a calm, loving manner, and not only exonerated himself, but won over those who had differed from him. So that we read—*

18 When they heard these things, they held their peace, and glorified God, saying, Then hath God also to the Gentiles granted repentance unto life. (*Would to God that all differences would end so sweetly. Probably they would, if all who are accused would defend themselves in as kindly a spirit as Peter did.*)

19, 20 Now they which were scattered abroad upon the persecution that arose about Stephen travelled as far as Phenice, and Cyprus, and Antioch, preaching the word to none but unto the Jews only. And some of them were men of Cyprus and Cyrene, which, when they were come to Antioch, spake unto the Grecians, preaching the Lord Jesus.

21 And the hand of the Lord was with them: and a great number believed, and turned unto the Lord. (*Getting into a new field they reaped large harvests. What a time it needed to teach*

these good men that Gentiles might be saved, and yet their Lord had told them expressly to preach the gospel to every creature.)

22—24 ¶ Then tidings of these things came unto the ears of the church which was in Jerusalem: and they sent forth Barnabas, that he should go as far as Antioch. Who, when he came, and had seen the grace of God, was glad, and exhorted them all, that with purpose of heart they would cleave unto the Lord. For he was a good man, and full of the Holy Ghost and of faith: and much people was added unto the Lord. (*This made him rejoice in the good which others had received, and also made him a fit medium for conveying good to many.*)

25 Then departed Barnabas to Tarsus, for to seek Saul:

26 And when he had found him, he brought him unto Antioch. And it came to pass, that a whole year they assembled themselves with the church, and taught much people. And the disciples were called Christians first in Antioch.

They were named not after the word Jesus, *for we cannot be joint saviours with him, but after* Christ, *the Anointed, for we also are anointed with the Holy Spirit.*

27, 28 And in these days came prophets from Jerusalem unto Antioch. And there stood up one of them named Agabus, and signified by the spirit that there should be great dearth throughout all the world: which came to pass in the days of Claudius Cæsar.

29, 30 Then the disciples, every man according to his ability, determined to send relief unto the brethren which dwelt in Judæa: Which also they did, and sent it to the elders by the hands of Barnabas and Saul. (*They not only wore the Christian name, but performed Christian actions: this act of true fellowship is one of the most beautiful things recorded in the Acts. The Jerusalem church sent a great teacher to Antioch, and the Antioch church, in return, showed its love by supplying the needs of their Judæan brethren. A munificent collection for a country suffering from famine would not astonish us now; but from men newly converted, while Christian love was yet a novelty, it was truly admirable. Let us be always ready to succour the Lord's poor.*)

NOVEMBER 1.—EVENING.

" The effectual fervent prayer of a righteous man availeth much."   [Or September 1.]

ACTS XII. 1—19.

NOW about that time Herod the king *(the grandson of Herod the Great)* stretched forth *his* hands to vex certain of the church. And he killed James the brother of John with the sword. *(Troubles seldom come alone; first the famine, then persecution; the church can endure all things.)*

3 And because he saw it pleased the Jews, he proceeded further to take Peter also. (Then were the days of unleavened bread.)

4 And when he had apprehended him, he put *him* in prison, and delivered *him* to four quaternions of soldiers to keep him; intending after Easter *(or rather after the Passover)* to bring him forth to the people.

5 Peter therefore was kept in prison: but prayer was made without ceasing of the church unto God for him. *(What a blessed "but"! Constant guards were baffled by constant prayer. Some would have said, "what can prayer do?" but the early church was not afflicted with such scepticism; they prayed on, and Herod was foiled.)*

6, 7 And when Herod would have brought him forth, the same night Peter was sleeping between two soldiers, bound with two chains: and the keepers before the door kept the prison. And, behold, the angel of the Lord came upon *him*, and a light shined in the prison: and he smote Peter on the side, and raised him up, saying, Arise up quickly. And his chains fell off from *his* hands.

8 And the angel said unto him, Gird thyself, and bind on thy sandals. And so he did. And he saith unto him, Cast thy garment about thee, and follow me. *(The Lord's deliverances are complete ones; Peter must not leave a shoe or a garment in prison, he is to come out with all that he took in.)*

9 And he went out, and followed him; and wist not that it was true which was done by the angel; but thought he saw a vision.

10 When they were past the first and the second ward, they came unto the iron gate that leadeth unto the city; which opened to them of his own accord: and they went out, and passed on through one street; and forthwith the angel departed from him.

11 And when Peter was come to himself, he said, Now I know of a surety, that the Lord hath sent his angel, and hath delivered me out of the hand of Herod, and *from* all the expectation of the people of the Jews.

12 And when he had considered *the thing*, he came to the house of Mary the mother of John, whose surname was Mark; where many were gathered together praying. *(He knew where the brethren prayed, and expected to find them there, and so he did. If he were to come now would he find church members at prayer-meetings? Alas, many of them never go to what they wickedly call "only a prayer-meeting.")*

13, 14 And as Peter knocked at the door of the gate, a damsel came to hearken, named Rhoda *(or Rose)*. And when she knew Peter's voice, she opened not the gate for gladness, but ran in, and told how Peter stood before the gate.

15 And they said unto her, Thou art mad. But she constantly affirmed that it was even so. Then said they, It is his angel. *(If God wishes to surprise his people he has only to answer their prayers, such is their unbelief.)*

16 But Peter continued knocking: and when they had opened *the door*, and saw him, they were astonished.

17 But he, beckoning unto them with the hand to hold their peace, declared unto them how the Lord had brought him out of the prison. And he said, Go shew these things unto James *(the Lord's brother)*, and to the brethren. And he departed, and went into another place. *(This is a notable instance of the power of supplication, and those who will but try it will find prayer to be as mighty as ever.)*

18, 19 Now as soon as it was day, there was no small stir among the soldiers, what was become of Peter. And when Herod had sought for him, and found him not, he examined the keepers, and commanded that *they* should be put to death.

Wrestling prayer can wonders do,
Bring relief in deepest straits,
Prayer can force a passage through
Iron bars and brazen gates.

For the wonders God has wrought,
Let us now our praises give:
And, by sweet experience taught,
Call upon him while we live.

ACTS XIII. 1—16; 38—42.

NOW there were in the church that was at Antioch certain prophets and teachers; as Barnabas, and Simeon that was called Niger, and Lucius of Cyrene, and Manaen, which had been brought up with Herod the tetrarch, and Saul. As they ministered to the Lord, and fasted, the Holy Ghost said, Separate me Barnabas and Saul for the work whereunto I have called them. And when they had fasted and prayed, and laid *their* hands on them, they sent *them* away. *(Here we have the solemn setting apart of the first missionaries. Out of a living and flourishing church the Lord raised up fit men, and their brethren with humble prayer sent them forth.)*

4 ¶ So they, being sent forth by the Holy Ghost, departed unto Seleucia; and from thence they sailed to Cyprus. *(Here begin the voyages and travels of that greatest of missionaries, Saul of Tarsus, late an enemy of the cross. He chartered the first foreign missionary ship.)*

5 And when they were at Salamis, they preached the word of God in the synagogues of the Jews: and they had also John *(or John Mark)* to *their* minister *(or attendant).*

6, 7 And when they had gone through the isle unto Paphos, they found a certain sorcerer, a false prophet, a Jew, whose name *was* Bar-jesus *(or Son of Jesus)*: Which was with the deputy of the country, Sergius Paulus, a prudent man; who called for Barnabas and Saul, and desired to hear the word of God.

8 But Elymas the sorcerer (for so is his name by interpretation) withstood them, seeking to turn away the deputy from the faith.

9, 10 Then Saul, (who also *is called* Paul,) filled with the Holy Ghost, set his eyes on him, And said, O full of all subtilty and all mischief, *thou* child of the devil, *thou* enemy of all righteousness, wilt thou not cease to pervert the right ways of the Lord? *(He called himself "son of Jesus," but Paul called him "child of the devil;" he had also taken the name of Elymas, or wise, but he is rightly described as full of all subtilty and mischief.)*

11 And now, behold, the hand of the Lord *is* upon thee, and thou shalt be blind, not seeing the sun for a season. And immediately there fell on him a mist and a darkness; and he went about seeking some to lead him by the hand.

He who had refused spiritual light, now lost natural light; he tried to lead others astray, and became dependent upon the leading of others.

12 Then the deputy, when he saw what was done, believed, being astonished at the doctrine of the Lord.

13 Now when Paul and his company loosed from Paphos, they came to Perga in Pamphylia: and John departing from them returned to Jerusalem. *(John Mark deserted the two missionaries, and it would seem from the after history that he did so in an unsatisfactory manner. The toils and dangers of the enterprise were too much for him. If we have put our hand to the plough let us not look back.)*

14 ¶ But when they departed from Perga, they came to Antioch in Pisidia, and went into the synagogue on the sabbath day, and sat down.

15 And after the reading of the law and the prophets the rulers of the synagogue sent unto them, saying, Ye men *and* brethren, if ye have any word of exhortation for the people, say on.

16 Then Paul stood up, and beckoning with *his* hand said, Men of Israel, and ye that fear God, give audience. *(Then he went on to describe the rejection of king Saul and the choice of David, and in due order preached to them Jesus and his salvation, and added,)*

38—41 Be it known unto you, therefore, men *and* brethren, that through this man is preached unto you the forgiveness of sins: And by him all that believe are justified from all things, from which ye could not be justified by the law of Moses. Beware, therefore, lest that come upon you which is spoken of in the prophets; Behold, ye despisers, and wonder, and perish: for I work a work in your days, a work which ye shall in no wise believe, though a man declare it unto you. *(Paul preached free grace and full forgiveness, and contrasted it with the condemning law; this method of preaching is most admirable.)*

42 And when the Jews were gone out of the synagogue, the Gentiles besought that these words might be preached to them the next sabbath. *(The good news had won their attention, and they were anxious at once to know more of it. How happy are we that every Sabbath brings us the sacred word. Perhaps because it is so common we do not value it as we should.)*

652   "𝔥𝔦𝔰 righteousness hath he openly shewed in the sight of the heathen."   [*Or September* 3.]

NOVEMBER 2.—EVENING.

ACTS XIII. 43—52.

NOW when the congregation was broken up, many of the Jews and religious proselytes followed Paul and Barnabas : who, speaking to them, persuaded them to continue in the grace of God. *(These earnest people wished for private conversation upon the gospel. Ministers are always hopeful of such hearers. We must not be backward in speaking to God's servants concerning our souls.)*

44 And the next sabbath day came almost the whole city together to hear the word of God. *(So that there was much excitement. Those who speak slightingly of the power which draws large congregations should reflect that men cannot learn the gospel if they never hear it. What grand days we should see if almost the whole of our population would come together to hear the word of God.)*

45 But when the Jews saw the multitudes, they were filled with envy, and spake against those things which were spoken by Paul, contradicting and blaspheming.

46, 47 Then Paul and Barnabas waxed bold, and said, It was necessary that the word of God should first have been spoken to you : but seeing ye put it from you, and judge yourselves unworthy of everlasting life, lo, we turn to the Gentiles. For so hath the Lord commanded us, *saying,* I have set thee to be a light of the Gentiles, that thou shouldest be for salvation unto the ends of the earth.

48 And when the Gentiles heard this, they were glad, and glorified the word of the Lord : and as many as were ordained to eternal life believed. *(The gospel dove being driven away from one place found a congenial nest in another. We cannot force men to be saved, and therefore we must carry the gospel to others when those reject it to whom we have presented it ; by this means the eternal purposes of God will be fulfilled, and his own elect will be gathered in.)*

49 And the word of the Lord was published throughout all the region.

50 But the Jews stirred up the devout and honourable women, and the chief men of the city, and raised persecution against Paul and Barnabas, and expelled them out of their coasts. *These bigots imagined that the coming of new teachers into their city was a reflection upon*

themselves. *Were they not both honourable and devout already ? Therefore they joined the malicious Jews and chased Paul and Barnabas away. It is not often that we read in Scripture of women, and devout women too, opposing the gospel, yet it is no uncommon thing for formal self-righteous ladies to be very bitter against those who dare to differ from them.*

51 But they shook off the dust of their feet against them, and came unto Iconium.

52 And the disciples were filled with joy, and with the Holy Ghost.

ACTS XIV. 1—7.

AND it came to pass in Iconium, that they went both together into the synagogue of the Jews, and so spake, that a great multitude both of the Jews and also of the Greeks believed. But the unbelieving Jews stirred up the Gentiles, and made their minds evil affected against the brethren. *(Like the dog in the manger, they would not allow others to feed upon that which they rejected themselves. If they chose to be unbelievers, why need they be persecutors ?)*

3 Long time therefore abode they speaking boldly in the Lord, which gave testimony unto the word of his grace, and granted signs and wonders to be done by their hands.

4—6 But the multitude of the city was divided : and part held with the Jews, and part with the apostles. And when there was an assault made both of the Gentiles, and also of the Jews with their rulers, to use *them* despitefully, and to stone them, They were ware of *it,* and fled unto Lystra and Derbe, cities of Lycaonia, and unto the region that lieth round about :

7 And there they preached the gospel.

However much they are harassed, they keep to their life work : nothing can stop them, not even the fear of a cruel death. Do we in like manner speak of Jesus in every company ? If not, we fall short of our duty. Let us amend, and in every place show forth the Saviour's love.

Now will I tell to sinners round,
What a dear Saviour I have found ;
I'll point to thy redeeming blood,
And say, "Behold the way to God !"

ACTS XIV. 8—27.

AND there sat a certain man at Lystra, impotent in his feet, being a cripple from his mother's womb, who never had walked :

This represents the impotency of all men in spiritual things till the grace of God puts strength into them. When we were yet without strength Christ died for the ungodly.

9—11 The same heard Paul speak : who stedfastly beholding him, and perceiving that he had faith to be healed, Said with a loud voice, Stand upright on thy feet. And he leaped and walked. And when the people saw what Paul had done, they lifted up their voices, saying in the speech of Lycaonia, The gods are come down to us in the likeness of men. *(Even now-a-days foolish persons will speak of a new minister as if he were a god, and in a short time will turn round and oppose him.)*

12—17 And they called Barnabas, Jupiter ; and Paul, Mercurius, because he was the chief speaker. Then the priest of Jupiter, which was before their city, brought oxen and garlands unto the gates, and would have done sacrifice with the people. *Which* when the apostles, Barnabas and Paul, heard *of*, they rent their clothes *(We do not find that they rent their clothes when the people talked of stoning them, but when they spake of worshipping them, they could not bear it ; being more concerned for God's honour than their own)*, and ran in among the people crying out, And saying, Sirs, why do ye these things ? We also are men of like passions with you, and preach unto you that ye should turn from these vanities unto the living God, which made heaven, and earth, and the sea, and all things that are therein : Who in times past suffered all nations to walk in their own ways. Nevertheless he left not himself without witness, in that he did good, and gave us rain from heaven, and fruitful seasons, filling our hearts with food and gladness.

18 And with these sayings scarce restrained they the people, that they had not done sacrifice unto them.

19 And there came thither *certain* Jews from Antioch and Iconium, who persuaded the people, and having stoned Paul, drew *him* out of the city, supposing he had been dead.

This is popularity—a god yesterday, and a criminal to-day; garlands first, stones afterwards. How fickle is man !

20—22 *(Paul was left for dead.)* Howbeit, as the disciples stood round about him, he rose up, and came into the city *(Paul was a true hero, the garlands did not ensnare him, nor the stones defeat him ; he had young converts to cheer, and at all hazards he entered the city again)*: and the next day he departed with Barnabas to Derbe. And when they had preached the gospel to that city, and had taught many, they returned again to Lystra, and *to* Iconium, and Antioch, Confirming the souls of the disciples, *and* exhorting them to continue in the faith, and that we must through much tribulation enter into the kingdom of God. *(The apostles had themselves endured much tribulation, and they very candidly assured the converts that they must expect the same. If we reckon upon a smooth path to heaven we deceive ourselves.)*

23 And when they had ordained them elders in every church, and had prayed with fasting, they commended them to the Lord, on whom they believed. *(Churches must have pastors ; those assemblies which have no ministers are not according to the apostles' order.)*

24 And after they had passed throughout Pisidia, they came to Pamphylia.

25 And when they had preached the word in Perga, they went down into Attalia :

26, 27 And thence sailed to Antioch, from whence they had been recommended to the grace of God for the work which they fulfilled. And when they were come, and had gathered the church together, they rehearsed all that God had done with them, and how he had opened the door of faith unto the Gentiles.

The returned missionaries held one of the first missionary meetings. Their speeches consisted of the details of God's work through them, and made the saints in Antioch exceedingly glad.

As a family, do we help missions as we ought ? The heathens are perishing, are we clear of their blood ?

> The heathen perish : day by day
> Thousands on thousands pass away ;
> O Christians, to their rescue fly ;
> Preach Jesus to them ere they die.

ACTS XV. 1, 2; 4—20; 30, 31.

AND certain men which came down *(to Antioch)* from Judæa taught the brethren, *and said,* except ye be circumcised after the manner of Moses, ye cannot be saved. When therefore Paul and Barnabas had no small dissension and disputation with them, they determined that Paul and Barnabas, and certain other of them, should go up to Jerusalem unto the apostles and elders about this question. *It was time that this question was settled once for all, before division grew up as the result of it. The first question—" Can the Gentiles be saved?" had been answered; the second was the one before us—" Must they not be circumcised?"*

4 And when they were come to Jerusalem, they were received of the church, and *of* the apostles and elders, and they declared all things that God had done with them.

5 But there rose up certain of the sect of the Pharisees which believed, saying, That it was needful to circumcise them, and to command *them* to keep the law of Moses. *(The old leaven showed itself. How closely do old ways and thoughts cling to even regenerate men!)*

6 ¶ And the apostles and elders came together for to consider of this matter.

7—11 And when there had been much disputing, Peter rose up, and said unto them, Men *and* brethren, ye know how that a good while ago God made choice among us, that the Gentiles by my mouth should hear the word of the gospel, and believe, And God, which knoweth the hearts, bare them witness, giving them the Holy Ghost, even as *he did* unto us; And put no difference between us and them, purifying their hearts by faith, Now therefore why tempt ye God, to put a yoke upon the neck of the disciples, which neither our fathers nor we were able to bear? But we believe that through the grace of the Lord Jesus Christ we shall be saved, even as they. *(This is the vital doctrine of Christianity—salvation by grace, and that grace revealed in our crucified Lord. Luther says, "We must not yield nor give up this article though heaven and earth should perish." Peter's short and telling speech was a noble contribution to the Gentile cause.)*

12 Then all the multitude kept silence, and gave audience to Barnabas and Paul, declaring what miracles and wonders God had wrought among the Gentiles by them. *(These addresses would have great weight in the discussion.)*

13—17 ¶ And after they had held their peace, James answered, saying, Men *and* brethren, hearken unto me: Simeon hath declared how God at the first did visit the Gentiles, to take out of them a people for his name. And to this agree the words of the prophets; as it is written, After this I will return, and will build again the tabernacle of David, which is fallen down; and I will build again the ruins thereof, and I will set it up: That the residue of men might seek after the Lord, and all the Gentiles, upon whom my name is called, saith the Lord, who doeth all these things.

18, 19 Known unto God are all his works from the beginning of the world. Wherefore my sentence is, that we trouble not them, which from among the Gentiles are turned to God:

20 But that we write unto them, that they abstain from pollutions of idols, and *from* fornication, and *from* things strangled, and *from* blood. *(Thus James summed up the evidence, and the brethren saw their way clear to a decision which was hearty and unanimous. Barnabas and Silas were sent to Antioch with a letter containing the opinion which had been so ably stated by James and supported by the whole body of disciples. Oh, that all disputes among Christians could be settled in such a manner!)*

30, 31 So when they were dismissed, they came to Antioch: and when they had gathered the multitude together, they delivered the epistle: *Which* when they had read, they rejoiced for the consolation. *(And a great comfort it was, for the saints were confirmed in their freedom from the Jewish yoke, those who troubled them were silenced, and the Gentiles were still further encouraged to receive the gospel. The Antioch Christians had done well to seek a settlement of a vexed question.)*

Ye Gentile sinners, ne'er forget
  The wormwood and the gall;
Go—spread your trophies at his feet,
  And crown him Lord of all.

ACTS XV. 35—41.

PAUL and Barnabas continued in Antioch teaching and preaching the word of the Lord, with many others also.

36 And some days after Paul said unto Barnabas, Let us go again and visit our brethren in every city where we have preached the word of the Lord, *and see* how they do. *(An active spirit will not long be at rest. Love to Jesus sets a man at work for his cause, and leads him to stir up others, as Paul did Barnabas.)*

37 And Barnabas determined to take with them John, whose surname was Mark.

38 But Paul thought not good to take him with them, who departed from them from Pamphylia, and went not with them to the work.

He would not go out a second time with a faint-hearted deserter, and he was right. Barnabas, believing that John Mark was penitent for what he had done, and would henceforth be faithful, wished to give him another opportunity; and he was right. Now, since these two brethren had each right on his side, neither of them could yield the point without violating his honest judgment, and we do not therefore wonder that the contention grew hot. The Holy Spirit is very considerate in thus recording the difficulties which occurred even among inspired men. How can we expect always to see eye to eye, when Paul and Barnabas differed?)

39—41 And the contention was so sharp between them, that they departed asunder one from the other: and so Barnabas took Mark, and sailed unto Cyprus; And Paul chose Silas, and departed, being recommended by the brethren unto the grace of God. And he went through Syria and Cilicia, confirming the churches.

There was no help for it but to part. Barnabas went one way with his nephew, and Paul another with Silas. Mark turned out well, and so justified the opinion of Barnabas, but Paul could not foresee that, and is not to be condemned for acting upon the general rule that he who puts his hand to the plough and looks back has proved himself unworthy. This separation, though painful in its cause, was a most excellent thing. There was no need for two such men to be together, they were each able to lead the way alone, and by their doing so double good was accomplished.

ACTS XVI. 1—12.

THEN came he to Derbe and Lystra: and, behold, a certain disciple was there, named Timotheus, the son of a certain woman, which was a Jewess, and believed; but his father *was* a Greek: which was well reported of by the brethren that were at Lystra and Iconium. Him would Paul have to go forth with him; and took and circumcised him because of the Jews which were in those quarters: for they knew all that his father was a Greek. And as they went through the cities, they delivered them the decrees for to keep, that were ordained of the apostles and elders which were at Jerusalem. And so were the churches established in the faith, and increased in number daily.

6—9 Now when they had gone throughout Phrygia and the region of Galatia, and were forbidden of the Holy Ghost to preach the word in Asia, After they were come to Mysia, they assayed to go into Bithynia: but the Spirit suffered them not. And they passing by Mysia came down to Troas. And a vision appeared to Paul in the night; There stood a man of Macedonia, and prayed him, saying, Come over into Macedonia, and help us. *(This is the great missionary call, and it is by night as well as by day sounding in the ears of the church of God. Once Europe thus called to Asia, now all the world is crying to us, " Come over and help us.")*

10 And after he had seen the vision, immediately we endeavoured to go into Macedonia, assuredly gathering that the Lord had called us for to preach the gospel unto them. *(The change of person and the use of the words "we," and "us," show that Luke was now in Paul's company. Paul and Silas, Timothy and Luke, set forth to cross over into Macedonia as soon as the heavenly communication came. All servants of Christ should be thus prompt in obedience.)*

11, 12 Therefore loosing from Troas, we came with a straight course to Samothracia, and the next *day* to Neapolis; And from thence to Philippi, which is the chief city of that part of Macedonia, *and* a colony: and we were in that city abiding certain days. *(In this manner the gospel came to our quarter of the globe. Blessed be God that ever Paul was led to cross the sea; may other lands rejoice in missionaries of the cross who shall visit them from us.)*

"*In my name shall they cast out devils.*"

ACTS XVI. 13—24.

AND on the sabbath we went out of the city by a river side, where prayer was wont to be made; and we sat down, and spake unto the women which resorted *thither.*

All sorts of places have been consecrated to prayer, the field, the sea shore, a prison, and even the belly of a fish, and a fiery furnace. Among praying people the gospel is sure of a hearty welcome. It is well worthy of note that the first gospel address delivered in Europe, was heard at a prayer meeting. We ought therefore to prize this institution very highly.

14 ¶ And a certain woman named Lydia, a seller of purple, of the city of Thyatira, which worshipped God, heard *us:* whose heart the Lord opened, that she attended unto the things which were spoken of Paul. *(The apostle did not bring crowds to Jesus on this occasion, yet was he amply repaid by the conversion of this one woman, whom providence had brought there in the course of her business, on purpose that she might be saved. Observe that it was not Paul who converted her, but the Lord himself. Paul would have knocked at the door of her heart in vain, if he who has the key of all hearts had not opened it. Lord, open all our hearts to give attention to thy word.)*

15 And when she was baptized, and her household, she besought *us,* saying, If ye have judged me to be faithful to the Lord, come into my house, and abide *there.* And she constrained us. *(Lydia showed her faith by her humility of speech and generosity of act. She was probably a merchant in easy circumstances, and she desired that her beloved teachers should share the comforts of her house. A hundred years before a bloody battle had been fought at Philippi: the bloodless victory of Paul was far more glorious, and its fruits far more useful to coming generations.)*

16—18 ¶ And it came to pass, as we went to prayer, a certain damsel possessed with a spirit of divination met us, which brought her masters much gain by soothsaying: The same followed Paul and us, and cried, saying, These men are the servants of the most high God, which shew unto us the way of salvation. And this did she many days. But Paul, being grieved, turned and said to the spirit, I command thee, in the name of Jesus Christ to come out of her. And

he came out the same hour. *(This poor creature was regarded as a prophetess, even as some wicked gipsy women are regarded among the extremely ignorant in our own day. Satan used her as the means of deceiving the people. The unclean spirit pretended to praise Paul and his friends, either with the view of puffing them up with pride, or to disgust the better sort of people by leading them to identify the gospel with the ravings of the maniac girl. Much money was paid to this poor woman by superstitious persons for her soothsaying, just as at this day the ungodly will pay much for the telling of their fortunes, or admission to a spiritualist séance, and yet think believers extravagant if they subscribe largely for the spread of the gospel.)*

19—22 ¶ And when her masters saw that the hope of their gains was gone, they caught Paul and Silas, and drew *them* into the marketplace unto the rulers, And brought them to the magistrates, saying, These men, being Jews, do exceedingly trouble our city, And teach customs, which are not lawful for us to receive, neither to observe, being Romans. And the multitude rose up together against them: and the magistrates rent off their clothes, and commanded to beat them. *(The reward of these good physicians for the cure they wrought, was such as had been meted out to their Lord beforehand, yet we may be sure they would sooner be beaten than be praised by the devil.)*

23, 24 And when they had laid many stripes upon them, they cast *them* into prison, charging the jailor to keep them safely: Who, having received such a charge, thrust them into the inner prison, and made their feet fast in the stocks. *(So ended a day which began with a miracle; but Satan's brief victory was in a few hours turned into total defeat. Glory be to God, saints may be beaten, but they conquer still.)*

Paul and Silas were confined,
And their backs were torn with whips;
Yet, possessing peace of mind,
They could sing with joyful lips.

So the Christian, free from care,
May in chains or dungeon sing;
If the Lord be with him there,
He is happier than a king.

THE *battle of Philippi was not over yet, the enemy were yet to be vanquished by those whom they had taken prisoner.*

ACTS XVI. 25—40.

25 And at midnight Paul and Silas prayed, and sang praises unto God : and the prisoners heard them. *(They turned, as one has well said, even a porch of death and a gate of hell into a sanctuary and a gate of heaven. With bleeding backs and in a comfortless posture they sang like angels, and made the grim walls ring again. No groans and moans were heard, but a nocturnal jubilate such as that dungeon never echoed with before.)*

26 And suddenly there was a great earthquake, so that the foundations of the prison were shaken : and immediately all the doors were opened, and every one's bands were loosed. *(Such an earthquake was evidently supernatural, and was a great wonder; but greater wonders were yet to come, for hearts were to be opened also.)*

27 And the keeper of the prison awaking out of his sleep, and seeing the prison doors open, he drew out his sword, and would have killed himself, supposing that the prisoners had been fled. *(Death, coupled with dishonour, would have been his doom. Desperate and frenzied, he was on the borders of hell; but grace plucked him as a brand from the burning.)*

28 But Paul cried with a loud voice, saying, Do thyself no harm : for we are all here.
Stricken with awe at the miracle, no prisoner left his cell. God can hold men in their places without bonds or bolts.

29, 30 Then he called for a light, and sprang in, and came trembling, and fell down before Paul and Silas, And brought them out, and said, Sirs, what must I do to be saved ?

31 And they said, Believe on the Lord Jesus Christ, and thou shalt be saved, and thy house.
The answer was quickly given, and in a few words. Is salvation then so simple? Indeed it is! Have we believed, and have we obtained mercy for our house? If not, let us pray in faith.

32 And they spake unto him the word of the Lord, and to all that were in his house.

33 And he took them the same hour of the night, and washed *their* stripes ; and was baptized, he and all his, straightway.
All his house believed and all were baptized. Here the apostles saw who it was that had said " Come over and help us."

34 And when he had brought them into his house, he set meat before them, and rejoiced, believing in God with all his house. *(His faith brought forth fruit, which evidenced his change of heart, else this rough jailor would not so courteously have entertained his prisoners.)*

35 And when it was day, the magistrates sent the serjeants, saying, Let those men go.

36 37, And the keeper of the prison told this saying to Paul, The magistrates have sent to let you go : now therefore depart, and go in peace. But Paul said unto them, They have beaten us openly uncondemned, being Romans, and have cast *us* into prison ; and now do they thrust us out privily ? nay verily ; but let them come themselves and fetch us out.

38 And the serjeants told these words unto the magistrates : and they feared, when they heard that they were Romans.

39 And they came and besought them, and brought *them* out, and desired *them* to depart out of the city. *(Paul sets us an example of claiming our civil rights when to do so will further justice and teach oppressors that they cannot violate laws as they like; yet this example must be followed cautiously, · or else, like the apostle, we may appeal unto Cæsar, and lose more than we gain.)*

40 And they went out of the prison, and entered into the house of Lydia : and when they had seen the brethren, they comforted them, and departed. *(They did not leave the city at once, but called upon Lydia and relieved her mind with the recital of the work of God in the prison, and then, to prevent further tumult, they went on their way.)*

Just as I am—without one plea
But that thy blood was shed for me,
And that thou bidd'st me come to thee,
    O Lamb of God, I come.

Just as I am—and waiting not
To rid my soul of one dark blot,
To thee, whose blood can cleanse each spot,
    O Lamb of God, I come.

658   "Is He the God of the Jews only? Is He not also of the Gentiles."   NOVEMBER 5.—EVENING.

[*Or September 9.*]

WE *shall still follow Paul in his missionary wanderings. Silas and Timothy continued with him.*

ACTS XVII. 1—15.

1, 2 Now when they had passed through Amphipolis and Apollonia, they came to Thessalonica, where was a synagogue of the Jews: And Paul, as his manner was, went in unto them, and three sabbath days reasoned with them out of the scriptures.

3 Opening and alleging, that Christ must needs have suffered, and risen again from the dead; and that this Jesus, whom I preach unto you is Christ. (*The apostle's custom was to reason from the Scriptures, and surely there is no weapon so powerful as that which is taken from the armoury of inspiration.*)

4, 5 And some of them believed, and consorted with Paul and Silas; and of the devout Greeks a great multitude, and of the chief women not a few. But the Jews which believed not, moved with envy, took unto them certain lewd fellows of the baser sort, and gathered a company, and set all the city on an uproar, and assaulted the house of Jason, and sought to bring them out to the people. (*On a former occasion Satan employed the honourable to disturb the apostle's work, now he summons the low fellows of the markets; little does he care what tools he uses, so that he can compass his ends. The mob attacked Jason's house, supposing the preachers to be there. The story reads like a tale of the early Methodist times.*)

6, 7 And when they found them not, they drew Jason and certain brethren unto the rulers of the city, crying, These that have turned the world upside down are come hither also; Whom Jason hath received: and these all do contrary to the decrees of Cæsar, saying that there is another king, one Jesus. (*Earnest Christians have often been attacked with this handy weapon—they are innovators, and, of course, are the enemies of "our glorious constitution," causing infinite disturbance by their new-fangled ways. Verily, church history repeats itself.*)

8, 9 And they troubled the people and the rulers of the city, when they heard these things. And when they had taken security of Jason, and of the other, they let them go.

Honoured indeed was Jason to be surety for one against whom the world was enraged, but of whom the world was not worthy.

10 And the brethren immediately sent away Paul and Silas by night unto Berea: who coming *thither* went into the synagogue of the Jews. (*See how they persevere, they are at their old work again.*)

11 These were more noble than those in Thessalonica, in that they received the word with all readiness of mind, and searched the scriptures daily, whether those things were so. *The candour of these Bereans was their nobility, they did not condemn unheard. Knowing the Old Testament to be the word of God, they tested the gospel by it.*

12 Therefore many of them believed; also of honourable women which were Greeks, and of men, not a few. (*They proved all things, and then held fast what they had tested.*)

13 But when the Jews of Thessalonica had knowledge that the word of God was preached of Paul at Berea, they came thither also, and stirred up the people. (*Earnest saints have earnest enemies; pleased with their success at Thessalonica, the Jews used the same tactics at Berea; yet they only gave wings to the feet of the missionaries and kept the light moving on.*)

14 And then immediately the brethren sent away Paul to go as it were to the sea: but Silas and Timotheus abode there still.

15 And they that conducted Paul brought him unto Athens: and receiving a commandment unto Silas and Timotheus for to come to him with all speed, they departed. (*What Berea lost Athens gained, for Paul arrived there all the earlier. Let Satan do what he may, he only speeds on the cause which he desires to hinder. To God be all glory, for thus vanquishing evil with good.*)

Oh, how restless is the foe
Jesu's kingdom to o'erthrow!
Shall not we as zealous prove
To proclaim redeeming love?

Let us publish saving grace,
Scatter life in every place;
Dare the world's and Satan's frown,
Turn *his* kingdom upside down.

ACTS XVII. 16—34.

NOW while Paul waited for them at Athens, his spirit was stirred in him, when he saw the city wholly given to idolatry. *Was it not well that the troublesome Jews drove the apostle to Athens before his companions, that he might, by surveying that idolatrous city alone, find a fresh stimulus for his zeal?*

17 Therefore disputed he in the synagogue with the Jews, and with the devout persons, and in the market daily with them that met with him. *(In the market he met with idle loungers ready to listen to anything and everything new; and even upon such soil, like the sower in the parable, he scattered his seed.)*

18—21 Then certain philosophers of the Epicureans, and of the Stoicks, encountered him. And some said, What will this babbler say? other some, He seemeth to be a setter forth of strange gods: because he preached unto them Jesus, and the resurrection. And they took him, and brought him unto Areopagus, saying, May we know what this new doctrine, whereof thou speakest, *is?* For thou bringest certain strange things to our ears: we would know therefore what these things mean. (For all the Athenians and strangers which were there spent their time in nothing else, but either to tell, or to hear some new thing.) *Nothing could have pleased Paul better than to address so large and important an assembly as that which gathered on Mars' Hill. With a considerable amount of courtesy the philosophers invited him to speak, curiosity to hear his novel teaching being their leading motive. The doctrine of the resurrection seemed most to startle them. The immortality of the soul they had already known, but the resurrection of the body was a new idea. Paul addressed them both faithfully and prudently. Few could have coped with these educated men as he did. His beautiful address is somewhat spoiled in our version, and therefore we will a little revise it.*

22 ¶ Then Paul stood in the midst of Mars' hill, and said, Ye men of Athens, I perceive that ye are on all points very God-fearing.

23 For as I passed by, and beheld your sacred things, I found an altar with this inscription, TO AN UNKNOWN GOD. What, therefore, without knowing it, ye worship, that I announce unto you.

24—31 God that made the world and all things therein, seeing that he is Lord of heaven and earth, dwelleth not in temples made with hands; Neither is worshipped with men's hands, as though he needed any thing, seeing he giveth to all life, and breath, and all things; And hath made of one blood all nations of men for to dwell on all the face of the earth, and hath determined the times before appointed, and the bounds of their habitation; That they should seek the Lord, if haply they might feel after him, and find him, though he be not far from every one of us: For in him we live, and move, and have our being; as certain also of your own poets have said, For we are also his offspring. Forasmuch then as we are the offspring of God, we ought not to think that the Godhead is like unto gold, or silver, or stone, graven by art and man's device. And the times of this ignorance God winked at; but now commandeth all men every where to repent: Because he hath appointed a day, in the which he will judge the world in righteousness by *that* man whom he hath ordained; *whereof* he hath given assurance unto all *men*, in that he hath raised him from the dead. *(What could be more courteous, more cogent, more adroit? He points to their own altars, he quotes their own poets, he appeals to their common sense. He knew the way of putting the truth so as to attract and not repel; and though but few of the Areopagites were saved, yet a noble testimony was borne among men of intelligence, who would talk of what they heard in many a company where else the gospel would have been unknown.)*

32 And when they heard of the resurrection of the dead, some mocked: and others said, We will hear thee again of this *matter.*

33 So Paul departed from among them.

34 Howbeit certain men clave unto him, and believed: among the which *was* Dionysius the Areopagite, and a woman named Damaris, and others with them. *(Not many wise men after the flesh are called, but a few are, and if only one be saved the preacher is well rewarded for his pains. Paul spake not in vain in Athens, a church was formed and flourished even in that ungenial soil.)*

ACTS XVIII. 1—17.

AFTER these things Paul departed from Athens, and came to Corinth;

2, 3 And found a certain Jew named Aquila, born in Pontus, lately come from Italy, with his wife Priscilla; (because that Claudius had commanded all Jews to depart from Rome :) and came unto them. And because he was of the same craft, he abode with them, and wrought : for by their occupation they were tentmakers.

Probably at first they accepted Paul as a companion because of their common trade, and through his instrumentality were led to receive the common faith. It is well to turn association in business into a means for winning souls.

4 And he reasoned in the synagogue every sabbath, and persuaded the Jews and the Greeks.

5 And when Silas and Timotheus were come from Macedonia, Paul was pressed in the spirit, and testified to the Jews *that* Jesus *was* Christ.

He felt more earnest than ever, and with greater vehemence pressed upon the Jews the duty of believing in Jesus.

6 And when they opposed themselves, and blasphemed, he shook *his* raiment, and said unto them, Your blood *be* upon your own heads ; I *am* clean : from henceforth I will go unto the Gentiles.

7 ¶ And he departed thence, and entered into a certain *man's* house, named Justus, *one* that worshipped God, whose house joined hard to the synagogue. *(If he could not go inside the synagogue, he yet remained as near to it as possible, that those who wished to hear might know where to find him.)*

8 And Crispus, the chief ruler of the synagogue, believed on the Lord with all his house ; and many of the Corinthians hearing believed, and were baptized.

9, 10 Then spake the Lord to Paul in the night by a vision, Be not afraid, but speak, and hold not thy peace : For I am with thee, and no man shall set on thee to hurt thee : for I have much people in this city. *(Good news for the apostle. He was to preach fearlessly because the Lord intended to bless abundantly. Some have said, "If the Lord has an elect people, why need we preach to them?" but the answer is,—if the Lord had not determined to save some, preaching would certainly be in vain.)*

11 And he continued *there* a year and six months, teaching the word of God among them.

This was quite a long stay for him. During this time he probably wrote both the first and second epistles to the Thessalonians. His time was also well occupied in building up the Corinthian church, which became large and important. As the Christians worshipped next door to the Jewish synagogue, their growing numbers soon aroused the Jews, and they proceeded to prosecute Paul before the Roman proconsul.

12, 13 And when Gallio was the deputy of Achaia, the Jews made insurrection with one accord against Paul, and brought him to the judgment seat, Saying, This *fellow* persuadeth men to worship God contrary to the law.

14—16 And when Paul was now about to open *his* mouth, Gallio said unto the Jews, If it were a matter of wrong or wicked lewdness, O *ye* Jews, reason would that I should bear with you : But if it be a question of words and names, and *of* your law, look ye *to it ;* for I will be no judge of such *matters.* And he drave them from the judgment seat. *(He would not interfere in religious matters, but kept to his proper sphere, therein proving himself to be a far more enlightened ruler than many in modern times.)*

17 Then all the Greeks took Sosthenes, the chief ruler of the synagogue, and beat *him* before the judgment seat. And Gallio cared for none of those things. *(The Jews gained nothing by their attempt, but drew down upon themselves the indignation of the Gentiles. Gallio failed in his duty in not protecting Sosthenes from violence; though he was right in refusing to oppress the conscience of Paul, he was wrong in not securing the civil rights of his opponent. Happy will that day be when civil rulers neither overstep their sphere nor neglect their office. May God bless the Queen and all in authority over us.)*

> What though earth and hell united
>   Should oppose the Saviour's plan ?
> Plead his cause, nor be affrighted,
>   Fear ye not the face of man ;
>   Vain their tumult,
> Hurt his work they never can.

A FTER *the defeat of the Jews before the judgment seat of Gallio, Paul remained at Corinth for some time, and then sailed to Ephesus, where they desired him to remain ; but he thought fit to proceed by vessel to Cesarea, and onward to Jerusalem. Thence he travelled again to Antioch, and set out on another tour. This indefatigable apostle was always at work, spending and being spent for the Lord Jesus.*

ACTS XIX. 1—20.

1, 2 Paul having passed through the upper coasts came to Ephesus : and finding certain disciples, He said unto them, Have ye received the Holy Ghost since ye believed ? And they said unto him, We have not so much as heard whether there be any Holy Ghost.

There are even now professing Christians who know nothing of the Holy Ghost, of the spirit of repentance, of the new birth, of adoption, of holy joy, or of sanctified fellowship. What do we each one of us personally know of the Holy Spirit ?

3 And he said unto them, Unto what then were ye baptized ? And they said, Unto John's baptism.

4 Then said Paul, John verily baptized with the baptism of repentance, saying unto the people, that they should believe on him which should come after him, that is, on Christ Jesus.

5 When they heard *this*, they were baptized in the name of the Lord Jesus.

6--9 And when Paul had laid *his* hands upon them, the Holy Ghost came on them ; and they spake with tongues and prophesied. And all the men were about twelve. And he went into the synagogue, and spake boldly for the space of three months, disputing and persuading the things concerning the kingdom of God. But when divers were hardened, and believed not, but spake evil of that way before the multitude, he departed from them, and separated the disciples, disputing *(or discoursing)* daily in the school of one Tyrannus.

> " *Temple, or house, or barn, or school,*
> *(The gospel consecrates the place,)*
> *No matter where, so Jesus rule,*
> *And teach the lessons of his grace."*

10—12 And this continued by the space of two years ; so that all they which dwelt in Asia heard the word of the Lord Jesus, both Jews and Greeks. And God wrought special miracles by the hands of Paul : So that from his body were brought unto the sick handkerchiefs or aprons, and the diseases departed from them, and the evil spirits went out of them.

13 ¶ Then certain of the vagabond Jews, exorcists, took upon them to call over them which had evil spirits the name of the Lord Jesus, saying, We adjure you by Jesus whom Paul preacheth. *(Wretched is that man who uses the name of Jesus for his own ends, knowing nothing of its power in his own heart. It is to be feared that many do this even now.)*

14 And there were seven sons of *one* Sceva, a Jew, *and* chief of the priests, which did so.

How sad is it that when Satan wants tools he often finds them among the sons of ministers.

15, 16 And the evil spirit answered and said, Jesus I know, and Paul I know ; but who are ye ? And the man in whom the evil spirit was leaped on them, and overcame them, and prevailed against them, so that they fled out of that house naked and wounded.

The evil spirit laughs at those whom God has not sent forth into the ministry ; they may use pious words, but they are destitute of divine power, and will surely be the sport of hell.

17, 18 And this was known to all the Jews and Greeks also dwelling at Ephesus ; and fear fell on them all, and the name of the Lord Jesus was magnified. And many that believed came, and confessed, and shewed their deeds.

19 Many of them also which used curious arts brought their books together, and burned them before all *men :* and they counted the price of them, and found *it* fifty thousand *pieces* of silver. *(Or nearly £2,000. Bad books, and bad pictures, never look so much in their place as when blazing away in a bonfire.*

> " *Your cards, and foolish books disdain,*
> *And cast your plays into the flame."*)

20 So mightily grew the word of God and prevailed. *(May a like good work be done all around us, for there is great need of it.)*

> Spirit of Truth, be thou
> In life and death our guide !
> O Spirit of Adoption, now
> May we be sanctified !

PAUL was about to leave Ephesus and journey to Jerusalem, when a riot occurred, which is thus described :—

ACTS XIX. 23—41.

23, 24 And the same time there arose no small stir about that way. For a certain *man* named Demetrius, a silversmith, which made silver shrines for Diana, brought no small gain unto the craftsmen ; (*He employed a large number of artisans in making shrines, which were purchased by pilgrims, to be carried home with them as memorials of the goddess. Demetrius was afraid that his trade would be injured through the spread of Christian doctrine, and, therefore, stirred up his men.*)

25—27 Whom he called together with the workmen of like occupation, and said, Sirs, ye know that by this craft we have our wealth. Moreover ye see and hear, that not alone at Ephesus, but almost throughout all Asia, this Paul hath persuaded and turned away much people, saying that they be no gods, which are made with hands : So that not only this our craft is in danger to be set at nought ; but also that the temple of the great goddess Diana should be despised, and her magnificence should be destroyed, whom all Asia and the world worshippeth. (*How finely does he veil self-interest under the cloak of religion. Selfishness is the most powerful adversary to the cause of truth.*)

28 And when they heard *these sayings*, they were full of wrath, and cried out, saying, Great *is* Diana of the Ephesians. (*Yes, and greatly profitable was the trade of shrine-making !*)

29—31 And the whole city was filled with confusion : and having caught Gaius and Aristarchus, men of Macedonia, Paul's companions in travel, they rushed with one accord into the theatre. And when Paul would have entered in unto the people, the disciples suffered him not. And certain of the chiefs of Asia which were his friends, sent unto him, desiring *him* that he would not adventure himself into the theatre. (*Had it not been for these entreaties the heroic apostle would have faced the crowd.*)

32—34 Some therefore cried one thing, and some another : for the assembly was confused ; and the more part knew not wherefore they were come together. And they drew Alexander out of the multitude, the Jews putting him for-ward. (*If this man was Alexander the coppersmith, we can understand why the Jews pushed him forward as their representative, for he would be supposed to have weight with his brother craftsmen. The object of the Jews was to show that they were not connected with Paul, and also to cast more odium upon the Christians.*) And Alexander beckoned with the hand, and would have made his defence unto the people. But when they knew that he was a Jew, all with one voice about the space of two hours cried out, Great *is* Diana of the Ephesians. (*The mob confounded the Christians with the Jews, and were in no mood to hear any explanation.*)

35—40 And when the townclerk (*or recorder*) had appeased the people, he said, Ye men of Ephesus, what man is there that knoweth not how that the city of the Ephesians is a worshipper of the great goddess Diana, and of the *image* which fell down from Jupiter ? Seeing then that these things cannot be spoken against, ye ought to be quiet, and to do nothing rashly. For ye have brought hither these men, which are neither robbers of temples nor yet blasphemers of your goddess. (*Paul's language had been moderate and winning. He had used no opprobrious language in reference to the idol.*) Wherefore if Demetrius, and the craftsmen which are with him, have a matter against any man, the law is open, and there are deputies : let them implead one another. But if ye enquire any thing concerning other matters, it shall be determined in a lawful assembly. For we are in danger to be called in question for this day's uproar, there being no cause whereby we may give an account of this concourse.

41 And when he had thus spoken, he dismissed the assembly. (*Calmed by his judicious speech, the mob retired, and the danger for the Christians ended. The Lord can rule the raging of the people and preserve his own servants from imminent peril.*)

The waves of the sea when highest they rise
Are governed by thee, our Lord in the skies ;
Thy succour imploring, thy presence we find
To silence the roaring, and quiet the wind.

The fierceness of men who threaten so loud,
Thy word can restrain, and bridle the crowd ;
And when it represses their madness of will,
The hurricane ceases, the tumult is still.

ACTS XX. 1—16.

THE *riot at Ephesus had been quelled by the judicious words of the recorder of the city.*

1 And after the uproar was ceased, Paul called unto *him* the disciples, and embraced *them*, and departed for to go into Macedonia.

Not as a coward did the apostle flee from conflict, but after all danger was over in Ephesus, he carried the war into other regions. See with what affection he bade farewell to the brethren; embracing them as a father does his children.

2, 3 And when he had gone over those parts, and had given them much exhortation, he came unto Greece, And *there* abode three months. And when the Jews laid wait for him, as he was about to sail into Syria, he purposed to return through Macedonia. *(With unwearied energy he laboured to spread the gospel. The words of the historian are few, but we know from the epistles that each day was crowded with work for Jesus.)*

4—6 And there accompanied him into Asia Sopater of Berea; and of the Thessalonians, Aristarchus and Secundus; and Gaius of Derbe, and Timotheus; and of Asia, Tychicus and Trophimus. These going before tarried for us at Troas. And we sailed away from Philippi after the days of unleavened bread, and came unto them to Troas in five days; where we abode seven days. *(Paul, having seen his dear Philippian brethren, came over with Luke and joined his seven companions at Troas.)*

7 And upon the first *day* of the week, when the disciples came together to break bread, Paul preached unto them, ready to depart on the morrow; and continued his speech until midnight. *(He felt that he should never speak to them again, and, therefore, he prolonged his address.)*

8 And there were many lights in the upper chamber, where they were gathered together. *The place thus became heated, and being very crowded, the air was heavy, and it was not easy for the hearers to keep awake.*

9, 10 And there sat in a window a certain young man named Eutychus, being fallen into a deep sleep; and as Paul was long preaching, he sunk down with sleep, and fell down from the third loft, and was taken up dead. And Paul

went down, and fell on him, and embracing *him* said, Trouble not yourselves; for his life is in him. *(Remember, if we go to sleep during sermon and die, there are no apostles to restore us. The word of God deserves our wakeful attention.)*

11, 12 When he therefore was come up again, and had broken bread, and eaten, and talked a long while, even till break of day, so he departed. And they brought the young man alive, and were not a little comforted.

13 ¶ And we went before to ship, and sailed unto Assos, there intending to take in Paul: for so had he appointed, minding himself to go afoot. *(A quiet lonely walk of twenty miles suited Paul, it would give him space for prayer and meditation, and help him to shake off some of the depression which had gathered over his mind while he waited at Philippi. Those who labour much for the Lord must have their times of retirement for self-examination, prayer, communion with God, and preparation for future efforts.)*

14, 15 And when he met with us at Assos, we took him in, and came to Mitylene. And we sailed thence, and came the next *day* over against Chios; and the next *day* we arrived at Samos, and tarried at Trogyllium; and the next *day* we came to Miletus.

16 For Paul had determined to sail by Ephesus, because he would not spend the time in Asia: for he hasted, if it were possible for him, to be at Jerusalem the day of Pentecost.

By these descriptions of Paul's activity we are taught to be active and energetic for our Lord. We can never do enough for him to whom we owe our all. What are we doing? There is a sphere for each one of us, whether old or young: are we filling it? Are we in earnest, or are we incurring the guilt of unprofitable servants?

Awake, my soul, stretch every nerve,
    And press with vigour on;
A heavenly race demands thy zeal,
    And an immortal crown.

'Tis God's all-animating voice
    That calls thee from on high;
'Tis his own hand presents the prize
    To thine aspiring eye.

A cloud of witnesses around
    Hold thee in full survey;
Forget the steps already trod,
    And onward urge thy way.

664   *" It is more blessed to give than to receive."*   NOVEMBER 8.—EVENING.

[Or September 15.]

THE *apostle was hastening to Jerusalem, and as he knew that if he called at Ephesus he would be detained, he chose a ship which did not stop at that port. There happened, however, to be a delay at Miletus, which was twenty or thirty miles from Ephesus.*

ACTS XX. 17—38.

17 And from Miletus he sent to Ephesus, and called the elders of the church.

18—21 And when they were come to him, he said unto them, Ye know, from the first day that I came into Asia, after what manner I have been with you at all seasons, Serving the Lord with all humility of mind, and with many tears, and temptations, which befell me by the lying in wait of the Jews: *And* how I kept back nothing that was profitable *unto you*, but have shewed you, and have taught you publickly, and from house to house, Testifying both to the Jews, and also to the Greeks, repentance toward God, and faith toward our Lord Jesus Christ.

22, 23 And now, behold, I go bound in the spirit unto Jerusalem, not knowing the things that shall befall me there : Save that the Holy Ghost witnesseth in every city, saying that bonds and afflictions abide me.

24 But none of these things move me, neither count I my life dear unto myself, so that I might finish my course with joy, and the ministry, which I have received of the Lord Jesus, to testify the gospel of the grace of God.

25 And now, behold, I know that ye all, among whom I have gone preaching the kingdom of God, shall see my face no more.

26 Wherefore I take you to record this day, that I *am* pure from the blood of all *men*.

27 For I have not shunned to declare unto you all the counsel of God.

28—30 Take heed therefore unto yourselves, and to all the flock, over the which the Holy Ghost hath made you overseers, to feed the church of God, which he hath purchased with his own blood. For I know this, that after my departing shall grievous wolves enter in among you, not sparing the flock. Also of your own selves shall men arise, speaking perverse things, to draw away disciples after them.

31 Therefore watch, and remember, that by the space of three years I ceased not to warn every one night and day with tears.

32 And now, brethren, I commend you to God, and to the word of his grace, which is able to build you up, and to give you an inheritance among all them which are sanctified.

33, 34 I have coveted no man's silver, or gold, or apparel. Yea, ye yourselves know, that these hands have ministered unto my necessities, and to them that were with me.

35 I have shewed you all things, how that so labouring ye ought to support the weak, and to remember the words of the Lord Jesus, how he said, It is more blessed to give than to receive. *(The apostle's inmost heart is seen in this touching farewell. His whole care was for the dear ones to whom his ministry had been useful, but whom he must now leave to be sorely tried. He forgot his own troubles in his anxiety for the converts. What a challenge he was able to give to these elders when he bade them bear witness to his labours and his tears ! Such an example could not fail to arouse them to diligence; ought it not to stir us up ? Are we living in Paul's fashion ? We owe as much to Jesus as he did. What are our returns ? May the Lord make us ashamed of ourselves, and lead us to a great amendment in the matter of consecration to his glory.)*

36 ¶ And when he had thus spoken, he kneeled down, and prayed with them all.

37 And they all wept sore, and fell on Paul's neck, and kissed him.

38 Sorrowing most of all for the words which he spake, that they should see his face no more. And they accompanied him unto the ship.

If the sorrow is so great to part for a while from those whom we love, how much sharper will the pangs be of those who will for ever be parted from their godly friends at the last day ! How terrible will it be to be separated eternally ! God grant it may not be our lot, for Jesus' sake.

Come, Christian brethren, ere we part,
Join every voice and every heart ;
One solemn hymn to God we raise,
One joyful song of grateful praise.

Perhaps we here may meet no more,
But there is yet a happier shore ;
And there, released from toil and pain,
Dear brethren, we shall meet again.

WHAT *plans of usefulness were in Paul's mind at this time, and what he did after the uproar at Ephesus, we gather from—*

ROMANS XV. 18—33.

18, 19 For I will not dare to speak of any of those things which Christ hath not wrought by me, to make the Gentiles obedient, by word and deed. Through mighty signs and wonders, by the power of the Spirit of God; so that from Jerusalem, and round about unto Illyricum, I have fully preached the gospel of Christ.

20, 21 Yea, so have I strived to preach the gospel, not where Christ was named, lest I should build upon another man's foundation: But as it is written, To whom he was not spoken of, they shall see: and they that have not heard shall understand. *(His was an aggressive policy, he pushed into the enemy's territory, as all God's servants should endeavour to do, for multitudes are still ignorant of the name of Jesus.)*

22—24 For which cause also I have been much hindered from coming to you. But now having no more place in these parts, and having a great desire these many years to come unto you; Whensoever I take my journey into Spain, I will come to you: for I trust to see you in my journey, and to be brought on my way thitherward by you, if first I be somewhat filled with your company. *(Little did he know in what manner he would enter Rome. He thought to journey thither at his own cost as a free man, but the Lord had other plans for him: he would enter Rome, but only as a prisoner.)*

25, 26 But now I go unto Jerusalem to minister unto the saints. For it hath pleased them of Macedonia and Achaia to make a certain contribution for the poor saints which are at Jerusalem. *(It seems that his business at Jerusalem was, for a second time, to carry help to the needy brethren. Such generous tokens of love from the new converts would greatly tend to break down the prejudice against the Gentiles, which still lingered in the Jewish capital.)*

27 It hath pleased them verily; and their debtors they are. For if the Gentiles have been made partakers of their spiritual things, their duty is also to minister unto them in carnal things. *(We are all debtors to believing Jews, and ought to be always doubly ready to relieve their necessities. To despise or think harshly of a Jew is very unbecoming in those who adore " The King of the Jews.")*

28, 29 When therefore I have performed this, and have sealed to them this fruit, I will come by you into Spain. And I am sure that, when I come unto you, I shall come in the fulness of the blessing of the gospel of Christ. *And in this he was not disappointed. His minor expectations failed, but the major were fulfilled; so shall it be in our own cases as we journey through life. Our essential interests will be safe, though in many a matter of less moment we shall experience failure.*

30—32 Now I beseech you, brethren, for the Lord Jesus Christ's sake, and for the love of the Spirit, that ye strive together with me in *your* prayers to God for me; That I may be delivered from them that do not believe in Judæa; and that my service which *I have* for Jerusalem may be accepted of the saints; That I may come unto you with joy by the will of God, and may with you be refreshed. *(Even an apostle craved the supplications of saints, and that, too, about temporal matters. Never can we attach too much importance to prayer. Everything should be gone about in the spirit of prayer, if we desire it to prosper. Yet how strangely is prayer answered; for Paul went to Rome, but it was as an ambassador in bonds. His wish was granted, but not in such a manner as he would have preferred.)*

33 Now the God of peace *be* with you all. Amen. *(Sweet benediction. Lord, fulfil it to us at this hour.)*

Now may the God of peace and love,
　Who from th' imprisoning grave
Restored the Shepherd of the sheep,
　Omnipotent to save;

Through the rich merits of that blood
　Which he on Calvary spilt,
To make the eternal covenant sure
　On which our hopes are built;

Perfect our souls in every grace,
　To accomplish all his will,
And all that's pleasing in his sight
　Inspire us to fulfil!

666   "𝔉𝔬𝔩𝔩𝔬𝔴 𝔞𝔣𝔱𝔢𝔯 𝔱𝔥𝔢 𝔱𝔥𝔦𝔫𝔤𝔰 𝔴𝔥𝔦𝔠𝔥 𝔪𝔞𝔨𝔢 𝔣𝔬𝔯 𝔭𝔢𝔞𝔠𝔢."   November 9.—Evening.

[Or September 17.]

LUKE describes Paul's interview with the brethren at Jerusalem as follows :—

ACTS XXI. 17—24; 26—28 ; 30—36.

17 And when we were come to Jerusalem, the brethren received us gladly.

18 And the *day* following Paul went in with us unto James ; and all the elders were present.

19 And when he had saluted them, he declared particularly what things God had wrought among the Gentiles by his ministry. *(He did not ascribe anything to himself, but modestly and truthfully spoke of what the Lord had wrought through him.)*

20—22 And when they heard *it*, they glorified the Lord, and said unto him, Thou seest, brother, how many thousands of Jews there are which believe; and they are all zealous of the law : And they are informed of thee, that thou teachest all the Jews which are among the Gentiles to forsake Moses, saying that they ought not to circumcise *their* children, neither to walk after the customs. What is it therefore ? the multitude must needs come together : for they will hear that thou art come. *(Even the Jewish Christians were prejudiced against Paul, how much more would the unbelieving Jews be irritated at his presence! The elders, therefore, proposed that he should show himself to be friendly to the law of Moses by joining in one of those actions which were hardly ever performed except by the zealous.)*

23—24 Do therefore this that we say to thee : We have four men which have a vow on them ; Them take, and purify thyself with them, and be at charges with them, that they may shave *their* heads : and all may know that those things, whereof they were informed concerning thee, are nothing ; but *that* thou thyself also walkest orderly, and keepest the law.

26 Then Paul took the men, and the next day purifying himself with them entered into the temple, to signify the accomplishment of the days of purification, until that an offering should be offered for every one of them.

It is an open question whether he was justified in this course of action. He was certainly carrying the principle of being all things to all men quite as far as it could be defended. He must have felt that legal purifications were out of date, and he could only have consented to practise them

in order to please the Jewish brethren. We ought to admire his desire for peace ; yet we cannot shut our eyes to the fact that peace was not the result after all ; on the contrary, this conciliatory act led to the apostle's imprisonment, and to his being carried in bonds to Rome.

27—28 And when the seven days were almost ended, the Jews which were of Asia, when they saw him in the temple, stirred up all the people, and laid hands on him, Crying out, Men of Israel, help : This is the man, that teacheth all *men* every where against the people, and the law, and this place : and further brought Greeks also into the temple, and hath polluted this holy place. *(The charges against the apostle were utterly false. Never had he spoken against the Jews, nor their temple, and so far from polluting the holy place he was doing it too much honour. Servants of God must expect to be misunderstood, and, perhaps, all the more so when for the sake of promoting harmony they yield to compromises.)*

30 And all the city was moved, and the people ran together : and they took Paul, and drew him out of the temple : and forthwith the doors were shut. *(To prevent the defiling of the place with riot and murder.)*

31—33 And as they went about to kill him, tidings came unto the chief captain of the band, *(or tribune of the cohort),* that all Jerusalem was in an uproar, Who immediately took soldiers and centurions, and ran down unto them *(out of the castle of Antonia which overlooked the temple),* and when they saw the chief captain and the soldiers, they left beating of Paul. Then the chief captain came near, and took him, and commanded *him* to be bound with two chains; and demanded who he was, and what he had done.

34 And some cried one thing, some another, among the multitude : and when he could not know the certainty for the tumult, he commanded him to be carried into the castle.

35, 36 And when he came upon the stairs, *(which led up from the temple to the fortress,)* so it was, that he was borne of the soldiers for the violence of the people. For the multitude of the people followed after, crying, Away with him. *(But he was safe from their fury. The Lord has ways of rescuing his servants out of the most perilous circumstances.)*

W E *left the apostle in the hands of the chief captain and his soldiers, who were carrying him away to their quarters.*

ACTS XXI. 37—40.

37, 38 And as Paul was to be led into the castle, he said unto the chief captain, May I speak unto thee? *(The request uttered in the Greek language startled the captain.)* Who said, Canst thou speak Greek? Art not thou that Egyptian, which before these days madest an uproar, and leddest out into the wilderness four thousand men that were murderers?

39 But Paul said, I am a man *which am* a Jew of Tarsus, *a city* in Cilicia, a citizen of no mean city: and, I beseech thee, suffer me to speak unto the people. *(The best of men are often mistaken for the very worst, nor need they wonder, for their Lord was condemned as a malefactor.)*

40 And when he had given him licence, Paul stood on the stairs, and beckoned with the hand unto the people. And when there was made a great silence, he spake unto *them* in the Hebrew tongue. *(The storm subsided into a lull, and Paul, the bravest of the brave, with the utmost composure proceeded to address the crowd.)*

ACTS XXII. 1; 3—18; 21, 22.

M EN, brethren, and fathers, hear ye my defence *which I make* now unto you.

3—5 I am verily a man *which am* a Jew, born in Tarsus, *a city* in Cilicia, yet brought up in this city at the feet of Gamaliel, *and* taught according to the perfect manner of the law of the fathers, and was zealous toward God, as ye all are this day. And I persecuted this way unto the death, binding and delivering into prisons both men and women. As also the high priest doth bear me witness, and all the estate of the elders: from whom also I received letters unto the brethren, and went to Damascus, to bring them which were there bound unto Jerusalem, for to be punished. *(He showed that he had once been as furious against the Christians as they themselves now were: this was intended to win their attention to the rest of his defence.)*

6—8 And it came to pass, that, as I made my journey, and was come nigh unto Damascus about noon, suddenly there shone from heaven a great light round about me. And I fell unto the ground, and heard a voice saying unto me, Saul, Saul, why persecutest thou me? And I answered, Who art thou, Lord? And he said unto me, I am Jesus of Nazareth, whom thou persecutest.

9 And they that were with me saw indeed the light, and were afraid; but they heard not the voice of him that spake to me.

10 And I said, What shall I do, Lord? And the Lord said unto me, Arise, and go into Damascus; and there it shall be told thee of all things which are appointed for thee to do.

11 And when I could not see for the glory of that light, being led by the hand of them that were with me, I came into Damascus.

12—16 And one Ananias, a devout man according to the law, having a good report of all the Jews which dwelt *there*, Came unto me, and stood, and said unto me, Brother Saul, receive thy sight. And the same hour I looked up upon him. And he said, The God of our fathers hath chosen thee, that thou shouldest know his will, and see that Just One, and shouldest hear the voice of his mouth. For thou shalt be his witness unto all men of what thou hast seen and heard. And now why tarriest thou? arise, and be baptized, and wash away thy sins, calling on the name of the Lord. *(When baptism is preceded by repentance, and is attended by a believing calling on the name of the Lord, it becomes a beautiful emblem of that washing away of sins, which is graciously given to all believers. Paul told his own conversion, for he well knew that God often blesses such personal confessions. He then proceeded to give his reason for preaching to the Gentiles.)*

17, 18 And it came to pass, that, when I was come again to Jerusalem, even while I prayed in the temple, I was in a trance; And saw him saying unto me, Make haste, and get thee quickly out of Jerusalem: for they will not receive thy testimony concerning me.

21 And he said unto me, Depart: for I will send thee far hence unto the Gentiles.

22 And they gave him audience unto this word, and *then* lifted up their voices, and said, Away with such a *fellow* from the earth: for it is not fit that he should live. *(Their national prejudice was aroused: they could not endure that the Gentiles should be spoken of as regarded by God. May the Lord save us from all bitterness and bigotry of spirit.)*

668   "The Lord stood by him."   NOVEMBER 10.—EVENING.

[*Or September* 19.]

THE *infuriated mob raved like madmen when Paul had spoken of the Lord's grace towards the Gentiles.*

ACTS XXII. 23—30.

23, 24 And as they cried out, and cast off *their* clothes, and threw dust into the air, The chief captain commanded him to be brought into the castle, and bade that he should be examined by scourging; that he might know wherefore they cried so against him.

25 And as they bound him with thongs, Paul said unto the centurion that stood by, Is it lawful for you to scourge a man that is a Roman, and uncondemned?

26 When the centurion *(who was appointed to scourge him),* heard *that,* he went and told the chief captain, saying, Take heed what thou doest: for this man is a Roman.

27, 28 Then the chief captain came, and said unto him, Tell me, art thou a Roman? He said, Yea. And the chief captain answered, With a great sum obtained I this freedom. And Paul said, But I was *free* born.

29 Then straightway they departed from him which should have examined him: and the chief captain also was afraid, after he knew that he was a Roman, and because he had bound him.

30 On the morrow, because he would have known the certainty wherefore he was accused of the Jews, he loosed him from *his* bands, and commanded the chief priests and all their council to appear, and brought Paul down, and set him before them.

ACTS XXIII. 1—11.

A ND Paul, earnestly beholding the council, said, Men *and* brethren, I have lived in all good conscience before God until this day.

2 And the high priest Ananias commanded them that stood by him to smite him on the mouth.

3 Then said Paul unto him, God shall smite thee, *thou* whited wall: for sittest thou to judge me after the law, and commandest me to be smitten contrary to the law? *(Paul's temper was roused by the unjust conduct of the high priest. His prophecy was fearfully fulfilled: almost at the commencement of the siege of Jerusalem Ananias fell by the daggers of his enemies.*

We cannot help noting the difference between the meek silence of Jesus, and the indignant reply of Paul.)

4 And they that stood by said, Revilest thou God's high priest?

5 Then said Paul, I wist not, brethren, that he was the high priest: for it is written, Thou shalt not speak evil of the ruler of thy people.

6, 7 But when Paul perceived that the one part were Sadducees, and the other Pharisees, he cried out in the council, Men *and* brethren, I am a Pharisee, the son of a Pharisee: of the hope and resurrection of the dead I am called in question. And when he had so said, there arose a dissension between the Pharisees and the Sadducees: and the multitude was divided.

8 For the Sadducees say that there is no resurrection, neither angel, nor spirit: but the Pharisees confess both.

9 And there arose a great cry: and the scribes *that were* of the Pharisees' part arose, and strove, saying, We find no evil in this man: but if a spirit or an angel hath spoken to him, let us not fight against God. *(The apostle obeyed the injunction, "Be ye wise as serpents and harmless as doves." He saw how hopeless it was to plead his cause before so prejudiced an assembly, and therefore he raised another issue. He knew that the Pharisees and Sadducees hated each other even worse than they hated him; and, therefore, he cast in a spark upon their combustible materials, and set them in a blaze. The two parties left their victim, and turned their weapons against each other.)*

10, 11 And when there arose a great dissension, the chief captain, fearing lest Paul should have been pulled in pieces of them, commanded the soldiers to go down, and to take him by force from among them, and to bring *him* into the castle. And the night following the Lord stood by him, and said, Be of good cheer, Paul: for as thou hast testified of me in Jerusalem, so must thou bear witness also at Rome. *(Amid the uncongenial sights and sounds of the barracks, the heart of the apostle would have sunk had it not been for the heavenly visitation. Jesus will not leave his faithful servants alone—he will reveal himself to us when we are in sore distress. Never let us despair, for the Lord has more work for us to do yet.)*

ACTS XXIII. 12—30; 34, 35.

AND when it was day, certain of the Jews banded together, and bound themselves under a curse, saying that they would neither eat nor drink till they had killed Paul. And they were more than forty which had made this conspiracy.

14, 15 And they came to the chief priests and elders, and said, We have bound ourselves under a great curse, that we will eat nothing until we have slain Paul. Now therefore ye with the council signify to the chief captain that he bring him down unto you to morrow, as though ye would enquire something more perfectly concerning him : and we, or ever he come near, are ready to kill him. (*They intended to assassinate him upon the stairs which led down from the fortress to the court. Seldom has a greater crime been contemplated in the name of religion. However, the Lord had a spy upon their secret conclave, and their stratagem was defeated. The deepest designs of hell are frustrated by the Lord.*)

16 And when Paul's sister's son heard of their lying in wait, he went and entered into the castle, and told Paul.

17, 18 Then Paul called one of the centurions unto *him*, and said, Bring this young man unto the chief captain : for he hath a certain thing to tell him. So he took him, and brought *him* to the chief captain, and said, Paul the prisoner called me unto *him*, and prayed me to bring this young man unto thee, who hath something to say unto thee.

19 Then the chief captain took him by the hand, and went *with him* aside privately, and asked *him*, What is that thou hast to tell me ?

20, 21 And he said, The Jews have agreed to desire thee that thou wouldest bring down Paul to morrow into the council, as though they would enquire somewhat of him more perfectly. But do not thou yield unto them : for there lie in wait for him of them more than forty men, which have bound themselves with an oath, that they will neither eat nor drink till they have killed him : and now are they ready, looking for a promise from thee.

22 So the chief captain then let the young man depart, and charged *him*, See thou tell no man that thou hast shewed these things to me.

23, 24 And he called unto *him* two centurions, saying, Make ready two hundred soldiers to go to Cæsarea, and horsemen threescore and ten, and spearmen two hundred, at the third hour of the night ; And provide *them* beasts, that they may set Paul on, and bring *him* safe unto Felix the governor. (*Forty had sworn to murder him, but five hundred protectors are found for him. The angels of the Lord are round about his people, and the Lord can use a band of soldiers for the same purpose. The apostle left Jerusalem attended like a prince: his enemies were powerless to touch a hair of his head. He went down to Cæsarea, and was out of reach of the daggers of his foes.*)

25 And *the chief captain* wrote a letter after this manner :

26—30 Claudius Lysias unto the most excellent governor Felix *sendeth* greeting. This man was taken of the Jews, and should have been killed of them : then came I with an army, and rescued him, having understood that he was a Roman. And when I would have known the cause wherefore they accused him, I brought him forth into their council : Whom I perceived to be accused of questions of their law, but to have nothing laid to his charge worthy of death or of bonds. And when it was told me how that the Jews laid wait for the man, I sent straightway to thee, and gave commandment to his accusers also to say before thee what *they* had against him. Farewell.

34, 35 And when the governor had read *the letter*, he asked of what province he was. And when he understood that *he was* of Cilicia ; I will hear thee, said he, when thine accusers are also come. And he commanded him to be kept in Herod's judgment hall. (*So that he was not put in a public prison, but kept in a room of a palace built by Herod the Great. How he must have admired the manner in which the Lord protected him! Let us trust in God, and be very courageous for the gospel, and the Lord himself will screen us from all harm.*)

From foulest plots and dangers dire,
When earth and hell in league conspire
The Lord preserves his own elect,
And none can harm if he protect.

The Lord will keep thy weakest powers
With his almighty arm ;
And watch thy most unguarded hours
Against surprising harm.

He guards thy soul, he keeps thy breath,
Where thickest dangers come ;
Go and return secure from death,
Till God commands thee home.

The love of Christ doth me constrain
To seek the wandering souls of men ;
With cries, entreaties, tears, to save,
To snatch them from the gaping grave.

For this let men revile my name ;
No cross I shun, I fear no shame :
All hail, reproach ! and welcome, pain !
Only thy terrors, Lord, restrain.

My life, my blood, I here present,
If for thy truth they may be spent :
Thy faithful witness will I be :
'Tis fix'd ! I can do all through thee.

O faint and feeble-hearted !
Why thus cast down with fear :
Fresh aid shall be imparted,
Thy God unseen is near.

His eye can never slumber ;
He marks thy cruel foes,
Observes their strength and number,
And all thy weakness knows.

Alarm'd in vain the truth he hears,
Repentance fatally defers,
And faith in Jesu's name ;
He fancies life is in his power,
Waits for a more convenient hour,
Which never, never came.

Beset with snares on every hand,
In life's uncertain path I stand :
Saviour divine, diffuse thy light,
To guide my doubtful footsteps right.

Engage this roving treacherous heart
To fix on Mary's better part,
To scorn the trifles of a day,
For joys that none can take away.

There's not a tint that paints the rose,
Or decks the lily fair,
Or streaks the humblest flower that blows,
But God has placed it there.

There's not a place on earth's vast round,
In ocean deep, or air,
Where skill and wisdom are not found,
For God is everywhere.

Around, beneath, below, above,
Wherever space extends,
There God displays his boundless love,
And power with mercy blends.

Lov'd of my God, for him again
With love intense I burn :
Chosen of him e'er time began,
I choose him in return.
Whate'er consists not with thy love,
Lord, teach me to resign :
I'm rich to all the intents of bliss,
If thou, O God, art mine.

Oh, to grace how great a debtor
Daily I'm constrain'd to be !
Let that grace, Lord, like a fetter,
Bind my wandering heart to thee.

Prone to wander, Lord, I feel it ;
Prone to leave the God I love—
Here's my heart, Lord, take and seal it,
Seal it from thy courts above.

Wake, harp of Zion, wake again,
Upon thine ancient hill,
On Jordan's long deserted plain,
By Kedron's lowly rill.

The hymn shall yet in Zion swell
That sounds Messiah's praise,
And thy loved name, Immanuel !
As once in ancient days.

For Israel yet shall own her King
For her salvation waits,
And hill and dale shall sweetly sing
With praise in all her gates.

Hasten, O Lord, those promised days,
When Israel shall rejoice ;
And Jew and Gentile join in praise,
With one united voice.

ACTS XXIV. 1—19; 22; 24—27.

AND after five days Ananias the high priest descended with the elders, and *with* a certain orator *named* Tertullus, who informed the governor against Paul.

2, 3 And when he was called forth, Tertullus began to accuse *Paul*, saying, Seeing that by thee we enjoy great quietness, and that very worthy deeds are done unto this nation by thy providence, We accept *it* always, and in all places, most noble Felix, with all thankfulness.

He flattered the detestable Felix, of whom it was hard to say a single good word. To gain their ends men stoop to anything.

4—9 Notwithstanding, that I be not further tedious unto thee, I pray thee that thou wouldest hear us of thy clemency a few words. For we have found this man *a* pestilent *fellow*, and a mover of sedition among all the Jews throughout the world, and a ringleader of the sect of the Nazarenes: Who also hath gone about to profane the temple: whom we took, and would have judged according to our law. But the chief captain Lysias came *upon us*, and with great violence took *him* away out of our hands, Commanding his accusers to come unto thee: by examining of whom thyself mayest take knowledge of all these things, whereof we accuse him. And the Jews also assented, saying, that these things were so.

10—16 Then Paul, after that the governor had beckoned unto him to speak, answered, Forasmuch as I know that thou hast been of many years a judge unto this nation, I do the more cheerfully answer for myself: Because that thou mayest understand, that there are yet but twelve days since I went up to Jerusalem for to worship. And they neither found me in the temple disputing with any man, neither raising up the people, neither in the synagogues, nor in the city: Neither can they prove the things whereof they now accuse me. But this I confess unto thee, that after the way which they call heresy *(or a sect)*, so worship I the God of my fathers, believing all things which are written in the law and in the prophets: And have hope toward God, which they themselves also allow, that there shall be a resurrection of the dead, both of the just and unjust. And herein do I exercise myself, to have always a conscience void of offence toward God, and *toward* men.

17 Now after many years I came to bring alms to my nation, and offerings.

18, 19 Whereupon certain Jews from Asia found me purified in the temple, neither with multitude, nor with tumult. Who ought to have been here before thee, and object, if they had ought against me.

22 And when Felix heard these things, having more perfect knowledge of *that* way, he deferred them, and said, When Lysias the chief captain shall come down, I will know the uttermost of your matter.

24, 25 And after certain days, when Felix came with his wife Drusilla, which was a Jewess, he sent for Paul, and heard him concerning the faith in Christ, And as he reasoned of righteousness, temperance, and judgment to come, Felix trembled, and answered, Go thy way for this time; when I have a convenient season, I will call for thee. *(This aged sinner had enticed Drusilla while a girl of about eighteen from her husband, and was living not only in open sin with her, but also in the commission of every other crime. Paul did well, therefore, to preach to him concerning the judgment: the cowardly voluptuary trembled, but continued in his sins.)*

26 He hoped also that money should have been given him of Paul, that he might loose him: wherefore he sent for him the oftener, and communed with him. *(He longed for bribes, and therefore retained his innocent prisoner. Men will do anything for gain. This man felt the power of Paul's sermon, but loved the wages of sin too well to repent. If we also are saying, " When I have a more convenient season I will call for thee;" is it not because we do not mean to give up our sins?)*

27 But after two years Porcius Festus came into Felix' room: and Felix, willing to shew the Jews a pleasure, left Paul bound.

And thus the apostle remained shut up for two whole years, and then was compelled to appeal unto Cæsar to avoid being taken up to Jerusalem, and murdered on the road. During the time that he waited to be sent to Rome, he was brought before Agrippa. Of his noble speech on that occasion we shall read in our next lesson.

672   " Turn you at my reproof."   NOVEMBER 12.—MORNING.

[*Or September* 22.]

ACTS XXVI.

THEN Agrippa said unto Paul, Thou art permitted to speak for thyself. Then Paul stretched forth the hand, and answered for himself: I think myself happy, king Agrippa, because I shall answer for myself this day before thee touching all the things whereof I am accused of the Jews: Especially *because I know* thee to be expert in all customs and questions which are among the Jews: wherefore I beseech thee to hear me patiently.

4 My manner of life from my youth, which was at the first among mine own nation at Jerusalem, know all the Jews;

5 Which knew me from the beginning, if they would testify, that after the most straitest sect of our religion I lived a Pharisee.

6, 7 And now I stand and am judged for the hope of the promise made of God unto our fathers: Unto which *promise* our twelve tribes, instantly serving *God* day and night, hope to come. For which hope's sake, king Agrippa, I am accused of the Jews.

8 Why should it be thought a thing incredible with you, that God should raise the dead?

9, 10 I verily thought with myself, that I ought to do many things contrary to the name of Jesus of Nazareth. Which thing I also did in Jerusalem: and many of the saints did I shut up in prison, having received authority from the chief priests; and when they were put to death, I gave my voice against *them.*

11 And I punished them oft in every synagogue, and compelled *them* to blaspheme; and being exceedingly mad against them, I persecuted *them* even unto strange cities.

12 Whereupon as I went to Damascus with authority and commission from the chief priests,

13, 14 At midday, O king, I saw in the way a light from heaven, above the brightness of the sun, shining round about me and them which journeyed with me. And when we were all fallen to the earth, I heard a voice speaking unto me, and saying in the Hebrew tongue, Saul, Saul, why persecutest thou me? *it is* hard for thee to kick against the pricks.

15 And I said, Who art thou, Lord? And he said, I am Jesus whom thou persecutest.

16 But rise, and stand upon thy feet: for I have appeared unto thee for this purpose, to make thee a minister and a witness both of these things which thou hast seen, and of those things in the which I will appear unto thee;

17 Delivering thee from the people, and *from* the Gentiles, unto whom now I send thee,

18 To open their eyes, *and* to turn *them* from darkness to light, and *from* the power of Satan unto God, that they may receive forgiveness of sins, and inheritance among them which are sanctified by faith that is in me.

19 Whereupon, O king Agrippa, I was not disobedient unto the heavenly vision:

20 But shewed first unto them of Damascus, and at Jerusalem, and throughout all the coasts of Judæa, and *then* to the Gentiles, that they should repent and turn to God, and do works meet for repentance.

21 For these causes the Jews caught me in the temple, and went about to kill *me.*

22, 23 Having therefore obtained help of God, I continue unto this day, witnessing both to small and great, saying none other things than those which the prophets and Moses did say should come: That Christ should suffer, *and* that he should be the first that should rise from the dead, and should shew light unto the people, and to the Gentiles.

24 And as he thus spake for himself, Festus said with a loud voice, Paul, thou art beside thyself; much learning doth make thee mad.

25 But he said, I am not mad, most noble Festus; but speak forth the words of truth and soberness.

26, 27 For the king knoweth of these things, before whom also I speak freely: for I am persuaded that none of these things are hidden from him; for this thing was not done in a corner. King Agrippa, believest thou the prophets? I know that thou believest.

28 Then Agrippa said unto Paul, Almost thou persuadest me to be a Christian.

29 And Paul said, I would to God, that not only thou, but also all that hear me this day, were both almost, and altogether such as I am, except these bonds.

30 And when he had thus spoken, the king rose up, and the governor, and Bernice, and they that sat with them:

31 And when they were gone aside, they talked between themselves, saying, This man doeth nothing worthy of death or of bonds.

ACTS XXVII. 1—26.

AND when it was determined that we should sail into Italy, they delivered Paul and certain other prisoners unto *one* named Julius, a centurion of Augustus' band. And entering into a ship of Adramyttium, we launched, meaning to sail by the coasts of Asia; *one* Aristarchus, a Macedonian, being with us. And the next *day* we touched at Sidon. And Julius courteously entreated Paul, and gave *him* liberty to go unto his friends to refresh himself.

4—8 And when we had launched from thence, we sailed under Cyprus, because the winds were contrary. And when we had sailed over the sea of Cilicia and Pamphylia, we came to Myra, *a city* of Lycia. And there the centurion found a ship of Alexandria sailing into Italy; and he put us therein. And when we had sailed slowly many days, and scarce were come over against Cnidus, the wind not suffering us, we sailed under Crete, over against Salmone; And, hardly passing it, came unto a place which is called The fair havens; nigh whereunto was the city *of* Lasea.

9—12 Now when much time was spent, and when sailing was now dangerous, because the fast was now already past, Paul admonished *them*. And said unto them, Sirs, I perceive that this voyage will be with hurt and much damage, not only of the lading and ship, but also of our lives. Nevertheless the centurion believed the master and the owner of the ship, more than those things which were spoken by Paul. And because the haven was not commodious to winter in, the more part advised to depart thence also, if by any means they might attain to Phenice, *and there* to winter; *which is* an haven of Crete, and lieth toward the south west and north west.

13, 14 And when the south wind blew softly, supposing that they had obtained *their* purpose, loosing *thence,* they sailed close by Crete. But not long after there arose against it a tempestuous wind, called Euroclydon.

15 And when the ship was caught, and could not bear up into the wind, we let *her* drive.

16, 17 And running under a certain island which is called Clauda, we had much work to come by the boat: Which when they had taken up, they used helps, undergirding the ship; and, fearing lest they should fall into the quicksands, strake sail, and so were driven.

18, 19 And we being exceedingly tossed with a tempest, the next *day* they lightened the ship; And the third *day* we cast out with our own hands the tackling of the ship.

20 And when neither sun nor stars in many days appeared, and no small tempest lay on *us,* all hope that we should be saved was then taken away.

21—26 But after long abstinence Paul stood forth in the midst of them, and said, Sirs, ye should have hearkened unto me, and not have loosed from Crete, and to have gained this harm and loss. And now I exhort you to be of good cheer: for there shall be no loss of *any man's* life among you, but of the ship. For there stood by me this night the angel of God, whose I am, and whom I serve, Saying, Fear not, Paul; thou must be brought before Cæsar; and, lo, God hath given thee all them that sail with thee. Wherefore, sirs, be of good cheer: for I believe God, that it shall be even as it was told me. Howbeit we must be cast upon a certain island.

For the sake of one good man all on board the vessel were preserved. May the Lord give to us, also, all who are with us. Paul was accompanied by Luke and other believers, there were also with him the courteous centurion, several prisoners, a crew of rough sailors, and a band of fierce soldiers, and God gave him all that sailed with him. We pray that all our family, our fellow church members, our servants, our neighbours, our work people, and even our enemies, may be saved. Are not our hearts large enough to pray for all? May the Lord give us faith to intercede for them, and what a joy it will be if all shall come safely through the tempests of this life to the shores of heaven! Grant it, O Lord! Amen and amen.

All that sail with us save, O Lord,
Yea, give us every soul on board;
Parents and children, servants, friends,
To all our fervent prayer extends.

Save from the tempests of this life,
From raging sin and Satan's strife,
Preserve us all by grace divine,
And all the glory shall be thine.

ACTS XXVII. 27—44.

BUT when the fourteenth night was come, as we were driven up and down in Adria, about midnight the shipmen deemed that they drew near to some country ; And sounded, and found *it* twenty fathoms : and when they had gone a little further, they sounded again, and found *it* fifteen fathoms.

29 Then fearing lest we should have fallen upon rocks, they cast four anchors out of the stern, and wished for the day.

30, 31 And as the shipmen were about to flee out of the ship, when they had let down the boat into the sea, under colour as though they would have cast anchors out of the foreship, Paul said to the centurion and to the soldiers, Except these abide in the ship, ye cannot be saved. (*The sailors, under pretence of casting out anchors from the bow, lowered the boat to make their escape, leaving the vessel and all the passengers to certain destruction ; but Paul saw through their cowardly purpose and prevented it. It is a shameful thing to leave others to perish while we can be of any service to them.*)

32 Then the soldiers cut off the ropes of the boat, and let her fall off.

33, 34 And while the day was coming on, Paul besought *them* all to take meat, saying, This day is the fourteenth day that ye have tarried and continued fasting, having taken nothing. Wherefore I pray you to take *some* meat : for this is for your health : for there shall not an hair fall from the head of any of you. (*Picture this one brave man, in the dim twilight, standing in the midst of nearly three hundred haggard faces, speaking so calmly, and giving them such sound advice. Faith ennobles believers, and makes them comforters of others.*)

35 And when he had thus spoken, he took bread, and gave thanks to God in presence of them all : and when he had broken *it*, he began to eat. (*Such calm devotion spreads courage on all sides. If Paul, even in a storm, gave thanks, what shall be said of those persons who rush upon their meals like swine, and never thank the Lord who provides for them ?*)

36 Then were they all of good cheer, and they also took *some* meat.

37 And we were in all in the ship two hundred threescore and sixteen souls.

38 And when they had eaten enough, they lightened the ship, and cast out the wheat into the sea. (*No longer abandoning themselves to despair, they adopted the last means for relieving the vessel, by throwing out the cargo, determining, when thus lightened, to run her on shore.*)

39, 40 And when it was day, they knew not the land : but they discovered a certain creek with a shore, into the which they were minded, if it were possible, to thrust in the ship. And when they had taken up the anchors, they committed *themselves* unto the sea, and loosed the rudder bands, and hoised up the mainsail to the wind, and made toward shore.

41 And falling into a place where two seas met, they ran the ship aground ; and the forepart stuck fast, and remained unmoveable, but the hinder part was broken with the violence of the waves.

42 And the soldiers' counsel was to kill the prisoners, lest any of them should swim out, and escape. (*They were responsible for their safe custody, and would forfeit their own lives if they allowed them to escape ; we need not therefore wonder at the soldiers' cruel proposition.*)

43, 44 But the centurion, willing to save Paul, kept them from *their* purpose ; and commanded that they which could swim should cast *themselves* first *into the sea*, and get to land : And the rest, some on boards, and some on *broken pieces* of the ship. And so it came to pass, that they escaped all safe to land.

Thus was the promise of God kept to the letter : the peril was great, but all were saved from death. God never did forfeit his word, and he never will. It is nothing more than right that we should, without wavering, believe his promises ; and if we do so, our lives will be free from care, and we shall have daily cause for rejoicing. This day may unbelief be cast out, and may childlike confidence rule our spirits.

Jesu, lover of my soul,
Let me to thy bosom fly,
While the nearer waters roll,
While the tempest still is high !
Hide me, O my Saviour, hide,
Till the storm of life be past ;
Safe into the haven guide ;
Oh, receive my soul at last.

ACTS XXVIII. 1—15.

AND when they were escaped, then they knew that the island was called Melita. *(Or Malta.)*

2 And the barbarous people shewed us no little kindness: for they kindled a fire, and received us every one, because of the present rain, and because of the cold. *(Compassion and kindness are such precious things, that the Spirit of God records them in favour of the barbarians: even thus will Jesus remember a cup of cold water given to his disciples. Should not kindness be yet more abundantly found in the followers of Jesus?)*

3 And when Paul had gathered a bundle of sticks, and laid *them* on the fire, there came a viper out of the heat, and fastened on his hand.

He was not too proud to gather sticks, nor should the most eminent Christian think any work beneath him by which he may minister to the comfort of others. It seemed strange that there should be but one viper, and that it should fasten upon the apostle's hand; serpent-bites will wound the most benevolent and holy hands.

4 And when the barbarians saw the *venomous* beast hang on his hand, they said among themselves, No doubt this man is a murderer, whom, though he hath escaped the sea, yet vengeance suffereth not to live. *(So readily do we interpret every accident into a judgment, but such a habit is cruelly unjust to good men. Such an instance as this ought to cure us of crying out "What a judgment!" whenever sudden calamities fall on men. God's judgments are reserved for another world, and are rarely seen in this life.)*

5, 6 And he shook off the beast into the fire, and felt no harm. Howbeit they looked when he should have swollen, or fallen down dead suddenly: but after they had looked a great while, and saw no harm come to him, they changed their minds, and said that he was a god. *(Paul remained unmoved amid the changes of human judgment. Though to men he was a murderer one moment and a god the next, in patience he possessed his soul, unmoved in holy faith. We must not allow the opinions of men to affect our minds, or we shall be changing as the wind.)*

7—9 In the same quarters were possessions of the chief man of the island, whose name was Publius; who received us, and lodged us three days courteously. And it came to pass, that the father of Publius lay sick of a fever and of a bloody flux: to whom Paul entered in, and prayed, and laid his hands on him, and healed him. So when this was done, others also, which had diseases in the island, came, and were healed:

10 Who also honoured us with many honours; and when we departed, they laded *us* with such things as were necessary. *(The shipwreck of the vessel had not shipwrecked the cause of the gospel; on the other hand, it had given to Malta a noble opportunity of hearing the gospel. The apostle well improved his stay.)*

11—14 And after three months we departed in a ship of Alexandria, which had wintered in the isle, whose sign was Castor and Pollux. And landing at Syracuse, we tarried *there* three days. And from thence we fetched a compass, and came to Rhegium: and after one day the south wind blew, and we came the next day to Puteoli: Where we found brethren, and were desired to tarry with them seven days: and so we went toward Rome. *(God has hidden ones everywhere, and there amid the excessive vice of such cities as Pompeii, Naples, Baiæ, and the like, were found saints who met Paul at the landing-place of Puteoli, near which commences the Appian Way, along which he marched towards Rome. The news of his arrival reached the brethren in Rome during the week of Paul's halting at Puteoli, and parties at once set out to meet him. This was thoughtful love, and showed that they were not ashamed to be identified with Christ's suffering servant.)*

15 And from thence, when the brethren heard of us, they came to meet us as far as Appii forum, *(about forty Roman miles from Rome,)* and The three taverns *(about twenty miles)*: whom when Paul saw, he thanked God, and took courage.

Plagues and deaths around me fly,
Till he bids I cannot die:
Nor can deadly serpents kill,
Till it is my Father's will.

O thou Gracious, Wise, and Just,
In thy hands my life I trust:
I am safe, for thou art near;
Wherefore should I yield to fear?

ACTS XXVIII. 16—31.

AND when we came to Rome, the centurion delivered the prisoners to the captain of the guard : but Paul was suffered to dwell by himself with a soldier that kept him. *(He, no doubt, had a house near the Prætorian barracks, and thus enjoyed more liberty than in a prison ; but he had a soldier fastened to his arm by a chain, a cause of constant discomfort, however courteous the soldier might be.)*

17—20 And it came to pass, that after three days Paul called the chief of the Jews together : and when they were come together, he said unto them, Men *and* brethren, though I have committed nothing against the people, or customs of our fathers, yet was I delivered prisoner from Jerusalem into the hands of the Romans. Who, when they had examined me, would have let *me* go, because there was no cause of death in me. But when the Jews spake against *it,* I was constrained to appeal unto Cæsar ; not that I had ought to accuse my nation of. For this cause therefore have I called for you, to see *you,* and to speak with *you :* because that for the hope of Israel I am bound with this chain.

21, 22 And they said unto him, We neither received letters out of Judæa concerning thee, neither any of the brethren that came shewed or spake any harm of thee. But we desire to hear of thee what thou thinkest : for as concerning this sect, we know that every where it is spoken against. *(This has always been the mark of real Christians ; and yet, for all that, they conquer the hearts of men. Christ is set for a sign which shall be spoken against, and to be called " a sect," has been the constant lot of his faithful church.)*

23 And when they had appointed him a day, there came many to him into *his* lodging ; to whom he expounded and testified the kingdom of God, persuading them concerning Jesus, both out of the law of Moses, and *out of* the prophets, from morning till evening. *(Such industry should shame us. Paul was not content with delivering a sermon every day, but kept his house open to inquirers, and poured out continually a stream of holy teaching.)*

24 And some believed the things which were spoken, and some believed not. *(That is always the case, whoever may be the preacher. On the stony ground the seed brings forth no harvest, even though an apostolic hand sows it. To which of the two classes do we belong ? Do we believe ? Or are we unbelievers still ?)*

25—28 And when they agreed not among themselves, they departed, after that Paul had spoken one word, Well spake the Holy Ghost by Esaias the prophet unto our fathers, Saying, Go unto this people, and say, Hearing ye shall hear, and shall not understand ; and seeing ye shall see, and not perceive : For the heart of this people is waxed gross, and their ears are dull of hearing, and their eyes have they closed ; lest they should see with *their* eyes, and hear with *their* ears, and understand with *their* heart, and should be converted, and I should heal them. Be it known therefore unto you, that the salvation of God is sent unto the Gentiles, and *that* they will hear it. *(If we also remain unbelieving, God may take the gospel from us, and send it to others who will accept it. That would be a dreadful thing indeed. How long will it be ere we believe in Jesus ? Do we mean to provoke the Lord to forsake us for ever ?)*

29 And when he had said these words, the Jews departed, and had great reasoning among themselves.

30, 31 And Paul dwelt two whole years in his own hired house, and received all that came in unto him, Preaching the kingdom of God, and teaching those things which concern the Lord Jesus Christ, with all confidence, no man forbidding him. *(Thus Luke, beginning at Jerusalem, closes his narrative at Rome, following the footprints of the gospel from the Mount of Olives to the City of the Seven Hills, and showing how the foundations of the church were laid both in Asia and Europe. What was begun with so much heroism ought to be continued with ardent zeal, since we are assured that the same Lord is mighty still to carry on his heavenly designs.)*

Christ and his cross is all our theme ;
  The mysteries that we speak
Are scandal in the Jew's esteem,
  And folly to the Greek.

But souls enlighten'd from above
  With joy receive the Word ;
They see what wisdom, power, and love
  Shine in their dying Lord.

THE *Epistle to the Romans is one of the greatest of Paul's writings, and is rather a treatise than a letter. It was probably written by him from Corinth, three years before he himself arrived at Rome. Dean Alford says, "There is not a grander thing in literature than this opening of the Epistle to the Romans."*

ROMANS I. 1—23.

1 Paul, a servant of Jesus Christ, called *to be* an apostle, separated unto the gospel of God,

2 (Which he had promised afore by his prophets in the holy scriptures,)

3, 4 Concerning his Son Jesus Christ our Lord, which was made of the seed of David according to the flesh; And declared *to be* the Son of God with power, according to the spirit of holiness, by the resurrection from the dead:

As to his flesh, he was of the seed of David, but his higher nature was by his resurrection manifested most powerfully to be divine. Had he not risen he could not have been God; his resurrection by his own power has made his Godhead plain.

5, 6 By whom we have received grace and apostleship, for obedience to the faith among all nations, for his name: Among whom are ye also the called of Jesus Christ:

7 To all that be in Rome, beloved of God, called *to be* saints: Grace to you and peace from God our Father, and the Lord Jesus Christ.

8 First, I thank my God through Jesus Christ for you all, that your faith is spoken of throughout the whole world.

9—12 For God is my witness, whom I serve with my spirit in the gospel of his Son, that without ceasing I make mention of you always in my prayers; Making request, if by any means now at length I might have a prosperous journey by the will of God to come unto you. For I long to see you, that I may impart unto you some spiritual gift, to the end ye may be established; That is, that I may be comforted together with you by the mutual faith both of you and me. (*Little did he dream that his prayers were to be answered by his being conveyed in chains to the great city. Very mysterious are the Lord's ways of granting our requests.*)

13 Now I would not have you ignorant, brethren, that oftentimes I purposed to come unto you, (but was let *(or hindered)* hitherto,)

that I might have some fruit among you also, even as among other Gentiles.

14 I am debtor both to the Greeks, and to the Barbarians; both to the wise, and to the unwise. (*His office and his gifts placed him in debt to mankind to labour for their conversion, and every Christian, according to his ability, is in the same condition. Are we paying the debts under which the Lord has laid us?*)

15 So, as much as in me is, I am ready to preach the gospel to you that are at Rome also.

He was not afraid of danger, and was willing to come right under the palace walls of Cæsar. In due time his desire became a fact.

16 For I am not ashamed of the gospel of Christ: for it is the power of God unto salvation to every one that believeth; to the Jew first, and also to the Greek.

17 For therein is the righteousness of God revealed from faith to faith: as it is written, The just shall live by faith.

18—20 For the wrath of God is revealed from heaven against all ungodliness and unrighteousness of men, who hold the truth in unrighteousness; Because that which may be known of God is manifest in them; for God hath shewed *it* unto them. For the invisible things of him from the creation of the world are clearly seen, being understood by the things that are made, *even* his eternal power and Godhead; so that they are without excuse.

21—23 Because that, when they knew God, they glorified *him* not as God, neither were thankful; but became vain in their imaginations, and their foolish heart was darkened. Professing themselves to be wise, they became fools, And changed the glory of the uncorruptible God into an image made like to corruptible man, and to birds, and fourfooted beasts, and creeping things. (*They must have known better. No man in his senses can worship birds and beasts without feeling degraded by so doing. Natural reason rebels against such an insult to God, and as they would not listen to its voice the heathen were left to fall into abominable vices. Let us never slight the checks of conscience, lest we should be given over to our own corrupt hearts. No doom could be more terrible.*)

WE shall read at this time a short but very precious portion, in which Paul writes of the high privileges and perfect security of believers.

ROMANS V. 1—11.

1 Therefore being justified by faith, we have peace with God through our Lord Jesus Christ: *Faith lays hold upon the righteousness of Jesus, and so makes us just before the Lord, and this brings a heavenly peace into the soul. No self-confidence can ever do this. Our own good works are faulty, and can neither make peace for us nor work peace in us. What a joy it is to be just before God, because " accepted in the Beloved!" No wonder that the man who is so favoured enjoys peace of soul.*

2 By whom also we have access by faith into this grace wherein we stand, and rejoice in hope of the glory of God. *(Being at perfect peace with God we are enabled to approach him, and in his presence we obtain a fulness of joy. Do we know anything about this ? Let us answer this question each one of us for himself.)*

3 And not only so, but we glory in tribulations also : *(Whatever privileges we enjoy, there are more to follow, and we may add, " and not only so." We come at length to find joy even in our sorrows, since they work our spiritual good.)* knowing that tribulation worketh patience ;

4, 5 And patience, experience ; and experience, hope : And hope maketh not ashamed ; because the love of God is shed abroad in our hearts by the Holy Ghost which is given unto us. *See how one fair stone is piled upon another, course upon course of priceless jewels ; a heavenly character is built up like the very temple of God, and then the love of God comes into it like the divine glory into the holy place, and lights it all up with a celestial splendour. Happy believer to be thus endowed with all the wealth of heaven !*

6 For when we were yet without strength, in due time Christ died for the ungodly. *This is a rich gospel verse in which every word drops fatness. We were powerless, but Jesus came to us, came at the right time, came to die for us, to die for us as godless beings, who had no merit and no fitness for his astounding love. Surely, we must praise him for this, or the very stones will cry out.*

7, 8 For scarcely for a righteous man will one die : yet peradventure for a good *(or benevolent)* man some would even dare to die. But God commendeth his love toward us, in that, while we were yet sinners, Christ died for us. *We were neither righteous nor merciful, we had no claim upon divine love, yet the Lord did all that even infinite love could do, he died for us while we were yet rebels and enemies. Was ever love like this ?*

9 Much more then, being now justified by his blood, we shall be saved from wrath through him. *(When we were enemies he died for us : will he now forsake us, and pour his wrath upon us ? Impossible.)*

10 For if, when we were enemies, we were reconciled to God by the death of his Son, much more, being reconciled, we shall be saved by his life. *(When we were sinners he justified us, will he now leave us ? He reconciled us when we were enemies, will he not save us now that we are his friends ? If his death has done so much, what will not his life do ? The threefold argument is overwhelming ; he cannot, he will not now suffer us to perish. His wrath is turned away, and his love is settled upon us for eternity, if we have believed in Jesus. Have we so believed ? There is the great point.)*

11 And not only so, but we also joy in God through our Lord Jesus Christ, by whom we have now received the atonement. *God himself is now our joy. We dreaded him once, but we do so no more. We are at one with him through Jesus, and the love of God is now the overflowing fountain of joy to us. Again let us each one ask, Is it so with me ? Parents, children, servants, is it so with you ?*

Firm as the earth thy gospel stands,
  My Lord, my hope, my trust ;
If I am found in Jesus' hands,
  My soul can ne'er be lost.

His honour is engaged to save
  The meanest of his sheep ;
All that his heavenly Father gave
  His hands securely keep.

Nor death, nor hell, shall e'er remove
  His favourites from his breast ;
In the dear bosom of his love
  They must for ever rest.

ROMANS VI.

WHAT shall we say then? Shall we continue in sin, that grace may abound? *Because salvation is all of grace shall we plunge into yet more sin? Some of the children of darkness have been vile enough to reason thus: shall the believer adopt the same base argument?*

2 God forbid. How shall we, that are dead to sin, live any longer therein? *(We are new men and cannot delight in sin. Our nature has undergone a change which has made the argument just mentioned most abhorrent to us. We are dead to sin, and have made an open declaration thereof in our baptism: we should be base indeed if we lived to sin as we once did.)*

3—5 Know ye not, that so many of us as were baptized into Jesus Christ were baptized into his death? Therefore we are buried with him by baptism into death: that like as Christ was raised up from the dead by the glory of the Father, even so we also should walk in newness of life. For if we have been planted together in the likeness of his death, we shall be also *in the likeness* of *his* resurrection:

6 Knowing this, that our old man is crucified with *him*, that the body of sin might be destroyed, that henceforth we should not serve sin.

7 For he that is dead is freed from sin.

8 Now if we be dead with Christ, we believe that we shall also live with him:

9 Knowing that Christ being raised from the dead dieth no more; death hath no more dominion over him.

10 For in that he died, he died unto sin once: but in that he liveth, he liveth unto God.

11 Likewise reckon ye also yourselves to be dead indeed unto sin, but alive unto God through Jesus Christ our Lord. *(We are one with Jesus, being both dead with him, and risen in him; ours therefore it is to live the new life, and view ourselves as dead to all the sinful joys of our former lives. Oh for grace to carry this out to the full.)*

12, 13 Let not sin therefore reign in your mortal body, that ye should obey it in the lusts thereof. Neither yield ye your members *as* instruments of unrighteousness unto sin: but yield yourselves unto God, as those that are alive from the dead, and your members *as* instruments of righteousness unto God. *(We cannot obey*

our old tyrant, sin: as citizens of a new kingdom, we must serve our glorious Monarch.)

14 For sin shall not have dominion over you: for ye are not under the law, but under grace. *Being under the law, it cursed you for your iniquity, and in return you transgressed the more; but now eternal love has set you free, and you cannot become again the slaves of sin.*

15 What then? shall we sin, because we are not under the law, but under grace? God forbid.

16 Know ye not, that to whom ye yield yourselves servants to obey, his servants ye are to whom ye obey; whether of sin unto death, or of obedience unto righteousness? *(If indeed we did run into evil because we believed in free grace, it would show that we were still the servants of sin, and not under grace at all.)*

17 But God be thanked, that ye were the servants of sin, but ye have obeyed from the heart that form of doctrine which was delivered you.

18, 19 Being then made free from sin, ye became the servants of righteousness. I speak after the manner of men because of the infirmity of your flesh: for as ye have yielded your members servants to uncleanness and to iniquity unto iniquity; even so now yield your members servants to righteousness unto holiness.

20 For when ye were the servants of sin, ye were free from righteousness.

21 What fruit had ye then in those things whereof ye are now ashamed? for the end of those things *is* death. *(How true is this! We served a bad master for bad wages: shall we not with far greater zeal devote ourselves to the delightful service of our Redeemer?)*

22, 23 But now being made free from sin, and become servants to God, ye have your fruit unto holiness, and the end everlasting life. For the wages of sin *is* death; but the gift of God *is* eternal life through Jesus Christ our Lord. *(Now we do not work for wages: every good thing comes to us as a free gift; therefore let gratitude move us to obedience, and constrain us to be in all things holy before the Lord. Self-interest makes the legalist work; gratitude for eternal love shall be a far stronger force in our hearts, and by the Holy Spirit's help we will abound in good works because grace abounds.)*

ROMANS VII.

KNOW ye not, brethren, (for I speak to them that know the law,) how that the law hath dominion over a man as long as he liveth? *(There is no deliverance from its power but by death; but, blessed be God, we were crucified with Christ, and as new creatures we are under the rule of grace and are not under the dominion of law.)*

2—4 For the woman which hath an husband is bound by the law to *her* husband so long as he liveth; but if the husband be dead, she is loosed from the law of *her* husband. So then if, while *her* husband liveth, she be married to another man, she shall be called an adulteress: but if her husband be dead, she is free from that law; so that she is no adulteress, though she be married to another man. Wherefore, my brethren, ye also are become dead to the law by the body of Christ; that ye should be married to another, *even* to him who is raised from the dead, that we should bring forth fruit unto God. *(Jesus is our husband, grace is the ruling principle of his house, and holiness is the fruit of the marriage. Glory be to God for this!)*

5, 6 For when we were in the flesh, the motions of sins, which were by the law, did work in our members to bring forth fruit unto death. But now we are delivered from the law, that being dead wherein we were held; that we should serve in newness of spirit, and not *in* the oldness of the letter. *(Law provoked our old nature to rebel, grace impels the new nature to obey.)*

7 What shall we say then? *Is* the law sin? God forbid. Nay, I had not known sin but by the law: for I had not known lust, except the law said, Thou shalt not covet.

8 But sin, taking occasion by the commandment, wrought in me all manner of concupiscence. For without the law sin *was* dead.

9, 10 For I was alive without the law once: but when the commandment came, sin revived, and I died. And the commandment, which *was* ordained to life, I found *to be* unto death. *The evil in us resented the divine command, and so the holy law aroused the enmity of our nature, and we rushed on to death. This was not the fault of the law, but of our depraved hearts; yet so it was.*

11 For sin, taking occasion by the commandment, deceived me, and by it slew *me*.

12 Wherefore the law *is* holy, and the commandment holy, and just, and good.

13,14 Was then that which is good made death unto me? God forbid. But sin, that it might appear sin, working death in me by that which is good; that sin by the commandment might become exceeding sinful. For we know that the law is spiritual: but I am carnal, sold under sin.

15 For that which I do I allow not: for what I would, that do I not; but what I hate, that do I. *(Such is our complex condition. We are new creatures, but the old man struggles within us to get the mastery.)*

16, 17 If then I do that which I would not, I consent unto the law that *it is* good. Now then it is no more I that do it, but sin that dwelleth in me. *(The new I sins not, but the old nature is sin, and remains what it always was.)*

18 For I know that in me (that is, in my flesh,) dwelleth no good thing: for to will is present with me; but *how* to perform that which is good I find not.

19 For the good that I would I do not: but the evil which I would not, that I do.

20 Now if I do that I would not, it is no more I that do it, but sin that dwelleth in me.

21 I find then a law *(or rule)*, that, when I would do good, evil is present with me.

22, 23 For I delight in the law of God after the inward man: But I see another law in my members, warring against the law of my mind, and bringing me into captivity to the law of sin which is in my members. *(This is the believer's riddle, which only regenerate men can understand. Do we know what it means?)*

24 O wretched man that I am! who shall deliver me from the body of this death?

25 I thank God through Jesus Christ our Lord. So then with the mind I myself serve the law of God; but with the flesh the law of sin. *(So that on the one hand he agonizes, and on the other hand he triumphs. Loathing sin and glorying in Christ are our daily experience. Groaning after holiness, and finding it in Jesus, we both sigh and sing, repent and rejoice, fight and conquer. This is not a past, but a present experience, and he is a true heir of heaven who feels it within.)*

H E *who comprehends the struggle of the seventh chapter is the man to enjoy the blessed elevation of the eighth. It is well to experience in due order the truths which God reveals, indeed they cannot be rightly known except in their relation the one to the other.*

ROMANS VIII. 1—18.

1 *There is* therefore now no condemnation to them which are in Christ Jesus, who walk not after the flesh, but after the Spirit.

They are not condemned and cannot be. They struggle, they mourn, they weep, but condemned they are not. These happy men are known by their character, the old nature does not rule them, the Holy Spirit guides their lives, both in their secret walk with God and in their public conversation among men.

2 For the law of the Spirit of life in Christ Jesus hath made me free from the law of sin and death.

3 For what the law could not do, in that it was weak through the flesh, God *(has done by)* sending his own Son in the likeness of sinful flesh, and for sin, condemned sin in the flesh :

4 That the righteousness of the law might be fulfilled in us, who walk not after the flesh, but after the Spirit. *(The principle of law produced no holiness in us, but Jesus has condemned sin and created a new life in our hearts, and thus he has brought forth in our lives the conformity to God which legal terrors never produced.)*

5 For they that are after the flesh do mind the things of the flesh; but they that are after the Spirit the things of the Spirit.

6 For to be carnally minded *is* death; but to be spiritually minded *is* life and peace.

7, 8 Because the carnal mind *is* enmity against God: for it is not subject to the law of God, neither indeed can be. So then they that are in the flesh cannot please God. *(Since their mind is enmity to him, their acts cannot please him ; renewed men are at peace with God, and their persons are acceptable to him, and hence their lives please him.)*

9, 10 But ye are not in the flesh, but in the Spirit, if so be that the Spirit of God dwell in you. Now if any man have not the Spirit of Christ, he is none of his. And if Christ *be* in you, the body *is* dead because of sin; but the Spirit *is* life because of righteousness. *(Though our inner nature is transformed, the body still suffers and tempts us to sin ; but even the body is the Lord's and is yet to be changed.)*

11 But if the Spirit of him that raised up Jesus from the dead dwell in you, he that raised up Christ from the dead shall also quicken your mortal bodies by his Spirit that dwelleth in you.

12 Therefore, brethren, we are debtors, not to the flesh, to live after the flesh.

13 For if ye live after the flesh, ye shall die : but if ye through the Spirit do mortify the deeds of the body, ye shall live.

14 For as many as are led by the Spirit of God, they are the sons of God.

15 For ye have not received the spirit of bondage again to fear; but ye have received the Spirit of adoption, whereby we cry, Abba, Father. *(A noble cry, with far more true eloquence in it than all the orations of Cicero and Demosthenes. Can we look up to God and cry "Abba, Father" ? Then are we miracles of divine grace.)*

16 The Spirit itself beareth witness with our spirit, that we are the children of God :

Our new nature claims kinship with God, the Holy Ghost confirms the claim, and hence comes our full assurance.

17 And if children, then heirs ; heirs of God, and joint heirs with Christ ; if so be that we suffer with *him*, that we may be also glorified together. *(This is a chain made of diamond links. It leads us from the cradle of regeneration to the perfection of glory, by sure steps, each one firm as the throne of God. Are we children ? Then we shall be glorified with Christ.)*

18 For I reckon that the sufferings of this present time *are* not worthy *to be compared* with the glory which shall be revealed in us.

Here the rule of proportion is calmly applied, and by heavenly arithmetic it is shown that our present griefs are hardly worth a thought, for eternal glory so infinitely transcends them. Blessed be the Lord God of our salvation for ever and ever. Amen.

> If in my Father's love
> I share a filial part,
> Send down thy Spirit, like a dove,
> To rest upon my heart.

682   " The Spirit also helpeth our infirmities."   NOVEMBER 17.—MORNING.

[Or October 2.]

WE *will now read the concluding verses of that glorious eighth of Romans.*

ROMANS VIII. 26—39.

26 Likewise the Spirit also helpeth our infirmities : for we know not what we should pray for as we ought : but the Spirit itself maketh intercession for us with groanings which cannot be uttered. *(Our ignorance shows itself in prayer, and is our great infirmity, we cannot tell what blessing we most require. What a mercy it is that the Holy Spirit knows all things, and moves us to ask for what is best. Before we pray we should wait upon the Spirit for his guidance, and then we shall go in unto the King with an acceptable petition.)*

27 And he that searcheth the hearts knoweth what *is* the mind of the Spirit, because he maketh intercession for the saints according to *the will* of God. *(So that he inclines our hearts to request the very blessings which the Father has determined to give, and hence our prayers are but the transcripts of the divine decrees.)*

28 And we know that all things work together for good to them that love God, to them. who are the called according to *his* purpose.

29 For whom he did foreknow, he also did predestinate *to be* conformed to the image of his Son, that he might be the firstborn among many brethren.

30 Moreover whom he did predestinate, them he also called : and whom he called, them he also justified : and whom he justified, them he also glorified. *(Like links in a golden chain, each one of the blessings of grace draws on another. The central links are within our view, and if we know them to be ours, we may be sure that the others which belong to the past and the future are securely fastened to them. He who is called is most assuredly predestinated, and shall, beyond all question, be in due time glorified.)*

31 What shall we then say to these things ? If God *be* for us, who *can be* against us ?

32 He that spared not his own Son, but delivered him up for us all, how shall he not with him also freely give us all things ? *This is the master argument in prayer. If we understand its force we shall not be afraid of asking too much.*

33 Who shall lay anything to the charge of God's elect ? *It is* God that justifieth.

34 Who *is* he that condemneth ? *It is* Christ that died, yea rather, that is risen again, who is even at the right hand of God, who also maketh intercession for us.

35, 36 Who shall separate us from the love of Christ ? *shall* tribulation, or distress, or persecution, or famine, or nakedness, or peril, or sword ? *(All these have been tried.)* As it is written, For thy sake we are killed all the day long ; we are accounted as sheep for the slaughter. *(But did they divide the suffering ones from Jesus ?)*

37 Nay, in all these things we are more than conquerors through him that loved us.

So far from being divided from the love of Jesus, the saints were in persecuting times driven closer to their Lord, so that they enjoyed yet sweeter communion with him. No earthly trial can make Jesus forget the souls for whom he died ; he changes not in the purpose of his mind or the affection of his heart.

38 For I am persuaded, that neither death, nor life, nor angels, nor principalities, nor powers, nor things present, nor things to come,

39 Nor height, nor depth, nor any other creature, shall be able to separate us from the love of God, which is in Christ Jesus our Lord.

The apostle began with No CONDEMNATION *and he ends with* No SEPARATION, *filling up the space between with priceless covenant blessings. No chapter in the Bible is more crowded with sublime and consoling teaching. Lord, grant us to know and enjoy all the inestimable privileges which it reveals.*

He lives, he lives, and sits above,
For ever interceding there ;
Who shall divide us from his love ?
Or what shall tempt us to despair ?

Shall persecution, or distress,
Famine, or sword, or nakedness?
He that hath loved us bears us through,
And makes us more than conquerors too.

Faith hath an overcoming power,
It triumphs in the dying hour :
Christ is our life, our joy, our hope ;
Nor can we sink with such a prop.

ROMANS XI. 1—12 ; 25—36.

I SAY then, Hath God cast away his people? God forbid. For I also am an Israelite, of the seed of Abraham, *of* the tribe of Benjamin. *(Personal evidence is best. Paul, as an undoubted Israelite, found in his own conversion the proof that the Lord had not utterly rejected the seed of Abraham.)*

2 God hath not cast away his people which he foreknew. Wot *(or know)* ye not what the scripture saith of Elias ? how he maketh intercession to God against Israel, saying,

3 Lord, they have killed thy prophets, and digged down thine altars ; and I am left alone, and they seek my life.

4 But what saith the answer of God unto him ? I have reserved to myself seven thousand men, who have not bowed the knee to *the image of* Baal. *(Things are often much better with the church of God than wise and good men think they are. They are ready to give up all for lost, when it is not so. God has a remnant still.)*

5, 6 Even so then at this present time also there is a remnant according to the election of grace. And if by grace, then *is it* no more of works : otherwise grace is no more grace. But if *it be* of works, then is it no more grace : otherwise work is no more work. *(This is the gospel in a nutshell. He who remembers these distinctions is on the right road to sound theology.)*

7, 8 What then ? Israel hath not obtained that which he seeketh for ; but the election hath obtained it, and the rest were blinded (According as it is written, God hath given them the spirit of slumber, eyes that they should not see, and ears that they should not hear ;) unto this day. *"It is a dreadful art that some acquire of having eyes and not seeing, of having ears and not hearing, of sleeping on when heaven, earth, and hell are making their souls a battle-field."*

9 And David saith, Let their table be made a snare, and a trap, and a stumbling-block, and a recompence unto them :

10 Let their eyes be darkened, that they may not see, and bow down their back alway.

11 I say then, Have they stumbled that they should fall ? God forbid : but *rather* through their fall salvation *is come* unto the Gentiles, for to provoke them to jealousy.

12 Now if the fall of them *be* the riches of the world, and the diminishing of them the riches of the Gentiles ; how much more their fulness ?

25 For I would not, brethren, that ye should be ignorant of this mystery, lest ye should be wise in your own conceits ; that blindness in part is happened to Israel, until the fulness of the Gentiles be come in. *(Though blindness has happened to Israel in part, yet not to all Israel. The Lord knoweth them that are his, and he will save them by his grace. Better times are, however, coming even for Israel after the flesh, for in the latter days they shall be converted to the Saviour.)*

26, 27 And so all Israel shall be saved : as it is written, There shall come out of Sion the Deliverer, and shall turn away ungodliness from Jacob : For this *is* my covenant unto them, when I shall take away their sins.

28, 29 As concerning the gospel, *they are* enemies for your sakes : but as touching the election, *they are* beloved for the fathers' sakes. For the gifts and calling of God *are* without repentance. *(He never repents of his choice, or changes his purposes of love.)*

30, 31 For as ye in times past have not believed God, yet have now obtained mercy through their unbelief : Even so have these also now not believed, that through your mercy they also may obtain mercy.

32 For God hath concluded them all in unbelief, that he might have mercy upon all. *He shuts them up as condemned by the law, that he may deal with them in a way of grace.*

33—35 O the depth of the riches both of the wisdom and knowledge of God ! how unsearchable *are* his judgments, and his ways past finding out ! For who hath known the mind of the Lord ? or who hath been his counsellor ? Or who hath first given to him, and it shall be recompensed unto him again ?

36 For of him, and through him, and to him, *are* all things : to whom *be* glory for ever. Amen. *(All things are of him, as the efficient cause ; through him, as the disposing cause ; to him, as the final cause. They are of him, without any other motive ; through him, without any assistance ; and to him, without any other end.)*

ROMANS XII.

I BESEECH you therefore, brethren, by the mercies of God, that ye present your bodies a living sacrifice, holy, acceptable unto God, *which is* your reasonable service.

As the pious Jew presented a bullock or a lamb upon the altar, so consecrate ye your whole selves unto the Lord, to live and to die for him. This is his due, and ought to be rendered to him.

2 And be not conformed to this world : but be ye transformed by the renewing of your mind, that ye may prove what *is* that good, and acceptable, and perfect, will of God. *(Mark well that the only way to escape being conformed to the world is to be transformed. The customs of society will lead us away unless the grace of God rules in us with divine power. We are set to prove to the world what the mind of God is : may we have grace to accomplish our mission.)*

3 For I say, through the grace given unto me, to every man that is among you, not to think *of himself* more highly than he ought to think ; but to think soberly, according as God hath dealt to every man the measure of faith.

4, 5 For as we have many members in one body, and all members have not the same office : So we, *being* many, are one body in Christ, and every one members one of another.

6, 7 Having then gifts differing according to the grace that is given to us, whether prophecy, *let us prophecy* according to the proportion of faith ; Or ministry, *let us wait* on *our* ministering : or he that teacheth, on teaching ;

8 Or he that exhorteth, on exhortation : he that giveth, *let him do it* with simplicity ; he that ruleth, with diligence ; he that sheweth mercy, with cheerfulness.

9 *Let* love be without dissimulation. Abhor that which is evil ; cleave to that which is good.

10—13 *Be* kindly affectioned one to another with brotherly love ; in honour preferring one another ; Not slothful in business ; fervent in spirit ; serving the Lord ; Rejoicing in hope ; patient in tribulation ; continuing instant in prayer ; Distributing to the necessity of saints ; given to hospitality. *(Paul writes at full length upon the doctrines, but he is very concise and pithy upon the precepts, for things of daily practice need to be short and easy of remembrance.*

Let us learn each one of these weighty sentences by heart and put them all in practice.)

14 Bless them which persecute you : bless, and curse not.

15, 16 Rejoice with them that do rejoice, and weep with them that weep. *Be* of the same mind one toward another. Mind not high things, but condescend to men of low estate. Be not wise in your own conceits.

17 Recompense to no man evil for evil. Provide things honest in the sight of all men.

18 If it be possible, as much as lieth in you, live peaceably with all men. *(Some people will quarrel, and it is barely possible to keep upon good terms with them. In their case we must do our best, and if, after all, we cannot live peaceably with them, it will be fortunate for us if we can move off and live without them.)*

19—21 Dearly beloved, avenge not yourselves, but *rather* give place unto wrath : for it is written, Vengeance *is* mine ; I will repay, saith the Lord. Therefore if thine enemy hunger, feed him ; if he thirst, give him drink : for in so doing thou shalt heap coals of fire on his head. Be not overcome of evil, but overcome evil with good.

It is recorded of a Chinese emperor that, on being informed that his enemies had raised an insurrection in one of his distant provinces, he said to his officers, " Come, follow me ; and we will quickly destroy them." He marched forward, and the rebels submitted upon his approach. All now thought that he would take the most signal revenge, but were surprised to see the captives treated with mildness and humanity. "How !" cried the first minister, " is this the manner in which you fulfil your promise ? Your royal word was given that your enemies should be destroyed ; and behold ! you have pardoned them all, and even caressed some of them." " I promised," replied the emperor, with a generous air, " to destroy my enemies. I have fulfilled my word ; for see, they are enemies no longer : I have made friends of them." This is a fit example for the Christian.

Forget not thou hast often sinned,
  And sinful yet must be :
Deal gently with the erring one,
  As God has dealt with thee.

ROMANS XIV.

HIM that is weak in the faith receive ye, *but* not to doubtful disputations.

Receive the weak but sincere believer into fellowship, but do not at once commence discussing knotty points with him, or quarrel with him upon matters of no importance.

2, 3 For one believeth that he may eat all things : another, who is weak, eateth herbs. Let not him that eateth despise him that eateth not; and let not him which eateth not judge him that eateth : for God hath received him.

4 Who art thou that judgest another man's servant ? to his own master he standeth or falleth. Yea, he shall be holden up : for God is able to make him stand. *(Matters of meat and drink are to be left to Christian liberty, and no one has any right to dictate to another how he shall act. It is, however, a good rule—" in all cases of doubt be sure to take the surer side.")*

5 One man esteemeth one day above another: another esteemeth every day *alike. (Some kept the Jewish festivals and some did not.)* Let every man be fully persuaded in his own mind.

6 He that regardeth the day, regardeth *it* unto the Lord; and he that regardeth not the day, to the Lord he doth not regard *it.* He that eateth, eateth to the Lord, for he giveth God thanks : and he that eateth not, to the Lord he eateth not, and giveth God thanks.

7 For none of us liveth to himself, and no man dieth to himself. *(No true Christian lives to himself, and therefore as he lives to God we have no right to judge his course of action.)*

8, 9 For whether we live, we live unto the Lord ; and whether we die, we die unto the Lord : whether we live therefore, or die, we are the Lord's. For to this end Christ both died, and rose, and revived, that he might be Lord both of the dead and living. *(The very design of our Lord's work is to make us live unto him and not as the servants of our fellow men ; we are therefore very wrong when we attempt to make our brethren the servants of our opinions and ideas. Let us leave them to serve the Lord as their consciences teach them.)*

10—12 But why dost thou judge thy brother? or why dost thou set at nought thy brother ? for we shall all stand before the judgment seat of Christ. For it is written, *As* I live, saith the Lord, every knee shall bow to me, and every tongue shall confess to God. So then every one of us shall give account of himself to God.

13 Let us not therefore judge one another any more : but judge this rather, that no man put a stumblingblock or an occasion to fall in *his* brother's way.

14 I know, and am persuaded by the Lord Jesus, that *there is* nothing unclean of itself: but to him that esteemeth any thing to be unclean, to him *it is* unclean. *(We must not violate our conscience. We may not do what we believe to be wrong because we see others do it. We must neither judge them nor excuse ourselves.)*

15 But if thy brother be grieved with *thy* meat, now walkest thou not charitably. Destroy not him with thy meat, for whom Christ died.

You have liberty to do as you please, but do not use that liberty if it would be mischievous to your brother in Christ. If your action, though right in itself, would have a tendency to destroy his soul, deny yourself for love's sake.

16, 17 Let not then your good be evil spoken of : For the kingdom of God is not meat and drink; but righteousness, and peace, and joy in the Holy Ghost.

18 For he that in these things serveth Christ *is* acceptable to God, and approved of men.

19 Let us therefore follow after the things which make for peace, and things wherewith one may edify another.

20 For meat destroy not the work of God. All things indeed *are* pure ; but *it is* evil for that man who eateth with offence.

21 *It is* good neither to eat flesh, nor to drink wine, nor *any thing* whereby thy brother stumbleth, or is offended, or is made weak.

22 Hast thou faith ? *(Do you feel quite sure upon such matters ?)* have *it* to thyself before God. *(Keep it within thine own bosom, but do not worry others with it.)* Happy *is* he that condemneth not himself in that thing which he alloweth.

23 And he that doubteth is damned *(or rather condemned)* if he eat, because *he eateth* not of faith : for whatsoever *is* not of faith is sin.

If you are not sure that a thing is right, let it alone, for it will be sin to you.

NOVEMBER 19.—MORNING.

686   "𝕽eceibe ye one another, as 𝕮hrist also receibed us."   [*Or October* 6.]

ROMANS XV. 1—16.

WE then that are strong ought to bear the infirmities of the weak, and not to please ourselves. *(If any course of action which would be safe to us would be dangerous to weaker brethren, we must consider their infirmity and deny ourselves for their sakes.)*

2—4 Let every one of us please *his* neighbour for *his* good to edification. For even Christ pleased not himself; but, as it is written, The reproaches of them that reproached thee fell on me. For whatsoever things were written aforetime were written for our learning, that we through patience and comfort of the scriptures might have hope. *(Jerome says, " Love the scriptures, and wisdom will love thee." Chrysostom says, " Is it not absurd, that in money matters men will not trust to others, but the counters are produced and the sum cast up ; yet, in their soul's affairs, men are led and drawn away by the opinions of others, and this when they have an exact scale and an exact rule, viz., the declaration of the divine laws ? Therefore, I entreat and beseech you all, that, not minding what this or that man may say about these things, you would consult the Holy Scriptures concerning them.")*

5 Now the God of patience and consolation grant you to be likeminded one toward another according to Christ Jesus ;

6 That ye may with one mind *and* one mouth glorify God, even the Father of our Lord Jesus Christ. *(Among Christians there must be unity, and especially in Christian families, so that all our powers may be undividedly employed in praising God. If we are jealous one of another, or use angry language, and quarrelsome words, we cannot glorify God as we ought.)*

7 Wherefore receive ye one another, as Christ also received us to the glory of God. *(If the Lord Jesus has indeed received us, and bears with our weaknesses and follies, well may we have patience with one another, and show pity to each other's infirmities.)*

8 Now I say that Jesus Christ was a minister of the circumcision for the truth of God, to confirm the promises *made* unto the fathers :

Jesus, our Lord, became the servant of the Jews, and preached among them in fulfilment of prophecy ; shall we not become the servants of others for their good ? Nor did his ministry end with Israel ; but we, who are Gentiles, share the blessing ; therefore, like our Lord, we should seek the good of all mankind and live to bless them.*

9 And that the Gentiles might glorify God for *his* mercy ; as it is written, For this cause I will confess to thee among the Gentiles, and sing unto thy name.

10 And again he saith, Rejoice, ye Gentiles, with his people.

11 And again, Praise the Lord, all ye Gentiles ; and laud him, all ye people.

12 And again, Esaias saith, There shall be a root of Jesse, and he that shall rise to reign over the Gentiles ; in him shall the Gentiles trust.

13 Now the God of hope fill you with all joy and peace in believing, that ye may abound in hope, through the power of the Holy Ghost.

14 And I myself also am persuaded of you, my brethren, that ye also are full of goodness, filled with all knowledge, able also to admonish one another.

· 15, 16 Nevertheless, brethren, I have written the more boldly unto you in some sort, as putting you in mind, because of the grace that is given to me of God, That I should be the minister of Jesus Christ to the Gentiles, ministering the gospel of God, that the offering up of the Gentiles might be acceptable, being sanctified by the Holy Ghost. *(As Paul was peculiarly the apostle of the Gentiles, he was the more anxious that in the Gentiles the gospel should produce the acceptable fruit of mutual love. Every man should give most attention to that part of the work with which the Lord has entrusted him, with the one pure motive that God may be glorified thereby. Paul was insatiable for the glory of God and the prosperity of the church ; let us be filled with the same zeal.)*

Lord, if thou hast made us strong,
Let us learn to help the weak ;
Bearing with each other long,
While the good of all we seek.

May we with one heart and mind
Seek the glory of thy name ;
In one sacred league combined,
All our aims and hopes the same.

ROMANS XVI.

I COMMEND unto you Phebe our sister, which is a servant of the church which is at Cenchrea : That ye receive her in the Lord, as becometh saints, and that ye assist her in whatsoever business she hath need of you : for she hath been a succourer of many, and of myself also. *(This godly woman laid herself out for usefulness, and even the apostle was indebted to her. Should not the sisters of the household imitate her ?)*

3—5 Greet Priscilla and Aquila my helpers in Christ Jesus : Who have for my life laid down their own necks : unto whom not only I give thanks, but also all the churches of the Gentiles. Likewise *greet* the church that is in their house. *(Both the heads of the family were saved, hence the household grew into a church.)* Salute my wellbeloved Epenetus, who is the firstfruits of Achaia unto Christ.

6 Greet Mary, who bestowed much labour on us. *(This is the third woman whom Paul commends in this chapter as working for the Lord: sex is no hindrance to service.)*

7 Salute Andronicus and Junia, my kinsmen, and my fellowprisoners, who are of note among the apostles, who also were in Christ before me. *These relatives of Paul were converted before he became a Christian. Did their prayers lead up to his call by grace ?*

8—10 Greet Amplias my beloved in the Lord. Salute Urbane, our helper in Christ, and Stachys my beloved. Salute Apelles approved in Christ. Salute them which are of Aristobulus' household. *(But not Aristobulus. It is sad to find the head of a gracious household himself unsaved.)*

11—13 Salute Herodion my kinsman. Greet them that be of the *household* of Narcissus, which are in the Lord. Salute Tryphena and Tryphosa, who labour in the Lord. *(Two sisters, and both believers. It is well when it is so.)* Salute the beloved Persis, which laboured much in the Lord. Salute Rufus chosen in the Lord, and his mother and mine. *(The mother of Rufus had no doubt been so kind to Paul that he calls her his mother. Love begets love.)*

14, 15 Salute Asyncritus, Phlegon, Hermas, Patrobas, Hermes, and the brethren which are with them. Salute Philologus, and Julia, Nereus, and his sister, and Olympas, and all the saints which are with them.

16 Salute one another with an holy kiss. The churches of Christ salute you.

17—20 Now I beseech you, brethren, mark them which cause divisions and offences contrary to the doctrine which ye have learned ; and avoid them. For they that are such serve not our Lord Jesus Christ, but their own belly; and by good words and fair speeches deceive the hearts of the simple. For your obedience is come abroad unto all *men.* I am glad therefore on your behalf : but yet I would have you wise unto that which is good, and simple concerning evil. And the God of peace shall bruise Satan under your feet shortly. The grace of our Lord Jesus Christ *be* with you. Amen.

21, 22 Timotheus my workfellow, and Lucius, and Jason, and Sosipater, my kinsmen, salute you. I Tertius, who wrote *this* epistle, salute you in the Lord. *(Tertius, the amanuensis, could not help putting in this line for himself. Christianity is the mother of courtesy. Kind words cost little, but are of great value.)*

23, 24 Gaius mine host, and of the whole church, saluteth you. Erastus the chamberlain of the city saluteth you, and Quartus a brother. The grace of our Lord Jesus Christ *be* with you all. Amen. *(Paul cannot finish. He writes postscript after postscript. Letter writing was a serious business in his day, and as he might never be able to write again, he wishes to say all he can. The last postscript is a delightful doxology in which we can heartily unite.)*

25—27 Now to him that is of power to stablish you according to my gospel, and the preaching of Jesus Christ, according to the revelation of the mystery, which was kept secret since the world began, But now is made manifest, and by the scriptures of the prophets, according to the commandment of the everlasting God, made known to all nations for the obedience of faith : To God only wise, *be* glory through Jesus Christ for ever. Amen.

To God the only wise,
Our Saviour and our King,
Let all the saints below the skies,
Their humble praises bring.

PAUL *loved the church in Corinth, but it caused him much pain and trouble through the evils which grew up in it, principally through the erroneous doctrines of Judaizing teachers, the fact that the church had more talent than grace, and that no pastor was raised up to conduct its affairs. We will now read a part of the first chapter of his first epistle.*

I. CORINTHIANS I. 1—17.

1, 2 Paul, called *to be* an apostle of Jesus Christ through the will of God, and Sosthenes *our* brother, Unto the church of God which is at Corinth, to them that are sanctified in Christ Jesus, called *to be* saints, with all that in every place call upon the name of Jesus Christ our Lord, both theirs and ours :

3 Grace *be* unto you, and peace, from God our Father, and *from* the Lord Jesus Christ.

4 I thank my God always on your behalf, for the grace of God which is given you by Jesus Christ ; *(It is always well to acknowledge and commend all the good which we see in our brethren, even though we may discern much to mourn over. They will all the more readily receive our reproofs, if we are just enough to admit and admire their excellencies.)*

5 That in every thing ye are enriched by him, in all utterance, and *in* all knowledge ;

6—8 Even as the testimony of Christ was confirmed in you : So that ye come behind in no gift ; waiting for the coming of our Lord Jesus Christ : Who shall also confirm you unto the end, *that ye may be* blameless in the day of our Lord Jesus Christ.

9 God *is* faithful, by whom ye were called unto the fellowship of his Son Jesus Christ our Lord.

10 Now I beseech you, brethren, by the name of our Lord Jesus Christ, that ye all speak the same thing, and *that* there be no divisions among you ; but *that* ye be perfectly joined together in the same mind and in the same judgment.

11 For it hath been declared unto me of you, my brethren, by them *which are of the house* of Chloe, that there are contentions among you.

If we bring a charge, we should be always willing to give our authority for it and mention the name of the accuser. Those who speak against others, and yet will not allow their names to appear, are unworthy of attention.

12 Now this I say, that every one of you saith, I am of Paul ; and I of Apollos ; and I of Cephas ; and I of Christ. *(Many of the Gentiles stood up for their own apostle; the Judaizers, on the other hand, cried up Peter; a third class were charmed by the eloquence of Apollos, and a fourth party separated from the other three under the professed object of following only Christ. These last appear to have been quite as censurable as the others. Party making in the church of Christ is always evil.)*

13 Is Christ divided ? was Paul crucified for you ? or were ye baptized in the name of Paul ?

14, 15 I thank God that I baptized none of you, but Crispus and Gaius ; Lest any should say that I had baptized in mine own name.

There are some baptized people who make us feel glad that we had no hand in their baptism ; as, for instance, those who rely upon the ordinance, those who live inconsistent lives, and those who sow strife among brethren.

16 And I baptized also the household of Stephanas : besides, I know not whether I baptized any other. *(This is a very singular passage. The apostle was inspired, and yet he made at first a statement which he afterwards corrected, and which he also modified with a hint that there might still be some others who had escaped his memory. This is intended by the Holy Spirit to teach us great carefulness in our statements, for even in small details we ought to speak the truth with the utmost accuracy.)*

17 For Christ sent me not to baptize, but to preach the gospel : not with wisdom of words, lest the cross of Christ should be made of none effect. *(Fine preaching feeds man's pride, plain preaching brings glory to God and benefit to men.)*

Let all the saints terrestrial sing,
    With those to glory gone ;
For all the servants of our King,
    In earth and heaven are one.

One family we dwell in him,
    One church above, beneath,
Though now divided by the stream,
    The narrow stream of death.

I. CORINTHIANS II.

A ND I, brethren, when I came to you, came not with excellency of speech or of wisdom, declaring unto you the testimony of God. For I determined not to know any thing among you, save Jesus Christ, and him crucified. (*This is the one thing needful for us to know. All our reading and studies will be in vain if we are ignorant of Christ and his atoning blood. If Paul the preacher determined to know nothing but this, we may be sure it is above all things important.*)

3—5 And I was with you in weakness, and in fear, and in much trembling. And my speech and my preaching *was* not with enticing words of man's wisdom, but in demonstration of the Spirit and of power : That your faith should not stand in the wisdom of men, but in the power of God. (*If men believed because of the preacher's grand speech, their faith would be good for nothing. If one man can convert you, another can unconvert you. God's power is needed ; no minister can give us faith.*)

6—8 Howbeit we speak wisdom among them that are perfect : yet not the wisdom of this world, nor of the princes of this world, that come to nought : But we speak the wisdom of God in a mystery, *even* the hidden *wisdom,* which God ordained before the world unto our glory : Which none of the princes of this world knew : for had they known *it,* they would not have crucified the Lord of glory.

Simple as the gospel is, it is wisdom itself— more philosophical than philosophy, and more reasonable than human reason's best conclusions.

9, 10 But as it is written, Eye hath not seen, nor ear heard, neither have entered into the heart of man, the things which God hath prepared for them that love him. But God hath revealed *them* unto us by his Spirit : for the Spirit searcheth all things, yea, the deep things of God. (*What reason and imagination could not have conceived, the Holy Spirit has revealed ; spiritual men have an inner eye and ear to which the Spirit grants discernment.*)

11 For what man knoweth the things of a man, save the spirit of man which is in him ? even so the things of God knoweth no man, but the Spirit of God.

12 Now we have received, not the spirit of the world, but the spirit which is of God ; that we might know the things that are freely given to us of God. (*Ours is a spiritual religion, which our new nature receives from the Spirit of God : it is not wrought in us by ceremonies which we can see with our eyes, neither are we persuaded into it by the fair speeches of men, but are taught it by the Holy Spirit himself.*)

13 Which things also we speak, not in the words which man's wisdom teacheth, but which the Holy Ghost teacheth ; comparing spiritual things with spiritual. (*As spiritual men receive the faith by a spiritual work, so they endeavour to spread it by spiritual means only. They reject the pride of learning and the pomp of oratory, and rely upon the Spirit and the truth.*)

14, 15 But the natural man receiveth not the things of the Spirit of God : for they are foolishness unto him : neither can he know *them,* because they are spiritually discerned. But he that is spiritual judgeth (*or discerneth*) all things, yet he himself is judged (*discerned*) of no man.

16 For who hath known the mind of the Lord, that he may instruct him ? But we have the mind of Christ. (*The whole of mankind may correctly be divided into natural and spiritual, and these are as distinct as the dead and the living. The natural man has no spirit, and cannot therefore discern spiritual things. In the new birth a spirit is implanted in us, and thus we gain spiritual faculties, we live in a spiritual atmosphere, and are capable of spiritual joys. Have we received this higher life? Have we the mind of Christ? Lord, work it in us, for Jesus' sake!*)

Mighty Redeemer ! set me free
From my old state of sin ;
Oh, make my soul alive to thee,
Create new powers within.

Renew mine eyes, and form mine ears,
And mould my heart afresh ;
Give me new passions, joys, and fears,
And turn the stone to flesh.

Far from the regions of the dead,
From sin, and earth, and hell,
In the new world that grace has made,
I would for ever dwell.

Teach me, my God and King,
In all things thee to see ;
And what I do in anything,
To do it as for thee.

All may of thee partake,
Nothing so small can be
But draws, when acted for thy sake,
Greatness and worth from thee.

If done beneath thy laws,
E'en servile labours shine ;
Hallowed is toil, if this the cause,
The meanest work, divine.

Allied to thee, our vital Head,
We act, and grow, and thrive :
From thee divided, each is dead
When most he seems alive.

Thy saints on earth, and those above,
Here join in sweet accord :
One body all in mutual love,
And thou our common Lord.

Thou the whole body wilt present
Before thy Father's face !
Nor shall a wrinkle or a spot
Its beauteous form disgrace.

There is a house not made with hands,
Eternal, and on high,
And here my spirit waiting stands,
Till God shall bid it fly.

Shortly this prison of my clay
Must be dissolved and fall :
Then, O my soul ! with joy obey
Thy heavenly Father's call.

'Tis he, by his almighty grace,
That forms thee fit for heaven ;
And, as an earnest of the place,
Has his own Spirit given.

Be not yoked unequally
With the unbelieving race ;
For what concord can there be
With the heirs of sin and grace ?

Sin opposes sanctity ;
Darkness, light doth ever shun,
Right and wrong can ne'er agree,
Christ and Belial ne'er be one.

Wherefore be ye separate,
Nor with sinners hold accord,
While ye in a holy state,
Bear the vessels of the Lord.

Bound by his word, he will display,
A strength proportion'd to our day ;
And, when united trials meet,
Will show a path of safe retreat.

Thus far we prove that promise good,
Which Jesus ratified with blood :
Still he is gracious, wise, and just,
And still in him let Israel trust.

Do I believe what Jesus saith,
And think his gospel true ?
Lord, make me bold to own my faith,
And practise virtue too.

Suppress my shame, subdue my fear,
Arm me with heavenly zeal ;
That I may make thy power appear,
And works of praise fulfil.

If men should see my virtue shine
And spread my name abroad,
Thine is the power, the praise be thine,
My Saviour, and my God.

What have I else whereof to boast ?
A sinner by myself undone,
And still, without thy mercy, lost,
I glory in thy cross alone.

Conform'd to my expiring Head,
I share thy passion on the tree ;
And now I to the world am dead,
And all the world is dead to me.

Go, you that rest upon the law,
And toil and seek salvation there ;
Look to the flame that Moses saw,
And shrink, and tremble, and despair.

But I'll retire beneath the cross ;
Saviour, at thy dear feet I'll lie ;
And the keen sword that Justice draws,
Flaming and red, shall pass me by.

I. CORINTHIANS III.

A ND I, brethren, could not speak unto you as unto spiritual, but as unto carnal, *even as unto babes in Christ. (Being more carnal than spiritual because so weak in grace.)*

2 I have fed you with milk, and not with meat : for hitherto ye were not able *to bear it,* neither yet now are ye able. *(The deeper doctrines cannot be received by the weak, and it is wise to teach such the simpler truths only.)*

3 For ye are yet carnal : for whereas *there is* among you envying, and strife, and divisions, are ye not carnal, and walk as men ?

4 For while one saith, I am of Paul; and another, I *am* of Apollos ; are ye not carnal ?

Every one thinks his party has the kernel, and others only the shell ; whereas they all are apt to let the kernel alone and dispute about the shell, as if that were the kernel.

5, 6 Who then is Paul, and who *is* Apollos, but ministers by whom ye believed, even as the Lord gave to every man ? I have planted, Apollos watered ; but God gave the increase.

7 So then neither is he that planteth any thing, neither he that watereth ; but God that giveth the increase. *(We must not rest in the best of men, or make idols of them ; they are instruments in God's hand, and nothing more. Let us look above the servants to their Master.)*

8 Now he that planteth and he that watereth are one : and every man shall receive his own reward according to his own labour.

9 For we are labourers together with God : ye are God's husbandry, *ye are* God's building.

10 According to the grace of God which is given unto me, as a wise masterbuilder, I have laid the foundation, and another buildeth thereon. But let every man take heed how he buildeth thereupon.

11 For other foundation can no man lay than that is laid, which is Jesus Christ.

12, 13 Now if any man build upon this foundation gold, silver, precious stones, wood, hay, stubble ; Every man's work shall be made manifest : for the day shall declare it, because it shall be revealed by fire ; and the fire shall try every man's work of what sort it is. *(Whatever work we do will be tested, by present opposition, by the lapse of time, by the advance of light, and especially by the judgment of the last great day.)*

14 If any man's work abide which he hath built thereupon, he shall receive a reward.

15 If any man's work shall be burned, he shall suffer loss : but he himself shall be saved ; yet so as by fire. *(Being a good man he shall be saved, but having wasted his life in mistaken work he will lose the fruit of his pains ; and having unwittingly caused injury to others, he will himself barely escape.)*

16, 17 Know ye not that ye are the temple of God, and *that* the Spirit of God dwelleth in you ? If any man defile the temple of God, him shall God destroy ; for the temple of God is holy, which *temple* ye are. *(The doctrine of the indwelling of the Spirit is very wonderful, and also very solemn. What condescension on his part to dwell in us ! How reverently should we entertain such a guest !)*

18 Let no man deceive himself. If any man among you seemeth to be wise in this world, let him become a fool, that he may be wise.

A sense of folly is the doorstep of wisdom. It is needful to leave the world's wisdom if we would know the wisdom of God.

19 For the wisdom of this world is foolishness with God. For it is written, He taketh the wise in their own craftiness.

20 And again, The Lord knoweth the thoughts of the wise, that they are vain.

21, 22 Therefore let no man glory in men. For all things are your's ; Whether Paul, or Apollos, or Cephas, or the world, or life, or death, or things present, or things to come ; all are yours ; *(True Christian teachers, whether Paul, or Apollos, or Cephas, Luther or Calvin, Wesley or Whitfield, belong to the whole church, and every member of the church derives benefit from their teachings. Thus the mind is expanded beyond party limits into a true catholicity.)*

23 And ye are Christ's ; and Christ *is* God's.

How vast the treasure we possess !
How rich Thy bounty, King of grace !
This world is ours, and worlds to come :
Earth is our lodge, and heaven our home.

All things are ours ; the gift of God,
The purchase of a Saviour's blood ;
While the good Spirit shows us how
To use and to improve them too.

692   "Let him that thinketh he standeth, take heed lest he fall."   NOVEMBER 21.—EVENING.

[*Or October* 11.]

I. CORINTHIANS X. 12—33.

IN *this tenth chapter of his epistle Paul mentions the sins and chastisement of ancient Israel, and then adds—*

12 Let him that thinketh he standeth take heed lest he fall.

13 There hath no temptation taken you but such as is common to man : but God *is* faithful, who will not suffer you to be tempted above that ye are able ; but will with the temptation also make a way to escape, that ye may be able to bear *it*. *(If our temptations were such as none else had ever endured, and there were no way out of them, we might give up in despair; but it is not so. The Lord will not try us too much, too long, or too often. Grace will bear us through.)*

14, 15 Wherefore, my dearly beloved, flee from idolatry. I speak as to wise men ; judge ye what I say. *(Idolatry in every form is to be avoided by us, and in these days especially we must avoid all participation in the Popish ritualistic idolatry which is becoming so common. All bowing before the cross or the wafer, and all attendance upon such idolatrous worship must be abhorred by the faithful.)*

16, 17 The cup of blessing which we bless, is it not the communion of the blood of Christ ? The bread which we break, is it not the communion of the body of Christ ? For we *being* many are one bread, *and* one body : for we are all partakers of that one bread.

18 Behold Israel after the flesh : are not they which eat of the sacrifices partakers of the altar ?

19, 20 What say I then ? that the idol is any thing, or that which is offered in sacrifice to idols is any thing ? But *I say*, that the things which the Gentiles sacrifice, they sacrifice to devils, and not to God : and I would not that ye should have fellowship with devils. *(As both among Christians and Jews the partaking of holy feasts involved fellowship, so if we join with idolaters we have fellowship with them and shall be sharers in their sin.)*

21 Ye cannot drink the cup of the Lord, and the cup of devils : ye cannot be partakers of the Lord's table, and of the table of devils.

22 Do we provoke the Lord to jealousy ? are we stronger than he ? *(Communion with the unholy is a challenge to Christ, an open defiance to his kingship.)*

23—26 All things are lawful for me, but all things are not expedient : all things are lawful for me, but all things edify not. Let no man seek his own, but every man another's *wealth*. Whatsoever is sold in the shambles, *that* eat, asking no question for conscience sake : For the earth *is* the Lord's, and the fulness thereof.

27 If any of them that believe not bid you *to a feast*, and ye be disposed to go ; whatsoever is set before you, eat, asking no question for conscience sake. *(There could be no harm in the meat itself, and the believer was free to eat what was set before him so far as he himself was concerned, but there were times when it would be better not to eat it, lest in the judgment of others the Christian should seem to have communed in an idolatrous sacrifice.)*

28, 29 But if any man say unto you, This is offered in sacrifice unto idols, eat not for his sake that shewed it, and for conscience sake : for the earth *is* the Lord's, and the fulness thereof : Conscience, I say, not thine own, but of the other : for why is my liberty judged of another *man's* conscience ?

30 For if I by grace be a partaker, why am I evil spoken of for that for which I give thanks ?

31 Whether therefore ye eat, or drink, or whatsoever ye do, do all to the glory of God.

(This is the rule at the table ; let us always observe it. Much evil may come out of eating and drinking : it was by eating that man first fell from innocence. The table must be watched lest it become a snare unto us.)

32, 33 Give none offence, neither to the Jews, nor to the Gentiles, nor to the church of God : Even as I please all *men* in all *things*, not seeking mine own profit, but the *profit* of many, that they may be saved. *(What we may do lawfully it will frequently be better not to do lest we injure others : for their sakes we must deny ourselves, for selfishness in a Christian is a grievous vice.)*

Gracious Lord, implant in me
Pure celestial charity ;
Let my every word and deed
From a loving heart proceed.

Let the touch of love divine
Make my meanest actions shine ;
That in all things I may be
Full of love, and like to Thee.

I. CORINTHIANS XII.

NOW concerning spiritual *gifts*, brethren, I would not have you ignorant.

2, 3 Ye know that ye were Gentiles, carried away unto these dumb idols, even as ye were led. Wherefore I give you to understand, that no man speaking by the Spirit of God calleth Jesus accursed: and *that* no man can say that Jesus is the Lord, but by the Holy Ghost.

> "'*What think you of Christ?' is the test*
> *To try both your state and your scheme;*
> *You cannot be right in the rest,*
> *Unless you think rightly of him.*"

4, 5 Now there are diversities of gifts, but the same Spirit. And there are differences of administrations, but the same Lord.

6 And there are diversities of operations, but it is the same God which worketh all in all.

7 But the manifestation of the Spirit is given to every man to profit withal. (*We are neither born nor born again for ourselves. Like bees, we must all bring honey to the common hive.*)

8—12 For to one is given by the Spirit the word of wisdom; to another the word of knowledge by the same Spirit; To another faith by the same Spirit; to another the gifts of healing by the same Spirit; To another the working of miracles; to another prophecy; to another discerning of spirits; to another *divers* kinds of tongues; to another the interpretation of tongues: But all these worketh that one and the selfsame Spirit, dividing to every man severally as he will. For as the body is one, and hath many members, and all the members of that one body, being many, are one body: so also *is* Christ. (*Meaning thereby, Christ mystical, or the church.*)

13 For by one Spirit are we all baptized into one body, whether *we be* Jews or Gentiles, whether *we be* bond or free; and have been all made to drink into one Spirit.

14—16 For the body is not one member, but many. If the foot shall say, Because I am not the hand, I am not of the body; is it therefore not of the body? And if the ear shall say, Because I am not the eye, I am not of the body; is it therefore not of the body? (*None of us, therefore, may despise another, because he does not happen to have our gifts. Variety in each is necessary to the completeness of the whole.*)

17—21 If the whole body *were* an eye, where *were* the hearing? If the whole *were* hearing, where *were* the smelling? But now hath God set the members every one of them in the body, as it hath pleased him. And if they were all one member, where *were* the body? But now *are they* many members, yet but one body. And the eye cannot say unto the hand, I have no need of thee: nor again the head to the feet, I have no need of you.

22, 23 Nay, much more those members of the body, which seem to be more feeble, are necessary: And those *members* of the body, which we think to be less honourable, upon these we bestow more abundant honour; and our uncomely *parts* have more abundant comeliness.

We cover with great care those parts of the body which are either tender or unsightly, and so those Christians who are feeble and faulty should receive the more of our kind care, lest the whole body should be injured through their means.

24, 25 For our comely *parts* have no need: but God hath tempered the body together, having given more abundant honour to that *part* which lacked: That there should be no schism in the body; but *that* the members should have the same care one for another.

26 And whether one member suffer, all the members suffer with it; or one member be honoured, all the members rejoice with it.

27 Now ye are the body of Christ, and members in particular.

28 And God hath set some in the church, first apostles, secondarily prophets, thirdly teachers, after that miracles, then gifts of healings, helps, governments, diversities of tongues.

29 *Are* all apostles? *are* all prophets? *are* all teachers? *are* all workers of miracles?

30 Have all the gifts of healing? do all speak with tongues? do all interpret?

31 But covet earnestly the best gifts: and yet shew I unto you a more excellent way.

What was that which was better than the best? Love to God and man. Graces are better than gifts. A heart full of holy love is a far better endowment than a head full of the clearest knowledge, or a tongue overflowing with utterance. Whatever way we cannot run in, let us make sure walking in the "more excellent way" of love.

694   " Watch ye, stand fast in the faith."   November 22.—Evening.

[*Or October* 13.]

THE *apostle had written that glowing chapter upon the resurrection which we have read on a former occasion, but he did not consider it at all unseemly to close his letter with a few words upon " the collection." To give of our substance to the poor, or to the cause of Jesus, if done in a right spirit, is one of the highest acts of worship—a deed of love which angels might envy us our power to perform. Is it not wonderful that God should condescend to receive a gift at his creatures' hands?*

I. CORINTHIANS XVI. 1, 2 ; 6—24.

1 Now concerning the collection for the saints, as I have given order to the churches of Galatia, even so do ye.

2 Upon the first *day* of the week let every one of you lay by him in store, as *God* hath prospered him, that there be no gatherings when I come. *(Weekly storing is a most healthful Christian practice. If we were to put a portion into the Lord's bag every Sabbath, we should always have money in hand to give to deserving objects.)*

6, 7 And it may be that I will abide, yea, and winter with you, that ye may bring me on my journey whithersoever I go. For I will not see you now by the way ; but I trust to tarry a while with you, if the Lord permit.

8 But I will tarry at Ephesus until Pentecost.

9 For a great door and effectual is opened unto me, and *there are* many adversaries.

10 Now if Timotheus come,.see that he may be with you without fear : for he worketh the work of the Lord, as I also *do*.

11 Let no man therefore despise him : but conduct him forth in peace, that he may come unto me : for I look for him with the brethren. *Timothy was young, and therefore some might slight him : it is pleasing to see how the apostle thus protects him, and requests respect for him. The old should be considerate for the young.*

12 As touching *our* brother Apollos, I greatly desired him to come unto you with the brethren : but his will was not at all to come at this time ; but he will come when he shall have convenient time. *(He does not blame Apollos for declining to grant his request, but puts a kind construction upon his action, and is sure that he will visit them when he can. Always think the best you can of others.)*

13 Watch ye, stand fast in the faith, quit you like men, be strong.

14 Let all your things be done with charity.

15, 16 I beseech you, brethren, (ye know the house of Stephanas, that it is the firstfruits of Achaia, and *that* they have addicted themselves to the ministry of the saints,) That ye submit yourselves unto such, and to every one that helpeth with *us*, and laboureth. *This would be one of the best cures for the disorders which had marred their church ! Watchful pastors are necessary to churches, and those are wrong who attempt to set up assemblies in which all rule, and none submit.*

17, 18 I am glad of the coming of Stephanas and Fortunatus and Achaicus : for that which was lacking on your part they have supplied. For they have refreshed my spirit and yours : therefore acknowledge ye them that are such.

19 The churches of Asia salute you. Aquila and Priscilla salute you much in the Lord, with the church that is in their house.

20 All the brethren greet you. Greet ye one another with an holy kiss. *(Not with a hollow kiss of hypocrisy, or an unholy kiss of wantonness. A shake of the hand is our western substitute for the kiss ; and a good hearty shake of the hand is a noble sign of Christian fellowship.)*

21 The salutation of *me* Paul with mine own hand. *(To prevent imposture the apostle took the pen out of the writer's hand, and wrote the last few lines himself.)*

22 If any man love not the Lord Jesus Christ, let him be Anathema Maran-atha *(or* ACCURSED WHEN THE LORD COMETH).

23, 24 The grace of our Lord Jesus Christ *be* with you. My love *be* with you all in Christ Jesus. Amen. *(A sweet conclusion. He had been obliged to write sharply, but it was all in love. May love be lord of this dear home.)*

Our God is love, and all his saints
   His image bear below ;
The heart with love to God inspired,
   With love to man will glow.

Oh, may we love each other, Lord,
   As we are loved of thee :
For none are truly born of God,
   Who live in enmity.

THE *Second Epistle to the Corinthians was written by Paul from Macedonia, after Titus had returned from Corinth, and informed him how the Corinthian church had received his first letter. The news was of a mingled kind, and caused him both joy and sorrow. The apostle seems at the time of writing it to have been much troubled and perplexed. We shall commence our reading with the fourth chapter.*

II. CORINTHIANS IV.

1, 2 Therefore seeing we have this ministry, as we have received mercy, we faint not; But have renounced the hidden things of dishonesty, not walking in craftiness, nor handling the word of God deceitfully; but by manifestation of the truth commending ourselves to every man's conscience in the sight of God. *(All underhand dealing and trickery Paul denounced. He said what he meant, and meant what he said. If we cannot spread the truth by plain speech, we cannot spread it at all.)*

3, 4 But if our gospel be hid, it is hid to them that are lost: In whom the god of this world hath blinded the minds of them which believe not, lest the light of the glorious gospel of Christ, who is the image of God, should shine unto them. *(If men do not understand the gospel, we must take care that the fault does not lie in our language; but wholly with their blinded carnal hearts.)*

5, 6 For we preach not ourselves, but Christ Jesus the Lord; and ourselves your servants for Jesus' sake. For God, who commanded the light to shine out of darkness, hath shined in our hearts, to *give* the light of the knowledge of the glory of God in the face of Jesus Christ.

7 But we have this treasure in earthen vessels, that the excellency of the power may be of God, and not of us. *(The weakness of the preacher only shows the power of God when he uses such poor means to accomplish so great an end. Never let us refuse to do good because our abilities are slender; let us the rather yield up our weakness unto the Lord that he may use it to his own glory.)*

8—11 *We are* troubled on every side, yet not distressed; *we are* perplexed, but not in despair; Persecuted, but not forsaken; cast down, but not destroyed; Always bearing about in the body the dying of the Lord Jesus, that the life also of Jesus might be made manifest in our body. For we which live are alway delivered unto death for Jesus' sake, that the life also of Jesus might be made manifest in our mortal flesh.

12 So then death worketh in us, but life in you. *(Paul rejoiced that good came to them by his sufferings. He loved them even as a mother who strips off her own raiment, and exposes herself to the cold to screen her child.)*

13, 14 We having the same spirit of faith, according as it is written, I believed, and therefore have I spoken; we also believe, and therefore speak; Knowing that he which raised up the Lord Jesus shall raise up us also by Jesus, and shall present *us* with you. *(He feared not death, for he expected resurrection.)*

15 For all things *are* for your sakes, that the abundant grace might through the thanksgiving of many redound to the glory of God.

16 For which cause we faint not; but though our outward man perish, yet the inward *man* is renewed day by day. *(His ruling passion was God's glory, and this sustained him under sickness, depression, and persecution.)*

17, 18 For our light affliction, which is but for a moment, worketh for us a far more exceeding *and* eternal weight of glory; While we look not at the things which are seen, but at the things which are not seen: for the things which are seen *are* temporal; but the things which are not seen *are* eternal. *(See how little Paul makes of trial; he calls it light and momentary; but how much he makes of glory! he labours for expressions, he cannot with the utmost exertion deliver himself. The way to live above trouble is to look up: we shall grow giddy if we look down upon earthly things, for they are tossed to and fro like waves of the sea.)*

Afflictions may press me, they cannot destroy,
One glimpse of his love turns them all into joy;
And the bitterest tears, if he smile but on them,
Like dew in the sunshine, grow diamond and gem.

A scrip on my back, and a staff in my hand,
I march on in haste through an enemy's land;
The road may be rough, but it cannot be long,
So I'll smooth it with hope, and cheer it with song.

696   " Willing rather to be absent from the body, and to be present with the Lord."   NOVEMBER 23.—EVENING.

[*Or October* 15.]

II. CORINTHIANS V.

FOR we know *(not we think or hope only, but we know)* that if our earthly house of *this* tabernacle were dissolved, we have a building of God, an house not made with hands, eternal in the heavens. *(Our clay cottage will come down, but our heavenly mansion is ready to receive us.)*

2—4 For in this we groan, earnestly desiring to be clothed upon with our house which is from heaven : If so be that being clothed we shall not be found naked. For we that are in *this* tabernacle do groan, being burdened : not for that we would be unclothed, but clothed upon, that mortality might be swallowed up of life. *(We cannot be satisfied here, for we are exiled from the glory land and compassed with infirmities. We await with expectation the summons, " Rise up and come away.")*

5 Now he that hath wrought us for the self-same thing *is* God, who also hath given unto us the earnest of the Spirit. *(God is preparing us for heaven, and has given us already a sure pledge of it in the possession of the Holy Ghost.)*

6, 7 Therefore *we are* always confident, knowing that, whilst we are at home in the body, we are absent from the Lord : (For we walk by faith, not by sight :)

8 We are confident, *I say,* and willing rather to be absent from the body, and to be present with the Lord. *(The exile longs to return, the child pines for his father's house, and so do we pant for our own dear country beyond the river, and sigh for the bosom of Jesus.)*

9 Wherefore we labour, that, whether present or absent, we may be accepted of him.

10 For we must all appear before the judgment seat of Christ ; that every one may receive the things *done* in *his* body, according to that he hath done, whether *it be* good or bad. *With this is view, we cannot afford to trifle or to sin. Every day should be viewed in the light of the last day, and then we shall live as we should.*

11 Knowing therefore the terror of the Lord, we persuade men ; but we are made manifest unto God ; and I trust also are made manifest in your consciences.

12 For we commend not ourselves again unto you, but give you occasion to glory on our be-half, that ye may have somewhat to *answer* them which glory in appearance, and not in heart.

13 For whether we be beside ourselves, *it is* to God : or whether we be sober, *it is* for your cause. *(The apostle did everything for Jesus and his church, and if any blamed his actions, he bade them remember that love to them was the sole motive of all he did.)*

14 For the love of Christ constraineth us ; because we thus judge, that if one died for all, then were all dead *(or rather, all died)* :

15 And *that* he died for all, that they which live should not henceforth live unto themselves, but unto him which died for them, and rose again. *(The death of Jesus for us has made us reckon ourselves dead to all but him, and for him alone would we exist.)*

16 Wherefore henceforth know we no man after the flesh : yea, though we have known Christ after the flesh, yet now henceforth know we *him* no more. *(Everything was spiritual, even his sight of Jesus with his mortal eyes was no longer cared for, in comparison with faith's view of him after a spiritual fashion.)*

17 Therefore if any man *be* in Christ, *he is* a new creature : old things are passed away ; behold, all things are become new.

18, 19 And all things *are* of God, who hath reconciled us to himself by Jesus Christ, and hath given to us the ministry of reconciliation ; To wit, that God was in Christ, reconciling the world unto himself, not imputing their trespasses unto them ; and hath committed unto us the word of reconciliation.

20 Now then we are ambassadors for Christ, as though God did beseech *you* by us : we pray *you* in Christ's stead, be ye reconciled to God.

21 For he hath made him *to be* sin for us, who knew no sin ; that we might be made the righteousness of God in him. *(Are we thus made righteous ? These verses are wonderfully weighty : do we understand them by personal experience ? Are we new creatures, reconciled by Jesus' blood, accepted in the Beloved, and one with him ? These are points which demand immediate inquiry.)*

II. CORINTHIANS VI.

WE then, *as* workers together *with him*, beseech *you* also that ye receive not the grace of God in vain. (For he saith, I have heard thee in a time accepted, and in the day of salvation have I succoured thee : behold, now *is* the accepted time ; behold, now *is* the day of salvation.) *(The apostle was therefore anxious that none should hear the gracious word of God without obtaining eternal life. He also longed to see the truly saved more and more fruitful, that it might not even seem that God's grace had been ineffectual in their lives and characters. No minister can be satisfied unless grace is seen to produce fitting results in those who profess to partake of it.)*

3 Giving no offence in any thing, that the ministry be not blamed :

4 But in all *things* approving ourselves as the ministers of God, in much patience, in afflictions, in necessities, in distresses,

5 In stripes, in imprisonments, in tumults, in labours, in watchings, in fastings ;

6, 7 By pureness, by knowledge, by long suffering, by kindness, by the Holy Ghost, by love unfeigned, By the word of truth, by the power of God, by the armour of righteousness on the right hand and on the left,

8 By honour and dishonour, by evil report and good report : as deceivers, and *yet* true ;

9 As unknown, and *yet* well known ; as dying, and behold, we live ; as chastened, and not killed ;

10 As sorrowful, yet alway rejoicing ; as poor, yet making many rich ; as having nothing, and *yet* possessing all things. *(Dr. Hawker, himself a minister of the Church of England, has beautifully said :—" What a lovely portrait the apostle hath here drawn of a minister of Jesus ! How totally dissimilar in every feature, from the rank and opulence of modern prelacy ! Who should have thought, when Paul wrote this epistle to the church at Corinth, that a time would come when state and grandeur would be considered suitable appendages to the sacred order ! Great part of what the apostle hath here said, concerning the 'all things,' in which he recommends the Lord's servants to approve themselves, as ministers of God, is done away. How is it possible, for such as the present hour furnisheth, to*

manifest whose servants they are, in stripes, in imprisonment, in tumults, labours, watchings, fastings, and the like ? But there are some of the characters of the ministry, which the apostle hath sketched in this picture, still to be found. 'By honour and dishonour, by evil report and good report : as deceivers, and yet true ; As unknown, and yet well known.' Some in every age of the world will be found to treat the distinguishing truths of the gospel with hatred and contempt ; and to dishonour the preachers of those truths, with evil report and reproach. While the highly-taught few, whom God the Holy Ghost teacheth, will honour his messengers. . . . . . Reader, learn from this portrait of the apostle's, and drawn under God the Spirit's direction, to form an estimate of the Lord's ministers: not by outward show, but by the inward illumination of the heart, and the blessing of God on their labours, both in word and doctrine.")

11 O *ye* Corinthians, our mouth is open unto you, our heart is enlarged.

12 Ye are not straitened in us, but ye are straitened in your own bowels.

13 Now for a recompence in the same, (I speak as unto *my* children,) be ye also enlarged.

14, 15 Be ye not unequally yoked together with unbelievers *(either in marriage or any other intimate union) :* for what fellowship hath righteousness with unrighteousness ? and what communion hath light with darkness ? And what concord hath Christ with Belial? or what part hath he that believeth with an infidel ?

16 And what agreement hath the temple of God with idols ? for ye are the temple of the living God ; as God hath said, I will dwell in them, and walk in *them ;* and I will be their God, and they shall be my people.

17 Wherefore come out from among them, and be ye separate, saith the Lord, and touch not the unclean *thing ;* and I will receive you,

18 And will be a Father unto you, and ye shall be my sons and daughters, saith the Lord Almighty. *(The great duty of believers in all ages is to maintain their character as a separate people, no more conformed to the world. May this family never fall into worldly fashions, amusements, or pursuits, but be distinguished as following the Lord fully ; so shall we be peculiarly dear to our heavenly Father.)*

698   *"Not unto us, O Lord, but unto Thy name give glory."*   NOVEMBER 24.—EVENING.

[Or October 17.]

II. CORINTHIANS XI. 1—9 ; 23—30.

WOULD to God ye could bear with me a little in *my* folly: and indeed bear with me. *(Paul was not pleased to have to speak of himself; he calls self-commendation folly, for so it usually is; but it was needful for him to vindicate his position and authority, in order that his letters might have weight with the Corinthian believers for their lasting good.)*

2, 3 For I am jealous over you with godly jealousy: for I have espoused you to one husband, that I may present *you as* a chaste virgin to Christ. But I fear, lest by any means, as the serpent beguiled Eve through his subtilty, so your minds should be corrupted from the simplicity that is in Christ. *(By the admixture of philosophy with the gospel, he feared that they would be seduced from the truth. Too much ground is there for the same anxiety about the churches of our own day.)*

4 For if he that cometh preacheth another Jesus, whom we have not preached, or *if* ye receive another spirit, which ye have not received, or another gospel, which ye have not accepted, ye might well bear with *him*.

If any man could bring us a better gospel, more sure, more full, more free, we might listen to his novelties; but so long as this is not attempted or pretended, we will abide by the old form of doctrine, and those men of God who preach it.

5, 6 For I suppose I was not a whit behind the very chiefest apostles. But though *I be* rude in speech, yet not in knowledge; but we have been throughly made manifest among you in all things.

7 Have I committed an offence in abasing myself that ye might be exalted, because I have preached to you the gospel of God freely?

8 I robbed other churches, taking wages *of them*, to do you service. *(He received nothing from the Corinthians, but allowed other churches to relieve his necessities that he might in no degree burden them; yet they were not grateful, but spoke of him disrespectfully. Gratitude is far too rare even among professing Christians.)*

9 And when I was present with you, and wanted, I was chargeable to no man: for that which was lacking to me the brethren which came from Macedonia supplied: and in all *things* I have kept myself from being burdensome unto you, and *so* will I keep *myself*.

The apostle, to vindicate his character and prove his apostleship, then mentioned what he had done and suffered.

23 Are they ministers of Christ? (I speak as a fool) I *am* more; *(He was called in a more remarkable way, had been more fully instructed, and enabled to accomplish more than any one of them.)* in labours more abundant, in stripes above measure, *(or far exceeding any one else,)* in prisons more frequent, in deaths oft.

24—27 Of the Jews five times received I forty *stripes* save one. Thrice was I beaten with rods, once was I stoned, thrice I suffered shipwreck, a night and a day I have been in the deep; *In* journeyings often, *in* perils of waters, *in* perils of robbers, *in* perils by *mine own* countrymen, *in* perils by the heathen, *in* perils in the city, *in* perils in the wilderness, *in* perils in the sea, *in* perils among false brethren; In weariness and painfulness, in watchings often, in hunger and thirst, in fastings often, in cold and nakedness.

28 Beside those things that are without, that which cometh upon me *(or rushes upon me)* daily, the care of all the churches. *(Which was a heavy burden; there were so many things to think about, that his mind was wearied.)*

29 Who is weak, and I am not weak? who is offended, and I burn not? *(He sympathized with all, and was the focus for all sorrows.)*

30 If I must needs glory, I will glory of the things which concern mine infirmities.

Surely after this recital these Corinthians would value the apostle, and trouble him no more with their criticisms. Better far is it for us to profit by good men than to find fault with them. Let not the Pauls among us now have to suffer for our unkindness.

When trials sore obstruct my way,
    And ills I cannot flee,
Oh, give me strength, Lord, as my day:
    For good remember me.

If on my face, for thy dear name,
    Shame and reproaches be,
All hail, reproach! and welcome, shame!
    If thou remember me.

II. CORINTHIANS XII. 1—19.

IT is not expedient for me doubtless to glory. I will come to visions and revelations of the Lord. (*The most modest man may be driven to speak his own praises if his usefulness is jeopardised by the depreciations of enemies.*)

2—4 I knew a man in Christ above fourteen years ago, (whether in the body, I cannot tell; or whether out of the body, I cannot tell: God knoweth;) such an one caught up to the third heaven. And I knew such a man, (whether in the body, or out of the body, I cannot tell: God knoweth;) How that he was caught up into paradise, and heard unspeakable words, which it is not lawful for a man to utter.

5 Of such an one will I glory: yet of myself I will not glory, but in mine infirmities.

Fourteen years he had kept the secret, so that clearly he was not given to boasting.

6 For though I would desire to glory, I shall not be a fool; for I will say the truth: but *now* I forbear, lest any man should think of me above that which he seeth me *to be*, or *that* he heareth of me.

7 And lest I should be exalted above measure through the abundance of the revelations, there was given to me a thorn in the flesh, the messenger of Satan to buffet me, lest I should be exalted above measure. (*From devout exaltation to self-exaltation is but a step, and that step our nature is prone to take. To be proud is one of the worst of calamities, and therefore to keep us humble the Lord sends us sharp trials. A thorn pierces, lacerates, festers, and yet it is but a little thing; very insignificant, yet very painful. Paul had a secret grief which cuffed him as schoolmasters punish boys, and the ignominy of it was its worst feature.*)

8 For this thing I besought the Lord thrice, that it might depart from me.

9 And he said unto me, My grace is sufficient for thee: for my strength is made perfect in weakness. (*One evening, as Bunyan was in a meeting of Christian people, full of sadness and terror, suddenly there "brake in" upon him with great power, and three times together, the words, "My grace is sufficient for thee; My grace is sufficient for thee; My grace is sufficient for thee." And "Oh! methought," says he, "that every word was a mighty word unto me,*

as 'My,' and 'grace,' and 'sufficient,' and 'for thee;' they were then, and sometimes are still, far bigger than others be.") Most gladly therefore will I rather glory in my infirmities, that the power of Christ may rest upon me.

10 Therefore I take pleasure in infirmities, in reproaches, in necessities, in persecutions, in distresses for Christ's sake: for when I am weak, then am I strong.

11 I am become a fool in glorying; ye have compelled me: for I ought to have been commended of you: for in nothing am I behind the very chiefest apostles, though I be nothing.

The Corinthians ought not to have required a defence from Paul, but should themselves have been among his warmest advocates.

12 Truly the signs of an apostle were wrought among you in all patience, in signs, and wonders, and mighty deeds.

13 For what is it wherein ye were inferior to other churches, except *it be* that I myself was not burdensome to you? forgive me this wrong.

14, 15 Behold, the third time I am ready to come to you; and I will not be burdensome to you: for I seek not yours, but you: for the children ought not to lay up for the parents, but the parents for the children. And I will very gladly spend and be spent for you; though the more abundantly I love you, the less I be loved. (*What a Christian spirit! He will not cease to seek their good, however base their conduct.*)

16—18 But be it so, I did not burden you: nevertheless, being crafty, I caught you with guile. Did I make a gain of you by any of them whom I sent unto you? (*He accepted nothing for himself, and he did not impose his friends upon them; he had served them in the most disinterested way.*) I desired Titus, and with *him* I sent a brother. Did Titus make a gain of you? walked we not in the same spirit? *walked we* not in the same steps?

19 Again, think ye that we excuse ourselves unto you? we speak before God in Christ: but *we do* all things, dearly beloved, for your edifying. (*It was shameful that so good a man as Paul should have been troubled by cavillers. May God grant that none of us may ever figure in the history of our church as discontented members and opposers of faithful ministers.*)

WE shall now read parts of the epistle to the Galatians, in which Paul stands in opposition to the *Jewish professors* who denied his apostleship, and strove to bring the church under the yoke of the law.

GALATIANS I.

1—5 Paul, an apostle, (not of men, neither by man, but by Jesus Christ, and God the Father, who raised him from the dead;) And all the brethren which are with me, unto the churches of Galatia: Grace *be* to you and peace from God the Father, and *from* our Lord Jesus Christ, Who gave himself for our sins, that he might deliver us from this present evil world, according to the will of God and our Father: To whom *be* glory for ever and ever. Amen.

Paul is very fond of writing doxologies. His heart was full of praise, and he could not help giving it vent. Would it not be well if every now and then, even in the midst of other things, we paused to bless the Lord? The apostle was answering opponents, but he sweetened the controversy with grateful adoration.

6, 7 I marvel that ye are so soon removed from him that called you into the grace of Christ unto another gospel: Which is not another; but there be some that trouble you, and would pervert the gospel of Christ.

8, 9 But though we, or an angel from heaven, preach any other gospel unto you than that which we have preached unto you, let him be accursed. As we said before, so say I now again, If any *man* preach any other gospel unto you than that ye have received, let him be accursed. *(Paul makes short work with new-fangled gospels. He was not one of the broad school whose wanton charity trifles with divine truth, as if it were a matter of no consequence what is preached, or what is believed.)*

10 For do I now persuade *(or seek to win the favour of)* men, or God? or do I seek to please men? for if I yet pleased men, I should not be the servant of Christ. *(Christ's ministers must never be men-pleasers, or they are false to their trust. Offend or please, their one business is to preach the truth, the whole truth, and nothing but the truth.)*

11, 12 But I certify you, brethren, that the gospel which was preached of me is not after man. For I neither received it of man, neither

was I taught *it*, but by the revelation of Jesus Christ. *(He was no retailer of other men's stuffs: he preached what he had been taught of the Holy Ghost in his own soul. Lord, send us more such ministries.)*

13, 14 For ye have heard of my conversation in time past in the Jews' religion, how that beyond measure I persecuted the church of God, and wasted it: And profited in the Jews' religion above many my equals in mine own nation, being more exceedingly zealous of the traditions of my fathers.

15, 16 But when it pleased God, who separated me from my mother's womb, and called *me* by his grace, To reveal his Son in me, that I might preach him among the heathen; immediately I conferred not with flesh and blood:

17 Neither went I up to Jerusalem to them which were apostles before me; but I went into Arabia, and returned again unto Damascus.

None could say that he was a copyist. In the solitudes of Arabia he had studied the Old Testament, communed with God, and obtained insight into the deep things of God; and his testimony was therefore fresh from heaven. More of God and less of man is what we all need.

18, 19 Then after three years I went up to Jerusalem to see Peter, and abode with him fifteen days. But other of the apostles saw I none, save James the Lord's brother.

20 Now the things which I write unto you, behold, before God, I lie not.

21—23 Afterwards I came into the regions of Syria and Cilicia; And was unknown by face unto the churches of Judæa which were in Christ: But they had heard only, That he which persecuted us in times past now preacheth the faith which once he destroyed. *(His remarkable conversion and independent course made him very decided in his teaching. The more certainly grace works in us, the more attached shall we be to the gospel of grace, and the more opposed shall we be to all those errors which rob God of his glory.)*

24 And they glorified God in me. *(May we so live that others may glorify God, because of his grace displayed in us.)*

IN our last reading we commenced Paul's summary of his early Christian life, we now continue the narrative.

GALATIANS II.

1, 2 Then fourteen years after I went up again to Jerusalem with Barnabas, and took Titus with *me* also. And I went up by revelation, and communicated unto them that gospel which I preach among the Gentiles, but privately to them which were of reputation, lest by any means I should run, or had run, in vain. (*He went up to Jerusalem lest he might be misrepresented and thought to be a teacher of some novel doctrine, and not one at heart with the rest of the brotherhood. We must be careful not to create misunderstandings by holding too much aloof from other believers.*)

3—5 But neither Titus, who was with me, being a Greek, was compelled to be circumcised: And that because of false brethren unawares brought in, who came in privily to spy out our liberty which we have in Christ Jesus, that they might bring us into bondage: To whom we gave place by subjection, no, not for an hour; that the truth of the gospel might continue with you. (*There were many who wished to make Paul exchange the liberty of the gospel for the yoke of the Jewish law, but he would not for a moment submit to them. We need to be equally staunch against Romanism in these days.*)

6—10 But of these who seemed to be somewhat, (whatsover they were, it maketh no matter to me: God accepteth no man's person:) for they who seemed *to be somewhat* in conference added nothing to me: But contrariwise, when they saw that the gospel of the uncircumcision was committed unto me, as *the gospel* of the circumcision *was* unto Peter; (For he that wrought effectually in Peter to the apostleship of the circumcision, the same was mighty in me toward the Gentiles:) And when James, Cephas, and John, who seemed to be pillars, perceived the grace that was given unto me, they gave to me and Barnabas the right hands of fellowship; that we *should go* unto the heathen, and they unto the circumcision. Only *they would* that we should remember the poor; the same which I also was forward to do.

11—14 But when Peter was come to Antioch, I withstood him to the face, because he was to be blamed. For before that certain came from James, he did eat with the Gentiles: but when they were come, he withdrew and separated himself, fearing them which were of the circumcision. And the other Jews dissembled likewise with him; insomuch that Barnabas was also carried away with their dissimulation. But when I saw that they walked not uprightly according to the truth of the gospel, I said unto Peter before *them* all, If thou, being a Jew, livest after the manner of Gentiles, and not as do the Jews, why compellest thou the Gentiles to live as do the Jews? (*Good men are sometimes afraid of a straight course of action because it may cause trouble, or appear to be too bold. In such a case we must not be silent out of respect for them, but openly oppose them. Dear is Peter, but dearer still the truth.*)

15, 16 We *who are* Jews by nature, and not sinners of the Gentiles, Knowing that a man is not justified by the works of the law, but by the faith of Jesus Christ, even we have believed in Jesus Christ, that we might be justified by the faith of Christ, and not by the works of the law: for by the works of the law shall no flesh be justified. (*How boldly is this stated! Faith alone and not works justify the soul before God. He who does not believe this rejects the gospel.*)

17 But if, while we seek to be justified by Christ, we ourselves also are found sinners, *is* therefore Christ the minister of sin? God forbid. (*Justification by faith does not make us think lightly of sin; on the contrary, it creates in us such love to God that we loathe the very idea of offending him.*)

18—20 For if I build again the things which I destroyed, I make myself a transgressor. For I through the law am dead to the law, that I might live unto God. I am crucified with Christ: nevertheless I live; yet not I, but Christ liveth in me: and the life which I now live in the flesh I live by the faith of the Son of God, who loved me, and gave himself for me.

21 I do not frustrate the grace of God: for if righteousness *come* by the law, then Christ is dead in vain. (*We cannot be saved by our own merits, for if so, the atonement was unnecessary, —a blasphemous idea not to be tolerated for a moment. Are we all believers in Jesus?*)

GALATIANS III. 1—5; 19—29.

O FOOLISH Galatians, who hath bewitched you, that ye should not obey the truth, before whose eyes Jesus Christ hath been evidently set forth, crucified among you?
What strange, Satanic influence has come over you? By what horrible deceit have you been entangled and held captive? You have heard and known the way of salvation by faith in the crucified Saviour—how could you then have been duped by legal teachers?

2 This only would I learn of you, Received ye the Spirit by the works of the law, or by the hearing of faith?

3 Are ye so foolish? having begun in the Spirit, are ye now made perfect by the flesh?

4 Have ye suffered so many things in vain? if *it be* yet in vain.

5 He therefore that ministereth to you the Spirit, and worketh miracles among you, *doeth he it* by the works of the law, or by the hearing of faith? *(Paul's argument is, that hitherto all the good they had received had come to them by grace and not by works, by the Spirit and not by the flesh, by faith and not by ceremonies, and he chides them for yielding in any degree to the delusive teaching of Judaizers. We have the best reason for keeping to the gospel, for no real good ever comes to men by the opposite teaching. The following testimony is only one of many, and establishes the point:—"I preached up sanctification very earnestly for six years in a former parish," says Mr. Bennet, in a letter, "and never brought one soul to Christ. I did the same at this parish for two years, without having any success at all; but as soon as ever I preached Jesus Christ, and faith in his blood, then believers were added to the Church, and the people flocked from all parts to hear the glorious sound of the gospel, some coming six, others eight, and others ten miles, and that constantly. The reason why my ministry was not blessed when I preached up salvation partly by faith and partly by works is, because the doctrine is not of God; and he will prosper no ministers but such as preach salvation in his own appointed way, namely, by faith in Jesus Christ.")*

19 Wherefore then *serveth* the law? *(If it cannot save, why was it given? It was given to discover and lay bare our sin to us. A sight of*

misery must go before a sense of mercy. Lex, lux, the law is a light, and shows us our need of a mediator. Therefore the apostle says—) It was added because of transgressions, till the seed should come to whom the promise was made; *and it was* ordained by angels in the hand of a mediator.

20 Now a mediator is not *a mediator* of one, but God is one. *(And this proves that God and men were opposed, or a mediator would not have been needed. Thus the giving of the law showed man's state of alienation.)*

21, 22 *Is* the law then against the promises of God? God forbid: for if there had been a law given which could have given life, verily righteousness should have been by the law. But the scripture hath concluded *(or shut up as prisoners)* all under sin, that the promise by faith of Jesus Christ might be given to them that believe. *(The law is not therefore the opponent of the promise, but an agent for putting men where they feel themselves to be in need of mercy, and therefore accept salvation by grace.)*

23 But before faith came, we were kept under the law, shut up unto the faith which should afterwards be revealed.

24—26 Wherefore the law was our schoolmaster *to bring us* unto Christ, that we might be justified by faith. But after that faith is come, we are no longer under a schoolmaster. For ye are all the children of God by faith in Christ Jesus.

27 For as many of you as have been baptized into Christ have put on Christ.
We are not baptized unto Moses, we have put off legal robes, and are dressed in the garments of grace.

28 There is neither Jew nor Greek, there is neither bond nor free, there is neither male nor female: for ye are all one in Christ Jesus.

29 And if ye *be* Christ's, then are ye Abraham's seed, and heirs according to the promise.
So that we obtain all the blessings of the law by faith, even in the same manner as Abraham became the heir of all things. Evermore in our hearts let us make a clear distinction between the law and the grace of God, so shall we be sound in doctrine and preserved from much bondage.

GALATIANS IV. 1—20.

NOW I say, *That* the heir, as long as he is a child, differeth nothing from a servant, though he be lord of all ; But is under tutors and governors until the time appointed of the father. Even so we, when we were children, were in bondage under the elements of the world : But when the fulness of the time was come, God sent forth his Son, made of a woman, made under the law, To redeem them that were under the law, that we might receive the adoption of sons. *(So that the Mosaic law of rites and ceremonies was only a temporary arrangement for the childhood of the church, which now, having reached full age, has come into possession of liberty in the truth, and rejoices in the free grace of the gospel. It would be ridiculous for a full-grown heir to go to school again, or continue under guardians, and so it is absurd to return to the service of forms and rituals, which are too childish for men in Christ Jesus.)*

6 And because ye are sons, God hath sent forth the Spirit of his Son into your hearts, crying, Abba, Father. *(Here is our true position, we are moved by the Spirit to claim our adoption, and we no more live in bondage to the law. Many even among Christians are afraid of being too sure of their sonship, lest they should be presumptuous ; this is very dishonouring to their heavenly Father.)*

7 Wherefore thou art no more a servant, but a son ; and if a son, then an heir of God through Christ. *(Therefore live as such. By faith possess and enjoy the treasures of divine grace. Cast doubts and tremblings to the wind, for why should heirs of God live like bondsmen ?)*

8, 9 Howbeit then, when ye knew not God, ye did service unto them which by nature are no gods. But now, after that ye have known God, or rather are known of God, how turn ye again to the weak and beggarly elements, whereunto ye desire again to be in bondage ?

How can ye go back to the things of your spiritual childhood? As well may full-grown men begin again to read their A B C, and learn from baby picture books !

10, 11 Ye observe days, and months, and times, and years. I am afraid of you, lest I have bestowed upon you labour in vain.

To keep holy days and practise symbolical ceremonies is contrary to the very spirit of Christianity ; and those who do so lead us to suspect that they do not know the gospel at all.

12—16 Brethren, I beseech you, be as I *am ;* for I *am* as ye *are (I am one with you in heart):* ye have not injured me at all. Ye know how through infirmity of the flesh I preached the gospel unto you at the first. And my temptation which was in my flesh ye despised not, nor rejected ; but received me as an angel of God, *even* as Christ Jesus. Where is then the blessedness ye spake of ? for I bear you record, that, if *it had been* possible, ye would have plucked out your own eyes, and have given them to me. Am I therefore become your enemy, because I tell you the truth ?

Bad teachers had weaned them from the apostle and led them into legal bondage.

17, 18 They zealously affect you, *but* not well ; yea, they would exclude you *(from us),* that ye might affect them *(and be of their party).* But *it is* good to be zealously affected always in *a* good *thing,* and not only when I am present with you.

19, 20 My little children, of whom I travail in birth again until Christ be formed in you, I desire to be present with you now, and to change my voice ; for I stand in doubt of you.

All his anxiety arose from their falling into ritualism and legalism. He wanted to see them living by faith upon Jesus, and worshipping God with free spiritual worship. The fashionable religion of the present day is overlaid with pompous forms, and the plain gospel of salvation by faith in Jesus is despised : nevertheless to the doctrine of grace let us steadfastly cleave, for it alone is truth, and in it alone is salvation.

In vain the trembling conscience seeks
Some solid ground to rest upon ;
With long despair the spirit breaks,
Till we apply to Christ alone.

Should all the forms that men devise
Assault my faith with treacherous art,
I'd call them vanity and lies,
And bind the gospel to my heart.

704   " 𝔎𝔣 𝔶𝔢 𝔟𝔢 𝔩𝔢𝔡 𝔬𝔣 𝔱𝔥𝔢 𝔖𝔭𝔦𝔯𝔦𝔱 𝔶𝔢 𝔞𝔯𝔢 𝔫𝔬𝔱 𝔲𝔫𝔡𝔢𝔯 𝔱𝔥𝔢 𝔩𝔞𝔴."   NOVEMBER 27.—EVENING.

[*Or October* 23.]

THE *apostle again expostulates with the Galatians for falling into legality, and points out to them the true path of the believer, namely, holiness produced by the Spirit of God.*

GALATIANS V. 7—26.

7, 8 Ye did run well; who did hinder you that ye should not obey the truth? This per-suasion *cometh* not of him that calleth you.

It is not of God, or it would be consistent with what you have been taught by his Spirit before.

9 A little leaven leaveneth the whole lump.

One man's influence may mislead thousands; one piece of false doctrine may taint our whole creed.

10, 11 I have confidence in you through the Lord, that ye will be none otherwise minded: but he that troubleth you shall bear his judg-ment, whosoever he be. And I, brethren, if I yet preach circumcision, why do I yet suffer persecution? then is the offence of the cross ceased. *(Some even said that Paul himself had preached ceremonialism, but he denies it, and backs up his declaration by the fact that men had not left off persecuting him, as they would have done had he diluted the gospel.)*

12 I would they were even cut off which trouble you. *(It were better that they were cut off from the church than remain to sow false doctrine. As lepers must be put out of the camp, so must evil teachers be cast out of the church.)*

13, 14 For, brethren, ye have been called unto liberty; only *use* not liberty for an occasion to the flesh, but by love serve one another. For all the law is fulfilled in one word, *even* in this; Thou shalt love thy neighbour as thyself.

This is more important than symbolic rites: to destroy love to preserve a ceremony is to kill a child in order to preserve its clothes.

15 But if ye bite and devour one another, take heed that ye be **not** consumed one of another.

16 *This* I say then, Walk in the Spirit, and ye shall not fulfil the lust of the flesh.

17 For the flesh lusteth against the Spirit, and the Spirit against the flesh: and these are contrary the one to the other: so that ye cannot do the things that ye would. *(Every new man is two men: there is a warfare within.)*

18 But if ye be led of the Spirit, ye are not under the law.

19—21 Now the works of the flesh are mani-fest, which are *these;* Adultery, fornication, un-cleanness, lasciviousness, Idolatry, witchcraft, hatred, variance, emulations, wrath, strife, sedi-tions, heresies, Envyings, murders, drunken-ness, revellings, and such like: of the which I tell you before, as I have also told *you* in time past, that they which do such things shall not inherit the kingdom of God. *(No matter what they profess, or what sacraments they may partake of, those who live in these sins are not alive unto God. What a list we have here! Surely sin is a prolific mother.)*

22, 23 But the fruit of the Spirit is love, joy, peace, longsuffering, gentleness, goodness, faith, Meekness, temperance: against such there is no law. *(For the works of the flesh there is no gospel, and against the works of the Spirit there is no law. Both God and man agree to com-mend such actions as those which are here men-tioned; let us abound in them.)*

24 And they that are Christ's have crucified the flesh with the affections and lusts.

25 If we live in the Spirit, let us also walk in the Spirit.

26 Let us not be desirous of vain glory, pro-voking one another, envying one another.

Our evil desires are nailed to the cross, but they are not yet dead; we have need therefore to abide under the influence of the ever-blessed Spirit, and we certainly have no ground for boasting or despising others. Be it ours under the divine guidance to cultivate love and peace, and flee from all pride and envy.

Jesus, take me for thine own;
To thy will my spirit frame;
Thou shalt reign, and thou alone,
Over all I have and am.

Making thus the Lord my choice,
I have nothing more to choose,
But to listen to thy voice,
And my will in thine to lose.

Then whatever may betide,
I shall safe and happy be;
Still content and satisfied,
Having all in having thee.

GALATIANS VI.

BRETHREN, if a man be overtaken in a fault, ye which are spiritual, restore such an one in the spirit of meekness ; considering thyself, lest thou also be tempted. *(Because men travel so slowly, sin overtakes them, overthrows them, and breaks their bones; believers who are in a better case must lovingly endeavour to heal their brethren, saying to themselves, " They fell yesterday, and we shall fall to-day unless the Lord shall hold us up.")*

2 Bear ye one another's burdens, and so fulfil the law of Christ.

3—5 For if a man think himself to be something, when he is nothing, he deceiveth himself. But let every man prove his own work, and then shall he have rejoicing in himself alone, and not in another. For every man shall bear his own burden. *(We have each one his own load of responsibility to bear, and therefore we do well to remember our own faults and sympathise with the infirmities of others. When tempted to condemn others, let us look at home.)*

6 Let him that is taught in the word communicate unto him that teacheth in all good things. *The preacher who zealously labours for our good in spirituals well deserves to partake of our temporals.*

7, 8 Be not deceived ; God is not mocked : for whatsoever a man soweth, that shall he also reap. For he that soweth to his flesh shall of the flesh reap corruption ; but he that soweth to the Spirit shall of the Spirit reap life everlasting.

9 And let us not be weary in well doing : for in due season we shall reap, if we faint not. *The rule of reaping what we sow is not changed under the gospel, but obtains an importance greater than before, for now we sow better seed, and through grace reap a richer harvest. At the same time, those who after hearing the word continue sowing to the flesh, will reap additional misery, because their sin is greatly increased by refusing the gospel light.*

10 As we have therefore opportunity, let us do good unto all *men*, especially unto them who are of the household of faith. *(Our kindness is to be general and yet special, like the redemption of our Lord Jesus, " who is the Saviour of all men, specially of them that believe.")*

11 Ye see how large a letter I have written

unto you with mine own hand. *(Probably his eyes were weak, and as he resolved to write with his own hand he used what an old divine calls "good great texthand letters." He mentions this little circumstance to show his earnestness in what he had written.)*

12, 13 As many as desire to make a fair shew in the flesh, they constrain you to be circumcised ; only lest they should suffer persecution for the cross of Christ. For neither they themselves who are circumcised keep the law ; but desire to have you circumcised, that they may glory in your flesh. *(They wanted to boast of their many followers and to curry favour with the Jews by showing that their converts to Jesus were also proselytes to circumcision. Paul cared not for such boastings.)*

14, 15 But God forbid that I should glory, save in the cross of our Lord Jesus Christ, by whom the world is crucified unto me, and I unto the world. For in Christ Jesus neither circumcision availeth any thing, nor uncircumcision, but a new creature.

16 And as many as walk according to this rule, peace *be* on them, and mercy, and upon the Israel of God.

17 From henceforth let no man trouble me : for I bear in my body the marks of the Lord Jesus. *(He cared nothing for the marks in his flesh which proved him to be a Jew, he valued far more those scars which he had received while engaged in the service of Jesus; these he looked upon as being the Lord's brand upon him, like the ear mark which was received by a Hebrew servant when he resolved to abide with his master for life. It is useless to oppose a man of Paul's order, he is too resolute to be turned aside, it is wisest for the enemy to let him alone.)*

18 Brethren, the grace of our Lord Jesus Christ *be* with your spirit. Amen.

When I survey the wondrous cross
On which the Prince of glory died,
My richest gain I count but loss,
And pour contempt on all my pride.

Forbid it, Lord, that I should boast,
Save in the death of Christ, my God ;
All the vain things that charm me most,
I sacrifice them to his blood.

THE *Epistle to the Ephesians is a complete body of divinity, treating of doctrinal, experimental, and practical godliness, in the most full and instructive manner. Its peculiar quality is sublimity. To be truly understood it must be spiritually discerned. O Lord, enlighten us.*

EPHESIANS I.

1 Paul, an apostle of Jesus Christ by the will of God, to the saints which are at Ephesus, and to the faithful in Christ Jesus :

2 Grace *be* to you, and peace, from God our Father, and *from* the Lord Jesus Christ.

Grace first, and peace as its consequence. That peace which does not come to us as the result of grace is false and dangerous. Note how he links the Father and the Lord Jesus together ; for neither grace nor peace can come to us, except through God in Christ Jesus.

3, 4 Blessed *be* the God and Father of our Lord Jesus Christ, who hath blessed us with all spiritual blessings in heavenly *places* in Christ : According as he hath chosen us in him before the foundation of the world, that we should be holy and without blame before him in love: (*All spiritual blessings come to us by the way of election, and have their fountain in eternal love ; but we are not chosen that we may live in sin, God has chosen us to holiness.*)

5, 6, Having predestinated us unto the adoption of children by Jesus Christ to himself, according to the good pleasure of his will, To the praise of the glory of his grace, wherein he hath made us accepted in the beloved.

Adoption and acceptance in Christ follow upon the divine choice. Do we possess these priceless blessings ?

7—10 In whom we have redemption through his blood, the forgiveness of sins, according to the riches of his grace ; Wherein he hath abounded toward us in all wisdom and prudence ; Having made known unto us the mystery of his will, according to his good pleasure which he hath purposed in himself : That in the dispensation of the fulness of times he might gather together in one all things in Christ, both which are in heaven, and which are on earth ; *even* in him : (*Jesus is the centre as well as the channel of all blessedness ; all the chosen in heaven and earth are to be gathered together in one in him.*)

11 In whom also we have obtained an inheritance, (*we have it even now in its price, in its first principle, and in the divine pledge and earnest of the Spirit,*) being predestinated according to the purpose of him who worketh all things after the counsel of his own will :

12 That we should be to the praise of his glory, who first trusted in Christ.

13, 14 In whom ye also *trusted*, after that ye heard the word of truth, the gospel of your salvation : in whom also after that ye believed, ye were sealed with that holy Spirit of promise, Which is the earnest of our inheritance until the redemption of the purchased possession, unto the praise of his glory. (*Have we the Holy Ghost? Then we have already a part of heaven ; yea, the very soul, mainspring, and glory of its infinite delights.*)

15—17 Wherefore I also, after I heard of your faith in the Lord Jesus, and love unto all the saints, Cease not to give thanks for you, making mention of you in my prayers ; That the God of our Lord Jesus Christ, the Father of glory, may give unto you the spirit of wisdom and revelation in the knowledge of him :

Where there was much good, the apostle prayed for more. We all need still further to advance in divine things. To stand still is impossible.

18—23 The eyes of your understanding being enlightened ; that ye may know what is the hope of his calling, and what the riches of the glory of his inheritance in the saints, And what *is* the exceeding greatness of his power to us-ward who believe, according to the working of his mighty power, Which he wrought in Christ, when he raised him from the dead, and set *him* at his own right hand in the heavenly *places*, Far above all principality, and power, and might, and dominion, and every name that is named, not only in this world, but also in that which is to come : And hath put all *things* under his feet, and gave him *to be* the head over all *things* to the church, Which is his body, the fulness of him that filleth all in all.

How enraptured the apostle is when he speaks of the glories of Jesus ; and well he may be, for it is a theme far excelling every other. Let us muse upon it till our hearts burn with love and our souls bow in adoration at his feet.

WE *have already seen how Paul describes what God's grace has done* for *us; we shall now hear him recite what it has wrought in* us *if we are indeed saved.*

EPHESIANS II.

1 And you *hath he quickened,* who were dead in trespasses and sins ; *(we were without spiritual life, but now we are made alive unto God; regeneration is as great a wonder as if the corpses in the churchyard should burst their graves and begin life again. Grace is life, sin is death, conversion is a resurrection.)*

2, 3 Wherein in time past ye walked according to the course of this world, according to the prince of the power of the air, the spirit that now worketh in the children of disobedience : Among whom also we all had our conversation in times past in the lusts of our flesh, fulfilling the desires of the flesh and of the mind ; and were by nature the children of wrath, even as others. *(What a humbling passage! The best of men were by nature no better than the worst. Satan found a willing servant in each one of us, and such we should still have been had not grace interposed.)*

4, 5 But God, who is rich in mercy, for his great love wherewith he loved us, Even when we were dead in sins, hath quickened us together with Christ (by grace ye are saved;)

That little sentence, " By grace ye are saved," is the key of true divinity. Study it well, and believe it thoroughly, and you will escape a thousand doctrinal errors. Carry this text in your heart, and you will be sound in the faith.

6 And hath raised *us* up together, and made *us* sit together in heavenly *places* in Christ Jesus :

We grovel in the dust by nature, but grace sets us up above all earthly things. What manner of persons ought we to be who sit with Jesus in heaven!

7 That in the ages to come he might shew the exceeding riches of his grace in *his* kindness toward us through Christ Jesus. *(In saved men the love of God is more clearly seen than in all the universe besides. The new creation is the crown of all the works of God.)*

8—10 For by grace are ye saved through faith ; and that not of yourselves : *it is* the gift of God : Not of works, lest any man should boast. For we are his workmanship, created in Christ Jesus unto good works, which God hath before ordained that we should walk in them.

11, 12 Wherefore remember, that ye *being* in time past Gentiles in the flesh, who are called Uncircumcision by that which is called the Circumcision in the flesh made by hands ; That at that time ye were without Christ, being aliens from the commonwealth of Israel, and strangers from the covenants of promise, having no hope, and without God in the world :

13 But now in Christ Jesus ye who sometimes were far off are made nigh by the blood of Christ. *(The distance was infinite, and the nearness is intimate. The blood of Jesus works marvels, it annihilates distance, breaks down partition walls, and transforms aliens into sons.)*

14, 15 For he is our peace, who hath made both one, and hath broken down the middle wall of partition *between us;* Having abolished in his flesh the enmity, *even* the law of commandments *contained* in ordinances ; for to make in himself of twain one new man, *so* making peace ;

16 And that he might reconcile both unto God in one body by the cross, having slain the enmity thereby :

17 And came and preached peace to you which were afar off, and to them that were nigh.

18 For through him we both have access by one Spirit unto the Father. *(Here we have the Trinity in one verse all uniting to help us to pray. All the three divine persons must aid us before we can offer a single acceptable petition.)*

19—22 Now therefore ye are no more strangers and foreigners, but fellowcitizens with the saints, and of the household of God ; And are built upon the foundation of the apostles and prophets, Jesus Christ himself being the chief corner *stone;* In whom all the building fitly framed together groweth unto an holy temple in the Lord : In whom ye also are builded together for an habitation of God through the Spirit.

The saints of God are not so many loose stones, but they are parts of a building, and it is for each one of us to fill his place in the church for the good of others and the glory of the Lord, who dwells within his church as a king in his palace. Let us remember this, and seek above all things to promote the unity, edification, and holiness of all our brethren in Christ.

708   "Let the word of Christ dwell in you richly."   NOVEMBER 29.—EVENING.

[*Or October* 27.]

PAUL *with the chain clanking upon his wrist writes most jubilantly of his position and office, counting it more honourable to be " the prisoner of the Lord" than to be the favourite of Cæsar.*

EPHESIANS III.

1 For this cause I Paul, the prisoner of Jesus Christ for you Gentiles,

2—5 If ye have heard of the dispensation of the grace of God which is given me to you-ward: How that by revelation he made known unto me the mystery; (as I wrote afore in few words, Whereby, when ye read, ye may understand my knowledge in the mystery of Christ) Which in other ages was not made known unto the sons of men, as it is now revealed unto his holy apostles and prophets by the Spirit;

6 That the Gentiles should be fellowheirs, and of the same body, and partakers of his promise in Christ by the gospel:

7 Whereof I was made a minister, according to the gift of the grace of God given unto me by the effectual working of his power.

8 Unto me, who am less than the least of all saints, is this grace given, that I should preach among the Gentiles the unsearchable riches of Christ; *(The greater the saint the less he thinks of himself. A very correct estimate of a man's worth may be gathered from his humility. Weighty materials sink, only " trifles, light as air" rise into the clouds.)*

9 And to make all *men* see what *is* the fellowship of the mystery, which from the beginning of the world hath been hid in God, who created all things by Jesus Christ:

10, 11 To the intent that now unto the principalities and powers in heavenly *places* might be known by the church the manifold wisdom of God, According to the eternal purpose which he purposed in Christ Jesus our Lord. *Even angels are to learn from us. Saints will be lesson-books in which the cherubim and seraphim will read with astonishment the wisdom and love of God; this was the eternal design of the great Lord of all, and he will not allow his purpose in any measure to be thwarted.*

12 In whom we have boldness and access with confidence by the faith of him.

13 Wherefore I desire that ye faint not at my tribulations for you, which is your glory.

See how he forgets himself, and is only anxious that they may not be distressed about him; after this manner ought we also to sink self, and live for the good of others.

14 For this cause I bow my knees unto the Father of our Lord Jesus Christ,

15 Of whom the whole family in heaven and earth is named, *(It is delightful to think of Paul pausing in the middle of his letter to kneel down and implore a blessing upon his friends, feeling himself, even in his prison, to be one of an august family, which had its dwelling-place not only on earth but in heaven also, and yet was one and indivisible. Let us devoutly listen to the apostle's prayer and offer it for all believers.)*

16—18 That he would grant you, according to the riches of his glory, to be strengthened with might by his Spirit in the inner man; That Christ may dwell in your hearts by faith; that ye, being rooted and grounded in love, May be able to comprehend with all saints what *is* the breadth, and length, and depth, and height;

19 And to know the love of Christ, which passeth knowledge, that ye might be filled with all the fulness of God. *(Having prayed, Paul now turns to praising; the two holy exercises are very near of kin, and the one naturally leads on to the other. We should sing more doxologies if we offered more intercessions.)*

20, 21 Now unto him that is able to do exceeding abundantly above all that we ask or think, according to the power that worketh in us, Unto him *be* glory in the church by Christ Jesus throughout all ages, world without end. Amen.

Come, dearest Lord, descend and dwell
By faith and love in every breast;
Then shall we know, and taste, and feel
The joys that cannot be express'd.

Come fill our hearts with inward strength;
Make our enlargèd souls possess
And learn the height, and breadth, and length
Of thine unmeasurable grace.

Now to the God whose power can do
More than our thoughts or wishes know;
Be everlasting honours done
By all the church, through Christ his Son.

SO far from being ashamed of being shut up in a dungeon like a felon, Paul again repeats, as his choice title of honour, the words, "the prisoner of the Lord." It is inexpressibly delightful to be allowed to suffer for him who suffered to the death for us. Paul uses his afflicted condition as an affectionate plea with the Ephesians to give heed to his counsel.*

EPHESIANS IV. 1—8 ; 11—32.

1—3 I therefore, the prisoner of the Lord, beseech you that ye walk worthy of the vocation wherewith ye are called, With all lowliness and meekness, with long suffering, forbearing one another in love ; Endeavouring to keep the unity of the Spirit in the bond of peace.

4 *There* is one body, and one Spirit, even as ye are called in one hope of your calling ;

5 One Lord, one faith, one baptism,

6 One God and Father of all, who *is* above all, and through all, and in you all.

True believers are one ; Christ has only instituted one church, he has quickened it with but one Spirit, and set before it one sole hope. The Lord is the alone Head of the church, she has not two Lords, neither has Jesus revealed more than one faith, or commanded any other than one baptism : hence believers should anxiously maintain unity, and endeavour each one to promote the good of the whole.

7 But unto every one of us is given grace according to the measure of the gift of Christ.

8 Wherefore he saith, When he ascended up on high, he led captivity captive, and gave gifts unto men.

11—13 And he gave some, apostles ; and some, prophets ; and some, evangelists ; and some, pastors and teachers ; For the perfecting of the saints, for the work of the ministry, for the edifying of the body of Christ : Till we all come in the unity of the faith, and of the knowledge of the Son of God, unto a perfect man, unto the measure of the stature of the fulness of Christ : (*All the ascension-gifts come to us for the building up, not of many sects, but of the Lord's one church. His choicest gifts are holy men, qualified for various gracious works, which they carry on for the perfecting of each believer, and of the whole body of the faithful.*)

14—16 That we *henceforth* be no more children, tossed to and fro, and carried about with every wind of doctrine, by the sleight of men, *and* cunning craftiness, whereby they lie in wait to deceive ; But speaking the truth in love, may grow up into him in all things, which is the head, *even* Christ : From whom the whole body fitly joined together and compacted by that which every joint supplieth, according to the effectual working in the measure of every part, maketh increase of the body unto the edifying of itself in love.

17—19 This I say therefore, and testify in the Lord, that ye henceforth walk not as other Gentiles walk, in the vanity of their mind, Having the understanding darkened, being alienated from the life of God through the ignorance that is in them, because of the blindness of their heart : Who being past feeling have given themselves over unto lasciviousness, to work all uncleanness with greediness.

20 But ye have not so learned Christ ;

21 If so be that ye have heard him, and have been taught by him, as the truth is in Jesus :

22, 23 That ye put off concerning the former conversation the old man, which is corrupt according to the deceitful lusts ; And be renewed in the spirit of your mind ;

24 And that ye put on the new man, which after God is created in righteousness and true holiness. (*Being made parts of a new body, of which the Lord Jesus is the head, we cannot act as we once did, or we should belie our profession altogether. Filthiness must be now abhorred, and holiness panted for ; is it so with us ?*)

25 Wherefore putting away lying, speak every man truth with his neighbour : for we are members one of another.

26 Be ye angry, and sin not : let not the sun go down upon your wrath : (*We may be angry at wrong without sinning thereby, but if anger be a selfish resentment, it is always sinful, and if it lives beyond a day it cannot be justified. One of the hardest things in the world is to be angry and not to sin.*)

27 Neither give place to the devil.

28 Let him that stole steal no more : but rather let him labour, working with *his* hands the thing which is good, that he may have to give to him that needeth. (*The cure for dishonesty is industry, and the remedy for a disposition to steal from others, is to learn to give to them.*)

29 Let no corrupt communication proceed out of your mouth, but that which is good to the use of edifying, that it may minister grace unto the hearers. *(Do we always attend to this? Are not some jests which are commonly heard very far from edifying?)*

30 And grieve not the holy Spirit of God, whereby ye are sealed unto the day of redemption.

31 Let all bitterness, and wrath, and anger, and clamour, and evil speaking, be put away from you, with all malice :

32 And be ye kind one to another, tenderhearted, forgiving one another, even as God for Christ's sake hath forgiven you. *(Let this be written up in our chambers, and practised in every room in the house. What a heaven will our family then become.)*

Fill every part of me with praise,
Let all my being speak
Of thee and of thy love, O Lord,
Poor though I be, and weak.

So shalt thou, Lord, from me—e'en me,
Receive the glory due;
And so shall I begin on earth
The song for ever new.

Lost in astonishment I see,
Jesus, thy boundless love to me ;
With angels I thy grace adore,
And long to love and praise thee more.

Still may I view thee on the cross,
And all beside esteem but loss ;
Here still be fixed my feasted eyes,
Enraptur'd with thy sacrifice.

Grace led my roving feet
To tread the heavenly road ;
And new supplies each hour I meet
While pressing on to God.

Grace taught my soul to pray,
And made my eyes o'erflow ;
'Twas grace that kept me to this day,
And will not let me go.

Grace all the work shall crown,
Through everlasting days ;
It lays in heaven the topmost stone,
And well deserves the praise.

Bless'd are the pure in heart,
For they shall see our God ;
The secret of the Lord is theirs ;
Their soul is Christ's abode.

The Lord, who left the heavens
Our life and peace to bring,
To dwell in lowliness with men,
Their Pattern and their King ;

He to the lowly soul
Doth still himself impart,
And for his dwelling and his throne
Chooseth the pure in heart.

Lord, we thy presence seek ;
May ours this blessing be ;
Give us a pure and lowly heart,
A temple meet for thee.

A fulness resides in Jesus, our Head,
And ever abides to answer our need ;
The Father's good pleasure has laid up in store,
A plentiful treasure to give to the poor.

Whate'er be our wants, we need not to fear ;
Our numerous complaints his mercy will hear ;
His fulness shall yield us abundant supplies ;
His buckler shall shield us when dangers arise.

When troubles attend, or danger or strife,
His love will defend and guard us through life ;
And when we are fainting and ready to die,
Whatever is wanting his hand will supply.

Worthy art thou, O dying Lamb ?
Worthy, O bleeding Lord ;
Eternal, Infinite, I AM,
Ceaseless to be adored !

Fulness of riches is in thee !
From thee all mercies spring :
And grace and love, divine and free,
And power enlivening.

Out of the deep of every heart,
Let praise to thee ascend :
Till thou to heaven shalt us translate,
Where praises never end !

EPHESIANS V. 1—21.

B E ye therefore followers *(or imitators)* of God, as dear children;

2 And walk in love, as Christ also hath loved us, and hath given himself for us an offering and a sacrifice to God for a sweetsmelling savour.

Here is a model at once so attractive and so perfect that we may love and copy it at the same time. We may not take the conduct of others for our model, and treat them as they treat us; the only pattern for a Christian is Christ.

3, 4 But fornication, and all uncleanness, or covetousness, let it not be once named among you, as becometh saints; Neither filthiness, nor foolish talking, nor jesting, which are not convenient: but rather giving of thanks. *(Sins of the tongue are fearfully common. Cheerfulness is a virtue, chaste pleasantries are the flowers of conversation, but those unholy allusions and unedifying jests which so often are commended as exceedingly clever should never obtain currency among the followers of the holy Jesus.)*

5 For this ye know, that no whoremonger, nor unclean person, nor covetous man, who is an idolater, hath any inheritance in the kingdom of Christ and of God. *(The covetous man is here placed in very disreputable company. This proves that the Holy Spirit judges lust for gold to be as vile a lust as any other; he sets the brand of Cain upon the brow of the greedy. We send missionaries abroad, and yet we do not sorrow over idolaters at home. If a man worships a god of gold, is he not quite as debased as if his idol were made of wood?)*

6 Let no man deceive you with vain words: for because of these things cometh the wrath of God upon the children of disobedience.

7 Be not ye therefore partakers with them.

8, 9 For ye were sometimes darkness, but now *are ye* light in the Lord: walk as children of light: (For the fruit of the Spirit *is* in all goodness and righteousness and truth;)

10 Proving what is acceptable unto the Lord.

11 And have no fellowship with the unfruitful works of darkness, but rather reprove *them.*

Avoid bad company. Choose only those for your friends who are also friends of God. How can we reprove sin if we take those who openly practise it to be our bosom friends?

12 For it is a shame even to speak of those things which are done of them in secret.

13 But all things that are reproved are made manifest by the light: for whatsoever doth make manifest is light.

14 Wherefore he saith, Awake thou that sleepest, and arise from the dead, and Christ shall give thee light. *(Death hides in darkness, life loves light. We, therefore, who have spiritual life should never do anything which we should be ashamed to have published to the whole world. Christ has given us light, let us not hide it, neither let us shut our eyes to it.)*

15 See then that ye walk circumspectly, not as fools, but as wise, *(Look all around, and be anxious that your conduct may do harm to no one, from any point of view.)*

16 Redeeming the time, because the days are evil.

17 Wherefore be ye not unwise, but understanding what the will of the Lord *is.*

18 And be not drunk with wine, wherein is excess; but be filled with the Spirit;

19 Speaking to yourselves in psalms and hymns and spiritual songs, singing and making melody in your heart to the Lord; *(Men filled with wine call for a song, and when believers are exhilarated by the divine Spirit they also should have their singing, but they must choose the songs of Zion, such as the Lord himself will account to be true melody.)*

20, 21 Giving thanks always for all things unto God and the Father in the name of our Lord Jesus Christ; Submitting yourselves one to another in the fear of God. *(To make God great and ourselves little is our peculiar occupation; we are to give him glory in all that we do, and seek no honour for ourselves, but willingly take the lowest place among our brethren for the Lord's sake.)*

Fill thou my life, O Lord my God,
  In every part with praise;
That my whole being may proclaim
  Thy being and thy ways;

Surrendering my fondest will,
  In things or great or small,
Seeking the good of others still,
  Nor pleasing self at all.

So shall each fear, each fret, each care,
  Be turnèd into song;
And every winding of the way
  The echo shall prolong.

WE are about to read a peculiarly beautiful passage, in which the apostle represents the believer as a soldier, and urges him to prepare for the battle by taking to himself all defensive and offensive arms.

EPHESIANS VI. 11—24.

11 Put on the whole armour of God, that ye may be able to stand against the wiles of the devil. *(Satan will assail every part of us, and therefore we need to be protected from head to foot, like the knights of old.)*

12, 13 For we wrestle not against flesh and blood, but against principalities, against powers, against the rulers of the darkness of this world, against spiritual wickedness in high *places.* Wherefore take unto you the whole armour of God, that ye may be able to withstand in the evil day, and having done all, to stand.

If we fought with men we might be less guarded; wrestling as we do with subtle and spiritual adversaries, whose weapons are as mysterious as they are deadly, it becomes us to be doubly watchful lest in some unguarded point we receive wounds which will bleed for years.

14 Stand therefore, having your loins girt about with truth, *(A girdle of sincerity keeps the whole man in marching order, and braces him up to meet the father of lies. An insincere man is a loose man, and a loose man is a lost man,)* and having on the breastplate of righteousness ; *(This will guard the heart. The righteousness of God, imputed and imparted, will protect the heart, and blunt the edge of Satan's temptations which he aims at the soul. Take notice that a breastplate is provided, but no backplate : we must never think of going back, we are bound to face the enemy, no provision is made for a retreat.)*

15 And your feet shod with the preparation of the gospel of peace : *(With a happy, calm, confidence, because the gospel has given us perfect peace, we shall march over the rough places of the way without becoming discontented or depressed. No pilgrim is so well booted and buskined as he who is at peace with God, his fellow-men, and his own conscience.)*

16 Above all, taking the shield of faith, wherewith ye shall be able to quench all the fiery darts of the wicked. *(Faith, like a shield, covers all and is therefore important above all. Look well to your confidence in God, for if this fails all fails.)*

17, 18 And take the helmet of salvation *(He who is truly saved and knows it will wear a "helm of health." The seat of thought and decision will be safe)* and the sword of the Spirit, which is the word of God : *(The Bible is a bright, keen, pointed, well-tempered weapon, for offence and defence, it cuts a way for us through all foes, slays sin, and chases away even Satan himself. "It is written" is the terror of hell.)* Praying always with all prayer and supplication in the Spirit, and watching thereunto with all perseverance and supplication for all saints ; *(This weapon of all-prayer will often serve our turn when all others are out of our reach. So long as we can pray we shall not be overcome.)*

19, 20 And for me, that utterance may be given unto me, that I may open my mouth boldly, to make known the mystery of the gospel, For which I am an ambassador in bonds : that therein I may speak boldly, as I ought to speak.

21, 22 But that ye also may know my affairs, *and* how I do, Tychicus, a beloved brother and faithful minister in the Lord, shall make known to you all things : Whom I have sent unto you for the same purpose, that ye might know our affairs, and *that* he might comfort your hearts.

23, 24 Peace *be* to the brethren, and love with faith, from God the Father and the Lord Jesus Christ. Grace *be* with all them that love our Lord Jesus Christ in sincerity. Amen.

He winds up with good wishes and prayers. A Christian should be known even by his letters ; when other men use empty compliments, he should abound in earnest prayers and holy wishes. Let us take note of this next time the pen is in our hand.

Soldiers of Christ, arise,
And put your armour on,
Strong in the strength which God supplies
Through His eternal Son :

Stand, then, in His great might,
With all His strength endued ;
But take, to arm you for the fight,
The panoply of God.

From strength to strength go on,
Wrestle, and fight, and pray,
Tread all the powers of darkness down,
And win the well-fought day.

WE *have now reached the Epistle to the Philippians, which has been well called the epistle of love and joy. In it we see most of the inner character of the apostle; there was the utmost mutual love between him and the brethren at Philippi.*

PHILIPPIANS I. 1—26.

1, 2 Paul and Timotheus, the servants of Jesus Christ, to all the saints in Christ Jesus which are at Philippi, with the bishops and deacons: Grace *be* unto you, and peace, from God our Father, and *from* the Lord Jesus Christ.

3—5 I thank my God upon every remembrance of you, Always in every prayer of mine for you all making request with joy, For your fellowship in the gospel from the first day until now;

They were the most generous and faithful of the churches, and gave the apostle much joy. Should we not all aim to cheer the heart of our ministers by our zeal and liberality?

6 Being confident of this very thing, that he which hath begun a good work in you will perform *it* until the day of Jesus Christ:

This delightful confidence is the crowning joy of the Christian life. If he who began the good work did not also carry it on we should be in a wretched plight, but, blessed be God, the work of grace is in the hands of one who never leaves his work unfinished.

7 Even as it is meet for me to think this of you all, because I have you in my heart; inasmuch as both in my bonds, and in the defence and confirmation of the gospel, ye all are partakers of my grace.

8 For God is my record, how greatly I long after you all in the bowels of Jesus Christ.

9—11 And this I pray, that your love may abound yet more and more in knowledge and *in* all judgment; That ye may approve things that are excellent; that ye may be sincere and without offence till the day of Christ; Being filled with the fruits of righteousness, which are by Jesus Christ, unto the glory and praise of God.

The one point in which the Philippians failed was love and unity among themselves; for this Paul prayed, for it is of the first importance.

12—14 But I would ye should understand, brethren, that the things *which happened* unto me have fallen out rather unto the furtherance of the gospel; So that my bonds in Christ are

manifest in all the palace, and in all other *places;* And many of the brethren in the Lord, waxing confident by my bonds, are much more bold to speak the word without fear.

15—18 Some indeed preach Christ even of envy and strife; and some also of good will: The one preach Christ of contention, not sincerely, supposing to add affliction to my bonds: But the other of love, knowing that I am set for the defence of the gospel. What then? notwithstanding, every way, whether in pretence, or in truth, Christ is preached; and I therein do rejoice, yea, and will rejoice. *(Sweet forgetfulness of self! So long as Christ is glorified, Paul minds not how he himself fares, nor what unkind motives towards himself may actuate other preachers. This is real Christianity.)*

19, 20 For I know that this shall turn to my salvation through your prayer, and the supply of the Spirit of Jesus Christ, According to my earnest expectation and *my* hope, that in nothing I shall be ashamed, but *that* with all boldness, as always, *so* now also Christ shall be magnified in my body, whether *it be* by life, or by death.

He hoped that the spread of the gospel would call Nero's attention to his case, and end his imprisonment one way or another, and little did he care whether he was set free by death, or by being allowed to resume his labours.

21—24 For to me to live *is* Christ, and to die *is* gain. But if I live in the flesh, this *is* the fruit of my labour: yet what I shall choose I wot not. For I am in a strait betwixt two, having a desire to depart, and to be with Christ; which is far better: Nevertheless to abide in the flesh *is* more needful for you.

25, 26 And having this confidence, I know that I shall abide and continue with you all for your furtherance and joy of faith; That your rejoicing may be more abundant in Jesus Christ for me by my coming to you again. *(He would even stay out of heaven a while for their sakes. Oh, to live only to do good! This is to live indeed.)*

Were the whole realm of nature mine
That were a present far too small:
Love so amazing, so divine,
Demands my soul, my life, my all.

714   "**Work out your own salvation with fear and trembling.**"   DECEMBER 2.—MORNING.

[*Or November* 1.]

PHILIPPIANS I. 27—30.

ONLY let your conversation be as it becometh the gospel of Christ: that whether I come and see you, or else be absent, I may hear of your affairs, that ye stand fast in one spirit, with one mind, striving together for the faith of the gospel;

28 And in nothing terrified by your adversaries: which is to them an evident token of perdition, but to you of salvation, and that of God. *(He was most anxious that they should be united in eager zeal for the spread of the gospel, and present a bold front to their persecutors. Men call the courage of the saints obstinacy, and reckon them to be hardened heretics; but such boldness is to believers a token of divine favour.)*

29, 30 For unto you it is given in the behalf of Christ, not only to believe on him, but also to suffer for his sake; Having the same conflict which ye saw in me, *and* now hear *to be* in me.

It would cheer the Philippian saints to remember that they suffered in good company, and were comrades with the apostle himself. Glad enough may we be to be ridiculed for Jesus' sake, since we are thereby made partakers with the noble army of martyrs.

PHILIPPIANS II. 1—16.

IF *there be* therefore any consolation in Christ, if any comfort of love, if any fellowship of the Spirit, if any bowels and mercies, Fulfil ye my joy, that ye be likeminded, having the same love, *being* of one accord, of one mind. *(How urgently he pleads! How he multiplies expressions! Love among Christians is so precious that he begs for it as if for his life. Be it ours never to fan the flames of party-feeling, but always to increase the holy affection of our Christian brethren.)*

3 *Let* nothing *be done* through strife or vainglory; but in lowliness of mind let each esteem other better than themselves.

4—11 Look not every man on his own things, but every man also on the things of others. Let this mind be in you, which was also in Christ Jesus: Who, being in the form of God, thought it not robbery to be equal with God: But made himself of no reputation, and took upon him the form of a servant, and was made in the likeness of men: And being found in fashion as a man, he humbled himself, and became obedient unto death, even the death of the cross. Wherefore God also hath highly exalted him, and given him a name which is above every name: That at the name of Jesus every knee should bow, of *things* in heaven, and *things* in earth, and *things* under the earth; And *that* every tongue should confess that Jesus Christ *is* Lord, to the glory of God the Father. *(Jesus is the divine example of love and self-denial, and as we hope to be saved by him we must diligently copy him. He is now exalted to the highest glory as the reward of his voluntary humiliation, and by the same means must his disciples rise to honour. We must stoop to conquer. He who is willing to be nothing shall be possessor of all things.)*

12, 13 Wherefore, my beloved, as ye have always obeyed, not as in my presence only, but now much more in my absence, work out your own salvation with fear and trembling. For it is God which worketh in you both to will and to do of *his* good pleasure. *(We work out what the Lord works in. The grace of God is not a reason for idleness, but for diligence. As both will and work are given us of God, let us will with firm resolution and work with dauntless perseverance; for so shall we fulfil the good pleasure of the Lord.)*

14, 15 Do all things without murmurings and disputings: That ye may be blameless and harmless, the sons of God, without rebuke, in the midst of a crooked and perverse nation, among whom ye shine as lights in the world;

We cannot be blameless if we murmur and dispute, for such things naturally lead to sin. Our lights cannot shine if instead of trimming them we occupy ourselves with blowing out the lamps of others.

16 Holding forth the word of life; that I may rejoice in the day of Christ, that I have not run in vain, neither laboured in vain.

We do not wish to rob faithful ministers of the result of their labours, and yet we shall do so unless we join heartily with our brethren in spreading the gospel, and do our best to live in holiness and Christian love.

PHILIPPIANS IV.

THEREFORE, my brethren dearly beloved and longed for, my joy and crown, so stand fast in the Lord, *my* dearly beloved.

2 I beseech Euodias, and beseech Syntyche, that they be of the same mind in the Lord.

He pleads with these two good women to end their differences. The worst results may arise from a quarrel, even when there are only two engaged in it, and those two are women.

3 And I entreat thee also, true yokefellow, help those women which laboured with me in the gospel, with Clement also, and *with* other my fellowlabourers, whose names *are* in the book of life.

4 Rejoice in the Lord alway : *and* again I say, Rejoice. *(We cannot have too much holy rejoicing ; we are to joy and re-joy, and then to rejoice again. See that this be done in this house all day long. Alas, none can truly rejoice but those who are in the Lord! Are we all in him?)*

5 Let your moderation be known unto all men. The Lord *is* at hand.

6 Be careful for nothing ; but in every thing by prayer and supplication with thanksgiving let your requests be made known unto God.

Be not careful, but prayerful. Prayer is the cure for care.

7 And the peace of God, which passeth all understanding, shall keep your hearts and minds through Christ Jesus.

8 Finally, brethren, whatsoever things are true, whatsoever things *are* honest, whatsoever things *are* just, whatsoever things *are* pure, whatsoever things *are* lovely, whatsoever things *are* of good report; if *there be* any virtue, and if *there be* any praise, think on these things.

Here is a mass of matter for thought. Take each word and study it, and then put it in practice. Every member of the family should learn this verse by heart ; it is much in little, a catalogue of the practical virtues.

9 Those things, which ye have both learned, and received, and heard, and seen in me, do : and the God of peace shall be with you.

10—13 But I rejoiced in the Lord greatly, that now at the last your care of me hath flourished again ; wherein ye were also careful, but ye lacked opportunity. Not that I speak in respect of want : for I have learned, in what-soever state I am, *therewith* to be content. I know both how to be abased, and I know how to abound : every where and in all things I am instructed both to be full and to be hungry, both to abound and to suffer need. I can do all things through Christ which strengtheneth me.

14 Notwithstanding ye have well done, that ye did communicate with my affliction.

Paul knew how to be poor, but he did not know how to be ungrateful. True ministers will work for the Lord, however badly their people may support them, yet it is well to treat them generously, and win their gratitude, for their Master is pleased when his servants are kindly used for his sake. Is there any deed of love which we can do for our pastor?

15, 16 Now ye Philippians know also, that in the beginning of the gospel, when I departed from Macedonia, no church communicated with me as concerning giving and receiving, but ye only. For even in Thessalonica ye sent once and again unto my necessity.

17 Not because I desire a gift : but I desire fruit that may abound to your account.

18 But I have all, and abound : I am full, having received of Epaphroditus the things *which were sent* from you, an odour of a sweet smell, a sacrifice acceptable, wellpleasing to God.

19 But my God shall supply all your need according to his riches in glory by Christ Jesus.

This is a grand assurance. God is the giver, his infinite glory is the store, Jesus is the channel, and the supply knows no limit. What more can the most expanded desires wish for? This promissory note from the Bank of Faith makes all believers rich beyond a miser's dream.

20 Now unto God and our Father *be* glory for ever and ever. Amen.

21 Salute every saint in Christ Jesus. The brethren which are with me greet you.

22 All the saints salute you, chiefly they that are of Cæsar's household.

23 The grace of our Lord Jesus Christ *be* with you all. Amen. *(Thus with an affectionate wish this fragrant letter of love comes to its close. May more of the tender spirit which it breathes be found in each one of us.)*

716

DECEMBER 3.—MORNING.

"It pleased the Father that in Him should all fulness dwell."

[*Or November* 3.]

IN *the epistle to the church at Colosse Paul had to deal with many dangerous errors and mischievous practices, hence it is more distinguished for earnest warning than for those tender expressions which abound in the epistle to the Philippians.*

COLOSSIANS I. 1—20.

1, 2 Paul, an apostle of Jesus Christ by the will of God, and Timotheus *our* brother, To the saints and faithful brethren in Christ which are at Colosse : Grace *be* unto you, and peace, from God our Father and the Lord Jesus Christ.

3—6 We give thanks to God and the Father of our Lord Jesus Christ, praying always for you, Since we heard of your faith in Christ Jesus, and of the love *which ye have* to all the saints, For the hope which is laid up for you in heaven, whereof ye heard before in the word of the truth of the gospel ; Which is come unto you, as *it is* in all the world ; and bringeth forth fruit, as *it doth* also in you, since the day ye heard *of it,* and knew the grace of God in truth.

7, 8 As ye also learned of Epaphras our dear fellowservant, who is for you a faithful minister of Christ ; who also declared unto us your love in the Spirit. *(It is delightful thus to hear one servant of God praise another. There is far too little of this in our day. True soldiers of Christ set high store by their comrades and are glad to advance their repute. Paul does not point out the failings of Epaphras to the Colossians ; this would have been destructive of the influence of that worthy brother, and so would have injured the cause of Christ.)*

9 For this cause we also, since the day we heard *it,* do not cease to pray for you, and to desire that ye might be filled with the knowledge of his will in all wisdom and spiritual understanding ; *(The Colossian church needed understanding as much as that of Philippi needed unity ; the brethren were too easily duped and decoyed from the gospel. We need in these days to know the gospel well, and hold it firmly ; for many deceivers are abroad who will mislead us if we permit them to do so.)*

10, 11 That ye might walk worthy of the Lord unto all pleasing, being fruitful in every good work, and increasing in the knowledge of God ; Strengthened with all might, according to his glorious power, unto all patience and longsuffering with joyfulness ; *(To labour, to suffer, and in both to rejoice, is the peculiar mark of a Christian. For this we need the all-sufficient grace of God ; nothing short of the glorious power of God can create a Christian, or maintain him when created.)*

12—14 Giving thanks unto the Father, which hath made us meet to be partakers of the inheritance of the saints in light : Who hath delivered us from the power of darkness, and hath translated *us* into the kingdom of his dear Son : In whom we have redemption through his blood, *even* the forgiveness of sins : *(Now that the apostle has touched this string we may expect sweet music, for never is his master-hand so much at home as when he is magnifying the Lord Jesus. Hear how he sounds forth the praises of the Son of God.)*

15—18 Who is the image of the invisible God, the firstborn of every creature : For by him were all things created, that are in heaven, and that are in earth, visible and invisible, whether *they be* thrones, or dominions, or principalities, or powers : all things were created by him, and for him : And he is before all things, and by him all things consist. And he is the head of the body, the church : who is the beginning, the firstborn from the dead ; that in all *things* he might have the pre-eminence.

19, 20 For it pleased *the Father* that in him should all fulness dwell ; And, having made peace through the blood of his cross, by him to reconcile all things unto himself ; by him, *I say,* whether *they be* things in earth, or things in heaven. *(If Jesus be not indeed God, such language as this is far-fetched, not to say blasphemous. What more could be said ? Is not language put to its utmost tension to set forth the Redeemer's glories ? Blessed be his name, he is all in all to us. We adore him as Creator, Head, Fulness, and Peacemaker ; and let others say what they will of him, we shall never cease to sing his praises. Happy will the day be when all those in heaven and earth for whom the Saviour died shall join in one happy band around his throne, united in one body through the atoning sacrifice. Even now we anticipate their victorious song, and sing, " Worthy the Lamb.")*

PAUL *continues to glorify the Lord Jesus, and to stir up his brethren to faithfulness. He shows how the death of Jesus has reconciled us to each other and to God.*

COLOSSIANS I. 21—29.

21, 22 And you, that were sometime alienated and enemies in *your* mind by wicked works, yet now hath he reconciled in the body of his flesh through death, to present you holy and unblameable and unreproveable in his sight : *(Thus the work of grace produces in us the highest degree of holiness : to be unblameable in man's sight is much, but to be unblameable even in the sight of God is absolute perfection. This will be the condition of every believer when the Lord's designs are accomplished in him.)*

23 If ye continue in the faith grounded and settled, and *be* not moved away from the hope of the gospel, which ye have heard, *and* which was preached to every creature which is under heaven ; whereof I Paul am made a minister ; *Steadfastness in the faith is an essential of true religion : a tree often transplanted cannot thrive. Since the gospel is assuredly the truth of God, it is foolishness in the extreme to be enticed from it by the novel teachings of men. Paul gloried in being a minister of the old unchanging gospel.*

24 Who now rejoice in my sufferings for you, and fill up that which is behind of the afflictions of Christ in my flesh for his body's sake, which is the church : *(All the body must suffer in order to have sympathy with the Head ; and in order to gather in all the Lord's chosen the church must undergo a measure of suffering and persecution ; in this Paul was glad to take his share. The atoning sufferings of Jesus were finished long ago, his sufferings in his mystical body are not for the expiation of sin, but arise out of our conflict with the powers of evil.)*

25—27 Whereof I am made a minister, according to the dispensation of God which is given to me for you, to fulfil the word of God ; *Even* the mystery which hath been hid from ages and from generations, but now is made manifest to his saints : To whom God would make known what *is* the riches of the glory of this mystery among the Gentiles ; which is Christ in you, the hope of glory :

28 Whom we preach, warning every man, and teaching every man in all wisdom ; that we may present every man perfect in Christ Jesus :

29 Whereunto I also labour, striving according to his working, which worketh in me mightily.

PAUL *a second time declares his call to the ministry.*

COLOSSIANS II. 1—7.

1—3 For I would that ye knew what great conflict I have for you, and *for* them at Laodicea, and *for* as many as have not seen my face in the flesh ; That their hearts might be comforted, being knit together in love, and unto all riches of the full assurance of understanding, to the acknowledgment of the mystery of God, and of the Father, and of Christ ; In whom are hid all the treasures of wisdom and knowledge.

What wisdom, therefore, it is to know Christ : however simple the gospel may appear to be, it is in very truth far superior in wisdom to all the systems of philosophy, or schools of " modern thought."

4, 5 And this I say, lest any man should beguile you with enticing words. For though I be absent in the flesh, yet am I with you in the spirit, joying and beholding your order, and the stedfastness of your faith in Christ.

6, 7 As ye have therefore received Christ Jesus the Lord, *so* walk ye in him : Rooted and built up in him, and stablished in the faith, as ye have been taught, abounding therein with thanksgiving. *(May the Lord grant us so to do. The gospel which has saved us will do to live by and to die by. To turn from it would be to forsake fulness for emptiness, the substance for the shadow, and the truth for falsehood. May the Holy Spirit continue to lead us yet further into the knowledge of Christ crucified, and never may we in any degree cease from earnest belief of the truth, or lose our thankfulness for it.)*

I rest upon thy word,
The promise is for me ;
My succour and salvation, Lord,
Shall surely come from thee.

But let me still abide,
Nor from my hope remove,
Till thou my patient spirit guide
Into thy perfect love.

THE *portion of scripture which we are about to read, ought to be well understood and earnestly observed by us, for it pleads for the purity and simplicity of the Christian faith, and deals heavy blows at those various additions of men which, under various pretences, are tagged on to the simple gospel. We need to stand fast to the plain, simple, gospel of Jesus; for to adorn it is to deface it, to add to it is to dishonour it.*

COLOSSIANS II. 8—23.

8 Beware lest any man spoil you through philosophy and vain deceit, after the tradition of men, after the rudiments of the world, and not after Christ. *(Pretendedly wise men would improve the gospel: as well might they dream of adding lustre to the sun or fulness to the ocean.)*

9 For in him dwelleth all the fulness of the Godhead bodily. *(What then can we need more? How can his gospel be improved?)*

10—12 And ye are complete in him, which is the head of all principality and power: In whom also ye are circumcised with the circumcision made without hands, in putting off the body of the sins of the flesh by the circumcision of Christ: Buried with him in baptism, wherein also ye are risen with *him* through the faith of the operation of God, who hath raised him from the dead. *(We have all things in Jesus, and want no Jewish or Popish rites: to all these we are dead and buried, our baptism teaches us that; and by faith we are risen from all dead formalities into a new spiritual life, which requires none of the ordinances of man to sustain it. We ought to beware of those gaudy rites with which Ritualists now mar the gospel of Jesus.)*

13—15 And you, being dead in your sins and the uncircumcision of your flesh, hath he quickened together with him, having forgiven you all trespasses; Blotting out the handwriting of ordinances that was against us, which was contrary to us, and took it out of the way, nailing it to his cross; *And* having spoiled principalities and powers, he made a shew of them openly, triumphing over them in it.

Christ on the cross has vanquished sin and ended the ceremonial law; let us not return to the bondage from which his death has set us free.

16, 17 Let no man therefore judge you in meat, or in drink, or in respect of an holyday, or of the new moon, or of the sabbath *days:* Which are a shadow of things to come; but the body *is* of Christ. *(From all human laws, as to holy days and fastings and ceremonies, we are free; they are vain shadows; Jesus is the true substance.)*

18, 19 Let no man beguile you of your reward in a voluntary humility and worshipping of angels, intruding into those things which he hath not seen, vainly puffed up by his fleshly mind, And not holding the Head, from which all the body by joints and bands having nourishment ministered, and knit together, increaseth with the increase of God. *(How plainly the angel-worship of the church of Rome is here condemned! What have we to do with adoring angels when we are already members of a body which has a divine head?)*

20, 21 Wherefore if ye be dead with Christ from the rudiments of the world, why, as though living in the world, are ye subject to ordinances, (Touch not; taste not; handle not;

22 Which all are to perish with the using;) after the commandments and doctrines of men?

Why bind yourselves with man's commands when you are dead to them all in Christ? Jesus gives you liberty, why put upon your shoulders a new yoke?

23 Which things have indeed a shew of wisdom in will worship, and humility, and neglecting of the body; not in any honour to the satisfying of the flesh. *(The precepts of men as to regarding different days, and rejecting certain kinds of food, appear to be wise and to foster humility, but it is only so in mere appearance, and Christians, being under the law of liberty, should refuse to bring themselves into bondage. One is our Master, even Christ; it is enough for us to obey his will and abide in the liberty which he has so dearly purchased for us, and so graciously given to us.)*

In thy promises I trust,
In thy precious word confide,
I am prostrate in the dust,
I with Christ was crucified.

Jesus lives—he fills my soul,
Perfected in him I am ;
I am every whit made whole,
Glory, glory to the Lamb

COLOSSIANS III.

IF ye then be risen with Christ, seek those things which are above, where Christ sitteth on the right hand of God.

2, 3 Set your affection on things above, not on things on the earth. For ye are dead, and your life is hid with Christ in God.

4 When Christ, *who is* our life, shall appear, then shall ye also appear with him in glory.

So completely are we renewed by regeneration that we are dead to the old life, and only live in Jesus. We cannot love the things of earth : our hearts are in heaven, our very life is there, where Jesus is, and until he comes we live a hidden life which worldlings cannot perceive or comprehend.

5—7 Mortify therefore your members which are upon the earth; fornication, uncleanness, inordinate affection, evil concupiscence, and covetousness, which is idolatry : For which things' sake the wrath of God cometh on the children of disobedience : In the which ye also walked some time, when ye lived in them.

8 But now ye also put off all these ; anger, wrath, malice, blasphemy, filthy communication out of your mouth. *(New men should have new manners, and new garments. The cast-off rags of our sinful estate must never be allowed to dishonour and defile us now.)*

9 Lie not one to another, seeing that ye have put off the old man with his deeds ;

The heathen gloried in clever deceits ; we have for ever done with falsehood of every kind.

10, 11 And have put on the new *man*, which is renewed in knowledge after the image of him that created him : Where there is neither Greek nor Jew, circumcision nor uncircumcision, Barbarian, Scythian, bond *nor* free : but Christ *is* all, and in all.

12 Put on, therefore, as the elect of God, holy and beloved, bowels of mercies, kindness, humbleness of mind, meekness, longsuffering ;

13 Forbearing one another, and forgiving one another, if any man have a quarrel against any: even as Christ forgave you, so also *do* ye.

14 And above all these things *put on* charity *(or love)*, which is the bond of perfectness.

15 And let the peace of God rule in your hearts to the which also ye are called in one body ; and be ye thankful. *(Sweet precept ! How often is it forgotten ! " Be ye thankful.")*

16 Let the word of Christ dwell in you richly in all wisdom ; teaching and admonishing one another in psalms and hymns and spiritual songs, singing with grace in your hearts to the Lord.

17 And whatsoever ye do in word or deed, *do* all in the name of the Lord Jesus, giving thanks to God and the Father by him.

A golden rule for all times, places, and duties. Life on earth would be like heaven below were this continually practised.

18 Wives, submit yourselves unto your own husbands, as it is fit in the Lord.

19 Husbands, love *your* wives, and be not bitter against them.

20 Children, obey *your* parents in all things : for this is well pleasing unto the Lord.

21 Fathers, provoke not your children *to anger*, lest they be discouraged.

22—25 Servants, obey in all things *your* masters according to the flesh ; not with eye-service, as menpleasers ; but in singleness of heart, fearing God : And whatsoever ye do, do *it* heartily, as to the Lord, and not unto men ; Knowing that of the Lord ye shall receive the reward of the inheritance : for ye serve the Lord Christ. But he that doeth wrong shall receive for the wrong which he hath done : and there is no respect of persons.

COLOSSIANS IV. 1.

1 Masters, give unto *your* servants that which is just and equal ; knowing that ye also have a Master in heaven. *(So that while we are free from the traditions of men, we are under law to Christ. Let us each one observe the precept which belongs to his condition. May the Spirit of all grace make all of us models, whether as parents or children, masters or servants, and to God shall be all the praise.)*

Be dead, my heart, to worldly charms ;
    Be dead to every sin ;
And tell the boldest foes without,
    That Jesus reigns within.

My life with his united stands,
    Nor asks a surer ground ;
He keeps me in his gracious arms,
    Where heaven itself is found.

I. THESSALONIANS II. 1—16.

THIS *is the first of the apostle's epistles, and was probably written by him from Corinth, when, having left Athens, he was joined by Silas and Timothy. Paul had founded the church at Thessalonica, and it had greatly flourished, but it had been subject to much persecution, hence he treats largely upon the second advent as affording the richest consolation to tried saints. The passage we shall read gives us a lovely picture of the apostle's earnestness for the good of souls, and it furnishes us with a grand example of how we also in our measure should serve the Lord.*

1, 2 For yourselves, brethren, know our entrance in unto you, that it was not in vain : But even after that we had suffered before, and were shamefully entreated, as ye know, at Philippi, we were bold in our God to speak unto you the gospel of God with much contention.

3, 4 For our exhortation *was* not of deceit, nor of uncleanness, nor in guile : But as we were allowed of God to be put in trust with the gospel, even so we speak ; not as pleasing men, but God, which trieth our hearts. *(If the preacher of the word be not bold and truthful he cannot expect a blessing. A trustee of the gospel must be faithful to his charge.)*

5, 6 For neither at any time used we flattering words, as ye know, nor a cloke of covetousness ; God *is* witness : Nor of men sought we glory, neither of you, nor *yet* of others, when we might have been burdensome, as the apostles of Christ.

7, 8 But we were gentle among you, even as a nurse cherisheth her children : *(Gentleness wins far more than severity. Many will be led who will not be driven).* So being affectionately desirous of you, we were willing to have imparted unto you, not the gospel of God only, but also our own souls, because ye were dear unto us. *(If we would do good to others we must be willing to sacrifice ourselves. Selfishness and soul-winning never go together. Love is power. What are we doing for our neighbours ? Have we an affectionate concern for their eternal welfare ? If not, how can we hope that we are ourselves converted ?)*

9—12 For ye remember, brethren, our labour and travail : for labouring night and day, be-

cause we would not be chargeable unto any of you, we preached unto you the gospel of God. Ye *are* witnesses, and God *also*, how holily and justly and unblameably we behaved ourselves among you that believe : As ye know how we exhorted and comforted and charged every one of you, as a father *doth* his children, That ye would walk worthy of God, who hath called you unto his kingdom and glory. *(Holy living is the great end of preaching. Hearing is nothing if it does not lead to this.)*

13—15 For this cause also thank we God without ceasing, because when ye received the word of God which ye heard of us, ye received *it* not *as* the word of men, but as it is in truth, the word of God, which effectually worketh also in you that believe. For ye, brethren, became followers of the churches of God which in Judæa are in Christ Jesus : for ye also have suffered like things of your own countrymen, even as they *have* of the Jews : Who both killed the Lord Jesus, and their own prophets, and have persecuted us ; and they please not God, and are contrary to all men : *(They had no love either for God or men. It is said of them that they would not even point out the way to a person of a different religion. Their bigotry had destroyed their humanity.) Nothing is more hardening to the heart than religious pride, it is the death of love.)*

16 Forbidding us to speak to the Gentiles that they might be saved, to fill up their sins alway : for the wrath is come upon them to the uttermost. *(Men cannot oppose the gospel without incurring great guilt. If they reject the Saviour who saves to the uttermost, they bring upon themselves "wrath to the uttermost," and that must be terrible indeed. May none of us bring such a doom upon our own heads.)*

Give tongues of fire and hearts of love,
To preach the reconciling word ;
Give power and unction from above,
Whene'er the joyful sound is heard.

Be darkness, at thy coming, light,
Confusion, order in thy path ;
Souls without strength inspire with might ;
Bid mercy triumph over wrath.

PAUL, *having spoken of the coming of the Lord, now tells the Thessalonians that they were not curiously to inquire as to the appointed date of the advent, but to live in daily preparation of the Lord's appearing.*

I. THESSALONIANS V.

1 But of the times and the seasons, brethren, ye have no need that I write unto you.

2 For yourselves know perfectly that the day of the Lord so cometh as a thief in the night.

3 For when they shall say, Peace and safety: then sudden destruction cometh upon them, as travail upon a woman with child; and they shall not escape.

4 But ye, brethren, are not in darkness, that that day should overtake you as a thief.

5, 6 Ye are all the children of light, and the children of the day: we are not of the night, nor of darkness. Therefore let us not sleep, as do others; but let us watch and be sober.

7 For they that sleep, sleep in the night; and they that be drunken, are drunken in the night.

8 But let us, who are of the day, be sober, putting on the breastplate of faith and love; and for an helmet, the hope of salvation.

9 For God hath not appointed us to wrath, but to obtain salvation by our Lord Jesus Christ,.

10 Who died for us, that, whether we wake or sleep, we should live together with him.

To others the advent will be an unexpected calamity, to us a long hoped for day of exultation. Ours it is to live with Jesus always, so that life or death shall make no difference. As a child both sleeping and waking is at home in his father's house, so whether here or in heaven we are still living together with Jesus.

11 Wherefore comfort yourselves together, and edify one another, even as also ye do.

Are we doing this? Mutual consolation and edification are very much too rare in these days.

12, 13 And we beseech you, brethren, to know them which labour among you, and are over you in the Lord, and admonish you; And to esteem them very highly in love for their work's sake. (*Be well acquainted with your minister, and esteem him for the sake of his work and his Master. He has many trials, and his work is arduous: endeavour to cheer his heart.*) *And* be at peace among yourselves.

14 Now we exhort you, brethren, warn them that are unruly, comfort the feebleminded, support the weak, be patient toward all *men.*

15 See that none render evil for evil unto any *man;* but ever follow that which is good, both among yourselves, and to all *men.*

16 Rejoice evermore.

17 Pray without ceasing.

18 In every thing give thanks: for this is the will of God in Christ Jesus concerning you.

Prayer comes in between two precepts of joy. Praise, pray, and then praise again; ring the changes upon the silver bells of devotion.

19 Quench not the Spirit. (*Resist not his sacred drawings, silence not his voice either in others or in your own soul.*)

20 Despise not prophesyings.

21 Prove all things; hold fast that which is good. (*Some are so busy with proving all things that they forget to hold fast that which is good; such persons use compasses with one foot, and so cannot complete the circle of holy duty.*)

22 Abstain from all appearance of evil.

You cannot be too careful: if there be any manifestation of evil, however slight, shun it at once. Flee from the lion's roar, and you need not dread his teeth.

23, 24 And the very God of peace sanctify you wholly; and *I pray God* your whole spirit and soul and body be preserved blameless unto the coming of our Lord Jesus Christ. Faithful *is* he that calleth you, who also will do *it.*

25 Brethren, pray for us. (*If the apostle asked for prayer, how much more does our pastor need it! We ought never to forget him, either in family prayer or on our knees alone.*)

26 Greet all the brethren with an holy kiss. (*Or as our western custom is, give them all a hearty shake of the hand. Christianity delights in sincere and loving courtesies.*)

27 I charge you by the Lord that this epistle be read unto all the holy brethren.

28 The grace of our Lord Jesus Christ *be* with you. Amen.

I am waiting for the coming
  Of the Lord who died for me;
Oh, his words have thrilled my spirit,
  "I will come again for thee."

I can almost hear his foot-fall
  On the threshold of the door,
And my heart, my heart is longing
  To be his for evermore.

722   *" Let no man deceive you by any means."*   DECEMBER 6.—MORNING.

[*Or November 9.*]

PAUL'S *first letter to the Thessalonians was misunderstood, and he therefore wrote them a second time. They had come to believe that the Lord would appear at once, whereas all that Paul had stated was, that the Lord would certainly come, that the time was unrevealed, and that, therefore, they should live in daily watchfulness. He here corrects their wrong impressions.*

II. THESSALONIANS II.

1, 2 Now we beseech you, brethren, by the coming of our Lord Jesus Christ, and *by* our gathering together unto him, That ye be not soon shaken in mind, or be troubled, neither by spirit, nor by word, nor by letter, as from us, as that the day of Christ is at hand.

3, 4 Let no man deceive you by any means; for *that day shall not come,* except there come a falling away first, and that man of sin be revealed, the son of perdition; Who opposeth and exalteth himself above all that is called. God, or that is worshipped; so that he as God sitteth in the temple of God, shewing himself that he is God. (*It is difficult to give this passage any other interpretation than the common one. The evil system of Popery was foreseen by the apostle, and it is every day developing itself. A few months ago the Pope claimed to be infallible, but long before he had been publicly adored, and spoken of as " our Lord God the Pope." The Popish system teaches that the priest creates his Creator, and thus it sets the son of perdition above God himself. If the Pope has not yet formally proclaimed himself actually to be God, we have only to wait a little and even this climax of blasphemy will be reached. Perhaps, when that last profanity shall have been perpetrated, the Lord will immediately come, but this we know not.*)

5 Remember ye not, that, when I was yet with you, I told you these things?

6 And now ye know what withholdeth that he might be revealed in his time.

7 For the mystery of iniquity doth already work: only he who now letteth *will let,* until he be taken out of the way. (*There were elements at work even in Paul's day, which only needed the removal of persecution to develop themselves. The traditions of men were beginning to mislead the church, and Paul saw that in after years, when the civil powers ceased their opposition,*

the pride of man would be rampant, and the church would yield to Antichrist.)

8—10 And then shall that Wicked be revealed, whom the Lord shall consume with the spirit of his mouth, and shall destroy with the brightness of his coming: *Even him,* whose coming is after the working of Satan with all power and signs and lying wonders, And with all deceivableness of unrighteousness in them that perish; because they received not the love of the truth, that they might be saved.

11, 12 And for this cause God shall send them strong delusion, that they should believe a lie: That they all might be damned who believed not the truth, but had pleasure in unrighteousness. (*It is hard to account for the apparent sincerity of Romish emissaries and their dupes, except upon the theory that they are given over to their delusions and justly left to perish in their own folly.*)

13, 14 But we are bound to give thanks alway to God for you, brethren beloved of the Lord, because God hath from the beginning chosen you to salvation through sanctification of the Spirit and belief of the truth: Whereunto he called you by our gospel, to the obtaining of the glory of our Lord Jesus Christ.

Electing love has called us out of the world and saved us from the vile priestcraft which slays its thousands: let us give thanks to God for this as long as we live.

15 Therefore, brethren, stand fast, and hold the traditions which ye have been taught, whether by word, or our epistle. (*Hold such traditions, but not the traditions of men.*)

16, 17 Now our Lord Jesus Christ himself, and God, even our Father, which hath loved us, and hath given *us* everlasting consolation and good hope through grace, Comfort your hearts, and stablish you in every good word and work. (*A blessed prayer. Comfort and stablish —two choice blessings; Lord grant them to us for Jesus' sake. Amen.*)

Hasten, Lord! the promised hour;
Come in glory and in power;
Still thy foes are unsubdued;
Nature sighs to be renewed.

Time has nearly reach'd its sum,
All things with thy bride say, " Come;"
Jesus, whom all worlds adore,
Come, and reign for evermore!

II. THESSALONIANS III.

FINALLY, brethren, pray for us, that the word of the Lord may have *free* course, and be glorified, even as *it is* with you :

2 And that we may be delivered from unreasonable and wicked men : for all *men* have not faith. *(Unreasonable men are almost as troublesome, and quite as dangerous, as those who are really bad; and men who are false and faithless are, above all, painful to deal with.)*

3 But the Lord is faithful, who shall stablish you, and keep *you* from evil. *(God is faithful; this is the great antidote for all the ills inflicted on us by evil and unfaithful men.)*

4 And we have confidence in the Lord touching you, that ye both do and will do the things which we command you.

5 And the Lord direct your hearts into the love of God, and into the patient waiting for Christ. *(They had been hasty in expecting the Lord to come at once, he now bids them be patient in their waiting. They were to look for the Lord soberly and patiently, and not as those fanatics did who ceased from their labours and neglected their lawful callings because they deemed that the end of the world was near.)*

6, 7 Now we command you, brethren, in the name of our Lord Jesus Christ, that ye withdraw yourselves from every brother that walketh disorderly, and not after the tradition which he received of us. For yourselves know how ye ought to follow us : for we behaved not ourselves disorderly among you; *(Paul and his friends had not acted in a fanatical manner and neglected sober, orderly labour, and he quotes his own example against the disorderly ones at Thessalonica. When men or women neglect their work on the pretence of religion they are acting improperly, and ought not to be countenanced by honest Christian people.)*

8—10 Neither did we eat any man's bread for nought; but wrought with labour and travail night and day, that we might not be chargeable to any of you : Not because we have not power, but to make ourselves an ensample unto you to follow us. For even when we were with you, this we commanded you, that if any would not work, neither should he eat. *(Laziness is sin. There is bread for the industrious, but none for the idle. May none in our household ever disgrace themselves and us by being sluggards.)*

11 For we hear that there are some which walk among you disorderly, working not at all, but are busybodies.

12 Now them that are such we command and exhort by our Lord Jesus Christ, that with quietness they work, and eat their own bread. *Some eat other people's bread almost all their lives. It is pleasant to help the needy, but it is a hard tax to have to support the indolent. Young people should strive to ease their parents as soon as possible of the task of supporting them, and receivers of the alms of the church should make conscience of never receiving a penny more than they absolutely need.*

13, 14 But ye, brethren, be not weary in well doing. And if any man obey not our word by this epistle, note that man, and have no company with him, that he may be ashamed.

15 Yet count *him* not as an enemy, but admonish *him* as a brother. *(Members of Christian churches have solemn duties to each other, for purposes of mutual discipline. If a man be regarded as a brother he is to be treated as such, but if he errs he is not to stand on the same footing as to converse and confidence as those who walk in an orderly manner. There must be love to him as a brother, but he must be made to feel that his sin grieves us.)*

16 Now the Lord of peace himself give you peace always by all means. The Lord *be* with you all. *(This devout wish seems even now to whisper over this family its gentle benediction. " The Lord be with you all" is a blessing fitly falling from an apostle's lips, and to it the holiest of men may joyfully say Amen from their very hearts.)*

17, 18 The salutation of Paul with mine own hand, which is the token in every epistle: so I write. The grace of our Lord Jesus Christ *be* with you all. Amen.

Enrich us with thy blessing Lord ;
Help us to feed upon thy word ;
All we have done amiss, forgive,
And let thy truth within us live.

Though we are guilty, thou art good :
Wash all our works in Jesus' blood ;
From every burden grant release,
And fill us all with perfect peace.

HITHERTO *we have only read portions from Paul's letters to churches; we now turn to one of his four epistles to individual Christians. It was written to Timothy, who was very dear to the apostle as one of the most affectionate, faithful, and gifted of his spiritual children.*

I. TIMOTHY I.

1, 2 Paul, an apostle of Jesus Christ by the commandment of God our Saviour, and Lord Jesus Christ, *which is* our hope; Unto Timothy, *my* own son in the faith: Grace, mercy, *and* peace, from God our Father and Jesus Christ our Lord.

3, 4 As I besought thee to abide still at Ephesus, when I went into Macedonia, that thou mightest charge some that they teach no other doctrine, Neither give heed to fables and endless genealogies, which minister questions rather than godly edifying which is in faith: *so do. (Jewish "teachers of the law" introduced into the churches a kind of mystic philosophy, made up of foolish legends, spiritualizings, and ascetical precepts, which Paul did not hesitate to call "old wives' fables" and "profane babblings." Timothy was stationed at Ephesus, to do battle with these mischief-makers, and to set the church in order. In these times there are tendencies to absurdities of the same kind, and we should be upon our guard against them. That which pretends to be wiser, deeper, or holier than the word of God must come from the father of lies.)*

5—7 Now the end of the commandment is charity out of a pure heart, and *of* a good conscience, and *of* faith unfeigned: From which some having swerved have turned aside unto vain jangling; Desiring to be teachers of the law; understanding neither what they say, nor whereof they affirm. *(Some teachers of our own day are for ever raising questions upon points of no practical value. Such vain jangling let us keep clear of, and follow the simple teachings of our Lord Jesus.)*

8—11 But we know that the law *is* good, if a man use it lawfully; Knowing this, that the law is not made for a righteous man, but for the lawless and disobedient, for the ungodly and for sinners, for unholy and profane, for murderers of fathers and murderers of mothers, for manslayers, for whoremongers, for them that defile themselves with mankind, for menstealers, for liars, for perjured persons, and if there be any other thing that is contrary to sound doctrine; According to the glorious gospel of the blessed God, which was committed to my trust.

12, 14 And I thank Christ Jesus our Lord, who hath enabled me, for that he counted me faithful, putting me into the ministry; Who was before a blasphemer, and a persecutor, and injurious: but I obtained mercy, because I did *it* ignorantly in unbelief. And the grace of our Lord was exceeding abundant with faith and love which is in Christ Jesus.

15 This *is* a faithful saying, and worthy of all acceptation, that Christ Jesus came into the world to save sinners; of whom I am chief. *This is a Christian proverb, an axiom of our creed, "familiar in our mouths as household words," and right well does it deserve to be repeated and received by all mankind.*

16 Howbeit for this cause I obtained mercy, that in me first Jesus Christ might shew forth all longsuffering, for a pattern to them which should hereafter believe on him to life everlasting.

17 Now unto the King eternal, immortal, invisible, the only wise God, *be* honour and glory for ever and ever. Amen. *(At thought of the grace which saved him, Paul broke forth into a doxology, and well he might.)*

18—20 This charge I commit unto thee, son Timothy, according to the prophecies which went before on thee, that thou by them mightest war a good warfare; Holding faith, and a good conscience; which some having put away, concerning faith have made shipwreck: Of whom is Hymenæus and Alexander; whom I have delivered unto Satan, that they may learn not to blaspheme. *(Perhaps they were left to follow out the natural tendency of their doctrines under the influence of Satan until they should see by actual experience where their teachings would land them, and would then have grace to repent. May the Lord keep us free from all false doctrine lest we come under the like condemnation.)*

Now to the God of victory,
Immortal thanks be paid,
Who makes us conquerors while we die,
Through Christ our living Head.

IN *this letter to Timothy Paul denounces many of those forms of error which have been the plague of the Christian church in all ages. Those who deal with spirits, or profess to do so, those who multiply forms and ceremonies, those who make religion to lie in meats and drinks, and those who attach importance to legends and traditions, are all heavily censured, as they deserve.*

I. TIMOTHY IV.

1 Now the Spirit speaketh expressly, that in the latter times some shall depart from the faith, giving heed to seducing spirits, and doctrines of devils : *(leading on to the worship of angels, fear of demons, and attempts at commerce with the dead. In every age some deceivers and deceived ones have wandered in this direction. Far from us be such darkness.)*

2 Speaking lies in hypocrisy ; having their conscience seared with a hot iron. *(As a hot iron deadens the part which it burns, so is their conscience no longer sensitive, and they can utter falsehood unblushingly.)*

3 Forbidding to marry, *and commanding* to abstain from meats, which God hath created to be received with thanksgiving of them which believe and know the truth. *(How well this describes the Church of Rome, which combines both superstitions. Other sects also have decried marriage, and issued laws as to eating and drinking, making that to be sin which is no sin.)*

4, 5 For every creature of God *is* good, and nothing to be refused, if it be received with thanksgiving : For it is sanctified by the word of God and prayer.

6 If thou put the brethren in remembrance of these things, thou shalt be a good minister of Jesus Christ, nourished up in the words of faith and of good doctrine, whereunto thou hast attained. *(To hold fast the true faith is one of our first duties. To be for ever chopping and changing is a most unhappy and dangerous condition.)*

7 But refuse profane and old wives' fables, and exercise thyself *rather* unto godliness.

8 For bodily exercise profiteth little : *(or a little ; it may, when rightly used, promote bodily health, but that is all):* but godliness is profitable unto all things, having promise of the life that now is, and of that which is to come.

9, 10 This *is* a faithful saying and worthy of all acceptation. For therefore we both labour and suffer reproach, because we trust in the living God, who is the Saviour of all men, specially of those that believe. *(All men derive some benefit from Jesus' death. They are spared, they enjoy the common blessings of providence, and they are placed under mediatorial rule ; yet redemption has its special design and effect, and these have to do only with believers. The Saviour has bought some good things for all men, and all good things for some men. Are we believers ? Then, in a special sense, Jesus is our Saviour.)*

11 These things command and teach.

12 Let no man despise thy youth ; but be thou an example of the believers, in word, in conversation, in charity, in spirit, in faith, in purity.

13 Till I come, give attendance to reading, to exhortation, to doctrine.

14 Neglect not the gift that is in thee, which was given thee by prophecy, with the laying on of the hands of the presbytery. *(Even when the miraculous gifts of the Spirit were in the church the most favoured ministers were to study and meditate : how much more then is it now their duty ! Those who speak without thinking seldom say anything worth thinking of.)*

15, 16 Meditate upon these things ; give thyself wholly to them ; *(Or " be thou wholly in them." Be absorbed in thy work,)* that thy profiting may appear to all. Take heed unto thyself, and unto the doctrine ; continue in them : for in doing this thou shalt both save thyself, and them that hear thee. *(Care as to our doctrine will both preserve the teacher himself from serious error, and keep his hearers from the same evil. This should lead us to be very prayerful, and careful as to what we receive, and what we communicate to others. Doctrines are not to be trifled with, they are life and death matters. Lord teach us thy truth.)*

Make me to understand
Thy precepts and thy will ;
Thy wondrous works on every hand,
I'll sing and talk of still.

THE *first epistle to Timothy concludes with a practical exhortation relating to various classes in the church, and with an earnest word to the young minister himself.*

I. TIMOTHY VI.

1, 2 Let as many servants as are under the yoke count their own masters worthy of all honour, that the name of God and *his* doctrine be not blasphemed. And they that have believing masters, let them not despise *them*, because they are brethren ; but rather do *them* service, because they are faithful and beloved, partakers of the benefit. These things teach and exhort. *(For Christian servants to take undue liberties because their employers are believers, is shameful, they ought rather to render them higher respect and more willing service.)*

3—5 If any man teach otherwise, and consent not to wholesome words, *even* the words of our Lord Jesus Christ, and to the doctrine which is according to godliness ; He is proud, knowing nothing, but doting about questions and strifes of words, whereof cometh envy, strife, railings, evil surmisings, Perverse disputings of men of corrupt minds, and destitute of the truth, supposing that gain is godliness : from such withdraw thyself.

6 But godliness with contentment is great gain. *(It makes us truly happy, by making our little into much and sweetening all the trials of life. "Poor and content is rich, and rich enough.")*

7, 8 For we brought nothing into *this* world, *and it is* certain we can carry nothing out. And having food and raiment let us be therewith content. *(Enough is as good as a feast, and frequently better, for it saves us from the ills of surfeit,—the sure punishment of greediness.)*

9, 10 But they that will be rich fall into temptation and a snare, and *into* many foolish and hurtful lusts, which drown men in destruction and perdition. For the love of money is the root of all evil : which while some coveted after, they have erred from the faith, and pierced themselves through with many sorrows. *Money can be used for the best of purposes, but the love of it is idolatry and the cause of countless evils. How is it that so many professed Christians live only to make money, and are just as eager after wealth as the avowed worldling?*

11, 12 But thou, O man of God, flee these things ; and follow after righteousness, godliness, faith, love, patience, meekness. Fight the good fight of faith, lay hold on eternal life, whereunto thou art also called and hast professed a good profession before many witnesses.

13—16 I give thee charge in the sight of God, who quickeneth all things, and *before* Christ Jesus, who before Pontius Pilate witnessed a good confession ; That thou keep *this* commandment without spot, unrebukeable, until the appearing of our Lord Jesus Christ : Which in his times he shall shew, *who is* the blessed and only Potentate, the King of kings, and Lord of lords ; who only hath immortality, dwelling in the light which no man can approach unto ; whom no man hath seen, nor can see ; to whom *be* honour and power everlasting. Amen.

17—19 Charge them that are rich in this world, that they be not highminded, nor trust in uncertain riches, but in the living God, who giveth us richly all things to enjoy ; That they do good, that they be rich in good works, ready to distribute, willing to communicate ; Laying up in store for themselves a good foundation against the time to come, that they may lay hold on eternal life. *(Having spoken to those who seek riches, he now admonishes those who possess them, that they must not hoard for themselves, but lay up treasure in heaven by generously distributing their goods on earth. Have we property ? Let us hold it as stewards of the Lord. It is both our duty and our happiness to use all that we have to glorify him who, though he was rich, yet became poor for our sakes. Is he truly ours ? Then let all ours be truly his.)*

20 O Timothy, keep that which is committed to thy trust, avoiding profane *and* vain babblings, and oppositions of science falsely so called :

21 Which some professing have erred concerning the faith. Grace *be* with thee. Amen.

O Lord, grant that grace may be with us also, this day and till the last great day. Amen.

Let us, in life and death,
Thy steadfast truth declare ;
And publish with our atest breath,
Thy love, and guardian care.

II. TIMOTHY I.

THE second epistle to Timothy is remarkable as being probably the last which the apostle wrote; it contains dying advice, written in the immediate prospect of martyrdom. Looking forward calmly to the grave, and with the executioner's axe in the foreground, Paul pens this letter to his favourite disciple, and solemnly charges him to abide faithful unto death.

1, 2 Paul, an apostle of Jesus Christ by the will of God, according to the promise of life which is in Christ Jesus, To Timothy, my dearly beloved son: Grace, mercy, and peace, from God the Father and Christ Jesus our Lord.

3—5 I thank God, whom I serve from my forefathers with pure conscience, that without ceasing I have remembrance of thee in my prayers night and day; Greatly desiring to see thee, being mindful of thy tears, that I may be filled with joy; When I call to remembrance the unfeigned faith that is in thee, which dwelt first in thy grandmother Lois, and thy mother Eunice; and I am persuaded that in thee also.

We see here the inmost heart of Paul. Deserted by many of his friends, and in the feebleness of old age, expecting a cruel death, he cherishes the memory of his beloved young disciple, and longs to look once more upon his face. With joy he remembers the holy mother and grandmother of his friend, and the unfeigned piety of Timothy himself. How natural and how touching!

6, 7 Wherefore I put thee in remembrance that thou stir up the gift of God, which is in thee by the putting on of my hands. For God hath not given us the spirit of fear; but of power, and of love, and of a sound mind.

8—10 Be not thou therefore ashamed of the testimony of our Lord, nor of me his prisoner: (Do not hesitate to come to Rome and bear with me the reproaches and dangers which belong to the ministers of Christ,) but be thou partaker of the afflictions of the gospel according to the power of God; Who hath saved us, and called us with an holy calling, not according to our works, but according to his own purpose and grace, which was given us in Christ Jesus before the world began, But is now made manifest by the appearing of our Saviour Jesus Christ, who hath abolished death, and hath brought life and immortality to light through the gospel:

"The old man eloquent" feels his soul kindling as he describes the glories of the gospel, eternal in its purpose, matchless in its achievements. He sits on the brink of the grave, and sings of one who hath abolished death. Faith in the resurrection could alone suggest such a triumphant exclamation.

11, 12 Whereunto I am appointed a preacher, and an apostle, and a teacher of the Gentiles. For the which cause I also suffer these things: nevertheless I am not ashamed: for I know whom I have believed, and am persuaded that he is able to keep that which I have committed unto him against that day.

13 Hold fast the form of sound words, which thou hast heard of me, in faith and love which is in Christ Jesus. (This is the main burden of the apostle's pleading with Timothy, "Hold fast." We have equal need of the same exhortation, for this is an evil day, and thousands hold everything or nothing as the winds of opinion may change.)

14 That good thing which was committed unto thee keep by the Holy Ghost which dwelleth in us.

15 This thou knowest, that all they which are in Asia be turned away from me; of whom are Phygellus and Hermogenes.

16—18 The Lord give mercy unto the house of Onesiphorus; for he oft refreshed me, and was not ashamed of my chain: But, when he was in Rome, he sought me out very diligently, and found me. The Lord grant unto him that he may find mercy of the Lord in that day: and in how many things he ministered unto me at Ephesus, thou knowest very well.

This good man is here immortalised. When he risked his life to find out and succour a poor despised prisoner, he little knew that he would live for ever on the page of the church's history. His cup of cold water given to an apostle has received an apostle's reward. Are there any yet alive like Paul to whom we might minister in love after the manner of Onesiphorus?

Stripp'd of my earthly friends,
I find them all in One;
And peace, and joy that never ends,
And heav'n, in Christ alone!

728

DECEMBER 9.—MORNING.

"𝕷𝖊𝖙 𝖊𝖛𝖊𝖗𝖞 𝖔𝖓𝖊 𝖙𝖍𝖆𝖙 𝖓𝖆𝖒𝖊𝖙𝖍 𝖙𝖍𝖊 𝖓𝖆𝖒𝖊 𝖔𝖋 𝕮𝖍𝖗𝖎𝖘𝖙 𝖉𝖊𝖕𝖆𝖗𝖙 𝖋𝖗𝖔𝖒 𝖎𝖓𝖎𝖖𝖚𝖎𝖙𝖞."

[*Or November* 15.]

II. TIMOTHY II.

THOU therefore, my son, be strong in the grace that is in Christ Jesus. And the things that thou hast heard of me among many witnesses, the same commit thou to faithful men, who shall be able to teach others also.

3 Thou therefore endure hardness, as a good soldier of Jesus Christ.

4 No man that warreth entangleth himself with the affairs of *this* life; that he may please him who hath chosen him to be a soldier.

Soldiers must be free from other business, and it is well for ministers not to encumber themselves with any other pursuit, but give themselves wholly to their Master's work. If so, their people must see that they are supplied with all they need, even as a nation sees that its soldiers have their rations and all other necessaries.

5 And if a man also strive for masteries, *yet* is he not crowned, except he strive lawfully.

6 The husbandman that laboureth must be first partaker of the fruits.

7 Consider what I say; and the Lord give thee understanding in all things.

8, 9 Remember that Jesus Christ of the seed of David was raised from the dead according to my gospel : Wherein I suffer trouble, as an evil doer, *even* unto bonds ; but the word of God is not bound. *(This was his consolation, he was bound, but the gospel was not.)*

10—13 Therefore I endure all things for the elect's sakes, that they may also obtain the salvation which is in Christ Jesus with eternal glory. It *is* a faithful saying : For if we be dead with *him*, we shall also live with *him* : If we suffer, we shall also reign with *him* : if we deny *him*, he also will deny us : If we believe not, *yet* he abideth faithful : he cannot deny himself. *(Here we have another Christian proverb, and in fact a hymn of the early church. It should be learned by heart, and often quoted by us.)*

14 Of these things put *them* in remembrance, charging *them* before the Lord that they strive not about words to no profit, *but* to the subverting of the hearers.

15 Study to shew thyself approved unto God, a workman that needeth not to be ashamed, rightly dividing the word of truth.

16 But shun profane *and* vain babblings : for they will increase unto more ungodliness.

We must keep clear of mystifyings, spiritualizings, traditions, and idle controversies. Plain sailing is best for Christian men.

17, 18 And their word will eat as doth a canker : of whom is Hymenæus and Philetus ; Who concerning the truth have erred, saying that the resurrection is past already ; and overthrow the faith of some.

19 Nevertheless the foundation of God standeth sure, having this seal, The Lord knoweth them that are his. And, Let every one that nameth the name of Christ depart from iniquity. *(The sentences inscribed upon the seal are precious and practical : there is the secret of the Lord, and the open manifestation of it. Election and holiness are bosom companions.)*

20, 21 But in a great house there are not only vessels of gold and of silver, but also of wood and of earth ; and some to honour, and some to dishonour. If a man therefore purge himself from these, he shall be a vessel unto honour, sanctified, and meet for the master's use, *and* prepared unto every good work.

Fit to be used of God ! Is not this a glorious condition ? Prepared not for some good work, but for every good work ! Is not this a grand attainment ? Let us aim at this, and never rest till we reach it.

22—26 Flee also youthful lusts : but follow righteousness, faith, charity, peace, with them that call on the Lord out of a pure heart. But foolish and unlearned questions avoid, knowing that they do gender strifes. But the servant of the Lord must not strive ; but be gentle unto all *men*, apt to teach, patient, In meekness instructing those that oppose themselves ; if God peradventure will give them repentance to the acknowledging of the truth ; And *that* they may recover themselves out of the snare of the devil, who are taken captive by him at his will.

Leave theories for those who like them, and by the grace of God, love and live the realities of religion, whatever they may cost you.

Grant, oh, grant thy Spirit's teaching,
　That I may not go astray,
Till, the gate of heaven reaching,
　Earth and sin are pass'd away !

II. TIMOTHY III.

THIS know also, that in the last days perilous times shall come.

2—5 For men shall be lovers of their own selves, covetous, boasters, proud, blasphemers, disobedient to parents, unthankful, unholy, Without natural affection, trucebreakers, false accusers, incontinent, fierce, despisers of those that are good, Traitors, heady, highminded, lovers of pleasures more than lovers of God ; Having a form of godliness, but denying the power thereof : from such turn away.

These persons will be in the church, and trouble it exceedingly. Many such are already around us, and they are on the increase: it is little use controverting with them, or seeking to set them right: we had better leave them to their own devices, and as they are in the Lord's hands he will know how to deal with them.

6, 7 For of this sort are they which creep into houses, and lead captive silly women laden with sins, led away with divers lusts, Ever learning, and never able to come to the knowledge of the truth. *(These deceivers acted like Jesuits, spreading their doctrine secretly among the weaker sort. Truth fears not the light, but falsehood is a night bird, and flies abroad by stealth. If any religious teacher asks us to conceal from our friends what he has told us, we may be sure that he is good for nothing.)*

8 Now as Jannes and Jambres, *(Pharaoh's magicians,)* withstood Moses, so do these also resist the truth : men of corrupt minds, reprobate concerning the faith.

9 But they shall proceed no further : for their folly shall be manifest unto all *men,* as their's also was. *(Paul laid bare the deceitful workings of the false teachers, boldy exposing them. However gentle we may be, we must not allow falsehood to be secretly spread, but must drag it to the light, and smite it till it dies.)*

10, 11 But thou hast fully known my doctrine, manner of life, purpose, faith, longsuffering. charity, patience ; Persecutions, afflictions, which came unto me at Antioch, at Iconium, at Lystra ; what persecutions I endured : but out of *them* all the Lord delivered me.

12 Yea, and all that will live godly in Christ Jesus shall suffer persecution. *(Christ's soldiers must expect hard blows. The cross is always to be* borne by those who trust in the Crucified : it is idle and mean to endeavour to escape it.

" Must I be carried to the skies,
On flowery beds of ease,
While others fought to win the prize,
And sailed through bloody seas ?")

13 But evil men and seducers shall wax worse and worse, deceiving, and being deceived. *There is no mending them, they must go on to the bitter end. Terrible will be their doom.*

14, 15 But continue thou in the things which thou hast learned and hast been assured of, knowing of whom thou hast learned *them ;* And that from a child thou hast known the holy scriptures, which are able to make thee wise unto salvation through faith which is in Christ Jesus. *(Happy Timothy to be thus prepared for the conflict with error ! Happier still to be enabled by grace to remain steadfast in that truth which from a child he had been taught. Yet he needed to be exhorted to steadfastness, and so do we. Never, never may any one of us give ear to false doctrine, but may we cling to the gospel with all our might.)*

16, 17 All scripture *is* given by inspiration of God, and *is* profitable for doctrine, for reproof, for correction, for instruction in righteousness : That the man of God may be perfect, throughly furnished unto all good works. *(Never let us forget this. The whole of the Bible is inspired, and is to be devoutly received as the infallible truth of God. Get away from this, and we have nothing left to hold by. Whatever we do, let us never give up the Bible. Those who would weaken our reverence for it are our worst enemies.)*

'Tis in cleaving to thee only,
  That my spirit finds its rest ;
'Tis while gazing on thy beauty,
  I am truly, fully blest.

Keep me then, Lord Jesus, near thee,
  Resting in thy precious love ;
Till thine unveiled presence cheer me,
  In thine own blest courts above.

II TIMOTHY IV.

THE *chapter opens with a most solemn charge to young Timothy. Coming from one who was so soon to seal his testimony with his blood, Timothy must have felt the power of it as long as he lived. Aged believers should impress upon the young the value of the gospel.*

1, 2 I charge *thee* therefore before God, and the Lord Jesus Christ, who shall judge the quick and the dead at his appearing and his kingdom; Preach the word; be instant in season, out of season; reprove, rebuke, exhort with all long-suffering and doctrine. (*A minister is never off duty: he is not only to win souls whenever an opportunity occurs, but he is himself to make opportunities. Sound doctrine and zeal must go together in equal proportions. Dr. Ryland well said, " No sermon is likely to be useful which has not the three R's in it—Ruin by the Fall; Redemption by Christ; Regeneration by the Holy Spirit. My aim in every sermon is to call sinners, to quicken the saints, and to be made a blessing to all.")*

3—5 For the time will come when they will not endure sound doctrine; but after their own lusts shall they heap to themselves teachers, having itching ears; And they shall turn away *their* ears from the truth, and shall be turned unto fables. But watch thou in all things, endure afflictions, do the work of an evangelist, make full proof of thy ministry.

6 For I am now ready to be offered, and the time of my departure is at hand. (*"I am already being poured out as a libation to God;" his sufferings had commenced, and he was ready to bear up under them even to death; yet how sweetly does he speak of his execution as a mere departure! He looked upon it only as a change of place, a removal to a better country.*)

7 I have fought a good fight, I have finished *my* course, I have kept the faith :

8 Henceforth there is laid up for me a crown of righteousness, which the Lord, the righteous judge, shall give me at that day ; and not to me only, but unto all them also that love his appearing. (*He looked on life as a battle, a race, and a trust, and having been faithful in all these he expected a gracious reward.*)

9 Do thy diligence to come shortly unto me :

10 For Demas hath forsaken me, having loved this present world, and is departed unto Thessalonica; Crescens to Galatia, Titus unto Dalmatia. (*As the leaves are gone in winter so do friends leave us in adversity.*)

11 Only Luke is with me. Take Mark, and bring him with thee : for he is profitable to me for the ministry. (*This proves that he had changed his opinion about Mark, concerning whom he had differed with Barnabas. The apostle was not like some who will never relent, he was as ready to praise, as once he was honest to censure.*)

12 And Tychicus have I sent to Ephesus.

13 The cloke that I left at Troas with Carpus, when thou comest, bring *with thee,* and the books, *but* especially the parchments.

Shivering in prison the poor and aged apostle needed his cloak. Desiring still to study the word of God he sent for his books and notes.

14, 15 Alexander the coppersmith did me much evil : the Lord reward him according to his works : Of whom be thou ware also ; for he hath greatly withstood our words. (*Paul spake as a prophet, not out of private anger, but because the man opposed the gospel.*)

16, 17 At my first answer no man stood with me, but all *men* forsook me : *I pray God* that it may not be laid to their charge. Notwithstanding the Lord stood with me, and strengthened me ; that by me the preaching might be fully known, and *that* all the Gentiles might hear : and I was delivered out of the mouth of the lion. (*Probably Nero, who well deserved this title. It was well for Paul that grace was given him under the terrible ordeal of facing such a monster of cruelty.*)

18 And the Lord shall deliver me from every evil work, and will preserve *me* unto his heavenly kingdom : to whom *be* glory for ever and ever. Amen.

God hath laid up in heav'n for me,
A crown which cannot fade;
The righteous Judge at that great day
Shall place it on my head.

Nor hath the King of grace decreed
The crown for me alone;
But all that love and long to see
Th' appearance of his Son.

TITUS *was another of Paul's sons in the faith, and is spoken of by the apostle as " my partner and fellow-helper." Paul wrote this epistle to give him instructions how to put in order the churches of Crete to which he had been sent.*

TITUS I. 1—9.

1—4 Paul, a servant of God, and an apostle of Jesus Christ, according to the faith of God's elect, and the acknowledging of the truth which is after godliness ; In hope of eternal life, which God, that cannot lie, promised before the world began ; But hath in due times manifested his word through preaching, which is committed unto me according to the commandment of God our Saviour ; To Titus, *mine* own son after the common faith : Grace, mercy, *and* peace from God the Father and the Lord Jesus Christ our Saviour.

5 For this cause left I thee in Crete, that thou shouldest set in order the things that are wanting, and ordain elders in every city, as I had appointed thee : *(The gospel had been preached in Crete, and converts made; but the churches needed to be properly constituted. Churches without elders are like an army without officers. Those err greatly who despise order.)*

6 If any be blameless, the husband of one wife, having faithful children not accused of riot or unruly. *(So that the Church of Rome has no right to forbid ministers to marry.)*

7—9 For a bishop *(or overseer, described in the fifth verse as an elder)* must be blameless, as the steward of God : not selfwilled, not soon angry, not given to wine, no striker, not given to filthy lucre ; But a lover of hospitality, a lover of good men, sober, just, holy, temperate ; Holding fast the faithful word as he hath been taught, that he may be able by sound doctrine both to exhort and to convince the gainsayers.

See what ministers ought to be, and pray that many such may be found for our churches.

TITUS II. 1—14.

BUT speak thou the things which become sound doctrine :

2 That the aged men be sober, grave, temperate, sound in faith, in charity, in patience.

Aged Christians are nearer heaven than others, and should be more heavenly-minded.

3—5 The aged women likewise, that *they be* in behaviour as becometh holiness, not false accusers, not given to much wine, teachers of good things ; That they may teach the young women to be sober, to love their husbands, to love their children, *To be* discreet, chaste, keepers at home, good, obedient to their own husbands, that the word of God be not blasphemed. *(The young woman's first duty is at home.)*

6—8 Young men likewise exhort to be sober minded. In all things shewing thyself a pattern of good works : in doctrine *shewing* uncorruptness, gravity, sincerity, Sound speech, that cannot be condemned ; that he that is of the contrary part may be ashamed, having no evil thing to say of you.

9, 10 *Exhort* servants to be obedient unto their own masters, *and* to please *them* well in all *things;* not answering again ; *(not disputing, or using impertinent language.)* Not purloining *(or stealing little things, whether under the name of perquisites or otherwise),* but showing all good fidelity ; that they may adorn the doctrine of God our Saviour in all things.

11—14 For the grace of God that bringeth salvation hath appeared to all men, Teaching us that, denying ungodliness and worldly lusts, we should live soberly, righteously, and godly, in this present world ; Looking for that blessed hope, and the glorious appearing of the great God and our Saviour Jesus Christ ; Who gave himself for us, that he might redeem us from all iniquity, and purify unto himself a peculiar people, zealous of good works. *(We have heard much of " the peculiar people," be it ours to be peculiarly holy.)*

When from the curse he sets us free,
He makes our natures clean ;
Nor would he send his Son to be
The minister of sin.

My Saviour and my King,
Thy beauties are divine ;
Thy lips with blessings overflow,
And every grace is thine.

Thy laws, O God, are right ;
Thy throne shall ever stand ;
And thy victorious gospel prove
A sceptre in thy hand.

THE EPISTLE OF PAUL TO PHILEMON.

THIS *has been called " the polite epistle," for Paul used great courtesy and tact in writing it. Onesimus, a slave, had robbed his master Philemon, and had then run away from him. Hoping to conceal himself best in the metropolis, Onesimus had fled to Rome, where he heard Paul preach and became converted. The apostle sent him back to his Christian master with the following letter of apology. Although its first object was only to restore a runaway slave to his master, it is a weighty letter, and every syllable has substance in it.*

1, 2 Paul, a prisoner of Jesus Christ, and Timothy *our* brother, unto Philemon our dearly beloved, and fellowlabourer, And to *our* beloved Apphia, and Archippus our fellowsoldier, and to the church in thy house :

3 Grace to you, and peace, from God our Father and the Lord Jesus Christ.

4—6 I thank my God, making mention of thee always in my prayers, Hearing of thy love and faith, which thou hast toward the Lord Jesus, and toward all saints ; That the communication of thy faith may become effectual by the acknowledging of every good thing which is in you in Christ Jesus. *(Paul knew Philemon was a true believer, and therefore prayed that others might feel the power of his piety, by seeing how he acted in the present case.)*

7 For we have great joy and consolation in thy love, because the bowels of the saints are refreshed by thee, brother.

8 Wherefore, though I might be much bold in Christ to enjoin thee that which is convenient,

9 Yet for love's sake I rather beseech *thee*, being such an one as Paul the aged, and now also a prisoner of Jesus Christ. *(This is the best of pleading. Philemon's heart would be sure to yield to it.)*

10 I beseech thee for my son Onesimus, whom I have begotten in my bonds :

11 Which in time past was to thee unprofitable, but now profitable to thee and to me :

12 Whom I have sent again : thou therefore receive him, that is, mine own bowels : *(who is so dear to me that he carries my heart with him wherever he goes.)*

13, 14 Whom I would have retained with me, that in thy stead he might have ministered unto me in the bonds of the gospel : But without thy mind would I do nothing ; that thy benefit should not be as it were of necessity, but willingly. *(Though he felt sure that Philemon would have been glad to spare his servant to care for his aged friend, yet Paul would not take the liberty of using his services, but gave Philemon the opportunity to do it of his own accord if he thought fit.)*

15 For perhaps he therefore departed for a season, that thou shouldest receive him for ever ;

16 Not now as a servant, but above a servant, a brother beloved, specially to me, but how much more unto thee, both in the flesh, and in the Lord ? *(Providence suffered him to run away that he might come under Paul's influence and become a Christian : the gracious purpose of God overrules evil for good.)*

17—19 If thou count me therefore a partner *(or true comrade in Christ)*, receive him as myself. If he hath wronged thee, or oweth *thee* ought, put that on mine account ; I Paul have written *it* with mine own hand, I will repay *it :* albeit I do not say to thee how thou owest unto me even thine own self besides.

20 Yea, brother, let me have joy of thee in the Lord : refresh my bowels in the Lord.

21 Having confidence in thy obedience I wrote unto thee, knowing that thou will also do more than I say. *(Is not this a graceful way of putting it ? Who could have the heart to resist such pleading ? Yet every word is gentle and quiet. Mild language is mighty.)*

22 But withal prepare me also a lodging : for I trust that through your prayers I shall be given unto you.

23, 24 There salute thee Epaphras, my fellowprisoner in Christ Jesus ; Marcus, Aristarchus, Demas, Lucas, my fellowlabourers.

25 The grace of our Lord Jesus Christ *be* with your spirit. Amen.

Our Father in heaven, we hallow thy name,
O'er earth may thy kingdom establish its claim !
Oh, give to us daily our portion of bread ;
It is from thy bounty that all must be fed.

Forgive our transgressions, and teach us to know
The humble compassion that pardons each foe ;
Keep us from temptation, from weakness, and sin,
And thine be the glory for ever. Amen.

WE *have now reached that wonderful part of Holy Scripture which is found in the epistle to the Hebrews. Fully to understand it we ought to study closely the Book of Leviticus. Diamonds only will cut diamonds ; the Word of God is its own expositor ; the New Testament is the key of the old.*

The epistle opens with the declaration that whatsoever was communicated by the prophets was spoken by God. He spoke whatsoever was uttered by his prophets. The Scriptures are very jealous on this subject ; how different from the language of many who seem desirous to exclude God from being the author of his own word !

HEBREWS I.

1, 2 God, who at sundry times and in divers manners spake in time past unto the fathers by the prophets, Hath in these last days spoken unto us by *his* Son, whom he hath appointed heir of all things, by whom also he made the worlds ; *(Ours is the clearest of all revelations. In Jesus we see far more of God than in all the teachings of the prophets.)*

3 Who being the brightness of *his* glory, and the express image of his person, and upholding all things by the word of his power, when he had by himself purged our sins, sat down on the right hand of the Majesty on high ; *(The priest stood while he performed service, and only sat down when his work was done. Jesus enthroned in glory enjoys the honours of his finished work.)*

4 Being made so much better than the angels, as he hath by inheritance obtained a more excellent name than they.

5 For unto which of the angels said he at any time, Thou art my Son, this day have I begotten thee ? *(But he does say this to Christ in the second Psalm.)* And again *(speaking to Solomon as the type of Christ in the Second Book of Samuel vii. 14),* I will be to him a Father, and he shall be to me a Son ?

6 And again *(in the ninety-seventh Psalm),* when he bringeth in the firstbegotten into the world, he saith, And let all the angels of God worship him. *(Or "worship him all ye gods," Jesus is by nature infinitely superior to the noblest created beings, for he is essentially God, and to be worshipped as Lord of all.)*

7—9 And of the angels *(in Psalm civ. 4)* he saith, Who maketh his angels spirits, and his ministers a flame of fire. But unto the Son *he saith (Psalm xlv. 6, 7),* Thy throne, O God, *is* for ever and ever : a sceptre of righteousness *is* the sceptre of thy kingdom. Thou hast loved righteousness, and hated iniquity ; therefore God, *even* thy God, hath anointed thee with the oil of gladness above thy fellows. *(Angels are servants and not kings, they fly upon the divine errands like flames of fire, but they do not sway a sceptre, neither have they a throne existing for ever and ever. Jesus is the anointed king, and though we share in the anointing yet is he far above us. Christ is infinitely greater than Christians. We are right glad to have it so.)*

10—12 And *(again we read in Psalm cii. 25—27),* Thou, Lord, in the beginning hast laid the foundation of the earth ; and the heavens are the works of thine hands : They shall perish ; but thou remainest ; and they all shall wax old as doth a garment ; And as a vesture shalt thou fold them up, and they shall be changed : but thou art the same, and thy years shall not fail. *(Since the Messiah is thus described as immutable and eternal he must be divine, and to deny the Godhead of the Saviour is a deadly error. Dr. Owen most comfortingly remarks :—" Whatever our changes may be, inward or outward, yet Christ changing not, our eternal condition is secured, and relief provided against all present troubles and miseries. The immutability and eternity of Christ are the spring of our consolation and security in every condition. Such is the frailty of the nature of man, and such the perishing condition of all created things, that none can ever obtain the least stable consolation but what ariseth from an interest in the omnipotency, sovereignty, and eternity of Jesus Christ.")*

13, 14 But to which of the angels said he at any time, Sit on my right hand, until I make thine enemies thy footstool ? Are they not all ministering spirits, sent forth to minister for them who shall be heirs of salvation ?

They are servants of God and our willing guardians ; but they are not to be worshipped. Jesus is Lord of all, and we are bound to adore him, and him only.

734   " It behoved Him to be made like unto His brethren."   DECEMBER 12.—MORNING.

[Or November 21.]

HEBREWS II.

THEREFORE we ought to give the more earnest heed to the things which we have heard, lest at any time we should let *them* slip. *(As if our apostle had said,—Seeing Christ is so excellent in his person, and seeing the gospel has such a glorious author, let us take great care that we esteem his person, revere his authority, reverence his ministry, and believe his message ; and let us take heed that our memories be not like leaking vessels, suffering the word at any time to slip or run from us.)*

2—4 For if the word spoken by angels was stedfast, and every transgression and disobedience received a just recompense of reward; How shall we escape, if we neglect so great salvation ; which at the first began to be spoken by the Lord, and was confirmed unto us by them that heard *him ;* God also bearing *them* witness, both with signs and wonders, and with divers miracles, and gifts of the Holy Ghost, according to his own will ? *(Let .that question ring in our ears, "How shall we escape ?" There will be no escape, there can be none if we refuse the Lord Jesus. Do we mean to be lost ? Dare we continue to neglect the great salvation ?.)*

5—9 For unto the angels hath he not put in subjection the world to come, whereof we speak. But one in a certain place testified, saying, What is man, that thou art mindful of him ? or the son of man, that thou visitest him ? Thou madest him a little lower than the angels ; thou crownedst him with glory and honour, and didst set him over the works of thy hands : Thou hast put all things in subjection under his feet. For in that he put all in subjection under him, he left nothing *that is* not put under him. But now we see not yet all things put under him. But we see Jesus, who was made a little lower than the angels for the suffering of death, crowned with glory and honour; that he by the grace of God should taste death for every man. *(Jesus died that to all men the message of salvation might be delivered, and that each one might be assured that upon his believing he will be pardoned. None are excluded from mercy but those who exclude themselves.)*

10—12 For it became him, for whom *are* all things, and by whom *are* all things, in bringing many sons unto glory, to make the captain of their salvation perfect through sufferings. For both he that sanctifieth and they who are sanctified *are* all of one : for which cause he is not ashamed to call them brethren, Saying, I will declare thy name unto my brethren, in the midst of the church· will I sing praise unto thee. *(This passage occurs in Psalm xxii., a psalm of Christ's sufferings, entitled " Upon Aijeleth Shahar," that is, The morning-stag, such an one as the huntsman singles out to hunt for that day. Christ thus hunted, praying for deliverance, promised to praise God's name amidst his brethren.)*

13 And again, I will put my trust in him. And again, Behold I and the children which God hath given me. *(All of which expressions denote nearness of relationship and likeness of nature, kindly recognised by the great head of the household of God.)*

14, 15 Forasmuch then as the children are partakers of flesh and blood, he also himself likewise took part of the same ; that through death he might destroy him that had the power of death, that is, the devil ; And deliver them who through fear of death were all their lifetime subject to bondage.

16 For verily he took not on *him the nature of* angels *(or he took not up angels) ;* but he took on *him* the seed of Abraham. *(Angels were passed by and men redeemed. Wondrous sovereignty this !)*

17, 18 Wherefore in all things it behoved him to be made like unto *his* brethren, that he might be a merciful and faithful high priest in things *pertaining* to God, to make reconciliation for the sins of the people. For in that he himself hath suffered being tempted, he is able to succour them that are tempted. *(Here is delightful encouragement to put our whole trust in him, and approach him without fear. Let us draw very near to him in prayer.)*

Jesus, who pass'd the angels by,
Assumed our flesh to bleed and die ;
And still he makes it his abode ;
As man, he fills the throne of God.

Our next of kin, our brother now,
Is he to whom the angels bow ;
They join with us to praise his name,
But *we* the nearest interest claim.

HEBREWS III. 12—19.

TAKE heed, brethren, lest there be in any of you an evil heart of unbelief, in departing from the living God. (*No good ever comes of carelessness. He who never examines himself is sure to be self-deceived.*)

13 But exhort one another daily, while it is called To day; lest any of you be hardened through the deceitfulness of sin. (*Sin slyly insinuates itself and by slow degrees prevails, therefore must we carefully guard against it.*)

14, 15 For we are made partakers of Christ, if we hold the beginning of our confidence stedfast unto the end; While it is said, To day if ye will hear his voice, harden not your hearts, as in the provocation. (*Continuance in faith is necessary to salvation, and only those who persevere to the end are indeed saved.*)

16—19 For some, when they had heard, did provoke: howbeit not all that came out of Egypt by Moses. But with whom was he grieved forty years? *was it* not with them that had sinned, whose carcases fell in the wilderness? And to whom sware he that they should not enter into his rest, but to them that believed not? So we see that they could not enter in because of unbelief. (*Want of true faith causes the religion of many to be shortlived. Those who are not sustained by faith soon weary of holiness and provoke the Lord.*)

HEBREWS IV. 1—6; 9—16.

LET us therefore fear, lest, a promise being left *us* of entering into his rest, any of you should seem to come short of it. For unto us was the gospel preached, as well as unto them: but the word preached did not profit them, not being mixed with faith in them that heard *it*.

3 For we which have believed do enter into rest, as he said, As I have sworn in my wrath, if they shall enter into my rest: although the works were finished from the foundation of the world.

4, 5 For he spake in a certain place of the seventh *day* on this wise, And God did rest the seventh day from all his works. And in this *place* again, If they shall enter into my rest.

6, 9 Seeing therefore it remaineth that some must enter therein, and they to whom it was first preached entered not in because of unbelief;

(*nor did Joshua lead the next generation into rest, or else David would not have spoken of another day*); There remaineth therefore a (*Sabbath*) rest to the people of God.

It is clear that there is a rest of God, and that some are to enjoy it, and as Israel did not attain to it, it still remains for God's people. Oh, that we might by faith be of that number!

10 For he that is entered into his rest, he also hath ceased from his own works, as God *did* from his. (*Resting in the finished work of Jesus we feel that our warfare is accomplished. The work we now do is of another kind from our own self-righteous work of former years. Our faith has introduced us into joyful rest.*)

11—13 Let us labour therefore to enter into that rest, lest any man fall after the same example of unbelief. For the word of God *is* quick, and powerful, and sharper than any two-edged sword, piercing even to the dividing asunder of soul and spirit, and of the joints and marrow, and *is* a discerner of the thoughts and intents of the heart. Neither is there any creature that is not manifest in his sight: but all things *are* naked and opened unto the eyes of him with whom we have to do. (*We should earnestly labour to be right, for no deceptions will avail. The Lord's word lays us bare and opens up our secret selves. Oh, to be clean before the Lord! This we can never be except by faith.*)

14 Seeing then that we have a great high priest, that is passed into the heavens, Jesus the Son of God, let us hold fast *our* profession.

Since salvation work is complete, let us hold to it and enjoy the consequent blessings. We should be foolish indeed to leave such riches of grace.

15, 16 For we have not an high priest which cannot be touched with the feeling of our infirmities; but was in all points tempted like as *we are, yet* without sin. Let us therefore come boldly unto the throne of grace, that we may obtain mercy, and find grace to help in time of need.

With joy we meditate the grace
Of our High Priest above;
His heart is made of tenderness,
His bowels melt with love.

Then let our humble faith address
His mercy and his power,
We shall obtain delivering grace
In the distressing hour.

DECEMBER 13.—MORNING.

736   "𝕳e became the author of eternal salbation to all them that obey 𝕳im."   [Or November 23.]

HEBREWS V.

FOR every high priest taken from among men is ordained for men in things *pertaining* to God, that he may offer both gifts and sacrifices for sins : Who can have compassion on the ignorant, and on them that are out of the way; for that he himself also is compassed with infirmity. *(An angelic priest for men would be out of place. Men need forbearance and sympathy, hence the priests of old were men of like passions with the people. This also is true of our Lord Jesus, who is most certainly and really a human being like the rest of mankind in all things except sin—that stain never defiled his holy nature.)*

3 And by reason hereof he ought, as for the people, so also for himself, to offer for sins.

This refers to the typical high priest, but our Lord had no sin of his own ; he bore our sin, but in him is no sin.

4 And no man taketh this honour unto himself, but he that is called of God, as *was* Aaron.

5 So also Christ glorified not himself to be made an high priest ; but he that said unto him, Thou art my Son, to day have I begotten thee.

6 As he saith also in another *place*, Thou *art* a priest for ever after the order of Melchisedec.

He was no unauthorised priest, self-appointed and unordained. What he does has the Father's decree to back it. "It pleased the Father to bruise him," and " it pleased the Father that in him should all fulness dwell." What solid ground we have for depending upon Jesus, the elect messenger of God, the ordained surety of the everlasting covenant !

7 Who in the days of his flesh, when he had offered up prayers and supplications with strong crying and tears unto him that was able to save him from death, and was heard in that he feared ; *(The cup was not removed, but he was strengthened to drink it. If the Lord does not answer his people one way he does another. Jesus understands our feelings in prayer even when we cannot express them except by strong crying and tears. Experience has made him the ready interpreter of anguished hearts.)*

8 Though he were a Son, yet learned he obedience by the things which he suffered ;

9 And being made perfect, he became the author of eternal salvation unto all them that

obey him ; *(A perfected Saviour presents all believers with a perfect and everlasting salvation. He was always perfect in character, but his sorrowful life below gave him a complete qualification for the office of Saviour, which nothing else could have obtained. Who would not obey a Master who has undergone all kinds of sorrow that he may be able to sympathise with his servants ? Who would not possess a salvation won for us by such condescending love?)*

10 Called of God an high priest after the order of Melchisedec. *(Here the apostle rises to a great height, and then suddenly pauses, remembering how unsuitable men's minds often are for the reception of mysterious truth.)*

11 Of whom *(namely, Melchisedec)* we have many things to say, and hard to be uttered, seeing ye are dull of hearing.

12 For when for the time ye ought to be teachers, ye have need that one teach you again which *be* the first principles of the oracles of God ; and are become such as have need of milk, and not of strong meat. *(Too often we learn and unlearn. Our progress is slow, and we remain babes when we ought to be full grown men in Christ. We draw upon the church's strength when we ought to be contributing to it.)*

13, 14 For every one that useth milk *is* unskilful in the word of righteousness : for he is a babe. But strong meat belongeth to them that are of full age, *even* those who by reason of use have their senses exercised to discern both good and evil. *(We should desire not only to be saved, and to know the elementary truths, but to be advanced scholars in Christ's school, so as to handle the deeper doctrines, and teach them to others. Good Master, have patience with thy servants, and teach us still !)*

It is my sweetest comfort, Lord,
   And will for ever be,
To muse upon the gracious truth
   Of thy humanity.

Oh joy ! there sitteth in our flesh,
   Upon a throne of light,
One of a human mother born,
   In perfect Godhead bright !

HEBREWS VI.

THEREFORE leaving the principles of the doctrine of Christ, let us go on unto perfection; not laying again the foundation of repentance from dead works, and of faith toward God, Of the doctrine of baptisms, and of laying on of hands, and of resurrection of the dead, and of eternal judgment. *(Children are to learn their letters in order that they may go on to higher branches of education, and believers are to know the elements of the faith, but are then to advance to the higher attainments, and endeavour to understand the deeper mysteries.)*

3 And this will we do, if God permit.

4—6 For *it is* impossible for those who were once enlightened, and have tasted of the heavenly gift, and· were made partakers of the Holy Ghost, And have tasted the good word of God, and the powers of the world to come, If they shall fall away, to renew them again unto repentance; seeing they crucify to themselves the Son of God afresh, and put *him* to an open shame. *If once the real work of grace fails it cannot be commenced again, the case is hopeless for ever. Hence the absolute necessity for persevering to the end. To draw back totally would be fatal.*

7, 8 For the earth which drinketh in the rain that cometh oft upon it, and bringeth forth herbs meet for them by whom it is dressed, receiveth blessing from God : But that which beareth thorns and briers *is* rejected, and *is* nigh unto cursing; whose end *is* to be burned. *When all that is possible is done for a piece of land, and yet it bears no harvest it must be given up. If, after all, the Holy Spirit's work in a man should prove fruitless, he must be given over to destruction, nothing else remains. Will any truly regenerated man ever come into this condition? The apostle answers this question in the next two verses.*

9 But, beloved, we are persuaded better things of you, and things that accompany salvation, though we thus speak.

10 For God *is* not unrighteous to forget your work and labour of love, which ye have shewed toward his name, in that ye have ministered to the saints, and do minister. *But this perseverance demands earnestness on our part, hence he adds—*

11, 12 And we desire that every one of you do shew the same diligence to the full assurance of hope unto the end : That ye be not slothful, but followers of them who through faith and patience inherit the promises. *(Those promises we shall inherit most surely, for we shall by grace be enabled to remain faithful until death.)*

13—15 For when God made promise to Abraham, because he could swear by no greater, he sware by himself, Saying, Surely blessing I will bless thee, and multiplying I will multiply thee. And so, after he had patiently endured he obtained the promise.

16—20 For men verily swear by the greater : and an oath for confirmation *is* to them an end of all strife. Wherein God, willing more abundantly to shew unto the heirs of promise the immutability of his counsel, confirmed *it* by an oath : That by two immutable things, in which *it was* impossible for God to lie, we might have a strong consolation, who have fled for refuge to lay hold upon the hope set before us : Which *hope* we have as an anchor of the soul, both sure and stedfast, and which entereth into that within the veil; Whither the forerunner is for us entered, *even* Jesus, made an high priest for ever after the order of Melchisedec.

The most solemn warnings against apostasy, and the declaration that total apostasy would be fatal, are not inconsistent with the great truth of the safety of all true saints. Safe they are, for the covenant promise and oath guarantee their security, their hope is placed where it cannot fail, and in their name Jesus has gone to take possession of heaven. Has he gone as a forerunner of those who may after all perish on the road? God forbid. Where our Head is, there must the members be ere long.

Raise, raise, my soul, thy raptured sight
With sacred wonder and delight;
Jesus, thine own forerunner see
Enter'd beyond the veil for thee.

Loud let the howling tempest yell,
And foaming waves to mountains swell,
No shipwreck can my vessel fear,
Since hope hath fix'd her anchor here.

HEBREWS IX. 15—28.

AND for this cause he is the mediator of the new testament, that by means of death, for the redemption of the transgressions *that were* under the first testament, they which are called might receive the promise of eternal inheritance. *(It was absolutely needful that guilt should be atoned for, and, therefore, Jesus became a mediator. Nothing short of this could secure the eternal inheritance for those who are called. Take away the atonement and you have robbed our Lord of his greatest reason for being a mediator at all. We love and live upon the truth of his atoning death.)*

16 For where a testament *is*, there must also of necessity be the death of the testator.

17 For a testament *is* of force after men are dead : otherwise it is of no strength at all while the testator liveth. *(Or it may be understood that a covenant is not of force till the victim is slain to ratify it with blood. In either sense the death of Jesus was necessary to secure to us the blessings of the gospel.)*

18—21 Whereupon neither the first *testament* was dedicated without blood. For when Moses had spoken every precept to all the people according to the law, he took the blood of calves and of goats, with water, and scarlet wool, and hyssop, and sprinkled both the book, and all the people, Saying, This *is* the blood of the testament which God hath enjoined unto you. Moreover he sprinkled with blood both the tabernacle, and all the vessels of the ministry. *(Blood was seen on all sides under the law, it was vital to its teachings. The blood of Jesus is the very life of the gospel; a ministry without the blood of Jesus in it is dead and worthless.)*

22 And almost all things are by the law purged with blood ; and without shedding of blood is no remission. *(This solemn truth needs to be well learned and remembered. Nothing can cleanse us but the blood of Jesus. Sacraments, prayers, repentances are all useless as a substitute for faith in the blood.)*

23 *It was* therefore necessary that the patterns of things in the heavens should be purified with these ; but the heavenly things themselves with better sacrifices than these. *(The blood of*

bulls would suffice to purge the types, but the realities must have a richer sacrifice to cleanse them.)*

24—26 For Christ is not entered into the holy places made with hands, *which are* the figures of the true ; but into heaven itself, now to appear in the presence of God for us : Nor yet that he should offer himself often, as the high priest entereth into the holy place every year with blood of others ; For then must he often have suffered since the foundation of the world : but now once in the end of the world hath he appeared to put away sin by the sacrifice of himself. *(Once has Jesus offered sacrifice, and only once. All attempts to offer him again, as the priests pretend to do in the mass, are blasphemous, and are an insinuation that the one offering was not sufficient. As for us, let us rest on the once offered atonement, and in humble faith know that we are fully accepted.)*

27, 28 And as it is appointed unto men once to die, but after this the judgment : So Christ was once offered to bear the sins of many ; and unto them that look for him shall he appear the second time without sin *(or without a sin-offering)* unto salvation. *(Every man's death day is his doomsday, all is settled then. So Jesus, when he died, finished his atoning work, and nothing remains for him but to come a second time, no more to die, to take his great reward.)*

O Christ, what burdens bow'd thy head !
  Our load was laid on thee :
Thou stoodest in the sinner's stead,
  To bear all ill for me.

Death and the curse were in our cup,
  O Christ, 'twas full for thee !
But thou hast drained the last dark drop,
  'Tis empty now for me.

Jehovah lifted up his rod,
  O Christ, it fell on thee !
Thou wast sore stricken of thy God ;
  There's not one stroke for me.

For me, Lord Jesus, thou hast died,
  And I have died in thee ;
Thou'rt risen ; my bands are all untied ;
  And now thou liv'st in me.

HEBREWS X. 1—31.

FOR the law having a shadow of good things to come, *and* not the very image of the things, can never with those sacrifices which they offered year by year continually make the comers thereunto perfect. For then would they not have ceased to be offered ? because that the worshippers once purged should have had no more conscience of sins.

3 But in those *sacrifices there is* a remembrance again *made* of sins every year.

4 For *it is* not possible that the blood of bulls and of goats should take away sins.

5—7 Wherefore when he *(that is, Jesus)* cometh into the world, he saith, Sacrifice and offering thou wouldest not, but a body hast thou prepared me : In burnt offerings and *sacrifices* for sin thou hast had no pleasure. Then said I, Lo, I come (in the volume of the book it is written of me,) to do thy will, O God.

8, 9 Above when he said, Sacrifice and offering and burnt offerings and *offering* for sin thou wouldest not, neither hadst pleasure *therein;* which are offered by the law ; Then said he, Lo, I come to do thy will, O God. He taketh away the first, that he may establish the second.

10 By the which will we are sanctified through the offering of the body of Jesus Christ once.

11—14 And every priest standeth daily ministering and offering oftentimes the same sacrifices, which can never take away sins : But this man, after he had offered one sacrifice for sins for ever, sat down on the right hand of God ; From henceforth expecting till his enemies be made his footstool. For by one offering he hath perfected for ever them that are sanctified.

15—17 *Whereof* the Holy Ghost also is a witness to us : for after that he had said before, This *is* the covenant that I will make with them after those days, saith the Lord, I will put my laws into their hearts, and in their minds will I write them; And their sins and iniquities will I remember no more. *(The Holy Ghost bears witness to the perfection of our Lord's sacrifice, for he declares that the believer's sins will be remembered no more.)*

18 Now where remission of these *is, there is* no more offering for sin *(and no need of any).*

19—22 Having therefore, brethren, boldness to enter into the holiest by the blood of Jesus, By a new and living way, which he hath consecrated for us, through the veil, that is to say, his flesh ; And *having* an high priest over the house of God ; Let us draw near with a true heart in full assurance of faith, having our hearts sprinkled from an evil conscience, and our bodies washed with pure water.

23—25 Let us hold fast the profession of *our* faith without wavering ; (for he *is* faithful that promised ;) And let us consider one another to provoke unto love and to good works : Not forsaking the assembling of ourselves together, as the manner of some *is ;* but exhorting *one another :* and so much the more, as ye see the day approaching.

26, 27 For if we sin wilfully after that we have received the knowledge of the truth, there remaineth no more sacrifice for sins, But a certain fearful looking for of judgment and fiery indignation, which shall devour the adversaries.

If we reject the atonement of Jesus now, there is no other sacrifice, and we must of necessity perish.

28 He that despised Moses' law died without mercy under two or three witnesses :

29 Of how much sorer punishment, suppose ye, shall he be thought worthy, who hath trodden under foot the Son of God, and hath counted the blood of the covenant, wherewith he was sanctified, an unholy thing, and hath done despite unto the Spirit of grace ?

30 For we know him that hath said, Vengeance *belongeth* unto me, I will recompense, saith the Lord. And again, The Lord shall judge his people.

31 *It is* a fearful thing to fall into the hands of the living God.

The ever-blessed Son of God
Went up to Calvary for me,
There paid my debt, there bore my load
In his own body on the tree.

'Tis finish'd all ; the veil is rent,
The welcome sure, the access free ;
Now, then, we leave our banishment,
O Father, to return to thee.

AFTER *that wonderful list of the heroes of faith of whom we read on a former occasion in Hebrews xi., Paul goes on to say :—*

HEBREWS XII. 1—14.

1 Wherefore seeing we also are compassed about with so great a cloud of witnesses, let us lay aside every weight, and the sin which doth so easily beset *us*, and let us run with patience the race that is set before us,

2 Looking unto Jesus the author and finisher of *our* faith; who for the joy that was set before him endured the cross, despising the shame, and is set down at the right hand of the throne of God. *(The eyes of onlookers stimulate the runners in a race, therefore since all heaven looks on, let us not flag till the goal is reached.)*

3 For consider him that endured such contradiction of sinners against himself, lest ye be wearied and faint in your minds. *(Let the grandest of all examples nerve us. Think how Jesus ran the race!)*

4—6 Ye have not yet resisted unto blood, striving against sin. And ye have forgotten the exhortation which speaketh unto you as unto children, My son, despise not thou the chastening of the Lord, nor faint when thou art rebuked of him: For whom the Lord loveth he chasteneth, and scourgeth every son whom he receiveth. *(Our trials are little compared with those of the martyrs of the olden times. Courage, brethren, these are small matters to faint about! Moreover, our chastenings are love tokens from God, let us not be alarmed at them.)*

7 If ye endure chastening, God dealeth with you as with sons; for what son is he whom the father chasteneth not?

8 But if ye be without chastisement, whereof all are partakers, then are ye bastards, and not sons. *(Yet no one should pray for troubles, or be anxious because he is without them: they will come fast enough and thickly enough ere long, and when they do, a blessing will be in them.)*

9 Furthermore we have had fathers of our flesh which corrected *us*, and we gave *them* reverence: shall we not much rather be in subjection unto the Father of spirits, and live?

10 For they verily for a few days chastened *us* after their own pleasure; but he for *our* profit, that *we* might be partakers of his holiness.

11 Now no chastening for the present seemeth

to be joyous, but grievous: nevertheless afterward it yieldeth the peaceable fruit of righteousness unto them which are exercised thereby.

While we are smarting, we cannot expect to feel the good result, but afterwards it will be seen. Let us wait and pray.

12—14 Wherefore lift up the hands which hang down, and the feeble knees; And make straight paths for your feet, lest that which is lame be turned out of the way; but let it rather be healed. Follow peace with all *men*, and holiness, without which no man shall see the Lord.

HEBREWS XIII. 16—21.

BUT to do good and to communicate forget not: for with such sacrifices God is well pleased. *(Give help in money, in comfort, and in instruction, as men require it.)*

17 Obey them that have the rule over you, and submit yourselves: for they watch for your souls, as they that must give account, that they may do it with joy, and not with grief: for that *is* unprofitable for you.

18, 19 Pray for us: for we trust we have a good conscience, in all things willing to live honestly. But I beseech *you* the rather to do this, that I may be restored to you the sooner.

20, 21 Now the God of peace, that brought again from the dead our Lord Jesus, that great Shepherd of the sheep, through the blood of the everlasting covenant, Make you perfect in every good work to do his will, working in you that which is wellpleasing in his sight, through Jesus Christ; to whom *be* glory for ever and ever. Amen. *(A rich benediction, fitly closing an epistle, in which the prominent theme is the perseverance of the saints. Lord, fulfil this blessing in us.)*

When my comforts fade and languish,
When bereaved of what was dear,
When the body faints with anguish,
And my bright hopes disappear:
Jesus only
Can my spirit soothe and cheer.

When in heaven I bow before him,
Trace his love's continued stream,
And in perfect songs adore him,
Where his unveiled glories beam;
Jesus only
Shall be my eternal theme.

THE GENERAL EPISTLE OF JAMES.

THIS *was probably written by that apostle who has been surnamed* THE JUST, *who presided over the council at Jerusalem. His epistle is practical rather than doctrinal. Alford remarks,—" The brother of him who opened his teaching with the Sermon on the Mount, seems to have deeply imbibed the words and maxims of it, as the law of Christian morals."*

CHAPTER I.

1 James, a servant of God and of the Lord Jesus Christ, to the twelve tribes which are scattered abroad, greeting.

2—4 My brethren, count it all joy when ye fall into divers temptations *(or trials);* Knowing *this,* that the trying of your faith worketh patience. *(And patience will be a crown of honour to you; therefore, viewing trial as an opportunity for proving your graces, you may rejoice in it.)* But let patience have *her* perfect work, that ye may be perfect and entire, wanting nothing.

5 If any of you lack wisdom, let him ask of God, that giveth to all *men* liberally, and upbraideth not; and it shall be given him.

6 But let him ask in faith, nothing wavering. For he that wavereth is like a wave of the sea driven with the wind and tossed.

7 For let not that man think that he shall receive any thing of the Lord.

8 A double minded man *is* unstable in all his ways.

9—11 Let the brother of low degree rejoice in that he is exalted: But the rich, in that he is made low: because as the flower of the grass he shall pass away. For the sun is no sooner risen with a burning heat, but it withereth the grass, and the flower thereof falleth, and the grace of the fashion of it perisheth: so also shall the rich man fade away in his ways.

12 Blessed *is* the man that endureth temptation: for when he is tried, he shall receive the crown of life, which the Lord hath promised to them that love him.

13—15 Let no man say when he is tempted *(or enticed to sin),* I am tempted of God: for God cannot be tempted with evil, neither tempteth he any man: But every man is tempted, when he is drawn away of his own lust, and enticed. Then when lust hath con-

ceived, it bringeth forth sin: and sin, when it is finished, bringeth forth death.

16 Do not err, my beloved brethren.

17, 18 Every good gift and every perfect gift is from above, and cometh down from the Father of lights, with whom is no variableness, neither shadow of turning. Of his own will begat he us with the word of truth, that we should be a kind of firstfruits of his creatures.

All our good is from God, but all our evil is from ourselves and Satan; let us always impute things to their true causes.

19, 21 Wherefore, my beloved brethren, let every man be swift to hear, slow to speak, slow to wrath: For the wrath of man worketh not the righteousness of God. Wherefore lay apart all filthiness and superfluity of naughtiness, and receive with meekness the engrafted word, which is able to save your souls.

22—24 But be ye doers of the word, and not hearers only, deceiving your own selves. For if any be a hearer of the word, and not a doer, he is like unto a man beholding his natural face in a glass: For he beholdeth himself, and goeth his way, and straightway forgetteth what manner of man he was.

25 But whoso looketh into the perfect law of liberty, and continueth *therein,* he being not a forgetful hearer, but a doer of the work, this man shall be blessed in his deed.

26 If any man among you seem to be religious, and bridleth not his tongue, but deceiveth his own heart, this man's religion *is* vain.

27 Pure religion and undefiled before God and the Father is this, To visit the fatherless and widows in their affliction, *and* to keep himself unspotted from the world. *(These are the best externals of worship—the rubrics of the only divine ritual. The more of daily prayers at sick beds, and offertories received by orphans, the better. Can we not, as a family, remember the orphans to-day and help to support them?)*

Jesus, poorest of the poor!
Man of sorrows! Child of grief!
Happy they whose bounteous store
Ministers to thy relief.

Happy they who wash thy feet,
Visit thee in thy distress!
Honour great, and labour sweet,
For thy sake the saints to bless.

742   " **ịatɧ not Ǥod chosen tɧe poor of this world rich in faith?** "   DECEMBER 16.—MORNING.

[*Or November 29.*]

JAMES II.

M Y brethren, have not the faith of our Lord Jesus Christ, *the Lord* of glory, with respect of persons.

2 For if there come unto your assembly a man with a gold ring, in goodly apparel, and there come in also a poor man in vile raiment;

3, 4 And ye have respect to him that weareth the gay clothing, and say unto him, Sit thou here in a good place; and say to the poor, Stand thou there, or sit here under my footstool: Are ye not then partial in yourselves, and are become judges of evil thoughts? *(The man is more than his clothes. A saint in vile raiment is not vile, neither is a wicked man honourable because of his goodly apparel.)*

5 Hearken, my beloved brethren, Hath not God chosen the poor of this world rich in faith, and heirs of the kingdom which he hath promised to them that love him? *(There can therefore be no reason for preferring the rich to the poor, since they are rarely the Lord's chosen.)*

6, 7 But ye have despised the poor. Do not rich men oppress you, and draw you before the judgment seats? Do not they blaspheme that worthy name by the which ye are called?

Most of the persecution against the gospel has been stirred up by the great: the church has, therefore, no excuse for flattering them.

8, 9 If ye fulfil the royal law according to the scripture, Thou shalt love thy neighbour as thyself, ye do well: But if ye have respect to persons, ye commit sin, and are convinced of the law as transgressors. *(You fail to act as Christians should do if you despise the poor. Whatever else you may do that is right and good, you ought not to err in this matter.)*

10 For whosoever shall keep the whole law, and yet offend in one *point,* he is guilty of all.

11 For he that said, Do not commit adultery, said also, Do not kill. Now if thou commit no adultery, yet if thou kill, thou art become a transgressor of the law.

12 So speak ye, and so do, as they that shall be judged by the law of liberty.

13 For he shall have judgment without mercy, that hath shewed no mercy; and mercy rejoiceth against judgment. *(Mercy reigns in our salvation, let it reign in our conduct to others.)*

To us it is not sweet to take vengeance, but to grant forgiveness.)

14—17 What *doth it* profit, my brethren, though a man say he hath faith, and have not works? can faith save him? If a brother or sister be naked, and destitute of daily food, And one of you say unto them, Depart in peace, be *ye* warmed and filled; notwithstanding ye give them not those things which are needful to the body; what *doth it* profit? Even so faith, if it hath not works, is dead, being alone.

18, 19 Yea, a man may say, Thou hast faith, and I have works: shew me thy faith without thy works, and I will shew thee my faith by my works. Thou believest that there is one God; thou doest well: the devils also believe, and tremble. *(So that they have a more practical faith than those who say they believe and yet live in sin without qualms of conscience.)*

20, 21 But wilt thou know, O vain man, that faith without works is dead? Was not Abraham our father justified by works, when he had offered Isaac his son upon the altar?

22 Seest thou how faith wrought with his works, and by works was faith made perfect?

23, 24 And the scripture was fulfilled which saith, Abraham believed God, and it was imputed unto him for righteousness: and he was called the Friend of God. Ye see then how that by works a man is justified, and not by faith only. *(Faith alone justifies, but not a faith which is alone and without works.)*

25 Likewise also was not Rahab the harlot justified by works, when she had received the messengers, and had sent *them* out another way? *(In any and every case suitable works attend upon saving faith, and it is idle to claim to be saved by faith, unless our lives are holy.)*

26 For as the body without the spirit is dead, so faith without works is dead also.

Come unto me, O come to me,
    Thou blessed Spirit, come;
To fill my heart with sanctity,
    And use it as thy home.
Thy pure and holy influence
    Grant, Lord, my soul within;
Expelling, by thy presence, thence
    The love and life of sin.

WE are generally too fond of talking, and are not always careful as to what we say; let us hear attentively what the Scriptures have to say of unholy tongues.

JAMES III.

1 My brethren, be not many masters (or teachers), knowing that we shall receive the greater condemnation. (Men are too ready to set up for teachers and censors, but if they knew the increased responsibility of the position they would prefer to be learners.)

2 For in many things we offend all (and this should make us slow to assume leadership). If any man offend not in word, the same is a perfect man, and able also to bridle the whole body.

3—5 Behold, we put bits in the horses' mouths, that they may obey us; and we turn about their whole body. Behold also the ships, which though they be so great, and are driven of fierce winds, yet are they turned about with a very small helm, whithersoever the governor listeth. Even so the tongue is a little member, and boasteth great things. (It walks through the earth, attacking the best of men, and even daring to assail heaven itself.) Behold, how great a matter a little fire kindleth! (If it be fire from heaven it brings a Pentecost; if fire from hell it makes a Pandemonium.)

6 And the tongue is a fire, a world of iniquity (not a nation, or a city of sin, but a whole world of evil): so is the tongue among our members, that it defileth the whole body, and setteth on fire the course of nature; and it is set on fire of hell. (Stella says an unruly tongue is worse than the fire of hell, for that torments only the wicked; but this afflicts all, both bad and good.)

7, 8 For every kind of beasts, and of birds, and of serpents, and of things in the sea, is tamed, and hath been tamed of mankind: But the tongue can no man tame; it is an unruly evil, full of deadly poison. (God alone can subdue it, and teach it to be silent, or to speak to his glory. This lion cannot be bound even by a Samson, but the Lord can transform it to a lamb.)

9, 10 Therewith bless we God, even the Father; and therewith curse we men, which are made after the similitude of God. Out of the same mouth proceedeth blessing and cursing. My brethren, these things ought not so to be.

Inconsistent language is monstrous. Our speech should be all of a piece, and altogether holiness unto the Lord. Is it so?

11, 12 Doth a fountain send forth at the same place sweet water and bitter? Can the fig tree, my brethren, bear olive berries? either a vine, figs? so can no fountain both yield salt water and fresh.

13 Who is a wise man and endued with knowledge among you? let him shew out of a good conversation his works with meekness of wisdom. (Holiness, meekness, and gentleness in conversation are the best signs of a really instructed mind. God alone by his Holy Spirit can give us this wisdom.)

14—18 But if ye have bitter envying and strife in your hearts, glory not, and lie not against the truth. This wisdom descendeth not from above, but is earthly, sensual, devilish. For where envying and strife is, there is confusion and every evil work. But the wisdom that is from above is first pure, then peaceable, gentle, and easy to be intreated, full of mercy and good fruits, without partiality, and without hypocrisy. And the fruit of righteousness is sown in peace of them that make peace.

Old Thomas Adams has wittily said: "It is a singular member. God hath given man two ears; one to hear instructions of human knowledge, the other to hearken to his divine precepts. Two eyes, that with the one he might see to his own way, with the other pity and commiserate his distressed brethren. Two hands, that with the one he might work for his own living, with the other relieve his brother's wants. Two feet, one to walk on common days to his ordinary labour, the other, on sacred days to frequent the congregation of saints. But among all, he hath given him but one tongue; which may instruct him to hear twice so much as he speaks; and to walk and work twice as much as he talks."

Words are things of little cost,
Quickly spoken, quickly lost;
We forget them, but they stand
Witnesses at God's right hand.

Grant us, Lord, from day to day,
Strength to watch and grace to pray;
May our lips, from sin set free,
Love to speak and sing of thee.

744   *" Speak not evil one of another, brethren."*   DECEMBER 17.—MORNING.

[*Or December 1.*]

JAMES IV.

FROM whence *come* wars and fightings among you? *come they* not hence, *even* of your lusts that war in your members?

Quarrels certainly do not come from heaven. If we always acted under the rule of grace, love would create perfect peace at home and abroad.

2 Ye lust, and have not: ye kill, and desire to have, and cannot obtain: ye fight and war, yet ye have not, because ye ask not.

Praying is better than fighting. If God will give us what we ask, why need we fight for it?

3 Ye ask, and receive not, because ye ask amiss, that ye may consume *it* upon your lusts.

If any say that they have prayed and not received, it is clear that their motive was selfish, and therefore God would not gratify them.

4. Ye adulterers and adulteresses, *(who give to worldly things the love which is due to Christ alone,)* know ye not that the friendship of the world is enmity with God? whosoever therefore will be a friend of the world is the enemy of God. *(How can you then love worldliness, and make earthly treasures your grand pursuit?)*

5 Do ye think that the scripture saith in vain, The spirit that dwelleth in us lusteth to envy?

6 But he giveth more grace. Wherefore he saith, God resisteth the proud, but giveth grace unto the humble. *(The testimony of Scripture concerning man's nature is manifestly true. We are by nature selfish and envious; but grace will enable us to conquer our inbred sins, if we humbly own them, and ask for help to overcome them.)*

7 Submit yourselves therefore to God. Resist the devil, and he will flee from you.

He is a coward, assail him boldly and he will quit the field.

8 Draw nigh to God, and he will draw nigh to you. Cleanse *your* hands, *ye* sinners; and purify *your* hearts, *ye* double minded.

9 Be afflicted, and mourn, and weep: let your laughter be turned to mourning, and *your* joy to heaviness. *(Voluntarily sorrow for sin, or you will have to suffer for it eternally. Mourn at the cross, or you will weep before the throne.)*

10 Humble yourselves in the sight of the Lord, and he shall lift you up.

11 Speak not evil one of another, brethren. He that speaketh evil of *his* brother, and judgeth his brother, speaketh evil of the law, and judgeth

the law: but if thou judge the law, thou art not a doer of the law, but a judge. *(The man who is severe upon his brother sets himself up to be a better judge than God. He would have those punished whom God has not punished; and thus he sits in judgment upon God, as though he were wiser than the Judge of all the earth.)*

12 There is one lawgiver, who is able to save and to destroy: who art thou that judgest another?

13, 14 Go to now, ye that say, To day or to morrow we will go into such a city, and continue there a year, and buy and sell, and get gain: Whereas ye know not what *shall be* on the morrow. For what *is* your life? It is even a vapour, that appeareth for a little time, and then vanisheth away. *(To count on life as if we had a lease of it is madness. If it be wrong to boast of to-morrow, what folly must it be to be plotting and planning for a great while to come? It is our duty and privilege to live by the day.)*

15 For that ye *ought* to say, If the Lord will, we shall live, and do this, or that.

This should be your general mode of speech. The mere use of the letters D.V. is an evasion of the rule: to live hour by hour, as those who will soon give an account, is the true mode of living.

16 But now ye rejoice in your boastings: all such rejoicing is evil.

17 *(Lest any should say, "We know all this, for we are fully persuaded that unless God lets us live we can do nothing," James adds, "Do you know so well? then you are all the more bound to do well, for knowledge involves responsibility.")* Therefore to him that knoweth to do good, and doeth *it* not, to him it is sin.

To-morrow, Lord, is thine,
Lodged in thy sovereign hand;
And if its sun arise and shine,
It shines by thy command.

The present moment flies,
And bears our life away;
Oh, make thy servants truly wise,
That they may live to-day.

To Jesus may we fly,
Swift as the morning light;
Lest life's young golden beams should die,
In sudden endless night.

DECEMBER 17.—EVENING.

[*Or December 2.*] " Stablish your hearts, for the coming of the Lord draweth nigh."

745

JAMES V.

GO to now, *ye* rich men, weep and howl for your miseries that shall come upon *you*. *The ungodly rich live only for this world as brutes do, and therefore the time shall come, when, like whipped or wounded beasts, they will howl in dismay. Those who by oppression cause the poor to weep shall themselves weep eternally.*

2, 3 Your riches are corrupted, and your garments are motheaten. Your gold and silver is cankered ; and the rust of them shall be a witness against you, and shall eat your flesh as it were fire. Ye have heaped treasure together for the last days. *(Goods ill gotten and greedily hoarded have heaven's curse upon them. Such treasure is only accumulated wrath. Who would wish to increase a heap which shall cause his own flesh to burn?)*

4 Behold, the hire of the labourers who have reaped down your fields, which is of you kept back by fraud, crieth : and the cries of them which have reaped are entered into the ears of the Lord of sabaoth. *(Covetousness is capable of any and every meanness, and will enrich itself even from the earnings of the poor. The Lord of Hosts is the Guardian of the needy, and he will avenge their wrongs.)*

5—8 Ye have lived in pleasure on the earth, and been wanton ; ye have nourished your hearts, as in a day of slaughter. Ye have condemned *and* killed the just ; *and* he doth not resist you. Be patient therefore, brethren, unto the coming of the Lord. Behold, the husbandman waiteth for the precious fruit of the earth, and hath long patience for it, until he receive the early and latter rain. Be ye also patient ; stablish your hearts : for the coming of the Lord draweth nigh. *(The great ones who wickedly persecute the righteous will soon be reckoned with, and the poor despised child of God shall speedily have his reward.)*

9 Grudge not one against another, brethren, lest ye be condemned : behold, the judge standeth before the door. *(Wrongs will so soon be righted that we may well bear with them a little longer.)*

10 Take, my brethren, the prophets, who have spoken in the name of the Lord, for an example of suffering affliction, and of patience.

11 Behold, we count them happy which endure. Ye have heard of the patience of Job, and have seen the end of the Lord ; that the Lord is very pitiful, and of tender mercy.

12 But above all things, my brethren, swear not, neither by heaven, neither by the earth, neither by any other oath : but let your yea be yea ; and *your* nay, nay ; lest ye fall into condemnation. *(Our word is our bond; and anything beyond it is forbidden. Let us shun swearing of all kinds.)*

13—15 Is any among you afflicted ? let him pray. Is any merry ? let him sing psalms. Is any sick among you ? let him call for the elders of the church ; and let them pray over him, anointing him with oil in the name of the Lord : And the prayer of faith shall save the sick, and the Lord shall raise him up ; and if he have committed sins, they shall be forgiven him. *Use the means and pray. Medicine and supplication should go together. We send for the doctor and his draughts, why not send for the elders and their prayers ?*

16—18 Confess *your* faults one to another, and pray one for another, that ye may be healed. *(This is not confession to a priest, but mutual acknowledgment of any wrong done to each other.)* The effectual fervent prayer of a righteous man availeth much. Elias was a man subject to like passions as we are, and he prayed earnestly that it might not rain : and it rained not on the earth by the space of three years and six months. And he prayed again and the heaven gave rain, and the earth brought forth her fruit. *(There are saints on earth whose prayers are equally prevalent. Why should we not be like them ?)*

19, 20 Brethren, if any of you do err from the truth, and one convert him ; Let him know, that he which converteth the sinner from the error of his way shall save a soul from death, and shall hide a multitude of sins.

> Behold the throne of grace!
> The promise calls me near,
> There Jesus shows a smiling face,
> And waits to answer prayer.
> My soul, ask what thou wilt,
> Thou canst not be too bold ;
> Since his own blood for thee he spilt,
> What else can he withhold ?
> Thine image, Lord, bestow,
> Thy presence and thy love ;
> I ask to serve thee here below,
> And reign with thee above.

OUR *present reading is taken from the first epistle of Peter, a letter full of pastoral teaching, but without a trace of a priestly, much less of a Papal, spirit. Those whose wicked legends set forth Peter as the first Pope find no countenance for their folly in either of his epistles.*

I. PETER I. 1—16.

1 Peter, an apostle of Jesus Christ, to the strangers scattered throughout Pontus, Galatia, Cappadocia, Asia, and Bithynia,

2 Elect according to the foreknowledge of God the Father, through sanctification of the Spirit, unto obedience and sprinkling of the blood of Jesus Christ: Grace unto you, and peace, be multiplied. *(Christians were not ashamed of the doctrine of election in the olden time, but styled each other " the elect." We are chosen to be holy, and who shall deny the Lord's right to choose men for such a purpose? Well may the apostle proceed to bless the Lord as he thinks of this choice favour.)*

3—5 Blessed *be* the God and Father of our Lord Jesus Christ, which according to his abundant mercy hath begotten us again unto a lively hope by the resurrection of Jesus Christ from the dead, To an inheritance incorruptible, and undefiled, and that fadeth not away, reserved in heaven for you, Who are kept by the power of God through faith unto salvation ready to be revealed in the last time.

Observe that the inheritance is kept for the saints, and the saints for the inheritance. Christ who has gone to prepare heaven for us has sent the Holy Ghost to prepare us for heaven.

6 Wherein ye greatly rejoice, though now for a season, if need be, ye are in heaviness through manifold temptations : *(It is not merely that we are in manifold troubles, but we are in heaviness through them ; the iron has entered into our soul. This is a needful part of those trials which are meant to chasten us. If the rod does not make the child smart, of what use is it ?)*

7—9 That the trial of your faith, being much more precious than of gold that perisheth, though it be tried with fire, might be found unto praise and honour and glory at the appearing of Jesus Christ : Whom having not seen, ye love ; in whom, though now ye see *him* not, yet believing, ye rejoice with joy unspeakable and full of glory : Receiving the end of your faith, *even* the salvation of *your* souls.

Peter's Master once bade him feed the sheep, and here he does so very sweetly : every word, yea, every letter, is full of an infinite sweetness. Jesus is with us, faith in him is our strength, and his love fills us with unutterable joy. All this we daily experience. Do we not ?

10 Of which salvation the prophets have enquired and searched diligently, who prophesied of the grace *that should come* unto you :

11 Searching what, or what manner of time the Spirit of Christ which was in them did signify, when it testified beforehand the sufferings of Christ, and the glory that should follow.

12 Unto whom it was revealed, that not unto themselves, but unto us they did minister the things, which are now reported unto you by them that have preached the gospel unto you with the Holy Ghost sent down from heaven ; which things the angels desire to look into.

13 Wherefore gird up the loins of your mind, be sober, and hope to the end for the grace that is to be brought unto you at the revelation of Jesus Christ ;

14—16 As obedient children, not fashioning yourselves according to the former lusts in your ignorance : But as he which hath called you is holy, so be ye holy in all manner of conversation ; Because it is written, Be ye holy ; for I am holy. *(Children should be like their parents. Nature itself prompts the son to imitate the father ; and shall not grace have equal power ? Shall not the new birth be even more influential than the first ? Shall not the children of the thrice holy Jehovah exhibit something of their great Progenitor's spirit and character ? It must be so, or we shall have serious reason to doubt whether we are children of God at all.)*

O Lord, with sorrow and with shame,
　We meekly would confess
How little we, who bear thy name,
　Thy mind and ways express.

Give us thy meek, thy lowly mind ;
　We would obedient be ;
And all our rest and pleasure find
　In fellowship with thee.

I. PETER III.

LIKEWISE, ye wives, *be* in subjection to your own husbands; that, if any obey not the word, they also may without the word be won by the conversation of the wives; While they behold your chaste conversation *coupled* with fear. Whose adorning let it not be that outward *adorning* of plaiting the hair, and of wearing of gold, or of putting on of apparel; But *let it be* the hidden man of the heart, in that which is not corruptible, *even the ornament* of a meek and quiet spirit, which is in the sight of God of great price. For after this manner in the old time the holy women also, who trusted in God, adorned themselves, being in subjection unto their own husbands: Even as Sara obeyed Abraham, calling him lord: whose daughters ye are, as long as ye do well, and are not afraid with any amazement. *(A woman's sphere is her home, her sceptre is love, her crown jewels are domestic virtues. She is most graceful who is most gracious, and she is best arrayed who is clothed with holiness.)*

7 Likewise, ye husbands, dwell with *them* according to knowledge, giving honour unto the wife, as unto the weaker vessel, and as being heirs together of the grace of life; that your prayers be not hindered. *(Tender love and affectionate honour must be rendered to the queen of the little kingdom of home, through whom God blesses the household so much.)*

8, 9 Finally, *be ye* all of one mind, having compassion one of another, love as brethren, *be* pitiful, *be* courteous: Not rendering evil for evil, or railing for railing: but contrariwise blessing; knowing that ye are thereunto called, that ye should inherit a blessing. *(We cannot wash off dirt with dirt, or cure evil by evil; let us not try to do so. If we are indeed believers, we are blessed, and we are yet to be more blessed, therefore let us bless others.)*

10—12 For he that will love life, and see good days, let him refrain his tongue from evil, and his lips that they speak no guile: Let him eschew evil, and do good; let him seek peace, and ensue it. For the eyes of the Lord *are* over the righteous, and his ears *are open* unto their prayers: but the face of the Lord *is* against them that do evil.

13 And who *is* he that will harm you, if ye be followers of that which is good?

14—16 But and if ye suffer for righteousness' sake, happy *are ye:* and be not afraid of their terror, neither be troubled; But sanctify the Lord God in your hearts: and *be* ready always to *give* an answer to every man that asketh you a reason of the hope that is in you with meekness and fear: Having a good conscience; that, whereas they speak evil of you, as of evildoers, they may be ashamed that falsely accuse your good conversation in Christ.

17 For *it is* better, if the will of God be so, that ye suffer for well doing, than for evil doing.

Yet we hear persons say, "I would not mind being blamed if I deserved it," which is very absurd, since it is the deserving of blame which ought to trouble us far more than the rebuke.

18—20 For Christ also hath once suffered for sins, the just for the unjust, that he might bring us to God, being put to death in the flesh, but quickened by the Spirit: By which also he went and preached unto the spirits in prison; Which sometime were disobedient, when once the longsuffering of God waited in the days of Noah, while the ark was a preparing, wherein few, that is, eight souls were saved by water.

This passage nobody understands, though some think they do. It is for our good to be made to feel that we do not know everything. The point which is clear is that as Jesus suffered though innocent, we also must be willing to suffer at the hands of the ungodly.

21, 22 The like figure whereunto *even* baptism doth also now save us (not the putting away of the filth of the flesh, but the answer of a good conscience toward God,) by the resurrection of Jesus Christ: Who is gone into heaven, and is on the right hand of God; angels and authorities and powers being made subject unto him.

Noah's deliverance in the ark, and our baptism, are figures of salvation. Both represent a living burial, a passage from the old world into the new, by death and resurrection. Was our baptism the answer of a good conscience toward God?

> Inured to poverty and pain,
> A suffering life my Master led;
> The Son of God, the Son of man,
> He had not where to lay his head.
>
> Since he is intimately nigh,
> Who, who shall violate my rest?
> Sin, earth, and hell, I now defy;
> I lean upon my Saviour's breast.

DECEMBER 19.—MORNING.

748   " 𝔦𝔣 any man suffer as a Christian, let him not be ashamed."   [*Or December* 5.]

I. PETER IV.

FORASMUCH then as Christ hath suffered for us in the flesh, arm yourselves likewise with the same mind: for he that hath suffered in the flesh hath ceased from sin ;

2 That he no longer should live the rest of *his* time in the flesh to the lusts of men, but to the will of God. *(We reckon the sufferings and death of Jesus to be ours. We cannot, therefore, love the sin for which such sufferings were endured. We have, in Jesus, been put to death for sin, and henceforth we are dead to it.)*

3—5 For the time past of *our* life may suffice us to have wrought the will of the Gentiles, when we walked in lasciviousness, lusts, excess of wine, revellings, banquetings, and abominable idolatries : Wherein they think it strange that ye run not with *them* to the same excess of riot, speaking evil of *you* : Who shall give account to him that is ready to judge the quick and the dead. *(Regeneration makes a marvellous change in men, and it generally happens that the ungodly see it, and at once begin to persecute the convert. Have we been converted? If so, we may expect opposition, but we need not be afraid of it, for the Lord is on our side.)*

6 For for this cause was the gospel preached also to them that are dead, that they might be judged according to men in the flesh, but live according to God in the spirit.

Our departed brethren heard the gospel to this end, that, though condemned to die by their cruel persecutors, they might win the immortal crown, and glorify God as his witnesses.

7 But the end of all things is at hand : be ye therefore sober, and watch unto prayer.

8 And above all things have fervent charity among yourselves : for charity shall cover the multitude of sins. *(Of love, the Christian poet sings,*

> "'Tis gentle, delicate, and kind,
> To faults compassionate or blind.")

9 Use hospitality one to another without grudging.

10 As every man hath received the gift, *even so* minister the same one to another, as good stewards of the manifold grace of God.

11 If any man speak, *let him speak* as the oracles of God *(trying to follow both the sense and spirit of the inspired Scripture);* if any man minister *(or render service), let him do it*

as of the ability which God giveth : that God in all things may be glorified through Jesus Christ, to whom be praise and dominion for ever and ever. Amen.

12 Beloved, think it not strange concerning the fiery trial which is to try you, as though some strange thing happened unto you :

13 But rejoice, inasmuch as ye are partakers of Christ's sufferings ; that, when his glory shall be revealed, ye may be glad also with exceeding joy. *(By such exhortations as these the heroes of the cross were trained to endurance, so that they defied death, and torments worse than death. Have we any of their brave spirit ?)*

14 If ye be reproached for the name of Christ, happy *are ye ;* for the spirit of glory and of God resteth upon you : on their part he is evil spoken of, but on your part he is glorified.

15, 16 But let none of you suffer as a murderer, or *as* a thief, or *as* an evildoer, or as a busybody in other men's matters. Yet if *any man suffer* as a Christian, let him not be ashamed ; but let him glorify God on this behalf.

17 For the time *is come* that judgment must begin at the house of God : and if *it* first *begin* at us, what shall the end *be* of them that obey not the gospel of God ?

18 And if the righteous scarcely be saved, where shall the ungodly and the sinner appear ?

A solemn question! Answer it, each one of you, if you are still unsaved. Where will you appear? Oh, be wise, and fly to Jesus; enlist beneath his banner, cost you what it may. May the Lord lead you to do so.

19 Wherefore let them that suffer according to the will of God commit the keeping of their souls *to him* in well doing, as unto a faithful Creator.

Press forward and fear not ! though trial be near :
The Lord is our refuge—whom then shall we fear ?
His staff is our comfort, our safeguard his rod ;
Then let us be steadfast and trust in our God.

Press forward and fear not ! we'll speed on our way ;
Why should we e'er shrink from our path in dismay ?
We tread but the way which our Leader has trod ;
Then let us press forward and trust in our God.

I. PETER V.

THE elders which are among you I exhort, who am also an elder (*He did not style himself Lord Bishop, much less Head of the Church; but though he was an apostle, he took the lowest room and called himself an elder*), and a witness of the sufferings of Christ, and also a partaker of the glory that shall be revealed: (*This last is best of all. It was an honour to be an elder, and a high distinction to have been an eye-witness of the sufferings of our Lord, but to be by faith an heir of the coming glory is far beyond both. It is a happy circumstance that we may all attain to this, though we cannot to the other two. If we believe in Jesus we are "partakers of the glory that shall be revealed."*)

2, 3 Feed the flock of God which is among you (*this is what the Lord Jesus bade Peter himself do*), taking the oversight thereof, not by constraint, but willingly; not for filthy lucre, but of a ready mind; Neither as being lords over God's heritage, but being ensamples to the flock.

Ministers may do more by their example than by their discourses. Let us pray for them that they may be upheld in the path of integrity.

4 And when the chief Shepherd shall appear, ye shall receive a crown of glory that fadeth not away.

5 Likewise, ye younger, submit yourselves unto the elder. Yea, all *of you* be subject one to another, and be clothed with humility: for God resisteth the proud, and giveth grace to the humble. (*In the olden times servants wore long white aprons, and the original word here used alludes to that dress. We are not to assume a lordly style, but stand apron-ed with humility, ready to serve our fellow Christians in all lowliness of mind.*)

6 Humble yourselves therefore under the mighty hand of God, that he may exalt you in due time: (*If it should seem hard to yield to others, do it for the Lord's sake, as under his hand, and he will in due time honour you.*)

7—9 Casting all your care upon him; for he careth for you. Be sober, be vigilant; because your adversary the devil, as a roaring lion, walketh about, seeking whom he may devour: Whom resist stedfast in the faith, knowing that the same afflictions are accomplished in your brethren that are in the world. (*If we were the only persons who were tempted of the devil we might be terrified; but since he is the common enemy of all believers, and has been defeated by them all in turn, let us show him a bold front, that it may be said of us as of Christian in "Pilgrim's Progress,"*

"*The man so bravely played the man
He made the fiend to fly.*")

10, 11 But the God of all grace, who hath called us unto his eternal glory by Christ Jesus, after that ye have suffered a while, make you perfect, stablish, strengthen, settle *you*. To him *be* glory and dominion for ever and ever. Amen.

12 By Silvanus (*or Silas*), a faithful brother unto you, as I suppose, I have written briefly, exhorting, and testifying that this is the true grace of God wherein ye stand. (*To exhort and to bear witness were the chief works of an apostle, especially the latter. By these Peter fed the sheep and lambs of Christ. We also can exhort and testify if we know the Lord, and have experienced his goodness. Are we doing so?*)

13 The *church that is* at Babylon, elected together with *you*, saluteth you; and *so doth* Marcus my son.

14 Greet ye one another with a kiss of charity. Peace *be* with you all that are in Christ Jesus. Amen. (*This blessing is given to all in Christ Jesus, but to none else. "There is no peace, saith my God, unto the wicked." Restlessness here, and woe for ever, are the portion of those who are out of Christ. O Lord, let none in this household remain without faith in Jesus.*)

When I can read my title clear
  To mansions in the skies,
I bid farewell to every fear,
  And wipe my weeping eyes.

Should earth against my soul engage,
  And hellish darts be hurl'd,
Then I can smile at Satan's rage,
  And face a frowning world.

Let cares like a wild deluge come,
  And storms of sorrow fall,
May I but safely reach my home,
  My God, my heaven, my all!

There shall I bathe my weary soul
  In seas of heavenly rest,
And not a wave of trouble roll
  Across my peaceful breast.

THE *second general epistle of Peter was written to warn the churches against the evil influence of certain teachers, erroneous in doctrine and impure in life. The style is earnest and tender, and is peculiarly marked by a solemn grandeur of imagery and diction.*

II. PETER I.

1 Simon Peter, a servant and an apostle of Jesus Christ, to them that have obtained like precious faith with us through the righteousness of God and our Saviour Jesus Christ :

2, 3 Grace and peace be multiplied unto you through the knowledge of God, and of Jesus our Lord, According as his divine power hath given unto us all things that *pertain* unto life and godliness, through the knowledge of him that hath called us to glory and virtue : (*Grace comes to us through the understanding; we grow in the knowledge of God, and of Jesus our Lord, and so obtain more grace : hence the importance of earnest thought, and diligent study of the Scriptures.*)

4 Whereby are given unto us exceeding great and precious promises : that by these ye might be partakers of the divine nature, having escaped the corruption that is in the world through lust. (*Precious faith lays hold on precious promises, and so raises the soul beyond mere nature into the highest conceivable condition, making it like to God in holiness and virtue. The phrase, "partakers of the divine nature," is a very remarkable one ; we cannot become divine, but we can be " partakers of his holiness."*)

5 And beside this, giving all diligence, add to your faith virtue ; and to virtue knowledge ;

6, 7 And to knowledge temperance ; and to temperance patience ; and to patience godliness ; And to godliness brotherly kindness ; and to brotherly kindness charity. (*Link these hand in hand as virgins in the dance, or place them one upon another, that like the stones of an arch they may yield mutual support.*)

8, 9 For if these things be in you, and abound, they make *you that ye shall* neither *be* barren nor unfruitful in the knowledge of our Lord Jesus Christ. But he that lacketh these things is blind, and cannot see afar off, and hath forgotten that he was purged from his old sins.

10 Wherefore the rather, brethren, give diligence to make your calling and election sure : for if ye do these things, ye shall never fall :

11 For so an entrance shall be ministered unto you abundantly into the everlasting kingdom of our Lord and Saviour Jesus Christ. *You shall enter grace and glory at flood tide, and not as those who are " saved so as by fire."*

12—14 Wherefore I will not be negligent to put you always in remembrance of these things, though ye know *them*, and be established in the present truth. Yea, I think it meet, as long as I am in this tabernacle, to stir you up by putting *you* in remembrance ; Knowing that shortly I must put off *this* my tabernacle, even as our Lord Jesus Christ hath shewed me.

15 Moreover I will endeavour that ye may be able after my decease to have these things always in remembrance.

16 For we have not followed cunningly devised fables, when we made known unto you the power and coming of our Lord Jesus Christ, but were eyewitnesses of his majesty.

17, 18 For he received from God the Father honour and glory, when there came such a voice to him from the excellent glory, This is my beloved Son, in whom I am well pleased. And this voice which came from heaven we heard, when we were with him in the holy mount.

19 We have also a more sure word of prophecy ; whereunto ye do well that ye take heed, as unto a light that shineth in a dark place, until the day dawn, and the day star arise in your hearts : (*The witness of Scripture is even surer than the voice heard in the mount. How much then ought we to prize it ! How well content may we be without visions and revelations.*)

20 Knowing this first, that no prophecy of the scripture is of any private interpretation.

21 For the prophecy came not in old time by the will of man : but holy men of God spake as *they were* moved by the Holy Ghost. (*We may not regard the Bible as the private word of Moses or Isaiah, but as the revelation of God to all time, most sure and infallible.*)

Come, Holy Ghost, our hearts inspire ;
   Let us thine influence prove,
Source of the old prophetic fire,
   Fountain of light and love.

God, through himself, we then shall know,
   If thou within us shine ;
And sound, with all thy saints below,
   The depths of love divine.

II. PETER II.

HOLY *men of old spake as they were moved by the Spirit.*

1, 2 But there were false prophets also among the people, even as there shall be false teachers among you, who privily shall bring in damnable heresies, even denying the Lord that bought them, and bring upon themselves swift destruction. And many shall follow their pernicious ways; by reason of whom the way of truth shall be evil spoken of.

3 And through covetousness shall they with feigned words make merchandise of you: whose judgment now of a long time lingereth not, and their damnation slumbereth not.

4—7 For if God spared not the angels that sinned, but cast *them* down to hell, and delivered *them* into chains of darkness, to be reserved unto judgment; And spared not the old world, but saved Noah the eighth *person*, a preacher of righteousness, bringing in the flood upon the world of the ungodly; And turning the cities of Sodom and Gomorrha into ashes, condemned *them* with an overthrow, making *them* an ensample unto those that after should live ungodly; And delivered just Lot, vexed with the filthy conversation of the wicked:

8 (For that righteous man dwelling among them, in seeing and hearing, vexed *his* righteous soul from day to day with *their* unlawful deeds;)

9 The Lord knoweth how to deliver the godly out of temptations, and to reserve the unjust unto the day of judgment to be punished:

Former judgments are the sure proofs that present sin will also meet with punishment.

10 But chiefly them that walk after the flesh in the lust of uncleanness, and despise government. Presumptuous *are they*, selfwilled, they are not afraid to speak evil of dignities.

11 Whereas angels, which are greater in power and might, bring not railing accusation against them before the Lord.

12 But these, as natural brute beasts, made to be taken and destroyed, speak evil of the things that they understand not; and shall utterly perish in their own corruption;

13 And shall receive the reward of unrighteousness, *as* they that count it pleasure to riot in the day time. Spots *they are* and blemishes, sporting themselves with their own deceivings while they feast with you;

14 Having eyes full of adultery, and that cannot cease from sin; beguiling unstable souls: an heart they have exercised with covetous practices; cursed children:

15, 16 Which have forsaken the right way, and are gone astray, following the way of Balaam *the son* of Bosor, who loved the wages of unrighteousness; But was rebuked for his iniquity: the dumb ass speaking with man's voice forbad the madness of the prophet.

17 These are wells without water, clouds that are carried with a tempest; to whom the mist of darkness is reserved for ever.

18 For when they speak great swelling *words* of vanity, they allure through the lusts of the flesh, *through much* wantonness, those that were clean escaped from them who live in error.

19 While they promise them liberty, they themselves are the servants of corruption: for of whom a man is overcome, of the same is he brought in bondage.

20, 21 For if after they have escaped the pollutions of the world through the knowledge of the Lord and Saviour Jesus Christ, they are again entangled therein, and overcome, the latter end is worse with them than the beginning. For it had been better for them not to have known the way of righteousness, than, after they have known *it*, to turn from the holy commandment delivered unto them.

22 But it is happened unto them according to the true proverb, The dog *is* turned to his own vomit again; and the sow that was washed to her wallowing in the mire. (*The apostles were most anxious that believers should persevere, and therefore they cautioned them as to the dire results of apostasy. These frequent warnings should make us watchful, and lead us to cry mightily to him who alone is able to keep us from falling. Only divine grace can preserve us from the seducing spirits which abound on all sides.*)

Jesus, the Lord, shall guard me safe
From every ill design;
And to his heavenly kingdom keep
This feeble soul of mine.

God is my everlasting aid,
And hell shall rage in vain:
To him be highest glory paid,
And endless praise—Amen.

II. PETER III.

THIS second epistle, beloved, I now write unto you; in *both* which I stir up your pure minds by way of remembrance:

2 That ye may be mindful of the words which were spoken before by the holy prophets, and of the commandment of us the apostles of the Lord and Saviour:

3, 4 Knowing this first, that there shall come in the last days scoffers, walking after their own lusts, And saying, Where is the promise of his coming? for since the fathers fell asleep, all things continue as *they were* from the beginning of the creation. *(They insinuate that there is no God, or that if there be he takes no interest in the affairs of men, or else surely he would have come to judge his enemies long ere this.)*

5, 6 For this they willingly are ignorant of, that by the word of God the heavens were of old, and the earth standing out of the water and in the water: Whereby the world that then was, being overflowed with water, perished:

They wilfully forget that there was one grand interposition of vengeance, and therefore it is not altogether true that the machinery of nature has from time immemorial moved on regardless of human sin. Once by water has the world been destroyed, and by another element it shall soon be overwhelmed.

7, 8 But the heavens and the earth, which are now, by the same word are kept in store, reserved unto fire against the day of judgment and perdition of ungodly men. But, beloved, be not ignorant of this one thing, that one day *is* with the Lord as a thousand years, and a thousand years as one day.

9 The Lord is not slack concerning his promise, as some men count slackness; but is long-suffering to us-ward, not willing that any should perish, but that all should come to repentance. *He waits that men may wait on him. He gives the race space to repent; but, alas, it abuses his longsuffering!*

10 But the day of the Lord will come as a thief in the night; in the which the heavens shall pass away with a great noise, and the elements shall melt with fervent heat, the earth also and the works that are therein shall be burned up.

11 *Seeing* then *that* all these things shall be dissolved, what manner *of persons* ought ye to be in *all* holy conversation and godliness,

12 Looking for and hasting unto the coming of the day of God, wherein the heavens being on fire shall be dissolved, and the elements shall melt with fervent heat?

13 Nevertheless we, according to his promise, look for new heavens and a new earth, wherein dwelleth righteousness.

14—16 Wherefore, beloved, seeing that ye look for such things, be diligent that ye may be found of him in peace, without spot, and blameless. And account *that* the longsuffering of our Lord *is* salvation; even as our beloved brother Paul also according to the wisdom given unto him hath written unto you; As also in all *his* epistles, speaking in them of these things; in which are some things hard to be understood, which they that are unlearned and unstable wrest, as *they do* also the other scriptures, unto their own destruction. *(Good doctrine can be twisted to bad purposes. This is not the fault of the doctrine, but of the foolish or wicked minds which pervert it. We must not neglect the study of those great truths which Paul treats of, for it is the ignorant who wrest them, and therefore we should not be of the number. If we are well acquainted with the deep things of God we shall, by God's grace, be all the less likely to abuse them.)*

17 Ye therefore, beloved, seeing ye know *these things* before, beware lest ye also, being led away with the error of the wicked, fall from your own stedfastness.

18 But grow in grace, and *in* the knowledge of our Lord and Saviour Jesus Christ. To him *be* glory both now and for ever. Amen.

Jesus, thy church with longing eyes,
For thy expected coming waits;
When will the promised light arise,
And glory beam from Zion's gates?

Yes, thou wilt speedily appear;
The smitten earth already reels;
And, not far off, we seem to hear
The thunder of thy chariot wheels.

Teach us, in watchfulness and prayer,
To wait for the appointed hour,
And fit us by thy grace to share
The triumphs of thy conquering power.

I. JOHN I.

THE *apostle John plunges at once into his subject, and begins to discourse upon the Word made flesh, in whom his soul delighted.*

1—3 That which was from the beginning, which we have heard, which we have seen with our eyes, which we have looked upon, and our hands have handled, of the Word of life ; (For the life was manifested, and we have seen *it,* and bear witness, and shew unto you that eternal life, which was with the Father, and was manifested unto us ;) That which we have seen and heard declare we unto you, that ye also may have fellowship with us : and truly our fellowship *is* with the Father, and with his Son Jesus Christ. *(How strong are John's expressions as to the certainty of our Lord's having appeared in the flesh. He had been heard, seen, studiously observed, and actually touched; his appearing was no fiction or pious legend, but a sure matter of fact, and he who appeared was none other than Jesus, the eternal life.)*

4 And these things write we unto you, that your joy may be full. *(Fellowship with Jesus and joy lie so .closely together, that the apostle could aim at both at the same time.)*

5 This then is the message which we have heard of him, and declare unto you, that God is light, and in him is no darkness at all. *These little words contain a mint of meaning. What a wondrous sentence,—"God is light !"*

6, 7 If we say that we have fellowship with him, and walk in darkness, we lie, and do not the truth : But if we walk in the light, as he is in the light, we have fellowship one with another, and the blood of Jesus Christ his Son cleanseth us from all sin. *(Only in truth and holiness can we have fellowship with God, and to render this possible to such sinful creatures as we are, the precious blood of Jesus must purge us from sin. Have we all been cleansed by it ?)*

8—10 If we say that we have no sin, we deceive ourselves, and the truth is not in us. If we confess our sins, he is faithful and just to forgive us *our* sins, and to cleanse us from all unrighteousness. If we say that we have not sinned, we make him a liar, and his word is not in us. *(God only acts according to the truth, he will meet us as sinners, for that is our true character ; but if we claim to be innocent, he cannot*

admit that falsehood, and will not conmune with us.)

I. JOHN II. 1—11.

MY little children, these things write I unto you, that ye sin not. And if any man sin, we have an advocate with the Father, Jesus Christ the righteous : *(This one sentence is worth the whole of the kingdoms of the world.)*

2 And he is the propitiation for our sins : and not for our's only, but also for *the sins of* the whole world. *(He did not die for Jews alone, but to all races the way of salvation is opened by his atoning blood.)*

3 And hereby we do know that we know him, if we keep his commandments. *(Our life and conversation are to ourselves as well as to others the best evidence as to our state.)*

4, 5 He that saith, I know him, and keepeth not his commandments, is a liar, and the truth is not in him. But whoso keepeth his word, in him verily is the love of God perfected : hereby know we that we are in him.

6 He that saith he abideth in him ought himself also so to walk, even as he walked.

7, 8 Brethren, I write no new commandment unto you, but an old commandment which ye had from the beginning. The old commandment is the word which ye have heard from the beginning. Again, a new commandment I write unto you, which thing is true in him and in you : because the darkness is past, and the true light now shineth. *(The love of our brother is in one sense an old command, for it is the substance of the second table of the law ; but the gospel sets it in a new light beneath the cross, and binds us to keep it by new and powerful obligations.)*

9—11 He that saith he is in the light, and hateth his brother, is in darkness even until now. He that loveth his brother abideth in the light, and there is none occasion of stumbling in him. But he that hateth his brother is in darkness, and walketh in darkness, and knoweth not whither he goeth, because that darkness hath blinded his eyes. *(Hatred is darkness, love is light ; the revengeful man is an heir of eternal midnight. Let us purge ourselves from all anger, malice, and envy, for these are evils of the darkest dye.)*

I. JOHN II. 12—28.

I WRITE unto you, little children, because your sins are forgiven you for his name's sake. (*Little children have sins; they need to be forgiven; and they may be forgiven at once. Should not every child go to Jesus and ask to be washed in his precious blood? To be little children in Jesus Christ is a great privilege, and to such the word of God is directed as much as to the more advanced saints.*)

13 I write unto you, fathers, because ye have known him *that is* from the beginning. (*These established saints, having a deeper knowledge of their Lord, were bound to lend the more earnest attention to his word, and to carry it out more fully.*) I write unto you, young men, because ye have overcome the wicked one. (*These young men are the flower of the army of the Lord of Hosts. By their victories already won the apostle summons them to new conflicts. The Spirit of God has a call for believers in all stages of the divine life.*) I write unto you, little children, because ye have known the Father.

14 I have written unto you, fathers, because ye have known him *that is* from the beginning. I have written unto you, young men, because ye are strong, and the word of God abideth in you, and ye have overcome the wicked one.

15 Love not the world, neither the things *that are* in the world. If any man love the world, the love of the Father is not in him. *He may use it, but love it he must not, unless he will renounce the love of God.*

16 For all that *is* in the world, the lust of the flesh, and the lust of the eyes, and the pride of life, is not of the Father, but is of the world.

17 And the world passeth away, and the lust thereof: but he that doeth the will of God abideth for ever.

18 Little children, it is the last time: and as ye have heard that antichrist shall come, even now are there many antichrists; whereby we know that it is the last time. (*The spirit of antichrist has many forms, and is present in every age. Everything which robs Christ of his glory is anti-christian.*)

19 They went out from us, but they were not of us; for if they had been of us, they would *no doubt* have continued with us: but *they went out*, that they might be made manifest that they were not all of us. (*Bad teachers leave the church of God because they never in truth belonged to it. When they go over to Rome they go to their own place.*)

20 But ye have an unction from the Holy One, and ye know all things. (*An experimental knowledge of the truth is the best preservative against error.*)

21 I have not written unto you because ye know not the truth, but because ye know it, and that no lie is of the truth.

22 Who is a liar but he that denieth that Jesus is the Christ? (*This is the greatest of all falsehoods, and it insults both the Father and the Son by doubting their testimony.*) He is antichrist, that denieth the Father and the Son.

23 Whosoever denieth the Son, the same hath not the Father: [*but*] *he that acknowledgeth the Son hath the Father also.*

24 Let that therefore abide in you, which ye have heard from the beginning. If that which ye have heard from the beginning shall remain in you, ye also shall continue in the Son, and in the Father. (*You cannot find a better gospel; persevere, then, in what you already know.*)

25 And this is the promise that he hath promised us, *even* eternal life.

26, 27 These *things* have I written unto you concerning them that seduce you. But the anointing which ye have received of him abideth in you, and ye need not that any man teach you: but as the same anointing teacheth you of all things, and is truth, and is no lie, and even as it hath taught you, ye shall abide in him.

28 And now, little children, abide in him; that, when he shall appear, we may have confidence, and not be ashamed before him at his coming. (*Being full of love he pleads with us never to desert our Lord, or listen to the false gospels which would lead us astray. Ever may this family be true to Jesus, to the gospel, and to holy living: and may none of us ever be deceived by false doctrine, or tempted into sin.*)

One there is to whom we're going,
One to whom we owe our all;
Daily grace is he bestowing,
He sustains us when we fall.
Precious Jesus!
Thou to us art all in all.

I. JOHN III.

BEHOLD, what manner of love the Father hath bestowed upon us, that we should be called the sons of God : therefore the world knoweth us not, because it knew him not.

2 Beloved, now are we the sons of God, and it doth not yet appear what we shall be : but we know that, when he shall appear, we shall be like him ; for we shall see him as he is.

3 And every man that hath this hope in him purifieth himself, even as he is pure.

4 Whosoever committeth sin transgresseth also the law : for sin is the transgression of the law.

5 And ye know that he was manifested to take away our sins ; and in him is no sin.

6 Whosoever abideth in him sinneth not : whosoever sinneth hath not seen him, neither known him. *(We understand by this not that believers are perfectly free from sinning, but that they do not sin habitually, wilfully, and openly as the unregenerate do. Their lives are holy, and when faults occur they grieve over them. The river of their lives runs towards righteousness, and though there are eddies in it these do not affect the main current.)*

7 Little children, let no man deceive you : he that doeth righteousness is righteous, even as he is righteous.

8 He that committeth sin is of the devil ; for the devil sinneth from the beginning. For this purpose the Son of God was manifested, that he might destroy the works of the devil.

9 Whosoever is born of God doth not commit sin ; for his seed remaineth in him : and he cannot sin, because he is born of God. *He cannot sin with his whole heart, or continuously, or finally, or as the main act of his life. Sin is not his element, or his delight.*

10, 11 In this the children of God are manifest, and the children of the devil : whosoever doeth not righteousness is not of God, neither he that loveth not his brother. For this is the message that ye heard from the beginning, that we should love one another. *(The beloved John seems to breathe out only love. Like the harp of Anacreon his heart resoundeth " love alone.")*

12, 13 Not as Cain, *who* was of that wicked one, and slew his brother. And wherefore slew he him ? Because his own works were evil, and his brother's righteous. Marvel not, my brethren, if the world hate you. *(That hatred has existed from the beginning. The very first man who died was martyred for the faith.)*

14 We know that we have passed from death unto life, because we love the brethren. He that loveth not *his* brother abideth in death.

15 Whosoever hateth his brother is a murderer : and ye know that no murderer hath eternal life abiding in him.

16 Hereby perceive we the love *of God*, because he laid down his life for us : and we ought to lay down *our* lives for the brethren.

17 But whoso hath this world's good, and seeth his brother have need, and shutteth up his bowels *of compassion* from him, how dwelleth the love of God in him ?

18 My little children, let us not love in word, neither in tongue ; but in deed and in truth.

He whose whole religion lies in words is a hypocrite worthy of the scorn of all mankind. Above all things let us be real in all that we do.

19 And hereby we know that we are of the truth, and shall assure our hearts before him.

20 For if our heart condemn us, God is greater than our heart, and knoweth all things.

21 Beloved, if our heart condemn us not, *then* have we confidence toward God.

22 And whatsoever we ask, we receive of him, because we keep his commandments, and do those things that are pleasing in his sight.

23, 24 And this is his commandment, That we should believe on the name of his Son Jesus Christ, and love one another, as he gave us commandment. And he that keepeth his commandments dwelleth in him, and he in him. And hereby we know that he abideth in us, by the Spirit which he hath given us.

Behold, what wondrous grace
The Father hath bestow'd
On sinners of a mortal race,
To call them sons of God !

Nor doth it yet appear
How great we must be made ;
But when we see our Saviour here,
We shall be like our Head.

If in my Father's love
I share a filial part,
Send down thy Spirit, like a dove,
To rest upon my heart.

I. JOHN IV.

BELOVED, believe not every spirit, but try the spirits whether they are of God: because many false prophets are gone out into the world.

2, 3 Hereby know ye the Spirit of God: Every spirit that confesseth that Jesus Christ is come in the flesh is of God: And every spirit that confesseth not that Jesus Christ is come in the flesh is not of God: and this is that *spirit* of antichrist, whereof ye have heard that it should come; and even now already is it in the world. (*This is a very useful test in many cases. If any form of doctrine denies or dishonours the Godhead or Messiahship of the Lord Jesus, or makes his incarnation to be a mere myth, it is to be rejected with abhorrence. Errors which touch the person or work of Jesus are fatal.*)

4 Ye are of God, little children, and have overcome them: because greater is he that is in you, than he that is in the world.

5 They are of the world: therefore speak they of the world, and the world heareth them.

6 We are of God: he that knoweth God heareth us; he that is not of God heareth not us. Hereby know we the spirit of truth, and the spirit of error. (*Every spirit which does away with Jesus or dishonours him in any degree we know to be the spirit of error. This test is very simple, but very accurate.*)

7, 8 Beloved, let us love one another: for love is of God; and every one that loveth is born of God, and knoweth God. He that loveth not knoweth not God; for God is love.

Love is the divine law of life, selfishness is sin; when grace restores us to our proper relationship with God and his creation, love is the very instinct of our renewed nature.

9, 10 In this was manifested the love of God toward us, because that God sent his only begotten Son into the world, that we might live through him. Herein is love, not that we loved God, but that he loved us, and sent his Son *to be* the propitiation for our sins.

11 Beloved, if God so loved us, we ought also to love one another. (*The master motive for benevolence is the love of God, it is an argument which will never lose its force.*)

12, 13 No man hath seen God at any time. If we love one another, God dwelleth in us, and his love is perfected in us. Hereby know we that we dwell in him, and he in us, because he hath given us of his Spirit.

14—16 And we have seen and do testify that the Father sent the Son *to be* the Saviour of the world. Whosoever shall confess that Jesus is the Son of God, God dwelleth in him, and he in God. And we have known and believed the love that God hath to us. God is love; and he that dwelleth in love dwelleth in God, and God in him.

17 Herein is our love made perfect, that we may have boldness in the day of judgment: because as he is, so are we in this world.

18 There is no fear in love; but perfect love casteth out fear: because fear hath torment. He that feareth is not made perfect in love.

Fear dwells upon the punishment deserved, and so has no rest. When perfect love assures the soul of pardoned sin, the heart has joyful rest.

19 We love him, because he first loved us.

20 If any man say, I love God, and hateth his brother, he is a liar: for he that loveth not his brother whom he hath seen, how can he love God whom he hath not seen?

An old Latin author says, " The eyes are our leaders in love." Juvenal wondered at one who loved a person whom he had never seen. If, then, we do not love those whom we see, is it likely that we really love the invisible God?

21 And this commandment have we from him, that he who loveth God love his brother also. (*A Christian is one who has a solemn awe of the commands of God, hence he labours to abound in deeds and words of love, because the Lord hath bidden him to do so.*)

Bless'd be the Father of our Lord,
From whom all blessings spring!
And bless'd be the Incarnate Word,
Our Saviour and our King!

We know and have believed the love
Which God through Christ displays;
And when we see his face above,
We'll nobler anthems raise.

I. JOHN V.

WHOSOEVER believeth that Jesus is the Christ is born of God: and every one that loveth him that begat loveth him also that is begotten of him. *(Dost thou believe in Jesus? Dost thou love thy Lord? Then thou art born again.)*

2, 3 By this we know that we love the children of God, when we love God, and keep his commandments. For this is the love of God, that we keep his commandments: and his commandments are not grievous. *(Obedience proves the truth of faith, especially obedience to the command which bids us love. It is idle to talk of being saved if we are not living unto God.)*

4, 5 For whatsoever is born of God overcometh the world: and this is the victory that overcometh the world, *even* our faith. Who is he that overcometh the world, but he that believeth that Jesus is the Son of God?

Faith, then, is the sure evidence of the new birth, and if we believe in the Lord Jesus we are born again, and shall overcome the world.

6 This is he that came by water and blood, *even* Jesus Christ; not by water only, but by water and blood. *(Cleansing from the power of sin, and delivering from its guilt.)* And it is the Spirit that beareth witness, because the Spirit is truth.

7, 8 For there are three that bear record in heaven, the Father, the Word, and the Holy Ghost: and these three are one. And there are three that bear witness in earth, the spirit, and the water, and the blood: and these three agree in one. *(Instead of all other heavenly signs, the church has for her standing miracles the energetic work of the Holy Ghost, the purifying influence of the gospel, and the peace-giving energy of the atonement. If there be no power of the Holy Ghost, no sanctification, and no pardon of sin, our religion is a delusion; but if these be facts, and they certainly are, our faith has solid grounds.)*

9 If we receive the witness of men, the witness of God is greater: for this is the witness of God which he hath testified of his Son.

10, 11 He that believeth on the Son of God hath the witness in himself: he that believeth not God hath made him a liar; because he believeth not the record that God gave of his Son.

And this is the record, that God hath given to us eternal life, and this life is in his Son.

12 He that hath the Son hath life; *and* he that hath not the Son of God hath not life.

13 These things have I written unto you that believe on the name of the Son of God; that ye may know that ye have eternal life, and that ye may believe on the name of the Son of God.

You do believe, but you may believe yet more. " Lord, increase our faith," is no needless prayer.

14, 15 And this is the confidence that we have in him, that, if we ask any thing according to his will, he heareth us: And if we know that he hear us, whatsoever we ask, we know that we have the petitions that we desired of him.

Answers to prayer are a powerful establishment of faith. The God who has an ear for our prayers is no fiction.

16—18 If any man see his brother sin a sin *which is* not unto death, he shall ask, and he shall give him life for them that sin not unto death. There is a sin unto death: I do not say that he shall pray for it. All unrighteousness is sin: and there is a sin not unto death. We know that whosoever is born of God sinneth not; but he that is begotten of God keepeth himself, and that wicked one toucheth him not. *(Whatever the unpardonable sin may be, the child of God shall be kept from it. We need not curiously inquire what that dark crime may be; it will be better to follow our Lord, and we shall be preserved from it.)*

19 *And* we know that we are of God, and the whole world lieth in wickedness.

20 And we know that the Son of God is come, and hath given us an understanding, that we may know him that is true, and we are in him that is true, *even* in his Son Jesus Christ. This is the true God, and eternal life.

21 Little children, keep yourselves from idols. Amen.

> For ever here my rest shall be
> Close to thy bleeding side;
> This all my hope and all my plea—
> For me the Saviour died.
>
> Th' atonement of thy blood apply
> Till faith to sight improve;
> Till hope in full fruition die,
> And all my soul be love.

758   " **This is love, that we walk after His commandments.** "   DECEMBER 24.—MORNING.

[*Or December* 15.]

THE SECOND EPISTLE OF JOHN.

HERE *we have a letter to a lady and her godly family, towards whom John felt a fervent Christian affection. Her name we do not know, nor is it of any consequence, for the epistle will suit any believing household.*

1, 2 The elder unto the elect lady and her children, whom I love in the truth; and not I only, but also all they that have known the truth; For the truth's sake, which dwelleth in us, and shall be with us for ever. (*John in his private letter does not mention that he is an apostle, but writes more familiarly as an elder of the church. The lady to whom he wrote was known to many, and beloved by all who loved the truth. The best and purest love arises out of common attachment to the gospel. Happy is that household which has gained the love of the saints by its zeal for God.*)

3 Grace be with you, mercy, *and* peace, from God the Father, and from the Lord Jesus Christ, the Son of the Father, in truth and love. *Such a blessing may the Lord pronounce on this family, and we shall be rich indeed.*

4 I rejoiced greatly that I found of thy children walking in truth, as we have received a commandment from the Father. (*The venerable old man's heart was more comforted by seeing family religion than by all else below the skies. How good and how pleasant it is to see a household loving the Lord.*)

5 And now I beseech thee, lady, not as though I wrote a new commandment unto thee, but that which we had from the beginning, that we love one another. (*John harps sweetly on this string. Being so aged a man none would misunderstand his affectionate words.*)

6 And this is love, that we walk after his commandments. This is the commandment, That, as ye have heard from the beginning, ye should walk in it. (*Obedience to Christ is love. "Be ye holy" is the most ancient rubric of the church; all lovers of God obey it.*)

7 For many deceivers are entered into the world, who confess not that Jesus Christ is come in the flesh. This is a deceiver and an antichrist. (*The world is bad enough, but deceivers come into it from Satan, and try to make it worse by their errors. Modern scepticism is by some praised and petted, but it is to be abhorred by all who abide in the truth.*)

8 Look to yourselves, that we lose not those things which we have wrought, but that we receive a full reward. (*Faithful ministers fear lest their converts should disappoint them by not remaining firm in the truth. If they go over to error their ministers have laboured in vain.*)

9 Whosoever transgresseth, and abideth not in the doctrine of Christ, hath not God. He that abideth in the doctrine of Christ, he hath both the Father and the Son.

10, 11 If there come any unto you, and bring not this doctrine, receive him not into *your* house, neither bid him God speed: For he that biddeth him God speed is partaker of his evil deeds. (*As he who aids and abets a thief cannot be an honest man, so he who encourages a false teacher is a sharer in his crime.*)

12 Having many things to write unto you, I would not *write* with paper and ink: but I trust to come unto you, and speak face to face, that our joy may be full. (*There are words of warning which are better spoken than written. In some cases it is wise even to make a journey to warn friends against insidious error.*)

13 The children of thy elect sister greet thee. Amen.

Oh that near the cross abiding,
  We may to the Saviour cleave!
Nought with him our hearts dividing,
  All for him content to leave.

May we still the cross discerning,
  To our Lord for comfort go;
And new wonders daily learning,
  More of Jesus' fulness know.

Walk in the light, so shalt thou know
  That fellowship of love
His Spirit only can bestow,
  Who reigns in light above.

Walk in the light, and sin abhorr'd
  Shall ne'er defile again;
The blood of Jesus Christ thy Lord
  Shall cleanse from every stain.

Walk in the light, and thou shalt own
  Thy darkness passed away;
Because that light hath on thee shone,
  In which is perfect day.

December 24.—Evening.
[*Or December 16.*]

"$\mathfrak{He}$ $\mathfrak{that}$ $\mathfrak{doeth}$ $\mathfrak{good}$ $\mathfrak{is}$ $\mathfrak{of}$ $\mathfrak{God}$."

759

THE THIRD EPISTLE OF JOHN.

OLD *Master Trapp says John wrote this letter " to a rich Corinthian, rich in this world and rich in good works, a rare bird anywhere, but especially at Corinth, where Paul found them far behind the poor Macedonians in works of charity."*

1, 2 The elder unto the wellbeloved Gaius, whom I love in the truth. Beloved, I wish above all things that thou mayest prosper and be in health, even as thy soul prospereth. *(It would not be safe to wish this for many, for if their bodies only prospered as their souls do, many would die, and most professors would be weak and withered, sick and sorry.)*

3, 4 For I rejoiced greatly, when the brethren came and testified of the truth that is in thee, even as thou walkest in the truth. I have no greater joy than to hear that my children walk in truth. *(John loved his converts as his children, and was glad when he found them sound in doctrine and in practice. What would he say to " modern doubt"? It would break the good man's heart. God's people should hold the truth more firmly than ever, for the professing church is idolising clever scepticism.)*

5 Beloved, thou doest faithfully whatsoever thou doest to the brethren, and to strangers ;

6, 7 Which have borne witness of thy charity before the church : whom if thou bring forward on their journey after a godly sort, thou shalt do well : Because that for his name's sake they went forth, taking nothing of the Gentiles.

Gaius kept open house for travelling preachers and poor saints. One of the greatest honours we can have is to entertain a servant of the Lord. The Master sets it down as done to himself.

8 We therefore ought to receive such, that we might be fellow-helpers to the truth. *(Gaius could not preach, but he lodged those who did, and so he obtained a prophet's reward.)*

9 I wrote unto the church : but Diotrephes, who loveth to have the preeminence among them, receiveth us not.

10 Wherefore, if I come, I will remember his deeds which he doeth, prating against us with malicious words : and not content therewith, neither doth he himself receive the brethren, and forbiddeth them that would, and casteth *them* out of the church. *(What ! Did*

men speak against the beloved John ? Then none of us can hope to escape opposition if we be faithful. We wonder at such a poor creature as Diotrephes impudently setting himself up against the great apostle. We must take heed that we do not imitate him by grieving any of the Lord's ministers.)

11 Beloved, follow not that which is evil, but that which is good. He that doeth good is of God : but he that doeth evil hath not seen God.

12 Demetrius hath good report of all *men*, and of the truth itself : yea, and we *also* bear record ; and ye know that our record is true.

John censured one but commended another. Where there is a Diotrephes there is generally a Demetrius ; the Lord neutralises the evil of one by the good of another, or churches could not exist.

13 I had many things to write, but I will not with ink and pen write unto thee :

14 But I trust I shall shortly see thee, and we shall speak face to face. *(Say little and write less. Speaking is better than writing, especially from preachers, who would do well to put away ink and paper and preach as the Lord gives them utterance.)* Peace *be* to thee. Our friends salute thee. Greet the friends by name.

Our religion is social and courteous. Let us not fail in kindly words and deeds.

Peace be to this favour'd dwelling,
    Peace to every soul therein ;
Peace of heavenly joy foretelling,
    Peace the fruit of conquer'd sin.

Peace that speaks its heavenly giver ;
    Peace to worldly minds unknown ;
Peace divine that flows for ever
    From its source, the Lord alone.

To God the only wise,
  Our Saviour and our King,
Let all the saints below the skies
  Their humble praises bring.

He will present our souls,
  Unblemish'd and complete,
Before the glory of his face
  With joys divinely great.

To our Redeemer God
  Wisdom and power belong,
Immortal crowns of majesty,
  And everlasting song.

DECEMBER 25.—MORNING.

760   " Earnestly contend for the faith which was once delivered unto the saints."   [Or December 17.]

THE GENERAL EPISTLE OF JUDE.*

JUDE, the servant of Jesus Christ, and brother of James, to them that are sanctified by God the Father, and preserved in Jesus Christ, *and* called : Mercy unto you, and peace, and love, be multiplied.

3 Beloved, when I gave all diligence to write unto you of the common salvation, it was needful for me to write unto you, and exhort *you* that ye should earnestly contend for the faith which was once delivered unto the saints.

4 For there are certain men crept in unawares, who were before of old ordained to this condemnation, ungodly men, turning the grace of God into lasciviousness, and denying the only Lord God, and our Lord Jesus Christ.

If, while the apostles were yet alive, errors crept into the churches, we need not wonder that they multiply in these last days. We must set our faces as a flint against them.

5, 6 I will therefore put you in remembrance, though ye once knew this, how that the Lord, having saved the people out of the land of Egypt, afterward destroyed them that believed not. And the angels which kept not their first estate, but left their own habitation, he hath reserved in everlasting chains under darkness unto the judgment of the great day.

If professors leave the gospel for unholy doctrine and impure living, he who cast down the angels for their sin will not spare them.

7 Even as Sodom and Gomorrha, and the cities about them in like manner, giving themselves over to fornication, and going after strange flesh, are set forth for an example, suffering the vengeance of eternal fire.

8—13 Likewise also these *filthy* dreamers defile the flesh, despise dominion, and speak evil of dignities. Yet Michael the archangel, when contending with the devil he disputed about the body of Moses, durst not bring against him a railing accusation, but said, The Lord rebuke thee. *(We do not know when this occurred, but the lesson of gentle speech is clear enough.)* But these speak evil of those things which they know not : but what they know naturally, as brute beasts, in those things they corrupt themselves. Woe unto them! for they have gone in the way of Cain, and ran greedily after the error of Balaam for reward, and perished in the gainsaying of Core. These are spots in your feasts of charity, when they feast with you, feeding themselves without fear : clouds *they are* without water, carried about of winds ; trees whose fruit withereth, without fruit, twice dead, plucked up by the roots ; Raging waves of the sea, foaming out their own shame ; wandering stars, to whom is reserved the blackness of darkness for ever.

14 And Enoch also, the seventh from Adam, prophesied of these, saying, Behold, the Lord cometh with ten thousands of his saints,

15 To execute judgment upon all, and to convince all that are ungodly among them of all their ungodly deeds which they have ungodly committed, and of all their hard *speeches* which ungodly sinners have spoken against him.

16 These are murmurers, complainers, walking after their own lusts ; and their mouth speaketh great swelling *words*, having men's persons in admiration because of advantage.

17, 18 But, beloved, remember ye the words which were spoken before of the apostles of our Lord Jesus Christ ; How that they told you there should be mockers in the last time, who should walk after their own ungodly lusts.

19 These be they who separate themselves, sensual, having not the Spirit.

20, 21 But ye, beloved, building up yourselves on your most holy faith, praying in the Holy Ghost, Keep yourselves in the love of God, looking for the mercy of our Lord Jesus Christ unto eternal life.

22, 23 And of some have compassion, making a difference : And others save with fear, pulling *them* out of the fire ; hating even the garment spotted by the flesh. *(Those who are in error are not all equally guilty : some are deceivers and others are dupes. We must restore all we can, but their error must be severely dealt with. Charity to error is cruelty to souls.)*

24 Now unto him that is able to keep you from falling, and to present *you* faultless before the presence of his glory with exceeding joy,

25 To the only wise God our Saviour, *be* glory and majesty, dominion and power, both now and ever. Amen.

* Those who observe Christmas Day should read the portion upon page 486.

THE REVELATION OF JOHN THE DIVINE.

ANDREW FULLER *has said concerning this mysterious book:—" It is that to the New Testament church which the pillar of the cloud was to the church in the wilderness, guiding it through the labyrinth of anti-Christian errors and corruptions. It must not be neglected under a notion of its being hard to be understood. As well might the mariner, amidst the rocks, neglect his friendly chart, under an idea of its being difficult to understand it."*

CHAPTER I.

1—3 The Revelation of Jesus Christ, which God gave unto him, to shew unto his servants things which must shortly come to pass; and he sent and signified *it* by his angel unto his servant John: Who bare record of the word of God, and of the testimony of Jesus Christ, and of all things that he saw. Blessed *is* he that readeth, and they that hear the words of this prophecy, and keep those things which are written therein: for the time *is* at hand.

" *To induce us to give the most serious attention to the subject, a blessing is pronounced on those who ' read, and hear, and keep,' the words of this prophecy, especially as the time of its fulfilment was at hand. There does not appear to be any other part of Scripture that is prefaced with such an inducement to read, and understand, and practically regard it.*"

4—6 John to the seven churches which are in Asia: Grace *be* unto you, and peace, from him which is, and which was, and which is to come; and from the seven Spirits which are before his throne; And from Jesus Christ, *who is* the faithful witness, *and* the first begotten of the dead, and the prince of the kings of the earth. Unto him that loved us, and washed us from our sins in his own blood, And hath made us kings and priests unto God and his Father; to him *be* glory and dominion for ever and ever. Amen.

7 Behold, he cometh with clouds; and every eye shall see him, and they *also* which pierced him: and all kindreds of the earth shall wail because of him. Even so, Amen.

8 I am Alpha and Omega, the beginning and the ending, saith the Lord, which is, and which was, and which is to come, the Almighty.

9 I John, who also am your brother, and companion in tribulation, and in the kingdom and patience of Jesus Christ, was in the isle that is called Patmos, for the word of God, and for the testimony of Jesus Christ.

He makes no mention of his being banished there by the persecutor: true virtue never boasts, or even invites others to admire it.

10, 11 I was in the Spirit on the Lord's day, and heard behind me a great voice, as of a trumpet, Saying, I am Alpha and Omega, the first and the last: and, What thou seest, write in a book, and send *it* unto the seven churches which are in Asia; unto Ephesus, and unto Smyrna, and unto Pergamos, and unto Thyatira, and unto Sardis, and unto Philadelphia, and unto Laodicea.

12, 13 And I turned to see the voice that spake with me. And being turned, I saw seven golden candlesticks; And in the midst of the seven candlesticks *one* like unto the Son of man, clothed with a garment down to the foot, and girt about the paps with a golden girdle.

14—16 His head and *his* hairs *were* white like wool, as white as snow *(to denote that he is the Ancient of days);* and his eyes *were* as a flame of fire; And his feet like unto fine brass, as if they burned in a furnace; and his voice as the sound of many waters. And he had in his right hand seven stars: and out his mouth went a sharp twoedged sword: and his countenance *was* as the sun shineth in his strength.

17—20 And when I saw him, I fell at his feet as dead. *(He was overwhelmed by the glory of his Lord's appearance. We are as yet incapable of beholding the full blaze of the Redeemer's glory: this corruptible must put on incorruption before we shall be able to endure the sight.)* And he laid his right hand upon me, saying unto me, Fear not; I am the first and the last: *I am* he that liveth, and was dead: and, behold, I am alive for evermore, Amen; and have the keys of hell and of death. Write the things which thou hast seen, and the things which are, and the things which shall be hereafter; The mystery of the seven stars which thou sawest in my right hand, and the seven golden candlesticks. The seven stars are the angels of the seven churches: and the seven candlesticks which thou sawest are the seven churches.

762

DECEMBER 26.—MORNING.

"To him that overcometh will I give to eat of the hidden manna." [*Or December* 19.]

REVELATION II. 1—17.

UNTO the angel *(messenger or minister)* of the church of Ephesus write ; These things saith he that holdeth the seven stars in his right hand, who walketh in the midst of the seven golden candlesticks ; I know thy works, and thy labour, and thy patience, and how thou canst not bear them which are evil : and thou hast tried them which say they are apostles, and are not, and hast found them liars : And hast borne, and hast patience, and for my name's sake hast laboured, and hast not fainted. *(Patient in labour, but impatient of error, the Ephesian church occupied a high position. Would to God that all believers were in as good a condition as the Ephesians were.)*

4 Nevertheless I have *somewhat* against thee, because thou hast left thy first love. *(Not* "lost" *it, as some say, as if it were a misfortune and scarcely a fault ; but left it, or departed from it. We ought to love Jesus better as we grow older and as we know more of him : to decline in love to him is to do him great dishonour.)*

5 Remember therefore from whence thou art fallen, and repent, and do the first works ; or else I will come unto thee quickly, and will remove thy candlestick out of his place, except thou repent.

6 But this thou hast, that thou hatest the deeds of the Nicolaitanes, which I also hate.

Probably these were men who preached up licentious freedom under the pretence of spirituality, like certain vicious sects in America. Uncleanness is very hateful to the Lord.

7 He that hath an ear, let him hear what the Spirit saith unto the churches ; To him that overcometh will I give to eat of the tree of life, which is in the midst of the paradise of God.

The imagery of this first blessing is taken from Paradise ; there was nothing in Eden which grace cannot restore to us.

8, 9 And unto the angel of the church in Smyrna write ; These things saith the first and the last, which was dead, and is alive ; I know thy works, and tribulation, and poverty, (but thou art rich) and *I know* the blasphemy of them which say they are Jews, and are not, but *are* the synagogue of Satan. *(This church was sorely persecuted, but remained faithful. It has*

been called " *sweet-smelling Smyrna, the poorest and the purest of the seven.*")

10 Fear none of those things which thou shalt suffer : behold, the devil shall cast *some* of you into prison, that ye may be tried ; and ye shall have tribulation ten days : be thou faithful unto death, and I will give thee a crown of life.

11 He that hath an ear, let him hear what the Spirit saith unto the churches ; He that overcometh shall not be hurt of the second death. *(They may die once, but not twice ; they shall inherit life eternal.)*

12, 13 And to the angel of the church in Pergamos write ; These things saith he which hath the sharp sword with two edges ; I know thy works, and where thou dwellest, *even* where Satan's seat *is :* and thou holdest fast my name, and hast not denied my faith, even in those days wherein Antipas *was* my faithful martyr, who was slain among you, where Satan dwelleth.

This church was faithful to the name of Jesus, yet there were evils within it.

14—16 But I have a few things against thee, because thou hast there them that hold the doctrine of Balaam, who taught Balac to cast a stumblingblock before the children of Israel, to eat things sacrificed unto idols, and to commit fornication. So hast thou also them that hold the doctrine of the Nicolaitanes, which thing I hate. Repent ; or else I will come unto thee quickly, and will fight against them with the sword of my mouth. *(Jesus will not tolerate filthiness in a church. He will sooner go to war with it than endure it.)*

17 He that hath an ear, let him hear what the Spirit saith unto the churches ; To him that overcometh will I give to eat of the hidden manna, and will give him a white stone, and in the stone a new name written, which no man knoweth saving he that receiveth *it. (Dr. Cumming says,* " *This is equivalent to triumphant acquittal. This will appear from Acts* xxvi., *where Paul says,* ' *I gave my voice against them ;' it is literally,* 'I gave my stone against them ;' that is, I put in the urn a black stone, denoting my vote for their condemnation. Our blessed Lord says, I will put in your urn a white stone ; that is, I will pronounce you absolved at the judgment seat, justified and accepted in me."*)*

REVELATION II. 18—29.

AND unto the angel of the church in Thyatira write; These things saith the Son of God, who hath his eyes like unto a flame of fire, and his feet *are* like fine brass;

19 I know thy works, and charity, and service, and faith, and thy patience, and thy works; and the last *to be* more than the first. *This church grew better and better, and did more and more for her Lord. Progress should be the constant characteristic of a church of God.*

20, 21 Notwithstanding I have a few things against thee, because thou sufferest that woman Jezebel, which calleth herself a prophetess, to teach and to seduce my servants to commit fornication, and to eat things sacrificed unto idols. And I gave her space to repent of her fornication; and she repented not.

22 Behold, I will cast her into a bed, and them that commit adultery with her into great tribulation, except they repent of their deeds.

23 And I will kill her children with death; and all the churches shall know that I am he which searcheth the reins and hearts: and I will give unto every one of you according to your works. *(Probably a party in the church led by a woman had taught that the sins of the flesh might be indulged in without evil. The Lord is most jealous of the purity of his church, and those who enter her midst and teach lasciviousness must expect condign punishment. No church ought to endure such, but should cast them out at once.)*

24, 25 But unto you I say, and unto the rest in Thyatira, as many as have not this doctrine, and which have not known the depths of Satan, as they speak; I will put upon you none other burden. But that which ye have *already* hold fast till I come.

26—28 And he that overcometh, and keepeth my works unto the end, to him will I give power over the nations: And he shall rule them with a rod of iron; as the vessels of a potter shall they be broken to shivers: even as I received of my Father. And I will give him the morning star. *(The grandest conqueror is the man who overcomes sin. He shall not only vanquish the world, but shall win the glory of heaven's eternal day. On him Jesus, the morning star, has shone, and the dawning must be near.)*

29 He that hath an ear, let him hear what the Spirit saith unto the churches. *(Ears are meant to hear with, but some have lost all power to hear the voice of the Spirit. If grace has opened our ear, let us attend to every word which the Spirit utters.)*

REVELATION III. 1—6.

AND unto the angel of the church in Sardis write; These things saith he that hath the seven Spirits of God, and the seven stars; I know thy works, that thou livest, and art dead. *(The bulk of the members were formalists and hypocrites, yet the church kept up its reputation, and it does not appear that any serious heresy had to be contended with. How beautiful may a fruit appear upon the outside and yet be rotten within.)*

2 Be watchful, and strengthen the things which remain, that are ready to die : for I have not found thy works perfect before God.

3 Remember therefore how thou hast received and heard, and hold fast, and repent. If therefore thou shalt not watch, I will come on thee as a thief, and thou shalt not know what hour I will come upon thee.

4 Thou hast a few names even in Sardis which have not defiled their garments; and they shall walk with me in white: for they are worthy. *(The Lord does not punish the righteous with the wicked; he discerns the pure in heart, and separates them from the unholy. Are we among those whose garments are unspotted?)*

5 He that overcometh, the same shall be clothed in white raiment; and I will not blot out his name out of the book of life, but I will confess his name before my Father, and before his angels. *(This is a choice reward. We are to be clothed like our Lord and to be owned by him. Who will not fight on till he conquers when such a prize is set before him?)*

6 He that hath an ear, let him hear what the Spirit saith unto the churches. *(We are not to hear what the churches say to us, but what the Spirit saith unto the churches. Be not satisfied with echoes, hear the grand original.)*

764   " As many as I love, I rebuke and chasten."   December 27.—Morning.

[Or December 21.]

REVELATION III. 7—22.

AND to the angel of the church in Philadelphia write; These things saith he that is holy, he that is true, he that hath the key of David, he that openeth, and no man shutteth; and shutteth, and no man openeth; I know thy works: behold, I have set before thee an open door, and no man can shut it: for thou hast a little strength, and hast kept my word, and hast not denied my name.

Sometimes the weakest may be the best. We shall not be called to account for the strength which we do not possess, but the Lord will commend us if we are faithful in that which is least.

9 Behold, I will make them of the synagogue of Satan, which say they are Jews, and are not, but do lie; behold, I will make them to come and worship before thy feet, and to know that I have loved thee. *(Those whom God loves, their bitterest foes shall be compelled to honour.)*

10 Because thou hast kept the word of my patience, I also will keep thee from the hour of temptation, which shall come upon all the world, to try them that dwell upon the earth.

11 Behold, I come quickly: hold that fast which thou hast, that no man take thy crown.

You have the crown of being found faithful, never lose it.

12 Him that overcometh will I make a pillar in the temple of my God, and he shall go no more out: and I will write upon him the name of my God, and the name of the city of my God, *which is* new Jerusalem, which cometh down out of heaven from my God: and *I will write upon him* my new name. *(The faithful will hold forth to wondering ages the records of divine love, even as pillars bear inscriptions. Happy souls to be thus devoted for ever to their Lord's glory.)*

13 He that hath an ear, let him hear what the Spirit saith unto the churches.

14—16 And unto the angel of the church of the Laodiceans write; These things saith the Amen, the faithful and true witness, the beginning of the creation of God; I know thy works, that thou art neither cold nor hot: I would thou wert cold or hot. So then because thou art lukewarm, and neither cold nor hot, I will spue thee out of my mouth. *(Lukewarmness is nauseous to the Lord. The bad may be*

reclaimed, but those who are neither one thing nor the other are in a hopeless condition, for they are too full of conceit to be led to repentance.)

17—19 Because thou sayest, I am rich, and increased with goods, and have need of nothing; and knowest not that thou art wretched, and miserable, and poor, and blind, and naked: I counsel thee to buy of me gold tried in the fire, that thou mayest be rich; and white raiment that thou mayest be clothed, and *that* the shame of thy nakedness do not appear; and anoint thine eyes with eyesalve, that thou mayest see. As many as I love, I rebuke and chasten: be zealous therefore, and repent.

When counsel is not sufficient, the Lord uses sharper means with his chosen, for he will not let them slumber on in indifference.

20 Behold, I stand at the door, and knock: if any man hear my voice, and open the door, I will come in to him, and will sup with him, and he with me. *(Jesus seeks fellowship with the church as the best means of restoring her. Communion with Jesus makes the heart burn with love, and effectually chases away the lukewarm spirit.)*

21, 22 To him that overcometh will I grant to sit with me in my throne, even as I also overcame, and am set down with my Father in his throne. He that hath an ear, let him hear what the Spirit saith unto the churches.

If we are growing chill, let us listen to this solemn rebuke. It will be terrible for us if we ever come to be loathed by our Lord on account of lukewarmness. This sin is common all around us, and we are very liable to it; let us pray for more grace, and, above all, let us open wide our hearts for Jesus to come in. One spiritual feast with him will be of more service to us than all the groaning and moaning in the world. Come, Lord Jesus, and sup with us even now!

When wilt thou come unto me, Lord?
Oh, come, my Lord most dear!
Come near, come nearer, nearer still;
I'm blest when thou art near.

Come spread thy savour on my frame,
No sweetness is so sweet;
Till I get up to sing thy name,
Where all thy singers meet.

REVELATION IV.

AFTER this I looked, and, behold,' a door was opened in heaven : and the first voice which I heard *was* as it were of a trumpet talking with me ; which said, Come up hither, and I will shew thee things which must be hereafter.

2, 3 And immediately I was in the spirit : and, behold, a throne was set in heaven, and *one* sat on the throne. And he that sat was to look upon like a jasper *(of a rich and brilliant colour)* and a sardine stone *(of blood red hue)*: and *there* was a rainbow round about the throne, in sight like unto an emerald. *(Lest the brightness indicated by the jasper, and the fiery justice symbolised by the sardine stone, should repel the gaze of faith, the throne is surrounded by the covenant rainbow, in which the predominating colour is the gentle green, the ensign of mercy.)*

4 And round about the throne *were* four and twenty seats : and upon the seats I saw four and twenty elders sitting, clothed in white raiment; and they had on their heads crowns of gold. *(These represent the church glorified in heaven. Royal ones, for they are crowned ; priestly ones, and therefore clothed in white. "He hath made us unto our God kings and priests.")*

5 And out of the throne proceeded lightnings and thunderings and voices : and *there were* seven lamps of fire burning before the throne, which are the seven Spirits of God.

6 And before the throne *there was* a sea of glass like unto crystal : and in the midst of the throne, and round about the throne *were* four beasts *(or rather* living creatures*)* full of eyes before and behind. *(Probably representing some noble order of creatures which are very near to God, and serve him with great watchfulness and ardour. Perhaps above all angels, cherubim and seraphim, these four orders of beings rise into greater nearness to God.)*

7 And the first living creature *was* like a lion, and the second living creature like a calf, and the third living creature had a face as a man, and the fourth living creature *was* like a flying eagle.

8 And the four living creatures had each of them six wings about *him ;* and *they were* full of eyes within : and they rest not day and night, saying, Holy, holy, holy, Lord God Almighty, which was, and is, and is to come.

9—11 And when those living creatures give glory and honour and thanks to him that sat on the throne, who liveth for ever and ever, The four and twenty elders fall down before him that sat on the throne, and worship him that liveth for ever and ever, and cast their crowns before the throne, saying, Thou art worthy, O Lord, to receive glory and honour and power : for thou hast created all things, and for thy pleasure they are and were created.

Adoration is the employment of heaven, and none can be desired more honourable or delightful. How happy shall we be when we too shall stand and bow before the throne in concert with that mighty host.

REVELATION V.

AND I saw in the right hand of him that sat on the throne a book written within and on the backside, sealed with seven seals.

The roll was full and written on both sides. The divine purposes are here intended.

2 And I saw a strong angel proclaiming with a loud voice, Who is worthy to open the book, and to loose the seals thereof ?

3, 4 And no man in heaven, nor in earth, neither under the earth, was able to open the book, neither to look thereon. And I wept much, because no man was found worthy to open and to read the book, neither to look thereon.

5 And one of the elders saith unto me, Weep not : behold, the Lion of the tribe of Juda, the Root of David, hath prevailed to open the book, and to loose the seven seals thereof.

6 And I beheld, and, lo, in the midst of the throne and of the four living creatures, and in the midst of the elders, stood a Lamb as it had been slain, having seven horns and seven eyes, which are the seven Spirits of God sent forth into all the earth. *(He possesses fulness of power, fulness of wisdom, and fulness of the Holy Spirit.)*

7 And he came and took the book out of the right hand of him that sat upon the throne.

No man knows the Father save the Son ; the Son alone can reveal the decrees of Jehovah.

8—10 And when he had taken the book, the four living creatures and four *and* twenty elders fell down before the Lamb, having every one of them harps, and golden vials full of odours, which are the prayers of saints. And they sung a new song, saying, Thou art worthy to take the book, and to open the seals thereof : for thou wast slain, and hast redeemed us to God by thy blood out of every kindred, and tongue, and people, and nation ; And hast made us unto our God kings and priests : and we shall reign on the earth.

The Lamb is, therefore, God, or he would not thus be adored. Jesus, our Saviour, is assuredly " God over all, blessed for ever. Amen."

11, 12 And I beheld, and I heard the voice of many angels round about the throne and the living creatures and the elders : and the number of them was ten thousand times ten thousand, and thousands of thousands; Saying with a loud voice, Worthy is the Lamb that was slain to receive power, and riches, and wisdom, and strength, and honour, and glory, and blessing.

13 And every creature which is in heaven, and on the earth, and under the earth, and such as are in the sea, and all that are in them, heard I saying, Blessing, and honour, and glory, and

power, *be* unto him that sitteth upon the throne, and unto the Lamb for ever and ever.

14 And the four living creatures said, Amen. And the four *and* twenty elders fell down and worshipped him that liveth for ever and ever.

Do all things thus worship Jesus ? then let us adore him. Oh for warm hearts with which to extol his precious name. All hail, Lord Jesus ! our very souls worship thee with lowliest and most loving reverence.

Who shall the Father's record search,
    And hidden things reveal ?
Behold, the Son that record takes,
    And opens every seal !

Hark how th' adoring hosts above
    With songs surround the throne !
Ten thousand thousand are their tongues ;
    But all their joys are one.

"Worthy the Lamb that died," they cry,
    "To be exalted thus ;"
"Worthy the Lamb," our lips reply,
    "For he was slain for us."

Now to the Lamb, that once was slain,
    Be endless blessings paid ;
Salvation, glory, joy remain
    For ever on thy head.

Thou hast redeem'd our souls with blood,
    Hast set the prisoners free;
Hast made us kings and priests to God,
    And we shall reign with thee.

Thou art the First, and thou the Last;
    Time centres all in thee,
The Almighty God, who was, and is,
    And evermore shall be.

Praise ye the Lord, exalt his name,
While in his holy courts ye wait,
Ye saints that to his house belong,
Or stand attending at his gate.

Praise ye the Lord ; the Lord is good,
To praise his name is sweet employ;
Israel he chose of old, and still
His church is his peculiar joy.

The Lord himself will judge his saints ;
He treats his servants as his friends ;
And when he hears their sore complaints,
Repents the sorrow that he sends.

Thou hast promised by the prophets,
    Glorious light in latter days ;
Come and bless bewilder'd nations,
    Change our prayers and tears to praise:
        Promised Spirit,
    Round the world diffuse thy rays.

All our hopes, and prayers, and labours,
    Must be vain without thine aid :
But thou wilt not disappoint us;
    All is true that thou hast said :
        Gracious Spirit,
    O'er the world thine influence spread.

In Gabriel's hand a mighty stone
Lies, a fair type of Babylon :
" Prophets, rejoice, and all ye saints,
God shall avenge your long complaints."

He said, and dreadful as he stood,
He sank the millstone in the flood :
" Thus terribly shall Babel fall,
Thus and no more be found at all."

REVELATION VII.

AND after these things I saw four angels standing on the four corners of the earth, holding the four winds of the earth, that the wind should not blow on the earth, nor on the sea, nor on any tree. And I saw another angel ascending from the east, having the seal of the living God : and he cried with a loud voice to the four angels, to whom it was given to hurt the earth and the sea, Saying, Hurt not the earth, neither the sea, nor the trees, till we have sealed the servants of our God in their foreheads. *(No leaf shall stir, nor ripple rise, until the redeemed are sealed and saved. The agencies of destruction shall lie down like lions in their dens till the elect are secure, and then they will leap forth to destroy the ungodly.)*

4 And I heard the number of them which were sealed : *and there were* sealed an hundred *and* forty *and* four thousand of all the tribes of the children of Israel. *(The Lord knows his own, their number is not left to chance. Jesus will see of the travail of his soul. The number mentioned represents the Jewish church, and is used to express greatness, definiteness, and completeness.)*

5—8 Of the tribe of Juda *were* sealed twelve thousand. Of the tribe of Reuben *were* sealed twelve thousand. Of the tribe of Gad *were* sealed twelve thousand. Of the tribe of Aser *were* sealed twelve thousand. Of the tribe of Nepthalim *were* sealed twelve thousand. Of the tribe of Manasses *were* sealed twelve thousand. Of the tribe of Simeon *were* sealed twelve thousand. Of the tribe of Levi *were* sealed twelve thousand. Of the tribe of Issachar *were* sealed twelve thousand. Of the tribe of Zabulon *were* sealed twelve thousand. Of the tribe of Joseph *were* sealed twelve thousand. Of the tribe of Benjamin *were* sealed twelve thousand. *(Last, but not least, for the smallest tribe is as favoured as royal Judah, or fruitful Manasseh.)*

9, 10 After this I beheld, and, lo, a great multitude, which no man could number, of all nations, and kindreds, and people, and tongues, stood before the throne, and before the Lamb, clothed with white robes, and palms in their hands ; And cried with a loud voice, saying, Salvation to our God which sitteth upon the throne, and unto the Lamb. *(The Lord has a chosen people among Gentiles as well as Jews, and these waving the palm of victory and wearing the robe of purity shall chant the song of sovereign grace.)*

11, 12 And all the angels stood round about the throne, and *about* the elders and the four living creatures, and fell before the throne on their faces, and worshipped God, Saying, Amen : Blessing, and glory, and wisdom, and thanksgiving, and honour, and power, and might, *be* unto our God for ever and ever. Amen. *(They use seven words of honour, for they render perfect praise both to the Lord God and to the Lamb. There are in heaven no deniers of the Deity of the Lord Jesus.)*

13 And one of the elders answered, saying unto me, What are these which are arrayed in white robes ? and whence came they ?

14—17 And I said unto him, Sir, thou knowest. And he said to me, These are they which came out of great tribulation, and have washed their robes, and made them white in the blood of the Lamb. Therefore are they before the throne of God, and serve him day and night in his temple : and he that sitteth on the throne shall dwell among them. They shall hunger no more, neither thirst any more ; neither shall the sun light on them, nor any heat. For the Lamb which is in the midst of the throne shall feed them, and shall lead them unto living fountains of waters : and God shall wipe away all tears from their eyes. *(What poetry is here, and yet all is true ! It makes one weep for joy to read the passage; but what bliss it must actually be to enjoy such blessings ! Shall we all be among that favoured throng ? Are we quite sure ?)*

Hunger and thirst are felt no more,
    Nor suns with scorching ray ;
God is their sun, whose cheering beams
    Diffuse eternal day.

The Lamb which dwells amidst the throne
    Shall o'er them still preside ;
Feed them with nourishment divine,
    And all their footsteps guide.

'Mong pastures green he'll lead his flock,
    Where living streams appear ;
And God the Lord from every eye
    Shall wipe off ev'ry tear.

REVELATION XIV. 6—20.

A ND I saw another angel fly in the midst of heaven, having the everlasting gospel to preach unto them that dwell on the earth, and to every nation, and kindred, and tongue, and people, Saying with a loud voice, Fear God, and give glory to him ; for the hour of his judgment is come : and worship him that made heaven, and earth, and the sea, and the fountains of waters. *(The gospel shall yet be preached in every part of the world. The day will come when the Holy Spirit will arouse the missionary spirit, and many shall go forth to preach the word. Would to God that the time were already come. Cannot we each do something to hasten it ?)*

8 And there followed another angel, saying, Babylon is fallen, is fallen, that great city, because she made all nations drink of the wine of the wrath of her fornication. *(The Babylon of Popery will soon fall when the gospel is everywhere proclaimed. She has a presentiment of this, and therefore endeavours to keep her victims from knowing the way of salvation.)*

9—11 And the third angel followed them, saying with a loud voice, If any man worship the beast and his image, and receive *his* mark in his forehead, or in his hand, The same shall drink of the wine of the wrath of God, which is poured out without mixture into the cup of his indignation ; and he shall be tormented with fire and brimstone in the presence of the holy angels, and in the presence of the Lamb : And the smoke of their torment ascendeth up for ever and ever : and they have no rest day nor night, who worship the beast and his image, and whosoever receiveth the mark of his name. *It will be a dreadful thing to be in any way identified with Popery. The warning here given is most terrible. Let us flee from every form of Popery, as Lot fled out of Sodom.*

12 Here is the patience of the saints : here *are* they that keep the commandments of God, and the faith of Jesus. *(Myriads were martyred by the Church of Rome, but their blood shall be avenged.)*

13 And I heard a voice from heaven saying unto me, Write, Blessed *are* the dead which die in the Lord from henceforth : Yea, saith the Spirit, that they may rest from their labours ; and their works do follow them.

Their persecutors cursed them, but the Lord writes them down as blessed, and their works shall live on to bless future ages. "To die for *the Lord, as well as* in *the Lord, is," says Latimer, " the greatest promotion in the world."*

14 And I looked, and behold a white cloud, and upon the cloud *one* sat like unto the Son of man, having on his head a golden crown, and in his hand a sharp sickle.

15, 16 And another angel came out of the temple, crying with a loud voice to him that sat on the cloud, Thrust in thy sickle, and reap : for the time is come for thee to reap ; for the harvest of the earth is ripe. And he that sat on the cloud thrust in his sickle on the earth ; and the earth was reaped. *(Jesus will trust no angel to gather in his wheat, he brings his people into his garner in person.)*

17, 18 And another angel came out of the temple which is in heaven, he also having a sharp sickle. And another angel came out from the altar, which had power over fire ; and cried with a loud cry to him that had the sharp sickle, saying, Thrust in thy sharp sickle, and gather the clusters of the vine of the earth ; for her grapes are fully ripe. *(Here is the judgment of the ungodly. The gathering of them is left to an angel, who cuts them off roughly when they are ripe for vengeance.)*

19, 20 And the angel thrust in his sickle into the earth, and gathered the vine of the earth, and cast *it* into the great winepress of the wrath of God. And the winepress was trodden without the city, and blood came out of the winepress, even unto the horse bridles, by the space of a thousand *and* six hundred furlongs.

By this terrible image the total crushing of the wicked is set forth, with special reference to the persecuting church of Rome. Foxe tells us that the Papists boasted that they would ride up to their saddle-girths in the blood of the Lutherans. How terribly will the Lord punish cruelty !

The Lord shall come ! but not the same
As once in lowliness he came ;
A silent lamb before his foes,
A weary man, and full of woes.

The Lord shall come ! a dreadful form,
With rainbow wreath and robes of storm ;
On cherub wings, and wings of wind,
Appointed Judge of all mankind.

AMONG *other visions, John was favoured to see the destruction of the evil system of Antichrist, which was foreshadowed before him under the image of a base and guilty woman. This mother of harlots we believe to be the Church of Rome. Certainly there is nothing upon earth so like to the description, and it is difficult to conceive that any future system could more fully answer to the prophecy.*

REVELATION XVII. 3—18.

3 So he carried me away in the spirit into the wilderness : *(Rome stands literally as well as spiritually in a wilderness.)* and I saw a woman sit upon a scarlet coloured beast, full of names of blasphemy, having seven heads and ten horns. *(Names of blasphemy are abundant in that church whose head dares to call himself* Infallible.)

4 And the woman was arrayed in purple and scarlet colour, and decked with gold and precious stones and pearls, having a golden cup in her hand full of abominations and filthiness of her fornication : *(Dr. Wordsworth remarks that in the description of the Pope's official dress mention is made of scarlet robes, a vest covered with pearls, and a mitre adorned with gold and precious stones.)*

5 And upon her forehead *was* a name written, MYSTERY, BABYLON THE GREAT, THE MOTHER OF HARLOTS AND ABOMINATIONS OF THE EARTH. *These words are like a photograph of the Papacy, no portrait could be more accurate.*

6 And I saw the woman drunken with the blood of the saints, and with the blood of the martyrs of Jesus : and when I saw her, I wondered with great admiration.

7 And the angel said unto me, Wherefore didst thou marvel ? I will tell thee the mystery of the woman, and of the beast that carrieth her, which hath the seven heads and ten horns.

8 The beast that thou sawest was, and is not ; and shall ascend out of the bottomless pit, and go into perdition : *(This beast is thought to be the old imperial power of Rome upon which the spiritual power rode as on a richly caparisoned steed.)* and they that dwell on the earth shall wonder, whose names were not written in the book of life from the foundation of the

world, when they behold the beast that was, and is not, and yet is. *(God's own chosen cannot be deluded by her, but myriads of others are.)*

9 And here *is* the mind which hath wisdom. The seven heads are seven mountains, on which the woman sitteth. *(Every schoolboy knows that Rome is built upon seven hills.)*

10 And there are seven kings : five are fallen, and one is, *and* the other is not yet come ; and when he cometh, he must continue a short space.

11 And the beast that was, and is not, even he is the eighth, and is of the seven, and goeth into perdition. *(Of this many interpretations have been given, but none seems to us to be clear.)*

12, 13 And the ten horns which thou sawest are ten kings, which have received no kingdom as yet ; but receive power as kings one hour with the beast. These have one mind, and shall give their power and strength unto the beast. *Probably these are the kingdoms which arose at the breaking up of the old Roman empire, and all became vassals of the Papal power.*

14 These shall make war with the Lamb, and the Lamb shall overcome them : for he is Lord of lords, and King of kings : and they that are with him *are* called, and chosen, and faithful.

15—17 And he saith unto me, The waters which thou sawest, where the whore sitteth, are peoples, and multitudes, and nations, and tongues. And the ten horns which thou sawest upon the beast, these shall hate her, and shall make her desolate and naked, and shall eat her flesh, and burn her with fire. For God hath put in their hearts to fulfil his will, and to agree, and give their kingdom unto the beast, until the words of God shall be fulfilled. *The Papacy will perish by the hands of the kings who once supported it. Already its temporal power is shorn away, and in almost every nation the rulers are resolved to curb its insolence.*

18 And the woman which thou sawest is that great city, which reigneth over the kings of the earth. *(This must be Rome, for no other city has exercised such imperial authority, and made the kings of the earth her vassals. May the fall of Romanism be speedy and overwhelming.)*

REVELATION XVIII. 4, 5; 8—13; 15—21; 24.

AND I heard another voice from heaven, saying, Come out of her, my people, that ye be not partakers of her sins, and that ye receive not of her plagues. *(Renounce the symbols of Rome, abhor her doctrines, and avoid her spirit. Come out, completely out.)*

5 For her sins have reached unto heaven, and God hath remembered her iniquities.

8 Therefore shall her plagues come in one day, death, and mourning, and famine; and she shall be utterly burned with fire: for strong *is* the Lord God who judgeth her.

Suddenness is a usual attendant of severity. Rome will be spared till her huge measure of sin is full, but not a moment longer. That period cannot be far distant, for it is barely within the power of imagination to conceive a more wicked system than popery, and especially popery intensified by the Jesuits. If a criminal so grossly guilty as the Church of Rome be not signally punished, where is the justice of God? Her end will astound all mankind.

9, 10 And the kings of the earth, who have committed fornication and lived deliciously with her, shall bewail her, and lament for her, when they shall see the smoke of her burning, Standing afar off for the fear of her torment, saying, Alas, alas that great city Babylon, that mighty city! for in one hour is thy judgment come.

The destruction of such an imperial system will astonish kings, but they will be both unable and unwilling to interfere.

11—13 And the merchants of the earth shall weep and mourn over her; for no man buyeth their merchandise any more: The merchandise of gold, and silver, and precious stones, and of pearls, and fine linen, and purple, and silk, and scarlet, and all thyine wood, and all manner vessels of ivory, and all manner vessels of most precious wood, and of brass, and iron, and marble, And cinnamon, and odours, and ointments, and frankincense, and wine, and oil, and fine flour, and wheat, and beasts, and sheep, and horses, and chariots, and slaves, and souls of men. *(Go into any of the rich Popish churches and see whether this is not an exact catalogue of what is to be seen there. It reads like an appraiser's list. When all these things cease to be*

used *in Popish worship it will make a great difference to trade, and hence this bitter lamentation of the merchants.)*

15—18 The merchants of these things, which were made rich by her, shall stand afar off for the fear of her torment, weeping and wailing, And saying, Alas, alas that great city, that was clothed in fine linen, and purple, and scarlet, and decked with gold, and precious stones, and pearls! For in one hour so great riches is come to nought. And every shipmaster, and all the company in ships, and sailors, and as many as trade by sea, stood afar off, And cried when they saw the smoke of her burning, saying, What *city is* like unto this great city!

In the middle ages foreign trade was greatly quickened by the luxury of the Popish Church, hence the wailing of mariners at her fall.

19 And they cast dust on their heads, and cried, weeping and wailing, saying, Alas, alas that great city, wherein were made rich all that had ships in the sea by reason of her costliness! for in one hour is she made desolate.

20 Rejoice over her, *thou* heaven, and *ye* holy apostles and prophets; for God hath avenged you on her. *(Merchants and shipmasters mourn, but saints and angels sing. O Lord, how long shall it be ere this desired end shall come?)*

21 And a mighty angel took up a stone like a great millstone, and cast *it* into the sea, saying, Thus with violence shall that great city Babylon be thrown down, and shall be found no more at all.

24 And in her was found the blood of prophets, and of saints, and of all that were slain upon the earth. *(This is her monster sin. The Romish Church is essentially persecuting. In every land she has been eager for the blood of the faithful people of God, and it is her boast that she never changes. Her doom is sealed, and glory be to God for it. The sooner such a system, with all its belongings, is swept from off the face of the earth, the better.)*

Come, in thy glorious might,
Come with thine iron rod,
Scattering thy foes before thy face,
Most Mighty Son of God.

Come and make error flee,
And Popish idols fall;
Let Rome's dominion cease to be,
And God be all in all.

REVELATION XIX.

AND after these things I heard a great voice of much people in heaven, saying, Alleluia; Salvation, and glory, and honour, and power, unto the Lord our God:

2 For true and righteous *are* his judgments: for he hath judged the great whore, which did corrupt the earth with her fornication, and hath avenged the blood of his servants at her hand.

3 And again they said, Alleluia. And her smoke rose up for ever and ever.

4 And the four and twenty elders and the four living creatures fell down and worshipped God that sat on the throne, saying, Amen; Alleluia. *(The utter overthrow of Popery will fill even heaven itself with superior gladness and bring new glory to God. Let us daily pray for it.)*

5—7 And a voice came out of the throne, saying, Praise our God, all ye his servants, and ye that fear him, both small and great. And I heard as it were the voice of a great multitude, and as the voice of many waters, and as the voice of mighty thunderings, saying, Alleluia: for the Lord God omnipotent reigneth. Let us be glad and rejoice, and give honour to him: for the marriage of the Lamb is come, and his wife hath made herself ready. *(When the false church is put away, the true church is revealed, and her time of glory comes.)*

8 And to her was granted that she should be arrayed in fine linen, clean and white: for the fine linen is the righteousness of saints.

9 And he saith unto me, Write, Blessed *are* they which are called unto the marriage supper of the Lamb. And he saith unto me, These are the true sayings of God.

10 And I fell at his feet to worship him. And he said unto me, See *thou do it* not: I am thy fellowservant, and of thy brethren that have the testimony of Jesus: worship God: for the testimony of Jesus is the spirit of prophecy.

11 And I saw heaven opened, and behold a white horse; and he that sat upon him *was* called Faithful and True, and in righteousness he doth judge and make war. *(After the revealing of the church comes the universal triumph of her king and his hosts.)*

12—14 His eyes *were* as a flame of fire, and on his head *were* many crowns; and he had a name written, that no man knew, but he himself. And he *was* clothed with a vesture dipped in blood: and his name is called The Word of God. And the armies *which were* in heaven followed him upon white horses, clothed in fine linen, white and clean.

15, 16 And out of his mouth goeth a sharp sword, that with it he should smite the nations: and he shall rule them with a rod of iron: and he treadeth the winepress of the fierceness and wrath of Almighty God. And he hath on *his* vesture and on his thigh a name written, KING OF KINGS, AND LORD OF LORDS.

17, 18 And I saw an angel standing in the sun; and he cried with a loud voice, saying to all the fowls that fly in the midst of heaven, Come and gather yourselves together unto the supper of the great God; That ye may eat the flesh of kings, and the flesh of captains, and the flesh of mighty men, and the flesh of horses, and of them that sit on them, and the flesh of all *men, both* free and bond, both small and great. *The birds of prey were summoned to devour the slain, for those who fight against Jesus will assuredly perish.*

19, 20 And I saw the beast, and the kings of the earth, and their armies, gathered together to make war against him that sat on the horse, and against his army. And the beast was taken, and with him the false prophet that wrought miracles before him, with which he deceived them that had received the mark of the beast, and them that worshipped his image. These both were cast alive into a lake of fire burning with brimstone.

21 And the remnant were slain with the sword of him that sat upon the horse, which *sword* proceeded out of his mouth: and all the fowls were filled with their flesh. *(However numerous or powerful the foes of Jesus, they must fall. Therefore let us be of good courage, and press forward in his name.)*

To thy great name, Almighty Lord,
We sacred honours pay,
And loud hosannahs shall proclaim,
The triumphs of the day.

Salvation and immortal praise
To our victorious King!
Let heav'n and earth, and rocks and seas,
With glad hosannahs ring.

REVELATION XX.

AND I saw an angel come down from heaven, having the key of the bottomless pit and a great chain in his hand. And he laid hold on the dragon, that old serpent, which is the Devil, and Satan, and bound him a thousand years, And cast him into the bottomless pit, and shut him up, and set a seal upon him, that he should deceive the nations no more, till the thousand years should be fulfilled : and after that he must be loosed a little season. *Does not this foretell that there shall come an age in which the agency of Satan in the world shall be suspended by divine power ? This will go far to make that period of a thousand years, which is commonly called the millennium, a time of peace and holiness. Glory be to God, the Prince of Darkness is under the power of the Prince of Light. He shall not always triumph.*

4 And I saw thrones, and they sat upon them, and judgment was given unto them : and *I saw* the souls of them that were beheaded for the witness of Jesus, and for the word of God, and which had not worshipped the beast, neither his image, neither had received *his* mark upon their foreheads, or in their hands ; and they lived and reigned with Christ a thousand years.

5, 6 But the rest of the dead lived not again until the thousand years were finished. This *is* the first resurrection. Blessed and holy *is* he that hath part in the first resurrection : on such the second death hath no power, but they shall be priests of God and of Christ, and shall reign with him a thousand years. *(Surely this is a literal resurrection, and it is clear that the blessed dead will rise before the wicked. Let us strive to attain unto this resurrection.)*

7 And when the thousand years are expired, Satan shall be loosed out of his prison,

8 And shall go out to deceive the nations which are in the four quarters of the earth, Gog and Magog, to gather them together to battle : the number of whom *is* as the sand of the sea.

9, 10 And they went up on the breadth of the earth, and compassed the camp of the saints about, and the beloved city : and fire came down from God out of heaven, and devoured them. And the devil that deceived them was cast into the lake of fire and brimstone, where the beast and the false prophet *are*, and shall be tormented day and night for ever and ever.

Satan will come out of his prison unchanged; hell is not a reformatory; but his determined pride will not avail him, he must feel the terror of divine wrath. Vain will be the last furious struggle of the hosts of evil.

11, 12 And I saw a great white throne, and him that sat on it, from whose face the earth and the heaven fled away ; and there was found no place for them. And I saw the dead, small and great, stand before God; and the books were opened : and another book was opened, which is *the book* of life : and the dead were judged out of those things which were written in the books, according to their works.

13 And the sea gave up the dead which were in it; and death and hell delivered up the dead which were in them : and they were judged every man according to their works. *(Good works will be cited as evidences of grace, and evil works as tokens of unbelief. This makes our daily conduct a solemn thing. How shall we bear to be thus weighed in the balances ?)*

14 And death and hell were cast into the lake of fire. This is the second death.

15 And whosoever was not found written in the book of life was cast into the lake of fire.

When, shrivelling like a parched scroll,
The flaming heavens together roll,
When louder yet and yet more dread
Sounds the high trump that wakes the dead ;

Oh, on that day, that wrathful day,
When man to judgment wakes from clay,
Be thou, O Christ, the sinner's stay,
Though earth and heaven shall pass away.

Lo ! what a glorious sight appears
To our admiring eyes !
The former seas have pass'd away,
The former earth and skies.

From heav'n the New Jerus'lem comes,
All worthy of its Lord ;
See all things now at length renew'd,
And paradise restor'd !

Attending angels shout for joy,
And the bright armies sing ;
Mortals ! behold the sacred seat
Of your descending King !

REVELATION XXI. 1—12; 14—16; 18—23; 25—27.

AND I saw a new heaven and a new earth : for the first heaven and the first earth were passed away ; and there was no more sea.

2 And I John saw the holy city, new Jerusalem, coming down from God out of heaven, prepared as a bride adorned for her husband. *(After the general judgment comes the full glory of the church, which is here represented as a heavenly city, or a bride in her marriage dress.)*

3, 4 And I heard a great voice out of heaven saying, Behold, the tabernacle of God *is* with men, and he will dwell with them, and they shall be his people, and God himself shall be with them, *and be* their God. And God shall wipe away all tears from their eyes ; and there shall be no more death, neither sorrow, nor crying, neither shall there be any more pain : for the former things are passed away.

5, 6 And he that sat upon the throne said, Behold, I make all things new. And he said unto me, Write : for these words are true and faithful. And he said unto me, It is done. I am Alpha and Omega, the beginning and the end. I will give unto him that is athirst of the fountain of the water of life freely.

7 He that overcometh shall inherit all things ; and I will be his God, and he shall be my son.

8 But the fearful *(or cowardly)*, and unbelieving, and the abominable, and murderers, and whoremongers, and sorcerers, and idolaters, and all liars, shall have their part in the lake which burneth with fire and brimstone : which is the second death.

9—11 And there came unto me one of the seven angels which had the seven vials full of the seven last plagues, and talked with me, saying, Come hither, I will shew thee the bride, the Lamb's wife. And he carried me away in the spirit to a great and high mountain, and shewed me that great city, the holy Jerusalem, descending out of heaven from God, Having the glory of God : and her light *was* like unto a stone most precious, even like a jasper stone, clear as crystal ; *(The city shone in dazzling light a vision of brightness, such as never before was seen of mortal eye.)*

12 And had a wall great and high, *and* had twelve gates, and at the gates twelve angels, and names written thereon, which are *the names* of the twelve tribes of the children of Israel.

14 And the wall of the city had twelve foundations, and in them the names of the twelve apostles of the Lamb.

15, 16 And he that talked with me had a golden reed to measure the city, and the gates thereof, and the wall thereof. And the city lieth foursquare, and the length is as large as the breadth : and he measured the city with the reed, twelve thousand furlongs. The length and the breadth and the height of it are equal.

The vision was inconceivably grand, the city seemed to stand on such an eminence, and its buildings reared their stately heads so high aloft, that it was as high as it was broad ; and yet its breadth was three hundred and seventy-five miles. This gives us a glimpse of inconceivable vastness and sublimity. The number of the redeemed must be immense to need such a dwelling-place.

18, 19 And the building of the wall of it was *of* jasper : and the city *was* pure gold, like unto clear glass. And the foundations of the wall of the city *were* garnished with all manner of precious stones.

21 And the twelve gates *were* twelve pearls ; every several gate was of one pearl : and the street of the city *was* pure gold, as it were transparent glass. *(The unutterable splendour and grandeur of the church triumphant blazes before us in these dazzling metaphors.)*

22, 23 And I saw no temple therein : for the Lord God Almighty and the Lamb are the temple of it. And the city had no need of the sun, neither of the moon, to shine in it : for the glory of God did lighten it, and the Lamb *is* the light thereof.

25 And the gates of it shall not be shut at all by day : for there shall be no night there.

26 And they shall bring the glory and honour of the nations into it.

27 And there shall in no wise enter into it any thing that defileth, neither *whatsoever* worketh abomination, or *maketh* a lie : but they which are written in the Lamb's book of life.

How repeatedly in this chapter is falsehood branded as a dreadful sin ! This should warn us to be truthful in all things, lest we be shut out of heaven.

REVELATION XXII.

AND he shewed me a pure river of water of life, clear as crystal, proceeding out of the throne of God and of the Lamb.

In the new Eden as in the old there is a river, but it does not take its rise from the springs of earth, its source is the throne of God.

2 In the midst of the street of it, and on either side of the river, *was there* the tree of life, which bare twelve *manner of* fruits, *and* yielded her fruit every month: and the leaves of the tree *were* for the healing of the nations.

Eden of old had but one such tree, but it is common in the new Jerusalem, and prevents the possibility of disease and death ever invading that happy city. Fallen man might not eat of its immortal fruit, but man restored shall feast upon it freely.

3—5 And there shall be no more curse: but the throne of God and of the Lamb shall be in it; and his servants shall serve him: And they shall see his face; and his name *shall be* in their foreheads. And there shall be no night there; and they need no candle, neither light of the sun; for the Lord God giveth them light: and they shall reign for ever and ever.

6 And he said unto me, These sayings *are* faithful and true: and the Lord God of the holy prophets sent his angel to shew unto his servants the things which must shortly be done.

7 Behold, I come quickly: blessed *is* he that keepeth the sayings of the prophecy of this book. *(How few are watching! How many trifle as if these things were mere dreams, or matters so remote as to deserve no consideration.)*

8—10 And I John saw these things, and heard *them.* And when I had heard and seen, I fell down to worship before the feet of the angel which shewed me these things. Then saith he unto me, See *thou do it* not: for I am thy fellowservant, and of thy brethren the prophets, and of them which keep the sayings of this book: worship God. And he saith unto me, Seal not the sayings of the prophecy of this book: for the time is at hand.

11 He that is unjust, let him be unjust still: and he which is filthy, let him be filthy still: and he that is righteous, let him be righteous still: and he that is holy, let him be holy still.

There is no hope of change of character in

another state. *Where death leaves us judgment finds us and eternity holds us.*

12 And, behold, I come quickly; and my reward *is* with me, to give every man according as his work shall be.

13 I am Alpha and Omega, the beginning and the end, the first and the last.

14, 15 Blessed *are* they that do his commandments, that they may have right *(or privilege to approach)* to the tree of life, and may enter in through the gates into the city. For without *are* dogs, and sorcerers, and whoremongers, and murderers, and idolaters, and whosoever loveth and maketh a lie.

16 I Jesus have sent mine angel to testify unto you these things in the churches. I am the root and the offspring of David, *and* the bright and morning star.

17 And the Spirit and the bride say, Come. And let him that heareth say, Come. And let him that is athirst come. And whosoever will, let him take the water of life freely.

18, 19 For I testify unto every man that heareth the words of the prophecy of this book, If any man shall add unto these things, God shall add unto him the plagues that are written in this book: And if any man shall take away from the words of the book of this prophecy, God shall take away his part out of the book of life, and out of the holy city, and *from* the things which are written in this book.

Omissions and additions are equally forbidden. Those who have committed this crime of tampering with the Bible, have generally professed to be Christians, hence their penalty is that their names shall be blotted out of that sacred register in which they believed them to be enrolled.

20 He which testifieth these things saith, Surely I come quickly. Amen. Even so, come, Lord Jesus.

21 The grace of our Lord Jesus Christ *be* with you all. Amen. *(As we close the year let us pray that our family reading may prove a blessing to us all. God grant that we may not read without profit, but may each one find Jesus in the Scriptures, as the merchant found the one pearl of great price hidden in the field.)*

PSALM CXIX. 129—136; 145—152; 169—176.

THY testimonies *are* wonderful: therefore doth my soul keep them. *(Tertullian said, "I adore the fulness of the Scriptures." This is well, but it is better still to stand in awe of their authority, and cheerfully yield obedience to their precepts.)*

130 The entrance of thy words giveth light; it giveth understanding unto the simple.

131 I opened my mouth, and panted: for I longed for thy commandments. *(When the word really enters the soul, it creates a strong desire for more holiness. Light outside may condemn, but light within works savingly upon the soul.)*

132 Look thou upon me, and be merciful unto me, as thou usest to do unto those that love thy name.

133 Order my steps in thy word: and let not any iniquity have dominion over me.

134 Deliver me from the oppression of man: so will I keep thy precepts. *(When others by their unkindness hinder us in the Lord's ways, our best course is to carry our case to the Lord, for he is the guardian of the oppressed.)*

135 Make thy face to shine upon thy servant; and teach me thy statutes.

136 Rivers of waters run down mine eyes, because they keep not thy law.

145 I cried with *my* whole heart; hear me, O Lord: I will keep thy statutes.

146 I cried unto thee; save me, and I shall keep thy testimonies.

147 I prevented the dawning of the morning, and cried: I hoped in thy word.

148, 149 Mine eyes prevent the *night* watches, that I might meditate in thy word. Hear my voice according unto thy lovingkindness: O Lord, quicken me according to thy judgment.

150, 151 They draw nigh that follow after mischief: they are far from thy law. Thou *art* near, O Lord; and all thy commandments *are* truth. *(When enemies are near, our Great Friend is near too, and therefore we do not fear.)*

152 Concerning thy testimonies, I have known of old that thou hast founded them for ever. *(Our faith does not waver, for the promises are immutable and eternal.)*

169—172 Let my cry come near before thee,

O Lord: give me understanding according to thy word. Let my supplication come before thee: deliver me according to thy word. My lips shall utter praise, when thou hast taught me thy statutes. My tongue shall speak of thy word: for all thy commandments *are* righteousness. *(Those who are well instructed by the Holy Spirit love prayer, praise, and holy conversation, all of which are mentioned here. Let us abound in all these.)*

173 Let thine hand help me; for I have chosen thy precepts.

174 I have longed for thy salvation, O Lord; and thy law *is* my delight.

175 Let my soul live, and it shall praise thee; and let thy judgments help me.

176 I have gone astray like a lost sheep; seek thy servant; for I do not forget thy commandments. *(In this humble, prayerful manner this long Psalm closes, and so will the believer's life-story end. Confession mourns a thousand faults, faith sees grace still alive within the soul, and prayer pleads for divine mercy. With such a prayer our earthly life will come to a fitting FINIS.)*

Father, I bless thy gentle hand;
How kind was thy chastising rod,
That forc'd my conscience to a stand,
And brought my wand'ring soul to God.

Foolish and vain, I went astray
Ere I had felt thy scourges, Lord;
I left my guide, and lost my way,
But now I love and keep thy word.

Jerusalem, my happy home,
　When shall I come to thee?
When shall my sorrows have an end?
　Thy joys when shall I see?

Thy walls are made of precious stones,
　Thy bulwarks diamond square;
Thy gates are of right orient pearl,
　Exceeding rich and rare.

Thy turrets and thy pinnacles
　With carbuncles do shine;
Thy very streets are paved with gold,
　Surpassing clear and fine.

FOR THE DAY OF A DEATH OR FUNERAL.

Job. i. 21.

THE LORD gave, and the LORD hath taken away; blessed be the name

I. Sam. ii. 6.
of the LORD. The LORD killeth, and maketh alive: he bringeth down to the

Ps. xxxix. 9.
grave, and bringeth up. I was dumb, I opened not my mouth; because thou

I. Sam. iii. 18.
didst *it*. It *is* the LORD: let him do what seemeth him good.

II. Cor. i. 3, 4.
Blessed *be* God, even the Father of our Lord Jesus Christ, the Father of mercies, and the God of all comfort; Who comforteth us in all our tribulation, that we may be able to comfort them which are in any trouble, by the comfort wherewith we ourselves are comforted of

Heb. xii. 6, 7, 10, 11.
God. For whom the Lord loveth he chasteneth, and scourgeth every son whom he receiveth. If ye endure chastening, God dealeth with you as with sons; for what son is he whom the father chasteneth not? For they verily for a few days chastened *us* after their own pleasure: but he for *our* profit, that *we* might be partakers of his holiness. Now no chastening for the present seemeth to be joyous, but grievous: nevertheless afterward it yieldeth the peaceable fruit of righteousness unto them which are exercised thereby.

Rom. viii. 28.
And we know that all things work together for good to them that love God, to them who are the called according to *his* purpose. For which

II. Cor. iv. 16, 17.
cause we faint not; but though our outward man perish, yet the inward *man* is renewed day by day. For our light affliction, which is but for a moment, worketh for us a far more exceeding *and* eternal weight of glory.

Lam. ii. 31—33.
The Lord will not cast off for ever: but though he cause grief, yet will he have compassion according to the multitude of his mercies. For he doth not afflict willingly, nor grieve the children

Isaiah lxiii. 9.
of men. In all their affliction he was afflicted, and the angel of his presence saved them: in his love and in his pity he redeemed them; and he bare them, and carried them all the days of old.

Psalm xxx. 5.
His anger *endureth but* a moment; in his favour *is* life: weeping may endure for a night, but joy *cometh* in the morning.

I. Thess. iv. 13, 14.
But I would not have you to be ignorant, brethren, concerning them which are asleep, that ye sorrow not, even as others which have no hope. For if we believe that Jesus died and rose again, even so them also which sleep in Jesus will God bring with him.

I. Cor. ii. 9.
But as it is written, Eye hath not seen, nor ear heard, neither have entered into the heart of man, the things which God hath prepared for them that love him.

I. Cor. xv. 55—57.
O death, where *is* thy sting? O grave, where *is* thy victory? The sting of death *is* sin; and the strength of sin *is* the law. But thanks *be* to God, which giveth us the victory through our Lord Jesus Christ.

Psalm. xc. 12—17.
So teach *us* to number our days, that we may apply *our* hearts unto wisdom. Return, O LORD, how long? and let it repent thee concerning thy servants. O satisfy us early with thy mercy; that we may rejoice and be glad all our days. Make us glad according to the days *wherein* thou hast afflicted us, *and* the years *wherein* we have seen evil. Let thy work appear unto thy servants, and thy glory unto their children. And let the beauty of the LORD our God be upon us: and establish thou the work of our hands upon us; yea, the work of our hands establish thou it.

Why do we mourn departing friends,
  Or shake at death's alarms?
'Tis but the voice that Jesus sends
  To call them to his arms.

Why should we tremble to convey
  Their bodies to the tomb?
There the dear flesh of Jesus lay,
  And left a long perfume.

The graves of all his saints he bless'd,
  And soften'd every bed:
Where should the dying members rest,
  But with the dying Head?

FOR A TIME OF TROUBLE.

Lam. iii.
22—26.

IT *is of* the LORD'S mercies that we are not consumed, because his compassions fail not. *They are* new every morning : great *is* thy faithfulness. The LORD *is* my portion, saith my soul ; therefore will I hope in him. The LORD *is* good unto them that wait for him, to the soul *that* seeketh him. *It is* good that *a man* should both hope and quietly wait for the salvation of the LORD.

Psalm
cxliii. 11.

Quicken me, O LORD, for thy name's sake : for thy righteousness' sake bring my soul out of trouble.

Isaiah
xxxiii. 2.

O LORD, be gracious unto us ; we have waited for thee : be thou their arm every morning, our salvation also in the time of trouble.

Isaiah
xli. 10.

Fear thou not; for I *am* with thee : be not dismayed ; for I *am* thy God : I will strengthen thee ; yea, I will help thee ; yea, I will uphold thee with the right hand of my righteousness.

Isaiah
xliii. 2.

When thou passest through the waters, I *will be* with thee ; and through the rivers, they shall not overflow thee : when thou walkest through the fire thou shalt not be burned ; neither shall the flame kindle upon thee.

Isaiah
liv. 7—10.

For a small moment have I forsaken thee ; but with great mercies will I gather thee. In a little wrath I hid my face from thee for a moment ; but with ever-lasting kindness will I have mercy on thee, saith the LORD thy Redeemer. For this *is as* the waters of Noah unto me : for *as* I have sworn that the waters of Noah should no more go over the earth ; so have I sworn that I would not be wroth with thee, nor rebuke thee. For the mountains shall depart, and the hills be removed ; but my kindness shall not depart from thee, neither shall the covenant of my peace be removed, saith the LORD that hath mercy on thee.

I. Peter
iv. 12, 13.

Beloved, think it not strange concern-ing the fiery trial which is to try you, as though some strange thing happened unto you : But rejoice, inasmuch as ye are partakers of Christ's sufferings ; that, when his glory shall be revealed, ye may be glad also with exceeding joy.

Romans
viii. 18.

For I reckon that the sufferings of this present time *are* not worthy *to be compared* with the glory which shall be revealed in us.

II. Corinth.
xii. 9.

And he said unto me, My grace is sufficient for thee : for my strength is made perfect in weakness. Most gladly therefore will I rather glory in my infir-mities, that the power of Christ may rest upon me.

Hebrews
ii. 18.

For in that he himself hath suffered being tempted, he is able to succour them that are tempted.

John
xiv. 27.

(Our Lord Jesus has said) Peace I leave with you, my peace I give unto you : not as the world giveth, give I unto you. Let not your heart be trou-bled, neither let it be afraid. *(Therefore*

Romans
viii. 35—
39.

do we confidently say :) Who shall sepa-rate us from the love of Christ ? *shall* tribulation, or distress, or persecution, or famine, or nakedness, or peril, or sword ? As it is written, For thy sake we are killed all the day long ; we are accounted as sheep for the slaughter. Nay, in all these things we are more than conquerors through him that loved us. For I am persuaded, that neither death, nor life, nor angels, nor princi-palities, nor powers, nor things present, nor things to come, Nor height, nor depth, nor any other creature, shall be able to separate us from the love of God, which is in Christ Jesus our Lord.

Sons of God in tribulation,
Let your eyes the Saviour view,
He's the rock of our salvation,
He was tried and tempted too ;
All to succour
Every tempted, burden'd son.

'Tis, if need be, he reproves us,
Lest we settle on our lees ;
Yet, he in the furnace loves us,
'Tis expressed in words like these ;
" I am with thee,
Israel, passing through the fire."

FOR A WEDDING.

SOLOMON'S *picture of a virtuous woman represents what we trust the bride of to-day will prove to be. May her husband be happy in her, and worthy of her, and may the great Father of spirits bless them both.*

PROVERBS XXXI. 10—31.

10 Who can find a virtuous woman? for her price *is* far above rubies.

11 The heart of her husband doth safely trust in her, so that he shall have no need of spoil.

12 She will do him good and not evil all the days of her life. *(Luther used to say, "The greatest gift of God is a pious amiable spouse, who fears God, loves his house, and with whom one can live in perfect confidence.")*

13, 14 She seeketh wool, and flax, and worketh willingly with her hands. She is like the merchants' ships; she bringeth her food from afar. *(She is not a religious recluse, shut out from the world; the virtuous woman is a sensible common-sense being, not at all ashamed to earn her living.)*

15 She riseth also while it is yet night, and giveth meat to her household, and a portion to her maidens. *(She knows that those who would thrive must rise at five.)*

16—19 She considereth a field, and buyeth it: with the fruit of her hands she planteth a vineyard. She girdeth her loins with strength, and strengtheneth her arms. She perceiveth that her merchandise *is* good: her candle goeth not out by night. She layeth her hands to the spindle, and her hands hold the distaff. *She is not afraid of hard and homely work, and is not too great a lady to soil her fingers.*

20 She stretcheth out her hand to the poor; yea, she reacheth forth her hands to the needy. *Her industry enables her to be charitable.*

21, 22 She is not afraid of the snow for her household: for all her household *are* clothed with scarlet. She maketh herself coverings of tapestry; her clothing *is* silk and purple. *Her thrift fills the home with comforts.*

23 Her husband is known in the gates, when he sitteth among the elders of the land. *His happiness is noticed and noted. His* honour contents her, she does not seek publicity herself.

24—26 She maketh fine linen, and selleth *it;* and delivereth girdles unto the merchant. Strength and honour *are* her clothing; and she shall rejoice in time to come. She openeth her mouth with wisdom; and in her tongue *is* the law of kindness. *(The tongue is a main point in woman. If her talk be wisely kind, she is a jewel indeed.)*

27, 28 She looketh well to the ways of her household, and eateth not the bread of idleness. Her children arise up, and call her blessed; her husband *also*, and he praiseth her.

29 Many daughters have done virtuously, but thou excellest them all. *(May such be the miniature biography of the new bride.)*

30, 31 Favour *is* deceitful, and beauty *is* vain: *but* a woman *that* feareth the LORD, she shall be praised. Give her of the fruit of her hands; and let her own works praise her in the gates. *(Religion is the root of happiness. Piety has charms which abide in all their freshness when mere fleshly beauty has given place to the wrinkles of old age. May the new household be founded in prayer, built up in holiness, and crowned with the divine blessing.)*

Since Jesus freely did appear,
To grace a marriage feast,
O Lord, we ask thy presence here,
To make a wedding guest.

Upon the bridal pair look down,
Who now have plighted hands;
Their union with thy favour crown,
And bless their nuptial bands.

With gifts of grace their hearts endow,
Of all rich dowries best;
Their substance bless, and peace bestow
To sweeten all the rest.

Friends who wish for a special passage for Christmas should read the portion upon page 486.

Those who regard Good Friday may read any of the portions from 608 to 614, or upon 616 or 34.

For Easter, read 617 or 621.

INDEX.

———◆———